W9-BUE-758

Contemporary Literary Criticism

Guide to Gale Literary Criticism Series

For criticism on	Consult these Gale series
Authors now living or who died after December 31, 1959	***CONTEMPORARY LITERARY CRITICISM (CLC)***
Authors who died between 1900 and 1959	***TWENTIETH-CENTURY LITERARY CRITICISM (TCLC)***
Authors who died between 1800 and 1899	***NINETEENTH-CENTURY LITERATURE CRITICISM (NCLC)***
Authors who died between1400 and 1799	***LITERATURE CRITICISM FROM 1400 TO 1800 (LC)*** ***SHAKESPEAREAN CRITICISM (SC)***
Authors who died before 1400	***CLASSICAL AND MEDIEVAL LITERATURE CRITICISM (CMLC)***
Black writers of the past two hundred years	***BLACK LITERATURE CRITICISM (BLC) AND BLACK LITERATURE CRITICISM SUPPLEMENT (BLCS)***
Authors of books for children and young adults	***CHILDREN'S LITERATURE REVIEW (CLR)***
Dramatists	***DRAMA CRITICISM (DC)***
Hispanic writers of the late nineteenth and twentieth centuries	***HISPANIC LITERATURE CRITICISM (HLC)***
Native North American writers and orators of the eighteenth, nineteenth, and twentieth centuries	***NATIVE NORTH AMERICAN LITERATURE (NNAL)***
Poets	***POETRY CRITICISM (PC)***
Short story writers	***SHORT STORY CRITICISM (SSC)***
Major authors from the Renaissance to the present	***WORLD LITERATURE CRITICISM, 1500 TO THE PRESENT (WLC)***
Major authors and works from the Bible to the present	***WORLD LITERATURE CRITICISM SUPPLEMENT (WLCS)***

ISSN 0091-3421

Volume 124

Contemporary Literary Criticism

Criticism of the Works of Today's Novelists, Poets, Playwrights, Short Story Writers, Scriptwriters, and Other Creative Writers

Jeffrey W. Hunter
EDITOR

Jennie Cromie
ASSOCIATE EDITOR

Justin Karr
Linda Pavlovski
ASSISTANT EDITORS

Detroit
New York
San Francisco
London
Boston
Woodbridge, CT

STAFF

Jeffrey W. Hunter, *Editor*

Jenny Cromie, Timothy J. White, *Associate Editors*
Justin Karr, Linda Pavlovski, *Assistant Editors*

Josh Lauer, *Contributing Editor*

Maria Franklin, *Permissions Manager*
Kimberly F. Smilay, *Permissions Specialist*
Kelly Quin, *Permissions Associate*
Erin Bealmear and Sandy Gore, *Permissions Assistants*

Victoria B. Cariappa, *Research Manager*
Corrine Boland, Wendy Festerling, Tamara Nott, Tracie A. Richardson, *Research Associates*
Tim Lehnerer, Patricia Love, *Research Assistants*

Mary Beth Trimper, *Production Director*
Cindy Range, *Production Assistants*

Barbara J. Yarrow, *Graphic Services Manager*
Sherrell Hobbs, *Macintosh Artist*
Randy Bassett, *Image Database Supervisor*
Robert Duncan and Mikal Ansari, *Scanner Operators*
Pamela Reed, *Imaging Coordinator*

Library of Congress Catalog Card Number 76-46132
ISBN 0-7876-3199-X
ISSN 0091-3421

Printed in the United States of America
10 9 8 7 6 5 4 3 2 1

Contents

Preface

A Comprehensive Information Source on Contemporary Literature

Named "one of the twenty-five most distinguished reference titles published during the past twenty-five years" by *Reference Quarterly,* the *Contemporary Literary Criticism (CLC)* series provides readers with critical commentary and general information on more than 2,000 authors now living or who died after December 31, 1959. Previous to the publication of the first volume of *CLC* in 1973, there was no ongoing digest monitoring scholarly and popular sources of critical opinion and explication of modern literature. *CLC,* therefore, has fulfilled an essential need, particularly since the complexity and variety of contemporary literature makes the function of criticism especially important to today's reader.

Scope of the Series

CLC presents significant passages from published criticism of works by creative writers. Since many of the authors covered by *CLC* inspire continual critical commentary, writers are often represented in more than one volume. There is, of course, no duplication of reprinted criticism.

Authors are selected for inclusion for a variety of reasons, among them the publication or dramatic production of a critically acclaimed new work, the reception of a major literary award, revival of interest in past writings, or the adaptation of a literary work to film or television.

Attention is also given to several other groups of writers—authors of considerable public interest—about whose work criticism is often difficult to locate. These include mystery and science fiction writers, literary and social critics, foreign writers, and authors who represent particular ethnic groups.

Format of the Book

Each *CLC* volume contains individual essays and reviews taken from hundreds of book review periodicals, general magazines, scholarly journals, monographs, and books. Entries include critical evaluations spanning from the beginning of an author's career to the most current commentary. Interviews, feature articles, and other published writings that offer insight into the author's works are also presented. Students, teachers, librarians, and researchers will find that the generous critical and biographical material in *CLC* provides them with vital information required to write a term paper, analyze a poem, or lead a book discussion group. In addition, complete bibliographical citations note the original source and all of the information necessary for a term paper footnote or bibliography.

Features

A *CLC* author entry consists of the following elements:

- The **Author Heading** cites the author's name in the form under which the author has most commonly published, followed by birth date, and death date when applicable. Uncertainty as to a birth or death date is indicated by a question mark.

- A **Portrait** of the author is included when available.

- A brief **Biographical and Critical Introduction** to the author and his or her work precedes the criticism. The first line of the introduction provides the author's full name, pseudonyms (if applicable), nationality, and a listing of genres in which the author has written. To provide users with easier access to information, the biographical and critical essay included in each author entry is divided into four categories: "Introduction," "Biographical Information," "Major Works," and "Critical Reception." The introductions to single-work entries—entries that focus on well known and frequently studied books, short stories, and poems—are similarly organized to quickly provide readers with information on the plot and major characters of the work being discussed, its major themes, and its critical reception. Previous volumes of *CLC* in which the author has been featured are also listed in the introduction.

- A list of **Principal Works** notes the most important writings by the author. When foreign-language works have been translated into English, the English-language version of the title follows in brackets.

- The **Criticism** represents various kinds of critical writing, ranging in form from the brief review to the scholarly exegesis. Essays are selected by the editors to reflect the spectrum of opinion about a specific work or about an author's literary career in general. The critical and biographical materials are presented chronologically, adding a useful perspective to the entry. All titles by the author featured in the entry are printed in boldface type, which enables the reader to easily identify the works being discussed. Publication information (such as publisher names and book prices) and parenthetical numerical references (such as footnotes or page and line references to specific editions of a work) have been deleted at the editor's discretion to provide smoother reading of the text.

- Critical essays are prefaced by **Explanatory Notes** as an additional aid to readers. These notes may provide several types of valuable information, including: the reputation of the critic, the importance of the work of criticism, the commentator's approach to the author's work, the purpose of the criticism, and changes in critical trends regarding the author.

- A complete **Bibliographical Citation** designed to help the user find the original essay or book precedes each critical piece.

- Whenever possible, a recent **Author Interview** accompanies each entry.

- A concise **Further Reading** section appears at the end of entries on authors for whom a significant amount of criticism exists in addition to the pieces reprinted in *CLC.* Each citation in this section is accompanied by a descriptive annotation describing the content of that article. Materials included in this section are grouped under various headings (e.g., Biography, Bibliography, Criticism, and Interviews) to aid users in their search for additional information. Cross-references to other useful sources published by The Gale Group in which the author has appeared are also included: *Authors in the News, Black Writers, Children's Literature Review, Contemporary Authors, Dictionary of Literary Biography, DISCovering Authors, Drama Criticism, Hispanic Literature Criticism, Hispanic Writers, Native North American Literature, Poetry Criticism, Something about the Author, Short Story Criticism, Contemporary Authors Autobiography Series,* and *Something about the Author Autobiography Series.*

Other Features

CLC also includes the following features:

- An **Acknowledgments** section lists the copyright holders who have granted permission to reprint material in this volume of *CLC*. It does not, however, list every book or periodical reprinted or consulted during the preparation of the volume.

- Each new volume of *CLC* includes a **Cumulative Topic Index,** which lists all literary topics treated in *CLC, NCLC, TCLC,* and *LC 1400-1800.*

- A **Cumulative Author Index** lists all the authors who have appeared in the various literary criticism series published by The Gale Group, with cross-references to Gale's biographical and autobiographical series. A full listing of the series referenced there appears on the first page of the indexes of this volume. Readers will welcome this cumulated author index as a useful tool for locating an author within the various series. The index, which lists birth and death dates when available, will be particularly valuable for those authors who are identified with a certain period but whose death dates cause them to be placed in another, or for those authors whose careers span two periods. For example, Ernest Hemingway is found in *CLC,* yet F. Scott Fitzgerald, a writer often associated with him, is found in *Twentieth-Century Literary Criticism.*

- A **Cumulative Nationality Index** alphabetically lists all authors featured in *CLC* by nationality, followed by numbers corresponding to the volumes in which the authors appear.

- An alphabetical **Title Index** accompanies each volume of *CLC.* Listings are followed by the author's name and the corresponding page numbers where the titles are discussed. English translations of foreign titles and variations of titles are cross-referenced to the title under which a work was originally published. Titles of novels, novellas, dramas, films, record albums, and poetry, short story, and essay collections are printed in italics, while all individual poems, short stories, essays, and songs are printed in roman type within quotation marks; when published separately (e.g., T. S. Eliot's poem *The Waste Land),* the titles of long poems are printed in italics.

- In response to numerous suggestions from librarians, Gale has also produced a **Special Paperbound Edition** of the *CLC* title index. This annual cumulation, which alphabetically lists all titles reviewed in the series, is available to all customers. Additional copies of the index are available upon request. Librarians and patrons will welcome this separate index: it saves shelf space, is easy to use, and is recyclable upon receipt of the next edition.

Citing *Contemporary Literary Criticism*

When writing papers, students who quote directly from any volume in the Literary Criticism Series may use the following general forms to footnote reprinted criticism. The first example pertains to material drawn from periodicals, the second to material reprinted in books:

[1]Alfred Cismaru, "Making the Best of It," *The New Republic,* 207, No. 24, (December 7, 1992), 30, 32; excerpted and reprinted in *Contemporary Literary Criticism,* Vol. 85, ed. Christopher Giroux (Detroit: Gale, 1995), pp. 73-4.

[2]Yvor Winters, *The Post-Symbolist Methods* (Allen Swallow, 1967); excerpted and reprinted in *Contemporary Literary Criticism,* Vol. 85, ed. Christopher Giroux (Detroit: Gale, 1995), pp. 223-26.

Suggestions Are Welcome

The editors hope that readers will find *CLC* a useful reference tool and welcome comments about the work. Send comments and suggestions to: Editors, *Contemporary Literary Criticism,* The Gale Group, 27500 Drake Rd., Farmington Hills, MI 48333-3535.

Acknowledgments

The editors wish to thank the copyright holders of the excerpted criticism included in this volume and the permissions managers of many book and magazine publishing companies for assisting us in securing reproduction rights. We are also grateful to the staffs of the Detroit Public Library, the Library of Congress, the University of Detroit Mercy Library, Wayne State University Purdy/Kresge Library Complex, and the University of Michigan Libraries for making their resources available to us. Following is a list of the copyright holders who have granted us permission to reproduce material in this volume of CLC. Every effort has been made to trace copyright, but if omissions have been made, please let us know.

COPYRIGHTED MATERIALS IN *CLC,* VOLUME 124, WERE REPRODUCED FROM THE FOLLOWING PERIODICALS:

American Literature, v. 63, December, 1991. Copyright © 1991 Duke University Press, Durham, NC. Reproduced by permission.—**Boundary 2**, v. 19, Spring, 1992. Copyright © 1992 by Duke University Press, Durham, NC. Reproduced by permission.—**Chicago Review**, v. 32, Spring, 1981. Copyright © 1981 by Chicago Review. Reproduced by permission.—**Christianity Today**, September 7, 1998 for "Still Surprised by Lewis" by J. I. Packer. © 1998 by Christianity Today, Inc. Reproduced by permission of the author.—**Commonweal,** December 9, 1977. Copyright © 1977 Commonweal Publishing Co., Inc. Reproduced by permission of Commonweal Foundation.—**Contemporary Review**, v. 260, March, 1992. Reproduced by permission.—**Critique: Studies in Contemporary Fiction**, v. XXXI, Spring, 1990. Copyright © 1990 Helen Dwight Reid Educational Foundation. Reproduced with permission of the Helen Dwight Reid Educational Foundation, published by Heldref Publications, 119 18th Street, N. W., Washington, DC 20036-1802.—**Critique: Studies in Modern Fiction**, v. XXVIII, Summer, 1987. Copyright © 1987 Helen Dwight Reid Educational Foundation. Reproduced with permission of the Helen Dwight Reid Educational Foundation, published by Heldref Publications, 119 18th Street, N. W., Washington, DC 20036-1802.—**The Dalhousie Review**, v. 60, Winter, 1980-81 for "Robert Lowell: The Problems and Power of Allusion" by Lauriat Lane, Jr. Reproduced by permission of the publisher and the author.—**First Things**, no. 85, August-September, 1998. Reproduced by permission.—**French Cultural Studies**, v. 8, February, 1997. Reproduced by permission.—**The French Review**, v. 60, October, 1986. Copyright 1986 by the American Association of Teachers of French. Reproduced by permission.—**L'Esprit Créateur**, v. XXXIII, Spring, 1993. Copyright © 1993 by L'Esprit Créateur. Reproduced by permission.—**Literature and Psychology**, v. XVII, 1967. © Editor 1967. Reproduced by permission of the publisher.—**The Massachusetts Review**, v. XVII, Autumn, 1976. © 1976. Reproduced from The Massachusetts Review, The Massachusetts Review, Inc. by permission.—**The Minnesota Review**, v. VIII, 1968 for "The Way Down to Wisdom of Louis-Ferdinand Céline" by Kingsley Widmer. © 1968 The Minnesota Review. Reproduced by permission of the author.—**MLN**, v. 107, September, 1992. © copyright 1992 by The Johns Hopkins University Press. All rights reserved. Reproduced by permission.—**Modern Age**, v. 33, Summer, 1991. Reproduced by permission.—**Modern Fiction Studies**, v. XVII, Spring, 1971; v. 32, Spring, 1986. Copyright © 1971, 1986 by Purdue Research Foundation, West Lafayette, IN 47907. All rights reserved. Both reproduced by permission of The Johns Hopkins University.—**Mosaic: A Journal for the Interdisciplinary Study of Literature**, v. XVII, Summer, 1984; v. XIX, Fall, 1986. © Mosaic 1984, 1986. Acknowledgment of previous publication is herewith made.—**The Nation**, New York, April 11, 1987; October 2, 1995. © 1987, 1995 The Nation magazine/ The Nation Company, Inc. Both reproduced by permission.—**The New Criterion**, v. 11, March, 1993 for "Camus Today" by Renee Winegarten. Copyright © 1993 by The Foundation for Cultural Review. Reproduced by permission of the author.—**The New England Quarterly**, v. LXVII, March, 1994 for "'One Gallant Rush': The Writing of Robert Lowell's 'For the Union Dead'" by William Doreski. Copyright 1994 by The New England Quarterly. Reproduced by permission of the publisher and the author.—**New England Review**, v. LXVIII, March, 1995 for "Surviving the Marketplace: Robert Lowell and the Sixties" by Hilene Flanzbaum; v. 16, Winter, 1996 for "Robert Lowell's Day by Day: 'Until the Wristwatch is Taken From the Wrist'" by Richard Tillinghast. Copyright © 1995, 1996 by Middlebury College. Both reproduced by permission of the respective authors.—**The New York Times Book Review**, July 28, 1968. Copyright © 1968 by The New York

Times Company. Reproduced by permission.—**Papers on Language and Literature**, v. 29, Winter, 1993. Copyright © 1993 by The Board of Trustees, Southern Illinois University at Edwardsville. Reproduced by permission.—**Partisan Review**, v. XLIX, 1982, for "Jean Rhys" by Linda Bamber. Copyright © 1982 by Partisan Review. Reproduced by permission of the author.—**PMLA**, v. 87, January, 1972. Copyright © 1972 by the Modern Language Association of America. Reproduced by permission of the Modern Language Association of America.—**Policy Review**, no. 68, Spring, 1994. Reproduced by permission.—**Polity**, v. XXIX, Spring, 1997. Reproduced by permission.—**The Romantic Review**, v. 87, May, 1996. © 1996 The Trustees of Columbia University. Reproduced by permission.—**The Sewanee Review**, v. CII, Winter, 1994. Copyright © 1994 by Richard Tillinghast. Reproduced with permission of the editor and the author.—**Signs: Journal of Women in Culture and Society**, v. 18 for "Gender and Subjectivity: Simon de Beauvoir and Contemporary Feminism" by Sonia Kruks. Reproduced by permission of the publisher and the author.—**The South Atlantic Quarterly**, v. 93, Spring, 1994. Copyright © 1994 by Duke University Press, Durham, NC. Reproduced by permission.—**The Southern Humanities Review**, v. XXVIII, Winter, 1994. Copyright 1994 by Auburn University. Reproduced by permission.—**Studies in American Fiction**, v. 17, Autumn, 1989; v. 22, Spring, 1994. Copyright © 1989, 1994 Northeastern University. Both reproduced by permission.—**Studies in the Literary Imagination**, v. XI, Fall, 1978; v. XXII, Fall, 1989. Copyright 1978, 1989 Department of English, Georgia State University. Both reproduced by permission.—**Studies in the Novel**, v. XVI, Summer, 1984; v. XVIII, Spring, 1986; v. 25, Spring, 1993. Copyright 1984, 1986, 1993 by North Texas State University. All reproduced by permission of the publisher.—**Symposium**, v. XXXV, Summer, 1981. Copyright © 1981 Helen Dwight Reid Educational Foundation. Reproduced with permission of the Helen Dwight Reid Educational Foundation, published by Heldref Publications, 1319 18th Street, NW, Washington, DC 20036-1802.—**The Virginia Quarterly Review**, v. 72, Autumn, 1996. Copyright, 1996, by The Virginia Quarterly Review, The University of Virginia. Reproduced by permission of the publisher.—**Women's Studies: An Interdisciplinary Journal**, v. 17, January, 1990. © 1990 Gordon and Breach Science Publishers. Reproduce by permission.—**Word & World I**, 1981. Reproduced by permission.—**World Literature Today**, v. 69, Winter, 1995. Copyright © 1995 by the University of Oklahoma Press. Reproduced by permission.—**World Literature Written in English**, v. 15, April, 1976; v. 17, April, 1978. © Copyright 1976, 1978 WLWE-World Literature Written in English. Both reproduced by permission.—**World Policy Journal**, v. XII, Winter, 1995/96. Reproduced by permission.—**The Yale Review**, v. 79, Winter, 1990. Copyright 1990, by Yale University. Reproduced by permission of the editors and Blackwell Publishers.

COPYRIGHTED EXCERPTS IN *CLC,* VOLUME 124, WERE REPRODUCED FROM THE FOLLOWING BOOKS:

Ascher, Carol. From "Women and Choice—A New Look at Simone de Beauvoir and The Second Sex" in **Faith of a (Woman) Writer**. Edited by Alice Kessler-Harris and William McBrien. Greenwood Press, 1988. Copyright © 1988 by Hofstra University. All rights reserved. Reproduced by permission of Greenwood Publishing Group, Inc., Westport, CT.—Britch, Carrol and Cliff Lewis. From "Growth of the Family in The Grapes of Wrath" in **Critical Essays on Steinbecks's The Grapes of Wrath**. Edited by John Ditsky. G. K. Hall & Co., 1989. Copyright © 1989 by John Ditsky. All rights reserved. Reproduced by permission.—Burns, Wayne. From "'I'll Protest If It Kills Me': A Reading of the Prologue to Death on the Installment Plan" in **Critical Essays on Louis-Ferdinand Céline**. Edited by William K. Buckley. G. K. Hall & Co., 1989. Copyright 1989 by William K. Buckley. All rights reserved. Reproduced by permission.—Cederstrom, Lorelei. From "The 'Great Mother' in The Grapes of Wrath" in **Steinbeck and the Environment: Interdisciplinary Approaches**. Edited by Susan F. Beegel, Susan Shillinglaw and Wesley N. Tiffney, Jr. The University of Alabama Press, 1997. Copyright © 1997 The University of Alabama Press. All rights reserved. Reproduced by permission.—McEntyre, Marilyn Chandler. From "Natural Wisdom: Steinbeck's Men of Nature as Prophets and Peacemakers" in **Steinbeck and the Environment: Interdisciplinary Approaches**. Edited by Susan F. Beegel, Susan Shillinglaw and Wesley N. Tiffney, Jr. The University of Alabama Press, 1997. Copyright © 1997 The University of Alabama Press. All rights reserved. Reproduced by permission.—Miles, Rosalind. From **The Female Form: Women Writers and the Conquest of the Novel**. Routledge and Kegan Paul, 1987. © Rosalind Miles 1987. All rights reserved. Reproduced by permission of the publisher.—Mistacco, Vicki. From "Mama's Boy: Reading Woman in L'Etranger" in **Camus's L'Etranger: Fifty**

Years On. Edited by Adele King. St. Martin's Press, 1982. Copyright © Adele King 1982. All rights reserved. Reproduced by permission of Macmillan, London and Basingstoke. In North American by St. Martin's Press, Incorporated and the author.—Nebeker, Helen E. From "The Artist Emerging" in **Critical Perspectives on Jean Rhys**. Edited by Pierette M. Frickey. Three Continents Press, 1990. Copyright © Three Continents Press, 1990. All rights reserved. Reproduced by permission.—O'Connell, David. From "Louis-Ferdinand Céline: An Introduction" in **Critical Essays on Louis-Ferdinand Céline**. Edited by William K. Buckley. G. K. Hall & Co., 1989. Copyright 1989 by William K. Buckley. All rights reserved. Reproduced by permission.—Ostrovsty, Erika. From "Louis-Ferdinand Céline: Creator and Destroyer of Myths" in **Critical Essays on Louis-Ferdinand Céline**. Edited by William K. Buckley. G. K. Hall & Co., 1989. Copyright 1989 by William K. Buckley. All rights reserved. Reproduced by permission.—Owens, Louis. From "The Culpable Joads: Desentimentalizing The Grapes of Wrath" in **Critical Essays on Steinbecks's The Grapes of Wrath**. Edited by John Ditsky. G. K. Hall & Co., 1989. Copyright © 1989 by John Ditsky. All rights reserved. Reproduced by permission.—Owens, Louis. From "The Story of a Writing: Narrative Structure in East of Eden" in **Rediscovering Steinbeck: Revisionist Views of His Art, Politics and Intellect**. Edited by Cliff Lewis and Carroll Britch. The Edwin Mellen Press, 1989. © Copyright 1989 The Edwin Mellen Press. All rights reserved. Reproduced by permission.—Piehler, Paul. From "Myth or Allegory? Archetype and Transcendence in the Fiction of C. S. Lewis" in **Word and Story in C. S. Lewis**. Edited by Peter J. Schakel and Charles A. Huttar. University of Missouri Press, 1991. Copyright © 1991 by The Curators of the University of Missouri. All rights reserved. Reproduced by permission.—Pilardi, Jo-Ann. From "Female Eroticism in the Works of Simone de Beauvior" in **The Thinking Muse: Feminism and Modern French Philosophy**. Edited by Jeffner Allen and Iris Marion Young. Indiana University Press, 1989. © 1989 by Indiana University Press. All rights reserved. Reproduced by permission of Jeffner Allen.—Satyanarayana, M. R. From "'And Then the Child Becomes a Man': Three Initiation Stories of John Steinbeck" in **John Steinbeck: A Study of the Short Fiction**. Edited by R. S. Hughes. Twayne Publishers, 1989. Copyright © 1989 by G. K. Hall & Co. All rights reserved. Reproduced by permission.—Simons, Margaret A. From "The Second Sex: From Marxism to Radical Feminism" in **Feminist Interpretations of Simone de Beauvoir**. Edited by Margaret A. Simons. The Pennsylvania State University Press, 1995. Copyright © 1995 The Pennsylvania State University. All rights reserved. Reproduced by permission of the publisher.—Solomon, Philip H. From **Understanding Céline**. University of South Carolina Press, 1992. Copyright © 1992 University of South Carolina. Reproduced by permission.—Ward, Julie K. From "Beauvoir's Two Senses of 'Body' in The Second Sex" in **Feminist Interpretations of Simone de Beauvoir**. Edited by Margaret A. Simons. The Pennsylvania State University Press, 1995. Copyright © 1995 The Pennsylvania State University. All rights reserved. Reproduced by permission of the publisher.

PHOTOGRAPHS AND ILLUSTRATIONS APPEARING IN *CLC,* VOLUME 124, WERE RECEIVED FROM THE FOLLOWING SOURCES:

Lewis, C. S., 1956, photograph. AP/Wide World Photos. Reproduced by permission.—Camus, Albert, photograph. The Library of Congress.—Celine, Louis F., Paris, France, 1951, photograph. Archive Photos, Inc. Reproduced by permission.—de Beauvoir, Simone, 1964, photograph. AP/Wide World Photos. Reproduced by permission.—Lowell, Robert, photograph. The Library of Congress.—Rhys, Jean, photograph by Jerry Bauer. © Jerry Bauer. Reproduced by permission.—Steinbeck, John, photograph. The Library of Congress.

Albert Camus

1913-1960

French-Algerian novelist, dramatist, essayist, short story writer, journalist, and critic.

The following entry presents an overview of Camus's career through 1997. For further information on his life and works, see *CLC,* Volumes 1, 2, 4, 9, 11, 14, 32, 63, and 69.

INTRODUCTION

A celebrated novelist and postwar intellectual, Albert Camus is considered one of the most important writers of the twentieth century. His short novel *L'etranger* (1942; *The Stranger*) and existentialist treatise *Le mythe de Sisyphe* (1942; *The Myth of Sisyphus*) are regarded as seminal works of "absurdism," a literary philosophy founded on the belief that human existence is inherently meaningless and futile. The long essay *L'homme révolté* (1951; *The Rebel*) and subsequent novels *La peste* (1947; *The Plague*) and *La chute* (1956; *The Fall*) fortified Camus's reputation as a formidable independent thinker and uncompromising artist. Public and critical interest in his work was renewed by the posthumous publication of his unfinished novel *Le premier homme* (1994; *The First Man*). His Nobel prize-winning novels, essays, and plays evince his commitment to social justice and the possibility of moral integrity in the modern world. Once hailed as the conscience of France, Camus is an internationally renowned literary figure whose poignant metaphysical concerns and arresting prose style exert a profound influence on contemporary letters.

Biographical Information

Born in Mondovi, Algeria, a French colony in North Africa until 1962, Camus was raised in poverty by his illiterate Spanish mother. His father, an itinerant laborer of French descent, was fatally wounded in the First World War before Camus reached his first birthday. In 1914 Camus moved with his brother and emotionally detached mother into a small apartment in Algiers which they shared with his uncle and grandmother. The adverse circumstances of his upbringing forged a lasting respect for his hardworking mother and the plight of the underprivileged. With the encouragement of Louis Germain, an elementary school teacher who early recognized Camus's abilities, he won a competitive grant to enter the Grand Lycée in Paris in 1924. At the Grand Lycée, Camus's intellectual mentor was philosophy teacher Jean Grenier, whom he later studied under at the University of Algiers. Shortly before enrolling at the University of Algiers at age sixteen, Camus suffered a near fatal bout with tuberculosis, a chronic illness whose physical and emotional effects haunted him for the remainder of his life. After a period of convalescence, he began studies in philosophy and literature at the University of Algiers, from which he graduated in 1936. While still a student, Camus married briefly and divorced; he remarried Francine Faure in 1940. Camus became increasingly involved in political activities during the 1930s. He joined the Communist Party in 1935, though resigned his membership in 1937 over ideological differences. He published his first two books, *L'envers et l'endroit* (1937; *The Right Side and the Wrong Side*) and *Noces* (1937; *Nuptials*), the same year. He also wrote and abandoned his first novel *La morte heureuse* (1971; *A Happy Death*). Between 1935 and 1938, Camus was active as an actor, writer, and producer with Theatre du travail (Labor Theater), renamed Theatre de l'equipe (Team Theater) after he abandoned the Communist Party. During the Second World War, Camus wrote *The Myth of Sisyphus* and *The Stranger* while living in France and Algeria. He also wrote for *Combat,* the clandestine newspaper of the French Resistance, through which he met existentialist philosopher Jean-Paul Sartre and Simone de Beauvoir. Upon the Allied liberation of Paris in 1944, Camus was awarded the Medal of the Liberation. Acclaim for *The Stranger* and his contributions to *Combat,* which he presided over as editor until 1947, quickly established Camus as a foremost French writer and intellectual of the postwar period. Over the next decade he produced *The Plague, The Rebel,* and dramatic works including *Caligula* (1944), *Le malentendu* (1944; *The Misunderstanding*), *L'etat de siege* (1948; *The State of Siege*), and *Les justes* (1949; *The Just Assassins*). During the 1950s, Camus's disdain for Soviet communism precipitated his highly publicized estrangement from Sartre and other Left Bank intellectuals. Camus's passivity during the Algerian struggle for independence also drew heavy criticism that damaged his reputation and plunged him into depression and writer's block. Despite such setbacks, he produced *The Fall,* the collection of essays *L'eté* (1954; *Resistance, Rebellion, and Death*), and the volume of short stories *L'exil et le royaume* (1957; *Exile and the Kingdom*). Camus was awarded the Nobel Prize for Literature in 1957. Three years later he was killed in an automobile accident near Paris. The manuscript for *The First Man* was found in his briefcase at the site of the wreck.

Major Works

Camus's fiction, discursive writings, and dramatic works revolve around the central themes of existential alienation, moral dilemma, and revolt. His first novel, *A Happy Death,* and early autobiographic essays in *The Right Side and the Wrong Side* and *Nuptials* adumbrate the lucidity, irony, and lyrical quality of his subsequent works. *The Right Side and the Wrong Side,* considered a pivotal early text, sheds light on Camus's experience with poverty and his relationship with his silent mother. His most important works are contained in two triptychs, each comprised of a novel, essay, and play. The first grouping, often referred to as the "cycle of the absurd," includes *The Myth of Sisyphus, The Stranger,* and *Caligula.* In the philosophical essay *The Myth of Sisyphus,* Camus examines the fundamental paradoxes of the human condition as evidence of the absurd. The title refers to Sisyphus of Greek legend who was condemned to repeatedly roll a massive stone up a hill only to roll it back down after reaching the crest. Dismissing suicide as a viable response to such futility, Camus suggests that consciousness of the absurd and vigilant resistance to its terms may facilitate the formation of personal identity and value. *The Stranger,* a novel set in Camus's native Algeria, features protagonist Meursault, a French-Algerian youth who impulsively guns down an Arab man on the beach while overcome by the blinding sun. Arrested, jailed, tried, and sentenced to death, Meursault begins to reflect on his actions and the absurdity of his situation. Emotionless over the recent death of his mother and unrepentant for the murder, Meursault welcomes his fate and resigns himself to his execution in open defiance of society and its imposed morality. In the play *Caligula,* Camus portrays the eponymous Roman emperor's tyrannical quest for unbridled individual freedom. Stunned at the death of his sister, who is also his lover, Caligula becomes cognizant of the absurdity of life, whereupon he initiates an orgy of random rapes, murders, and punishments to act out his disillusionment. In *The Misunderstanding,* another significant play from this period, Camus presents a variation of the Oedipus myth in which a man is mistakenly murdered by his mother and sister. Camus's second major triad, unified by the theme of revolt, includes *The Plague, The Just Assassins,* and *The Rebel. The Plague* recounts the impact of a fictitious epidemic on the populace of Oran, a city in Algeria. The protagonist and narrator is Dr. Bernard Rieux, a secular physician committed to the systematic treatment of the afflicted. His spiritual foil is Father Paneloux, a Jesuit priest who appeals to divine intervention and the promise of salvation. Though the pestilence is eventually brought under control by a medical, or human, solution, their cooperative effort suggests the importance of fraternity and courage in the face of oppression. Regarded as a allegory of the Nazi Occupation of France during the Second World War, the novel illustrates the imperative of revolt against agents of persecution. *The Just Assassins* dramatizes the human cost of political violence in the service of ideology or expediency. The play centers upon Kalayiev, an idealistic poet and revolutionary who volunteers to throw a bomb at the Grand Duke in a planned assassination. However, when he notices the Duke's niece and nephew beside him in the carriage, he changes his mind, realizing that for this act he would be a murderer rather than a "just assassin." Camus elucidates the history and varieties of revolution in *The Rebel,* an extended essay in which he attempts to formulate the ethical conditions for revolt free of murder or malefaction. Opposing the nihilistic, violent tendencies of mass revolutions, Camus concludes that the individual must revolt against injustice by simply refusing to be a part of it. Camus's last novels, though extensions of earlier investigations, reveal a new vitality and theological interest. The novel *The Fall* presents the enigmatic, hypocritical confessions of Jean-Baptiste Clamence, a successful trial lawyer who, through rambling, self-mocking conversation with an interlocutor, excoriates himself for his perversity and numerous transgressions. The title refers to his guilt at having once failed to rescue a drowning woman. In his unfinished novel *The First Man,* Camus began to reconstruct the story of his life in the experiences of autobiographic protagonist Jacques Cormery. The existing narrative, a fragmentary account of Jacques's childhood, reveals Camus's deeply personal search for self-identity and connection with his prematurely deceased father.

Critical Reception

Camus is widely recognized as one of the most provocative and enduring literary figures of the postwar period. He is consistently praised for his perceptive evocation of metaphysical despair, the stark intensity and natural imagery of his lyrical prose, and his unequivocal condemnation of political tyranny. A preeminent absurdist writer who captured the moral climate of his generation, Camus defined the philosophical and artistic sensibility of many contemporary authors, especially those affiliated with the Theatre of the Absurd during the 1950s and 1960s. His popular association with existentialism, a classification that he dismissed, is traced to the philosophical legacy of Fydor Dostoyevsky, Friedrich Nietzsche, and Soren Kierkegaard. While *The Stranger* and *The Myth of Sisyphus* are viewed as his greatest accomplishments, Camus is also highly regarded for *The Plague, The Fall,* and his examination of revolution in *The Rebel.* Critics note that *The First Man,* though incomplete, is further evidence of Camus's remarkable sensitivity and narrative gifts. *Caligula* and *The Misunderstanding* are generally considered Camus's most effective plays, however, his dramatic works as a whole are typically viewed as secondary to his novels and essays. *The Stranger,* his best known work and a brilliant study of modern alienation, continues to attract rigorous critical scrutiny directed at the moral and psychological motivations of its protagonist, particularly as informed by Camus's aversion to capital punishment and his relationship with his mother. Critics frequently comment on the significance of Camus's early poverty and the Algerian landscape in this and all his writings. Though Camus enjoyed a mercurial rise, he became the subject of ridicule following his notorious break with Sartre, intensified by his neutrality during the Franco-Algerian war. Camus's detractors, especially those allied with Sartre, cite egregious elements of political naivete, moral intransigence, and philosophical amateurism in his writing. Despite such criticism, Camus's literary reputation rests largely upon the power of his prose, his unshakable commitment to his art, and his compelling effort to fashion meaning out the absurd.

PRINCIPAL WORKS

L'envers et l'endroit [*The Wrong Side and the Right Side*] (essays) 1937
Noces [*Nuptials*] (essays) 1937
Le mythe de Sisyphe: Essai sur l'absurde [*The Myth of Sisyphus and Other Essays*] (essays) 1942
L'etranger [*The Stranger;* also published as *The Outsider*] (novel) 1942
Caligula (drama) 1944
Le malentendu [*The Misunderstanding;* also translated as *Cross Purpose*] (drama) 1944
La peste [*The Plague*] (novel) 1947
L'etat de siege [*The State of Siege*] (drama) 1948
Les justes [*The Just Assassins*] (drama) 1949
L'homme révolté [*The Rebel*] (essays) 1951
L'eté [*Resistance, Rebellion, and Death*] (essays) 1954
La chute [*The Fall*] (novel) 1956
Requiem pour une nonne [adaptor; from the novel *Requiem for a Nun* by William Faulkner] (drama) 1956
L'exil et le royaume [*Exile and the Kingdom*] (short stories) 1957
Caligula and Three Other Plays [contains *Caligula, Le Malentendu, L'Etat de Siege,* and *Les Justes*] (drama) 1958
Les possédés [adaptor; from the novel *The Possessed* by Fydor Dostoyevsky] (drama) 1959
Lyrical and Critical Essays [includes *L'envers et l'endroit* and *Noces*] (essays) 1967
La mort heureuse [*A Happy Death*] (novel) 1971
Le premier homme [*The First Man*] (unfinished novel) 1994

CRITICISM

Alan W. Woolfolk (essay date Summer 1984)

SOURCE: "The Dangers of *Engagement:* Camus' Political Esthetics," in *Mosaic,* Vol. XVII, No. 3, Summer, 1984, pp. 59-70.

[*In the following essay, Woolfolk discusses Camus's political sympathies and overriding artistic ideals. According to Woolfolk, Camus resisted participation in revolutionary causes due to his belief that political ideology limits the artist's experience and creative vision.*]

"True artists," Camus stated in his Nobel Prize acceptance speech, "force themselves to understand instead of judging." In this respect, he is not unlike his character Tarrou, the former political revolutionary in ***The Plague,*** who admits:

> For many years I've been ashamed, mortally ashamed, of having been, even with the best intentions, even at many removes, a murderer in my turn. As time went on I merely learned that even those who were better than the rest could not keep themselves nowadays from killing or letting others kill, because such is the logic by which they live; and that we can't stir a finger in this world without the risk of bringing death to somebody. Yes, I've been ashamed ever since; I have realized that we all have plague, and I have lost my peace. And today I am still trying to find it; still trying to understand all those others and not to be the mortal enemy of anyone. . . . I leave it to others to make history. I know, too, that I'm not qualified to pass judgment on those others.

Similarly, the title of the novel itself suggests Camus' critical attitude toward judgment, the "plague" being the ancient Biblical symbol of punishment for wrong-doing.

At the same time, however, Camus also sensed that understanding had its limits, and that it was necessary to preserve the ability to deny, to say *No* to experience, to judge or condemn those who committed violence in the name of history. And it is this recognition that is the key to his attitude toward the writer's role in society.

Despite Camus' unquestioned sympathy for the victims of social injustice and political exploitation, art did not encompass for him, as it did for many of his contemporaries, an overwhelming involvement in politics. Art might be required to limit politics, but never should politics limit art. Political commitment or *engagement* was for him an entanglement which led to contemporary nihilism. Accordingly, rather than the expression *engagement,* Camus chose with a note of irony the term *embarqué* to indicate his deep reluctance at finding himself, almost against his will, compelled to address political concerns. I say *almost* because Camus was anything but unmoved by "history's woes." For instance, his early and consistent theme of passionate indignation over the miseries of poverty was perhaps most openly expressed in his 1939 reporting for the leftist newspaper *Alger Républicain,* in a series entitled "*Misère de la Kabylie.*" Later, this indignation was overshadowed by his unflagging resistance to political violence and terror enacted in the name of abolishing such impoverishment in Algeria and elsewhere. In both cases his passionate rejection of misery precluded political commitment: "The only *really* committed artist is he who, without refusing to take part in the combat, at least refuses to join the regular armies and remains a freelance." Camus found that he could no more side with left-wing militants than with right-wing militarists, since both groups were prepared to engage in violent acts that would destroy art and ultimately all civilization.

At nearly the same time that Camus began writing during the early 1930s, the image of the *engagé* intellectual became popular in French culture. According to the leftist Catholic, Emmanuel Mounier, who was one of the first to reintroduce the idea to the educated French public after the Dreyfus case, "to be viable one's action must have both a will to be efficacious and a spiritual ingredient. It is a double polarity, prophetic and political, and a constant tension between the two poles must exist." Despite a brief membership in the Communist Party and two years of anti-government newspaper reporting, which resulted in his being evicted from Algeria, as a young man Camus rejected, albeit ambivalently, the criterion of political efficacy. In a prewar review of communist Paul Nizan's *La Conspiration,* he stated that "Nizan requires an *engagement* in which a man relinquishes himself, and with himself his prejudices and choices. . . . We cannot follow him on that terrain." Camus' reluctant attitude toward judgment, however, immediately moved him to equivocate: "But, all things considered, it is as futile a problem as that of immortality, an affair that a man solves for himself and upon which one should not pass judgment." He concluded, on this occasion, that in the case of the writer his work must serve as evidence for judging the effect of *engagement.*

Building upon this criterion in his later writings, Camus grew to oppose political commitment precisely because it threatened to overwhelm the higher discipline that art represented in the distracting immediacies of the struggle for power. It was not simply a matter, as he wrote nearly twenty years after the Nizan review, of art being "threatened by the powers of the state." It was "more complex, more serious too," as soon as it became "apparent that the battle is waged within the artist himself." Art loses from such a "constant obligation." It loses that "ease, to begin with, and that divine liberty so apparent in the work of Mozart." Camus thought it obvious "why we have more journalists than creative writers, more boyscouts of painting than Cézannes, and why sentimental tales or detective novels have taken the place of *War and Peace* or *The Charterhouse of Parma.*" Implicitly, he understood that all genuine art, as higher culture, lives only if it can successfully discipline the momentary imperative to become engaged.

Camus did not escape unscathed from the conflict between politics and art. His statement on the occasion of accepting the Nobel Prize that "to create today is to create dangerously" reflects his recognition that the literary imagination had come loose from its traditional forms and was opening itself to dangerous creative possibilities. Elsewhere, too, he stated that "if we bring ourselves as artists into the positions we take up as men the experience will, in an unseen but powerful way, weaken our power of speech." In his role as artist, he recognized the danger of incoherence first of all within himself. Yet, like Marx and Engels in nineteenth-century London and the revolutionaries of eighteenth-century Paris, Camus found it impossible to avert his eyes from the misery and unhappiness of the masses: "What characterizes our time, indeed," he stated, "is the way the masses and their wretched condition have burst upon contemporary sensibilities."

In the course of his lifelong response to the social question, Camus developed a bold and perhaps fatal artistic strategy: he returned to the fundamental demands for justice underlying modern politics in its revolutionary form and swallowed them whole into his art, on the gamble that successful incorporation would allow for a more meaningful and less violent externalization of emotions. Thus, the imperative of responding to raw physical suffering and biological need witnessed in "*Misère de la Kabylie*" reappears again and again in his writings. Prompted by what Hannah Arendt has called passion in its noblest form, "compassion," Camus stubbornly refused to let go of the theme of abject suffering. Implacable, he insisted on recruiting what he thought was the *raison d'être* of Marxist and socialist politics into the camp of literature rather than allowing them to subsume art: "We writers of the twentieth century . . . must know that we can never escape the common misery and that our only justification, if indeed there is a justification, is to speak up, insofar as we can, for those who cannot do so." Caught between the demands of his art and the demands of political commitment, Camus attempted to work out an apology for the relevance of art in the twentieth century. As in the case of the Christian apologists, the crucial question, from the perspective of all higher, ennobling culture, hinged on whether he could successfully close the abyss of possibilities that he dared to open.

There have been several notable attempts within European literature to broaden the imagination to the point where it might control or at least contain the involvement of thought and action in modern politics. George Orwell's *Nineteen Eighty-Four* is perhaps the best known example, but it is notable in particular because of Orwell's attitude of total acceptance toward the corruptions of political power. Winston Smith, after all, does not symbolically triumph over O'Brien. In the end Winston has moved beyond personal despair because he has been so completely emptied of any memory and the capacity for love that there is nothing left to do but consummate his totalitarian surrender and "love" Big Brother. Winston's acquiescence to the ultimate political regime imaginatively represents what Orwell elsewhere predicted in a mood of total despair: "The autonomous individual is going to be stamped out of existence. But this means that literature, in the form in which we know it, must suffer at least a temporary death."

Another political novel of the same era, Arthur Koestler's *Darkness at Noon,* is almost as pessimistic in that it ends with the sacrifice of the old Bolshevik, Rubashov, to the totality of the Party. Yet it extends beyond what Orwell himself described as the unusual ability of a good political writer—"to imagine oneself as the victim"—to what Rubashov calls the evil of the Bolshevik mind: "We have thrown overboard all conventions, our sole guiding principle is that of consequent logic: we are sailing without ethical ballast." Ignazio Silone's *Bread and Wine* goes still further in its attempt to dominate and transform the meaning of political commitment. Just as Rubashov expresses his speculation about the nature of the Party evil in the privacy of his diary, so the committed Marxist Pietro Spina asks in the privacy of his jottings whether his denial of "petit bourgeois prejudices" is not the source of his error. But, as Camus once pointed out in a review of *Bread and Wine,* Silone's lesson represents a "return from an abstract philosophy of the revolution to the bread and wine of simplicity." In consequence, Silone stands closer to Camus' goals of assigning limits to revolutionary thought and establishing the supremacy of artistic insight.

These goals are most clearly expressed in Camus' own interpretation of Martin du Gard's *Les Thibault,* which he considered one of the first novels to have mastered the dangers of political commitment. Camus makes his case for the superiority of artistic over political meaning by arguing for the symbolic strength of the rebellious Antoine over his revolutionary socialist brother, Jacques. While both men are deeply moved enough by the existence of human misery to leave the narrowness of their private lives for a broader world of public purpose, Jacques' character transformation is "less significant," less profound, less persuasive because he adheres to the reason of revolutionary doctrine. In Camus' analysis, the unreality of revolutionary ideas introduces a shallow thought-world that uproots and destroys lives. Their emptiness is betrayed in the impatience of Jacques "who can be satisfied only by action" and who dies, finally, as a terrorist. In contrast, Antoine proves to be the "true hero" precisely because he is the deeper or "richer character" when compared with his politically committed brother. Politics does not consume his social relationships. The revulsion he feels at "the recognition of a common misery" extends beyond politics into his profession of medicine, which, Camus implies, helps both to deepen and to order his life. In the end Antoine is the more uncertain but stable, even when confronting death, for having rejected the ideological passions of political commitment.

Camus' rejection of political commitment, intellectually and emotionally, rests upon the argument that revolutionary doctrine corrupts the original feeling of indignation and revulsion over the perceived injustices of the world by narrowing their expression to the political realm alone. As to the desirability of having these feelings in the first place, Camus simply took this for granted, implicitly invoking the insights of the modern novel in particular. As he saw it, Dostoevsky had established beyond a doubt the justification for intense and passionate revolt in the face of human misery through the character of Ivan in *The Brothers Karamazov.* Ivan's fault lay not in his revolt against creation but in the rationalization of his rebellion to the point of imagining that "everything is permitted." Intellectualization marked his fall into the political temptations expressed by the Grand Inquisitor.

Camus thought it quite clear that *not* "everything is permitted." But he was not about to appeal to a vision of sacred order to narrow the possibilities that the imperatives of suffering and misery raised. If any created order existed, it was created by men; hence, the importance of the artist. As an exemplary rebel, the artist represented a disciplining of creative energies, a tempering of experience, because of a loyalty to the very forms on which art depends. "Both the historical mind and the artist seek to remake the world," Camus wrote, "but the artist, through an obligation of his very nature, recognizes limits the historical mind ignores." As to where this "nature" came from, Camus, except on rare occasions, did not deign to ask.

Camus' case against Marxist thought repeats many familiar points concerning its questionable scientific basis, the inaccuracies of its economic-historical predictions, its bourgeois prejudice in favor of economic-technological development, and its similarity to certain aspects of Christian thought. But the crux of Camus objections pertains to the subordination of the personality to historical demands, especially the demands of faith. Since Marxism, like Christianity, places man within a historical rather than a natural universe, Camus sees Marxist doctrine as suppressing both the opportunity for spontaneous revolt and the achievement of self-limitation by the autonomous personality. It is only insofar as Marxism envisions a release from the demands of history that he is sympathetic: "the aims, the prophecies are generous and universal," Camus writes of Marxism, "but the doctrine is restrictive, and the reduction of every value to historical terms leads to the direst consequences." More specifically, these serious consequences result from the denial of "ethical demands that form the basis of the Marxist dream." According to Camus, Marx himself was a rebel: "he rebelled against the degradation of work to the level of a commodity and of the worker to the level of an object." He affirmed the natural dignity of man. But Marx corrupted his original ethical demands when rebellion against injustice gave way to prophetic demands, not so much the prophecy of release from history into the Communist community of true individuals, as the prophecy of a protracted historical development that places the meaning of history at its end. In Camus' terms, Marx was a "fatalist," for by accepting the necessity of class struggles and economic progress, Marx accepted the necessity of misery and violence, of punishment in the name of the future. It no longer matters that the Kingdom of Ends is established by dictatorship and violence, that suffering becomes merely provisional and will be forgotten. And even if the "New Jerusalem" is achieved, "echoing with the roar of miraculous machinery," Camus asks, "who will still remember the cry of the victim?"

Despite the fact that Marxism is built upon what Camus sees as the Hegelian destruction of transcendence, parallels between the Old Jerusalem and the New Jerusalem run throughout Camus' analysis. Behind the historical interpretation of social reality, Camus ultimately finds the demands of faith. The punishing consequences of the fatalistic acceptance of misery result from neither an economics nor a science of history but from a religion of history imposed by a doctrinal faith. While he finds much to criticize in Marx's economic predictions and his submission to "the economic imperative" in a world governed by "the cult of production," it is the subordination of economic and scientific reasoning to the prophecy of an end to history that turns reason toward the rationalization of terror and violence. Doctrinal faith, in the form of Marxism, repeats the mistake of Christianity, which subjected "living reason to dead faith and freedom of the intellect to the maintenance of temporal power." Intellectualization corrupts the original moral demands associated with the virtues of revolt and leads to the quest for power. Because Camus operates from the assumption that there are no final or religious answers to the misery of living, he links all doctrines proclaiming such saving answers to the tendency toward "intellectual Caesarism." All authority is seen as a consequence of this bad habit of intellectualizing, which, if it is not simply a mask for power, certainly is a metaphor for the same.

Camus' reading of Western cultural history responds with an acute sensitivity to the problem of legitimacy in the modern state that Max Weber most clearly identified. He simply could not accept an ordinary answer to the extraordinary problem of justifying the use of violence. But his sensitivity to the violence at the root of the modern state—which will not be resolved, as he grasped in his anguish, by the intellectual trick of equating authority with legitimate power—was complicated by his anarchistic revolt against any theory of public authority. Having pointed to the crippled capacity to distinguish right from wrong peculiar to our times, Camus proceeded to call into question all authoritative standards of judgment, traditional and otherwise, by suggesting that they are a "plague" without purpose. The terror of power asserts itself not merely through intellectual creeds but especially by means of the repressive judgments, the *thou shalt nots,* against the spontaneous expressions of the human spirit. Camus compounded a variety of irreconcilable theories of the decline of Christianity to arrive at the charge that it is the Judaic heritage in Western culture that has led to the punishing demands of history and to the destruction of the Greek concept that man lives in a natural universe. Frightened by the injustice of the modern state, Camus simply projected his sense of injustice backward into the Western traditions that he otherwise recognized as having been decisively rejected by modern revolutionaries, with the result that he accented the continuity of religious and revolutionary traditions at the same time that he questioned their unity.

Camus' confusion of religious and revolutionary motifs can be directly traced to his concept of the *sacred.* He assumes that "only two possible worlds can exist for the human mind: the sacred (or, to speak in Christian terms, the world of grace) and the world of rebellion." As a consequence, the revolutionary thought-world of Marxism is assimilated to the realm of the sacred. But under the category of the sacred he conflates two contradictory motifs. The world of the Old Testament, for example, is antinomian. It is simultaneously controlling and violative, interdictory and transgressive, resulting in a violence that always subverts but never subserves traditional judgments. Themes of gratuitous violence, hatred, frenzy and massive infliction of injustice dominate any possibility of impulse control. Punishment is meaningless, senseless, absurd: ***The Plague*** "shows that the absurd *teaches nothing*" because the Biblical symbol of repressive control punishes without purpose. God prefers Abel's sacrifice over Cain's and demands Abraham's sacrifice of Isaac. Likewise, the Christian God permits the sacrifice of Ivan's innocent children for no apparent reason, just as Marxism in practice demands sacrifices in the name of the future. Camus' understanding of judgment completely ignores the notion of punishment as a sanction that supports controls upon experience. But even more significantly, his understanding closes off the possibility of revelation. There is no revelation of criminal possibilities in the heart of man and, therefore, no opportunity to repent and live under a new collective and individual order.

Prophecy is a dead tradition as seen through the eyes of Camus. Its remoteness from urban-technological culture is explicit in the sermons of Father Paneloux in ***The Plague*** and in the inverted apologetics of the false prophet Jean-Baptiste Clamence in ***The Fall,*** and implicit in Camus' conception of prophecy as a literal prediction about the future unrelated to an inner return to the past in ***The Rebel.*** In the latter work, especially, Camus overlooks the fact that the Western prophetic traditions were a recall to the repressive limits of the past, which were revolutionary only insofar as they were culturally conservative. To the Jewish prophets, for example, punishment was a revelation of violation of the Commandments. Camus' linking of Judaic and Christian traditions with Marxist prophecy obscures the complete break with traditional conceptions of man envisioned by Marx: for the Marxist prophecy of the future Communist identity liberated from traditional necessities carries powerful anti-repressive implications for the personality. When Camus states that "by demanding for the workers real riches, which are not the riches of money but of leisure and creation," Marx reclaimed the "dignity of man," he assumes the continuation of an ascetic personality type which Marx did not. For Camus, "creation" and "leisure" involved repressive necessities that mandated withdrawal from the world. A literary vocation was no leisure time activity worked in between some morning hunting and afternoon fishing, but rather an exclusive act of devotion which opened the way into a meaningful life. Fixation of activity was the very precondition of the achievement of identity.

Camus did not subscribe to the Marxist and humanist conception in which a person becomes fully human only through liberation from specific vocational, communal, national and religious identities. Yet his rejection of Western religious traditions inevitably pushed him toward the abstract humanist language of "humanity" and "mankind" (which Marx transformed into the "proletariat"), conceptually cutting him loose from the moorings of particular commitments. Camus' great admiration for Simone Weil, however, betrays the conservative assumptions implicit in his idea of human dignity. In *The Need for Roots,* for instance, Weil makes quite explicit the theological grounding of her defense of restraining commitments to vocation, community and nation. Camus simply ignored any such theologizing while exemplifying in much that he said and did the importance of particularity, of the need for roots, even though the demand for *engagement* pulled him toward an abstract, rootless conception of mankind and justice. Ungrounded in either an explicit or implicit theology, Camus found his roots in his literary vocation and French-Algerian homeland.

Unconsciously, at first, and then by conscious design, Camus became increasingly obedient to what he saw as the demands of the French literary tradition in modern society. Much the same pattern of return to constraining demands linked to the past repeats itself, but at a slower pace, with regard to Camus' commitment to French Algeria. Distraught over the increasing terror and violence of both "liberation" and colonial forces during the 1950s, Camus adamantly rejected the policies of both sides. Despite his protests against the irresponsible conduct of French colonial rule, Camus' sympathy with the misery-stricken population of Algeria precluded "a policy of surrender that would abandon the Arab people to an even greater misery, tear the French in Algeria from their century-old roots, and favor, to no one's advantage, the new imperialism now threatening the liberty of France and of the West."

Increasingly, the binding character of communal-national origins became a significant aspect of Camus' thought, progressing to the subject of Camus' own origins in his unfinished autobiographical novel, ***Le Premier Homme.*** But Camus followed the conservative theorizing of theologists such as Weil only so far, for in his conception writing was a "man's trade" and not a "gift of grace." The background of ***Le Premier Homme*** was to have been "those lands without a past" of which he wrote in ***L'Été,*** "lands of imagination, composed of a mixing of races." He imagined "a 'first man' who starts at zero, who can neither read nor write, who has neither morality nor religion." It was to have been the story of the creation of human culture, but this time without the antinomian excesses of historical doctrines.

Conservative modern theorists from Burke and Tocqueville to Arendt have assumed that people can become and remain human only to the extent that they identify with, and thereby limit themselves by means of, binding communal commitments. These commitments have been *public* commitments to vocation, community, class, nation and religion. Because Camus refused to articulate a public doctrine to oppose the radical break with traditional commitments explicit in Marxist doctrine, he frequently emphasized the importance of personal commitments, especially friendship, as the basis of social order. For him, justice, morality and social order were the consequence of personal loyalties, close to what American sociologist Charles Horton Cooley called primary relationships. Denial of binding affective ties permitted the excesses of nihilism. For this reason, Camus underscored the nihilistic significance of Nechave's sacrifice of friendship and love for the revolution. (Paragraph 6 of the *Revolutionary Catechism* reads: "Hard with himself, he must be hard towards others. All the tender feelings of family life, of friendship, love, gratitude and even honour must be stifled in him by a single cold passion for the revolutionary cause.") Camus assumed that political commitment suppresses the personal experiences necessary to the creation of public life, that it prevents their diffusion into society by destroying the private life of love and friendship itself.

The same basic charge is at the heart of Camus' argument that Lenin "never ceased to fight mercilessly against the sentimental forms of revolutionary action." Although Camus has in mind anarchism and syndicalism, the sentiments to which he refers spring from the affections of private existence. But in the case of Lenin, Camus openly admits what is elsewhere unstated—that Lenin "wanted to abolish the morality of revolutionary action because he believed, correctly, that revolutionary power could not be established while still respecting the Ten Commandments." Here, Camus not only acknowledges the importance of traditional controls to his conception of the private sphere, but he also specifically refers to prohibitions that are at the center of what he rather vaguely calls "the Judaic heritage" and "the God of the Old Testament." Plainly, if Lenin was despotic because he opposed the Commandments, then despotism must not result from traditional judgments. Camus' very understanding of the spontaneous expressions of the private life was so deeply imbued with traditional assumptions about the hierarchical nature of man that he could not imagine human nature without them.

Camus' continual opposition of theory and spontaneity, doctrine and nature, then, is misleading. It assumes the unqualified rejection of neither traditional controls nor the intellect, but rather the denial of theories of the state and public authority. Only in the closing pages of ***The Rebel*** does he begin to make clear that the history of our time is the history of "the struggle of German ideology against the Mediterranean mind"—of the "Caesarian revolution" against trade-unionism, the State against the commune, absolutist society against concrete society: "The profound conflict of this century is perhaps not so much between the German ideologies of history and Christian political concepts, which in a certain way are accomplices, as between German dreams and Mediterranean traditions, between the violence of eternal adolescence and virile strength, between nostalgia, rendered more acute by knowledge and by books and courage reinforced and enlightened by the experience of life—in other words, between history and nature." What is *natural* is a world without the power politics of the State, without the sometimes terrible demands of public authorities. While profoundly anti-political, Camus' vision of society may also be seen as culturally conservative. The "irrepressible demand of human nature" is not for a life without impulse repression, but against a life of political suppression. Camus expresses the anarcho-syndicalist dream in which the State is itself the dream of historical theorists.

Camus rightly points to Lenin as a key figure in understanding the modern state. However, he fixes upon Lenin's subordination of the spontaneity of the masses to a theoretical vanguard in *What is to be Done?* as further confirmation that the heart of the Bolshevik evil is located in theory or doctrine. While recognizing that Lenin "jettisons economic fatalism and embarks on action," Camus makes nothing of the fact that Marxist, like Hegelian, doctrine is heavy with the hidden purposes of history, and that therefore Lenin's moral indifference, and especially his activism, may be more the product of doctrinal subservience to the Party than doctrinal discipline. This shift from the superiority of doctrine to organizational tactics, which Camus overlooks, is clear, for instance, in Lenin's use of the term *ideology.* According to a strict Marxist definition, ideology refers to false consciousness, to conscious expressions that mask unconscious responses to the imperatives of a particular economic-historical circumstance. Lenin eliminates the weight of this unconscious element. By writing of a choice between either bourgeois or Socialist ideology, he shifts focus to the importance of consciousness alone.

This does not mean that the culpability of Marxist doctrine can be dismissed, for the Marxist concept of ideology itself functionalizes away the very possibility of moral, intellectual and religious opposition. With his transformed concept of ideology, Lenin simply took this denial one step further by making it a matter of organizational rather than doctrinal discipline. He pushed the Marxist denial of traditional commitments toward its logical conclusion, making the leap from theory to practice with disastrous consequences. Commitments to Party and then State replaced all others, with the result that not merely private sentiments but public purposes, such as nationality, were denied. As Solzhenitsyn has recently made clear, the Soviet Communists have never been nationalists. From Stalin to the present, they have systematically suppressed and destroyed all evidence of national culture, loyalties and affections, driving a wedge between Nation and State. Similarly, the committed Communist Pietro Spina in Silone's *Bread and Wine* is not only alienated from the simplicity of the private life by his commitment to the Party, as Camus thought, he is also dangerously close to the Fascists whom he opposes in his rejection of communal purposes that transcend Party interest.

Not simply doctrinal commitment but doctrinal subordination defines the problem. "Man takes refuge in the permanence of the party in the same way that he formerly prostrated himself before the altar" *only* after doctrine has failed in its highest function from a sociological perspective, which is to preserve the capacity to resist inwardly the corruptions of the established social order. Writing during an era in which the professional revolutionary, like the clergy of an earlier day, could no longer claim moral superiority and spiritual leadership, Camus exemplifies the anti-creedal idealism of a culture suffering from a disenchantment with public commitments from which we have not recovered.

Robert Greer Cohn (essay date October 1986)

SOURCE: "The True Camus," in *The French Review,* Vol. 60, No. 1, October, 1986, pp. 30-8.

[*In the following essay, Cohn provides an overview of Camus's literary career. Cohn praises Camus as "beyond all intellectual fashions and ideological factions, the finest, most authentic voice of his age."*]

Let us start modestly, as Albert Camus did. By the time he was stopped, when he died brutally in his forty-seventh year, he was widely regarded as the most important literary figure in the Western world.

He could hardly have come from humbler circumstances. His French father, who died in World War I almost as soon as Albert was born, was an agricultural worker in Algeria. His Spanish mother could not read, seldom spoke, and was partially deaf. Her mother was a straight-laced old lady who raised Albert and his older brother with strictness and, at times, the whip. Camus grew up in Belcourt, a working-class neighborhood of Algiers. As he looked back on it later, his childhood seemed happy despite the hardships. He loved the life of the streets and the beaches in the sun. A dedicated teacher took an interest in him and encouraged him in his studies. Camus worked with fierce concentration and went on with scholarships to the University of Algiers, where he specialized in philosophy. But at age 17, he contracted the tuberculosis which never really left him, though it came and went. He dropped out of school and took a series of odd jobs. At age 20, he married but divorced a year later; his first wife, Simone Hié, was a beautiful drug addict who betrayed him and wounded his psyche deeply. Camus's affair with the Communist Party shortly after this was rather similar; youthful hopes and swift disenchantment. Simultaneously, he founded a politically-inspired theater group which attracted some local attention. He did some writing as well as acting and directing for it, loved it all passionately. He had meanwhile recovered enough to go back and get a diploma in philosophy. In 1937, he published his first little book, ***L'Envers et l'endroit.***

This bring us to the literary Camus who most concerns us, for it is a marvelously honest and tender piece of writing about his early years, and when it was republished shortly before his death, he said that unless he returned to the unspoiled simplicity and piety of that book he would never do anything worthwhile. So let us have a look at it, remarking only that what happened to Camus after that is quite well known: how he fought for justice to the Arabs in the local press, went on to help edit and write for the Resistance paper *Combat* during the war; how he remarried and had twins, how he became famous with ***L'Etranger, Le Mythe de Sisyphe, La Peste, L'Homme révolté,*** and so on; the quarrel with Sartre; the Nobel prize; his dismay at his fame; and at the Algerian conflict in which he refused to take sides, out of loyalty to his mother; his stupefying death in a car accident in 1960. We will return to some of these items later.

The title ***L'Envers et l'endroit*** refers to the deep, honest ambivalence that runs throughout Camus; typically for him, particularly in his first manner, love and hate, beauty and ugliness, life and death go hand in hand. Eventually, this total cancellation will be identified with the absurd, referring especially to the tension between the mind's quest for unity or meaning and the world's chaotic refusal of it. One would speak too of heaven and hell, if it were not for the fact that Camus, like his parents, had little use for organized religion though he was baptized a Catholic. But he was a profoundly religious man in his own way and said "God is beauty" to an intimate friend. Later, he will reintroduce into a world threatened by valuelessness the moderate religious concept of "the sacred." Altogether, a pantheism not unlike that of the other great artists of modern France or Europe, or Emily Dickinson here, is close to his untrumpeted belief. But the God of beauty, or of the wistful sacred, is remote indeed from often-grim human affairs, and in these pieces we see an old woman whom no one is interested in staying with any more. The young folks go off heedlessly to the movies and leave her alone with her cold crucifix. Young Camus goes off too, but with a stab of concern in his heart, and we see him, in a sense, betraying those other young'uns, becoming himself with his deeper awareness. There is another sketch about an old man, similarly avoided in a café, going home alone in the dusk toward his eventual death.

There is a scene where Camus is sitting in an Arab café overlooking the twinkling port alone, listening to the foghorns in the night and wondering about his future itinerary through life. The key notes are sounded in the darkness of his love for his strange "indifferent" mother—she never caressed him but they were utterly in league and he knew it—and his need to be a man.

This is a telling point. He was fatherless like his Stranger, of whom it is said tersely "He had never known his father." In ***La Chute,*** equally tersely, Clamence laments "Il n'y a plus de père, plus de régles!" It is suggestive to note that any number of France's greatest writers, from Du Bellay and Racine through Baudelaire, Rimbaud, and Sartre were orphaned or otherwise deprived of their fathers. The impact is fairly obvious. The normal father provides a role model which mediates the boy's struggles to manhood. Failing that, the process of dissociating oneself from the mother becomes quite problematic, and an excessive pattern is apt to develop of "proving oneself as a man." This is confirmed by Ernesto Guarner (revealed to me by Charles McCabe), a Spanish psychiatrist whose clientele was exclusively matadors. Without exception, they were fatherless. Before I had learned that, I had spoken in print of Camus's bullfighter psychology, mindful of his Spanish inheritance as well as Michel Leiris' essay, "De la littérature considérée comme une tauromachie" (in *L'Age d'homme* [Paris: Gallimard, 1939]). I was naturally pleased when Herbert Lottman's biography disclosed the fact that one of his closest friends thought of Camus in just that way. The fact that Patrick McCarthy in his recent book dismisses this notion loftily causes me no particular pain. McCarthy's book (*Camus* [New York: Random House, 1982]) is often hasty and insensitive, though it has its uses and is cleverly packaged.

In another scene, Camus stares for hours at a mother cat that has just devoured some of her kittens. This is the other side of his special courage and one which I particularly admire. He describes in an unbearably powerful understatement of tenderness a night he spent lying next to his mother after she had been frightened by an unknown assailant, breathing in her perspiration and her silent anguish. In this daring to *stay* with the unmediated mother, he resembles Proust whom he, unlike Sartre, worshiped. We know about Proust's stubborn relation to his mother; few normal people are honest about their deepest affections and anxieties as this pair of artists were.

Further, as in the case of Proust whose mother could become an object of fierce hatred out of jealousy, in *Jean Santeuil* to the point of wishing her death, so too Camus sees in the mother cat the hideous "wrong side" of his total attachment, what Jung refers to as the "terrible mother." The Stranger tells the examining magistrate that his indifference before the death of his mother can be partly explained by the fact that everyone desires the death of loved ones at times. This is repeated elsewhere in Camus, and it is an important theme of ***La Chute.*** Camus' play ***Le Malentendu*** is about a mother who, with the help of her daughter, strangles the incognito traveller who turns out to be her son.

No doubt the betrayal by Simone Hié has something to do with all this and with the well-known don Juanism of Camus, but of course, beneath all that, there are universal facts of life, which some people are more candid about than others. Not that one should wallow in them; Camus thought of his ***Misunderstanding*** as a modern tragedy, and that, one feels, is the proper way to handle these matters, just as Sophocles did with his *Oedipus.* But let there be no misunderstanding here: woman is at the core of Camus' earthly world, where the mother securely is in ***La Peste.***

In ***L'Etranger,*** which came out in 1942 and made his reputation, Camus' protagonist seems dazed at first. He has been inwardly stabbed by a new awareness, as we gradually learn with him; he is "on to something," the absurd. The consolations of religion had departed from lots of lives in his time, but it is another thing to feel in depth that the world is made of a profound cleavage between mind and reality. The fact of mortality alone when it hits you truly can make mockery of the quest of meaning; or the simple confrontation of self too close-up in a mirror when you see a sort of alien moonlandscape. Where is our identity, or anything fixed in this fleeting, ephemeral existence? But all that *Angst* is familiar by now, and I would like rather to emphasize that this is one of those dazzling, infinite half-truths of which reality is obviously made, such as freedom and determinism, continuity and discontinuity, heredity and environment. Since each is infinite, one can get hooked on it as on an infinity-opening drug and Camus did for a youthful while, as did a lot of young people in his time, partly through reading him. As a result of the impact of World War II which, as he said, "made me modest," he discovered or rediscovered the other half-truth, that life is not absurd. From then on, those two half-truths *together* interested him more in what he described as a "higher balance," in connection with his doctrine of limits and moderation. One infinite balances off and limits the other in his more mature perspective.

But for the moment, his hero is stuck in his half-truth of the absurd which Camus will further explore in ***Le Mythe de Sisyphe.*** The vertical posture of the young matador can usefully characterize this steep excessive and one-sided honesty which leads or allows him to commit murder. Everyone remembers the scene where he yields to a sort of universal indifference under a dazzling sun on the beach and numbly shoots the Arab who was harassing his friend, Raymond. The fact that he shoots one shot and then four more has been often explained: his honesty dictates that he, as it were, *endorse* his dazed act, take fully responsibility in a sort of Nietzschean mood of superman suspension of ordinary morality. The Stranger becomes, it is widely agreed, the full conscious absurdist at this fateful juncture. But the usual comments are less sure of the puzzling accompanying thought which runs through Meursault's head, that he was aware that he had "unbalanced the day". Though nothing can be proven here, I submit that this is the germ of the movement to maturity in the "higher balance" I alluded to earlier. The Stranger's steep, vertical, infinite honesty is tentatively crossed by a ghostly dimension of other-relatedness, equally infinite as he will discover later, in ***La Peste*** and ***L'Homme révolté*** and which moderates our individual juvenile-omnipotent drives.

This dimension had already existed in his play ***Caligula,*** written a few years earlier, in the mouth of his spokesman for decency and sanity, Cherea. But Camus had gone on to get smitten by the new kind of awareness which, as he said in the preface to ***Le Mythe de Sisyphe,*** he had found on the "street corners of his time."

In that essay, published in 1943, Camus accepts practically as axiomatic—though he hedges a little in the preface about its being merely a tentative proposition—the manifold contradictions he finds throughout western culture from Zeno and Aristotle on to the existential exponents, such as Kierkegaard, Jaspers, Heidegger and Chestov, of "humiliated thought." So taken is he by this view that he seriously considers whether suicide might not be the proper response to the universal absurdity of our lives, and that is the subject of his essay. To explore, as he puts it, a logic to its extreme consequences even if it dictates our death. A Spanish stubbornness, which Camus was known for, is at work here, very clearly, and I think a succinct comment might be: *Olé*. Fortunately, he finds for life. Suicide, it turns out, would be a sort of evasion, a copout or "leap." This is a term he applies to a number of thinkers such as Kierkegaard, Chestov, Jaspers, Husserl, who accept the absurd to a point and then find a way out through religious salvation or some equivalent resolution. In this sense, they abort the unending tension which is the essence of absurd contradiction. Suicide would obviously do the same thing. But for this Camus the absurd is our only reality, our only good and must be lived with all the bittersweet way, with passion, lucidity, revolt—by this last term, he means never giving in, as in suicide or consoling religion. It is equivalent to consciousness or high consciousness. In other words, suicide would take away all we have, bitter as it is at times, and even in essence. A long, lucid, and intensely indifferent life is the defiant *révolté* answer to such a fate, and he imagines Sisyphus, rolling his eternal rock up the hill only to have it roll back down again, as being happy, as he says at one decisive point.

All this can bear another look. What is really going on underneath is this: at the point where Camus considers suicide as a solution to the absurd, he is confronted with another kind of absurdity, namely that it makes no sense to end a life to solve a life's dilemma because at the moment you die, the very problem disappears; at death, you have solved nothing since there is no more problem. Or if one imagines a tiny instant *between* life and death and the *wavering* that would occur between a problem to be solved and a no-problem (in death), then you have what can be seen as the absurd formula folded back or turning on itself. The absurd, which is a contradiction, can—as a total proposition of truth—be seen itself as contradictory. The absurd is both true and not true or, as I said earlier, it is a *half*-truth.

In the case of Meursault, a *tilt* from the vertical bullfighter dimension to the horizontal dimension of other-relatedness occurred at least in his mind: it would have provided a balance, the "balance of the day," which he sensed he had broken. Here too, an excessive drive to honesty, a kind of mortal logic which could dictate his death is providentially moderated by a tilt or pivoting: the logic of the absurd, and the suicide which might result from it, give way to an illogical, merely human impulse. Incidentally, even in his early lyrical essays, we find that promising, humane giving-in in terms of tenderness and, at times, a flow of tears. If suicide turns out to be the problematic, wavering solution we just saw it to be, then there is no point committing suicide. Rather, one does nothing drastic in that self-canceling direction but just keeps on living impulsively, which is what we all do all the time. Camus' "logic" has encountered a limit in the breakdown of the absurd, contradicted by its own self, fortunately. It is precisely such a tilt which characterizes the "happiness" of Sisyphus, which is not at all warranted within the absurd. In fact, it looks suspiciously like what he accused others of: a leap into another dimension of existence, away from the too-perfect logic of the "absurd." This is also true of the statement the good-hearted Camus makes at one point in his essay. Although theoretically his absurdist heroes accept no conventional morality, at that point Camus, obviously frightened of some of the implications, says that there is no reason to commit a crime any more than there is not to commit it, adding that to perform evil would be "childish." If that is not an arbitrary "leap" in his terms, what is it?

Still, the whole doctrine had an immense appeal, as we know, and set the tone of Camus's reputation at that time. Even recently, one heard William Styron speaking of Camus as his guide to whatever replaced religion for him.

But for those who followed Camus into his later phase, during and after and occasioned by the war, we find something quite altered. The tilt to the horizontal of other-relatedness is fully described and accepted in the preface to ***L'Homme révolté*** in 1951.

Partly because his reputation was so bound up with it, Camus at this point is at some pains to square his new view with his previous absurdist "logic." But now he clearly states what I have stated a few moments ago: the "profound ambiguity of the absurdist position," or what we have seen as the absurdity or arbitrariness of the absurd. Camus is left quivering at a crossroads: between the two horns of the original absurd contradiction in one direction, the vertical, and between its acceptance and rejection in another direction, the horizontal. At this crucifying juncture, he throws up his hands and sees himself bereft of all but a blind "impulse," life itself just going on at this crossing of dilemma and protesting against the mess. Moreover, the protest is against a world which has seen murder on such a staggering scale in World War II. Indeed, the book ***L'Homme révolté,*** which he is prefacing, is an attempt to answer the problem of mass murder in his time, just as ***Le Mythe*** was supposed to deal with individual suicide. So he is left only with the protest, this "impulse" which he now calls "revolt." Earlier, you will recall, revolt was the expression of a defiant response to life's absurdities and it just kept you living in the absurd, not copping out. That revolt led to no solution to anything. But now it is his answer to murder, as follows: a "révolté," or rebel, is a person who says no to an unacceptable situation, for example, an exploitative master. But he says "no" in terms of a right, a right to be free of exploitation or injustice. This right is a "yes" which goes with the "no." In other words, a true rebel revolts in the name of a principle which is universal, a right. Since a principle is by definition not just for one individual but a general law, the tilt to the horizontal occurs here, of which I spoke earlier. Since that right encompasses all men, one has no justification for murdering anyone in the name of rebellion, Camus claims. One may well sympathize, as I do, and still see that this pivoting or tilt is just another impulse with no real foundation in logic, absurd or otherwise. It is just the feeling one can have that I and you are all bound up and one slides into the other easily, as in life. There is, indeed, a great mystery of reality here—the problem of identity and intersubjectivity—but it is obvious that people who do not feel it just go ahead and murder anyway, and by the millions, in wars. Camus is sensitive and does feel the connection and compassion, just as he did for the old woman in the early essay we spoke of. He wants us all to feel it and stop killing each other. He is singularly good-hearted. Alas, his notion that we must in true revolt always balance the "no" and the "yes" as well as the I and the we—the striking and the caring or scrupulosity—is not easily observed in the heat of *action* which is *not* simultaneous, balanced, but serial or successive. Typically, one will strike and then regret it, or mourn a dead enemy if it comes to that; but not both together.

In a section of ***L'Homme révolté*** Camus alludes to Ivan Kaliaev, a Russian poet who insisted on giving his own life to pay for the life of the tyrant which he took. Camus called him "an innocent assassin" and wrote an admiring play about him, called ***Les Justes.*** Well, not too many will emulate him and it is clear that there is no sure-fire formula here. Yet, I think Camus is doing as well with all this as one can. By adding the horizontal dimension to his earlier perspective and maturing into his doctrine of limits and "higher balance," he has powerfully and convincingly shown at least what is desirable. He knows that this impulse toward The Other, including an enemy, is just that, an impulse. It is a *tilt* to the side and The Other and on-going life, even as you radically revolt in depth and cut through (vertically) a status quo. But, *knowing* that, he *nudges* us in the humane direction, and that is a good thing. In this way, he gives comfort to all those who would temper the ruthless revolts of Marxism by a limit, a cross-cutting dimension of humanity, as in the views of Silone and Gramsci in Italy and the modern Socialists in Western Europe generally, including France under Mitterrand.

If you look at this another way, viewing history along a time-line—seeing a ruthlessly goal-directed drive in the modern totalitarians, a deification of history as leading to a final justice for all, then Camus's good heart and sense of balance tell him, in ***L'Homme révolté,*** that we must limit the drive of that "horizontal religion" by a perspective of the sacred, which cuts across it in the name of individual (vertical) human rights, a *value* outside of history. In this sense, he contests the Sartrean doctrine of existence always preceding essence, and a constantly open relativistic "situation." Rather, he rediscovers that man has a nature after all, a sort of moderated essence which can serve as a value; this or that man is infinitely precious in himself, stemming from the sacred, and history has no right to treat him as a mere pawn toward some utopian end in a remote future.

In this way and others, I believe Camus got the better of Sartre in their famous quarrel. I totally disagree with Patrick McCarthy as to the value of ***L'Homme révolté*** and Camus' thought in general. ***L'Homme révolté*** is a heart warming attempt to figure out what went wrong in our Western culture to the extent of the massive atrocities of the twentieth century. He traces our sins of imbalance and hubris from the roots in Judeo-Christianity, which is too obsessively judgmental and goal-oriented as compared to the temperate and relatively now-oriented Greek view of life. His investigation and analysis take him through numerous figures of our tradition, up through the Hegels, Marxes and Nietzsches. He does not always do them full justice—though he is usually generous in admitting this too—but he tries to, and mightily, and for me this is the key book of modern historico-political theory. Camus is not a philosopher and says so, but he is a non-specialized thinker, a poetically visionary, intuitive one, rather like Heidegger's *Denker.* The wrestling with the absurd dimensions which I noted is right in line with the most sophisticated patterns of thought such as we find in Lacan, Foucault, and Jakobson. If he gets no final answers, it is because there are none, for these others as well.

The new social concern and the mature higher balance were already evident in ***La Peste*** of 1947. There is now a definite tilt away from the perfect tension or ambivalence of the absurd in the new formula: "There is more to admire in man than to despise"; such a tilt is, also, sideways, into the flow of time and humane emotion. The hero, Dr. Bernard Rieux, is described as being square-jawed, aged 35, and stocky. It would be hard to be more four-square balanced than that . . . Because of the new emphasis, Rieux is a doctor, and the people who are too individualistically concerned about (vertical) salvation, such as the Jesuit Paneloux and even the philosophical Tarrou, are somehow doomed and succumb to the plague, whereas an ordinary guy, the journalist Rambert who just wants to be happy with his girl, makes it. For similar reasons, the artist-figure Joseph Grand is cut radically down to humanity in that his art is risible though his decency is great; he too survives, partly because in the midst of the crisis he burns his manuscripts, which is a surefire way to lower your hubris. The later Camus was much concerned about his reputation, pride, and ego getting in the way of breathable life and creativity. Everything in ***La Peste*** moves in this direction in emphasis, though the vertical is preserved too in proper proportion through Rieux's meditative depth and even Grand's renewed art, in the end. The very tone of the novel is moderated, cool, a chronicle, with a new objectivity and workaday calm befitting the doctor narrator. The emphasis is collective, and the events of the chronicle are seen from several viewpoints. Fraternity, unpretentious struggle against a still-absurd fate which brings plagues that come and go when they want, courage with refusal of heroics, just life wanting to go on and be normally happy, all this had a considerable appeal to young people who were looking for guidance in a world without much belief after the second World War.

One of his last books, and some think his best, was ***La Chute,*** of 1957. It is a bitterly funny portrait of a former Parisian lawyer living in Amsterdam. He had a golden youth and thought very highly of himself as a lover of his fellow man until one day he failed to respond to a dangerous call for help from a drowning woman in the Seine, and then his whole ego-structure collapsed. "The lights went out" on the party, as it did for Salinger's girls in *Uncle Wiggly in Connecticut* or, really, all of us privileged people. No longer being able to keep up an image of his goodness and innocence, he resorts to a stratagem of spreading universal sense of guilt; "misery loves company." This was his fall from a sort of grace, and his name and much of the symbolism allude to Saint John the Baptist and the theme of baptism which the plunge into the nocturnal river would have been, a sacrificial descent leading to salvation, rebirth. So he calls himself a "false prophet," living in duplicity like all the rest of existence, and this is the constant, searingly amusing theme: all our little self-deceptions and hypocrisies are paraded before us. And there is the higher duplicity of the Hegelian notion that evil is just a part of the on-going synthesis of good and evil, which Kierkegaard trenchantly revolted against with his either-or. Camus is solidly, underneath, on the side of Kierkegaard here, though he is never mentioned. The muddy, verbose dialectics of his own time, Sartre's included, are being subtly invoked. But the pure light of the Greek islands stands for that clear innocence we can never find again in our northern mists amid the hustling, hassling, self-seeking, lobbying, conniving, half-lying millions in our semi-polluted cities like Amsterdam, the site of one of the greatest crimes in history, as Camus puts it, the genocide of the Dutch Jews. But the protagonist, Jean-Baptiste Clamence, goes rattling on about this and that, always worrying about his own self-justification. He even tries to pull Jesus down to his all-too-human size, seeing him as guilty because of his awareness of the children of Rachel, the slaughter of the Innocents killed for his sake, and he hears the cries of Rachel refusing to be consoled. Here, Camus and Clamence want us to break through at least for an imagined instant, a flash. There is not the slightest question of Clamence speaking for Camus, as some (like Simone de Beauvoir) thought; Camus denied this roundly in an interview, and poured scorn on Clamence. No, but in those break-through moments, we see the original Camus whom Patrick McCarthy and others rightly deem a deeply religious man without a church—a man who could reject organized religion and the afterlife again and again and, yet, say to an interviewer "The anti-religious view is vulgar," or "God is beauty", and speak of the sacred as the *only* resource—a Value—against the ruthless nihilistic plunge into merely secular history. A beggar who comes up to Clamence in the street whispers humbly "We have lost the light." Those few words are quite sufficient for those who have eyes to glimpse with.

Camus in an interview put truth above all other values, but as we noted, he was a good-hearted decent man and, on the whole, he was a sort of higher centrist. He stayed in the middle of controversies such as the Algerian war for independence, and at the end of ***L'Homme révolté*** he comes out for a whole series of mid-positions: moderation in revolt, the mild, reasonable Mediterranean, and an idea of Europe as being humanly in-between excesses in Russia and technology-driven America (as he saw it then); the village as opposed to big cities—he rather loathed New York and did not often care for Paris—or rural emptiness on the other side; the season, as of the harvest, between overambitious teleological or eschatological reaches of time or the too short sighted daily perspectives; the trade-union movements in politics; and so on. He spoke for the centered literary work, e.g., the novel, as against formalistic art on one hand and journalism on the other; and it was supposed to be balanced between private concerns and public. As a novelist, he was a daring innovator, and yet he spoke again and again of his love for the French classic era and style: Pascal, Molière,

Madame de LaFayette. He wanted to write a modern tragedy, and, in a fine essay, he saw tragedy as arising on its two august occasions, in Greece and Renaissance Europe, between an age of faith declining and a rising age of reason. Altogether he was a sublime muddler-through, in the enlightened middle as it were. That is not a comfortable position to be in, especially when everyone else is taking sides as they usually do. You get hit by both parties at times, like a referee. Politics is not carried on this way and he can be said, in brief, to be largely apolitical despite his struggles to pitch into his time. McCarthy calls him "indifferent" in contradiction to the popular image of Camus as a moral leader, but that is excessive. No, he was a fiercely caring man, but in his own far-seeing and superior way. At times, of course, these higher syntheses drop into a dreadful opposite of nothingness, indifference in that sense, and Camus with his recurring tuberculosis, certainly had his black or zero moments; his friend, Martin du Gard, even spoke of his misanthropy. But taking that with the sacrificial and deep concerns, still, all in all, including the sensitivity, the courage, the lucidity, the culture, the style, the sense of humor, he was probably what we Americans all along tended to think he was: beyond all intellectual fashions and ideological factions, the finest, most authentic voice of his age.

Vicki Mistacco (essay date 1992)

SOURCE: "Mama's Boy: Reading Woman in *L'Etranger,*" in *Camus's L'Etranger: Fifty Years On,* edited by Adele King, St. Martin's Press, 1992, pp. 152-69.

[*In the following essay, Mistacco offers a psychoanalytical feminist reading of* The Stranger, *drawing attention to elements of femininity in the pre-oedipal relationship between Meursault and his mother.*]

In his last interview, when asked what he felt critics had most neglected in his work, Camus replied: 'La part obscure, ce qu'il y a d'aveugle et d'instinctif en moi.' Many have since sought to approach this dark, enigmatic side from the perspective of psychoanalysis, emphasising, as Freudian and Lacanian orthodoxy requires, the oedipal moment, and in so doing repressing or devaluing the maternal bond, giving primacy to the phallus and the threat of castration. To my knowledge, however, no sustained effort has been made to view Camus's writing from the perspective of psychoanalytic *feminism,* stressing rather the importance of the *pre*-oedipal stage in which the primary figure is not the father but the *mother* and the primary relationship is a dual not triangular one, between mother and child. Feminist critics have most often adopted this approach to study the mother/*daughter* dyad in *women* writers. Shifting the context, I propose here to effect a kind of 'naive' reading, to 'overread' Camus, as if he were a woman writer, for traces of the relationship between the feminine and text production, bracketing psychoanalytic orthodoxy to allow the 'underread,' the feminine maternal, to emerge from the shadows of critical repression and be seen in Meursault's revolt in ***L'Etranger,*** the text's ambiguities, and the author's concept of the Absurd. By referring positively to Meursault as a 'mama's boy,' I am drawing upon the hero's infantile vocabulary to suggest the transgressive potential in this relationship and to question the term's pejorative cultural connotations of a somehow 'effeminate' boy whose excessive attachment to the mother extends scandalously beyond the 'normal' time.

It is difficult to appreciate the consequences of this critical move without a sense of the constraints of previous masculinist psychoanalytic interpretations. These have instituted and reinforced a kind of *doxa,* a rigid hermeneutic grid that only permits repetition of the same, phallocentrism, and generates the greatest degree of critical excitement around the ideas of incest and castration.

The standard procedure among the Freudian critics is to interpret all of Camus, and especially ***L'Etranger,*** in the light of ***L'Envers et l'endroit,*** a collection of autobiographical essays first published in 1937 just prior to the composition of ***L'Etranger,*** then republished in 1958 with an all-important preface in which Camus points to the childhood world of poverty they evoke—and above all the silent mother—as the source of his work. These critics then focus on two features of the mother/son relationship as portrayed in one of the essays, **'Entre oui et non,'** the boy's ambivalence toward maternal silence and an incident in which the mother is attacked by a male intruder and the son, called in to tend to her in her state of shock, ends up spending the night on her bed watching over her. Camus uses the third person to refer to the son in the recollected past, distancing himself from what may in fact be fiction or fictional transposition of lived experience for aesthetic ends, something most Freudian critics tend to overlook, keen as they are to (re)discover the 'events' determining Camus's psyche and writing that will allow them to replay the usual gynophobic Freudian scenarios.

Let us first consider maternal silence. Camus's mother as depicted in ***L'Envers et l'endroit*** was nearly deaf, practically mute, inarticulate, feeble-minded, illiterate. Conversation between mother and son was sparse as the mother withdrew into a solitary, immobile, and unreflective world of silence. On the one hand, her silence is described in positive terms as a form of presence and plenitude ('"A quoi tu penses?" "A rien," répondait-elle. Tout est là, donc rien'), timelessness ('un temps d'arrêt, un instant démesuré') and knowledge ('A se taire, la situation s'éclaircit. Il est son fils, elle est sa mère. Elle peut lui dire: "Tu sais"'). On the other hand, it inspires fear and pain in the young boy and is presented negatively as 'mutisme', 'irrémédiable désolation,' 'silence animal' and as a form of indifference reinforced by deprivation of maternal caresses and linked with feelings of estrangement and strangeness (*'L'indifférence de cette mère étrange!'*).

According to Costes, Gassin, Lazere, and other Freudian critics, this ambivalence and the frustrations that the mother's seeming indifference 'must have' (a key phrase in these analyses) caused the child, led to a splitting of her imago as a defence mechanism. She thus becomes both Good Mother and Bad Mother and is endowed with both maternal (good) and paternal (bad) characteristics, including in the latter instance, a phallus. What is interesting is that although Camus stresses in these essays ambivalence and tension *maintained* between opposing notions which ultimately revert back to the mother ('Entre cet endroit et cet envers du monde, je ne veux pas choisir, je n'aime pas qu'on choisisse'), for all these critics the scales definitely tip toward the Bad or Phallic Mother whose phallus is her silence. Costes goes so far as to say that the Phallic Mother presides, 'en maîtresse absolue' over the early cycle of the Absurd. Clearly, this type of simplification is commanded by the critic's own desire for unity, an unproblematised unity which, unlike the one I see at work in Camus, enables interpretive mastery of the author's psyche and writings and a repetition of the same, the masculine, the valorised term. The Good Mother and the positive attributes of her silence are essentially dismissed as an idealisation, a defence wrought by castration anxiety. The persecuting phallus turns out to be nothing but a mask for the mother's lack and her silent mouth none other than a castrating *vagina dentata.* Critical gynophobia is transformed into the hermeneutic key that will unlock the secrets of Camus's work protecting us all (all of us men) from the enigmatic Sphinx who devours young men: 'l'oeuvre entière de Camus n'avait d'autre fonction-de son seul point de vue inconscient, évidemment-que de combler ce silence maternel, véritable gouffre à fantasmes.' The threatening hole must be filled, repressed, covered up with a phallus, lest the 'nothing' be acknowledged to harbour a something and the 'admirable silence' that Camus sets forth in the preface as the centre of his work and an ethical model be viewed positively. Contradictions must be swept aside by the 'symbolisme latent et négatif' of the Mother psychoanalysis relentlessly rediscovers.

The second critical move, involving slippage from the pre-oedipal to the oedipal, from positive symbiosis to incest, and from maternal discourse to 'incestuous language,' may be discerned in the standard Freudian interpretations of the scene of the attack on the mother and the ensuing night with her son. Gassin and Costes are essentially in agreement that this is Camus's version of the primal scene fantasy—that of the child's witnessing of parental intercourse—with its accompanying panoply of sadism, masochism, and guilt. It is an anxiety-inducing scene in which the mother appears to castrate the father and incorporate his penis. The son's identification with the aggressor, here seen as his taking the place of the aggressor/father in his mother's bed, yields guilty incestuous feelings as well as anxiety about his own potential castration by father and mother combined. Only Lazere suggests that the night shared by mother and son on the same bed may be interpreted as a fantasy of the womb, a pre-genital fantasy of symbiotic union with the mother, although, retrospectively, he too shifts to a negative oedipal interpretation in analysing the remainder of the essay. Incest is clearly but one possible interpretation of the scene which may also be read in a way that highlights pre-oedipal union where vivid memories of the womb subsist and where the simultaneous breathing, the solitary bonding of mother and child against the rest of the world ('Seuls contre tous. Les "autres" dormaient, à l'heure où tous deux respiraient la fièvré'), even abolishing the outside world ('Le monde s'était dissous'), and 'les liens qui l'attachaient à sa méré,' are most important. To view ***L'Etranger*** 'dans son ensemble,' not to mention all of Camus's *oeuvre,* in the exclusive light of an oedipal and primal scene interpretation of this one episode is to blind oneself to the workings of the maternal in Camus and to foreclose all possibility of a hermeneutics of the feminine. It is hardly surprising, then, that Costes should fail to recognise a crucial distinction in his own terminology when he conflates 'la langue maternelle' with 'le language incestueux' as the aim of Camus's literary discourse.

Barthes pondered in *The Pleasure of the Text,* 'Doesn't every narrative lead back to Oedipus?' I suggest we reformulate the question, asking 'does every narrative *have* to lead back to Oedipus, even if the subject is male?' Perhaps the oedipal perspective is not, as Freud would have it, 'the only angle on the pre-oedipal.' Freed from the oedipal grid, would we not also be freed from the requisite remarks about Camus's fear and hostility toward the mother and therefore toward women in general? Would we not then be able to see beyond obvious thematics—Meursault's treatment of Marie, his participation in Raymond's sordid scheme of revenge, his apparent indifference to his mother—and come to a more nuanced appreciation of the novel's ambiguities? And as feminists, to escape repetition of the same, must we not propose a feminist reading that is first and foremost a reading of the feminine?

What does this mean? To read the feminine is not primarily to psychoanalyse the hero or the author, but rather to draw attention to traces of maternal discourse, to the workings of the pre-oedipal in the signifying system of the novel. This frame of reference makes it possible to recontextualise previous critical findings and illuminate the text otherwise. Take, for example, the famous opening paragraph:

Aujourd'hui, maman est morte. Ou peut-être hier, je ne sais pas. J'ai reçu un télégramme de l'asile: 'Mère décédée. Enterrement demain. Sentiments distingués.' Cela ne veut rien dire.

Maman died today. Or yesterday maybe. I don't know. I got a telegram from the home: 'Mother deceased. Funeral tomorrow. Faithfully yours.' That doesn't mean anything. Maybe it was yesterday.

This text represents the first cut, a disruption of undifferentiated pre-narrative existence that sets the story in motion. As such, it figures not so much a death as a birth, the cutting of the umbilical cord which precipitates the child into a first, pre-oedipal, signifying process not structured by the phallus, into a *process of differentiation* between self and other (Julia Kristeva on maternity, discussed in Jacobus). The first emblem of this process is lexical: 'maman.' In the absence of a father he never knew, Meursault seems to prolong into adulthood the pre-oedipal phase and the early linguistic relationship to the mother. Whether or not this is by choice, as his remark about abandoned studies suggests, is not immediately relevant. Many have noted Meursault's childish, simple vocabulary, his elementary syntax, his childlike attitudes, and infantile occupations (the games he plays to pass the time, his long hours of sleep). What interests me here is that, by ironic juxtaposition with the formal, stilted language of the telegram, a first incursion of the symbolic, the language of patriarchy, Meursault's infantile vocabulary and syntax reinscribe the pre-oedipal in much the same way as feminist theoreticians such as Kristeva, as both a marginal space and a space of dissidence, projecting into meaning lessness language as we know it: 'cela ne veut rien dire.' The feminine maternal thus becomes the vantage point for the crisis in language that is evidenced throughout the novel and for the crisis in meaning it engenders. The pre-oedipal archaic mother presides over a narrative of non-mastery, of meaning decontextualised and deferred, of unresolved enigmas: 'peut être . . . , je ne sais pas.'

At the threshold and in the margins of the narrative, the mother's body unsettles the border between absence and presence, inside and outside, beginnings and endings, perturbing, by this liminality, identity, representation, and truth. We never actually 'see' the mother's body: 'J'ai voulu voir maman tout de suite. Mais le concierge m'a dit qu'il fallait que je rencontre le directeur.' Paternal figures intervene to screen it. The concierge explains: 'On l'a couverte, mais je dois dévisser la bière pour que vous puissiez la voir.' Later the director reiterates the invitation to view the body in the casket. What this amounts to is maternal repression. From the point of view of the Symbolic Order, to look at the mother can only mean to see death—or lack, as the director's expression 'veiller la disparue' suggests. Above all, for patriarchy to function smoothly, the maternal body must simply be *buried,* for it is only after the burial, Meursault concludes, that 'tout aura revêtu une allure plus officielle.'

Situating the mother's absence differently, Meursault's refusal to view the body draws attention to society's repression of the maternal and rewrites feminine lack as dissidence. This is the real crime for which he is punished by the judicial system, the most ostentatious manifestation of the Law of the Father in the novel. In the words of the prosecutor: 'j'accuse cet homme d'avoir enterré une mère avec un coeur criminel.' This symbolic 'matricide' turn out to be in society's eyes the equivalent of patricide: Meursault has threatened patriarchy by killing its body-effacing image of the mother.

The pre-oedipal attachment to the mother is not without contradiction and attempts at distancing, however, just as her procreating body itself marks a space of differentiation. By putting her in an old-people's home, Meursault has reenacted an infant's primal distancing from the mother as not-yet-object. To explain his impassiveness at the funeral, he tells his lawyer: 'Tous les êtres sains avaient plus ou moins souhaité la mort de ceux qu'ils aimaient.' We need not invoke the oedipal drama, incest, maternal indifference or rejection to account for these apparently negative moments in the son's relationship to the mother. They are part of the self-differentiating process that brings about subject-formation and therefore a pre-symbolic type of signification, a process Julia Kristeva has called 'abjection': 'A massive and sudden emergence of uncanniness, which, familiar as it might have been in an opaque and forgotten [pre-natal?] life, now harries me as radically separate, loathsome.' The 'abject' or maternal pseudo-object represents a first attempt to distinguish ourselves from the maternal entity even before we exist outside her through the autonomy granted by language. The mother in this perspective is same-but-different and the mother/child relationship is one of estrangement as well as union. It seems difficult not to recognise in these the ambivalent terms of the mother/son relationship in ***L'Envers et l'endroit*** also, and not to read a reference to abjection in that ur-text of the maternal in Camus, the first entry in the ***Carnets:*** 'le sentiment bizarre qu'un fils porte à sa mère constitue *toute sa sensibilité.* Les manifestations de cette sensibilité dans les domaines les plus divers s'expliquent suffisamment par le souvenir latent, matériel de son enfance (une glu qui s'accroche à l'âme).' '*The bizarre feeling that a son has for his mother constitutes* all his sensitivity. *The expressions of this sensitivity in the most varied spheres can be sufficiently explained by the latent, material memory of his childhood (a glue that sticks to the soul)*'. Union and estrangement/abjection at once, not only are these the basis of Camus's art, they also anticipate the fundamental contradiction of the Absurd.

Neither fully absent nor present, dispersed and disseminated, the mother's body returns with insistence throughout the novel. During the vigil, Meursault unconsciously discerns its every presence everywhere, from the Arab nurse with her back to him whom he imagines knitting and whose face is covered except for her eyes, to the silent old women with their huge, bulging stomachs protruding under their aprons. These are all anonymous, marginal figures of subordinate otherness with respect to the dominant white, French male colonialists represented here by the paternalistic director and to a certain degree by the concierge—both refer to the old people as 'the others.' But seen through the eyes of Meursault these enigmatic characters recast difference as differentiation rather than polar opposition reducible to the dominant term, just as they multiply and disperse, same and different, the body of the mother—silent, gazing, or pregnant—from whom the child has been severed. Similarly, the old woman's crying and the toothless old people's bizarre sucking sounds displace the infant's instinctual behaviour after being torn from the womb. In this entire episode of the vigil, Camus is calling attention to the originary trauma of birth which creates a space at once separating and linking mother and child where otherness and dissidence may eventually find a voice. The mother's body and her body language—her silence, her gaze ('Quand elle était à la maison, maman passait son temps à me suivre des yeux en silence'), replicated in the judgmental looks and silent intimacy of the old people—become the potential site of an alternative non-symbolic discourse of vigilance, repressed anger, and truth that would unsettle the institutions of patriarchy.

A less obvious attack originating in the maternal takes place on the level of naming. 'Maman' may be buried, but her name surfaces everywhere confounding identity and blurring gender distinctions. The already reduplicated 'ma' reappears in the names or designations of other female characters; *Marie,* 'la *Ma*uresque,' 'l'infir*m*ière *a*rabe,' 'la petite femme auto*m*ate,' 'la femme de *Ma*sson.' But, more importantly, the infant's rhythmic, pre-discursive signifier is disseminated in the names of practically all of the *male* characters as well: Em*ma*nuel, *Ma*sson, Sala*ma*no. In the case of R*aym*ond, as if to compensate for the reversal of phonemes, the maternal is inscribed in Sintès, Camus's own mother's maiden name. The feminine maternal surfaces as non-expressive rhythm, word-play, traversing the symbolic and displacing the founding opposition of female to male upon which the entire oppressive dialectics of patriarchy rests. Summing up this subversive gesture by which sexual difference and the categories it supports are confused and exceeded is the name of the mother's fiancé: Tho*mas Pérez,* 'maman/père,' mama/father.

An apparently marginal figure, Thomas Pérez is nonetheless present at two strategic moments: the beginning where Meursault's lingering fascination yields perhaps the most elaborate, if repugnant, physical portrait in the novel and the climactic final revelation in which he comes to understand why, on the eve of death, his mother had taken a fiancé. This and the fact that a substantial portion of the opening chapter is devoted to Thomas Pérez suggest that this figure merits even more scrutiny than his name alone would warrant. The director's embarrassed dismissal of his relationship with Mme Meursault as 'childish' intimates that here too we might look for subversive traces of the feminine maternal or, more generally, Woman. What is 'embarrassing' to the director and fascinating to Meursault is the intimation by way of Pérez of the mother's sexuality, her existence as woman, both sexual and maternal.

Beyond the surface, in between or outside the categories of the symbolic, the most deeply repressed figure of the orgasmic mother points enigmatically to a truth other than man's, the half-herd truth of woman's *jouissance.* Thus, the text forges an elusive link between the mother, Pérez, the landscape, and truth. Meursault observes Pérez while the director explains that often Pérez and Meursault's mother would take evening walks to the village.

> Je regardais la campagne autour de moi. A travers les lignes de cyprès qui menaient aux collines près du ciel, cette terre rousse et verte, ces maisons rares et bien dessinées, je comprenais maman. Le soir, dans ce pays, devait être comme une trêve mélancolique.

> *I was looking at the countryside around me. Seeing the rows of cypress trees leading up to the hills next to the sky, and the houses standing out here and there against that red and green earth, I was able to understand Maman better. Evenings in that part of the country must have been a kind of sad relief.*

Access to maternal truth-*jouissance* will be indirect, via the landscape and/or Pérez. The mother earth figure, which others have discussed in Camus, is actually not a figure, a substitute for the mother's body that erases it. The conjoining of mother and earth is, in my view, a manifestation of the confusion of boundaries, of the mingling of same and other in non-contradictory synthesis, that Lacanian and feminist psychoanalysis attributes to feminine *jouissance.* The feminist psychoanalyst Luce Irigaray analogises this feature of woman's *jouissance* from her body:

> As for woman, she touches herself in and of herself without any need for mediation, and before there is any way to distinguish activity from passivity. Woman "touches herself" all the time . . . for her genitals are formed of two lips in continuous contact. Thus, within herself, she is already

two—but not divisible into one(s)—that caress each other.

In this light, the mother earth connection represents the insistence in the text of the mother's body as the locus of a non-figural truth beyond meaning and mastery. Thus, Meursault's final revelation, precipitated by sense impressions from the landscape, reconvenes the same elements, including some of the same phrases, that are linked in this passage:

> j'ai pensé à maman. Il m'a semblé que je comprenais pourquoi à la fin d'une vie elle avait pris un 'fiancé', pourquoi elle avait joué à recommencer. Là-bas, là-bas aussi . . . le soir était comme une trêve mélancolique. Si près de la mort, maman devait s'y sentir libérée et prête à tout revivre.'
>
> *I thought about Maman. I felt as if I understood why at the end of her life she had taken a 'fiancé,' why she had played at beginning again. Even there . . . evening was a kind of wistful respite. So close to death, Maman must have felt free then and ready to live it all again.*

Mersault's reading of Woman justifies his refusal of patriarchy and culminates in rejection of the binary oppositions that support it. Endings, of novels and of lives, are also beginnings, and in this non-hierarchical imbrication of opposites lie truth, freedom, and the real unity sought in Camus's writings. As we shall see, these are not the only traces of the feminine in the last pages of the novel.

Truth is in neither term of the opposition, but in between, 'entre', 'inter-dit.' Unlike the lighting at the vigil described by the concierge as 'tout ou rien,' 'she-truths' burst forth where contradiction is maintained. In 'Le vréel' ('she-truth' or 'true-real') Julia Kristeva theorises that in this space where the symbolic falters the pre-oedipal archaic mother surfaces and reclaims her right to language, pointing to ineffable *jouissance* and causing the real to appear as a jubilant enigma. This perspective is strikingly close to Camus's when he meditates on truth in **'L'Enigme'** (1950):

> Tout se tait . . . De nouveau, une énigme heureuse m'aide à tout comprendre . . . Le soleil . . . coagule l'univers et ses formes dans un éblouissement obscur . . . cette clarté blanche et noire qui, pour moi, a toujours été celle de la vérité.
>
> *Everything grows quiet . . . Once again, a happy enigma helps me to understand everything . . . the sun . . . coagulates the universe and its forms into a dazzling darkness . . . the white and black clarity that, for me, has always been the sign of truth.*

In the inscrutable, unimaginable space between alternatives in Camus's writing may be glimpsed an elusive 'mother's truth' whose roots are buried in childhood:

> Si ce soir, c'est l'image d'une certaine enfance qui revient vers moi, comment ne pas accueillir la leçon d'amour et de pauvreté que je puis en tirer? Puisque cette heure est comme un intervalle entre oui et non, . . . recueillir seulement la transparence et la simplicité des paradis perdus: dans une image.
>
> *If, this evening, the image of a certain childhood comes back to me, how can I keep from welcoming the lesson of love and poverty it offers? Since this hour is like a pause between yes and no . . . only to capture the transparency and simplicity of paradises lost: in an image.*

'She-truths' or the lost paradise of maternal *jouissance,* these represent both the source ('image') and the aim ('image') of Camus's thought and art. When it refuses to repress otherness, when it affirms non-hierarchically both elements of an opposition ('oui et non'; 'Il n'y a pas d'amour de vivre sans désespoir de vivre'), the discourse of the Absurd approximates a discourse of the feminine. By the same token, Meursault's celebrated indifference—apparent in such formulas as 'cela m'était égal,' 'dans un sens . . . dans un autre,' 'd'un côté . . . d'un autre côté'—may be understood not as difference annulled but rather as an illustration of this 'feminine' kind of difference.

Most important for their implications of alterity and for Meursault's evolution with respect to otherness are the Arabs. In much the same way as the mother the Arabs contribute to Camus's myth of utopian otherness. 'Ils nous regardaient en silence, mais à leur manière, ni plus ni moins que si nous étions des pierres ou des arbres morts.' These are the same silent looks as the mother's, looks of the oppressed/repressed whose silence may signify anger. They recall the alternative discourse of dissidence suggested in the attitude of the old people during the vigil and the blend of familiarity and estrangement we have traced to the pre-oedipal relationship to the mother. Marginalised, colonised, depersonalised, presented anonymously as 'Arabes' or 'groupes d'Arabes' or more exotically as 'Mauresques,' from an abstract semiotic point of view—though not, as many of Camus's critics have observed, a pragmatic, political one—they serve in ***L'Etranger*** to critique Western notions of identity and the self. In Part 2, the murmured communication between the crouching Arab prisoners and their visitors beneath the din of their French counterparts forms a 'basso continuo' that suggests the repressed semiotic subtext of the symbolic, a non-figural (hence the musical comparison to convey the impression their Arabic makes on Meursault) and more authentic form of communication ('malgré' le tumulte, ils parvenaient à s'entendre en parlant très bas').

Camus reinforces the association with the semiotic or dissident maternal discourse by juxtaposing the Arabs' conversation with the silent communication between two other characters, an old woman and her son, who stare intensely at each other. At parting their silent looks are seconded by gesture and the pre-discursive 'maman,' the only time it does not refer to Meursault's own mother: 'Il a dit: "Au revoir, maman"' et elle a passé sa main entre les deux barreaux pour lui faire un petit signe lent et prolongé.' Meursault describes the son as 'un *petit* jeune homme *aux mains fines,*' (italics mine) as if to emphasise his childlike relationship to the mother and a feminine trait that evokes the sameness-in-difference preceding the oedipal cut and the constitution of sexual difference.

If the Arabs carry all these positive, maternal connotations, then what does it mean to murder an Arab? As others have noted, this is the oedipal moment. Raymond has progressively dragged the passive Meursault into man's world: 'il m'a déclaré . . . que moi, j'étais un homme,' 'Raymond . . . m'a dit qu'entre hommes on se comprenait toujours.' Reflecting the Symbolic Order, this world of the white Western colonist grants Arabs and women existence only as subordinate others. Thus, Meursault is becoming more 'normal.' He agrees to marry Marie and recognises in the conventional Masson couple an image of his own conjugal future. In the murder chapter there is strong emphasis on traditional gender roles: the men go for a walk while the women do the dishes, the men get into fights and the women cry. Furthermore, Meursault is uncharacteristically patronising: 'Là, nous avons trouvé *nos* deux Arabes' (italics mine).

This process culminates in the murder. Raymond's revolver, itself emblematic of his phallocentric world, is symbolically related to the sun, the primary paternal symbol in the episode. The sun glints on the gun when he hands it to Meursault. But in this second encounter with the Arabs Meursault remains poised in a quasi-maternal world of equilibrium and suspended choices, of silence and water: 'tout s' arrêtait ici *entre* la mer, le sable et le soleil, le double silence de la flûte et de l'eau. J'ai pensé qu' *on pouvait tirer ou ne pas tirer*' (italics mine). '*Everything came to a stop there* between *the sea, the sand, and the sun, and the double silence of the flute and the water. It was then that I realised that* you could either shoot or not shoot.' When he returns to the beach alone, he is both rejecting Raymond's world with its stereotyped femininity and trying to shake off the 'blinding' sun which opposes his advance to the shade, repose, and the cool maternal spring ('je me tendais tout entier pour triompher du soleil'). The play of the sun of the Arab's knife becomes more obviously a metaphor for the threat of castration. The paternal sun in fact *prevents him from turning back* and pushes him toward the constitution of the Arab—and Woman—as polar Other. The associations between the Arab and Woman are numerous. Not only does the Arab occupy a space connoted maternal, he is lying in a 'feminine', almost seductive pose. And he is there to exact revenge on behalf of his sister. Finally, the sun here recalls the primal separation from the mother's body at the funeral: 'C'était le même soleil que le jour où j'avais enterré maman.' With the passive firing of the first shot under the influence of the sun, Meursault has destroyed 'l'équilibre du jour' and happy silence. He now fully enters the Symbolic Order, firing four more shots with Raymond's gun to complete the repression of Arab and Woman as Other.

Cut from the pre-oedipal by this act, Meursault will (re)discover in it a positive rhetoric of dissidence. The prison visit represents an important turning point in this development. Camus builds on the implications of maternal semiosis in the scene by devoting the rest of the chapter of Meursault's infantile regression. The prison cell becomes a womblike environment returning him to maternal wisdom ('C'était d'ailleurs une idée de maman . . . qu'on finissait par s'habituer à tout') and unsettling adult temporality, antinomy, fixed boundaries, as well as language: 'Je n'avais pas compris à quel point les jours pouvaient être *à la fois longs et courts* . . . ils finissaient par *déborder* les uns sur les autres. Ils y *perdaient leur nom.* Les mots hier et demain étaient les seuls qui gardaient un sens pour moi' (italics mine). '*I hadn't understood how days could be* both long and short at the same time . . . *they ended up* flowing *into one another.* They lost their names. *Only the words "yesterday" and "tomorrow" still had any meaning for me.*' But these pages also suggest the dangers of pure silence through the cautionary tale of the Czech who fails to speak his identity when he returns to his village after twenty-five years and ends up being killed by his mother and sister who have not recognised him.

Not until the final chapter, however, does Meursault emerge from his characteristic 'rien à dire' to speech. Before his outburst against the priest, his efforts at symbolisation are striking. He tries, for example, to represent the unrepresentable, the moment his heart will stop beating. More importantly, there is a long meditation on the guillotine, the core of which is the memory of a story his mother used to tell about the father he never knew. Access to the father occurs only via the mother who does not embody here the 'feminine' stereotype of a mute presence whose silence may be rich with meaning. She assumes rather the 'masculine' role of speaking subject, of storyteller, and in her story the father, unlike all the other paternal figures in the novel, appears in a positive light. For in his openness to the man whose execution he witnessed, in his refusal to perceive the assassin as absolute Other, in his bodily protest against death and the horror of the guillotine—he vomits, a reaction not unlike the body language of female hysterics—the father transcends traditional gender roles. Like Thomas Pérez, he mingles the maternal and paternal, the feminine and masculine, just as by speaking the mother embodies both masculine and feminine. In playing out sexual differentiation rather than difference, in suggesting a process, a back-and-forth movement between same and other rather than rigid divisions, the mother's discourse opens a space for the unrepresentable and offers in its form as in its content a model for an authentic language—and literature—of dissidence.

Assuming a feminine maternal posture, Meursault puts this discourse of dissidence into effect against the priest and in his climactic nocturnal vision. His revolt against the priest turns a passionate outcry into a reasoned rejection of the hierarchised world of Fathers and Others. The pre-oedipal origins of this revolt are suggested in the introduction to his tirade: 'Alors, je ne sais pas pourquoi, il y a *quelque chose qui a crevé en moi. Je me suis mis à crier à plein gosier* et je l'ai insulté' (italics mine). '*Then, I don't know why, but* something inside me snapped. I started yelling at the top of my lungs, *and I insulted him.*' Meursault identifies with the self-differentiating mother's body. He is both mother and child. The waters break and he gives birth to the cry, the semiotic of the infant converted into the language of protest of the adult. 'J'étouffais en criant tout ceci. . . .' '*All the shouting had me gasping for air.*'

By far the most spectacular feminisation of Meursault and the most far-reaching identification with the mother occur after the priest's departure in the closing paragraph of the novel. Calling upon those elements of nature already connoted maternal, Camus presents Meursault's revelation as an opening up to the mother: 'Des odeurs de *nuit,* de *terre* et de *sel* rafraîchissaient mes tempes. La merveilleuse paix de cet été endormi entrait en moi comme *une marée* . . . Je m'ouvrais pour la première fois à la *tendre indifférence* du monde' (italics mine). '*Smells of* night, earth, *and* salt air *were cooling my temples. The wondrous peace of that sleeping summer flowed through me like* a tide . . . *I opened myself to the* gentle indifference *of the world.*' If in the scene with the priest he identifies with the *procreating* mother, here his identification is with the *orgasmic* mother. Opening up to the maternal brings understanding of the mother's taking a fiancé and experience of the limitlessness and confusion of boundaries in maternal *jouissance:* 'maman devait s'y sentir libérée et prête à tout revivre . . . Et moi aussi, je me suis senti prêt à tout revivre.' '*Maman must have felt free then and ready to live it all again . . . And I felt ready to live it all again too.*' The world allows Meursault to reenact this positive movement between same and different, self and other: 'De l'éprouver si pareil à moi, si fraternel enfin, j'ai senti que j'avais été heureux, et que je l'étais encore.' '*Finding it so much like myself-so like a brother, really-I felt that I had been happy and that I was happy again.*' Maternal and fraternal, the world confounds feminine and masculine, just as Meursault figures in non-contradictory synthesis his mother, his mother's son, and his mother's daughter. Rather than a reversal of the sexual hierarchy with Woman in the dominant position, feminisation entails the displacement of opposition and 'results in an excess, a spilling over of categories and an ambiguous surplus of meanings.'

Meursault has learned to 'read' ambiguous maternal signs 'cette nuit chargée de signes et d'étoiles'—and in dying commits to turning his own body into an equally enigmatic Woman-sign capable of inciting revolt: 'il me restait à souhaiter qu'il y ait beaucoup de spectateurs le jour de mon exécution et qu'ils m'accueillent avec des cris de haine.' With death imminent, Meursault can never really translate feminisation and reading Woman into effective action in his own life. This can lead one to interpret the ending as a death-wish signifying pre-oedipal escapism rather than heroic dissidence. But if Meursault is viewed as *a sign to be read* and not just a character to be psychoanalysed, then like Janine in **'La Femme adultère'**—a more explicit figuration of Woman who also identifies with the orgasmic mother in a nocturnal ecstasy—he can be interpreted as an expression of Camus's own repressed feminine and as the positive outcome of his concerted effort to symbolise the maternal in art and praxis. However surprising it may seem to those who view him chiefly as the proponent of virile fraternity, Camus appears in fact to be one of those rare male writers of whom Héléne Cixous writes, who are 'able to venture onto the brink where writing, freed from law, unencumbered by moderation, exceeds phallic authority, and where subjectivity inscribing its effects becomes feminine.'

This gesture is not without its own ambiguity and I wouldn't be much of a feminist reader if I didn't end by problematising it. For in the long run we have to ask ourselves some questions. Does Meursault/Camus speak *for* or *with* the mother? Is the mother effaced as usual as subject and her discourse finally appropriated by man? Is this yet another instance of symbolic 'matricide' and a male fantasy of self-engenderment after all? But ambivalence toward the mother as enabling/engulfing, as eliminated subject yet object of a sustained quest, is as much a feature of women's writing (see, among others, [Marianne] Hirsch). Camus's artistic dilemma, so poignantly voiced in the preface to ***L'Envers et l'endroit,*** namely, to find a discourse of love that would 'balance' yet incorporate admirable maternal silence, reflects many women writers' entanglement with the maternal. Not until we approach the writing of men with the insights into the maternal and the critical tools gained from studying women writers will we begin to appreciate the primordial role played by Woman in the generation of literary texts.

Renee Winegarten (essay date March 1993)

SOURCE: "Camus Today," in *The New Criterion,* Vol. 11, No. 7, March, 1993, pp. 35-42.

[*In the following essay, Winegarten provides analysis of* Caligula *and Camus's literary preoccupations and career.*]

Camus, after Kafka, a fellow sufferer from tuberculosis, was haunted by judgment, by those who judge, and by the question of their right to do so. "Before the bar of history, Caligula, the bar of history!" cries Camus's odious yet fascinating Roman emperor. Caligula's very last words in the play, uttered with a gasping laugh as he is being struck down, are—astonishingly—"I am still alive!" Like so much of Camus's writing, with its deceptive surface of classical clarity, these words resonate with mystery as well as savage irony.

Caligula is still conscious of life, still full of life, when he is stabbed to death by the conspirators he awaits in a form of "superior suicide"; he is defiant and triumphant at the very moment when he is overcome and breathes his last. Does it mean that the spirit of this aspiring monster, who tests and goes beyond every limit on human conduct, is alive in the world and even in ourselves? That is what Camus once implied. Is Caligula one aspect of the plague that Camus later suggested can never be totally eliminated? What values remain, what embargo is there on violence and cruelty, if all is nothingness? Unable to pass beyond good and evil as a proper disciple of Nietzsche should, and obsessed with violence all his life, Camus hovered about the problem of inner and outer darkness, which somehow he could not elude. In this regard, Camus's work remains as central to the accumulating horrors of our age as ever.

In the first sketch of the conclusion of the play, which was to be entitled, tellingly, *Caligula or the Awareness of Death,* the emperor appears at the end saying, "No, Caligula is not dead. He is there, and there. He is in each one of you. If you were given power, if you had courage, if you loved life, you would see this monster or this angel that you bear within you break out." So wrote the young Camus in his early notebooks in 1937, with all his yearning for personal happiness, for the absolute, for the unattainable—together with his confrontation of danger within and without. Caligula was the role that Camus the actor and actor-manager originally wrote for himself to perform with the theater company he ran in Algiers as a young man.

Like all his work, even the most seemingly detached, the play is intimately bound to his own personal concerns. Even Caligula's weird anguished reach for the moon could derive from personal reminiscence for, according to Camus's brother Lucien, their frustrated and dominating grandmother used to speak of "having the moon." In **"Le Vent à Djémila"** (**"The Wind at Djémila"**), Camus declared: "You live with a few familiar ideas. Two or three. As a result of chance encounters with worlds and men, you polish and transform them. It takes ten years to have an idea that is really your own—one you could possibly speak about." Then he added with characteristic irony, "Naturally, it is a little discouraging." His imagination returns constantly to a few vital experiences and images.

The mirror is one recurring image. The reflection of himself in the mirror that endlessly fascinates Caligula is and is not the true self, that goal of authenticity for the artist and actor whose sense of alienation and solitariness Camus identified in his notebooks. "Et tout m'est étranger, tout . . ." ("And everything is foreign to me, everything . . ."), owned the author of ***L'Etranger*** (***The Stranger***). Added to this feeling of estrangement was the detachment of the creative artist, of the observer of human conduct, and of the actor (as defined by Camus in ***Le Mythe de Sisyphe*** [***The Myth of Sisyphus***]). Brought up under the French educational system to seek horizons beyond his working-class origins, Camus was an Algerian-born Frenchman who afterwards never felt quite at home either in Algeria or among the Parisian literary and intellectual élite.

Like his Caligula, Camus himself now stands before the bar of history: he, too, over thirty years after his death in a stupid car accident at the age of forty-seven, is very much alive. Among the signs of his enduring presence are two recent productions of ***Caligula,*** one of them given at the Comédie Française. The probing texts of a conference on Camus's theater, the most controversial part of his literary output (as distinct from his politico-cultural essays and journalism), have been published. The fiftieth anniversary of that widely read novel, ***L'Etranger,*** influenced by the American "though guy" school of James M. Cain, and first published in 1942 during the Occupation, has been duly celebrated in France.

Camus's fiction has long attracted filmmakers with intellectual pretensions like Luchino Visconti, who made a movie of ***L'Etranger,*** and Ingmar Bergman, who apparently regrets not having transferred ***La Chute*** (***The Fall***) to the screen. A new film has just been made of that strange allegory, ***La Peste*** (***The Plague***)—a work inspired by Kafka and Melville—by the Argentinian film director Luis Puenzo, who seems to have found similarities between Camus's Oran in the grip of the plague and the situation under dictatorship in his own country. One prospective filmmaker who wanted to film ***La Peste*** professed to see a link between the nihilism of Camus's era and that of the present day.

In addition to this activity, a selection of Camus's journalistic writings from 1944-47 in the Resistance newspaper *Combat* is now presented in English translation, with the evident conviction of their relevance to present-day affairs. In his sharp account of the aberrations of French intellectuals, few of whom escape whipping, Bernard-Henri Lévy declares: "I am fond of Camus. . . . A writer who is scarcely ever found wanting in nobility and courage is exceptional. Besides, I am sure he was amusing." (Like Kafka, Camus had a humorous side, and he himself once remarked that people did not take sufficient note of his sense of humor.) Given all this interest in his work in the spheres of stage, screen, and the written word, it looks as if the end of the Cold War has not dimmed Camus's reputation. Instead, this epoch-making upheaval has perhaps moved the angle from which the writer can now be viewed.

To return to ***Caligula,*** first performed in 1945: it marks—along with Camus's adaptation of William Faulkner's *Requiem for a Nun,* staged in 1956—a rare highpoint of his popular success in the theater. Each play offers an attempt to wrestle with the problem of evil in a life shorn of values. These dramas also reflect Camus's tireless (and possibly misguided) concern with the creation of a modern form of tragedy in an age that he found deeply tragic. (He though that Faulkner's powerful baroque novel, composed in semi-dramatic form, was "one of the rare modern tragedies.") It is well known that the original production of ***Caligula*** owed much of its impact to the début of the young Gérard Philipe in the demanding title role. Delicate and vulnerable in appearance, with the innocent air of a perverse adolescent, and endowed with the inimitable musicality of his voice, Gérard Philipe (all who saw him agree) has proved without equal as Caligula in conveying charm, vanity, cruelty, and ambivalence. By common consent, his successors, in France and elsewhere, however talented in other respects, have mostly been competent but ordinary, lacking charisma, unable to efface the original image of a unique presence that can still be felt even in theatrical photographs.

So it was with the recent staging of ***Caligula*** at the Comédie Française. The production there, under the aegis of the noted Egyptian film director Youssef Chahine, took the form of an elaborate conflation of ancient and modern in the current fashion, a mélange of togas and motorbikes, Rome and North Africa—visually striking and even cinematographic where perhaps simplicity might have fared better. The producer was not averse to changing the order of scenes to suit his own purpose. But which is the "correct" text? There are several versions of the play, which occupied Camus at different moments between 1937 and 1958, as he moved the emphasis of Caligula's revolt from the sphere of the cosmic and metaphysical, where it was placed originally, to that of the political and social, from solitariness to the implication of solidarity with humankind.

Shattered by the sudden death of his sister-mistress Drusilla, the all-powerful young Caligula embarks on a series of arbitrary acts of folly and cruelty. He (like his creator), and not only when he is impersonating the goddess Venus, is an actor-manager of considerable talent. His destructive indifference to human life and human suffering springs, paradoxically, from a passion for life. His monstrous madness has a certain absurd literal logic to it, breaking the hypocrisy of conventionally accepted norms and forms. If, for instance, the Treasury is to be regarded as all-important, then clearly human life is not. He shares the bitter sardonic humor of the atheist Meursault, condemned to death in ***L'Etranger,*** who rejects the spiritual comfort offered by the priest by saying that he is not interested in the things that do not interest him. Caligula's one merit is that he tries to force people to think about the truth of their condition, though finally he is driven to acknowledge that, in acting against other human beings, "I have not taken the proper path, I have achieved nothing. My liberty is not the right kind." On the stage, the play remains dark, difficult, disconcerting, and challenging.

What did Camus see in this catalogue of horrors to occupy him for so long? The simple commonplace that human beings die and that they are not happy sets the young Caligula on his frenzied path to make life give up its secrets, to change life as it is commonly lived unthinkingly. Camus was only about seventeen, fond of swimming and playing football, when he was struck down by tuberculosis: he thought he was going to die; he dreaded nothingness with "that physical fear of the animal who loves the sun." He was to suffer recurrent attacks of this illness for the rest of his life—a matter that is often overlooked. Latterly, much has been made of the fact that—like André Malraux—he came late to the Resistance. Where Malraux's commitment took the form of armed resistance, Camus's involvement was moral, in the shape of clandestine journalism for *Combat.* As "Albert Mathé" he was also engaged in underground activity that carried considerable risks of imprisonment, deportation to the camps, death. Given the state of his health, his conduct should seem creditable enough.

Camus's early years in Algeria had been marked by extreme poverty. His father, of French ancestry, was killed in the battle of the Marne in 1914 before the boy was a year old. His illiterate mother, of Spanish descent, found work as a cleaning woman to try to hold the family together. Yet such poverty, one possible source of his ill health, did not by his own account bring unhappiness, or preclude his profoundly sensuous and lyrical enthusiasm for the Algerian landscape, for the violent sun and radiant sea, the Roman ruins of Tipasa, the palimpsest of Djémila, all those life-enhancing elements of his youth that he would encapsulate in what he later liked to call the Mediterranean spirit. This was less an idea—to be scorned by academic philosophers—than a personal experience or response transformed into a value that would help to guard him (and, possibly, others) against the fearful destructive consequences of the powerful nihilistic ideologies that tempted him and his contemporaries.

It was not long before Camus's reputation was hedged about with misunderstandings. He was taken for the conscience of his age—a sort of French George Orwell—because he came to defend certain humane principles, and to advocate measure and the recognition of human limitations. Most notably he stood out against racialism, against the death penalty, against the criminality of "the end justifies the means," against the bloodshed of the would-be utopia of "the new man," against institutionalized murder on the grounds of "necessity" or for the supposed benefit of future generations. The Swedish Royal Academy, in awarding Camus the Nobel Prize for literature in 1957, cited his treatment of the problems facing the conscience of humanity at the time. Camus would scarcely have been human if he had not felt some gratification at his celebrity, at the path he had traversed from the poor district of Algiers. Yet he also knew that his fame as a kind of "secular saint" was a millstone around his neck, irritating some (notably one-time friends like Sartre and Simone de Beauvoir) and generally preventing people from seeing him as he truly felt himself to be.

Protest as he might, though, few appeared to pay much attention to his disclaimers. In a manuscript note to ***L'Homme révolté*** (***The Rebel***), Camus the Don Juan complained about the painful misunderstanding under which he labored: "I bear the weight of a reputation for austerity at once undeserved and rather ridiculous. If I have fought so firmly and uncompromisingly against those who legislated or killed in the name of the absolute, it is because I was aware of my own shortcomings and because I found only in them the permission to say that nobody is sufficiently just or pure to arrogate the right to judge without appeal. . . . Neither in my work nor in myself has there been an attempt to convert people to virtue but a logic that derives from frailty and a difficult struggle to attain to greater light. That is all." Years later, in an interview with the novelist and playwright Jean-Claude Brisville, published in 1959, Camus was still elaborating the same theme, declaring that his name as a guide and guru made him laugh.

Even in the very last interview he gave, in December 1959, he went on insisting that "I don't speak for anyone else: I've enough trouble to find my own manner of speech. I don't guide anybody: I don't know, or scarcely know, where I'm going. I don't live on a pedestal: I walk like everybody else in the streets of the day. I ask myself the same questions as men of my generation, that's all." In his acceptance speech in Stockholm he had quietly talked of being gifted with his doubts alone. "Why am I an artist and not a philosopher? It is because I think in accordance with words not ideas," he had once observed in his notebooks.

This tendency to work slowly and with no little effort toward a position that he can regard as true and just—one that is then held firmly and is publicly defended—may be traced throughout his life. What separates him from the "German friend" to whom he addressed those powerful "letters" in 1943-44? From an intellectual point of view, very little, it would seem, since they both derive from the same masters of nihilism, from Nietzsche and the rest. And yet it turns out to be a great deal, when Camus finally opposes the Nazi and his like, offering resistance in the name of humanity and justice. "I have chosen justice . . . so as to stay faithful to the earth," he wrote. "I continue to believe that this world has no supernatural meaning. But I know that something in it has meaning, and that is man, because he is the only being who demands meaning for himself." The determination to resist, to take a stand, has no sacred sanction, it is not rooted in some philosophical system. It is a free choice made from an inner propulsion ("I know"). Here, Camus's debt to André Malraux (in their photographs, even down to the manly cigarette ever hanging between the lips) is evident, in his attempt to rescue "man" from the forces that would destroy him. Camus's vocabulary derives from that of Malraux, in its assumption (characteristic of the day) that there is no need to mention woman in the definition of humankind.

Equally plain is Camus's debt to Henry de Montherlant's aristocratic view of "qualité" or nobility and a kind of Spanish point of honor. He shared Montherlant's reliance on scorn, and his distaste for the "shopgirl's morality" that in his opinion flourished under the Third Republic. Literature could still inculcate some of the attitudes of aristocracy even in those who were not born aristocrats. The seductiveness of Montherlant's writings lay in his prose, in his hedonism and his death-oriented nihilism. Yet ultimately Camus drew away from Montherlant. He came to reject Montherlant's stress on equivalence. For Camus, life cannot be regarded from the point of view of eternity.

A similar kind of slow development or revelation is to be found in the matter of the excesses of the purge at the Liberation. In the exaltation of the moment, in *Combat* on October 20, 1944, Camus could justify the purge in the name of a terrible law which obliged Frenchmen "to destroy a still living part of this country to save its very soul." Gradually, though, Camus moved away from his rallying call to revolution, from being the new "Saint-Just issuing alive from Malraux's *L'Espoir,*" as a contemporary expressed it, in the immediate post-Resistance period. He turned into the journalist who wanted neither victims nor executioners. It is clear, then, that when in 1951 Camus published ***L'Homme révolté,*** his influential critique of revolution (as indeed with ***Caligula*** in 1945), he was not composing a detached study or work but was writing out of his own temptations as well as those he witnessed among leading fellow writers and intellectuals.

It is from this angle that we should now view ***L'Homme révolté,*** that mine which many writers have since worked and reworked, a book once seen as integral to the polemics of the Cold War. (Indeed, this influential book would soon connect with the horrors of the Franco-Algerian War, which raged from 1954 until two years after Camus's death, with the use of torture on the French side and terror on the other.) The notorious polemic instituted by Sartre and his spokesman, Francis Jeanson (who even today expresses no regrets), on the subject of ***L'Homme révolté*** remains central to the history of ideas and to the culture of our age. The tone of Sartre's reply to Camus, criticizing the loftiness of Camus's objections to Jeanson's review, is not just deeply wounding, it intends to wound. It would be tough on someone unknown to the author: addressed to a sensitive friend whose every vulnerable spot is familiar, it is cruel. Whenever afterward Camus declares that he does not seek to put himself on a pedestal, one can be sure that he is still smarting from Sartre's accusation that he carries a kind of "portable pedestal" around with him.

Camus's working-class origin is coldly discounted by Sartre, who levels at him the deadly charge of turning "bourgeois" and of betraying the proletariat and the Left. Unlike Sartre, he was not prepared to defend Communism and the USSR at all costs, supposedly in order to save the workers from the loss of hope, from the harsh truth of what was going on there. The one-time ardent young Communist of 1935-37, who grew indignant when the party line changed and the Algerian Moslems were left to their fate, and who was expelled for his pains, would always see himself as a man of the Left. He was neither a liberal (in the European sense) nor had he gone over to the Right Wing whose luminaries sought to co-opt him. Moreover, during the Cold War, despite his loathing of Soviet tyranny, he could not give his whole-hearted faith to the United States because of the notion of "my enemy's enemy is my friend," and the policy of support for dictators, most notably for General Franco. Camus was extremely keen on his Spanish heritage through his mother, and he treasured his debt to it; he was emotionally attached to the distinguished actress Maria Casarès (daughter of Santiago Casares Quiroga, former prime minister of the Spanish Republic), who played leading roles in several of his plays; and his greatest friends in Paris were to be found among the Spanish Republican exiles.

Where Camus sought to take his stand was on truth and justice as he understood them: these were the great rocks that, like Sisyphus, he was endlessly pushing up the hillside to see them roll down again. His concern for them, and for moderation, came to save him from the self-righteous intransigence of Sartre, Simone de Beauvoir, and their allies as they favored first the USSR, and then Mao's China and each new and usually murderous revolutionary "utopia" in turn, in the name of a changed world and "the new man." In this way Camus eluded the deception, the lies, the passion for the extreme and, above all, the advocacy of the use of violence and the condonation of terror which besmirch the reputation of Sartre, Genet (if the word reputation may be used of him), and the Maoist intellectuals who followed.

This is not to say that Camus was lacking in a certain "nostalgia" (as his editor Roger Quilliot calls it) for the nineteenth-century Russian terrorists, like Ivan Kaliayev, who was responsible for the assassination of Grand Duke Serge in 1905—but then much of our culture is rooted in nostalgia for violence. Here was another contemporary temptation (see the celebrated opening pages of Malraux's *La Condition humaine,* with the terrorist's murder of a sleeping man). Camus depicted Kaliayev and his associates as "fastidious assassins" in ***L'Homme révolté,*** on which he was working when his play on the same theme, ***Les Justes*** (***The Just***), was first staged in 1949. They are seen as "fastidious," admired as pure, noble, and honorable because—unlike the terrorists of Camus's day and our own—they are ready to yield up their own lives after killing in the name of an ideal. As has been pointed out with regard to this specious view, murder is murder, no matter how refined the scruples of the assassin.

Certainly, by the time of the Algerian revolt, and the indiscriminate terror practiced by the FLN (the Algerian Front de Libération Nationale)—keenly supported and justified by Sartre and his circle—Camus made no secret of his opposition to political murder. He particularly scorned intellectuals who advocated terror and who sympathized with terrorists from the comfort of their armchairs. In a much commented-upon observation, he said that he put the life of his mother, who was still living in Algiers, first. In the end, with him as a writer and a human being, it was not just words but people that came before ideas.

A good deal of ink has been spilt over Camus's attitude to French colonialism in Algeria, especially by his judges on the Left or by the politically correct. Camus found himself in a cleft stick. By origin descended from settlers, he would have liked to keep a reformed, democratic Algeria linked to France. In his youth he had favored the reforms proposed by the Léon Blum-Maurice Vialatte bill, reforms that were stymied by powerfully entrenched French colonial interests. As a young journalist he had written a moving report on poverty among the inhabitants of the Kabylie region. He was outraged by the terrible repression of the uprising at Sétif in 1945, which left many dead. After all, he was brought up among Algerian Moslems, some of them future political leaders, who counted among his friends and acquaintances.

What he did not seem to take into account was the driving force of fanatical nationalism which, once unleashed, would inevitably propel Algeria to full independence, democratic or no. There was a certain naïve idealistic strain in Camus, one-time supporter of Gary Davis, the now long forgotten would-be citizen of the world. Camus tried to do what he could for peace and reconciliation: in January 1956 he went to Algiers to speak in favor of a truce. Events outstripped him. Thenceforward, fearing to aggravate the situation by public declarations, he intervened constantly behind the scenes on behalf of numerous Algerian Moslems who were on trial or in prison awaiting execution. The list of those he tried to save is long.

It was inevitable that the Franco-Algerian tragedy would leave Camus torn with ambivalent feelings. Central to his impassioned self-inquiry is the masterly monologue ***La Chute*** of 1956. There, Camus probed the theme of "Judge not, that ye be not judged," with its religious connotations. Now, after the Fall, nobody can be innocent. The work is a cry of critical and self-critical irony, issuing from his own profound self-dissatisfaction as well as from his acute perception of the self-righteousness and self-deception of his pontificating fellow intellectuals on the Left who judged him to be a traitor to the cause. That super-subtle former lawyer, Jean-Baptiste Clamence, heir to Diderot's eccentric personage, Rameau's nephew, has left France for Amsterdam, abandoning his profession, spending his time there in button-holing strangers, like the one whose responses can only be gleaned from the words of Clamence himself.

Clamence's sustained sardonic confession provides at the same time a way of accusing everyone else. The details of his disquisition or indictment are left deliberately vague, and are constantly being called into question, so that his words have a wide reference. Are all of the utterances of this womanizing self-styled actor really true? There is reason to doubt it. The great sin of omission that (he claims) changed his life as a do-gooder of repute, his failure to respond to the cries of a drowning woman, can stand for all sins of omission and commission, all the acts that obsess the human conscience with the burden of guilt and destroy the virtuous self-image. The piece is a sustained dramatic parable where the judge-penitent flays human weakness in himself and in others: ". . . I am concocting a portrait which is that of everyone and no one. All things considered, a mask. . . . Yet, as the same time, the portrait I offer my contemporaries turns into a mirror," says Clamence. Here is a later version of Caligula's mirror—the reflection of the darkness within.

Where does Camus stand today now that the Cold War, in whose intellectual or cultural history he figured so largely, has come to an end? The collapse of the Communist system in the USSR and its former satellites has not actually eliminated die-hard Communism and the many shades and varieties of radical Left Wing sympathy. (The ability of members of extreme movements of Left and Right to shed skins in renewal, like the snake, has been witnessed countless times.) That collapse has merely shown up the bankruptcy and bad faith of the intellectuals who championed Stalin, Mao and the rest, and who whitewashed terror as a political instrument. Certainly, the cry of violent revolution as a substitute faith or a fashionable shibboleth is not being heard at the moment. In this sense, the mature Camus has been vindicated.

Yet to regard the end of the Cold War between the superpowers as a victory for liberal democracy and a new world order would surely be premature. Camus well knew that freedom—like truth and justice—has to be conquered. Violence and terrorism have not been erased from the imagination or from actuality. A Pandora's box of moral, political, and economic ills has now been opened: extreme nationalism, racialism, religious zealotry, "ethnic cleansing," together with Fascism and Nazism, have reappeared in late-twentieth-century Europe. An idea, however perverse, cannot be killed. It goes underground to re-emerge when times are ripe. In *Le Monde* of December 5, 1992, that well-known authority on Sartre, Michel Contat, could inquire whether Marxism has taken refuge in the catacombs.

Toward the end of Camus's allegory ***La Peste,*** there is a shatteringly resonant passage: "But he knew nonetheless that this chronicle could not be that of the conclusive victory. It could only be the witness of what had had to be accomplished and what, doubtless, all men . . . would still have to accomplish against terror and its tireless weapon. . . . For he knew what this joyous crowd did not know: . . . that the bacillus of the plague never dies or disappears, that it can remain dormant for dozens of years in furniture and linen, that it waits patiently in rooms, cellars, trunks, handkerchiefs and bundles of papers, and that, perhaps, the day would come when, for the misfortune and the education of men, the plague would reawaken its rats and would send them to die in a fortunate city." In ***La Peste*** the plague is not only Fascism and Nazism, perverse ideology, violence, injustice, inhumanity, dictatorship, and the Occupation of France: in one of its aspects, the plague is life itself and all the ills and evils that flesh is heir to. The warnings of Camus are there to remind us of a never-ending struggle where we are not granted to complete the work.

As Camus wrote in 1950 in an essay entitled **"L'Enigme"** (**"The Enigma"**): "In the darkest moment of our nihilism, I looked only for reasons to go beyond that nihilism." Not, he added, out of virtue or loftiness of soul but out of a passion for light and life. In Aeschylus, he suggested, there is an enigma, a meaning deciphered with difficulty because it dazzles the view. Something of that kind of enigma is to be found in his own works. Indeed, it is neither as a "secular saint" nor as the partisan of a particular cause that Camus should be viewed today, but as a fallible human being who made mistakes and was aware of many of his own shortcomings, who struggled for justice and decency, and whose writings stand as moving testimony to that struggle. He could be wrong at times, of course, but the amazing thing is how often he was in the right, and how much he still has to say to us in a dark hour.

Robert R. Brock (essay date Spring 1993)

SOURCE: "Meursault the Straw Man," in *Studies in the Novel,* Vol. 25, No. 1, Spring, 1993, pp. 92-100.

[*In the following essay, Brock provides an overview of critical interpretation of* The Stranger. *According to Brock, scholarly debate centered upon psychoanalytical speculation obscures the novel's primary significance as a treatise against capital punishment.*]

Although d'Ormesson was referring to the critic's approach to literature in general, it should be obvious to anyone reading learned articles on ***L'Etranger*** that he could have had their treatment of Camus' short masterpiece specifically in mind. This desire to explain, rather than to understand, means that the book will not be discussed as a whole, as an entity, but as a series of all but unrelated segments. There may well be some discussion of the story as a manifestation of the *absurde,* as well as arguments over just what that word entails, but the book will be examined primarily as an expression of some political, social or psychological cant based on a subjective reading of one or two scenes.

For most critics, the book is either an indictment of the French judicial system that deprives the proletariat of an effective voice by stealing its language, or it is the case-study of a man with more Oedipal problems than even Freud ever dreamed of. One doesn't have to spend much time in a musty library to verify my charge: Ben Stoltzfus has already done the essential legwork for his article "Camus' *L'Etranger:* a Lacanian Reading." Perusing it will prove d'Ormesson's point, and mine; some scenes will be "explained," but the basic message of ***L'Etranger*** will not be noticed, let alone understood.

Stoltzfus's research shows that Meursault is either a nihilistic juvenile delinquent (René Girard) or a man of rigorous honesty (Germaine Brée). He could have been condemned to the guillotine because he won't play the game (Sartre and Robert Champigny) or because he is inept and wants to die (Monique Wagner). The death of the Arab was either an accident (Louis Hudon) or a *crimen ex machina* (Girard). On the other hand, perhaps the judges condemn Meursault in order to "destroy the truth he embodies" (Albert Maquet). Of course, the whole thing might be a *fatum* as in ancient Greek literature (Carl Viggiani).

As to the four extra shots that baffle the judge, J. H. Mathews says they might be the first manifestation of Meursault's will, while Hudon sees them as an expression of exasperation. However, Julian L. Stamm is certain that Meursault was really a homosexual and that the shots on the beach were ejaculations. In his article, Stoltzfus goes on to note that Brian T. Fitch has covered these and various other interpretations of ***L'Etranger*** in his study and concludes by citing Alain Robbe-Grillet's comment, "I am the stranger." (*L'étranger, c'est moi*). Stolzfus then comes to the very dangerous conclusion that the book is "a work that reads the reader." In other words, "We each read the book with our own unconscious desire."

The unfortunate thing here is that he is right. It is unfortunate in that a too personal identification with the work, or its hero, leads to readings that are then presented to us not as one person's very subjective interpretation of, in this case, ***L'Etranger,*** but rather as objective, self-evident truth. The book becomes then *not* what the author wrote in fact, but what the critic would have written/meant given his/her personal bent had he/she written it. The critic does not say, for instance, this scene makes me think that Camus may have wanted to supplant his father in his mother's bed, but that it is perfectly obvious that he wished to do so. As Hudon wrote in his essay on ***L'Etranger,*** "Many put their nickel in the philosophical slot, and existentialism comes out of everywhere, others in the new critical slot, and it rains symbols."

Critics are willing to quote authors on any given subject save one: what the authors think of critics. Stoltzfus, whose article presents a highly personal view of ***L'Etranger,*** takes Freudians to task and insists that his approach is the only valid one. (For those who do not subscribe to either dogma, the difference between them is not all that obvious.) In any event, perhaps all critics should read, or reread, what Sartre had to say about literary criticism.

> When I picked up a book, it made no difference if I opened it and closed it twenty times, I could see that it didn't change. Sliding over this uncorruptable surface: *the text,* my sight was only a minuscule surface accident, it disturbed nothing . . . I left my bureau, turned off the light: invisible in the darkness, the book continued to

> glow; for itself alone. (*Quand je prenais un livre, j'avais beau l'ouvrir et le fermer vingt fois, je voyais bien qu'il ne s'altéait pas. Glissant sur cette substance incorruptible le texte, mon regard n'était qu'un miniscule accident de surface, il ne dérangeait rien . . . je quittais le bureau, j'éteignais: invisible dans les ténèbres, le livre étincelait toujours; pour lui seul.*)

In other words, the reader has no part to play in the work. It exists independently of him and must be approached on its own terms and not as a mirror or manifestation, of "our own unconscious desire." *L'Etranger,* then, must be seen as a mirror of Camus' soul, not the critic's, a point to which I shall return.

Stoltzfus also quotes Robbe-Grillet's statement, "each of us has a tendency to conceive a history of literature that is his own story." (*chacun d'entre nous a tendance à concevoir une histoire de la littérature qui est sa propre histoire.*) That is, we tend to see literature as a reflection of ourselves. Stoltzfus gives this quote in order to shore up his argument for a Lacanian reading. He is correct in citing Robbe-Grillet, since this innovative author has based some of his method of writing, not his philosophy, on Camus, as evidenced in his critical essays. However, Robbe-Grillet does not approve of this sort of interpretation. He also wrote that there is no connection between man and things, where Stoltzfus, and others, see the word *lame,* used to describe both the waves and the knife blade, as being highly significant. (Has any such critic seriously wondered what choice of vocabulary items Camus had to describe knife blade and wave, [lame], or sea and mother, *mère* and *mer*? As the French say, there aren't thirty-six.) One must also wonder why such psychological interpretations are always predicated on the most morbid and/or prurient readings possible.

Robbe-Grillet, in any case, does not see things the same way that Stoltzfus and the partisans of psychological interpretations do. For Robbe-Grillet, man is man and things are things and things do not have human qualities. This attitude will be seen as antihumanist and therefore criminal and—be ignored.

> The crime is to affirm that something exists in the world that is not man, that addresses no sign to him, that has nothing in common with him . . . he sees these things, but he refuses to appropriate them, he refuses to enter into any shady understanding with them, any complicity; he asks nothing of them. (*Le crime c'est d'affirmer qu'il existe quelque chose, dans le monde qui n'est pas l'homme, qui ne lui adresse aucun siqne, qui n'a rien de commun avec lui . . . il les* [*les choses*] *voit, mais il refuse de se les approprier, il refuse d'entretenir avec elles aucune entente louche, aucune connivence; il ne leur demande rien.*)

This statement is clearly counter to the Freudian and Lacanian approaches to literature.

Moreover, the difficulty of a conventional psychological interpretation of ***L'Etranger*** was noted by John K. Simon in his article in *Yale French Studies.* He considers the book to be the first successful novel in a contemporary movement that will lead to Robbe-Grillet and Claude Simon, a movement marked by its refusal of conventional social and psychological readings.

Critics who are partial to such interpretations have claimed that the beach scene that leads to the shooting is the first outburst of poetic writing in a book previously most noteworthy for its resolutely pedestrian narration and that it must therefore have special significance. Forgetting the wake, the funeral procession and their figura, such critics should at least look at the afternoon and evening Meursault spent on the balcony watching life in the streets. Even students reading their very first novel in French and struggling mightily with the simplest language, are struck by the sheer beauty of Camus' description. As Sunday came to an end, the streets were filled with strutting elegant young men and coquettish women meeting, flirting and joking. There were also the streetlamps and streetcars and their lights reflecting off damp pavement, bracelets and smiles. Camus describes the trees, the paling stars and all "until the first cat slowly crossed the again deserted street" (*jusqu'à ce que le premier chat traverse lentement la rue de nouveau déserte.*) What great psychological horror story are we to make of that?

It the description of the beach scene, the burning sun and the death of the Arab are more emotionally charged, is it really because Meursault is being pursued by some evil Mother? (Just why do critics who insist that he is being so pursued, and identify the Mother as being Meursault's, i.e. Camus', never speak of the loving relationship between Dr. Rieux and his mother in ***La Peste?*** Or did someone else write that book?) The style that an artist chooses normally corresponds to the events that he is describing. Thus the beach scene is in a more electrifying style simply because the act that will lead to Meursault's execution is more emotionally, and dramatically, charged than his spending a quiet day on his balcony and then going down to a now empty street to buy bread and pasta.

Robbe-Grillet speaks of ***L'Etranger*** in *Pour un nouveau roman* because Camus' hero resembles his own "heroes" in *Les Gommes* and *Le Voyeur,* heroes that were inspired, at least in part, by Meursault. Even though the literary goals of the two authors have nothing in common, Meursault embodies much of what Robbe-Grillet feels the new hero should be: a single name, no real, detailed past history, no face or physical description, no clearly defined profession or character. In short, none of the standard literary tactics that allow us to identify with the hero and vicariously share in his trials and tribulations. Comparing Meursault to any hero of Balzac or Stendhal should suffice to convince all but those most incurably wedded to the new criticism that no serious links exist between the two schools of writing and that Camus must have had something else in mind when he wrote this book. In the same way, Robbe-Grillet's affinity for Camus' technique, not for his philosophy, came from his belief that Camus had created a "new" literary hero. He had not, of course; he had simply re-invented the hero of the *conte philosophique*. In any event, Camus' influence can best be seen by comparing Wallas (from *Les Gommes*) and Mathias (from *Le voyeur*) to Rastignac or Julien Sorel, a comparison that should convince most that Robbe-Grillet also had something other than the conventional psychological novel in mind. If the doubters need further proof of Robbe-Grillet's thinking, they should read what he wrote in *La Jalousie*.

Two of the protagonists, A . . . and Franck, are reading a novel that takes place in Africa. The narrator, who listens and comments to himself but does not speak in the novel, notes that they never talk about the qualities of the text. "On the other hand, they often reproach the heros themselves for certain acts, or certain character traits, as they would for mutual friends." (*En revanche il leur arrive souvent de reprocher aux héros eux-mêmes certains actes, ou certains traits de caractère comme ils le feraient pour des amis communs.*) The same is true for the critics' treatment of ***L'Etranger*** even though they and Meursault are *not* mutual friends. Some, Girard, for instance, will condemn Meursault for his "crime" even though it is more than obvious that Camus does not. Camus' sympathy, if not affinity, for the accused and against the judges is a constant theme in ***L'Homme révolté.*** This attitude may well make some of Camus' admirers very uncomfortable. Nonetheless, he did write that if one cannot prove one's own virtue, an impossible task, the prisons must be opened. That statement is a reflection of his soul, his thinking, and his position on the question of punishment. As such, it is the only opinion that critics should take into account when discussing his works. The critics are free to disagree with his beliefs, but they have no right to falsify or to ignore them.

The major problem with standard political, psychological and sociological interpretations of ***L'Etranger*** is that they are by literary people who are in the business of seeking, and finding, learned interpretations of literary works. In his novel of student unrest at the University of Nanterre, Robert Merle, who, like Camus, was born in Algeria, presents us with a non-literary person. And an Arab at that. The Arab, Abdelaziz, is a laborer, not a university student. As such, he is interested in mathematics, not literature, since a simple night-school certificate will allow him to get a better job, while studies in literature will not. His would-be helper, a French student, and therefore an intellectual, insists that he read ***L'Etranger*** and *L'Immoraliste.*

As Abdelaziz knows, and points out, despite all the talk about the "absurd," the only thing that is really absurd is the story itself. As both Camus and Abdelaziz knew, there is simply no possibility that a respectable, gainfully-employed European would ever have been arrested, much less tried, convicted and executed, for having killed an Arab armed with a knife. At least not in the Algeria of 1940. (Let us not forget the Arab prisoners' reaction at finding Meursault, a European, among them.) But since the critics do not live in that place and that period, they have chosen to ignore that simple fact. They should have started by wondering why Camus would base his novel on an impossible situation.

In the same way, the critics have agonized over why he had Meursault kill an Arab. Camus has even been accused of being anti-Arab, an accusation that he probably found too grotesque to bother to refute even though some then mistook his silence for an admission of guilt. He could have cited the articles he wrote attacking the government for its mistreatment of Arabs in pre-war Algeria. But he didn't. Nor did he bother to cite the difficulties he had had with press censors, and the Communist Party, which, for political reasons, backed the government's anti-Arab actions. (How many of the new critics remember that Dr. Rieux refused to cooperate with the journalist, Rambert, when the latter informed him that he could not, or would not, print the whole truth on the Arabs' condition in Algeria?)

Moreover, in a footnote to a discussion of Hitler's Germany and the savage destruction of Lidice, Camus wrote. "We should note that atrocities which could remind us of these excesses were committed in the colonies (India, 1857, Algeria, 1946 etc.) by European nations who obeyed the same irrational belief in racial superiority." (*Il est frappant de noter que des atrocités qui peuvent rappeler ces excès ont été comises aux colonies* [*Indes, 1857, Algérie, 1945, etc.*] *par des nations européenes qui obéissaient au même préjugé irrational de supériorité raciale.*) That statement alone should put to rest all charges of his alleged racism.

But, as some critics continue to look for "proof" of his hatred of Arabs, we are asked to note that there is no Arab culture, such as mosques and souks, in the book. This argument assumes that Camus should have wished to be a latter-day Pierre Loti but I can see no reason for such an assumption. We are also asked to consider the alleged attack on his mother as a motive for the killing of the Arab. If one dares ask the question, "Why, if he hated Arabs to that point, did he not then indulge in language that would cast them in an unfavorable light?", one will simply be ignored, as the student ignored Abdelaziz's objections. The question that should have been asked is not "why did he kill an Arab?", but "Why did he *not* kill a European?"

Sartre was the first one to note that the book is not really a novel since there is no development in the character of Meursault. (He does come to a certain self-knowledge in prison, but that he has changed is very debatable.) He comes to us pretty much a fullblown figure such as we would find in a story by Voltaire. From this, Sartre deduced, logically, that the story is rather a *conte philosophique* in the same way that *Zadig* and *Micromégas* are. This type of literary work does not have as its primary goal the simple telling of a story. Rather, it has a point to prove or at least to demonstrate. Why should Camus have defended himself against those who read the book as an expression of their own unconscious desires or racism? Did Voltaire ever explain what he meant in his *contes?* Of course not. He assumed enough intelligence on the part of the reader to be able to determine that without his further help.

In any examination of ***L'Etranger,*** one must start with the question, why did Camus write the book? Certainly not for money, since he had no reputation that would lead to serious sales. Just as certainly not to tell a story, since there is no development in Meursault's character or conduct that could lead to a real story. Certainly not, and for the above reasons, to arrive at a philosophical position as Sartre did in *La Nausée.* As with Voltaire, there must have been such a position already determined. Since the one common bond of any importance between this work and, say, ***La Peste, Réflexions sur la guillotine, L'Homme révolté,*** etc., is the question of the death penalty, let us consider that to be the real subject of the book and see if such a conclusion can be justified. (If we wish to drag his father into the story, let us also remember that his father, who was in favor of capital punishment, witnessed an execution and was sickened by it. As was, finally, Tarrou of ***La Peste.***) In chapter five of ***L'Etranger,*** Meursault thinks about his father who had been, in contrast to Camus' own father, obliged to witness an execution and had also been revolted by it. At the time, Meursault was disgusted by his father's reaction, but now he understands him. "How had I not seen that nothing was more important than an execution and that, all in all, it was the only truly interesting thing for a man." (*Comment n'avais-je pas vu que rien n'était plus important qu'une exécution capitale et que, en somme, c'était la seule chose vraiment intéressante pour un homme.*) Moreover, in ***L'Homme révolté.*** Camus wrote, "We will know nothing as long as we do not know if we have the right to kill this individual who stands before us or to accept that he be killed." (*Nous ne saurons rien tant que nous ne saurons pas si nous avons le droit de tuer cet individu devant nous ou d'accepter qu'il soit tué.*) It is obvious, at least to me, that these quotes justify my reading of the novel as a pamphlet against the death penalty.

But, since the majority of people, at any given time, are in favor of capital punishment, how can one write a book against it and make it seem a despicable and unacceptable punishment? The answer, I feel, is by setting up a straw man.

As I said, the question that should have been asked is why Meursault did not kill a European. The answer is, because the European would have to be a "real" person and the Arab would not. That is, since Arabs had no real rights, and often no real identity, in the Algeria of Camus' youth, certain weaknesses in his story would go unnoticed if only because other Europeans, not Arabs, would read the book. If this reasoning bothers you, or seems specious, answer the following questions. Why does the Arab have no name? Why does he not have a face or age or profession? Why has he no family, no friends? Who speaks for him at the trial? No one! He simply does not exist other than as a means to get Meursault condemned to the guillotine. Even in *Le Grand dadais,* by Poirot-Delpech, a brilliant novel sometimes compared to ***L'Etranger,*** the victim had a name, if only Freddy, and two relatives, if somewhat remote. Here, there is nothing. O. Zero.

Why? Because it forces the reader to concentrate on Meursault, the alleged murderer. It shows him at work, at play. It talks of his friends, his dead mother, his loves, his future both before and after the shooting. He has neighbors, good and bad. (Raymond, too, exists only to get Meursault into a position where he will kill a non-person.) In short, it gives us a "murderer" but no victim, and the reader, Camus hopes, will be properly horrified at his unjust conviction and death sentence. And no one will notice that the Arab doesn't exist because Camus wants it that way. A European "victim" would demand, if not equal time of the author, at least a semblance of existence. Even the most minimal, the lowliest European would have what the Arab does not: family, friends, face, character, social position. A European victim might well have gotten the reader's sympathy and that would have drawn attention away from Meursault and his plight. Camus could not take that chance. A *conte philosophique* must always be played out with a stacked deck.

In a sense, it was the same in ***La Peste,*** a parable of the Second World War, that has only victims and no guilty. In that book, the rats came on their own, without a leader. There was no evil dictator or his minions to send people to the death camps and the incinerators. In both books, then, there is no one to really hate, no one to blame, no one to castigate, except, of course, the system itself that causes both death by war and death by guillotine. How very tidy.

In *Le Grand dadais,* our hero, Alain, accidentally kills a contortionist who works in a strip-joint. Freddy, as I said, had a name, a job and at least two relatives who testified, falsely it would seem, that his death was an irreparable loss. Poirot-Delpech really doesn't spend any time detailing Freddy's life because it simply is not relevant to the story, even if his death is. It is the same for Camus' treatment, or rather, his non-treatment, of the Arab whose sole contribution to the book is his death. But at least, unlike the Arab, Freddy is there, he speaks and participates, albeit minimally, in the story. Like Meursault, Alain also is tried and convicted, but with a difference. Reflecting on the events that got him into prison, Alain says to himself, "Like all criminals, I deserved a spanking or the guillotine. But these two extreme punishments, the only ones that I could have understood, ran the risk of shocking public opinion." (*Comme tous les criminels, je méritais la fessée ou la guillotine. Mais ces deux punitions extrêmes, les seules que j'eusse comprises, risquaient de heurter l'opinion.*) Instead, Alain got five years and Meursault the guillotine.

Where Poirot-Delpech is not really trying to prove a philosophical point and presents his characters honestly. Camus is, and, in a sense, cheats. After all, had Meursault gotten even an impossible five years in prison instead of the guillotine, can anyone seriously believe that this slim book would have had a second printing? As Judge Orthon put it in ***La Peste,*** "It's not the law that counts, it's the sentence," (*Ce n'est pas la loi qui compte, c'est la condamnation.*) And Cottard, a criminal, tells Rieux that the judge is public enemy number one.

There is much that is admirable in ***L'Etranger,*** but this subterfuge is not, because it fails to consider that there are at least two sides to the debate over the death penalty. But then, it didn't really matter since the central question was overlooked in the rush to analyze the hero's non-existent childhood and psyche.

Adele King (review date Winter 1995)

SOURCE: "*Le premier homme:* Camus's Unfinished Novel," in *World Literature Today,* Vol. 69, No. 1, Winter, 1995, pp. 83-5.

[*In the following review, King discusses Camus's literary legacy and the publication of* The First Man.]

When Albert Camus died in a car crash in January 1960, the manuscript of part of a novel on which he had been working was found in his briefcase. Thirty-four years later his daughter Catherine Camus, the literary executor of her father's estate after the death of her mother Francine in 1979, has edited this uncompleted novel, ***Le premier homme,*** and allowed it to be published. It became a major publishing event of 1994 in France, with over 100,000 copies sold within the first few months following its release. There were articles, sometimes many pages in length, devoted to discussion of the text in all the major newspapers and weekly magazines.

Publication of ***Le premier homme*** is also an event for the scholarly community. The international Société des Etudes Camusiennes organized its annual meeting in May, only six weeks after the novel was published, as a discussion, "First Impressions of ***The First Man.***" Already in France there are Master's theses being written on the novel, which had previously been the subject of an unpublished thesis based on the manuscript. The interest in the general community and among scholars can be partly explained by the continuing reputation of Camus as one of the most widely read novelists of this century (***L'Etranger*** is the best selling novel on Gallimard's list and has been for many years). Studies of Camus are numerous. There are also more specific reasons, both in terms of Camus's biography and in terms of politics, for the wide discussion of ***Le premier homme*** at this time.

Before he died, many felt that Camus's inspiration had dried up. He had not published an original creative work since ***L'exil et le royaume*** in 1957. After winning the Nobel Prize in Literature in 1957, he had seemed obsessed with the problems raised by the Algerian war of independence. He told Robert Gallimard, for example, that he could no longer write, but would work in the theater. His enemies on the left, and they were numerous following his famous quarrel with Sartre after the publication of ***L'homme révolté*** in 1952, used his lack of new work as another stick with which to attack him. Even many critics favorable to Camus wondered if he had the creative stamina to continue. Catherine Camus waited to allow publication of ***Le premier homme*** partly because she felt the style of this first draft might be used to confirm doubts about her father's artistic ability.

For years Camus's refusal to embrace the cause of Algerian independence was considered an act of treason by the French left. The Algerian rebellion was by far the major political event in France during the 1950s, until de Gaulle finally granted the colony independence in 1962. The attitude toward Algeria of Camus, who describes the *pied-noir* culture of his youth with considerable admiration and love in his earlier work, always aroused controversy in France. After Camus's death, for example, some even read ***L'Etranger*** as a "racist," anti-Arab novel. Catherine Camus waited until the political climate was less hostile toward her father. Undoubtedly as well, she was reluctant to go against the wishes of her mother, who knew that Camus himself would have been unwilling to let an unfinished work be printed. ***Le premier homme,*** in fact, is not even an unfinished novel, but merely a draft of some chapters, with notes for additional material to be added. Some of the autobiographical material, particularly references to Camus's love affairs, may also have influenced Francine Camus's initial decision.

There were also by the 1990s other reasons to allow publication. In the present political situation, France is trying to maintain contact with the government of Algeria, the successors of the FLN against which France fought, but now the group which France has supported in its decision to annual the elections that gave a majority to the violently anti-French Islamic fundamentalists. With this political situation in the headlines almost every day, Camus's thoughts on Algeria seem of contemporary relevance and not necessarily politically suspect.

Since Camus's death, many critics and scholars have looked for more texts. Scholarly interest in Camus has been intense. Six of the seven volumes in the Cahiers Albert Camus series are previously unpublished or uncollected writings by Camus. The unpublished early novel ***La mort heureuse*** was printed in the series in 1971. A collection of early, mostly unpublished stories appeared in 1973. Articles from *Combat* were collected. An early version of ***Caligula*** was published. Catherine herself became involved in editing the uncollected articles from *Alger-Républician.*

Considerable work was needed to make this early draft available. Francine Camus had typed the handwritten manuscript, which contains many additions and marginal corrections and which is written in what seems to the reader looking at the sample pages included in this edition a handwriting almost impossible to decipher. In addition to the draft manuscript of thirteen chapters, ***Le premier homme*** includes loose notes for insertion found in the briefcase, and Camus's plans and general notes for the novel. Catherine also added correspondence between Camus and Louis Germain, his primary-school teacher and first important mentor in Algiers and the model for a central character in the draft chapters that exist.

Le premier homme is closely autobiographical, relating the childhood of a character modeled on Camus himself, though named Jacques Cormery. It was, however, intended as a novel, in fact the first work to which Camus presumably meant to give the label "roman." (***L'Etranger*** and ***La Chute*** are called "récits"; ***La Peste*** is a "chronique.") In the existing draft, characters are occasionally called by their real names—an indication of how the writer had only begun to fictionalize his material. While Camus himself would have been very reluctant to let this work be published, many today will read it as much for its biographical interest as for its confirmation of Camus's ability as a writer.

Readers of Camus will initially be surprised by the wealth of detail, the capturing of a precise place, the realism of this work, in comparison with everything Camus wrote earlier. (Some of the notes, composed in the epigrammatic style of Camus's notebooks, are closer to what readers of Camus might expect than are the draft chapters themselves.) The Algeria of ***L'Etranger*** and ***La Peste*** is a Mediterranean country, but with little description to make it specifically North African. When Camus wrote descriptively, particularly in the early ***Noces,*** it was with a poetic intensity not suited to his fiction, in which the narrative voice is a principal organizing element. Another stylistic difference from the earlier work is the presence of a number of extended, page-long sentences, often beautifully written, a bit Proustian.

Le premier homme is divided into two sections: "Recherche du père" and "Le fils." Neither, however, is complete. The father for whom the hero searches died, as did Camus's own father, fighting in World War I for a country he had never seen before he was drafted. Jacques's search for some understanding of his father is rendered particularly difficult by the limited ability of his mother to tell him anything. She is illiterate, speaks little, suffers silently in a life of extreme poverty, supporting her children by doing housework, while dominated at home by her equally uncultured but tyrannical mother. As one commentator has noted, however, the very fact that the father chose to marry this woman should be of interest to the son, although he never mentions this.

Apart from a realistic description of the birth of the hero, in which his father is introduced as the new supervisor of a vineyard in Mondovi (Camus's actual birthplace), who arrives with his pregnant wife just prior to the birth of their second son, both sections of the novel are recounted in the third person but from the perspective of the hero. When he is forty, he visits his father's grave in France, only to realize that there is little he can learn about a man who died at the age of only twenty-nine and who, as a poor Algerian, left little trace. Some of those to whom Jacques turns are substitutes for his father: the schoolteacher based on Louis Germain, or the intellectual to whom the adult Cormery speaks and who is clearly based on the philosopher Jean Grenier, Camus's mentor from his lycée days.

In the childhood sections, which are the most complete, the sensual detail, and particularly the descriptions of the odors of poverty, are exceptionally vivid. The characters are to some extent familiar from earlier texts: the silent mother, the domineering grandmother, the deaf uncle. Interestingly, the older brother is almost never mentioned. The poverty of Cormery's childhood (and of Camus's) is more extreme than has usually been realized. While the essays in ***L'Envers et***

L'Endroit, Camus's first published work, give some indication of his cultural isolation at home, this becomes clear in ***Le premier homme***'s descriptions of Jacques's mother and grandmother attending school prize days with no understanding of the ceremony. Several French critics have commented on the vast difference between the childhood Sartre described in *Les Mots* and that of Camus. French literary discussion seems never to get beyond contrasting Sartre and Camus.

In the draft chapters relating the adult Cormery's search for his father, Camus sometimes appends marginal notes such as "make Jacques more of a monster," without indicating in what way the character is monstrous. He does comment, however, that he feels himself to be a monster. The bitter self-examination of ***La Chute*** has not been forgotten.

The title has already been a subject of much discussion. Is either father or son "the first man"? One explanation of the title is Catherine's: the first man is the Algerian, either European or Arab, the poor man without a past, whose life is completely forgotten on his death: "C'est tous ceux qui passent sur la terre sans apparemment laisser de trace mais qui quand même construisent ce monde dans lequel nous vivons." Like several other commentators, Catherine took pains to stress that, for Camus, both Arabs and *pieds-noirs* are of equal importance in an Algerian culture often at odds with that of the metropolis. There are indications that Camus considered both the Arabs and the *pieds-noirs* as new men, without roots in cultures of the past and sharing a life of poverty, but it is clear from this manuscript that he also considered the Arabs as fundamentally different from himself.

More often the "first man" seems to be Jacques Cormery (or Camus) himself, the son without a father to help him find his way in the world, to transmit a tradition. He describes himself as the "first inhabitant or the first conqueror." A similar theme that recurs is the dual world of Jacques, defined sometimes as the split between this hard, empty, traditionless Algeria and a Europe of measured spaces filled with centuries of culture; at other times the two worlds of Jacques are those of the family without books, where he must read the titles of silent films for his illiterate grandmother, and of the school and lyceé, where books are the sustenance of his imaginative life.

The chapter relating a conversation with the (unnamed) Grenier character, stylistically one of the least successful, is labeled by Camus in a marginal note: "To write and then to omit." The notation, illustrating how Camus planned to work through his autobiographical material, should make us wary of thinking that the more realistic and detailed style in ***Le premier homme*** was necessarily one that Camus intended to keep. In fact, some of the notes suggest what might have been a radical revision of the text: "Alternate chapters would give the voice of the mother. Comments about the same facts but with her vocabulary of 400 words." This possible organization sounds to me much closer to the earlier Camus, finding the tone for his fiction through the voice of an individual character.

Some draft material on the early history of the French colonization in Algeria, based on documentation of, for example, the number of deaths from disease among the first settlers, would presumably have been related to the search for a father who could hardly be known except as an example of this settler community. Other draft material, about terrorism in the 1950s, is not integrated into the story successfully in the existing manuscript. At one point Camus's marginal note suggests he was unsure whether or not to include one long passage about a terrorist attack.

Beyond the impressive description of his poor childhood, Camus was going to evoke a whole life close to his own, including (it appears from the general notes and plans) a passionate love affair, the discontent of a life in Paris, the impossibility of accepting terrorism in support of independence when it might hurt his family, and admiration for many Arabs who are contrasted to those fighting in the revolution. But it is perhaps impossible to speak about the themes of a work which is so incomplete. As it stands, ***Le premier homme*** is a tribute to Camus's mother (surely one of the few illiterate parents of any Western artist in this century), an impressive evocation of a childhood in Algiers, and a tantalizing glimpse of what Camus might have revealed of his adult life through a fictional form that he did not have time to finish.

Elizabeth Hawes (review date 2 October 1995)

SOURCE: "Sunlight and Silence," in *The Nation,* October 2, 1995, pp. 358-60.

[*In the following review, Hawes discusses Camus's artistic and thematic concerns in* The First Man.]

Back in 1960, the sudden death of Albert Camus at the age of 46 was a tragic event for young intellectuals, like the breach of a promise, the end of then and the beginning of now. Memories of the day still remain—the photograph of the Facel Vega wrapped around a tree, the muddy briefcase in a field, the sense of personal loss, the unbearable Absurdity of it all. "Rarely have the nature of a man's work and the conditions of the historical moment so clearly demanded that a writer go on living," Jean-Paul Sartre mourned. "No modern writer that I can think of, except Camus, has aroused love," Susan Sontag wrote from America.

More than Sartre or Gide or even Malraux, Albert Camus had become the cultural hero of the postwar generation. From the early 1940s, when the young journalist from French Algeria raised a singular voice in the Resistance newspaper *Combat,* then published, in rapid succession, the novel ***The Stranger,*** the play ***Caligula*** and the essay ***The Myth of Sisyphus***—his triptych of the Absurd—critics had spoken of *le phénomène Camus.* Almost overnight, Camus had risen to a celebrated role as "the moral conscience of his times." Like Meursault and Sisyphus, he was *l'homme engagé, l'homme sans autre avenir que lui-même,* committed to finding meaning in the modern world. In the next decade, he produced ***The Plague*** and ***The Fall,*** the long essay ***The Rebel,*** plays, translations, short stories and political essays, an *oeuvre* that was crowned with the Nobel Prize for Literature for 1957. By that time, however, Camus was *en panne,* estranged from Sartre and his old literary crowd by their criticism of ***The Rebel,*** anguished over the explosion of war in Algeria, suffering from writer's block and his own success, as silent as if he were in exile. When he died, he left behind only the rough beginnings of a new work he had described as the novel of his maturity and entitled ***Le premier homme.***

Last year, after prolonged deliberation, Camus's family decided to publish the manuscript he was working on at the time of his death; it created a literary sensation in France. This unfinished novel, now translated into English as ***The First Man,*** has resurrected the author as dramatically as a revisitation.

As early as 1951, Camus spoke in his journals of his plans for an epic novel on the model of *War and Peace.* It would be his *éducation sentimentale,* he said later, the story of his Algeria, recounted for mainland France. ***The First Man*** is the beginning of this historical saga, told through the lives of a poor family named Cormery, which unfolds between the birth of a son, Jacques, on the eve of World War I and his nostalgic return home in the violent days of the Front de Libération Nationale in the late 1950s. It is also an astonishing piece of autobiography, for in name, chronology and virtually every important aspect of his life, Jacques Cormery is Albert Camus transposed to the third person. Like Cormery (the family name of his paternal grandmother), Camus had a father who was mortally wounded in the battle of the Marne and buried in Saint-Brieuc in Brittany, a strong silent illiterate mother whom he adored, a near-mute uncle and a tyrannical grandmother who ruled the household; grew up in poverty in the Belcourt neighborhood of Algiers; and was saved by a primary school teacher who introduced him to books, proposed a scholarship to the *lycée* and "opened for me the door to everything I love in the world." Like the adult Cormery, who speaks of "the secret exultation" of leaving Paris for Africa ("with the satisfaction of one who has made good his escape and is laughing at the thought of the look on the guards' faces"), he always rejoiced in the physical pleasures of his land. And like Cormery, he too, after visiting his father's grave in his middle age, set out in quest of the man he never knew and found himself back in his childhood.

Although ***The First Man*** was meant to be a full portrait of his life and times—the author's notes preserved in the appendix include references to sports, politics, morality, terrorists, farmers, old friends, lovers, children, Tipasa, Paris, Provence—Camus was able to complete only the first third of that work, which describes his search for his father and, more expansively, his childhood. Dedicated to his mother, the Widow Camus "who will never be able to read this book," ***The First Man*** is dominated by this humble figure isolated by semi-deafness and illiteracy, who did not hear the words of the officer who came to announce her young husband's death in France, "who had no idea what history and geography might be." Camus, who had earlier spoken of putting at the center of a work "the admirable silence of a mother and the effort of a man to find some form of justice or love which could counterbalance this silence," writes with poignant detail and a perceptible ache about the fearful and submissive woman he so loved, of the hollow in her neck that "to him had the scent of a tenderness all too rare in his young life," of her life that "by dint of being deprived of hope, had become also a life without any sort of resentment," of the shame of feeling shame when he had to describe her as a *domestique* in his *lycée* application.

As a portrait of poverty, ***The First Man*** is lyric in its illuminations. The most humdrum details of Jacques's youth are revealing—the single pair of pants pressed nightly, the nails in his shoes to preserve the soles and to prevent him from playing soccer, the street games with apricot pits; they describe a life of bare necessities, "among things named with common nouns," a life in the present tense. "Remembrance of things past is just for the rich," Jacques observes; "in order to bear up well one must not remember too much, but rather stick close to the passing day, hour by hour, as his mother did." In the search for his own heritage, Jacques confronts "the mystery of poverty that creates beings without names and without a past." Algeria is "the land of oblivion," he concludes, where men try to learn to live without roots, "where each one is the first man."

As a portrait of Algeria, ***The First Man*** is passionate and troubled. No one has written more evocatively of the North African landscape than Camus in his youthful essays, which brim with the joys, and freedom of the sun and the light, and, here, twenty years later, he luxuriates in recollections of swimming in the sea, hunting in the mountains, roaming the streets of the poor quarter where the houses smell of spices, the terraces of honeysuckle and jasmine. Algeria emerges as even more than physical sensations and childhood ways, as Camus describes the settling of the harsh and hostile land by waves of poor European immigrants; the primitive fraternity that exists between Frenchmen and Arabs—"We were made to understand each other. Fools and brutes like us, but with the same blood of men"; the menace in the air and "this soft unbearable burden on the heart" as the era of decolonization dawns. Camus, who had spoken out for colonial reforms and indigenous rights all his life, and consistently refused to justify terrorism in the name of revolution, still believed in the future of a multicultural Algeria, even as Arab bombs exploded under his mother's window. That was his dilemma in the last days of his life, the "night inside him," the "tangled hidden roots," and it called into question both his politics and his identity.

The First Man is Camus's own quest for identity. Like his father and Jacques Cormery and the European in Algeria, he is that eponymous first man, rootless, traditionless, creating his own history, threatened with anonymity and oblivion. "I am going to tell the story of an alien," the author reminded himself in his notes. This is the theme he first sounded in ***The Stranger,*** but here it becomes a personal saga that resonates with details—the shell fragment from his father's head that is kept in an old biscuit tin behind the towels, the elderly smell of his grandmother's flesh during one of their dreaded afternoon naps, the taste of the leather strap of the school satchel he chews during lessons. It is difficult to read this book as other than autobiography, because in its very nature as an unedited and unpolished first draft it has both a spontaneity and a transparency that are made even more obvious by the occasional slips into the first person, and the corrections and explanations included in the text. (In the French edition, the addition of facsimile manuscript pages, covered with Camus's small, tight, almost indecipherable script, adds a further sense of veracity to the work.) Camus's prose intensifies the sense of immediacy and purpose, for it moves in primal rhythms, magnificent surges of long sentences that seem like searches in themselves and consume whole pages before ending. If the short, blunt sentences of ***The Stranger*** reflected a world without connections or hope, the sweeping lyricism of ***The First Man*** speaks of something new.

Camus originally titled his novel *Adam.* Coming as it did several years after the confessional ***The Fall*** and at a time of personal decline and depression, it represented a new beginning for him. Even incomplete, it is the most ambitious and compassionate of his books. It is also an integral and important part of his whole *oeuvre,* both a continuation and an illumination of his thought. There is a story about his father's violent reaction to a public hanging that speaks to Camus's own strong opposition to the death penalty. There is a passage about "the secret of the light, of the warm poverty that had enabled him to survive and to overcome everything," that explains his humanism. "For all his life it would be kindness and love that made him cry, never pain or persecution, which on the contrary only reinforced his spirit and his resolution," Camus writes of Cormery, and thus of himself, in retrospection. In the last sentence of this last work, he also contemplates his own death—"he, like a solitary and ever-shining blade of a sword, was destined to be shattered with a single blow and forever"—and expresses "the blind hope" that he will grow old and die without rebellion.

Stanley Hoffmann (review date Winter 1995-96)

SOURCE: "Passion and Compassion: The Glory of Albert Camus," in *World Policy Journal,* Vol. 12, No. 4, Winter, 1995-96, pp. 83-90.

[*In the following review, Hoffmann provides critical analysis of* The First Man. *According to Hoffmann, "Rough and raw as it is, it is a splendid work of art, and it helps us to understand Camus—the man and his work—better and more profoundly."*]

The First Man is the final, unfinished work of Albert Camus. The manuscript—144 handwritten pages—was found in the car in which he died at the age of 46 on January 4, 1960. It was published in France only in 1994. One can see why Camus' widow hesitated to release it. It was almost impossible to decipher (as the reproductions of several pages show), devoid of commas, full of corrections and additions. Many words are missing and many remain illegible, many sentences are incomplete, several characters are given different names. And it is only a fragment of what was intended as a much bigger book, covering most of the life of the main character. Jacques Cormery, who is none other than Camus. The manuscript ends when he is 14, an adolescent who has just kissed his first girl.

According to Catherine Camus, the author's daughter, there was another reason why her mother, who died in 1979, had been reluctant to publish it. Camus' reputation had fallen dramatically—at least in the French intelligentsia, which he had never liked. (The public continued to buy his books, and high school students continued to study them.) French authors, after their death, often drop into a kind of purgatory from which they later emerge and move, finally, either to the paradise of the classics or to the hell of the forgotten. Gide is still in purgatory, and Malraux seems to keep him company there. Camus' purgatory felt very much like an antechamber of hell. He was denounced for his moralism, for his lack of understanding of politics, for his rejection of Algerian independence, for the amateurishness of his philosophical essays, for the grandiloquence of his plays, for the gray abstraction of ***The Plague.***

The intelligentsia that decides on reputations had declared him the loser in the famous 1952 debate with Sartre over ***The Rebel,*** when Sartre denounced Camus as a *belle âme* who refused to dirty his hands and whose moral attitudes barely concealed the bourgeois sin of anticommunism. Camus, defending his work, had replied that Sartre had never done more than place his directorial chair at *Les Temps Modernes* in the direction of history. When the Algerian war broke out, Sartre, championing not only independence but the cleansing virtues of violence against the colonizers (in his famous, frantic preface to Frantz Fanon's *The Wretched of the Earth*), filled the long years of the war with his vociferous support of the Front de Libération Nationale (FLN). Camus condemned terrorism and torture on both sides and—I paraphrase a famous sentence of his, pronounced when he received the Nobel Prize in 1957—found it difficult to prefer the justice of the Arab rebels, who fought to free their people, to his mother, who could have fallen victim to guerrilla terror. He lapsed into silence.

Sartre's embrace of complete independence for Algeria even if it meant killing or expelling all Europeans appeared far more realistic than Camus' occasional endorsements of schemes aimed at keeping Algeria French, while granting equal rights to the Europeans and to the Arabs.

"In these circumstances," according to Catherine Camus, "to have published an unfinished manuscript might well have given ammunition to those who were saying that Camus was through as a writer. His friends and my mother decided not to run that risk." But "between 1980 and 1985, voices began to be heard saying that perhaps Camus had not been so wrong." The twin children of Camus decided to publish the manuscript even though he "would never have published [it] as it is"—because of its importance as an autobiographical document. They were right. Rough and raw as it is, it is a splendid work of art, and it helps us to understand Camus—the man and his work—better and more profoundly.

The Poor Boy

It is not the first time that Camus tells us about his childhood in Algiers—about the death of his French father at the battle of the Marne in 1914, when Albert was still a baby; about the terrible poverty in which he (and his slightly older brother) lived, brought up by a partly deaf, illiterate, silent, and overworked mother who exhausted herself as a cleaning woman and by her stern, often brutal mother; about his adoration for this affectionate but somehow unreachable mother; about his love for the sun and the beaches of Algiers. We knew that, in an archetypical French way, his gifts had been noticed and nurtured by his teacher in primary school, and that thanks to him, he was able to continue to study in a *lycée* (where, later, the philosopher and writer Jean Grenier was going to encourage him again). But two things are distinctive about ***The First Man.*** One is the intensity of Camus' recollections and reflections, to which I will return. The other is the timing of this work and its purpose.

Camus, who had, in the 1930s, become, for a very brief period, a member of the Communist Party, and a lucid and sharply critical reporter on Algerian affairs (particularly on the plight of the Arabs), had moved—reluctantly—to metropolitan France, in order to get treatment for tuberculosis, just as the Second World War was engulfing Europe. He burst upon the literary scene in 1942, with the ***Myth of Sisyphus*** and ***The Stranger.*** After the liberation, as editor and star of the Resistance paper *Combat,* for which he wrote trenchant editorials—demanding purges against collaborationists and denouncing nationalism and any return to France's prewar political diseases—he became one of the most fashionable and celebrated intellectuals in Paris. Much of this giddy, golden period is described (and somewhat distorted) in Simone de Beauvoir's *Mandarins.*

But the poor boy from Algiers never felt at home in gray and rainy Paris or at ease among the sophisticates of the intelligentsia, with their clans, mutual excommunications, sarcasms, and settlements of accounts. And then his popularity declined in the 1950s. ***The Fall,*** published in 1956, marked the end of his era as a Parisian guru. This sardonic, dark, and brilliant tale, written in a style that was far different both from the lyrical vein of some of his early stories and of his essays, and from the more austere style of his philosophical writings and of ***The Plague,*** has been interpreted very differently by critics. Some, like Conor Cruise O'Brien recently, see it as an exercise in self-criticism in which Camus rejected "his own role of Camus *le juste,* and also his role as a contemporary Saint-Just," and denounced the hypocrisy of his own moralism.

I do not doubt that Camus, insofar as he had participated in the glitter and clatter of Parisian intellectual café life, had wanted to make fun of his part in it. But I do believe that his target was Sartre, and that J.B. Clamence, the lawyer who says "I" in ***The Fall,*** and who becomes a judge-penitent pursued by the memory of the woman whom he has failed to rescue after she had jumped into the Seine, was a fictional representation of Sartre, the writer who felt guilty about his bourgeois origins and his apolitical youth, and who beat his breast, so to speak, on the breasts of others—all those whom he denounced as guilty cowards or stinkers. (It would be fascinating to compare Clamence with Sartre's own fictional character Frantz in Sartre's play *The Condemned of Altona.*)

Having turned his back on the Paris scene, demoralized by the atrocities of the Algerian war, torn between the desire to speak out on the ethical and political issues that were plaguing his contemporaries and the fear of compromising his integrity as an artist if he crossed the line that separates concern from commitment, and elucidation from *engagement,* Camus expressed his dilemma in the sad and lovely story of the painter Jonah who, when he dies, leaves an unfinished painting, an empty canvas on which one can find one word scribbled, but it is not clear whether it is *solitaire or solidaire.* Camus now suffered from a writer's block, which lasted several years.

The First Man was Camus' attempt to overcome this block by going back to his origins and by trying to make sense of his whole life. For Camus, unlike for Sartre, *l'absurde* was not the human condition, but the gap, the discrepancy, between an often beautiful but indifferent nature and human desires and aspirations that can never be fulfilled because, as Caligula puts, it, "men die and are not happy."

Camus wanted to understand himself, to see where his desires and passions had come from and where they had led him—an exercise far removed from the highly complacent and narcissistic self-criticism (mixed, as usual, with a denunciation of some of his bourgeois family members) in Sartre's *Words* but comparable to Proust's own gigantic quest for time past.

It is clear from the "notes and sketches" that accompany the text of ***The First Man*** that Camus would have been unsparing in his introspection of the adolescent and adult Camus, of his machismo, of his fickleness. Just as Sartre's attempt at a total "reconstruction" of Flaubert remains unfinished, Camus' effort to understand the person to whom he several times refers to as a "monster" was aborted. But the fragment he left is miraculously complete, and it has been very well translated by David Hapgood—not an easy task, since Camus' prose is often so (spontaneously, abundantly, intoxicatingly) poetic.

The Son or the First Man

It is divided into two parts. In the first, "Search for the Father," Camus tells the story of his father's arrival in the fall of 1913 in the hinterland of Bône, where he was going to manage a farm, and of his own birth during the night of this arrival. Then, abruptly, he takes us to Saint Brieuc in Brittany, where the father is buried. His son visits the grave in 1954 and, realizing that he is much older than his father was when he was killed, feels like an adult in front of a murdered child.

Attempts at finding out more about his father from his mother, or from settlers who had known him, bring out very little. Jacques only remembers his father's return in horror from having witnessed the execution of a murderer, an anecdote that Camus had elsewhere cited as the root of his own horror of capital punishment and that he links here to his father's violent death.

What Jacques discovers is the story of the French who settled in Algeria after the 1848 Revolution, attracted by the promise of land and work, which they did not have in metropolitan France. His father's family had come from Alsace after 1871, his mother's from Spain: poor devils uprooted by misery or persecution and driven to a land where they would disappear without leaving any trace, a "land of oblivion where everybody is the first man." Jacques, returning to Algeria from Saint Brieuc, feels that "he too was a member of the tribe," despite his attempt to escape from it.

The chapters about the missing father are interspersed with chapters about the games played by Jacques as a child and about the family in which he was brought up. The formidable grandmother who had had nine children, the mother who was hard of hearing, and her brother Etienne (also often called Ernest in the text), who was deaf and explosive, and whom his old mother treated with surprising gentleness because he was handsome: "it is our weakness for beauty" that "helps make the world bearable."

These chapters about Jacques as a child continue in the second part of the manuscript, "The Son or the First Man." They are the most moving and vivid. In one of his notes, he wrote: "Free oneself from any concern with art and form. Regain contact, without intermediary, thus innocence. To give up art here is to give up one's self. Renouncing the self, not through virtuousness. On the contrary, accept one's hell."

This is exactly what he accomplishes here. There is a constant, and constantly successful, effort to recapture the sensations, sounds, smells, and feelings of his childhood, which give his prose, full of long sentences that try to encompass a whole bygone world, a richness and lyrical precision he had never reached before. And it is made even more resonant by the fact that the man who thus brings the past back to a startlingly vibrant life at the same time reflects on it and on his feelings for it from the perspective of middle age, with the bitter wisdom of someone who had escaped from the past because he could not stand living in it any longer, yet felt forever after "exiled" from the miserable "kingdom" of his Algerian childhood.

Hence the peculiar lyricism of this rough draft, a lyricism both celebratory and desolate. Passion and compassion are fused in his evocation of those who brought him up, of his relation to them, of the relationship between his mother and her brother, of his love for his mother and for M. Bernard his schoolteacher—in real life, M. Germain, to whom Camus wrote a lovely note after receiving the Nobel Prize, and who replied in a letter that seems to come straight from the annals of the Third Republic, full of affection and admiration for his pupil and of worry for the future of *l'école laique* (they are published in an appendix). What could easily have been gloomy or *misérabiliste* is transfigured by the light of the Mediterranean, by the sun that made it all bearable, and that turned his condition into a "warm poverty that had enabled him to survive and to overcome everything."

A Fortress without Drawbridges

Indeed, ***The First Man*** is a kind of pious tribute to all those who live in poverty—not in what has sometimes been called, pompously, the culture of poverty, because the poor, as he shows, are deprived of culture. In a life entirely eaten up by the need to work so as to earn just enough money to keep going, there is no room for objects except the most indispensable, no room for art, no time for religion, no connection "to traditional values and stereotypes." "Poverty is a fortress without drawbridges."

When little Jacques escapes to the beach or uses up his shoes playing soccer, he gets whipped by his grandmother, he should have been working. "Poor people's memory is less nourished than that of the rich; it has fewer landmarks in space because they seldom leave the place where they live, and fewer reference points in time throughout lives that are gray and featureless. . . . Remembrance of things past is just for the rich. For the poor it only marks the faint traces on the path to death. And besides, in order to bear up well one must not remember too much."

When Jacques resents his uncle because Etienne kept his sister away from a man for whom she seemed to have some affection, he—or rather the writer—comments that "the poverty, the infirmities, the elemental need in which all his family lived . . . made it impossible to pass judgment on those who were its victims."

The heart of this book is the portrait of young Jacques, of Camus, as a child, and what it tells us about the experiences that shaped his values. Unlike most other works of Camus, it is not about ideas; here, we are soaked in sensations and feelings. What we find, above all, is this extraordinary bond to the silent mother, whom he describes with a heartbreaking tenderness, whom he never blames for allowing her mother to beat her boy, and whom he reveres for her life of endurance, her lack of resentment, her gentleness. When Camus writes about the child's "despairing love for something in his mother that did not belong or no longer belonged to the world and to the triviality of the days," or describes himself endlessly watching "her in the shadows with a lump in his throat, staring at her thin bent back, filled with an obscure anxiety in the presence of adversity he could not understand," the depth and immediately of his feeling leads to the purest form of art.

His Ambivalence

What Camus also tells us is the story of a child whom poverty condemns to repeated humiliations. He keeps a few pennies from the money that his grandmother had given him to buy groceries and pretends to have dropped them in the hole that serves as a toilet. When the old woman goes looking for them in it, he feels ashamed to have deprived his family of the coins, which he had wanted to use to go watch a soccer game. When he goes to the *lycée* and has to indicate his mother's profession on a form, he is ashamed of having to write "domestic." When he has to seek a summer job—so that he will be able to compensate his family for failing to earn any money while studying at the *lycée*—he discovers that he cannot get one if he does not lie about his intention to return to the *lycée* in the fall, and he suffers bitterly for having "to lie for the right to have no vacation, to work far from the summer sky and the sea he so loved."

What gives the book its tension and keeps it from ever slipping into sentimentality is the drama of Jacques' ambivalence. He is tied forever to his mother and to his milieu by "two or three favorite pictures that joined him to them, made him one with them." But at the same time, the boy had a thirst for learning and a "hunger for discovery." School provided him both with an escape from his "destitute home" and with a "powerful poetry," which Camus describes minutely—the smell of the ink, the "varnished rulers and pen cases," the joy of finding out about the world in textbooks. If M. Bernard had not come pleading to Jacques' home, the grandmother would not have allowed him to go on to the *lycée.*

But as a result, Jacques was torn between two completely different universes. When he gained admittance to the *lycée,* "a child's immense anguish wrung his heart, as if he knew in advance that this success had just uprooted him from the warm and innocent world of the poor—a world closed upon itself like an island in the society—to be hurtled into a strange world, one no longer his." The world he belonged to was stifling, the one he escaped to would turn out to be cruel and deceitful. He felt as if he had betrayed the world of the poor for a false glory, but also that he could not have stayed in it.

The intensity of Camus' feelings, the delicacy and beautiful aptness with which he renders them, make one realize that the reason why they had been either expressed obliquely or fleetingly or else transposed and "distanced" in his fiction and plays was because he struggled between a flood of passionate emotions and the drive to control and master them, a drive inculcated by the school, but also by the need not to let himself be engulfed by his love for his mother and by his empathy, his pity, for his family's condition.

Camus describes himself as a mixture of life-long attachments to those he loves and indifference, as a man who felt at ease only with "what was inevitable . . . everything in his life he had not been able to avoid, his illness, his vocation, fame or poverty . . . The heart, the heart above all is not free. It is inevitability and the recognition of the inevitable."

This fervent desire to escape from poverty and from his mother's "life of blind patience, without words, without plans," and to live as an artist indifferent to the world, he expressed in his first novel, ***A Happy Death,*** which was published only after his own death. But the world diverted Camus from his dream of indifference, and he felt that he needed forgiveness from his mother—"but you do not understand me and cannot read me": all she could do was "smile on me."

The Roots of His Thought

The First Man is both a familiar story—the story of emancipation through learning and of the mix of innocent pleasure and obscure guilt that is childhood—and a revelation of the roots of Camus' thought. It is not a book about politics, and those who, one more time, attack Camus for his views on Algeria are the victims of their own obsessions. The Algerian tragedy was going to be dealt with in a part of the book Camus never got to.

This does not mean that we do not find here some essential clues about his feelings for Algeria. When he deals with the past—the arrival of the *colons,* and the life of the *pieds noirs* at the time of his childhood, he expresses, again, mainly compassion for the settlers who came from many lands and disappeared after having lived and toiled without roots. He mentions the xenophobia of the workers, afraid of losing their jobs to the Spaniards, the Jews, or the Arabs, and fighting for "the privilege of servitude." There are few Arabs in this story: to young Jacques, they are companions. The real divide is the one that separates all those born in Algeria from those born in France, like Jacques' *lycée* friend Didier, whose fervent patriotism astonishes Jacques, for whom France is an abstraction (in one of his notes, Camus wrote that "what they did not like in him was the Algerian").

In the brief passage where the older Jacques, having returned to an Algeria torn by the war, reports both on his reactions and on the reactions of some of the settlers, Camus makes clear his revulsion against the FLN's violence, and he tells the story of a settler who decides to destroy his vineyards and move to France after having heard the *préfet* denounce the way the *colons* had treated the Arabs; but the farmer who reports this story to Jacques says that the *colons* and the Arabs are "made to understand each other. Fools and brutes, like us, but with the same blood of men. We'll kill each other a little longer . . . And then we'll go back to living as men together."

Jacques himself, visiting his mother, hears a huge explosion in Algiers and protects an innocent Arab from the wrath of vengeful workers. We know now that the legacy of colonialism and the war itself destroyed that solidarity of Algerians, European and Arab, living on the same land and under the same sun that Camus dreamed about.

But it was always a mistake to read Camus as a political thinker or as a philosopher. He was haunted by the issues that *l'absurde* raised: suicide, murder, the impossibility of communicating fully even (or especially) with those one loves. But metaphysical questions and philosophical systems were not his domain. Insofar as public life was concerned, it was the ethical preconditions for political action that bothered him. He had no solutions to offer, only barriers he wanted to erect. He had one obsession, like Proudhon, with whom he shared enthusiasm for the artisan's work and hatred for work that is boring, work "so interminably monotonous that it made the days too long and, at the same time, life too short." He wanted fairness for human beings and, especially, for the poor.

This meant that politics had to be modest: grand salvationist schemes always led to more misery and oppression and deprived people of their right to their private lives; ideologies that subordinate means to ends and the present to a distant dubious future are evil; and the state is no more than a tool, not the culmination of history. What Camus taught was limits: do not do anything that adds to human misery, such as terror, torture, wanton violence.

On all these points, he clashed with Sartre, and this child of the poor resented especially Sartre's embrace of a proletariat he knew nothing about. Camus' rejection of Marxist and communist philosophies of history, his refusal to sanctify history, his advocacy of a kind of rebellion against servitude and injustice that says "we" and proclaims its solidarity with the downtrodden, his nausea at all forms of murder that add to the unhappiness and hasten the death that are our fare—all this comes directly from the childhood of a boy who had lost his father to the mindless massacre of Europe's Great War, who had experienced poverty and injustice but was singularly free of resentments and utterly devoid of hatred, for whom games, love, and learning, all the addictions of private life, took precedence over public affairs, who was entirely outside the ideological and class trenches of metropolitan France, and who sought solace in the light. When ***The Rebel*** was published, many scoffed at the fuzziness of that plea for both revolt and moderation, and especially of that hymn to *la pensée de midi* that comes at the end. ***The***

First Man shows where it all originated. "The nobility of the writer's occupation lies in resisting oppression, thus in accepting isolation."

Rehabilitation

Camus has, in recent years, regained much of his earlier prestige: the demise of Soviet totalitarianism, the fading of old ideologies, the advent of a kind of pragmatic centrism in France, the rediscovery of the virtues of liberalism (with its recognition of human rights, the limits it puts on state power, and the virtues it finds in rational discussion and compromise), the collapse of the FLN state and the tragedy of the independent Algeria, all of this has led to a rehabilitation of Camus. He finds himself now in the same pantheon as Raymond Aron (who liked him but saw him as an amateurish thinker).

However, this new fame may well rest on one more misreading, which would not have surprised the author of that elliptical and gruesome play, ***Le malentendu*** (a play that should be compared to Sartre's *No Exit:* for Camus, hell is not "the others," it is our inability to reach them).

France's new liberals tend to be close to America's neoconservatives. They worry more about sound finance than about social reforms and have very little to say about the poor. In their enthusiasm for the death of messianism, they have tended to bury the hope of a better life for the underprivileged with it. Camus would not be comfortable in their midst.

Indeed, Camus was above all an artist with a "very great vision" of art: "not because I see art to be above everything, but because it does not separate itself from anyone" (a sentence from one of the notes that has been dropped in the English translation). It is as an artist that he will survive—an artist whose view of life was far more complex, and often more somber, even despairing, than was suggested by the cartoon-like image of Camus as a kind of "Red Cross moralist" so fashionable in the 1960s. What saved him from despair and restored his bruised serenity was the memory of the Algerian sun and that bond beyond words to his mother.

When Jacques flew back from Saint Brieuc to Algiers, "he knew from the bottom of his heart that Saint Brieuc and all it represented had never been anything to him" and acknowledged "with a strange sort of pleasure that death would return him to his true homeland. With its immense oblivion, death would obliterate the memory of that alien [the French text says *monstrueux*] and ordinary man who had grown up, had built in poverty, without help or deliverance, on a fortunate shore in the light of the first mornings of the world, and then alone, without memories and without faith, had entered the world of the men of his time and its dreadful and exhausted history."

To those of us for whom Camus' voice, in the 1940s and 1950s, was always the voice of refined beauty, deep and humane wisdom, controlled passion, and noble art, the publication of ***The First Man*** is an invaluable gift.

V. C. Letemendia (essay date Spring 1997)

SOURCE: "Poverty in the Writings of Albert Camus," in *Polity,* Vol. XXIX, No. 3, Spring, 1997, pp. 441-60.

[*In the following essay, Letemendia explores Camus's early experiences with poverty, as revealed in* The First Man, *and his outrage over society's indifference toward the plight of the poor. According to Letemendia, Camus viewed poverty as "both a moral and political crime against humanity."*]

Albert Camus approached the understanding of poverty from the viewpoint of both an internal and an external witness. He had experienced poverty in his youth, as he describes in his autobiographical novel, **Le premier homme,** *but acknowledged that education, financial security and fame had distanced him from the poor, and did not consider that his own experience gave him the authority to speak for other poor people. Unlike some on the French left, he saw freedom as equally essential to a fully human life as material well-being: the poor and working-class could not be denied basic liberties in the name of social justice, just as they could not be treated as an abstraction to be fitted into revolutionary theory. While Camus regarded himself as an outside witness to the devastating effects of poverty, he maintained that those who suffered silently must be given a context in which they could speak out with their own authentic voices.*

Albert Camus is famous not only for his works of fiction and theatre, but as an active member of the Resistance, as a commentator on the political problems of his age, and as the friend and later intellectual opponent of Jean-Paul Sartre and his circle. Camus's warnings about the destructive nature of fanaticism have lost no relevance in the last decades of the twentieth century, nor yet has his passion for individual freedom. His pained and angry denunciations of social injustice serve as a reminder that people still suffer from avoidable ills, despite the many political and social changes that have occurred since his untimely death in 1960. The publication in April 1994 of ***Le premier homme,*** Camus's incomplete semi-autobiographical novel, has awakened new interest in his life and work. The extant manuscript, a fraction of the planned novel, offers the first detailed account of his experience of a poor childhood in Algeria and the marks it left upon the man, no longer poor or unknown, who looked back to recall it. This intimate record of Camus's early years is fascinating to read for both literary and autobiographical reasons, but it has also attracted fresh attention to a crucial though frequently neglected theme in his writings: his commentary on poverty.

Camus named poverty as one of the initial and most fundamental influences upon his awareness of the world, and once said that he had learned about freedom not from Marx, but from poverty. His approach to the understanding of poverty was compelling and remarkably contemporary. He saw it not as a single, uniformly lived condition that could be comprehended easily by any external observer, but as a condition that spanned a scale from tolerable discomfort to utter deprivation of the necessities of life. Each degree of poverty gave birth to a separate and specific experience of destitution. Because of this, poverty could not be externally measured or described only as a state of systematic political and social disadvantage. It assaulted its victims on an individual level, psychologically and morally, at its very worst curtailing human expression and communication, and destroying individual and collective dignity. In short, severe poverty threatened all that Camus found to be most precious about human existence.

Existence itself, he argued, brought forth a metaphysical form of suffering, arising from an acknowledgement of mortality and other inevitable, natural ills. Though still experience as an injustice, metaphysical suffering was an inherent aspect of the human condition. Preoccupied with the problem of how, in the absence of religious belief, we might discover values by which to live as individuals and as common members of humanity, Camus identified metaphysical suffering as consequent to a recognition of the absurd, and grounded in this suffering his definition of what he saw as both precious and changeless about individual human life. Yet he identified another form of suffering, inflicted by people upon each other, as neither inevitable nor natural. Poverty was one of these afflictions and as such, in the eyes of Camus, was both a moral and political crime against humanity. Outraged by the ignorance or indifference of society toward the fate of the poor, he found it unacceptable that they should remain condemned to suffer in silent misery from a condition that could be significantly alleviated, if not fully eradicated.

Although he did not consider himself to have suffered its worst ravages, Camus had tasted many of the bitter injustices of poverty during his childhood and youth. And while he could and did describe from the inside how poverty had affected him, he laid no personal claim to the stories of other poor people. These he described from the viewpoint of a keen and sympathetic witness, rather than an omniscient outsider, acknowledging the distance that now lay between himself and material deprivation, and respecting the exclusive nature of every poor person's experience. For Camus was quick to recognize that his past provided him only with a certain sensitivity towards the misery of others, not a firm knowledge. He was eager to speak, from his position of privilege, for the poor who had been denied a voice, but restrained himself with characteristic *pudeur,* or modesty, from mistaking his voice for theirs.

I. Camus as an External Witness to Poverty

Even Camus's earliest published efforts reveal his interest in observing and commenting upon social injustice, and poverty in particular. He was active with more than his pen: at university he participated in the activities of the Popular Front in Algeria, and before completing his studies he joined the Communist Party, not because he had been converted to Marxism by his reading of theory, but because of what he had witnessed and lived. In his words, "it seems to me that, more than ideas, life itself often leads to Communism. . . . I have such a strong desire to reduce the sum of unhappiness and bitterness which poisons mankind." With his friends on the left, he formed a co-operative political theatre group and a "people's university" to provide adult education for workers, and helped organize a *Theatre du Travail* in Algiers. Subsequently, as a reporter on the new, left-leaning *Alger Républicain,* he addressed himself to exposing the misery of some of the poorest members of his community, the Arabs and the indigenous Berber population of Kabylia.

Camus knew well that the Arabs suffered disproportionately when compared even to very poor European families such as his own, for he had long been able to observe their situation at first hand. Well acquainted with the Arab quarter of Algiers, which he had frequented since boyhood, he had gone to school with Arab children, had close contact with left-wing Moslem intellectuals through the Communist Party, openly supported the cause of Arab nationalists, and as a journalist gave sympathetic coverage to a number of political trials involving Arab defendants.

His disgust and indignation at the plight of the poor emerges most forcefully in his reports on famine-struck Kabylia. These articles, written in the first person, relay the statistics of poverty, search for the underlying economic, political, and demographic reasons for the famine, and describe the devastation wreaked upon at least half of the Kabylia population, driven to feed their families on grasses and roots until administrative handouts of grain arrive. Can anyone, he asks, have an easy conscience after seeing such suffering, about which almost nothing has been done? Perhaps it is impossible to convey the extremity of the misery, he writes,

> but I know that on the return from a visit to the

> "tribe" of Tizi-Ouzou, I went up with a Kabyle friend into the heights which tower over the town. There we watched night fall. And at that hour when the shadow descending from the mountain over this splendid earth brings respite to the most hardened human heart, I knew all the same that there was no peace for those who, on the other side of the valley, were gathering together around a cake of bad barley. I knew also how sweet it would be to abandon oneself to an evening so amazing and magnificent, but that the misery whose fires glowed before us made the beauty of the world a forbidden thing. "Let's go down, shall we?" my companion said to me.

Just as his companion urged him, Camus urges his reader to go down into the valley. If you think it is an inevitable state of affairs, he writes, then say so; if you think it is an outrage, then *act;* if you do not believe that it is happening, come and take a look. For Camus, the most despicable thing to say is that the situation has something to do with the "Kabyle mentality," and that these people do not have the same needs as us, and can adapt to anything. Even the French President, if he were given only two hundred francs a month to live on, would get used to living under bridges, to dirt, and to crusts of bread found in dustbins, for "there is something stronger in a man's attachment to life than there is in all the miseries of the world." Camus did not hesitate to stress that the Kabylian situation originated in a far larger pattern of systematic political disadvantage imposed upon this population by the French government. He argued that temporary or partial solutions could not change the circumstances of the Kabyle, whose education, employment opportunities, political representation and general standard of living required urgent, fundamental reform.

If he had restricted himself to describing his own horror at the conditions he witnessed, and to decrying the ignorance and inhumanity which could permit such misery to continue, the articles would still remain a powerful indictment of colonial rule. Yet he went further, emphasizing above all that even though, to French eyes, these people might be mere Berbers enured to a life of hardship, the Kabyle could not go on being treated worse than animals. Their suffering was just as terrible for them as it would be for any European, and was actually far worse than the misery endured by Algeria's European poor. To borrow Camus' compelling phrase, one had to come down from the mountain to learn what was happening, and it was not enough merely to observe. Once you agreed that the suffering was utterly unacceptable, there was a large measure of hypocrisy in still doing nothing to remove it.

The Communist Party, which Camus had joined earlier, now appeared to be shifting away from its support for the Arab cause, associating itself instead with the pro-colonial Radical Socialist Party. Camus was expelled from the CP in 1937 when he openly objected to this association; he had anyway become increasingly disturbed by the CP's authoritarian tendencies. But he was very far from embracing bourgeois moral values and political policies, which he always considered inadequate to the task of eliminating social and economic injustice. By the end of the war, in his editorial writing in the Resistance newspaper *Combat,* he demanded that people not become resigned to the return of the old pre-war bourgeois society. He had commented over-optimistically in 1944 that "'social justice needs no complicated philosophy,'" and in the first open edition of *Combat* called for the destruction of trusts and other financial monopolies, so that a genuine popular working-class democracy might be built, the middle-class should hand over power to the workers, and accept instead the role of "witness to a greatness it could not create itself."

Bread was essential to survival, in Camus's view, but so also was a certain dignity and quality of life. It was not enough only to satisfy the immediate physical wants of underprivileged people when they were still systematically deprived of full participation in society and treated, as a consequence, without understanding or respect, particularly by certain left-wing intellectuals who claimed to understand their best interests. In his foreword to a novel by the working-class writer Louis Guilloux, Camus makes the point that most French writers who talk about the working-class come from comfortable or well-off backgrounds. Though he regards this as no stain on them, but as the luck of the draw, he nevertheless confesses, "I have always preferred that one should bear witness . . . after having had one's throat under the knife. Poverty, for example, leaves behind in people who have experienced it an intolerance which doesn't take well to someone who speaks of a certain kind of destitution without knowing what they're talking about." The proletariat, he observes, is often discussed as though it were a tribe with strange customs, in a way that would nauseate proletarians themselves if only they had the time to read these specialists' studies in order to be informed about the happy march of progress. Camus finds it hard to decide which is the most insulting in such sermons, the disgusting flattery or the open disdain, which he paraphrases in the following exchange: "proletarians would not cherish the small amount of freedom which they have at their disposal. Bread alone interests them and, without bread, what would they do with formal liberties? How vulgar they are!" And, for the working-class reaction: "'What do you like best, man, the fellow who wants to take your bread away in the name of freedom, or the one who wants to take your freedom away to make sure you have your bread?' Answer: 'Who should get spat on first?'" In contrast, writers born of the working-class know that "if one can lend a kind of nobility to poverty, the slavery which almost always accompanies it will never be justified," for they understand how excessive poverty impoverishes even the most intimate of passions: "Fifteen thousand francs a month, life in the workshop, and Tristan has nothing to say to Iseult any more. Love also is a luxury, there lies the condemnation."

Camus argued that the chasm between the outlook of the working-class and the left intelligentsia would deepen if the latter continued to accept the sacrifice of vital social freedoms in the pursuit of ultimate social justice. In his view, the liberal position, offering freedom without justice, would perpetuate the oppression of the many by the few who owned wealth, but bread without freedom was an insult to individual human dignity. The task ahead lay in finding an equilibrium between the two claims rather than in painting them as antagonistic, possibly irreconcilable forces, as was all too often done by both liberals and radicals: freedom and justice were opposite sides of the same coin existing in a creative balance, not an antagonism. For Camus, this balance could only be maintained by socialism, a socialism which preserved and cherished democratic liberties, most important of all freedom of expression. As he confessed in a letter to his friend, Roger Quilliot, "it is quite true that I would no longer have any fondness for living in a world from which what I will call the Socialist hope would have disappeared."

No revolution, whatever justice it might promise, could be bought at the expense of basic humanity: injustice in the name of some future human condition would betray the very people whom the revolution sought to liberate. In his play, ***Les justes*** and in ***L'homme révolté,*** Camus explores this painful lesson of history, searching for an alternative form of political action that could fight for social justice without devastating human life. The "scrupulous murderers" of ***Les justes*** acknowledge from the outset that they must be prepared to give their own lives in payment for their targeted acts of political violence, yet circumstances force them inevitably to confront a further question: can their revolution justify the taking of innocent life? The answer, for Camus, is clearly no: even in destruction there must be limits, for as the simplest of peasants could tell any intellectual, to kill children is contrary to honor, and honor is not a luxury, but "the last of the poor's riches."

With ***L'homme révolté,*** Camus unfolds, as a tentative beginning, his view of an alternative politics. He proposes, in place of the revolutionary's messianic spirit, the attitude of the rebel, whose political action is limited always by a sense of the sacredness of human life, requiring a constant balance between relative freedom and relative justice. Camus offers the trade union movement as an example of rebellion translated into effective political action. Libertarian syndicalism, he argues, has long struggled against bourgeois oppression, and it is to this movement, rather than to Marx, that the proletariat owes its most basic victory, the reduction of a sixteen-hour working day to a forty-hour week. In such political action, as in the wise use of technology, he sees the opportunity to alleviate the misery of working-class life without increasing injustice and crushing freedom. The nature of a union collective, organized by and for the workers to address their own problems, can give the working-class an authentic political voice in its successful, as in its unsuccessful struggles.

Camus's short story, **"Les muets,"** from ***L'exil et le royaume,*** describes one of these unsuccessful struggles. Set in an Algerian town, the tale concerns the aftermath of a failed strike at a cooper's workshop. After being forced back on the job out of the need to put food in their families' mouths, the workers express their bitterness by refusing to speak when addressed by their boss. The irony is obvious: rather than a sign of impotence, the curse of the oppressed, their silence has become a non-violent weapon, a last defense of outraged dignity. When they learn later that the boss's little daughter has been taken seriously ill, their silence becomes a painful one in the face of a common human tragedy. However barren their lives, the workers have not lost their compassion, then, but nor have they lost their sense of solidarity, demonstrated even toward the one Arab who works with them. Although they are simple men, they communicate through a language of mutual respect and show a delicacy of feeling toward one another that contrasts strongly with the insensitivity and awkwardness of the boss in his dealings with them. Their nobility in silent rebellion exemplifies, in Camus's terms, what it means to affirm one's companionship with all of humanity.

If Camus's hopes for a post-war working-class democracy went unfulfilled, his radical tone did not change, as may be observed in his somewhat neglected editorials for *L'Express* written in 1955-56. He frequently used the editorials to draw notice to specific instances of poverty and oppression that had been comfortably ignored or tolerated by the bourgeois establishment. One such small, overlooked tragedy noted by Camus is that of two roofers, still working at well over retirement age, who fell to their deaths while on the job. In another piece, Camus discusses a settlement made at the Renault company, without a strike, between workers and management. It was good that there was no strike, he says, if you know what a strike can do to a working-class family. And it is *not* true that an improvement in their standard of living would diffuse the fighting force of the workers, for it is often the poorest who are most resigned. But the main problem, as yet unresolved, he identifies as "that internal exile which separates millions of men from their own country" through miserable wages and suburban ghettoes. If this injustice continues, Camus argues, the working-class will remain, "against its will, a state within a state." Reforms should not be despised, but nor should the end of reform be forgotten: "the re-integration of the working-class with all of its rights and the abolition of wage labour."

His review for *L'Express* of an inquiry into the condition of the Parisian working-class bluntly calls working-class misery the disgrace of this civilization, for which bourgeois society has only come up with one remedy: silence. To be poor in the presence of wealth, Camus adds, is an especially bitter fate: for all those who own luxury cars, there are women holding themselves back from leaving the job to go to the toilet, so as not to lose their three franc bonus. What the inquiry illustrates, in his words, is "a solitary world deprived of any immediate hope." He quotes a miner as saying poignantly, and with particular significance to one such as Camus himself, born under Mediterranean skies, "when our boys first go down the mine, they start to cry: they can't see the sun any more."

Another of Camus's editorials concerns a true-life example of working-class oppression remarkably close in flavor to **"Les muets."** He describes how two trade union members were condemned to do time in a correctional institution for having refused to shake the hand of their perfect, or local government administrator: "their reserve," he explains, "constituted an outrageous attitude, according to the judges. He who doesn't say a word insults." Yet refusing to shake hands, Camus suggests, is really a peaceful way of showing that one disapproves of something: "unable to dignify the social morality that had been outraged in this affair, [the workers] wanted at least to substitute for it a sort of cleanliness. Not to compromise oneself, wasn't that the rule of true nobility? And besides, what would our hand be, for those we love, if we gave it to the first comer?"

In Camus's opinion, then, the misery and humiliation of poverty, and of discrimination against the working class, remained ill-disguised cankers polluting society, and little had been done to remove them. His editorials point uncompromisingly at the conclusion that freedom alone could not end social injustice, and that bourgeois liberals, blinded either by their nature or by choice, would *not* come to recognize the misery of the working class or of the indigenous population in their colonies as an urgent, unacceptable tragedy. At the same time, the editorials consistently demand a shift in the position of the left toward a new emphasis on the importance of freedom. For if certain people on the left considered servitude an excusable path to justice, while others on the right continued to hide the realities of poverty and economic oppression under cloak of constitutional liberties, the struggle to shape a better society could not be won.

Camus saw the Communist left as condescending to the working class, offering social justice at the terrible price of liberty, and advocating revolutionary violence without considering, or without revealing, that the poor, who had no political voice, would have to pay for it most dearly. How ironic it was, indeed, that working-class consciousness should be so exalted by those who knew nothing about it, yet thought of themselves as most qualified to judge how the working class should pursue its struggles. Bourgeois liberals and Communist left were, it seemed, curiously united in their emphasis on some form of future social well-being, though their respective panaceas differed. But for Camus, who believed in no heavenly reward for suffering on earth and considered the future an unpredictable affair, to accept the ruin of a life lived today was criminal, whether that life were devastated in an urban slum or in a forced labor camp. Whoever saw fit to excuse or even to tolerate the exclusion of the greater part of society from full enjoyment of its benefits became themselves impoverished in human terms. The supreme arrogance of such an attitude could only warp any kind of politics that it might produce. For the politics of fighting poverty required, in his view, a fundamental recognition of a common human condition and a shared destiny. If poverty could attack its victims psychologically, the psychology of the fortunate could act equally as a barrier to understanding the world of the poor. So whatever social and economic policies might be adopted to tackle the problem of poverty, there had also to be a change of consciousness, both morally and politically, on the part of those more privileged members of society, or else the poor would still be condemned to internal exile in their own land. As may be seen in the pained irony of his editorials for *L'Express,* Camus sought urgently to convince his readers that the occasional sense of pity or act of charity was an insufficient, even insulting, answer to such suffering. Political action had to be accompanied by individual moral integrity on the part of those involved, arising from a genuine realization that it was a crime to treat the poor as if they were a breed apart, and had no need of justice, freedom, and dignity. He demanded, in place of the insincerities and inhumanities of both Communist left and bourgeois politics, a socialism distinguished by its defense of human solidarity and communication, a socialism that would assure all members of society an equal freedom to cultivate their individuality.

Camus did not forget that as a successful writer he himself was no longer poor, and he worried that material comfort might exert a damaging influence upon his own moral integrity: he comments regretfully in a notebook entry, "it is in poverty that I have found and always will find the necessary conditions such that my guilt, if it exists, should at least not be shameful, and remains proud." He retained a strong sense of solidarity with the working class from which he had come: "French workers," he writes, "are the only people I feel good around, that I want to get to know and to 'live.' They are like me." Although, during the acrimonious debate in *Les temps modernes* following the publication of ***L'homme révolté,*** Sartre put forward the argument that Camus was now just as much a bourgeois as Francis Jeanson and himself, Camus could claim justifiably to have come *from* the working class and hence to possess a certain sensitivity toward it that could not easily be gained from reading books. His angry retort to his critics who had "never placed anything but their armchairs in the direction of history" surely stemmed in large part from his frustration at hearing the working class discussed by people who had no more than a theoretical grasp of its problems and declared their commitment to revolutionary change in writing only, from the safety of cafe terraces. The suffering of the poor he considered to be similarly misunderstood by existentialists: "according to [them], every man is responsible for who he is. This explains the complete disappearance of compassion from their universe of aggressive old men. And yet they pretend to fight against social injustice. So there do exist, then, people who aren't responsible for what they are; the poor man is innocent of his poverty." The innocence of the poor man Camus could certainly claim to know about from personal experience: if he was no longer innocent, living the life of a bourgeois intellectual, he had been touched by poverty, remembered its injustices, and identified passionately with those who still endured it.

II. Camus's Experience of Poverty

Throughout his career as a writer, Camus repeatedly turned back to his childhood and youth in Belcourt to retrieve and to explore artistically the internal experience of poverty. ***Le premier homme*** offers the most continuous and detailed of these explorations. In comparison to his commentary on working-class poverty in France or on the tragedy of Kabylia, it might seem at first glance that Camus had a nostalgic, even romantic, attitude toward his own poverty, mitigated as it was for him by the natural wealth of Algeria's climate and landscape. Poverty and the sun, he writes, were the twin sources of his artistic vision, poverty reminding him that not all is well under the sun and history, and the sun teaching him that history is not everything. In ***Noces,*** an early work, Camus celebrates the beauty of nature and youthful bodies, describing lyrically the sensual pleasures of sea and sun, and the direct, spontaneous attitude to life of the young working—class Algerians among whom he grew to manhood. But his lyricism is tempered by a sober warning: youth is short for those who are poor, and any idea of self-improvement, or of virtue, means little if one must enjoy existence so passionately, so swiftly. Without religious sense and without myths to disguise the brutality of their existence, these people have their own moral code, which he recalls in spare terms: "You don't let your mother down. You make sure your wife is treated respectfully in the street. You show consideration for a pregnant woman. You don't come two to one upon your enemy, because that's 'pulling a dirty move.' Anyone who fails to respect these basic rules is 'not a man,' and that's it."

In ***Le premier homme,*** Camus's lyricism is equally tempered by his description of the consequences of poverty: there is no change of heart regarding its crushing indignities, despite the recollected pleasures and moments of human tenderness in the novel. The internal experience of poverty is stripped naked, quite without romance or sentimentality, to reveal a universe closed in upon itself, clinging to its own particular values born not of religion or theory, but of simple hardship. Camus writes movingly about the terrible vulnerability of the poor European community from which he came, not just as it might be in the violent Algeria of the 1950s, but as it had been from its first tenuous and tortuous attempts to establish a livelihood in a strange land. ***Le premier homme*** thus illustrates with particular acuity why Camus might refuse to condone wholesale Arab nationalist violence against the French presence in Algeria: he sought to defend the poor Europeans, themselves in a sense silent victims of colonial rule, for they would be the ones to suffer helplessly if random terrorism became widespread, not the wealthy *colons* who could afford to protect themselves or to move elsewhere. His avowed intent in writing ***Le premier homme*** was precisely to "tear his poor family away from the destiny of poor people, which is to disappear from history without leaving a trace," and the title of the novel reflects a double meaning. Jacques Cormery, Camus's fictional counterpart, is the first man, having had to bring himself up alone, fatherless and poor, and navigate a new course far beyond the limited universe of his family. He came, however, from immigrant stock, people who had fled poverty and oppression in their own countries; so in his family history, too, were "first men," uprooted often unwillingly from their European origins and driven to plant new roots in African soil.

Poverty, Camus remarks, is "a fortress without drawbridges"; and as ***Le premier homme*** unfolds, it becomes more and more remarkable that he himself managed to find a way out of the fortress. For his family were not just badly off but constantly on the edge of indigence, and without the intervention of a primary school teacher who recognized his promise, he would have disappeared into the workforce at the age of thirteen. Instead, as a scholarship student at the Lycée, he began to discover a whole world outside his own small one that would be forever closed to his family. The home of Jacques Cormery (Camus's fictive name) was a small world indeed, curtailed by lack of education born of scant opportunity, and by the grinding effects of a constant struggle to secure the minimum for survival. Jacques had never known his father: Henri Cormery died in France during the Great War before Jacques was two years old. He is described as a "hard man, bitter, who had worked all his life, had killed on command, had accepted everything that he could not avoid, but who, in some part of himself, refused to be tamed. In short, a poor man. Because poverty does not choose itself, but it can look after itself." And if Henri Cormery had left his family in poverty to fight for a land he had never even seen, how much less did his wife understand the cause that would eventually claim his life. Hampered by partial deafness, illiterate, and without the least sense of geography, she could not vaguely imagine what France might be like. She knew that her own family had fled Minorca because they were starving, and knew that it was an island, but she had no conception of what an island was because she had never seen one. She had no idea of history beyond that of her family, and the orders that came for her husband to join up were as mysterious to her as the written notice she received of his death: since neither she nor her mother, who lived with the family, could read, the very notice of death had to be read aloud to them. So it was useless for Jacques to try and talk at home about what he was studying because his family members had no points of reference in their own lives through which to give coherence to his discoveries: For them,

> Latin, for example, was a word that had absolutely no meaning. That there might have been (apart from savage times, which they could, on the contrary, imagine) a time in which nobody spoke French, that civilizations (and the very word meant nothing to them) might have succeeded each other whose customs and language were different: these truths had not reached as far as them. Not picture, nor written word, nor spoken information, nor the superficial culture that comes from everyday conversation had reached them: In this house where there were no newspapers, until Jacques brought them in, no radio either, where there were only objects of immediate usefulness, where only family was received, a family one rarely left—and always to meet members of the same ignorant family—what Jacques brought back from school was impossible to assimilate, and the silence grew between him and his family.

The poverty of Jacques's family had other consequences difficult to imagine for someone from a more fortunate home. His own home, for example, was so naked of objects that things had no special names; and only in a richer house containing a multiplicity of vases, cups, statuettes and pictures did the young Cormery come to know that things can have proper names. The ability of poor people such as the Cormery family to recall past events was similarly affected. For, as Camus explains, the memory of the poor is

> less nourished than that of rich people, it has fewer points of demarcation in space because they rarely leave the place in which they live, fewer landmarks also in the time taken up by a uniform, grey life. Of course, there is the memory of the heart that is said to be the most reliable, but the heart gets worn out by burdens and hard work; it forgets more quickly under the weight of tiredness. Past time is only discovered by rich people. For the poor, it marks only the vague traces of the road toward death. And after all, to be able to bear things well, it's better not to remember too much; you have to stick close to the days, hour by hour.

Proust's madeleine, Camus appears to suggest, is a luxury not enjoyed by poor households.

While the Cormerys could not understand the new intellectual wealth Jacques had gained at high school, it was just as difficult for him to explain his family's world to his classmates and teachers. The shocking poverty of his household was sometimes a source of outright embarrassment for a boy gradually becoming sensitive to the differences in background between himself and his peers. For example, he could quite acceptably tell the class, when asked at the beginning of the new term, that his father had been killed in the war. Yet when he came to fill out a form which required him to state his parents' professions, he was at a loss. At first he wrote, for his mother, "housewife," but Pierre, a schoolfriend, explained that this implied his mother had no profession at all and stayed at home to keep house. Jacques revealed that his mother looked after other peoples' houses; "'Oh well, then,' said Pierre, hesitating, 'I think you'd better put maid.'" Jacques was surprised, never having thought of his mother as someone who worked for other people, but as someone who worked for her own family. As he was about to write the word "maid," "he stopped and suddenly felt . . . ashamed, and the shame of having been ashamed." And he copied the word out boldly. On another occasion, he was asked that his parents sign a form, the sophisticated language of which he had to unravel for his mother and grandmother. His mother had learned from a neighbor how to write her name so that she could obtain her war-widow's pension, but she left early for work having forgotten to sign the form, and his grandmother could not write even her own name. So he faced further embarrassment before his teacher when he was asked whether anyone at home could not have signed it apart from his mother. He realized, from his teacher's surprise at his answer, that "his situation was less common than he had imagined until then." On prize-giving day, the Cormery women arrived embarrassingly early for the ceremony, "as the poor always are," Camus remarks, "having few social obligations and pleasures, and worrying about not being on time." For "those whom fate has served badly can't help, in some part of themselves, believing that they are responsible, and they feel that this general guilt should not be added to by small lapses."

Poverty, Jacques also discovered, tried his desire to be honest, as much as it did his pride. At the age of thirteen, he had to start earning to contribute to the household's meager income, even though he would only be able to work over the summer holidays. Knowing that the boy would not be hired by anyone just for such a short period, his grandmother falsely told his prospective employer that he had left school for good because his family was too poor for him to continue studying. Jacques was left to explain the lie on his dreaded last day of work before the new term; and his irate boss could not be made to realize that it was the Cormery's poverty that had required the lie in the first place. His financial contribution to the Cormery household nonetheless marked an important transition in his life: in their eyes, he was now a man.

Jacques was lucky to escape the drudgery of work during school-time: the rest of his family enjoyed no such luxury. There could never be a break, for such a thing would mean less to eat for everybody. The poor would only stop working in the case of an accident on the job when their sick-leave was paid by company insurance. Unemployment not covered by insurance was their worst nightmare. Camus explains this to be the reason

> why workingmen . . . who in their everyday lives were ever the most tolerant of men, were always xenophobes when it came to questions about work, accusing in succession the Spanish, the Jews, the Arabs, and finally the whole world of stealing their work away from them—a disconcerting attitude, certainly, for intellectuals theorizing about the proletariat, and at the same time extremely human and understandable. It wasn't for world domination or for the privileges of money and leisure that these unexpected nationalists got into disputes over other nationalities, but for the privilege of slavery. Work in this quarter was not a virtue but a necessity which, for the sake of survival, carried you on to death.

Death was a frequent visitor in Cormery's neighborhood, to be greeted without sentimentality or fuss: his grandmother, upon hearing that a person had died, would only say, "'Ah well, he won't fart any more,'" or in the case of someone closer to her, "'Poor fellow, he was still young,' even if the deceased had been of a dying age for a long while. It was not a lack of awareness on her part. Because she had seen a lot of people die around her. . . . But precisely, death was as familiar to her as work or poverty; she did not think about it but lived it in some way." Meanwhile, with "the terrible wear and tear of poverty, it became hard to find a place for religion. . . . One was Catholic as one was French, and that entailed a certain number of rites . . . baptism, first communion, the sacrament of marriage (if there were a marriage) and the last sacraments. Between these ceremonies, by their nature very far apart, one was busy with other things, and primarily with surviving."

The world Jacques Cormery so narrowly escaped was one of a daily struggle which could not for a moment be abandoned, whether to rest, to gain education or simply to contemplate the larger questions about human existence. There was no comfortable padding between these poor people and three grim facts: a brief youth, hard work, and an early death. Like victims of tuberculosis, they lived in the constant presence of their own mortality, unable to afford the relief of either romance or sentimentality. Nevertheless poverty, in all of its humiliating nakedness, nourished a kind of ethic, teaching the boy what it was "to be a man," and to carry on with as much pride and dignity as might be salvaged after the hours of drudgery. "It is . . . among these humble or proud people," Camus states unreservedly, "that I have most surely touched that which seems to me to be the true meaning of life."

In spite of what he might have learned from his Belcourt years, Camus nowhere suggested that poverty was worth suffering because it was a condition that encourage virtue. On the contrary, at its worst it was an experience salutary for neither soul nor body. Poverty limited human intercourse with the world just as his mother's deafness restricted her to a lonely and silent universe. To be poor was to be entrapped in an unceasing cycle of work from birth to death, with the fear of unemployment and hunger hanging overhead like a sword of Damocles. Poverty shortened the memory, dampened the imagination, wore down friendships and loves, ate away at youthful vigor and promised no reward after death but the curt sympathy of a neighbor or family member. It permitted of no time for sickness, idleness, or self-development, and demanded of its victims the kind of solidarity and endurance required of an army under attack: one slip, and everyone would be exposed to suffering.

Poverty had given Camus his initial, personal experience of human solidarity, but he was clearly aware that such solidarity was not exclusive to the experience of the poor: he encountered it also sharing in the struggles of the Resistance movement under the Nazi occupation. His metaphorical use of the plague and its effects upon the citizens of Oran, in ***La peste*** is evidence of this awareness: his protagonist, Dr. Rieux, bears witness to both human solidarity and human weakness in the face of a desperate common plight. Never did Camus propose that everyone should suffer the deprivations and humiliations of poverty, or the misery and terror of an occupying totalitarian power in order to be acquainted at first hand with the true meaning of life. Rather, he was proposing that because such experiences strip our existence of its sheltering illusions, testing our moral fortitude as much as our capacity for compassion, they can remind us powerfully and directly of our shared human fate.

Through his literary art, Camus attempted to offer both the suffering and the solidarity to the imagination of his readers who might not or could not experience the world of poverty for themselves. His great achievement in ***Le premier homme*** lies exactly in his ability to portray what to many of them might as well be the landscape of some alien universe. Although he had escaped the barren and shuttered life of poverty, he had not forgotten even its most intimate details, nor its greatest injustices. His escape was not a source of self-congratulation for the adult looking back, but a sobering reflection: so many others were left behind, and it was for these people that he felt driven to speak. His experience, while not the desperate misery of the Kabyles, gave him a bitter taste of the extreme: to use his own phrase, it shortened his descent into the other side of the valley.

Poverty was an urgent political issue for Camus because it concerned those who did not suffer it as much as those who did: to tolerate its presence passively was to perpetuate actively a gross inhumanity. Though he never elaborated a comprehensive and detailed social policy regarding poverty, he did indicate the direction that might be taken by government and society to relieve some of its most conspicuous hardships. He voiced the need for a socialism that would protect all members of society from political and economic injustice, while assuring them free expression as individuals. He demanded also an awakening of consciousness on the part of people who did not live under the burden of poverty, so that their political actions could be informed by genuine moral integrity, rather than theory or self-interest. Camus acknowledged that he himself had become distanced from the experience of poverty, not so much by an emotional gulf as by his material and intellectual circumstances. Still, he could at least bear witness with sympathy and honestly to its devastating effects, and employ his art with caution and respect to "say a little about eternal human suffering." The tragedy of the poor was that, unlike dumb animals, they knew very well that they were victims of injustice, but their lives were so draining, so monotonously absorbing, and so isolating that they might not be able to act to change them, let alone find the opportunity to speak out about their plight. Yet in the end, for Camus, all those who suffered mutely had to be encouraged to tell their story with their own authentic voices, no longer dismissed, organized, or condescended to by more fortunate outsiders, even such acutely sympathetic outsiders as he. And while these outsiders could not speak for the poor, Camus argued that it was their duty in human solidarity to provide a context in which the silence might finally be broken.

FURTHER READING

Aciman, André A. "Of Things Past." *Commentary* 101, No. 3 (March 1996): 60-3.

Provides positive analysis of *The First Man.*

Chaitin, Gilbert D. "The Birth of the Subject in Camus' *L'Etranger.*" *The Romanic Review* 84, No. 2 (March 1993): 163-80.

Explores the development of Meursault's subjectivity and alienation in *The Stranger.*

Chaitin, Gilbert D. "Narrative Desire in *L'Etranger.*" In *Camus's L'Etranger: Fifty Years On,* edited by Adele King, pp. 125-38. New York: St. Martin's Press, 1992.

Examines the narrative voice and temporal structure in *The Stranger.*

Davis, Colin. "Interpreting *La Peste.*" *The Romanic Review* 85, No. 1 (January 1994): 125-42.

Examines critical reception of *The Plague* and overlooked elements of narrative and linguistic ambiguity in the novel.

Erickson, John. "Albert Camus and North Africa: A Discourse in Exteriority." In *Critical Essays on Albert Camus,* edited by Bettina L. Knapp, pp. 73-88. Boston: G. K. Hall, 1988.

Discusses Camus's portrayal of North Africa in his novels and short stories.

Golsan, Richard J. "Spain and the Lessons of History: Albert Camus and the Spanish Civil War." *Romance Quarterly* 38, No. 4 (November 1991): 407-16.

Examines Camus's view of the Spanish Civil War as reflected in the plays *Révolte dans les Asturies* and *State of Siege.*

Lazere, Donald. "Camus and His Critics on Capital Punishment." *Modern Age* 38, No. 4 (Fall 1996): 371-80.

Explores critical debate surrounding Camus's opposition to capital punishment.

O'Brien, Conor Cruise. "The Fall." *The New Republic* (16 October 1995): 42-7.

Provides critical discussion of Camus's late career and the publication of *The First Man.*

Peyre, Henri. "Presence of Camus." In *Critical Essays on Albert Camus,* edited by Bettina L. Knapp, pp. 15-26. Boston: G. K. Hall, 1988.

Offers an overview of Camus's literary career and critical reputation.

Scheir, Donald. "The Warm and Innocent World of the Poor." *The Sewanee Review* 104, No. 3 (Summer 1996): lxvi-lxviii.

Provides positive evaluation of *The First Man.*

Sterling, Elwyn F. "Albert Camus's Adulterous Woman: A Consent to Dissolution." *Romance Quarterly* 34, No. 2 (May 1987): 155-63.

Explores the source of infidelity and guilt in "The Adulterous Woman."

Stoltzfus, Ben. "Camus's *L'étranger:* A Lacanian Reading." *Texas Studies in Literature and Language* 31, No. 4 (Winter 1989): 514-35.

Provides critical analysis of *The Stranger* based on the psychoanalytic theory of Jacques Lacan.

Zepp, Evelyn H. "The Popular-Ritual Structural Pattern of Albert Camus' *La Chute.*" *Modern Language Studies* 13, No. 1 (Winter 1983): 15-21.

Examines the ritual pattern of carnival "crowning" and "discrowning" in *The Fall.*

Additional coverage of Camus's life and career is contained in the following sources published by Gale: *Contemporary Authors,* Vols. 89-92; *Dictionary of Literary Biography,* Vol. 72; *DISCovering Authors; DISCovering Authors: British; DISCovering Authors: Canadian; DISCovering Authors Modules: Dramatists, Most-Studied, and Novelists; Drama Criticism,* Vol. 2; *Major Twentieth Century Writers,* Vol. 1; *Short Story Criticism,* Vol. 9; and *World Literature Criticism.*

Louis-Ferdinand Céline
1894-1961

(Pseudonym of Louis-Ferdinand Destouches) French novelist, pamphleteer, and dramatist.

The following entry presents an overview of Céline's career through 1996. For further information on his life and works, see *CLC,* Volumes 1, 3, 4, 7, 9, 15, and 47.

INTRODUCTION

A highly influential prose stylist and controversial polemicist, Louis-Ferdinand Céline is widely regarded as one of the most important European novelists of the twentieth century. His first two novels, *Voyage au bout de la nuit* (1932; *Journey to the End of the Night*) and *Mort à crédit* (1936; *Death on the Installment Plan*), earned immediate critical admiration and established his reputation as a daring literary innovator and iconoclast. Distinguished for his acerbic misanthropy, black humor, and apocalyptic vision of modern civilization, Céline broke from conventional French literature with his "style télégraphique," a fragmented, elliptical prose style infused with convulsive obscenity, neologism, lower-class slang, and delirious diatribe. Though condemned as a vehement anti-Semite and Nazi collaborator—unfortunate biographical facts that have long maligned his literary reputation—the startling intensity and nihilism of his early novels exerted a pervasive and lasting influence on contemporary European and American literature.

Biographical Information

Born Louis-Ferdinand Destouches in Courbevoie, France, Céline was an only child raised by his mother, a lace merchant, and father, an insurance businessman, in a lower middle-class Paris suburb called the Passage Choiseul; his pseudonym derives from the first name of his maternal grandmother. Céline was educated at local schools and, during his early adolescence, sent abroad to study in England and Germany, where it was hoped he would acquire marketable language skills for a business career. After working a series of odd jobs, in 1912 he enlisted in the French calvary and attained the rank of sergeant. During the First World War, Céline sustained serious arm and head wounds in the line of duty, for which was hospitalized and bestowed a medal of honor. He was he was reassigned to the French consulate in London in 1915. While in London, he met and unofficially married his first wife, Suzanne Nebout, a barmaid. Upon his discharge from the military in 1916, Céline abandoned London and his wife for West Africa, where he worked for a trading company in Cameroon. He returned to France the next year after contracting malaria and dysentery. Following employment with Henri de Graffigny, publisher of the inventor's magazine *Eurêka,* Céline worked for the Rockefeller Foundation as a traveling lecturer on tuberculosis in 1918. The next year he began his medical studies at the University of Rennes and married Edith Follet, daughter of the school's director. Céline completed his medical degree in 1924, along with his first published work, a doctoral dissertation entitled *La Vie et l'oeuvre de Philippe-Ignace Semmelweis* (1924; *The Life and Work of Semmelweis*). In 1925 Céline left his wife and daughter, as well as a lucrative medical career under his father-in-law, to work as a doctor for the League of Nations, a position that took him to Africa, Canada, Cuba, and the United States. With his divorce made final in 1926, Céline began an affair with American dancer Elizabeth Craig, the first of several dancers with whom he was involved. In 1928 he resettled in Clichy, France, where for the next decade he worked as a physician for the poor, in private practice and at a local clinic, and began to write. With the 1932 publication of his first novel, *Journey to the End of the Night,* Céline won instant acclaim and a nomination for the prestigious Goncourt Prize; he was awarded the lesser Théophraste Renaudot Prize due to jury politics. The next year he published his only drama, *L'Eglise* (1933), a satirical rendering of his medical experiences in Africa, America, and postwar France; the work, completed in 1927, represents a preliminary version of *Journey to the End of the Night.* After the 1936 publication of *Death on the Installment Plan,* Céline traveled to Russia to collect his royalties and reacted strongly against the hypocrisy and exploitation of the communist system, which he denounced in his first polemical tract *Mea Culpa* (1936; published with *The Life and Work of Semmelweis*). Céline published several additional political texts, including the venomous anti-semitic pamphlets *Bagatelles pour un massacre* (1937; Trifles for a Massacre), *L'Ecole des cadavres* (1938; School for Corpses), and *Les Beaux Draps* (1941; A Nice Mess), in which he alleged an international Jewish conspiracy to bring war, professed his own pacifism, and criticized French society. During the Second World War, Céline worked as a doctor on a French arms transport ship, published the first volume of *Guignol's Band* (1944), and contributed writings to collaborationist journals under the Nazi Occupation of France. Labeled a traitor and fearful of reprisal from the Resistance, Céline fled France in 1944 with Lucette (Lili) Almanzor, a former ballet dancer whom he married in 1943. Upon their arrival in Copenhagen, Céline was arrested by Danish officials at the insistence of the French government and incarcerated for fourteen months. After his release, due to poor health, he remained in Denmark for the next five years. In 1951 a French court found Céline guilty of treason, though a military tribunal granted him amnesty, whereupon he returned to France with Lili and settled in the Paris suburb of Meudon. During the remainder of his life, Céline practiced medicine among the poor and continued to write. He completed several additional novels, *Féerie pour une autre fois* (1952) and its sequel *Normance* (1954), and the trilogy *D'un château l'autre* (1957; *Castle to Castle*), *Nord* (1960; *North*), and *Rigodon* (1969; *Rigadoon*). His affinity for dance is also reflected in compositions for ballet contained in *Bagatelles pour un massacre* and *Ballets san musique, sans personne, sans rien* (1959; *Ballets Without Music, Without Dancers, Without Anything*). Céline suffered a fatal stroke at his Meudon home in 1961, a day after completing *Rigadoon.* A sequel to *Guignol's Band, Le Pont de Londres* (1964; *London Bridge*), was discovered among his papers and posthumously published.

Major Works

Céline's picaresque fiction recounts the author's childhood, wartime experiences, foreign travels, and medical career through the episodic misadventures of rogue protagonists whose first-person narratives are an amalgam of autobiography, invective, social satire, hyperbole, and hallucinatory paranoia. *Journey to the End of the Night* features Ferdinand Bardamu, a disillusioned French soldier who is seriously wounded during the First World War. After convalescing in various hospitals, reflecting on the horror and absurdity of war, and suffering a nervous breakdown, Bardamu embarks for Africa, where he witnesses the greed and exploitation of European colonialism as a trade representative deep in the jungle—an episode that resembles Joseph Conrad's *Heart of Darkness.* Disgusted with his position and the oppressive climate, he abandons his post to travel to America, where he experiences alienation and poverty in New York and Detroit. While in Detroit he takes a mindless factory job with Ford Motor Company and falls in love with a benevolent prostitute named Molly. Bardamu finally returns to France, signifying his resolve to confront rather than flee reality, where he completes his medical degree and works as a doctor among the working-class poor then at a private insane asylum. The novel is punctuated by recurring encounters with Bardamu's alter ego Léon Robinson, whom Bardamu meets during the war, in Africa, America, and again in France where, after becoming entangled in an assassination plot that results in his blindness, Robinson is shot to death by his estranged fiancée. *Death on the Installment Plan* is a *bildungsroman* based on Céline's traumatic childhood and adolescence prior to his military enlistment. Amid the poverty and squalor of suburban Paris, the protagonist, Ferdinand, endures the derision, lunacy, and physical abuse of his father, a feckless insurance clerk, and tenacious mother, a crippled lace peddler who operates a small shop below their apartment. After leaving public school, Ferdinand works several menial jobs and is dismissed in disgrace from each. Through the intervention of his kindly uncle, he is sent to a boarding school in England, where he has an affair with the headmaster's suicidal wife. Back in France, Ferdinand finds employment with Courtial des Pereires, a quack inventor and publisher of pseudo-science manuals. When Courtial's office is destroyed by defrauded subscribers, Ferdinand accompanies Courtial to the countryside to pursue an ill-conceived agricultural scheme that ends in police intervention and Courtial's suicide. Ferdinand is returned to his family and the novel ends with his decision to join the army. Ferdinand reappears in *Guignol's Band,* which centers upon Céline's experiences in London during the First World War. The word "guignol" is a double reference to a children's marionette show and a ridiculous person or buffoon. While in London, Ferdinand becomes involved in the underworld of prostitution and drugs through dealings with Cascade, a pimp who heads a large criminal operation. When Ferdinand is implicated in the death of a pawnbroker, he is pursued throughout the city by the police and Cascade's henchmen. At the French Consulate, where he seeks to rejoin the army, Ferdinand meets Hervé Sosthène de Rodiencourt, a mysterious occult explorer who is hired by an eccentric military officer to design a new gas mask for the British army. In the end, Sosthène's takes Ferdinand on as his assistant. *London Bridge,* the second part of *Guignol's Band,* picks up where the first leaves off.

While working on the gas mask with Sosthène under the direction of Colonel J. F. C. O'Colligan, Ferdinand remains in hiding and falls in love with the colonel's young niece, Virginia. The project is eventually abandoned when the colonel disappears and Ferdinand plans to flee the country with Virginia and Sosthène, who experiments with magical powers. A reconciliation with Cascade causes Ferdinand to miss a ship bound for Argentina and, in a final scene, he crosses London Bridge on the way to new adventures. Céline's wartime trilogy—*Castle to Castle, North,* and *Rigadoon*—recounts his desperate flight from France via Germany to Denmark at the end of the Second World War. Abandoning the pretense of a fictional protagonist, Céline writes openly as himself in these works, though takes great liberties in the presentation of time, place, and nonfactual episodes as he dramatizes events between June 1944 and the spring of 1945. In *Castle to Castle* Céline describes the middle stage of his journey, during which he lived and worked as a doctor in the French colony of Sigmaringen while seeking entry into Germany. After a long prologue in which he rails against the false accusations and hardships imposed upon him, the novel centers upon activities in and around the resort town which attracted many refugees of the notorious Vichy government. *North* revolves around Céline's stay in Baden-Baden and war-ravaged Berlin, where he witnessed the disintegration and chaos of the collapsing Third Reich, and *Rigadoon* traces his travels through northern Germany and finally to short-lived freedom at his destination in Denmark. Céline's additional novels, *Féerie pour une autre fois* and its sequel *Normance,* are transitional works that deal primarily with his imprisonment in Copenhagen and experiences prior to his arrival in Denmark. In *Entretiens avec le professeur Y* (1955; *Conversations with Professor Y*) Céline delineates his literary principles and techniques, which he compares to the work of Impressionist painters, through a mock interview with a hostile and inept questioner.

Critical Reception

Considered among the first rank of twentieth-century French novelists, Céline is highly regarded as a radical literary innovator whose manic prose, savage humor, and accusatory pessimism inspired a generation of writers and introduced new possibilities for the novel form. As David O'Connell reports, "In the last twenty years, Louis-Ferdinand Céline has emerged and, in the opinion of most major critics, joined Proust as one of the two greatest novelists of the twentieth century." Céline's wide-reaching influence is evident in the work of Samuel Beckett, Jean-Paul Sartre, and numerous major American authors, including Henry Miller, Jack Kerouac, William S. Burroughs, Joseph Heller, Ken Kesey, Kurt Vonnegut, Jr., and Thomas Pynchon. According to O'Connell, "In the United States, the number of writers clearly influenced by Céline is greater than for any other European writer, living or dead." While *Journey to the End of the Night* and *Death on the Installment Plan* are widely viewed as his most important works, Céline has also attracted critical praise for his trilogy *Castle to Castle, North,* and *Rigadoon.* Both *Journey to the End of the Night* and *Death on the Installment Plan* were immediately embraced by representatives of the political left and right, however Céline's anti-Semitism and fascist sympathies caused his work to fall into silent disrepute for several decades. His reputation was partially reinstated during the 1960s as critics regained appreciation for his lyrical rage and demystification of hypocritical institutions and popular sentiments, particularly military valor, middle-class respectability, and industrial prosperity. Philip H. Solomon writes, "Céline wields his pen like a scalpel (he was, after all, a doctor by vocation). He dissects the human condition, exposing its malignancies, but he offers no treatments or cures." As Jane Carson notes, "Céline writes with a purpose: to show us that the world does not conform to the structure we conventionally give it, that we are in fact surrounded by anarchy."

PRINCIPAL WORKS

La Vie et l'oeuvre de Philippe-Ignace Semmelweis [*The Life and Work of Semmelweis*] (dissertation) 1924

Voyage au bout de la nuit [*Journey to the End of the Night*] (novel) 1932

L'Eglise, comédie en 5 actes (drama) 1933

Mea Culpa, suivi de La Vie et l'oeuvre de Semmelweis [*Mea Culpa* and *The Life and Work of Semmelweis*] (pamphlet and dissertation) 1936

Mort à crédit [*Death on the Installment Plan*] (novel) 1936

Bagatelles pour un massacre (pamphlet and ballet) 1937

L'Ecole des cadavres (pamphlet) 1938

Les Beaux Draps (pamphlet) 1941

Guignol's Band (novel) 1944

Casse-pipe (prose sketches) 1949

Féerie pour une autre fois (novel) 1952

Normance: Féerie pour une autre fois II (novel) 1954

Entretiens avec le professeur Y [*Conversations with Professor Y*] (fictional interview) 1955

D'un château l'autre [*Castle to Castle*] (novel) 1957

Ballets san musique, sans personne, sans rien [*Ballet Without Music, Without Dancers, Without Anything*] (ballet) 1959

La Naissance d'une fée (pamphlet) 1959

Voyou Paul, pauvre Virginie (pamphlet) 1959

Nord [*North*] (novel) 1960

Le Pont de Londres: Guignol's Band II [*London Bridge: Guignol's Band II*] (novel) 1964

Rigodon [*Rigadoon*] (novel) 1969

CRITICISM

Kingsley Widmer (essay date 1968)

SOURCE: "The Way Down to Wisdom of Louis-Ferdinand Céline," in *Minnesota Review,* Vol. VIII, No. 1, 1968, pp. 85-91.

[*In the following essay, Widmer offers analysis of Céline's misanthropy and pessimism in* Journey to the End of the Night *and* Death on the Installment Plan. *According to Widmer, "Those who see nothing but humor and rancor in Céline miss the existential wisdom."*]

Céline's writings have a special relevance to contemporary American literature. While that should not be, given the usual adumbrations of our culture as arising from optimistic innocence and pragmatism and affluence, we may now be more willing to revise the bright theories than deny the dark facts of the American psyche. From the start of his literary career, with ***Journey to the End of the Night*** (1932), Céline appealed to the yearning for extremity so basic to American writers. Henry Miller, for example, was revising *Tropic of Cancer* in Paris when he enthusiastically read Céline's foray into new depths of the autobiographical novel of despair and outrage. The effects on Miller's best work, even including passages of verbal imitation, are evident. With the translation of ***Journey,*** and the following ***Death on the Installment Plan*** (1936), Céline became a more generally available standard for the American need of enraged disgust. To our *revoltés* of the 1950s he became a master. This continues, with that sachem of hyperbolic invective, Allen Ginsberg, recently proclaiming (in an interview in *Paris Review*) the greatness of Céline. And sentimentally sour Jack Kerouac recently acknowledged (in *Desolation Angels*) that he is, in part, imitating Céline. William Burroughs, an explicit admirer of Céline, attempted in *Naked Lunch* to outdo his master in the rhetoric of self-hatred, as did Sartre in *Nausea.* This emphatic, if peculiar, accolade has been repeated by several current American novelists of the urban inferno. More generally, not only is Céline undergoing an American revival, including new translations and academic studies, but his pertinence to our literary pursuit of apocalyptic grotesquery becomes pervasive.

Yet most of the American discussions of Céline seem tangential to the coherence of his best work. At least initially, we respond to the energy of his anger but not to the rigor of his pessimism. Partly this may be because of the difficulty of taking a disinterested view. Not only was it an avowed purpose of Céline's style to achieve a "gut" reaction, which it does, but the man, in and out of his writings, seems obstreperously unpleasant. Céline's anti-Semitism understandably cripples Milton Hindus' angry-awed pioneering study, *The Crippled Giant.* Irving Howe, dedicated to viewing literature in terms of ameliorist political moralisms, can only find unpleasant extremity in works that "lead to nothing" and illustrate no "yearning for good" (*A World More Attractive*). David Hayman does somewhat better in a cursory discussion (his Columbia essay, *Louis-Ferdinand Céline*) which emphasizes the author as a "comic genius" who is a master of "farce" and "verbal slapstick." Certainly there is much frenzied humor in Céline's work, though most dominant in the least integral scenes (and in the most fragmentary books, such as ***Guignol's Band***). But to see the violence of feeling as primarily farce and the negations as mostly humorous can serve as a defense, by way of nasty laughter, from the savage perceptions and sense of the art.

Because of its peculiar wisdom as well as its novelistic achievement, ***Journey to the End of the Night,*** I believe, provides the author's most significant work. (It is not, I suppose, accidental that the first novels of rebellious writers are usually their best work, as also with Henry Miller, J. P. Sartre, J. P. Donleavy, Ken Kesey, and many others.) That so many (including Hindus, Howe and Hayman) prefer his second novel, ***Death on the Installment Plan,*** may partly be explainable by that work's destructive "purity." This violent assault on petit bourgeoise life, by way of narrating the monstrous miseries of a shopkeeper's son in schools and various apprenticeships in and around pre-World War I Paris, remains unilateral. Any exaggeration in this comedy of nausea simply comes from a rhetorical extension of the undeniable realities of lower-middle class life. Céline's real "excess" here is the refusal to carry his autobiographical anti-hero out of that mean and resentful way of life. His Ferdinand, unlike the heroes of almost all novels of maturation, never "rises," and we are shocked to realize that the one grace of lower-middle class life is to leave it.

Death on the Installment Plan insists that its reality is hopeless and our shock of recognition comes in realizing that Stendahl and Dickens and Lawrence and other documentors of growing-up from mean origins also said this but allowed their heroes to escape. Not Céline, and therefore he can announce early in the book that "it was having been born that was such a mistake"; and by the book's end and his adolescent's despairing maturity, he can coolly conclude that "Growing up's a damn dirty break." In between come perhaps the most emphatically elaborated scenes of anxious grubbing and perpetual puking in literature which stays this side of nightmare. All pleasurable moments are illicit and merely preludes to scabrous despair. Sensitivity and intelligence speed up death's collections. The zest of the invective and the piling on of sordid details provide an antiphonal mode for the explicit moral: "Nothing mattered." Nothing, that is, but recognizing fully the stinking and cheating malice of a mean life-style from which there can be no escape.

Even Céline's sentimentality about the despoiled feminine, from the crippled and self-sacrificing mother through a series of good-hearted whores and other degraded-angel surrogates, serves only to re-enforce the negation and the characteristic grotesqueness of the feelings. For "life isn't a question of heart." But grotesquery cannot distract from the main theme that this social order makes life a petty accumulation of deathly payments. His most expansively brilliant grotesque, Courtial—a mad inventor, showman-rogue, philosopher-fraud—comes to the messiest accounting of all in a world of vicious bookkeeping. This *lumpen* Homais ends bankrupt, pursued, starving, head blown off, brains literally stuck in the filth. No ironic detachment here, even with the confidence man that traditionally calls it forth (as in Melville and Mann), for Céline rigorously denies the pleasant solace that one ever separates himself from his origins. In effect, Céline says, I hate myself—and with good reason.

Only rarely in ***Death on the Installment Plan*** does the exacerbated drubbing of a funkishly miserable lot reach an aphoristic brilliance, as in Céline's most quoted *bon mot:* "I piss on it all from a considerable height. . . ." Cathartic rage seeks such wisdom but cannot grant it, for memory and self remain all too true. The viewpoint is adolescence recollected with a total refusal of tranquility. ***Death*** remains an exhausting rubbing of a one-sore reality, a kind of *ne plus ultra* of the "social novel," the final downward push into an hallucinatory realism of the Balzac-Flaubert-Zola tradition of savage detailing of lower-middle class life. It is monumental, no doubt, but may also mark the final logic of such literary efforts. Later attempts to go beyond ***Death*** in disgust and nausea and self-hatred—including some of Céline's own later works—not only must break with the specific social reality but inevitably become fragmented and fantastic. The monomaniacal purity of that frenzied recall of an anxiously miserable childhood and society creates a mortuary document without range or reversal.

Not so with ***Journey to the End of the Night,*** the far less fixed and one-dimensional precursor to ***Death on the Installment Plan.*** The sick and desperate young protagonist of *Death* is preparing to enlist in the army, and that is the starting point of ***Journey.*** (The life-sequence of the two autobiographical novels is in reverse order.) He comically runs down the street to join up, and that starts him "on the road to nothing at all." The enlistment of the narrator, Bardamu, is casually tossed off as a total irrationality. The very lack of development of the crucial choice becomes one of the keys to the purpose of ***Journey;*** it is incomprehensible for the cynical anti-patriot introduced in the opening pages to enlist in the cavalry but, then "the war, in fact, was everything one didn't understand." And since modern society is simply war by other means, any journey through it is irrational violation of meaning and self.

The war scenes, such as that of the Colonel getting his stomach ripped open or those of the malicious absurdity of the officers (one's own army is the real enemy), are also casually deployed. None of it makes human sense, as with the off-hand summary of the death of a friend: they were in the wrong place and attacked by their own side, which was also in the wrong place and mistook them for someone else. Only by repeatedly undercutting traditional drama and meaning can we recognize our reality. "A lot of things, a lot of very cruel things, have got to happen to a fool before his mind can change its thoughts."

Journey rather raggedly covers about fifteen years in the thought changing of Bardamu-Céline as soldier, convalescent, colonial trader, drifter, American immigrant, doctor to the poor, marginal rogue and director of a mental sanitarium. While for Céline, as for so many others, a world war provides the path for disillusionment, he also searches for something much larger, for the "Truth" at the end of all this darkness. "Wisdom! That's what's essential. . . ." For this it is necessary to voyage into misery, the night side of life, the black places of the heart just because this "frightens all these bloody people" and they flee the truth. In both understanding and fact, "You don't climb upwards in life; you go down."

The end of the journey is the knowledge of his own failure. He arrives at no adequate compassion, "no great conception of humanity," to counter the reality of "a truly appalling, awful world." He reflects at the end that he knows his failure because his feelings won't do when confronted with death; he "hadn't acquired one single good solid idea," a "beautiful idea . . . to die with," an idea that could bring "joy and insouciance and courage." Ideas are not games to Céline, as to most moderns, but ultimately serious. And so was his journey into the darkness—a will to truth. The effort, then, however perversely, is to "wisdom literature."

In spite of the alternately raging and side-of-the-mouth tones of the narrative, Céline employs some artful ways in ***Journey.*** Underplayed but recurrent allegorical scenes heighten the narrative, such as the tawdry carnival in filthy weather (the state of human solaces) and the insane asylums (the normative madness of the world). Parallel family scenes in different places bitterly point up domesticity as commercial conspiracy and sexual torture. Surreal close-ups of sore mouths and fragments of inane conversation recur to remind us that Bardamu's truth is not to be found in the absurdities of human talk, nor in, as he says, "knowing too much," which confuses intellectuals. "Truth is a pain which will not stop."

One of the ways to hold to the pain of truth is to disrupt the usual logic of the world. The central experiences of the protagonist, from a traditional narrative view, would be his serious wounding during an heroic action in the war, his getting a job as a commercial trader in the African colonies, his becoming a doctor in Paris, and so on. Yet none of these are described at all in the book. Céline literally jumps over the center of an action or sequence, closely analogous to the "jump cutting" in contemporary cinema, to insist on the gratuitous fate that leads to the trap of worldly choice and to lay out the corpse in the heart after the trap has been implacably sprung. Since the usual narratives, and the usual analyses of character as an historical accumulation of actions, assume the coherent significance of reality, they cannot serve to tell the truth in a drastically irrational world.

Bardamu reflects at the end that what one actually remembers of his life is a series of regrets. Even memory, then, depends on pain. More extremely put: it takes a "protracted death agony, in which your brain is lucid . . . [to make it] impossible to comprehend anything but the absolute truths." Lucid pain: this is the nihilistic version of the traditional tragic argument that suffering brings wisdom.

With the detachment achieved from burnt-out rage, Céline often treats the truth- from-pain as grotesque comedy. The above pronouncement incongruously leads to several burlesque love affairs. Spending a convalescent leave in Paris, in which he must grossly feign patriotism to cover-up his feigned insanity to save himself from the grossly insane war world, he carries on with a pretty and fatuous American Red Cross Girl. Here Bardamu necessarily discovers the practical wisdom of reverse morality—the advantages of lying, leeching and lechery—and its general principle: "Morals, in fact, were a dirty business." As to his "pilgrimage," the stupid American's fine body provides the geography of his future; it was from the American's "backside that a message from a new world came to me." His American literary imitators have returned the compliment.

Céline's misanthropic gestures seem to mislead some readers. Certainly they provide crucial responses, wafted forth on the odors—he had a nose as fastidious as Shakespeare's—of bad breath, urine, feces, rot, dirt and disease. That is nature. So are his insect images: most men "are poisoned by themselves, like scorpions." And the metamorphoses of human ideals merely twist nature so that butterflies become maggots. For Céline, the misanthropic gestures are an answer to moral rhetoric and sentimentality: "Since we are nothing but packages of warm and rotten tripes, we shall always have difficulty with sentiment."

Certainly there are positive moments, the brief lapses when "one has disgusted Fate." In such energetic disillusionment, a meaningless universe threatens to become a malignant one, though Céline's anger at a false world keeps him from demoniacally respiritualizing the universe, as against some of the surrealists and Norman Mailer. The misanthropy must be understood as counterattack. His aesthetic derives from "retribution to fit the selfishness of the world."

Céline's sentimentality raises similar difficulties. The rough sergeant Bardamu finds in an African outpost rotting his life away to keep his crippled niece in a "nice" school, the generously loving whore in Detroit, and the other kindly waifs and outcasts, get exalted as they who "hobnobbed with the angels" and offer "tenderness enough to make a world anew." No doubt the good heart under the despised surface too easily transforms, for the moment, "a world that has no meaning." Just as often, of course, Céline's protagonist discovers false feeling, as when he notes that everyone has a good heart—"sods, with so much love inside . . . they die of love—still inside." For Céline's "angels" go beyond sentiment to bring forms of great though unrecognized ideas. Sophie, for example, the last of the angelically accepting women in ***Journey,*** prophesies in her open sexuality "the era of living delights of the great incontrovertible physiological harmonies yet to come." We see in such passages the positive basis of the nihilism, the antinomian vision, the radical prophecy of the heterodox artist. The good-hearted whores of rough male fantasy provide a local and defiant guise for transcendent demands.

To Céline's peculiar uses of misanthropy and sentimentality we must add his immorality as a trap for the literal reader. ***Journey*** certainly is an education in how to be a moral sod. Bardamu, for instance, learns how to jettison self-esteem: "While this humiliating trial [of groveling before vicious colonial officials] lasted, I felt my self-respect . . . slipping still further from me . . . it's a very pleasant sensation. After this incident I've always felt infinitely light and free; morally, I mean, of course. Perhaps fear is what you need most in life to get you out of a hole. Personally, since that day I've never wanted any other weapon, or any other virtues." ***Journey*** amply demonstrates cynical self-disgust as the most useful morality. But as long as he keeps journeying, Céline's hero never finds himself to be an adequate sod, despite the knowledge that this is what the world demands.

To be a fraud as well as to discover that most of the world is fraudulent are not quite the same thing, though, as Céline comments, to be an honest fraud rather than a righteous one is a considerable decency. Bardamu learns that he "must choose: either dying or lying." He chooses lying; yet, in terms of ***Journey***'s dramatic unfolding, that was clearly the wrong choice. Robinson, the rather shadowily developed but crucial alter-ego of the narrator, enforces the awareness of Bardamu's failure. When Bardamu is not yet conscious that he should desert the army, Robinson appears for the first time and announces he is going to surrender to the "enemy." With the same clarity, Robinson appears, a moral step ahead of Bardamu, scrounging in Paris, fleeing the commercial outpost in Africa, lamenting a stupid job and miserable loneliness in America, despairing of money and health in suburban Rancy, conniving at crime in Toulouse and (half-patient, half-keeper) in the mental sanitarium. Robinson, "that most unlucky man," is the narrator's "bad dream" and black-luck totem. He comes to represent to Bardamu the man who goes "all the way," completely opting out of a bad world and its rationalizations, the brave one who never shirks the journey into the night.

For Robinson did have what the narrator finally lacked: a "single good solid idea" to die with. That idea is simply negation, the certitude of "no." A lumpenish Bartleby, he endlessly prefers not to do what is demanded of him. The rather flat development of Robinson might be explained by the author's insistence that the character is drastically ordinary except for his saving idea. Crude, unreflective, Robinson lives his idea instead of arguing it—for "to philosophize is only another way of being afraid."

As archetypal victim and scapegoat, Robinson is seen externally; as Bardamu reluctantly recognizes, where he has it bad, Robinson has it worse. But not until the end does the narrator acknowledge the exceptional idea of Robinson, the man he should have been. For Bardamu has sold out. Hired as a medical hack in a private hospital for the insane, he curries favor with the director, such as agreeing with him that those who believe "in justice . . . are the most deranged." He also gives the Director lessons in English. Ironically, the exploiter acquires from the study of English literature and history an idea of individual freedom. So the Director gives up his nasty career and starts journeying, literally, down the insouciant dark road! Bardamu, however, sinks into anxious comfort and successful complacency as the new director of the insane. Robinson found a parallel choice with a little business and a girl who loves him in Toulouse. But Robinson refuses, and flees. Tracked down to the asylum by the girl, he continues to refuse, even when her love turns into a series of threats. As Robinson explains, what she calls "love" is but a "sauce covering the rot," and Robinson will not accept the rotten world. She finally shoots him for refusing her "love." Robinson painfully but bravely dies. With this, Bardamu recognizes his own failure to follow his journey to the end of the night, his own lack of an existential idea unto death, his inadequate refusal of the rotten world and its lying sauces of love.

Once the courage of refusal is recognized as the central wisdom of ***Journey to the End of the Night,*** the novel's irregular episodes become more than misanthropic and grotesque gestures. For example, some readers show puzzlement over Céline's treatment of the poor in various episodes of ***Journey,*** which seems rather "anti-liberal" in its cynicism. But those scenes continue the basic argument of the book. The "lower classes," the narrator notes, do not need moral charity. "When you've no money to offer the poor, you might as well shut up" for otherwise "you are almost invariably tricking them." (Many in our "Great Society" still don't get the point.) The only "job" for the exploited and defeated, indeed their only real hope for human dignity, "is to overcome that feeling of obedience" which the established in society demand. If the exploited have truly denied complicity in and acceptance of the vicious and fraudulent social authority, "then they can boast of not having lived in vain." The basic idea: the nobility of refusal.

Essentially similar points arise from Céline's satiric burlesques. Immune to little ideas, such as those of conventional religion and science, he elaborates this in the mocking scenes of a conniving, smelly, sore-mouthed priest and in the scenes of a nymphet-lusting scientist who specializes in hemorrhoids because those who give the rewards are likely to have them. Granted, the burlesques of America, as of the "debauchery" of our toilets and the promising but undeveloped satire of a Detroit mass-production factory, seem too easy and thin. (The scenes of the "Gay Calvin" Hotel of luxuriously desperate loneliness make their point more effectively.) With proper savagery, Céline builds identifications of patriotism and insanity, imperialism and accountancy, wealth and narcissism, morality and hatred. Only refusal is relevant.

The proper pilgrimage consists of a life of such refusal. His narrator in ***Journey*** wanders, picquantly and picaresquely, through the quasi-solaces of vice and nastiness. That is how things are. But even as he wonders in his grotesqueries, he also notes the peace and perception to be found outside. Only then does one truly know, "maddeningly realize how completely men are walled off from each other." With sad exhilaration, he discovers "it's during the little interval that you aren't known in a place that life's most bearable." Insight fuses with paranoia. But his Bardamu did not stay outside and so sank into petty comfort and yearnings which led to the denouement. Perhaps life, then, is only "lie, copulate and die." That remains the innocent truth for a Céline, until proved otherwise. But by the very energy of his bitter questioning and his refusal of the given world he remains a proponent of life until he comes to the end of the night.

It is that will to truth and the willingness to descend to death-in-life to find it which carries ***Journey to the End of the Night*** beyond Céline's roughness, his sometimes paranoic hatreds and cynical revulsions. Though sometimes a gross mode, novelistically and morally, it reaches through grotesquery to a fine old point—an idea for dying well. Those who see nothing but humor and rancor in Céline miss the existential wisdom. Certainly some of the doing is overdone, but an authentic art remains. Caught in the modern nihilist's dilemma of trying to make something—truth—out of nothing—an awful world—only the passion for refusal gives him strength and direction. He well knows that which must be denied (not least in the literary sense, as in his burlesques of Montaigne's and other traditional rhetorics of acceptance). Perhaps we can conclude with a prescriptive suggestion: those who would make use of Céline, including quite a number of contemporary American writers, must take with his social rages and literary violations his ancient questionings and his rigor of refusal. For the way down reveals its wisdom only when it does not pretend to be the way up.

Paul A. Fortier (essay date Spring 1971)

SOURCE: "Marxist Criticism of Céline's *Voyage au bout de la nuit,*" in *Modern Fiction Studies,* Vol. XVII, No. 1, Spring, 1971, pp. 268-72.

[*In the following essay, Fortier examines Marxist themes, interpretation, and critical reaction to* Journey to the End of the Night.]

Voyage au bout de la nuit, from its publication in 1932, created around itself an atmosphere of mystery and controversy. The author, who called himself Céline, was unknown. The grammar used in this text resembles that of factory workers, taxi drivers, and hoodlums—an idiom hardly considered to be a fit vehicle for art. The vocabulary is a curious mixture of neologisms, medical terms, and slang, frequently too coarse for mixed company. Yet the language of this novel bears the stamp of high artistic achievement; it moves swiftly and evokes powerful images with an economy of means rarely found in literature, let alone in the lower-class conversations which it imitates.

The setting of this strange and powerful novel shifts from wartime France—both at the front and in the hospitals behind the lines—to an equatorial African colony, then to an American automobile plant, and finally to various lower class milieux around Paris. Bardamu, the narrator, provides a unifying thread with his virulent criticism which spares nothing, least of all himself.

Immediately after the publication of ***Voyage au bout de la nuit*** Léon Daudet a founder of *Action Française* began a campaign to have this novel awarded the Goncourt prize. Daudet's efforts were seconded by George Altmann's laudatory article in the *Monde.* The Goncourt Jury announced informally that its coveted prize would be awarded to Céline. But a last minute manoeuvre deprived the author of official recognition—a disappointment ironically noted by Jean Fréville in *L'Humanité* and by Georges Bernanos in *Le Figaro,* among others. Céline was not the loser in this affair. The different political orientations of the four newspapers mentioned indicate the wide range of outlook among critics who admired his work.

A novel written in an approximation of working class style, set in the disadvantaged sectors of society, and generally recognized as great art, would certainly appeal to Marxist critics, all the more so because it roundly condemns all aspects of the capitalist society which it depicts. It is not surprising, then, that Louis Aragon and Elsa Triolet translated the novel into Russian. But after the short articles written when the novel appeared such as those by Paul Nizan and Jean Fréville, several years elapsed before the appearance of two more serious Marxist interpretations—both by Russian Marxists.

By 1935, the *Atlantic Monthly* published a study entitled "Novelist and Politician" by Leon Trotsky. Immediately identifying the "novelist" as Céline, Trotsky notes the artistic maturity of ***Voyage au bout de la nuit*** and predicts—quite accurately: "Céline has written a book which will survive, independently of whether he writes other books, and whether they attain to the level of his first." Trotsky notes that the novel is full of black pessimism, and—with obvious relish—he rapidly summarizes Céline's debunking of such sacred cows as military valor, the white man's burden, mechanized efficiency, scholarly altruism, petty bourgeois frugality, patriotism, love, motherhood.

Taking his transition from an allusion to Poincaré in Céline's novel, Trotsky shifts his attention to Poincaré's *Memoirs,* singling out examples of poor taste and hypocrisy. Trotsky suggests that these faults result from the politician's fervent belief in a bourgeois liberalism which has long since ceased to be a liberating force and has hardened into conventionality, or worse. Céline, we are told, rips away such sham to show bourgeois society in all its horror and depravity. Trotsky explains this in part by the novelist's truculent pessimism, but also by the nature of his art: "Céline's style is subordinated to his receptivity of the objective world. In his seemingly careless, ungrammatical, passionately condensed language there lives, beats, and vibrates the genuine wealth of French culture, the entire emotional and mental experience of a great nation, in its living context, and its keenest tints." According to Trotsky, the moving power of ***Voyage au bout de la nuit*** derives mainly from the fact that the novel is a faithful artistic re-expression of reality. But he points out that "hopelessness ever leads to docility." The novelist's pessimism, which also contributes to his success, is a threat to his originality: "By rejecting not only the present but also what must take its place, the artist gives his support to what is. To that extent Céline, willy-nilly, is the ally of Poincaré."

Trotsky's adroit use of dialectic leads to what seems to be the main point of his article: the difficulty for a non-Marxist to formulate a valid criticism of society. Trotsky uses Céline's novel, and Poincaré's *Memoirs,* merely to build up a highly sophisticated bit of propaganda.

The Russian language edition of ***Voyage au bout de la nuit*** appeared in 1936 with a critical preface by Ivan Anissimov. The second paragraph of this study suggests the critic's point of view: "Louis Céline a écrit une véritable encyclopédie du capitalisme agonisant." An encyclopedia, in spite of what Anissimov seems to think, does not usually contain the same amount of creative fiction as a novel.

Anissimov finds Céline's point of view somewhat ambivalent: "Céline n'est pas un adversaire conscient du capitalisme, mais seulement un grand artiste qui ne cache pas la vérité." The critic goes on to analyse the "truth" revealed by the author using a double-edged approach. A brief synopsis turns each section of the novel into an encyclopedia article on different aspects of capitalist society—war, African colonies, American industry, Parisian slums; each synopsis is followed by a critique of the author's presentation. After summarizing Céline's vision of wartime Paris, for example, Anissimov comments: "Il s'est figé dans l'horreur. L'idée de lutte ne lui vient même pas à l'esprit. L'indignation à laquelle il est en proie, est sans but. Il ne réfléchit pas au mécanisme social qui a engendré la monstruosité qui s'étale à ses yeux." These statements are entirely off the point. Céline was no immobilized by horror or overcome with aimless indignation; he undertook the difficult enterprise of writing a novel. We do not know what Céline thought about fighting capitalism, but obviously a novel is not a weapon to fight an entire social and economic system. The most it can do is satirize, which is precisely what Céline's novel does, as Anissimov himself pointed out. Finally, the novelist constructs a work coherent in artistic terms; he cannot shift his aim and comment convincingly on social structure. That is the job of the critic. Anissimov's study suffers from a basic misunderstanding of the difference between art and reality.

Whatever it might be, ***Voyage au bout de la nuit*** is not a fully developed Marxist analysis of the capitalist system. Yet, because of this, Anissimov condemns the novel for being passive, philistine, cynical, hypocritical, sterile, nihilistic, and abstract. So that the reader may be fully warned, the critic expresses such condemnation sixty-four times in eight pages. At the beginning of his study, Anissimov pointed out that Céline was not a Marxist; the effort involved in going through his novel and condemning it, because this is true down to matters of detail, is pointless. Anissimov's study seems important mainly as an example of the difficulty for a Marxist to interpret foreign literature in Russia during the height of the Stalinist era.

Céline travelled to the Soviet Union in 1936 to spend the royalties on the Russian translation of his novel. A year later in a pamphlet, ***Mea Culpa,*** he proclaimed his disgust with Russia and with the communist system. In 1938 and 1939 he poured out violently anti-communist opinions in two virulent polemical works. Trotsky's cavalier treatment of Céline and Anissimov's outright condemnation were fortunate in the short run. The Marxist world was spared the embarrassment of singing Céline's praises, only to have him turn anti-communist.

Trotsky had predicted that ***Voyage au bout de la nuit*** would be an enduring work of literature, and time has borne him out. He and Anissimov agree that this novel—in which Céline, not unlike Balzac, creates a model of an entire society—accurately reflects conditions in the capitalist world. The text of the novel presents, for example, in the war situation a strange division of roles. The ordinary soldiers like Bardamu or Robinson bear the greatest hardships, without believing in the struggle. Officers encourage the soldiers, more or less subtly, to continue their pointless efforts. Above them are the shadowy beings who profit from the war: the press, the organizers of "benefits" for the soldiers, the faceless Argentinians. In Africa the natives are doubly oppressed by the disease-ridden climate and by the rapacious European soldiers and traders. The whites—from the lowliest clerk, like Bardamu, to the Director General of the trading company himself—inflict suffering on the natives, but are exposed to the rigors of the climate and are exploited by the stockholders of that company, who, safe in Paris, only profit. Bardamu's description of the factory in Detroit fits into the same pattern. There are workers like himself, the foreman, and the doctor who help keep the system going, and Ford, an impersonal entity that somehow controls everything and profits from it. Each one of these situations is characterized by excessive noise and by violence. These two themes highlight the parallel inherent in the tripartite structure of each of the three situations mentioned.

A tentative explanation of these parallels could be found in Marxist theory which has long pointed out that a developed industrial system requires colonies or spheres of influence for markets, raw materials, and investment of surplus capital. Rivalry over colonies or spheres of influence is, in the Marxist approach, seen as a prime cause of war, specifically of the First World War—which Céline describes. Similarly the stratification of war society, colonial society, and industrial society ties in with a statement by Lenin:

> It is characteristic of capitalism in general that the ownership of capital is separated from the application of capital to production, that money capital is separated from industrial or productive capital, and that the rentier, who lives entirely on income obtained from money capital, is separated from the entrepreneur and from all

who are directly concerned in the management of capital.

The foregoing may suffice to suggest that Céline's novel could be interpreted from a Marxist viewpoint.

Céline, the author of ***Voyage au bout de la nuit,*** was not, had never been, and was never to become a communist or a Marxist of any kind. But his novel presents a microcosm of early twentieth-century society. It should be possible for a Marxist critic—fully realizing the difference between Céline's ideas and his own—to put aside controversy and analyse this novel in terms of one of the great critical and ideological systems of our age. The model for such a treatment can already be found in George Lukacs' studies of Balzac. Lukacs points out quite clearly that the royalist utopian vision, on which Balzac based his novelistic world, had been singled out for special irony by Marx, then he goes on to illuminate both Balzac's art, and the society from which the author drew his material, by analysing the texts in Marxist terms. A similar study of ***Voyage au bout de la nuit*** could promote understanding of a novel which, almost forty years after its publication, remains both powerful and mysterious.

Colin W. Nettelbeck (essay date January 1972)

SOURCE: "Journey to the End of Art: The Evolution of the Novels of Louis-Ferdinand Céline," in *PMLA: Publications of the Modern Language Association of America,* Vol. 87, No. 1, January, 1972, pp. 80-9.

[*In the following essay, Nettelbeck examines the evolution of ethical and aesthetic concerns in Céline's oeuvre. "Despite his reputation as a hate-filled iconoclast," writes Nettelbeck, "the central thrust of Céline's literary works . . . is, on the contrary, toward affirmation."*]

During the last fifteen years of his life, Céline reflected a great deal about his art. In his correspondence (particularly the 1947 letters to Milton Hindus), in the several interviews which he gave after his return from exile in 1951, and in his satirical self-interview ***Entretiens avec le Professeur Y*** (1955), there are many signs of a highly conscious esthetic theory. Yet these statements are limited in that they take no account of the *development* of the author's code which, far from being static, follows the evolution of his actual writing. Furthermore, analysis of the opus as a whole reveals that esthetic considerations are closely allied to ethical problems, so that by confining most of his comments to the stylistic aspect of his work, he actually obscures some of his most positive and ambitious intentions. Despite his wide reputation as a hate-filled iconoclast, we shall see that the central thrust of Céline's literary works, with the single exception of ***Voyage au bout de la nuit,*** is, on the contrary, toward affirmation. This does not mean, of course, that the negative side of his vision is unimportant, but rather that, from the tension created between the perception of death as the most potent reality, and the almost simultaneous intuition of the beauty of life, Céline seeks resolution in the direction of life. It is in this context that his more theoretical remarks on his art find their proper place.

Voyage au bout de la nuit differs essentially from the later works in both form and impact. It is the only novel in which Céline attempts to present a total synthesis of his vision, and the only one whose effect on the reader is unequivocally negative.

In the first section of this binary-structured novel, each of the major episodes is dominated by Bardamu's fear and hatred, and by multiple images of death and putrefaction. Any moments of tenderness quickly turn to disappointment or a sense of futility. It is only when he meets Molly that he finds a semblance of peace: "Pour première fois un être humain s'intéressait à moi, du dedans, si j'ose le dire, à mon égoïsme."

By forsaking the personal happiness offered by Molly in order to become a doctor, in the second half of the novel Bardamu takes on a social dimension that saves him from the fate of his double Robinson, whose undeviating egoism turns his rebellion into a revolt against life itself, leading to murder and self-obliteration. At the same time, Bardamu's "socialisation" does not imply liberation. On the contrary, it merely widens his despair. The protagonist sees the reason for this in his own lack of what he calls "l'amour de la vie des autres." In other words, despite the enlargement of his social awareness, he remains a prisoner of his ego, and the "qu'on n'en parle plus" that closes the novel suggests nothing more than a hopeless, mute survival. For the reader also, there is no possibility of catharsis, and the book is an intensely depressing experience. As Céline himself says of his opus, ***Voyage*** is "le send livre vraiment méchant."

At the same time, however, ***Voyage*** is a necessary foundation for Céline's self-definition as an artist. It is by expressing the extent of his negative vision that he prepares the way for affirmation. In the first half of the novel, Bardamu's characteristic response to experience is escapism. More specifically, he frequently becomes ill: "Moi, j'avais la vocation d'être malade, rien que malade." In the second half, however, the protagonist is first a doctor, then the director of a lunatic asylum. This change of role symbolizes the creation of an esthetic distance, which depends on an underlying faith in life. Not, certainly, in any individual human life, nor even perhaps in human life in general: the power of death is recognized in Bardamu's failure to save a single patient, and entertains no hope of curing the madness of the microcosmic society of the asylum. But life as a biological mystery—described by the narrator as "la vraie maîtresse des véritables hommes"—is perceived as beauty, and will henceforth become an increasingly positive pole in Céline's vision. At this stage, the perception remains relatively crude and ineffectual. Bardamu's glimpses of the beauty of life come mainly through his contact with women, particularly Molly and Sophie. He extols the vitality of Molly's legs—"magnifiquement déliées et musclées"—and of. Sophie's body: "Quelle musculature! Quelle excuse! Elastique! Nerveuse! Etonnante au possible!" At the same time, however, his egoism prevents him from really participating in this life. With Molly: "On s'embrassait. Mais je ne pas bien, comme j'aurais dû, à genoux en vérité." Sophie's body becomes "une divinité tripotée par mes mains honteuses." For real contact with life to be made, egoism has to be transcended to a greater degree than in Bardamu, for the ego contains the principle of death. Céline's subsequent artistic evolution hinges on this realization.

On the level of style and language, too, ***Voyage*** important. As Marc Hanrez points out, this novel is richer in linguistic and stylistic invention. Many of the following ones. Even though Céline, in retrospect, criticizes it as being too "well-written," his rejection of the traditional French distinction between the written and spoken language is clearly established, and the ground prepared for a new kind of language which, while retaining the flexibility and subtlety of literary expression, is deeply rooted in the vocabulary and syntax of popular speech. Céline's use of language is not a gratuitous rebellion; it is an attempt to prevent stereotyped reactions, to produce in the reader a raw emotional response. The novelist is explicit about this purpose in the Meudon speech 1933: "Nous travaillons à présent par la sensibilité et non plus par l'analyse, en somme 'du dedans.' Nos mots vont jusqu'aux instincts." In ***Voyage*** he uses his language as a weapon, but later this will not be the case.

In the next three novels Céline abandons the synthesizing form of ***Voyage,*** and adopts a more directly autobiographical approach. Bardamu disappears, replaced by a closer-to-real-life Ferdinand. Within this framework, Céline is able to pursue more systematically his exorcising of egoism, by reaching its sources in himself. And in doing so, he gets beyond the constructs of his own civilization to the submerged spring of man's myth-making poetic nature.

The title of ***Mort à crédit*** suggests a continuation of the death-dominated vision of ***Voyage,*** and to a large extent this is true. Both in the prologue and in the narrative proper, there are many images of death. At the same time, however, neither of the structural high points of the novel—Ferdinand's attempt to kill his father and the suicide of Courtial des Pereires—is entirely negative.

In view of the protagonist's uniformly soul-destroying apprenticeship in life, his attack on his father must be seen less as a mere psychological response to a miserable childhood than as an organic rebellion against all the forces that are crushing life out of him. On the personal level, it is an attempt to throw off the immediate source of repression and guilt, but it is also a revolt against the whole social superstructure. To this extent, it is an affirmation of life, at least on a visceral level, and it frees Ferdinand for the encounter with Courtial des Pereires.

As in the second half of ***Voyage,*** the Courtial episode of ***Mort à crédit*** marks the introduction of a new dimension, a move from the subjective adventure of the protagonist to a more universal plane. Courtial is an archetypal figure, incarnating Western man's thirst for knowledge of the cosmos. When Ferdinand begins to work for him, however, Courtial's destiny is already on the decline, as is witnessed by his farcical balloon ascents, his bankrupt journal, the fraudulent competitions that he launches to raise money, and the sexual orgies and flagellation which he uses to distract himself from the image of death. His final undertaking, the attempt to grow giant potatoes by using electric current as a stimulus, is a grotesque betrayal of nature and his own ideals: "Ça pouvait très bien se propager à toutes les racines de la France . . . Bouffer complètement la campagne! . . . Qu'il reste plus rien que des cailloux sur tout le territoire! . . . Que nos asticots rendent l'Europe absolument incultivable . . . Plus qu'un désert de pourriture!" Inevitable on the personal level, Courtial's suicide becomes a symbol of the suicidal tendencies of a civilization whose scientific spirit has been completely undermined and given over to materialism.

To this point, ***Mort à crédit*** reflects the binary structure of ***Voyage,*** with a similar widening of the vision of death. On the other hand, because of its symbolic repercussions, Courtial's destiny is profoundly tragic, and prepares the catharsis which occurs during the last few pages of the novel, where it becomes apparent that his decline has been accompanied by a corresponding ascent on the part of Ferdinand: "Ça m'atténuait les malaises de relever la tête . . . le ciel était d'une grande clarté . . . Je crois que jamais je l'avais vu si net . . . Ça m'a étonné ce soir-là comme il étoiles découvert . . . Je reconnaissais toutes les étoiles . . . Presque toutes en somme . . . et je savais bien les noms!" What Ferdinand has learned from Courtial amounts to an initiation into the ways of Nature, and even though it magnifies his knowledge and fear of death, it also liberates his consciousness.

By this "epilogue," which provides the mechanism for release of tension, Céline reveals an important change in his attitude toward the reader, as well as in his art. These changes are actually contained embryonically in the fragmented legend of King Krogold which takes up much of the prologue, but it is not until the upswing of the ending that the artistic significance of the elliptical Krogold myth becomes clear. In this respect, the themes of the legend—death, betrayal, vengeance—although they are also major themes in the novel, are less relevant than the fact that Céline is casting an image of the novelist as a teller of tales that ennoble and transcend reality, and elevate the spirit of the listener by their poetic vision.

This metaphor also evokes the notion of an essentially *oral* art, brought out in ***Mort à crédit*** when the narrator recounts fragments of his legend to Gustin, Mireille, and André. Significantly, the language of the novel, while less rich than in ***Voyage,*** is also less literary. It is here that Céline establishes his characteristic use of the "trois points," a key factor in his transposition of the rhythms and vitality of the spoken language. This is the beginning of the "style émotif" of which he writes in ***Entretiens avec le Professeur Y:*** "Le lecteur qui me lit! il lui semble, il en jurerait, que quelqu'un lui lit dans la tête! . . . dans sa propre tête!"

The storyteller image will continue to be an important reference point throughout the rest of Céline's work. In ***Guignol's Band I,*** the novelist presents himself as "Ménéstrel pour tous précipices . . . Baladin faridondant aux Antres du Monde." In the Hindus correspondence, he calls himself "un rêvasseur bardique." The title of ***D'un château l'autre*** continues the metaphor, as does the image of the protagonist in this and the last novels, wandering through time and making legends from history. If the metaphor is later enriched with others, it already reveals in ***Mort à crédit*** a far greater esthetic distance than in ***Voyage,*** and although death continues to dominate the author's vision of reality, the notion of "crédit" implies a certain reprieve. The time that kills is also the artist's entrance into the continuum of life.

It can be assumed that ***Casse-pipe*** would have continued the path opened by ***Mort à crédit.*** The fragments extant indicate a direct chronological sequel, dealing with Ferdinand's life in the army. Just how much Céline wrote of this novel is not known, and probably never will be, since the manuscript was among the papers scattered when his apartment was seized and pillaged during the Liberation. If, as Jean Ducourneau suggests ***Casse-pipe*** was begun immediately after ***Mort à crédit,*** then Céline interrupted it—and possibly abandoned it—in order to write his notorious pamphlets.

The anti-Semitism of ***Bagatelles pour un massacre, L'Ecole des cadavres,*** and ***Les Beaux Draps*** is not directly germane to this study. Without wishing to excuse Céline's treatment of the Jews which he himself later admitted to be indefensible, it could well be argued that the Jews as such are not his prime target. The main object of his hostility would seem to be French society with its widespread alcoholism, its atrophied education system, its sterile formalistic literature, its social injustices—all of which tend to transform people into robots: "L'Imagination matérialiste nous condamned à l'infini dans la destruction, la philosophies matérialiste, la poésie matérialiste nous mènent au suicide par la matière, dans la matière . . . Les hommes épris de la matière sont maudits. Lorsque l'homme divinise la matière il se tue."

On this level, the pamphlets tend toward the same end as the novels: a regeneration of the spirit of life. This is manifested in the ballet scenarios which begin and end ***Bagatelles,*** in the dedication of ***L'Ecole des cadavres*** to Julian the Apostate, the emperor who ejected the corrupt Christian power structure and restored the cult of the ancient pagan gods, and finally in ***Les Beaux Draps:*** "Il faudrait réapprendre à danser. France est demeurée heureuse jusqu'au rigodon. On dansera jamais en usine, on chantera plus jamais non plus. Si on chante plus on trépasse, on cesse de faire des enfants, on s'enferme au cinéma pour oublier qu'on existe."

Apart from its polemical content, ***Bagatelles*** furnishes considerable information about Céline's art. First, the ballet scenarios indicate a passionate interest in the dance, which has not been present in his writing since the end of ***L'Eglise,*** but which will become an increasingly important symbol of life in his work. Secondly, there is a prolonged attack on academic literature as a purveyor of secondhand emotions, with a strong statement on the necessity of a style that transposes into literature the living forms of the spoken language. In itself this is not a new discovery, as we have seen from our discussion of ***Mort à crédit,*** but it does show that Céline was working on a conscious level. Finally, Céline recognizes two influences that are well worth exploring: Barbusse and Léon Daudet's *Le Rêve éveillé.*

The connections with Barbusse are fairly obvious. The autobiographical form, concern for the common people, and de-mystification of war which characterize *Le Feu* are bound to have found affinity in Céline's temperament. But the greatest impact is on the stylistic level, with the possibilities which Barbusse opens up for literary use of the spoken language. *Le Feu* is almost completely composed of dialogue, of which the following sentence is typical: "Faut que j'cherche la voiture-dentiste, à cette fin qu'on m'accroche c'râtelier et qu'ils m'ôtent les vieux dominos qui m'restent." The structures and vocabulary of slang and popular speech, widely present in Barbusse, are at the base of Céline's own style. Of course, Céline goes much further than his predecessor. Barbusse is a realist, concerned with *reproducing* the language of his "poilus." His only transposition is in the typography, and this, too, is an attempt to approximate actual pronunciation. Céline both exploits his source more fully and enriches it with literary usage and invention. His aim is not to write the spoken language, but to give the reader the *impression* of a speaking voice.

The Daudet influence is much more fundamental. Daudet's main thesis is that man's dreaming is a constant process, which is most often masked during waking hours by the functioning of the rational faculties. To produce the dream state in oneself, one has only to suspend one's judgment, and limit oneself to watching what is projected into the consciousness. The dream itself is composed of an influx of concentric waves, moving from the outside to the center, bringing various impressions, images, fragmented memories, desires, and premonitions. At the center, the waves are condensed into a single theme: "Ce thème c'est le 'être ou ne pas être' de Shakespeare, et l'on peut dire de lui qu'il est, pour les trois quarts du temps, le lieu géométrique de notre personnalité toute entière."

Daudet goes on to analyze the dream as the source of artistic creation. From the initial dream state, the subject moves into a state of "distraction," and from there to a feeling of the sublime. This brings about a renunciation of self and leads in turn to meditation, which, with an act of will, becomes creation. Within the meditative state, free reign is given to what Daudet calls "hereditary memory" (a concept not unlike Jung's collective unconscious, which first alternates, then mingles with individual memory in an ascent toward the universal).

Although this synopsis does little justice to the subtlety of Daudet's analysis, it is sufficient to show that *Le Rêve éveillé* played a powerful role in the elaboration of Céline's art. It is at the basis of the atmosphere of delirium that pervades the novels, of the extensive use of personal memories, of the creation of archetypal figures, and of the frequent elliptical references to events and personages of the past. It is certainly no accident, either, that to express the life-death dualism, in the last novels Céline, like Daudet, makes frequent use of Hamlet's words. In a way, it is hardly an exaggeration to say that Daudet's essay describes the whole of Céline's evolution, for the novels, beginning with the very subjective vision of ***Voyage,*** ascend toward an ever greater degree of universality and detachment. Although it is not possible to ascertain exactly when Céline read Daudet (*Le Rêve éveillé* was published in 1926), certain references to the dream in the Meudon speech of 1933 make it probable that it was before then, and it is altogether possible to place the influence before ***Voyage,*** in which delirium, as Michel Beaujour has shown, is a conscious technique for evading an intolerable reality. The substantive influence, however, comes with ***Mort à crédit*** and the following works, where the dream is no longer used merely as a personal escape (this function is fulfilled in the prologues which precede the narrative of all the novels after ***Voyage***), but as a progressively more selfless liberation of the reader.

Guignol's Band completes the childhood-adolescence cycle opened by ***Mort à crédit,*** and brings Céline's art to the threshold of maturity. As in ***Mort à crédit,*** the narrative proper is preceded by a prologue that reveals an unlivable present reality—in this case the bombing of Orléans at the beginning of World War II—and works up to a frenzy of delirium, followed by a plunge into the past. The pattern of the narrative here is, however, more complex than in ***Mort à crédit:*** the binary movement with a sudden upswing at the end is replaced by a clear ternary structure, through which the novelist achieves a definitive victory over the ego-centered, death-dominated vision of the earlier works. Furthermore, all the major figures in this novel have the richly archetypal qualities of Courtial des Pereires, so that the entire action takes place on a much more universal level.

In the first section of the narrative, Céline extends the scope of the superego figure represented by Ferdinand's father in ***Mort à crédit*** to include the whole of French culture: Cascade and his band are an unmistakable allegory of the degenerate French society already portrayed in ***Bagatelles.*** Similarly, Ferdinand's rebellion against this milieu, which culminates in his attempted murder of Mille-Pattes—a symbol of Cascade's power—is a widening of Céline's own revolt against readymade superstructures. As we shall see, however, the rebellion is not a total rejection, but an effort to establish a more equitable balance between the individual and the collective. Such a balance is possible only if the potential of the individual has been determined and realized.

This is the function of the second part of the novel, which explores the two major areas of experience needed to complete Ferdinand's initiation: the spiritual and the esthetic.

The spiritual dimension is created through Sosthène de Rodiencourt. Sosthène embodies the religious mode of knowing the harmony of the universe, which, as Céline presents it, is a mixture of genuine mystery, superstition, and mummery. Like his scientific counterpart Courtial, Sosthène is on the decline when Ferdinand encounters him: from a traveling magician with genuine powers he has degenerated into an exotic confidence man more interested in money than in the spirit. Yet Sosthène's false spirituality is relevant, for it prepares Ferdinand for the real spiritual dimension represented by Virginia: it is through Sosthène that he meets her.

With her youth, her beautiful legs, and her transcendent laughter, Virginia is the incarnation of life in its purest form. It is important to note that this life is at first inaccessible to Ferdinand however, and it is only with the incursion of Cascade's band into the idyllic life of Virginia's house, and particularly with the return of Mille-Pattes, that he is able to seduce her and release her potential fertility. In other words, if the esthetic principle is perceived initially as a spiritual value, it is only within the cultural context that creation—symbolized by Virginia's pregnancy—becomes possible. Through the Virginia episode, Céline also points toward the form that his subsequent creation will take, namely, the dance. Virginia's dancing and laughter mark her as a prototype for Lili, the ethereal dancer of the last novels. Significantly, it is Sosthène's lack of the spirit of the dance that is seen as his greatest weakness, and Ferdinand's possession of it that enables him to outstrip his "master" in the realm of the spirit.

The last section of the novel draws the spiritual and cultural themes together, and, in dissolving the tensions between them, emphasizes their interdependence in sustaining the creative act. The climactic scene—the celebration, with all the major characters present, of the "feast of Saint Ferdinand"—resolves itself into an apotheosis for the protagonist, the Chaotic revelry being the final initiation rites after which he experiences the ecstacy of liberation: "C'est le moment de respirer! Humez-moi ce souffle! . . . C'est vrai . . . c'est de la bouffée marine . . . ça vous déferle au parapet. . . ça vous arrive en sautes rafales . . . vou débarbouille" (***Pont de Londres***).

The freedom is not unqualified, however, London is Cascade's territory, and to that extent Ferdinand remains a prisoner of his culture. Moreover, as the last pages of the novel show, his relationship to the spiritual and esthetic principles represented by Sosthène and Virginia is essentially one of responsibility. In line with Daudet's analysis of the dream, Céline sees his inspiration as coming from outside of him, and limits his role as artist to that of protector and guide for the life forces in which he participates. An analogous notion is expressed a few years later in the Hindus correspondence: "Je ne crée rien à vrai dire—je nettoye une sorte de médaille cachée, une statue enfouie dans la glaise—*Tout existe déjà* . . . Tout est fait hors de soi—dans les ondes je pense—Aucune vanité en tout ceci—c'est un labeur bien ouvrier—ouvrier dans les ondes— . . ."

The humility reflected here is a far cry from the hostile attitude represented in ***Voyage,*** and must be seen as a result of Céline's evolution away from egocentricity. The apparent paradox of transcending the ego through autobiography is resolvable in Jungian terms, the descent into subjectivity leading eventually to the archetypal domains of the collective unconscious. Similarly, it is through submission to time—as represented by the autobiographical form as a whole, and the Cascade myth in particular—that the novelist is able to reach an extratemporal perspective, his own fate diminishing in importance as his perception of archetype becomes firmer. The catharsis afforded by the last part of ***Guignol's Band*** stems directly from the merging of Ferdinand's destiny into the larger frame of reference provided by the Cascade group, Sosthène, and Virginia. And with this increase in distance between the reader and the protagonist, life is perceived not in its turmoil, but as the beautiful movement of pure forms.

The pattern of narration in ***Guignol's Band*** corresponds closely to Céline's idea of the "métro émotif." This metaphor which the novelist (first in the Hindus letters, then in ***Entretiens***) uses to describe his art is built around the image of a descent from the surface, followed by a nerve-racking journey through the emotional underground of life. Characteristically, Céline does not say what the destination is. Erika Ostrovsky suggests that it is the dream, but, as Céline points out, the dream is part of the journey itself. The ending of ***Guignol's Band*** would seem to indicate that the point of arrival is a more elevated position, from which a peaceful contemplation of the surface is possible.

As the first of the novels of maturity, ***Féerie pour une autre fois*** definitively establishes both the mythical dimension of Céline's vision and the positive direction of his art. This is accomplished partially through the structure, which remains the same as before, and partially through the interplay of the major characters, whose archetypal dimensions are now made explicit.

Beyond his personal betrayal of Ferdinand, the sculptor Jules appears as an incarnation of universal evil: his leglessness is diametrically opposed to the positive value of the dance; his workshop in an obscure subbasement suggests a sort of hell; and during the bombing, he is specifically described as "l'empereur des flammes" (***Normance***). As myth, Jules is the embodiment of all energy that is oriented toward destruction.

At the other extreme, Lili (Arlette), the narrator's dancer-wife, incarnates the good: "La noblesse toute harmonie, la danseuse en l'âme et au corps, noblesse toute!" (***Féerie***). Lili represents total transcendence. To her, the bombing appears as so much ballet, and in the battle between the angels (both Jules and Lili are thus described), it is obvious that Lili is the victor. At the end of the novel, Jules is effectively stripped of his power, while Lili is as ethereal and carefree as ever.

As narrator, Céline presents himself from the double point of view of doctor and chronicler. In both roles he is on a lower plane than either Jules or Lili. Where they appear as angels, the narrator is part of the degraded and depraved civilization symbolized in the concierge's lodge, and embodies the anxiety and suffering of man.

The doctor metaphor asserts the preservation of life, and the fact that Céline is reduced to impotency in his role as doctor makes the forces of death seem all the more powerful. In the early part of the narrative, it is Jules, a quasi-supernatural force, who is responsible for preventing him from going to his medical duties. But the novelist reserves the bulk of his disgust for his fellow men, those who, within the lodge, act as impediments to the forces of life. Normance, an archetype of materialism who blocks the way to his dying wife Delphine, is described as being worse than Jules: even misdirected energy is preferable to inertia. The other people in the lodge are another aspect of the same degenerateness, reflecting the moral and spiritual atrophy which Céline detected in France at large. On another level, all the people in the lodge, including Normance and Delphine, may be considered as an image of the novelist's public. Given the futility of the doctor's attempt to help Delphine (which symbolizes the novelist's attempt to revive the dying spirit of his civilization), it is not surprising that Céline should have implied by the title of his fantasy that it would be more accessible to readers of another time.

The sense of being misunderstood in his own time also partially explains the image of the chronicler: Céline is suggesting that even if his contemporaries are too degraded to take an interest in the "deluge" that is destroying them, he should at least record it for future generations. We cannot take him too literally, however, for although the last novels do constitute a kind of chronicle of the end of the war, and although some episodes, such as the scenes of Sigmaringen in ***D'un château l'autre,*** may actually be valuable as history, Céline's imagination always eclipses the dispassionate observer in him. This is particularly true in ***Féerie,*** where it is perfectly obvious that Céline is not concerned with any real events—the bombing of Montmartre, for example, never took place—but with conveying an emotional impression of the reality of his time. The principal meaning of the chronicler image must rather be seen as a continuation of the immersion-in-history concept already discussed in respect to ***Guignol's Band:*** subjection to time leads to victory over time. What is new here is that in portraying himself as a chronicler, Céline is presenting his credentials as one who has personally experienced what he is writing, in order to draw the reader into the same journey. If the reader can recognize in Céline's presentation of the deluge a reflection of the underlying anguish of his time, he can be released from it.

Release, in ***Féerie,*** as in ***Guignol's Band,*** is effected through an increase in the distance between the reader and the narrator, but in ***Féerie*** the process is more complex and more markedly an esthetic one. After the bombing, the narrator is a complete wreck, and it takes the return of Ottavio to bring him back to Lili and safety. On the highest level of interpretation, Ottavio is an emanation of the novelist's own creative energy. If Lili, as spirit of Life, is the source of Céline's inspiration—"heureusement que j'ai Lili dites, pour faire un livre! en faire un livre! . . . plutôt!" (***Normance***)—he can remain in contact with her only through Ottavio, that is, creation. In breaking through the wall of the destroyed building to the intact twin that adjoins it, Ottavio also underlines the power of art to unify or restore an otherwise disparate experience. The presence in the intact apartment of the actor Norbert Loukoum (Le Vigan in the following novels) illustrates the transposition of reality necessary to the process, while the actor's fixed pose evokes a form capable of transcending the movement of time.

The balance achieved here is a delicate one. Even the power of art cannot abolish the presence of death, as is shown by the corpse that Ferdinand finds in the otherwise limpid water of the bathtub. Also, the failure of Loukoum's attempt to retain Lili reveals the incapacity of any fixed form to "capture" life, and perhaps, as well, the ultimate primacy of life over art. Nonetheless, as the narrator's suffering humanity merges into the wider perspective afforded by Lili's spirit, Ottavio's energy, and Loukoum's purity of form, the tension built up during the novel is relaxed. With the final image of Céline's writings, instead of bombs, falling from the sky, the work's therapeutic purpose is accomplished: the unbearable has been made bearable.

The doctor-patient relationship between the novelist and his reader, suggested in ***Féerie,*** is brought out explicitly in ***D'un château l'autre*** through Mme Niçois. It is from her window that he first sees Charon's boat, the image of death that acts as a catalyst for the beginning of the narrative, and the "2cc" of morphine which he injects to alleviate her pain are evocative of the trance-like state that he needs to induce for his "therapy" to be effective. When she appears again at the end of the novel, Mme Niçois is half-paralyzed and dying, but at the same time she is accompanied by a double, Mlle Armandine, equally old, but endowed with astonishing vitality. This illustrates the twosided effect which Céline expects to produce: on the one hand, in imposing his vision of a collapsing civilization, he tends to generate the paralysis of despair; on the other, the narrative acts as a purge that restores energy and lightness.

The main narrative uses many of the same devices as in ***Féerie.*** If the Charon's Barque hallucination seems to prefigure a journey toward death, the presence among the crew of the actor Le Vigan—established as a symbol of artist form in ***Féerie***—announces the possibility of transcendence. Again, as in ***Féerie,*** the action under the guise of a chronicle, takes place in a deliberately microcosmic setting, this time the city of Sigmaringen.

The symbol of destructive energy in ***D'un château l'autre*** is Aïcha von Raumnitz. Although a lesser demon than Jules, she is equally indiscriminate: anything that disturbs her order produces the same swift and deadly reaction. Against this image of Death, Céline pits the spirit of Life, and Aïcha and her hounds are opposed by Lili and Bébert. Lili plays much the same role as before, her instinctive serenity and total freedom of movement providing the impetus and direction of transcendence. In particular, she is Céline's key to all the secret corners of the castle: "Lili allait où elle voulait dans tout l'Hohenzollern-Château . . . d'un dédale de couloir à l'autre . . . du beffroi de tout en l'air, des cloches, à la salle d'armes, à fleur du fleuve . . . un itinéraire que d'instinct!"

Entry to the castle is essential. The castle allows an overview impossible elsewhere: ". . . tous les toits du bourg, et la forêt . . . on comprend la vie de château . . . la vue de là-haut et de loin . . . le détachement des seigneurs. . . . la grande beauté de pas être villains." Although his status as a human being places him among the villeins, through Lili, through creation, the artist can reach detachment and tranquillity. Furthermore, through his contacts in the castle, Céline is able to participate in the train journey to Bichelonne's funeral, which resumes the whole novel, and gives it its final direction. Beginning, as the novel does, as a journey toward death, and going through the same vicissitudes of hunger, cold, and the struggle to survive, when the funeral ceremonies abort, the voyage turns back on itself, and with the presence of the children and the pregnant women taken on as passengers in Berlin, it becomes a journey toward new life.

The regeneration suggested here is confirmed by the epilogue. Through Mlle Armandine, the reader is released from the tension that comes from identification with the narrator: at the end, she, not he, is at the center of our attention, and we are able to share her benevolent scorn for him. It is in this context that one can explain the numerous interruptions in the narrative, where Céline comes back to the surface to complain about his publishers and his other woes. It is possible that these passages, in their genesis, reflect a real fatigue in the author, but he exaggerates the scope of his personal troubles, deforming his own image in order to prepare and facilitate the separation from him that is necessary to the final catharsis. In the prologue, the narrator, half ironically, presents himself as a universal scapegoat—"coolie de l'ouest." At the end of the novel, Céline is seeking a similar exorcising power for this art.

In ***Nord,*** Céline pushes the idea of a salutary art to its extreme. Early in the text, he compares himself to Jesus, a comparison that is picked up by the Le Vigan figure, who is consistently presented as Christ and savior. (In this context, the indication that Le Vigan used to play *Le Misanthrope,* but has long since ceased to do so, is very significant as a sign of Céline's own evolution.)

The positive force of art is brought out once more through the Lili figure. As before, in the battle between life and death, Lili is made to represent life and the esthetic ideal. Her frequent dancing in Marie-Thérèse's tower (again Céline carefully notes the overview) marks her superiority over the web of hostile relationships and dangerous events that threaten the protagonists' lives at Zornhof.

Nord differs from the previous novels, however, in that the esthetic symbols are more closely woven into the texture of the narrative. Le Vigan and Lili, instead of being episodic figures, are constant companions of the narrator, and for the most part they act as a community. In molding direct experience (the narrator), transposition (Le Vigan), and the spirit of creation (Lili) into a unity, Céline is able to maintain throughout a greater distance from the sources of tension than in any of the previous novels. This procedure obviates the necessity of a release of tension at the end, and allows Céline to use that important structural position for another purpose, to clarify the relationship between his writing and his medicine.

He does this through Harras. In the composition of the novel, Harras has a position similar to Mme Niçois' in ***D'un château l'autre:*** his two appearances act as a frame for the major part of the action, and thus provide the perspective in which the novel should be considered. There are two particularly striking aspects of Harras in himself: the fact that he is an *Oberartz*—a "supra-doctor"—and his enormous laughter. As *Oberartz,* he is above the vicissitudes of history: in the midst of war, for example, he can travel freely to international conferences, in the peaceful pursuit of world health. His laughter is the outward sign of this transcendency. He can laugh when Lili accidentally sets off all the Berlin antiaircraft defenses, just as he can mock his own role as Nazi judge at the end of the novel.

In respect to the protagonists, Harras acts as protector by constantly assuring their safety. On another level, in obtaining the narrator's permit to practice medicine, he also has the function of justifier. In the microcosm of Zornhof, Harras is the power that gives Céline his very raison d'être: the supra-doctor becomes the spirit of medicine. (The end of the novel brings a refinement of this notion, when Harras is eclipsed by the psychopathologist Goring, suggesting that the physical preventive medicine practiced by Harras is inadequate in the modern world, whose most urgent diseases are of the mind.) In specifically placing his writing under the patronage of medicine, which at its highest degree of perfection is an attempt to reestablish natural harmony, Céline makes quite explicit the positive intention of his work.

The progression toward total transcendence is brought to its conclusion in ***Rigodon.*** Although the exterior structure of this novel remains the same as before, it is characterized throughout by a gentle serenity. Even in the prologue, where the narrator indulges in his customary attacks on his publisher and predicts the imminent destruction of the white race, the angry tone is gone, replaced by a constant sparkling humor. Furthermore, instead of the usual delirium around the theme of death, the prologue ends with a metaphor of the novelist's art.

Borrowing his initial image from Bergson, Céline explains that a punch into a box of iron filings will produce the shape of a funnel, and that although a human intelligence can be satisfied by a simple description of the phenomenon, he, in his writings, has chosen the viewpoint of an ant: ". . . l'intelligence de la fourmi toutéberluée, qui se demande par quel miracle un autre insecte, fourmi comme elle, a pu faire tenir tant de limaille, brin par brin, en tel équilibre, en forme d'entonnoir." The idea of working so close to his material is basically the same as we have seen before. In ***Entretiens*** he compares himself to an impressionist painter, thereby suggesting in yet another way the distance that must exist between the actual narrative—the process of "painting"—and the position from which the work should be "viewed." What is particularly interesting in the funnel image, however, is that from the ant's viewpoint, the direction of the form is toward the top, that is, the wider, open end of the funnel. In this metaphor, Céline reaffirms, more clearly than ever before, the positive orientation of his writing.

The main body of the narrative bears this out. Once again in the form of a pseudo-chronicle, the action appears as a sequel to ***Nord,*** consisting of a series of train journeys across the ruins of Germany to Copenhagen. The first section follows a downward trend, both geographically and emotionally, the southward journey from Rostock to Sigmaringen coinciding with a multitude of images of death and disintegration. On the symbolic level, the two most significant indications are the fact that Harras, in his brief reappearance, has lost his laughter, and Le Vigan's leaving of the group in Sigmaringen. It appears at first that Céline has been stripped of his two most precious projections: medicine and art. In fact, as the second half of the novel reveals, it is he who is abandoning them.

The northward journey from Sigmaringen to Copenhagen, though not without its tensions and images of death, follows a steadily upward direction. Le Vigan is replaced by a group of children: art has been transcended by life. Although Céline depicts the children as cretins, their role is clearly positive: they save the group from starvation by finding food, and, later, they become Céline's passport to Denmark. They are always happy, and toward the end the novelist specifically designates them as a symbol of hope: ". . . je pense là à eux, trente ans plus tard, s'ils vivent toujours foutre ils sont grands l'heure actuelle, là-haut . . . aussi peut-être qu'ils ne bavent plus, qu'ils entendent très bien, absolument rééduqués . . . des vioques rien à espérer, n'est-ce pas? mais des mômes tout."

Just as the children's vitality more than compensates for the loss of Le Vigan, the loss of Harras' laughter is overcome by the narrator's own entry into the level of laughter. Throughout the second part, even in the gravest circumstances, he laughs at himself, at others, at the whole situation.

The arrival in Copenhagen is nothing less than an epiphany. It is springtime, and the city is a haven of peace in the midst of war. The final episode is a return to Eden. The narrator and Lili go to the countryside on the outskirts of the city to verify that they still have their "treasures": their real passports, their marriage certificate, and their cyanide. Each of these items is rich with symbolism. The passport, as proof of identity, signifies that Céline has arrived at the end of his life-journey intact. The marriage certificate symbolizes the total merging of the narrator with Lili, the marriage of experience with the spirit of the dance: hence the title of the work. Beyond history, beyond art, apotheosis has been reached. But total liberation is only possible in death, which explains the presence of the cyanide. Death, here, is no longer the negation of Life, but the peaceful end for one whose work has been completed. That Céline put the final touches on this novel the day he died is poignantly significant: there could be no reason for writing anything more. ***Rigodon*** is his *Nunc dimittis,* and, as such, is a fitting epilogue for the whole opus.

Beginning with the perception and fear of his own death, magnified by the sense, so common to the twentieth-century artist, of the stagnant decrepitude of Western civilization, Céline's ethos, in the context of the two world wars that form the backdrop to his novels, takes on the proportions of an apocalypse. His art, an organic outgrowth of his struggle against egocentricity, in which he saw the underlying causes for the paralyzing fear of death, is initially self-exorcism. But as the work develops it becomes an increasingly altruistic attempt to free the reader from his anguish. On this level, his literary and medical careers coincide: Destouches, the author of ***Semmelweiss,*** and Céline, the novelist, become one. Precisely because his work is so organic, however, it is almost imperative for the reader to consider the opus as a whole. The initiation provided by the early novels into the "emotional underground" is indispensable to the liberating effect of the later works. Because of their progressively more elliptical nature, these can seem a nightmarish and often blurred vision of disintegration, but when viewed from the proper perspective, they appear as a gradual spiraling away from the cataclysm to a point where death is no longer a reason for sterile fear, but a promise of renewed life and a stimulus for creation.

Jane Carson (essay date Summer 1981)

SOURCE: "Céline: The Fire in the Night," in *Symposium: A Quarterly Journal in Modern Foreign Literatures,* Vol. XXXV, No. 2, Summer, 1981, pp. 117-30.

[In the following essay, Carson examines picaresque themes and the metaphorical significance of fire in Céline's fiction. "In Céline's novels," Carson writes, "the images of fire reveal many of the author's ideas about creativity and the act of writing."]

The narrators of Céline's novels, from Bardamu in ***Voyage au bout de la nuit*** to the doctor of ***Rigodon,*** share a desire to recount a journey which, as they are the first to point out, leads to no magic solution, no shining Grail. From the opening of the first novel the dominant image in Céline's fiction is black and hopeless night. It is not strictly true, however, that "nothing" shines. Night is frequently brightened by fires, sometimes to the extent that it turns into day. Beyond this, in a figurative sense, the story itself may be considered a bright spot in the writer's night.

The journey here compared to life is the aimless wandering of the *picaro,* the search his sustained and perilous effort to survive. The picaresque novel is a peculiar elaboration of the quest theme as we know it in Western literature, and, since its first appearance in Spain, this episodic pseudo-autobiographical form has inspired innumerable imitations and variations. Unlike the hero of myth, the *picaro* is no better endowed than other people, he does not cross the threshold into the other world, and the only boon he gains to pass on to his fellows is the tale of his own adventures. In this respect his "quest" is an archetypal failure. Although he lacks a sense of sacred mission, the *picaro,* driven by a desire to rise in society, still seems to be engaged in a search. Inasmuch as he usually rejects, in the end, the goal of wealth he has been pursuing, the only result of his journey is a need to communicate his peripatetic history to a reader. The *picaro*'s history is varied, scatological, darkly humorous, morally ambiguous. He narrates it himself. The outcome of his quest is the writing of his novel.

A. A. Parker insists on the following four points as essential to the true picaresque: the *picaro* is of disreputable origin, he has a profound desire to rise and become a gentleman, instead he becomes a social delinquent, and after sinking to the depths of depravity he experiences a religious conversion. Céline's work is almost a parody of these points: his protagonist is of respectable middle-class parentage, his greatest desire is to descend to the depths of human experience, he becomes not an outlaw but a moral delinquent, and he denies the possibility of a spiritual exaltation. Step by step, Céline's narrators follow this distorted version of the picaresque, with the result that his assembled novels may be taken as the history of the inverted picaresque adventure of the future novelist. The frustrated quest forms the basis for each of Céline's novels, some of which adhere to the picaresque pattern more closely than others. The point that each novel makes, and for which the succession of novels stands as evidence, is that the protagonist gains nothing from life but a story to tell.

In the thirty years (1932-61) during which the narrator gradually becomes the doctor/novelist identified as the writer, the quest theme in its picaresque variant remains predominant. The *picaro* is a thief, and one of his archetypal predecessors is Prometheus. The narrators of these novels are the purveyors of a stolen flame, the work of art they have somehow seized in their travels, the story they have culled from life. Fire is a metaphor for the novel. In Céline's novels, the images related to fire reveal many of the author's ideas about creativity and the act of writing. The narrator sees himself as a fire-maker, and the light of his work fitfully illuminates a world of otherwise unrelieved blackness.

Early in ***Voyage au bout de la nuit,*** shortly after Bardamu discovers the horrors of war and the loneliness of night, he finds consolation in watching villages burn. The weather is dry, and every night some burning village can be found to brighten the darkness and provide some distraction from the constant fear Bardamu and his men feel riding about looking for their regiment: "Un village brûlait toujours du côté du canon. On en approchait pas beaucoup, pas de trop, on le regardait seulement d'assez loin le village, en spectateurs pourrait-on dire." There seem to be no people in these villages, no sense of disaster, just flames to light up the night. "Ça se remarque bien comment ça brûle un village, même à vingt kilomètres. C'était gai. Un petit hameau de rien du tout qu'on apercevait même pas pendant la journée, au fond de'une moche petite campagne, eh bien, on a pas idée la nuit, quand il brûle, de l'effet qu'il peut faire!" The men watch churches, barns, and haystacks burning and collapsing as if they were watching a movie; they fall asleep with a sense of security unique in the novel's war episodes. The fire makes the night bearable: "Mais quand on a des feux à regarder la nuit passe bien mieux, c'est plus rien à endurer, c'est plus de la solitude."

Fires, both large and small, from candles to full-scale flaming bombardments, reappear frequently in Céline's novels, generally at night. They are not always reassuring, but they always provide light and a better look at the night. All through ***Voyage*** Céline compares life to a night-journey; fire is a positive element in this journey. Furthermore, according to Gilbert Durand, fire can be equated with the word: "le feu est très souvent assimilé à la parole." This same image appears in the opening words of John's gospel. The written word, or the novel, is the fire in Céline's night, and an analysis of fire imagery shows the role of verbal art in Céline's imaginative space. The four works from which examples are drawn here—***Voyage au bout de la nuit, Guignol's Band, Normance,*** and ***Nord***—span his writing life from his first novel to the last published during his lifetime.

Fire consumes garbage. This is not one of the more widely recognized functions of the work of art, but the action of fire is very similar to the act of digestion, a ready metaphor for reading, and for writing as well. Digestion is generally believed to remove the useful parts of food and eliminate the remainder as waste, whereas, as everyone knows, "fire purifies"; what is unconsumed must be "pure." If the act of writing is seen to be related to fire, the experience is presumably cleansing. If the work itself is like fire, it is apt to burn those who come in contact with it. Fire often becomes liquid in Céline's novels and flows like lava. There are also many explosive, eruptive scenes. The volcano is an important image. However, this deluge of fire is not a form of divine retribution, for it is often man-made. It is the human race's attempt at self-destruction. The third aspect of fire to be examined is its power to attract and kill, like a lantern drawing moths at night. People are drawn by the flickering light on a movie screen because it makes the night a little brighter, life a little easier. The work of art is in fact a suicide on the part of the artist, for to fix anything is to kill it, and to fix one's dreams is to kill oneself.

Bardamu in ***Voyage*** falls ill in Africa and decides to leave his post in the jungle. Before leaving, he takes a lesson from his experience at war and sets a match to his hut to light up the night. "Cela se passait après le coucher du soleil. Les flammes s'élevèrent rapides, fougueuses." Just as the fire is a form of speech and represents the written word, so the fire-maker is the writer. Jules in ***Normance*** and Borokrom in ***Guignol's Band*** are outstanding examples: Jules calls down a bombardment and Borokrom throws bombs. Through the images of fire we see the artist's view of himself; he is an incendiary, a pathfinder, a Cassandra crying on the ramparts, a prophet, a sorcerer unconsumed by his own flames. The fire-maker sees himself at least as a prophet, if not a god. He denounces the evil he sees around him and reveals what is to come. The news is not cheering.

The incendiary and the arsonist are intent on destroying by fire. The writer who sees himself in such terms—as the kindler of a destructive fire—writes to destroy something, illusion perhaps, as well as literary convention. The wandering writer, the *picaro,* will see much in society about which his audience must be disabused.

Fire cleanses, as Bardamu points out in ***Voyage:*** "Ma mère n'avait pas que des dictons pour l'honnêteté, elle disait aussi, je m'en souvins à point, quand elle brûlait chez nous les vieux pansements: Le feu purifie tout!" We notice at once that Bardamu's mother is not purifying anything whatsoever, unless it be a world full of soiled bandages, in which case she has a long way to go. She is in fact destroying, and might have said more aptly. "Le feu nous débarrasse des saletés." Bardamu quotes her presumably to justify his odd behavior when, in the middle of a drenching nocturnal rain, he sets fire to his hut and sets off into the forest with a raging fever:

> Le moment vint. Mes silex n'étaient pas très bien choisis, mal pointus, les étincelles me restaient surtout dans les mains. Enfin, tout de même, les premières marchandises prirent feu en dépit de l'humidité. C'était un stock de chaussettes absolument trempées. Cela se passait après le coucher du soleil. Les flammes s'élevèrent rapides, fougueuses. . . . Le caoutchouc nature qu'avait acheté Robinson grésillait au centre et son odeur me rappelait invinciblement l'incendie célèbre de la Société de Téléphones, quai de Grenelle, qu'on avait été regarder avec mon oncle Charles, qui chantait lui si bien la romance. L'année d'avant l'Exposition ça se passait, la Grande, quand j'étais encore bien petit. Rien ne force les souvenirs à se montrer comme les odeurs et les flammes. Ma case elle sentait tout pareil. Bien que détrempée, elle a brûlé entièrement, très franchement et marchandises et tout. Les competes étaient faits. La forêt s'est tue pour une fois. Complet silence.

This passage contains repeated references to the past—to the narrator's childhood, to his predecessor Robinson, to his fear of the forest, which dates from the war. Flames, like odors, bring back memories, says Bardamu, reducing the Proustian concept of involuntary memory to a hazy nostalgia for childhood which is just barely comforting, and which certainly does not transcend temporality. Bardamu has surrendered to a childish impulse to destroy the hut which gave him painful memories, to protest against the company which had exploited him, against Robinson who had stolen all the money and left him alone in the jungle, against the jungle which surrounded him and held him prisoner. He does not seek to regenerate the past in order to stand outside time; he destroys memory's dirty bandages, leaving a cleaner past in which little Bardamu and his uncle watch the telephone company burn down. He has recreated a childhood experience already purified by faulty memory. The action of the flames, like writing, wipes out the unpleasant present, reinstates an agreeable but inaccurate past.

Bardamu enjoys the odor of the fire because it brings back memories. But the purifying quality of fire, as Bachelard tells us, is at least partly due to its ability to deodorize. Instead of deodorizing, Bardamu is creating a voluminous quantity of malodorous smoke. In the same way Céline's writing kindles a flame which creates the unpleasant smell of vomit, defecation, war and disease. The novels themselves, the product of a *picaro*'s observations, are full of odors.

The bombardment in ***Normance*** creates an odor of burning people mixed with gunpowder and tar—a scene from hell:

"l'odeur! . . . Je suis assez sensible aux odeurs . . . c'est de la poudre là-dessous et du feu . . . et du reste . . . du goudron aussi . . . c'est ça les Déluges, des odeurs et puis encore d'autres . . . des trouvailles . . . oh, un relent de viande grillée!" The opening scene in ***Guignol's Band,*** also a bombardment, brings out the roasted meat image again with a baby "tout cuit à point."

In ***Nord*** we meet the prostitutes who build a fire in a hole in the plain to roast the Rittmeister's horse: "que ça sent si fort!" The scene is a grotesque caricature of the underground *Reichsgesundt* in which the doctor and his party took refuge earlier, with a filthy pond full of horse entrails in place of the Finnish bath, screaming prostitutes instead of smiling secretaries. The doctor's role is reversed: he is not expelled from the hole as he was from the *Reichsgesundt*; he invades it to save the count and the Revizor, who are being beaten. The hole is also a distorted transposition of the count's basement kitchens. The count himself is not able to join the villagers as they feast on the singed horsemeat left by the fleeing women. Formerly a hoarder, he watches his rescuers eating the remains of his own mare. The scene is one of near-cannibalism, with the horse substituted for the count, the "Rittmeister," who later dies from brutal treatment. The distribution of meat is accompanied by a parody of civilized manners, as if the action were set in an expensive restaurant: "un romani qui découpe . . . petites tranches? minces? . . . ou des épaisses? . . . il nous demande notre goût?"

Céline's fire departs from both of the purifying qualities noted by Bachelard (deodorizing and cooking) because his fire creates odors and the flesh that is cooked was not originally intended to be eaten. "La viande cuite représente avant tout la putréfaction vaincue." Cooking facilitates digestion and achieves a civilized victory over food's swift decay. But "la personne cuite" interrupts the natural process of putrefaction without benefiting people in any way. Fire harms people; they are not meant for burning. Céline's novels deliberately attack people, serve them up to themselves "tout cuits à point." These works are fiery, and they sear. At the same time, the novels have a purifying quality. By transforming garbage and distasteful subjects into art, Céline somehow exalts humankind's dirty linen, even if he does not destroy it. People are evil, but a novel about people is good. This is true alchemy: from such stuff to create literary flames of lasting value.

Céline's writing may have accomplished this very object on a personal level. To burn away the trash of memory, to protest against all the companies and encircling forests which have enslaved us and held us prisoner—who would not set fire to a houseful of soaked socks with that in mind? As we have seen, the flame is the word. Other writers have professed more openly the cathartic value of writing (Henry Miller, Anaïs Nin, Simone de Beauvoir). Céline offers the cleansing experience as an excuse for pyromania.

Céline's love for the ocean, boats, harbors, and rivers has been noted: Danièle Racelle-Latin sees the boat as the dominant image in ***Voyage;*** Gilbert Schilling considers water the dominant element. "He who dreams water cannot dream fire," says Bachelard, and it must be admitted that in Céline's water-ruled world fire behaves much like water. Even taking into consideration that certain metaphorical combinations of fire and water are literary conventions (a flood of light, a rain of fire, sunset over the ocean), Céline's novels include an unusually large number of fire/water couplings and, in ***Normance,*** repeated references to the bombardment as a modern-day Deluge. The flames cascade, inundate, splash, surge. The sky melts, the Seine boils, molten cataracts pour down at Jules's command. "C'est une inondation de feu," "des vraies cataractes de lumière!" "les cascades du ciel!" "de vrais torrents," "un fleuve," "tout Paris en mer de feu!"

The doctor hypothesizes in ***Nord*** that Berlin is under heavy attack, and the underground *Reichsgesundt* has probably been destroyed: "Grünwald doit être un lac de feu." The lake of fire reminds us of the Finnish baths which formerly occupied the same place and contributed to a womblike atmosphere; by now they have been transformed into their antithesis, a volcano: "le cratère des bains finlandais" All of Berlin, the doctor supposes, has become a volcano: "l'impression . . . que Berlin est tourné volcan."

The flood from the sky in ***Normance*** resembles nothing so much as a volcanic eruption, Céline does not hesitate to say so: "au moins quatre immeubles qui sautent! . . . qui rejaillit! une lave, des torrents de lave qui fusent! haut! haut! éclaboussent autour! tout le quartier! . . . et le métro! submergés! . . . il doit faire chaud sous le tunnel! . . . ils y sont tous! . . . toute la Place bouillonne de <<Bengale>> . . . un volcan d'éclaboussures!" These repetitions of the words volcano, lava, crater show this latest flood to be one of fire, for Céline's world is not destroyed by a long hard rain. The rain is of fire, the flood of molten rock. War images are fire images. War is essential to his fictional universe. War erupts, spreads out, devastates like a volcano.

The first hint of the importance of the volcano image is the dedication of ***Normance:*** à Pline l'Ancien. Frédéric Vitoux points out that the dedication makes a flattering comparison between Céline and Pliny the Elder, emphasizing the author's innocence as a dedicated chronicler. As the doctor explains, "Saquez pas le probe chroniqueur! . . . regardez un peu Pline l'Ancien, il a fallu des années qu'il se décide à son grand moment . . . qu'il aille renifler le Vésuve!" Pliny's curiosity led him to examine Vesuvius, and when he warned the people of their danger, he himself died asphyxiated by the fumes. That the doctor should cite him as an example implies that he sees himself as a latter-day martyr, a chronicler of disaster—specifically, of a volcanic eruption—who has suffered from his devotion to scientific observation. One of the problems, of course—and one that he recognizes fully when he insists that he is inventing nothing, simply reporting—is whether the chronicler only observed the eruption, as he claims, or whether, like Jules, he actually provoked it. The problem is a crucial one for Céline, repeatedly accused of collaborating. The doctor may place the responsibility for the cataclysm on a perfectly unadmirable character—Jules—still, it is not only clear that Jules is performing the work of the artist (as is the doctor), but it is also obvious that the doctor identifies with him: "C'est pas une petite histoire de faire raffluer les Déluges, de nous faire foncer dessus charges sur charges des quatre horizons! au doigt! . . . zessayez! zessayez un peu! Vous allez dire que je me régale, que je suis un cataclyste aussi." The entire novel justifies the label. To mitigate his condemnation and enhance the role of "cataclyste," the doctor compares Jules to Noah, pointing out that the Flood was nothing next to this inundation of fire. Noah is a savior; we can only hope the artist is too.

Bardamu's burning of his jungle hut is a reply to a deluge, and he compares himself to Noah. The combination of the drenching rain and Bardamu's fever makes everything appear to be melting. Everything is losing its shape, its rigidity, its solidity. Everything is returning to the state of primal chaos: "Tout fondait en bouillie de camelotes, d'espérances et de comptes et dans la fièvre aussi, moite elle aussi. Cette pluie tellement dense qu'on en avait la bouche fermée quand elle vous agressait comme par un bâillon tiède. Ce déluge n'empêchait pas les animaux de se rechercher, les rossignols se mirent à faire autant de bruit que les chacals. L'anarchie partout et dans l'arche, moi Noé, gâteux. Le moment d'en finir me parut arrivé." Feverish, Bardamu finds it hard to distinguish between things; the fire in his body shows everything about him in its chaotic state, although the hut still forms an artificial barrier between him and the rain. Taking the situation into his own hands, this false Noah burns the ark, the partition between him and anarchy. By burning the hut, he burns the rain's "bâillon tiède," and his fire is a form of speech. His message is that nothing but illusion separates us from chaos. The night rain is life, the fire a flicker illuminating the flood, which otherwise might not be seen. The novel is the fire, really a torch in the darkness. Céline writes with a purpose: to show us that the world does not conform to the structure we conventionally give it, that we are in fact surrounded by anarchy. In any case this is the structure of his fictional space, the imaginary landscape through which his *picaro* journeys and from which he gathers the material for the fire in the night his books represent.

"Pendant que nous parlions des nègres, les mouches et les insectes, si gros, en si grand nombre, vinrent s'abattre autour de la lanterne, en rafales si denses qu'il fallut bien éteindre," we read in ***Voyage.*** One insect fluttering around a lamp at night is a nuisance, but a cloud of them, drawn by the light and falling dead in droves, is more than inconvenient; eventually the light must be put out. People, too, are drawn to fire, even when it means their own death. Bardamu admits that it was a suicidal attraction to fire that made him join the army: "A présent, j'étais pris dans cette fuite en masse, vers le meurtre en commun, vers le feu. . . ." Inevitably, fire attracts large numbers of insects seemingly bent on self-destruction. War has the same effect on humans. People are often compared to insects in ***Voyage,*** but never more appropriately than in the description of their mindless rush to war. It is not the fire alone that attracts people; they are actually drawn to death-their own or someone else's. Friends and relatives gather to watch a man die, and their swarms under the lights remind one of flies: "Et comme il y en avait des parents! Des gros et des fluets agglomérés en grappes somnolentes sous les lumières des <<suspensions>>." The fascination of fire is at least partially the fascination of death.

The fundamental image of ***Voyage au bout de la nuit*** is that life is a journey through night; the secondary image of art as a flame reinforces the idea that the work gives another perspective, illuminates the night in at least a limited way. This does indeed bestow a certain conventional immortality on the work: it is a torch that can be rekindled long after the death of the author. In this respect the fascination with the work of art is also linked to death.

Céline's remarks on the cinema reveal a tendency to regard it as escapist, but he has much more respect for the illusions of the movie theater than for the commonly accepted illusions of love. As Bardamu watches a film, he feels again the fatal attraction of the moth to the lantern: "Alors les rêves montent dans la nuit pour aller s'embraser au mirage de la lumière qui bouge." The film, like a novel, is the fire that sets the dream ablaze. It is not like life. The well-lighted theater is compared to a cake, the people pressing about it to larva. "C'était comme tout le contraire de la nuit." The movie is illusion, but it sheds some light on reality. "Ce n'est pas tout à fait vivant ce qui se passe sur les écrans, il reste dedans une grande place trouble, pour les pauvres, pour les rêves et pour les morts." The cinema is unquestionably a positive dream-producer. It gives courage to face the darkness outside. It is the part of the film that is "not quite alive" that makes these dreams possible.

For its creator as well, the work has the fascination of death. Writing is like dying. The writer is spearing something within himself and fixing it at the end of his pen. Showing it to a reader has some of the morbid quality of exhibiting the corpse of a suicide to the public. Not only does the writer feel himself bleeding as he writes; he feels that every phrase, once set down, destroys the possibilities for growth in another direction; the possibilities become fewer and fewer until the whole work is pinned down, no longer palpitating, to become what each reader chooses to make of it. The reward for the grisly business is that the work has the power to light up the night.

After all, fire is not always fatal; it also warms, like the war in ***Voyage*** "La guerre avait brûlé les uns, réchauffé les autres, comme le feu torture ou conforte, selon qu'on est placé dedans ou devant." The author is inside, the reader happily toasting himself in front of the fire. It is significant that although the work burns, it is not consumed. One of the few things not damaged by the thorough bombing in ***Normance*** is the doctor's book. The apartment building is a shambles, fire is everywhere, but his papers did not burn: "et que ça avait pas brûlé! . . . le plus drôle!" The concierge gathers together the papers which are blowing in the street: chapters from various books mixed in with old bills and letters. This is Céline's final comment on the book; it is a disconnected and intensely personal mixture of odd papers blowing down the street for anyone to catch hold of. We may discard them or use them to light a fire (literally or spiritually), as we choose.

Almost by definition, the *picaro* is an apprentice. Bardamu had prepared for the hut-burning in ***Voyage*** by an apprenticeship in the art of fire-making, just as any artist practices his craft. "Malgré que je fusse maladroit naturellement, après une semaine d'application je savais moi aussi, tout comme un nègre, faire prendre mon petit feu entre deux pierres aigües." He lacked the time to become adept at striking the stones: "Beaucoup d'étincelles me sautaient encore dans les yeux." With sparks in his eyes, Bardamu is building a fire, as if the coruscating eyes themselves made the fire catch. The fire-maker is in a position of great power; the writer who sees himself as a fire-maker is not belittling his role.

Jules, in ***Normance,*** has more than shining eyes; his entire body gleams: "le moulin brille à présent, luit! . . . Jules aussi luit sur sa plate-forme! reluit!" Jules looks as if he is on fire. He sends off sparks; he has caused the conflagration. "Regardez-le done! ses doigts! les bouts! vous voyez pas les étincelles?" Jules appears to be a sorcerer cursing the city. Jules "empereur des flammes," Jules pointing a flaming finger at the clouds and calling down a rain of fire shows us an imposing picture of the artist-prophet. The doctor-narrator also sees himself as a prophet, one of the denouncing variety. "Y a des dénonceurs de périls! je suis de ceux!"

The doctor's excuse for his flamboyant, jerky, repetitive style is that the nature of his material—catastrophe—and his role as universal scapegoat require just such an emotional style. "J'ai pas de cinéma personnel pour vous faire voir le tout assis . . . confortable . . . ou comme dans un rêve . . . ni de <<bruitage>> non plus . . . ni de critiques rémunérés aptes à me vous tartiner mille louanges du tonnerre de Dieu de mes génies! . . . j'ai que l'hostilité du monde et la catastrophe! . . . je perds la catastrophe je suis perdu!" Without cinematic effects or critics to persuade the public to like him, the writer must rely on showmanship, and disaster makes a good show. In any case, his message of denunciation is perfectly sincere. He does not need Jules's power to summon disaster to be able to see catastrophe in Europe's future. He believes that his fire enables him to foresee what is to come, particularly the consequences of war.

The writer's clairvoyance makes him an excellent leader and pathfinder. Such is the position of the doctor in the last novels, as he wanders through Germany in search of refuge. He organizes the journey and protects his little band (wife, friend, cat) from the sometimes contained, sometimes savage hostility surrounding them. His expression of the loneliness and uncertainty of his position in ***Nord*** can be poignant: "Vous diriez de l'encre notre sousbois . . . y a là-haut les nuages qui sont illuminés, brillants . . . des pinceaux des cent projecteurs et des reflects d'autres explosions . . . nord . . . est . . . mais dans notre parc nous, rien . . . l'encre . . . deux pas . . . trois pas . . . vous vous sentez devenir tout ouate, tout nuit, vous-même. . . un moment vous êtes étonné de chercher encore, quoi? . . . vous ne savez plus. . . ." The use of the second-person pronoun and the sense of dissolving into the night universalize the experience described and include the reader, even though the repeated "encre" implies that Céline is describing the loneliness of the writer. We are all seekers. Although he recognizes that he is not the only one looking for something—a path, an answer, Céline nevertheless remains convinced that of all those seeking, he alone knows in which direction to go. In this he is descended from a long line of poets and writers who sincerely believed the role of the artist is to point the way. Victor Hugo's radiant poet in "Fonction du poète" is just one example. His luminous brow is the only bright spot in a night of total darkness. "Il rayonne! il jette sa flamme / sur l'éternelle vérité!" Flooding with his light the entire world, he leads the people to God. Céline's purpose is not to reveal God, but to force people to recognize the reality and finality of death. His position as Cassandra ("dénonceur de périls") is not likely to win him great popularity, but he is upheld by the certainly that he is right. For Hugo, poet, message, and medium all cast light, illuminate the future, point the way. For Céline too the writer is a pathfinder, flamethrower, seer, and wizard.

Borokrom, the piano player of ***Guignol's Band,*** got his name from his ability to make bombs: "Enfin on l'appelait Borokrom à cause de son savoir chimique, des bombes qu'il avait fabriquées, paraît-il, au temps de sa jeunesse." His propensity to throw them is another matter. The first incident takes place in a bar, where Joconde is responsible for a brawl. "C'est elle qu'incendiait." She inflames the dockers gathered there; under the impression she is being mistreated, they attack Cascade and begin to destroy the bar. Boro starts the barrel organ to add to the din, then throws a grenade. "Wrroung! . . . le tonnerre de Dieu! La tôle qu'explose! Quelque chose alors! et ces flammes! . . . Ah! merde! J'ai vu! Merde! C'est lui! . . . Dans les flammes là! . . . Dans le feu jailli! Il a jeté le truc!" The explosion effectively breaks up the fight and all escape.

Boro turns on the organ and throws the grenade at the same time because he uses them to the same effect: to create a diversion, and the key word is *create.* Borokrom makes music and bombs; both inspire an intense emotional reaction in his companions. His task, as a performing artist, like the writer's, is to create an emotional response. Céline himself insisted that conveying emotion was the main purpose of his writing. Borokrom is an incendiary—so is Céline, in his way.

The second bomb also permits Boro to escape, and especially to destroy the evidence of Claben's murder. He shuts Delphine and Ferdinand in the basement with the dead body. Just as Ferdinand forces the trap-door open, an object is thrown inside and explodes: "Au moment pflof! . . . plein dans la pêche! . . . je prends un caillou . . . en pleine gueule! pflam!!! je dingue! . . . je culbute! . . . à la renverse! . . . Brrouum!! . . . Un tonnerre qu'éclate dans le noir! . . . là en pleine cave! . . . en même temps! . . . en plein bazar! . . . Ah! c'est féerique! . . . plein la gueule!. . . Je suis écroulé sous les décombres . . . C'est lui qu'a jeté le truc! Maudit chien . . . une explosion formidable! . . . Encore lui!"

We are struck by the parallel between Borokrom, the bomb-throwing piano player, and Jules, the bombardment-provoking painter of ***Normance.*** Borokrom obviously used bombs to help him escape, but one wonders why Jules chose to make a holocaust of Montmartre. The doctor suggests that Jules is a frustrated ceramicist looking for a kiln: "lui qui parlait toujours de son four! qui souffrait de pas avoir un four . . . un four <<grand-feu>>! je le trouvais servi! . . . qu'il nous montre un peu sa maîtrise s'il était si artiste au four!"

Jules is, in fact, displaying his artistry with a colossal flame-show—the light beams sweeping across the sky are, after all, "pinceaux." The doctor himself exercises his artistry in describing the light show. Page after page is filled with colors; the lights are compared to jewels, flowers, and delicate lace. At this point the creative arts of the painter and writer fuse: the bombardment is their masterpiece. The doctor tells us, "faudrait être artiste pour vous faire voir les couleurs . . . la palette. . . ." Modestly, the narrator professes to be a simple "chroniqueur," unequal to the task of rendering the "féerie" in the sky. Any of a number of brilliant quotations would give him the lie:

> Le ciel crève à gauche, là juste! . . . *brrac*! au Sud! . . . une cataracte d'or d'en haut . . . un fleuve des nuages . . . jaune . . . et puis vert . . . c'est pas commun comme masse de feu ce qui cascade, rejaillit, inonde . . . je vous ai raconté pourtant . . . mais là vraiment c'est le ciel entier qu'on dirait qui fond . . . et puis d'en bas on voit des rues qui s'élèvent . . . s'enlèvent . . . montent en serpents de flammes . . . tourbillonnent . . . tordent d'un nuage à l'autre . . . une église entière qui part, se renverse, tout son clocher pointu, brulant, en espèce de pouce! . . . c'est extraordinaire! renversé sur nous! . . . l'Église d'Auteuil . . . je vous l'ai raconté . . . à l'envers . . . mais elle, pas si flambante tout de même . . . plutôt en reflects . . . ah vous voyez c'est pas semblable . . . vogue! s'envole . . . c'est que je suis pas artiste peintre, je vous rends mal l'effet. . . . . . j'ai que du petit don de chroniqueur. . . .

The writer writing about the painter painting produces an extraordinary work of art. At one point the doctor compares Jules's real painting unfavorably to his sky painting; as an ironic condemnation of surrealistic painting, the intent—and the effect—is to form a highly laudatory word-picture couched in derogatory language: "Je l'avais vu vernisser ses toiles . . . moi parfait plouc, aucune autorité d'art, je m'étais dit à moi-même: il le fait exprès! il bluffe le bourgeois! il leur peint des autobus sur la mer de Glace . . . et les Alpes elles-mêmes en neiges mauve, orange, carmin, et les vaches paissant des couteaux! . . . des lames d'acier! des poignards en fait d'herbe tendre! . . . maintenant il nous sorcelait autre chose! . . . c'était plus terrible que ses gouaches! c'était un petit peu plus osé!" The sky-painting is indeed bolder, but not significantly different in style. The upside-down church, the sky melting into a golden cataract, the streets mounting in serpentine flames to the clouds, are the living, moving, colorful offspring of the bus on the sea of ice and the cows grazing on steel blades. The difference in medium is, however, significant. By substituting fire for paint, the artist attributes divine qualities to himself, especially when he uses fire to paint the heavens, where only the sun or Zeus' lightning bolts should provide color. Since fire can be equated with the word, the sky-painting is essentially a linguistic image, and we have not merely a writer describing a painting, but a writer describing the artistic scope of language. The visual effects alone are spectacular. When the writer becomes incendiary, his novel will have an explosive effect.

Jules's work of art is not just a display of fireworks for people to gape at on the fourteenth of July; it is an air attack, part of a war. The bombing is a form of expression. Jules, the id-figure, creates a very beautiful work of art expressing anger, aggression, and the urge to destroy. Certainly Céline does nothing less with his novel. He sees himself as a painter of destruction. Not only does he depict the destructive forces already existing (war, poverty, death); he sees creation as stemming from destruction: he is Jules calling the bombers, directing them, setting the fire. Fire consumes; destruction is the subject and, in a sense, the work of the artist. Céline's novels directly attacked French literary conventions of vocabulary, syntax, and, of course, punctuation. He did not see the writer as the staid guardian of the purity of French letters, but rather as a bomb-thrower.

The novelist's journey takes place in the metaphorical darkness of nihilism, but the written word is a kind of fire lighting up the night. The functions of the work of art and the roles of the artist are implicit in the images related to fire and the fire-maker. Fire cleanses by consuming garbage. It flows like lava, and Céline's version of the apocalypse is a deluge of fire. Fire draws insects to their own destruction. The fire-maker is an incendiary or a prophet; inasmuch as the prophet uses fiery language and flings bomb-like prophecies, the two roles are perhaps indistinguishable. Céline's *picaro,* as represented in his successive narrators, wants to keep moving and light fires. His final gesture, the summing up of his life and experience, is the novel which he casts like a bomb in the face of his public. This is the endpoint of the journey, the final twist he gives to the picaresque form, his distorted version of a version of the quest. From heroes seeking the Holy Grail, through little boys stealing grapes from blind men, we have come to the artist hurling his brimstone-filled prophecies at the reader. In its journey, the quest itself has been transformed.

William K. Buckley (essay date Spring 1986)

SOURCE: "Louis-Ferdinand Céline's Novels: From Narcissism to Sexual Connection," in *Studies in the Novel,* Vol. XVIII, No. 1, Spring, 1986, pp. 51-65.

[*In the following essay, Buckley examines Céline's treatment of sexual desire and love in* Journey to the End of the Night *and* Death on the Installment Plan.]

> "Ah, Ferdinand . . . as long as you live you will always search for the secret of the universe in the loins of women!"
> (***L'Eglise***)

> . . . the female mystery doesn't reside between the thighs, it's on another wave-length, a much more subtle one.
> (***Castle to Castle***).

After Freud, modern novelists grew more conscious of not only their own literary expression as a kind of narcissism, but also of the narcissism in the characters they created. Distress about narcissism, therefore, can be easily detected in modern novels. "The psychoanalytic concept of narcissism," says Russell Jacoby in his study *Social Amnesia* (1975), "captures the reality of the bourgeois individual; it expresses the private regression of the ego into the id under the sway of public domination. . . . it comprehends the dialectical isolation of the bourgeois individual—dialectical in that the isolation that damns the individual to scrape along in a private world derives from a public and social one. The energy that is directed toward oneself, rather than toward others, is rooted in society, not organically in the individual. . . . The mechanism of this shift is not the least the society that puts a premium on the hardening of each individual—the naked will to self-preservation." This *naked will* to self-preservation, this *hardening* of oneself is an apt description of most protagonists in our modern novels. These terms are an especially good description of Céline's main character in his first two novels: the young Ferdinand.

Still creating their storm of interest and influence after fifty years, Céline's ***Journey to the End of the Night*** (1932) and ***Death on the Installment Plan*** (1936) are good examples of modern novels which use a narrator who expresses his hardened feelings over both his narcissistic and crushed ego-ideals, and over his careful love choices. Ferdinand, like so many in modern fiction, is a character who has withdrawn his libido from the outer world because his contact with that world has brought mostly economic and emotional disaster; and, in defense, he has directed his libido to his ego. Major American scholarship on Céline has not explored the sexual behavior of Céline's characters as closely as it needs to do. Of course there have been important discussions of Céline's views on sex by many. McCarthy gives us a rather negative assessment of the author's views in his biography *Céline* (1975), as does J.H. Matthews in his book, *The Inner Dream: Céline as Novelist* (1978). In comparing Céline's views on sex to Baudelaire's views in *Journaux intimes,* McCarthy claims that ***Journey*** shows women as "predatory," that Céline suggests "women need to destroy men because there is a link between female sexuality and cruelty," and that, in the final analysis—because of the behavior of Musyne and Lola—"sex turns out to be disgusting" for Ferdinand, reflecting Céline's personal view that the male loses himself in orgasm with a woman because he is "weary" to have done "with himself." J. H. Matthews offers an equally negative view of sex in ***Death on the Installment Plan.*** He points to several episodes in the novel which support his point that sex "brings no consolation of any kind, no sense of release. It is a heightened form of terror. . . . Ferdinand's sexual contacts revitalize the cliche that represents sex as a form of death and likens the ecstasy of orgasm to dying." The client who early in the novel invites the young Ferdinand to engage her in oral sex; the sexual demands made upon Ferdinand by Madame Gorloge, and her theft of a jewel from the young boy's pocket; Gwendoline, the sex partner Ferdinand meets after crossing the Channel, and whom Matthews calls the *vagina dentata;*

Nora's desperate actions with Ferdinand at Meanwell College; the astonishing scene between Antoine and his wife, to which Ferdinand and his friend Robert are voyeurs: all these scenes are examples of what Matthews calls Céline's linking of violence and eroticism. Matthews further maintains that even masturbation is "marked by terrorism" in this novel, especially when the boys at the English boarding school cruelly beat and masturbate the retarded Jongkind for getting penalties during a soccer match. Therefore since at "no time in his life has Ferdinand felt capable of trusting women enough to love any of them," masturbation becomes the "significant feature" of his early life. "It is a direct expression of his profound need to change his destiny in a world ruled by violence and predatory sexuality, where [Ferdinand] is alternately victim and pariah." I agree with Matthews that in most of these scenes "tenderness has no place," and that masturbation, sodomy, and rape become the clear but worst examples of narcissism in this novel. One could argue, for example, that Gorloge's seduction of the little Ferdinand is an example of emotional exploitation born out of the economic brutalities which exist between the classes in Paris, or that Antoine's attempt to copulate with his wife using butter, while Ferdinand and Robert look on and laugh, is an illustration of common but secret sexual hilarities. Ferdinand's laughter in this scene, and our mix of laughter and uncomfortable surprise, is to free us from pompous judgment, to suspend our surprise in humor—much as Chaucer does in his tales on sex. And yet I believe that Ferdinand's experience with Nora, as I will show, is the exception to what Matthews and McCarthy call the predatory nature of sex in Céline's novels. In fact, his feelings over Nora are very exceptional indeed, for they begin Ferdinand's emotional education, his learning to see women as affirmations of beauty and life.

In her *Céline and His Vision* (1967), Erika Ostrovsky sees Céline as debunking sex, but for a very special reason: "Céline tends to blacken most descriptions" of sexual gratification, but in a "spirit of mockery," because the author "finds this business of 'I lo-o-ve you' vulgar, heavy-handed, and cheaply sentimental." As a result, she says, Céline intends to show us that eroticism is also "quite frequently linked to violence": witness Hilda, the sixteen-year-old, who waits for troop trains in ***Castle to Castle,*** Frau Frucht, addicted to sexual perversion, in ***Castle to Castle,*** Ferdinand's escape from a brawl with women on board the *Bragueton* in ***Journey,*** or Céline's comment in ***North*** that the more cities burn the more crazy for sex women become. Ostrovsky is quick to point out, however, that Céline can also be quite positive about sex, can even see sex as regenerative. She points to the author's descriptions of Lola, Molly, Madelon, and Sophie in ***Journey,*** Nora in ***Death on the Installment Plan,*** and Virginia in ***Pont de Londres***—all characters reflecting, perhaps, Céline's comment in a letter to Eveline Pollet: "I love the physical perfections of women almost to the point of madness. It's a truth I reveal to you. It governs all the others." Moreover, Ostrovsky comments on Céline's astonishingly positive description of Sophie in ***Journey,*** that "if anywhere in Céline's work there is a glimpse of hope and beauty, of sun and joy, it is in the sight of such women . . . only the physical perfection of a woman, an animal, a gesture, can offer affirmation or a momentary respite from horror."

Wayne Burns and Gerald Butler go even further in their positive estimations of Céline's treatment of sex. In his essay "***Journey to the End of the Night:*** A Primer to the Novel," (from the recently published anthology of essays edited by James Flynn entitled *Understanding Céline* [1984]), Burns says that "Through loving the woman's body—Sophie's, Tania's, Molly's, even Madelon's—[Ferdinand] comes to love the woman herself. Much as Céline would have disliked having Ferdinand compared with Mellors (Céline once described *Lady Chatterley's Lover* as 'a gamekeeper's miserable prick for six hundred and fifty pages') Ferdinand's attitude towards women is essentially Lawrentian in that he comes to the woman herself through her body." Burns also reminds us of Céline's long "lyrical description" of Sophie in ***Journey.*** In his essay "The Feeling for Women in Céline and His American Counterparts," (also from *Understanding Céline*), Gerald Butler not only maintains that Céline's view of women is one of adoration when compared to the way women are seen in Miller and Kerouac, but also "that it is *not* true," as Julia Kristeva claims (in her chapter on Céline entitled "Females Who Can Wreck the Infinite," from her book *Powers of Horror: An Essay on Abjection*) that Céline's fiction "shows all women as of only two kinds: desexualized and delightful on the one hand and sexual and terrifying on the other, so that beauty is what wards off the sexual." "Sophie," Butler says, "is both sexual and, in her sexuality, a miracle of delight for Ferdinand." Her "presence and Ferdinand's reaction to it is enough to give the lie to the 'heroism' of Robinson that is the epitome of that bitterness and 'sense of superiority' and 'heaviness' that the world. . . . teaches." And in his essay "The Meaning of the Presence of Lili in Céline's Final Trilogy," he says that Lili is "put forth in the novels as a guiding light for humanity," that even "her animal qualities, in the positive sense that Céline gives to 'animal'" (and here Butler means Lili is on the same "wave-length" as animals—she tunes in only those who are helpless) "do not detract from her comparison to a heroine from Dickens, for Lili's 'heart' does not exclude the 'animal' but seems to be profoundly connected with it. If that is so, then all the sexuality of human beings that Céline does not at all present in these novels in a favorable light is not an expression of animality in the sense that Lili is like an animal. Rather, the implication, the message for human beings is that they should have real animality above all by having hearts, as Lili does."

These are the important discussions of Céline's view of sexual feeling. My intention here is not to further discuss Dr. Destouches' views on sex and love, interesting and shadowy as this topic is turning out to be. (See, for example, Céline's own definition of love and sex in Marc Hanrez's *Céline* [1961].) Rather, my intention is two-fold: first, to describe how the young Ferdinand came to feel that women are regenerative, worthy of trust, and beautiful (how he learned about what Ostrovsky, Burns, and Butler are calling the *positive* aspects of sexual experience); and second, how the older Ferdinand came to realize that the sheer naked force of his will and the hardening of his heart would not help him be less narcissistic, would not help him gain sexual satisfaction. My goal is to open a more detailed investigation into those scenes of Céline's novels which describe modern sexual behavior, to look more closely at the sexual needs, desires, and secrets of Céline's characters.

In ***Death on the Installment Plan,*** young Ferdinand, already hardened to real connection from his brutal experiences in Paris as the son of a mother and father who want him to be a success, retains an erotic fantasy for Nora, the wife of an English school master. He has been sent by his parents to Meanwell College, in England, in order to learn English for business purposes so that when he returns to Paris he will start his business career off on the right foot. Badgered by an embittered and humiliated father, watching his mother work herself to death in their lace and furniture shop, and seduced by their female customers, Ferdinand is a tight-lipped adolescent, unable to connect with anyone, and full of childhood memories that are violent and sad. He is a classic self-preservative personality. And in this novel his masturbation preserves gratification in fantasy. He compliments his fantasies for Nora this way: "I can still see her. . . . I can bring back her image whenever I please. At the shoulders her silk blouse forms lines, curves, miracles of flesh, agonizing visions, soft and sweet and crushing. . . . The kid that came around to lap me up had his money's worth on Sunday night . . . But I wasn't satisfied, it was her I wanted. . . . Beauty comes back at you in the night . . . it attacks you, it carries you away . . . it's unbearable . . . I was soft in the head, from jerking off on visions . . . The less we had for meals, the more I masturbated. . . ." Ego regresses into id under the power of parental domination, fantasy masturbation, and the sheer weight of poverty at the bankrupt English boarding school. Ferdinand's ego-libido creates Nora as his "object-choice." In one scene he masturbates with a school friend, while thinking of Nora, and, as the angry narcissist, fuels his mild sadism with attacks on sentimentality in love. *At the same time,* however, his attack on sentiment exhibits a deep desire for real connection, and this is what gives this novel a complexity rarely found even in our best modern British and American fiction.

> "We did each other up brown . . . I was ruthless, I couldn't stop, my imagination kept winding me up . . . I devoured Nora in all her beauty. . . . I'd have taken all her blood, every drop . . . Still it suited me better to ravage the bed, to chew up the sheets . . . than to let Nora or any other skirt take me for a ride. . . . To hell with all that stinking mush! . . . Yak! yak! I love you. I adore you! Sure, sure! . . . Why worry, it's a party. Bottoms up! It's so lovely! It's so innocent! . . . I'd wised up when I was a kid! Sentiment, hell! Balls!. . . . I clutched my oil can. . . . You won't catch me dying like a sucker . . . with a poem on my lips."

When Nora does, at last, come to Ferdinand's room, out of her own mad loneliness and lack of connection to her husband, and abruptly flattens him out with her caresses, giving him, as Céline says, "an avalanche of tenderness," young Ferdinand does surprisingly well in responding. In bed with her he is beginning to reject, I believe, his narcissism—if only for a moment:

> I try to soothe her pain, to make her control herself . . . I caulk wherever I can . . . I knock myself out . . . I try my best . . . I try the subtlest tricks . . . But she's too much for me . . . She gives me some wicked holds . . . The whole bed is shaking . . . She flails around like crazy . . . I fight like a lion . . . My hands are swollen from clutching her ass! I want to anchor her, to make her stop moving. There. That's it. She's stopped talking. Christ almighty! I plunge, I slip in like a breeze! I'm petrified with love . . . I'm one with her beauty . . . I'm in ecstacy . . . I wriggle. . . . On her face I go looking for the exact spot next to her nose . . . the one that tortures me, the magic of her smile."

In feeling "love," and in "looking for the exact spot" which tortures him, Ferdinand replaces his fantasy of Nora with her reality. Unfortunately Nora "breaks loose" from Ferdinand, and runs from the school to make her way to a bridge, where she will jump into a river to her death, a "nightgown fluttering in the wind." This whole scene is charged with the helpless desperation of human behavior. "I knew it," says Ferdinand, "she's "off her rocker! . . . Dammit to hell . . . Could I catch her? . . . But it's none of my business . . . There's nothing I can do . . . The whole thing is beyond me . . . I listen . . . I look out through the hall door . . . to see if I can see her on the waterfront . . . She must be down by now . . . There she is again . . . still screaming . . . 'Ferdinand! Ferdinand!' . . . her screams cut through the sky . . . ." It is Céline's intention, as Wayne Burns has pointed out in *Understanding Céline,* "to make the reader hear cries he has never heard before; to make him realize that there is no end to these cries (in either time or circumstance), for they are cries which cannot be remedied by religion or philosophy or morality—much less by the paltry palliatives of social reform or even social revolution."

Ferdinand does go after her, but feels helpless and endangered as he stands on the bridge with the retarded boy both he and Nora had been taking care of at the school. We hear more of her pleas as she "flits" like a "butterfly" from one street lamp to the next. Sirens and whistles blow, rescue squads arrive, but nothing has helped. She is a "little white square in the waves. . . . caught in the eddies. . . . passing the breakwater!" It is Céline's intention, as he later has Ferdinand say in ***Journey to the End of the Night,*** "to go deeper and hear other cries that I had not heard yet or which I had not been able to understand before, because there seems always to be some cries beyond those which one has heard." This need to hear the "cries" of humanity is not the impulse of a narcissist, for he is not, as Freud says in "On Narcissism: An Introduction" (1914), "plainly seeking" himself "as a love-object." Nor is Ferdinand seeking a Nora as males would seek women to "save," those who would fulfill the male's desire to believe that "without him she would lose all hold on respectability." Even though Nora's behavior could trigger the *narcissistic* impulse in Ferdinand to rescue her, "justified by her untrustworthy temperament sexually and by the danger to her social position" (as Ferdinand might say it), it does not do so, neither in fantasy nor in reality. For there has been no "skill in argument" to win Nora, to save her from Meanwell College, no real seduction on Ferdinand's part. In fact, his *self-preservative* impulse remains defiant and hostile after her death, for he fears he will take the rap for it. Freud has it that "the attitude of defiance in the 'saving' phantasy far outweighs the tender feeling in it, the latter being usually directed towards the mother. . . . in the rescue phantasy, that is, he identifies himself completely with the father. All the instincts, the loving, the grateful, the sensual, the defiant, the self-assertive and independent—all are gratified in the wish to be *the father of himself*. . . . When in a dream a man rescues a woman from the water, it means that he makes her a mother . . . his own mother." Yet Nora is not rescued. The drowning is no *phantasy.* And Ferdinand, after hearing Nora's cries and feeling he was sure to get caught and blamed, runs back to the school to wake Nora's old husband out of his own torpor. The scene we see then is painful: the old man, drunk on the floor, making masturbatory gestures with the flesh on his stomach; and Ferdinand, observing, and finally giving up, leaving to pack his bags for Paris "at the crack of dawn."

Despite the suicide, both Nora and Ferdinand had freed themselves, momentarily, from their environments, fixed as they were to their economic realities: Ferdinand to his petit-bourgeois Paris background and Nora to her bankrupt English middle-class. Without moralizing or sentimentalizing their encounter, Céline shows us Nora and Ferdinand achieving a moment of difficult tenderness. "It seems very evident," Freud says in "On Narcissism," that "one person's narcissism has a great attraction for those others who have renounced part of their own narcissism and are seeking after object-love." As an adult, Nora has rejected part of her narcissism, and a kind of vulnerable, nervous, but tender compassion remains. She is no Madame Gorloge, who, as the wife of Ferdinand's boss, *orders* Ferdinand to take his clothes off and make love to her. "She grabs me by the ears . . . She pulls me down to mother nature . . . She bends me with all her might. . . . 'Bite me, sweet little puppy . . . Bite into it!'"

Ferdinand *plays* "the ardent lover," and charges into her, as he had seen her husband Antoine do when he and Robert were spying on them, "but much more gently." "She squashed me against her tits! She was having a hell of a good time . . . It was stifling. . . . She wanted me to work harder. . . . to be more brutal. . . . 'you're ripping me apart, you big thug! Oh rip me' . . . ." Ferdinand did not have to play the "ardent lover" with Nora; nor could their lovemaking be called "ripping." She was not, as he characterized Gorloge, a "vampire." She was a "mirage of charm." Neither was Nora a Gwendoline, Ferdinand's "Greasy Jone," the English fish and chips girl he meets on the docks before finding Meanwell College. "She kept repeating her name. She tapped on her chest . . . Gwendoline! Gwendoline! . . . I heard her all right, I massaged her tits, but I didn't get the words . . . To hell with tenderness . . . sentiment! That stuff is like a family. . . . She took advantage of the dark corners to smother me with caresses. . . . We could have done our business, we'd certainly have had a good time . . . But once we'd had our sleep out, then what?" "Anyway I was too tired . . . And besides, it was impossible . . . It stirred up my gall . . . it cramped my cock to think of it . . . of all the treachery of things . . . as soon as you let anybody wrap you up. . . . That's all I had on my mind in the little side streets while my cutie was unbuttoning me . . . She had the grip of a working girl, rough as a grater, and not at all bashful. Everybody was screwing me. O well . . . ."

Rather, when Ferdinand sees Nora for the first time, he is astonished at his reaction to the *gentleness* in her face: "the special charm she had, that lit up on her face when she was speaking. . . . It intimidated me . . . I saw stars, I couldn't move." Ferdinand's narcissism is under attack by such powerful gentleness, tenderness, and charm because it is responding to it, needing it, and weakened by it in its self-preservative inner life. For all through the Meanwell College scene, Nora will be tending to the needs of a helpless retarded boy. And even though Ferdinand's young narcissism is interested in the idealized Nora—the Nora of his dreams, the picture of her which helps him adjust to his bitterness—he still responds, physically to *her,* and not to her manipulations, as he did with Gorloge and Greasy Jone. This is especially remarkable when you consider Ferdinand's characterization of himself earlier in the novel: "you'll never know what obsessive hatred really smells like . . . the hatred that goes through your guts, all the way to your heart . . . Real hatred comes from deep down, from a defenseless childhood crushed with work. That's the hatred that kills you." Even more remarkably, it may be said that Ferdinand gets a bit of compassion from Nora, learns from her, as he too walks with the retarded boy Jongkind, who "whines like a dog" after Nora's death.

> I got to get the brat home . . . I give him a poke in the ass. . . . He's worn out from running . . . I push him . . . I throw him . . . He can't see a thing without his glasses . . . He can't even see the lamp posts. He starts bumping into everything . . . He whines like a dog . . . I grab him and pick him up, I carry him up the hill . . . I toss him into his bed . . . I run to the old man's door. . . . He blinks a little, his eyelids flutter . . . He don't know from nothing . . . 'She's drowning! She's drowning!' I yell at him. I repeat it even louder . . . I shout my lungs out . . . I make motions . . . I imitate the glug-glug . . . I point down . . . into the valley . . . out the window!

Ferdinand's heart and naked self-will are now less hardened to women, and to those who are victims of biology.

In ***Journey to the End of the Night,*** Ferdinand, as an adult, is the eloquent spokesman of revulsion from European colonialism and modern warfare, the voice of revulsion from our traditional beliefs in brotherhood, marriage, and love. He does not believe in our modern love, which is, for him, a "poodle's chance of attaining the infinite." His travels in the novel from the front lines of World War I, to Paris, to New York City and Detroit, to Africa, and back to Paris, have given him an anti-idealistic view of human behavior. "The great weariness of life," he says near the end of the novel, "is maybe nothing but the vast trouble we take to remain always for twenty or forty or more years at a time reasonable beings—so as not to be merely and profoundly oneself, that is to say, obscene, ghastly, and absurd." His first relationship with a woman in this novel is with Lola, an American nurse who believes in the existence of the soul and in patriotism, and it is a relationship characterized by a weariness because Ferdinand believes only in survival after coming home from the war. The understanding between them is of the body not the heart because the hardened heart cannot be trusted during war time. At first he accepts Lola for what she is, and this is even more of a step forward for his self-preservative personality, even less narcissistic than his relationship with Nora, for he no longer needs to see the female body in idealized images: "If I had told Lola what I thought of the war, she would only have taken me for a depraved freak and she'd deny me all intimate pleasures. So I took good care not to confess these things to her. . . . she hadn't only a fine body, my Lola,—let us get that quite clear at once; she was graced also with a piquant little face and grey-blue eyes, which gave her a slightly cruel look, because they were set a wee bit on the upward slant, like those of a wildcat." When Ferdinand does admit that he is not going back to the front, Lola leaves him, furious at his lack of ideals, and returns to New York. But when Ferdinand arrives in New York, he meets Lola again.

> she inquired after my genital lapses and wanted to know if I hadn't somewhere on my wanderings produced some little child she could adopt. It was a curious notion of hers. The idea of adopting a child was an obsession with her. . . . what she wanted was to sacrifice herself entirely to some "little thing." I myself was out of luck. I had nothing to offer her but my own large person, which she found utterly repulsive.

"Really, it's a pity, Ferdinand," Lola says, "that you haven't a little girl somewhere. . . . Your dreamy temperament would go very well in a woman, whereas it doesn't seem at all fitting in a man . . . ." This is an interesting description of female narcissism, to which Ferdinand responds with some of his own. Lola's attitude toward Ferdinand is cool, but now she has found a way to object-love: through a child she could possess the ideal of what she thinks Ferdinand should be. The desire Lola has for Ferdinand is not based on a need to tend him, nor is the desire Ferdinand has for Lola based on a need to protect her. There is, therefore, no *anaclitic* object-choice here. Rather, Lola looks at Ferdinand as a lover who should be what she wants him to be. And Ferdinand looks at Lola as a source for adventure in America. Her body to him was a endless source of joy because of its "American contours"; she is "a type" that appeals to him. Only when Lola gives him money and he takes off for Detroit to work in the Ford plant, do we see a strong and more radical change in Ferdinand's desires for women. The mechanisms involved in his new object-choice—Molly, the Detroit prostitute—are now *more* anaclitic than narcissistic, more dependent than independent, and not so much concerned about being with an "American type." And although Ferdinand's relationship with Molly shows remarkable similarities with Freud's description of male love for the *grande amoureuse* (especially when Freud describes the childhood experiences, the mother-complex, and youthful masturbatory practices of those who have "love for a harlot"), I believe that the following remarks show Ferdinand freeing himself of narcissistic self-absorption, and combining, if only for a time, his feelings of sex *and* tenderness, despite the fact that he is eventually fonder of his longing to "run away from everywhere in search of something."

> I soon felt for Molly, one of the young women in

> this place, an emotion of exceptional trust, which in timid people takes the place of love. I can remember, as if I'd seen her yesterday, her *gentleness and her long white legs,* marvellously lithe and muscular and noble. . . . (emphasis added)
>
> "Don't go back to the works!" Molly urged me, making it worse. "Find some small job in an office instead. . . . Translating, for example; that's really your line . . . you like books. . . ." She was very sweet giving me this advice; she wanted me to be happy. . . . if only I'd met Molly. . . . Before I lost my enthusiasm over that slut of a Musyne and that horrid little bitch Lola!"

At the end of the Detroit chapter, we begin to understand the causes of Ferdinand's narcissism, and his possible solutions for his troubles:

> Molly had been right. I was beginning to understand what she meant. Studies change you, they make a man proud. Before, one was only hovering around life. You think you are a free man, but you get nowhere. Too much of your time's spent dreaming. You slither along on words. That's not the real thing at all. Only intentions and appearances. You need something else. With my medicine, though I wasn't very good at it, I had come into closer contact with men, beasts, and creation. Now it was a question of pushing right ahead, foursquare, into the heart of things.

No longer do we have a character at the mercy of narcissism—like the young Ferdinand—because the narcissist would never want to plunge "into the heart of things." Rather, the adult Ferdinand sees conventional love (i.e. egocentric romantic love) as doomed to fail in a world where so many people have to scrape and crawl just to get by, in a world where Nature's lessons are hard to swallow, where "sex is the poor man's pocket gold mine."

> To love is nothing, it's hanging together that's so hard. . . . All our unhappiness is due to having to remain Tom, Dick, and Harry, cost what it may, throughout a whole series of years.

And near the end of ***Journey,*** when Ferdinand visits a bistro for some cheap fun, living, as he says, a "capitalist's existence without capital," we hear him comment with irony and compassion on a female singing group from England, who are bawling out their little songs of love: "They were singing the defeat of life and they didn't see it. They thought it was only love, nothing but love; they hadn't been taught the rest of it, little dears. . . ." Ferdinand finally realizes that conventional love, the kind we see today everywhere in American culture, richly narcissistic as it is, fails to help anyone—especially him.

What *would* help he tries to describe for us at the end of the novel, after seeing the death of his friend Robinson at the hands of a romantic lover. Ferdinand says about himself that he is just "a quite real Ferdinand who lacked what might make a man greater than his own trivial life, a love for the life of others." This "love for the life of others" is not at all narcissistic, and it is the kind of love which the young Ferdinand began to achieve when he took Jongkind back to the school the night Nora died, and when he banged on the door to tell Nora's old, drunken husband that she was dying. It is the kind of love which would allow death to be

> imprisoned in love along with joy, and so comfortable would it be inside there, so warm, that Death, the bitch, would be given some sensation at last and would end up by having as much fun with love as every one else. Wouldn't that be pretty? Ah, wouldn't that be fine? I laughed about it, standing there alone on the river bank, as I though of all the dodges and all the tricks I'd have to pull off to stuff myself like that full of all-powerful resolves. . . . A toad swollen out with ideals!

But Ferdinand dismisses even these ideas as hopelessly idealistic for a man like him.

What *does* help him are not resolves, but what he finds in Sophie, the Slovak nurse who works at the lunatic asylum with him. In his relationship with Sophie, I believe, we see a man nearly free of narcissism. For Sophie is a woman

> who still from time to time caught me to her, her whole body strong with the strength of her concern for me and tenderness and a heart full also and overflowing and lovely. I felt the directness of it myself, the *directness of her tender strength.* (emphasis added)

Male narcissism could never feel the directness of *tender strength* in a woman's body, the kind of strength Ferdinand now finds that he desires to have not only for himself, but also for women. It is this tender strength in a woman's body, this sex-tenderness and a full heart, which can ease the hardened heart and cruel naked self-will of a man.

I have been looking at scenes which show Ferdinand as an individual seeking meaning and sexual fulfillment. Yet there are other kinds of scenes in Céline's novels which do not emphasize individual sexual action, but rather mass sexual action. These scenes are astonishing in their impact, and they need further study—for they show Céline as a keen observer of herd psychology. Questions, therefore, remain to be answered.

For example, what is the function of Céline's *délire* and exaggeration in the episode from ***Death on the Installment Plan,*** where, in the Bois de Boulogne, Ferdinand and Mireille make love in public, and an orgy of sexual chaos moves and surges a crowd up to the Arc de Triomphe, where they are routed by "twenty-five thousand" policemen? Or what is the meaning of that scene in ***Guignol's Band,*** where Virginia and Ferdinand are swept up in a chaos of orgy, violence, and delight in the night club, where people are copulating in a jumble of arms and legs? There are similar scenes of mass, violent delight in ***North*** and ***Castle to Castle.*** Are these "little narcissistic eccentricities," as Céline labels his writing in ***Guignol's Band?*** Or are they scenes which tell us to: "Palpitate, damn it! That's where the fun is! . . . Wake up! Come on, hello! You robot crap! . . . Shit! . . . Transpose or it's death! I can't do any more for you. Kiss any girl you please! If there's still time!" Perhaps these mass scenes expose the flimsiness of even our most sophisticated ideas about love, or perhaps they speak of what Céline thought to be some ancient longing in sex, the "quite bestial act" of it, as he said. Ferdinand (and later Céline himself in his World War II trilogy) are both swept up by such sights and crowds in every one of the novels—as if this author, as a physician, wants us to understand that he sees impulses which repeat themselves on a huge scale, as if all of human life is joyously trapped into having such feelings out of the sheer biological surgings of the species, as well as out of our small motivations, brutalized as they are by war and stupid economies. Witness this description from ***Castle to Castle,*** where in a railway station, Céline's favorite locale for the mob's sexual *délire,* we see that:

> sadness, idleness, and female heat go together . . . and not just kids! . . . grown women and grandmothers! obviously the hottest ones, with fire in their twats, in those moments when the page turns, when History brings all the nuts together and opens its Epic Dance Halls! . . . you've got to have phosphorus and hunger so they'll rut and sperm and get with it without paying attention! pure happiness! no more hunger, cancer, or clap! . . . the station packed with eternity!

Are these scenes of mass erotic action in direct conflict with Ferdinand's lessons about tenderness? Or do they, then, in their juxtaposition with Ferdinand's raptures, for example, over Sophie, show us the value of individual, sexual tenderness in the face of "History"?

More comment is also needed on the intriguing relationship between what Ferdinand enjoys about women (their astonishing bodies, their compassion and intelligence, their ability to have orgasms, and their "wave-lengths"), and what Céline says about sex for men ("it allows a guy a few seconds delirium which permits him to communicate with her"). How do we square Céline's striking portraits of what women have to offer men with this statement from ***Rigadoon*** (1961):

> all our theater and literature revolve around coitus, deadly repetition! . . . the orgasm is boring, the giants of the pen and silver screen with all the ballyhoo and the millions spent on advertising . . . have never succeeded in putting it across . . . two three shakes of the ass, and there it is . . . the sperm does its work much too quietly, too intimately, the whole thing escapes us . . . but childbirth, that's worth looking at! . . . examining! . . . to the millimeter! fucking . . . God knows I've wasted hours! . . . for two three wiggles of the ass!

And lastly, careful analysis is needed on the relationship between what we see as the positive aspects of sexuality in Céline, what Burns calls "the essentially Lawrentian attitude" Ferdinand gains in coming to the woman, and Céline's personal comment that "(coitus is delirium): to rationalize that delirium with precise verbal maneouvers seems to me silly." Perhaps Céline sees deeper than my critical phrase "positive aspects of sexuality"—a "precise verbal maneouver" if ever I could invent one. Just how deeply and broadly Céline sees can be detected as early as 1916, the date he wrote a poem for his parents in his early twenties, while traveling to Africa. Even at this early date we see that Céline's vision of sexuality is much like the "town crier's," who remains perched in a minaret:

> Stamboul est endormi sous la lune blafarde
> Le Bosphore miroite de mille feux argentés
> Seul dans la grande ville mahométane
> Le vieux crieur des heures n'est pas encore couché—
>
> Sa voix que l'écho répète avec ampleur
> Announce à la ville qu'il est déjà dix heures
> Mais par une fenêtre, de son haut minaret
> Il plonge dans une chambre, son regard indiscret
>
> Il reste un moment, muet, cloué par la surprise
> Et caresse nerveux, sa grande barbe grise
> Mais fidèle au devoir, il assure sa voix

This indiscreet glance, which plunges into a bedroom, and yet remains mute, frozen with surprise, is a remarkable description of not only our reaction to the sexual scenes we see in Céline's works, but it also characterizes the young Ferdinand's sights of sex behavior in ***Death on the Installment Plan,*** as well as the eventual mature view of sexual behavior in the later novels. For as an author, Céline continues to sing that our odd sun rises, despite what he has seen either in or out of his *délire,* and no matter how many times "History brings all the nuts together and opens its Epic Dance Halls." At every reading of his novels, Céline continues to plunge us "into the heart of things."

Wayne Burns (essay date 1989)

SOURCE: "'I'll Protest If It Kills Me': A Reading of the Prologue to *Death on the Installment Plan,*" in *Critical Essays on Louis-Ferdinand Céline,* edited by William K. Buckley, G. K. Hall, 1989, pp. 180-92.

[*In the following essay, Burns discusses incongruities between the narrator of* Journey to the End of the Night *and the narrator of the prologue to* Death on the Installment Plan. *According to Burns, the later work "is a distinct and separate novel that makes its own demands in order to express its own intentions."*]

> The novel of adventures, the tale, the epic are [an] ingenuous manner of experiencing imaginary and significant things. The realistic novel is [a] second oblique manner. It requires something of the first: it needs something of the mirage to make us see it as such. So that it is not only *Don Quixote* which was written against the books of chivalry, and as a result bears the latter within it, but the novel as a literary genre consists essentially of that absorption.
>
> —José Ortega y Gasset

> I'm first of all a Celt—*daydreamer, bard.* I can turn out legends like taking a leak—with disgusting ease. Scenarios, ballet—anything you like—just while talking. That's my real talent. I harnessed it to realism because I hate man's wickedness so much; because I love combat.
>
> —Céline in a letter to Milton Hindus, 29 May 1947

I

The first thing to be said about ***Death on the Installment Plan*** is that it is not a prolongation of ***Journey to the End of the Night***—not, as it may initially seem to be, first a prolongation forward (for thirty-two pages) into the life of the mature Ferdinand who appears in ***Journey*** and then one backward (for more than 540 pages) into the childhood of the same Ferdinand. The mature Ferdinand of ***Death*** is not the mature Ferdinand of the end of ***Journey,*** nor is the eighteen-year-old at the end of ***Death*** the same Ferdinand who enlists in the army at the beginning of ***Journey.*** For all their fundamental likenesses, the Ferdinand of ***Journey*** and the Ferdinand of ***Death*** are, in both character and function, quite distinct, and they render the two novels quite distinct.

Why distinctions so primary have not been generally recognized I have difficulty understanding. Perhaps it is because most readers and critics read ***Journey*** first, since it is better known and more widely discussed and is, in the opinion of most critics, Céline's best novel. Then, if they go on to read ***Death,*** they may be inclined, for obvious reasons, to see it as a backward extension of Ferdinand's adventures in which Céline draws upon his boyhood to repeat, even more savagely, everything that he has said in ***Journey.*** Approached in this way, ***Death*** may well appear to be a lesser novel, despite the fact that nearly all critics concede its superiority in matters of structure and style. But to read ***Death*** in this way is like reading *Great Expectations* as a revision of *David Copperfield.* ***Death*** is neither a greater nor a lesser ***Journey;*** it is a distinct and separate novel that makes its own demands in order to express its own intentions. The similarities are always there. They are bound to be there in any two novels of any novelist. But they are there with variations and developments that make ***Death*** a quite different and, in my judgment, a much greater novel.

II

In the first thirty-two pages of ***Death,*** which have come to be designated the prologue, Céline introduces Ferdinand Bardamu, the mature "I" who stands behind the boy "I" who then, in the succeeding five hundred forty-one pages, tells the story of his growing up. Or, put another way, the boy "I" is the "I" the mature "I" conjures up from his memories in order to present the fullest possible account of what he was like as a boy and what he went through in growing up. It therefore follows that if we, as readers, are to understand the boy we must first understand the man: whether he is the same Ferdinand who narrated ***Journey,*** a few years older but otherwise essentially unchanged, or whether he is a Ferdinand who has, in growing older and becoming a writer as well as a doctor, taken on a somewhat different character.

As the novel opens, Ferdinand is mourning the death of "Madame Bérenge, the concierge . . . a good friend, gentle and faithful." Alone again, he has no one left to mourn with him:

> Those people are all so far away . . . They've changed their souls, that's a way to be disloyal, to forget, to keep talking about something else.
>
> Poor old Madame Bérenge; they'll come and take her

> cross-eyed dog away . . . Someone will have to put out the fire in the lodge. Whom will I write to? I've nobody left. No one to receive the friendly spirits of the dead . . . and let me speak more softly to the world . . . I'll have to bear it all alone.

Now these words, I submit, could not have been spoken as Ferdinand here speaks them by the Ferdinand of ***Journey.*** While there may be lines in ***Journey*** that approximate these, when Ferdinand is speaking of Molly or Bébert or Aleide or Robinson, the tone is different, the expressions of sentiment more guarded. The Ferdinand of ***Journey*** could hardly bring in Bérenge's "cross-eyed dog" as unashamedly as Ferdinand does here; nor could he then add, as Ferdinand does here, the line about putting out "the fire in the lodge." And the Ferdinand of ***Journey*** could never, under any circumstances, acknowledge that he might wish "to speak more softly to the world."

In the paragraph that follows, as Ferdinand speaks of Madame Bérenge's final moments, he does lapse into the kind of bitterness he so often expresses in ***Journey.*** Yet even here the tone is different. While he knows that he can talk about his hatred, and promises to do that "later on if they don't come back," he would rather "tell stories . . . stories that will make them come back, to kill me." This final phrase, "to kill me," can neither be erased nor denied. It is there, prophetically there. It has to be, since the stories he proposes to tell them (and us) are not stories that anyone wishes to hear, and he must therefore be killed for telling them. "Then," he concludes, in a voice more resigned than defiant, "it will be over and that will be all right with me."

In the passages that follow Ferdinand continues to speak more softly, and seemingly with more self-assurance. In talking with his cousin Gustin, who is also a doctor, he is affectionate, at times even playfully affectionate, and always compassionate. And if he says scathing things about his patients en masse he is kindness itself, for all his ferocious grumbling, when he treats them individually. But then Ferdinand could never, even in his worst moments in ***Journey,*** be unkind to his patients—not even when, by his own admission, he behaves "in that stupid way" in treating a sick child:

> I had been feeling very strange in mind and body, and the screams of this little innocent made a ghastly impression on me. What screams, my God, what screams! I couldn't bear it another second.
>
> No doubt something else too made me behave in that stupid way. I was so furious I couldn't help expressing, out loud, the rancour and the disgust I had been feeling, too long, inside myself.
>
> "Hey," I said to this little screamer, "don't you be in such a hurry, you little fool! There'll be plenty of time yet for you to yell. There'll be time, don't you worry, you little donkey! Pull yourself together. There'll be unhappiness enough later on to make you cry your eyes out and weep yourself silly, if you don't look out!"

When Ferdinand suffers the same kinds of provocation in a comparable scene in ***Death*** he reacts altogether differently—not because he suppresses his feelings of rancor and disgust but because he no longer has such feelings to express or suppress. After putting up with the antics and lamentations of a drunken mother and father, he does everything he can for their sick little girl; then, in a gesture "that was better than talking," he tries to cheer her up by making a swing for her doll. Conceivably the Ferdinand of ***Journey*** might have done something like this, although I can't recall an instance in which he actually does, but—and this is the crucial point—he could never, having done such a thing as making a swing for a child's doll, go on to observe: "I thought I'd cheer her up. I'm always good for a laugh when I put my mind to it." In ***Journey*** Ferdinand is never good for a laugh—at least not for this kind of a laugh, with no trace of bitterness or satiric bite in it. These are the words of a gentler, more relaxed, more self-assured Ferdinand—a Ferdinand much like the real-life Céline who appears in the reminiscences of his friends of these years.

III

In mentioning the real-life Céline I am not, I hasten to add, trying to validate my interpretation by an appeal to biography. Whether the Ferdinand of ***Death*** is more like Céline than the Ferdinand of ***Journey*** is of no real consequence here. What matters is that passages such as this—and they recur throughout the early pages of the novel—tend to modify Ferdinand's character in just those ways that lend credibility to his becoming, like Céline himself, a writer who is at once a "daydreamer, bard" and a relentless "realist." Although Ferdinand has not, like Céline, won fame and fortune with his first novel ("I wasn't making enough money yet to go off and write full time"), he has been writing "big fat books," and he is presumably the author of ***Journey:*** "a little pimp, Bébert . . . He ended up on snow. He'd been reading the ***Journey*** . . . ." At any rate Gustin's remarks, when Ferdinand first mentions his writing, echo the critical refrain that ***Journey*** gave rise to: "'You could talk about something pleasant now and then.' That was Gustin's opinion. 'Life isn't always disgusting.'"

Against this opinion Ferdinand offers no defense. Instead he concedes that Gustin may, in part at least, be right:

> In a way he's right. With me it's kind of a mania, a bias. The fact is that in the days when I had that buzzing in both ears, even worse than now, and attacks of fever all day long, I wasn't half so gloomy . . . I had lovely dreams . . . Madame Vitruve, my secretary, was talking about it only the other day. She knew how I tormented myself. When a man's so generous, he squanders his treasures, loses sight of them. I said to myself: "That damn Vitruve, she's hidden them some place . . ." Real marvels they were . . . bits of Legend, pure delight . . . That's the kind of stuff I'm going to write from now on. . . .

Although Ferdinand's manner is playful—as, for instance, when he is talking about squandering his treasures—he is nevertheless responding seriously to Gustin's criticism. "I might," he remarks a bit later, "have consulted some sensitive soul . . . well versed in fine feelings . . . in all the innumerable shadings of love. . . ." But, he adds, "sensitive souls are often impotent." And so, when he rediscovers the "bits of Legend" that he had written earlier, "the kind of stuff I'm going to write from now on," he again turns to Gustin:

> I wanted to talk to him about my Legend. We'd found the first part under Mireille's bed. I was badly disappointed when I reread it. The passage of time hadn't helped my romance any. After years of oblivion a child of fancy can look pretty tawdry . . . Well, with Gustin I could always count on a frank, sincere opinion. I tried to put him in the right frame of mind.
>
> "Gustin," I said. "You haven't always been the mug you are today, bogged down by circumstances, work, and thirst, the most disastrous of servitudes . . . Do you think that, just for a moment, you can revive the poetry in you? . . . are your heart and cock still capable of leaping to the words of an epic, sad to be sure, but noble . . . resplendent? You feel up to it?"

Gustin's response to Ferdinand's affectionate banter is wonderfully appropriate: he dozes on without saying a word. But that doesn't stop Ferdinand, who proceeds to read the part of his legend that recounts the death of "Gwendor the Magnificent, Prince of Christiania." And while Gwendor's death is a mixture of gore and sentimentality, the rhetoric with which he expresses it is truly impressive, as Ferdinand himself points out when, at a climactic moment, he interjects, "Get a load of this." Nevertheless Gustin, who may still be dozing, remains unimpressed:

> Gustin's arms dangled between his legs.
>
> "Well, how do you like it?" I asked him.
>
> He was on his guard. He wasn't too eager to be rejuvenated. He resisted. He wanted me to explain the whole thing to him, the whys and wherefores. That's not so easy. Such things are as frail as butterflies. A touch and they fall to pieces in your hands and you feel soiled. What's the use? I didn't press the matter.

Yet if Ferdinand does not press the matter he still continues to read—until Gustin, in what may be taken as his ultimate critical statement, falls "sound asleep." And his later expressions of kindly tolerance, when Ferdinand is about to read more of his legend, are equally discouraging: "Go on, Ferdinand, go ahead and read, I'll listen to the damn thing. Not too fast, though. And cut out the gestures. It wears you out and it makes me dizzy."

IV

While there is, by this time, no mistaking Gustin's response to *King Krogold,* Ferdinand's attitude remains ambiguous. From the time when he and Vitruve and Mireille find the first part of the legend "under Mireille's bed," where she not only sleeps but earns her living, there is a tone of mockery in just about everything he says about the legend—a tone which belies his seeming sincerity in defending his "masterpiece," particularly when his defense ("Such things are as frail as butterflies") seems almost as absurd as the "masterpiece" he is defending. For that matter the legend is riddled with lines totally out of keeping with its overall mood and tone—as, for instance, in the following passages:

> Gwendor's army has just suffered a terrible defeat . . . King Krogold himself caught sight of him in the thick of the fray . . . and clove him in twain . . . *Krogold is no do-nothing king* . . . He metes out his own justice. . . . (my italics)
>
> After the battle King Krogold, his knights, his pages, his brother the archbishop, the clerics of his camp, the whole court, went to the great tent in the middle of the bivouac and dropped with weariness. The heavy gold crescent, a gift from the caliph, was nowhere to be found . . . Ordinarily it surmounted the royal dais. The captain entrusted with its safekeeping *was beaten to a pulp.* The king lies down, tries to sleep . . . He is still suffering from his wounds. He wakes. Sleep refuses to come . . . He reviles the snorers. He rises. He steps over sleepers, *crushing a hand here and there,* leaves the tent. . . . (my italics)

That the italicized lines are intentional seems beyond question. But are they to be understood as the inadvertent slips of a hopelessly naive Ferdinand? Or of a Ferdinand who cannot quite stomach the rhetoric of his "romance"? Or are they direct authorial intrusions on the part of Céline in which he is playfully undercutting the pretensions of the legend? The truth is, unless I have somehow been remiss in my reading, the novel provides no satisfactory answer to these questions.

Equally puzzling, though in a somewhat different sense, is the passage in which Gwendor meets Death:

> "O Death! Great is my remorse! Endless my shame . . . Behold these poor corpses! . . . An eternity of silence will not soften my lot . . ."
>
> *"There is no softness or gentleness in this world, Gwendor, but only myth! All kingdoms end in a dream . . ."*
>
> "O Death, give me a little time . . . a day or two. I must find out who betrayed me . . ."
>
> "Everything betrays, Gwendor . . . The passions belong to no one, even love is only the flower of life in the garden of youth."
>
> And very gently Death gathers up the prince . . . He has ceased to resist . . . His weight has left him . . . And then a beautiful dream takes possession of his soul . . . The dream that often came to him when he was little, in his fur cradle, in the Chamber of the Heirs, close to his Moravian nurse in the castle of King René. . . . (my italics)

The words of Death that I have italicized express Céline's titular theme so eloquently that they might stand as an epigraph to the entire novel. But why, if this is true, are they tucked away in the middle of the gory legend, then encased in the rhetorical trappings that Gustin, and Ferdinand too at times, find either boring or funny? Are the italicized words another disguised authorial intrusion in which Céline is mocking the pretensions of the legend from a still different angle—by inserting lines more appropriate to the death of his old teacher, Metitpois, than to the poeticized death of Gwendor? Or is the entire passage a virtuoso performance in which Céline, via Ferdinand, is exercising his literary prowess ("I could make alligators dance to Pan's flute") by demonstrating that he can, when he chooses, imbue his high-flown rhetoric with significant meaning? To these and related questions the novel once again provides no clearcut answers.

But—and I know this question will, to many critics, seem dangerously heretical—does this lack of certainty really matter that much? Do we, as readers, have to know exactly how much Ferdinand the writer knows at any given moment about his own writing—especially when the effects of that writing are not dependent on how much Ferdinand knows? Do we, in reading *Don Quixote,* have to know exactly how much Don Quixote knows at any given moment when the effects of what he is saying and doing are not dependent on how much he knows? Nevertheless, it may be objected, Sancho Panza is always there to let Don Quixote (and the reader) know just how foolish he is being. Where is Ferdinand's Sancho?

The obvious answer is Gustin, who plays a straightforward Panzaic role throughout Ferdinand's readings. Vitruve also functions Panzaically, as does her niece Mireille. But it is Ferdinand himself, in his real or assumed naïveté, who most effectively undercuts his own dreams of what is "noble . . . resplendent." Up to the time of his delirium, Ferdinand is a divided personality: on his Quixotic side, he tries to believe in and defend his romance even as, on his Panzaic side, he can't help revealing how his own life and the lives of all those around him give the lie to all his idealistic fancies—just as Metitpois's death gives the lie to "his classical memories, his resolutions, the example of Caesar . . ." The effect of these Panzaic revelations is therefore to permit us, as readers, to see clearly what Ferdinand has only begun to see dimly, namely, that the gory agonies in his legend are but rhetorical fantasies he has concocted in a vain attempt to escape what he and the people around him are going through; that his legend is to him what drinking is to Gustin, what Mireille's dirty stories are to her, what his mother's memories of his father are to her.

V

Toward the end of the prologue Céline sends Ferdinand into a fever or delirium in which he comes close to madness before he finally resolves his inner conflicts. The delirium is brought on by his trip to the Bois with Mireille, the girl with the "sumptuous ass." "Christ Almighty, what a rear end. That ass of hers was a public scandal." Yet this is not, he explains, what attracts him: "What attracts me is your imagination . . . I'm a voyeur. You tell me dirty stories . . . And I'll tell you a beautiful legend . . . Is it a bargain? . . . fifty-fifty . . . you'll be getting the best of it." Ferdinand then tells her the story, complete with settings and costumes, of "Thibaud the Wicked, a troubadour." "The tone appealed to Mireille; she wanted more." But on the way home they abandon his "beautiful Legend for a furious discussion about whether what women really wanted was to shack up with each other"—a discussion that ends up with Ferdinand talking about dildoes and Mireille, going still further, talking about girls growing phalluses "so they can rip each other's guts out." At this point, apparently feeling that Mireille has not only outdone him but will tell the whole world that he has "behaved like a beast," Ferdinand first resorts to violence and then goes off into a delirium that ends with the words: "It was hell."

When he comes to, after being brought home by an ambulance, he is in bed, and his mother and Vitruve are in the next room waiting for his fever to go down. But fever is not all he is suffering from: "Fever or not, I always have such a buzzing in both ears that it can't get much worse. I've had it since the war. Madness has been hot on my trial . . . no exaggeration . . . for twenty-two years." But he outruns her; he raves faster than she can: "That's how I do it. I shoot the shit. I charm her." Yet it isn't easy: "My thoughts stagger and sprawl . . . I'm not very good to them. I'm working up the opera of the deluge . . . I'm the devil's stationmaster . . . The last gasp is very demanding. It's the last movie and nothing more to come. A lot of people don't know. You've got to knock yourself out. I'll be up to it soon . . . ." By the time he gets to the last few lines Ferdinand's near madness has been transformed into near sainthood, and he is once more the Ferdinand he was in the opening pages. He is knocking himself out—for us—so that we can know what we don't yet know: the truth about life and death. And he does this knowing full well that we, his readers, will come back to kill him.

In putting Ferdinand back together again as a near saint who is writing (as well as doctoring) in order to save us, Céline comes as close to revealing Ferdinand's deeper motives as he ever comes in the prologue. For his compassion, though always disguised, is always there. It is there when he is mourning Madame Bérenge's death; when he walks blocks out of his way because a stray dog is following him and he has to feed it and try to save it; when he speaks so tenderly to Gustin, as he always does, and excuses his looking "to the bottle for forgetfulness"; when he says, "I wouldn't want to be too hard on Vitruve. Maybe she has had more trouble than I have"; when he looks at his mother's crippled leg "as skinny as a poker" and says, "I've seen it all my life." Céline cannot, however, permit Ferdinand to remain a near saint—either as doctor or writer. No one would believe in him then. He cannot even permit him to be a near hero. Heroes can only feel and see and know what Gwendor knows, or what Metitpois knows, "with his classical memories, his resolutions, the example of Caesar"; whereas Ferdinand feels and sees and knows what Death knows, what Death tells Gwendor: that "there is no softness or gentleness in this world . . . but only myth! All kingdoms end in a dream."

In bringing Ferdinand to a full understanding of these words Céline renders him forever incapable of being heroic, or for that matter, of acting, or speaking, or writing heroically—except in play or jest. When Ferdinand can no longer believe in dreams and myths he can no longer be a hero. He may perform actions that outwardly correspond to those of a hero; he may even risk his own life to save others; yet so long as he performs these actions without believing that they will somehow make people or the world better, without, in short, believing that they have any meaning beyond their material consequences, his actions cannot possibly be heroic. To be heroic they would have to derive from, or express, beliefs or faiths or dreams or myths that evade or deny the real world. For Céline as for Ortega y Gasset "materiality" contains a "critical power which defeats the claim to self-sufficiency of all idealizations, wishes and fancies of man . . . the insufficiency of all that is noble, clear, lofty." In the novel, Ortega explains, "reality, the actual can be changed into poetic substance" but only "as destruction of the myth, as criticism of the myth. In this form reality, which is of an inert and insignificant nature, quiet and mute, acquires movement, is changed into an active power of aggression against the crystalline orb of the ideal. The enchantment of the latter broken, it falls into fine, iridescent dust which gradually loses its colors until it becomes an earthy brown. We are present at this scene in every novel."

I have quoted Ortega at such length because his critical argument so closely anticipates the dramatic argument with which Céline concludes the prologue—as he brings Ferdinand, still in bed, and still so feverish that he intermittently lapses into delirium, into direct conflict with his mother's idealized account of her life with his dead father:

> She's telling Madame Vitruve the story of her life . . . Over and over again, to make it clear what a time she's had with me. Extravagant . . . irresponsible . . . lazy . . . nothing like his father . . . he so conscientious . . . so hardworking . . . so deserving . . . so unlucky . . . who passed on last winter . . . Sure . . . she doesn't tell her about the dishes he broke on her bean . . . how he used to drag her through the back room by the hair . . . Not one word about all that . . . nothing but poetry . . . Yes, we lived in cramped quarters, but we loved each other so. That's what she was saying. Papa was fond of me, he was so sensitive about every little thing that my behavior . . . so much to worry about . . . my alarming propensities, the terrible trouble I gave him . . . hastened his death . . . all that grief and anguish affected his heart. Plop! The fairy tales people tell each other . . . they make a certain amount of sense, but they're a pack of filthy stinking lies. . . .

Ferdinand here defines it all, both for himself and for the reader: "Nothing but poetry," or "a pack of filthy lies." Enough to make Ferdinand leave his sick-bed to vomit. And when the lies continue he "can't stand it," and takes refuge in his legend: "If I've got to be delirious, I'd rather wallow in stories of my own." If, in other words, he has to wallow, he would rather wallow in his own "pack of lies" than in his mother's. And that is what he immediately proceeds to do:

> I see Thibaud the Troubadour . . . He's always in need of money . . . He's going to kill Joad's father . . . Well, at least that will be one father less in the world . . . I see splendid tournaments on the ceiling . . . I see lancers impaling each other . . . I see King Krogold himself . . . He has come from the north . . . He had been invited to Bredonnes with his whole court . . . I see his daughter Wanda, the Blonde, the Radiant . . . I wouldn't mind jerking off, but I'm too sticky . . . Joad is horny in love . . . Oh well, why not. . . .

In his interjected comments, Ferdinand is jerking off to, or trying to jerk off to, his own stories in much the same way that his mother, as he sees her, has been jerking off to hers. But his mother's fantasies, as he listens to her talking to Vitruve, overwhelm his own: "I can't stand the sight of her anymore, she gives me the creeps. She wants me to share in her fantasies . . . I'm not in the mood . . . I want to have my own fantasies . . . ."

At this point Ferdinand lapses into another delirium in which he sees himself in his "gallant ship" on "a long tack across the Etoile," only to come to as his mother says: "Ah, if only your father were here"—words that so inflame Ferdinand's feelings of hatred that he yells them straight at his mother: "My father, I say, was a skunk! I yell my lungs out . . . "There was no lousier bastard in the whole universe! from the Galeries-Lafayette to Capricorne. . . .'" At first his mother is "stupefied. Transfixed . . . ." After that she attacks—with words, fits, and finally the umbrella, which she breaks across his face. But Ferdinand refuses to give way. In a finale that is at once a prevision of the rest of the novel and a restatement of the artistic commitment with which he opens the prologue, he declares that he will not put up with his mother's idealized memories: "I'll protest if it kills me. I repeat that he was a sneak, brute, hypocrite, and yellow in every way."

Everything Ferdinand says or does in his battle with his mother reveals his powerful Oedipal jealousy: "The deader he is the more she loves him. Like a she-dog that can't get enough . . . But I won't put up with it . . . ." And when she starts up again and is "ready to die for her Auguste," he threatens to "smash her face," but instead, "in a blind rage," he smashes her, as well as himself, with gestures and words that come straight from the depths of his Oedipal agony: "I bend over and lift up her skirt. I see her calf as skinny as a poker, without any flesh on it, her stocking all sagging, it's foul . . . I've seen it all my life . . . I puke on it, the works . . ." Unnerved finally, his mother backs away and runs for the stairs, while Ferdinand—and this is the final touch—hears "her limp all the way down."

VI

This is the mature Ferdinand who is, in the guise of the boy Ferdinand, about to tell the story of his growing up. And he has, through his words and actions, foreshadowed the nature of the story that he feels he must tell, the way that he feels he must tell it—or, more accurately, he has foreshadowed the first 325 pages of the story that he feels he must tell; namely, the story of his inability to deny his feelings in order to become like his parents. And because both his father and mother, along with nearly everyone else in their world, are mired in middle-class poverty and ideals that sustain people in that condition, it is to be the story of his struggle to overcome the neglect and even hatred, disguised as love and sacrifice and virtue, to which he is constantly subjected. And because he has come to realize that "there is no softness or gentleness in this world," that the myths in which these ideals are enshrined are like his own legend, or on another level, Mireille's "dirty stories," or the fairy tales his mother tells about his father, his story is to be not a legend or a fairy tale, but a protest against all "the fairy tales people tell each other"—all the fairy tales that people jerk off to.

What Ferdinand's words do not foreshadow, however, is the latter or Courtial half of the novel, which is something of a legend or fairy tale in itself, though of a totally different kind. Courtial, the fatherly Quixote, takes the sixteen-year-old Ferdinand as his Panzaic son, and together they defy the world's lies with hopes and dreams of their own—until the world finally catches up with them and reduces their "crystalline orb" to an "earthy brown." Céline's choosing not to foreshadow or in any direct way acknowledge or anticipate this latter half of the novel raises a number of questions for which once again, I have no very satisfactory answers. Possibly he felt that he could not allow Ferdinand to speak directly about that part of his life in which he was happy without lessening the intensity of the tragic outlook he is trying to establish. Or possibly Céline felt that everything Ferdinand says about his legend and about the stories he is going to tell actually does apply to the second half of the novel, since it too ends on a note of despair. It can even be argued that Courtial is present in spirit if not in name when Ferdinand tries to speak more softly to the world, or when, more specifically, he remembers the pitiful dreams of Auguste, his dead father: "I think of Auguste, he liked boats too . . . He was an artist at heart . . . He had no luck . . . he drew storms now and then on my blackboard."

Yet Ferdinand's softness never impairs his vision. Auguste's dreams, unlike Courtial's, are but impotent fantasies. For him there is nothing in this world but the lies he tries to live by and would have others live by. He, along with almost everyone else, has become like the people Ferdinand described earlier in ***Journey:*** "they really have got love in reserve . . . Only it's a pity people should still be such sods, with so much love in reserve." The distinction Ferdinand draws here is critical. For if he can pity people for being such sods he cannot pity what they do, as sods, to themselves and one another, in the name of some fairy tale or another. What they do, as sods, he hates; the fairy tales that provide them with both impetus and justification for doing what they do he hates even more. And he is determined to express his hatred so forcefully that he will, as he promises in the very beginning of the prologue, "tell stories that will make them come back, to kill me, from the ends of the world."

Having revealed so much about himself and the stories he will tell, the mature Ferdinand makes his final exit by first asking Emilie, the maid, who is still there beside his bed, to lie down with him in her clothes, so that she can accompany him on a make-believe cruise (presumably a continuation of the cruise he embarked on earlier in his delirium). The significance of the ports of call on this cruise Emilie "doesn't get," although her response indicates that she understands the lying down part: "'Tomorrow,' she says, 'Tomorrow. . . .'" With only this promise to sustain him, Ferdinand is "really alone," as he was at the opening of the prologue; and he sees, as he returns to his delirious state, "thousands and thousands of little skiffs returning high above the Left Bank . . . Each one had a shriveled little corpse under its sail . . . and his story . . . his little lies to catch the wind with." And these are the same "dead" (now corpses and in skiffs), the same "lies" ("the fairy tales people tell each other . . . a pack of filthy stinking lies") Ferdinand encounters at the beginning of his cruise: "The whole town is on deck. All those dead—I know them all . . . The pianist has caught on . . . He's playing the tune we need: 'Black Joe' . . . for a cruise . . . to catch the wind and weather . . . and the lies . . . ."

David O'Connell (essay date 1989)

SOURCE: "Louis-Ferdinand Céline: An Introduction," in *Critical Essays on Louis-Ferdinand Céline,* edited by William K. Buckley, G. K. Hall, 1989, pp. 100-10.

[*In the following essay, O'Connell provides an overview of Céline's literary career, novels, and critical reception.*]

In the last twenty years, Louis-Ferdinand Céline has emerged and, in the opinion of most major critics, joined Proust as one of the two greatest novelists of the twentieth century. This change in his literary fortunes is one of the most interesting stories in modern literature, and is understandable if one remembers that Céline's work was surrounded by what amounts to a conspiracy of silence by French (mostly leftist) intellectuals from the end of World War II until about the mid-sixties. Having been accused of collaborating with the Nazis during the war, it took almost twenty years for his name to be cleared. Once it became apparent that despite his vocal anti-Semitism of the late thirties he had not been a Nazi collaborator during the Occupation, there was no way to stop the frustrated and widespread desire of younger Frenchmen to read Céline and to know more about his life and work.

Louis-Ferdinand Destouches was born on 27 May 1894 in Courbevoie, a suburb of Paris. His father worked for an insurance company and his mother, to make ends meet, ran her own retail establishment, a soft goods store in the Passage Choiseul near the Place de l'Opéra on the Parisian Right Bank. Beginning in 1899, the family lived at the same address as Mme Destouches's store and young Louis, an only child, attended local schools before being sent by his parents in the years 1907-9 for protracted stays in both Germany and England in order to learn the languages of these two countries. In his mother's thinking, such knowledge would eventually come in handy in the lace business. This early exposure to foreign languages and cultures was unusual for a young French boy of this period, especially for one from his less than privileged petit bourgeois social class.

After his return from aboard, he took odd jobs during 1909-12, working for various small businesses in his neighborhood. Although he later claimed that the desire to study medicine had come to him early in life, he still did not attend school through these adolescent years. Not long after reaching the age of eighteen, in 1912, he joined a cavalry regiment and attained a rank equivalent to that of sergeant by the time the war began. He was seriously wounded in the arm while carrying out his duties at the front in Flanders and was operated on shortly thereafter. Fearful that army doctors would take the easy way out and remove his arm, he insisted on being treated without anesthesia. Thus he kept his arm, the loss of which would have impeded his later medical career. Awarded the Médaille Militaire for his bravery in battle, he was sent back to Paris to rest and recuperate. His disability for the arm injury and damage to his ear drums was rated at 75 percent, so there was no chance of his being sent back to the front.

A year later, in May 1915, he was assigned to the French consulate general in London, where he worked in the passport office. During the year that he spent there, he married Suzanne Nebout, a French bar girl working in one of the local nightclubs that he frequented, but he did not register the marriage with the French Consulate. When he left London a year later, having been definitively released from military service, he left his wife behind. In search of adventure and to earn a living, he spent the next year in West Africa working as a trader in the bush for a French forestry company. His stay in the Cameroons was shortened when, due to ill health caused by the harsh climate, he had to return home. Back home in France in May 1917, he seemed ready to settle down. Taking accelerated course work, he completed his baccalaureate degree in 1919. Enrolling at the medical school of the University of Rennes in that same year, he completed his medical degree in 1924 and, in the process, married Edith Follet, the daughter of the school's director. The marriage to Nebout was disregarded under French law.

With his doctoral dissertation, entitled ***La Vie et l'oeuvre de Philippe-Ignace Semmelweis*** (1818-65) (***The Life and Works of Philippe-Ignace Semmelweis***), published by the medical school, and good connections in the medical profession thanks to his marriage, he seemed to have a bright professional future ahead of him. But this very perspective, a bourgeois life of privilege, did not appeal to him. On the contrary, he felt restricted by it. For this reason, he left his wife and daughter in 1925 to take a job as a doctor with the League of Nations. Thanks to this new post, he was able to travel to Geneva and Liverpool, and even back to West Africa. He also made a trip to the United States, Canada, and Cuba that lasted more than two months in 1925 and that took him to a number of cities, as well as to Detroit, where he took a particular interest in the social, psychological, and medical problems of assembly line workers in the Ford plant located there. These wanderings continued until 1928 when he finally settled in Clichy, a dreary working-class suburb of Paris. Divorced in 1926, he spent the next ten years there, the first three in private practice and, beginning in 1931, as an employee of the local town clinic.

It is at this point, at the age of about thirty-two, that Céline began to write. He devoted most of his free time during the next four years to the composition of his first novel, ***Voyage au bout de la nuit*** (***Journey to the End of the Night***). Its publication in 1932 was by far the major literary event of the year. As Leon Trotsky, a great admirer of the book, but much less so of Céline the man, put it: "Louis-Ferdinand Céline walked into great literature as other men walk into their own homes". The novel is a startling one to read, its bitter pessimism affecting readers in a powerful way even today, more than a half-century after publication. It is impossible to be indifferent to ***Voyage*** and, by extension, to its author.

Léon Daudet, at the time a member of the Goncourt jury and an ardent admirer of the novel, sought to have ***Voyage*** awarded the prestigious Goncourt Prize. The other members of the jury were frightened, however, by the idea of awarding the prize to such a bitterly pessimistic work. Thus, as a matter of simple politics, the award went to the now totally forgotten and insignificant writer Guy Mazeline for his novel *Les Loups* (*The Wolves*). Instead, and as a kind of consolation prize, Céline's first novel was awarded the Renaudot Prize.

Voyage opens with young Ferdinand Bardamu talking with his friend and fellow medical student, Arthur Ganate. The point of view of the novel, from the beginning, is that of a first-person narrator. Bardamu sees a parade passing by and, in a fit of patriotism, decides to join the army. From here we follow him to the front and then back to Paris where he convalesces. This section of the novel contains some of the strongest antiwar passages ever written. In the process, it attacks the stupidity of professional military men, the cupidity and mendacity of politicians, the plundering and exploitation of civilians behind the front lines, and the docility with which the average citizen accepts his fate. After this, Bardamu goes off to Africa where he works in the bush for a French company. Here we see colonialism at work, with black natives being systematically exploited by the whites as well as by each other. Although the narrator clearly feels that the natives are inferior to whites, he still displays sympathy for their woes, since the white colonials are only creating more problems for them. At the end of this section, as during the previous section in France, the hero lapses into a state of delirium brought on by the stress of living. Delirium to Céline is an escape from the stressful reality of modern life, and it is only through delirium that he escapes from Africa.

When he awakens, he is in New York, and from here his travels will take him to Detroit, where he falls in love with Molly, a local whore, and works in a Ford factory. While in the United States, he comes in contact with modern, unrestrained capitalism and the worship of money and material comfort as reflected in modern American life. At the same time, he sees how people at the bottom of the social ladder live in comparison to the rich. Here, in Detroit, he meets up again with a certain Léon Robinson, his alter ego, whom he had already met in other stressful situations, at the front in France, in Paris, and even in Africa. Partly in order to get away from Robinson and partly to put his own life in order, Bardamu leaves the United States and returns to France where he decides to study medicine.

Here, about a third of the way through this 500-page novel, begins what can be called the second part of the work. Now, instead of running away from reality, he vows to attempt to meet it head on. First, his life as a doctor in the working-class suburb of Rancy is chronicled. Caring for the sickest and least educated segment of society, Bardamu descends into the lowest circles of the hell of modern life. Inevitably, he again runs into Robinson, who is living in the neighborhood. When Robinson tells him that he has been hired to assassinate a neighbor, Old Lady Henrouille, who has become a nuisance to her son and daughter-in-law, both of whom want to get rid of her, Bardamu tries to stay out of it. As Robinson is setting the bomb that he hopes will detonate later and kill the old lady, it suddenly goes off in his face, blinding him. At this point, Bardamu gets involved with the Henrouilles and helps them arrange for both the old lady and Robinson to work in the crypt of a church in Toulouse where they serve as guides for tourists interested in seeing the mummies preserved there. Finally, after the trip to Toulouse, Bardamu returns to Paris where he works in a privately run mental institution. Here, he seems to conclude at the end of the novel, he will be safe from man, the most dangerous predator in the universe. Living among the insane, he has finally found his place in the world.

This second part of the novel, which some critics have found slower to read than the first part, is highlighted by the author's strong social protest against poverty and ignorance as well as against some of the tools that, in his view, society uses to maintain the social status quo: alcohol, the press, and modern cinema.

Although this description offers only an overview of the plot of ***Voyage,*** it should be clear that the overriding concern of the novelist is to depict the conditions of modern life. The words of the great Catholic novelist of the interwar years, Georges Bernanos, still apply to ***Voyage:*** "Pour nous la question n'est pas de savoir si la peinture de M. Céline est atroce, nous demandons si elle est vraie. Elle l'est" ("For us the question is not to decide if Céline's view of life is horrible, but whether it is true. It is)".

As the first part of the novel is characterized by flight and a search for self and for meaning to existence, the second part is static and shows the hero willing to stay in place, to compromise if necessary, while awaiting death and attempting to find out what meaning he should eventually assign to that event. Living and working among the poor, Bardamu, like Céline himself, comes to the realization that life for most people in our modern consumer societies is humdrum and boring. The major difference between the rich and poor is that the former have the means to buy forgetfulness, while the poor, whom Céline knew all too well, do not have any such opportunity. Much has also been written about the Bardamu/Robinson relationship, but Merlin Thomas's assessment is probably the most sensible. To him, each of these characters represents a different view of death. Bardamu, who has a role to play in life, is still struggling to go on living. Robinson, however, who has no role to play, is happy to have his life ended. Murdered by Madelon, he "had decided upon his own death: he could have avoided it. . . . it all amounts to a question of ultimate acceptance of the lot of humanity." As the novel ends, Bardamu has clearly decided to go on living. He knows that death is what awaits him at the end of the night, but his time has not yet come.

Céline showed that his knack for inventing catchy titles was no accident when his next book, ***Mort à crédit*** (***Death on the Installment Plan***), appeared in 1936. Like ***Voyage***—and all the novels that would follow—this book is adapted from the author's own experiences. It goes back in time to the period that precedes the action recounted in ***Voyage,*** to Céline's childhood and adolescence.

Although he enjoyed publicly poking fun at Proust, Céline nonetheless admired his ability to fashion an imposing multivolume novel out of the stuff of memory. As if to mimic Proust, Céline begins ***Mort à crédit*** by showing us the mature Ferdinand at work as both a doctor and a writer. But when he lapses into a state of delirium brought on by both an attack of malaria contracted in Africa and a recurrence of dizziness caused by war wounds, we cannot help thinking of Proust and of the privileged moments, like the one provoked by the dipping of a butter cookie, the famous *madeleine,* that brought back understanding of past events through the process of involuntary memory. Here though, Céline, who was always proud of his war record and, through the darkest days of exile after World War II would always consider himself to be a true patriot, stresses his difference from Proust. Whereas the latter always wrote in long, highly stylized periodic sentences about upper bourgeois and aristocratic characters, Céline used this fit of delirium to summon up recollections of his working-class past and express them in a slang that is even more daring than the one experimented with in ***Voyage.*** Furthermore, the style relied more and more on what he later called his "style télégraphique," little bits of sentences, divided and punctuated by three or more dots. The reason for this technique, he claimed, was that in order to achieve the emotional effect that he sought, he had to write the way people talk, adapting oral speech slightly so that the reader, even though reading, would still have the impression of being in the presence of genuine working-class speech. Beginning with his childhood in the fictional Passage des Bérésinas, the transposed Passage Choiseul of his youth, where the family lives and his mother works, the first-person narrator, Ferdinand, paints a bleak picture. His father, a loser stuck in a dead-end job, takes out his frustrations by beating his son. His mother, unfortunately, is not much better, and the family eats only noodles for most of their meals because his mother is afraid that anything else will leave odors in the lacework that she has for sale. The relatives are just as bad, with the exception of his grandmother, Caroline, who dies in due course, and his uncle, Edouard, who understands, helps, and consoles him.

Leaving school in his early teens, long before finishing his *baccalauréat* degree, he works at two different jobs and is fired from each one. His Uncle Edouard luckily intervenes and suggests that the boy be sent to England for language study. Enrolling for a year in Meanwell College in England, Ferdinand eventually has an affair with the headmaster's young wife, Nora, and returns home. Like Molly of ***Voyage,*** Nora is treated with sensitivity and warmth and stands out in Céline's fiction for this reason. Back home, Uncle Edouard once again comes to the rescue and introduces Ferdinand to an inventor and con man, Courtial des Pereires. Just as Robinson had slowly assumed more and more importance in the earlier work, now Courtial, with his quacky experiments and projects, becomes a major character as the novel progresses. But when he finally commits suicide near the end of the work because his idealistic vision cannot be achieved (just as Robinson had been killed off by his creator because there was no place for him in life), Ferdinand realizes that, like Bardamu in ***Voyage,*** he will have to go ahead on his own and make sense out of life.

Returning to Paris from the experimental farm that Courtial had organized, he decides that he will have to get away from his family and seek true independence. Ironically, he seizes upon the army as the place to find this fresh start in life, and it is with this intention in mind—joining the army—that we leave him at the end of the novel.

Mort, although a successful novel by any criterion, did not achieve the same overwhelming success as ***Voyage.*** It did, however, solidify Céline's reputation as a pessimistic writer with a generally negative view of family and social relationships. Despite the warm feelings that the narrator expresses for his Uncle Edouard (and some of the warmest pages that Céline ever wrote concern this character), it is difficult to disagree with this assessment. Like ***Voyage, Mort*** was immediately translated into all the major European languages and kept Céline's name alive as an important author (seemingly, but not really, of the Left) in a world about to go to war.

Céline's royalties from the publication of ***Voyage,*** in France and around the world, were substantial. He used them to buy a house in Saint-Malo, but he still continued to live in his shabby Paris apartment and never stopped working among the poor and dispossessed. The translation of his work into Russian resulted in the accumulation of a vast sum of money held in his account in the Soviet Union. Since the Soviets would not send him the money, he accepted an invitation in 1936 to visit what the French Left held as an article of faith to be the workers' paradise and to spend his money there. As a result of that trip, Céline published the first of four political pamphlets that appeared during 1936-41. ***Mea Culpa*** (Through my fault), the first of them, attacked Russia as a brutal dictatorship organized on the philosophical basis of materialism. Its citizens he announced, live in filth and depravation and are exploited by a new ruling class—the Party. The title of the work is obvious: Céline repented for having allowed people to believe that he was sympathetic to the organized political Left in France.

His next pamphlet, ***Bagatelles pour un massacre*** (Trifles for a massacre), exploded on the political landscape. In this work, Céline's political consciousness, comparatively subdued in his two novels, where he makes extensive use of understatement, and only beginning to show itself in ***Mea Culpa,*** now directs itself in a frontal assault on international Jewry. Claiming that the Jews in France, with their brothers in London and New York, are planning another war in which they intend to wipe out the Aryans, he calls for the neutralizing of Jewish power in France. Reaction to the work, which runs on for over 400 pages, was mixed in France, and in fact many intellectuals, including André Gide, the reigning pontiff of French letters, thought that he was kidding, that the anti-Semitic tone was so exaggerated that it could not be sincere and must be ironic. But when, in the following year, 1938, Céline published another pamphlet, entitled ***Ecole des cadavres*** (School for cadavres), that picked up where the first one left off, going so far as to propose a Franco-German alliance against Russia and the Jews as the only way for Europe's Aryans to survive, there could be no doubt about his intentions. As a result of these pamphlets, Céline found himself politically isolated from both the Left and the Right, and he remained in this state for the rest of his life. The last of the four pamphlets, ***Les Beaux Draps*** (A nice mess), was published during the Occupation in 1941 and castigates the French army for running away from the Germans. The basic proposition of the work is that France ought to institute what Céline thought would be a true form of communism in which everyone would receive the same salary no matter what form of work he did. In this book he drops the anti-Semitism of the years 1937-38 and presents himself as a true patriot and a decorated hero of the Great War. In fact, after the outbreak of hostilities, Céline served on board a French vessel in the Mediterranean that was shelled by the German Navy. Although he openly called for a Franco-German alliance in 1938 to counter what he took to be Soviet, British, and Jewish attempts to start a new war, he rallied to the defense of his country once the Germans attacked.

Céline's major literary projects during the Occupation were his two-part novel ***Guignol's Band,*** and the fragments of what may have been a large novel entitled ***Casse-Pipe*** (***Kick the Bucket***).

The word "guignol" in French usually refers to a kind of marionnette show, the "Grand Guignol," that inspires deep emotion in children because of the extremes of human behavior that it can depict. The word can also be used to refer figuratively to a human being who is comic and ridiculous, and it is this meaning that Céline presumably wanted to give to the novel. The old narrator, who is in fact none other than Ferdinand himself, gazes back over the course of the next 900 pages and reflects on the foolish and laughable youth that he once was and of the "band" of characters that he came to know while residing in London for a year during World War I.

Guignol's Band I, published in Paris in 1944, deals with the underworld characters—pimps, prostitutes, and the like—that Céline knew during his year in London. Various adventures in the first volume culminate in a flight to the French consulate where Ferdinand demands to be reintegrated into the French Army, since he has concluded that service at the front could not be more dangerous than life in the London underworld. It is here, however, that he meets Sosthène de Rodiencourt, a would-be magus who seeks access to the fourth dimension of existence. Ferdinand falls under his spell, much like the earlier Ferdinand of ***Mort*** had been bemused by Courtial. As part 1 ends, we find them going off together in search of adventure. In the second part of the novel, which was not published until 1964, two years after Céline's secretary had accidentally come upon it, the quack inventor, Colonel J.F.C. O'Calloghan, who is working on a new type of gas mask, and his lovely niece Virginia, become major characters. The same type of unbelievable and far-fetched events take place throughout this second part, which culminates, once again, with Ferdinand's symbolic crossing of London Bridge in order to leave these characters behind and seek more adventures elsewhere. The plot line of the two parts is generally incoherent, and most critics have found that the novel fails for this reason. However, J. H. Matthews contends that this failure of narrative was a deliberate strategy on the part of Céline. In this novel, "plot is downgraded," he claims, "so that readers will not concentrate upon narrative incident so much as on the manner in which Ferdinand gives an account of events." This might well be the case; but it does not make this tedious novel any easier to read.

Casse-Pipe, preserved in a few fragments that constitute less than 200 pages of text, is centered on barracks life in the cavalry during the period of 1912-14. Chronologically, it fits into Céline's life between ***Mort*** and ***Voyage,*** just as the two parts of ***Guignol's Band*** may be read as an insert in ***Voyage*** between the episode in Paris after Bardamu is wounded and his trip to West Africa. The sections of the novel that remain are all that survived the plunder of Céline's Paris apartment after his departure in May 1944. Remaining fragments of it may be rediscovered at a future date.

Féerie pour une autre fois (Fairy tale for another time), which appeared in two volumes in 1952-54, is generally considered to be Céline's weakest work of fiction. It must be admitted, however, that in comparison to the critical attention devoted to his other novels it has not yet been closely studied. Ostensibly written during his exile in Denmark, where he fled in 1945 and remained until 1951, when he was granted amnesty and allowed to return to France, this book is best considered as a transitional work that shows Céline moving from the transformation of his lived experiences into the form of a novel, as in ***Voyage, Mort*** and ***Guignol's Band,*** to what will become, in his last three books, chronicles that do not seek to fool the reader any more, and where the first-person narrator is Céline himself. In the opening pages of ***Féerie,*** part 1, we find the embittered narrator in Paris, but throughout most of the book he is in prison in Copenhagen lamenting his fate, pointing out, among other things, that there are many real collaborators freely walking the streets of Paris, while he is in prison and in exile. The action of ***Féerie,*** part 2, written before the first part but published after it, is set in Paris and revolves around an Allied air raid on the French capital. The word "féerie," which denotes a form of entertainment that includes an element of magic and supernatural, is essentially Céline's ironic fantasy about himself. It fails as a novel, if that is what it is supposed to be, but is perhaps redeemed by the fact that it points the way to Céline's last three works, generally hailed by critics as masterpieces.

Once the Allies had landed in France, Céline realized that it was only a question of time until Paris would be liberated and he would be called to account for his prewar writings. Convinced that he stood virtually no chance of receiving a fair trial from the Communist-dominated Resistance, he decided to flee. In July 1944, he left Paris with his wife Lucette, the former ballet-dancer whom he had married the year before, his friend the actor Le Vigan, and his now-famous cat, Bébert. After a short stay in Baden-Baden, he made a trip to Berlin to visit hospitals and then remained for several months in Kränzlin, in Brandenburg, northwest of Berlin. When the Vichy government, by now in exile, retreated to Sigmaringen, Céline moved there and joined the French colony in November 1944. He stayed on with them as a kind of house physician until March 1945. At that time, and allegedly to recover money he had hidden in a friend's back yard in Copenhagen before the war, he left for Denmark. He arrived there safely three weeks later.

The events of this nine-month period were to become the subject matter of Céline's last three works: ***D'un château l'autre*** (***Castle to Castle***), published in 1957, ***Nord*** (***North***), which he brought out in 1960, and ***Rigodon*** (***Rigadoon***), which he completed the morning of the day he died, 1 July 1961. This last text was not published, however, until 1969.

The events of Céline's life during this period of flight are not recounted in order in the trilogy. Nor does he seek strict verisimilitude, as would a professional historian. The subject matter, while based on the author's personal experience, includes a certain amount of fiction and fantasy. The end result, however, is that we have over a thousand pages that describe life in the closing days of the Third Reich. The Allied bombardments, the reactions of the French puppets to their inevitable fate, and the growing awareness of the general population that their cities will soon be overrun by the enemy are all vividly recounted.

These three books are also remarkable in that they reflect Céline's contempt for the Germans. The same man who had sought a Franco-German alliance in 1938 now scoffs at them and their leaders. Another recurrent theme is that of the corruption of leadership, for the masters in the Third Reich never seem to lack any of the creature comforts so absent from the lives of ordinary citizens. A third continuing theme is that of the collapse of Germany itself, the confusion and disintegration of a whole society. Finally, what is perhaps the most important theme of the three works, and which links up with ***Voyage*** in this regard, is that of sheer survival. Céline will do anything, flatter any person, do whatever is asked, merely to go on living, to survive until another day when the conditions of normalcy will finally be at hand. Both the fright and desperation that he experienced, and the cunning required to overcome them, are recounted by Céline in his usual self-deprecating way. Convinced of his own political innocence, for which he argues throughout these pages, he also strikes a note for the poor and dispossessed, with whom now more than ever he identifies. These three volumes, properly called chronicles rather than novels, are the last works of Céline's literary career.

In April 1945, a French court issued a warrant for Céline's arrest as a collaborator, but it was only eight months later that French officials in Copenhagen demanded his immediate extradition. The Danes responded by imprisoning both Céline (for fourteen months) and his wife (for two months). In February 1947, Céline's declining health caused him to be hospitalized. After another four months, his health restored, he was allowed to go free on condition that he not leave Denmark. He thus remained in that country until his amnesty in France was declared in April 1951. The last ten years of his life were lived in quiet and seclusion on the outskirts of Paris where he earned his living, as always, by practicing medicine. As mentioned above, his last three books, the chronicles, were composed during this period.

In the United States, the number of writers clearly influenced by Céline is greater than for any other European writer, living or dead. Henry Miller for years was fond of telling anyone who would listen how much he owed to Céline. Jack Kerouac, in the frenzied, breathless flight of *On the Road* (1957) and in the analysis of the effect of drugs on his heroes, took his cue from Céline's famous delirium scenes in which his hero, overcome by the pain of living, escapes from reality into a kind of therapeutic dreamworld. Joseph Heller, in *Catch-22* (1961), took the whole idea for his novel from the first part of Céline's ***Journey.*** As Bardamu learns in the opening pages of the novel, while serving at the front in the late summer of 1914, there is nothing more insane than war between two civilized nations. Wounded and rehabilitated in Paris, Bardamu decides that the only way to avoid returning to the combat zone is to act crazy. But French doctors know that anyone insane enough not to want to do his patriotic duty is really sane, and this is precisely the "catch" that Heller places at the heart of his own novel. Ken Kesey, in *One Flew Over the Cuckoo's Nest* (1962), expanded on the theme of the man who voluntarily decides to live in a madhouse. In this, too, he follows Céline, for if Bardamu is forcefully interned in an asylum early in ***Journey,*** by the end of the novel he is a doctor in charge of one. Finally, the most interesting Céliniste to surface in recent years has been Kurt Vonnegut, Jr. Céline's influence in him, however, does not grow out of ***Journey,*** but rather from the later novels, mentioned above, that chronicle among other things the Allied destruction of a large part of Germany's civilian population in 1944-45. As Céline's prestige grows, more American disciples will no doubt emerge.

Céline's future reputation as one of the two great novelists of twentieth-century France seems secure. Although the linguistic fireworks found in his novels obviously suggest a comparison with James Joyce in English, scholars are only now analyzing his prose to discover the secrets that make it work. As no great novelist or school of fiction has arisen in France in the quarter century that has elapsed since the death of Camus, Céline and his work have to a large extent filled the vacuum.

Erika Ostrovsky (essay date 1989)

SOURCE: "Louis-Ferdinand Céline: Creator and Destroyer of Myths," in *Critical Essays on Louis-Ferdinand Céline,* edited by William K. Buckley, G. K. Hall, 1989, pp. 92-100.

[*In the following essay, Ostrovsky examines Céline's adaptation and subversion of myth themes and patterns in his novels.*]

Céline has elicited so much critical commentary—especially in the past decade—the corpus of interpretations devoted to him is so rich and varied, that one might well ask what still remains to be said. Yet his work, by its extraordinary complexity and vitality, constantly inspires, even demands, new explorations. Among these, the treatment of myth elements in his fictions suggests itself as a fecund although (to date) insufficiently used approach. This essay, while necessarily limited in scope, will attempt to make at least an initial incursion into that challenging domain.

At the very outset, however, a clarification is mandatory: the analysis of myth elements here will not deal with factors immediately visible, such as the use of characters, situations, or sites from mythology or the recreation of ancient myths in modern form (as found in the works of many contemporary French writers, for example, Anouilh, Butor, Cocteau, Giraudoux, Sartre, and Wittig). True, mythological figures do at times appear in Céline's fictions (Charon, the Minotaur, Jupiter, Neptune, Venus, centaurs, and sirens), and, on occasion, the author claims the title of mythographer or creator of legends. But these phenomena are only of minor interest for the present undertaking. Matters far less evident and thus—characteristically—much more fundamental in Céline's writings are those that are based on his recognition of the plight of modern man who lives in a desacralized world, yet feels a profound (though hidden) nostalgia for legend or myth. This nostalgia, also observed by one of the great specialists in the field—Mircea Eliade—translates itself, according to the latter, into what he terms "mythological behavior" manifesting itself in a variety of ways in our lives dominated by the profane. Since, however—and this is essential for the purposes of the present analysis—this "mythological behavior" finds its essential expression in the domain of the imaginary, it demands, for its discovery and analysis in literature, the study of myth patterns that are evident in some aspects of a fiction and follow specific models with which specialists of mythology are well acquainted.

Three of these patterns, representing a choice determined by the richness of the material found in Céline's major fictions as well as by their importance in any consideration of myth structures, will furnish the principal areas of exploration in this essay: (1) Initiation; (2) The Modalities of Time; and (3) Cosmogony and *Eschaton.* It must immediately be added, however, that, although Céline's *adherence* to myth patterns is of great interest, his *subversion,* truncation, or suspension of them is just as fascinating and speaks equally of the author's profound originality. Both as creator and destroyer, Céline remains here—as elsewhere—one of the most innovative of contemporary French writers.

Our point of departure will be Initiation—the point of departure par excellence. Traditionally, the pattern it follows consists of a certain number of motifs and stages: separation of the novice or candidate for initiation from his birthplace, native soil, or the maternal domain; segregation in a place both distant and unknown; crossing of a threshold; encounter with a guardian, guide, double, or spirit; trials (frequently in the form of torture); symbolic death (mutilation, sacrifice, circumcision, subincision); a night journey or visit to the underworld/otherworld; a radical transformation in his mode or level of being; the acquisition of a different name; the revelation of a fundamental truth or mystery; the triumphant return of the initiate, now in the possession of important secret knowledge; the transmission of this knowledge to the community.

Even when seen by itself, this list of motifs and phases in the initiation scenario already reveals many striking parallels with the itinerary of ***Journey to the End of Night*** (whose very title, of course, suggests the motif of the night journey): the protagonist, Bardamu, like the traditional neophyte, is separated from his native world (Paris, the Place Clichy) and will proceed to a series of distant and unknown places (battlefields, Africa, America); he crosses the first threshold (represented by the image of an empty space obscured by rain but also—perhaps even more powerfully—through stylistic means such as a brutal change of rhythm, the suspension of punctuation, a different lexical register); he encounters a guide or double (Robinson) who will appear at every important turning point, or crossing of another threshold, in the novel; Bardamu undergoes trials, torture, and mutilation, as well as a radical change in his mode of being. Most important of all, a fundamental truth is revealed to him. This occurs in two stages: the first marks his passage into adulthood (which, in the traditional initiation, introduces the neophyte both to death and sexuality) and is here expressed in the famous sentence: "One is as virgin to Horror as to sensuality"; the second, after this loss of virginity and the progressive discovery that occurs throughout the novel (in a pattern repeated several times), is summed up in the formula: "The truth of this world is death."

It is at this point that Céline's fiction ceases to adhere to the mythological model and its subversion begins. After having explored and left the "Other World" (at the exact center of the novel), the initiate, Bardamu, does not return triumphant, although in possession of important secret knowledge. On the contrary, he remains a stranger, an outsider, fixed in a pose of failure at the conclusion of his long night journey. And the transmission of the fundamental truth acquired (usually the final stage of the initiation scenario) is completely reversed, for ***Journey to the End of Night*** ends in an appeal for silence: "Let's speak no more about it."

While the Initiation pattern illuminates many aspects of Céline's early novels (for one could, space permitting, trace similar parallels in ***Death on the Installment Plan*** and ***Casse-pipe***), a much more dramatic (although related) scenario is applicable to the later works, from ***Le Pont de Londres*** onward: that of the shaman. The mythological model in question contains the following elements: illness, seizures, possession, disintegration of personality, as signs of vocation, of being chosen; tortures (even involving the symbolic dismemberment of the body or its reduction to a skeletal state); manifestations of furor, heat, trance, ecstasy; ascension or levitation; astral voyages or descents into hell; extraordinary powers in the realm of poetry, prophecy, medicine; visionary states; a prodigious memory; the discovery of a new language; communication with animals, especially birds; the transmission of illuminations to the members of the tribe.

It will certainly have become apparent to those who know

Céline's works well, how many parallels can be found between these attributes and those of the narrators (and their companions or doubles) in his later fiction, such as Sosthène de Rodioncourt and Mille-Pattes in ***Le Pont de Londres*** or Jules in ***Féerie pour une autre fois.*** The first enters repeatedly into trance states; the second is, in effect, reduced to a skeletal shape and performs vertiginous acts of levitation at the *Touit-Touit-Club* (a place whose very name suggests, among other things, the sound of a bird-call); the third, whose body has undergone dismemberment (he is a double amputee) ascends to the top of the Moulin de la Galette (an image of the *Axis Mundi?*) and directs an infernal round. Descents into hell occur quite frequently in Céline's last trilogy and are represented by entry into subterranean labyrinths, tunnels, room no. 36, and bomb craters, or assemblies of monsters and demons in ***Castle to Castle, North,*** and ***Rigadoon.*** The protagonists of these novels also manifest others of the shaman's unusual powers: that of prophecy (for example, the "extra-voyant" narrator of ***Castle to Castle***); of poetry (such as the writer-doubles of almost all the narrators); of communication with animals (the cat, Bébert, chief among them) and especially with birds (the role of "bird-charmer" had already been attributed to Sosthène and will revert to the narrator at the end of Céline's last novel, ***Rigadoon***); of medical skills (which make the protagonist of almost all the later fiction a witch doctor or medicine man, in the truest sense of the word).

In this case, as in the previous one, it can be seen that the subversion of the mythological model (as powerful as adherence to it) operates at the moment of the scenario where the triumphal stage usually begins. Thus, ascension inevitably ends in a fall or a derisive failure—for Mille-Pattes as well as for Jules. (Of course, this pattern had already been prefigured by the grotesque end of Courtial des Pereires' balloon in ***Death on the Installment Plan,*** but it becomes more dramatic in the later works.) Ecstasy, if it occurs at all, leads to nothing (as in the case of Sosthène); the discovery of a new language is limited to that of an apocalyptic Esperanto or the sign language of cretins; the transmission of an illumination to the members of the tribe either ends in disaster or never takes place at all.

Let us now proceed to the second stage of our itinerary: the Modalities of Time. According to mythological thinking, there are two kinds of time: profane time—linear, chronological, irreversible—which leads to degeneration, decrepitude, and death; the time of origins, of absolute beginnings—primordial, auroral, infinitely recuperable—characterized by strength, purity, perfection. For modern man, who considers himself defined by history, it is the former that dominates, creating a profound sense of anguish that is the result of his "fall into time" and the temporal flow that leads, inevitably, toward death. It is this kind of time that is so powerfully evoked in a passage of ***Death on the Installment Plan*** (a work whose very title translates this obsession): "Ah! it's really terrible . . . how one loses people along the way . . . pals one never sees again . . . never . . . who've vanished like dreams . . . it's all over . . . gone . . . then one will also be lost . . . in the dreadful torrent of things . . . of days. . . ." An attempt, overwhelming in its futility, to halt the flow of time, follows this pronouncement: "A mad desire took hold of me . . . to jump into the fray . . . to block their path . . . to stop them in their tracks . . . so they wouldn't move at all anymore! . . . so they'd stand still . . . once and for all! . . . So I wouldn't see them leave anymore!" But the "dreadful torrent of . . . days" cannot be halted nor turned from its course. One cannot be cured of the ravages of time. At most, one can attempt to nullify it by projecting oneself out of the temporal. Bardamu had already expressed this wish in his cry: "To leap out of Time!" and had momentarily succeeded by various forms of escape—the cinema, voyages, eroticism, delirium. But they provided only a short respite and rapidly gave way to an awareness of temporality and its accompanying anguish. It is of no avail either to circumnavigate the globe and to visit the "other world." For once one stops running, "one picks up the thread of the days again, the way one has left it dragging here, filthy, precarious. It waits for you."

If, according to mythological thinking, the return to the Origin is the only way to kill the dead time that leads to death and if, by ritually returning to the beginning of the world one can re-create the paradisial state which preceded our fall into time, then in Céline's fiction, any attempt to break the temporal flow fails in the final analysis. At most, what remains is a nostalgia, an unslated thirst for such a state and some frenetic attempts to attain the Time of Origins (i.e., a Golden Age when a strong, pure race of supermen peopled the earth). The latter seem to lead to the monstrous pronouncements made by the narrators of the pamphlets that coincide (both temporally and historically) with Aryan myths and the racist theories of the Nazis.

The only true means of escaping linear and destructive time (according to nearly all mythologies) is by a repetition of the act of creation—or cosmogony. Such an act is possible for the creator of fiction even if it is impossible for his creatures. First of all, because any construction (in this case, that of a book) is a repetition of the act of Creation, an absolute beginning and, as such, a way of restoring the initial instant, the plenitude of a present without any trace of history. Second, because the writer (and the reader) can move outside of historical and personal time and gain access to an ahistorical and transpersonal dimension: the time of the imaginary that contains all the liberty lacking in the temporal realm of living—a time that is expanded or contracted and where one can, once again, experience all things with the same intensity as when they occurred at the very first instance. The writer can also refuse linear time in his fiction and, by means of structures, suggest a world sheltered from the ravages of chronological time. In his early novels, Céline seems to have undertaken this task by a relatively simple chronological reversal of episodes or of entire works (such as ***Journey to the End of Night, Death on the Installment Plan, Guignol's Band,*** parts 1 and 2). In his late works however, fictional time itself is expanded or contracted; it even exists simultaneously (for example, in ***Rigadoon*** where, in numerous passages, verbs in the past, present, and future tense are found in the same paragraph, even in the same sentence); it is exploded, winds back upon itself, and finally becomes so chaotic that it no longer seems to exist at all. It is then no more the representation of a leap out of time but the very annihilation of time itself. This state of nothingness, this regression or return to the amorphous and to original chaos, is the point where what one could term *Endzeit* rejoins the *Urzeit* that figures in all the myths of the End of the World.

This brings us to the last stage of our exploration: Cosmogony and *Eschaton.* Traditionally, the order of these two terms would be reversed, for the *Eschaton* supposes the total destruction of the cosmos and its return to chaos—to the primordial *massa confusa*—in order to subsequently permit the renewal or absolute regeneration of the world. Whether it is a question of the diurnal and nocturnal cycle, the round of the seasons, or the Great Year of the cosmos, the pattern remains the same.

In the case of Céline's fiction, the eschatological phase is, of course, the most evident. According to most critics, he is an "apocalyptic" writer, the destroyer par excellence of an existing (literary) universe, a specialist in the reduction to zero. He himself reinforces this impression by the pronouncements of many of his narrators: "I am the thunder, the cataclysms," one of them says; "I write the opera of the Flood," another adds. All of this might lead one to think that the mythological model would constantly be subverted or sabotaged and that, in his works, cosmogony would never follow the *eschaton.* It will be seen, however, that even this subversion would be subverted by Céline on occasion.

Naturally, readers of Céline are well aware of the fact that the stages of the destructive phase are painted in great detail and occupy the predominant place in his fictions and that, from ***Journey to the End of Night*** to ***Rigadoon,*** an apocalypse of human origin is taking place. All the motifs of the *eschaton* are present: destruction by fire due to criminal acts of war; floods of all kinds, often tragic but at times comical—such as the deluge of vomit during the Channel crossing in ***Death on the Installment Plan*** or the flooding of toilets in ***North;*** the reign of demons and the resurrection of the dead, in ***Death on the Installment Plan*** or in ***Castle to Castle;*** the ruin of entire civilizations and the destruction of humanity as a whole, in the last trilogy and especially in ***Rigadoon.*** Not only on the mimetic but also on the stylistic level, this annihilation is reflected. The latter is expressed by the fragmentation of the novels' structures, the atomization of syntax, the deluge of words, the chaotic nature of fictional time and space.

However, and this is most important, the subversion of the mythological model— exceptionally—does not take place at the moment when Céline's life and work come to an end. For, if one closely examines the second part of ***Rigadoon*** (from the moment the narrator suffers a head wound), one sees that a transformation takes place and a turning point has been reached: the end of the world allows a new creation to take place. The first indication of this is that the "infernal music" that has pursued the narrator ever since the initiatory head wound inflicted during World War I (described also as "excruciating noises," "the opera of the Flood," "the small song of Death") undergoes a metamorphosis the instant the final head wound is suffered during World War II. The music now heard is: "A song! . . . magnificent! as magnificent as the panorama . . . a song like a symphony for this ocean of ruins . . . crazy ruins . . . 'waves of little flames' . . . pink . . . green . . . and small crackling bouquets . . . the souls of the house . . . far . . . very far away . . . dancing. . . ." Noises have changed into a "magnificent song," "a symphony"; the Flood image has given way to that of the "ocean" and of the "wave" (symbols of birth and becoming); the harsh and brutal colors of destruction have become tender tints of "pink" and "green"; flames have changed into flowers; the round of demons and witches has been transformed into a dance.

From this moment on, a sense of calm and peace will reign; a pause occurs that is neither emptiness nor absolute ending, but rather a time of rest before something takes place. This something, ushered in by inexplicable laughter (the laughter of creation), is the birth of a new world. In the beginning, the seeds of primordial life appear, breaking forth from the original and most primitive substance—clay (or mud)—in the form of creatures existing on the simplest level, beings in a larval state, animallike, functioning on a preverbal level: the "little cretins" with whom "everything is possible" and "everything begins again." Together with the author-*accoucheur* we witness the birth of new life which, truly, arises from its own ashes.

Thus, not only does cosmogony follow the *eschaton* but, in the last part of ***Rigadoon,*** there is a brief yet extraordinary passage in which one sees a kind of garden of Eden where the narrator and his wife (resembling the first human couple) are surrounded by fabulous birds that eat from their hands (in the presence of Bébert, the cat) as trusting as the animals at the dawn of creation, before the Fall.

This renewal out of the void takes place not only on the

level of mimesis, however. Céline, after having submitted literary style to eschatological action, assures us (parodying Genesis of Judeo-Christian mythology) that "In the beginning was emotion" and to re-create style from the base of emotion. And, although the narrator of his final work announces that "each creation carries within itself, with itself, its birth as well as its end," we might add that each end (and this is substantiated by all his novels) carries within it its own birth or rebirth. And, although the title, ***Rigadoon,*** contains the image of a target riddled with bullet holes (and thus, of death), it contains at the same time a reference to creation through dance, by dancing.

Thus, Céline, in the work completed at the moment of his death before entering into absolute silence, gives us a brief glimpse of dawn at the end of cosmic night.

Philip H. Solomon (essay date 1992)

SOURCE: "Reading Céline," in *Understanding Céline,* University of South Carolina Press, 1992, pp. 5-15.

[*In the following essay, Solomon provides an overview of the major themes and characters in Céline's novels.*]

Céline preferred to think of himself as a stylist, but it would be more appropriate to consider his writings in terms of a particular vision of the human condition. Vision is a crucial concept in Céline's novels. Several of his novels begin with a unique pattern of opening signals. The narrator finds himself in a set of circumstances articulated by a mythologized head wound which results in his having perceptual distortions. These distortions self-consciously announce that the reader is entering the realm of fiction, whatever similarities—and there are many—will emerge between the author, the protagonist-turned-narrator, and the protagonist. In ***D'un château l'autre*** (1957, ***Castle to Castle),*** the narrator will refer to himself as a visionary, a "lucid super-seer," one who sees clearly, by means of heightened perception, beyond or through surface appearances. Beginning with ***Féerie pour une autre fois*** (1952, Enchantment for Another Time), the reader may begin to question the focus and scope of that lucidity as a kind of double vision sets in. Céline's condemnation as a Nazi collaborator for his anti-Semitic writings and his subsequent prosecution (Céline would consider it persecution) become an integral part of his novels' subject matter. These latter narratives serve, among other things, as a means of self-defense and self-exculpation. How, one might wonder, could such a visionary be so shortsighted with respect to his support of an ideology that would lead to genocide?

But first, by way of introduction, let us explore what the seer sees. All of Céline's novels are marked by the presence of war. Céline's fear and hatred of war is conditioned not only by his own circumstances—he was a disabled veteran of World War I (and served briefly as a ship's doctor and ambulance driver during World War II)—but also by the devastation of his country in the so-called "war to end all wars." As the principal battleground of World War I as well as one of its major participants, France incurred staggering losses—1.4 million dead, an entire generation wiped out. For Céline, war has no geopolitical justification. It is a grotesque mockery in which misguided, incompetent, and callous leaders, political and military, countenance the slaughter and maiming of millions of ordinary citizens to further their dubious goals.

Céline chooses to focus not so much on the fighting itself but on the landscapes of war, external and subsequently internalized as traumatic memories. The battlefields of Flanders in World War I become deceptive landscapes in which the ordinary hum of insects is replaced by the whine of bullets, deadly expanses on which, viewed from a distance, tiny uniformed figures shoot at one another for reasons they are unable to comprehend. As for World War II, with its saturation bombings, it leaves in its wake a world turned upside down—cities transformed into necropolises, asphyxiated soldiers still guarding their posts, multicolored fires whose seemingly cheerful flames make one forget their origin, buildings reduced to numbered bricks as if they were about to be constructed. Céline depicts the horrors of war but also its perverse beauty. When survival at any price becomes one's chief concern, "normal" values are no longer applicable. Cowardice is transformed into a virtue. The insane seem reasonable in the midst of universal insanity. When Céline's protagonist leaves the front, he remains haunted and obsessed by the carnage he has witnessed, by the specter of death.

But if war, as Céline presents it, is antiheroic, it is, nonetheless, a desirable activity for its participants. It liberates, as it legalizes, an inherent human predilection for killing. Céline represents daily existence as a struggle to maintain a coherent identity, some semblance of civilized behavior, in the face of a natural tendency, accelerated by war, for such constraints to collapse. Spite, cruelty, hatred, exploitation, and various forms of brutality ooze through that protective envelope, even in the absence of war. Céline adds an element of geographical determinism to this volatile mixture. Warmer climates bring such nefarious elements to the surface more readily than do colder climates; the Southerner is thus more unstable than the Northerner.

All of Céline's protagonists—successive versions of the same figure, designated as Bardamu in his first novel, Ferdinand in those that follow—are engaged in the apprenticeship of life. They lose their illusions along the way and are transformed into older and wiser, if not more cynical, narrators. They are shaped not only by their experience with war and all it connotes but, in a more general sense, by the realities of an existence marked by disintegration, disorder, and death. Throughout the novels they experience and bear witness to the passage from order to disorder as structures of all kinds crumble away. Societies fragment under the pressure of war, relationships and personalities erode, and the advance of technology turns individuals into anachronisms. They discover that surface appearances are deceptive, masking only temporarily the dangers lurking behind them. Their plans and dreams are transformed into absurd fantasies. Beauty is revealed to be a veneer for the ugly and grotesque, and virtues can no longer be distinguished from vices. Céline's universe is a place of confusion (in the literal sense of a "running together"), heteroclite, in which hierarchies and categories no longer hold. Céline wields his pen like a scalpel (he was, after all, a doctor by vocation). He dissects the human condition, exposing its malignancies, but he offers no treatments or cures.

Céline's fictions are haunted by the ubiquitous presence of death, for that is where disintegration and disorder ultimately lead: death as an immediate settling of accounts, and death "on the installment plan." War takes care of the former; disease, poverty, despair, and a gamut of deleterious instincts and emotions will eventually help to pay off the latter. Some characters, like Robinson in ***Journey to the End of the Night,*** become death's willing accomplices, driven to despairing acts by their inability to create a meaningful existence for themselves. Ferdinand, for his part, cheats death, if for no other reason than to bear witness to the truths, however unpleasant, that experience reveals, to transmit the disorder of life through the order of art. We are meant to admire his cleverness and his tenacity in that effort.

What one might term the nobler sentiments—love, tenderness, self-sacrifice—rarely counterbalance the panoply of destructive tendencies that surround the protagonist and from which, given his privileged role, he is largely exempt. Ferdinand's infatuation with Virginia in ***Guignol's Band II*** is a parody of romantic love that transforms him into a buffoon but also, and here he shares the common penchant for violence toward others, into a brutal rapist who assaults his idolized beloved and makes her pregnant. For Céline's protagonists, sexual love is usually either a masturbatory fantasy or the expression of a brute instinct that weakens a man and makes him an easy prey for the devouring female. There is a fear of women in Céline's novels that transforms them into ogres or into self-effacing, and thus non-menacing, dependents. Even Lili, Ferdinand's wife in the later novels, is a vaguely defined background figure, the incarnation of the dancer. Her existence is subsumed by her husband's.

Children receive special treatment in Céline's fiction by virtue of their contrast with adults. According to Céline's concept of reverse metamorphosis, children are the butterflies that will become "maggots" (Céline prefers the more negative designation to the relatively innocuous "caterpillar") once they reach adulthood and begin to assume the noxious personality that is inherent to the species. The narrator of ***Guignol's Band I*** remembers with great fondness and tenderness the groups of children playing in the wet, gloomy streets of London. Their games and their songs endow those streets with a gaiety and light they would otherwise not possess. Animals, perforce innocent, also receive their share of affection. One of the companions of the journey traced in the wartime trilogy is the cat Bébert, to whom his master demonstrates an exemplary kindness.

How does one cope with existence, as Céline depicts it? Delirium is one way. One of its forms is the simple delusion, entertained at least briefly, that things are not as bad as they seem or will get better. In ***Death on the Installment Plan,*** Ferdinand's mother Clémence insists that honesty and hard work—time-honored middle class values—will permit her commerce in handmade old lace to return to prosperity, despite the increasing popularity of machine-made goods and the growing dominance of the department store. A more extreme form of delirium is insanity, a permanent withdrawal behind the walls of one's own mind, an abdication of responsibility for oneself and the world. The journey, one of the major themes in Céline's novels, can itself be a form of escape, each new place bearing with it new possibilities. But such opportunities quickly evaporate. They were, after all, but a mirage, since existence is everywhere the same, since one cannot leave one's self behind. Movement becomes yet another delusion, a rigadoon (the title of Céline's last novel) in which one stays, despite the appearance of progress, in the same place. Ferdinand is fascinated by ships. But his reveries of distant shores are short-lived. The only satisfactory voyages are those of the imagination. The journey of life must, of course, end with death. Ferdinand, modern picaro, ironic Ulysses, learns to travel underground, picking his way through the interstices of existence and observing its tragicomedy.

Although they convey a pessimistic view of the human condition, Céline's novels are by no means humorless. But their humor is most often black and bitter. Verbal wit in the service of iconoclasm, satire, and demystification exposes the ludicrousness of individual and societal pretentiousness. Neither the narrator nor the protagonist are immune from such scrutiny—to which they frequently respond with self-deprecating irony or sarcasm. There is a comical incongruity in the protagonist's clumsy but determined efforts to order an existence that becomes, in the face of such attempts, that much more problematical. That we know the protagonist's survival is never in doubt permits us to be both apprehensive about the defeats he suffers and convinced he will devise the necessary stratagem that will permit him to recover before moving on to the next catastrophe. His resiliency is amusing as is that of the cartoon character who, flattened or shattered, reconstitutes itself before another devastating encounter takes place. The wartime trilogy is replete with such incidents as Ferdinand stumbles, sometimes literally, from one obstacle to another in his fitful progress toward Copenhagen. There is a good deal of humor as well in Céline's depiction of those individuals whose larger-than-life idiosyncrasies shape their own equally eccentric universes. In ***Guignol's Band II,*** Sosthène de Rodiencourt (the aristocratic name does not match the behavior of its bearer), mystic and illusionist, believes he has appropriated the strength of a demon and decides to demonstrate his new powers by zigzagging through the traffic on Piccadilly Circus—transforming it into a literal circus. The comedy comes to an end when the clown is beaten into submission under the clubs of the police.

There are several secondary characters like Sosthène, and they constitute one of the salient aspects of Céline's novels. Their brand of delirium transcends simple insanity. They are obsessed with a variety of manias that are magnified to an epic scale. Like massive force fields, they bend the universe around themselves so it becomes an extension of their own personalities, a closed system that is, at least temporarily, impermeable to the contingencies of external reality. Eventually, such systems break down, with far more catastrophic results than the thrashing Sosthène received from the Bobbies. In ***Death on the Installment Plan,*** Courtial, inventor and polymath, blows his brains out when his mind can no longer conceive and, above all, verbalize the schemes that have been his refuge.

Certain secondary characters are fascinating in the ways they serve as doubles for the protagonist. These individuals embody conflicting or alternative aspects of the protagonist's psyche. Their autonomous yet dependent existences dramatize the protagonist's or narrator's awareness of his own complexity. Jules, the legless painter in the two volumes of ***Guignol's Band,*** incarnates the dark side of the artist, the perversion of creative ability for personal satisfaction. In the wartime trilogy, Le Vigan, film actor and collaborator, represents by his sinking into insanity the temptation to abdicate lucidity in the face of harsh reality. Doubles like Robinson and Le Vigan also serve a necessary function vis-a-vis the protagonist: they can take the journey of life beyond the limits imposed upon the latter. The protagonist must survive, must remain lucid, in order to fulfill his dual function: to bear witness to his and others' experiences and, having become the narrator, to transform memory into text.

One cannot read Céline without taking into account his anti-Semitic writings. Although one could suppose that Céline, having heard as a young boy his father read anti-Semitic literature aloud at the dinner table, simply espoused the views of the elder Destouches, it is more reasonable to assume that he chose to be an anti-Semite (the earliest evidence for his prejudice dates from 1916). The choice was not difficult to make or to sustain. Although a previous wave of anti-Semitism in France, generated by the Dreyfus Affair (1894-1906), had waned by the early 1920s, a second, far more powerful, surge took place in the 1930s. Many factors contributed to this renewal of anti-Jewish sentiment. In the late 1920s and into the 1930s there was a considerable immigration to France of Eastern European Jews, particularly from anti-Semitic Poland.

Many of these immigrants were manifestly Jewish in dress and speech, and thus stood out from their more assimilated French brethren. As Nazi racist policies grew more rigorous (Hitler had become chancellor in 1933), a number of German Jews fled to nearby France. Jews, as well as other immigrant groups, competed with the French for relatively scarce jobs in a weak national economy. A sense of the decline of democratic political and social institutions gave new vitality to such right-wing organizations as the Action Française, always ready to blame the Jews for France's troubles. The coming to power of the leftist Popular Front government (1936-38), under the leadership of the Jew Léon Blum (1872-1950), drew the wrath of the anti-Semites, convinced that the Popular Front was proof of an international Jewish conspiracy and, concomitantly, that France was in need of a New Order like that of Germany.

One must remember that during that during these years anti-Semitism in France was not associated with what we would designate today as the "lunatic fringe." Respected national figures were infected by the disease, and anti-Jewish literature was inexpensive and readily available. In short, there was no stigma attached to being an anti-Semite and expressing such views publicly, in speech or in writing. That situation would change in 1939 with the passage of the Marchandeau law making it illegal to defame a particular religious or ethnic group and subsequently with the German occupation of France, when anti-Semitic publications served to support Nazi racial policies and would justify an accusation of treason. Céline's first two pamphlets, ***Bagatelles pour un massacre*** and ***L'Ecole des Cadavres,*** were both published before the war, withdrawn from circulation following a suit for defamation, and then republished during the Occupation. His third pamphlet, ***Les Beaux Draps,*** appeared initially in 1941. The views expressed in the pamphlets were seconded by Céline's letters to collaborationist newspapers and his presence at various anti-Semitic functions.

Even a very cursory reading of Céline's pamphlets (***Bagatelles pour un massacre*** is briefly examined in the final chapter of this study) reveals the familiar cliches of the anti-Semitism of the period. Although Céline claimed they were pacifist in intent, directed only against those Jews who were supposedly leading France into another catastrophic war with Germany, the pamphlets condemn all Jews as racially inferior, as conspiring to take control of the world for their own power and profit, as parasites infecting an otherwise healthy Aryan society. Céline does not call specifically for violence against the Jews, although he does express his admiration for Hitler's racist policies. However, his message is clear: arouse hatred and disgust for the Jews by exposing their true nature and intentions so that they will be restricted, as second-class citizens, to the most limited role possible. Céline would later deny that the Holocaust had ever taken place.

Apart from some stray remarks, Céline's novels are free from the anti-Semitism he displays elsewhere. However, Céline's condemnation and prosecution as a traitor for his anti-Semitic pamphlets and contributions to collaborationist newspapers shape the protagonists of the later novels, beginning with ***Féerie pour une autre fois I.*** Protesting his innocence, claiming he had composed the pamphlets to save his country from going to war and had not written a line for pro-Nazi newspapers, Ferdinand sees himself as an innocent victim of persecution, a scapegoat for a humiliated nation. He has recourse to the Romantic myth of the writer pursued for his unpopular views—and generating new art as a result of that pursuit. Crossing the war-ravaged German landscape, he makes no connection between the events of history and the course of his personal life. In fleeing to the presumed safety of Denmark, he attempts to outrun history and then, having failed to do so, cannot understand why he was jailed. The "lucid super-seer" has somehow become blind to the nature and consequences of the ideology he espoused and publicly defended.

The apprenticeship of life for Céline's protagonists is inseparable from the relating of their experience, from its transformation into a text. The temporal distance between the protagonist-turned-narrator and the protagonist is the "space" within which the fictions are generated. For Céline, so long as the two do not coincide, there are further stories to be related. Mobility—the voyage as coterminous with the journey of life—leads to immobility, the protagonist becoming the narrator, and then the voyage is reiterated through words. In ***Féerie I,*** the narrator, confined to a cell in a Danish prison, frees himself through the medium of his narration and in his text ranges unencumbered over time and space.

Céline describes his style at length in a mock interview entitled ***Entretiens avec le professeur Y*** (1955, ***Conversations with Professor Y***), which will be analyzed in the last chapter of this book. His point of departure for the definition of that style is his rejection of written French, a language that he considered lifeless and artificial. In one of his pamphlets he criticizes the French schools for imposing that sort of language upon generations of students, using the models furnished by the half-Jewish writers Montaigne (1533-1592) and Proust (1871-1922). Putting aside Céline's anti-Semitism, one must remember how influential the highly centralized French educational system was, and still is, as the purveyor of an elitist linguistic standard. One should note as well a more carefully maintained separation between written French and spoken French than is the case with English, particularly in America.

Céline turned to spoken French as a repository of emotion and energy, as well as of more colorful expressions. But Céline rejects any notion of a simple recording of that spoken language. He seeks, paradoxically perhaps, to transmit those qualities through the medium of a (re)written language, carefully arranged for maximum effect, so that it will be capable of expressing a given content while creating an emotional resonance in the reader. Céline refers to his style as a "métro émotif," an "emotional subway," trains packed with the heteroclite materials of his fictions, plunging along the twisted tracks of his phrases. The ties supporting the tracks are constituted by his use of ellipsis points that permit him to cut away the dead tissue of standard syntax, leaving behind the essential aspects of the phrase to explode upon the reader's sensibility.

It is obvious that the impact of Céline's style can best be felt by the reader fluent enough in French to appreciate the texts in their original language. Fortunately, for those American readers not having the requisite command of French there exist the superlative English translations by Ralph Manheim. Céline's readers, whatever their language, will find that their trip on his "métro émotif" is a unique experience, an exhilarating ride on an underground rollercoaster rather than on a sedate subway. Reading Céline is sometimes tiring but never tiresome.

Sally M. Silk (essay date September 1992)

SOURCE: "Caught in the Dialogic: The Célinian Narrator Silenced," in *Modern Language Notes,* Vol. 107, No. 4, September, 1992, pp. 795-805.

[*In the following essay, Silk discusses the effect of cultural alienation on the protagonist's ability to communicate in* Journey to the End of the Night.]

Introduction

Dialogism's emphasis on an interplay of voices is grounded in Bakhtin's conception of the word as social material. Because "all words have the 'taste' of a profession, a genre, a tendency, a party, a particular work, a particular person, a generation, an age group, the day and hour," the notion of a word of one's own becomes impossible. Privacy and the word are incompatible in a way that recalls Geertz's view of culture as a symbolic system that can be characterized by its public nature. Although Bakhtin affirms everywhere in his writings that all words belong to the public domain (this is, after all, dialogism's most salient characteristic), nowhere does he explore the dynamics behind a textual subject's relationship to culture. Therefore a fundamental question remains unanswered, one that comes directly out of his work, but is never addressed therein: What happens to the relationship between culture and dialogism when a subject is forced into discursive marginalization by another voice in a text? How is dialogical activity problematized when the self is litera(ri)lly invaded by an other?

To begin to examine this issue, it is useful to locate where the mutual attraction resides between culture and the word. Geertz's view of culture suggests we start by looking closely at Lacan's concept of the Symbolic Order. Because it is precisely the place where desire is rearranged and laws are erected in order to allow a subject access to language, the Symbolic Order can be regarded as the place where culture and the word intersect.

If Lacan's theory is going to be useful in helping us get at the problematics of dialogism, it must be noted that while the Symbolic Order is the place where a subject gains entry into language, it is also the place where a loss occurs, in view of the subject's mediation through an other necessary to the process of acquiring language. How does dialogism account for the acquisition of language as well as the loss of self? I argue that this question can be answered by projecting the Symbolic Order on to a spatial plane, imagining it as an area possessing both a center and a periphery, with the center giving full primacy to the public and the word, while the periphery designates virtual isolation and alienation from language.

Enlisting Lacan to contend with problems of dialogism is an idea that emerged from a reading of Céline's ***Voyage au bout de la nuit.*** The loquacious narrator Bardamu, despite his remarkable manipulation of language, remembers his travels to Africa and becomes entangled in a colonial discourse that he is unable to master. He undergoes a discursive decentering so complete that the narrative voice, known for its skill with words, is ultimately silenced. Bardamu, in resisting culture as it is embodied in the Symbolic Order, becomes a marginalized subject as he moves farther and farther away from the center of the Symbolic Order. When he arrives at what I have conceptualized as the periphery, he is left without a voice. To understand how he copes with this prospect of an endangered relationship to the word, the role of the other (on whom the subject depends for a definition of self) needs to be foregrounded.

In Céline's text the other incarnates the "public" from which the subject grows increasingly isolated as it approaches the boundaries of the Symbolic Order. Despite conflict between the two, the subject actively goes in search of the other. This complicated dynamic between self and other grows so intense that the subject must actually do violence to the silence he suffers in order to ensure dialogical engagement in the realm circumscribed by the Symbolic Order.

Bardamu's stay in Africa represents the only time in the novel when he is without language; the episode functions as a key textual moment that positions him at the periphery of the Symbolic Order. I shall demonstrate that when the self is forced into discursive marginalization by an other, when it is pushed to the limits of the Symbolic Order, from a dialogical perspective, the narrator suffers dramatic consequences.

The Narrative Voice: Colonizer Turned Colonized

Bardamu's marginal cultural position in the Symbolic Order is revealed in his confrontation with colonialism in Africa. Sent to man a tiny provisions store in the jungle, he has difficulty adjusting to the colonial behavior that his fellow countrymen slip into so effortlessly. Before arriving at his own little store deep in the jungle, he stops in a town where he observes a fellow countryman exploiting a group of natives. He nervously describes how this French entrepreneur takes complete advantage of an African family wishing to sell a basket of raw rubber. When the entrepreneur pays the family by wrapping a dirty handkerchief around the neck of one of the children instead of giving them a few coins, Bardamu comments: "La famille sauvage contemplait à présent le petit orné de cette grande chose en cotonnade verte . . . Il n'y avait plus rien á faire puisque le mouchoir venait d'entrer dans la famille." Although he appears cynically indifferent to the incident, Bardamu does, in effect, demonstrate his complicity in an imperialist discourse. For just as the child wears this symbol of civilization around his neck, so too does Bardamu occupy the voice of the ethnographer, a role that authoritatively describes the handkerchief's introduction into the family as if he understood the natives' symbolic systems.

The ethnographic voice assumed here by Bardamu silences the other. For when the bewildered family leaves the store, their lack of understanding is interpreted in the text as silence. Discursively, Bardamu embodies what Said terms "the power of culture," a force that maintains its stronghold "by virtue of its elevated position to authorize. The power of culture is an agent of, and perhaps the main agency for, powerful differentiation within its domain and beyond it too."

Bardamu's voice is legitimized, and "powerful differentiation" is brought to a dramatic climax when he ends the scene with a description of the African father receiving "un grand coup de botte en plein dans les fesses" from the shopkeeper. Literally kicked *out* of the shop, the native sets into relief Bardamu's own inside position, both *in* the shop and *in* the authoritative discourse of colonialism.

Bardamu is firmly ensconced in the Symbolic Order, for colonialism owes its discursive strength to the Symbolic Order's function as the place where desire is repressed and laws erected. But Bardamu is not at all prepared for what will happen to him when he leaves the entrepreneur to run his own shop in a remote corner of the country. His place in the Symbolic Order, which up to this point has guaranteed him access to language, is about to be overthrown. It is in the tiny village of Bikomimbo that the constitution of the subject becomes a completely traumatic operation.

We have seen that Bardamu's unwillingness to recognize the natives as a legitimate other allows him to appropriate a colonial discourse that silences them. One might think that by denying the natives a voice, he simultaneously denies himself an addressee, thereby compromising his position in the Symbolic Order. Curiously, however, the natives in Bikomimbo do not threaten his secure position in the Symbolic Order; instead, a westerner very much like himself encroaches upon his space in the Symbolic Order. In Bikomimbo he meets up with his alter ego Robinson, the character that he unexpectedly keeps running into throughout the novel and actually begins to seek out. We shall see that what Bardamu has done to the natives, i.e. silence them discursively, Robinson will do to Bardamu. The disturbing confrontation between Bardamu and his alter ego Robinson propels discourse in a centrifugal direction so that in the end Bardamu is left completely voiceless, as silent as the natives he portrayed only several scenes earlier. Before proceeding further, it would be useful to examine how the concept of silencing an other involves the co-opting of discursive space.

In a study of nineteenth-century travel writing about Africa, Mary Louise Pratt explains that the narrating western voice codifies the other because the "eye/I" that looks and speaks "commands what falls within its gaze." Houston Baker comments that her conclusions demonstrate "a writing of the 'Other' out of relationship to his or her native ground and into the sexual, commercial voyeuristic fantasies of imperialism." Bardamu's narrative is undoubtedly a product of the power of this ethnographic "eye/I" and is dialogically engaged with it. However, an important difference is that Bardamu never wishes to impose himself on the native. He is there not because of an active desire to participate in the colonial apparatus, but rather, like many colonists, in self-exile from France. He does not possess "the will to intervene" that characterized the travel writing explored by Pratt. She explains that this nineteenth century "will"

> emanates from an unknown site behind the speaking 'I'—behind the periphery of what is seen, from a seat of power that should probably be identified with the state, [. . .] the current conception of state [being] a form of public power separate from both ruler and ruled, constituted most basically by the exclusive right to exercise legitimate violence within a certain defined territory.

In the previous scene in which the native family is "kicked out" of the shop, Bardamu simultaneously accepts and resists the colonial "eye/I." He accepts it insofar as he allies himself with the petty colonial entrepreneur and thus feels he should view the situation from his perspective; but he resists it in that he is uncomfortable interpreting a world he himself does not comprehend. Therefore Bardamu is forced to adopt the privileged voice that Pratt calls the "eye/I" at the same time that he enters into conflict with it.

Bardamu's discomfort with the western monopoly on discourse suggests that he is also ill at ease with the traditionally western concept of blackness as a sign of absence, negation, and silence, as explained by Henry Louis Gates in *Figures in Black.* Bardamu, the colonialist cum deserter, writes about Africa, the continent shrouded in a myth of darkness. Maintaining resistance to the ethnographic authority behind the "eye/I" means he must also penetrate this darkness. Doing so requires confrontation with the "Signifying Monkey," who, Gates explains, is "he who dwells at the margins of discourse, ever punning, ever troping, ever embodying the ambiguities of language." In other words, in the jungle where Bardamu will meet his alter ego Robinson, he is surrounded by others (i.e. the natives) who, like him, also function on the margin. This is likeness intensified. In Bikomimbo Bardamu will thus literally see versions of himself *everywhere.* Colonial exploitation performed by Bardamu at the level of theme thus occurs in discourse as well. A close reading of the scene itself will reveal how the feeling of oppression that accompanies exploitation is discursively played out.

Robinson, starved for interlocutors, consistently reads Bardamu's thoughts, forces Bardamu to listen to his longwinded pronouncements about the natives, and exploits Bardamu's presence to keep talking. Bardamu finds him disturbing, and although he writes "Je cessai de converser avec ce forban," it becomes obvious that Bardamu seeks to appropriate the self-assured status represented for him by Robinson's voice, even though he is simultaneously afraid of it.

The animals in the vicinity of the hut make so much noise that Bardamu writes: "On en finissait par ne plus s'entendre entre nous dans la case. Il me fallait gueuler à mon tour par-dessus la table comme un chat-huant pour que le compagnon me comprît." By substituting "chat-huant" in the original French expression "gueuler comme un veau," Bardamu plays with a cliché and, consequently, a traditionally secure position in the Symbolic Order. Moreover, reduced to an animal-like state, verbal communication begins to fade between them, an indication of his increasing distance from the center of the Symbolic Order.

Bardamu, becoming desperate in his need to shed some light on the fast approaching darkness, asks his predecessor: "Comment vous appelez-vous? N'est-ce pas Robinson que vous venez de me dire?" Bardamu doesn't understand him the first time, and never receives an answer the second time. This unfulfilled desire to know Robinson's name, to be able to assign the primary signifier to a referent amidst all this confusion, dramatizes Bardamu's now more than ever questionable relationship to discourse.

His connection to the Symbolic Order deteriorates as both the outside noise and Bardamu's own inability to understand Robinson grow stronger. Even the simplest metaphor on the part of Robinson throws Bardamu into a discursive situation that the latter is apt to misunderstand.

> Vous n'avez pas du coton pour vos oreilles? me demanda-t-il encore . . . Si vous n'en avez pas, faites-en donc avec du poil de couverture et de la graisse de banane. On réussit ainsi des petits tampons très bien . . . Moi je veux pas les entendre gueuler ces vaches-là!
>
> Il y avait pourtant de tout dans cette tourmente, excepté des vaches, mais il tenait à ce terme impropre et générique.

Focusing on the alter ego's language, Bardamu, a master with words, tries to create a superior position for himself by drawing attention to this particular use of "vache." However, by reading Robinson literally, Bardamu demonstrates his inability and/or unwillingness to deal with the highly valorized rhetorical device of metaphor, a sign that he has difficulty coping in the Symbolic Order. Moreover, he reinforces his vulnerability to the presence of this alter ego so that semantic play takes on threatening overtones.

Bardamu is lost because he misreads his alter ego. Discursively, his position has become so unstable that he even discards a literal understanding of Robinson's words in favor of a symbolic reading of the latter's advice to use earplugs. Bardamu writes:

> Le true du coton m'impressionna subitement comme devant cacher quelque ruse abominable de sa part. Je ne pouvais plus m'empêcher d'être possédé par la crainte énorme qu'il se mette à m'assassiner là.

Paranoia grows so intense here that Robinson's advice is portrayed in terms of a plot against Bardamu, who even goes so far as to use the word "assassiner." Bardamu's suspicion of this resourceful combination of banana oil and animal hair demonstrates his unwillingness to "stick Africa in his ear." Unlike the fantastic Rabelaisian play with this part of the body, Bardamu's paranoia about tampering with his ear demonstrates a rejection of all that is playful in language in order to keep every line of communication open. In his desperation, Bardamu requires a more direct link with language, one that can assure him the decisive orientation of the Symbolic Order rather than the *mis*orientation suggested by his inability to reconcile his body with its surroundings (witness his resistance to Robinson's advice to use earplugs).

Confronting his alter ego in the jungle has resulted in the desire for guaranteed communication, that is, communication without mediation. Robinson's subversive earplug advice requires Bardamu to shut out communication entirely while what he desires more than anything in Bikomimbo is the opposite. Robinson advocates transgression of the rules of the communicative act as it is embodied in *la parole intermédiaire;* but Bardamu, throughout the story admittedly less daring than his alter ego, does not have the courage to block the receiving end of an enunciative act so that he may sleep undisturbed. He is too sensitive to language to plug his ears. If Bardamu transgresses in the way he plays with conventions of language, he resists going so far as to transgress its very properties in terms of enunciative positions. If "transgression is both positive and desirable," if "it breaks, frees, opens, makes possible fictional construction and reconstruction, and guarantees *authentic literariness,*" then Robinson's presence in Africa causes Bardamu *not* to see a reflection of himself in the alter ego but rather to engage in a confrontation with his writerly self.

Is it any wonder, then, that Bardamu's dilemma turns into one concerning being heard/read? When he explains anxiously: "Mais que faire? Appeler? Qui? Les anthropophages du village? . . . Disparu? je l'étais déjà presque en vérité!," the reader is actually the only one who can recognize his predicament because Robinson is gone and Bardamu does not deem the natives acceptable as illocutionary partners. Even though he rejects Robinson's advice to use earplugs and therefore stop listening, Bardamu himself is not listened to because no one can hear him from his position in the jungle.

One might assume that Bardamu's connection to the Symbolic Order is problematic because of the conflict he experiences with the only one who can guarantee him an entry into language, i.e. the alter ego Robinson. I shall demonstrate, however, that it is because of Robinson that Bardamu's confrontation with his writerly self calls into question his relationship to the Symbolic Order.

For if the Symbolic Order marks the point at which the subject gains entry into language, then Bardamu appears to be teetering on the edge of such a space. Does his peripheral position in the Symbolic Order suggest then that he is not subject to the division of self that accompanies any entry into language? Can Bardamu be considered a unified subject exempt from the "negative imperatives" that characterize the Symbolic Order as a site of disconnection and repression?

In order better to answer this question, it is useful to return to Pratt's concept of the "eye/I." It was demonstrated earlier that Bardamu both accepted and resisted this imperialist position; now, however, the western ethnographic voice no longer attempts to describe its surroundings. Instead, the "eye/I" seeks recognition by an other.

The pivotal moment in the African episode occurs at this point: Robinson disappears without a trace in the middle of the night, his absence affecting Bardamu's search for an addressee. Bardamu is debilitated by the very fact that the power of his western language is now superfluous in the jungle. Without an interlocutor to guarantee communication, Bardamu lacks the proper environment for an enunciative act. If the natives were silenced as others, Bardamu is himself silenced in the jungle because he refuses to accord them any illocutionary rights. We learn that he ends up being discursively assimilated to the natives:

> Les noirs petits et grands se décidèrent à vivre dans ma déroute en complète familiarité. Ils étaient réjouis. Grande distraction. Ils entraient et sortaient de chez moi (si l'on peut dire) comme ils voulaient. Liberté. Nous échangions en signe de grande compréhension des signes.

Bardamu and the natives communicate exclusively through nonverbal signs. But we soon learn that he cannot abandon language for silence. He grows feverish, and in his delirium decides to set on fire the hut in which the natives feel at home. The smell of burning rubber reminds Bardamu of when he was a small child in Paris witnessing a dramatic fire at the telephone company. Should it come as a surprise that the memory of burning telephone wires in France is triggered by his attempt in Africa to put an end to a hated enunciative situation? Like the telephone company fire, signs exchanged with the natives represent a threat to language. This episode opened with the abuse of an African family as they tried to sell a basket of rubber to a western entrepreneur; the scene ends with Bardamu, desperate for the western voice of his alter ego, setting the same material on fire. At the beginning when the family selling rubber is mocked by westerners, Bardamu is planted firmly in the Symbolic Order; by the end, when he is silenced by the absence of a western other, he has been pushed to the edge of the Symbolic Order so that it is now he himself who sets fire to the very material that introduced him to Africa.

Conclusion

Bardamu's status as a subject with regard to his now marginal position in the Symbolic Order raises an important question. Do we conclude that he is *not* a split subject because he has moved away from the censorship necessary to keep the Symbolic Order functioning smoothly? I would argue that the Symbolic Order's drive to reorganize and repress desire in a way that culture is then produced keeps Bardamu very much on the *inside* of the boundaries of the Symbolic Order. Bardamu and the natives do communicate by signs, but where the natives have their own language and culture, Bardamu is dispossessed by the loss of a western interlocutor, the other without whom there is no self. He is denied verbal communication and, positioned at the edge of the Symbolic Order, is left discursively homeless.

The natural reaction is therefore to leave Africa and go in search of Robinson who, as alter ago, holds out the only possibility of identity for Bardamu. The Symbolic Order, as the promise of a move towards language, becomes the mechanism by which Robinson's status as reified other silences Bardamu. When Jameson speaks of the Symbolic Order's power to humiliate the subject, one can look to the role of the western other embodied here by Robinson to see how it operates. Pushed to the limits of the Symbolic Order, Bardamu sets fire to his silence in order to regain language. The consequence of this destructive act is to pursue the other that is Robinson, thereby deciding Bardamu's status as a split subject unable to survive without the Symbolic Order.

Bardamu embodies the Symbolic Order's characteristic trait of continually ensuring the infinite division of the subject within culture, the guaranteed separation of self from other. Juliet Flower MacCannell notes that the *modus operandi* of the Symbolic Order is just this, that it "reminds us that the drive of culture is neither benevolent nor malevolent; it is a mindless, inexorable drive towards division, splitting. It is aimed, but only at producing, through this fission, the energy and the power to perpetuate itself."

The energy so vital to the Symbolic Order derives its heat from the "warm[th]" inherent in the tensions of the dialogical word. Bakhtin's work on dialogism has made possible this analysis of alterity in culture as it is represented by the Symbolic Order. Throughout his writings he speaks of the "boundary," perhaps nowhere more eloquently than in the following statement:

> The realm of culture has no internal territory; it is entirely distributed along the boundaries, boundaries pass everywhere, through its every aspect, the systematic unity of culture extends into the very atoms of cultural life, it reflects like the sun in each drop of that life. Every cultural act lives essentially on the boundaries: in this is its seriousness and its significance; abstracted from boundaries, it loses its soil, it becomes empty, arrogant, it degenerates and dies.

The emphasis Bakhtin places on the importance of boundaries to dialogical activity has been held up to a different light in this reading of ***Voyage au bout de la nuit.*** When examined discursively in Céline's text, the edges of the Symbolic Order's "drive of culture" resound with properties that define the ensnaring space of dialogism.

Andrea Loselle (essay date Spring 1993)

SOURCE: "Fading Images: The Touristic Itinerary and Spatial Representation in Céline's German Trilogy," in *Symposium: A Quarterly Journal in Modern Foreign Literatures,* Vol. XLVII, No. 1, Spring, 1993, pp. 16-35.

[*In the following essay, Loselle examines the narrative presentation of time and space in* Castle to Castle, North, *and* Rigadoon, *and Céline's role as a chronicler of historical reality and postwar tourist.*]

> *Imagine, Amalia, you're sitting in a room screening a film and the projector jams. Right in the middle of a cross fade between scenes. You see double. The frozen images of the scene just past, and the not-quite formed images of the next scene. If you live in changing times,* querida, *you get two of everything (diplostathmos). You get Ayatollahs and video cassettes. The sexual revolution and the Moral Majority. You bottle Coca Cola in Athens and you load Ritz Crackers on a 747 cargo jet headed to Montevideo.* (Chrono Jasuel, letter to his niece, translated from Esperanto, 41) . . .

In 1917, Hachette issued a reprint of its Guides-Joanne to Paris. Its editors stated in the introduction that they had hoped, as many had in 1914, that the war would be short lived, but the complete exhaustion of their stock of Paris guides had forced them by 1917 to issue a reprint during wartime. Except for minor changes to statistics and the addition of a few new museums and monuments, the editors took care to retain the guide as it was before World War I. They did, however, add a supplement "sur feuilles roses" dated April 15, 1917 with information on curtailed transportation services, higher tarifs, closed museums, and a more current point of interest, the Invalides, where one could view, among other war trophies and souvenirs on display, a "bombe jetée par un zepplin le 29 janvier 1916, et carte du théâtre de la guerre." The supplement does not say where the bomb had actually been dropped; all one is certain of is that it managed to land intact, as a defused museum artifact, within the walls of the Invalides.

One smiles at the mental picture of a war raging without a museum's walls and its harmless, touristic representation within, a feckless redundancy of what could at any minute fall from the sky and blast such displayed serenity to smithereens. But this image is also a retrospective bird's eye view of history in the making. The war as a past event was already being integrated into everyday life and would figure as another kind of spectacle staged behind glass. This observation is more palpable in light of the fact that the supplement is dated no later than nine days *after* the Americans officially declared war on Germany (April 6, 1917), a positive sign to the editors, perhaps, that the war might soon be brought to an end. An isolated, historical artifact representing two articulations, the guide approximates Chrono Jasuel's much later and more radical perception of changing times—a blurring of cultural difference—as a film frozen between two screens. Unlike the guide, the film's medium is a sign of technological advancement. Only stopping the film strip enables one to read, and thus reterritorialize, all the contradictory cultural juxtapositions.

The war in 1917 would figure prominently in the actual use of the guide, because the seventeen "promenades" mapped out in it could hardly be expected to function smoothly when most museums had closed and stored their treasures elsewhere for safekeeping, and transportation was irregular or, as in the case of the bus service, nonexistent; still, it would have been understandably impossible, the editors wrote, to tailor the guide "d'après l'état des choses actuel qui n'a d'ailleurs qu'un caractère transitoire, et varie d'un jour à l'autre." War and tourism are not, it would appear, concurrent activities despite the overlapping "feuilles roses," because war is transient, and tourism is its immobilized monumentalization. It would be difficult to map out and measure distances in the guide without the transportation channels and sites. The war would thus make the guide as a set of signs and markers uncommunicative and purposeless, prefiguring, perhaps, with the supplement itself a remapping, a new organization. The supplement, though originally a temporary representation of present conditions, nevertheless ends up in its own way on permanent display like the bomb and the map of the war theater. From this perspective, tourism makes war, after the fact, eminently "visitable" as an inert spectacle, a concept to which the Hachette guide caught between two states bears testimony.

Then again, whereas war and tourism are separate, consecutive activities, the tourist industry would gain much of its momentum from the war, because it boosted France's weakened, postwar economy. Furthermore, the war in its aftermath greatly enhanced the tourist trade through the creation and development of new paths and roads, and improved technology. Michelin launched its lucrative series of *guides verts* with a guide to the battlefields of the Great War. Tourism, then, was parasitic on the war's networks and sites. Realizing the great economic profits to be reaped from the tourist trade, the French government finally placed the Office National du Tourisme under the change of an Under Secretary of State for Tourism, Gaston Gérard, in 1928. More than ever before, tourism was, like war, a national concern. Tourism and war, therefore, are seen to coincide not on the level of event but on that of their organization and movement.

Turning to the aftermath of another war, the second, one finds the same dynamic of double images (war and tourism) of which this article's epigraph and the 1917 guide to Paris are exemplary but frozen parables. Nowhere is this more evident than in the context not of a guide but of a series of three novels, the German trilogy (***D'un château l'autre, Nord, Rigodon***), L. F. Céline's autobiographical narrative of his flight from Paris through Germany to Denmark at the close of the Second World War. Writing in the postwar France of the 1950s, Céline imagined war and tourism as intimately linked. They constitute two readings so parallel that they are often confused; the numerous references to war and tourism in the trilogy tend, for example, to obscure the narrator's identity. He is both an avowed chronicler (an anachronized historian) and a reluctant tourguide/tourist to the events and places of his history. Oscillating rapidly between his historical narrative and digressions into the present, the narrator registers confusion as to the nature of his narrative when he states: "maintenant nous voici en tourisme et pleine Histoire! . . ." Even though he consciously attempts to increase the temporal distance between his wartime experiences and their capitalist, touristic representation by taking on the identity of the "feudal" chronicler, the narrator has no control over changing times. For the reader, the temporal blurring, as in the example of the jammed projector, leads both to isolating and comparing frozen, past and present images, and to making him and her aware of a cultural acceleration that cannot be arrested.

If one compares the German trilogy to the Paris guide, it appears that the transition from war to tourism may have accelerated from one war to the next, making it thus possible for Céline to identify them more closely with one another. This is equally evident if one also reads the trilogy side by side with Céline's first novel, ***Voyage au bout de la nuit,*** which opens with the narrator's experience of the first war. Its style is far less fragmented and fast-paced, and its narrative structure is an uncomplicated chronological progression without shifts from past to present. The narrator, Bardamu, belongs to the cavalry and, although airplanes were a significant, new presence in World War I, they play no role in the novel. Subsequent chapters involve Bardamu's travels; these are not vacations, or even "working vacations," but travel based either on necessity (a job in Africa or at the Ford factory in Detroit) or on *discovery* (Bardamu arrives by boat in America). The trilogy's rapid style and temporal oscillations show that, as life accelerates through technological innovation, the world appears to shrink. And, as speed effaces space, it effaces the history of a time when space was strategic and invasions meant crossing and appropriating boundaries, not flying over them. Time as "contemplative" space, or as the distance one needs to perceive difference, disappears for both the chronicler and the tourist. Video cassettes next to Ayatollahs and Ritz Crackers loaded on a 747 jet headed for Montevideo are scrambled images caused by technological speed. Similarly, the confusion between chronicler and tourguide/tourist is predicated on acceleration.

Articulating the relationship between time and space through its representation in war and tourism uncovers the problematic of speed that lies at the core of the German trilogy. In the early 1950s, at the same time Céline was beginning the trilogy, a new field of study called "time-geography" appeared. Time-geography analyzes lifespans (or "biographies") as paths in temporal space; space, therefore, is "space over time." It maps out how much an individual accomplishes in the course of a day, a week, a year, and by what means one can "intensify" his or her temporal "paths" through speed and frequency. Just as speed is erasing space, tourism as a degraded speed aesthetic in the trilogy is, as I shall argue, not war immobilized, but it is based on war's organized form of "mobilization." It overtakes the narrative, that is, history itself.

The trilogy recounts the narrator's four-month stay at Sigmaringen, locus of the displaced Vichy government in 1944, his extended stay at "Zornhof," which he locates in northern Germany, and other short stops along the way. This flight is unavowedly motivated by the author's/narrator's anticipated prosecution by a military tribunal for wartime collaboration in France prior to his flight and stay at Sigmaringen. Neither pure fact nor fiction, Céline's chronicle is both a novelistic autobiography and a history related out of chronological sequence. The first book, ***D'un château l'autre,*** on the narrator's stay at Sigmaringen would, if placed in its proper chronological sequence, appear after the passage through Ulm in the third book, ***Rigodon.*** And the second book, ***Nord,*** with its major stops at Baden-Baden, Berlin, and "Moorsburg" ("Zornhof") would take the place of the first book, because these are the first stops in the narrator's itinerary.

Cut up into mostly short sections (not chapters), the trilogy entertains its readers with amusing anecdotes about Pétain's daily walks, his conversations with Pierre Laval, with other French collaborators (Paul Marion, Abel Bonnard, Fernand de Brinon, Alphonse de Chateaubriant), and with German officials (Otto Abetz), and doctors (Harras). But it also describes sudden bombardments, fire-bombed cities, masses of panic-stricken peoples, and carbonized victims. Like the narrator and his traveling companions—his wife Lili, the actor Robert Le Vigan, and the cat Bébert—everyone is frantically fleeing the Allies, either by hiding or by boarding overcrowded trains headed north beyond the reach of the Allies. As it crumbles beneath the Allied invasions and is gradually strangled by her ever shrinking defense lines, Nazi Germany becomes a shifting map of scurrying peoples of all nationalities, who can no longer make sense of their surroundings, who all carry false identity papers, and who, out of hunger and fear, become more and more "dislocated." They are all possessed, being literally dispossessed of their identities. When Céline, Lili and Le Vigan have new identity photos taken in Berlin, they discover that they no longer resemble their peacetime selves but rather disjointed, upside-down Picassos. Le Vigan, the actor, starts losing his mind when he repeatedly replays one of his film roles, Christ on the cross. Another character, Pretorius, thinks he can still hear Hitler's Nuremberg rally speeches. Lepers, madmen and professional assassins are also encountered on the way to Denmark and, toward the end of the journey, the narrator is even saddled with a band of nameless, retarded children.

Woven into the lighthearted anecdotes and hallucinatory confusion, the narrator constructs his self-defense. According to his version of the story, other compromised writers such as Montherlant and Morand escaped "persecution" (= prosecution); but Ferdinand alone is the sacrificial lamb, the "bouc providentiel," "la seule vraie ordure: Ferdinand!" as he writes his history, he laments that public opinion is "'anti-moi'." But, why Ferdinand must bear such seemingly excessive persecution appears to have very little to do with the virulent anti-Semitic pamphlet, ***Les Beaux draps,*** which he wrote and published in 1941 during the Occupation—not to mention the Occupation reprintings of the other two anti-Semitic pamphlets, ***Bagatelles pour un massacre*** (1937) and ***L'Ecole des cadavres*** (1939). Here he temporally obviates his crimes in the telling of events in that he only admits to a first crime that excludes his pamphlet-writing activities before his flight: "mais d'avoir quitté notre patrie qu'était notre fatal premier crime . . . le premier pas toujours qui compte! . . ." This step not only begins the trilogy but also negates the real motives behind his leaving France. The earlier "written" transgressions are blurred by this "first" step across the border, a physical, hence more seemingly obvious, political transgression.

Time also colors the way Céline states his case, which is, an accusation against his past and present treatment with a few nasty prophecies ("avec mes 'Nostradamus'") thrown in for good measure on the bleak future of the French race. The trilogy, then, provisionally breaks down into two oscillating moments: the narrative of the past flight and the discursive passages on present trials and tribulations. These intercalated discursive passages, or digressions, remind the reader that the narrative of past events falls under the category of "souvenirs payés," an expression which the reader must interpret in two ways: (1) as the memory of the narrator's personal sufferings coupled with his assertion that he has done his time in prison; (2) as the advances Brottin Achille (= Gaston Gallimard) has given the narrator for his "memoirs," that is, the trilogy. The narrator receives no *congés payés* for his labor: "que je lui [Achille] dois des sommes et des sommes, qu'il dit! *homo deliquensis,* j'ai dit! . . ." He is perpetually indebted to his editor, who at various points in the trilogy, sends emissaries (Norbert Loukoum [= Jean Paulhan] and Roger Nimier) to check up on his progress. The economic, temporal doubling in *souvenirs payés* further relieves the narrator of the burden of his guilt, because it leads the reader away from the other possible telling of history centered on cause and effect (he fled *because* he knew he was guilty) and substitutes in its place a personal chronology characterized by eyewitness testimony, succession of events, and digression. The gist of the chronicler's temporal indebtedness—real Nietzschean *Schuld*—is that writing history is an interpretive strategy of power and, as we shall see later, such a strategy would ideally be one that succeeds in maintaining a stable place not to be consumed by the passing moment and against which one is not forced to pay installments: "les dettes, si vous êtes ministre, ne comptent pas . . . ." Only the victors appear to have won the right to institute and live comfortably off their history. As one of the vanquished, the narrator is faced with the threat of being economically excluded from the ruling or official version of history and thus makes it clear that he intends to tell his story in another way: through the anachronistic voice of the feudal chronicler, an historian who has lived the history he recounts. He emphatically writes, "moi chroniqueur des Grands Guignols, je peux très honnêtement vous faire voir le très beau spectacle que ce fut, la mise à feu des forts bastions. . . ."

The models Céline uses and cites, both in the trilogy and in the numerous interviews conducted as he was writing his work, come from the Middle Ages and the Renaissance as well as from the seventeenth century. At that time memoirs and histories were still not clearly differentiated. As "exemplary" histories, chronicles and memoirs would come to be considered as too subjective and moralizing, and therefore less objectively reliable than the "scientific" histories representative of nineteenth-century historiography. Céline's chosen chroniclers and memorialists, Froissart, Joinville, Commynes, Montluc, Tallemant de Réaux and their sources and models, Caesar and Tacitus, all left ample room for what Céline in one interview calls "affabulation," obliging him, he concedes, to call his work a novel. "L'air du temps," which the trilogy's chronicler struggles to convey, will be construed as subjective.

To make the reader see the spectacle in modern day, post-war France, Céline relies not so much on the mere power of literature to re-present past events as on a strategy to make literature theorize (as spectacle) "historical reality" as a contemporary cultural construct. For the "truth" of evidence is subsumed by another—tautological—proof, the chronicler's own inability to prove that the people he remembers were real: "la preuve le mal que j'ai moi-même à vous donner un petit peu de preuves, que ces personnes furent bien réelles et agissantes, plaignez le pauvre chroniqueur! . . ." The rare, strategic appearance of the literary tense of the *passé simple* makes it even clearer that the chronicler's history is so remote that it lacks the weight of live memory and becomes no more than an object, a dusty *souvenir* of forgotten times. His evidence is his memory, which has no official place precisely because it is deemed subjective. Memory is more literary than literature, which, in the first instance, was like a self-defensive maneuver explicitly pitted against cause-and-effect history. The spectacle cannot therefore accede to the level of event as historical evidence but only to the level of potential touristic spectacle, which Céline sees as a spectacle degraded by capitalist organization and appropriation. Ultimately, seeing the spectacle is seeing a defenseless self-defense. The chronicler's history is doomed to be misread, because his strategy against historical knowledge as instituted event is simultaneously undermined by modern history's often unacknowledged double, tourism.

Tourism is the pervasion of historical spectacle at its most formal and controlled. As Dean MacCannell's book shows, tourism functions semiotically, relating sites to their markers. Furthermore, like written historical interpretation, tourism is oriented toward monumentalization; and it will be the trilogy's acknowledged task to maintain, if it can, the difference between its own monumentalization as authentic, lived experience, and tourism's monumentalization as staging and simulation. Tourism will, therefore, threaten to invade the trilogy and make it something else. The inevitability of this struggle lies in the fact that it is the modern tourist, the narrator's interlocutor, who reads the history. The reader as tourist (and vice versa) is not, however, to be construed as a superficial reader of cultural and historical artifacts; on the contrary, he is a participant in a cultural practice: "The tourist comports himself 'as if' he has seen the things he has visited. It is through sightseeing that he enters into a relationship to society." The cultural and historical artifacts that the tourist visits reaffirm in their organization and presentation the social context that places the tourist not in the past, but in the present (reading as recognition).

This "reading" (a "spectacular" theory) will undermine the chronicler's account, which as a genre, according to Hayden White, "represents it [historical reality] as if real events appeared to human consciousness in the form of unfinished stories." Although the absence of closure would appear to safeguard living memory against the dead souvenir, the trilogy radicalizes White's *as if* and closes it, because the chronicle is an avowed generic fiction, an anachronism having no place in the present. Consequently the tourist's formal "as if," emphasized in MacCannell's semiotic study, is forced both to collide and to coincide with the chronicler's lived "as if." What precludes the success of the chronicler's labors, one notes, is the present, which White describes in temporal terms as an unfinished story. Danto points out, however, that "a statement about the past is a covert prediction of the outcome of an historical inquiry." As the outcome posited by the trilogy, tourism, a new history, privileges spatial organization over time so that the chronicle will be both denied and given a place. Finally, tourism will end up theorizing literature as semiotic leisure instead of work.

On the one hand the chronicler pits his fading, anachronistic world against the vulgar tourist world: "le tourisme, l'aventure sont des ornements de la Paix, qu'on m'en parle pas en ce temps de guerre! . . . ; "Tout n'a pas toujours été touristique, hélicoptère et salles de bains, hôtesses 'pin-up' comme de nos jours. . . ." On the other hand, writing on the past turns the chronicler into a guide and the reader into a tourist, so that even the chronicler's history is ultimately touristic: "Ça vaut la peine, puisque nous sommes en touristes, que je vous parle un peu des trésors tapisseries, boiseries, vaisselles, salles d'armes . . . ." Only through tourism, it seems, is the reader able to "relate" to the chronicler's experience of the collapse of Nazi Germany. In referring to his subsequent incarceration in Denmark, the chronicler will have to insist that he has done some tourism, too: "j'ai même fait du tourisme tel quel, en autobus grillagé. . . ." He even calls the handcuffs he had to wear *"sight-seeing* menottes." Statements blurring the distinction between chronicler and tourist/tourguide far exceed those attempts to retain the distinction partly because, as mentioned earlier, the chronicler uses the confusion to effect transitions between the past and the present. In addition, addressing *us* puts the chronicler in the compromised position of being chronicler and guide at once. Nevertheless, these transitions are fraught with implied differences in that two visual values are presented in the guises of the eyewitness and the sightseer (*"sight-seeing* menottes" is within this context an oxymoron). The chronicler and the tourist are also two different economic types of traveler: the wartime traveler (*souvenirs payés*) and the off- time, vacation traveler (*congés payés*). Furthermore, two different speeds predicated on the difference between authentic and reproducible semiotic experience explicitly distinguish the past from the present: the war-torn chronicler's meticulous process of the "remémoration" of his old-fashioned war and the tourist's accelerated, package tour. As two different readings, the chronicle and tourism are consequently two separate representations. They meet where the identification between chronicler and tourist forms the figural "deterritorialization" of the chronicler's history spurred by the problematic of writing history in the modern present.

Thus, the trilogy's history does not encompass just the chronicler's past but France's past, from the time of Caesar, Tacitus, and the Crusades to the present. Repeatedly opposing his cumbersome genealogy to the tourist's quick, superficial "take" on it, the chronicler is weighed down by his origins, the tradition out of which he writes and the long, repetitive histories of the campaigns of the "hunters" and the "hunted" criss-crossing the map of western Europe. Yet, if tourism is pervasive, then the chronicle can only be read as a tour guide and historical monument to the past sights/ sites of collision and bloodshed, like the first post-WWI Michelin guide. Thus, the chronicler and his companions keep turning into tourists of their own flight, if only because tourism consistently invades the narrative of the past: "Moi, mes cannes, Lili, Bébert, nous voici touristes. . . ." Bombed-out Berlin is more like a Hollywood stage set ("c'était une ville plus qu'en décors . . .") or a fantasized re-presentation of the war, where all the peoples passing through are tourists and not participants: "où sont les autres voyageurs? . . . '*sight-seeing*'? . . . *new-Berlin*? . . ." Pretorius asks Ferdinand and his companions if they are in Berlin "'en touristes.'" A getaway train headed north is "ce tourisme 'stratégique spécial'. . . ." Writing and reading history are equivalent to the secondary invasion of the tourist industry: first the barbarian hordes and war, then the tourist hordes. Touristic secondary invasion in the history itself turns the chronicler's memories into signs that no longer correspond to history, that is, the "real" events, but to a touristic reading that is perceptible in the difference the chronicler draws between, for example, two pictorial representations or "spectacles": the tapestry and the comic strip.

The tapestry is his preferred visualization of what writing history is: "le mieux je crois, imaginez une tapisserie, haut, bas, travers, tous les sujets à la fois et toutes les couleurs . . . tous les motifs! . . . tout sens dessus dessous! . . . prétendre vous les présenter à plat, debout, ou couchés, serait mentir . . . la vérité: plus aucun ordre en rien du tout à partir de cet attentat [the attempt on Hitler's life] . . . ." The experience of disorganized simultaneity juxtaposed to the linear organization of a chronology makes the chronicler wonder why he cannot "coudre tout de traviole" as painters and musicians do. He would like his history to be more an unmediated spectacle than a reading. Roger Nimier, the persistent editor from Gallimard, will later give the despondent, overworked chronicler a solution both to writing his memoirs more quickly and to making them sell better in modern France. He tells him to use the comic strip in his chronicle to replace large chunks of his writing: " 'trois . . . quatre images par chapitre . . . chapitres 'contractés' . . . trois lignes pour cinquante des vôtres, habituelles . . . .'" The chronicler listens sceptically to the solution, and then rejects it because a popular, fragmented style *à trois points* is the chronicler's trademark. His rapid, exclamatory style would, in effect, be an element guaranteeing the authenticity and labor behind his history.

A comic strip, a linear series of pictures, is the literature of the future: "'*comics! comics*! pas dix ans que tout sera *aux comics!* . . . sens unique! . . . , exclaims Nimier, and not, as the chronicler wishes, "tout sens dessus dessous! . . ." It would also be a trivialized modern version of one of the functions of the tapestry, the commemoration of an event—like the popular assumption that the relatively belated appearance of Vietnam comics meant that the American public had finally learned to put behind itself the shame of defeat and mythologize its experience of that war. Such commemorative tapestries, like the comic strip, would sometimes consist of a series of panels telling the story of a particular historical or mythological event (e.g., the Bayeux tapestries); but for Céline, the tapestry stands for the chronicler's privileged representation of his singular experience of events in his style, whereas the comic strip is a metaphor for changing times. Through the tapestry the chronicler attempts to create a spatial, nonchronological dimension to time. What happens to the chronicler, however, is that no sooner does he call up the example of the tapestry, than his carefully embroidered history turns into a comic strip, a secondary invasion: "fines tapisseries, broderies d'astuces, le style, j'en suis! (. . .) je vous laisse en plan, et mes *comics!* . . . ." His "comic" irony uncovers the fatality of his imagery and style. Since the tapestry was posited as a model of simultaneity and style, the threatened confusion of comics with the tapestry appears to bring the representation of time and chronology back into focus as the advent of a stripped down "'style étiquette,'" a comic pastime and not tragic, time past.

As Roger Nimier well understands, the consequence of the confusion is "capital." The problem for the feudal chronicler, as he looks with dismay upon capitalist modernity, is that history, the one he lived, has turned into tourism. The economic principle dictating the use of the old battlegrounds for the tourist armies is parallel to the transition between the time-consuming, meticulous creation of the one-of-a-kind tapestry and the mass-produced, infinitely reproducible comic strip. Tourism feeds off history by transforming it into an economic value. The transition from war maneuvers, flight, wandering hordes of refugees, or any kind of war travel to tourist travel is accelerated with a speed commensurate with the escalation of the cost of living. The chronicler too, needs hard cash, because he has some real debts to pay off. As much as he may critique the tourist world, he is nevertheless capitalizing on it through his history and making value exchanges in the form of his *souvenirs payés.* Caught up in the momentum of his needs and the comic strip world, his fear that his account will become pure appearance and disappear is justified: he, too, is actively participating in the system of fetishized values that effaces and deterritorializes his own history.

The ironic originality of the trilogy's critique of tourism as part of an escalating movement, and this just as the trilogy is becoming touristic, is that it consistently brings tourism in to succeed and to precede war. Each interval of touristic peacetime promises a technologically more advanced war and new invasions of foreign hordes, like the Chinese "invasion" prophesied by the chronicler. Similarly, each war promises a technologically more effective tourist industry: after the Franco-Prussian War, the massive World Exhibition of 1900; World War I, and trench warfare bring the airplane and the *guide vert,* better organized and faster tourism; World War II and Blitzkrieg are followed by superjets, helicopters and "pinup" stewardesses. Travel and speed are the key elements supporting this hypothesis because wars, from the chronicler's point of view, are first of all travel: "Dans les très vieilles chroniques on appelle les guerres autrement: voyages des peuples . . . ." The two terms, war and voyage, are interchangeable because they belong to the same principle of invasion. "Peoples" travel either in economic warfare or in armed warfare.

For Céline, the proof of this continuation is travel and speed, because peoples are always on the move. The reasons for war, then, are pure inventions: "ce qui n'existe pas ils l'inventent! on a inventé les Croisades n'est-ce pas?" Europe, the chronicler keeps repeating, is nothing but a vast Roman arena of gratuitous massacre, where participation is mandatory because the civilian in modern warfare is also a target. Total participation is underscored by the use of the word "peuples"; for, despite the posited effacement of territorial boundaries, peoples are representations of cultural boundaries and territories to be invaded and conquered. Yet, each war employs a newer, more efficient technology, which in peacetime is rationalized into ideological progress as the (touristic) abolition of boundary: " 'Mais c'est pour ça que les guerres existent! . . . le progrès! plus de distances! plus de passeports!'" War, the first motive for travel, a prime mover, is the true progressive factor, not peace: "En vrai, un continent sans guerre s'ennuie . . . sitôt les clairons, c'est la fête! . . . grandes vacances totales! et au sang! . . . de ces voyages à plus finir! . . ." More efficient strategies and technological inventions emerge from war, only to organize touristic warfare in peacetime on the same disputed battlefields, "les Arènes d'Europe!"

The oscillation between past and present in the trilogy serves this dual critique of war and tourism. The title of the first book of the trilogy, ***D'un château l'autre,*** for example, reflects the series of rapid, temporal transitions between war and tourism that occurs within the narrative, because a *château* is either a prison or a castle: from prison (Sigmaringen, where Pétain's Vichy government was held against its will) to castle (the chronicler's tour of the treasures and portraits in the Hohenzollern castle), to prison (the laborers and the chronicler are prisoners of Zornhof), to castle (not a place the chronicler says that he would recommend to tourists because it is not picturesque), to prison (Vestre Faegnsel prison in Denmark), to castle ("*sight-seeing* menottes"). These transitions would closely resemble the recent conversion of the Berlin "no-trespassers" Wall into the Berlin "welcome" Wall. But modern war, the chronicler adds, has gained too much momentum. This assertion is represented by the chronicler's own transitional speed where even the preposition *à* is absent from the title of the first book to reflect the intensification of the quick changeovers. There can be no contemplative moments, no intervals of inert time, no space and no place to hide when nuclear Vesuviuses can be set off and multiplied at great speed with the mere push of a button:

> dans un autre genre, bien mémorable, j'ai vu ce qu'on ne reverra jamais: les grandes manoeuvres de cavalerie, 1913, du camp de Cercottes, déploiements, mouvements tournants en fourrageurs, sept divisions! . . . à la trompette! . . . l'héros de l'avenir sera envoyé immobile, ficelé au poteau, bâillonné, lancé dans la stratosphère, aura juste le temps de faire pipi, tour de la terre! et hop! . . . chez lui! . . . plus fera de tours, plus sera héros!

At Zornhof (= the House of Wrath) in the second book, ***Nord,*** the chronicler writes that only the rich and powerful have the luxury of endless space and contemplation. Musing on the mansion's vantage point over a vast, nondescript terrain where he can watch hordes of refugees traveling from the East, West and South, he writes: "y avait un certain envoûtement à regarder ces étendues, ces terres ocre, un charme . . . on massacre ses heures . . . il faut être riche et tranquille pour s'occuper de l'horizon . . . ." This is also the economically liberated vantage point from which the chronicler would ideally like to write his history. It is, in fact, from a similar (but much less exalted and needy) position that the chronicle is launched: from the window of Madame Niçois, his patient, overlooking the Seine. The chronicler establishes himself at the outset as a voyeur, a stationary eye. Yet, he still faces the problem of how to write his chronicle when the momentum of the modern world consumes and effaces it as it is being written:

> transposez alors! . . . poétisez si vous pouvez! mais qui s'y frotte? . . . nul! . . . voyez Goncourt! . . . là la fin de tout! . . . de toutes et tous! . . . 'ils ne transposaient plus' . . . à quoi servaient les croisades? . . . ils se transposaient! . . . depuis ils se font éjecter, de Passy, leur seizième étage, par super-jet conditionné, direct Golgatha . . . sept minutes . . . photographiés aux 'Oliviers' . . . Monsieur en Joseph . . . Madame en Marie (. . .) retour avant l'apéritif! . . . depuis que chaque homme moteur au cul, va où il veut, comme il veut, sans jambes, sans tête, il n'est plus qu'une baudruche, un vent . . . il ne disparaîtra même pas, c'est fait. . . .

Literature, war, tourism, and speed are all triggered by "transposer," a term Céline has used before—beginning with his first pamphlet, ***Bagatelles pour un massacre*** (1937)—to describe his *style émotif.* This time, the word "transposer" serves as a global critique. The crusades were travel (transposition as displacement), and the old chroniclers transposed these displacements, that is, wrote about them with style. Transposition, therefore, also means being able to take one's time to invent a style. Touristic displacements are not true transpositions, because speed consumes the space and time needed to write an authentic, lived experience. Instead, people are disappearing into a speed zone as the motors that carry them off eliminate any necessity for physical exertion and thought. Paradoxically, movement is an immobilizing force, in that it makes space and time not relative but irrelevant, like watching a film from a stationary position. The car, for example, "c'est une façon de sortir du Temps, des gens, et de l'espace . . . ." The trilogy's chronicler is caught somewhere in the middle, transposing his transpositions in an intensified speed zone where style is disappearing. The result, like the instance of the comic strip, appears comic rather than tragic. The chronicler envies tragedians such as Racine and Sophocles, because their tragedies could take their time to reach a tragic end with just a little incest plot to go on. Then he adds: "les anciens temps étaient jouisseurs (. . .) maintenant je vous demande: un continent à effacer? . . . affaire de deux . . . trois minutes! . . . Here once again, the chronicler begins with a discussion of style and literature and ends with a comment on the antithetical nature of speed and style.

Commenting on the relationship between speed and the writing of history, Paul Virilio has underlined the temporal significance of the chronicler's time when history and its writing were complementary:

> In fact, history progresses at the speed of its weapons systems. At the end of the fifteenth century, it is still for Commynes a stable memory, a model to be reproduced. Annals are seasonal, like the war that returns every year in springtime. Linear time is eliminated, as it was from the ancient fortress in which "the enemy Time" was beaten by the static resistance of the construction materials—by duration.

Memory and monument are counterposed to linear time, calling up once again the tapestry metaphor for style and simultaneity and the comic strip as the suggested means to replace parts of the narrative. Linearity is disrupted in the trilogy so that its history might sustain its monumentality; a strict adherence to chronology would, like a film, play into speed's momentum. Unlike the touristic monument, the trilogy, as a monument threatened with becoming touristic, is more actively strategic (Céline the self-proclaimed pacifist is, in his own way, always at war). Disrupting the chronological sequence of events will paradoxically stabilize and "spatialize" the chronicler's memory by turning it into the model of history as a repetitive, *cyclical* phenomenon.

Thus the chronicler's memory is not so much that of human consciousness, as Hayden White argues, but rather of the conversion of the chronicler into a fixed point of historical density, into a timeless geography that circumscribes a space from which the chronicler can attack and retreat at will. The effect of recounting the itinerary of his flight out of chronological sequence—and the reader is frequently reminded that the order was deliberately changed—is the isolation of the two *places* where the chronicler stayed the longest, Sigmaringen and Zornhof, which occupy nearly all of the first two books, ***D'un château l'autre*** and ***Nord.*** The third book, ***Rigodon,*** however, proceeds rapidly from one train station to the next, skipping over the comparatively lengthy stay at Sigmaringen; and it is in this book that, predictably, many of the chronicler's observations on speed and tourism occur. Such a strategy is what one could not see were one to see a map of the trilogy's itinerary. That is, perhaps, one reason why no one, especially Céline, has ever made one. A map would be a comic strip "correcting" the narrative by reinterpreting and metrically measuring it into a strict itinerary. This would be the very opposite of what the chronicler wishes to do, which is to "sew" everything "de traviole."

The absence of the map stems from the familiar opposition in Céline's work (beginning with the pamphlets) between authentic and inauthentic experience. In ***Bagatelles pour un massacre,*** Céline draws a distinction between *lycéens* whose emotions are merely *lues* and students of the *école* *communale* whose emotions are lived hence *vues*. To describe the mediated emotions of the *lycéens*, Céline uses the metaphor of the road map. Using a road map to culture, as would a tourist, means that emotion has not been experienced firsthand. Even though one must *read* the trilogy to get a sense of the chronicler's particular *vue*, the opposition between things seen and things read is retained in the trilogy. The absence of a map suppresses the touristic, semiotic reading that favors the rhetorical metaphor of history as a disorganized, simultaneous set of events experienced first hand. Céline's style is geared to resist appropriative representation as touristic transposition.

What the map cannot reflect, in addition, is the strategic *viewpoint* (a spatial rhetoric) that Sigmaringen and Zornhof share in common: the former is a castle from which a dynasty once ruled its fief ("repaire berceau du plus fort élevage de fieffés rapaces loups d'Europe!"; the latter is a mansion overlooking a modern fief where *bibelforscher* (Jehovah's witnesses or conscientious objectors), gypsies and prisoners of scattered nationalities are forced to farm the endless beet fields and where the quixotic Rittmeister disappears with his trusty mare on an ill-fated, imaginary campaign. The Hohenzollern castle at Sigmaringen and the Zornhof mansion have dominion over their fiefs and are centers from which their dominion is enforced. As Virilio writes in *Speed and Politics*, a fief is an ancient battleground upon which the Frankish conqueror erected his castle as a kind of look-out tower. The Crusades, the Hundred Years' War, and civil wars such as the Thirty Years' War are all feudal troops on the march with stopping points: from castle to castle. Thus space was regulated as a strategic element of war so that dispersion could always be centralized or centralization could always be dispersed.

In any case, the maneuvers, like the chronicler's nostalgic reference to the maneuvers of the French cavalry of World War I, were stable and repeatable. The power-to-invade schema appears to hold the same through the centuries, but modern technology disrupts the stability of the schema without annihilating the power by subtracting space or territory from its functioning. Movement is no longer tactical, a question of strategic view-points and terrains, but technical, a question of who will get there first. In this dynamic, space is always convertible, emptiable or fillable. One might conclude from this analysis of speed and space that Céline, ever the unrepentant, racist reactionary, would favor a return to feudalism to counter the capitalist predicament of his indebtedness. But this hasty conclusion would forestall investigating the fate of his style, if only because the chronicler's half-serious prophecies of France being invaded by Asiatic hordes do not suggest that he is susceptible to such "utopic" idealism.

If space used to be a safety net, a viewpoint from which one could transcend the course of history and write, then the state of speed without space, that is, "deterritorialization," suggests, too, that language has been let loose (deterritorialized) to follow a course of proliferating, detachable signs to be emptied or filled according to need. For in the trilogy "true" writing is always nostalgically associated with an anchored style and having a contemplative space in which to develop that style. Language is a bygone look-out tower, an example of which can be verified in a saying—itself a viewpoint found in a book of "detached" sayings—by Anatole France: "La géographie et la chronologie sont les deux yeux de l'histoire" (*Dictionnaire des proverbes, sentences et maximes,* Larousse). The chronicler would lament that one of these eyes has been poked out, so that what the saying says no longer functions as a stabilizing look-out tower and topples over. In other words, both language *and* travel (historical and touristic) are now principles of pure, intensified movement.

By their very movement, war and tourism set the conditions for the possibility of another kind of communication which, in its banality, takes on a "reality" of its own. This reality, the ideology one takes for reality, would be none other than progress itself as the kind of accelerated movement inherent in the approach of "time-geography." One notes that, in the trilogy, the original, feudal meaning of "banal" (pertaining to the suzerain's district or his "ban") has ironically lost all boundary and definition, spreading into undifferentiated, convertible space as touristic "banalization." "Biographies" in this regard are a suppression of the event in favor of metrically measurable life-span paths. Faced with this predicament, in his equally fast and escalating style, Céline predicts the advent of an accelerated war of the "same": "demain vous verrez les mêmes, rassemblés en souks au Kremlin, Russie, à la Maison-Blanche, U.S.A., une autre guerre en plein! . . . dix, vingt Hiroshima par jour . . ." or "comme demain re-ici! . . ." The power of language, like its power to say ten, twenty Hiroshimas a day, is trivializing, not stabilizing. This particular power makes tourism in the trilogy a logical counterpart to modern war. Thus it follows that, if tourism is the new history, history is caught up in progress, thus converting this once-stable field, at least from Céline's embittered point of view, into an organized, touristic war machine: "Histoire! Géotechnie! . . ."

In a present that tends to invent—like Céline, with a certain morbid delight—its temporal "end" in nuclear disaster (even though the world has yet to experience a nuclear war), it seems strange that the loss of space does not carry as significant an affective charge. In narratives involving travel (flight, adventure, journey, epic) organized by an itinerary, space is usually less important than the temporal progress of the itinerary. Time does not really change even though journeys take less time. What has changed is space; and the less space there is over time the more porously touristic the experience of space becomes. Céline's German trilogy allows itself to become touristic so that we, as tourists, might take the time to become readers of irredeemable space and not of our temporal fictions. If, as the chronicler claims, style is an endangered species, the life of his work, as labor and not leisure, depends upon space.

Yves Pagès (essay date Spring 1994)

SOURCE: "Céline and Anarchist Culture," in *South Atlantic Quarterly,* Vol. 93, No. 2, Spring, 1994, pp. 321-31.

[*In the following essay, Pagès examines right-wing extremism and libertarian discourse in Céline's writing. According to Pagès, "the momentum of anarchic subversion that surfaces in Céline's fiction almost imperceptibly valorizes certain ethical or existential perspectives that are by nature antiauthoritarian."*]

It is important to remember one's first impressions of a book. When I first read ***Voyage au bout de la nuit*** at the age of sixteen, I felt as though I were entering into an uncensored language, one that bypasses the usual split between the spoken and the written; above all, I felt as though I had encountered a work whose rebellious nature and resistance to social norms had more confused the boundaries between poetry and politics. Soon after, I learned that the author, who had described ***Voyage*** as a text that was "too anarchistic," if not the only novel of the century to have a "communist soul," had, since 1937, also written three anti-Semitic pamphlets and had thus effectively collaborated, at least by writing these impassioned tracts, in the xenophobic massacre of the 1940s. From then on, we needed only to choose our side. For some people, Céline was the inspired destroyer of the dominant order, the acerbic critic of "the end of the night" of modern misery. For others, he was the filthy loudmouth, author of racist slurs and herald of the imminent massacre. It was thus necessary to forget one or the other, if not to reclaim one instead of the other, since his work seemed to be forever irreconcilable with itself. Unlike Rimbaud, who destroyed his pen so that he could become an arms dealer, Céline left us an oeuvre that is neither incomplete nor repudiated. On the contrary, it oscillates between several incompatible impulses that Céline, the genius of one or two books, would definitely have subordinated to the level of unresolvable ideological debates. After reading ***Guignol's Band,*** however, it seemed to me that this schematic view of the Célinean dilemma missed the essential point. Published in 1944, just a few years after his racist pamphlets, Céline's English saga continued the insidious undermining initiated in ***Voyage;*** this was accomplished by the double critique of dominant social norms and of the registers of literary writing. Thanks to his obsessive rhetoric, the emergence of anti-Jewish, anti-black, anti-homosexual, anti-communist banalities did not diminish the rebellious spirit of his first book. The anti-Semitic ranter did not replace the iconoclastic novelist; from beginning to end, they more or less coexisted, constructing, work by work, an ambivalent oeuvre that was often contradictory and wrought by political turmoil.

As ambivalent as it may be, this Célinean ideological jumble is not timeless; it belongs to a very specific period. Its reactionary or leftist temptations are related to an important historical time lag produced by World War I. In his fiction, Céline never stopped reproducing the frozen, nostalgic image of the early 1900s as an Eden, in addition to feeding his racist obsession with a visionary pacificism taken from his apocalyptic lessons in murderous bellicosity. In other words, he polemically interpreted and fictionally transposed the epochs through which he lived not according to the political divisions of the 1930s and 1940s, but by means of a double psychic universe: the idealism of the pre-1914 world and the trauma of the Great War.

If we were to try to locate the links between, for example, Drieu la Rochelle's or Barbusse's ideology and Céline's, we would run the risk of missing the true stakes of the latter's ideology. By returning to the sources of the extremist discourses specific to the years 1871-1914, however, we can examine the raw forms of the two original tropes in Céline's political statements. The first comes from an ultra-right-wing discourse that enjoyed a brief popularity amidst the racist fervor of the Dreyfus affair and was given a second wind during the early 1900s by numerous ultra-patriotic, corporatist, and racist movements. The second evolves within a composite libertarian discourse driven by a variety of forces, from anarchic unionism to radical individualism, which attained its moment of glory in the 1890s before gradually declining during the belle époque. The resurgence of a pre-1914 xenophobic and generally reactionary discourse in Céline's pamphlets of 1937-41 and in his post-1945 novels is clear. This discourse contributes to a fundamental coherence in Céline's work that is impossible to ignore. It still remains to be seen whether the libertarian resurgence of the early 1900s, the relatively unknown side of the pre-Célinean political universe, furnishes his work with another sort of coherence.

We can discern three axes within the remnants of libertarian thought: the *critique of normative knowledge,* which is based on the denunciation of the dominant scholarly and academic cultures; *the critique of the notion of progress,* which is characterized by a certain defiance toward the cult of mechanized and alienating work; and *the critique of the working class* and its proletarian messianism, which is linked to a rejection of the oppressive laws of social conformity and of the idea of class consciousness. But this schematic classification poses a new problem. These three axes essentially resume beating, term for term, the dead horses specific to the themes found in pre-1914, ultra-right-wing discourse: anti-intellectualism, which critiqued the decadence of the democratic intelligentsia in the name of a more or less aristocratic elitism; reactionary antiprogressivism, which rejected Enlightenment thought and applauded the return to ancien régime values; and moralistic antimaterialism, which denied class antagonism in the name of a systematic and corporatist conception of national community. The convergence of anarchic and ultra-right-wing foundations in Céline's work is not simply a coincidence. The referential ambivalences of his extremisms seem to share a single ideological core, which the historian Zeev Sternhell labels "pre-fascist" in his book *Ni droite, Ni gauche.* One could say that, thirty years later, Céline returned to the sources of the revolutionary right's laboratory of ideas by going down the same convoluted paths of this initial synthesis between the antidemocratic left of the post-Dreyfus era and the moral neocorporatism of the Action Française. Céline in turn used the pretext of rhetorical anarchy in order to camouflage the ultra-right-wing essence of his texts. His seemingly ideological contradictions thus conform to the framework of a superseding coherence, that of the "national populism" of the turn of the century.

This a priori, seductive hypothesis seems nonetheless to omit an essential aspect of Célinean ambiguity. In Céline's work, fascinating polemical filiations tend to become purely backward-looking, conservative, and racist litanies without giving rise to any new, right-wing system of values. His reactionary babbling does not become truly Pétainist or pro-Nazi enthusiasm, giving his blessing to family, work, and triumphant Aryanism. The only gesture that his satirical verve borrows from ultra-right-wing thought is that of a totally self-contained, redundant denunciation: "a system of hostilities with no way out." Céline does not follow this positive element found within the fascist agenda, the Spartan utopia that for certain people included the notions of eugenics and pan-Europeanism; in fact, he embraces only their rage for nihilist devalorization. It is thus essential that we ask ourselves if the libertarian affinities of his discourse do not also feed a voracious, critical negativity. It is not a question of simply detecting the slightest "revolutionary" positivity in the sense of a collective, social emancipation; however, it does seem that the momentum of anarchic subversion that surfaces in Céline's fiction almost imperceptibly valorizes certain ethical or existential perspectives that are by nature antiauthoritarian.

The critique of scholarly and academic norms of knowledge manifested in all of Céline's work seems at first to exist for the sake of a socio-literary exchange value: authenticity. In opposition to the professional dilettante, Céline offers the model of an "authentic" author who attempts to reconcile the existence of the narrator with the idealized life of his characters. This model closely resembles that of the proletarian writer glorified in the late 1920s by Barbusse or Poulaille. But, in the final analysis, we see that Céline's work does not follow this agenda of social realism, which is supposed to represent the misery of working-class conditions while actively participating in its fight for emancipation. A stranger to this literary valorization of class consciousness, Céline, like the Paris Commune writer Jules Vallès before him, uses authenticity as a stylistic weapon. As antibourgeois as it may claim to be, this weapon challenges only a single experience, either marginal or "irregular," which is in perpetual opposition to the classical, mimetic, and conformist uses of the dominant language. This is where Céline gets his repeated praise—that is to say, for "direct emotion"—which, associated with his verbal lynching of the so-called sophisticated intelligentsia in ***Bagatelles,*** tends to be mistaken for the irrational and anti-intellectual rhetoric of a Barrès and his fascistic spiritual sons. However, in Céline's novels, on the periphery of the pamphleteer's diatribes against the dominant cultural cartels, we sense the emergence of figures who can be seen as alternatives to knowledge: the "bohemians" and "inventors" of ***Death on the Installment Plan;*** the visionaries and street musicians of ***Guignol's Band;*** or the wanderers and vagabonds who appear throughout his work. These contrasting silhouettes converge in the virtually clandestine model of the autodidact, the person who has reappropriated culture without passing through the mediation of a uniform, scholarly knowledge. It is in this way that the characterization of the intellectual, who is systematically deconstructed, does not culminate in a purely "emotional" nihilism, but rather in the covert revalorization of a type of apprenticeship without master—the autodidacticism that was one of the characteristic traits of the anarchic ideas in circulation at the beginning of the century. Within the unofficial culture of these libertarian spheres, it is possible to distinguish three particular pre-Célinean cases: the artisans, who acquire partial savoir-faire; the vagabonds, who, in pursuing their itinerant experiences, survive by means of an eclectic knowledge; and the orphans and social outcasts, who waver between various skewed registers of knowledge. We must add that slang, the corporate language of laborers, the idiom of hoboes, and the debased linguistic register of all marginal people, constituted a privileged, minor art of anarchic discourse during the belle époque. The critique of normative knowledge thus leads to a principal model that is subversive in a constructive way: the autodidact's existential fusion of knowledge.

In Céline's work, like that of Vallès, the satire of intellectual conformity is fomented by a violent diatribe against the educational system. For the anarchists of the early 1900s, school was like an "antechamber of the barracks," a place for "licking into shape," a place of "pesky, puritan, and sullen oppression"; for Céline, school emblematizes "the disaster of enchantment [*féerie*]." These parallel attacks inevitably conclude in a purely negative critique, which closely resembles, once again, the ultra-right-wing harangues against "state education." Nevertheless, a number of Céline's novels depict the childlike extravaganzas that seem to survive the wreckage of this failed academic space: the "Meanwell College" episode in ***Death on the Installment Plan;*** that of the "Orphans of the Red Cross" in ***Castle to Castle;*** or that of the "idiotic kids" in ***Rigadoon.*** The apparent nihilism in his critique of school allows a space for intermediary communities "peopled by children who are at their games and little nothings and giddy pleasures and showy stuff," which reminds us of the atmosphere of the "free areas" that the anarchists established during the belle époque. We know that the young Destouches, as a cavalryman stationed at Rambouillet, had an opportunity to come into contact with "La Ruche" (The Beehive), established by the libertarian pedagogue Sebastien Faure according to the principles of "integral" education propagated by the Fourierists. The episode of the "agricultural phalanstery" in ***Death on the Installment Plan,*** inspired by this experience, allows Céline to revalorize another type of playful, eclectic, and noncoercive apprenticeship to knowledge: the "passionate" pedagogy of the utopian socialist Charles Fourier. The emancipated brats of Blême-le-Petit, who "discipline themselves" and "no longer understand obedience," like the "little hordes" of "phalangette" Fourierists, are the New Men of one of the rare utopias that Céline spares from his apocalyptic polemics.

The critique of the illusion of a working class begins with a meticulous deconstruction of the concept of the proletariat: "The misfortune in all this is that there are no 'common people' in the poignant sense that you understand. . . . The heroic, egalitarian proletariat *does not exist,*" Céline concludes in a letter to Elie Faure dated March 1935. This pithy remark defines the alleged proletariat as an obvious expression of the nothingness of human nature, a pure dynamic of voluntary submission, and a collective "hypnotic" violence. By reducing the popular entity to the level of vicious proles, to a subservient mass or hallucinating crowd, without proposing in return the slightest aristocratic relief, Céline engages only in an exercise of purely nihilistic devalorization. It nevertheless seems that certain unspoken anarchic/individualistic assumptions within this denunciation of proletarian messianism harbor some ethical outlets at the heart of a social space that Céline describes as a game of the "Roman arena" and of "massacre."

In the moralizing satire concerning public cowardice and voyeurism—which, as M. C. Bellosta notes in *Céline ou l'art de la contradiction,* is borrowed from a profoundly reactionary version of neo-Jansenism—Céline isolates several rare exceptions to the rule of human nature's false virtues. These exceptions, as in the case of the soldiers Bardamu and Robinson, or their insubordinate and self-mutilated alter egos of the years 1914-18, demand the right to "fear," that is to say, the right to an active cowardice. While watching villages burn, they practice a "voyeurism" that distances them from the insane bellicosity. Princhard's monologue at the beginning of ***Voyage*** establishes the minimum agenda for this ethical alternative: it consists of an opposition between collective cowardice and a simple, passive resistance "without ideal," between the honors earned via social struggle and a "fundamental unworthiness," between a "formal disgrace" and an "automatic dishonor." Permitting oneself to "stink" in order to remain "pacifist," to be "disgusting enough to disgust the Nation"—these are the paradoxically positive principles of Célinean *resistant stoicism* that we also find in the writings of André Colomer, the insubordinate libertarian who wrote in 1916:

> I was not fleeing the battle by deserting, rather, I was looking for it. Staying in the melee would have been, in every way, a cowardice for me. . . . By denying myself to the Nation, I was eliminating the possibility of all effects and all repairs. I was declaring my own state of war. I was positioning myself not merely outside their melee, but against their melee.

Behind Céline's satire of mass servility, reactualized in the pseudo-Freudian form of a "sadico-masochistic" death drive, lay another critical reference, to *Discours de la servitude volontaire,* written by Montaigne's friend, the humanist Estienne de La Boétie. In this text, which lays bare the masses' "unrelenting will to serve," we find Céline's principal insight: "Men cling . . . to all of their sadness, and we cannot coax them to let go." For the sixteenth-century humanist, the "decision to be a serf" is a direct result of the familiar custom of "cretinization" through the games of the Roman arena and of the reproduction of despotic relations throughout the social pyramid. By stigmatizing the sadomasochistic inertia of the masses in accordance with these same principles, Céline reappropriates one of the most characteristic positions of attack within the individualist anarchy of the belle époque. Interestingly enough, during this period, La Boétie's *Discours* was paradoxically transformed into a bible for the call to rebellion. In the final analysis, we can see that the Célinean critique of the proletariat's desire for bondage does not attempt in any way to justify a natural social hierarchy, but instead seeks to revalorize an alternative subversion that rejects both the revolutionary illusions of the workers' movement and the Stations of the Cross of state reform. In his own way, Céline reappropriates the spirit of provocation that emblematized certain belle époque "outlaws/scofflaws" who were similar to the anarchist Jules Bonnot; in April 1912, Bonnot converted his own death into a war machine to be deployed against the double rule of tyranny and servitude after he was besieged at Choisy-le-Roi by hundreds of police and gawking vigilantes. As early as 1910, the young libertarian and Nietzschean Victor Serge explained this pre-Célinean *politics of the worst,* in all its positivity, as a need "to make the ignominy of masters, or even the ignominy of subjugation, felt through our obstinate independence."

Céline's critique of the idea of the proletariat was inspired by Gustave Le Bon's early version of sociology; beginning in 1895, Le Bon proposed the theory of a "psychology of the crowd" in opposition to that of Marxist materialism. According to this psycho-sociologist, the masses are incapable of both initiative and rebellion and are thus nothing but a mob displaying "irrational" behavior, which, in the end, does nothing but unconsciously follow the "suggestions" of a "leader." This theory would become reactualized by the massive tyrannies of the twentieth century, all of which, from Leninism to Nazism and on through the fascisms of Mussolini and Sorel, developed an intimidating manual of totalitarian propaganda out of the art of governing by "collective hypnosis." It is true that Céline's work constantly divides the proletariat into "hallucinating" hordes, but it does not culminate in a celebration of the leader or the modern Prince of Public Opinion. Instead, Céline celebrates a "transversal" perspective, which aligns the charisma of the leader with the manipulated crowd so as to emphasize an *individual path that goes against the current* of the dominant order's commands and the slavish imitation of the dominated; this is the perspective that the Stirnerian anarchist Albert Libertad summarized in 1905: "We love the man, we hate the crowd. We reiterate the cry of this pamphlet: *Against the shepherds, against the flocks.*"

If Céline's harangues against the shams of the intellectual and the proletariat have much in common with the critical nihilism of right and left-wing extremists, they do not lead to an enthusiasm for the national populism of the belle époque, but rather to the paradox of ethical and existential figures who exhibit underlying affinities with libertarian thought: the autodidact, who embodies a notion of apprenticeship without a master and the pedagogical utopias of the Fourierists; and the *resister,* who glorifies pacifist counter-heroism and active neutrality when confronted by the dead ends of voluntary servitude and the obedience of the masses. We could carry out the same analysis with respect to Céline's critiques of the idea of progress and of the symptoms of social "degeneracy"; these also present unusual individual alternatives. Two examples would be Doctor Semmelweis's experimental skepticism, which haunts Céline's entire oeuvre, and, among others, Mère Henrouille's "gay knowledge," which suggests the glorification of categorical idiocy. It is only in terms of this theoretical agenda that we can distinguish his anti-Semitism, which does not generate any covert libertarian perspective and does not reveal the underside of the utopian setting. Céline's anti-Semitism is not the departure point for all of his political uncertainties, as has often been said, but, on the contrary, it signifies the specific moment when Céline silenced his creative uncertainties at their source and sentenced himself to a racist univocality that closed in on itself, an ideological rhetoric that henceforth became a shield, blocking all the outlets that his antiauthoritarian affinities had previously unlocked.

It is important to reiterate the way in which Céline literally reappropriated fragments of libertarian sensibility; their significant substance was derived from perspectives that did not present themselves as a doctrine of political concepts, but rather as marginal, partial, and eccentric figures, actors in an interior phantasmagoria who are like ethical or existential indices immersed in a fictional space. Anarchy was never more than potential ideological material, a series of banalities that needed to be reenergized with the help of a subversive imagination and writing. The reactionary side of Céline's work, culminating in the pamphlets of the late 1930s, expressed itself in an ostentatiously political way, which tended to radically simplify Céline's system of thought, to subsume his imagination within a univocal ideological paradigm. In this Célinean game of hide-and-seek between politics and literature, we need to read beyond the evidence or proof of supposedly "engaged" texts and look instead to the political unspoken, which probably engages the mental universe of the writer even more profoundly than that which is stated: those liberating scenarios that a literary oeuvre creates, and not the declarations of ideological faith, which essentially serve as decoys for the work; those norms and conventions that the oeuvre cunningly subverts under the guise of certain motivating norms and prejudices—the utopias of intimate asides masked by official slogans.

Rosemarie Scullion (essay date Spring 1994)

SOURCE: "Céline in Cross-Cultural Perspective," in *South Atlantic Quarterly,* Vol. 93, No. 2, Spring, 1994, pp. 513-22.

[*In the following essay, Scullion discusses Céline's depiction of American capitalist society, his literary influence on American writers, and his often problematic critical interpretation.*]

Reminiscing on his world travels in postwar conversations with Robert Poulet, Louis Ferdinand Céline derided the boundless "commercial optimism" he found animating life in the United States during his visits in the 1920s and 1930s: Americans "tend not to revel in the morose. . . . When they realize they're no longer perky, they check their pulse and temperature." One might think that the moroseness in which Céline typically wallowed and the irksome cheeriness with which he saw early twentieth-century America engaging in its mercantile endeavors would have made the encounter between two such incompatible temperaments necessarily brief and therefore inconsequential. But ***Voyage au bout de la nuit***'s extended account of New York's urban Darwinism and Detroit's industrial alienation, the author's duplicitous dance with Hollywood, and the entwining of his professional, personal, and literary identities with such figures as Henry Ford, Elizabeth Craig, and Milton Hindus indicate that a distinct American presence asserted itself in Céline's life and writings. And as the scholars and authors in this issue skillfully demonstrate, Céline, the quintessentially French modernist, has also left his mark on American intellectual and literary life.

The modern tourist, Roland Barthes remarked, suffers from the "virus of essences," which narrows the scenic scope of his ethnological inquiry to a cluster of easily assimilable clichés. In seeking to "know" a foreign land and its people, Barthes's typically middle-class travelers follow guidebook selections of the monuments that reveal essential truths about the culture being observed. Although Céline's trips to the United States were largely of a professional nature, the knowledge he gleaned from these excursions—which later found its way into ***Voyage***'s literary depiction of American life—has much in common with the touristic essentialism that Barthes indicts. Céline can, of course, be credited with redescribing the American Dream of unlimited material wealth and human productivity in decidedly more nightmarish terms than the dominant ideology at the time would have allowed its subjects to fathom. But the monuments around which his narrative gravitates in ***Voyage***—New York's towering sky-scrapers and Detroit's industrial colossus—flatten rather than bring into relief the great complexity and heterogeneity of American society.

To be sure, Bardamu's conception of America is from the outset rather limited, inspired as it is by the anatomical mystique and promise of a New World mapped from the contours of Lola's American behind. His later "pilgrimage" to the capitalist mecca does little to make that vision any less sketchy. Those with a broader understanding of the American body politic will notice, for instance, that except for the flashing appearance of a bomb-toting servant during his visit to Lola's New York apartment, all of the individuals Bardamu encounters are—or at least are assumed to be—of European descent. This selective view of America's demography is especially striking when one considers the mass migration of African Americans to industrial centers in the North during the interwar period when Céline—and later, presumably, Bardamu—would have had ample opportunity to observe New World racism in its modernizing forms. In textual hindsight, Céline's elision of black America is perhaps not all that surprising, given the swipe he seems to be taking at American jazz in his pejorative reference to "Negro-Judeo-Saxon" music early in the novel. In a similarly reductionist mode, workers at Ford's Detroit plants are cast as pathetic simpletons who are unable and unwilling to defend themselves against their collective dehumanization. Transformed into robotic cogs in the machinery of Taylorist rationalization, they have neither the physical nor the mental wherewithal to assert their agency in a labor process designed to control their every move. While Céline insightfully identifies some of the strategies that Ford and other manufacturing giants adopted to ensure the compliance of their labor force, this important episode of ***Voyage*** bears not the slightest signifying trace of the considerable resistance mounted by American labor in the early decades of the century to the introduction of such deadening production techniques. Instead, the narrative emphasis is placed on matters of hygiene and health, reflecting Céline's own abhorrence of corporeal degeneracy and his obsession with anatomical perfection, an ideal that the wretched conditions under which workers were obliged to live and labor during this period did little to promote. Ironically, for all of his antibourgeois bluster, Céline's hygienist discourse in the Detroit episode of ***Voyage*** actually dovetailed with the aesthetic sensibilities and class-based contempt that middle- and upper-middle-class America expressed in the eugenics-inspired discourse projected onto the working poor of the early twentieth century. Céline glides subtly, though incontrovertibly, toward the condescending and elitist right in his novelistic account of class domination and exploitation, revealing deeply conservative ideological impulses that are often eclipsed in discussions of his much-touted anarchism. The following description of the prostitute Molly, the winsome angel of mercy who rescues Bardamu from the crushing monotony of the Ford assembly line, succinctly illustrates Céline's inability to think beyond the limits not only of biology but, more importantly, of hierarchy—a notion whose legitimacy was vigorously contested in the egalitarian thought of late nineteenth and early twentieth-century European and American anarchists.

> Toward Molly, one of the lovely girls there, I soon developed an uncommon feeling of trust, which in frightened people takes the place of love. I remember her kindness as if it were yesterday, and her long, blond, magnificently strong, lithe legs, noble legs. Say what you like, the mark of true aristocracy in humankind is the legs.

Race, gender, and class are marked in a thoroughly conventional manner in this morsel of Célinean text, one that happens to introduce a passage in which a shadow erotic economy appears to subvert the productionist logic presented in both the Detroit and the New York episodes as the essence of America—precisely the impression left when the protagonist abandons Ford's employ for the idle existence which Molly's prostitution affords him. But in the end, Bardamu's brush with this monument of capitalist modernity is not as seditiously anticonformist as it appears to be. As is often the case with middle-class sightseers, or so Barthes contends, Céline's literary vision "mask[s] the spectacle of real conditions" in industrial America, transforming the entire Ford adventure into a crude sociological surface onto which he projects his own bourgeois hygienist anxieties before taking refuge from that specter of decay in a regal, flaxen body symbolizing the hierarchy of values that ideologically anchor his white male subjectivity.

The American writers who were apparently most influenced by Céline in the late 1930s and especially in the postwar years—Henry Miller, Thomas Pynchon, Kurt Vonnegut, Philip Roth, Joseph Heller—were largely oblivious to the subtle forms of conservatism and conventionality that Céline evinces here and elsewhere in his novels. The sense of Céline that appears to prevail among these writers and many readers is that of a clamorous voice of cultural and political dissidence, an impression that stems, of course, from his assaults—especially in ***Voyage au bout de la nuit*** and ***Mort à crédit***—on an array of societal institutions: the military, the family, the medical profession, the school, the industrial factory, and, ultimately, the modern liberal State itself. In addition, he expressed that dissent in a style that released the novel from its conventional grammatical and syntactical strictures and allowed raw human emotion to surge through textual space. Introduced into a culture whose dominant modes of speech and comportment actively discouraged unseemly displays of human emotion—a product of what Bardamu contemptuously refers to as "Anglo-Saxon puritanism"—Céline's style must have had a great emancipatory appeal for these American authors.

As Morris Dickstein notes, the Célinean presence in American literary life was especially palpable in the late 1950s and early 1960s, when the author became something of a cult figure for the Beat generation. He also influenced such writers as Roth and Heller, whose anticonformist, antimilitarist novels imaginatively fostered the anti-establishment sensibilities underlying the protests that erupted on college campuses across America in the late 1960s. Céline's disdain for humanity, and for what he saw as its intrinsic depravity, surely acted as a powerful counterforce to the imagery of consumer euphoria and domestic bliss plastered on billboards across the landscape in the postwar rush to suburbanize America. His dim view of modern technological progress and his unsettling portraits of the inane human violence that sustained such institutions as the military and the family—two key elements in the American postwar social order—lent an oppositional force not only to experimentation with new literary forms, but to other expressions of cultural discontent as well.

As instructive and engaging as such analyses of Céline's influence on American literary practices are for me, I find myself left with a nagging sense that terribly important historical, cultural, and political meaning is being dropped from the Célinean text in its transmission to the United States. As an American who is one generation removed from the countercultural appropriation of Céline, I listen with keen interest to witnesses and students of that process describing the effect that he and the writers he influenced had on my own culture. Particularly in a critical age that has so radically diminished the significance of the author, I also delight in hearing American writers present their work and discuss the ways in which Céline's contentious style has shaped their own artistic practice. Having studied French literature, history, and politics of the 1930s and 1940s for some time, I am also, however, acutely aware that Céline's rebellion against institutionalized aesthetic and societal norms is far more ideologically complex than the decontextualized reading of his work leads one to believe. Philip Watts's analysis of the Célinean resonance in Kurt Vonnegut's *Slaughterhouse-Five,* which focuses, as does Céline's German trilogy, on the Allied bombing of Germany at the end of the war, skillfully brings important aspects of this complexity to the critical fore. Generally speaking, however, Céline's postwar readers have tended to abstract his ideological discourse and aesthetic practice from the strife-ridden and trauma-laden context of the 1930s and 1940s, which greatly influenced the reception of his first two novels, impelled the writing of his pamphlets, and informed the content of his last five novels. This is particularly true in the United States, where knowledge of France's bitter internecine political struggles during the 1930s, the Occupation years, and the postwar purge is quite limited. In glossing over that context, do we not run the risk of engaging in forms of intellectual and cultural tourism that blind us to the "spectacle of real conditions" behind the literary monument Céline has become? What happens, for instance, to a timelessly subversive Céline when his writing is considered in its full historical and political specificity, a specificity that generates meanings more closely aligned with the politics of reaction and the hierarchical status quo than with the democratizing forces of his time, which so energetically sought to level that order? What emerges is no longer simply the profile of a great modernist whose seditious literary voice gleefully menaces all institutional authority, but rather a more sobering perspective on the vicious face of human intolerance.

In the course of the discussions about Céline's influence on American writers and writing, I found myself reconstructing my first encounter with Céline and the dizzying paradoxes in his writing. As a graduate student in search of a term paper topic and with an interest in European history and politics of the 1930s, I was directed by one of my teachers toward Céline—a great novelist who also happened to be—I was told—a notorious fascist. With images of goose-stepping, muscle-flexing, order-obsessed SS types in mind, I was astonished to find, first in ***Mort à crédit*** and then in ***Voyage au bout de la nuit,*** wrenching representations and what seemed to be a wholesale condemnation of the abuses of patriarchal power in a vast range of modern institutions—all of which was difficult to reconcile with what I knew to be fascism's authoritarian logic. And, as an American schooled in the history and sociology of the complex processes that leave class oppression largely occluded in the signifying practices of my own culture, Céline's focus on the effects of class violence spoke poetically to my own knowledge of similar suffering and despair in a presumably classless America—an experience whose very unrepresentability is part and parcel of that oppression. In a less cognitive mode, there was also something intangibly alluring about his irreverent, populist speech, no doubt the desemanticizing poetic voice that, as Julia Kristeva so astutely observes, issues "a call to rhythm and joy, beyond the crippling constraints of a society ruled by monotheistic symbolism." Things were, I was quickly forced to conclude, significantly more complex than I had been led to believe by the conventional academic wisdom surrounding Céline.

Figuring out how Céline got from the ingeniously comical disaffection of ***Voyage au bout de la nuit*** to the frothing aggression of ***Bagatelles pour un massacre*** five years later has been a most enlightening critical venture that has taken me far afield of my initial, admittedly reductive, perceptions of both Céline and European fascism. Closer analysis of the various hierarchies configured in his texts began to reveal a more embedded ideological accommodation of the institutional authority that Céline appears to indict, thus rendering more intelligible the evolution from ***Voyage*** to the unequivocally reactionary ***Bagatelles.*** My exploration of the intricacies of European fascism and Céline's ambivalent relation to it began overlapping with my questions about racial, ethnic, gender, and national identity, leading me to consider how Céline's textual construction of these differences—most often seen by mainstream culture as outrageously aberrant—actually mark the Other it strives to exclude in ways that are strikingly paralleled by the cultural and discursive norms of his time. Examining how Céline himself was Othered in turn by postwar literary elaborations of collaborationist evil opens a veritable Pandora's box of political projections, displacements, and massive historical denial, which allowed the society at large to focus with such righteousness on the deplorable bigotry of a writer like Céline, while dispensing with a thorough-going critique of the more refined and naturalized articulations of Western ethnocentrism and racism that contributed to the mass genocide perpetrated during the war and, in its aftermath, that continued to drive colonial policy. In extending the scope of analysis beyond the limits of Céline's literary identity, meanings begin to proliferate that not only implicate the extremist forms of misogynistic white supremacy with which Céline can clearly be identified, but that also involve the more extensive binary, phallogocentric foundations of Western thought on which our exploitative patriarchal and racist structures have continued to thrive in the postwar era. That critics are now moving well beyond what Alice Kaplan has termed the "separatist" moment in Célinean studies—the inveterate tendency to bifurcate the aesthetic and the political, the literary and the ideological, the dazzling style and the appalling racism—and toward a more "integrationist" understanding of the coherence of these facets of Céline's texts offers some hope that their intersection with and dependence on more mainstream forms of discursive Othering will be more fully elucidated in the years to come.

This special issue of *SAQ* and the conference on which it is based illustrate splendidly that, rather than leading to the cul-de-sac of misunderstanding and oversimplification that so often mar cross-cultural exchanges, the encounter between Céline and American intellectual, literary, and cultural life has opened up an intersubjective space abounding not only with projections and counter-projections, but also with exciting possibilities for understanding one of the "great" figures of European modernism and for generating readings of what Jonathan Culler terms "previously unseen inscriptions." While most of his postwar readers have at least some sense that Céline's writing is marked by scandal of an often ill-defined historical and political nature, many walk away with the distinct impression that he is merely a cantankerous cuss who glories in literary rebellion against the powers that be. Candid and informed discussion about the various dimensions and implications of the American presence in Céline and the Célinean presence in American writing can greatly nuance that perception, peeling back layers of historical and ideological complexity to reveal the genesis of his racist discourse and, correspondingly, the traditions of ethnocentrism that his political texts have come to emblematize. Moreover, a consideration of gender issues introduces into the debate questions concerning the production of sexual difference and Céline's willfully masterful—though everfoundering—male narrative subjectivity: questions that are far-reaching in their political and cultural implications for patriarchal institutions on both sides of the Atlantic. Ironically, it is a writer who sought so stridently to fortify the boundaries of linguistic, racial, ethnic, and sexual identity, aggressively marking the Other and struggling to flush it from his field of vision, whose texts provide the opportunity half a century later to deconstruct the cultural codes that proved to be so injurious to minority groups in Céline's day, codes that have since then demonstrated their remarkable tenacity and efficacy in keeping oppressed segments of society relegated to the margins of power. While I may be succumbing here to a characteristically American reflex of attempting to turn a lemon into lemonade, we may nevertheless come to see as one of Céline's most important cultural contributions his unwitting complicity in unraveling the sign systems propelling the West's ascendancy in the modern era, signifying practices whose essential violence he categorically refused to mediate through the refinements of "civilized" speech.

Sally Silk (essay date May 1996)

SOURCE: "Céline's *Voyage au bout de la nuit:* The Nation Constructed Through Storytelling," in *Romanic Review,* Vol. 87, No. 3, May, 1996, pp. 391-403.

[*In the following essay, Silk examines the fictional invention of national identity in* Journey to the End of the Night. *According to Silk, "it is in Bardamu's relationship to the bourgeois patriotism of wartime France that one can locate a link to Céline's later embrace of fascism."*]

Céline's oeuvre, like those of numerous other twentieth-century writers, is strongly marked by the problematic status of the writer's fiction vis-à-vis his politics. For some critics, Céline's anti-semitism and his avowed fascism raise questions about the "quality" of his writings, these overtly ideological works of the late thirties being viewed as the point towards which the works before the fascist "period" move and as the position from which his post-war work emerges. While these questions are of course important, their significance depends entirely on the way they are posed. On the one hand, they can drastically oversimplify the connection between the text and the writer's reactions to the configuration of political forces that surround him and in which his life is embedded. They can imply the kind of uninterrupted continuity of the author's consciousness over time that much recent critical work problematizes. On the other hand, such inquiries can open avenues of investigation into the development of ideological positions and the complex interrelationship of narrative, history, and ideology.

Céline's first novel, ***Voyage au bout de la nuit*** (1932), does not reveal any direct connection to the fascist writings of the late thirties; in fact, the book's abject humor, as well as the reader's consistent and enduring sympathy for Bardamu, seem to undercut the kinds of violence one might expect in the text of such a controversial writer. This obviously does *not* mean that questions of ideology are not relevant to a critical reading of the novel; it has been demonstrated that protofascist ideology permeates the novel in ways that, although they operate quietly, are nonetheless significant for scholars of Céline, as well as for historians studying the rise of fascism in France in the 1930s. The novel's central ideological tension lies in Bardamu's alienation from the ways of life and structures of feeling of bourgeois France during the Third Republic. This alienation is played out in a number of spheres (in the alienation of the wage laborer, in the terrifying loneliness of the agent of imperial commerce) whose cumulative momentum takes Bardamu on a kind of quest that gives the novel its title. I have shown elsewhere that this alienation occurs not only on a thematic level, but, more significantly, on a discursive one as well: the text is itself a highly charged manifestation of Bardamu's "homelessness."

With regard to the bourgeois world, one of the text's most intractable problems is with that most mythical and powerful "home" of bourgeois invention: the nation. And it is in Bardamu's relationship to the bourgeois patriotism of wartime France that one can locate a link to Céline's later embrace of fascism. While the narrator relentlessly parodies this patriotism, the glorification of the nation that lies at its heart is something he cannot escape. To the extent that in fascist ideology the nation belongs to another discourse, standing in radical opposition to the categories of bourgeois nationalism, and to the extent that the fascist nation is less a "nation" than a primeval collectivity gathered in the mists of romantic historiography, perhaps we can hypothesize a development in Céline's oeuvre. His support for the fascist nation was made possible by another phenomenon: the discursive power of the nation could be escaped only though the embrace of another discourse, the counter-discourse of fascism.

This, then, is the framework into which I would like to fit a close reading of several crucial scenes in ***Voyage au bout de la nuit.*** I shall demonstrate that Bardamu becomes inextricably bound to the processes by which the category of nation is both performed and taught. Furthermore, ***Voyage au bout de la nuit*** offers insight into the discursive constitution of the "nation" itself.

Bardamu and Storytelling Gone Awry

Current work on the relationship between the nation and writing suggests that the nation is constituted in the potentially violent space opened up by the process of narration itself. Céline's ***Voyage au bout de la nuit*** is a useful context in which one can observe the volatile nature of the construction of nation hood because the protagonist's heroic tales of war reveal a contestatory space in which the nation is to be constituted. Contestatory, not simply because his stories are lies, but also because they are eventually retold by others, for their ends, at his expense. When Bardamu, who is both protagonist and narrator, constructs a vision of the French nation through his stories, it is always represented as an idea that enjoys the self-assured status of epistemological truth. However, the nation is exposed as a severely problematic concept precisely at the moment when it appears so hermeneutically safe.

Thematically, ***Voyage au bout de la nuit*** never seriously ponders the question of nationhood. This is not to say that characters do not discuss the issue, for indeed, they do; but such action often appears simplistic, even predictable at times. Yet, discursively, the issue is played out in great seriousness, to the point where it becomes so complicated that the reader can practically feel every desperate breath taken by the narrator as he painstakingly reconstructs his past role as an actor in the unfolding story of the French nation.

Storytelling is Bardamu's strength. He is so gifted at it, however, that he is eventually taken in by the power of his own tales. He prefers telling stories to any other activity, not out of *jouissance* in Barthes's sense, but rather as a means for dealing with the weighty ugliness of the past. He explains:

> Quand on sera au bord du trou faudra pas faire les malins nous autres, mais faudra pas oublier non plus, faudra raconter tout sans changer un mot, de ce qu'on a vu de plus vicieux chez les hommes et puis poser sa chique et puis descendre. Ça suffit comme boulot pour une vie tout entière.

The text we hold in our hands then, is Bardamu's way of making a virtue of necessity by telling stories.

The episode under discussion here is easily summarized: twenty years old and confined as a patient in a psychiatric hospital for fleeing the battlefield during World War I, Bardamu exploits the power of storytelling by using the text to frame stories within stories. He does so not because it helps him pass the time, but because it guarantees him visitors, and one visitor in particular. What attracts his audience is the content of his stories: he tells of the battles he fought and the love of France that kept him going. The irony here is that Bardamu, unbeknownst to his visitors, has been brought to the psychiatric hospital because he was stricken with cowardice on the battlefield, hiding behind trees whenever possible. He deceives his listeners with stories that nourish their vision of the *patrie*. At the end of this episode, the tables have been turned and it is Bardamu who is the true victim.

This essay will reveal, through a close reading of the passage in question, the positions occupied by a textual subject embroiled in the disruptive act of narrating the nation. I shall argue that the act of embedding war stories within the larger narrative not only completely confounds the text, but, more significantly, tells us a great deal about the problematics involved in the act of writing the nation.

Bardamu Displaced: From Battlefield to Hospital

Bardamu and his fellow patients are visited by prominent Parisian figures, as a sort of social call, because they are now "présentables et pas dégoûtants du tout moralement" to the outside world that represents the bourgeois nation. Fully aware that "on se le répéta dans les salons, que le centre neuromédical du professeur Bestombes devenait le véritable lieu de l'intense ferveur patriotique, le foyer, pour ainsi dire," he also realizes that he was an object of curiosity for all of Paris; remembering himself helpless in front of their glare, he makes fun of this society that justified its visits as taking up the cause of patriotism. As is carefully pointed out in previous chapters, Bardamu is not only terrified of war, but repelled by "[la] ferveur patriotique" as well. Thus, while the patients understand their visitors, they do not share their values and find themselves in the hospital precisely because of their improper patriotic behavior. But in reporting Parisian salon gossip ("on se le répéta . . ."), Bardamu is at once aware of this discrepancy *and* taken in by the idea that it has become fashionable to visit local mental patients in the service of one's country. Madness and patriotism are supposed to mutually exclude one another in the confines of the hospital, the former being the state one is thought to suffer if the latter cannot be experienced. But the two are constantly being played off of one another in Bardamu's narrative, to the point where they merge completely when he works himself into a mad, patriotic frenzy at the Comédie Francaise, a state that can be calmed only back at the hospital.

The narrator portrays the hospital as a theater stage on which a variety of characters play their roles: "des évêques, [. . .] une duchesse italienne, un grand munitionnaire, et bientôt l'Opéra lui-méme et les pensionnaires du Théâtre-Français. On venait nous admirer sur place." While Bardamu and the other patients are the object of a theater-like gaze, he also finds them thoroughly entertaining, portraying them to the reader as if it is they who are on stage. Having taken the position of his audience and occupied it, Bardamu turns those who are curious into an object of curiosity that achieves a comic result contrary to that intended by his visitors. The narrative turns the tables on patient and society, on stage and audience, producing a caving in of hierarchical difference that recalls Bakhtin's observation that carnival eliminates the separation between actor and spectator. But there is a disturbing quality to this scene that Bakhtin's work does not account for: the joyful freedom that characterizes the Bakhtinian conception of carnival is nowhere present. The narrator's memory of his confinement consists of a procession-like vision of figures that he at once mocks and is impressed by. It is not clear where he stands in relationship to this image. Bardamu may be entertained by the scene, but he is nevertheless unable to distance himself from the idea of the nation as it is embodied in this privileged group of visitors come to ogle outcasts from the war. This is the claustrophobia of the bourgeois nation-state.

The discursive effect here becomes disquieting, not celebratory. One of the salient characteristics of an abject voice, this quality can be characterized as manifesting a "strain of hysteria" that "infect[s] the comic as much as the socially 'corrective' thrust of the Abject Hero's" utterances. Bardamu demonstrates his talent for storytelling in the psychiatric hospital; yet this power can only be realized in the textual narration where he counts on his reader to notice his skill. Because the latter does not know how to read this playing with roles, Bardamu the narrator only reinforces his position of confinement and the accompanying failure to find a subject-centered voice. As a result of the utterance, the narrator's position is further shaken; the only thing that he affirms is a possible misreading of his text. Bardamu as textual subject is produced by the utterance rather than vice versa. "Democratic truth" is not only wanting here, but impossible to cultivate as well.

The image of the spectacle that opens this passage gains strength as it becomes central to the action in the story. Of the "petit ballet mondain" that visits the hospital, an actress from the Comédie-Française, impressed with Bardamu's war stories, develops a rapport with him. He guarantees himself attention by relating certain juicy details that will keep her coming back. She enjoys his stories so much that she asks permission to relate "les plus intenses passages de [ses] récits" to a poet who would then put them into verse so that she may recite them during a special performance at the Comédie-Française. Bestombes, the director of the hospital and a character given to patriotic excess, addresses the press about the upcoming event. This character, whose inflated language and aw(e)ful clichés illustrate "l'intense ferveur patriotique" that Parisian society clamors to see, is represented by his ex-patient through reported speech, a technique Bardamu uses here to satirize not only a character's discourse, but epic language as well. It would lend the narrator some authority were it not for the character of the poet (the actress's friend who turns Bardamu's stories into performance material for her) who will later in the passage decisively eliminate any promise of discursive centering. These intricate layers of mediated storytelling vis-à-vis the nation (marked by Bardamu's fabrications in the first place and ending with the poet's fabulous verses) point to the fictional status of the idea of nationhood as elaborated in Anderson's *Imagined Communities.* Bardamu's representation of Bestombes indicates a point of confrontation, a place at which the outside world of glorified French patriotism meets the inside world of institutionalized cowards; as madness and patriotism begin to resemble one another, the latter's claims that it is based in the real are undermined. Bestombes's epic language plays an important role because Bardamu negotiates a place for it in his hierarchy of constructing the nation purely through stories. Bestombes may be mocked here, but the effect of his speech on the patients foreshadows the disembodied voice that the narrator will occupy once the poet artistically puts into verse Bardamu's stories.

Afraid of losing "la palme de l'héroïsme" that he assumes the actress has bestowed upon him, the narrator writes that his younger self becomes involved in a never-ending game of storytelling with the other patients. A mood of solidarity prevails among them as they unite to make fun of the visitors:

> Nous vivions un grand *roman de geste,* dans la peau de personages fantastiques, au fond desquels, dérisoires, nous tremblions de tout le contenu de nos viandes et de nos âmes. On en aurait bavé si on nous avait surpris au vrai. La guerre était mûre. (emphasis mine)

In the same way that Bestombes's noble speech about the epic functions satirically, so too does Bardamu's description of patients doing battle for the most dramatic war story. But there is one overwhelming difference: where the narrator was confident playing with Bestombes's language, here he is caught up in his own epic-like description of the patients' storytelling efforts. He has significantly moved from satirizing the epic in the previous scene to a situation that he himself can only, albeit ironically, describe in epic language. Although in the satire portrayed here Bestombes is naïve and the patients are not, the narrator is so affected by the irony used to treat the discourse of the other as represented by Bestombes that he will soon be unable to distinguish between the ingenuous and the disingenuous in his own discourse. Bardamu, although he recognizes Bestombes's words as empty and artistically second-rate, is nonetheless unable to resist the powerful concept of the nation that bolsters Bestombes's soaring metaphors. His only solution is to appropriate Bestombes's language in a way that outdoes him. Bardamu makes fun of Bestombes's vision of the nation, yet becomes thoroughly involved in cultivating the fictions necessary to its representation.

The climax of the satire occurs here: the *chanson de geste* suggested by the doctor's speech is transformed into a "*roman* de geste" appropriate to the genre of this text. The significance of the tension between these two can be understood in light of the following comment about the reading process:

> The text has not only an intertextual relationship to previous texts but also an intertextual relationship to itself as canonized text. The responsibility is ours for making this relation one of difference from itself, of self-estrangement, rather than of conformity with itself.

The reader cannot help but see that the narrator's text recalls a different time, a different genre; but the complicitous relationship between the narrator and his reader is broken off as the latter observes that Bardamu can no longer keep such associations at a distance. Intertextual activity operates here in such a way as to bring out the relationship between the nation and telling: what we have here is a setting into place of the conflict between what Homi Bhabha calls the pedagogical and the performative in the ambivalent writing of the nation, a conflict that will erupt once Bardamu's stories, put into verse by the poet, are recited on stage by the actress. Pedagogical temporality transforms people into objects whereby discourse derives its authority from a "pregiven or [already] constituted historical origin or event"; performative strategy, on the other hand, positions people as subjects "of a process of signification that must erase any prior or originally presence of the nation-people." The growing tension between the pedagogical and the performative introduces the problematic site of writing the nation, a site that comes into view once Bardamu's war stories leave his mouth. That is, they are first related by him to the actress, then retold by her to her poet friend, who then rewrites them for the actress, only to be further mediated by her on stage at the long-awaited performance at the Comédie-Française. Bestombes's announcement of the performance to the press who, importantly, resides outside of the hospital, marks the point at which the narrative voice enters into the struggle between the performative and the pedagogical. The reader knows that his stories are powerful because they deny his conspicuous absence on the battlefield. Bardamu the storyteller deceives his visitor, but Bardamu the narrator lets us in on his ironic joke. Bestombes's announcement, however, produces tension where there wasn't before: it introduces the "ambivalent double-writing" of the pedagogical and the performative into the narrative voice, pedagogical because the *raison d'être* of the upcoming performance derives its authority from the supposed historic greatness of France, and performative because the event is a spectacle (both well-publicized and well-attended), bearing witness to the idea that when subjects actively participate in national life, they renew and reproduce the "process of cultural identification." In other words, in the marginal space of the hospital, discourse is safe from the crisis represented by the split between the pedagogical and the performative; once moved to center stage, literally, the narrative voice is subject to all the problems that inhere in this double-time of writing the nation.

Stories Misplaced: From Hospital to Stage

In the final scene of this episode, Bardamu's unexpected enchantment at the performance indicates a move away from the self. For it is upon hearing the actress recite the poet's version of his own story that Bardamu is profoundly moved

> en l'entendant vibrer, exhorter de la sorte, cette superbe amie, gémir même, pour rendre mieux sensible tout le drame inclus dans l'épisode que j'avais inventé à son usage. Son poète décidément me rendait des points pour l'imaginative, il avait encore monstrueusement magnifié la mienne, aidé de ses rimes flamboyantes, d'adjectifs formidables qui venaient retomber solennels dans l'admiratif et capital silence. Parvenue dans l'essor d'une période, la plus chaleureuse du morceau, s'adressant à la loge où nous étions placés, Branledore et moi-même, et quelques autres blessés, l'artiste, ses deux bras splendides tendus, sembla s'offrir au plus héroïque d'entre nous. Le poète illustrait pieusement à ce momentlà un fantastique trait de bravoure que je m'étais attribué.

The emphasis here is on the *delivery* of a story that originally belonged to Bardamu. The colloquial, familiar style characteristic of Bardamu's language is absent from the poet's version, yet Bardamu is transported by his rival's words precisely because it is in the poet's language that he can lose himself. Sensitive to the poet's "rimes flamboyantes," "adjectifs formidables" and "solennels," and "l'essor d'une période," he is moved by a style so foreign to him that he imagines himself as the most heroic patient there; the narrator anxiously lets his reader know that the poet's "fantastique trait de bravoure" was really his own. Bardamu confuses his own invented tales with the poet's artistic renderings of them; unable to reconcile the pedagogical and the performative aspects of narrating the nation, Bardamu is caught in the conflict of relinquishing his original playful fabrications in favor of the poet's more stylized ones. In both cases, the story is inauthentic, yet it is most powerful when it is furthest removed from its original fictional point: total submission to the poet's creation means that Bardamu has completely identified with the most fictional account of the nation. Indeed, the concept of nation derives its power from the very fact that it is rooted in the shared imagination of many, a condition that is beyond the narrator's control. The nation is at its strongest here, fascinating and discursively seductive as it sweeps Bardamu up in its path.

Bardamu's *récit ennobli* is a fake on all counts. Through multiple levels of deception (his invented tales, the actress's recounting of them to the poet, the poet's version, the actress's mediated delivery), the narrator has turned heroism on its head and, more significantly, been brought down with it in the process. For when the actress gestures to the audience that the original teller of the tale is seated in the balcony, the other patients clamor over seats to accept their applause, concealing Bardamu from view. Eager for recognition and desperate for praise, he is defeated this time by his fellow patients, who succeed in excluding him from appearing in what is already the marginal space of the theater. When he writes "'Mais c'est de moi qu'il s'agit! ai-je failli crier à ce moment. De moi seul!,'" it is the narrator's only attempt to represent his younger storytelling self through the authoritative marks of direct discourse. The attempt fails, however, because these words are actually uttered for the reader's ears, not for other characters in the story ("ai-je *failli* crier") for whom they were supposedly destined; we are the only ones who hear the frustration intended for his fellow patients. What is important here, and of course ironic, is that he is now willing to identify with his own fictions of heroism. This reflects the effective force of the nation as a concept as well as the success of the poet's work, which, according to the narrator's need for verisimilitude, represents Bardamu's original story as told to the actress; for even this first version was pure invention that was then subjected to further change by the actress, then the poet, and finally, again, by the actress. In other words, it is impossible for the narrator to portray his younger storytelling self through direct discourse because the fictions cannot be authenticated: there is too much deception circulating to occupy fully a voice. Indeed, the very notion of origins or authenticity is unthinkable here.

This idea of telling as act of deception becomes central to the discursive space delineated by the relationship between nation and narration in ***Voyage au bout de la nuit.*** On the one hand, we see the pedagogical at work since the poet's glorious poem furnishes the narrator with a narcissistic pleasure as he sees his own story reflected within, a state that results from "the process of identity constituted by historical sedimentation"; but on the other hand, the representation of misery and inferiority caused by the success of a poem that is not really his is indicative of the "loss of identity [that occurs] in the signifying process of cultural identification" that inheres in the performative.

These contradictions are inextricably linked to the fact that the narrator has been victimized by a situation that was written into the initial enunciative act itself. As Nietzsche explains, telling by its very nature is deceptive:

> The danger of the direct questioning of the subject *about* the subject and of all self-reflection of the spirit lies in this, that it could be useful and important for one's activity to interpret oneself *falsely* . . . The will to logical truth can be carried through only after a fundamental *falsification* of all events is assumed.

Telling is a fiction in its own right. So when Bardamu the storyteller jockeys for the position of hero alongside his rivalrous companions who have since done the same, he also finds himself in competition for that position with the poet himself, his alter ego who is the incarnation of the otherness of his discourse. The narration thus reveals an ironic parable of sorts, one that demonstrates the Nietzschean point that 1) narrative is always already false; and 2) this falsity is what subjects identify with as their "truth."

Just as fiction represents a distortion that puts "truth" in question, so too does this scene represent the refraction of a performance supposedly based on the lived experience of a brave soldier. For both Bardamus are at once spectator and spectacle, the younger Bardamu because at the gesture of the actress, all eyes turn from the stage to the audience to view the hero, and the older Bardamu because his confessional style reveals him watching a former self at the same time that he draws the reader's attention to the older one. If telling is deception, it also results in transgression because the narration has toyed with the rules of theater, with the very idea of positions as defined by Pêcheux.

> Nous dirons que *la forme-sujet du discours,* où coexistent indissociablement interpellation, identification et production de sens, réalise *le non-sens de la production du sujet comme cause de soi sous la forme de l'évidence première.* Nous avons affaire à une détermination qui s'efface elle-même dans l'effet nécessaire qu'elle produit sous la forme du rapport entre sujet, centre et sense, ce que nous avons condensé en parlant d' <<effet Münchhausen.>> (emphasis Pêcheux)

Bardamu's narration of his storytelling antics has literally overturned the notion of "fixed" points from which an utterance is emitted. If the narrator's voice is both laughable and pathetic, if only his addressee hears his frustration, then this performance gone awry proves to be his most efficacious attempt to find a center. An overturned enunciative situation is the only one that gives him hope for ideal communication that can never be realized. His stories are mediated through others so such an extreme degree that he depends on the skills of the actress and the poet for an affirmation of self. The nation can only be told then through discourse that is always a little off. Telling stories about the glory of France becomes a textual phenomenon that overwhelms Bardamu and challenges him to participate in it, despite the fact that he holds his country in contempt. The power of fiction that inheres in the act of narrating the nation is what forces Bardamu to explode at the end of this passage. What began as parody (with Bestombes and society's visits to the hospital) has turned into something more desperate. Although Bardamu's stories are applauded for their "nationness," they are nothing more than a site of pure conflict devoid of the thing itself.

The ultimate outcome of this performance gone wrong is reflected in the fact that the actress he longs for chooses instead "cet harmonieux inverti." Her preference for the homosexual poet over the heterosexual war hero is the biggest blow yet and draws attention to Bardamu's involvement in impossible situations (the performance at the theater, an affair with the actress, a relationship with the poet), ones that can only dissolve without closure, leaving him as trapped as ever in discourse that offers him no way out. Desire for the actress is transformed into narrative desire as Bardamu is unable to complete the scene in a way he finds satisfying; in the final paragraph of the episode his "Récapitulons" announces to his reader that he will return to the scene again. Bardamu can recuperate his invented tales, but he must still submit to the illusion of the signifier that obliges the textual self to depend on an other in order to be heard. Bardamu loses himself as he speaks through the poet and the actress, even if both are inaccessible to him. His highs and lows, his continual repositioning throughout the episode, demonstrate indeed that the nation is "an ambivalent agency of narration." The removal of Bardamu's glorious stories from their originally marginal location in the hospital to center-stage in the Comédie-Française underscores the novel's obsession with speaking the nation. Representation itself is privileged over both truth and falsehood so that the narrator has no means by which to guarantee himself a secure position in the narrative.

This episode can be read in a variety of ways, but I have chosen to focus on the various storytelling positions it occupies when caught up in the act of representing the nation. Critical work on ***Voyage au bout de la nuit*** has paid little attention to the importance of storytelling, to the relationship between the exchange-value of Bardamu's stories and the completely deceptive character of fiction. His tales would appear to be worth a great deal in light of the fact that they guarantee him, in return, the repeated visits of the actress that he desires; but when the poet gets hold of his stories in order to rewrite them, Bardamu derives great pleasure from them precisely because they no longer resemble the stories he had originally told to the actress. His original stories are deprived of any exchange-value whatsoever because he is eventually completely humiliated by a situation that has backfired on him. Bardamu has been blinded by the power inherent in narrating the nation.

The Nietzschean theory that telling in and of itself is deception calls into question the very subject that got Bardamu into so much trouble: France as *patrie.* Although a coward on the battlefield in World War I, Bardamu is bold with words yet unable to hold onto them literally. The idea of French nationhood is exposed as a completely discursive one, created by the text itself rather than by the character's very unbrave actions. His antics and abject position at the end of this episode bring about a dismantling of the concept of *patrie* from the perspective of the textual subject. Yet the concept itself loses none of its potency, and indeed, is reinforced all the more because he is clearly vanquished by the fictions that allow the nation to continue to be so convincingly imagined.

FURTHER READING

Criticism

Buckley, William K. "Céline: The Rumble Under Our Floorboards." *Studies in the Novel* 21, No. 4 (Winter 1989): 432-9.

Provides an overview of contemporary critical response to Céline's fiction, noting the persistence of reactionary and outdated interpretations of his work.

Clemmen, Yves W. A. "Travel, Fiction, and the Cross-Cultural: Céline and Tournier Experiencing the Other." *CLA Journal* XXXVIII, No. 1 (September 1994): 46-58.

A comparative study of travel themes and transcultural encounters in *Journey to the End of the Night* and Michel Tournier's *Les Meteores.*

Dickstein, Morris. "Sea Change: Céline and the Problem of Cultural Transmission." *South Atlantic Quarterly* 93, No. 2 (Spring 1994): 205-24.

Examines the transformation of Céline's literary legacy among American authors, including Henry Miller and the Beat writers.

Kristeva, Julia. "Céline: Neither Actor Nor Martyr." *Powers of Horror: An Essay on Abjection,* translated by Leon S. Roudiez, pp. 133-9. New York: Columbia University Press, 1982.

Discusses the ambiguous combination of comedy, compassion, and morality of Céline's literary style.

Jameson, Fredric. "Céline and Innocence." *South Atlantic Quarterly* 93, No. 2 (Spring 1994): 311-9.

Examines Céline's narrative strategies of observation and detachment, drawing comparison between the conventions of detective fiction and Céline's physician protagonists.

Kaplan, Alice, and Philippe Roussin. "Céline's Modernity." *South Atlantic Quarterly* 93, No. 2 (Spring 1994): 421-43.

Explores Céline's depiction of American industrial society, urban life, and disillusionment in *Journey to the End of the Night* and the novel's influence on subsequent American literature.

Luce, Stanford. "Why Professor Y?" In *Critical Essays on Louis-Ferdinand Céline,* edited by William K. Buckley, pp. 243-51. Boston: G. K. Hall, 1989.

Traces the origins of *Conversations with Professor Y* and the symbolism of the letter "Y" to Céline's correspondence with Milton Hindus.

Nettelbeck, Colin W. "Historical Vision in Céline's Last

Novels." In *Critical Essays on Louis-Ferdinand Céline*, edited by William K. Buckley, pp. 268-78. Boston: G. K. Hall, 1989.

Reconsiders the significance of Céline's postwar fiction, particularly the interplay of historical and autobiographic elements in *Féerie pour une autre fois I* and *II, Castle to Castle, North,* and *Rigadoon.*

Roussin, Philippe. "Getting Back from the Other World: From Doctor to Author." *South Atlantic Quarterly* 93, No. 2 (Spring 1994): 243-64.

Examines the significance of Céline's dual self-identity as a practicing physician and author, particularly as related to his utopian medical perspective during the 1920s.

Roussin, Philippe. "The Logic of the Reception of Céline's Works in the Thirties." In *Critical Essays on Louis-Ferdinand Céline*, edited by William K. Buckley, pp. 111-21. Boston: G. K. Hall, 1989.

Examines initial critical reaction to *Journey to the End of the Night*, contemporary literary norms against which the novel was evaluated, and the influence of critical interpretation on the social context and meaning of the text.

Spear, Thomas C. "Céline and 'Autofictional' First-Person Narration." *Studies in the Novel* 23, No. 3 (Fall 1991): 357-70.

Explores distinctions between autobiography and autofiction and Céline's conflation of fact and fiction, nonlinear presentation, and narrative identity in his novels.

Thiher, Allen. "Céline's *Journey to the End of the Night:* From One Asylum to the Next." In *Critical Essays on Louis-Ferdinand Céline*, edited by William K. Buckley, pp. 144-54. Boston: G. K. Hall, 1989.

Examines the elements of Cartesian duality and Renaissance folly in the parodic reversal of reason and madness in *Journey to the End of the Night.*

Additional coverage of Céline's life and career is contained in the following sources published by Gale: *Contemporary Authors*, Vols. 85-88; *Contemporary Authors New Revision Series*, Vol. 28; *Dictionary of Literary Biography*, Vol. 72; and *Major Twentieth-Century Writers*, Vol. 1.

Simone de Beauvoir
1908-1986

French philosopher, nonfiction writer, novelist, autobiographer, short story writer, essayist, and playwright.

The following entry presents an overview of Beauvoir's career through 1997. For further information on her life and works, see *CLC,* Volumes 1, 2, 4, 8, 14, 31, 44, 50, and 71.

INTRODUCTION

Among the most prominent French intellectuals of the twentieth century, Simone de Beauvoir is recognized as a pioneering feminist thinker and leading proponent of existentialist philosophy. Her groundbreaking sociological treatise *La deuxième sexe* (1949; *The Second Sex*), in which she delineates the historical and cultural structures of patriarchy, is often credited with establishing the theoretical underpinnings of modern feminist scholarship. Along with philosopher Jean-Paul Sartre, her lifetime companion, and Albert Camus, Beauvoir helped define and popularize the principles of existentialism in her novels and nonfiction works such as *Pour une morale de l'ambiguité* (1947; *The Ethics of Ambiguity*) and later writings on aging and death. Her best known novels, including the award-winning *Les mandarins* (1954; *The Mandarins*), are noted for their lively portrayal of Parisian social and intellectual milieus of the 1930s and 1940s. Eschewing marriage and motherhood, Beauvoir served as a living model of female liberation and artistic commitment. Her observations concerning the social construction of female inferiority and the primacy of self-determination are central to her series of autobiographic volumes, including *Mémoires d'une jeune fille rangée* (1958; *Memoirs of a Dutiful Daughter*), regarded as an important personal testament to the plight of women in a male-dominated world.

Biographical Information

Born Simone Lucie Ernestine Marie Bertrand de Beauvoir in Paris, France, Beauvoir was raised by her watchful Catholic mother and agnostic father, a lawyer, in an upper-middle-class home. The pleasant security of Beauvoir's childhood ended, however, with the outbreak of the First World War, during which the family fortune dissipated. A precocious student and zealous reader of forbidden books, Beauvoir received a strict, limited education at a Catholic school for girls. As an adolescent she struggled against the strictures of religion and social expectations that discouraged intellectual pursuits among women. The 1929 death of her best friend Elizabeth (Zaza) Mabille, whose manipulative parents refused to allow her to marry a fellow student, later marked a turning point in Beauvoir's hostility toward bourgeois institutions. Defying her parents' wishes, Beauvoir announced her ambition to teach and enrolled at the Instit Saint-Marie in 1925, where she studied philosophy and literature. Continuing her education at the Sorbonne, she received the *agrégation de philosophie* in 1929. While at the Sorbonne, Beauvoir met Jean-Paul Sartre, an intellectual equal and intimate whose existentialist philosophy influenced much of her own thought and writing. Dismissing conventional morality in favor of principles of honesty and freedom, Beauvoir and Sartre never married, although they maintained a lifelong open relationship that permitted "contingent" loves. After receiving her degree, graduating second only to Sartre, Beauvoir taught at several French lycées from 1931 to 1943 while writing fiction and associating with Left Bank intellectual circles habituated by Camus, André Malraux, Raymond Queneau, and Michel Leiris. Beauvoir's previously unpublished short stories from this period are contained in *Quand prime le spirituel* (1979; *When Things of the Spirit Come First*).

Though notably apolitical during the 1930s, she and Sartre became involved in the French Resistance while living under Nazi Occupation in Paris during the Second World War. Beauvoir also published her first book, the novel *L'invitée* (1943; *She Came to Stay*), and the philosophical tract *Pyrrhus et Cinéas* (1944), during the war. In 1945 Beauvoir and Sartre founded *Les Temps modernes,* a literary and political journal devoted to existentialism. Beauvoir also produced her only play, *Les bouches inutiles* (1945; *Who Shall Die?*), and two additional novels, *Le sang des autres* (1945; *The Blood of Others*) and *Tous les hommes sont mortels* (1946; *All Men Are Mortal*). After a visit to the United States in 1947, Beauvoir published *L'Amérique au jour le jour* (1948; *America Day by Day*), a volume of anti-capitalist observations dedicated to Richard Wright and his wife. Her first full-length philosophical work appeared as *The Ethics of Ambiguity* in 1947, followed by *The Second Sex* in 1949. Among the leading figures of the French left-wing intelligentsia, Beauvoir was politically active during the 1950s as a supporter of Marxist causes in the Soviet Union and China—communist China is the subject of *La longue march* (1957; *The Long March*)—and as an outspoken critic of French military involvement in Algeria and Indo-China. She also produced *The Mandarins,* winner of the prestigious Prix Goncourt in 1954, and the first of her autobiographic works, *Memoirs of a Dutiful Daughter,* continued over the next two decades with *La force de l'âge* (1960; *The Prime of Life*), *La force des choses* (1963; *Force of Circumstance*), and *Tout compte fait* (1974; *All Said and Done*). Her reminiscences in *Une morte trèd douce* (1964; *A Very Easy Death*) relate her anguish over her mother's illness and death in 1963. Beauvoir published additional fiction in the 1960s with *Les belles images* (1966) and *La femme rompue* (1968; *The Woman Destroyed*). Though reluctant to assume a feminist label, during the 1970s Beauvoir became an important advocate of women's issues and reproductive rights as a member of the Mouvement de la Libération des femmes (MLF) and as president of the feminist groups Choisir and Ligue du droit des femmes. *La vieillese* (1970; *The Coming of Age*), regarded as a companion volume to *The Second Sex,* deals with the appalling treatment of the elderly. In her last published work, *La céremonie des adieux* (1981; *Adieux*), Beauvoir records her final conversations with Sartre and reflects upon her painful witness to his decline. Beauvoir died of pneumonia in Paris six years later at age seventy-eight.

Major Works

Beauvoir's existentialist investigations, autobiographic writings, and fiction center largely upon her preoccupation with the nature of personal freedom, moral action, and, in particular, the alienation of women in a society defined by men and male attributes. In *The Ethics of Ambiguity,* her first major philosophical work, Beauvoir addresses the absurdity of the human condition and the possibility of self-definition and transcendence. Influenced by the existentialist theories of Sartre, Beauvoir describes human life as an inherently ambiguous process of becoming that depends upon relationships with others for meaning. Turning her attention to the particular situation of women in *The Second Sex,* Beauvoir asserts that female sexual identity is predominately a social construct built upon oppressive male definitions of femininity. As Beauvoir famously observed, "One is not born, but rather becomes, a woman." Drawing broadly upon existentialist philosophy, psychoanalytic theory, and historical research in this expansive two-volume study, Beauvoir exposes the modalities of female subordination embedded in myth, cultural practices, biological facts, and gender stereotypes that cast women as weak, alienated objects of masculine ideals and desires. According to Beauvoir, women are relegated to a secondary existence of dependency and passivity because they are defined in relation to men rather than as autonomous subjects themselves. Beauvoir's four volume autobiographic series chronicles her personal and intellectual development over six decades. *Memoirs of a Dutiful Daughter* recounts her happy childhood and disillusioning formative years, including her close relationship with her sister, intense friendship with Zaza, and introduction to Sartre. *The Prime of Life* documents her unconventional relationship with Sartre beginning in 1929 and their experiences during the Nazi Occupation of France. *The Force of Circumstance* covers events in her life from the Liberation of Paris to 1963, including somber reflection upon the French-Algerian War and the subjects of aging and death. In *All Said and Done* Beauvoir abandons the chronological presentation of the previous three volumes to contemplate alternate paths that her life may have taken and to discuss her dreams and international travels, leaving the reader with an open-ended summary of her life. Much of Beauvoir's fiction explores the existentialist tenets of freedom and contingency with heavy autobiographic overtones. Her first novel, *She Came to Stay,* examines destructive emotional dynamics in a love triangle consisting of a man and two women. Set in Paris at the outbreak of the Second World War, the story involves Pierre and Françoise, a committed though unmarried couple, and Xavière, a younger woman whom they invite to stay with them. Tension mounts as Pierre and Xavière grow closer, alienating Françoise until, consumed with hatred and jealousy, she finally murders Xavière. In *The Blood of Others,* one of the first novels ever written about the French Resistance, Beauvoir explores the individual's moral obligation to society through the guilt-wracked recollections of Jean Blomert, a member of the Resistance who abandons his bourgeois family for the Communist party, and his lover, Hélène Bertrand, a Resistance fighter who is killed in action against the Nazis. As Jean struggles to reconcile the deaths of several familiar people and friends, including Hélène, whom he feels responsible for, he realizes that a life untainted by social guilt is impossible, affirming the belief that the only moral response to injustice is personal engagement on the side of freedom. In *All Men Are Mortal* Beauvoir traces the peregrinations of Raymond Fosca, an immortal thirteenth century Italian prince who attempts to direct the course of European history through his interventions over several centuries. Juxtaposing Fosca's solitude and ennui with the political commitment and urgency of mortal actors, Beauvoir suggests that a meaningful human existence depends upon the prospect of death and its attendant joys and anguish, without which freedom and action have no value. Beauvoir's most acclaimed novel, *The Mandarins,* involves a coterie of disillusioned French intellectuals immediately after the Second World War. Once united in purpose and action in the Resistance movement, the small circle of friends soon find their grand hopes for the future shattered by divisive allegiances to the vying postwar ideologies of communism and capitalism. Though Beauvoir denied that the novel was a *roman à clef,* the four main characters—Anne Dubreuil, Henri Perron, Robert Dubreuil, and Lewis Brogan—bear strong resemblance to herself, Sartre, Camus, and American author Nelson Algren, with whom Beauvoir was romantically involved at the time. As in earlier works, in *The Mandarins* Beauvoir examines the competing interests of individualism and political commitment and the intellectual's responsibility to act. Beauvoir's last two volumes of fiction, *Les Belles Images* and *The Woman Destroyed,* feature modern professional women who struggle to find meaning and acceptance amid the decadent materialism and shifting political fortunes of the 1960s. *Les Belles Images,* translated as "advertisements," centers upon Laurence, a wife, mother, and advertising producer who maintains a façade of success and satisfaction to mask her own deep-seated metaphysical fears. She is eventually forced to confront reality and her feelings when her ten-year-old daughter expresses serious concerns about social injustice and human suffering. *The Woman Destroyed* consists of three novellas. The first, *Age of Discretion,* is narrated by an aging mother, wife, and left-wing intellectual who encounters changing contemporary values when her writing is dismissed by critics and her son abandons his political principles for a lucrative position with the government. In the second story, *Monologue,* the female narrator is a forty-three-year-old woman who angrily decries her martial misfortunes and the suicide of her daughter while alone in her apartment on New Year's Eve. The final story, *The Woman Destroyed,* is narrated by Monique, a middle-aged woman who discovers that her husband, a successful doctor, is having an affair with a younger, professional woman. Monique rues her decision to forgo her own medical studies to marry and have children, underscoring the consequences of female dependency and self-sacrifice in contrast to the independence of her husband's lover.

Critical Reception

Beauvoir is highly regarded for her important contributions to the development of postwar existential philosophy and her systematic examination of women's issues and patriarchal institutions. Best known for *The Second Sex,* widely considered a classic of feminist literature, Beauvoir is praised as one of the earliest and most perceptive twentieth century feminist theorists. Since its original publication in 1949, *The Second Sex* has generated heated controversy and remains the focus of critical writing on Beauvoir to this day. Though once a revered staple of feminist reading, *The Second Sex* has fallen out of favor among many postmodern feminist writers over the last several decades, largely due to what critics consider Beauvoir's disdain for the female body and biological reductionism. As Sonia Kruks notes, "Beauvoir has been criticized, with considerable justification, for her horror of the female body and its functions. There are indeed many passages in *The Second Sex* where women's bodily functions are identified with animality, passivity, and lack of freedom and are denigrated from the masculinist standpoint of an apparently disembodied reason and freedom." Critics also note that Beauvoir's reliance on phallocentric concepts derived from Freudian psychology and Sartre's existentialism limit her ability to conceive of new forms of freedom outside of patriarchal language and ideologies. Despite such objections, Beauvoir is considered a formidable philosophical thinker and critics continue to laud the importance of her original insights into the socialization of gender and the alienation of women. Margaret A. Simons concludes, "Beauvoir, in *The Second Sex,* laid the theoretical foundations for a radical feminist movement of the future and defined a feminist political philosophy of lasting importance." While *The Mandarins* remains Beauvoir's most acclaimed work of fiction, she has received considerable praise and popularity for *She Came to Stay, The Blood of Others, Les Belles Images,* and *The Woman Destroyed.* These works, and her four autobiographic volumes, continue to be regarded as important sources for the understanding of Beauvoir's existentialist theories, the historical context of her feminist perspective, and mid-century French intellectual activity.

PRINCIPAL WORKS

L'invitée [*She Came to Stay*] (novel) 1943
Pyrrhus et Cinéas (nonfiction) 1944
Le sang des autres [*The Blood of Others*] (novel) 1945
Les bouches inutiles [*Who Shall Die?*] (drama) 1945
Tous les hommes sont mortels [*All Men Are Mortal*] (novel) 1946
Pour une morale de l'ambiguité [*The Ethics of Ambiguity*] (nonfiction) 1947
L'Amérique au jour le jour [*America Day by Day*] (nonfiction) 1948

L'existentialisme et la sagesse des nations (nonfiction) 1948
La deuxième sexe [*The Second Sex*] 2 vols. (nonfiction) 1949
Faut-il brûler Sade? [*Must We Burn Sade?*] (essay) 1953
Les mandarins [*The Mandarins*] (novel) 1954
Privilèges (essays) 1955
La longue marche: Essai sur la Chine [*The Long March*] (nonfiction) 1957
Mémoires d'une jeune fille rangée [*Memoirs of a Dutiful Daughter*] (autobiography) 1958
Brigitte Bardot and the Lolita Syndrome (essay) 1960
La force de l'âge [*The Prime of Life*] (autobiography) 1960
La force des choses [*Force of Circumstance*] (autobiography) 1963
Une morte très douce [*A Very Easy Death*] (reminiscences) 1964
Les belles images (novel) 1966
La femme rompue [*The Woman Destroyed*] (short stories) 1968
La vieillesse [*The Coming of Age;* also translated as *Old Age*] (nonfiction) 1970
Tout compte fait [*All Said and Done*] (autobiography) 1974
Quand prime le spirituel [*When Things of the Spirit Come First: Five Early Tales*] (short stories) 1979
La céremonie des adieux: Suivi de entretiens avec Jean-Paul Sartre [*Adieux: A Farewell to Sartre*] (reminiscences) 1981

CRITICISM

Terry Keefe (essay date 1979)

SOURCE: "Psychiatry in the Postwar Fiction of Simone de Beauvoir," in *Literature and Psychology,* Vol. XXIX, No. 3, 1979, pp. 123-33.

[*In the following essay, Keefe examines Beauvoir's interest in psychiatry and psychoanalysis in* The Mandarins, Les Belles Images, *and* The Woman Destroyed. *According to Keefe, "Beauvoir's broad view of the development of the individual and of family life has very obviously been much influenced by psychoanalytic theory and modern psychiatry in general."*]

In a review recently published in *Literature and Psychology,* Dr. Simon Grolnick reminded us of some of the complexities of Jean-Paul Sartre's attitude towards psychoanalysis. As one of the contributors to the reviewed volume points out, 'One day the history of Sartre's thirty-year-long relationship with psychoanalysis, an ambiguous mixture of *equally* deep attraction and repulsion, will have to be written'. An interesting side-light is already thrown upon aspects of that history, however, by the postwar fiction of Sartre's life-long companion, Simone de Beauvoir. In this matter as in certain others, Beauvoir's writings, fascinating and valuable in their own right, constitute a most useful complement to those of Sartre, for whilst he has published no novels since the third volume of his wartime series, *The Roads to Freedom,* three fictional works by Beauvoir appeared in the fifties and sixties, each in part giving imaginative expression to her own intense and lasting interest in modern psychiatry.

Since the Second World War Beauvoir has written one long novel, ***The Mandarins*** (published and awarded the Prix Goncourt in 1954), a shorter novel, ***Les Belles Images*** (1966), and a collection of three stories, ***The Woman Destroyed*** (1967). The narrative of ***The Mandarins*** alternates systematically between the viewpoints of Henri Perron, a journalist and author, and Anne Dubreuilh, a successful psychiatrist. Through Anne, in one half of the book the profession of psychiatry regularly comes under scrutiny from the inside, and serious questions and doubts are raised about the underlying principles of all psychotherapy. One of the principal characters linking the two halves of the narrative, moreover, has a breakdown in the course of the story and undergoes a psychoanalytical 'cure'. On the other hand, whilst the central figure of ***Les Belles Images*** has a long and continuing history of mental disturbance, the climax of the story is her firm decision to take her favorite daughter *out of* the care of a psychiatrist. In ***The Woman Destroyed,*** the main character and narrator of the second tale (**'Monologue'**) is beyond any doubt a psychopathological case; and the heroine of the long third story (which gives its name to the collection) is driven to a psychiatrist by the breakdown of her marriage. In other words, in only one of the five separate stories she has published since the war (namely, **'The Age of Discretion'**) does Beauvoir fail to bring mental illness and psychiatry quite prominently into the plot in one form or another. And this, of course, takes no account of numerous passing references to psychiatry and psychoanalytical methods in the books, or of the fact that Beauvoir's broad view of the development of the individual and of family life has very obviously been much influenced by psychoanalytical theory and modern psychiatry in general.

Early on in ***The Mandarins*** we learn that Anne Dubreuilh became a psychiatrist because she wished to help people to rid themselves of the obstacles they place in the way of their happiness. Her Marxist husband, Robert, had never accepted the unfavourable Communist-Party line on psychiatry and fired her with enthusiasm at the prospect of rethinking classical psychoanalysis in the light of Marxism.

She has always acknowledged that it is possible to question the worth of any one person's equilibrium within an essentially unjust society, but has responded to the challenge of finding an answer in each individual case, believing that to relieve patients of their personal nightmares is to enable them to face up to the real problems of the world. The central purpose of the novel as a whole, however, is to depict the dilemmas experienced by French left-wing intellectuals after the war, and when the story opens (Christmas 1944) it is clear that the experiences of the Occupation have marked Anne profoundly and have already changed in certain respects the nature of her relationship with her patients. Personally, she feels that to allow herself to forget the worst incidents of the war would somehow be to betray those who suffered and died, and yet her professional life is now dominated by the task of encouraging others to set aside the horrors of the past and to adjust to the present and the future.

Anne, therefore, begins to entertain rather far-reaching doubts about the nature of her work as a psychiatrist. She wonders whether, at least in these circumstances, there is not something intrinsically wrong with an attempt to assist people to forget the past. Is she right, for instance, to try to drive out of the mind of one of her child patients (Fernand) the memory of his father, who died two years earlier in Dachau? It is certain that nothing she may do to 'help' will bring the dead back to life or efface past evils, but above all she now lacks the faith in the future that formerly enabled her to believe it appropriate to aid patients to 'neutralize' their past: her pre-war assumption that 'every sane man had a role to place in a history that was leading mankind on towards happiness' is one that she can no longer accept. Yet in that case, looking only to the present, since the future is in doubt, what difference does it make whether little Fernand becomes cheerful and carefree like other children?

Since Anne's professional life continues as before in spite of her acknowledgement that, if this is what she really believes, she ought to stop treating certain patients or even give up her work altogether, we may reasonably assume that the doubts assailing her do not yet amount to complete conviction that psychiatry is an unjustified activity. And indeed, although she periodically experiences great frustration and fatigue in dealing with people who cope reasonably well as adults but virtually revert to being children in her consulting-room, she regains some of her earlier faith in her profession when the first war-deportees begin returning to France. These 'ghosts' bring back more horrifying stories of the war years than ever and they can gain no rest from their past. They are represented by one of Anne's patients in particular, a young woman whose hair is completely white. Faced with cases like this, Anne feels ashamed at not having suffered enough herself and temporarily loses some of her earlier doubts about the value of therapy: 'the questions that I had asked myself now seemed quite idle ones; whatever the future might hold, these men and women had to be helped to forget, had to be cured. She throws herself wholeheartedly into her work once more and enjoys a certain limited success, not just with children like Fernand, but even with patients like the young white-haired woman: 'the equilibrium she had achieved wasn't marvelous, but at least she was sleeping well'. Before long, however, some of her doubts seem to return, for she is soon saying to Henri Perron that she finds it rather futile to be treating individual states of mind in the prevailing circumstances. Once more she claims that she no longer has enough faith in the future to believe that every life can have a purpose.

As far as we are able to tell, this is more or less where things stand when Anne goes to America at the beginning of the second part of the novel. Her reputation as a 'brilliant doctor' is apparently already established, though she admits that she has a great deal to learn about the latest developments in American psychoanalysis. In fact, other matters (outstandingly, a lengthy love-affair with an American writer, Lewis Brogan) preoccupy her much more than her work in the second half of the book. Yet if we now learn less about her relations with her own patients, we gain a new kind of insight into her attitude towards psychoanalytical 'cures' as she observes at close quarters the breakdown and treatment of her friend Paule. Anne is clear that the ethics of her profession preclude the possibility of treating Paule herself, but although this makes matters somewhat awkward for her as Paule actually goes into decline, its effect is to allow Anne to follow in great detail the impact of psychoanalysis upon someone that she knows very well indeed. That is, she is not involved in the usual doctor-patient relationship here but is, as a result of her professional expertise and her intimate knowledge of Paule, in a privileged position from which to judge the case.

It is Anne who takes Paule to the eminent analyst, Murders, yet from the first we find her wondering exactly what Paule will be cured of, and what she will be like afterwards. And in a stance paralleling her attitude towards suffering in general earlier in the book we also see her initially reacting to Paule's cure by suggesting that it has somehow cancelled out Paule's earlier pain and rendered it pointless. She seems sympathetic to Paule's own view that her 'madness' was associated with a richness of perception and a sensitivity that are now lost, but in any case she explicitly claims that there is an element of inauthenticity in Paule's new personality: 'for the rest of her life she would probably play the part of a normal woman, but it was a task that scarcely inclined her towards sincerity'. Paule, she says, seems more alien to her now than when she was mad. More significant still is Anne's view of the explanation of Paule's troubles that Mardrus has persuaded his patient to accept (that she felt guilt over her infantile jealously of her brother, who died at the age of fifteen months, and had therefore become masochistic in her long love-affair with Henri, who was a kind of brother-substitute):

> I kept quiet. I was very familiar with explanations of the kind that Mardrus had used. I, too, made use of them on occasion and I appreciated them for what they were worth. Yes, in order to cure Paule, one had to reach back into the past to destroy her love. But I could not help thinking of the sort of microbe that can be killed only by destroying the organism that it is feeding on.

Anne, who admitted early on that she had always been aware that 'to cure is often to mutilate', finds the destruction of Paule's past increasingly difficult to accept: 'I wanted to weep with her over the love that for ten years had been the pride and meaning of her whole life, and which had now been transformed into a shameful ulcer'. She sees that many of the concerns with which Paule has replaced her love for Henri are foolish, and she cannot avoid relating all of this to her own case, refusing to believe that her feelings are ailments. She would rather go on suffering than have her past scattered to the winds, and when her affair with Brogan breaks up painfully she draws some consolation from the fact that it will continue to live in her memory. She is so saddened by Paule's resignation to her new state, moreover, that she becomes disgusted with her own work as a psychiatrist and wants to tell her patients: '"Don't try to get better. We always get better soon enough"'. All of her earlier doubts are now intensified: 'I could no longer understand why it is a good thing that people should sleep well at nights, make love easily, be capable of acting, choosing, forgetting, living'. Although she is still having successes with some difficult cases, she is now going through the motions more than anything else; she becomes more and more like her own patients, with their misfortunes and obsessions, and she can see no urgent need to 'cure' them. At the end of the novel, however, Anne is portrayed as being in the depths of an intense personal crisis which affects the way in which she sees *everything,* so that it is not clear how complete and permanent we should regard her disillusionment with psychiatry as being.

More important for present purposes is the fact that in the course of ***The Mandarins*** Beauvoir has used Anne's profession as a way of raising many points about the philosophical and moral implications of psychotherapy that have a particular modern ring. In the way in which the nature of Anne's work (and thereby her own reactions to it) changes with the precise political and historical circumstances in the immediate postwar years, we see Beauvoir's sharp awareness of how psychiatry is related to the state of the society within which it is operating. And the point, of course, is taken one stage further than this when Anne is made to question the validity of helping the patient to adjust to a life of 'normality' when the norms themselves may be anything but admirable. Beauvoir stops a little short of suggesting, as R. D. Laing was subsequently to do, that the schizophrenic is a kind of prophet in whose hands the salvation of society may ultimately lie, but she must surely, in 1954, have been among the first to express in memorable fictional terms doubts about the psychiatric concept of normality in the context of modern society. Furthermore, the way in which Anne's approach to her work is shown to be intimately linked with her personal life and circumstances is also very much in line with recent emphasis on the nature of the psychiatrist's own experience with his patient and the phenomenon of counter-transference. In general, the broad aims and the narrative sweep of a novel like ***The Mandarins*** provide an excellent context for the airing of fundamental and vital questions about mental illness and its treatment, since the interaction between individual and society which lies at the heart of the matter can be explored so tellingly in fiction. It is also quite clear that Beauvoir, at this stage, has mixed feelings about psychiatry, and the novel-form undoubtedly gives her rather more scope for expressing her hesitations and doubts than would the philosophical essay.

The ambiguity in her attitude is equally discernible in her subsequent works of fiction, where no major character is a psychiatrist, but where we see that Paule was simply the first in a line of case-studies in which Beauvoir continues to explore major aspects of the theory and practice of psychotherapy. The case of Monique in **'The Woman Destroyed',** in fact, runs quite closely parallel to that of Paule. Monique, too, (though in different circumstances and in an entirely different way from Paule) has allowed herself to become over-dependent upon her man and eventually needs psychiatric help when it becomes clear that he is going to leave her after twenty-two years of marriage. We do not observe her crisis through the eyes of another as we do with Paule, however, for the story is narrated from her own viewpoint. Hence we notice that she records in her diary various physical symptoms that suggest the onset of some kind of breakdown—loss of weight, fainting, mid-cycle bleeding—and we see both a friend and then her husband suggesting that she should see a psychiatrist. The friend claims that Monique needs only minor help rather than a full analysis but Monique cannot at first see what a psychiatrist could possibly do to help her, and she resists very strong pressure to consult one from her husband, who is himself a doctor. Yet she has to admit that she may be making herself ill 'with the unacknowledged intention of moving him to pity' and, perhaps mainly because she is afraid of the continuous bleeding, she soon gives way. As she ironically notes, she begins to pay a psychiatrist to listen to her.

From this point onwards, most of the parallels with Paule's

case fall away: the respects in which Monique's situation is different come more to the fore and, in any case, it is suggested that Monique is in no danger of becoming deranged. But precisely because her case is a less extreme one, the whole question of what effect psychiatric treatment has upon her is more difficult to resolve—a difficulty only compounded by the fact that we never see Monique from the outside and have to read between the lines of her own comments. Taking at face value the totality of her remarks about the efforts of her psychiatrist, Dr. Marquet, we could easily believe that he does nothing at all for her: she soon abandons the work she has taken up on his advice ('What a joke their ergotherapy is! I've given up that idiotic job'); at one point she suspects him of being in league with Maurice; she is often scathing about his analyses; and her last reference to her treatment in the diary implies that Marquet may only have made matters worse. Yet a careful reading of the story indicates that the picture is a more complicated one than this. At least the hemorrhage stops and Monique begins eating again within three days of her first consultation, and she does take up her diary once more on Marquet's advice. In a number of instances, moreover, the accuracy of his comments about Monique is confirmed by what we already know of her *in spite of herself.* Monique is blind to certain things about her own life and is an arch self-deceiver, so that we are perfectly ready to accept the psychiatrist's view that her intelligence has been stultified by her obsessions and that she must be prepared to consider her own responsibility for the situation as well as that of Maurice and his mistress.

In principle, of course, Monique's psychiatrist is trying to do with her much the same as Mardrus did with Paule: to ease her away from preoccupations with one man and to restore her sense of individual identity. Yet in the context of the story as a whole his attempt is presented in a far more sympathetic light than is that of Mardrus. Monique overtly belittles what he is doing ('Then he began to muddle me with talk of a lost and regained personality, of distance to be adopted, of returning to myself. Claptrap'), but she admits that she wants to collaborate, wants to try to find herself again. Moreover, when Marquet approaches the matter 'from the other end' from Monique and wants to talk not about her husband and mistress but about Monique's mother and father and her father's death, the attentive reader already has reason to suppose that this is appropriate, since many earlier references buried in her diary suggest that much of her current difficulty with her husband stems from her attempt to make him conform to an ideal that her father, himself a doctor, embodied for her. In other words, the psychiatrist's deep analysis of Monique's problem has a great deal of plausibility for us and is not made to appear out of the blue as a kind of *deus ex machina* as does Mardrus's explanation of Paule's state. Yet having said all of this, we cannot be absolutely sure to what extent psychiatry is effective in Monique's case. The consultations certainly *appear* to help her, contrary to her own expectations and claims, but she is still in a very bad state at the end of the story and, in any case, we have no means of knowing how well she would have coped without such help.

Much of the emphasis that Beauvoir placed, in ***The Mandarins,*** on the psychiatrist-patient relationship and on the nature and implications of psychiatric treatment as such comes to fall, in all of her subsequent stories, on the way in which the structure and quality of the original family situation lies at the roots of mental disturbance. Indeed, Beauvoir acknowledged in ***All Said and Done:*** 'I am much more concerned than I used to be with the problems of childhood'. In some respects, therefore, the reported comments of Monique's younger daughter, Lucienne, near the end of **'The Woman Destroyed',** may well express the author's own views:

> According to her, what counts in childhood is the psychoanalytical situation as it exists without the parents' knowledge, almost in spite of them. Education, in so far as it is conscious and deliberate, is quite secondary.

It is unlikely, however, that Beauvoir would wholly subscribe to Lucienne's inference that someone like her mother accordingly bears no responsibility at all for the development of her children. In fact, part of the point of the preceding story in the collection, **'Monologue',** is to show how, in spite of all her protestations that she was a perfect mother, Murielle actually *drove* her daughter to suicide.

In any case, Murielle is in every respect a fascinating case from the psychiatric point of view. In spite of the fact that, again, no point of view other than the heroine's own is adopted anywhere in the story, there is no shadow of doubt that she is mentally sick, and seriously so. Beauvoir herself has referred to Murielle's 'distortion of reality' and claimed that she can scarcely envisage any future for her except madness or suicide. And technical concepts seem far more appropriate here than is usually the case with characters in fiction: Beauvoir talks of 'paraphrenia' for instance, and it is almost impossible to describe Murielle without using the term 'paranoia'. Indeed, irrespective of any comment by the author, Murielle's obsessions are plain for any reader to see: she not only has a persecution complex, but is also (despite her denials) preoccupied with sex in the most unhealthy way, as well as with the theme of purity and filth. It is also apparent that most or all of those around her consider her deranged, which is not in the least surprising in view of the type of conduct she engages in. Furthermore, her mental disturbance manifests itself in both real physical symptoms and an excessive concern with her own state of health; and we know that when she had to visit the doctor about serious loss of weight after her daughter's suicide, her illness was described as 'psychosomatic'.

Yet as far as we can tell, the nearest that Murielle has come to receiving psychiatric help is in a clinic following this psychosomatic disorder. In **'Monologue'**, that is, Beauvoir goes still further than she does in **'The Woman Destroyed'** in dropping her earlier emphasis on psychiatric treatment as such and stressing the family origins, or at least the family context, of mental illness. According to Murielle's account of her childhood, whilst her father loved and cherished her, her mother much preferred and favoured her brother, Nanard, thereby ruining Murielle's upbringing and her whole life. The evidence of Murielle's intense hatred of her mother is quite plain in the text and if the mother is guilty of only a small proportion of the misdeeds that Murielle charges her with, then it is certainly not without foundation. The difficulty is, of course, that it is impossible to know how much objective 'truth' we must take to lie behind Murielle's version of the past. But in certain respects the question is an unimportant one, since the link *in Murielle's mind* between her present parlous state and her early family life is a vital one. As R. D. Laing has pointed out, real patterns of relationship within the family have to be 'internalized' by each member and this can bring into being a 'family as a fantasy structure' which is at least as influential as the objective situation. The most interesting feature of **'Monologue'** for present purposes is the sensitivity that Beauvoir shows to considerations of just this kind and the great skill with which she enables, or even forces, the reader to enter into Murielle's fantasy world. Moreover, the character's own level of awareness of the forces at work and of what we saw Lucienne describe as 'the psychoanalytical situation as it exists without the parents' knowledge' adds yet another dimension to the complex picture and to the fascination of the story. Murielle claims (though doubtless with distorting hindsight) that although her own jealously of her brother was normal ('all the books say so'), she had the exceptional merit of being prepared to acknowledge it. And although she perverts them for her own ends, she displays certain other items of psychoanalytical knowledge in referring to her own daughter ('She was at the age when young girls detest their mother. They call it ambivalence, but it is hatred'), and in insisting that the children of broken marriages develop complexes. In short, adopting Murielle's own voice, the author in various detailed and subtle ways makes us see her character in psychiatric terms, yet offers no positive suggestion at all that any form of psychotherapy might help her. In its own manner, **'Monologue'** again reveals at one and the same time Beauvoir's dependence upon, and reservations about, the general discipline of psychiatry.

But it is, in fact, in ***Les Belles Images,*** published the year before, that we see most distinctly that whilst Beauvoir's indebtedness to psychoanalytical theory had undoubtedly increased by the mid-sixties, her doubts about psychiatric practice were at least as strong as in ***The Mandarins.*** Like Murielle, Laurence, the central figure and 'narrator' of the story, provides more than enough material for a complex psychiatric case-study. Piecing together fragmentary comments, we learn not only that she experienced some kind of severe disturbance at the age of eleven, but also that there is a certain cyclical pattern to her depressions and that she underwent a crisis five years before the events of the book take place, as well as a near-crisis only three years before. More than this, as we watch Laurence in the story she is having serious difficulties in relating to those around her, feeling alienated from everything and everyone except her children and being unable to experience the emotions that she believes she ought to. Events build up to a new major crisis—this time concerning her elder daughter, Catherine—which constitutes the climax of the book. This particular crisis, like the earlier ones, is portrayed as relating in certain ways to the state of modern Western society. (Laurence believes that just as there were 'reasons' for being disturbed in 1945, so there are in 1965, in abundance; she is therefore much more sympathetic to her daughter's anxieties about the world than are her husband and parents.) In this respect ***Les Belles Images*** takes up and develops the theme already broached in connection with the different historical and political circumstances described in ***The Mandarins,*** that mental illness and its treatment are intimately bound up with the social context in which they are set: if society itself is 'sick', how can mental health consist in successfully adapting to it? But Laurence's main preoccupations in the story and the extremes to which she is driven by them are shown, above all, as stemming once more from her own upbringing, from the 'psychoanalytical situation as it exists without the parents' knowledge'.

While our situation as readers of ***Les Belles Images*** is basically similar to that in **'Monologue'**—we have only Laurence's views to base our judgements upon—here we do in fact see her with both her father and mother and, most important of all, we watch her eventually lose faith in her apparently crucial relationship with her father. Laurence is one of a surprisingly high number of characters in Beauvoir's later fiction who are said or seen to have an unresolved Oedipus complex. It is hinted in the story that this is at the root of any difficulties in her relations with her husband and other men, but in any case her breakdown at the end of the book comes after a trip to Greece with her father (they actually visit the crossroads where Oedipus is said to have killed Laius), when Laurence fails to make the kind of spiritual contact with him that she desires. More specifically, her final crisis (which like those of Murielle and

Monique expresses itself in severe physical symptoms, notably anorexia and vomiting) is precipitated by the surprise announcement that her father and mother are to begin living together again after a lengthy separation and Laurence's consequent acknowledgement that she has become *disillusioned* with her father. Equally important to the story is the fact that in her attitude towards the particular issue that provides the point of focus for the conflict at the end of the book—how Laurence's daughter Catherine should be handled—Laurence is reacting strongly against the way in which she herself was brought up by her dominant mother. Like Murielle, she claims with regret that although she was closer to her father, it was her mother who 'formed' her, and she is quite determined by the end that Catherine shall not be forced to toe the line in the way that she was.

What is particularly intriguing about the ending of ***Les Belles Images,*** however, is that the particular form taken by Laurence's reaction against a childhood that we are encouraged to see in psychoanalytical terms directly brings into the picture the other main strand of Beauvoir's views on psychiatry, that is her reservations about certain aspects of psychiatric *treatment.* Laurence, despite her claim at one point that she does not know what to think about psychoanalysis, is shown as having firm opinions about psychiatry in general. She is instantly opposed to her husband's suggestion that Catherine be taken to see a 'psychologist' and, although we probably sense that there is some truth in his retort that 'parents are immediately jealous of psychologists who deal with their children' (Laurence later admits as much), her rational justification of her distrust is one already familiar to us from ***The Mandarins:*** '"Isn't as it should be": what does that mean? In my opinion, things aren't altogether "as they should be" with the people you consider normal'. Like Monique, however, she eventually gives way and allows Catherine to begin going to a psychiatrist, Mme. Frossard, before she goes off to Greece with her father. But even during that trip Laurence expresses doubts about her decision. Again, ideas already present in ***The Mandarins,*** like that of 'mutilation' in psychiatric treatment, are right to the fore: 'On the pretext of curing Catherine of the "sentimentality" that bothered Jean-Charles, they were going to mutilate her'. When Laurence returns from Greece she at first appears willing to accept Mme. Frossard's analysis and the advice that Catherine needs to be gently separated from her best friend, Brigitte. Yet she soon begins to resist and in the end, to her husband's great surprise, makes an issue of the matter, insisting that Catherine shall not be 'mutilated', shall not be deprived of the friend that she, Laurence, never had, and shall stop seeing the psychiatrist.

It might be argued that Laurence's attitude towards psychiatry at the end of ***Les Belles Images*** is, like Anne's at the end of ***The Mandarins,*** something of a special case, in that she is in a very singular, disturbed state of mind and that her central preoccupation with the welfare of her daughter has little to do with psychiatry as such. But it is important to recognize that Laurence's resistance to psychotherapy is not confined to the case of Catherine or to the end of the novel. If we study her comments on her own past problems we learn that she is really rather proud of having tackled her difficulties without professional aid: 'Naturally, her depression had deeper causes, but she did not need to be psychoanalysed to come out of it; she took a job that interested her; she recovered'. This does not, of course, prevent us from having doubts whether she is a good advertisement for the brand of self-help that she is implicitly advocating, even though her commendable stand at the end seems to be the result of a deliberate process of self-analysis ('I have drawn the curtains and, lying down with my eyes closed, I shall go over the trip again, image by image, word by word). More important here, however, is the point that, like Murielle, Laurence is portrayed as having assimilated certain Freudian insights, so that anything that she manages to do for herself is undoubtedly already dependent upon psychoanalytical theory and method: 'I am aware of the real reasons behind me: crisis and I have put them behind me: I brought out into the open the conflict between my feelings for Jean-Charles and those for my father and it no longer tears me apart'. Yet altogether much of her thinking about herself takes psychoanalytical concepts like the Oedipus complex as a starting-point, something—presumably her distrust of how psychiatrists actually treat their patients—makes her oddly wary of accepting the full implications of the type of explanation involved: 'I am simply jealous. An unresolved Oedipus complex, with my mother remaining my rival. Electra, Agammemnon: is that why I found Mycenae so moving? No. No. Nonsense. Mycenae was beautiful; it was its beauty that moved me . . . I am jealous, but above all, above all . . . . In other words, through the hesitations and contradictions of her heroine, Beauvoir can once more be seen to adopt in ***Les Belles Images*** the ambiguous, uneasy stance towards psychiatry that we have detected in other stories. She invokes theories of mental illness with varying degrees of conviction, but resists, for the most part, the notion that psychiatric treatment as it is professionally conceived is a desirable or appropriate procedure for dealing with it.

Although examination of further detailed evidence from the stories considered would produce nothing to modify this general account, we do, of course, need to bear in mind the existence of Beauvoir's many essays and autobiographical works. Scrutiny of these would undoubtedly refine our understanding of her attitude towards psychoanalytical theory, but it would not be likely to add to our knowledge of her reservations about psychotherapeutic practices, since she has said little about the latter in her non-fictional writings. Indeed, one of the tangible advantages of specifically studying the fictional expressions of Beauvoir's views is that it brings out the importance of this distinction and enables us to see the whole matter in a broader perspective.

When Sartre describes himself as a 'critical fellow-traveller' to psychoanalysis, he uses a description that fits Beauvoir just as well as himself, and it is in the very ambivalence implied that the importance of their continuing dialogue with Freudian theory resides. The interest of Sartre's attempt to assimilate psychoanalysis into his own philosophy at the different stages of his career has long been apparent, but those of Beauvoir's fictional works written when Sartre was producing no novels can now be seen to give the topic an additional density or resonance at two levels. Both in the author's own process of creating her characters and in the struggles of particular individuals in the stories to understand themselves and those around them, we see the vacillations and unease that result from using certain psychoanalytical concepts and methods without a wholehearted belief in, or commitment to them. And, perhaps above all, we see very closely linked with this a distrust of therapeutic practices as employed by professional psychiatrists which varies in strength and even in nature but never quite disappears. In all of these respects Beauvoir's stance in her fiction is very much in line with (and may well, via Laing and others, have actually *influenced*) recent attitudes towards psychiatry. Her stories themselves never go beyond a broad identification of psychiatry with psychoanalysis proper, but it is quite clear from them that her sympathies lie with modern attempts to break wholly new ground in both the theory and practice of psychiatry. In the latest volume of her autobiography Simone de Beauvoir reveals that she has read with great attention the works of Szasz, Cooper, Laing and others: it is interesting to speculate what fictional embodiments of 'anti-psychiatry' this may yet produce from her pen.

Carol Ascher (essay date 1988)

SOURCE: "Women and Choice—A New Look at Simone de Beauvoir and *The Second Sex*," in *Faith of a (Woman) Writer,* edited by Alice Kessler-Harris and William McBrien, Greenwood Press, 1988, pp. 173-8.

[*In the following essay, Ascher examines Beauvoir's views concerning freedom, morality, and women's oppression as delineated in* The Second Sex *and* The Ethics of Ambiguity.]

How does the individual responsibility and choice that we assume for each woman dovetail with our belief that failure, disease, and psychological crippling are caused by oppression? In recent years, the women's movement has tended to accept the liberal connection between caring and an assumption of determinism. Because of this, we focus on the oppression side of the issue when we reach out to help a battered wife or someone who has just been raped. As if our sympathy might be blown away, we shout, "you're blaming the victim" at anyone who dares to raise the issue of choice. Though it may not seem useful to debate the abstract concepts of free will and determinism, the implications of these ideas live in the way we view, as well as act on, our lives.

These issues have crystallized for me in writing my book, *Simone de Beauvoir; a Life of Freedom,* and talking to other women across the country about her ideas. Though she has been called the mother of this wave of the women's movement the interest of American feminists in her existentialism has been negligible. In discussing ***The Second Sex,*** women have marveled at, or been exhausted by, her encyclopedic detailing of the patriarchy as it has shaped history as well as the chronological life of each female. But the dialectic of choice which is an integral (though imperfectly realized) part of that book has been almost totally ignored.

Freedom, as those who have read the memoirs know, has been a catapulting notion for Simone de Beauvoir throughout her life. As a personal vision, it has pulled at her as the wish for love or harmony might draw another. It has also been a tool by which she has judged (harshly at times) her life.

Reading the memoirs, however, one notes an idiosyncratic manner in which necessity and freedom combine at moments of particular contentment. She feels most free when she is at one with what she is doing and can't imagine doing or being anything else—that is, an inner necessity imparts her very feeling of freedom. For example, she writes of her pleasure as a child in being just who she was, inside her own family, with her younger sister Poupette at her side. It was all perfect; she couldn't imagine another life. Being a devout, bourgeois Catholic in the early years of this century was, of course, all part of this self-satisfied perfection. Or later, starting at the age of nine, her friendship with Elizabeth Mabille gave her a sense of freedom because of its feeling of being necessary to her existence. And when she met Sartre at the Sorbonne a dozen years later, she felt that, like Zaza, he too would "impose himself upon me, prove he was the right one otherwise I should always be wondering: why he and not another?" A second quote about her early relationship with Sartre conveys this same overlay of freedom and necessity:

> When I threw myself into a world of freedom, I found an unbroken sky above my head. I was free of all shackling restraint, and yet every moment

> of my existence possessed its own inevitability. All of my most remote and deep-felt longings were now fulfilled.

Now de Beauvoir is being self-conscious and not a little self-ironic when she writes this (though she is also clear about the pleasure of her emotion), for the God who once granted her necessity is gone, and only the primitive wish to replace that necessity thrives on.

For the same reasons, philosophically speaking, de Beauvoir's most anguished moments are those when inner or outer necessity stands at the door, but is not answered by a freedom imported through either her acquiescence or circumstance. A moment alone on a train when she experiences the raw unfulfilled needs of her sexuality is one example from early adulthood. During World War II, and again during the French-Algerian War, the "force of circumstance" is unbearable to her because of the multitude of personal and political acts which go against her wishes and are beyond her control.

In reading Simone de Beauvoir, whether it is fiction, sociological treatise, or autobiography, however, one must remember that she is a philosopher at base, and words like freedom, even if ironically intended, convey the richness of a philosophical view. During the first decade of her relationship with Sartre (1929-39), their understanding of freedom was highly personal. With God unmasked as merely a "useless passion," society, as created by individual human beings, had nothing sacred about it. It could be changed to suit those individuals by mere acts of decision and will. As she writes of herself and Sartre:

> The working plan which Sartre and I were pursuing for the annexation of the world around us did not fit in with those patterns and taboos established by society. Very well, then; we rejected the latter, on the supposition that man would have to create his world again from scratch. (***The Prime of Life***)

In fact, in their view, the pretense that there was either a sacred quality to social laws or something immutable about them was an act of "bad faith."

Though the choice to be free was an individual one, it obviously had social repercussions. "Our liberties support each other like the stones of an arch," de Beauvoir argued in an early philosophical essay, ***Pyrrhus et Cinéas.*** The choice had to be made. One had a moral duty to oneself and others to make it.

The war, and particularly her direct experience with the German occupation of France, gave to de Beauvoir the beginnings of a more complex view of the power of the world as it is and what might be needed for social change. Sartre, as she writes in her memoirs, was coming to consider himself an activist; and he would begin to try to reconcile his existentialism, for a short time, with the views of the French Communist Party and, in the long run, with a Marxist perspective.

The Ethics of Ambiguity, despite de Beauvoir's critical evaluation to the contrary, stands among her most interesting works. In this long philosophical essay, she began to speak to how oppression might curtail freedom—when an act of freedom "is condemned to fall uselessly back upon itself because it is cut off from its goals," this constitutes oppression—as well as to imagine how one might develop an ethics of revolution. (What does one do when one cannot convince the oppressor to yield his power; how does one evaluate violence?) One of the major contributions of this work is her distinction between freedom and liberation. Understanding that oppression for some people was such that they could not simply choose to be free, she argued that in those cases there had first to be social liberation. A slave, for example, might not even be aware of his or her servitude, and it would be "necessary to bring the seed of his liberation from the outside" (***Ethics***). In this book, too, de Beauvoir tried to establish the criteria by which to distinguish oppression from acts of bad faith. "The less economic and social circumstances allow an individual to act upon the world, the more the world appears to him as given. This is the case of women who inherit a long tradition of submission, and those who are called 'the humble'" (***Ethics***). Yet, she warns, "There is often laziness and timidity in their resignation; their honesty is not complete" (***Ethics***). Thus, though oppression was internalized in the individual, there were in a sense still free zones which could be called accountable to act.

In late 1946, at the age of 38, de Beauvoir began to write ***The Second Sex.*** She completed the book—1,000 pages in French—in 2 1/2 years, taking out time to travel to the U.S. and to write her journalistic account, ***America Day by Day.*** To add to the accomplishment, it should be noted that, although women had recently been given the vote in France, and so the question of female emancipation was surely in the air, in the context of the devastation and deaths of World War II, news of Stalin's camps, the beginning of a nuclear world with the bombing of Hiroshima and Nagasaki, and the arming of Europe in the Cold War between the United States and Russia, a discussion of women from the beginning of civilization to the present did not appear on the front burner in the world of left Parisian intellectuals—or anywhere. Nor did de Beauvoir have a women's group, or even a woman friend, with whom to share her efforts.

The Second Sex opens with three sections focusing on theories of women's condition that to de Beauvoir are deterministic: biologism, psychoanalysis, and Marxism. To the first, she argues basically that, though our being finite and physical has an effect on how we see the world, the details of our body make no difference, and that "One is not born but becomes a woman." To the second, she offers two arguments: that a Freudian explanation (penis envy) reduces to physiology what could be explained by power; and that psychoanalysis designates transcendence or freedom as normal for men, while condemning women to the "normalcy" of immanence and oppression. As for Marxism, the advent of private property is, to de Beauvoir, an insufficient explanation for women's oppression. In fact, class conflict itself need not exist and must be accounted for. Thus dispensing with the popular explanations for women's oppression, de Beauvoir would seem at the point of asserting a freedom which has merely been waiting to be acted upon. For if nothing has made the patriarchy a necessity, then why not simply lift it off?

Yet de Beauvoir does finally offer a grounding for men's power over women: it lies in what she sees as a basic category, "the other," and the primitive desire to dominate this other. Now this philosophical category has followed de Beauvoir through her early novels and theoretical works. (It is central to Sartre's *Being and Nothingness.*) The wish to dominate—or, at times, annihilate—the other is part of the same "bad faith" that makes some long for Gods and others want to be God. The lonely, separate, finiteness of the mortal individual is too hard to bear. Dominating and being dominated offer the escape from freedom into necessity. If men solve their fear of freedom by assuming power over women, women solve theirs by being that "other" which is dominated. In fact, with the introduction of this existentialist category of the Other, we are back, or still, in the realm of choice.

In ***The Second Sex,*** de Beauvoir expands the analysis of oppression, freedom, and morality she began in ***The Ethics of Ambiguity.*** "Every time transcendence falls back into immanence, stagnation, there is a degradation of existence into the 'en soi'—the brutish life of subjection to given conditions—and of liberty into constraint and contingence. At one time, in early civilization, there were material reasons for men becoming the dominators and women the dominated, but these reasons have long been obsolete. This downfall represents a moral fault if the subject consents to it; if it is inflicted upon him, it spells frustration and oppression" (***Second Sex***). Women who want to be the subject of their lives as much as do men, are confined to immanence, to being an object: "What particularly signalizes the situation of woman is that she—a free and autonomous being like all human creatures—nevertheless finds herself living in a world where men compel her to assume the status of Other" (***Second Sex***). Unable to reach out toward new liberties through projects in the world, women live unduly tied to their bodies, their physiology; through narcissism, they make projects of themselves, but they thereby only increase their situation as the Other.

In their status as Other, women are like Blacks and Jews—or any other oppressed people. "The eternal feminine corresponds to 'the black soul' and the Jewish character'" (***Second Sex***). Although the Jew is not so much inferior as the evil enemy, both women and Blacks "are being emancipated today from a like paternalism, and the former master class wishes to 'keep them in their place'" (***Second Sex***). The "good Negro" is childish, merry, submissive. The "true woman" is frivolous, infantile, irresponsible. By definition, the Other is not worthy of the responsibilities and benefits of full citizenship.

Still, de Beauvoir does not conceive of women's activities as fully determined. "I shall place woman in a world of values and give her behavior a dimension of liberty," she says. "I believe that she has the power to choose between the assertion of her transcendence and her alienation as object; she is not the plaything of contradictory drives; she devises solutions of diverse ranking in the ethical scale" (***Second Sex***). Rather than her situation being imposed on her, as it is upon a child or a slave, "the western woman of today chooses it or at least consents to it" (***Ethics***). This means that, unlike children or absolutely oppressed peoples, who have no opportunity to choose change, "once there appears a possibility of liberation, it is a resignation of freedom not to exploit the possibility, a resignation which implies dishonesty and which is a positive fault" (***Ethics***). In fact, because all our liberties are mutually interdependent, de Beauvoir implies that women's complicity in their own oppression is also thwarting the liberty of men. Because women have some access to freedom, judgments about their acts should be based, not on "normalcy," but on "moral invention." These judgments should be positive, about where and when women have made choices within the confines of their circumstances.

Unfortunately, this enormously creative project of determining women's "moral inventiveness" within the framework of oppression is only unevenly accomplished. (In fact, more than thirty years later, the project awaits furthering by any writer.) Instead, ***The Second Sex*** has a lumpiness, in which oppression is described with great vigor for paragraphs or pages on end, and only at times interspersed with sections in which one sees how women choose or act upon their (greatly constricted) freedom, pushing it beyond its previous borders. Of course, the overweighting of the oppression side of the dialectic has also been emphasized in the English edition (and in the most current French edition, as well) by the omission of the lives of fifty French painters, writers, soldiers, doctors, etc., who pushed beyond the borders of their world and so created greater freedom for themselves and others. Still, the integration of freedom and oppression doesn't work perfectly on every page. One can imagine de Beauvoir in the Bibliothèque Nationale. She had begun the project, she says, not out of being a feminist, but merely to try to understand what it meant to be a woman. The impressions caused by her reading must have bowled her over! It must have been hard to remember the sense of freedom and choice she had sought to keep alive.

Simone de Beauvoir's pleasure in her memoirs when inner freedom and necessity seem contained within each other show both that she (like most others) finds comfort in being in harmony with herself, and that in her youth and early adulthood this inner harmony seemed most likely to be produced by loving someone who gave her life direction. Yet her life has not been one geared toward comfort; on the contrary, she had often sacrificed the least of the known in order to think and act in ways that grant herself and others greater freedom. If there is the anguish of this discomfort in her fiction and later memoirs, it is an honest anguish—of the price that everyone must pay.

In my talks about de Beauvoir I have been asked as often, "But she really hates men, doesn't she?" as "Don't you think she finally blames women for it all?" Like most books, ***The Second Sex*** may be seen as a Rorschach, for people do read what they want in it. And I must admit, ten years ago when I first read the book I saw the detailing of women's oppression only; I would have been astounded and disbelieving had someone pointed out the recurrent theme of choice. Yet de Beauvoir's requirement of determining oppression is a demanding one; if, and only if, one has *tried* to reach toward a goal, and that attempt has been definitively thwarted, can one speak of being oppressed. At a time when women are being asked to pull in the enlarged boundaries they have fought for over the past decade, it seems particularly important to hold onto this active notion of oppression, with its implications for responsibility and choice.

Jo-Ann Pilardi (essay date 1989)

SOURCE: "Female Eroticism in the Works of Simone de Beauvoir," in *The Thinking Muse: Feminism and Modern French Philosophy,* edited by Jeffner Allen and Iris Marion Young, Indiana University Press, 1989, pp. 18-34.

[*In the following essay, Pilardi explores Beauvoir's philosophical investigations into female eroticism and passivity in* The Second Sex. *According to Pilardi, "in* The Second Sex *and elsewhere, a woman is described by Beauvoir as so totally merged with her erotic experience that her own body seldom appears to her as anything but a fevered 'receiving machine.'"*]

The canon of Western literature is filled with lectures by men about female sexuality, from Ovid to Diderot to Freud. To create and maintain the myth of male superiority, patriarchy has required that the "other" voices on eroticism be silent, or be reduced to silence through ridicule and omission. Yet that is hardly surprising. Erotic experience is an important dimension of human life. Indeed, some would argue that it is a dimension more fundamental than any other. It is, thus, inevitable that women's erotic experience, like every other dimension of women's lives, has been structured—constrained—by patriarchal society.

Simone de Beauvoir's is the sole female voice to be heard among the first generation of existentialists and phenomenologists of twentieth-century France. In ***The Second Sex,*** Beauvoir struggled to create a theory of women's oppression from an existentialist philosophy of subjectivity and freedom. Her analysis of female eroticism in that book was constrained by patriarchal conceptualizations as much as it was by the limits of existentialism. The problems she met with in that work provide a good example of how difficult it is to create an "other" to the patriarchal ideology. Yet it is critical that women do so. The effort of women to reclaim our bodies must include an intellectual reclaiming as well as direct physical control. It must include women's own descriptions and analyses of our own sexuality.

In this essay I trace the development of Simone de Beauvoir's thought on female eroticism from her early novels, through ***The Second Sex,*** to two later essays, **"Must We Burn Sade?"** and **"Brigitte Bardot and the Lolita Syndrome."** In such a study, ***The Second Sex*** will remain of central importance, however, because there she directly presents her analysis of eroticism. Yet the directness of Beauvoir's analytical method in ***The Second Sex*** is offset by a certain indirectness, since the analysis of eroticism appears scattered throughout the work. Beauvoir's analysis of eroticism is at base existentialist and phenomenological, although she makes use of the work of other contemporary French thinkers and, of course, adds to this her own unique vision and sensitivity about woman's situation.

Although Beauvoir claimed more than once that an analysis of women's eroticism was necessary, it remains unfinished in ***The Second Sex.*** In that work Beauvoir adopts a position that remains problematic in two ways: (1) it is an analysis of female eroticism that is traditional and phallocentric in that it describes women's experience as passive and men's experience as active, and (2) it "betrays" the existentialist analysis that is the work's announced philosophical foundation in that it focuses on, indeed describes, the determining factors that limit women. In spite of Beauvoir's occasional calling women to task for not insisting on our freedom, freedom is overshadowed by limitation, determination, or in Sartrian language, "facticity." Women's situation is spelled out, from prehistory to mid-twentieth century, as one of confinement and oppression within a patriarchal world.

Eroticism

Following the existential-phenomenological tradition, Beauvoir maintains that eroticism is that dimension of human existence that has to do with the sexual, but always insofar as it denotes a situation and a lived experience, not a collection of genital facts. "The body is not a thing, it is a situation," she says, acknowledging a debt to Heidegger, Sartre, and Merleau-Ponty. Eroticism cannot be reduced to mere energy, or reflex, but should be understood as a form of *desire,* which is the choice of a human consciousness. The essential character of eroticism, for Beauvoir, is a movement toward the other. What will be discovered in this movement is not only that I am flesh, but that I am an active consciousness as well—in short, I discover the "ambiguity" of the human condition.

The concept of "ambiguity" had already been discussed by Beauvoir in ***The Ethics of Ambiguity,*** published in 1947. The term "ambiguity," functioning on two levels, first carries the existentialist claim that human life is ambiguous, not ever fixed, i.e., human existence has no nature, neither participating in a universal human nature nor having an individual but fixed nature. It is "ambiguous"—uncertain and undefined. Second, ambiguity besets those "truths" of the human condition which have a contradictory nature: freedom and servitude, solitude and the bond with others, life and death, and the insignificance as well as importance of the human being. Thus understood in an existential and ethical sense, ambiguity is the mark and the tension of the human condition within the self-other configuration:

> . . . each is bound to all; but that is precisely the ambiguity of one's condition: in one's surpassing toward others, each one exists absolutely as for one's self; each is interested in the liberation of all, but as a separate existence engaged in one's own projects.

Because our existence is lived out in relation to our being flesh so differently than men's, an understanding of women's eroticism is central to an existential-phenomenological understanding of women.

The erotic may include, but certainly need not include, love. In Beauvoir's novels, the emotion of love is a favorite topic, most often in the form of the dependency relationship of a woman upon a man. Although some claim that Beauvoir is a didactic writer, Merleau-Ponty's assertion that she is not morally but metaphysically or ontologically didactic is more precise. A lesson that Beauvoir teaches well—particularly in her novels—is the evil of the dependency of women and, relatedly, how perfect a medium the emotion of love is for this. She finds a woman in love a necessarily conflicted human being, first because of the nature of love itself, and second because of the ease with which love entraps a woman, to the extent that it provides her with a reason for being satisfied with less than freedom. So "love represents in its most touching form the curse that lies heavily upon woman confined in the feminine universe, woman mutilated, insufficient unto herself."

The Novels

Beauvoir's first novel, ***She Came to Stay*** (***L'Invitée***), investigates love, but not eroticism, in the relationship of a romantic triangle that is based on the hope of the development of "a real trio, a well-balanced life for three, in which no one was sacrificed." The main character, Françoise, experiences greater and greater anxiety as the important distinction blurs between essential and contingent love, and her primacy to her lover Pierre weakens. As Françoise becomes convinced that her own existence is threatened, coexistence with the other woman seems impossible and she is driven at the end to kill her. In so doing, we are told, she "had chosen at last. She had chosen herself." This woman in love had no other alternative but to destroy the other woman, an end to the primacy she enjoyed with her lover being unbearable in that it would involve her "suicide," for her own existence was so marked by her dependence on him. Thus the Hegelian malediction Beauvoir uses as epigraph for this novel is realized: "Each consciousness seeks the death of the other." In ***Les Belles Images,*** a much later work, we find a similar theme: women living unsatisfactory and unsatisfied lives not only because they are members of a degenerate bourgeoisie, but also because they are mere reflections, mere dependencies, of the men through whom they live.

In ***The Blood of Others,*** an early novel set in the period of the French Resistance, we find described not only love but eroticism. Beauvoir metaphorically renders one woman's erotic experience as a gradual metamorphosis from woman, to plant, to spongy moss, to jellyfish, enveloped always in darkness and vapors, becoming less and less capable of voluntary movement. The female erotic subject she describes becomes more uncomfortable as she finds herself becoming like an object in the natural world, a status particularly threatening to a woman, and consequently she fights against this "naturizing" process. To continue her metaphors, we could say that the woman seeks to retain the stark light of subjectivity against the dark and spongy forest world of the female flesh. For this woman, carnality and subjectivity at once will be no easy task. The hardest fight, clearly, involves her subjectivity.

Eroticism in *The Second Sex*

The Second Sex contains extensive comments on female eroticism, primarily in the chapters on psychoanalysis (chapter 2), and sexual initiation (chapter 14). Beauvoir relies heavily on the existential categories of transcendence and immanence to define the relationship of female to male sexuality. Her analysis of female eroticism focuses on heterosexuality, except in one chapter on lesbianism.

Transcendence, the forward movement into the future of a willing subject, struggles with the urge toward immanence that also tempts the subject, the urge toward passivity, toward the being of a thing. This struggle Beauvoir had analyzed in ***The Ethics of Ambiguity.*** In ***The Second Sex,*** she writes: "Every subject plays his part as such specifically through exploits or projects that serve as a mode of transcendence; he achieves liberty only through a continual reaching out toward other liberties. . . . Every time transcendence falls back into immanence, stagnation, there is a degradation of existence."

Beauvoir's description of women carries out the existentialist approach mentioned earlier in regard to her notion of eroticism. A woman is defined as "a human being in quest of values in a world of values, a world of which it is indispensable to know the economic and social structure." The body itself is described as a situation, that particular situation which makes possible our grasp on the world. A person is a sexual body, better, a "sexuate" body, because sexuality is not a part of the person, is not "appended" to a human being. The human being is, rather, a totality, and sexuality is one dimension of that totality.

The constraint which women suffer due to social and cultural oppression is a denial of choice—i.e., our own projects, through which the self transcends itself. To be a woman is to be "other," but also still to be a subject, even given the subjection under which that particular subjectivity usually functions, for subjection is never total enough to force the for-itself to give up transcendence. The result is immanence, rather than transcendence, the being of the *en-soi* (in-itself, the thing), and not the *pour-soi* (for-itself, human consciousness). Such is a woman's "drama," her conflict. And if she manages to overcome external male-imposed constraints, she is caught in internal conflict, in that insofar as she succeeds, she defeats her *feminine* self as a subject-self. An autonomous existence for women conflicts with women's "objective self," i.e., self as "other," for to be feminine is to be nonautonomous, passive.

This conflict between being "other" and being a subject is incarnated in the body. Within the existential phenomenological perspective of ***The Second Sex,*** the body which the subject "is" is not a thing; its existence is never merely factual: ". . . if the body is not a *thing,* it is a situation, as viewed in the perspective I am adopting—that of Heidegger, Sartre and Merleau-Ponty: it is the instrument of our grasp upon the world." Directly related to the for-itself's existence-as-body is the body as sexual, erotic existence. The general condition which, as we saw, meets a female self, in that her success as self means the realization of transcendence, or subjectivity, and at the same time means her failure as a female (other/object), also meets the female self in sexual experience, but doubly so. According to Beauvoir, erotic experience itself intensely reveals the ambiguity of the for-itself, both as subject and as object for another. But the female self begins by feeling itself as object. Hence its subject status is twice in question in sexuality, or rather, its message of its own immanence is intensified, doubled.

From the point of view of a strict existentialist, one might be tempted to say that Beauvoir's notion of the self in ***The Second Sex*** is philosophically flawed, because it places too much emphasis on the constraints on freedom in "situation." In Sartrian existentialism, the subject's situation is constituted from two moments, freedom and facticity. The existentialist philosophy in Beauvoir's early work, ***The Ethics of Ambiguity,*** stresses the use of one's freedom and the respect for the freedom of others as the core of morality. The philosophy of ***The Second Sex,*** on the other hand, stresses facticity. Due to its stress on the individual subject, the Sartrian existentialism of *Being and Nothingness* neglects consideration of the long-term historical situation of a group. In ***The Second Sex,*** Beauvoir suggests that the "situation" of a certain group, women, is so impressed upon the individual as to hamper or prevent the use of freedom, that is, the individual's transcendence of her facticity. In the "Introduction to Book II" of ***The Second Sex*** Beauvoir says, "It is not our concern here to proclaim eternal verities, but rather to describe the common basis that underlies every individual feminine existence." Such a statement not only radically undercuts the notion of freedom relative to "every individual feminine existence," since through that common basis a woman is "confined," it also radically changes the focus of the analysis of existence that existentialist philosophy had made from Kierkegaard to Sartre.

A general analysis of the commonalities of any *group* of individual existents does not make the use of existentialist categories impossible by any means, though it changes the emphasis of the analysis. Each individual human being experiences facticity, according to Sartre in *Being and Nothingness,* whether or not we would call this being "confined." The innovation represented by Beauvoir in ***The Second Sex*** is twofold: not only is the analysis focused on facticity but individual facticity does not remain individual; it is generalized—genderized—since Beauvoir describes the common basis of the lives of all women, a basis provided by education and custom.

The chapter on psychoanalysis in ***The Second Sex*** reflects the tension between these twin elements of Sartrian existentialism, freedom and facticity, and displays the shift toward facticity that Beauvoir's thinking was taking (a shift Sartre's thinking made later as well). In this chapter Beauvoir claims that psychoanalysis lacks the existential perspective of the human being as a totality, a perspective that disallows the notion of sheer fact. Beauvoir claims that for psychoanalysis, sexuality is an irreducible datum, and human existence is mistakenly understood in terms of this irreducible datum rather than in terms of the transcendence that can be accomplished by a human being which is a totality, that is, in terms of an existential choice.

But Beauvoir's rejection of Freudianism is hardly complete. In order to retain some of its notions concerning sexuality in women, she uses the idea of the "constant," that is, "certain factors of undeniable generality and repetition," which can be found in every individual case. These "constants" are not "eternals." They last as long as any particular epoch, according to Beauvoir. We might call them "epochal," not eternal, truths. Thus within the patriarchal epoch, it is a "truth" that the phallus is a symbol of transcendence. It is in keeping with the power of men within a patriarchal society that the male sexual organ "means" liberty, and symbolizes the flight from facticity, from immanence, which is the human enterprise. Within patriarchal society, men are not unique in engaging in transcendence, but because they are the sex in power, they become the sex in which the properly human—transcendence—and the genital symbolically merge. Woman, a transcendent being also in that she is human, is continually denied access to subjecthood through her life situation in general. For a woman, then, transcendence will be seen as a personal *and* cultural triumph.

Further, for Beauvoir this sexist oppression has turned woman into an "imperfect being," to use Thomas Aquinas's phrase, and this means sexual as well as intellectual, metaphysical, and psychological imperfection. A woman within patriarchal society is a creature "intermediate between male and eunuch," Beauvoir says, not a fully but only a partially sexed being, because she is not a phallic creature.

Beauvoir claims that it is to Freud's credit that he maintains that for women, unlike men, there are two distinct erotic systems at work: the clitoral and the vaginal. With this fact, a woman's erotic history, as well as her erotic problems, commence. Before a woman reaches sexual maturity, she must not only pass through the narcissistic phase (at puberty) but she must also go through a second transition, from the clitoral to the vaginal. Beauvoir's notion of "constant" is at work here again, in her acceptance of the Freudian analysis of a general path of psychogenital development for women—for all women.

The phallocentrism of Freudian thinking is destructive to a thorough analysis of women, but not simply because it is modeled on male sexuality. It has, according to Beauvoir, prevented the study of female eroticism in its own right. The male libido has become not only the model of sexuality; it has also acted as the *mask* over the female libido.

Within the pages of ***The Second Sex,*** Beauvoir indeed attempts a description of female eroticism. The starting point for her analysis, an existential-via-Hegel one, is the idea that eroticism is, in its essential character, "a movement toward the Other." But this creates a problem for a woman, because she is continually made, or making herself, object, not subject. In a striking statement of this fact, Beauvoir tells us, "Woman, like man, is her body; but her body is something other than herself." Yet as an erotic creature she will have to extend herself to the Other. This amounts to a kind of "aggressiveness"—a will to be more than passive flesh, more than immanence. A woman still has an ability to be aggressive erotically, because she is never reduced finally and forever to the status of object, yet her eroticism becomes, and can remain, a source of ontological confusion to her, due to her being-made-object and not being-made-subject. She is required to *be* passively, but must at the same time *be* actively, in an erotic experience. Carnality and subjectivity simultaneously will be no easy task for woman. The hardest fight, clearly, involves her subjectivity.

A woman's erotic experience, Beauvoir maintains, is nearly always the experience of passivity. The strength of Beauvoir's assertion of women's passivity cannot be underestimated. It is extreme. A woman feels the "shame of her flesh." when gazed at, more than a man, and she "feels trespassed upon in her flesh." "She always feels passive; she is caressed, penetrated; she undergoes coition, whereas the man exerts himself actively," Beauvoir says. A woman requires a man to reveal to her own body; she is therefore more reliant on him than he on her. She is from the beginning not her own sexual being, but becomes her own through being his—to the extent that she ever becomes her own.

We can understand easily enough the source of Beauvoir's assertion that the phallus is a symbolic organ of transcendence, and, for woman, of domination as well, but she is not careful enough, so that occasionally it seems she wants to claim that the phallus is both a symbolic and a *real* organ of domination, both a symbolic and a *real* organ of transcendence. The contrast continues. We read elsewhere: "The sex organ of a man is simple and neat as a finger; it is readily visible . . . but the feminine sex organ is mysterious even to the woman herself, concealed, mucous, and humid as it is . . . Woman does not recognize herself in it."

Beauvoir provides a striking metaphor to carry her theory. "Feminine sex desire is the soft throbbing of a mollusk," thus it is similar to an animal that lacks a backbone, and with a soft and unsegmented body. I discovered that Sartre had said, six years earlier in *Being and Nothingness,* "I desire a human being, not an insect or a mollusk." Beauvoir seems to be replying, "What one receives, however, is a mollusk!" A woman's erotic experience is thus characterized by Beauvoir as primarily vaginal—for the "soft throbbing of a mollusk" is a clear reference to the vulva, and it is from this that all female eroticism is claimed to emanate. ***The Blood of Others,*** as mentioned earlier, contains a fascinating and similarly biological description of one woman's erotic experience.

It is disappointing that Beauvoir never acknowledges, to any extent, the other erotic areas of a woman's body. The dependence on the "mollusk" metaphor is what leads her to the cliché that a woman's sexuality is inward, mysterious, and unlocalized. By calling attention to the more inward and "invisible" nature of a woman's genitalia, Beauvoir claims that, sexually, a woman is something she can neither see nor understand. Her "wetness" and her bleeding—both signs of her sexuality, erotic and non-erotic (or reproductive)—are dismissed as alienations from, not realizations of, her sexuality.

> Woman lies in wait like the carnivorous plant, the bog, in which insects and children are swallowed up. She is absorption, suction, humus, pitch and glue, a passive influx, insinuating and viscous; thus, at least, she vaguely feels herself to be. Hence it is that there is in her not only resistance to the subjugating intentions of the male, but also conflict within herself.

And this conflict within herself will bring about, on more than one occasion, considerable disgust, even physical disgust, both at her own erotic being and at sex in general, Beauvoir claims.

But we need to call Beauvoir's descriptions into question. If woman's eroticism is "unsegmented" in quality, like a mollusk, it is because it has not been "segmented" intellectually, and verbally, by a culture that treats female sexuality as, precisely, mystery. And this is exactly the way Beauvoir herself treats it. Because Beauvoir fails to go beyond cultural stereotypes of woman's eroticism, she leaves us no richer on this topic than we were prior to reading ***The Second Sex.*** Stopping at the wall of mystery that has been built around woman's sexuality, she articulates for us only the message of a patriarchal culture: passivity, immanence, oppression lived in the erotic night, as well as in the day.

The generalized, unlocalized sexuality and consequent passivity that a woman is forced into leads Beauvoir, dialectically, to assert that a woman's general erotic experience is characterized by its stronger intensity than a man's. She says that, in lovemaking, a woman "loses her mind." Because the very goal of eroticism for a woman is in itself uncertain, according to Beauvoir, so too her enjoyment as it occurs "radiates throughout her whole body," that is, her enjoyment is not localized, nor is a woman conscious that her genital organs are the center of this experience.

Because female eroticism is distinctively a general, totalized body state, unlike men's, Beauvoir says that women are often repulsed by the too obvious attempts to help women achieve orgasm. Due to a woman's own special form of eroticism, she wants the achievement of a spell: "She would abolish all surroundings, abolish the singularity of the moment, of herself, and of her lover, she would fain be lost in a carnal night." In Beauvoir's novel, ***The Mandarins,*** one can find described such a generalized, unlocalized female eroticism, and the corresponding desire for the creation and maintaining of a "spell." Sexuality becomes a form of mindlessness.

Although early in ***The Second Sex*** Beauvoir denies that anything human is totally innate or totally "natural," she comes dangerously close, in her descriptions of female eroticism, to affirming what she should be denying by her own standards. At a point where we would expect Beauvoir to suggest social, historical, or cultural explanations for behavior, we find she avoids them.

Clearly, there are a variety of ways in which an individual may *actively* object to societal oppression—whether it is the oppression of a particular system of morality, as Beauvoir shows in her essay **"Must We Burn Sade?"** or the political oppression felt by a proletariat that eventually revolts, or the oppression of women, whose oppression/situation is unique within human history. We need to understand if women's erotic passivity, suitable behavior for a patriarchal culture, is not also a protest—a political action—similar to the actions American slaves took, through their listless movements and pretended incompetencies. Is women's erotic passivity a dimension of women's political rebellion? Beauvoir does not ask the question in ***The Second Sex.*** Further, one might place the body and sexuality in a cultural context, taking account of historical changes and political movements, like feminism, which have had tremendous effects on how a woman lives her body, and consequently, her sexuality.

According to Beauvoir, a woman may overcome the erotic passivity that men and culture require of her in two ways. The first way is by rejecting men permanently, by a woman living out her erotic life with women, thus satisfying her sexuality as well as her ontological need to exercise her subjectivity, for she will be engaging her eroticism within an experience in which the roles are not always, already, determined according to gender. Beauvoir claims that all women are *naturally* homosexual. Women experience the female body as desirable largely because it is the locus of their first experience of sensuality—the mother—and because the culture has made of it the erotic object par excellence. In addition, lesbianism is the form which an active eroticism may take because:

> Woman is an existent who is called upon to make herself object; as subject she has an aggressive element in her sensuality which is not satisfied on the male body; hence the conflicts that her eroticism must somehow overcome. . . . Woman's homosexuality is one attempt among others to reconcile her autonomy with the passivity of her flesh.

The second way a woman may overcome the erotic passivity she experiences within patriarchal culture is through the creation, within heterosexual couples, of a *reciprocal* relationship between female and male, in order that a woman's subjectivity be permitted and acknowledged, as her body is desired. Beauvoir displays too cavalier an attitude about the ease of achieving this state. Its content is also unclear. She provides a simplistic answer through her evocation of existentialist categories, which seem to operate merely as rhetoric. We must ask: How can one become an erotic subject if one is not a genuine subject already, that is, within the culture? And how does one escape the fear of cultural male domination, even in order to allow for the production of generosity and reciprocity in sexual intercourse?

Nonetheless, Beauvoir provides for the possibility of our thinking through human sexuality as one species differentiated into two "subsets"—female and male—rather than into two separate species. She asserts: "As a matter of fact, man, like woman, is flesh, therefore passive, the plaything of his hormones and of the species, the restless prey of his desires. And she, like him, in the midst of the carnal fever, is a consenting, a voluntary gift, an activity; they live out in their several fashions the strange ambiguity of existence made body."

Focusing as it does on the mutuality of the difficulties and pleasures of human sexuality, this passage beautifully and succinctly demystifies heterosexual sexuality. But it is, of course, only comprehensible as a utopian description of heterosexuality because it requires a state of equality between the sexes which does not yet exist, although among "verbal" political acts no work has done more than ***The Second Sex*** to bring about such a state.

Sade and Bardot: Beyond *The Second Sex*

In her essay **"Must We Burn Sade?"** Beauvoir contends that insofar as Sade's sexual aberrations were acts of cruelty directed at individuals, they are to be condemned, but insofar as his fundamental enterprise was to challenge some of his society's most basic values, he should be understood and appreciated as a type of social and moral critic, one who chose to work out his argument with society through erotic experience. (The extent to which he differs from the "ordinary" sex criminal in this is an important question, though not to be taken up here.) "It is not the object of debauchery that excites us, but rather the idea of evil," he said, his design being (in a kind of pre-Nietzschean spirit) to oppose evil to good, to will evil in his actions as well as in his writings, as a form of active objection to the societal oppression embodied in a particular system of morality.

The Marquis de Sade did not simply torture, and thereby produce his pleasure; he dramatized his eros within the framework of a play. Beauvoir asserts that fundamental to Sade's delight in the screams of his victims, the desire for the play, really only a desire for control, was entrenched. By creating a spectacle within which the erotic can happen, the classic sadist seeks control of the other, but more important, of himself. To maintain the sovereignty of the erotic subject, too easily lost in the ecstasy of the erotic moment, that moment is mapped out in advance, scripted to protect the still un(self)mastered master. Nietzsche had said that the true man loves woman as "the most dangerous plaything," but for Sade it was not woman but erotic ecstasy which was loved, desired, as the most dangerous plaything, and for that reason he sought control over it.

For the reader of ***The Second Sex,*** two related questions arise from Beauvoir's analysis of sadistic eroticism. First, does woman's eroticism as understood by Beauvoir carry out woman's argument with society, as Sade's carried out his, and if so, how? Second, can we discover a reason for Beauvoir's interest in Sade, one related to the development of a female erotic?

First, in ***The Second Sex*** and elsewhere, a woman is described by Beauvoir as so totally merged with her erotic experience that her own body seldom appears to her as anything but a fevered "receiving machine." She is "there" carnally, like a bog, like a mollusk, darkly and slowly feeling her own sensuality, waiting not only for a man but for herself, to be overtaken by her own sensuality—hardly the "lived body" that Merleau-Ponty, another French existential-phenomenologist whom Beauvoir cites, had described.

Unquestionably, we need to advance from this standpoint, an overgeneralized, simplistic assertion of female erotic passivity. The particular erotic behavior Beauvoir is describing, passive female behavior, must be seen as only one possible form of a woman's erotic life, a Beauvoirian "bog," or Freudian "dark continent," only for those who choose to limit their own sight—and insights—of it. Such behavior is only one way in which a woman's sexuality can and has been lived out—even within the patriarchal epoch, though it may indeed be, or have been, the most common. Further, and with reference to Beauvoir's analysis of Sade, it can be claimed that this passive sexuality may indeed carry out, for women at least, their argument with society, as Sade's did his. Although in one sense this passive behavior hinders the development of a woman's subjectivity and active sense of self, in another sense, i.e., if it is a *choice* in response to patriarchy, it is the exercise of subjectivity within an unjust world, a response of protest or rebellion in the same sense that certain actions of black American slaves were indirect forms of protest. Perhaps in "the passive form" of erotic behavior, as Beauvoir says in another context, a woman "refuses to play the game because she knows the dice are loaded."

Second, what led Beauvoir to study Sade? If the foregoing is correct, this becomes clearer. The Sade essay may have been derived from her will to study how a connection may be made between subjectivity and eroticism. Sade had combined a will to evil with a will to mastery and carried these out within a totally controlled erotic experience. A woman's erotic enterprise must be nearly the reverse. For a woman there can be no pretense of mastery, since she is always cast in the role of erotic object, Beauvoir says, and denied the state necessary to mastery, that of subject. But things are not always what they seem, she reminds us, for "there is in her . . . resistance to the subjugating intentions of the male."

Beauvoir's analysis leads me to suggest that women's will to be something more than erotic object has led women to develop a control system of passivity within erotic experience. That is, we need to question whether erotic passivity, to the extent it does exist in women, has been developed as a survival tactic. But ultimately, erotic passivity is useless, just as the sadist's tactics for control are useless. The moment of erotic ecstasy, if attained, is precisely the moment in which women are uncontrolled. Moreover, erotic passivity in women is inadequate as a response to cultural domination.

The spectacular achievement of an eroticism not founded in domination will not be easy. It presupposes societal changes, as well as changes made directly by a woman upon her own eroticism. In ***Brigitte Bardot and the Lolita Syndrome,*** published in 1960, Beauvoir claims that the real basis for Bardot's appeal lies in the new quality of female eroticism she displays: an aggressiveness. Bardot, in film after film, is every bit as much the erotic hunter as the male—a self-conscious being, innocent of tricks and, in fact, oblivious to the opinions of others. Her eroticism is intimidating to men, particularly French men, because it is so unconventionally aggressive. Bardot—the ingenue with a woman's body and a sexual appetite we supposedly find only in men. The result of Bardot's presence on the screen in this role of erotic hunter is a "debunking of love and eroticism," according to Beauvoir, which has tremendous implications for the demystification and humanization of women's eroticism.

The age of Bardot has passed, and Beauvoir's analysis seems problematic. The sixties brought a sexual revolution via the increased practice of free love. The availability of sex outside the strictures of marriage certainly increased for women. Whether the quality of a woman's sexual experience also increased, and her erotic "passivity" decreased, is questionable. In any case, if there was a lessening of female erotic "passivity," the women's movement of the late sixties and seventies would, I think, have to be granted more than a little responsibility for this.

In the conclusion to ***The Second Sex,*** Beauvoir tells us that "there will always be certain differences between man and woman; her eroticism, and therefore her sexual world, have a special form of their own and therefore cannot fail to engender a sensuality, a sensitivity, of a special nature. This means that her relations to her own body, to that of the male, to the child, will never be identical with those [of] the male." It is at this point, the last full page of the book, that Beauvoir is on the verge of concretely connecting for us a woman's body/form and a woman's eroticism.

In her novels after ***The Second Sex,*** Beauvoir continues to dwell on female characters, but she never gives more than a fleeting look at the peculiarly female erotic experience which she claims in ***The Second Sex*** needs a spokeswoman. She continues in her novels, as she had done earlier, to pay great attention to love, in particular to women in love and problems resulting from that experience, but nowhere will one find the descriptions of female eroticism she implied should be made. It was not via existential phenomenological description, but through autobiographical narration, the telling of the story of her own life, that she intended to concretize the analysis of woman that she had begun earlier. In an interview with Alice Schwarzer in 1978, Beauvoir expressed dissatisfaction with her memoirs, specifically on this point:

> I would have liked to have given a frank and balanced account of my own sexuality. A truly sincere one, from a feminist point of view; I would like to tell women about my life in terms of my own sexuality because it is not just a personal matter, but a political one, too.

It is important to keep in mind that Beauvoir's descriptions of the passivity of "carnal fever" into which a woman submerges are meant to be descriptions of a *specific historical* woman—i.e., patriarchalized woman, rather than some "*eternal* woman," doomed in an "innate" or "determined" sexuality of passivity. Beauvoir ends not with female passivity, in ***The Second Sex,*** but with *difference:* "There always will be certain differences between men and women; woman's eroticism and therefore her sexual world have a specific form and therefore a special sensuality."

Thus we need to begin at the point to which Beauvoir led us, and where she unfortunately leaves off: with a description of a female erotic, a description of a woman's "special sensuality," and with a comprehension of the relationship to this of human consciousness and human history. The specific task confronting feminist thinkers now is a comprehension of women's lived body, which might include: (1) the sensory systems of the clitoral and vaginal areas, (2) the breasts, for women, as zones of erotic pleasure in themselves and as instruments within an erotic drama in which men participate, and are manipulated, (3) female experience of the male body, (4) female experience of the female body, and (5) women's "unlimited" sexuality, as well as whether and how this is diminished through the controls and regularization of marriage, as Beauvoir has claimed. Some of this has been addressed already in feminist poetry and novels, but more needs to be done.

Women's victimization within a patriarchal society includes an elaborate intellectual system of silences constructed against the simple fact of our existence, which ignores women's manner of being and invalidates our experience. We need to create, and it is a political act to do so, precise descriptions to "inform" the silences surrounding all aspects of female human existence. In particular, discovering what in women's eroticism derives directly from situations of oppression, what is derived from and determined by our bodily structures, and what dimensions women's eroticism can hope to take on in a nonsexist world, become basic issues of a feminist theory of eroticism.

Niza Yanay (essay date January 1990)

SOURCE: "Authenticity of Self-Expression: Reinterpretation of Female Independence Through the Writings of Simone de Beauvoir," in *Women's Studies,* Vol. 17, January, 1990, pp. 219-33.

[In the following essay, Yanay examines Beauvoir's interpretation of female dependency, interpersonal connection, and autonomy as suggested in her autobiographic writings. According to Yanay, Beauvoir invites an alternate notion of female independence based on "themes of spontaneity and authenticity of expression."]

Based on the autobiographical writings of Simone de Beauvoir, this paper reinterprets the concepts of "dependency" and "independence" with respect to women's experiences. De Beauvoir, considered a strong and independent woman, continuously struggled for emotional independence, a struggle which she conceived as being against the need that drove her "impetuously toward another person". However, a careful examination of de Beauvoir's inner voice as it is reflected in the subtext of her autobiographical writings, suggests that her true struggle revolves around a desire for authentic expression of her feelings and needs—rather than for separation from others.

As an adolescent de Beauvoir was caught between the expectations of her parents and her own needs, remaining the "dutiful daughter" at the expense of being false to her own self. This pattern of dependency reappears in her adult life, when she seems to be incapable of validating her feelings of jealousy and anger in her relationship with Sartre. Her means of coping with this problem is by giving it a literary expression, hence, she seems to gain a sense of freedom and independence by giving her repressed feelings an authentic outlet.

The re-reading of de Beauvoir's autobiography in a new light of feminist criticism reveals a concept of dependency different from the need to rely on, receive help from, and be influenced by another. When one examines the meanings of dependency and independence through the female language of connectedness and women's values of care and involvement, the essential meaning of dependency shifts from the lack of self-reliance to suppression of self-expression, and from struggles for separation to struggles for one's personal truth and for authenticity in one's relations with others.

This paper aims to reopen discussion of the meaning of "dependence" and "independence" as they reflect the experiences of women. This desire to reexamine and revise accepted concepts and terms in light of principles of female experience is prompted by the work of feminist scholars, who have suggested the adoption of a new language with which to conceptualize accepted values.

Psychology treats the concept of "dependency" as a tendency to rely on and seek attention, care, or help from close others. Thus, dependence is often equated with affiliation or with the need for affection, reassurance and approval. Along these same lines, the concept of "autonomy" or "independence" is often associated with self-reliance and needing no one else—accomplishing things on the basis of one's own efforts in response to one's own interests and in an attempt to reach self-fulfillment.

This conception of autonomy has only recently been challenged by feminist scholars who explore the masculine attributes of the very nature of scientific thought. [J. B.] Miller (1976), [C.] Gilligan (1982), [E. F.] Keller (1985) and others have pointed out that the prevailing meaning of autonomy is alienating to women because it excludes passion, love, and desire, the very dynamics of interpersonal relations, which, as [O.] Kerenberg (1974) argued, require the crossing of ego boundaries. Miller (1976), for example, claims that the concept "autonomy" derives from male development, as it bears the implication that "one should be able to give up affiliations in order to become a separate and self-directed individual." Similarly, Gilligan (1982) believes that the word "autonomy" has become so closely associated with separation that "separation itself becomes the model and the measure of growth." Keller (1985) points to the correlation between the accepted meaning of autonomy and masculinity in Western culture, which she attributes to certain paradigmatic changes in the nature of scientific thinking. She claims that the transition from hermetic science, characterized by metaphors of sexual unity with nature, to a mechanical science, characterized by masculine metaphors of power and domination of nature, has shaped a concept of autonomy separate from desire and dominated by images of impersonality. At the same time, feminist scholarship in psychology (Miller, 1976; Gilligan, 1982) has demonstrated the different values around which women's selves emerge and the importance of inclusiveness and affiliation to their self-concept and identity.

My own contribution to this argument is to explore the concepts of dependency and independence as they are reflected in the autobiographical writings of Simone de Beauvoir. Not only are these works of recognized literary and intellectual merit, but they deal with "a relatively large number of lines of experience, giving a picture of variety, roundness and inter-relatedness in the life from which the structure of life as a whole emerges" ([C.] Allport, 1951). Moreover—and perhaps most importantly—they mirror a substantial portion of the author's experiences of emotional dependency, and these stand in sharp contrast to the woman herself, who has become a symbol of independence and strength in her own lifetime: "She is a woman who refuses to accept her role passively, who has taken a stand, flouting all convention and opposition" ([A.] Schwarzer, 1985). While accepting her femininity, de Beauvoir has never used her womanhood as an alibi and, moreover, she recognizes emotional dependency on men as "a curse that weighs upon most women" and a condition she has had to struggle with and to defend herself against through most of her youth and adult life. Her autobiographical works are a testimony to an unresolved struggle to reconcile her longing for independence with the love that drove her "impetuously toward another person."

However, though de Beauvoir perceives her struggle as a conflict between unity with another and separatedness—a perception based on the conventional interpretation of "dependence"—it seems that in actuality it revolved around the need to maintain a very close relationship without being false to her innermost needs and feelings. Thus, by drawing out the themes of dependency and independence of de Beauvoir's writings and interpreting them in terms of the development of the feminine self-identity, feminine values, and feminine conceptions of relationships, we challenge accepted definitions of independence and dependency in Western society, particularly the culturally perceived contradiction between love and independence. In this new light, the accepted distinction between emotional "symbiosis" or unity and individual autonomy appears conceptual and culture-bound rather than ontological and absolute. The reflexive reading of de Beauvoir's autobiographical writings through the prism of feminist conceptualizations of autonomy, with the aim of uncovering the author's most inner feelings as a woman, lends new meaning to the concepts of dependency and independence.

Setting the Stage for Reinterpretation

Simone de Beauvoir perceives the struggle for independence as the core experience in a woman's life. In her four-volume autobiography—***Memoire of A Dutiful Daughter*** (**MDD**) (1958), ***The Prime of Life*** (**PL**) (1960), ***Forces of Circumstance*** (**FC**) (1963), and ***All Said and Done*** (**ASD**) (1972)—and her first autobiographical novel, ***She Came to Stay*** (1943), she consciously and subconsciously reveals an ongoing struggle to escape "women's doomed destiny of dependent existence" and to reconcile independence and intimacy, a struggle which is also characteristic of her fictional characters (Ann in ***The Mandarins,*** Francoise in ***She Came to Stay,*** and the heroine of her short story ***The Woman Destroyed***).

The earliest signs of this inner conflict appear in her childhood memories. Even as a little girl, de Beauvoir rejected traditional feminine values (but not her own womanhood): "When we played games, I accepted the role of the mother only if I were allowed to disregard its nursing aspects. Despising other girls who played with their dolls in what seemed to us a silly way, my sister and I had our own particular way of treating our dolls" (**MDD**). The young de

Beauvoir felt that femininity limited a woman's existence, establishing her position as "other," while masculinity offered endless possibilities of intellectual excitement and freedom. Her male teachers were, in her opinion, clever, even brilliant, but the women who taught her were "comical old church hens." Even though the majority of boys she knew seemed of limited intelligence, she recognized intuitively that "they belonged to a privileged category." The world of men appeared to her as free, imaginative, and full of adventure. As an adolescent, de Beauvoir believed that men were the great writers, the finest thinkers, and that women were tied to family conventions, salon smiles, and to small talk. "My education, my culture, and the present state of society all conspired to convince me that women belonged to an inferior cast" (**MDD**).

De Beauvoir's adolescent years were marked by the contradictory expectations of her father, who projected onto his first-born daughter (he had hoped for a son) not only his pride and bourgeoise aspirations, but also his economic and social failure:

> The war had ruined him, sweeping away all his dreams, destroying his myths, his self-justifications, and his hopes. I was wrong to think he had resigned himself to the situation: he never stopped protesting against his condition . . . he was trying to show, by his aggressive exhibitionism, that he belonged to a superior class . . . I was not just another burden to be borne: I was growing up to be the living incarnation of his own failure (**MDD**).

At the same time, though he "liked intelligent and witty women and . . . was of the opinion that a woman should be well read and a good conversationalist," and though he was pleased by de Beauvoir's early scholastic success, he also believed in the myth of femininity and the cult of the family: "When I entered the 'difficult age,' he was disappointed in me: he appreciated elegance and beauty in women. Not only did he fail to conceal his disillusionment from me but he began showing more interest than before in my sister, who was still a pretty girl" (**MDD**). So while praising his daughter for her academic achievements, he was exasperated by what he considered her childish scribblings.

Notwithstanding her father's ambivalence toward her, the adolescent de Beauvoir adored and idolized him. "I could not imagine a more intelligent man than my father . . . As long as he approved of me, I could be sure of myself." At times her love for him seems incestuous: "But my real rival was my mother. I dreamed of having a more intimate relationship with my father. But even on the rare occasions when we found ourselves alone together we talked as if she was there with us" (**MDD**).

De Beauvoir's mother was a traditional woman; religious, with a strong sense of duty, she remained in the background, moderating her desires, making no demands on life, and teaching her children austerity and unselfishness. She treated her daughter with tenderness, care and understanding and gave her the acceptance that she sought and needed. "I wanted to be noticed: but fundamentally I needed to be accepted for what I was, with all the deficiencies of my age; my mother's tenderness assured me that this wish was a justifiable one . . . Without striving to imitate her, I was conditioned by her" (**MDD**).

Exposed to her father's "individualism and pagan ethical standards" on the one hand, and her mother's "rigid moral conventionalism" on the other, and torn between dependency on her mother and admiration for her father, the young de Beauvoir struggled to reconcile her intellectual life with her growing female sensibility. In this imbalanced atmosphere "I grew accustomed to the idea that my intellectual life—embodied by my father—and my spiritual life—expressed by my mother—were two radically heterogeneous fields of experience which had absolutely nothing in common" (**MDD**).

De Beauvoir's high esteem for the independent masculine mind and her disparagement of femininity were rooted thus in rebellion, as well as submission, to the image she had of her parents. She internalized their contradictory expectations of herself, particularly her father's ambivalent attitude: "I was obeying his wishes to the letter, and that seemed to anger him: he had destined me to a life of study, and yet I was being reproached with having my nose in a book all the time . . . I kept wondering what I have done wrong" (**MDD**). It was by her father's rules—and against them—that de Beauvoir the child seems to have set her ideals and developed her aspirations for freedom. It was also from those early contradictory experiences of affection, idealization and unexpressed inner resentment towards her parents that her conflict between dependency and independence emerged.

Although she idealized her father and was influenced by his literary preferences and intellectual aspirations, she was deeply wounded by his attitude towards the "fair sex" in general and toward her own femininity in particular. Similarly, although needful of her mother's acceptance, she disparaged her religiosity and traditional femininity. As an adolescent de Beauvoir was caught between the world of her parents and that of herself, and though she was developing her own sense of self and identity, she was unable to express it. She therefore remained the "dutiful daughter," being false to her true self:

> I accepted their verdict while at the same time I looked upon myself with other eyes than theirs.

> My essential self still belonged to them as much as to me: but paradoxically the self they knew could only be a decoy now; it could be false. There was only one way of preventing this strange confusion: I would have to cover up superficial appearances, which were deceptive **(MDD)**.

Even while preparing herself for graduation from school, a few years later, her outward behavior did not change: "I still didn't dare disobey or tell any outright lies. I still used to tell my mother what my plans were for the day; in the evening I had to give her a full account of how I had passed my time. I gave in. But I was choking with fury and vexation" **(MDD)**. Hence, de Beauvoir silenced her inner fury and suppressed her true needs. The gap between her real feelings, needs and wishes, on the one hand, and the de Beauvoir she showed to the outside world on the other, seems to signify a pattern of dependency on others, a pattern which continued into her adult life.

By outward appearances the adult de Beauvoir was strong-willed and independent, determined to establish her place in the world: "My own particular enterprise was the development of my life, which I believed lay in my own hands" **(PL)**. Throughout her adult life she was economically independent and never suffered the constraints of marriage or of motherhood ([D. K.] McCall, 1979). She often took long trips by herself to places "no living soul would ever pass through." She was also daring and unconventional in her teaching, standing unsupported against the values and beliefs of the provincial middle-class community in which she worked. Risking her position, she sacrificed neither her freedom of ideas nor her ideals.

Yet, despite this outward appearance of autonomy, it seems that de Beauvoir was continuously striving for emotional independence, struggling against her imperious need for others: "The existence of otherness maintained a danger for me, one which I could not bring myself to face openly" **(PL)**. Describing Francoise, the heroine of ***She Came to Stay,*** she writes: "Now another danger threatened her, one which I myself had been endeavouring to exorcise ever since my adolescence. Other people could not only steal the world from her, but also invade her personality and bewitch it" **(PL)**. This threat is particularly salient in de Beauvoir's desire and need for absolute emotional and physical unity with her friend and lover, Jean-Paul Sartre.

[C.] Ascher (1981), following the normative assumption that separatedness, individualism, self-contentment and self-reliance constitute the essence of independence, sees this relation as evidence of an unresolved dependency. In this spirit she has claimed that de Beauvoir's usage of the pronoun "we" in her memoire indicates an unsettled tension between her developing individuated self and developing intimate relationships: "With a relationship to God ended absolutely, a major theme in ***The Prime of Life*** is the tension between de Beauvoir's sense of herself as an "I" and as part of a "we," that is, the working out of her autonomy and aloneness within the context of her strong ties to Sartre" (Ascher, 1981).

It seems, however, that these "we relations" (which she had not only with Sartre, but also with others, male and female alike, whom she loved dearly) did not necessarily threaten her self-identity and autonomy. The story of her relation with Zaza is a case in point.

At the age of ten, de Beauvoir experienced the emotion of love for the first time. Elizabeth Mabille, or Zaza as she called her, was a small, dark, thin-faced girl, who was seated next to the young de Beauvoir in their fourth grade. With Zaza she talked about books, schoolwork, their teachers, and their friends. "She at once seemed to me a very finished person" and "everything she had to say was either interesting or amusing." Zaza appeared to her a fascinating person and de Beauvoir's attitude toward her, as later to Sartre, was one of admiration and total devotion. De Beauvoir was drawn to Zaza's courage and spirit of independence, as well as to her originality and talent, characteristics which attracted her also to Sartre. A simple word of praise from Zaza overwhelmed her with joy and a sarcastic smile would cause her terrible torment; her happiness, indeed her very existence, lay in Zaza's power. "Zaza didn't suspect how much I idolized her, nor that I had adjusted my pride in her favor," reflects de Beauvoir **(MDD)**. Nonetheless, her all-encompassing feeling toward Zaza did not prevent her from recognizing their individual places in the world, and her sense of "we" in this case did not compromise her recognition and acceptance of their differences. "If it had been suggested that I should be Zaza, I would have refused" **(MDD)**.

With Sartre, the "we identity" was somewhat different. De Beauvoir, like Sartre, perceived their relationship as a single unity: "I settled the anomaly of Sartre by telling myself that we formed a single entity placed together at the world's center" **(PL)**. Indeed, feeling one with Sartre was most essential to her inner harmony. However, this oneness of identity represented a value and an ideal to de Beauvoir, not a "problem" as is often suggested by her critics.

The strong feelings of closeness and affiliation that de Beauvoir shared with Zaza and later with Sartre should not be confused with dependence upon them. It is true that the accepted definition of dependency includes affiliation with another—as opposed to separatedness—as a major component, and indeed psychology as yet lacks the terminology to distinguish between connectedness and purely negative aspects of dependence, such as experience of inequality (Miller, 1976). Yet the positive and negative aspects of dependency need to be separated. Miller (1976), [L.] Stiver (1984) and others have pointed to the positive elements of dependency, such as its providing conditions for growth and enrichment. Along similar lines, [A.] Memmi (1984) considers dependency an ontological need: "On the whole, dependence is one of the basic elements of the bond that ties one member of a society to another," and the fear of dependency is a fear of others.

In an attempt to focus only on the negative aspects of dependency, the present paper pursues a new interpretation of the concept which isolates those components that reflect inequality and that have been inhibiting to women's expression of self. Underlying this quest is the assumption that women are governed by different rules of psychological development than men (Gilligan, 1983).

Authenticity of Expressed Feelings as Reflecting Independence

Simone de Beauvoir's admitted need to hide her true feelings in order to be a dutiful daughter has already been discussed, this need seems to have persisted into her adult life and to have been highly salient in her relationship with Sartre. Indeed, her tendency to mask her actual feelings is even apparent in her autobiographical works, where an inner voice seems to express feelings which are quite different from, and even contradictory to, her explicit statements. It is around this striving for authentic expression of her feelings and beliefs—rather than for separateness from others—that the true struggle for independence seems to revolve.

One clue in her autobiographical works to this struggle for authenticity of expression is the sharp contrast between the stated conception of freedom and autonomy proffered by de Beauvoir the philosopher and the intellectual and that which may be inferred from the voice of de Beauvoir the woman. The first voice advocates a conception of freedom in keeping with Sartre's existentialism. Like him, she believes that autonomy has to be attained through one's own actions, and, going further, that any woman can escape her destiny of dependence through her own efforts. Shifting one's responsibilities onto another, she feels, is immoral, and, what is more, in the absence of a God, it is a flight from freedom. According to this existential moral ontology, one transcends animal nature by a continuous affirmation of self. The voice of de Beauvoir the woman, however, suggests a different interpretation of independence, one which is closely linked to authenticity of feelings and needs.

The nature of de Beauvoir's struggle for independence is gleaned from a specific example of the way in which she coped with a triadic love arrangement involving herself, Sartre, and Olga, a young student of hers with whom she became intimate friends. Early on in their relationship, Sartre had explained to de Beauvoir his "philosophy" of attachments: "What we have is an essential love, but it is a good idea for us also to experience contingent love affairs . . . We reflected on this problem a good deal [says de Beauvoir] during our walks together" **(PL)**. Despite her ostensibly neutral intellectual tone, de Beauvoir's inner voice seems to project jealousy of the lovers and doubts as to her own worth. At the same time "the need to agree with Sartre on all subjects outweighed the desire to see Olga through eyes other than his" **(PL)**. Unable to bear the anxiety, but worse, unable to even consider diverging from Sartre's ideals, de Beauvoir chooses to glorify the trio and foster its well-being: "From now on we could be a trio rather than a couple. We believed that human relationships are a matter of constant fresh discovery" **(PL)**. Nevertheless, she admits to feelings of anger: "I was vexed with Sartre for having created this situation and with Olga for taking advantage of it."

Eventually, as is clear from her remarks in ***The Prime of Life,*** de Beauvoir deals with this love triangle by giving indirect expression to her feelings of jealousy and anger in her first autobiographical novel, ***She Came to Stay:*** "I exposed myself so dangerously [in that novel] that at times the gap between my emotions and the words to express them seemed insurmountable" **(PL)**. The novel portrays a love triangle between Francoise the heroine "whom I endowed with my own experiences" **(PL)**, her lover Pierre and a young woman Xavierre. Slowly, before the reader's eyes, Francoise is transformed from "a position of absolute and all-embracing authority" to "an utterly transparent creature without features of individuality" who betrays her own truth. With no more than a faded image of herself, Francoise becomes obsessively involved in Xavierre's affections, hatreds, and caprices, and with Pierre's desire for Xavierre. She conceals her true feelings and allows Pierre to dictate her desires because she feels lonely experiencing needs different from his. Hence, she permits herself to express only sympathy for Pierre and understanding of the triangular relationship. Even when she clearly sees Pierre as "a man fighting desperately for his masculine triumph," she sacrifices her emotional harmony for the sake of his freedom. Hurting herself is less threatening, easier, clearer, more acceptable. But her support is equivocal and not without conflict; she despises her role of benevolence. In times of "weakness" she challenges her own behavior: "She had always disregarded her dreams and her desire . . . why would she not make up her mind to will what she hoped for?" After all, "she need only say one word to herself, she need only say 'it is I.' But she would have to believe in that word; she would have to know to choose herself." Yet, Francoise continues to attribute her (unexpressed) anger, anxiety, and confusion to her own mistrust, and to her inability to transcend human pettiness. She is incapable of validating her feelings of jealousy and anger in the face of Pierre's higher, more noble emotions.

In the final analysis, however, Francoise chooses to be true to her own feelings and so to achieve the "ultimate" freedom: "Her own image became so loathsome to Francoise that she was faced with two alternatives: A lifetime of self-disgust, or to shatter the spell by destroying her who cast it. This latter course she took, and thus remained, triumphantly, true to herself" (**PL**). And it is this fictional murder of Xavierre that gains de Beauvoir her freedom; killing Olga on paper "purged every twinge of irritation and resentment I had previously felt toward her and cleansed our relationship . . ." (**PL**). Moreover, destroying Olga in a projected literary act was more than a cathartic experience. It was also a means of extracting and displaying her innermost feelings. "By releasing Francoise, through the agency of crime, from the dependent position in which her love for Pierre kept her, I gained my own personal autonomy" (**PL**).

The act of crime represents in de Beauvoir's writing the epitome of both individualism and immersing oneself into the whole of society. It is one means albeit an admittedly extreme one, of achieving independence. Indeed, in discussing her feelings of dependence upon Sartre, de Beauvoir makes an explicit connection between crime and personal autonomy:

> The only solution would have been to accomplish some deed for which I alone, and no one else, must bear the consequences. But this would have meant society as a whole taking charge of the matter, since otherwise Sartre would have shared the responsibility with me. Nothing, in fact, short of an aggravated crime could bring me true independence. I often amused myself by a more or less close interweaving of these related themes. (**PL**)

Perhaps that is why the metaphysical aspects of crime have always fascinated de Beauvoir and captured her imagination: ". . . crime figured regularly as an element in my dreams and fantasies. I saw myself in the dock, facing judge, prosecutor, jury, and a crowd of spectators, bearing the consequences of an act which I recognized as my handiwork, and bearing it alone" (**PL**). As de Beauvoir could not actually commit a crime—"Francoise, as I have depicted her, is just as incapable of murder as I am" (**PL**)—she gained her freedom through a literary projection. The philosophical and ontological ties between the primordial state of "being true to oneself" and the act of murder has long historical roots. The connotative meaning of the Greek "authento" simultaneously reflects the virtue of power over someone or something and the act of committing a murder ([L.] Trilling, 1972). Similarly, "[S.] Miller (1973) traces the 'politics of the true self' back to the poet William Blake and shows that violence is conceived of as the ultimate form of self-expression and self-discovery in the writings of Fanon and Sartre" (in [R.] Turner, 1976).

Much like Raskolikov's murder of the old woman in *Crime and Punishment,* which was a psychological assertion of his freedom and authenticity, even if momentary, so was de Beauvoir's literary solution of killing Xavierre. This was not merely a philosophical stand, but rather a means of recovering her autonomy and reaching as very deep emotional and psychological resolution. Francoise's real crime, then, was having refused to accept responsibility for her inner needs. Indeed, by justifying, rationalizing and suppressing her emotions, and thereby relinquishing her independence, she had been untrue to herself. Ironically, she purges herself of this sin with an act of extreme violence:

> Francoise has given up looking for an ethical solution to the problem of coexistence. She endures the Other as an inevitable burden and then defends herself against this invasion by accomplishing an equally brutal and irrational act herself: murder. The rights and wrongs of her individual case do not concern me. (**PL**)

This should not be construed to mean that any expression of needs and emotions short of crime lacks authenticity. On the contrary, the ultimate solution of murdering Xavierre is employed by de Beauvoir to depict an act of psychological inversion, to indicate how unnecessary the act would have been if only Francoise had accepted and expressed her true emotions and needs. Authentic expression of needs and emotions through language is, according to de Beauvoir, a viable substitute for violence directed toward the self or the other. "The paradoxical thing is that [gaining my autonomy] did not require an unpardonable action on my part, but merely the description of such an action in a book" (**PL**).

Interesting enough, the more accepted solution (by social standards) of having Francoise leave Pierre does not seem adequate to be Beauvoir, although it would have relieved her of an "awkward" ending, which has been frequently criticized by her readers, and which she herself recognized to be "beyond any doubt the weakest aspect of the book" (**PL**). Yet she insists on this conclusion, as it conveys a personal truth which she desperately needed to express.

In de Beauvoir's autobiographical writings the need for another person (excessive as it may be) is distinct from dependency. Her ardent need for unity with Sartre is congruent with her desire for an absolute and essential existence. Similarly, it was not Francoise's need for unity with Pierre which condemned her to a life of servitude. What drove Francoise from her independent self was the lack of spontaneity and authenticity of her emotions and needs.

In summary, the re-reading of de Beauvoir's autobiography in a new light of feminist criticism, reveals a concept of dependency different from the need to rely on, receive help from, and be influenced by another. When one examines the meanings of dependency and independence through the female language of connectedness and women's values of care and involvement, the essential meaning of dependency shifts from lack of self-reliance to suppression of self-expression, and from struggles with separation to struggles with one's own truth and authenticity with respect to relations with others.

It may not be surprising, within de Beauvoir's philosophical framework of the ontological opposition between self and other, that spontaneity of desire and authenticity of expression are the intrinsic values of a dignified human existence, as well as those qualities which distinguish otherness and alterity from autonomous existence. This is not to say that de Beauvoir did not attach an utter importance to the economic and material condition of women. She continuously argued that a woman can achieve true autonomy only through the practice of an independent profession. However, authentic expression of needs is a necessary mediation between love and autonomy.

With all its philosophical connotations, the connection between authentic self-expression and independence ring intimate and psychologically close. It reveals an unspoken dimension of human experience which needs to be further explored and understood.

Whether inhibited self-expression indeed captures the core of women's inner experience of dependency in our society is an empirical question for another study. Nonetheless, de Beauvoir's autobiography does demand our reconsideration of the concept of independence defined as self-reliance and dependency defined as its lack, and calls our attention to the themes of spontaneity and authenticity of expression both in our interpersonal relations and in our sense of independence.

Toril Moi (essay date Summer 1992)

SOURCE: "Ambiguity and Alienation in *The Second Sex,*" in *Boundary 2,* Vol. 19, No. 2, Summer, 1992, pp. 96-112.

[*In the following essay, Moi discusses Beauvoir's philosophical analysis of female oppression in* The Second Sex. *"For Simone de Beauvoir," writes Moi, "women are fundamentally characterized by ambiguity and conflict."*]

> Divided, torn, disadvantaged: for women the stakes are higher; there are more victories and more defeats for them than for men.
>
> —Simone de Beauvoir, ***The Force of Circumstance*** (translation amended)

Preliminary Note

The article that follows is an excerpt from a much longer discussion of alienation and the body in ***The Second Sex,*** taken from chapter 6 of my forthcoming book on Simone de Beauvoir. The excerpt printed here is preceded by a discussion of the relationship between ***The Second Sex*** and ***The Ethics of Ambiguity,*** and by an analysis of the rhetoric—the language—of philosophy in ***The Second Sex.*** It is followed by a detailed study of Beauvoir's analysis of female desire. Drawing these threads together, the chapter concludes by examining the philosophical implications of Beauvoir's analysis of what I like to call *patriarchal femininity.* One of my conclusions in this chapter is that Beauvoir actually succeeds in dismantling the patriarchal paradigm of universal masculinity in philosophy. I am afraid that the excerpt published here only forms one of the steps on the way to that conclusion. I nevertheless hope that it can be read on its own as a close textual analysis of the concept of alienation in Beauvoir's theory. As this excerpt makes clear, this concept is bound up with the idea of the body: it is imperative to integrate any discussion of alienation with an exploration of Beauvoir's understanding of the body. I should perhaps also say that in my own readings of Beauvoir I try to produce a dialectical understanding of her contradictions and ambiguities. It follows that I don't consider every contradiction to be unproductive. It also follows that any single concept, such as that of alienation, should be examined in its interaction with other crucial concepts in Beauvoir's texts. This is why Beauvoir's account of female sexuality—or female psychosexual development—should not be taken to represent the whole of her analysis of women's oppression. In order to grasp the political implications of her epochal essay, it is also necessary to explore the strength and limitations of her understanding of freedom. That is the task I try to carry out in chapter 7 of my book.

Ambiguity

In ***The Ethics of Ambiguity*** (1947) Beauvoir presents a general philosophy of existence. Her fundamental assumptions in this book also form the starting point for her next essay, ***The Second Sex*** (1949). According to Beauvoir's 1947 essay, men and women share the same human condition. We are all split, all threatened by the "fall" into immanence, and we are all mortal. In this sense, no human being ever coincides with him- or herself: we are all lack of being. In order to escape from the tension and anguish (*angoisse*) of this ambiguity, we may all be tempted to take refuge in the havens of bad faith. Starting where ***The Ethics of Ambiguity*** ends, ***The Second Sex*** launches its inquiry into women's condition by focusing on the question of difference:

> Now, what specifically defines the situation of woman is that she—a free and autonomous being like all human creatures—nevertheless discovers and chooses herself in a world where men compel her to assume the status of the Other. They propose to turn her into an object and to doom her to immanence since her transcendence is for ever to be transcended by another consciousness which is essential and sovereign. The drama of woman lies in this conflict between the fundamental aspirations of every subject—which always posits itself as essential—and the demands of a situation which constitutes her as inessential.

This is perhaps the single most important passage in ***The Second Sex,*** above all because Beauvoir here poses a radically new theory of sexual difference. While we are all split and ambiguous, she argues, women are *more* split and ambiguous than men. For Simone de Beauvoir, then, women are fundamentally characterized by *ambiguity* and *conflict.* The specific contradiction of women's situation is caused by the conflict between their status as free and autonomous human beings and the fact that they are socialized in a world in which men consistently cast them as Other to their One, as objects to their subjects. The effect is to produce women as subjects painfully torn between freedom and alienation, transcendence and immanence, subject-being and object-being. This fundamental contradiction, or split, in which the general ontological ambiguity of human beings is repeated and reinforced by the social pressures brought to bear on women, is *specific to women under patriarchy.* For Beauvoir, at least initially, there is nothing ahistorical about this: when oppressive power relations cease to exist, women will be no more split and contradictory than men. As I will go on to show, however, Beauvoir's analysis implies that while the major contradictions of women's situation may disappear, women will in fact always remain somewhat more ambiguous than men.

Again Beauvoir's theory is clearly metaphorical: the social oppression of women, she implies, *mirrors* or repeats the ontological ambiguity of existence. Paradoxically enough, on this point Beauvoir's analysis gains in potential strength from its metaphorical structure: it is precisely the absence of any purely logical link between the two levels of analysis that leaves us free to reject the one without having to deny the other as well. In this way, Beauvoir's careful account of women torn between freedom and alienation under patriarchy may well be experienced as convincing, even by readers radically at odds with Sartre's theory of consciousness.

The oppression of women, Beauvoir argues, is in some ways similar to the oppression of other social groups, such as that of Jews or American blacks. Members of such groups are also treated as objects by members of the ruling caste or race. Yet women's situation remains fundamentally different, above all because women are scattered across *all* social groups and thus have been unable to form a society of their own: "The bond that unites her to her oppressors is not comparable to any other," Beauvoir insists. The effect of this social situation is that women tend to feel solidarity with men in their own social group rather than with women in general. This is why, unlike every other oppressed group, women have been unable to cast themselves as historical subjects opposing their oppressors: under patriarchy, there are no female ghettos, no female compounds in which to organize a collective uprising: "Women," Beauvoir writes in 1949, "do not say 'We' . . . they do not authentically posit themselves as Subject." The specificity of women's oppression consists precisely in the absence of a female collectivity capable of perceiving itself as a historical subject opposed to other social groups. This is why no other oppressed group experiences the same kind of contradiction between freedom and alienation. Beauvoir, in other words, is not interested in producing a competitive hierarchy of oppression. Her point is not that women necessarily are *more,* or *more painfully,* oppressed than every other group but simply that the oppression of women is a highly specific *kind* of oppression.

Rich and varied, Beauvoir's own vocabulary of ambiguity and conflict ranges from ambivalence, distance, divorce, and split to alienation, contradiction, and mutilation. But every ambiguity is not negative: as readers of ***The Second Sex,*** we must not make the paradoxical mistake of taking the value of ambiguity to be given once and for all. For Beauvoir, the word ambiguous often means "dialectical" and describes a fundamental contradiction underpinning an apparently stable and coherent phenomenon. In ***The Second Sex,*** every conflict is potentially both productive and destructive: in some cases, one aspect wins out; in others, the tension remains unresolved. The advantage of Beauvoir's position is that it enables her to draw up a highly complex map of women's situation in the world, one that is never blind to the way in which women occasionally reap paradoxical advantages from their very powerlessness. As a whole, however, ***The Second Sex*** amply demonstrates that such spurious spin-offs remain precarious and unpredictable: for Beauvoir, the effects of sexism are overwhelmingly destructive for men as well as for women.

Every one of the descriptions of women's "lived experience" in ***The Second Sex*** serves to reinforce Beauvoir's theory of the fundamental contradiction of women's situation. Unfortunately, the sheer mass of material makes it impossible to discuss the whole range of her analyses: her brilliant account of the antinomies of housework, or the absolutely stunning defense of abortion rights (see the chapters entitled "The Married Woman" and "The Mother"), for instance, ought still to be required reading for us all, yet they will not be discussed here. Instead, I have chosen to explore the single most important—and by far the most complex—example of contradictions and ambiguity in ***The Second Sex:*** Beauvoir's account of female sexuality. By *sexuality* I understand the psychosexual, as well as the biological, aspects of female sexual existence, or, in other words, the interaction between desire and the body.

Alienation

"One is not born a woman, one becomes one," Beauvoir writes. The question, of course, is *how.* How does the little girl become a woman? In her impressive history of psychoanalysis in France, Elisabeth Roudinesco credits Simone de Beauvoir with being the first French writer to link the question of sexuality to that of political emancipation. Beauvoir's interest in the various psychoanalytic perspectives on femininity was so great, Roudinesco tells us, that a year before finishing her book, she rang up Lacan in order to ask his advice on the issue: "Flattered, Lacan announces that they would need five or six months of conversation in order to sort out the problem. Simone doesn't want to spend that much time listening to Lacan for a book which was already very well researched. She proposes four meetings. He refuses." It is not surprising that Lacan was flattered by Beauvoir's request: in Paris in 1948, Beauvoir possessed much more intellectual capital than he; in other words, she was famous, he was not.

Given this highly Lacanian disagreement on timing, the tantalizingly transgressive fantasy of a Lacanian ***Second Sex*** has to remain in the imaginary. Although she never sat at Lacan's feet, Beauvoir nevertheless quotes his early work on *Les Complexes familiaux dans la formation de l'individu,* and much of her account of early childhood and femininity reads as a kind of free elaboration on Lacan's notion of the alienation of the ego in the other in the mirror stage.

The term *alienation,* in fact, turns up everywhere in ***The Second Sex.*** Mobilized to explain everything from female sexuality to narcissism and mysticism, the concept plays a key role in Beauvoir's theory of sexual difference. It is unfortunate indeed that this fact fails to come across in the English translation of ***The Second Sex.*** In Parshley's version, the word *aliénation* tends to get translated as 'projection', except in passages with a certain anthropological flavor, where it remains 'alienation'. *Aliénation,* however, also shows up as 'identification', and on one occasion it even masquerades as 'being beside herself'. As a result, English-language readers are prevented from tracing the philosophical logic—in this case particularly the Hegelian and/or Lacanian overtones—of Beauvoir's analysis. In my own text, I amend all relevant quotations, and I also signal particularly aberrant translations in footnotes.

According to Beauvoir, the little child reacts to the crisis of weaning by experiencing "the original drama of every existent: that of his relation to the Other." This drama is characterized by existential anguish caused by the experience of *délaissement,* or what Heidegger would call *Überlassenheit,* often translated as 'abandonment' in English. Already at this early stage, the little child dreams of escaping her freedom either by merging with the cosmic all or by becoming a thing, an in-itself:

> In carnal form [the child] discovers finiteness, solitude, abandonment in a strange world. He endeavours to compensate for this catastrophe by alienating his existence in an image, the reality and value of which others will establish. It appears that he may begin to affirm his identity at the time when he recognizes his reflection in a mirror—a time which coincides with that of weaning. His ego blends so completely into this reflected image that it is formed only through its own alienation [*il ne se forme qu'en s'aliénant*]. . . . He is already an autonomous subject transcending himself towards the outer world, but he encounters himself only in an alienated form.

Initially, then, all children are equally alienated. This is not surprising, since the wish to alienate oneself in another person or thing, according to Beauvoir, is fundamental to all human beings: "Primitive people are alienated in mana, in the totem; civilized people in their individual souls, in their egos, their names, their property, their work. Here is to be found the primary temptation to inauthenticity." But sexual difference soon transforms the situation. For little boys, Beauvoir argues, it is much easier to find an object in which to alienate themselves than for little girls: admirably suited to the role as idealized *alter ego,* the penis quickly becomes every little boy's very own totem pole: "The penis is singularly adapted for playing this role of 'double' for the little boy—it is for him at once a foreign object and himself," Beauvoir claims. Projecting themselves into the penis, little boys invest it with the whole charge of their transcendence. For Beauvoir, then, phallic imagery represents transcendence, not sexuality.

A little girl, however, has a more difficult time. Given that she has no penis, she has no tangible object in which to alienate herself: "But the little girl cannot incarnate herself in any part of herself," Beauvoir writes. Similar in many respects to Freud's analysis of femininity, Beauvoir's account differs, as we shall see, in its explicit denial of *lack* and in its emphasis on the tactile rather than the visual. For Freud, girls experience themselves as inferior because they see the penis and conclude that they themselves are lacking; for Beauvoir they are different (not necessarily inferior) because they have nothing to *touch.* Because her sex organs are impossible to grab hold of (*empoigner*), it is as if they do not exist: "in a sense she has no sex organ," Beauvoir writes:

> She does not experience this absence as a lack; evidently her body is, for her, quite complete; but she finds herself situated in the world differently from the boy; and a constellation of factors can transform this difference, in her eyes, into an inferiority.

Deprived of an obvious object of alienation, the little girl ends up alienating herself in herself:

> Not having that *alter ego,* the little girl does not alienate herself in a material thing and cannot retrieve her integrity [*ne se récupère pas*]. On this account she is led to make an object of her whole self, to set herself up as the Other. The question of whether she has or has not compared herself with boys is secondary; the important point is that, even if she is unaware of it, the absence of the penis prevents her from becoming conscious of herself as a sexual being. From this flow many consequences.

Objects for themselves, regardless of whether they know about the penis's existence or not, little girls are radically split, yet irredeemably caught up in their own alienated self-image. But this is not all. On the evidence of this surprising passage, little girls are forced *by their anatomy* to alienate themselves in themselves. Furthermore, Beauvoir claims, they fail to "recover" or "retrieve" (*récupérer*) themselves. In my view, these remarks offer a condensed version of the whole of Beauvoir's theory of alienation. As such, they have a series of wide-ranging and complex implications that I will now go on to explore.

Much like Lacan, Beauvoir casts the moment of alienation as constitutive of the subject, but, unlike Lacan, she believes that the subject only comes into authentic being if it completes the dialectical movement and goes on to *recover* (*récupérer*), or reintegrate, the alienated image of itself (the double, the *alter ego*) back into its own subjectivity. Drawing on this Hegelian logic, Beauvoir insists that little boys easily achieve the required synthesis, whereas little girls fail to recover themselves. Why, then, do little boys easily "recover" their own transcendence? For Beauvoir, the answer is to be found in the anatomical and physiological properties of the penis. Eminently detachable, the penis is nevertheless not quite detached from the body. Projecting his transcendence into the penis, the boy projects it into an object that is part of his body yet has a strange life of its own: "the function of urination and later of erection are processes midway between the voluntary and involuntary," Beauvoir writes; the penis is "a capricious and as it were foreign source of pleasure that is felt subjectively. . . . The penis is regarded by the subject as at once himself and other than himself." Not so foreign and distant as to appear entirely without connections with the boy, yet not so close as to prevent a clear-cut distinction between the boy's subjectivity and his own projected transcendence, the penis, according to Beauvoir, enables the boy to *recognize* himself in his *alter ego:* "Because he has an *alter ego* in whom he recognizes himself, the little boy can boldly assume his subjectivity," she writes, "the very object in which he alienates himself becomes a symbol of autonomy, of transcendence, of power."

In my view, the word *recognition* here must be taken to allude to the Hegelian *Anerkennung.* Loosely inspired by Hegel, Beauvoir would seem to imply that there can be no recognition without the positing of a subject and an other. By being relatively other (thus allowing the positing of a subject-other distinction), yet not quite other (thus making recognition of oneself in the other easier), the penis facilitates the recuperation of the boy's alienated transcendence back into his subjectivity. Recuperating his sense of transcendence for himself, the boy escapes his alienation: his penis totem becomes the very instrument that in the end allows him to "assume his subjectivity" and act authentically.

To say that there is something Hegelian about Beauvoir's argument here is not to claim that she is being particularly orthodox or consistent. Freely developing the themes of recognition and the dialectical triad, Beauvoir entirely forgets that for Hegel recognition presupposes the reciprocal exchange between two *subjects.* As far as I can see, however, Beauvoir never actually claims that the penis speaks back. Confronted with the alluring idea that it is not only the little boy who must recognize himself in his penis, but the penis that must recognize itself in the boy, Hegel himself might have had some difficulty in recognizing his own theory.

Whatever the vicissitudes of the penis may be, little girls have a harder time of it. As we have seen, Beauvoir holds that the girl's anatomy makes her alienate herself in her whole body, not just in a semi-detached object, such as the penis. Even if she is given a doll to play with, the situation doesn't change. Dolls are passive things representing the whole body, and as such they encourage the little girl to "alienate herself in her whole person and to regard this as an inert given object," Beauvoir claims. In her alienated state, the little girl apparently becomes "passive" and "inert." Why is this the outcome of the girl's alienation? The "alienated" penis, after all, was perceived by the boy as a proud image of transcendence. Why does this not happen to the girl's whole body? Where does *her* transcendence go?

On this point, Beauvoir's text is not particularly easy to follow. I take her to argue that the girl's alienation sets up an ambiguous split between herself and her alienated image of herself. "Woman, like man, *is* her body," Beauvoir writes about the adult woman, "but her body is something other than herself." This, one may remember, is an exact quotation of her description of the boy's alienated penis. The adult woman, then, has still not achieved the dialectical reintegration of her transcendence. The reason why she fails to do so is that, paradoxically, she wasn't alienated enough in the first place. Precisely because her body *is* herself, one might say, it is difficult for the girl to distinguish between the alienated body and her transcendent consciousness of that body. Or, in other words, the difference between the whole body and the penis is that the body can never be considered simply an object in the world for its own "owner": the body, after all, *is* our mode of existing in the world: "To be present in the world implies strictly that there exists a body which is at once a material thing in the world and a point of view towards this world," Beauvoir writes.

Alienating herself in her body, the little girl alienates her transcendence in a "thing" that remains ambiguously part of her own original transcendence. Her alienation, we might say, creates a murky mixture of transcendence, thingness, and the alienated *image* of a body-ego. The very ambiguity of this amalgam of the in-itself and the for-itself recalls Sartre's horrified vision of the "sticky" or "slimy," as that which is eternally ambiguous and always threatening to engulf the for-itself. Permitting no clear-cut positing of a subject and an other, this ambivalent mixture prevents the girl from achieving the dialectical reintegration of her alienated transcendence which, apparently, is so easy for the boy. For her, in other words, there is no unambiguous opposition between the two first moments of the dialectic: this is what makes it so hard for her to "recover" her alienated transcendence in a new synthesis.

It does not follow from this that the little girl has no sense of herself as a transcendence at all. If that were the case, she would be *entirely* alienated, which is precisely what she is not. Instead, Beauvoir appears to suggest that there is an ever present tension—or even struggle—between the little girl's transcendent subjectivity and her complicated and ambivalent alienation. On this theory, the girl's psychological structures must be pictured as a complex and mobile *process* rather than as a static and fixed *image.* But on this reading, Beauvoir's account of the girl's alienation transforms and extends her own highly reified initial concept of alienation: rather unwittingly, I think, Beauvoir here manages to challenge the limitations of her original point of departure. The result is that her theory of female subjectivity is far more interesting and original than her rather too neat and tidy account of male psychological structures.

Towards the end of ***The Second Sex,*** Beauvoir argues that the process of alienation is constitutive of narcissism. (On this point, one may add, her position is entirely compatible with that of Lacan.) "Narcissism is a well-defined process of alienation," Beauvoir writes, "in which the ego is regarded as an absolute end and the subject takes refuge from itself in it." For the narcissistic subject, her ego or self is nothing but an alienated and idealized *image* of herself, another *alter ego* or double in danger in the world. As far as I can see, the difference between the narcissistic and the non-narcissistic woman is that the latter conserves a sense of ambiguity or contradiction, whereas the former persuades herself that she *is* the image projected by her alienation. This is why narcissism, according to Beauvoir, represents a supreme effort to "accomplish the impossible synthesis of the *en-soi* and the *pour-soi*": the "successful" narcissist really believes that she is God.

For Beauvoir as for Sartre, alienation is transcendence attempting to turn itself into an object. Alienating ourselves in another thing or person, we deprive ourselves of the power to act for or by ourselves. Deprived of agency, our alienated transcendence is defenselessly delivered up to the dangers of the world. For Beauvoir, there is thus no need to mobilize a specific theory of castration anxiety to explain why little boys feel that their penis is constantly endangered. To worry about the safety of one's penis, however, is infinitely preferable to feeling obscurely threatened in one's whole person, as little girls do:

> The diffuse apprehension felt by the little girl in regard to her "insides" . . . will often be retained for life. She is extremely concerned about everything that happens inside her, she is from the start much more opaque to her own eyes, more profoundly immersed in the obscure mystery of life, than is the male.

In this passage, as everywhere else in ***The Second Sex,*** Beauvoir's subtle and incisive exploration of women's situation is juxtaposed to a far too sanguine view of masculinity. In the light of her own belief in the influence of social factors on the development of sexual difference, she hugely overestimates the convenience of the penis as a foolproof instrument of alienation and reintegration. Every little boy or every adult male does not, after all, come across as an authentically transcendent subject. Beauvoir's admiration of masculinity is such that she even assumes that girls brought up by men rather than by women "very largely escape the defects of femininity."

While there are strong biographical reasons for her misjudgment on this point, rhetorically speaking, the main source of Beauvoir's idealization of the penis would seem to be metaphorical. Littered with references to the powerful symbolic effects of urination from a standing rather than from a crouching position, her text repeatedly emphasizes the penis's capacity for quasi-independent motion, as well as for the projection of liquids over a certain distance. What fascinates her above all is the idea that the male organ moves and, moreover, that it is *upwardly mobile,* particularly in its grandiose projection of urine: "Every stream of water in the air seems like a miracle, a defiance of gravity: to direct, to govern it, is to win a small victory over the laws of nature," Beauvoir claims, quoting Sartre and Bachelard to substantiate her point.

Strikingly original in her approach, Beauvoir in fact sees sexual difference as the result of different modes of alienation. At first glance, however, it looks as if the development of different forms of alienation depends entirely on the anatomical presence or absence of the penis. The question is whether this really is a correct reading of Beauvoir's position. Insisting that hers is a theory of the *social* construction of femininity and masculinity, Beauvoir herself categorically refuses the idea of a biological "destiny". On the contrary, she argues, it is the social context that gives meaning to biological and psychological factors: "True human privilege is based upon anatomical privilege only in virtue of the total situation [*la situation saisie dans sa totalité*]." It is only when the girl discovers that men have power in the world and women do not that she risks mistaking her difference for inferiority: "She sees that it is not the women, but the men who control the world. It is this revelation—much more than the discovery of the penis—which irresistibly alters her conception of herself."

Given the right social encouragement, Beauvoir argues, girls may still manage to recover their transcendence. While the penis is a privileged possession in early childhood, after the age of eight or nine it holds onto its prestige only because it is socially valorized. Social practices, not biology, encourage little girls to remain sunk in passivity and narcissism, and force little boys to become active subjects. It is because little boys are treated more harshly than girls, and not because they intrinsically are less self-indulgent, that they are better equipped to project themselves into the competitive world of concrete action. In my view, Beauvoir's theory of alienation actually implies that social factors have *greater* influence on girls than on boys: precisely because girls' transcendence is precariously balanced between complete alienation and authentic subjectivity, it doesn't take much to push the girl in either direction. Less pronounced in boys, one might argue, this ambiguity makes girls particularly susceptible to social pressure:

> Along with the authentic demand of the subject who wants sovereign freedom, there is in the existent an inauthentic longing for resignation and escape; the delights of passivity are made to seem desirable to the young girl by parents and teachers, books and myths, women and men; she is taught to enjoy them from earliest childhood; the temptation becomes more and more insidious; and she is the more fatally bound to yield to those delights as the flight of her transcendence is dashed against harsher obstacles.

I take her constant appeal to social factors to be one of the strongest points of Beauvoir's position. But when it comes to explaining exactly how we are to understand the relationship between the anatomical and the social, Beauvoir's discourse becomes curiously slippery. Not to have a penis, for instance, is not necessarily a handicap: "If woman should succeed in establishing herself as subject, she would invent equivalents of the phallus; in fact, the doll, incarnating the promise of the baby that is to come in the future, can become a possession more precious than the penis." Dolls, it now appears, do not necessarily cause alienated passivity after all: "The boy, too, can cherish a teddy bear, or a puppet into which he projects himself [*se projette*]; it is within the totality of their lives that each factor—penis or doll—takes on its importance." There is something circular about Beauvoir's argument here. For if the very form of the little girl's body encourages a sticky and incomplete mode of alienation in the first place, the little girl will find it difficult, indeed, to "establish herself as a subject." If "equivalents of the phallus" are what is needed in order to become an authentic subject, it is hard to see why women would want them *after* they have managed to become subjects in their own right anyway. In my view, Beauvoir's hesitations over the subject of dolls signal her own uneasy feeling that her original formulation of the girl's alienation privileges anatomy more than she would wish. Her contradictory feelings about the role of dolls, then, reveal a deeper theoretical difficulty: that of finding a way of linking an anatomical and psychological argument with a sociological one.

The fact that Beauvoir fails explicitly to raise this problem causes her to overlook an important gap in her own account of alienation. Attentive readers may already have noticed that her text moves directly from the Lacanian idea of the alienation of the child in the gaze of the other to the rather different idea that boys and girls alienate themselves in their bodies. Unfortunately, Beauvoir makes no attempt to relate Lacan's theory to her own. For her, apparently, the two simply coexist. Failing to perceive this as a problem, Beauvoir also misses out on a crucial opportunity to bridge the gap in her own theory, for instance by suggesting that it is the gaze of the other that originally invests the child's alienated image of itself with the phallocentric values it then goes on to repeat in its own work of alienation. By giving her own theory a slightly more Lacanian twist on this point, she would have managed, at least in my view, to produce a better account of the relationship between the biological and the psychosocial than she actually does.

It is unfortunate, to say the least, the Beauvoir makes her subtle theory of femininity function as a foil to her rather less sophisticated theory of masculinity. It is not difficult to show that Beauvoir's idealization of the phallus in fact contradicts Sartre's own account of masculine desire and transcendence. Nowhere is she on a greater collision course with Sartre than in her idealized account of masculinity: there is a nice paradox in the fact that in the very passages where she unconsciously seeks to pay tribute to Sartre, she entirely betrays his philosophical logic.

In Beauvoir's theory of alienation, I appreciate above all her effort to think dialectically, her courageous attempt fully to grasp the contradictions of women's position. The strength of Beauvoir's theory of alienation as constitutive of sexual difference is not only that it manages to suggest—albeit somewhat imperfectly—that patriarchal power structures are at work in the very construction of female subjectivity but also that it attempts to show exactly *how* this process works. Emphasizing the social pressures brought to bear on the little girl, Beauvoir also indicates that different practices will yield different results: hers is not at all a theory of intrinsic sexual differences. Providing the basis for a sophisticated analysis of women's difficulties in conceiving of themselves as social and sexual subjects under patriarchy, Beauvoir's theory also implies that it is both unjust and unrealistic to underestimate the difficulty involved in becoming a free woman. Given Beauvoir's logic, for a woman to be able to oppose the order that oppresses her is much harder than for a man to do so; under patriarchy, women's achievements therefore become rather more impressive than comparable male feats. As she puts it in ***The Force of Circumstance:*** "For women the stakes are higher; there are more victories and more defeats for them than for men."

Sonia Kruks (essay date Autumn 1992)

SOURCE: "Gender and Subjectivity: Simone de Beauvoir and Contemporary Feminism," in *Signs: Journal of Women in Culture and Society,* Vol. 18, No. 1, Autumn, 1992, pp. 89-110.

[*In the following essay, Kruks offers a reexamination of Beauvoir's view of female subjectivity and her relationship to contemporary postmodern and feminist thought.*]

Theoretical debate among North American feminists in the last decade has been widely influenced by postmodernism. Indeed, some have gone so far as to claim that feminist theory is inherently postmodern, its very project necessarily challenging such "Enlightenment myths" as the existence of a stable self or subject and the possibility of attaining objective truth about the world through the use of reason. They argue that feminist theory, with its deconstruction of what appears natural in our society, its focus on difference, and its subversion of the stable phallocentric norms of Western thought, "properly belongs in the terrain of postmodern philosophy" and that "feminist notions of the self, knowledge, and truth are too contradictory to those of the Enlightenment to be contained within its categories" ([Jane] Flax 1987).

I am not convinced, however, that such claims can be substantiated. For one thing, they presuppose a binary opposition, Enlightenment/postmodern, that is itself both historically and conceptually questionable. For another, we do not have a sufficiently clear consensus on what we might mean by "feminist" notions of "the self, knowledge, and truth" to permit us to be able to claim that they "properly" belong anywhere in particular. Most important, feminism is much more than a field of scholarship, and it is when we come to the terrain of feminist politics that postmodernism arguably presents the greatest difficulties.

In a spate of recent articles, authors such as Wendy Brown (1987), Nancy Hartsock (1987), and Linda Alcoff (1988) claim that postmodernism depoliticizes feminism and urge feminists to have virtually no truck with it. Such authors argue that the problems that postmodernism presents for feminist practice, its radical nominalism or constructivism (including a constructivist account of the body) and its discourse-boundedness, preclude a grasp of the objective conditions of women's lives. Most significantly, they hold, the postmodern refusal to conceive of the self or subject as a knowing and volitional agent—a conception of agency that has underpinned most prior feminist visions of political action—implies an unacceptable passivity: women are reduced to no more than the effects of discursive practices, products of the play of signifiers, victims of a "discourse determinism." No place, they charge, is left in the postmodern account of social change for the organized and conscious struggle of groups or individuals. For postmodernists erroneously claim that change takes place through a suprahuman play of discourses over which we can have little or no influence.

Though such writers portray postmodernism as irremediably

flawed and inimical to effective feminist politics, others who share some of their concerns also believe that it is still worth attempting to work toward a rapprochement with postmodernism. Sandra Harding, for example, has recently argued that feminist epistemology needs both Enlightenment and postmodern agendas and that neither agenda can be constructed to the total exclusion of the other (1990). Mary Poovey has neatly summed up the problem this way: "The challenge for those of us who are convinced both that real historical women do exist and share certain experiences *and* that deconstruction's demystifying of presence makes theoretical sense is to work out some way to think both women and 'woman.' It isn't an easy task" (1988).

My own view, while critical of the more grandiose claims sometimes, made in the name of postmodernism—including those for the "death of the subject," for the impossibility of any totalizing or continuous account of history, and for the irrelevance of biology to sexuality (let alone gender)—is that, at a more modest theoretical altitude than that to which its adherents usually aspire, postmodernism offers valuable tools and techniques to feminism. The best of what postmodern feminism has developed so far is not "high theory" so much as a series of radical glosses on the now classic starting point proposed by Simone de Beauvoir: "one is not born a woman, one becomes one." Postmodern deconstructive techniques and genealogical methods, like the work of Beauvoir, may help us to de-essentialize and de-naturalize the concept of "woman."

What we have learned (or perhaps re-learned) from postmodern theories is the very real power of discourse and the lack of transparency of language: there is no returning to a simple realism today. Yet I share with Poovey a concern that we remain able to talk about "real historical women" and that we do not embrace a kind of postmodern hyperconstructivism in which the very category of "women" can disappear (as, e.g., in [Denise] Riley [1988]).

Similarly, what we have learned from the postmodern critique of the Enlightenment subject is that we should not attribute to consciousness the absolute power to constitute its own world: subjectivity is never "pure" or fully autonomous but inheres in selves that are shaped by cultural discourses and that are always embodied—selves that thus are also gendered. Yet to acknowledge all of this does not mean that we are obliged to proclaim definitively "the death of the subject." It is important for feminist politics (as Alcoff and others have argued) that we remain able to grant a role to individual consciousness and agency, to insist even on a notion of individual responsibility for our actions. But we must do so while also acknowledging the ways in which subjectivity is discursively and socially constructed. In particular, we need to be able to account for gender as an aspect of subjectivity, but to do so without either essentializing or dehistoricizing it.

As a contribution to such an attempt to re-construct the subject, this article sets out to re-examine the work of an earlier thinker: Simone de Beauvoir. For it is not the case that before postmodernism there was only the Enlightenment or modernity. Indeed, if ever there was a binary opposition that needs deconstructing, it is that between modernity and postmodernity. Fortunately, we do not have to choose between the unhappy alternatives of an Enlightenment subject (i.e., an autonomous or self-constituting consciousness) on the one hand and the attempt, as Michel Foucault pithily put it, "to get rid of the subject itself" on the other ([1977] 1980). In the work of Beauvoir, I want to argue, we find a nuanced conception of the subject that cannot be characterized as either Enlightenment or postmodern: rather, it is a conception of the subject as situated.

In her account of women as subjects "in situation," Beauvoir can both acknowledge the weight of social construction, including gender, in the formation of the self and yet refuse to reduce the self to an "effect." She can grant a degree of autonomy to the self—as is necessary in order to retain such key notions as political action, responsibility, and the oppression of the self—while also acknowledging the real constraints on autonomous subjectivity produced by oppressive situations. As I suggest later, Beauvoir's account of situated subjectivity is one from which we could begin to develop an account of the gendering of subjectivity that can avoid both essentialism and hyperconstructivism.

It will perhaps be helpful to return to Beauvoir through a brief overview of recent intellectual history, recalling that, like the main proponents of postmodernism, Beauvoir wrote in a distinctly French intellectual milieu. Postmodernism and the existential phenomenology that shaped Beauvoir's thought form (to write old-fashioned narrative) part of the same history. Although the postmodern critique of modernity can be traced back to Nietzsche or to the later work of Heidegger, what has been imported into American feminist theory in the last decade under the rubric of postmodernism is a cluster of ideas formulated primarily in France from the late 1960s onward. I would argue, however, that these ideas do not constitute the profound epistemic or epistemological break their authors frequently claim for them but, rather, are both absorptions of and reactions against the work of earlier generations of French thinkers.

Postmodernism emerged in France above all as a radicalizing critique of 1960s structuralism, as "poststructuralism." In spite of its objectivist stance and claims to scientificity, structuralism easily passed into post-structuralism through their shared hostility to the classical notion of the subject. What links structuralism and poststructuralism in France is what may be summed up as their antihumanism. From the insistence of Claude Lévi-Strauss that the aim of the human sciences is "to dissolve man" and the claims of Jacques Lacan and Louis Althusser that "the subject" is a mere "effect," to Jacques Derrida's attacks on the metaphysics of "presence" and Foucault's arguments that subjects are "constituted" as a function of discourse, what has been under attack are those notions of autonomous subjectivity and agency that have indeed been central to philosophy since the Enlightenment.

Although this attack can, if one so chooses, be located in the broad historical sweep from modernity to postmodernity, the emergence of French antihumanism was in its origins also a far more parochial phenomenon: a Parisian-based reaction against the hegemony exercised by humanistic existential phenomenology and Marxism in postwar France. It was, above all, against Jean-Paul Sartre that the battle was waged. Indeed, the "dissolution of man" was first proclaimed by Lévi-Strauss in 1962 in the context of a chapter-length attack on Sartre's *Critique of Dialectical Reason* ([1962] 1968, chap. 9). In the late 1970s, Foucault still bluntly stated his agenda as the attempt to use genealogy to displace not only Marxism but also the phenomenology of his student days: the phenomenological subject, in any form, had to be destroyed, he insisted. Long after we might have thought phenomenology dead in France, Foucault felt it necessary to insist on killing it yet again:

> I don't believe the problem can be resolved by historicizing the subject, as posited by the phenomenologists, fabricating a subject that evolves through the course of history. One has to dispense with the constituent subject, to get rid of the subject itself, that's to say, to arrive at an analysis which can account for the constitution of the subject within a historical framework . . . [Genealogy] is a form of history which can account for the constitution of knowledges, discourses, domains of objects etc., without having to make reference to a subject which is either transcendental in relation to the field of events or runs in its empty sameness throughout the course of history. [(1977) 1980]

This statement opposes as stark alternatives a conception of the subject as "constituent" (or constituting) and as "transcendental" to history, on the one hand, and a conception of the subject as constituted and to be analyzed as an "effect" of its historical framework, on the other. In it we find posed those oversimple choices between humanism and antihumanism, between Enlightenment or modernity and postmodernity that postmodernists frequently tend to present us with because of the dichotomizing lenses through which they view the history of philosophy. In order to account for the weight of social structures, discourses, and practices in the shaping of subjectivity and yet still to acknowledge that an element of freedom is intrinsic to subjectivity—an element that allows us to talk, as I think we must, of individual human agency and responsibility—we need a far more complex, indeed dialectical, account of the subject than Foucault's work would grant us. Ironically, such an account is be found in the work of some of the very French phenomenologists Foucault dismissed, including Beauvoir and Maurice Merleau-Ponty. It is also to be found in Sartre's later works, such as *Critique of Dialectical Reason* ([1960] 1976) and his monumental study of Flaubert. As I have argued elsewhere, however, it was not yet present in his 1940s "existentialism," of which *Being and Nothingness* (1943) was the fullest formulation: a work that still asserted (albeit paradoxically) a version of the classic Enlightenment subject.

Simone de Beauvoir, the "Mother" of second wave feminism ([Carol] Ascher 1987), was, of course, closely associated with Sartre personally and philosophically. When ***The Second Sex*** (1949) was adopted by American feminists in the late 1960s, its insight that one is not born but becomes a woman, that femininity is a social construct and not an unchangeable essence or a biological destiny, seemed a revelation. But although this insight remains central to postmodern feminism, by the late 1970s ***The Second Sex*** began to seem rather passé. It was not only that Beauvoir's descriptions of women's experiences increasingly applied to a bygone age and to women of a narrow social stratum. Her solutions—the book ended with a call for a "fraternal" collaboration of men and women in establishing "the reign of liberty in the midst of the world of the given"—seemed to deny the female difference that many feminists now valorized. Her notion of liberation arguably implied making women conform to a male ideal. Her persistent use of sexist language (the Sartrean language of "man" and "his" world) demonstrated how insensitive she had been to male dominance in her own intellectual milieu.

Moreover, since Beauvoir was said to share with Sartre not only a misogynist dislike of the female body but the entire philosophical baggage of "existentialism," including the Sartrean conception of the subject, postmodern feminism has come to dismiss her as methodologically naive. Today Beauvoir is generally treated as a venerable ancestor, but she is no longer regarded as having anything of significance to contribute to the on-going development of feminist theory. Rather than consigning her to ancestor worship, however, I want to argue that Beauvoir remains highly relevant to current theoretical concerns. In particular she still speaks to the problem of developing an adequate feminist theory of the gendering of subjectivity.

Both in her ethical essays of the 1940s and in ***The Second***

Sex, Beauvoir developed a somewhat submerged account of "being-in-situation," or situated subjectivity, that was radically different from Sartre's. To claim that Beauvoir departs significantly from the notion of the autonomous subject is also, of course, to say that Beauvoir was far more philosophically independent from Sartre than has generally been recognized. I will begin from this last point, to show that Beauvoir's work is not as consistently rooted in Sartrean philosophy as has been commonly supposed and that it departs from Sartre's identification of subjectivity with an inviolable, autonomous consciousness. I will then suggest, in the final section, what it is about Beauvoir's conception of the subject that makes it of enduring significance for the project of reconstructing our account of the gendering of subjectivity.

It was Beauvoir herself who insisted that her work was philosophically derivative of Sartre's. Repeatedly, and until the last years of her life, Beauvoir said that she lacked originality and was merely Sartre's disciple in matters philosophical. She was willing to claim originality for herself in the field of literature, but in the more hallowed field of philosophy she could not compete but only follow. "On the philosophical level," she insisted, "I adhered completely to *Being and Nothingness* and later to *Critique of Dialectical Reason.*" Too many scholars and commentators have taken Beauvoir at her word. Most assume that, as one author recently put it, she simply uses Sartre's concepts as "coat-hangers" on which to hang her own material, even to the point where it can be said that "Sartre's intellectual history becomes her own" ([Judith] Okely 1986). Yet such a view, even though embraced by Beauvoir herself, is misleading. For although Beauvoir doubtless tried to work within a Sartrean framework (i.e., the framework of *Being and Nothingness*), she did not wholly succeed. Many of the leaps and inconsistencies one can find in her work reflect, I believe, a tension between her formal adherence to Sartrean categories and the fact that the philosophical implications of her work are in large measure incompatible with Sartreanism.

For Sartre, subjectivity or "being-for-itself" is wholly autonomous and, because unconditioned, free. Man is an "absolute subject." Each subject, although existing "in situation" and thus encountering the facticity of the world of things (or "being-in-itself"), always freely and autonomously constitutes the meaning of its own situation through the capacity for transcendence. Moreover, in relations between human beings, which Sartre characterizes as the fundamentally conflictual relation of Self and Other, this absolute autonomy of the subject always remains intact. Thus, for Sartre, relations of unequal power have no bearing on the autonomy of the subject. "The slave in chains is as free as his master," Sartre tells us, because each is equally free to choose the meaning he gives his own situation. The question of material or political inequality between master and slave is simply irrelevant to their relation as two freedoms, as two absolute subjects. In the same vein, Sartre is able to write—in the middle of World War II!—that the Jew remains free in the face of the anti-Semite because he can choose his own attitude toward his persecutor.

In his delineation of the absolute subject, Sartre remains within what many feminists have suggested is a typically male conception of the subject. He presents a version of what Nancy Hartsock has characterized as the "walled city" view of the self, which conceives of the self as not only radically separate from others but also as always potentially hostile. As Hartsock has observed, Hegel's account of the emergence of self-consciousness "seeks the death of the other"—an account that Sartre appropriates as the relation of self and other in *Being and Nothingness*—restates a common masculine experience: "The construction of a self in opposition to another who threatens one's very being reverberates throughout the construction of both class society and the masculinist world view and results in a deep-going and hierarchical dualism" (Hartsock 1985). Moreover, Sartre's notion of the subject shares the abstract universalism that others have suggested comes with a specifically male notion of reason (see, e.g., [Genevieve] Lloyd [1984] and Harding [1986]). To be master or slave, anti-Semite or Jew—or male or female—has, for Sartre, no bearing on the absolute and inviolable subjectivity of which each of us is the bearer.

Given these arguably masculinist elements of the Sartrean notion of the subject, his philosophy would not seem to provide a hospitable framework within which to develop feminist theory. Insofar as Beauvoir tries to remain within it, she does appeal to a predominantly male notion of abstract, universal freedom as the goal for the liberated woman. Existing in unhappy antagonism with the Sartrean framework, however, is a significantly different notion of the self from which Beauvoir operates. This is a less dualistic and more relational notion of the self, such as Hartsock and others have argued often emerges from the particularities of women's life experience (Hartsock 1985). It involves, contra the early Sartre, a tacit rejection of the notion of the "absolute subject" for a situated subject: a subject that is intrinsically intersubjective and embodied, thus always "interdependent" and permeable rather than walled.

Beauvoir had already begun to develop a notion of the subject different from Sartre's well before she wrote ***The Second Sex.*** This is apparent in the summary in her autobiographical volume, ***The Prime of Life,*** of a series of conversations she had with Sartre in the spring of 1940. In these conversations, Sartre set out for her the main lines of the argument of what was to become *Being and Nothing-*

ness. Their discussions, Beauvoir recalled in 1960, centered above all on the problem of "the relation of situation to freedom." On this point they disagreed:

> I maintained that, from the point of view of freedom, as Sartre defined it—not as a stoical resignation but as an active transcendence of the given—not every situation is equal: what transcendence is possible for a woman locked up in a harem? Even such a cloistered existence could be lived in several different ways, Sartre said. I clung to my opinion for a long time and then made only a token submission. Basically I was right. But to have been able to defend my position, I would have had to abandon the terrain of individualist, thus idealist, morality, where we stood.

Beauvoir was right that her "submission" was no more than "token." Although she was never willing to challenge head-on Sartre's conception of freedom, or the notion of the impermeable "walled city subject" that it implied, she quietly subverted them. This becomes clearer in two essays on ethics she wrote prior to ***The Second Sex: Pyrrhus et Cinéas*** (1944) and ***The Ethics of Ambiguity*** ([1947] 1967). In ***Pyrrhus et Cinéas,*** written while *Being and Nothingness* was in press, Beauvoir begins from the Sartrean autonomous subject but ends by putting in question the theory of fundamentally conflictual social relations that Sartre develops from it. Although Beauvoir presents freedoms as separate, she argues that, paradoxically, they are also intrinsically interdependent. If one tries to imagine a world in which one is the only person, the image is horrifying, she insists. For everything one does would be pointless unless there were other subjects to valorize it: "A man [*sic*] alone in the world would be paralysed by the self-evident vanity of all his goals; he could not bear to live."

Moreover, for others to valorize one's project, Beauvoir argues, it is not enough that they are free merely in Sartre's sense; it is not sufficient for them to be subjects each of whom constitutes, like the master and the slave, the meaning of his or her own discrete situation. Freedom for Beauvoir, far more than for Sartre, involves a practical subjectivity: the ability of each of us to act in the world so that we can take up each other's projects and give them a future meaning. And for this to be possible, we also require an equal degree of practical freedom:

> The other's freedom can do nothing for me unless my own goals can serve as his point of departure; it is by using the tool which I have invented that the other prolongs its existence; the scholar can only talk with men who have arrived at the same level of knowledge as himself . . . I must therefore endeavour to create for all men situations which will enable them to accompany and surpass my transcendence. I need their freedom to be available to use me, to preserve me in surpassing me. I require for men health, knowledge, well being, leisure, so that their freedom does not consume itself in fighting sickness, ignorance, misery.

Already, then, Beauvoir is aware of the interdependence of subjectivities and, in ways that Sartre is not, of the permeability of the subject. She arguably takes the first step here toward adequately linking Sartre's individualistic existentialism with their shared commitment to the solidaristic and communal values of socialism. In ***The Ethics of Ambiguity,*** she went a step further. There she suggests that oppression can permeate subjectivity to the point where consciousness itself becomes no more than a product of the oppressive situation. The freedom that Sartre had associated with subjectivity can, in a situation of extreme oppression, be wholly suppressed, even though it cannot be definitively eliminated. In such a situation, the oppressed become incapable of the project of resistance, unable to maintain the reflective distance necessary to be aware that they are oppressed. In such a situation, "living is only not dying, and human existence is indistinguishable from an absurd vegetation." The oppressed—and this is a point Beauvoir will later return to in her analysis of woman's situation—live in an "infantile world" of immediacy, with no sense of alternative futures. Freedom is no longer the capacity to choose how to live even the most constrained of situations, which Sartre had claimed it to be. Freedom is here seen as reducible to no more than a suppressed potentiality. It is made "immanent," unrealizable. Yet, for all this, freedom, is still not a "fiction" or an "imaginary" for Beauvoir. For should oppression start to weaken, freedom can always reerupt.

In ***The Second Sex,*** Beauvoir's break from Sartre's version of the walled city subject becomes even more marked. She begins ***The Second Sex*** on what appears to be firmly Sartrean ground. "What is a woman?" she asks, and answers initially that woman is defined as that which is not man—as Other: "She is determined and differentiated with reference to man and not he with reference to her; she is the inessential as opposed to the essential. He is the subject, he is the Absolute: she is the Other."

Some commentators have used this and other similar passages to accuse Beauvoir of taking on board the Sartrean (and Hegelian) notion of the self-construction of subjectivity through conflict. Very early in the book, however, Beauvoir relativizes the notion of otherness by introducing a distinction not found in *Being and Nothingness,* and whose originality needs emphasizing. We can, she argues, distinguish two significantly different kinds of relations of otherness: those between social equals and those that involve social inequality. Where the relation is one of equality, she suggests that otherness is "relativized" by a kind of "reciprocity": each, as she had said in ***Pyrrhus et Cinéas,*** recognizes that the Other is an equal freedom. Where, however, otherness exists through relations of inequality, there reciprocity is to a greater or lesser extent abolished, replaced by relations of oppression and subjection. When one of the two parties in a conflict is privileged by having some material or physical advantage, then, "this one prevails over the other and undertakes to keep it in subjection." It is not, then, woman's otherness per se but her subjection—the nonreciprocal objectification of woman by man—that Beauvoir sets out to explain. It is not only that woman is the Other; she is the unequal Other. The question is, if this inequality is not inscribed in nature, how does it occur?

The short answer for Beauvoir is, of course, that "being a woman" is a socially constructed experience; it is to live a social situation that men have, for their own advantage, attempted to impose on women. Beauvoir's discussion of the varying degrees to which women choose or are forced to accept this imposition suggests a continuum of different possible responses. Some—the "independent" women she describes in the last part of the book—consistently, if unsuccessfully, attempt to resist it. Some choose to accept it in what Sartre termed "bad faith" (a strategy to evade the pain and responsibility that come with freedom) because of the security and privilege it brings. Others, unable to conceive of real alternatives, accept it while engaging in forms of passive resistance and resentment. For yet others, as for the oppressed whom Beauvoir had described in ***The Ethics of Ambiguity,*** freedom is suppressed to the point where they cease to be capable of choice or resistance. What is of interest here is that in describing the most oppressed end of the continuum Beauvoir departs even more sharply from the Sartrean notion of the subject than in her earlier essays. In so doing, she also breaks free of any kind of Enlightenment notion of the subject, although (as we will see) she certainly does not thereby intend to "get rid of the subject itself."

Once again Beauvoir relativizes Sartre's ideas in ways that significantly transform them. She begins by appearing to agree with Sartre that there is a radical disjuncture between the human and the natural realms, with freedom and subjectivity characterizing the human. Indeed, this claim is the basis for her rejection of deterministic biological explanations of the female condition. However, yet again, Sartre's dualistic ontology rapidly becomes transmuted in her hands. While biology is not itself "destiny," the oppressive situation that men across the ages have imposed on women and justified in large part on the grounds of real biological difference can function analogously to a natural force. Women can have a man-made destiny; indeed, she says at one point, "the whole of feminine history has been man made." If a woman is oppressed to the point where her subjectivity is suppressed, then her situation is de facto her "destiny" and she ceases to be an effective or morally responsible agent. "Every subject," she writes,

> continually affirms himself through his projects as a transcendence; he realizes his freedom only through his continual transcendence toward other freedoms; there is no other justification for present existence than its expansion towards an endlessly open future. Each time that transcendence falls back into immanence there is a degradation of existence into the 'in-itself,' of freedom into facticity; this fall is a moral fault if the subject agrees to it; it takes the form of a frustration and an oppression if it is inflicted upon him.

Woman, then, is locked in immanence by the situation man inflicts upon her—and she is not necessarily responsible for that condition. Although the language in the passage is Sartrean, the argument is not. A consistent Sartrean position would make woman responsible for herself, no matter how constrained her situation. But for Beauvoir, women are not the primary source of the problem even though some comply with their oppressors in "bad faith." For many, there is no moral fault because there simply is no possibility of choice. In the notion that freedom can "fall back into the 'in-itself,'" that the "for-itself" can be turned through the action of other (i.e., male) freedoms into its very opposite, Beauvoir has radically departed from the Sartrean notion of the absolute subject. For Sartre, there can be no middle ground. Either the for-itself, the uncaused upsurge of freedom, the "absolute subject," exists whatever the facticities of its situation, or else it does not exist at all. In the latter case, one is dealing with the realm of nature or inert being. Insofar as Beauvoir's account of woman's situation as one of immanence involves the claim that freedom, the for-itself, can be penetrated and modified by the in-itself, it implies another notion of the subject than Sartre's. Beauvoir is trying to describe human existence as a synthesis of freedom and constraint, of consciousness and materiality that, finally, is incompatible with Sartre's version of the walled city subject.

Indeed, so far has Beauvoir moved that one might even be tempted to formulate her position, albeit only at this extreme end of the spectrum, in Foucault's terms: woman is a historically constituted, not a constituting, subject. For not only does woman fail freely to choose her situation, according to Beauvoir, she is in the most extreme situation its product: "When . . . a group of individuals is kept in a situation of inferiority, the fact is they are inferior . . . yes, women on the whole *are* today inferior to men, which is to say that their situation gives them less possibilities."

Yet unlike Sartre's postmodern critics, Beauvoir never

wholly discards a notion of free subjectivity. Even when it is suppressed, reduced to immanence, subjectivity remains a distinctly human potentiality. Thus, for example, while much of her painstaking and detailed account of the young girl's *formation* could be retold in the Foucauldian mode of "the political technology of the body" and of "discipline," Beauvoir would never have agreed to abandon the notion of a repression of freedom. However suppressed, however disciplined, it is still freedom-made-immanent that distinguishes even the most constituted human subject from a trained animal. For Beauvoir, a real repression or oppression of this subject is also always possible, unlike for Foucault. However socially constructed its identities may be, for Beauvoir the subject is still something other than the "effect" of its conditionings. Although she avoids the essentialism of the subject as, for example, a Cartesian cogito, she also rejects the hyperconstructivism of the Foucauldian account, which presents the subject as discursively produced, to be "stripped of its creative role and analysed as a complex and variable function of discourse" (Foucault [1969] 1977).

How then does Beauvoir develop this account of a situated subject that can be characterized neither as an autonomous walled city nor as uniquely a construct of discursive practices? Two fundamental insights orient the development of her account of situated subjectivity. The first is her recognition of what I will call the intersubjectivity of the subject. By this is meant something more than the interconnectedness of subjects. What is meant is the impossibility of a subjective self-constitution that is not always socially and culturally permeated. If all that took place between an individual man and woman was a struggle of consciousnesses between two human beings, one of whom happened to be male and one female, then we could not anticipate in advance which of them would objectify the other. If, however, we examine the relations of a husband and a wife, then it is very different. For the social institution of marriage in all its aspects—legal, economic, sexual, cultural, etc.—has formed in advance for the protagonists their own relation of inequality. As Beauvoir points out in a strikingly unSartrean passage, "*It is not as single individuals that human beings are to be defined in the first place;* men and women have never stood opposed to each other in single combat; the couple is an original *Mitsein;* and as such it always appears as a permanent element in a larger collectivity" (emphasis added).

Although subjectivity is individually lived, it is never, then, simply an individual constitution of existence. Rather, according to Beauvoir, it is both constituting and constituted. It is, to use Sartre's later terminology, "singular universal." Thus it follows (as Beauvoir had already made clear in her ethical essays) that oppression of any kind affects more than its immediate victims and that liberatory struggles cannot be other than collective. That Beauvoir herself did not apparently see at the time she wrote ***The Second Sex*** that she should explicitly apply these conclusions to women (as she was already doing in the late 1940s to colonial peoples) is an indication of the isolation in which she wrote her book and of the limits to her own political imagination. But this failure should not blind us to the implications of her argument.

Beauvoir's later assessment of ***The Second Sex*** was that it was not a "militant" book. Insofar as it presents no call for a concerted resistance by women to their oppression, she was justified in this judgment. But if not militant, the book is in its implications deeply political—and it is here that much of its continuing relevance lies. For in her insistence that freedoms are interdependent and that freedom, however suppressed, however immanent, is an enduring potentiality, Beauvoir affirms that women's oppression is real and that political struggle is indeed possible. While eschewing the naive assumptions of individual free agency and responsibility that are central to the Enlightenment conception of subjectivity, she also insists that subjectivity cannot be accounted for solely in terms of the effect of the apparently autonomous power of structures, technologies, or discourses.

I turn now to Beauvoir's second insight. This concerns the inherence of subjectivity in the body: the idea, which she borrows from Merleau-Ponty, that the subject is always properly called a "body-subject." It is toward the specificities of embodied subjectivities that Beauvoir orients us to grasp the oppression of women. If the couple is an "original *Mitsein*" (Heidegger's term, meaning a fundamental "being with"), this is because of its reproductive significance. By stressing that reproduction and sexuality are socially and culturally constituted phenomena, Beauvoir avoids the essentialism of biological reductionism. But she also avoids hyperconstructivism by arguing that reproduction is ontologically fundamental. If (as she had argued in ***Pyrrhus et Cinéas***) we need others to take up our projects and overcome our finitude, then each individual freedom requires "the perpetuation of the species." Thus, she now argues, "we can regard the phenomenon of reproduction as ontologically founded." In an argument that is neither realist nor constructivist but dialectical, Beauvoir insists that although biological "facts" have no significance outside the values that human beings give them, they do still have an objective reality: there are real limits to the significations we can choose. It is helpful to contrast Beauvoir with Foucault here. According to Foucault, "nothing in man—not even his body—is sufficiently stable to serve as the basis for . . . self-recognition." For Beauvoir, however, although the body is not a stable essence, it still is encountered by the self as an objective given. And whether or not a woman decides to procreate, it is an inescapable fact that of the two biological sexes her physiology is geared to the more extended and physiologically demanding role in perpetuating the species. Although a woman's body "is not itself sufficient to define her as woman," it is, Beauvoir argues, "an essential element of the situation she occupies in the world."

Beauvoir has been criticized, with considerable justification, for her horror of the female body and its functions. There are indeed many passages in ***The Second Sex*** where women's bodily functions are identified with animality, passivity, and lack of freedom and are denigrated from the masculinist standpoint of an apparently disembodied reason and freedom. There is, however, another reading of woman's body to be found in Beauvoir's text as well. This reading, which I intend to pursue here as the more fruitful one for feminism, tells us that it is as body that human subjectivity both encounters and gives meaning to its own inescapable rootedness in objective reality. In Beauvoir's account, women encounter this in a particularly intense form, one whose alienating aspects she most emphasizes: "Woman, like man, *is* her body," she says, but immediately adds, "but her body is something other than herself."

The important point that is lodged here against Enlightenment or walled city conceptions of the subject is that subjectivity is not given in closed contradistinction to a realm of objective entities that it oversees or contemplates in detachment. Rather, it is through the body that we each inhere in one and the same world. Moreover, this common inherence may form the basis for an overlapping or for an even fuller sharing of experience on which common action may be based. Beauvoir's woman is not, then, a Sartrean for-itself for whom the body is merely a facticity. But neither, contra Foucault, is she merely a "soul . . . produced permanently around, on, the body, by the functioning of a power that is exercised on . . . those one supervises, trains, corrects." Rather, for Beauvoir, we need to explore what she calls "the strange ambiguity of existence made body." For "to be present in the world implies strictly that there exists a body which is *at the same time* a thing in the world and a point of view on this world" (emphasis added).

For Beauvoir, subjectivity is corporally constituted; it is coextensive with the body, while being simultaneously "a point of view." This account is significantly different from Sartre's, for whom "my body forme" and "my body for-others"—that is, the body as object—are on "different and incommunicable levels of being." She holds that biological difference itself, as well as the socially constructed significations that adhere to that difference, permeates subjectivity, but it is not reducible to their effect. Thus, rather than accepting either a realism of the kind that posits an inevitable feminine essence grounded in the body and in mothering or the position of much postmodern theory in which the body itself becomes no more than a discursive construct, Beauvoir suggests a less dichotomized account of subjectivity. Such an account allows us to acknowledge the sameness of women as biologically sexed and socially constructed females without pinning an immutable essence of womanhood onto "real historical women" whose lives may also be radically divergent, shaped also by class, race, ethnicity, age, sexual orientation, and many other factors. Biological sex is always present as a given in the "lived experience" of the body. Yet our lived experience of the body is never "natural." It is, for Beauvoir, one of the always socially mediated experiences we have of the objective givens of our lives. Thus Beauvoir would, I think, approve of postmodern feminist projects to contest the discursive constructions of gender, even though she would reject the hyperconstructivist epistemology upon which they generally rest.

Thus, against the hyperconstructivism incipient in postmodernism, in which subjectivity itself can become but a fiction and everything, including the category of woman, can cease to be real, Beauvoir sketches an account of the gendering of subjectivity that can best be characterized as a dialectical realism. By this I mean an account in which not only discourse but also a discursively mediated "beyond" of discourse is acknowledged. This "beyond" of discourse includes, on the one hand, the existence of objective parameters to human life, such as sex, birth, disease, malnutrition, and death and, on the other hand, an always-present potentiality for that margin of autonomous thought and action in situation that Beauvoir calls "freedom." For unless we grant that real historical women live and die, that they do decide and act, and that they can in varying degrees be oppressed or free, we risk becoming our own grave diggers. If we need to seek a way between hyperconstructivism and essentialism, Beauvoir's work remains richly suggestive as to how we might set about it.

Elizabeth A. Houlding (essay date Spring 1993)

SOURCE: "Simone de Beauvoir: From the Second World War to *The Second Sex*," in *L'Esprit Créateur*, Vol. XXXIII, No. 1, Spring, 1993, pp. 39-51.

[*In the following essay, Houlding discusses the influence of the Nazi Occupation of France on Beauvoir's intellectual development and philosophical insights in* The Second Sex. *According to Houlding, "Through her exposure to the nature of women's everyday lives during the Occupation, Beauvoir first began to perceive the active construction of femininity."*]

In her memoirs, Simone de Beauvoir referred to the Second World War as a pivotal moment in her life, a time when her ways of interacting with the world underwent permanent transformations. Until 1939, Beauvoir had refused to believe that the trauma of war could come to interrupt the life she had so carefully constructed: "Je refusai furieusement d'y croire; une catastrophe aussi imbécile ne pouvait pas fondre sur moi." It was through the war that Beauvoir came to perceive her "historicity," that is, the force of history in the shaping of individual lives. Years later, in a 1985 interview with her biographer Deirdre Bair, Beauvoir would criticize her pre-war attitude: "À vrai dire, je ne suis pas fière de ce que j'étais alors—trente ans et toujours égocentrique. Je regrette qu'il ait fallu la guerre pour m'apprendre que je vivais dans le monde, pas en dehors."

The Occupation and the Second World War precipitated a generation of French intellectuals toward political engagement. ***Le Deuxième sexe*** was published only four years after the war in 1949. Beauvoir undertook her study of the feminine ideal in the wake of the Occupation. In this paper, I will consider what led Beauvoir to incorporate questions of gender within the post-war project of engagement in the world.

Commenting on the reception of ***Le Deuxième sexe,*** Toril Moi has remarked upon what she terms the "political isolation" of the book in 1949, finding it

> curiously out of step with its own historical moment, written as it was at a time when Western capitalism was kicking women out of the factories in order to hand their jobs over to the boys back from the war, and published just as the West was about to embark on that most antifeminist of decades, the 1950s.

Within this global representation of Western capitalism, Moi's transposition of Rosie the Riveter from the United States to France is misleading, since the particular conditions of occupied France had not transformed the traditionally agrarian French economy into the booming American model of industrialized military production.

In addition, French women had not played as prominent a role in the wartime workplace as their American counterparts. In direct contrast to the American model, women in France were actively recruited as workers after the war in order to shore up the depleted national workforce and the desperate national economy. Among the political measures taken toward national recovery by liberated France, women "were finally granted the right to vote and to run for public office, and the Constitution of the Fourth Republic enshrined the right to work in its articles." The Liberation was seen as "the moment to bring women into full participation in the polity and equality of the workplace." It must be said, though, that postwar social programs were implemented under the assumption that women's true place was within the family, where wives remained subordinate to their husbands, the legal *chefs de famille.*

Moi's second displacement, that in which she projects ***Le Deuxième sexe*** forward into the 1950s, is more central to my argument here, however. Because of the enormous impact of ***Le Deuxième sexe*** in its American incarnation as ***The Second Sex*** in 1953, there has been a tendency to date the work and its influence from that time. Yet, in observing that the text central to the elaboration of late twentieth-century feminism appears oddly out of step with the 1950s, we do not account for the fact that ***Le Deuxième sexe*** stepped into history directly out of World War II and the German Occupation of France. It is precisely the genesis of ***Le Deuxième sexe*** in occupied France, with its specific gender conditions and historical configurations, that we have overlooked.

Rather than an eery prediction of the house-bound 50s, or a clarion call to the women's movement of the 70s, ***Le Deuxième sexe*** responded above all to the experience of the 40s. Closing the French decade in 1949, it is literally a post-war work, a work that Beauvoir could not have written before the lessons of the war years. For France, this was a decade defined by war, defeat, and occupation by the eternal enemy. For French women, it was a decade in which it was virtually impossible to avoid what Denise Riley has termed "gendered self-consciousness," that is, the (self-) recognition that results when women are consistently "named as a sex" within social discourse. In what might now be interpreted as attempts to counter the crisis in masculinity occasioned by the French defeat, the Occupation was the site of relentless attempts to define women's social function and to circumscribe the dangers posed by femininity in a nation controlled by a foreign and unremittingly masculine presence. As recent feminist criticism on women and war has demonstrated, "war throws gender into sharp relief." In an extremely dramatic way, the German Occupation of France exacerbated conventional notions of femininity and politicized the traditionally "feminine" networks of everyday life.

Humiliated by the *exode,* feminized by the rapid defeat, and by the signing of the Armistice with the Nazis, France did in fact appear to be a country of women in the early years of the Occupation. While the recurrent image of France-as-fallen-woman haunted Vichy discourse, many men, an estimated 1.6 million, were held as prisoners after the defeat, while 92,000 had died in combat. For all its focus on the rights of the family, Vichy legislation actually limited the rights of women as individuals, since the effect of such conservative ideology bound women as wives and mothers even more forcefully to the home. To this day, French families have Philippe Pétain's traditional Catholic leadership to thank for the national holiday known as "La Fête des Mères." Vichy also underwrote the legislation of specific pro-family laws: aid to families was significantly increased; divorce was prohibited for couples married less than three years; adoption laws were broadened in order to reduce the number of childless homes; husbands who abandoned their families were charged with having committed a misdemeanor; and in keeping with this pro-natalist policy, the performing of abortions was punished as a form of treason against the state.

For Simone de Beauvoir, who had scrupulously rebelled against the life of a dutiful French daughter until this point, the Occupation provided an obvious working example of the social and historical construction of gender. Through her exposure to the nature of women's everyday lives during the Occupation, Beauvoir first began to perceive the active construction of femininity. Writing daily letters to Sartre (who was absent from Paris on military duty and then in prison camp until March 1941), waiting in food lines, preparing meals, and attempting to secure the continuity of life for those within her care, Beauvoir herself lived more "like a woman" during the Occupation than at any other time in her life.

Beauvoir briefly discussed the factors which led her to undertake a study of women's condition in ***La Force des choses.*** As an admirer of Michel Leiris's *L'Âge d'homme,* Beauvoir was moved to write an autobiographical work after the war. With Leiris's text serving as a masculine model, she began with a personal question: "Qu'est-ce queça avait signifié pour moi d'être une femme?" At this time, Beauvoir did not feel that being a woman had hindered her in any way: "ma féminité ne m'avait gênée en rien." When Sartre pointed out that she had nonetheless not been raised in the same manner as a boy, Beauvoir realized that the question deserved more thought and, characteristically, took herself off to the Bibliothèque Nationale to study it further. It was then that Beauvoir had the following revelation concerning the "myths of femininity":

> Je regardai et j'eus une révélation: ce monde était un monde masculin, mon enfance avait été nourrie de mythes forgés par les hommes et je n'y avais pas du tout réagi de la même manière que si j'avais été un garçon. Je fus si intéressée que j'abandonnai le project d'une confession personnelle pour m'occuper de la condition féminine dans sa généralité.

I want to argue, beyond Beauvoir's analysis, that it was her Occupation experience which led her to pose the initial question of the meaning of sexual difference in her own life, and to seek its answer in the theoretical exploration of gender in ***Le Deuxième sexe.***

In reading Beauvoir's personal texts concerning the war years, it becomes clear that Beauvoir's confrontation with the nature of women's daily lives under the extreme conditions of the Occupation supplied the key impulse to the writing of ***Le Deuxième sexe;*** through her wartime encounters and experiences, Beauvoir began, however unconsciously, to take the measure of what she terms in her memoirs a certain "condition *féminine.*" A work of the magnitude of ***Le Deuxième sexe*** draws on various origins, among which we must include Beauvoir's first trip to the United States in 1947, her encounters with American women and visits to several women's colleges, her readings on the system of slavery, and the traditional aspects of her love affair with Nelson Algren. Virginia M. Fichera's study of ***Les Bouches inutiles*** has also identified Beauvoir's only play, written during the Occupation, as a definite precursor to ***Le Deuxième sexe.*** The role played by women's Occupation experiences in the elaboration of ***Le Deuxième sexe*** has remained a missing piece around which these other essential elements must be reassembled.

Severe practical hardships did not end for the French with the Liberation nor with the end of the war in 1945. The winter of 1944-45 was the coldest of the war thus far, with supplies of coal and clothing reaching their lowest level. Food rationing continued well beyond 1945, while prices for the basics rose. Bread rationing was reintroduced in December 1945, with the daily allotment decreased to 300 grams, a lesser amount than during the Occupation. A newspaper estimated that the average Parisian diet consisted of 1400 calories per day in March 1946, with this figure also representing a decrease since previous years. In September 1947, women in Le Mans rioted in protest against bread shortages. At the end of the war and for several years afterward, France represented the hungriest and least well-supplied European country other than Italy. Naturally, the everyday hardships occasioned by this lack of necessities fell upon the shoulders of women. This was the atmosphere in which Beauvoir was researching and writing ***Le Deuxième sexe.***

With the mobilization of her two closest male friends Sartre and Jacques-Laurent Bost in the fall of 1939, Beauvoir found herself in familiar but somewhat depleted surroundings. During the *drôle de guerre* and the Occupation, Beauvoir was to spend a significant amount of her time in the company of women. Her most constant companions, all members of the extended Family constructed around the Beauvoir-Sartre couple, were drawn from the circle of young women who revolved around the couple in their various roles as lovers, friends, students and protégées. Much of Beauvoir's memoirs of the time, her recently published journals, and the letters to Sartre involve the intrigues created by the shifting configurations of these relationships.

Perhaps the most striking thing about Beauvoir's recording of her daily life during the early months of the war is her breathtaking level of activity. For Beauvoir, as for most of the proverbial "women who wait," the previously impressive demands on her time and attention increased with the coming of war. Beauvoir continued to carry out her teaching duties until 1943. With the absence of many male teachers from Paris in the fall of 1939, her workload was significantly increased while her salary did not change. As she recalled in conversation with Bair:

> Le bon peuple de Paris devait continuer à éduquer ses enfants et, maintenant que tous les hommes étaient appelés à se battre, on attendait des femmes qu'elles fassent leur devoir patriotique et assument les postes des hommes sans aucune compensation financière. Je me rappelle m'être dit que ce n'était pas juste que j'aie une telle surcharge d'élèves sans toucher un franc de plus.

Bair reminds us that as many as eight people often depended upon Beauvoir's salary for their well-being during the war.

Perhaps due to the feminine company in which she necessarily found herself, even the seemingly indifferent Beauvoir came to realize more fully the meaning of a woman's public appearance during the war. In its very restrictions, the Occupation drew attention to the demands and the significance of women's fashion. As Dominique Veillon notes in her study of the French fashion industry under the Occupation, the first winter of the war occasioned the birth of the adjective "utilitaire" to describe the element of practicality that now governed certain fashion choices. Upon the death of her father in 1941, Beauvoir and her mother made use of his clothing coupons and old clothes. For herself, Beauvoir had an unflattering dress and coat made up out of a heavy overcoat of her father's. Each one of the few items in her wardrobe was threadbare from use by the end of the war. As many women took to wearing men's trousers during the winter months, Beauvoir wore her ski pants and ski boots as daily apparel. However, even during the record cold temperatures of 1942-43, female instructors were required to wear dresses in the classroom.

Beauvoir was one of many women who learned how to ride a bicycle during the war. Still, these utilitarian aspects of the Occupation years were recuperable within the fashion system: for example, in the summer of 1941, the newspaper *Paris-Midi* sponsored a contest for the most beautiful cycling outfits. With each new development in women's wear, the magazines of the day debated the fine line between reason and fashion. In June 1942, *Marie-Claire's* "Ten Commandments for the Parisienne" warned female readers: "La jupe-culotte, tu porteras à bicyclette seulement." Beauvoir's trademark turban was yet another sign of the practical times, as trips to the beauty salon became increasingly expensive and shampoo increasingly rare. Here too, French unwillingness to sacrifice femininity entirely during wartime is illustrated by a striking double photograph taken by Lee Miller: as women at the Salon Gervais sit under hairdryers with manicurists in attendance, two young men—"les forçats du bigoudi"—ride bicycles in the basement to generate electricity for the dryers above. Images such as this, with its division of labor along gender lines, demonstrate the degree to which it was essential that the notion of femininity and the sacrifices made in the name of Parisian glamor survive during a time of national crisis.

Accustomed to an austere lifestyle, Beauvoir confided in her journal on 5 September 1940 that she adapted easily to the restrictions of Occupation life: "Personnellement, ça m'amuse un peu la modicité des ressources qui me sont offertes; j'ai toujours aimé imaginer des situations où il fallait arranger sa vie presque sans matière: extrême pauvreté, ou maladie, ou village, ou province." Despite this initial enthusiasm, Beauvoir discovered over the next five years that the "challenges" of women's lives during wartime could prove to be exhausting and demoralizing. With Sartre's release from prison camp in the spring of 1941, he and Beauvoir resumed their communal life by renting rooms in the same hotel and meeting for meals together. As dining in restaurants became unaffordable, Beauvoir took on the ever more challenging tasks of purchasing and preparing food for herself, Sartre, and various members of the Family. The Occupation was the only moment of her life during which Beauvoir actively participated in the daily concerns of a typical French housewife:

> J'avais peu de goût pour les tâches ménagères et pour m'en accommoder je recourus à un procédé familier: de mes soucis alimentaires, je fis une manie dans laquelle je persévérai pendant trois ans. Je surveillais la sortie des tickets, je n'en laissai jamais perdre un; dans les rues, par-delà les étalages factices des magasins, je cherchais à découvrir quelque denrée en vente libre: cette espèce de chasse au trésor m'amusait; quelle aubaine si je trouvais une betterave, un chou!

As she sat in her room writing while dinner simmered on the burner, Beauvoir momentarily shared in the modest pleasures afforded by the interiority of women's domestic lives:

> Je me rappelle, au début de décembre, une fin d'après-midi où le couvre-feu—fixé à 6 heures, à la suite d'un attentat—me claquemurait dans ma chambre. J'écrivais; dehors c'était le grand silence des déserts; sur le fourneau cuisait une soupe de légumes qui sentait bon; cette odeur engageante, le

> chuintement du gaz étaient une compagnie; je ne partageais pas la condition des femmes d'intérieur, mais j'avais un aperçu de leurs joies.

Wartime conditions made Beauvoir more aware of "la condition des femmes d'intérieur," although she herself had deliberately chosen to live outside of the restrictive domestic space by avoiding both matrimony and maternity. Within these passages, Beauvoir is also sure to maintain her distance from the "joys" of housekeeping by implying that her glimpse of domesticity's fleeting pleasures did not still the pen in her hand.

If Beauvoir often appears in her memoirs to be innocently playing at the role of French housewife, referring half-ironically to these years as her "femme de charge" period, she does not go so far as to glamorize the labor and sacrifices involved. In the first months of the Occupation, she was infuriated by her father's complaints of hunger and hardship because she knew that it was taken for granted that "it was [her] mother who stood in the queues all day long trying to find enough for him to eat, shorting herself to give him more." It is also clear that, with Beauvoir fulfilling her "wifely" duties, Sartre was never expected to share household responsibilities and indeed was often shielded from certain realities of Occupation life: "Quant à Sartre, nous lui dissimulâmes la vérité." While Beauvoir did her best to disguise the unsavory food that she was obliged to put on the table, packages of food sent from the provinces often arrived with the meat in an advanced form of decay. Beauvoir attempted to salvage what she could, cleaning maggots out of pork, rinsing beef in vinegar, heavily seasoning the stewpot so as to camouflage any telltale signs: "D'ordinaire, je réussissais mon coup; j'étais mortifiée quand Sartre repoussait son assiette." On one particular day, however, Sartre arrived home to discover Beauvoir unwrapping a piece of rotting rabbit, seized it from her hands and rushed downstairs to throw it out. Unbeknownst to Sartre, Beauvoir was to retrieve it later, soak it in vinegar, cover it in herbs, and serve it to him for dinner.

In 1985, Beauvoir also admitted that, in spite of Sartre's vehement principles against black-market dealing, she was sometimes forced by hunger and necessity to purchase goods there without his knowledge. While she clearly enjoyed the special occasions on which she acted as hostess for friends such as Michel and Louise Leiris, Camus, and Picasso, Beauvoir also recognized the costs of taking on such a role permanently. Bair writes that after the war ended Beauvoir never cooked again, a highly unusual accomplishment for any woman, and especially so for a woman born in 1908.

Until the Second World War, Beauvoir had considered herself an exception in her discontent with the roles of wife and mother traditionally accorded to women. When the Occupation brought her into contact with a slightly older group of women whose lives were more conventional than her own, Beauvoir began to take stock of the similar obstacles they had each encountered along the way:

> Soudain, je rencontrai un grand nombre de femmes qui avaient passé la quarantaine et qui, à travers la diversité de leurs chances et de leurs mérites, avaient toutes fait une expérience identique: elles avaient vécu en "êtres relatifs."

Although Beauvoir felt at the time that, as an unmarried woman without children, she had escaped being trapped within the traditional model, her interest in the socially-determined patterns of women's lives had nonetheless been focused.

Beauvoir makes another vital connection in this passage of ***La Force de l'âge*** concerning the extent to which the war years transformed prewar abstractions into concrete realities:

> Sur bien des points, j'avais réalisé combien, avant la guerre, j'avais péché par abstraction: qu'il ne fût pas indifférent d'être juif ou aryen, à présent je le savais; mais je ne m'étais pas avisée qu'il eût une condition féminine.

Beauvoir had learned during the war years that whether one was Jewish or Aryan could matter immensely, and that such distinctions were not mere abstractions. Although she would not articulate her wartime intuition until after the Liberation, Beauvoir had also witnessed the difference gender made during the Occupation.

The ideological connections between anti-semitism, racism and sexism would prove to be essential to Beauvoir's opening argument in ***Le Deuxième sexe.*** During the war, Sartre drafted a "Constitution" for the post-war period to be sent to Charles de Gaulle, which included the protection of religious, cultural and linguistic rights for Jews. Whereas Beauvoir felt at that time that no individual or culture should benefit from "special" treatment, Sartre argued that the specificity of "le fait juif" must be recognized and protected. Beauvoir was eventually to agree with him on this. Both Sartre's work on "the Jewish question" and Beauvoir's project on "the Woman question" reflect this change in attitude toward oppression which the war had provoked.

In the introduction to ***Le Deuxième sexe,*** Beauvoir makes numerous references to cultural stereotypes surrounding European Jews, African American slaves, and women:

> Refuser les notions d'éternel féminin, d'âme noire, de caractère juif, ce n'est pas nier qu'il y ait

> aujourd'hui des Juifs, des Noirs, des femmes: cette négation ne représente pas pour les intéressés une libération, mais une fuite inauthentique. Il est clair qu'aucune femme ne peut prétendre sans mauvaise foi se situer par-delà son sexe.

Beauvoir makes clear distinctions between forms of oppression in terms of race, class, and gender. However, for today's reader, certain similarities remain powerful and telling. The Holocaust and slavery were both systems in which no "after" could be envisioned, in which the fundamental assumption was that European Jews and African American slaves would not go on to testify to the conditions of their lives. Jews were not to have survived. Slaves were not considered capable of constructing a meaningful narrative. How then would these stories be told? What form would the witness's testimony take? Regarding female testimony, Beauvoir could not have foreseen when writing this introduction that her readers would come to speak in terms of "before" and "after" ***Le Deuxième sexe*** itself. Nor could she have known that her decision to study "la condition féminine" rather than herself alone would so undeniably result in a work that set generations of women's testimony and writing in motion. ***Le Deuxième sexe*** provided precisely an analysis of women's condition through which female testimony could occur.

In the recent *Yale French Studies* issue devoted to her work, Beauvoir is celebrated as the "witness to a century," in recognition of the fact that "her autobiography 'begins' back in 1908 with ***Memoirs of a Dutiful Daughter*** and goes up to 1970 with ***All Said and Done,***" continuing through to 1980 with the account of Sartre's last years in ***Adieux.*** In considering ***Le Deuxième sexe*** as Beauvoir's first contribution to twentieth-century feminism, we are obliged to rethink the role of the war years in the decades of women's history that followed. ***Le Deuxième sexe*** draws on her position as an eyewitness to the Occupation years. It was at this time that Beauvoir witnessed the process through which women become a gender, a process compellingly identified in ***Le Deuxième sexe:*** "On ne naît pas femme: on le devient." The Second World War did not just make of Beauvoir a historical subject, it made her a woman as well.

Margaret A. Simons (essay date 1995)

SOURCE: "*The Second Sex:* From Marxism to Radical Feminism," in *Feminist Interpretations of Simone de Beauvoir,* edited by Margaret A. Simons, Pennsylvania State University Press, 1995, pp. 243-62.

[*In the following essay, Simons explores elements of Marxist, socialist, and psychoanalytic theory in Beauvoir's feminist philosophy. According to Simons, "Beauvoir, in* The Second Sex, *laid the theoretical foundations for a radical feminist movement of the future and defined a feminist political philosophy of lasting importance."*]

Despite the acknowledgment by radical feminist theorists of the women's liberation movement in the 1960s that Simone de Beauvoir provided a model for their theorizing, ***The Second Sex*** (1949) has yet to find a secure place in the history of political philosophy. The feminist philosopher Alison Jaggar, for example, whose pioneering work defined the categories of feminist political philosophy (i.e., liberal, socialist, and radical feminism), does not include a discussion of ***The Second Sex*** in her definitive text, *Feminist Politics and Human Nature,* despite her recognition of the "historical significance" of ***The Second Sex*** as "a forerunner of the contemporary women's liberation movement."

Jaggar omits "religious and existentialist conceptions of women's liberation" (including Beauvoir's) because they fall "outside the mainstream of contemporary feminist theorizing" and she finds them "implausible" from her socialist feminist perspective. But I shall argue in this paper that far from being outside the mainstream of feminist philosophy, Beauvoir provides the very foundation for radical feminism in ***The Second Sex,*** where the historical importance of radical feminism to both socialist and radical black theorizing of racial oppression is apparent.

Demonstrating the foundational relationship of ***The Second Sex*** to radical feminism addresses one of Jaggar's fundamental criticisms of radical feminism: that it lacks a "comprehensive theoretical framework" and in particular any psychological explanation of male behavior. Ignoring Beauvoir's work in ***The Second Sex,*** Jaggar traces the roots of radical feminism to a "contradictory heritage" in "the basically liberal civil rights movement and in the Marxist-inspired left." Liberal feminism and socialist feminism, in contrast, have strong foundations in the philosophies of Mill and Marx, respectively. But a recovery of Beauvoir's philosophy in ***The Second Sex*** can both reveal the philosophical foundation for radical feminism, and challenge the conception of the civil rights movement as "basically liberal," since Beauvoir drew upon the challenge to Marxist reductionism in radical black theorizing of racial oppression in formulating her theory. Her work thus challenges the definition of the feminist "mainstream" by affirming the interconnections of different forms of oppression while challenging the reductionism of identity politics.

In the discussion that follows I draw upon the definition of radical feminism provided by the feminist historian, Alice Echols (1989), author of *Daring To Be Bad: Radical Femi-*

nism in America, 1967-1975, the first comprehensive historical study of the radical feminist movement. Echols, unlike Jaggar, makes a helpful distinction between radical feminism and "cultural feminism," the movement that followed it in the 1970s. Jaggar charges radical feminism with falling back on biological determinism for an explanation of men's behavior, defining women's oppression under patriarchy as seamless and absolute with women as absolute victims, and focusing on the construction of a womanculture as the sole political strategy. But Echols differentiates these "cultural feminist" positions from earlier radical feminism, which was "a political movement dedicated to eliminating the sex-class system." According to Echols, radical feminists were both "typically social constructionists who wanted to render gender irrelevant," and at least "implicitly" "anti-capitalists" who "believed that feminism entailed an expansion of the left analysis." Cultural feminists, in contrast, "conceived of feminism as an antidote to the left," "dismissed economic class struggle as 'male' and, therefore, irrelevant to women," and sought to establish a womanculture where "'male values' would be exorcized and 'female values' nurtured."

In Echol's view Jaggar's analysis of radical feminism reflects a misreading of the movement common to socialists: "Most leftist and socialist-feminists mistakenly characterized radical feminism as apolitical. To them radical feminism involved changing the 'cultural super-structure' and developing alternative life-styles, rather than effecting serious economic and political change. . . . So when radical feminism began to give way to cultural feminism, socialist feminists simply did not notice." Echols can provide convincing evidence for the existence of a radical feminist movement that was social-constructionist and leftist in its critique of racism and economic class oppression. But her focus on American movement history prevents her from identifying Beauvoir's contribution to radical feminism in writing ***The Second Sex*** in France some twenty years earlier. To do that, it is most useful to adopt a methodology more akin to Jaggar's own philosophical analysis.

Echol's history of the movement reminds us that radical feminism was born out of dissatisfaction with both liberal feminism and socialism, and inspired by the transformation of the liberal civil rights struggle into the radical black power movement, a development that Jaggar does not acknowledge. In obvious parallels with radical black criticisms of the civil rights movement, radical feminists criticized liberal feminists for pursuing "formal equality within a racist, class stratified system, and for refusing to acknowledge that women's equality in the public domain was related to their subordination in the family." Much like the radical black theorists who defended the specificity of the African-American experience against Marxist reductionism, radical feminists also differed from socialists "who attributed women's oppression to capitalism, whose primary loyalty was to the left, and who longed for the imprimatur of the 'invisible audience' of male leftists." For radical feminists "male supremacy was not a mere epiphenomenon."

In ***The Second Sex*** Beauvoir rejects liberalism and its legalistic model of society as a public sphere governed by a social contract, and accepts instead a Marxist model of history as shaped by material factors and class struggle. Beauvoir recognized in 1949 the importance of the hard-fought battle for legal equality but saw it as insufficient. "Abstract rights . . . have never sufficed to assure woman a concrete hold on the world." Women have yet to attain "the union of abstract rights and concrete opportunities" without which "freedom is only a mystification." Even with many legal rights won, "the institutions and the values of patriarchal civilization have largely survived." Liberal individualism is no solution: "The success of a few privileged women can neither compensate for nor excuse the systematic degradation on the collective level." The analysis of the causes of women's oppression would have to go much deeper.

In an important theoretical step toward radical feminism—one paralleled by the radical African-American writer Richard Wright, whose work Beauvoir read and published in the 1940s—Beauvoir begins with a Marxist historical-materialist analysis of oppression and class struggle. In ***The Second Sex*** she argues that economic and technological developments provided the conditions for a women's liberation struggle. The industrial revolution "transformed women's lot in the nineteenth century and . . . opened a new era for her" by enabling her "to escape from the home and take a new part in production in the factory," thus "winning again an economic importance lost to her since the prehistoric era." Developments in technology made this possible by "annulling the difference in physical strength between male and female workers in a large number of cases."

New methods of birth control "permitted the dissociation of two formerly inseparable functions: the sexual function and the reproductive function." Reproductive technology will provide the material conditions for further gains by women: "By artificial insemination the evolution will be achieved which will permit humanity to master the reproductive function. . . . [Woman] can reduce the number of her pregnancies, and integrate them rationally into her life instead of being a slave to them. . . . It is by the convergence of these two factors: participation in production and emancipation from the slavery of reproduction that the evolution of woman's condition is to be explained."

When economic developments in advanced capitalist societies freed bourgeois women from dependence on their families, the material conditions were laid for the collective struggle by women, across economic classes, for their liberation. Beauvoir's feminism is activist: the only recourse for women is the collective struggle for their own liberation. "Freedom remains abstract and empty in woman, and can be authentically assumed only in revolt. . . . There is no other issue for woman than to work for her liberation. This liberation can only be collective, and it demands before all else that the economic evolution of the feminine condition be achieved."

An analogy with racism was important to both 1960s radical feminists and Beauvoir, as is evident in this passage:

> Whether it's a question of a race, of a caste, of a class, of a sex reduced to an inferior condition, the processes of justification are the same: "the eternal feminine" is the homologue of "the black soul" and "the Jewish character." . . . [T]here are profound analogies between the situation of women and that of Blacks: both are emancipating themselves from a same paternalism and the formerly master caste wants to keep them in "their place," that is to say in the place the master caste has chosen for them.

Beauvoir's analysis of the underlying paternalism common to justifications of both sexism and racism bears striking resemblance to an essay by Alva Myrdal, "A Parallel to the Negro Problem," included as an appendix to the classic text on American racism *An American Dilemma: The Negro Problem and Modern Democracy* (Myrdal, Sterner, and Rose 1944), a book Beauvoir consulted while writing ***The Second Sex.***

For Beauvoir ethnocentrism seems to encompass sexism historically in the experience of alterity. Women were not the original, or the only Other: "[Woman] has not represented the sole incarnation of the Other for [man], and she has not always kept the same importance in the course of history." Drawing on the structuralism of Lévi-Strauss, Beauvoir argues that: "The category of the *Other* is as original as consciousness itself. In the most primitive societies, in the most ancient mythologies, one finds the expression of a duality—that of the Same and the Other. This duality was not originally attached to the division of the sexes. . . . Jews are 'others' for the antisemite, Blacks for the American racists, indigenous peoples for the colonialists, the proletariat for the class of owners."

According to Jaggar, the defining feature of radical feminist theory, which set it apart from liberal and Marxist theories "was a conviction that the oppression of women was fundamental: that is to say, it was causally and conceptually irreducible to the oppression of any other group." Echols agrees that radical feminists "expanded the left analysis" of oppression and "argued that women constituted a sex class, that relations between women and men needed to be recast in political terms, and that gender rather than class was the primary contradiction." Beauvoir's support for this fundamental claim is evident in the following passage from ***The Second Sex,*** where she acknowledges Marxist insights into the historically changing role of technology and economic factors in shaping women's lives, but criticizes Marxism for failing to recognize the irreducible nature of women's oppression: "Engels does not recognize the singular character of this oppression. He tried to reduce the opposition of the sexes to a class conflict. . . . It's true that the division of work by sex and the oppression that results from it evokes the class division on certain points. But one must not confuse them. . . . The situation of the woman is different, singularly due to the community of life and interests that renders her in solidarity with the man, and by the complicity which he meets in her." For Beauvoir, "the bond that attaches [woman] to her oppressors is comparable to no other."

To expand Marxism to include an analysis of gender oppression, and to argue on one level for the primacy of gender contradiction, as later radical feminists would, Beauvoir returns to the philosophical roots of Marxism in Hegel's distinction between immanence and transcendence and his analysis of the master/slave relation. Turning Hegel against himself, Beauvoir argues that his description of the relationship of men, whose warfare and inventions create values that transcend the mere repetition of Life, and women, whom biology destines to immanence, to the passive and dependent reproduction of Life, is more reflective of the absolute opposition of the master/slave relationship than any relationship between men: "Certain passages of the dialectic by which Hegel defines the relation of the master to the slave would better apply to the relation of the man to the woman. . . . Between the male and she there has never been combat. Hegel's definition applies singularly to her."

Beauvoir described the relationship between men and women as a "caste" relationship defined by struggle: "All oppression creates a state of war; this is no exception." "[W]oman has always been, if not the slave of man, at least his vassal." In the past,

> the woman confined to immanence tried to keep the man in this prison as well. . . . She denied his truth and his values. . . . Today, the combat takes on another face. Instead of wanting to enclose man in a dungeon, woman is trying to escape from it herself. She no longer attempts to drag him into the regions of immanence but to emerge into the light of transcendence. . . . It is no longer a question of a war between individuals each enclosed in their sphere. A caste with demands mounts an assault and it is held in check by the privileged caste.

For Beauvoir, a historical analysis is necessary to understand the differences between women and other oppressed groups, and explain why women's liberation has been so long in coming:

> [Women] have no past, no history, no religion of their own; and they have no such solidarity of work and interest as that of the proletariat. They are not even promiscuously herded together in the way that creates community feeling among the American Blacks, the ghetto Jews, the workers of Saint-Denis, or the factory hands at Renault. They live dispersed among the males, attached through residence, housework, economic condition, and social standing to certain men—fathers or husbands—more firmly than they are to other women.

This situation elicits woman's moral complicity with her oppression, a willingness to accept dependence as a way of fleeing the responsibility of freedom facing any existent. Women are not simply victims in Beauvoir's analysis, as Jaggar charges of radical feminism. Beauvoir argues, in anticipation of the later radical feminist "pro-woman line," that women find both material and ontological advantages from their dependence on men.

But unlike many radical feminists, Beauvoir also holds women morally responsible for complicity with their own oppression once an alternative is presented to them:

> To decline to be the Other, to refuse complicity with the man, would be for women to renounce all the advantages conferred upon them by their alliance with the superior caste. Man-the-sovereign will provide woman-the-liege with material protection and will undertake the justification of her existence; thus she can evade at once both economic risk and the metaphysical risk of a freedom which must invent its ends without aid. . . . The man who makes woman an Other will then meet profound complicities in her. Thus, woman may fail to claim herself as subject because she lacks the concrete means to do it, because she feels the necessary bond that ties her to man regardless of reciprocity, and because she is often well pleased with her role as *Other.*

The complexity of Beauvoir's analysis of gender difference and women's oppression is evident in her critiques of Marxism and psychoanalysis. Both theories attempt, unsuccessfully, to apply a model derived from men's experience to women. Beauvoir's version of existential phenomenology provides her with the ontological and methodological grounds for reclaiming the specificity of women's experience while avoiding the essentialism of identity politics. Her criticism of the Marxist analysis of woman's situation is both existentialist and feminist. She charges Marxist economic reductionism with denying the reality of woman's lived experience.

Engels's attempt to reduce woman's situation, including her reproductive role, to economic production is "not tenable." Sexuality and maternity are dramas in the lives of individual women that defy integration into society and control by the State. "One cannot without bad faith consider woman uniquely as a worker. Her reproductive function is as important as her productive capacity, as much in the social economy as in individual life. . . . Engels evaded the problem; he limited himself to declaring that the socialist community will abolish the family: it is an abstract solution indeed."

The practice in the Soviet Union reveals the limits of such a reductionist theory, which fails to recognize the patriarchal power of the State as oppressive to women. "Suppressing the family is not necessarily to emancipate the woman: the example of Sparta and the Nazi regime prove that by being directly bound to the State she can be no less oppressed by the males." In the interest of rebuilding its population, the Soviet Union was trying to once again "enclose her in situations where maternity is for her the only outlet. . . . These are exactly the old patriarchal constraints that the USSR is resuscitating today. . . . This example shows well that it is impossible to consider the woman uniquely as a productive force."

For Beauvoir a true socialist revolution must affirm, not deny individualism, and thus acknowledge gender difference in individual experience and the uniqueness of women's situation. "For a democratic socialism where class will be abolished but not individuals, the question of individual destiny will keep all of its importance: sexual differentiation will keep all its importance. The sexual relation which unites the woman to the man is not the same as that which he sustains with her; the link which bonds her to the child is irreducible to every other. She was not created only by the bronze tool, the machine will not suffice to abolish her. Demanding for her all the rights, all the chances of the human being in general does not signify that one must blind oneself to her singular situation. And to become acquainted with it one must go beyond historical materialism that sees in man and woman only economic entities."

So Marxism, by imposing a male theoretical model of economic production on women's experience, falsifies the experiences of individual women and fails to provide the grounds for challenging patriarchal oppression of women by a male-dominated socialist state. Beauvoir's rejection of the mystification of gender difference by antifeminists and cultural feminists thus does not entail the denial of gender differences in the lives of individual women.

Beauvoir argues that psychoanalysis as well as Marxism reduces women's experience to that of men, thus silencing women. Her argument against essentialist reductionism reflects an existentialist ontology that links her with the new left's "politics of experience" and 1960s radical feminism. It also differentiates her position from that of cultural feminism, and in its combination of cultural critique and celebration of spontaneity and the transgressing of boundaries, aligns her with postmodernism.

Beauvoir criticizes Freud's psychoanalytic theory for attempting to impose a male model onto female experience: "Freud concerned himself little with the destiny of the woman; it is clear that he modelled it on the description of the masculine destiny of which he limited himself to modifying several traits." Freud "admitted that woman's sexuality is as evolved as man's; but he scarcely studied it in itself. He wrote: 'The libido is in a constant and regular fashion essentially male, whether it appears in a man or a woman.' He refused to pose the feminine libido in its originality." By relying on a reductive male model of female sexuality, Beauvoir argues, Freud was unable to explain either penis envy or the Electra complex, primary features of his psychology of woman. Freud "supposed that the woman felt herself to be a mutilated man. But the idea of mutilation implies a comparison and a valorization . . . it cannot be born from a simple anatomical confrontation. . . . Freud took [this valorization] for granted when it was necessary to account for it."

An adequate explanation of both penis envy and the Electra complex, in which Freud accounts for women's heterosexuality, would require that one leave the confines of the psychoanalytic model and examine the larger social, historical, and ontological dimensions of individual life and woman's oppression: "Psychoanalysis can only find its truth in the historical context." "The fact that feminine desire focussed on a sovereign being [as it does in the Electra complex] gives it an original character; but [feminine libido] is not constitutive of its object, it submits to it. The sovereignty of the father is a fact of the social order, and Freud fails to account for it."

Thus for Beauvoir a primary feature of the development of female heterosexuality and the transference of a girl's attraction from her mother to her father, is the father's sovereignty, that is, the social context of woman's oppression. Here we see Beauvoir extending social constructivism to sexuality. Her alternative description of the female libido further undermines the assumption of normative female heterosexuality by postulating an original resistance and repulsion toward men. Psychoanalysts who have approached the female libido only from the male libido, "seem to have ignored the fundamental ambivalence of the attraction that the male exerts on the female. . . . It is the indissoluble synthesis of attraction and of repulsion that characterizes it." Psychoanalysis has failed to acknowledge gender difference in female sexuality: "The idea of a 'passive libido' disconcerts because one has defined the libido on the basis of the male as drive, energy; but neither could one conceive *a priori* that a light could be at once yellow and blue; it's necessary to have the intuition of green." Beauvoir's social constructivist analysis of sexual difference, and her challenge, albeit limited, to normative female heterosexuality anticipates the later radical feminist critiques of "compulsory heterosexuality."

But in arguing for gender difference, Beauvoir avoids essentialist claims. She lays the groundwork for an appreciation of differences among women in arguing against the reductionism of Freudian psychoanalytic theory: "One must not take sexuality as an irreducible given. . . . Work, war, play, art define manners of being in the world which do not allow themselves to be reduced to any other." Sexuality is one manner among others of ontologically discovering the world. Thus Beauvoir, unlike the radical feminists described by Echols, rejects the a priori primacy of sexual difference. An individual woman establishes a unity among her activities as she chooses herself through her work, play, struggles, and sexuality.

Beauvoir criticizes psychoanalytic theory for reducing women to passive objects in the world and for denying women the possibility of authentic choices. "We will situate woman in a world of values and we will give to her actions a dimension of freedom. We think that she has to choose between the affirmation of her transcendence and her alienation as an object; she is not the plaything of contradictory drives; she invents solutions between which exist an ethical hierarchy." In describing a subject's failure to effect a transference or a sublimation (and surely the most obvious example here is in the "failure" of a woman to become a heterosexual), a psychoanalyst, Beauvoir argues, "does not suppose that they perhaps refused it and that perhaps they had good reasons for doing so; one does not want to consider that their conduct could have been motivated by ends freely posed."

Freedom is a central theme of ***The Second Sex.*** If "one is not born a woman," then with the reality of social intervention comes the possibility of individual action, as Butler argues. Beauvoir is celebrating woman's freedom, the expansion of her choices, not confinement in a role, whether defined by Freud, or by implication here, essentialist identity politics. In her critique of psychoanalytic theory Beauvoir rejects as inauthentic the pursuit of Being, of a substantive self, which was to become prominent in cultural feminism.

> In the psychoanalytic sense "to identify oneself" with the mother or the father is to *alienate one-*

> *self* in a model; it is to prefer an alien image to the spontaneous movement of her own existence, to play at being. One shows us woman solicited by two modes of alienation; it is indeed evident that playing at being a man will be a source of failure for her. But playing at being a woman is also a trap. To be a woman would be to be an object, the *Other;* and the Other remains subject in the heart of its abdication. The real problem for woman is refusing these flights in order to accomplish herself as transcendence.

Beauvoir's description of the contemporary struggle as one in which women claim the values of "transcendence" and refuse the limits of "immanence" differentiates her from the cultural feminist position Echols describes as seeking a womanculture where "'male values' would be exorcized and 'female values' nurtured." For Beauvoir, women's "demand is not to be exalted in their femininity; they want transcendence to prevail over immanence for themselves as for all of humanity."

> In truth women have never opposed female values to male values. It is men desirous of maintaining the masculine prerogatives who have invented this division. They have claimed to create a feminine domain—realm of life and immanence—only in order to enclose woman there. It is beyond all sexual specification that the existent seeks her justification in the movement of her transcendence. . . . What [women] are demanding today is to be recognized as existents as men are and not to subjugate existence to life, man to his animality.

But Beauvoir's theory of gender difference is complex. She rejects both the mystification of gender difference and the abstract, gender-free nominalism of liberal modernity as well.

Some feminist critics, such as Iris Young (1990) have charged ***The Second Sex*** with typifying a nineteenth-century "humanist feminism" that, leaving gender largely unexamined, calls on women to assume men's public roles. Beauvoir does reject the mystification of gender difference typical of both nineteenth-century antifeminists, who argued that women's intellectual and physical inferiority and sensitive natures warranted their exclusion from public life and confinement to the private sphere, and their contemporaries, the "domestic feminists," who argued that women should have access to both education and the vote in order to improve and extend the influence of their special moral sense. But Beauvoir does not deny there are differences.

In the introduction to ***The Second Sex,*** Beauvoir differentiates her position from modernism, from "the philosophy of the enlightenment, of rationalism, of nominalism; women, to them, are merely the human beings arbitrarily designated by the word *woman*. . . . But nominalism is a rather inadequate doctrine. . . . Surely woman is, like man, a human being; but such a declaration is abstract. The fact is that every concrete human being is always singularly situated. To decline to accept such notions as the eternal feminine, the black soul, the Jewish character, is not to deny that Jews, Blacks, women exist today—this denial does not represent a liberation for those concerned, but rather a flight from reality. It is clear that no woman can claim without bad faith to situate herself beyond her sex."

Beauvoir is a social constructionist who sees women's liberation as requiring the dismantling of the male cultural construct of woman as Other. She certainly wants women to gain access to the public sphere, to escape the confines of women's traditional role of wife and mother, to emerge as an individual. But the public sphere will be transformed in the process: "The future can only lead to a more and more profound assimilation of the woman into the *formerly* masculine society" (my emphasis). She describes how philosophy, for example, has been distorted by men who have taken their own unique perspective as absolute. Her alternative is not to argue for the possibility of an absolute perspective without differences, that is, a return to the nominalism of modernity, but to both critique the male claim to objectivity and to begin constructing a knowledge based on a phenomenological description of women's experience. Hence the title of the second volume "Lived Experience," where Beauvoir tries to move outside the context of men's constructions of woman as Other, which are primarily useful in understanding not women but the men themselves, into women's ways of knowing their own experience.

Beauvoir does not demand access to a gender-free objectivity of modernity, but rather challenges the objective/subjective dualism itself and provides a phenomenological description of how men's perspectives shape their views of women, and reality. Laying the groundwork for women's studies in her feminist cultural critique, Beauvoir argues that men, in defining knowledge from their own point of view, have mistaken that perspective as absolute: "[Man] seizes his body as a direct and normal connection with the world, which he believes he apprehends in its objectivity, whereas he regards the body of woman as an obstacle, a prison, weighed down by what specifies it." "She is defined and differentiated with reference to man and not he with reference to her; she is the inessential as opposed to the essential. He is the Subject, he is the Absolute—she is the Other."

According to Beauvoir, Lévinas exemplifies this masculinist view in his essay *Le Temps et l'Autre* where he writes that: "'Otherness reaches its full flowering in the feminine, a term of the same rank as consciousness but of opposite meaning.' I suppose that Lévinas does not forget that woman is also consciousness for herself. But it is striking that he deliberately takes a man's point of view, disregarding the reciprocity of subject and object. . . . Thus his description, which is intended to be objective, is in fact an assertion of masculine privilege." Beauvoir would have men, as well as women, claim the subjectivity of their situated consciousness, rather than lay claim to false objectivity.

Beauvoir's psychological explanation of men's behavior is derived from her close reading of myths and male-authored texts with which she began her research for ***The Second Sex.*** Her analyses of the images of women in the works of Montherlant, D. H. Lawrence, Claudel, Breton, and Stendhal provided the model for Millett's cultural critique in *Sexual Politics.* Psychologically, men's oppression of women is, in Beauvoir's existential analysis, an inauthentic attempt to evade the demands of authentic human relationships and the ambiguous realities of human existence. For men who would define themselves as pure spirit, women represent an odious link to the absurd contingency of a man's own life: his birth, embodiment, and death. "In all civilizations and in our own day, [woman] inspires horror in man: it is horror of his own carnal contingence which he projects onto her."

Woman as Other also seems a privileged prey of men desirous of the confirmation of self found in relationships with others, and yet fearful of the dangers in relationships with their peers. "[Woman] opposes to him neither the enemy silence of nature, nor the hard exigencies of a reciprocal recognition; by a unique privilege she is a consciousness and yet it seems possible to possess her in her flesh. Thanks to her, there is a means of escaping the implacable dialectic of master and slave which has its source in the reciprocity of freedom."

Authentic human relationships, on the contrary, must be constantly created. Beauvoir's vision does not offer a comforting if static social order, but a future of ceaseless struggle in morally challenging relationships. According to Beauvoir, the master/slave dialectic can be surmounted, but only by

> the free recognition of each individual in the other, each posing at once himself and the other as object and as subject in a reciprocal movement. But friendship, generosity, which realize concretely this recognition of freedoms, are not easy virtues. They are assuredly the highest accomplishment of man, the means by which he finds himself in his truth. But this truth is that of a struggle forever opening up, forever abolished; it demands that man surmount himself at each instant. One could say also in another language that man attains an authentic moral attitude when he renounces *being* in order to assume his existence.

"One is not born, but rather becomes a woman." This familiar quotation (eloquently translated by Parshley) which opens volume 2 of ***The Second Sex,*** indicates Beauvoir's social constructionism, a position Echols sees as key in differentiating radical feminism from the biological determinism of cultural feminism. In fact Jaggar unknowingly points toward Beauvoir as a theoretical source for the social constructivism of radical feminism in recognizing Monique Wittig as one of the few radical feminists to reject biological determinism; Jaggar cites Wittig's influential 1979 essay "One is not born a woman"—clear reference to Beauvoir.

Judith Butler has argued that Beauvoir's concept of the body as situation "suggests an alternative to the gender polarization of masculine disembodiment and feminine enslavement to the body." For Beauvoir, Butler writes, "any effort to ascertain the 'natural' body before its entrance into culture is definitionally impossible, not only because the observer who seeks this phenomenon is him/herself entrenched in a specific cultural language, but because the body is as well. The body is, in effect, never a natural phenomenon." Butler draws our attention to the conclusion of the biology chapter in ***The Second Sex,*** where Beauvoir writes: "it is not merely as a body, but rather as a body subject to taboos, to laws, that the subject takes consciousness of himself and accomplishes itself. . . . It is not physiology that can found values; rather, the biological givens assume those that the existent confers upon them."

If Beauvoir's view, Butler argues, is that the body exists as a locus of cultural interpretations, "then Simone de Beauvoir's theory seems implicitly to ask whether sex was not gender all along," a view radicalized in the work of Monique Wittig and Foucault who both "challenge the notion of natural sex and expose the political uses of biological discriminations in establishing a compulsory binary gender system." Butler, it should be noted, claims that Foucault, a student of Merleau-Ponty, was not influenced by Beauvoir. But an indirect influence is not unlikely given Merleau-Ponty's long association with Beauvoir.

Beauvoir "suggests," according to Butler, "that a binary gender system has no ontological necessity." In fact, Beauvoir argues explicitly against the ontological necessity of sexual dimorphism earlier in the biology chapter. Beauvoir argues there against Hegel that "it is in exercising sexual activity that men define the sexes and their relations as they create the sense and the value of all the functions that they accomplish: but [sexual activity] is not necessarily implied in the nature of the human body." "The perpetuation of the species appears as the correlative of individual limitation. One can thus consider the phenomenon of reproduction as ontologically founded. But we must stop there. The perpetuation of the species does not entail sexual differentiation. If [sexual differentiation] is assumed by existents in such a manner that in return it enters into the concrete definition of existence, so be it. It nonetheless remains that a consciousness without a body and an immortal man are rigorously inconceivable, while one can imagine a society reproducing itself by parthenogenesis or composed of hermaphrodites."

Butler's analysis provides an alternative reading of existentialist concepts of freedom and choice found in radical feminism, which Jaggar discredits as liberal and idealist (as in one "choosing a sex role" from a transsocial standpoint). For Butler:

> In making the body into an interpretive modality, Beauvoir has extended the doctrines of embodiment and prereflective choice that characterized Sartre's work. . . . Simone de Beauvoir, much earlier on and with greater consequence [than Sartre himself], sought to exorcise Sartre's doctrine of its Cartesian ghost. She gives Sartrean choice an embodied form and places it in a world thick with tradition. To "choose" a gender in this context is not to move in upon gender from a disembodied locale, but to reinterpret the cultural history which the body already wears. The body becomes a choice, a mode of enacting and reenacting received gender norms which surface as so many styles of the flesh.

Beauvoir's rejection of the mystification of gender difference evident in her ontology is based, in part, on her analysis of the historical deployment of an ideology of difference in women's oppression. She concludes from her historical analysis in ***The Second Sex*** that: "Those epoques that regard woman as the *Other* are those that refuse most bitterly to integrate her into society as a human being. Today she is becoming a fellow *other* only in losing her mystical aura. Antifeminists are always playing on this equivocation. They gladly agree to exalt woman as *Other* in order to constitute her alterity as absolute, irreducible, and to refuse her access to the human *Mitsein* [being-with]." Beauvoir's intent, here as elsewhere, is not to deny gender difference as women experience it concretely, but to demystify it.

In the nineteenth century, glorification of woman's difference was common to both antifeminists such as Comte and Balzac, as well as utopian socialists such as the Saint-Simonians, who, in a foreshadowing of the goddess worship of contemporary cultural feminism, awaited the advent of the female messiah. But neither, according to Beauvoir, served well the interests of women's liberation: "The doctrines that call for the advent of the woman as flesh, life, immanence, as the Other, are masculine ideologies that in no way express feminine demands." Beauvoir's analysis of the historical relationship of socialism and goddess worship provides an interesting context for reading the critiques of cultural feminism in both Jaggar and Echols. Some utopian socialists of the nineteenth century such as Saint-Simon, Fourier, and Cabet called for an end to all slavery and for the ideal of the "free woman." But later followers of Saint-Simon, "exalted woman in the name of her femininity, which is the surest means of her disservice." Enfantin "awaited the coming of a better world from the woman messiah, and the Companions of the Woman embarqued for the Orient in search of the female savior." But for all the glorification of the feminine, with few exceptions, "women held only a secondary place in the Saint-Simonien movement." The socialist Flora Tristan, we learn later, also "believed in the redemption of the people by the woman, but she interested herself in the emancipation of the working class rather than in that of her own sex." Thus socialism, which Jaggar argued could provide the only clear alternative to goddess worship and cultural feminism, is, ironically, itself a historically problematic root of both.

Beauvoir's historical analysis reveals other limitations of socialism for feminists, problems still apparent in contemporary socialism. There was Fourier, for example, "who confused the enfranchisement of women with the rehabilitation of the flesh. . . . He considered woman not in her person but in her amorous function." But the most serious problem for socialist feminism stems from the reductive Marxist analysis that conceives of women's liberation as contained within the proletariat revolution instead of, as Beauvoir argues, requiring women's own collective struggle as a separate development.

In arguing for the importance of recognizing gender difference in experience, Beauvoir does not maintain that the relationship between men and women has been historically unchanging. Her analysis of women's oppression is not a simple analogy, neither trivializing other forms of oppression nor asserting that gender is always the primary contradiction. Class differences figure prominently in Beauvoir's analysis of how the historically different situations of bourgeois and proletariat women have undermined feminist solidarity and activism. For example, in her analysis of the bourgeois French Revolution, Beauvoir argues that neither working-class women, "who experienced, as women, the most independence," nor bourgeois women were able to make many gains: "The women of the bourgeoisie were too integrated into the family to know any concrete solidarity among themselves; they did not constitute a separate caste able to impose their demands: economically, their existence was parasitic. Thus the women who, despite their sex, would have been able to participate in the events were prevented from doing so by their class, while those of the activist class were condemned as women to remain at a distance." No analysis that ignores class differences can understand the history of women's oppression and the problems of feminist activism.

Beauvoir criticized the so-called independent French feminist movement at the turn of the twentieth century for reflecting bourgeois interests. But the "revolutionary feminism" of the same era, which "took up the Saint-Simonien and Marxist tradition," also contributed to the internal divisions that were the source of the "weakness of feminism." "Women lacked solidarity as sex; they were first linked to their class; the interests of the bourgeois women and those of the proletariat women did not intersect. . . . Louise Michel pronounced herself against feminism because this movement only served to divert forces which ought to be in their entirety employed in the class struggle; women's lot will find itself well ordered by the abolition of capital." "Since it is from the emancipation of workers in general that women await their freedom, they only attach themselves in a secondary manner to their own cause."

Beauvoir reserves her highest praise for the Woman's Social and Political Union established in Britain by the Pankhursts around 1903. Progressive without putting women's issues second; it was "allied with the laborist party," and "undertook a resolutely militant action." "It is the first time in history that one sees women try an effort as women: that is what gives a particular interest to the adventure of the 'suffragettes' in Britain and America." In a detailed account, deleted by Parshley from the English edition, Beauvoir pays tribute to their inventiveness: "During fifteen years they led a campaign of political pressure which recalls on certain sides the attitude of a Gandhi: refusing violence, they invented more or less ingenious substitutes."

Identifying with an earlier feminist movement, drawing on insights of radical African-American theorists of racial oppression, Beauvoir, in ***The Second Sex,*** laid the theoretical foundations for a radical feminist movement of the future and defined a feminist political philosophy of lasting importance.

Julie K. Ward (essay date 1995)

SOURCE: "Beauvoir's Two Senses of 'Body' in *The Second Sex*," in *Feminist Interpretations of Simone de Beauvoir,* edited by Margaret A. Simons, Pennsylvania State University Press, 1995, pp. 223-42.

[In the following essay, Ward examines Beauvoir's views concerning the nature of the female body and gender roles. Rejecting the view that Beauvoir's feminism is guided by principles of biological determinism, Ward contends that Beauvoir "should be seen as developing a social-constructivist view of the body."]

It was Beauvoir's dictum that one *becomes* but is not *born* a woman and her broad analysis of the reality behind that statement that charted the course for most contemporary currents in modern Western feminism and for which she has been hailed in the past as an emancipator. Yet in the wake of a gynocentric wave in feminist thinking, Beauvoir's work has increasingly come under scholarly scrutiny, with the result that Beauvoir, far from being hailed as a liberator, is reviled as a turncoat. Some of the more trenchant criticism centers on Beauvoir's discussion of woman's body and related subjects such as sexual intercourse, pregnancy, and maternity ([Mary] O'Brien 1981, [Charlene] Seigfried 1984, [Mary] Evans 1987, [Céline] Léon 1988). Almost uniformly, these critics have found her analysis of these areas to reflect a negative attitude about the female body, and so her view has been labeled "masculinist" and essentialist. In a sense, the evidence for their claims is not difficult to find: Beauvoir's descriptions of females as more enslaved to the species than males, of women as less transcendent than men and as alienated from their bodies in the course of normal processes such as menstruation, pregnancy, and childbirth seem tailored to fit the critics' charges. And so, some have gone on to conclude that Beauvoir, perhaps unknowingly, has adopted a hostile, "masculine" stance toward women, and toward the female body in particular. Others have maintained that Beauvoir assumes that female characteristics are fixed by nature so as to doom her to inferiority. Judith Okely, for example, finds that Beauvoir's account is deterministic: "Despite Beauvoir's formal rejection of biological determinism, when the details of her arguments are closely examined it can be seen that she contradicts any claim that biological factors are irrelevant or arbitrary. Again and again she slips into biological reductionism to explain the primary cause of women's subordination." First, it should be pointed out that, as far as the critics' charges are concerned, biological determinism does not coincide with biological reductionism: the latter is a weaker view than the former in the sense that it reduces human abilities like thinking to biological properties, but it does not entail the further view that these capacities are subject to deterministic biological laws. However, in spite of Okely's contrary implication—since the two positions are not logically equivalent—for the purposes of this essay, I shall offer arguments against both sorts of objections to Beauvoir's account of women's oppression and of the body. So, while one cannot deny that readers of ***The Second Sex*** encounter a host of negative remarks about woman's biology, the question to address is whether these claims constitute biological reductionism or determinism. I contend that they do not, and that Beauvoir clearly rejects both these positions. It would, in fact, be surprising for Beauvoir to embrace any incompatibilist position that would preclude the possibility for individual choice and responsibility, as does biological determinism. In order to make this case, I argue that one has to take seriously Beauvoir's claim that it is her intention to consider the body not as a *thing,* but as a *situation,* about which more will be said in the following section. Briefly, if we follow her suggestion, we see in her theoretical analysis of woman's body at least two different perspectives from which the discussion about the body is conducted, so that we must put her comments in their proper context by noting the perspective from which she makes them. By differentiating between these levels, I contend that neither the charge of biological determinism (or reductionism), nor that of "masculinism" has a firm foundation. The charge of "masculinism" will be displaced by showing that Beauvoir is not committed to the negative views about woman's body that she mentions—which is why she distinguishes the "biological" treatment of the body from her own way of accounting for it.

As a general observation, the method of philosophical analysis Beauvoir employs in ***The Second Sex*** is fundamentally nonreductionist in the sense that it depends on a synthesis of social, economic, and historical factors to one perspective she sometimes calls the "existential" perspective, which is her preferred stance in comprehending the full reality of woman's oppression. Once the theoretical complexity of Beauvoir's perspective is acknowledged, two obvious objections to the reductionist interpretation of Beauvoir emerge. First, the possibility that we could reduce the intrinsically heterogeneous analyses of female experience—psychological, biological, economic, etc.—to a single kind of analysis looks to be slight. Second, even supposing that we could achieve this reduction, why should we be inclined to think that for her the biological explanations, rather than historical ones, say, are the most fundamental? These two basic objections warrant against the reductionist program.

But, so her critics would maintain, even though Beauvoir's overall analysis of woman is multifaceted, her account of woman's body is seriously flawed: Beauvoir herself succumbs to some of the well-worn, patriarchal myths about the female body. I reject this criticism, finding that Beauvoir's distinction between the two senses of the body, and of the physical generally, has been overlooked or not addressed adequately by her critics. Briefly, my interpretation of Beauvoir's position is this: she appears to make neutral statements about females and biology in chapter 1, and so looks to be making essentialist statements about women's bodies; in fact, this is not true. For, as Beauvoir points out, one cannot make neutral, aperspectival claims about female biology since the physical capacities of either sex gain meaning only when placed in a cultural and historical context—this, I argue, is what Beauvoir means by saying that the body is to be seen as a *situation.* In the rest of this essay, I shall contend that if Beauvoir takes seriously the notion that the body is itself a situation, as I believe she does, she must reject the idea of the body as a purely biological mechanism, contrary to her critics' charge. For these same reasons, I shall also find that Beauvoir is not fundamentally opposed to typically female functions, such as maternity. Instead of being cast as holding some form of biological reductionism or determinism, she should be seen as developing a social-constructivist view of the body. In this vein, I generally agree with Judith Butler's view of Beauvoir. In the last section, I shall argue that Beauvoir's claim about the body as situation may be taken as rejecting the notion of a natural, sexed body. So interpreted, we may comprehend Beauvoir's dictum that one only *becomes* a woman to imply not only that gender, but the body itself, is socially constructed.

Putting Biology in Context

> "the body is not a thing, it is a situation"

In coming to general conclusions about Beauvoir's view of woman's body, I have followed two heuristic principles. The first is that when confronted with apparent contradictions among an author's claims, one needs to look deeper for some means of reconciling them. The second principle consists in taking the structure of the work as central to its interpretation. On this latter point, it is useful to note that the initial three chapters of the work, on biology, psychoanalysis, and historical materialism, preface the chapters on history and myths about women. Together these chapters constitute the volume entitled "Les Faits et Les Mythes" (Facts and myths), which precedes the second volume entitled "L'Expérience Vécu" (Lived experience). By naming them thus, the two halves of the work suggest distinct yet interrelated levels of analysis, the first half emphasizing abstract constructs with which male thinkers have theorized about woman, the second what woman's experience under patriarchy has been like. This order, then, suggests a "top-down" approach to her discussion: a mode of analysis such that the current myths and theories detailed in her first volume are to be regarded as part of the conceptual apparatus presupposed in the lived histories of women in the second volume. Since the theories and myths detailed in volume 1 constitute part of the theoretical framework of patriarchy, it would be naive to think that that which is said about women and their experience is necessarily affirmed by Beauvoir herself. For example, in chapter 1, Beauvoir asserts that the theoretical justification in biology of the male as the sole creator of the offspring coincides with the advent of patriarchy. Additionally, Beauvoir ends each of the three initial chapters with critical comments detailing the inadequacies of each theoretical approach. We must infer, then, that Beauvoir is open to rejecting either part or all of the conceptual analyses of women given in volume 1. In this regard, we may note that she rejects psychoanalysis for its partiality and ahistoricity, specifically faulting the theory for its failure to explain, rather than merely assert, the supremacy of male as against female power as it is reflected in the sovereignty of the phallus. Beauvoir's comment that "representation of the world, like the world itself, is the work of men . . . which they confuse with absolute truth" is instructive here: she clearly acknowledges the dominant myths and ideologies that men have created about women, but she by no means thereby subscribes to them. This said, it is highly improbable to think—as her critics maintain—that the traditional view of woman merely as a reproductive vessel, such as is expressed in the opening lines of chapter 1, can be identified with Beauvoir's own view: "Woman? very simple, say the fanciers of simple formulas: she is a womb, an ovary, she is a female—this word is sufficient to define her." While even her critics may acknowledge that such a line does not express Beauvoir's position it seems to me that the critics have charged her with holding views as improbable as this one—largely by overlooking the fact that since much of the theoretical discussion in volume 1 is the product of male theorizing about women, it will inevitably be subject to some criticism by Beauvoir. If true, it follows that when we encounter various apparently essentialist statements about woman's body in the chapter on biology, we cannot thereby conclude that Beauvoir is uncritically accepting them. In general, any reductive account of woman, such as what Beauvoir calls the "sexual monism" of Freud or the "economic monism" of Engels, clearly runs contrary to her own foundations since the whole thrust of Beauvoir's analysis of woman is to appreciate the complexity of being feminine. For the same reasons, one can imagine Beauvoir calling the simplistic view that woman is merely "a womb, an ovary" as a kind of "biological monism" and dispensing with it.

Although Beauvoir has been faulted for opening her work with a chapter on biology, in fact the chapter involves a complex task. It aims to set out a nonreductive, nondualistic account of human beings. So, while Beauvoir rejects the notion that woman can be reduced to her reproductive organs, she wishes to mark the importance of the physical by emphasizing the central role that the body plays in human experience. She reflects a strongly anti-Cartesian, or antidualist, perspective in her general conception of human beings, claiming: "the body [is] the instrument of our grasp upon the world." She then goes on to claim that women and men do not "grasp" the world in the same terms, for differences in body entail differences in experience. Now, when she summarizes the differences between the sexes, she says that the two biological traits that characterize woman are that her grasp upon the world is less "extended" than man's ("sa prise est moins étendue que celle de l'homme"), and that she is more narrowly enslaved to the species ("elle est plus étroitement asservie a l'espèce"). Presumably, what Beauvoir has in mind here are various physiological differences she details in chapter 1, for example, the relatively smaller musculature of women to men, and the possession of fewer red blood corpuscles so that the gross muscular effort is lower.

Do these and related comments entail she is being "masculinist" in her view of the female body as her critics charge? I think not, although it is easy enough to see in her descriptions of woman as having "a less extended grasp," and as being "enslaved to the species" the basis for the criticism that she is mixing biological facts with value judgments. However, Beauvoir is in fact not unaware that "factual" descriptions are insignificant in themselves and acquire meaning by being placed in a cultural context. As she notes at the opening of chapter 3: "these facts [above-mentioned] take on different values according to the economic and social context. In human history, grasp upon the world has never been defined by the naked body . . . on the contrary, technique may annul the muscular inequality of man and woman." Consequently, although she acknowledges physical differences such as the relatively greater musculature of men over women, she correctly points out that this difference in itself signifies nothing. In fact, as she here argues, the large part of human history has been concerned with the improvement of technology, the historical effect of which has been to negate all the advantages of brute strength. Thus, she is arguing precisely contrary to what she ought to be if she were in fact holding some form of biological determinism. Again, in a related passage, Beauvoir astutely comments that the notion of "weakness" one presupposes depends upon both one's instruments and one's goals; in any case, bodily force alone is hardly the sole criterion for determining what power is. Even if one sums up all the physical differences between men and women, including the apparent inequalities, one cannot infer any truths about female experience from this "data." For, as Beauvoir is quick to note, the so-called biological facts do not set an inevitable destiny for woman, contrary to the Freudian estimation. Rather, she maintains that woman's physical and physiological characteristics are themselves the effect, or result, of woman's social and material conditions, and so, they are inadequate to explain her subordinate social status. So, while Beauvoir asserts that woman's biological characteristics place a kind of constraint on her experience, it does not follow that these characteristics stand as the explanatory determinants of her experience, for they are themselves accounted for in terms of social, economic, and cultural conditions, at the level which Beauvoir refers to as *situation*.

Before looking more closely at the significance of Beauvoir's term *situation* and how it relates to her view of the body, one needs to make mention of two fundamental threads of her analysis of woman. She subscribes, first, to the existentialist notion of humans as conscious beings able to shape themselves through freely chosen projects, and second, to some form of historical materialism. Both of these commitments are evident in chapter 3, "The Point of View of Historical Materialism," where she embraces the notion of humans as subject to historical material conditions, yet maintains that the Marxist theory itself is inadequate to explain the concrete situation for human beings: "to comprehend that situation we must look beyond the historical materialism that perceives in man and woman no more than economic units." One may conclude that Beauvoir thinks that humans as conscious beings have the ability to transform their environment, yet as social beings they should be considered primarily in relation to the historical and economic conditions that to some extent determine them.

Although it may appear to some that existentialism and historical materialism are opposed on the issue of the extent to which human beings may choose their actions— with the former emphasizing individual freedom and the latter determination by material conditions—yet in both views there exists a combination of indeterminacy or freedom, and determinacy in the sense of being subject to certain unchosen conditions. Thus, Beauvoir's attempt to synthesize the two views should not be viewed as prima facie implausible. But leaving aside the larger issue of whether one can strike a precise balance between the existentialist and historical materialist conceptions of human beings, I find that Beauvoir tries to combine these two views in her general notion of situation. The task may appear less daunting to us once we note that Beauvoir embraces a form of existentialism that does not insist on the radical and fundamental freedom of human beings to the exclusion of deterministic factors like race, class, or gender; she finds, instead that humans are only partly free because they are partly determined by various internal and external factors. In her introduction, Beauvoir actually points out several kinds of limiting factors on human freedom: here she insists on the seriousness of gender discrimination, likening it to forms of racial and ethnic discrimination. In her words: "whether it is a race, a caste, a class, or a sex that is reduced to a position of inferiority, the methods of justification are the same." Especially striking evidence of the latter in her analysis of women is the analogy Beauvoir draws between racial and gender discrimination: "there are deep similarities between the situation of woman and that of the Negro. Both are being emancipated today from a like paternalism, and the former master class wishes to 'keep them in their place'—that is, the place chosen for them." So, it may be said that in her analysis of women, Beauvoir eschews the radical freedom sometimes attributed to existentialists. Yet having stated this one cannot conclude thereby that woman for Beauvoir is not also responsible for her actions due to oppressive institutions and customs. On the contrary, it is precisely because she is free to some extent that Beauvoir criticizes the middle-class woman for her complicity in various patriarchal and sexist institutions which she can use to her advantage.

We may conclude that, on the one hand, Beauvoir claims that women as human beings are transcendent—able to choose their own projects—and yet, on the other hand, are often caught up in social and economic forces beyond their control, forced into *immanence.* So we see Beauvoir attempting to correct the extreme voluntarist form of existentialism with her insistence that we take a broader, historical view of human beings, as exemplified here in a passage from chapter 3: "The theory of historical materialism has brought to light some important truths. Humanity is not an animal species; it is a historical reality. Human society is an *antiphysis*—in a sense, it is against nature; it does not submit to the presence of nature but rather takes over the control of nature on its own behalf. This arrogation is not an inward, subjective operation; it is accomplished objectively in practical action." We may draw a parallel, then, between Beauvoir's view of the position of human beings and of woman's situation in particular: both are culturally and historically bound, yet are not wholly subject to the social and economic constraints placed upon them. It is fitting, then, for Beauvoir to deny that any one set of given conditions, in this case, biological characteristics, could ever be fully determinative of feminine experience. Thus, she demurs in giving undue importance to physical or sexual properties in her explanation of woman: "Thus, woman could not be considered simply as a sexual organism, for among the biological traits, only those have importance that take on concrete value in action. Woman's awareness of herself is not defined exclusively by her sexuality; it reflects a *situation* that depends upon the economic organization of society, which in turn indicates what stage of technical evolution mankind has attained." Beauvoir's point here is that biological characteristics are not themselves explanatory of feminine experience; rather, women's status and self-identity is constituted by the set of external, social conditions in which women find themselves. But if woman's self-awareness cannot be said to be determined by a natural, sexual identity, then it becomes untenable to claim Beauvoir subscribes to some form of biological reductionism.

We may now turn to our examination of Beauvoir's term "situation," a word that appears often in ***The Second Sex*** and one that has special significance in her analysis of the body. In general, Beauvoir uses "situation" to signify the specific historical and social contexts in which women find themselves to be *Other,* that is, relegated to a subordinate status relative to men. In these occurrences, the word clearly signifies the set of social, economic, and in general, material conditions that give rise to the psychological, subjective condition of being a woman. Significantly, she also chooses to analyze the concept of the body in terms of situation, the effect of which is to reconceive the body as a social construction, as opposed to a physical thing. In fact, we find both senses of "body" alluded to in the chapter on biology where Beauvoir asserts her preference for the constructivist conception of the body, in spite of her long discussion of the "alienating" aspects of female biological functions. Notwithstanding such comments, she employs the notion of situation to explain the sense in which the biological statements about "body" are to be considered. She distinguishes between two conceptions of "body": in one sense, it may be said to signify the body conceived of as inert matter or stuff, "a thing," as she terms it; in another sense, it signifies how the physical body is experienced, given the social and economic conditions, and here her term is situation. Now the body conceived of in the first sense is roughly equivalent to the Cartesian *res extensa,* extended matter lacking all thought, whereas in the second sense the notion presupposes thought and consciousness, and so, is anti-Cartesian. And it is just this latter sense of body that Beauvoir embraces in chapter 1, rejecting the Cartesian notion.

It should be clear that seen from the perspective of situation, what "body" signifies is not an entity with certain invariant characteristics, but an entity whose features can change since the nature and value of bodies depends upon the social, historical, and economic context within which embodied individuals exist. In surprising fashion, Beauvoir then weaves the existentialist notion of human beings as incomplete in their nature with the Marxist view of human beings as subject to historical variants into the notion of the human situation:

> As Merleau-Ponty very justly puts it, man is not a natural species, he is an historical idea. Woman is not a completed reality, but rather a becoming, and it is in her becoming that she should be compared with man; that is to say, her *possibilities* should be defined. What gives rise to much of the debate is the tendency to reduce her to what she has been, to what she is today, in raising the question of her capabilities; for the fact is that capabilities are clearly manifested only when they have been realized—but the fact is also that when we have to do with a being whose nature is transcendent action, we can never close the books.

The passage illuminates Beauvoir's existentialist notion of humans as dynamic beings, in her term, "transcendent," that create themselves through their activities. Yet more striking is her insistence upon marrying this view with historicism in considering the meaning of woman's physical attributes. Thus, in spite of the fact that she claims woman's body to be weaker, less muscular, less stable, and to possess less lung capacity than a man's, she also argues that when interpreting the female body on the "basis of existence," such weakness is incomplete, without meaning. For, it is only within the context of certain social norms and values that differences in lung capacity and muscular mass have any significance. As Beauvoir rightly observes:

> "weakness" is revealed as such only in the light of the ends that man proposes, the instruments he has available, and the laws he establishes. . . . In brief, the concept of *weakness* can be defined only with reference to existentialist, economic, and moral considerations. . . . Thus, while it is true that in the higher animals the individual existence is asserted more imperiously by the male than by the female, in the human species individual "possibilities" depend upon the economic and social situation.

The direction of Beauvoir's analysis of woman's body, then, is toward subjecting the biological statements concerning the body to further historical and material analysis. For, as she consistently points out in the first three chapters, human biology is incomplete: biological "facts" about human beings cannot be interpreted in isolation from the relevant social and economic conditions in relation to which they take on value. She argues, for example, "these facts [biological facts] take on different values according to the economic and social context. In human history, grasp upon the world has never been defined by the naked body." Rather, "the value of muscular strength, of the phallus, of the tool can be defined only in a world of values." So, at the close of the chapter on biology, she notes, "we must view the facts of biology in the light of an ontological, economic, social, and psychological context."

Beauvoir thus sets forth a standard for assessing biological claims. But does she herself follow it? At first glance, it would appear that she does not carry out the promised broad analysis of biology in terms of social, economic, and existential factors. As previously noted, chapter 1 contains a number of statements that appear to be a historical and essentialist, such as that in intercourse, as in fertilization, woman experiences a "profound alienation," and that since the embryo requires the woman to become "other than herself," she becomes alienated from her body. Or, again, we find that in morning sickness we see "the revolt of the organism against the invading species." I suggest, however, that it is unnecessary to read these claims as essentialist and masculinist. After all, it is only if we expect Beauvoir to be making ahistorical claims that we find this is the only possible interpretation. If, on the other hand, we acknowledge that she is not limited to describing the body as a *thing,* there is no need to read these statements as essentialist. Instead, as [Kristana] Arp demonstrates, Beauvoir's claim that the female is alienated from her body has to be interpreted as a description about the body as "situation," not about the body as a thing. I suggest that once we acknowledge the legitimacy of analyzing the body as situation, we need not find her comments about woman's body as essentialistic and misogynistic. Instead of reading enslavement to the species, for example, as a description of the female body outside of social and historical context, I suggest that we consider it as a description of the female body under various patriarchal periods. Under this interpretation, the above-mentioned objections leveled against her discussion of the body are perhaps understandable, if unjustified. For it may be admitted that when Beauvoir makes these essentialist-sounding comments, she is not always careful to explain at which level she is speaking, and so sometimes invites confusion. As a consequence, some of what Beauvoir says about the female body appears to have escaped her critical lens and so, her work has achieved the reputation of evincing an aversion to "femininity" and specifically, to the female body.

Situating Maternity

> "the close bond between mother and child will be for her a source of dignity or indignity according to the value placed upon the child—which is highly variable"

Of all the female experiences Beauvoir critically observes, perhaps her most controversial account is that of pregnancy and maternity. Mary O'Brien (1981), for example, finds that Beauvoir's account of motherhood simply repeats the traditional view that women are doomed by their biology: since maternity prevents women from participating in social, public life, women should refrain from becoming mothers, according to Beauvoir. Where Beauvoir errs, as O'Brien sees it, is in the initial assumption that female reproduction and birth is alienating; according to O'Brien, it is men who, in lacking the continuity between sexual intercourse and birth, are alienated from sexual reproduction. And so, O'Brien argues, since Beauvoir begins with the wrong premise about women's reproductive experience, she necessarily comes to the wrong conclusion about maternity. This criticism raises the question whether Beauvoir is, in fact, taking the position that women's biology necessarily entraps them so as to prevent their attaining equal status in society.

There is, as noted above, the appearance of a conflict in the text insofar as one interprets Beauvoir's comments ahistorically. So, for example, much has been made of the fact that Beauvoir describes the female reproductive capacity as making the woman the "prey to the species," and that she seems to denigrate the usual functions of motherhood. But when Beauvoir speaks of the female's subordination to the species she is usually thinking of the host of unfavorable conditions under which women, lacking adequate food, health care, and contraceptive control, become pregnant and bear many children to the detriment of their well-being. In addition, she points out that regarding children as an universal panacea for one's happiness can be naive and harmful.

But having said this, we are not compelled to think that Beauvoir finds maternity always to have negative value for women. Beauvoir clearly wants to argue that the value of maternity, like pregnancy, depends upon the *situation* of the woman: the attitude she takes toward these experiences, her social and economic condition, and whether they are freely chosen acts or states imposed upon her. Depending on the external conditions, as well as the psychological attitude of the mother, the experience of birth is variable among women, Beauvoir finds. Some women, she notes, find birth an enriching experience, one that gives them "a sense of creative power; [that] they have accomplished a voluntary and productive task," while for others the experience of birth makes them feel like passive instruments. So, too, with the experience of child-rearing: Beauvoir argues that the mother's relations to her child are not univocal, but vary according to the "situation." Some women feel alone and empty following birth, others welcome and find delight in the child, as Colette's description of her own feelings toward her daughter in *L'Etoile Vesper* which Beauvoir quotes: "I marvelled at the assemblage of prodigies that is the newborn child: her fingernails transparent as the pink shrimp's convex shell, the soles of her feet, which had come to us without touching the ground. The feathery lightness of her eyelashes, lowered on her cheeks or interposed between the scenery of the earth and the pale-blue dream in her eyes." Beauvoir, in choosing to quote this and many other positive passages about motherhood, indicates her openness to the rewards of maternity. As she claims in her chapter on the mother, "the fact remains that unless the circumstances are positively unfavorable the mother will find her life enriched by her child."

Beauvoir's general point in the discussion of motherhood has been overlooked by her critics in the presence of cer tain negative remarks. In this chapter, her theoretical objective is to restore the plurality of women's experience. By bringing together all kinds of accounts of motherhood, both literary and "scientific," Beauvoir effectively demonstrates: first that it is of necessity a heterogeneous experience, and second that since the former is true, there is no such thing as "maternal instinct." It is true that she thereby seeks to dispel a familiar assumption, namely, the notion that maternity is an univocal experience for women and one that in some way is a guarantee of their happiness, but for women living without contraception and adequate wealth, this would hardly seem to be controversial. So it is that Beauvoir dares to question whether one can say that human beings possess a maternal instinct, concluding that "the mother's attitude [toward the child] depends upon her total situation and her reaction to it . . . [which] . . . is highly variable." So, although Beauvoir is hardly averse to pointing out the problems and pitfalls of maternity, neither is she blind to its potential as a source of positive experience. Rather, her point is to reveal two basic misconceptions about maternity: first, that it is not sufficient in itself to ensure woman's happiness; and second, that a child is not certain to be happy in its mother's arms. Not only is her discussion adequate to this goal, but Beauvoir is surely right in arguing for these two premises. For the related notions that women are necessarily fulfilled by motherhood and that they are naturally good mothers ignores the role that negative conditions such as poverty, ignorance, and general deprivation play in the experience of mothers and children. Beauvoir is highly sensitive to these external conditions that may definitively color the experience of motherhood for women. So, while some feminists charge Beauvoir with classism, it is instead the feminists who insist on the primary place and value of motherhood who may themselves be guilty of a classist assumption, one that assumes that all women are able to undertake pregnancy voluntarily, in comfortable economic situations and supportive surroundings, enjoying good health care throughout. Of course, as Beauvoir admits, under favorable conditions, children are bound to be highly positive experiences for the woman, but society can hardly choose to disdain women as human beings, give them no economic support for being mothers, exclude them from public life and then expect them to find motherhood rewarding.

Nor do children raised under the conditions of inequality mentioned flourish, as the myth maintains. Instead, as Beauvoir notes, the social contempt for women is often played out in the relations among the family members, with the result that children suffer. Since there is nothing "natural" about maternal love, according to Beauvoir, there is the possibility that there be bad mothers, a point illustrated in her fiction with dramatic examples of mothers like Madame Blomart in ***The Blood of Others*** (1945) who is at once the passive, submissive martyr and a mother who causes both guilt and resentment in her son. Yet Beauvoir's criticism of such mothers does not lie, as some think, with the relation itself, but rather with its present expression in society. Beauvoir's recommendation in ***The Second Sex*** is that society come to care for its children and help its mothers by furthering them in careers. She is right, I believe, in rejecting talk about the "sacred rights of the mother" and its attendant notion that through motherhood in the abstract woman somehow attains the social and political equality of men. However, having said this, she also holds that there is no essential conflict between woman's transcendence and maternity: "In a properly organized society where children would be largely taken in charge by the community and the mother cared for and helped, maternity would not be wholly incompatible with careers for women. . . . The woman who enjoys the richest individual life will have the most to give to her children and will demand the least from them, she who acquires in effort and struggle a sense of true human values will be best able to bring them up properly." The emphasis in this discussion, then, lies in the social and economic context surrounding maternity, not in the institution in itself. Thus, the objection that Beauvoir deprecates motherhood misses the mark in failing to appreciate the historicized stance she adopts toward maternity. O'Brien's criticism that Beauvoir errs in neglecting the role of motherhood in the path toward woman's emancipation is thus flawed since Beauvoir eschews taking an ahistorical perspective in her analysis of maternity. Furthermore, it appears that O'Brien confuses two senses of alienation that are at work in Beauvoir's discussion, one biological, one social, so that even if O'Brien is correct to dispute the idea sometimes suggested by Beauvoir that woman is biologically alienated in reproduction, she has not thereby disproved Beauvoir's other contention that woman is socially alienated in reproduction. But as I have noted, even Beauvoir in her more careful moments rejects biological determinism as untenable, preferring to analyze woman's biological capacities in light of what she calls "the total situation."

Constructing the Body

> "it is not the body-object described by biologists that actually exists, but the body as lived by the subject"

As Judith Butler has pointed out, Beauvoir's insight that one *becomes* a woman ought to be interpreted as related to another, less familiar idea, that there is no "natural" body. The argument for this conclusion would be that just as for Beauvoir there is no gender identity that one is born with, so, too, there is no sexual identity that one is born with. Thus, the body itself should, on Beauvoir's grounds, come to be seen as a cultural and historical idea, not as a natural fact. Yet the notion of the physical body as a social artifact may strike some as implausible; they would argue that the biological body is simply something natural or given. Yet it is precisely this notion with which Beauvoir has tried to take issue in her distinction between the two senses of "body," arguing that the relevant sense for understanding woman's oppression is the sense in which the body is experienced by the subject, and this body, surely, is a product of social and cultural meanings. Then it becomes comprehensible how one must set aside the idea of a "natural body"; that is, a body whose features are capable of being "neutrally" or "scientifically" described, in order to understand how the body can be socially constructed. If we approach Beauvoir's statement in volume 2 that one is not born but becomes a woman with her idea that the body should be conceived of as a situation, we would not be led into thinking that she intends that a "natural" body comes to take on a gendered identity, or equally, that a genderless subject pre-exists the acquisition of gender. As Butler points out, it is incorrect to think that Beauvoir's dictum implies either that some mysterious "I" exists apart from the gendered subject or that an ungendered subject exists prior to becoming female, since Beauvoir never assumes the existence of a natural, ahistorical body.

As I have argued, Beauvoir's biological discussion needs to be interpreted in relation to the historical comments with which she flags such discussion. So, for example, when she claims that woman of all mammals is the one most alienated by her biology, that her body dooms her to immanence, she should be read as intending to say that because woman's social and economic status throughout history has been subordinate to men's, as a consequence her body has been despised and derogated to the level of something shameful. Consequently, Beauvoir's descriptions of women's biology should be interpreted in light of her further analysis of the roots of women's oppression, noting well that for her these roots are historical and cultural. So conceived, the claim that, for example, woman is "alienated" from her body should be taken as asserting a true proposition about women's bodies as conceived within patriarchal societies; biology thus repeats culture.

On the interpretation I have proposed of how to read her claims about the female body and its biological capacities, Beauvoir is far from thinking that biology determines destiny in any straightforward sense. By the same reasoning, Beauvoir is not committed to maintaining that gender acquisition, that is, coming to be feminine or masculine, is a wholly deterministic process, although it may be limited by the social, historical, and economic conditions that place constraints on what counts as femininity and masculinity. Thus, if one were to place Beauvoir's position on the spectrum of determinist and indeterminist views, one would have to locate it on the end conventionally termed "indeterminist" since she maintains the reality of choice, although I do not find her holding that we possess the kind of contra-causal freedom characteristic of the libertarian position. In contrast to my reading of Beauvoir, Butler places more emphasis on the indeterminacy of gender and thereby upon the freedom that the individual has in attaining some gender identity. Butler even suggests that we may conceive of a wide spectrum of genders, expanding Beauvoir's insight that gender is culturally constructed so as to provide for a multiply gendered society. That is, Butler takes Beauvoir's fundamental insight that one becomes a woman to suggest that gender is, or should be, a fluid category. So, Butler reads Beauvoir as saying that although there is cultural constraint as to the general "shape" of gender that one becomes, one is nevertheless free to realize it in various ways. Concerning the relation of gender to body, one may say that the body becomes the stage, as it were, upon which one acts out one's gender identity. In this respect, gender is not a process that happens to the mute, static body—like poaching an egg—but it is an activity consciously engaged in by the subject, and one over which the subject herself can exert considerable control. Butler makes the point that "gender is a corporeal style, a way of acting the body, a way of wearing one's own flesh as a cultural sign," such that to become a woman means "to execute, institute, produce, reproduce, wear, flaunt, hide, and always stylize [one's womanhood] in one way or another." If one can interpret the descriptions such as "acting the body" and "wearing one's own flesh" as nondualistic metaphors for the agency implicit in gender expression, I concur. Furthermore, the idea that gender is nondeterministic, or fluid, in the sense that it is historically and culturally contingent strikes me as both true and liberating, rather than defeatist or "masculinist." Beauvoir's account of how an apparently nonsocial thing, the human body, is in fact itself the product of profound social and historical forces is highly original, no feminist before Beauvoir thinking to analyze our very ideas about the body in this way. Furthermore, her account concerning the social and historical roots of the ideas about woman's body yields both a description of the malady and the suggestion for a cure. Insofar as she pinpoints certain prevalent Western cultural myths and assumptions about the female body that affect our present reasoning about women's bodies, she correctly diagnoses the problem, and insofar as she expresses the need for universal dignity and self-creation, she indicates the direction for social change to allow women to participate fully in the human arena.

Terry Keefe (essay date February 1997)

SOURCE: "Commitment, Re-Commitment and Puzzlement: Aspects of the Cold War in the Fiction of Simone de Beauvoir," in *French Cultural Studies,* Vol. 8, No. 22, February, 1997, pp. 127-36.

[*In the following essay, Keefe discusses Beauvoir's political perspective during the Cold War and attitudes concerning the United States and the U.S.S.R. as reflected in* Le sange des autres, Les mandarins, Les belles images, Le femme rompue *and "Malentendu à Moscou."*]

In two novels having a kind of continuity that is not always recognized, Simone de Beauvoir creates fictional worlds that closely mirror major phases and events of two decades of modern French history. But whereas ***Le Sang des autres*** reaches back some way before focusing on the build-up to

World War Two and the Occupation, a distinctive feature of ***Les Mandarins*** is that it treats a very short period of time in considerable depth. Portraying the dilemmas and reactions of French left-wing intellectuals in the immediate post-Liberation years, it tells a story beginning in December 1944 and ending in summer 1948, thereby encompassing the world's movement into Cold War, which forms an integral feature of the political framework of the novel. Long sequences set in America, although centring on a love-affair, also reflect the way in which French intellectuals like Sartre, Camus and Beauvoir discovered that country at a time when they were obliged to take serious account of it in their political thinking, with the emergence of the 'superpowers'. Beauvoir's final two works of fiction, ***Les Belles Images*** and ***La Femme rompue,*** contain few references to the Cold War, but, intriguingly, a story written though discarded by her in 1966 and recently published for the first time, **'Malentendu à Moscou',** turns out to be set wholly in the Soviet Union in that year. It forms a counterpart to certain aspects of ***Les Mandarins*** and enables us to examine a wider and more balanced treatment of the Cold War in Beauvoir's fiction as a whole—a treatment that supplements in interesting ways her account in the third and fourth volumes of her memoirs.

In spite of its over-schematization, one of the continuing fascinations of ***Le Sang des autres*** is the way in which it shows a variety of characters drawn into political commitment. Jean Blomart's evolution, of course, is relatively complex. He becomes involved in politics very early, but is so troubled by his part in the violent death of a young friend that he leaves the Communist Party and falls back upon a version of 'le vieux syndicalisme français' that permits only non-violent political action. In spite of the pressure of events, he clings onto his pacifism throughout the late 1930s, passes a very brief period as a soldier, then during the Occupation comes to advocate Resistance sabotage and killing even more strongly than most of those around him. His young girl-friend Hélène, who at first takes her political indifference to the point of mild collaboration with the German occupier, undergoes an equally abrupt and radical conversion. Moreover, by the time she is fatally injured while working for Blomart's group, they have been joined by a range of characters who seemed most unlikely to make common political cause—including Marcel, the previously uncommitted artist, his socially ambitious wife Denise, the Communist Paul, and even Blomart's bourgeois father. The novel ends as a kind of hymn to such unity around the ideal of freedom.

This unity can be seen as the starting-point of ***Les Mandarins.*** In various ways, the reader is constantly reminded of the Resistance, and the sole political goal of one minor character, Luc, is to 'sauver l'unité de la Résistance'. But what is more striking is that the central figures Henri and Dubreuilh both deride Luc's objective as ridiculous ('Tout ça c'est des conneries!'), suggesting that Resistance activities were essentially negative or destructive. This raises the question of exactly what Resistance groups were committed to. They were clearly anti-fascist, but the very composition of Blomart's team constituted a warning against any simple notion that they uniformly supported the political left. In any case, from the very beginning of ***Les Mandarins,*** the matter of whether the left itself is entirely united is brought under scrutiny. In the first chapter, the Russian émigré, Scriassine, who has also lived in the United States, questions the assumption that unity of action with the Communists is desirable, and shows that he is far from regarding the Soviet Union as a model, or as a country holding the future of the working classes in its hands—a belief shared by most of the other major left-wing characters and constituting a major element of their commitment. Precisely because ***Les Mandarins*** concentrates so strongly upon the French political dilemmas that *internalize* international conflict, it is worth emphasizing that Scriassine's prophecies—of massive technological and economic change, the emergence of the superpowers, and the Cold War—hang over the whole novel, and that the reader is often given cause to remember them.

Of the two narrative focalizers, Anne is the more disturbed by Scriassine's vision, because it implies a bleak future for her husband Dubreuilh. But it is Henri, above all, who is shown as learning the hard way that the world is indeed polarizing around the great powers of the U.S.A. and the U.S.S.R. He is reminded of the influence of America, 'le grand pays libérateur', when he discovers that it is indirectly helping to maintain fascism in Portugal, and when the American Preston tries to attach political conditions to his offer of extra paper for Henri's newspaper, *L'Espoir.* Yet he is still taken aback when a former Resistance leader argues that France counts for nothing in the world any more: 'Soudain, il découvrait qu'il habitait la capitale moribonde d'un tout petit pays . . . Henri n'était plus que le citoyen négligeable d'une puissance de cinquième ordre'. Considering the world to be hesitating between the new war that Scriassine has predicted and peace, he develops a growing sense of impotence, which leads him to doubt the value of writing novels—'Les Russes étaient en train de saccager Berlin, la guerre s'achevait ou une autre commençait: comment pouvait-on s'amuser à raconter des histories qui ne sont jamais arrivées?'—and eventually to put his newspaper at the service of Dubreuilh's new independent political party. For some time the threat from America in particular is shown as increasing, but everything else, of course, is eclipsed by the exploding of the first atomic bombs. Henri is clearer than ever at this point where he stands in relation to the U.S.A. and the Soviet Union:

> L'hégémonie américaine: c'est la sous-alimentation, l'oppression à perpétuité pour tous les pays d'Orient: leur seule chance, c'est l'U.R.S.S.: la

> seule chance d'une humanité délivrée du besoin
> de l'esclavage et de la bêtise, c'est l'U.R.S.S; alors
> il faut tout faire pour l'aider.

Scriassine's further warning that, while those on the left in France are always ready to attack the U.S.A., they will not say a word against the Soviet Union, seems justified when the first serious evidence of the existence of an extensive system of labour camps in the U.S.S.R. comes to light, since a row ensues over whether to make this publicly known. Quite apart from the consequences for internal French politics, Henri is especially deeply affected by the worry that what he had always assumed—that a socialism reconciling freedom and justice would finally come into being in the Soviet Union—is false. It may turn out to be like every other country: 'Impossible de le nier: en U.R.S.S. aussi des hommes exploitaient à mort d'autres hommes!' Perhaps the end justifies the means, but he sees that everything now needs to be reconsidered, and is entirely bemused by the implications of the new situation.

Placed exactly at the mid-point of ***Les Mandarins,*** the discovery of the Soviet labour camps is a major turning-point in the political developments of the story as a whole. As far as fictionalization is concerned, what is of interest is the time-shift that Beauvoir operates in the novel, situating in the middle of 1946 in her story a controversy that flared up at the end of 1949. To that extent, with the benefit of hindsight, she forces certain dilemmas of the Cold War upon her characters much sooner than they were actually experienced. As in ***Le Sang des autres,*** she is concerned with the interaction of the private and the political in the lives of her characters, and wishes to foreground the general moral as well as political confusion that came to prevail, as well as to dwell upon a subsequent period of disengagement, even irresponsibility, on the part of both Henri and Anne. After denouncing the camps in his newspaper, Henri is accused of furthering the American cause, but in fact he is still perfectly clear that he will always continue to defend the U.S.S.R. against the U.S.A., which he sees as a country that systematically takes the side of the privileged rather than the people. When he and Dubreuilh bury their differences barely a year later, Scriassine's earlier claim that one is obliged to accept one or the other of the two world blocs in its entirety looks more plausible, in that Dubreuilh argues that they could only achieve anything by throwing in their lot with the Communists.

There is little mention of the Cold War in those sections of ***Les Mandarins*** recounting Anne's first trips to America, but towards the end of her affair with Brogan she sees the country in a threatening light: 'Maintenant l'Amérique, ça signifiait bombe atomique, menaces de guerre, fascisme naissant', and in summer 1948 she argues that, if her American friends go on doing nothing, they will have no right to complain when their country becomes fascist and brings about war. Philippe's answer that, unless one is prepared to withdraw from the battle altogether, the fanaticism of the U.S.S.R. has to be answered in kind by America is an important one in its way, since it ushers in the last phase of the novel, where Dubreuilh and eventually Henri snap out of their fatalistic stage and return to the political fray.

Deciding that the French left is not so completely powerless as he had believed—for instance, America's attempt to arm Europe could be resisted—Dubreuilh claims to be reverting to a position very close to his original political commitment in the 1930s, using any means at hand in order to fend off a particular danger. He acknowledges that the Soviet Union is far from perfect, but says it has the advantage over other possible forms of socialism that it exists. Henri himself is not wholly convinced, and when he looks back to the Christmas party in 1944, with which the story began, he is struck not only by his naïvety about America, but also by continuing uncertainties concerning the Soviet Union: 'la secourable Amérique se préparait à asservir l'Europe, et quant à ce qui se passait en U.R.S.S. il valait mieux ne pas y regarder de trop près'. Nevertheless, with a new war looking imminent, Henri finally agrees to resume the political struggle. If the circumstances of World War Two led to commitment, one could say that, after a period of withdrawal characterized by confusion and a strong sense of powerlessness, the circumstances of the Cold War lead to *re-commitment.* And just as the nature of the original commitment was in some respects clear, but in other respects not, so the re-commitment has its certainties and its obscurities. In global terms, however, what is involved is undoubtedly opposition to the U.S.A., in conjunction with resolute but qualified approval of the Soviet Union.

It is unsurprising that, with a gap of twelve years between ***Les Mandarins*** and ***Les Belles Images,*** the latter should not resume, politically, from exactly the position reached at the end of ***Les Mandarins,*** in the way that the former picked up the ending of ***Le Sang des autres.*** Interestingly, the central figure of ***Les Belles Images,*** Laurence, is presented as having undergone in 1945, at the age of 11, a crisis related to the desperate state of the world, but there is no significant notion of political commitment in the novel. Moreover, it contains remarkably little mention of Cold War phenomena. And the only exception to a similar pattern in the short stories published a year later as ***La Femme rompue*** is that André, the husband of the central woman figure of **'L'Âge de discrétion',** is shown—in contrast to his wife—as still active politically at around the age of 60, at least to the extent of working on behalf of the persecuted anywhere in the world. But again there is no general preoccupation with the Cold War as such in the story, and, unlike his mother, André seems to have lost the will to go on struggling for the eventual triumph of socialism. He will do his utmost to help suppress human suffering, but admits that 'pratiquement aucune cause n'est tout à fait la nôtre: nous ne sommes pas pour l'U.R.S.S. et ses compromissions; pas non plus pour la Chine'. However, a major theme of the story as a whole is ageing, and André visibly allows any remaining political commitment he may have to be weakened by the fact that there are goals that he now knows he will never see attained in his own lifetime. Since in the second story of ***La Femme rompue,*** **'Monologue',** virtually everything said by Murielle is discredited, it contains no substantive references at all to politics. And in the final story of the collection, **'La Femme rompue',** neither of the two central figures has any political involvement whatever. Indeed, there is scarcely any indication at all of the political context in which this essentially private, domestic story takes place.

By contrast, **'Malentendu à Moscou',** the story that Beauvoir left unpublished, has quite strong political content. A retired French couple, André and Nicole, are visiting the Soviet Union in 1966, for the first time for three years, to see André's daughter, Macha, who lives and works in Moscow. At the beginning we learn that Nicole is anxious about the possibility of a third world war, and André later confirms that the Cold War anxieties that emerged in ***Les Mandarins*** are now greater than ever: 'La bombe, en 45, ce n'était qu'une menace assez abstraite: aujourd'hui elle était devenue une angoissante éventualité'. As is usual in a Beauvoir text, however, it is André who is much the more involved in politics. We see from the first that he is particularly anxious to learn more about a country that has meant more to him politically than any other. Like Henri and Dubreuilh (and the other André), he has never joined the Communist Party, but 'à travers les remous de l'espoir et du désespoir il avait toujours pensé que l'U.R.S.S. détenait les clés de l'avenir, donc de cette époque et de son propre destin'. Beauvoir has no occasion to refer to all that has happened between the late 1940s and the mid-1960s, but she indicates how far things have moved on by having André acknowledge of the U.S.S.R. that 'jamais, même dans les noires années du stalinisme, il n'avait eu l'impression de si mal la comprendre'. The political content of the rest of the story will, effectively, expand upon this point.

The context of André's remark—although this is sketched in rather than explained—turns out to be some kind of disillusionment that set in *after* any re-commitment that he might be assumed to have made. He claims not to be exactly engaged in the political struggle any more: 'J'essaie de rendre des services, ce n'est pas pareil. Par dessus le marché, c'est toujours vain'. And, as is the case in **'L'Âge de discrétion',** whatever change has taken place is somehow associated with the Algerian War, for André believes he has lost 'toute prise sur le monde' since 1962 and regards his own (new) powerlessness as that of the French left as a whole. He is essentially in a state of confusion that is bound up with the difficulty of understanding what is happening in other countries, including the U.S.S.R., so that it is above all that country's commitment to socialism and its foreign policy—and to this extent the Cold War—that becomes the subject of heated exchanges between himself and his daughter. Macha claims that the U.S.S.R. does not want war: André suggests that, although no one else does either, it may come about if American 'escalation' is allowed to continue. Macha says that the Soviets cannot take the chance of American retaliation if their bases are bombed: André asks whether they will act when America attacks China. Finally, he responds to Macha's point that the U.S.S.R. is trying to reconcile two imperatives, 'aider le socialisme à travers le monde, et sauver la paix', by acknowledging that the situation is not a simple one and reiterating his disillusionment:

> si l'U.R.S.S. s'installait dans la coexistence pacifique, le socialisme n'était pas pour demain. Que d'espoirs déçus! En France, le front populaire, la résistance, l'émancipation du Tiers Monde, qui n'avait pas fait reculer d'un pouce le capitalisme. La révolution chinoise: elle aboutissait au conflit sino-soviétique. Non, jamais l'avenir n'avait paru à André aussi désolant.

In general, André discovers that the Soviet Union has moved more towards capitalism, as well as peaceful co-existence, since his previous visit in 1963. When the three of them go to Leningrad, he is struck even more forcefully by a kind of westernization, and has to fall back upon a sort of speculation in order to preserve any of the hopes that he had on arriving in Moscow. His uncertainty, and, specifically, his feeling that, even if the Soviet Union is still on track for genuine socialism, he will not live to see it come about, increases in the later part of the story, as ageing becomes more of a central theme. When Macha almost convinces him that he is seeing no more than a kind of backward surge in the Soviet Union, which will eventually be replaced by a new phase, a new generation who will fight for a brand of socialism that excludes neither happiness nor freedom, his reaction is entirely consistent with the stance of his counterpart in **'L'Âge de discrétion':**

> à Moscou et à Leningrad il no trouvait pas ce qu'il avait espéré. . . . Bien sûr, il y avait uno grande différence entre l'U.R.S.S. et l'Occident. . . . Le socialisme finirait par devenir une réalité. Un jour il triompherait dans le monde entier. . . . C'était possible, c'était probable. Une probabilité qu'André ne vérifierait jamais. . . . Il avait compté sur l'histoire pour justifier sa vie: il n'y comptait plus.

Since **'Malentendu à Moscou'** was certainly written before **'L'Âge de discrétion'**, it is possible to trace or reconstruct in Beauvoir's fiction a long and sinuous line of political development that passes through Jean Blomart, Henri Perron, the André of **'Malentendu à Moscou'**, and finally terminates in the André of **'L'Âge de discrétion'**. Textual indications suggest that all four characters were born at much the same time, so that the continuity and coherence of their experience in relation to relevant twentieth-century historical events can be maintained. Only Henri and the two Andrés, of course, are shown as seeing anything at all of the Cold War. And many of its vital stages which the latter must be presumed to have lived through are not touched upon at all in Beauvoir's stories. Her memoirs are naturally much fuller in this respect, addressing the same and additional aspects of the Cold War explicitly. Nevertheless, just as Henri speculates in ***Les Mandarins*** that, in personal matters, literature is in some ways truer than life, so we can suggest that some of the patterns in Beauvoir's fiction may be clearer and bring sharper insights into her experience than accounts in her non-fictional writings. Certainly, the broad movement of the characters' political involvement after World War Two in the stories examined is one of great interest.

The way in which it is always the *male* characters who are engaged in politics, with the women figures drawn in only on the margins—and then reluctantly—is especially prominent. So is the fact that, at least on the global scale, the issue of *whether* to be politically committed or not rather prevails over that of what to be committed *to.* Or, better, one could say that certain assumptions or constants in the political attitudes involved—like the basic faith in the Soviet Union that is at the root of most of the phases described—are so strong that, in difficult circumstances of a particular kind, they bring about a paralysing puzzlement. Hence the dominant pattern of commitment, confusion/withdrawal, re-commitment, confusion/withdrawal, which—albeit in a different way—even stretches back beyond wartime commitment, since in Blomart's case this was preceded by a period of confusion/withdrawal, which itself followed an initial commitment. . .

Moreover, within this general pattern, which, together with the earlier gender point, raises obvious questions about the relationship between Beauvoir's own political involvement and that of Sartre, other, more specific areas of interest come to the fore. References to Algeria serve as a useful reminder that France had its own war (indeed, wars, if one thinks of Indo-China) in the middle of the Cold War, and one that probably eclipsed the latter for many French intellectuals for a long period. And, perhaps above all, as a result of the belated publication of **'Malentendu à Moscou',** the vexed matter of later perceptions of the Soviet Union comes into sharp focus. It was clearly during the trip that Beauvoir made with Sartre in May 1966 that she gathered many of the impressions registered in the story, yet in it she barely records anything at all in relation to their central concern during that and earlier visits, namely freedom of expression and the fate of writers and other artists. It is even possible that any unease about the state of the U.S.S.R. that this betrays may lie behind her decision to replace, in ***La Femme rompue,*** a story set in Russia by one in which virtually the only substantive reference to the Soviet Union expresses disapproval of its 'compromissions'. **'Malentendu à Moscou'** was written in the second half of 1966, but by 1967 Beauvoir and Sartre had become sufficiently disillusioned with aspects of the U.S.S.R. to refuse to go back. It is quite possible, therefore, that the portrayal of the country in that story came to seem too favourable. However that may be, the kind of confusion surrounding Beauvoir's attitude towards the U.S.S.R. from the mid 1960s onwards is scarcely different in principle from the perplexity experienced by Henri in the mid 1940s. The Cold War appears once more to have brought the wheel full circle.

Of course, this pattern, based just upon her fiction, amounts to no more than one perspective on Beauvoir's political stance as a whole, but it is a helpful and suggestive one. In any case, any totalized account of her view of the Cold War could only ever be a fragment of a larger picture. In considering this even stranger type of 'war', we do well to bear in mind Mathieu's paradoxical comments on the elusive nature of World War Two in Sartre's *Le Sursis:*

> C'était un drôle de corps, proprement impensable . . . Elle est là, elle est partout, c'est la totalité de toutes mes pensées, de toutes les paroles d'Hitler, de tous les actes de Gomez: mais personne n'est là pour faire le total. Elle n'existe que pour Dieu. Mais Dieu n'existe pas. Et pourtant la guerre existe.

FURTHER READING

Criticism

Adamowski, T. H. "Death, Old Age, and Femininity: Simone de Beauvoir and the Politics of *La Vieillesse.*" *Dalhousie Review* 50, No. 3 (Autumn 1970): 394-401.

Provides critical analysis of Beauvoir's views on aging and the elderly in *La Vieillesse.*

Davis, Colin. "Simone de Beauvoir's *Le Sang des autres* and the Ethics of Failure." *Modern Language Review* 93, No. 1 (January 1998): 35-47.

Examines the significance of violence and uncertainty in *La Sang des autres* as a commentary on the risk associated with political engagement and decision-making.

Davis, Mary G. "Introduction: Debating Simone de Beauvoir." *Signs: Journal of Women in Culture and Society* 18, No. 1 (Autumn 1992): 74-88.

Provides an overview of contemporary feminist response to *The Second Sex* and the significance of Beauvoir's theories for feminist scholars.

Hughes, Alex. "Murdering the Mother: Simone de Beauvoir's *Mémoires d'une jeune fille rangée.*" *French Studies* XLVIII, No. 2 (April 1994): 174-83.

Provides a psychoanalytic reading of *Mémoires d'une jeune fille rangée* focusing on Beauvoir's relationship with her mother, Zaza, and Sartre.

Kuykendall, Eléanor H. "Simone de Beauvoir and Two Kinds of Ambivalence in Action." In *The Thinking Muse: Feminism and Modern French Philosophy,* edited by Jeffner Allen and Iris Marion Young, pp. 35-50. Bloomington: Indiana University Press, 1989.

Offers linguistic analysis of Beauvoir's existentialist ethics and feminist vocabulary in *The Second Sex.*

McCall, Dorothy Kaufmann. "Simone de Beauvoir, *The Second Sex,* and Jean-Paul Sartre." *Signs: Journal of Women in Culture and Society* 5, No. 2 (Winter 1979): 209-23.

Offers reevaluation of Beauvoir's feminist perspective through examination of her complex relationship with Sartre and the influence of Sartre's existentialism in *The Second Sex.*

Moi, Toril. "Beauvoir's Utopia: The Politics of *The Second Sex.*" *South Atlantic Quarterly* 92, No. 2 (Spring 1993): 311-60.

Provides an overview of Beauvoir's feminist perspective and philosophical ideals in *The Second Sex.*

Pilardi, Jo-Ann. "The Changing Critical Fortunes of *The Second Sex.*" *History and Theory* 32, No. 1 (1993): 51-73.

Examines the critical reception and publishing history of *The Second Sex* and the lasting significance of Beauvoir's ideas for feminist scholarship.

Powrie, Phil. "Rereading Between the Lines: A Postscript on *La Femme rompue.*" *Modern Language Review* 87, No. 2 (April 1992): 320-9.

Discusses Beauvoir's presentation of unstable female characters in *Le Femme rompue* as a reflection of the difficulty women authors encounter when creating their own fictions within male literary tradition.

Simons, Margaret A. "Lesbian Connections: Simone de Beauvoir and Feminism." *Signs: Journal of Women in Culture and Society* 18, No. 1 (Autumn 1992): 136-61.

Examines Beauvoir's romantic attachments to women and the significance of her bisexuality for feminist interpretation of her gender identity and writing.

———. "Sexism and the Philosophical Canon: On Reading Beauvoir's *The Second Sex.*" *Journal of the History of Ideas* 51, No. 3 (July-September 1990): 487-504.

Discusses Beauvoir's important contributions to existentialism and her problematic status as a woman philosopher in the male-dominated canon of Western philosophical literature.

Sturm, Douglas. "Natural Law and the Ethics of Simone de Beauvoir." *Bucknell Review* XIII, No. 2 (1965): 88-101.

Offers analysis of *The Ethics of Ambiguity* and elements of Beauvoir's existentialism that correlate with principles of natural law theory.

Suleiman, Susan Rubin. "Simone de Beauvoir and the Writing Self." *L'Esprit Créateur* XXIX, No. 4 (Winter 1989): 42-51.

Explores issues surrounding sexual identity and authorship in *The Second Sex,* Beauvoir's autobiographical writings, and fiction.

Interviews

Jardine, Alice. "Interview with Simone de Beauvoir." *Signs: Journal of Women in Culture and Society* 5, No. 2 (Winter 1979): 224-36.

Beauvoir discusses her intellectual relationship with Sartre, contemporary feminism, and *The Second Sex.*

Simons, Margaret A., and Jessica Benjamin. "Simone de Beauvoir: An Interview." *Feminist Studies* 5, No. 2 (Summer 1979): 330-45.

Beauvoir discusses her role in the feminist movement and the influence of psychoanalytic theory and literature on her own writings and ideas about women.

Additional coverage of Beauvoir's life and career is contained in the following sources published by Gale: *Contemporary Authors,* Vols. 9-12R, 118; *Contemporary Authors New Revision Series,* Vols. 28, 61; *Dictionary of Literary Biography,* Vol. 72; *Dictionary of Literary Biography Yearbook,* Vol. 86; *DISCovering Authors; DISCovering Authors: British; DISCovering Authors: Canadian; DISCovering Authors Modules: Most-Studied and Novelists; Major Twentieth Century Writers,* Vol. 1; and *World Literature Criticism.*

C. S. Lewis
1898-1963

(Also wrote under pseudonyms Clive Hamilton, N. W. Clerk, and Nat Whilk; full name Clive Staples Lewis) English novelist, short story writer, nonfiction writer, essayist, children's writer, critic, and poet.

The following entry presents an overview of Lewis's career. For further information on his life and works, see *CLC,* Volumes 1, 3, 6, 14, and 27.

INTRODUCTION

The prolific author of persuasive religious polemics, allegorical fiction, and literary criticism, C. S. Lewis is considered among the most brilliant and influential Christian writers of the twentieth century. He is revered by religious thinkers, particularly in the United States, as a Christian apologist, lecturer, and essayist whose intelligence and provocative insight into the nature of divinity and human spirituality has won both the faith and devotion of legions of admirers. While his science fiction and didactic novels, particularly *The Pilgrim's Regress* (1933), *The Screwtape Letters* (1942), and *Till We Have Faces* (1956), enjoyed popular and critical esteem, his classic fantasy series, "The Chronicles of Narnia," is widely regarded as a landmark in children's literature. As a professor of literature Lewis also produced respected commentaries on medieval literature. His ability to write compelling narrative fiction and witty, accessible religious commentary caused his reputation to grow even after his death in 1963.

Biographical Information

Born in Belfast, Ireland, Lewis was the younger son of Albert James Lewis, a solicitor, and Flora Augusta Hamilton Lewis, an accomplished mathematical scholar. After his mother died when Lewis was nine, he spent some unhappy years at boarding schools before becoming the private pupil of W. T. Kirkpatrick, whom Lewis admired greatly and who exerted a profound influence on his intellectual development. Lewis entered Oxford University in 1917, though soon left to serve in the army in World War I. He was wounded in 1918 and returned to Oxford in 1919. That year he published *Spirits in Bondage* (1919), poetry written under the pseudonym Clive Hamilton. Around this time he began an unusual association with Mrs. J. K. Moore, twenty-seven years his senior and the mother of an army friend killed in the war. Lewis established a household with Mrs. Moore, her young daughter, and his older brother Warren at The Kilns, his house near Oxford. Mrs. Moore continued to live with him until her death in 1951. Lewis taught philosophy and English literature at Oxford from 1925 until 1954, when he left for a professorship in Medieval and Renaissance English at Cambridge University. At Oxford, Lewis was the first president of the Oxford Socratic Club, which served as a forum for debates on Christianity. He also founded the Inklings, an informal literary group whose members included two friends, the writers J.R.R. Tolkien and Charles Williams. The defining event of Lewis's life and work was his conversion to Christianity in 1929. Until this period, Lewis had professed strictly atheist beliefs for most of his intellectual life, but he became convinced that his studies and personal experience led him incontrovertibly towards a belief in theism. In his autobiography, *Surprised by Joy* (1955), Lewis described his reluctant conversion: "I gave in, and admitted that God was God, and knelt and prayed: perhaps, that night, the most dejected and reluctant convert in all of England." In 1941 and 1942 Lewis broadcast four series of radio programs on Christian issues on the BBC. These programs, which were later published in *Broadcast Talks* (1942), *The Case for Christianity* (1943), *Christian Behaviour* (1943), and *Mere Christianity* (1952), made Lewis famous in Britain as a Christian justifier and speaker. His radio talks and the 1942 publication of *The Screwtape Letters* earned him great demand as a lecturer, writer, and debater for the rest of his life. His fame grew in the next decade when he published "The Chronicles of Narnia," a series of children's fantasy books. Lewis married Joy Davidman Gresham, an American writer, in 1956. Gresham was diagnosed with cancer shortly afterwards and despite a remission died in 1960. Lewis was shattered by the loss of his wife and chronicled his bereavement in *A Grief Observed* (1961), which he published under the name N. W. Clerk. Lewis died at The Kilns of heart failure following a long illness on November 22, 1963.

Major Works

Lewis's extensive body of work comprises literary criticism, poetry, religion, and fiction. After his conversion, all of Lewis's fiction and most of his nonfiction writings reflected his study of and faith in Christianity. Lewis's work addresses conflicts between rationalism and faith and Christians' never ending quest to gain knowledge and grace and to move closer to God. He owed literary debts to a wide range of writers and thinkers including Plato, Milton, John Bunyan, Jonathan Swift, George MacDonald, G. K. Chesterton, and Tolkien. In his capacity as a scholar of literature Lewis wrote several respected works of literary criticism, including *The Allegory of Love* (1936), which studies the development of the idea of romantic love and the use of allegory in literature. Lewis was one of the first to espouse the idea that romantic love is strictly a modern construct and did not exist as modern society knows it until fairly recently. Lewis's religious nonfiction was typically directed towards lay people who wish to explore issues faced by contemporary Christians. Written in a lucid, conversational style, Lewis's religious writings are known for their incisive use of language and metaphors that make complicated ideas easy to understand. For example, *The Problem of Pain* (1940) discusses why God allows people to suffer and evil to exist if he is good. Lewis concludes that suffering is often vital to spiritual growth and that pain is sometimes essential to human existence. *Surprised by Joy* is an autobiographical account of the events leading to Lewis's religious conversion in which he explains how the atheist beliefs he held as a young man slowly gave way to a belief in God; particularly influential was Chesterton's *Everlasting Man* (1925). In *A Grief Observed*, Lewis recorded his odyssey through the stages of grief and his ensuing struggles with faith. Lewis's fiction spans genres as diverse as allegory, myth, science fiction, and children's fantasy. Present throughout all is his supernatural view of a higher power: God is everywhere, present in every aspect of his characters' lives. Typically at least one of the characters denies God's existence or betrays him, but cannot find fulfillment until he embraces the higher power's presence. In the allegory *The Pilgrim's Regress,* influenced by Bunyan's *Pilgrim's Progress,* the character John wanders the land searching for The Landlord. During his travels he meets characters representing schools of thought that attempt to steer him away from his path. These characters, including Mr. Enlightenment, Mr. Broad, and Mr. Sensible, satirize modern beliefs such as rationalism and subjectivism that Lewis disagreed with and sought to discredit. As John travels and encounters these characters, he finds he must go to back to his starting point and begin again where he lost his way before he can find the Landlord—God. Lewis's science fiction trilogy, *Out of the Silent Planet* (1939), *Perelandra* (1943), and *That Hideous Strength* (1945), follows the travels of a human named Dr. Elwin Ransom to Mars, Venus, and back to Earth. In *Out of the Silent Planet*, Ransom is kidnapped by the evil Dr. Devine and his partner Weston and brought to Mars, known by its inhabitants as Malacandra. There he encounters the various beings of Malacandra. The planet is overseen by Oyarsa, the God figure, and *eldila*, angel-like beings. This contrasts sharply with Earth, which Ransom learns is known as Thulcandra, the "Silent Planet," because it is controlled by an entity the Malacandrans call The Bent One rather than Oyarsa. The other Malacandrans are the *hrossa*, poet-farmers, the *sorns*, scholar-philosophers, and the *pfiltriggi*, the artisans. Ransom is astonished to find that they all live in harmony, in contrast with Earth. He lives among the Malacandrans and grows to like them. When Devine and Weston kill a Malacandran, he helps the Malacandrans capture and try them. In *Perelandra*, Ransom goes to Venus, or Perelandra, to prevent a Perelandran Fall and expulsion from Eden. The part of the tempter is played by Weston, who has followed Ransom to the planet. An intense intellectual tug-of-war between the two ends in flight, pursuit, and Weston's Death. Ransom has saved the Perelandran Eve from temptation and Perelandra retains its Paradise. In the final book of the trilogy, *That Hideous Strength*, a young sociologist and his wife, Mark and Jane Studdock, become involved in Earth's struggle between good and evil. Mark is recruited by a group known as NICE, the National Institute of Coordinated Experiments, led by Devine in a new incarnation as Lord Feverstone, while Jane becomes involved with a group headed by Ransom which fights NICE and its malevolent intentions. Lewis uses the now familiar metaphor of the bureaucracy as hell, depicting the bureaucracy NICE as an evil entity. He carried this metaphor further in *The Screwtape Letters*, an epistolary novel composed of correspondence from Screwtape, a senior devil, to his nephew Wormwood, a young devil. Screwtape sends Wormwood advice on tempting his first soul, making a number of observations about modern society, culture, marriage and family. Ultimately, Wormwood's mission fails when his target dies a heroic death with his soul intact. Lewis's most famous fictional works are a seven-volume series of children's fantasies, "The Chronicles of Narnia": *The Lion, the Witch, and the Wardrobe* (1950), *Prince Caspian* (1951), *The Voyage of the "Dawn Treader"* (1952), *The Silver Chair* (1953), *The*

Horse and His Boy (1954), *The Magician's Nephew* (1955), and *The Last Battle* (1956). The books revolve around Narnia, another world with doorways into our world. Aslan, a benevolent lion and Christ-like figure, watches over Narnia. They are saturated with Christian symbolism blended with Greek and Roman mythical influences and Arthurian battle scenes. The narrative is fast-paced and compelling—although the books are allegorical, Lewis wished children to be able to read them simply to enjoy the story, without being conscious of being taught a lesson in the process. The Chronicles begin with the four Pevensie children, Peter, Susan, Edmund, and Lucy. In *The Lion, the Witch, and the Wardrobe*, the four children are visiting the Professor, a family friend, when Lucy finds a door into the world of Narnia inside an old wardrobe. Narnia, which is populated by talking animals and mythical creatures such as fauns, centaurs, and dryads, is frozen in winter because it is ruled by the evil White Witch. Edmund falls under the Witch's spell and betrays Narnia and his siblings. Edmund is later forgiven and the children save Narnia, although Aslan must sacrifice himself in order to save his people. The children become Kings and Queens of Narnia but must eventually return to their own world where time runs differently to live out their lives there as ordinary children. In turn they become too old to return to Narnia and two new children, the Pevensies' cousin Eustace Scrubb and his schoolmate Jill Pole, join the story. The adventures culminate with *The Last Battle*, a Narnian account of the Book of Revelation. All the characters except Susan—whom we learn has rejected Narnia and its teachings—are brought to Narnia on its last day. Aslan welcomes them on the last day of Narnia's existence and the reader learns that they have all been killed in a train accident in Britain and are present at Narnia's judgment day. The series ends with the end of Narnia's existence and the characters' joyous passage to Paradise. *Till We Have Faces* (1956), a retelling of the Cupid and Psyche myth, was Lewis's last work of fiction. Orual, Queen of Glome, narrates her story in the first person. Her tale begins as a complaint against the gods for their ill treatment of her. Orual is Psyche's older sister, and her ugliness stands in sharp contrast to Psyche's beauty. Orual makes up for the lack of affection in her life by smothering her sister with a jealous love. As the novel progresses, Orual sees that the gods are not to blame for her unhappiness. She comes to realize that she must abandon her bitterness and possessiveness in order to be cleansed.

Critical Reception

Many scholars of English literature consider Lewis's literary criticism, particularly *The Allegory of Love* and *English Literature in the Sixteenth Century, Excluding Drama* (1954) to be among the finest commentaries on medieval literature in existence. Lewis's religious essays earned him enormous popular recognition and a number of critics echoed this sentiment, praising his extraordinary ability to use witty language, colloquialisms, anecdotes and simple metaphors to make moral precepts and theological issues easily comprehensible to lay persons from varied backgrounds. Though some religious critics fault Lewis for failing to construct a comprehensive theological framework for his beliefs, Lewis often stressed that he did not claim to be a theologian. He wanted to explore and explain religious issues that confronted ordinary people, and most thinkers of the time felt he accomplished that goal quite well. Some critics considered Lewis's work too imitative of other writers. His essays owe a great literary debt to Chesterton, whose work was instrumental in Lewis's conversion to Christianity, while the inspiration for *The Pilgrim's Regress* came directly from Bunyan's *Pilgrim's Progress*. Lewis's fiction was generally well received by critics. Though his science fiction trilogy is more "fiction" than "science," his ability to combine myth and religious archetypes into a compelling narrative generally pleased reviewers. While some reviewers reserved the most praise for the last and most ambitious installment of the trilogy, *That Hideous Strength*, others felt it reached too far and became mired in the moral framework Lewis constructed to tell his story. Devotees of children's literature consider "The Chronicles of Narnia" one of the finest fantasies ever created. Although some critics, including Lewis's friend and "Lord of the Rings" author Tolkien, disliked Lewis's use in Narnia of a pastiche of Western characters from Greek mythological figures to St. George to Father Christmas, most critics praise Lewis's inventive retelling of Christian stories. In "C. S. Lewis and the Tradition of Visionary Romance," John D. Haigh regards Lewis as an author of classic romances rather than a novelist proper. According to Haigh, "the limitations of story do not preclude memorable moments in which the visionary romance succeeds in illuminating our inner being and its divine context. At these moments the romance enters regions of experience which are normally closed to the mundane patterns of the realistic novel." Lewis's contributions to the world of mythical and fantasy literature and his extensive writings on Christian theology make him a respected and controversial author in contemporary literary circles.

PRINCIPAL WORKS

Spirits in Bondage: A Cycle of Lyrics [as Clive Hamilton] (poetry) 1919

Dymer [as Clive Hamilton] (poetry) 1926

The Pilgrim's Regress: An Allegorical Apology for Christianity, Reason and Romanticism (novel) 1933

The Allegory of Love: A Study in Medieval Tradition (criticism) 1936

Out of the Silent Planet (novel) 1938

Rehabilitations and Other Essays (essays) 1939

The Problem of Pain (nonfiction) 1940
The Screwtape Letters [revised edition published as *Screwtape Proposes a Toast and Other Pieces,* 1965] (novel) 1942
Broadcast Talks: Right and Wrong; A Clue to the Meaning of the Universe and What Christians Believe [republished as *The Case for Christianity,* 1943] (broadcasts) 1942
A Preface to "Paradise Lost" (criticism) 1942
Christian Behaviour: A Further Series of Broadcast Talks (broadcasts) 1943
Perelandra (novel) 1943
The Abolition of Man; or, Reflections on Education with Special Reference to the Teaching of English in Upper Forms of Schools (nonfiction) 1943
Beyond Personality: The Christian Idea of God (essays) 1944
That Hideous Strength: A Modern Fairy-Tale for Grownups (novel) 1945
The Great Divorce: A Dream (novel) 1945
Miracles: A Preliminary Study (nonfiction) 1947
Transpositions [republished as *The Weight of Glory*] (essays) 1949
The Lion, The Witch and the Wardrobe (juvenilia) 1950
Prince Caspian: The Return to Narnia (juvenilia) 1951
The Voyage of the "Dawn Treader" (juvenilia) 1952
Mere Christianity (nonfiction) 1952
The Silver Chair (juvenilia) 1953
The Horse and His Boy (juvenilia) 1954
English Literature in the Sixteenth Century, Excluding Drama (criticism) 1954
The Magician's Nephew (juvenilia) 1955
Surprised by Joy: The Shape of My Early Life (autobiography) 1955
The Last Battle (juvenilia) 1956
Till We Have Faces: A Myth Retold (novel) 1956
Reflections on the Psalms (nonfiction) 1958
Studies in Words (criticism) 1960
The Four Loves (nonfiction) 1960
The World's Last Night and Other Essays (essays) 1960
A Grief Observed [as N. W. Clerk] (autobiography) 1961
An Experiment in Criticism (criticism) 1961
They Asked for Paper: Papers and Addresses (criticism) 1962
The Discarded Image: An Introduction to Medieval and Renaissance Literature (criticism) 1964
Letters to Malcolm: Chiefly on Prayer (correspondence) 1964
Poems (poetry) 1964
Studies in Medieval and Renaissance Literature (criticism) 1966
Of Other Worlds: Essays and Stories (essays and short stories) 1966
Spenser's Image of Life (criticism) 1967
Christian Reflections (essays) 1967
A Mind Awake: An Anthology of C. S. Lewis (essays) 1968
Narrative Poems (poetry) 1969
Selected Literary Essays (essays and criticism) 1969
God in the Dock: Essays on Theology and Ethics [published in England as *Undeceptions: Essays on Theology and Ethics,* 1971; republished as *First and Second Things,* 1985] (essays) 1970
Fernseed and Elephants and Other Essays on Christianity (essays) 1975
The Dark Tower and Other Stories (short stories) 1977
The Joyful Christian: 127 Readings from C. S. Lewis (essays) 1977
Boxen: The Imaginary World of the Young (sketches) 1985
Present Concerns (essays) 1986
The Seeing Eye and Other Selected Essays from Christian Reflections (essays) 1986
All My Road Before Me: The Diary of C. S. Lewis, 1922-1927 (diary) 1991

CRITICISM

William G. Johnson and Marcia K. Houtman (essay date Spring 1986)

SOURCE: "Platonic Shadows in C. S. Lewis' Narnia *Chronicles,*" in *Modern Fiction Studies,* Vol. 32, No. 1, Spring, 1986, pp. 75-87.

[*In the following essay, Johnson and Houtman examine references to the philosophical investigations of Plato in Lewis's* Chronicles of Narnia. *According to the critics, Lewis frequently incorporates Platonic concepts found in* The Republic, *in particular the famous Allegory of the Cave.*]

As a literary critic, science fiction writer, Christian apologist, and creator of the ***Chronicles of Narnia,*** in the last several decades C. S. Lewis has attained a reputation and following enviable in size and amazing in diversity. In many ways the quiet Oxbridge professor's achievements have assumed an air of authority, an aura of credibility, difficult to explain; Lewis, after all, is not an "apologist" in the same sense as Merton, nor a critic with a comprehensive system such as McLuhan. He is not, likewise, a fiction writer whose "science" background even begins to parallel that of Asimov, whose characterizations approach those of Faulkner, whose ethical dilemmas rival Greene's, and whose epic sweep is as broad as Tolkien's.

What Lewis' fiction has, however, and what captures his readers, is a sense of "story"—not just "story" as plot, but "story" as myth, as archetype, as dreams recalled. And what Lewis succeeds in doing so well is creating in the fiction a reality that draws readers into worlds seemingly more real than those in which the readers live. Behind Lewis' process and method of the "real" fiction set in opposition to the "fictionalized" world of reality is a long tradition of Platonized Christianity with which Lewis was very familiar and from which he selected elements to incorporate into his personal beliefs.

In his scholarly works Lewis makes quite clear his knowledge of, and familiarity with, Plato's works. Indeed, it is Lewis the critic of Medieval and Renaissance literature who was prominent in affirming the "Platonic" nature of those two literary-historical periods. His ***Allegory of Love, The Discarded Image, English Literature in the Sixteenth Century, A Preface to "Paradise Lost,"*** and ***Spenser's Images of Life*** make clear how extensively Plato and the Neo-Platonists influenced the Christian humanist writers of those respective literary periods. In Lewis' own fiction some elements of the Christian Platonism are easily identifiable, whereas others are so intermingled with Lewis' own theology that they are almost overlooked or, at least, hardly recognizable as being Greek in origin. At times Lewis himself not only points the way to such sources but even allows characters to point them out.

Such is the case with Lewis' character Digory Kirke, the professor who appears in five of the seven Narnia ***Chronicles.*** Variously depicted as the one "very wise grown-up" to whom the adventurous children can entrust their story of Narnia, as a young boy in ***The Magician's Nephew*** and as a rejuvenated, handsome Lord Digory in ***The Last Battle,*** Digory Kirke is also presented as being human enough to have all the foibles and failings of a middle-aged professorial bachelor. In ***The Magician's Nephew,*** for example, it is a younger Digory, with his uncontrolled curiosity, who wanders too far and loses the path back to earth; in the same book it is Digory who falls under the spell of Jadis, the White Witch, whom he finds the most beautiful woman he ever saw—refusing to recognize her terrible power and evil intent (which even the children can see). Yet it is an older Digory, motivated so often by the love of his sick mother, who is both transformed into a handsome young lord in ***The Last Battle*** and proffers his "explanation" for the apocalypse just witnessed in Narnia: "It's all in Plato, all in Plato: bless me, what *do* they teach them at these schools!"

But the professorial Digory goes too far in such a hasty glossing as this. Certainly some of what has just occurred in ***The Last Battle*** is "in Plato" and can be explained by Platonic concepts; but just as certainly much of what the earth travelers have just seen has little or no base in the Greek philosophies. Lewis' own Platonism is highly selective and highly diffused, and although he was quite familiar with the corpus of Plato's writings, the application of Plato's ideas is through Lewis' Platonized Christianity (more so than through any Christianized Platonism).

If put to the test one might find Platonic "sources" in a variety of Lewis' writings. Most obvious would be the use of the *Republic,* with its famous Allegory of the Cave, its exposition of the doctrine of Forms, and its ur-Freudian doctrine of dreams as submerged wishes. The *Phaedo* is also evident, particularly because of its discussions of immortality and the unchanging reality behind the mutable Forms; the *Timaeus* also develops the nature of Forms and Ideas, but does so with a developed myth or story about a scheme of creation in which the world is described as a work of art crafted by a beneficent creator. In the *Timaeus* Plato treats the subject of sense perceptions, and in the *Symposium* one finds the famous presentation of the ascendancy of love, a topic of great significance in Lewis' work but which is more closely connected to the Neo-Platonists—particularly Ficino and Pico—than to Plato. One might also point to the theodicy, or principles of natural religion, of Plato's *Laws,* as well as to the refutation of dogmatic atheism contained in that work, as background for Lewis' various universes (notably in ***Perelandra***). Finally, and especially as they prepare readers for Lewis' depictions and descriptions of *Sehnsucht,* both the *Meno* and the *Phaedrus* discuss more than passingly Plato's theory of recollection.

Yet one can read Lewis' fiction without the background in Plato, although, like the children, one must be wary of Digory's offhanded remark—wary because it is spoken with authority by a respected professor and therefore can too readily be assumed to be "true." What Digory blithely refers to as "Plato" might much more accurately be described as "Plato as his doctrines are filtered through St. Paul, Augustine, the Florentine Neo-Platonists, and the Christian Humanists." Furthermore, considering that the observation about Plato is Digory's attempt to explain how the "New Narnia" is the "real thing" and that what had previously been thought to be Narnia was actually only "a shadow or a copy of the real Narnia, which has always been here and always will be here" (***The Last Battle***), a much more evident "source" (as well as explanation) is Paul's famous statement in I Corinthians that "when that which is perfect is come, then that which is in part shall be done away."

For another reason the reader must also be wary of Digory's source reference: it is too easy to forget that no one "source," even Plato, could possibly account for the artistic, theoretical, cosmological, and theological mélange Lewis presents within the seven books depicting Narnia's genesis, history, and destruction. As John D. Cox suggests, "a beginning list of sources for [even] *The Last Battle* would include the biblical Apocalypse, Malory's *Morte D'Arthur,* Wagner's *Ring,* the *Enneads* of Plotinus, George MacDonald's sermons, ancient Roman religion, and probably Aesop's *Fables*." Although the temptation is strong to add vast compilations of other "sources" used in depicting Narnia—Homer, Virgil, Ovid, Augustine, Dante, Chaucer, Medieval bestiaries, Spenser, Milton, Bunyan, Chesterton, Carroll, Potter, Milne, Tolkien, Williams, to name a few—the fact remains that Lewis was an enormously well-read writer who freely adapted, adopted, and altered to suit his purposes. In most cases it is only of passing interest to note a "source"—as when Glimfeather in *The Silver Chair* flies off to the Parliament of Owls (an amusing reference to Chaucer's *Parliament of Fowls*). What really matters "is the use made of these hints, ideas and inspiration . . . now arranged in a new pattern."

Nonetheless, Plato does play a strong role in Narnia—sometimes directly, sometimes not. Lewis himself never quibbled about his admiration for this philosopher. In ***Miracles*** he refers to Aristotle and Plato being at "the peak" of Greek philosophy, and in the same work refers later to "the old, richly imaginative thought which still survives in Plato." Earlier he had written in his diary entry for 8 February 1927 about Plato's "delightful civilized imagination," and at one time Lewis declared that he loved Plato before he even knew Augustine (***God in the Dock***). As Robert Houston Smith indicates, there was within Lewis "a deep-rooted affinity for Platonism" that enabled him to enfold "Platonism into his Christianity, not simply as an intellectual system but as a satisfying window upon reality."

Although Lewis' fiction is liberally sprinkled with Platonic elements, it is primarily in the ***Chronicles,*** and specifically in ***The Last Battle,*** that Plato's influence is most clearly observed in the controlling images and in the philosophy with which the work is imbued. In this work Lewis pictures the differences between the New Narnia and the Narnia of the previous six ***Chronicles;*** he likewise differentiates between the "Shadowlands" and the Real World (Earth and the old Narnia for the former, the New Narnia for the latter), noting that the one is like dreaming in the night and the other like waking to the morning.

It is also in the final chapters of ***The Last Battle*** that several of the Narnian characters, along with Jill and Eustace, pass through the Stable Door from a dark and crumbling Narnia into a bright world where they are met by their old friends, the Pevensies. And it is at this point that Digory explains to young Peter and the others that the Narnia they had known was "only a shadow or a copy of the Real Thing, as different as waking life is from a dream." And all of it, he adds, is in Plato.

The most obvious place in Plato to which Digory might be referring is Book Seven of the *Republic* with its famous Allegory of the Cave. Or, as Walter Hooper suggests, one might look as well to the *Phaedo,* in which Plato discusses immortality and the unchanging reality behind the changing Forms. As it is, there are so many scattered hints, clues, and references it hardly pays to look to one Platonic work at all. It takes little literary or philosophical acumen to discern in the eschatological upheaval that destroys the Old Narnia and in the resulting movement into the unchanging Real Narnia Lewis' adaptation both of the Platonic view of the real world of Forms behind the instantial world of shadows and the Christian concept of the New Jerusalem replacing the temporary, insubstantial, mutable Old Earth.

But long before the dissolution of the Old Narnia and the Old Order, Lewis raises Platonic questions about the nature of reality; he fills the pages of ***The Last Battle*** with examples of the mistaken identification of the "shadows," or insubstantial, for the Real. In the last days of Narnia the distortions become even greater than they were earlier. For example, Puzzle, the gentle but simple donkey, succumbs to the wishes of the clever monkey, Shift, dons the lionskin, and presents himself as Aslan. Ludicrous as the imitation is, there are those who actually confuse Puzzle with Aslan; many of the dwarfs, for example, are led to fatal misconceptions because of their insisting on the reality of what is only a shadow.

And "shadow" is precisely the association Lewis creates for Tash, the bloodthirsty god of the Calormenes in ***The Last Battle.*** A cruel deity appeased by blood sacrifice, Tash is presented as the antithesis of Aslan's good qualities. His arrival in Narnia is one of the most terrifying in all the ***Chronicles:***

> In the shadow of the trees on the far side of the clearing something was moving. It was gliding very slowly Northward. At first glance you might have mistaken it for smoke, for it was grey and you could see things through it. But the deathly smell was not the smell of smoke. Also, this thing kept its shape instead of billowing and curling as smoke would have done. It was roughly the shape of a man but it had the head of a bird; some bird of prey with a cruel, curved beak. It had four arms which it held high above its head, stretching them out Northward as if it wanted to snatch all Narnia in its grip; and its fingers—all twenty of them—were curved like its beak and had long, pointed, bird-like claws instead of nails. It floated on the grass instead of walking, and the grass seemed to wither beneath it.

Such shadows and shadowy figures are not uncommon the closer one gets to the last days of the Old Narnia; they remind one of the shadows that Plato's Cave prisoners mistake for reality. In Plato, as in Lewis, one cannot be sure about the shadows—until the time when one leaves the cave and literally sees the light. A prisoner released from the cave, Plato suggests, would be blinded by the light and would, for a time, see shadows more clearly than real things. He would distrust these unfamiliar "real" things and cling to his old belief in "reality," only gradually replacing the old view with a new. Only after this kind of adjustment would the prisoner come to understand that even the greatest honors in his old world would be nothing compared to life even as a slave in the new. Any attempts to convince those still in the Cave of their error would be met with resentment, refusal, and rejection.

This is precisely the situation in ***The Silver Chair*** where the Queen of the Underland (a projection of Spenser's Lucifera) has imprisoned and enchanted Prince Rilian. Paul Ford interprets Rilian's movements as a progress of the soul, which "in its depths knows that its present bodily existence is a fall from a sunny overworld of truth into a shadowy underworld of shifting appearances. This fall, however, is simultaneously a fall in consciousness. The soul forgets its immortal identity." The witch convinces Rilian and the others sent to his rescue that the Overworld and Aslan exist only in their minds and only as a "copy" of her Underland and its inhabitants. After asking the Prince to explain what the sun is (Plato's ultimate example of the bright light of reality), the Queen turns to her own purposes his attempt to define the sun by comparing it to the overhead lamp:

> When you try to think out clearly what this *sun* must be, you cannot tell me. You can only tell me it is like the lamp. Your *sun* is a dream; and there is nothing in that dream that was not copied from the lamp. The lamp is the real thing; the *sun* is but a tale, a children's story.

Even Aslan is, she tells them, only a copy, an imaginary "bigger and better cat." The Queen "is the archetypical reductionist, trying to convince the cave-dwellers that the shadows of their immediate experience are all there is." She only fails because the very practical Puddleglum dis-spells her evil effects by stamping out the fire creating the Underland illusions (exactly as the fire in Plato's allegory casts the shadows on the Cave wall).

The famous Cave is itself cleverly presented in ***The Last Battle,*** although the falsehood of the shadow world is more pronounced because of the Ape's manipulation of light and image. One recalls that in Plato the light is behind the insubstantially bound prisoners, whereas the shadows are projected on the wall before them. The *son et lumière* presented to Tirian, last King of Narnia, relies on a distortion of a different sort:

> Far away there appeared a red light. Then it disappeared for a moment and came back again, bigger and stronger. Then he could see dark shapes going to and fro on this side of the light and carrying bundles and throwing them down. He knew now what he was looking at. It was a bonfire, newly lit, and people were throwing bundles of brushwood on it. Presently it blazed up and Tirian could see that it was on the very top of the hill. He could see quite clearly the stable behind it, all lit up in the red glow, and a great crowd of Beasts and Men between the fire and himself.

Here, in the "false Narnia," even the light deceives; the good Tirian "could not make out very clearly" what the objects were and "couldn't be sure that what he saw was not the real Aslan. . . . How could one be sure?"

Sureness never comes in the shadow world although eventually the real light is shown to everyone. It then becomes a matter of accepting the "real" light or rejecting it as false. Lewis believes that even the cave dwellers have some longings, dreams, intimations of immortality for a world beyond the shadows. This longing (a form of Plato's doctrine of the soul's longing for the real Forms behind the instantial shapes of this world) Lewis calls *Sehnsucht.* An important, even key, element of Lewis' thought, *Sehnsucht* describes "the desire for God and Heaven [which Lewis] thought was part of every person. . . . *Sehnsucht,* for Lewis, can only be filled by God, and is similar to the desire described by Blaise Pascal as a cross-shaped hole in the heart of man." In his ***English Literature in the Sixteenth Century*** Lewis staunchly defends *Sehnsucht* in the works of one of his heroes and models, Edmund Spenser, noting that *Sehnsucht* would "logically appear as among the sanest and most fruitful experiences we have" because the object of the longing "really exists and really draws us to itself."

Yet Lewis is only partially Platonic in his repeated references to *Sehnsucht.* Taken in their full expression, the longings Plato describes (particularly in the *Phaedo*) are part of his argument for immortality of the soul, a belief already affirmed in Greece by Pythagorean and Orphic mystics. Still, Plato was the "first great prose writer to enforce it by philosophical arguments, or impress it upon the imagination by vivid eschatological myths. . . . Plato's name was the symbol and rallying point of the entire religious and philosophic opposition to the dogmatic materialism of the Epicureans and of the positive wing of the Peripatetics." But these same "proofs of immortality" in the *Phaedo* are inextricably interconnected with, and depend on the logical consequences of, the theory of Ideal Forms.

In the first part of the *Phaedo* two proofs are given for immortality, the first being that all processes or changes are transitions between contraries. If life changes into death, death must therefore change into life. The soul must exist after death because it must pass into life. Yet the second argument, which Lewis develops only in part and which is significant to his view of *Sehnsucht,* is the theory of recollection and reminiscence (also discussed in the *Meno* and *Phaedo*). This theory not only implies a transcendent world of reality (the Forms) but the possibility of preexistence, or of a nonincarnate soul that has experiences in a prior existence and which prior experiences are then recollected at various times, causing the soul in this world to long for the perfect world it once knew.

Lewis never seems to have been concerned that what he develops in his discussions of *Sehnsucht* was only half a Platonic theory. The soul's longing is important for Lewis; it is this longing that ultimately gets the Narnia "pilgrims" to the Real Narnia, and it is this longing that is described by Jewel the Unicorn (in ***The Last Battle***) when exclaiming about the real Narnia:

> I have come home at last! This is my real country! I belong here. This is the land I have been looking for all my life, though I never knew it till now. The reason why we loved the old Narnia is that it sometimes looked a little like this.

In one sense Lewis is playing with the idea of one world "looking a little" like the real world, for in each of the reminiscences "recollected" is the germ of the whole image. As with Blake's grain of sand, in which one can see a world and thus hold eternity in one's hand, and as with Dame Julian's image of the universe seen as a hazelnut in her own hands, so Lewis depicts small things containing larger things inside. Digory explains to the assembly that in the New Narnia "its inside is bigger than its outside," and Lucy adds the metaphysical paradox that "in our world too, a Stable once had something inside it that was bigger than our whole world."

Such is the longing Lewis himself reveals in ***Mere Christianity:***

> Most people, if they had really learned to look into their own hearts, would know that they do want, and want acutely, something that cannot be had in this world. There are all sorts of things in this world that offer to give it to you, but they never quite keep their promise. The longings which arise in us when we first fall in love, or first think of some foreign country, or first take up some subject that excites us, are longings which no marriage, no travel, no learning can really satisfy. . . . I must keep alive in myself the desire for my true country, which I shall not find till after death. . . . I must make it the main object of life to press on to that other country and to help others do the same.

In other words, what is seen in this life as some kind of ultimate fulfillment turns out, like Don Quixote's windmills, to be an insubstantial shadow, a False Florimell, a mere suggestion of that for which a person is actually longing.

What Lewis does not touch on, at least in Platonic terms, is the preexistence of the souls, which state draws those in the shadow world of this life to return to their "true country." For Lewis the explanation for the longing and for the reminiscences is a different one, one that marks a major distinction between Plato's distant, removed Demiurge and Lewis' Hebraic-Christian depiction of an involved God. In Plato the Demiurge created the Forms as well as the insubstantial worlds; the preexistent souls of people recall the bright shapes of the Forms and long for a return to the world beyond this one. The Demiurge has little or nothing to do with the real or the unreal worlds after their creation. For Lewis, however, as for all orthodox Christians, God is intimately involved with the creation, and the "intimations of immortality" are both recurring gifts and an ongoing means (as with Marvell's drop of dew) to draw the created world to a heavenly "home." As Lewis notes when writing about himself: "If I find in myself a desire which no experience in this world can satisfy, the most probable explanation is that I was made for another world. . . . Probably earthly pleasures were never meant to satisfy it, but only to arouse it, to suggest the real thing."

Not everyone, as Lewis suggests in various places, wants the gifts, and not everyone is lured from the instantial world of shadows to the substantive reality of true Forms (such as those represented by the Real Narnia). The most poignant depiction of this is in ***The Great Divorce,*** where the "Bright Spirit" Reginald tries to convince his shadowy sister Pam that she must make some vital changes in her viewpoint if she hopes to remain in heaven and have the chance to see her beloved son Michael. Reginald explains gently to Pam that Michael

> won't be able to see or hear you as you are at present [an insubstantial dweller in the shadowlands]. You'd be totally invisible to Michael. But we'll soon build you up. . . . As soon as it's possible for him to see you, of course he will. You need to be thickened up a bit. . . . But the whole thickening treatment consists in learning to want God for His own sake.

This "thickening treatment" is the result of moving out of the cavelike world of shadows into the wider, deeper world of reality, Narnia, Heaven; it is, as it were, the putting on of reality—a process that hurts "at first, until your feet are hardened. Reality is harsh to the feet of shadow," as the omnibus travelers' in ***The Great Divorce*** discover when "two of the ghosts screamed and ran for the bus. The rest . . . huddled closer to one another."

The reaction of the ghosts to the solid people is echoed in the reaction of the disloyal renegade dwarfs in ***The Last Battle.*** Like the prisoners in Plato's Cave who refuse to respond to the knowledge of another world outside the Cave, the shadow-blinded dwarfs huddle together "in a little circle facing one another" immediately before the same Stable Door that has just allowed Tirian, the children, and the loyal Narnians to move into a beautiful, dazzlingly bright land. The dwarfs, however, are blind to their surroundings despite the futile campaign of Tirian and the others to convince them that a brave and bright new world can open for them also. As the group approaches the dwarfs, the harsh voice of a dwarf reprimands them:

> "Look out!" said one of [the dwarfs] in a surly voice. "Mind where you're going. Don't walk into our face!"
>
> "All right!" said Eustace indignantly. "We're not blind. We've got eyes in our heads."
>
> "They must be darn good ones if you can see in here," said the same Dwarf whose name was Diggle.
>
> "In where?" asked Edmund.
>
> "Why you bone-head, in *here* of course," said Diggle. "In this pitch-black, poky, smelly little hole of a stable."
>
> "Are you blind?" said Tirian.
>
> "Ain't we all blind in the dark!" said Diggle.
>
> "But it isn't dark, you poor stupid Dwarfs," said Lucy. "Can't you see? Look up! Look round! Can't you see *me*?"
>
> "How in the name of all Humbug can I see what ain't there? And how can I see you any more than you can see me in this pitch darkness?"

No matter what the children and the true Narnians do, the dwarfs will not be convinced. To the "blind" dwarfs, the violets Lucy offers are only "filthy stable litter," and the feast Aslan lays before them consists only of things one would normally expect to find in a "smelly little hole of a stable." Tirian, in frustration, cries, "There is no black hole, save in your own fancy, fool!" and picking Diggle up "swung him right out of the circle of Dwarfs." But Diggle only rubs his nose, howls, and runs back to his place in the tight little circle.

Even the appearance of Aslan, depicted as "huge and real," has no effect on the dwarfs. Lucy pleads with him to help them, but he explains that there is only so much he can do:

> They will not let us help them. They have chosen cunning instead of belief. Their prison is only in their own minds, yet they are in that prison; and so afraid of being taken in that they can not be taken out. But come, children. I have other work to do.

Harsh as it might seem to contemporary readers, Aslan leaves the dwarfs and moves on. All efforts have been made to bring them into the new, Real Narnia—but the dwarfs themselves have chosen the world of shadow. They have, as with Milton's Satan, "made a hell of heaven" in which the mind is its own place. Aslan's response to move on is precisely that of Plutarch's Ulysses to the unrepentant Gryllus, of Spenser's Guyon when he commands, "Let Grill be Grill, and have his hoggish mind," and of Dante's Virgil when he describes the "cieca vita" (blind lives) of the Neutrals damned to a shadowy limbo outside the gates of heaven as well as outside the gates of hell—"non ragioniam di lor, ma guarda e passa" (let us not talk further of them; look and pass on).

Whereas the blindness of the dwarfs is metaphoric, Plato treats "sight" as literal and figurative; and in the *Republic* he indicates an area in which sight is distinguished from the other senses. In order that sight may occur not only must there be an object to see and an eye capable of seeing, but there must also exist light playing on the object. In the best cases this light will be that of the sun. For Plato, the light and the sun become major images. Just as the eye sees most clearly when its object is bathed in sunlight, so "the mind apprehends most clearly when it views its object in the light of the Idea of good. It is this that 'gives to objects of knowledge their truth, and to him who knows them his power of knowing.'"

Translated into traditional literary imagery, light brings enlightenment; transformed into traditional Christian imagery, the light of the "Son" enlightens with eternal life. Life in the shadowy Cave gives way to a world so big it cannot be comprehended, and so wonderful it cannot be described. In ***Till We Have Faces*** Lewis has Psyche explain to Orual that in some of the Greek masters "death opens a door out of a little dark room (that's all the life we have known before it) into a great, real place where the true sun shines. . . ." King Tirian's password—"The light is dawning, the lie broken"—succinctly describes both cause and effect and in one word, "lie," represents the shadow world for what it is. The ascent "farther up and farther in," a phrase repeated numerous times (particularly in ***The Last Battle,*** where this is precisely the direction the travelers take), reminds us again of the mystical ascent into the great Rose of the *Paradiso,* where all is suffused with an ever-increasing brightness of light. It is, as Lucy notes, a "world within world, Narnia within Narnia," literally ad infinitum, and it is the same movement into the real light and the real world of Forms Plato's prisoners must make if they ever leave the dark Cave.

It is with light that Lewis culminates both ***The Great Divorce*** and ***The Last Battle*** in both of which the process of moving from the instantial and insubstantial world to the solid and real world of Heaven/Narnia is completed with the drawing of a new day. In the former the light comes "like solid blocks," bringing with it a chorus of woods, men, and angels all singing together "It comes! It comes! . . . Sleepers awake!" The narrator, realizing that he has not yet completed his lessons in preparation for a new life in the new world, is compelled by the first rays of the sun shooting over the horizon to bury his head into the folds of his Teacher's robes and scream, "The morning! The morning! I am caught by the morning and I am a ghost."

But in ***The Last Battle,*** the reader observes characters who have completed their lessons and are ready to understand fully that they have reached heaven, the place of ultimate reality. As the light before them grows stronger, Aslan himself comes to greet the group. Though they are overwhelmed with the joy of their new discoveries and their reunion with Aslan, their knowledge is not quite complete. However, Aslan's words give them all the reassurance they will ever need:

> "You do not yet look so happy as I mean you to be."
>
> Lucy said, "We're so afraid of being sent away, Aslan. And you have sent us back into our own world so often."
>
> "No fear of that," said Aslan. "Have you not guessed?" Their hearts leaped and a wild hope rose within them.
>
> "There *was* a real railway accident," said Aslan softly. "Your father and mother and all of you are—as you used to call it in the Shadow-Lands—dead. The term is over: the holidays have begun. The dream is ended: this is the morning."

Recollections of other worlds, movements from shadowy worlds to brightly illuminated ones, the dangers of sense perceptions in a world of changing shapes and forms, the reality of an immutable world beyond this one and of an immortal life that replaces this instantial and insubstantial present one (which actually exists only as a dream): these are themes to which Lewis repeatedly returns. His fictionalized worlds and his nonfiction works reveal his treating these topoi as serious, fundamental ones. And all of these are treated as well in the various dialogues of Plato. Although the analogies to the Cave story are fairly explicit, it is impossible to ascertain how much else Lewis takes directly from Plato, how much is "second hand" through the Church Fathers, Neo-Platonists, and Renaissance Christian Humanists, and how much is merely an amalgam developed by Lewis as part of his own creative processes. As much an overstatement as Digory's words are, the fact remains that much of what one finds in Lewis' fiction *is* in Plato— though certainly not "all." It is sufficient to note that the Platonic elements are there throughout Lewis' works, and for those readers who recognize them, there is added a dimension to the readings that both broadens and deepens the literary experience.

Sally A. Bartlett (essay date Fall 1989)

SOURCE: "Humanistic Psychology in C. S. Lewis's *Till We Have Faces:* A Feminist Critique," in *Studies in the Literary Imagination,* Vol. XXII, No. 2, Fall, 1989, pp. 185-98.

[In the following essay, Bartlett provides a feminist reading of Till We Have Faces *from the theoretical perspective of humanistic psychology. According to Bartlett, feminists and humanistic psychologists would object to Lewis's presentation of "self-effacing women" who submit to male control.]*

C. S. Lewis writes in his concluding note in ***Till We Have Faces,*** "The central alteration in my own version [of the Psyche myth] consists in making Psyche's palace [the palace given her by the god Amor] invisible to normal eyes. . . . This change, of course, brings with it a more ambivalent motive and a different character for my heroine [one of Psyche's sisters] and finally modifies the whole quality of the tale." I believe Lewis is correct in his analysis of this change, for, as I shall demonstrate, the protagonist's inability to see the palace mirrors her inability to see and understand her own inner conflicts.

Yet, while I feel Lewis has masterfully illustrated Orual's psychological dilemma, the vision of reality I see presented in this text appears confused, for Lewis asserts an Archetypal Christian ontology and then proceeds to impose that ontology on his mimetically constructed characters in an attempt to fuse the moral requirements of his religious belief system with what he intuitively perceives and accurately presents as the psychological motivations of human behavior. While Lewis's moral recommendations seem to work for the characters in his text, these ideals may or may not work so well for the book's readers, whose reality does not necessarily validate such recommendations. Bernard Paris, in *Character and Conflict in Jane Austen's Novels,* speaks of a clash between the structural requirements of a novel and the demand for accuracy in mimetic representation. ***Till We Have Faces*** presents just such a difficulty. If Lewis's characters lived in our world rather than in their own world, the resolutions they find for their emotional and moral dilemmas would not work.

Paris proposes the application of the concepts of humanistic psychology for describing the nature of mimetic characterization and for explaining this conflict between verisimilitude and the formal structure of a book. This article will use the terminology of psychologists Abraham Maslow and Karen Horney in discussing the emotional development of Lewis's extremely complex protagonist Orual as well as in describing and accounting for the conflict between her accurate portrayal and Lewis's avowed Christianized vision of reality as manifested in the archetypal structure of the novel. While Lewis may not have been aware of these psychologists' writings, he was sufficiently acute in his perception of human nature to demonstrate accurately (though perhaps unwittingly) much of their theory in his mimetic characterizations.

Maslow has said that what is commonly called Humanistic Psychology is more accurately named "Third Force Psychology," for it is a "viable third alternative to objective, behavioristic . . . psychology and to orthodox Freudianism." According to Maslow, a hierarchy of five basic types of needs exists for human beings. These (in order from lowest to highest) are the physiological needs, the safety needs, the love and belonging needs, the esteem needs, and the need for self-actualization. The physiological needs are met through food, shelter, and clothing; the safety needs require security, stability, and freedom from fear; the love and belonging needs require affectionate interpersonal relationships; the esteem needs require self-respect and the respect of others; and self-actualization is the ongoing development of one's unique personhood, so as to become all that one can be.

While Maslow's concept of self-actualization does not point ultimately to a transcendent God, Maslow does speak of transcendence when describing moments of truest self-actualization or "peak-experiences." Thus his secular psychology is compatible with what William J. Bouwsma has called "Christian adulthood." In contrast to the Greek view of a gender-specific ideal of rational "manhood," Bouwsma identifies the "normative Christian" concept of a non-gender-specific "adulthood," using a term suggestive of process from its Latin root *adolescere,* "to grow up." He sees the Christian life "as indefinite growth, itself the product of a full engagement with temporal experience involving the whole personality." We can see Lewis drawing on this normative Christian concept of adulthood in ***The Great Divorce,*** where the bright and solid people of heaven spend eternity moving closer to God, continually growing in their awareness of "him" and of their true natures. In this story, Lewis demonstrates an understanding of the need for continuous growth in the human personality. One is never fully grown in Lewis's or in Maslow's vision of the human condition.

In Lewis's retelling of the Psyche myth, Orual, Psyche's older half-sister, feels the effect of deprivation at the level of love and belonging on Maslow's hierarchy. Though she is a princess in the barbaric state of Glome, it seems that almost everyone rejects her because she is ugly. She remembers her father's words to her at the coming of her tutor, the Fox, in this way:

> "Now, Greekling," said my father to this man, "I trust to beget a prince one of these days and I have a mind to see him brought up in all the wisdom of your people. Meanwhile practice on *them.*" (He pointed at us children.) "If a man can teach a girl, he can teach anything." Then, just before he sent us away, he said, "Especially the elder. See if you can make her wise; it's about all she'll ever be good for." I didn't understand that, but I knew it was like things I had heard people say to me ever since I could remember.

Orual's account of her father's words indicates two reasons for his rejection of her: (1) she is a woman and (2) she is ugly. Bernard Paris, in *A Psychological Approach to Fiction,* describes the results of such rejection by attributing to the individual who is not adequately fulfilled in his lower needs a consequential fixation at an earlier stage of development. In Orual's case, because she does not feel loved and accepted by others, she spends her life searching for the affection and approval she seldom receives.

Karen Horney, in *Neurosis and Human Growth,* provides the terminology for describing Orual's method of coping with her loneliness when she speaks of "neurotic solutions." Paris explains the use of such solutions by telling us that a person abandons the real self as a means of self-preservation. His statement implies that individuals try to actualize not what they really are but what they think they should be. Horney calls this new and fictitious image of the self an idealized image, and accounts for it as the individual's attempt to counteract self-hate. But because inner conflicts produce contradictory values in the idealized self, this self is impossible to actualize; so self-hate remains to torment its victim. The "despised self" is Paris's term for what Horney describes as this equally imaginary hated self. Orual's despised self is an ugly woman not worth loving. As this essay will illustrate, in an effort to banish her self-hate, Orual claims the beautiful Psyche as her own, and thus unconsciously unites Psyche's beauty with herself, consequently becoming, in her mind, lovable. Also we shall see that because Orual is ashamed of her womanhood, her idealized image demands that she be motherly toward Psyche and yet masculine at the same time.

The sacred story told by Psyche's priest at the end of the book reveals to Orual the true nature of her demands on Psyche:

> But now all the dreamlike feeling in me suddenly vanished. I was wide awake and I felt the blood rush into my face. He was telling it wrong—hideously and stupidly wrong. First of all, he made it that both Psyche's sisters had visited her in the secret palace of the god (to think of Redival going there!).

The priest continues to tell Orual that the sisters could see Psyche's palace and were jealous because "Her husband and her house were so much finer than theirs." Consequently, according to the priest, the sisters attempted to ruin Psyche by convincing her to light a lamp and view her husband, an act which he had forbidden her.

The retelling of her life's story from this perspective drives Orual to write her case against the gods, which constitutes Book One of ***Till We Have Faces.*** Horney would call this attack on the gods an "expansive solution," for the expansive personality, says Horney, identifies with an idealized self and is therefore very sensitive to criticism and failure. The Priest's story has threatened her self-deception, and she must prove his tale false in order to continue believing that she embodies her idealized self.

Horney also describes a solution which relies on self-effacing behaviors rather than on expansive ones. According to Horney, self-effacing individuals feel no conscious superiority and unwittingly exaggerate whatever helplessness and suffering they experience. They long for "help, protection, and surrendering love." Their method of externalizing self-hate is to believe that others are accusing and despising them. Thus, they deny their expansive feelings, which actually remain repressed by the dominant solution. They become what Horney calls their "subdued" selves, hoping to appease others and therefore attract love. Yet, because no amount of love from others will convince self-effacing people that they are lovable, they make unjust claims on these others as the proof of affection. Self-effacing individuals feel their suffering is so exceptional that they are entitled to the excessive devotion they demand. Instead of expressing rage (as the expansive-types would do) when denied these demands, they absorb their rage and make others feel guilty as a means of revenge. Often, self-effacers become morbidly dependent on others, trying, through loving, to "develop to the full the loving attributes" of their idealized selves.

Orual begins her self-alienation with all of these self-effacing characteristics, when, at Psyche's birth, she takes over the child's care, relieving the nurse of her duties:

> Batta was only too pleased to have her work done for her and the king knew and cared nothing about it. The Fox said to me, "Don't wear yourself out, daughter, with too much toil, even if the child is as beautiful as a goddess." But I laughed in his face. I think I laughed more in those days than in all my life before. Toil? I lost more sleep looking on Psyche for joy of it than in any other way. And I laughed because she was always laughing. She laughed before the third month. She knew me for certain (though the Fox said not) before the second.

Orual's exceptional care of Psyche is a means of merging with Psyche's person, thus taking the child's beauty into herself. Her peculiar devotion to Psyche is also an attempt to make the girl totally dependent on Orual and thus eternally grateful as well. This particular devotion, Orual unconsciously feels, will satiate her insatiable need for love. In fact, when trying to persuade Psyche to leave her divine mate, Orual says, "if anyone is to care for you or counsel you or shield you . . . it can only be I."

Despite this self-effacing care for Psyche, Orual, like all individuals who rely on this particular neurotic solution, has latent aggressive tendencies which reveal themselves when Orual batters her sister Redival for hitting Psyche:

> Then I hardly knew myself again till I found that I was astride of Redival, she on the ground with her face a lather of blood, and my hands about her throat. It was the Fox who pulled me off and, in the end, some kind of peace was made between us.

Since childhood, Orual has been forced to compete with Redival, whose beauty, though not equal to Psyche's, is far greater than her own, and therefore Orual uses the excuse of retaliation on Psyche's behalf to vent her vindictive anger at Redival.

Expansive trends are evident in her feelings for Psyche, as when Orual threatens to kill Psyche if she will not light a lamp and view her husband. Orual's threat to kill Psyche is a desperate expansive attempt to force the girl to obey her wishes. In inflicting Psyche with guilt rather than physical wounds, Orual still attempts to dominate her. But, with these words, Psyche calls her sister's bluff:

> You are indeed teaching me about kinds of love I did not know. It is like looking into a deep pit. I am not sure I like your kind better than hatred. Oh, Orual—to take my love for you, because you know it goes down to my very roots, and cannot be diminished by any other newer love, and then to make it a tool, a weapon, a thing of policy and mastery, an instrument of torture—I begin to think I never knew you. Whatever comes after, something that was between us dies here.

While Psyche loves Orual, she does not appreciate this "loving" blackmail, and thus she loses trust in Orual's intentions. Because neither the expansive solution nor the self-effacing solution brings Psyche's complete surrender in action *and* emotional assent to her sister's unrealistic demands, Orual suffers great disappointment and terror. She says of Psyche, "I found I was becoming afraid of her." Psyche has removed herself emotionally at this point, and when the whole valley is destroyed by the wrath of the god, Psyche becomes an outcast in some unknown realm, farther from Orual than she was while she remained in the god's valley.

Horney describes a third neurotic solution which suppresses both the expansive and the self-effacing trends we have been examining in Orual's behavior. Horney calls one who uses such a solution the resigned personality. Such individuals give up struggling to achieve their goals and settle for less than they could achieve. They convince themselves that they do not want love, companionship, or success, believing that what they do not want, they cannot lack. Emotional detachment distances resigned types from others and thus protects them from the emotional pain often present in interpersonal relationships. In fact, they usually resent any type of influence, pressure, or coercion.

"It's a strange, yet somehow a quiet and steady thing," writes Orual, "to look round on earth and grass and the sky and say in one's heart to each, 'You are all my enemies now. None of you will ever do me good again. I see now only executioners.'" Because the other two neurotic solutions have failed her, Orual takes on the characteristics of the resigned personality as she distances herself emotionally from the universe. Because she expects only the worst from the world about her, she guards herself against its influence and asks nothing at all from her environment. As we shall see, because Psyche is further from her than ever, Orual grits her teeth and waits on the gods' supposedly vindictive judgment. She writes, "I looked on things about me with a new eye. Now that I'd proven for certain that the gods are and that they hated me, it seemed that I had nothing to do but wait for my punishment." Yet, as day after day passes with no punishment forthcoming, Orual must resign herself, not to punishment, but to life. She writes, "I began to see, at first unwillingly, that I might be doomed to live, and even to live an unchanged life, some while longer."

Realizing that she must go on living, Orual protects her emotions by locking away her memories of Psyche. Upon returning to Psyche's room, she restores everything as it had been in Psyche's childhood:

> I found some verses in Greek which seemed to be a hymn to the god of the Mountain. These I burned. I did not choose that any of that part of her should remain. . . . I wished all to be so ordered that if she could come back she would find all as it had been when she was still happy, and still mine. Then I locked the door and put a seal on it. And, as well as I could, I locked a door in my mind. Unless I were to go mad I must put away all thoughts of her save those that went back to her first, happy years.

Orual admits in this passage that her defense against madness is to lock in some secret recess of her mind the pain she feels because of Psyche's rejection of her. Later readers discover that because the Fox grieves openly for his loss of the adult Psyche, Orual finds little comfort in his company.

However, she still finds him useful to her in her efforts to bury her emotions, for by questioning him often upon matters of "the physical parts of philosophy, about the seminal fire, and how soul arises from blood," she hopes to learn "hard things . . . and to pile up knowledge." In this way, she can stifle her softer moods with hard facts. Her softer moods are identified with the mothering, womanly part of her idealized self-image and the discredited neurotic solution, self-effacement. Although she has wounded her arm in her attempt to coerce Psyche into lighting the lamp, she returns to the fencing lessons she had been taking from Bardia, the captain of the king's guards, even before her arm has healed. She tells her readers, "My aim was to build up more and more of that strength, hard and joyless, which had come to me when I heard the god's sentence; by learning, fighting, and labouring, to drive all the woman out of me." Womanhood has always been a burden to her because she has always been ugly. This is a chance to do away with her womanhood and thus the source of her pain. Her first defense emphasized a part of womanhood which requires no beauty. A child of necessity loves its mother, whether she is beautiful or not, for she is the source of nourishment. When this kind of behavior no longer brings her the devotion she craves, Orual must deny her craving in order to hide from herself her own self-hate and her sense that she does not deserve this love she now must believe she does not need.

Because masculinity and a lack of emotion are frequently equated, stifling her emotions allows Orual to satisfy the masculine side of her idealized image. Her womanhood embarrasses her, for it is the reason her father rejects her. Being masterful in the knowledge the Fox imparts and skillful (if not strong) in the fencing Bardia teaches provides a way for Orual to be like a man, even though she cannot become one. This satisfaction is only temporary, however, for as her comment on Bardia's well-meaning words indicates, after she becomes queen and assumes her father's manly role, Orual finds that she cannot "drive all the woman out of" her:

> "We've had scores of matches together. The gods never made anyone—a man or woman—with a better natural gift for it. Oh, Lady, Lady, it's a thousand pities they didn't make you a man." (He spoke it as kindly and heartily as could be; as if a man dashed a gallon of cold water in your broth and never doubted you'd like it better.)

Orual has masculine talent but also the need to develop her feminine potential. When she tries to actualize her idealized image of masculinity without her real self's womanhood entering in, she frustrates this very acute need. It is interesting to note that, because of her unseemly countenance, her earlier tendencies toward motherliness ignore the sexual component of motherhood. She is a sexless mother, and therefore one who, because she has symbolically dried up her own breasts, cannot nourish Psyche in any way. The conflict in her idealized image, then, is between these two poles. She must be a mother without a mate *and* be a man, but not a woman. In order to be self-actualizing, she must integrate these contradictory needs. She must allow herself to develop her manly talents and her womanly tendencies as well. She must also become a mother who is able to create an atmosphere of growth for the beloved which will foster the beloved's self-actualizing tendencies. But she cannot foster growth if she continues to perpetuate her own barren idealized self.

In the following passage, Orual sums up the purpose of her resigned solution:

> Ever since Arnom had said hours ago that the King was dying, there seemed to have been another woman acting and speaking in my place. . . . I was taking to queenship as a stricken man takes to the wine-pot or as a stricken woman, if she has beauty, might take to lovers. It was an art that left you no time to mope. If Orual could vanish altogether into the queen, the gods would almost be cheated.

Here Orual attempts to rid herself of the pain she feels because of Psyche's rejection, as she takes on duties associated with her father, thus becoming manly, and in the process ridding herself of womanhood. Thus, she can isolate herself from rejection by rejecting feeling before she can feel rejected.

Her desire to be rid of this "despised" self is clearly demonstrated when she permanently dons a veil to cover her face. Here again, she has resigned herself to her "fate":

> Hitherto, like all my countrywomen, I had gone bareface; on those two journeys up the Mountain I had worn a veil because I wished to be secret. I now determined that I would go always veiled. I have kept this rule, within doors and without, ever since. It is a sort of treaty made with my ugliness. . . . The Fox, that night, was the last man who ever saw my face; and not many women have seen it either.

Orual's resignation, far from allowing her to cope with her environment, only makes it possible for her to hide from herself. The veil she wears over her face to mask her ugliness before the world, she has already had intact internally for years, acting as a protective barrier between her and her despised self. She perpetuates a self-deception, believing that, in fact, "Orual" is dying; but she soon finds "Orual" will not die. Here the image of pregnancy in reverse aptly describes how she perceives what is happening to her despised self:

> I must now pass quickly over many years (though they made up the longest part of my life) during which the Queen of Glome had more and more a part in me and Orual had less and less. I locked Orual up or laid her asleep as best I could somewhere deep down inside me; she lay curled there. It was like being with child, but reversed; the thing I carried in me grew slowly smaller and less alive.

It is in the midst of this self-deception that she is confronted with the sacred story in the temple of Istra. Because it is a true story, it pierces her psychological defenses, causing her to see the uselessness of her resigned solution. Her counterattack is a return to expansive behavior as she writes her "case against the gods," and we, the readers, are to affirm her idealized self-image by agreeing that the gods have dealt unfairly with her. As she puts it in her final expansive assertions at the end of the volume:

> Now, you who read, judge between the gods and me . . . Why must holy places be dark places?
>
> I say, therefore, that there is no creature (toad, scorpion, or serpent) so noxious to man as the gods. Let them answer my charge if they can. It may be that, instead of answering, they'll strike me mad or leprous or turn me into beast, bird, or tree. But will not all the world then know (and the gods will know it knows) that this is because they have no answer?

While at this point Orual feels the gods cannot answer her accusations, as the following passage from her second book points out, her own words provide a response:

> Since I cannot mend the book, I must add to it. To leave it as it was would be to die perjured; I know so much more than I did about the woman who wrote it. What began the change was the very writing itself. Let no one lightly set about such a work. Memory, once waked, will play the tyrant. I found I must set down (for I was speaking as before judges and must not lie) passions and thoughts of my own which I had clean forgotten. The past which I wrote down was not the past that I thought I had (all these years) been remembering.

Writing down her own motives forces Orual to think about them. Because her idealized image demands that she have the justice she requires of the gods, Orual is driven to an honesty of which she is not capable under different circumstances. Thus, her unrealistic demands upon herself prove to be the catalyst for her self-discovery. As she relates her self-deceptions, she becomes aware that she has been deceived and therefore meets herself face to face. In this way, her book, which was originally meant as an attack on that which threatens her neurotic solutions, is the very thing which begins the breakdown of those solutions.

Now that Orual's wall of defense has a crack in it, a harsher stroke comes from the individuals around her. Orual learns that Redival had felt hurt and lonely when the Fox and Psyche began to dominate Orual's attention. "I had never thought at all how it might be with her when I turned first to the Fox and then to Psyche," says Orual, "For it was somehow settled in my mind from the very beginning that I was the pitiable and ill-used one. She had her gold curls, hadn't she?" This is Orual's first glimpse of what Redival was really thinking and the reasons for her antagonism toward both the Fox and Psyche: they had stolen Orual's love.

While the Fox and Psyche may have unwittingly stolen Orual's love from Redival, shortly after Bardia's death, Ansit, his wife, accuses Orual of stealing Bardia's energies and devotion:

> "Oh, I know well enough that you were not lovers. . . . You left me my share. When you had used him, you would let him steal home to me; until you needed him again. After weeks and months at the wars—you and he night and day together, sharing the councils, the dangers, the victories, the soldiers' bread, the very jokes—he could come back to me, each time a little thinner and greyer and with a few more scars, and fall asleep before his supper was down, and cry out in his dream, 'Quick, on the right there. The Queen's in danger.' And next morning—the Queen's a wonderful early riser in Glome—the Pillar Room again. I'll not deny it; I had what you left of him."

The queen, who has secretly loved Bardia for years and had begrudged his sickness because it had kept him from the palace, knows Ansit's words are true. She has devoured all those for whom she cares by taking all and giving back nothing. She has drained Bardia of his life's blood, consuming him in order to satisfy her own voracious needs.

Orual comes to understand her motivations even more clearly through a series of visions which she attributes to the gods. In her first vision her dead father returns and forces her to dig down through the floor of the Pillar (or throne) Room into another Pillar Room just like the original, only smaller, where the air is warmer and harder to breathe. This room, "floor, walls, and pillars," is made all of "raw earth." Then she must dig again through this earthen floor until she comes to still another Pillar Room, even smaller than the last, and made of "living rock." This room is darker, signifying the darkness of Orual's soul. It is dark because (despite her cries for understanding and her dislike for the darkness of the goddess Ungit's house) she has refused to see what is in her own soul. Just as her soul shrinks within her, so the roof of this small room closes in on them, and as it does, her father asks, "Who is Ungit?" Her answer, "I am Ungit," signifies her recognition of her despised self, for, like this all-devouring faceless stone goddess, Orual returns nothing to her devotees and reveals none of herself. The darkness of the temple is the same darkness with which Orual cloaks her own motives.

Lewis's belief in original sin is evident here for he presents Orual as actually embodying her Ungit-like despised self; yet if we as readers look objectively at Orual's life, we see that the only reason she acts as she does is that bitterness has been provoked by her environment from childhood. Horney would urge her to recall these circumstances and ask her to realize that while she is not her idealized self, neither is she her despised self. Lewis seems to interpret the information he presents in a way that conflicts with what Horney would call therapeutic.

Orual's next encounter with her inner self occurs in a dream when she meets holy sheep in the pasture of the gods and is overrun by them as they come to greet her. They demonstrate the beauty of being true to one's self, for, in Lewis's created world, the gods and the things of the gods cannot act contrary to their own natures. This vision, as Horney would see it, *is* therapeutic, for it provides Orual with a model for self-actualization and a hope for the discovery of her real self.

In Orual's final visionary encounter, she at last reads her case against the gods. Through its reading she relates, not the book she has written, but the very substance of her thoughts. As she says, "I looked at the roll in my hand and saw at once that it was not the book I had written. It couldn't be; it was far too small." As she begins to read, she sees that her real motivations have been all the jealousies, hatreds, and fears that we have discussed earlier:

> There was utter silence all round me. And now for the first time I knew what I had been doing. While I was reading, it had, once and again, seemed strange to me that the reading took so long, for the book was a small one. Now I knew that I had been reading it over and over—perhaps a dozen times. I would have read it forever . . . if the judge had not stopped me.

Thus, Orual reads her own mind and knows her own motives; yet Horney would argue that she remains too harsh with herself, for this psychologist would say that we cannot accept another's forgiveness until we are willing to forgive ourselves. Lewis does, however, demonstrate an awareness of the redundancy of neurotic claims, for Orual repeats in her vision the neurotic claims she has repeated time and time again in the extra-visionary world.

Now that Orual is aware of her Ungit-like despised self (though she still does not see that it is a false self), she comes to understand that all the effort in the world will not produce the perfection of her idealized image. Therefore, she is ready to reach out to her possible self in an effort to actualize her true potential.

> Two figures, reflections, their feet to Psyche's feet and mine, stood head downward in the water. But who were they? Two Psyches, the one clothed, the other naked? Yes, both Psyches, both beautiful (if that mattered now) beyond all imagining, yet not exactly the same.
>
> "You also are Psyche," came a great voice. I looked up then, and it's strange that I dared. But I saw no god, no pillared court. I was in the palace gardens, my foolish book in my hand. The vision to the eye had, I think, faded one moment before the oracle to the ear. For the words were still sounding.

Because Orual becomes a second Psyche at the end of the novel, we can safely say that, for Lewis, Psyche is a role model for both Orual and his readers. Because Orual is equally as beautiful, yet not the same as the original Psyche, we can say that Lewis appears to see the need for some kind of individuality in emotionally healthy individuals.

Yet Horney and many Feminists as well would reject Psyche as a model for the healthy human being. Peter Schakel, in *Reason and Imagination in C. S. Lewis: A Study of Till We Have Faces*, makes the following statement which will help to explain their objections:

> We are not to assume, therefore, that Psyche's loving attitude, self-giving concern for others, responsiveness to spiritual urgings, and understanding of divine matters reflect something unique and unattainable; rather, they exemplify what all of us could be and indeed should be.

This aspect of Lewis's message is what Horney, who has been described as the originator of much Feminist thought, would not accept. Psyche, when sacrificed to the god of the Mountain, becomes a Pagan symbol for the Incarnate Christ. As we shall see, in her marriage to the anthropomorphic deity, she becomes the model for the Christian wife. When Orual cites the opinions of those in Glome in an attempt to persuade Psyche to light a lamp and gaze on her husband, Psyche's response emphasizes the human nature of her marriage to the god of the mountain. Later she refers to her sister's virginity and thus emphasizes the sexual physicality of her own relationship with her mate. Psyche also mentions that she would be ashamed to disobey him. Because the god is anthropomorphic, he, not Psyche, becomes the role model for males, and Psyche's behavior toward him is the model for female relationships with men. Psyche's submissive example recommends a self-effacing solution as the goal for feminine behavior, and the authoritarian position of the god glorifies the expansive solution in men. Feminists as well as the psychologists we have been discussing would agree that such a model for human interaction can work only within the confines of fiction, for the world of the readers, as Paris points out, does not confirm the effectiveness of such exclusive reliance on one model for human relations.

While Lewis's Psyche shows great inner strength in resisting Orual's neurotic claim that Psyche be totally surrendered to Orual's insatiable desire for undivided allegiance, Lewis nevertheless presents as the only appropriate alternative allegiance, devotion to a masculine mate who demands an identical amount of control over Psyche's behavior. Psyche is not even permitted to view her husband's countenance. Readers see that although Lewis appears to admire Orual's intellect, he ultimately condemns her search for knowledge and its inherent power, through his presentation of Psyche's willingness to remain ignorant as a virtue. A recent analysis of the Psyche myth presents a psychologically healthier interpretation in which the goddess discovers her true identity when she leaves the oppression of Amor's cave.

Feminists would argue that women must resist Lewis's solution to the problem of communication between the sexes, for they would see Lewis's idealized image of heterosexual relationships, not as one of communication, but as one of domination of the male over the female, a model which Horney, Maslow, and Paris also would find unacceptable. It seems that the remedy Lewis provides for Orual's inner conflict is what Horney would call another neurotic solution. Though this self-effacement works within the confines of the novel, humanistic psychologists and Feminists alike would say that in the world outside Lewis's text, self-effacing women who allow men to set limits to their personal knowledge or efforts toward other achievements severely hinder their own self-actualization. Also, they would agree that though Lewis demonstrates in Orual's portrayal a deep understanding of much of the female experience, he fails in his attempt to provide a pragmatic solution to the emotional crises many women face. Feminists and humanistic psychologists would explain that only in insisting upon her right to define her self-worth as something which does not depend upon someone else's opinion can any woman discover her full feminine potential. They would add that in this way, and this way alone, will she be able to come "face to face" with her real self.

Peter J. Schakel (essay date Fall 1989)

SOURCE: "The Satiric Imagination of C. S. Lewis," in *Studies in the Literary Imagination,* Vol. XXII, No. 2, Fall, 1989, pp. 129-48.

[In the following essay, Schakel examines elements of satire in Lewis's fiction. Schakel asserts that "Lewis's success as a satirist, which has not been sufficiently taken into account in previous studies of Lewis, must be given attention if Lewis's works, and his literary imagination, are to be fully understood."]

Although satire appears prominently in many of C. S. Lewis's works and is an important part of his thought and style, it has been largely neglected, at the cost of a full understanding of his works. Lewis is usually thought of as having the imagination of a romantic and a writer of fantasy, not that of a satirist. Yet, until late in his life, he wrote more and better satire than fantasy, and showed as much of the neoclassical spirit as of the romantic. To examine his attention to and use of satire in his criticism and fiction reveals a good deal about his imagination and the movement of his thought through his career.

Although better known for his work on medieval and Renaissance literature, Lewis read, enjoyed, and wrote perceptively on satire. His section on satire in the 1590s in ***English Literature in the Sixteenth Century*** is well informed and judicious. Better still are his essays on the great age of English satire, 1660-1800: that on Addison, with its comparisons to Jonathan Swift, is among the finest of his literary essays. Lewis understood satire in Webster's terms, "the literary art of holding vices, follies, stupidities, abuses, etc. up to ridicule and contempt," or, "a literary manner which blends a critical attitude with humor and wit for the purpose of improving human institutions or humanity," and found it well suited to his taste and temperament.

Lewis points out that "satire as a literary kind must be distinguished from the satiric, an element which can occur (like the pathetic, or the heroic) in almost any composition." Thus *Gulliver's Travels* could be considered a satire, since its main focus and purpose is the humorous exposure and undercutting of folly and evil; *Pride and Prejudice* contains a satiric element, but it is not a satire because exposure and undercutting of evil are not predominant in it. Lewis himself wrote no satires, but many of his works include the satiric as an important element, and they will be the focus of this essay. The satiric adds a light, often witty, usually trenchant edge to his stories through its use of a mocking tone or spirit, established by such devices as mockery, reversal of normal expectations, exaggeration, and belittlement—and through irony.

Satiric Model: *The Pilgrim's Progress*

Satire forms an important part of Lewis's earliest two published works of fiction, ***The Pilgrim's Regress*** (1933) and ***Out of the Silent Planet*** (1938)—in each case influenced by the work which Lewis used as his main source and model. Lewis's title and form point to the work which shaped ***The Pilgrim's Regress,*** John Bunyan's *The Pilgrim's Progress* (Part I, 1678; Part II, 1684). Like Bunyan's story, Lewis's uses allegorical form to warn against the evils of the world which will lead to damnation, and to illustrate the journey the sinner must follow to reach salvation.

Overt satire in *The Pilgrim's Progress* is rare, with a passage describing the Pope being a notable exception: "I espied a little before me a Cave, where two Giants, *Pope* and

Pagan, dwelt in old time . . . But I have learnt since that *Pagan* has been dead many a day; and as for the other, though he be yet alive, he is by reason of age, and also of the many shrewd brushes that he met with in his younger dayes, grown so crazy and stiff in his joynts, that he can now do little more then sit in his Caves mouth, grinning at Pilgrims as they go by." Such humorous undercutting of positions appears likewise in wry choices of names, such as Talkative, the son of Saywell from Prating-row, Mrs. Bat's-eyes, and Mr. Linger-after-Lust. There is a great deal of irony—especially of the "he who shall save his life will lost it" variety—but it is mostly serious irony, not humorous; and, although Bunyan frequently levels attacks at social and theological evils, they lack the wit and humor typical of satire: "Mr. *Gripe-man,* a Schoolmaster in *Love-gain,* . . . taught them [Mr. *Hold-the-World,* Mr. *Money-love,* and Mr. *Save-all*] the art of getting, either by violence, cousenage, flattery, lying or by putting on a guise of Religion."

The greater part of ***The Pilgrim's Regress,*** like *The Pilgrim's Progress,* is serious, even expository and philosophical for extended stretches. Of greatest significance in understanding Lewis's message, and Lewis's own pilgrimage in the faith, are the long discourses delivered to John by Reason (who shows him how to dissect the fallacies on which modern thinking is based), by Mr. Wisdom (explaining how philosophy can take a seeker partway to faith), and by History (who puts John's experiences into perspective). These discourses, however, are heavy going. They carry many evidences of having been written by a student with a recent first-class degree in philosophy, recounting the intellectual and spiritual struggles he experienced on the road to Christianity.

The more enjoyable parts of ***The Pilgrim's Regress,*** the parts one looks forward to as one rereads it, are the ironic and satiric portions. Many of these follow Bunyan, though in a lighter, more humorous vein. Lewis, more witty than Bunyan by nature, infuses Bunyan's serious traits with humor and satire. Lewis's names, like Bunyan's, are comic even as they thrust at specific notions, features, and fashions of his day. Nineteenth-century rationalism, under "Mr. Enlightenment," has built the city of "Claptrap" from a village of forty inhabitants to a metropolis of "twelve million, four hundred thousand, three hundred and sixty-one souls, who include, I may add, the majority of our most influential publicists and scientific popularizers." Lewis jibes at the flappers of the '20s by calling them the "Clevers," and describing them in disparaging terms: "The girls had short hair and flat breasts and flat buttocks so that they looked like boys: but the boys had pale, egg-shaped faces and slender waists and big hips so that they looked like girls—except for a few of them who had long hair and beards." And he gives liberal theology the name "Mr. Broad," and satirizes him through word-play contrasting what he does believe and what he does not: "'Listen!' said Mr. Broad, 'it is a thrush. I really believe it is a thrush,'" though he has trouble really believing any dogmas of Christianity ("as I grow older I am inclined to set less and less store by mere orthodoxy. . . . It is those things which draw us together that I now value most—our common affections, our common delight in this slow pageant of the countryside, our common struggle towards the light").

Irony is much more pervasive and central in Lewis's story than in Bunyan's. There is a grim humor in John and Vertue's rejection of Mother Kirk, the only person who can gain for them what they desire. More laughably ironic are Mr. Sensible's conviction that he is self-sufficient and independent and Wisdom's children's belief that they are living on the spare diet of Philosophy. In fact both he and they feast on food and drink from other sources. Underlying the entire story is a more powerful irony—that when John reaches his destination, he must regress, go back, return to where he started, for the island he sought is the other side of the mountains a few miles from his home in Puritania. And irony permeates the return journey, as John sees the things he encountered before, but sees them as they really are, sees the pride, ignorance, and indulgence which had been covered over when he passed by them the first time.

As there is more irony in Lewis than in Bunyan, so too there is more satire. ***The Pilgrim's Regress*** opens with some delightful satire on puritanism, as the Steward (or clergyman) hands young John a big card with small print all over it and says, "'Here is a list of all the things the Landlord says you must not do. You'd better look at it.' So John took the card: but half the rules seemed to forbid things he had never heard of, and the other half forbade things he was doing every day and could not imagine not doing: and the number of the rules was so enormous that he felt he could never remember them all." According to his first biographers, Lewis was "furious" when the blurb on the Sheed and Ward edition implied that Lewis was satirizing Ulster Protestantism: "The hero, brought up in Puritania (Mr. Lewis himself was born in Ulster), cannot abide the religion he finds there." This biographical interpretation is too limited, considering such passages as the Steward's "pointing out that the Landlord was quite extraordinarily kind and good to his tenants, and would certainly torture most of them to death the moment he had the slightest pretext."

The handling of nineteenth-century and twentieth-century rationalism is similarly satiric, undercut by reductive simplifications aimed to render them absurd. Thus, when John asks Mr. Enlightenment how he *knows* there is no Landlord (God), the rationalist answer is "'Christopher Columbus, Galileo, the earth is round, invention of printing, gunpowder!!'", expressed "in such a loud voice that the pony shied." John doesn't understand.

"Why, it's as plain as a pikestaff," said the other.

"Your people in Puritania believe in the Landlord because they have not had the benefits of a scientific training. For example, now, I dare say it would be news to you to hear that the earth was round—round as an orange, my lad!"

"Well, I don't know that it would," said John, feeling a little disappointed. "My father always said it was round."

"No, no, my dear boy," said Mr. Enlightenment, "you must have misunderstood him. It is well known that everyone in Puritania thinks the earth flat."

Freudian thought is satirized in part by labelling it the offspring of nineteenth-century rationalism—Sigismund Enlightenment is the son of Old Mr. Enlightenment—and in part by Sigismund's casual dismissal of everything desirable as wish-fulfillment, all "things people *wish* to believe." Both father and son endeavor to "see through" things, to take nothing at face value. Lewis uses exaggeration and literalization to ridicule them, as John, having fallen under their way of thinking, looks at a woman: "But he did not know it was a woman, because, through the fact, he saw the skull and through that the brains and the passages of the nose, and the larynx, and the saliva moving in the glands and the blood in the veins: and lower down the lungs panting like sponges, and the liver, and the intestines like a coil of snakes."

The satire on twentieth-century thought continues in John's encounter with the "Three Pale Men" in Book 6, chapters 2-4.

"You will fare badly here," said one of the three men. "But I am a Steward and it is my duty according to my office to share my supper with you. You may come in." His name was Mr. Neo-Angular.

"I am sorry that my convictions do not allow me to repeat my friend's offer," said one of the others. "But I have had to abandon the humanitarian and egalitarian fallacies." His name was Mr. Neo-Classical.

"I hope," said the third, "that your wanderings in lonely places do not mean that you have any of the romantic virus still in your blood." His name was Mr. Humanist.

In this case Lewis was satirizing individuals as well as intellectual trends; he wrote later, "What I am attacking in Neo-Angular is a set of people who seem to me . . . to be trying to make of Christianity itself one more high-brow, Chelsea, bourgeois-baiting fad" and "T. S. Eliot is the single man who sums up the thing I am fighting against." Similarly, any knowledgeable reader in the '30s would have recognized Mr. Neo-Classical as Irving Babbitt and Mr. Humanist as George Santayana. Lewis attacks them together because their thought is marked by denial of the romantic and a negativism typical, Lewis believed, of modern analytical thought. As he put it in the headings he added to the third edition, "These men are interested in everything not for what it is but for what it is not and talk as if they had 'seen through' things they have not even seen and boast of rejecting what was never in fact within their reach." In such passages, George Sayer suggests, we come closer than in his other works to hearing Lewis's voice: "No other book of his is written-with such a light touch, and few are so often witty and profound. . . . The polemic has a sharpness often present in Jack's conversation but rarely in his later writings." Wit and satire, then, deserve attention, not just as aspects of Lewis's writing style, but because they were deeply embedded in the way he thought and talked.

Satire Model: *Gulliver's Travels*

As *The Pilgrim's Progress* formed a model for ***The Pilgrim's Regress,*** so Swift's *Gulliver's Travels* (1726) provided a model for ***Out of the Silent Planet.*** It is not the only model (H. G. Wells and David Lindsay are others), but it is a more pervasive and influential one than has generally been recognized—in overall concept as well as satiric details. Like Gulliver, Ransom is taken to a world that is not perfect (the upper regions have been devastated and the warmth and oxygen needed for life are available only in the valleys), but the lives of the residents have significant advantages over life as he had known it. Most notable is the harmony and cooperation. Although inhabitants of Malacandra are unlike each other in appearance, language, and interests, they are able to live together supportively. The farmers (*hrossa*), academics (*sorns*), and artisans (*pfifltriggi*) respect and value each other's work and accept each other as equals: Ransom tries to discover which species "was the real master" over the others, but in vain, for only "Oyarsa rules." No one profits from another's need: "If the other *hnau* wanted food, why should we not give it to them? We often do." Work is an enriching, fulfilling activity; no one is forced into mindless, repetitive drudgery so others can work creatively: "All keep the mines open; it is a work to be shared. But each digs for himself the thing he wants for his work. What else would he do?" No one must work to satisfy the "needs" of others: the *pfifltriggi* like making things but they are not forced, for survival, to manufacture useful things: the other Malacandrians accept the fact that "they have not patience to make easy things however useful they would be." All Malacandrians accept and follow the laws that all rational beings know, "of pity and straight dealing and shame and the like."

As we view Malacandra and hear Ransom express surprise and confusion over its differences from our world, we grasp an implicit critique of our world—as one does in reading *Gulliver's Travels.* As Gulliver talks to the Brobdingnagian King about the English political and social system, the King asks probing questions about legislators, judges, the national debt, and political and religious wars; Swift has him reply with an outsider's assessment of what he heard: the King protests that recent English history "was only an Heap of Conspiracies, Rebellions, Murders, Massacres, Revolutions, Banishments; the very worst Effects that Avarice, Faction, Hypocrisy, Perfidiousness, Cruelty, Rage, Madness, Hatred, Envy, Lust, Malice, and Ambition could produce." Gulliver tries to soften the evidence: "I artfully eluded many of his Questions; and gave to every Point a more favourable turn by many Degrees than the strictness of Truth would allow." In spite of that, the King concludes, in one of the harshest lines in the *Travels:* "I cannot but conclude the Bulk of your Natives, to be the most pernicious Race of little odious Vermin that Nature ever suffered to crawl upon the Surface of the Earth."

Lewis uses the same technique as Ransom talks to the *hrossa* and the *sorns.* As the *hrossa* informs him about the spiritual beings on Malacandra, he "found himself being treated as if *he* were the savage and being given a first sketch of civilised religion"; and the descriptions of the compatibility of the different species on Malacandra make him feel similarly uncivilized socially. "He [then] had to repay them with information about Earth"—and his reply sounds very Gulliverian: "He was hampered in this both by the humiliating discoveries which he was constantly making of his own ignorance about his native planet, and partly by his determination to conceal some of the truth. He did not want to tell them too much of our human wars and industrialisms." The *hrossa,* true to their natures, devise poetry rather than analytical conclusions from what Ransom says; conclusions are left for the *sorns* after a similar question and answer session with Augray and his pupils:

> They were astonished at what he had to tell them of human history—of war, slavery and prostitution.
>
> "It is because they have no Oyarsa [planetary archangel]," said one of the pupils.
>
> "It is because every one of them wants to be a little Oyarsa himself," said Augray.
>
> "They cannot help it," said the old *sorn.* "There must be rule, yet how can creatures rule themselves? Beasts must be ruled by *hnau* [rational beings] and *hnau* by *eldila* [angelic beings] and *eldila* by Maleldil [Christ]. These creatures have no *eldila.* They are like one trying to lift himself by his own hair."

And the Oyarsa's later conclusion that Weston had broken all the laws of nature and reason except one, which he had bent to his own purposes, is closely similar to the conclusion of the Houyhnhnm master after lengthy question and answer sessions with Gulliver: "He looked upon us as a Sort of Animals to whose Share, by what Accident he could not conjecture, some small Pittance of *Reason* had fallen, whereof we made no other Use than by its Assistance to aggravate our *nature* Corruptions, and to acquire new ones which Nature had not given us."

The fiercest satire in ***Out of the Silent Planet*** also draws on Swift and involves direct imitation of specific passages in the *Travels.* When Gulliver arrives in Houyhnhnmland, he finds the most disagreeable animal he has encountered on his travels. Later, in a satire of sudden exposure, Gulliver realizes he is seeing creatures very like himself: Swift satirizes the human form, or rather human pride in physical form, by the shock of seeing that form in its sheer physicalness. Lewis uses much the same technique when a procession of *hrossa* approaches Ransom, some of them guarding two creatures he did not recognize.

> They were much shorter than any animal he had yet seen on Malacandra, and he gathered that they were bipeds, though the lower limits were so thick and sausage-like that he hesitated to call them legs. The bodies were a little narrower at the top than at the bottom so as to be very slightly pear-shaped, and the heads were neither round like those of *hrossa* nor long like those of *sorns,* but almost square. They stumped along on narrow, heavy-looking feet which they seemed to press into the ground with unnecessary violence. And now their faces were becoming visible as masses of lumped and puckered flesh of variegated colour fringed in some bristly, dark substance . . . Suddenly, with an indescribable change of feeling, he realised he was looking at men. The two prisoners were Weston and Devine and he, for one privileged moment, had seen the human form with almost Malacandrian eyes. (ellipsis in the original text)

Lewis gently pokes fun at the human body (he followed St. Francis in calling his own "Brother Ass"), making us see what is so familiar in a fresh way. Gulliver, repelled by the human form, finds grace and beauty instead in horses and even tries to become a horse himself. Swift thus turns the satire on Gulliver, poking fun at his inability to distinguish between human folly and human worth, illustrated in the Portuguese sea captain, Don Pedro de Mendez. Lewis similarly has Ransom find grace and beauty in the bodies of the Malacandrians, who initially seemed repulsive or fearsome, but in his case it is an evidence of Ransom's growth in openness and understanding.

That openness and understanding are illustrated further in another episode borrowed from Swift. When Gulliver attempts to describe human attitudes and activities to his Houyhnhnm Master, he has difficulty finding terms in Houyhnhnm language. The simplifications and reductions effected by explaining English affairs in Houyhnhnm terms are a key part of the satire against human abuses of reason, as when Gulliver explains the causes of wars:

> Differences in Opinions hath cost many Millions of Lives: For Instance, whether *Flesh* be *Bread,* or *Bread* be *Flesh:* Whether the Juice of a certain *Berry* be *Blood* or *Wine:* Whether *Whistling* be a Vice or a Virtue: Whether it be better to *kiss* a *Post,* or throw it into the Fire: What is the best Colour for a *Coat,* whether *Black, White, Red,* or *Grey*; and whether it should be *long* or *short, narrow* or *wide, dirty,* or *clean*; with many more.

Lewis achieves a similar effect when Weston, Devine, and Ransom appear before the Oyarsa on the sacred island Meldilorn. As Gulliver struggled to express human evil and folly in Houyhnhnm terms, so Lewis has Ransom struggle to translate Weston's unreasonable philosophy into Old Solar:

> "Life is greater than any system of morality; her claims are absolute. It is not by tribal taboos and copybook maxims that she has pursued her relentless march from the amoeba to man and from man to civilisation."
>
> "He says," began Ransom, "that living creatures are stronger than the question whether an act is bent or good—no, that cannot be right—he says it is better to be alive and bent than to be dead—no—he says, he says—I cannot say what he says, Oyarsa, in your language. But he goes on to say that the only good thing is that there should be very many creatures alive."

It is brilliant satire, mocking an unreasonable and foolish philosophy by reducing it to absurdity.

Out of the Silent Planet, thus, is not "a satire"—criticism of our world is not its main shaping purpose; but such criticism is a very important aspect of it. A satiric spirit is evident in much of the work, as Lewis criticizes the competitiveness, greed, pride, and selfishness he found all around him. ***Out of the Silent Planet*** is enjoyable reading as a fantasy, as an imaginary voyage to a new and fascinating place and people. But much of its strength and durability arise from the satiric strain which runs through the voyage.

Ironic Inversion: ***The Screwtape Letters***

The strength and durability of Lewis's next narrative work, ***The Screwtape Letters,*** are similarly derived. Published serially in *The Guardian* from 2 May through 28 November 1941, the letters were subsequently collected into a book, which first made Lewis well known, in America as well as Britain, as a popular writer. The work is based on ironic inversion. To have a senior devil writing letters of advice to his junior-level nephew reverses our normal expectations and values. The first letter, originally presented in *The Guardian* without announcing its approach, signals the irony subtly, but skillfully. The greeting—"My Dear Wormwood"—supplies the first clue, though for most readers it can be appreciated only in retrospect: "Wormwood" combines the visual element of "serpent" with the overtone of madness from the second-meeting the word carried for the Elizabethans (Lewis would have remembered the famous line "wode within this wood" from *A Midsummer Night's Dream,* 2.1.192, for example).

The word "materialist" in the first sentence indicates something of the values underlying the work, but as yet their application is not evident: "I note what you say about guiding your patient's reading and taking care that he sees a good deal of his materialist friend." Similarly the word "patient" turns deeply ironic once one realizes that it refers to the victim being subjected to Wormwood's temptations—and satiric if "patient" establishes an implicit parallel between the devil and physicians or psychiatrists. Even in sentence three, for new readers—like those reading it originally in *The Guardian*—the irony still is only latent: "It sounds as if you supposed that *argument* was the way to keep him out of the Enemy's clutches." One's reading remains necessarily ambivalent through the next several sentences: one wants to believe in the connection of "thinking with doing," and not having dozens of abstract and incompatible philosophies in one's head, but customarily or initially at least, one tends to accept a speaker's words as authoritative.

Finally, in the tenth sentence, the speaker's unreliability comes through explicitly: "Jargon, not argument, is your best ally in keeping him from the Church." And, a few sentences later, the juxtaposition of "the Enemy" with "Our Father Below" makes the ironic reversal fully evident. By the time the speaker recounts his earlier experience of preventing the mind of a scholar in the British Museum from going "the wrong way," one knows that such statements invert the serious values of the work, and that argument, reason, and reality—because they are deprecated by the speaker—are to be held onto as sound and desirable.

What makes ***The Screwtape Letters*** successful, however, is that it does not involve just, or wholly, a simple ironic inversion. Much of the time what Screwtape writes is accurate description, straightforward statement of fact: the irony comes not through reversal, but in seeing the truth for what it is—as for example impediments to true worship and spiritual growth (whether they arise from a personal tempter or the disquiet of our own minds):

> When he gets to his pew and looks around him he sees just that selection of his neighbours whom he has hitherto avoided. . . . Provided that any of those neighbours sing out of tune, or have boots that squeak, or double chins, or odd clothes, the patient will quite easily believe that their religion must therefore be somehow ridiculous.

In such passages Lewis evinces the keen psychological insights that characterize so many of his works; here the context turns the insights into satire—light, humorous ridicule of the folly of our tendency to allow trivialities and externals to dominate over crucial internal issues.

Screwtape's straightforward statements are accurate summaries of Christian truths, expressions of what Lewis believed and regarded as important teaching. Screwtape's description of Christian humility and self-acceptance illustrates:

> The Enemy . . . wants each man, in the long run, to be able to recognise all creatures (even himself) as glorious and excellent things. He wants to kill their animal self-love as soon as possible; but it is His long-term policy, I fear, to restore to them a new kind of self-love—as charity and gratitude for all selves, including their own; when they have really learned to love their neighbours as themselves, they will be allowed to love themselves as their neighbours. For we must never forget what is the most repellent and inexplicable trait in our Enemy; He *really* loves the hairless bipeds He has created.

Older satiric traditions—the Roman satires of Juvenal, Horace, and Persius, and the seventeenth- and eighteenth-century British satires of Dryden, Swift, Pope, and Fielding—almost always included positive alternatives to the values attacked; twentieth-century satire typically does not, but is just negative, comprised wholly of attack and exposure. Lewis does include positives (since Lewis intends the book for spiritual instruction, it is essential that he get beyond ironic reversals) and he even improves on Swift as he does so. In Swift's satire, it seems inconsistent when a speaker utters straightforward truths, it breaks the spell for a moment; but in ***The Screwtape Letters*** it seems entirely necessary and believable that Screwtape should utter truths as part of the process of educating Wormwood in essentials he missed at Training College.

Ironic Inversion: ***That Hideous Strength***

Lewis's next strongly satiric work seems closely related to, even owes some debt to, ***The Screwtape Letters.*** The Hideous Strength in the third volume of the Ransom trilogy is the power of evil incarnate in ambitious humans. What seems initially to be an attempt by the National Institute of Coordinated Experiments to seize control of a nation turns out to be a cover for an attempt by Screwtape's secret service to infiltrate and take over the world. The ultimate horror in the book occurs when the reader, with the central character Mark, discovers that the Head of the evil empire is not just a human head severed from its body and sustained by machines, but devils referred to as Macrobes.

That Hideous Strength is indebted to ***The Screwtape Letters*** first for its treatment of bureaucratic structures. Basic to ***Screwtape*** is its social satire of the bureaucratic system which is today even more pervasive than when Lewis was writing. To depict hell as a bureaucracy places a powerful judgment against a system we have come to take for granted, but which is, in the words of the Preface Lewis added to a later edition, "held together entirely by fear and greed." Initially the bureaucracy in ***The Screwtape Letters*** sounds like part of the industrial or business world, but it later emerges as a dictatorial governmental structure, with striking anticipations of the N.I.C.E.: Screwtape refers to the Secret Police and the Infernal Police, which resemble Miss Hardcastle's security police force; the Screwtapian bureaucracy, like the N.I.C.E., has a "Philological Arm"; and the N.I.C.E., like the Screwtapian bureaucracy, regards its victims as "patients"—Feverstone says, in describing N.I.C.E.'s goals, "a real education makes the patient what it wants infallibly."

Even more telling than the debt ***That Hideous Strength*** owes to Screwtapian bureaucracy is the purpose shared by the individuals within the bureaucracies. Screwtape early on reminds Wormwood that "to us a human is primarily food; our aim is the absorption of its will into ours, the increase of our own area of selfhood at its expense." The point is closely similar to Wither's, though his expression is typically less direct, when he and Frost discuss initiating Mark into the secrets of their organization: "Of course . . . nothing is so much to be desired as the greatest possible unity. . . . Any fresh individual brought into the unity would be a source of the most intense satisfaction—to—ah—all concerned. I desire the closest possible bond. I would welcome an interpenetration of personalities so close, so irrevocable, that it almost transcends individuality. You need not doubt that I would open my arms to receive—to absorb—to assimilate this young man."

In view of these similarities, it is not surprising to find ***That Hideous Strength*** as heavily dependent on satire and irony as ***The Screwtape Letters.*** The satire seems to stand out more in ***That Hideous Strength*** than in ***Out of the Silent Planet,*** perhaps because the action occurs not in space, but in a small English university town that reminds one of Oxford. Much of the pleasure offered by the story—beyond the simple "what will happen, how will it turn out" level—derives from Lewis's satiric attacks on various aspects of the modern world. Because much of the satire is political-sociological and advocates conservative social values, however, it has given rise to objections from some readers who endorse his satire on broad personal traits.

Most obvious of this sort is the satire on Jane's intellectual pretensions as she struggles with her doctoral dissertation; the placement of two lines from Donne, "Hope not for minde in women; at their best / Sweetness and wit, they are but *Mummy* possest" juxtaposed with her subject, "Donne's 'triumphant vindication of the body'," sharply undercuts not only her efforts, but the capability of women generally for such efforts. The irony that this modern woman can write about the body but is not at ease with her own sexuality (hates "being kissed," to use Mrs. Dimble's euphemism) undercuts her further. And though Lewis presumably offers Mrs. Dimble as a more desirable alternative to such modernism, to have her say "husbands were made to be talked to. It helps them to concentrate their minds on what they're reading" is not helpful in rebuilding the case for women.

Similarly offensive, potentially, to twentieth-century readers brought up to reverence the social sciences, is Lewis's satire on sociology, first through the words of the good scientist Hingest: "There *are* no sciences like sociology . . . I happen to believe that you can't study men, you can only get to know them, which is quite a different thing. Because you study them, you want to make the lower orders govern the country and listen to classical music, which is balderdash. You also want to take away from them everything which makes life worth living, and not only from them but from everyone except a parcel of prigs and professors." Hingest's opinion is confirmed when Cosser, a sociologist helping Mark expose the abuses and anachronisms of a small village, comments on a local pub: "I should have thought it was just the sort of thing we wanted to get rid of. No sunlight, no ventilation. . . . If people have got to have their stimulants, I'd like to see them administered in a more hygienic way." And the general attack on sociology as a discipline continues, less humorously, in the description of Mark's training: "It must be remembered that in Mark's mind hardly one rag of noble thought, either Christian or Pagan, had a secure lodging. His education had been neither scientific nor classical—merely 'Modern.' The severities both of abstraction and of high human tradition had passed him by. . . . He was a man of straw, a glib examinee in subjects that require no exact knowledge."

More important and less controversial is the larger, sustained satire on autocratic regimes and especially the socio-scientific "expertise" which has come to be used to support them. The acronym N.I.C.E. for an institution dedicated to "sterilisation of the unfit, liquidation of backward races, . . . [and] selective breeding" is one of the best satiric touches: humorous, reductive, and ironic simultaneously. The N.I.C.E. is the imaginative version of what Lewis described straightforwardly in his essay "Willing Slaves of the Welfare State," "the first-fruit of that constructive fusion between the state and the laboratory on which so many thoughtful people base their hopes of a better world." It marks the beginning of a new era, "the *really* scientific era," and will "put science itself on a scientific basis." It initiates a committee system which can be recognized by anyone involved in a major strategic planning study for any large organization, and its methods of inter-committee communication are easily recognizable today, though rendered much faster and easier through the advent of the computer: "There are to be forty interlocking committees sitting every day and they've got a wonderful gadget . . . by which the findings of each committee print themselves off in their own little compartment on the Analytical Notice-Board every half-hour. Then that report slides itself into the right position where it's connected up by little arrows with all the relevant parts of the other reports." It creates the ultimate in bureaucratic isolation: "The secretary's office was next door. When one went in one found not the secretary himself but a number of subordinates who were cut off from their visitors behind a sort of counter."

To make the N.I.C.E. not only repulsive but also ridiculous, Lewis directs a good deal of its attention toward "our rivals on this planet." As Feverstone puts it, "There's far too much life of every kind about, animal and vegetable. We haven't really cleared the place yet." The practical implications of what he says become clear only later, as Filostrato explains at dinner why he has ordered a grove of fine beech trees cut down: "The forest tree is a weed. But I tell you I have seen the civilised tree in Persia. . . . It was made of metal. . . . No leaves to fall, no twigs, no birds building nests, no muck and mess . . . no feathers dropped about, no nests, no eggs, no dirt. . . . It is simple hygiene." That principle of hygiene must be applied as well to human beings: "The real filth is what comes from organisms—sweat, spittles, excretions. . . . We must get rid of [the body]. . . . Learn how to reproduce ourselves without copulation." In the story line, all this sets up the revelation to Mark of the "real Man," the guillotined head of Alcasan seemingly kept alive by machines. For the reader well-versed in Lewis, it also makes literal the castration metaphor he uses as warning in ***The Abolition of Man:*** the horror of a totalitarian state becomes explicit through the satire as Filostrato concludes, "You would understand if you were peasants. Who would try to work with stallions and bulls? No, no; we want geldings and oxen. There will never be peace and order and discipline so long as there is sex. When man has thrown it away, then he will become finally governable."

Inseparable from the satire on the N.I.C.E. is the humorous depiction of its Deputy Director, Mr. John Wither, especially his use of language. His first words to Mark, clarifying Mark's position if he joined the organization, illustrate nicely his constant manner of expression: "I assure you, Mr. Studdock, . . . that you needn't anticipate the slightest . . . er . . . the slightest difficulty on that point. There was never any idea of circumscribing your activities and your general influence on policy, much less your relations with your colleagues and what I might call in general the terms of reference under which you would be collaborating with us, without the fullest possible consideration of your own views and, indeed, your own advice" (ellipses in the original text). Wither has brought the technique of bureaucratese to ultimate indeterminacy; as Miss Hardcastle puts it, "Making things clear is the one thing the D.D. can't stand," and as Wither himself says to Frost, "It is one of the disadvantages of that extreme simplicity and accuracy with which you habitually speak (much as we all admire it) that it leaves no room for fine shades." It is ironic, then, that, in contrast to the Deputy Director of N.I.C.E., the Director of the company at St. Anne's is a philologist, author of *Dialect and Semantics,* one who himself speaks with great clarity and precision. And even more ironic, the destruction of the N.I.C.E. is the result of Merlin's use of Old Solar, the original language which expresses things precisely as they are, to reduce Wither's talk, along with that of his entire organization, to gibberish, the inevitable culmination of the bureaucratese he cultivated with such care.

Focus on the Satirist

Neglect of Lewis's irony and satire has led, in some cases, to misreading his works. For example, some readers have regarded ***The Great Divorce*** as a book about heaven and hell as places, despite Lewis's warning that it is not, but is about the way choices lead to salvation or damnation. ***The Great Divorce*** is based on ironies of the lack of self-recognition. As the Ghosts from hell who have come for a day's outing in heaven talk, each reveals the self it has developed through its choices: most of them have put themselves in a hellish condition by not getting beyond self in thoughts and concerns. What a Spirit asks of one ghost applies to all of them, "Could you, only for a moment, fix your mind on something not yourself?" The running irony is that readers see through the empty claims and self-congratulation as each ghost talks, though the ghosts themselves cannot—they do not see their antagonisms, arrogance, hatred, and possessiveness for the consuming evils they are. Thus they cannot open themselves to the Love which would free them from evil and put someone else ahead of self. As one Ghost puts it in a line loaded with double meanings and ironies, "I'm not asking for anybody's bleeding charity"; but that of course is exactly what he must ask for to find freedom from self and salvation.

Individual ironies abound in the book. There is verbal irony as the Big Ghost refuses to stay in heaven: "Tell them I'm not coming, see? I'd rather be damned than go along with you" and as the fashion-conscious Ghost claims "I'd rather die" than go around heaven looking the way she does. This is situational irony as the Episcopal Ghost, on holiday from hell and standing in heaven, laughs at the way his friend, before they both died, had been "coming to believe in a literal Heaven and Hell!" and as tub-thumping Ghosts, in thin, batlike voices, urge the blessed spirits "to shake off their fetters, to escape from their imprisonment in happiness, to tear down the mountains with their hands, to seize Heaven 'for their own.'" There is a sort of theological irony that a repentant murderer is in heaven while one who "done his best all his life" is in hell, and a cosmic irony as the Episcopal Ghost laments the crucifixion as a disaster: "What a tragic waste . . . so much promise cut short" (ellipsis in the original text). And there is the ultimate irony that hell, which initially seemed so huge as inhabitants live millions of miles from each other and frequently decide to move further still, actually is smaller than an atom at the bottom of an almost invisible crack in the soil: that is room enough, "for a damned soul is nearly nothing: it is shrunk, shut up in itself."

Through the book also runs a line of satire, not the political-societal satire of ***That Hideous Strength*** but an intellectual-social satire on personal follies that disturbed Lewis throughout his life. There is satire on the tendency to blame our problems on economic systems and on others, as the Ill-Used Ghost does at length; and satire on materialism, as Ikey tries to bring solid "things" back from heaven (which, ironically, could not fit into hell anyway) in order to create "Needs" as the proper basis for economic life; there is satire on domineering wives, in the wonderfully ironic five-page dramatic monologue delivered by Hilda's friend, and the satire on stifling, possessive parenthood, which Michael's mother can recognize in Winifred Guthrie but not in herself. Most powerful, however, is the lengthy satire on liberal theologians, especially unbelieving church officials, in the depiction of the Episcopal Ghost, which recalls the satire on Mr. Broad in ***The Pilgrim's Regress.*** In framing his exposure of unbelieving clergy and their failure to leave the church when they no longer accept what is fundamental to the church's existence, Lewis may well have had in mind the last Bishop of Birmingham, E. W. Barnes, author of *Rise of Christianity,* in which he tried to explain away the miraculous. Later, however, Lewis would say similar things of John Robinson, Bishop of Woolwich, author of *Honest to God,* as he presumably would now of the Bishop of Durham; what he complains of elsewhere in straightforward terms, here he ridicules and renders laughable through exaggeration and comic inconsistency.

To the Episcopal Ghost, God is "purely spiritual," heaven and hell are superstitious or mythological, and stagnation is the most soul-destroying of intellectual errors. All this he came to, his friend asserts, not through honest intellectual searching, but by plunging into a modern and successful current of ideas; his rejection of orthodox doctrines was not honest and risky, but a sure road to success: "What was at all likely to come of it except what actually came—popularity, sales for your books, invitations, and finally a bishopric?" He eventually decides not to remain in heaven because it lacks "an atmosphere of free inquiry" and requires belief in God as "Fact," and because he has to be back in hell that Friday to read a paper to a theological society on what Jesus's mature views would have been if his life had not been cut short tragically by the crucifixion. He strolls away, "humming softly to [him]self 'City of God, how broad and far.'"

Satire, therefore, forms a major part of tone and theme in Lewis's stories through the mid '40s, and a full understanding of Lewis's work and his literary imagination requires giving attention to it. Assessing its importance, however, requires looking not just at works in which satire is present, but also at those from which it is absent. There is no satire in ***Perelandra,*** very little in the ***Chronicles of Narnia,*** and none in ***Till We Have Faces.*** Thus the works which are the most mythical are the least satiric. The imagination which gives rise to myth or fantasy and that which creates satire commonly seem to run in opposite directions. The former, the "romantic" imagination, identifies with its subject, appreciates it, and infuses it with personal emotion; the latter, the "antiromantic" imagination, stands back from, analyzes, and critiques. When Lewis is fully engaged in the type of imagination necessary in depicting a different world, there seems to be no room for the analytical, dissecting imaginative activity involved in satire.

I have argued elsewhere that a change in Lewis's thought and writing occurs in the late 1940s, partly at least as a result of Elizabeth Anscombe's attack on Lewis's argument in the third chapter of ***Miracles.*** As he recorded in ***Surprised by Joy*** Lewis lived much of his life in a tension between his reason and his imagination—drawn to the imagination by his romantic longings, but held back by his reason from yielding himself unreservedly to the imagination. In the late '40s a shift seems to have occurred, a lessening of the strong reliance on reason which marked his writing in the '30s and '40s and a greater use of and trust in the imagination. The pattern of satire in his works tends to confirm that movement. Although the creation of satire requires imaginative activity of the highest order, satire retains a significant involvement of the intellect in literature; that Lewis wove satire into most of his creative works in the '30s and '40s substantiates his unwillingness or inability—whether consciously or unconsciously—to give himself wholly to the imagination. The disappearance of satire from his stories in the '50s reflects trust in imagination, a readiness to allow his stories to work on readers wholly through the imagination and emotions.

It should be noticed, however, that, though satire largely disappears from Lewis's prose after 1947, it finds expression elsewhere, in his poetry. Satire was too deeply engrained in him to be given up completely even though full commitment to the mythical imagination forced it from the stories. Lewis's early poetry—that in the volume ***Spirits in Bondage*** (1919), that included in ***The Pilgrim's Regress,*** and much of that printed in Part I of the volume of poetry edited by Walter Hooper—was mostly serious in tone, but many of the poems published in the mid-'50s are satiric. He has great fun in **"Evolutionary Hymn"** (1957), for example, twitting intellectual follies he had satirized earlier, in works discussed above:

Lead us, Evolution, lead us
  Up the future's endless stair:
Chop us, change us, prod us, weed us.
  For stagnation is despair:
Groping, guessing, yet progressing,
  Lead us nobody knows where.

Similarly amusing, and biting, is the satire on literary critics in **"Odora Canum Vis"** ("Come now, don't be too eager to condemn / Our little smut-hounds if they wag their tails") and on the space program in **"Science-Fiction Cradlesong"** ("From prison, in a prison, we fly; / There's no way into the sky"). Lewis had an affinity for the epigram and epigrammatic expression, which have always been closely associated with satire. If these poems gave an outlet for Lewis's satiric wit, they also result in some of the most entertaining verse he wrote.

Lewis may have been a romantic at heart, but he had a neoclassical head. He has been appreciated for his achievements in the genres of myth and fantasy; he deserves recognition also for his achievements in the mode of satire. Lewis's success as a satirist, which has not been sufficiently taken into account in previous studies of Lewis, must be given attention if Lewis's works, and his literary imagination, are to be fully understood.

Gilbert Meilaender (essay date 1991)

SOURCE: "Theology in Stories: C. S. Lewis and the Narrative Quality of Experience," in *Word and Story in C. S. Lewis*, edited by Peter J. Schakel and Charles A. Huttar, University of Missouri Press, 1991, pp. 147-56.

[*In the following essay, Meilaender discusses the significance of Christian storytelling and the human longing for divine communion in Lewis's fiction. According to Meilaender, "Lewis offers not abstract propositions for belief but the quality, the feel, of living in the world narrated by the biblical story."*]

At the outset of ***The Voyage of the "Dawn Treader,"*** Lucy, Edmund, and Eustace have been whisked magically off into Narnia and are now sailing with King Caspian and his crew on a quest. Caspian is seeking some lost lords of Narnia as well as the end of the world ("the utter East"). They have many adventures—some merely strange, others dangerous. The adventure which concerns us comes when they arrive at the island of the Dufflepuds. These strange creatures (who have one large foot on which they hop about and who are not particularly intelligent) have, for reasons we need not concern our-selves with, been made invisible. In order to become visible again they need a young girl to go into the Magician's house, up to the second floor, and find the proper spell in the Magician's book. And they are determined not to permit Caspian's party to leave their island until Lucy consents to undertake this task.

Since it seems they have little choice—battling invisible antagonists is rather hard to do—Lucy agrees to brave the frightening house. She finds the book and begins turning pages looking for the spell. As she does so, however, she becomes engrossed in the various spells she finds there and reads large portions of the book. At one point she finds a spell "for the refreshment of the spirit."

It turns out to be "more like a story than a spell." She begins to read, and "before she had read to the bottom of the page she had forgotten that she was reading at all. She was living in the story as if it were real." When she finishes it, she feels that it is the loveliest story she has ever heard and wishes she could have gone on reading it for ten years.

She decides that she will, at least, read the story again but discovers that the pages will not turn backwards. "'Oh, what a shame!' said Lucy. 'I did so want to read it again. Well, at least, I must remember it.'" But she finds, unfortunately, that she cannot really remember the plot of the story. It all begins to fade in her memory. "And she never could remember; and ever since that day what Lucy means by a good story is a story which reminds her of the forgotten story in the Magician's Book."

I

We will not, I think, fully understand the wide appeal of Lewis's writings until we think carefully about the importance of stories for communicating Christian belief. Lewis often depicts the whole of life in terms of the Christian story of creation, fall, incarnation, redemption, and resurrection. Beyond that, however, Lewis has, I believe, a strong sense of what Stephen Crites has called "the narrative quality of experience." The very nature of human existence—conceived in Christian terms—is best understood within narrative.

Anyone who has read very far in Lewis will have encountered his characteristic theme of "romantic longing," or *Sehnsucht*. It is, in many ways, Lewis's restatement of the Augustinian theme of the restless heart. We are, as Lewis says, always trying to capture something, trying to "get in." We want to ride time, not be ridden by it, "to cure that always aching wound . . . which mere succession and mutability inflict on us." The human being is, we may say, both finite and free: a bodily creature living in space and time, yet desiring to transcend such finite limitations and rest in God.

The crucial question, of course, is whether such a creature is an absurdity or whether this desired fulfillment is attainable. If fulfillment of the longing integral to our being is impossible, then we really are absurd creatures, and we would be better simply to acknowledge the search as futile and endless, to vow with Faust never to say to any moment, "Stay a while, you are so lovely." Lewis is concerned with this question, concerned to know whether finite creatures such as we are can find any spell which offers genuine "refreshment of the spirit"—lasting refreshment of which we cannot be deprived by the corrosive powers of time.

The spell, if there is one, is not available in abstract, theoretical reasoning. Built into our thinking is a kind of frustration: a gap always exists between experiencing a thing and thinking about that thing. In thinking "about" anything we abstract ourselves from it, begin to separate it into its parts, and lose it as an object of contemplation. That is, while thinking about it we are cut off from experiencing it. A man cannot, as Lewis points out, experience loving a woman if he is busy thinking about his technique.

Lewis searches, therefore, for some other way, some means other than abstract thought to find the "refreshment of the spirit" for which human beings seem to be made. One way to such refreshment, a way which always attracted Lewis, lies in myth. In his somewhat stipulative definition, myth is extraliterary. The fact that it must be communicated in words is almost accidental, for it is not so much a narration as it is a permanent object of contemplation—more like a thing than a story. That is to say, in myth we experience something timeless. Experiencing a myth is more like tasting than thinking, concrete rather than abstract. Yet it is also very different from other tastings, for it seems to bring experience not of some isolated tidbit of life which passes away but of what has timeless, universal significance.

We can, of course, also think "about" the universal and in that way move beyond isolated particulars of life. But this gives no *experience* of what is timeless, no experience of anything which may satisfy the longing of the human spirit to transcend the constraints of our finite condition. Instead, thinking about what is universal and timeless—which simultaneously cuts us off from experiencing it—is merely one more testimony to thought's built-in frustration. Myth provides, if only for a moment, what we desire: to break through to some great truth in which the heart can rest and which can give coherence to the isolated particulars of life. It offers what no other experience can, an actual tasting of a reality which transcends our finite existence. It brings us briefly into a world more real than our own, so real that any talk "about" it would have to be metaphorical.

However, myth offers no permanent peace for the quarrel between the two sides of our nature—our freedom and finitude. For a brief moment finitude is transcended, we are free of temporal constraints, and the transcendent is comfortingly passive. But the truth we are given in myth is not really a truth to live by in our here and now, for we live as creatures both free *and* finite. Because this is the case, Lewis looks elsewhere, away from myth to story, to find that "refreshment of the spirit" we desire. Although story cannot in any single moment of experience overcome the tension between finitude and freedom in the human being as completely as can myth, it points toward a more lasting peace, a peace we can live.

Lewis discusses the genre in his essay **"On Stories."** We can begin at the literary level of his ideas about story and move toward the theological. The story is, Lewis thinks, different from the novel, which concerns itself with delineation of character, criticism of social conditions, and so forth. The story is not merely, as some think, a vehicle of excitement and danger—anxious tension and then relief when the moment of danger passes. Lewis suggests that, at least for some readers, something more is going on when they read a story: a sense of atmosphere is conveyed; we feel that we have come close to experiencing a certain state or quality.

At the same time, there is frustration or tension in the structure of story, a frustration which story never fully overcomes. For a story is a net with which we try to catch something else, something timeless, something more like a state or quality—a grand idea like homecoming, or reunion with a loved one, or the simple idea of otherness. The tension arises because the story is also narrative, involving temporal succession and plot. A story must involve a series of events; it must move on. But the thing we are seeking is timeless. What we really seek to take hold of can never last in a story, and the storyteller is, therefore, doomed to frustration. The medium, the story, is inherently temporal; yet the storyteller is trying to catch something which is not really a process at all—what Lewis calls "theme." The art of the storyteller is to break through the mere succession of particular experiences and to catch theme by means of plot.

What Lewis describes in his essay **"On Stories"** is essentially Lucy's experience on the island of the Dufflepuds. The story is a spell which brings "refreshment of the spirit." It brings one close to, if not directly into contact with, something entirely beyond time. But this all fades and is soon gone; for story is narrative. The spirit is both refreshed and frustrated because it has temporarily been drawn out of the constraints which time places upon us and yet has been so drawn by a literary form which is itself inherently temporal. Thus story—more than myth—unites the temporal and eternal as intimately as plot and theme.

II

This is Lewis's literary theory. Near the end of his essay **"On Stories,"** however, Lewis makes a comment which carries us beyond literary considerations alone. "Shall I be thought whimsical," he writes, "if, in conclusion, I suggest that this internal tension in the heart of every story between the theme and the plot constitutes, after all, its chief resemblance to life?" Life, Lewis suggests, is frustrating in the same way a story is: "We grasp at a state and find only a succession of events in which the state is never quite embodied." The author of a story uses the net of temporal plot to try to catch a timeless theme. Life is the same sort of net, amenable to being understood within the narrative genre: a net of successive experiences seeking to catch something which is not temporal at all. Lewis's literary theory and his belief that the human heart is restless until it rests in God meet here.

What I have described might *almost* be said to be Lewis's metaphysic. Certain human experiences take us beyond—or almost beyond—the finite boundaries of life. But they never last; they pass us by and are gone. Still, they are clues, if we will follow them. How do we do so? Not by constructing a completely explanatory theory which will itself attempt to be a timeless product, for our theories do not participate in the timelessness which we momentarily experience. The theorist is also a pilgrim; the theorist's own life has a narrative quality. As Stephen Crites has put it, every moment of experience is itself in tension, for memory and anticipation are the tension of every moment of experience. Past and future, memory and anticipation, are themselves present. Hence, the present moment is "tensed." Tensed and therefore filled with tension. As long as we remain within history we cannot escape that. We are limited to the present, yet in that very present both memory and anticipation serve as signals of transcendence.

Crites suggests that only narrative can contain the full temporality of our experience within a unity of form. And Lewis, I believe, is suggesting something similar. The human creature, made for fellowship with God, can touch the Eternal but cannot (within history) rest in it. Our experience is inherently narrative, relentlessly temporal. We are given no rest; the story moves on. Hence, the creature who is made to rest in God is in this life best understood as a pilgrim whose world is depicted in terms of the Christian story. This may explain why stories are sometimes the most adequate form for conveying the "feel" of human existence.

Most particularly, it is in stories that the quality—the feel—of creatureliness may be most adequately conveyed. Lewis himself suggests on one occasion that "if God does exist, He is related to the universe more as an author is related to a play than as one object in the universe is related to another." By way of illustration, Lewis suggests that we think of looking for Shakespeare in his plays. In one sense, Shakespeare is present at every moment in every play, but not in the same way that Hamlet or King Lear is present. Yet we would not fully understand the plays if we did not understand them in relation to Shakespeare, as the product of his creative genius.

Even more important, narrative is the form which does justice to the experience of creatures who are embodied spirits. Crites has stressed the point that story does not isolate body and mind. Lewis, likewise, seems to suggest that the narrative genre is most appropriate for creatures who are finite yet free. By trying to catch in its net what is not temporal at all, story recognizes that we are made to transcend our present condition. At the same time, story is not just this grasping after a transcendent theme. Its bodily structure, plot, always moves on. It is relentlessly temporal, just as historical life is. Because story gives no lasting rest, we may try to escape its limitations. Lewis thinks we ought not. He suggests that being a pilgrim involves a willingness to accept the temporality of human experience, a willingness to understand ourselves in terms of narrative structure and to accept the tension of the "tensed present."

In his essay on the narrative quality of experience, Crites describes two ways in which we may try to escape the temporality of our existence and find a rest in some false infinite of our own making. A reader of Lewis's ***The Pilgrim's Regress*** will recognize a striking similarity to the Northern and Southern ways which the pilgrim John must avoid as he travels the road. On the one hand, Crites believes, we may try to escape from narrative by abstraction. We may seek refuge in some theory which pretends to be timeless. Abstraction has an intellectual character, isolating mind from body. This is Lewis's North, where all is arid, austere, bodiless, and finally sterile. The other attempted escape which Crites depicts is that of constriction: narrowing our attention to dissociated immediacies and disconnected particulars. In this case one assumes that feeling and sensation are irreducible in our experience. We accept our finite condition as the whole meaning of life and purchase timelessness by giving up the quest for the universal. We focus on the present, ignoring memory and anticipation, and do not see that particular experience calls us out beyond itself. This way is all body. It is Lewis's "South"—where the pilgrim can find himself present at an orgy.

The first way is content to talk "about" the universal but gives up the quest to experience it. The second refuses to notice how particular experience calls us away from itself toward something which transcends all particularity. Lewis's pilgrim, an embodied spirit, is to eschew both ways of escape. His is to be a "feeling intellect." Lewis says in his preface to ***The Pilgrim's Regress*** that we were "made to be neither cerebral men nor visceral men, but Men"—things both rational and animal, creatures who are embodied and ensouled. We can neither abstract from the temporal flow of our experience nor reduce it to immediate experience without ignoring something important in our nature.

III

If up to this point I have managed to convey my message at all successfully, its irony must certainly be clear; for in rather abstract fashion I have been suggesting that such abstract argument cannot convey a quality like creatureliness successfully. This raises, quite naturally, a problem for the theorist, in particular the theologian. If the quality of our experience through time is narrative, no theory—itself an abstraction from experience—can fully capture the truth of reality. There may be occasions when abstraction is important and necessary; nevertheless, it is no accident that Lewis writes stories instead of a *Summa.* The story is, on his account, the form most true to our experience. Its form makes clear that we grasp after what is not fully given.

There are certain features of our experience, essential to serious discussion of the Christian life, which cannot be adequately conveyed by theological treatment, however careful and precise. Thus, for example, Christians have commonly wanted to say that our commitment to God must be freely and willingly given. Yet at the same time, they have wanted to say that we are of ourselves incapable of making this commitment, that it must be "worked in us" by God's grace. By abstracting, isolating, and emphasizing the divine activity, one ends up with irresistible grace, election of some to condemnation, and the suspicion that it is something of a sham to speak about our free and willing commitment. By abstracting, isolating, and emphasizing our own free commitment, one ends up with Pelagianism, having made grace superfluous. If one constructs instead, however, a narrative of one's own commitment (as Lewis does, for example, in ***Surprised by Joy***), it may make good sense to say *both* "I might not have made this commitment which I now freely and willingly make" *and* "I could not have so committed myself had I not been drawn by God, and it is really his doing." That is what believers are likely to say in telling the story of how grace has abounded in their own commitment.

Within the narrative it seems to make sense to speak this way. Lewis writes in similar terms of the Oedipus story, in which, despite his efforts to avoid it, Oedipus kills his father and marries his mother: "We have just had set before our imagination something that has always baffled the intellect: we have *seen* how destiny and free will can be combined, even how free will is the *modus operandi* of destiny. The story does what no theorem can quite do. . . . It sets before us an image of what reality may well be like at some more central region." To take an example from the history of Christian thought, there are, I think, few who would deny that St. Augustine's *Confessions* offers a more compelling picture of the relation of creature and Creator and conveys better the paradox of a freely given commitment, elicited solely by God's grace, than even the best of his more abstract treatises on the grace of Christ and on the predestination of the saints. However important and necessary those treatises are in certain contexts, they cannot convey the quality, the feel, of creatureliness in the way the *Confessions* do.

But the treatises *are* still necessary in certain contexts. The theologian's task is not superfluous. In one of his brief essays, Lewis distinguishes nicely between ordinary language, scientific language, and poetic language. He gives these illustrations of each: "(1) It was very cold (2) There were 13 degrees of frost (3) 'Ah, bitter chill it was! The owl, for all his feathers was a-cold; The hare limped trembling through the frozen grass, And silent was the flock in woolly fold: Numb'd were the Beadsman's fingers.'" Theological language tries to bring to religion the technical precision of scientific language. It is an attempt to provide what scientific language offers in different contexts—a precise test which can end dispute. It is language, as Lewis says, on which we can take action. We can, for example, use it to guard against mistaken understandings of our beliefs. But this is not the language the believer naturally speaks, for such language cannot convey the quality of religious belief and experience. Believers, when questioned, are usually more likely to tell their story.

My theme is by now becoming familiar: abstraction, however important, means a loss of immediacy—a loss, for example, of the sense of what it feels like to be a creature. To see this theme in Lewis's writings is to begin to understand the wide appeal those writings continue to demonstrate. He appeals far less to theoretical argument than many of his readers (and critics) have imagined. Rather, he tells stories which expand the imagination and give one a world within which to live for a time. Like Lucy, the reader can almost forget he is reading a story at all and can be "living in the story as if it were real." Lewis offers not abstract propositions for belief but the quality, the feel, of living in the world narrated by the biblical story. In stories we do not have to divide our treatment into separate *loci*—to talk first about the creature, then God (or the reverse, on which distinction a good many theological arguments can be constructed). Instead, we are permitted to see God and the creature as they really are—in a narrative in which it makes little sense to think of human beings abstracted from either time and history or from the God-relation.

We may grant that there will still be something dissatisfying about this. The relentlessly temporal character of human life will tempt us to try to make our peace by separating theme and plot, dividing the feeling intellect into its parts. We may seek to view ourselves as all body, finding significance only in isolated present experiences and perhaps regarding the longing for something more as an absurdity. Or we may seek to view ourselves as all intellect, all free, self-transcending person—as, in effect, one like God. But when we take either of these ways, we are not talking about human beings, creatures known properly only when known in relation to God, made for a destiny they cannot at present fully experience. The point is not, in the first instance, a religious one for Lewis. It is simply a claim about what rings true to our experience of what it means to be human. Of course, it leads on to a religious claim. If we understand ourselves as creatures, we will recognize the narrative quality of our experience and may perhaps find a way to make peace with it.

IV

How make that peace between the two sides of our nature? Like Lewis, who was always something of a Platonist, one might be drawn to myth, that permanent object of contemplation which, he believed, brings us into contact with a "more real" world. In myth one might transcend the limits of thought and "taste" the universal. However, this is a solution which temporarily eclipses but does not bridge the gap between time and eternity. We fall back from the mythic universal into our finitude and have no truth to live by *there.* We want and need more, or so Lewis thinks.

> In life and art both, as it seems to me, we are always trying to catch in our net of successive moments something that is not successive. Whether in real life there is any doctor who can teach us how to do it, so that at last either the meshes will become fine enough to hold the bird, or we be so changed that we can throw our nets away and follow the bird to its own country, is not a question for this essay.

Elsewhere, however, Lewis takes up the question and suggests that incarnation—for him the central turning point in the Christian story—surpasses even myth. The Christian story affirms that in one human being that other and more real world has entered our history and we need not transcend our finitude in order to find that more real world. The universal is particularized, located in time and space. The author has written himself into the play. As Augustine found the Word made flesh in the gospel but not in the Platonists, so Lewis has turned here from myth to story and found the story which promises to satisfy the longing of the restless heart while acknowledging, even affirming, the relentless temporality of a pilgrim existence.

Paul Piehler (essay date 1991)

SOURCE: "Myth or Allegory? Archetype and Transcendence in the Fiction of C. S. Lewis," in *Word and Story in C. S. Lewis,* edited by Peter J. Schakel and Charles A. Huttar, University of Missouri Press, 1991, pp. 199-212.

[*In the following essay, Piehler examines Lewis's critical study of allegory, historical varieties of allegory, and the use of allegory in Lewis's fiction.*]

I sometimes find myself bothered by the recollection that in Lewis's Oxford it was fashionable to say things like "Of course his academic work is quite brilliant, but why on earth does he waste everyone's time with all this religious stuff?" Since I was at that time enough of a hireling of Giant Zeitgeist to make that kind of remark myself without even having taken the trouble to read any of his religious writings, apologetic or fictional, I welcome the opportunity to recant for such shallow timeserving.

Nor can I be accused of attempting to revive a dead issue. The horse is alive and could stand some more flogging. A few years ago, a famous student of Lewis's who was a successful candidate for that Oxford Professorship of Poetry denied to Lewis, in the course of a handsome tribute to Lewis's greatness as a scholar, inserted the comment, "Setting aside his novels, which I take it are simply bad—he developed in later years a telltale interest in science fiction, which is usually a reliable sign of imaginative bankruptcy."

John Wain's casual phrasing here would seem to imply that his views are so widely accepted among intelligent people that any actual argument to justify his contumely would be quite superfluous. Nonetheless, my own reading of Lewis's work leads me to quite opposite conclusions: in respect of Lewis's quite central interests in allegory and myth, his fictional works have been undervalued, and his scholarship has been in some respects overvalued. And since all discussions of allegory tend to involve reference to at least two levels of reality, and thus to become somewhat complex, I shall, for the sake of clarity, summarize my conclusions in the form of four propositions:

First, Lewis's most famous scholarly work suffers from a strange critical flaw. The writer of ***The Allegory of Love*** never quite produced a sustainable definition of allegory.

Second, the problem of definition arises from a failure to make a necessary distinction between two diametrically opposed forms of the genre, the allegory of vision and the allegory of demystification.

Third, the outcome of this failure to resolve what is in fact a quite ancient critical dilemma is reflected not only in inconsistency in his theoretical position, but also in a constriction of scope in his own attempt at an allegory of demystification, ***The Pilgrim's Regress.***

Fourth and most important, Lewis's readings in medieval visionary allegory inspired not only his academic scholarship but his literary imagination and are powerfully reflected in the structures and imagery of his own fiction.

As a scholar C. S. Lewis is deservedly most famous for ***The Allegory of Love.*** Although it appeared relatively early in his career, it was never equalled, in scope or authority, by any of his later works, brilliantly successful as they have been. Yet, paradoxically enough, Lewis himself had a surprisingly low opinion of allegory, as opposed to what he saw as the alternate or rival mode of symbolism. He writes, for example, "There is nothing 'mystical' or mysterious about medieval allegory; the poets know quite clearly what they are about and are well aware that the figures which they present to us are fictions. Symbolism is a mode of thought, but allegory is a mode of expression." Thus, for Lewis "the allegorist leaves the given—his own passions—to talk of that which is confessedly less real, which is a fiction." He does not see himself as "reaching after some transcendental reality which the forms of discursive thought cannot contain." The symbolist, on the contrary, "leaves the given to find that which is more real." Allegory then would seem to be no more than a way of dressing up prettily what the poet and presumably his audience already know, so that if he wishes to explore and communicate new or transcendent truths he must have recourse to symbolism.

If this is all there is to allegory, it would hardly be worth discussing as anything more than a deservedly obsolete literary device, in no way relevant to the understanding of Lewis's fiction. But when we turn from his theories of allegory to actual interpretations, we discover hints that it may well be more important than his theoretical discussions imply. Considering *The Romance of the Rose,* for instance, he warns us not be misled by modern allegory into thinking that "in turning to Guillaume de Lorris we are retreating from the real world into a shadowy world of abstractions." Nor do allegory and symbolism, or at least myth, seem so far apart in his elucidation of Lord Mirth's park in the same work:

> But, of course, its classical and erotic models only partially account for it. Deeper than these lies the world-wide dream of the happy garden—the island of the Hesperides, the earthly paradise, Tirnanogue. The machinery of allegory may always, if we please, be regarded as a system of conduit pipes which thus tap the deep, unfailing sources of poetry in the mind of the folk and convey their refreshment to lips which could not otherwise have found it.

Lewis's sharp theoretical distinction between allegory and symbolism is by no means original with him but goes back as far as the critical writings of Coleridge, who doubtless based his views on the relatively trivial allegories of eighteenth-century classicism, as opposed to the new symbolism characteristic of Romantic poetry.

But we shall not need to explore any further the well-known but all too misleading distinction Lewis made between allegory and symbolism, for it goes nowhere unless it is applied to actual allegorical texts. And then it will turn out that the relationship between the two is almost the exact opposite of what the theory would lead us to expect. At all events Lewis makes no use of this distinction in his actual analysis of medieval allegories.

Nonetheless a useful theoretical division of this type can be made—even given practical application to actual allegories—but in rather different terms. While the majority of medieval allegories, as we shall see, do consistently reach after myth, archetype, and transcendence, there is another type equal in antiquity (if not in dignity) to the main tradition, a type which specifically and deliberately turns away from the evocation of spiritual realities. In fact this feature is its chief *raison d'être.* Let us take a look at this poor cousin, for she has an important role to play, and let us name her the allegory of demystification.

The great example of this secondary type is Prudentius's fourth-century Christian poem of the wars of the Virtues and Vices, the *Psychomachia.* These battles within the soul were depicted in terms of gory but repetitious clashes between ponderous, all too vociferous, allegorized warriors, modeled on the battle descriptions of Vergilian or Statian epic. Today, for most readers, these epic combats seem quite repugnant when they are not simply boring. And most notably the persons and locales are totally deficient in the numinous or archetypal aura characteristic of true visionary allegory. Nonetheless, the *Psychomachia* was an immensely popular work for over a thousand years and the subject of innumerable imitations, as well as sculptural and mural illustrations.

What, then, accounts for the intense and long-lived popularity of the work? The reason is not hard to find if we look at the kind of "psychoanalysis" that preceded Prudentius's work. Prior to the knock-'em-down style battles between Anger and Patience, Lust and Modesty, hacking each other about in their greaves and corslets, we find earlier heroes assaulted by infinitely more sinister powers. One sees them at work in Aeschylus's *Oresteia,* in the form of the Furies—they whom the Greeks, in their anxiety to speak inoffensively of such dread avengers of crimes and sin, named the Eumenides, the "Kindly Ones."

Thus, when the early Christian reader of Prudentius work up in the small hours quivering in the cold sweat of some nightmare encounter with the Eumenides or Hecate, the sinister queen of darkness, he could take comfort from this new psychology. Prudentius had replaced such mysterious and terrifying beings with figures like *Cultura Veterum Deorum,* "Cult of the Ancient Gods," a scarcely intimidating daytime warrior who is ruthlessly smashed down by a single barehanded blow from the redoubtable Lady Fides.

This allegorical procedure, tedious as it sounds today, was extremely significant in an age when mankind desperately needed a method of coping with the negative forces that assault and over-whelm the reason. Thus Prudentius's allegorical procedures effected a separation between the sin itself, the punishment of the sin, and the supernatural terror which bonded these fears together, constituting an act of psychological analysis and demystification fundamental to the control of these dark irruptions from the underworld.

The spirit and style of Prudentius's *Psychomachia* survived the iconoclasm of the Reformation, which put an end to the old style of numinous visionary allegory. It prevailed in the tepid rationalistic allegorizations of the eighteenth century and was thus indirectly influential in forming Coleridge's and Lewis's low opinion of allegory as a genre.

Moreover, when we turn to Lewis's ***The Pilgrim's Regress,*** the only work he explicitly acknowledged as allegory, we find it to be largely composed in the limited psychomachia style, but written for an age when the urgency of such apotropaic demystification had long passed. It fits very well the definition of allegory Lewis made in a letter of 1958, where it is described as "a composition . . . in who immaterial realities are represented by feigned physical objects." In terms of this definition, ***The Pilgrim's Regress*** is a highly successful, indeed brilliant, work. Every character or scene encountered by the hero constitutes an ingenious representation of such assorted "immaterial realities" as Virtue, the Spirit of the Age, the Heroic Ideal, Philosophical Idealism, Mother Church, the Sin of Lust, and, finally, Death itself—all designed to constitute a convincing semi-autobiographical account, in allegorical terms, of Lewis's own intellectual and psychological journey from childhood credulity, through many phases of skepticism or apostasy, to genuine religious conversion.

Of course, there is something not quite satisfactory about ***The Pilgrim's Regress,*** and doubtless it merits no more than its relatively minor place in the Lewis canon. Why? Lewis himself gave us some indication of the problem in his preface to the second edition of 1943, where he clarifies, among other things, his system of psychological geography. North, for example, stands for excessive rigidity of thought, emotion, and belief, and South for excessive laxity. However, he goes on to confess, "But it remains true that wherever the symbols are best, the key is least adequate. For when allegory is at its best, it approaches myth, which must be grasped with the imagination, not with the intellect." But in fact the intellectual significance of the allegory is at once so precise and so obscure that Lewis was prompted to emulate the editors of the original *Pilgrim's Progress* by putting explanatory "running heads" at the top of each page.

The point is a crucial one. Compared to his later fiction, ***The Pilgrim's Regress*** is remarkable for its high proportion of "feigned physical objects" intellectually translatable into "immaterial realities" and equivalently for its low degree of that elusive but infinitely attractive "mythic" quality, which appeals primarily to the imagination and constantly challenges while constantly eluding cogent translation into intellectual terms.

The Pilgrim's Regress, therefore, works very well as an allegory of demystification, indeed as an allegory satirical of contemporary intellectual life, as its hero, John, visits the various schools of heresy or worldliness north or south of the true road. But it lacks a transcendent dimension. Unlike the true visionary allegory that inspired his later fiction, but faithful to the limited, reductionistic tendency of the psychomachia tradition, ***The Pilgrim's Regress*** does not, for instance, grant us more than the briefest glimpse of the landlord's castle on the other side of the stream of death. The work seems best defended as a legitimate but preliminary intellectual reconnaissance to discover and mark out the best routes to the place of transcendence.

Lewis does not seem to have changed his theoretical position on allegory, though in his later writings we find the role he previously attributed to symbolism being taken over by myth. In a letter to Peter Milward written in 1956, he says: "My view wd. be that a good myth (i.e. a story out of which ever varying meanings will grow for different readers and in different ages) is a higher thing than an allegory (into which one meaning has been put). Into an allegory a man can put only what he already knows; in a myth he puts what he does not yet know and cd. not come by in any other way." The weakness of this rather shaky polarity between allegory on the one hand and symbolism or myth on the other becomes clearer when we take a closer look at the way in which allegory actually functions in the Middle Ages. At the same time we shall see how Lewis's own fiction is itself largely based on the themes and structures of medieval allegory.

Confusion often arises concerning the term "allegory" because the word can refer either to a certain method of writing or to a complete work written in this allegorical style—in other words, to a mode of writing or to a genre. In ***The Pilgrim's Regress*** it is easy to miss the distinction, for it both functions as an allegory in the sense of genre and is written in the *mode* of allegory throughout. Indeed, the very thoroughness with which Lewis infused allegory of mode into his allegory of genre turns out to be its major limitation.

This odd situation in which allegory fails, it seems, by remaining too faithful to its own definition makes a good case for changing either the genre or the definition. Fortunately, the second, less drastic solution is available to us. If we turn our attention to great medieval visionary allegories which Lewis revived for the modern imagination, we find they contain a much higher proportion of myth than is perceptible in ***The Pilgrim's Regress.*** Moreover, the distinction between mythic and allegorical creation turns out to be not at all so hard and fast as it was to become in later centuries.

At the outset of *The Divine Comedy,* the type and pattern of all visionary allegories, the reader finds himself in the most famous of allegorical landscapes, Dante's *selva oscura.* With respect to this dark and fearsome forest, it would be much more difficult than in ***The Pilgrim's Regress*** to distinguish the specific roles of the literary forms, the myth, allegory, and symbolism that underline and shape its imagery. In Dante's experience of mortal terror when he comes to realize he has lost his way in the wilderness, the surface allegorical significance of wandering from the true path merges seamlessly into the traditional mythic adventure of the dreadful encounter with the dark forest and its monsters experienced by almost every mythic hero from Gilgamesh to Frodo. Long before Dante, classical philosophers had made an allegorical identification of the forest with chaos—that is, matter in that unthinkable, fearful condition before it receives the imprint of form. But such different levels of meaning are distinguishable only through the prisms of analysis. It would surely be inappropriate to Dante's intention (and to a proper experience of the poem) if we were to become overly conscious of these distinct elements as we read the text, whereas in reading ***The Pilgrim's Regress*** we should on the contrary be missing an essential part of the experience if we failed to remain alert to the separate but parallel lines along which story and interpretation are progressing. Indeed, the "running heads" are there to prompt the forgetful.

There is nothing precisely equivalent to Dante's dark wood in Lewis's fiction. But if we think about the way in which the experience of the wood prepares us for the reading of Dante's adventures in the afterworlds, the structural function of the wood if you like, then we can find many equivalences. As Dante and Lewis would be sufficiently aware, their readers will almost inevitably come to these works in a "normal" state of mind—that is, they will be clenched firmly in the grip of the prevailing, rarely questioned assumption that everyday experience gives us all we know or need to know of the true reality of things.

How then to break the spell of this existential inertia? What happens in the dark wood is what one might term a "disorientation experience," a disturbance of the normal postulates of everyday life sufficiently severe and sustained to cause the hero and, through him, ourselves (insofar as we participate imaginatively in the experience) to doubt the coherence of our familiar world as a sole or sufficient reality.

Such experiences of disorientation seem an essential preliminary to acceptance of the very different postulates of visionary realities shortly to be revealed to the hero. They occur, moreover, in just about every serious medieval vision. Not surprisingly, there is nothing similar at the opening of ***The Pilgrim's Regress.*** On the other hand, Lewis's later fiction abounds in such allegorical motifs, despite the fact that, in his view, these works are in no way to be thought of as allegories. Writing of the Narnian stories in a letter dated as late as 1958, he describes them rather as "suppositions," distinguishing them from allegory as follows:

> Allegory and such supposals differ because they mix the real and the unreal in different ways. Bunyan's picture of Giant Despair does not start from supposal at all. It is not a supposition but a *fact* that despair can capture and imprison a human soul. What is unreal (fictional) is the giant, the castle, and the dungeon. The Incarnation of Christ in another world is mere supposal; but *granted* the supposition, He would really have been a physical object in that world as He was in Palestine and His death on the Stone Table would have been a physical event no less than his death on Calvary.

Important as this distinction is, it is nonetheless these fictional, "suppositional" works that resemble and indeed appear to be inspired by the visionary allegories Lewis became familiar with during his writing of ***The Allegory of Love.*** It is in these that we find, for example, the preliminary disorientation experiences we have already identified. Thus, the first of the Narnian histories opens with young Lucy exploring the mysterious wardrobe, which she discovers would on occasion transform its dark recesses into the enticing, if somewhat menacing entrance, to a Narnian forest. In ***The Magician's Nephew,*** the "wood between the worlds" functions as a similar though rather more complex "locale of disorientation." In later stories, where the children are more accustomed to the Narnian reality (as, presumably, are most of Lewis's readers), we find fewer of these disorientation experiences, though in ***The Voyage of the "Dawn Treader"*** the shock of being plunged into the great ocean swells of the Narnian seas in the opening scene acts as a requisite and effective preliminary disorientation for benefit of the obnoxiously skeptical Eustace.

In the case of the planetary trilogy, Ransom's experiences upon arriving on Malacandra constitute a powerful and unusual disorientation experience, as he strives to make conceptual sense of the dizzyingly elongated vegetation, the near perpendicular mountains, and the grotesquely distorted appearance of the terrifying *sorns*—all baffling to his system of perceptions, nurtured on earthy Thulcandran landscapes. At the opening of ***Perelandra,*** on the other hand, we encounter a quite brilliant use of a contrary technique, the familiar made strange, when Lewis takes what should have been a tranquil evening stroll from the railway station to Ransom's cottage and transforms the gentle south-country scenery, in some uncanny fashion, into a landscape of nightmare.

Nonetheless, no instance of this disorientation experience compares with the intensity of confusion and terror experienced in the shifting, chaotic landscape of Dante's dark wood. Dante was of course reporting a more massive account of an otherworld experience than anything attempted by Lewis—or anyone else for that matter. None of Lewis's heroes is ever depicted as being in the intensity of spiritual peril Dante experiences at the start of his visionary journey, and the disorientations in the novels are appropriately milder experiences.

The most important of the allegorical motifs Lewis has in common with Dante is the earthly paradise. Almost every major work treated in ***The Allegory of Love*** embodies a striking instance of this motif, usually in a position of great importance in the story. Its occurrence in myth is equally pervasive, and, as in the case of all such major archetypes, when medieval allegory took over the motif, it acquired not only a Christian dimension but a greatly enhanced rational or explanatory element that nonetheless leaves the original power of the myth intact.

So far as Lewis's own fiction is concerned, the focal image of the earthly paradise similarly constitutes a focal point of almost all his work. But there is a striking difference in the nature of the paradise archetype as opposed to that of the dark wood. The disorientation and subsequent panic consequent upon getting lost in a forest are quite comprehensible experiences. But to the rational mind, it must seem hardly credible that anyone has ever encountered in normal waking experience an earthly paradise of the type that appears so frequently in the myths and allegories of every culture. These paradises, moreover, appear not as the setting for incidental adventure but as the ultimate goal of a sustained heroic quest, frequently comprising an underworld journey, the ascent of a sacred mountain, and the penetration of some formidable protective wall or similar barrier. Dante himself has to descend to the very lowest circles of hell and then make the painful ascent of Mount Purgatory before reaching the portals of the earthly paradise. And these, he tells us, have to be entered through a wall of flame so fierce that he would have leaped into molten glass to cool himself (*Purgatorio,* 27.7-51).

Thus *The Divine Comedy* and other medieval allegories had a primary role in supplying motif and inspiration for such Lewisian paradises as Meldilorn in Malacandra, the holy mountain of Perelandra, the country of heaven in ***The Great Divorce,*** the Narnian garden of Aslan, and the palace of Psyche in ***Till We Have Faces.*** Significantly, however, in ***The Pilgrim's Regress*** the hero never attains more than a brief and obscure vision of paradise, though his whole journey is inspired by his longing to find the source of the "sweet desire" that has haunted his life from his earliest childhood. This omission is characteristic of a work whose images tend to represent one-dimensional, intellectualized versions of the ancient archetypal patterns we have been describing. But only ***That Hideous Strength,*** with its grim, back to "the silent planet" theme, lacks a paradise. Its sacred grove, Bragdon Wood, at once eerie *selva oscura* and protoparadise, is desecrated by man's malice, greed, or indifference, and is finally destroyed in an apocalyptic cataclysm. This act of destruction echoes, perhaps, Milton's rationale for God's iconoclastic obliteration of the earthly paradise in *Paradise Lost:* "To teach thee," as Michael puts it to Adam, "that God attributes to place / No sanctity, if none be thither brought / By Men who there frequent, or therein dwell."

Curiously enough, the sources Lewis specifically acknowledged were all relatively modern. One might instance William Morris's heart-stirring but ultimately inconclusive paradise quests, the eerily unpredictable wanderings of George MacDonald's heroes (who do, however, finally attain the land of heart's desire rather than merely go in quest for it), and the brilliantly imagined wanderings of Maskull on Tormance in David Lindsay's *Voyage to Arcturus* (perhaps the most profound, surely the most provocative antiparadise romance ever written). One could also trace lesser debts to the early Yeats, to H. G. Wells, even to E. M. Forster perhaps. But apparently Lewis never alluded directly to his major debts to the medieval paradise visions as sources of inspiration.

What is the psychological significance of this paradise archetype, which, by definition, can never be encountered in normal experience? In terms of the psychology of landscape, man has dwelt, since the dawn of what we think of as human consciousness, in tense polarity between the settlement or city he has constructed and the other landscape, against and in defiance of which the city has been built—the wilderness, the unknown outerness. Since that dawn, man's energies have been persistently and in the main successfully directed to extending the area of the city at the expense of the wilderness, both in geographical and in concomitant psychological terms.

But consider the paradox underlying this expansion of the city: the more successful it is, the more diminished the power of the wilderness and the less, therefore, the energizing stimulus of this tension on the peoples who have pushed the wilderness back too far. Finally, today, the wilderness survives at all only as the result of the extraordinary efforts of such groups as the Sierra Club. Or in specifically psychological terms, the city is the very manifestation and representation of man's capacity for reason and order, while the wilderness manifests deep and awesome *potentiality*—in modern terms, the subconscious. Again, normal consciousness is totally dependent on a healthy balance between these mighty opposites, city and wilderness, reason and the subconscious.

But for the romantic, the lover of myth and allegory, the admirer of Lewis's fiction, this is hardly the whole story. From the intuition, that faculty of man which preeminently mediates between reason and subconscious, comes the message, the "Sweet Desire," from that land beyond the dark forest where the tension between the mighty opposites of city and wilderness is finally resolved and transcended. For this garden is the place where one may find the aching awesome beauty of the wilderness ordered and harmonized, walled and protected by the rationality we associate with the city. Psychologically, therefore, in this place reason and the subconscious are finally reconciled, the psyche reintegrated, and perfected.

Thus, as we might expect, if we look at the medieval allegories that embody this motif, we find that in such works as Bernardus's *Cosomographia,* John of Hanville's *Architrenius,* Dante's *Purgatorio,* Chaucer's *Parliament of Fowls,* Spenser's "Mutability Cantos," the garden is the place where the intellectual and emotional problems raised by the work find their solution, as intellect, emotion, and intuition achieve a harmony transcending all other expectations of happiness.

But in an age where commercial and political spokesmen tend to encourage expectation of instant gratification of desires, we can hardly avoid the question of why the hero has to endure such long, arduous, and quite frequently terrifying experiences on his wilderness journey before reaching his goal. Psychologically, however, these preliminary ordeals seem essential. In the first place, the ordeal of disorientation, the dark wood experience, purges the hero of what one might call the epistemological parochialism of his city, his tendency to think of the reality conventions of his civilization as prevailing in the universe as a whole.

In this way he becomes attuned to function in a region where external forms and inner realities have a startlingly close relationship, as compared to the city where the divisive analytical consciousness keeps the connections between mental and physical events to a minimum. Once this is achieved, the qualities of rationality and mental stability he has acquired in the city will be tested against the horrors and seductions manifesting out of the untamed forces of the subconscious. Thus, the final experience of paradise will synthesize and transcend both civic and wilderness elements of his existence. For each of these powerfully opposed forces must be fully manifested and reconciled within him before the external goal of paradise can become an inner reality.

The rationality of the city will not be sufficient in itself, however, for there will come to him on his journey spiritual beings who will bestow upon him the advice without which his journey could not be made nor his experiences comprehended. These spiritual beings may take such forms as gods, angels, or revered ancestors. In medieval allegory they frequently appear as personifications but by no means resemble the rather pallid figures of modern allegory. With all the dignity of their poetic ancestors, the gods of classical Rome, or the Platonic ideas from which they derive philosophically, they are usually so numinously awesome that the hero is liable to lose consciousness at the mere sight of their manifestation, suffering the kind of perturbation that Lewis reports of his own—one presumes fictional—account of his meeting with the Malacandrian Oyarsa in the opening chapter of ***Perelandra.*** He will also frequently have to discriminate against the advice or seductions of spiritual powers that would lure him from the true way. Finally, even after attaining paradise itself, there will be illuminating dialogue with the benevolent powers of that place, so that the experience may be comprehended intellectually as well as emotionally and the fullest possible integration of the faculties of the soul be attained.

But how is it that the rational wisdom of our great civilizations is so strangely inadequate that the hero has to undertake such an appalling journey to remedy its defects? For an answer we can turn to the greatest paradise myth, which describes the precise opposite of the psychic integration we have been discussing—the history of psychic disintegration and loss of paradise we find related in the book of Genesis. The consequence of eating the fruit of the forbidden tree is that one gains knowledge of good and evil only as separate entities that wage war against each other in endless patterns of polarity. No longer in that paradisal serenity where thought, will, and action remain in their original perfection, we form the habit of judging all events as internal or external, better or worse, active or passive, progressive or conservative, or whatever criteria one chooses.

The resulting mental fluctuations produce the transient fragmented hopes and anxieties, the cycle of malaise and satisfaction which the turns of Fortune's Wheel constantly inflict upon us. In terms of Lewis's ***Perelandra,*** this is the fate of those who allow themselves to fall into the state of separation from Maleldil that the Unman urges upon Tinidril, in the Perelandran version of the temptation of Eve. In this way, the story of the Fall provides an explanation in mythic terms of how the hero gets into the world of turbulent relativities which in the end must make it impossible to find interests or purposes in human existence other than the long journey back to absolute life.

What about the biographical implications in all of this? We are all familiar with the astonishing scope of Lewis's mental activity, ranging from ruthless rationalistic polemics to the most intense of searches for supranational transcendence. Owen Barfield, speaking of ***The Great Divorce*** as "itself a kind of myth," commented, "In that book, as perhaps not quite in any other, this ever diverse pair—atomically rational Lewis and mythopoeic Lewis—I will not say unite, but they do at least join hands."

Lewis has himself evidently trodden the way of the archetypal hero, enduring, as he has, a life in constant tension between these mighty opposites, as the romantic artist always participates in the aesthetic worlds he creates. Out of respect for Lewis's views on the "personal heresy," however, I shall say no more than that, when it comes to his own book, the author is really no more than a special type of reader.

After his experiment with "pure" allegory of demystification in ***The Pilgrim's Regress,*** Lewis achieved a remarkable degree of success in reviving the medieval visionary form and, like the medieval allegorist, in inviting his readers not merely to play the role of noncommitted observers but to be themselves participants in a healing of the soul. In this respect Lewis's work might be described in terms of the intentions that Dante attributed to his own *Comedy* to remove those living this life from the state of misery and to bring them to the state of felicity (*Epistolae,* 10.15). It is for this reason as much as any other, I believe, that Lewis's books not only enjoy extraordinary and still increasing worldwide popularity but also engender in their readers a curious kind of loyalty, a sense of commitment to they know not quite what—even if at the same time provoking the profoundest misgivings among those who do not share such hopes of transcendent routes to human perfection.

The view I am putting forward here is that Lewis's contributions to the theory and practice of allegorical writing cannot be regarded as limited to ***The Allegory of Love*** and a few passing remarks in letters and prefaces. Although his study of allegory clearly ranks among the major scholarly works of the century in its field, its most significant achievement is its description and interpretation of actual medieval allegories, interpretation which, ironically enough, is far more advanced in its implied theoretical basis than the explicit theory the book puts forward. But Lewis's most important contribution to the history of allegory goes beyond either his theorizing or his specific interpretations. It is to be seen in his fictional work, where one may experience and enjoy an extraordinary revival of what is arguably the greatest collective achievement in literary history, the visionary allegory of the Middle Ages as a mode of psychic integration and healing of soul.

James E. Person, Jr. (essay date Summer 1991)

SOURCE: "The Legacy of C. S. Lewis," in *Modern Age,* Vol. 33, No. 4, Summer, 1991, pp. 409-11.

[*In the following essay, Person discusses the enduring popularity, major themes, and critical reception of Lewis's writings.*]

On Friday, November 22, 1963, at about the same time as President John F. Kennedy prepared to enter the black limousine that would take him through downtown Dallas to his violent death, another life was coming to a far less dramatic close across the Atlantic in England. It was late afternoon in the village of Headington Quarry, a few miles outside Oxford, as a retired and infirm university professor, having just taken his afternoon tea, collapsed on the floor of his bedroom with a crash.

"C. S. Lewis is dead," announced F. R. Leavis to his English literature students at Cambridge University a few days later, while the world mourned for Kennedy. American novelist and essayist D. Keith Mano, then studying at Cambridge, remembers Leavis continuing his brief commentary on Lewis' passing as follows: "They said in the *Times* that we will miss him. We will *not.* We will *not.*"

It is perhaps uncharitable to repeat this brief anecdote, revealing as it does the words of an honorable man—and Lewis' longtime foe in theories of literary criticism—in what surely was not his finest hour. Yet it bears repeating if only because it illustrates something of the strong reaction, favorable or unfavorable, C. S. Lewis could evoke—and continues to evoke—from his readers.

Despite the denial of some critics, Lewis is recognized worldwide as an outstanding Christian lay apologist, a writer of children's books already deemed classics in their field, an adept novelist and fantasist, and a formidable literary scholar and logician. In the years since his death his books have attracted an ever-growing number of readers and are the subjects of increasing critical study. Lewis' ***Mere Christianity*** (1952), for example, is considered one of the cornerstones of Christian literature written in this century and has helped numerous people to an understanding of the Christian faith. Meanwhile, the soundness of his theories of story-writing has been affirmed by authors of such various interests and outlooks as J.R.R. Tolkien and the rising American writer of horror fiction, Thomas Ligotti. Lewis has had his opponents and detractors as well, with Leavis being, if not the first or latest, among the foremost of his critics who have wished that the reputation and influence of "Screwtape Lewis" (as Wyndham Lewis called him) would simply disappear.

Today it is readily clear that Lewis' popularity refuses to wane. Indeed, approximately two million copies of Lewis' books are sold each year in the United States and the United Kingdom—six times the number sold in the author's lifetime. This is not to suggest that statistics alone are the surest measure of an author's greatness, else some of the nation's foremost pulp-writers would, by such a standard, be considered our premier literary artists. No, in the case of Lewis the numbers reflect to a great extent the widespread appeal of his skill at delighting readers while instructing them in those essential truths and values which we ignore or challenge at our peril—"the permanent things" as T. S. Eliot called them. For in both his fiction and nonfiction Lewis, like Eliot, affirmed such norms as the rightness of order, not anarchy; the desirability of cultural change coming about slowly and organically; and the high value of custom, convention, and continuity. He also stressed the importance of individual responsibility for one's decisions and actions; the necessity of recognizing man as a flawed creature, and of mistrusting the naked human ego and all utopian talk of men being like gods; and the overarching imperative of recognizing a transcendent order in the Person of God, the Author of Joy as revealed in the doctrines of orthodox Christianity.

At the foundation of Lewis' major writings are godly Joy and the verities which the reader recognizes as squaring with his or her perceptions and conceptions of what is true. 'Lewis' works bring into agreement one's understanding gained of reasoning, personal experience, custom, and—if one has been so fortunate as to have acquired it in any measure—Scriptural knowledge. As one writer has well remarked somewhere, in Lewis' books the materialist, the militant atheist, and the garden-variety sneerer suffer having their own long-trusted weapons of logic, ridicule, and irony turned back upon them, with devastating effect to their own orthodoxies and a heartening effect upon the pursuer of Joy. As Eugene McGovern has written, Lewis' readers feel that their author

> . . . has encountered their difficulties and dealt with them, that he has anticipated their objections and has articulated them better than they could. It is not too much to say that (as has been said of Dr. Johnson) he convinces his readers that however far back they go he has been there before them and they are meeting him on his way back, back from having addressed these subjects that matter most and having thought them through to the end, to "the absolute ruddy end."

Out of all of Lewis' works, the permanent things are discussed and defended perhaps most directly in the essay **"The Poison of Subjectivity"** and in one of the slimmest of the author's many books, ***The Abolition of Man*** (1943). In the latter, Lewis warns of the creeping destruction of all values through progressive education designed to eliminate traditional concepts of objectivity, dictating instead the belief that there is no truth other than the fact that there is no truth. Lewis begins by taking to task a single English-grammar textbook's coauthors, whom he identifies only as "Gaius" and "Titius." Using examples drawn from their book, he attacks what he perceives as a growing trend in educational material: that of presenting all feelings, thoughts, and moral concepts as simply matters of opinion—all equally true or untrue depending upon one's point of view. Lewis proceeds to flatten this argument, invoking what he terms the *Tao:* the natural moral law common to all cultures, which (he claims) came to full fruition in Christianity and which he illustrates with supporting quotations in the appendix to his book.

All of which is a cheap, grandstanding performance, hostile critics have claimed. ***The Abolition of Man,*** they say, is merely the simplistic work of a traditionalist crank, and it is based on a dubious premise, to boot. For "Gaius" and "Titius" are only two textbook authors, and to present their prejudices as typical and then destroy their alleged position is straw-man brawling at its shabbiest. But many other critics—among them a substantial number of public school teachers and university professors—believe otherwise. They assure us that if "Gaius" and "Titius" are straw men, they are straw men whose veins flow with warm, red blood, and that they are nowhere near as isolated as Lewis' attackers maintain. With the followers of these alleged straw men striding by the thousands beneath the banners of values clarification and political correctness, "Gaius" and "Titius" might be cloaked more suitably in the joint pseudonym of "Legion," for they are many. All of which suggests that the arguments of Lewis' hostile critics sometimes reflect more unwise prejudice and condescending bluster than thoughtful substance.

The Abolition of Man, in fact, has been praised as Lewis' best book by such a distinguished scholar as the author's longtime friend and influence, Owen Barfield, and deemed an important work by the noted Christian thinker Francis A. Schaeffer. Likewise, Russell Kirk has affirmed the work's value, writing, "I believe ***The Abolition of Man*** is Lewis' book most pertinent to our present discontents." The book can be read as a most appropriate and worthwhile introduction to Kirk's own *Enemies of the Permanent Things* (1969) and to the more recent *The Closing of the American Mind* (1987) by Allan Bloom, and *A World without Heroes* (1988) by George Roche.

"Every age has its own outlook. It is specially good at seeing certain truths and specially liable to make certain mistakes," wrote Lewis in 1944. "We all, therefore, need the books that will correct the characteristic mistakes of our own period. And that means the old books." Little did Lewis know, when he wrote those words, that the day would come when his own books would be valued as such—and much more. To many readers Lewis is the soldering-point between a belief in God and the sense of joy and wonder they experience reading Tolkien. Since Lewis' death, the world has not seen an orthodox Christian apologist of his persuasiveness and influence. Meanwhile such classics as ***The Screwtape Letters*** (1942), ***Mere Christianity, The Chronicles of Narnia*** (1950-56), and the science-fantasy "Ransom trilogy"—***Out of the Silent Planet*** (1938),

Perelandra (1943), and ***That Hideous Strength*** (1945)—have found new generations of readers and influenced many writers; read, for example, Frank E. Piretti's novel *This Present Darkness* (1986), a work which combines some of the spiritual insights of ***The Screwtape Letters*** with an apocalyptic story line reminiscent of ***That Hideous Strength.*** These and Lewis' other books continue to provide hours of entertainment, instruction, and joy to millions.

In his book ***Letters to Malcolm*** (1964), finished shortly before his death, Lewis concluded his final letter to the fictional Malcolm with the promise of an impending weekend visit, signing off with the confident words, "Till Saturday." Or, in other words, till we meet on the old Sabbath. Till we reach and know the rest of God. Until that time, appearances seem to indicate of Lewis' work what Eliot wrote in his own final poem: that

> *. . . the communication*
> Of the dead is tongued with fire beyond
> the
> *language of the living.*

"Think of me," Lewis once wrote in a letter, "as a fellow-patient in the same hospital who, having been admitted a little earlier, could give some advice." Those in search of spiritual guidance, thoughtful essays on far-ranging subject matter, and entertaining fiction, could do little better than turn to the books of C. S. Lewis. To borrow and alter the ending of Evelyn Waugh's famous essay on P. G. Wodehouse: Lewis' joyful world can never stale. He will continue to release future generations from a captivity that may be grayer and altogether worse than our own. For the benefit of us all, he has made vivid The Word and a world for us to live in and delight in.

Ann Bonsor (essay date March 1992)

SOURCE: "'One Huge and Complex Episode': The Diary of C. S. Lewis," in *Contemporary Review,* Vol. 260, No. 1514, March, 1992, pp. 145-9.

[*In the following essay, Bonsor discusses Lewis's personal life and relationships as revealed in* All My Road Before Me.]

'If Theism had done nothing else for me, I should still be thankful that it cured me of the time-wasting and foolish practice of keeping a diary' wrote C. S. Lewis in 1955. This is an interesting and not altogether unexpected statement when one considers Lewis's complicated and secretive personality, and although it is true that the 'huge and complex episode' he refers to in his autobiography ***Surprised by Joy*** almost certainly concerns his relationship with Mrs. Moore, one might say the phrase describes as well as any other the extraordinary contradictions and complexities of C. S. Lewis's whole life—itself a huge and complex episode indeed.

C. S. Lewis's Diary for the years 1922-1927 has now been ably and compendiously edited by Walter Hooper and entitled ***All My Road Before Me.*** In it we are given information we would certainly not otherwise have had of Lewis's attitudes, prejudices and opinions on a variety of subjects and about a considerable number of people. Above all we discover what at the time almost no one, not even his closest friends were aware of, how those years were, one might say obsessively, concerned with Mrs. Janie Moore, a woman 27 years older than 'Jack' Lewis, who was himself a mere nine years older than Maureen, Mrs. Moore's only daughter. Mrs. Moore was the mother of a close friend and fellow officer of Lewis's who was killed in the First World War. Lewis remained faithful to his promise to look after Mrs. Moore, who had separated from her husband in Ireland. It was Maureen who completed that curious little household which has so puzzled and fascinated Lewis's many biographers, admirers and critics. Some years ago Maureen, now Lady Dunbar of Hempriggs, said to me whilst discussing the impact made upon the young Jack Lewis by the death of his mother when he was only nine years old: 'And that was where my mother came in'.

Referred to as she is in Lewis's Diary as 'D', Mrs. Moore most probably should be regarded primarily as a mother-figure, but what a mother-figure the young intellectually aggressive, yet emotionally naive C. S. Lewis met when he was only 18 years old!

It was Lewis's nature to be critical in the view he took of people, of men, and especially of women. He was intolerant and dismissive of anybody and almost everybody with whom he came in contact. His attitude to and relationship with his own father is ambivalent to say the least; love/hate is the psychological cliché that has been used to describe it; and this even though Albert Lewis seems from Jack's own descriptions of his dealings with his father, to have been generous and conciliatory in his efforts to remain on terms with a son who can only have appeared to him as wayward, secretive and difficult, even if academically brilliant.

How then can we account for the infinite patience, understanding and sympathy that Lewis so consistently demonstrated in almost everything that he wrote between the age of 23 and 28 about Mrs. Janie Moore?

She appears at the best to have been not very intelligent. She seems to have had distinctly hypochondriacal tendencies. She was also a convinced workaholic and a bossy and difficult woman. Mrs. Moore must have been exceedingly awkward to live with—and yet Lewis not only lived with her, but from the age of 23 he supported her, cherished her, and hardly ever did more than evince the mildest exasperation or displeasure at her autocratic treatment of him. (It must be remembered, of course, that the diary was written, partly at least, at her instigation, and that she had access to it. Often the two of them read the latest entries together.)

For us to read C. S. Lewis's Diary from a domestic point of view is to be regaled with a catalogue of his chores. These ranged from scraping turnips to putting up curtains, laying linoleum, going to the shops, mowing the grass, doing endless washing-up, and very, very often indeed, ministering to 'D', suffering from one of her headaches, migraines, fits of indigestion or colds in the head. Through these years and in spite of distractions which included acting as father rather than brother to Maureen, interviewing her music teachers, watching school plays and taking her to concerts, Lewis was also occupied in getting a First in Greats in 1923 and a First in English in 1924. He was as well exceedingly active in various university debating clubs and societies, and immersed in the writing of ***Dymer***—an epic poem of which one reader to whom it was sent remarked: 'The metrical level is good, the vocabulary is large, but Poetry—not a line'. ***Dymer*** was, in fact published in 1926, and maybe the best that can be said for it is that very little has ever been said. Lewis is not a poet, hard though he worked to become one; although it is fair to remark that he did write a handful of pleasant and sometimes moving verses—**"The Apologist's Evening Prayer"** being one that must rank high by any rating:

From all my lame defeats and oh! much more
From all the victories that I seemed to score;
From cleverness shot forth on Thy behalf
At which, while angels weep, the audience laugh;
From all my proofs of Thy divinity,
Thou, who wouldst give no sign, deliver me.

Thoughts are but coins. Let me not trust, instead
Of Thee, their thin-worn image of Thy head.
From all my thoughts, even my thoughts of Thee,
O Thou fair Silence, fall, and set me free.
Lord of the narrow gate and needle's eye,
Take from me all my trumpery lest I die.

'Trumpery' is not a word that springs to mind when considering C. S. Lewis: scholar, man-of-letters, Christian-apologist and creator of Narnia and it is interesting to read in his Diary not only of his strong personal antipathies and prejudices but also of his intellectual and literary judgements as these developed during those five to six incredibly formative years between 1922 and 1927.

C. S. Lewis read prodigiously throughout his whole life and in his Diary he records what he is reading and how it strikes him. 'Gusto' is a word that has been used about his attitude to almost everything and it was with gusto that Lewis read omnivorously, dealt with his pupils at Magdalen, and at University College before that, and argued with his colleagues and his friends; 'argued to win' as it has also been remarked; and in groups such as the Martlets, the Coalbitars, and above all in his own creation, the Inklings, argument, discussion and critical evaluation continued as a driving force throughout his life.

C. S. Lewis was combative in his twenties and remained combative in his fifties and sixties. By temperament and by training he relished what, referring to his treatment of pupils in tutorials, Professor John Wain has called 'The Socratic approach in Spades'—and no undergraduate who was taught by Lewis or attended his lectures could possibly have regarded him as other than brusque, scholarly, direct and straight-forward. Of him one might have supposed 'le style, c'est l'homme même', and in many aspects it was; but not in all. For Lewis was secretive to the point of being, in his private life, downright deceitful; and whilst 'economy with the truth' has become in these days a phrase somewhat overworked, Jack Lewis in his Diary and in his life was frequently more (or is it less?) than economic. He often abandoned truth entirely for falsehood.

This is especially the case in his dealings with his father, and it is not surprising that Albert Lewis, and Jack's elder brother, Warnie, worried about the relationship with Mrs. Moore, Albert finding the situation in Oxford, or what he knew of it 'uncomfortable', and Warnie calling it 'freakish'.

I am not sure how much is to be gained by attempting to add to the discussion about Mrs. Moore's and Jack's sexual relationship, if indeed there was one. Probability must be that for some years, at least, it was not for nothing that Maureen was packed off to church on Sunday mornings and was not accompanied by her mother. What is perhaps more interesting than this however, is the sheer dependence revealed by Jack in his need for and total acceptance of a situation which would have been intolerable for most people; a dependence upon Janie Moore that presumably gave him a stability he might not otherwise have known, but for which he paid a heavy price. For some years at least Jack Lewis seems to have needed the emotional support of a woman 27 years older than he. For many more years a more mature C. S. Lewis had the still greater responsibility of a domineering and demanding woman who depended in her physical and mental decrepitude upon him. He did indeed look after her stoically and constantly until she died at the age of 78, and it may or may not be relevant that for approximately 25 of their 31-year relationship Lewis was a Christian. No one who reads his Diary or has read ***Surprised by Joy*** need be surprised if his conversion in 1929 brought about certain changes of attitude and behaviour to many aspects of C. S. Lewis's life, changes which Janie Moore herself may not have appreciated.

The diarist in Lewis has long been supplanted and the poet and perhaps mystic has found his place. In the latest of his many services to Lewis scholarship, Walter Hooper has shown us the daily life and frustrations of the young Lewis who would develop into one of the great Christian writers of our time.

If C. S. Lewis did change in certain fundamentals as his life progressed many of his earlier interests and pleasures never altered. As we discover in the Diary he always loved walking, and walked considerable distances most days, whether during term or vacation, and whether in and around Oxford or further afield. He had a deep feeling for nature and a sense of natural beauty, though this, one gathers, did not result in later years in his acquiring much of an aesthetic appreciation indoors or at home. He had, when young, to be careful with money. As he grew older he continued to be just as careful. It was reported many years later that when paper began to peel from the walls at 'The Kilns', his house in Headington, the offending strips were torn off but not replaced! Parsimony ruled, according to, amongst others, the late Fred Paxford, the gardener and handyman who worked for Lewis from the early 1930s until the latters death in 1963. To offset this miserliness it must be added that Lewis was immensely generous with the royalties from his books, and contributed lavishly to charities of many sorts.

'The things I assert most vigourously are those that I resisted long and accepted late.' C. S. Lewis made this revealing comment about himself in ***Surprised by Joy,*** and it is interesting, as we study the older Lewis in relation to the younger man who wrote the Diary, to see just how true that statement is. It is certain that Lewis did nothing by halves. He lived with intensity; he worked with a single-minded concentration, he admired whole-heartedly and disliked with ferocity. Of those aspects of life for which he had no time he was ruthlessly dismissive. In his later years he read no newspapers, listened to no radio, had probably not heard of television. If there was to be a war someone he was sure would tell him about it! How can we admire, and perhaps we do not, such insulated self-sufficiency?

Joy Gresham, *nee Davidman,* certainly did, and her entry into Lewis's life and to The Kilns during the early 1950s was catalystic, if not, from some points of view, catastrophic. The story of her relationship with Jack has in it something of legend and perhaps something of farce and has been much speculated about and sometimes over-romanticized (e.g. Bill Nicholson's play *Shadowlands*). Not many of those who were allowed to meet Joy seem to have liked her; some of Lewis's closest friends scarcely knew of her existence until the two of them had married. Once again Lewis had more or less secretly acquired dependants, a wife and two stepsons—and once again Warnie, the loyal and devoted but alcoholic brother was forced into third place in a house which he had hitherto shared with Jack.

History throughout C. S. Lewis's life, if not repeating itself, does seem to achieve a certain regularity of pattern, and this pattern starts to emerge during his earliest years at Oxford. That his relationship with Mrs. Moore gave him stability we cannot doubt, and that his marriage to Joy Davidman was a source of enrichment and fulfilment is also not in question. The courage with which Joy herself, and Jack, faced and endured her long and dreadful illness, and the fortitude Lewis managed to acquire after Joy's death and also during his own painful and protracted physical decline,—all this impresses and indeed moves us.

How then are we to sum up this remarkable man's remarkable life and his no less remarkable literary achievement? C. S. Lewis it must be emphasized has been a force to be reckoned with since ***The Allegory of Love*** was published in 1936, the ***Preface to Paradise Lost*** in 1941 and ***English Literature in the Sixteenth Century*** in 1954, as well as the countless other essays, articles and reviews on an immensely wide range of subjects.

Outside academic circles I suppose Lewis is better known for his popular and religious writings such as ***The Screwtape Letters,*** and for his Christian-orientated science-fiction novels, ***Perelandra*** and the others. For more people still it will be the Narnia books beginning with ***The Lion, the Witch and the Wardrobe*** that have helped to make him not only famous but also a cult-figure in the USA. One could add to this list and mention later and specifically religious works such as ***Letters to Malcolm: Chiefly on Prayer, The Four Loves,*** and ***A Grief Observed*** amongst many others, but there is no need. The point that has to be stressed is that C. S. Lewis, against a background of more or less complicated domestic circumstances, remained constant throughout his life to his quest for Joy—a spiritual Joy that he mentions frequently in his early Diary, that he defines in ***Surprised by Joy*** and many of his other writings, and that was for him 'the stab, the pang, the inconsolable longing'. Joy in the sense of mystery, of splendour and of glory,—a Christian Joy, after C. S. Lewis's conversion, which he described as 'brightness, splendour, luminosity', when he told his listeners, in an address given in The University Church in Oxford as early as 1941: 'We are to shine as the sun, we are to be given the Morning Star.'

John G. West, Jr. (essay date Spring 1994)

SOURCE: "Politics from the Shadowlands: C. S. Lewis on Earthly Government," in *Policy Review,* No. 68, Spring, 1994, pp. 68-70.

[*In the following essay, West discusses Lewis's views on government, political action, and public morality. According to West, "Lewis championed the time-honored idea of natural law—the belief that the fundamental maxims of civic morality are accessible to all human beings by virtue of their God-given reason."*]

Even before the film *Shadowlands,* C. S. Lewis was probably the most widely recognized Christian thinker of the 20th century. By the end of the 1980s, his works—including ***Mere Christianity, The Screwtape Letters,*** and ***The Chronicles of Narnia***—had sold more than 70 million copies, an achievement that surely places Lewis among the best-selling authors of all time.

Lewis is most appreciated today for his superlative imagination and his lucid defense of Christian orthodoxy. But he also was a keen observer of social and political affairs. As Americans struggle to define the proper relationship between religious faith, moral principle, and political action, there is much that they might learn from this inimitable British academic.

PERMANENT IN THE POLITICAL

Turning to C. S. Lewis for advice about politics is undeniably a bit paradoxical. According to stepson David Gresham, Lewis was skeptical of politicians and not really interested in current events. He even observed that he had no use for the "great issues" of his day. "Lord! How I loathe great issues," he wrote in 1940. "Could one start a Stagnation Party—which at General Elections would boast that during its term of office no event of the least importance had taken place?"

Lewis likewise avoided making partisan commitments. During the 1930s, he told a student that he refrained from donating money "to anything that had a directly political implication"; in 1951, he declined a title offered him by Prime Minister Winston Churchill (whom he greatly admired), because he feared that critics would seize upon the honor as evidence that his "religious writings are all covert anti-Leftist propaganda."

Despite this seeming indifference to political life, Lewis wrote about a variety of political topics, including crime, war, censorship, capital punishment, conscription, socialism, vivisection, the welfare state, and the atomic bomb. When he discussed these matters, however, his primary concern was not public policy. Political problems of the day interested him only insofar as they involved matters that endured. Seen in this light, Lewis's habit of writing about politics and his simultaneous detachment from the political arena are perfectly understandable. Uninterested in the partisan passions of the moment, he always tried to find the permanent in the political. As a result, much of what he has to say about public life remains acutely relevant. Indeed, it is the very timelessness of his writings that makes them so timely.

GOD-GIVEN REASON

Of all the political lessons we can learn from Lewis, perhaps the most important is that public morality should be founded squarely upon public principles. Unlike some Christian conservatives, he did not believe that civic morality ultimately had to be grounded in the Bible to be legitimate. Nor did he believe that arguments about social morality were fundamentally arguments about religion.

Instead, Lewis championed the time-honored idea of natural law—the belief that the fundamental maxims of civic morality are accessible to all human beings by virtue of their God-given reason. This natural moral code cannot be escaped, he said; it is the source from which all moral judgments spring. Its cardinal virtues—justice, honesty, good faith, magnanimity, beneficence, mercy—are known to be true independently of experience. According to Lewis, these basic precepts form a moral common ground that undergirds all civilized societies. He illustrated this point in his book ***The Abolition of Man*** by cataloguing similar ethical injunctions from some of the world's major civilizations.

Lewis was aware that some Christians objected to natural law because they thought it detracted from the dignity of revealed religion. But he could not accept their view. Far from contradicting Christianity, he argued, natural law is actually presupposed by it. Pointing out that a convert to Christianity "accept[s] the forgiveness of sins," he asked:

> But of sins against what Law? Some new law promulgated by the Christians? But that is nonsensical. It would be the mockery of a tyrant to forgive a man for doing what had never been forbidden until the very moment at which the forgiveness was announced. The idea that Christianity brought an entirely new ethical code into the world is a grave error. If it had done so, then we should have to conclude that all who first preached it wholly misunderstood their own message: for all of them, its Founder, His precursor, His apostles, came demanding repentance and offering forgiveness, a demand and an offer both meaningless except on the assumption of a moral law already known and already broken.

Lewis agreed that Christianity, with its claim to revealed truth about the human condition, deepened one's ethical understanding. But he was insistent that "Christian ethics" not be regarded as "a radically new thing." The practical political consequences of Lewis's understanding of morality are considerable. The present controversy over religion in politics largely hinges on the assumption that the morality espoused by conservative Christians cannot be justified apart from the Bible, and hence it is illegitimate as a guide to secular policy. But according to Lewis, this is a red herring. One does not need to accept the authority of the Bible to know that theft and slander are wrong, or that honoring one's commitment to a spouse or child is a good thing. Civic morality is not the peculiar domain of religion, and Christians who wish to be politically effective (as well as theologically sound) should drive this point home. It is one of the best ways for them to disarm their critics.

IMPORTANCE OF PRUDENCE

Natural law provides a common moral ground for all citizens to enter politics as equals, but it does not provide simple-minded solutions to specific political problems. Nor did Lewis claim that it would. He understood that being morally right is not the same thing as being politically bright. Translating moral principles into public policy requires something more than merely the right moral principles. It requires the virtue of prudence, which Lewis aptly defined as "practical common sense, taking the trouble to think out what you are doing and what is likely to come of it." The importance of prudence is his second lesson about politics.

Lewis lamented that "nowadays most people hardly think of Prudence as one of the 'virtues,'" and he chided fellow Christians for being especially guilty of this offence. "Because Christ said we could only get into His world by being like children, many Christians have the idea that, provided you are 'good,' it does not matter being a fool. But that is a misunderstanding." In Lewis's view, consequences matter, and one of the problems with idealists in politics is that they often don't comprehend this fact. They crusade for perfect health, universal employment, or everlasting peace, but they don't bother to pay any attention to the disastrous effects their policies, if enacted, would likely bring about.

Fundamental to C. S. Lewis's conception of prudence was an unflinching realism about the human condition. He believed human beings are both limited and sinful. They are limited in their knowledge about the world around them. They are limited in their ability to do anything about the knowledge they have. And in those cases where they should know what to do—and are able to do it—their judgment is often derailed by their selfishness. As a result, earthly perfection is unobtainable. Political utopians who think otherwise deceive themselves. Their kind of thinking, said Lewis,

> . . . assum[es] that the great permanent miseries in human life must be curable if only we can find the right cure . . . But I have received no assurance that anything we can do will eradicate suffering. I think the best results are obtained by people who work quietly away at limited objectives, such as the abolition of the slave trade, or prison reform, or factory acts, or tuberculosis, not by those who think they can achieve universal justice, or health, or peace. I think the art of life consists in tackling each immediate evil as well as we can.

Lewis thought that Christians in politics needed to heed the hard lessons of human imperfection just as much as the secularists. This is particularly so in a society where many people were no longer Christians. In such a situation, Christians ought to recognize the futility of using the government to promote distinctively Christian standards of behavior—as opposed to the shared dictates of the natural law.

Writing about efforts to teach Christianity in state schools, Lewis pointed out that if non-Christian teachers were charged with inculcating Christianity in their pupils, unbelief would be the most likely result. "As the teachers are," he observed, "so they will teach. Your 'reform' may incommode and overwork them, but it will not radically alter the total effect of their teaching . . . if we were permitted to force a Christian curriculum on the existing schools with the existing teachers we should only be making masters hypocrites and hardening thereby the pupils' hearts."

Another facet of Lewis's prudent realism was his emphasis on political humility. Echoing Aristotle in the *Ethics,* he more than once explained that specific applications of moral principles "do not admit of mathematical certainty." The more specific the application of a moral principle, the greater the possibility of error—especially when fallible humans are involved. Hence, political partisans should be wary of being too dogmatic. Those who proclaim their political program with absolute certainty are flirting with despotism. If ever they begin to take their exalted rhetoric seriously, they will be tempted to stop at nothing—even tyranny—to push their agenda forward.

This was one reason Lewis opposed the creation of an explicitly Christian political party. Such a group, he feared, would raise the political stakes too high. "The danger of mistaking our merely natural, though perhaps legitimate, enthusiasms for holy zeal, is always great," he said, but a Christian party would make the temptation irresistible. "The demon inherent in every party is at all times ready enough to disguise himself as the Holy Ghost; the formation of a Christian Party means handing over to him the most efficient make-up we can find."

Lewis added that attaching divine certitude to a party platform is a theological blunder as well as a political one. It takes the Lord's name in vain by "pretending that God has spoken when He has not spoken. He will not settle the two brothers' inheritance: 'Who made Me a judge or a divider over you?' [Luke 12:14]. By the natural light He has shown us what means are lawful: to find out which one is efficacious He has given us brains. The rest He has left to us."

BEWARE THE OMNICOMPETENT STATE

A final political lesson to be learned from Lewis is the moral necessity of limited government. An unrepentant critic of what he termed the "omnicompetent" state, Lewis believed that civil society's chief task was the defense of individual liberties so that citizens could live their lives in their own way. No doubt part of Lewis's support for limited government sprang from his prudent assessment of human nature. "I am a democrat because I believe in the Fall of Man," he remarked in the *Spectator*. "Mankind is so fallen that no man can be trusted with unchecked power over his fellows."

However, Lewis also had a positive reason for defending limited government. Good societies depend upon virtuous individuals, and he knew that individual virtue could never be produced by government decree. Government can make people behave, but ultimately it cannot make them good. That is because virtue presupposes free choice. The society where all acts are compelled is a society where no act can be virtuous. Lewis acknowledged that the freedom required for virtue to flourish also "makes evil possible." But this is the price that must be paid for "any love or goodness or joy worth having."

The problem with the modern welfare state is that it operates on premises antithetical to human freedom and the private institutions that help secure it. Lewis summarized why in an essay in *The Observer* in 1958: "The modern State exists not to protect our rights, but to do us good or make us good—anyway, to do something to us or to make us something. Hence the new name 'leaders' for those who were once 'rulers.' We are less their subjects than their wards, pupils, or domestic animals. There is nothing left of which we can say to them, 'Mind your own business.' Our whole lives *are* their business."

Lewis, who lived through Europe's flirtation with both Communism and Nazism, understood the lure of the omnicompetent state. Confronted by the sheer volume and extent of human misery, people naturally look for an earthly savior; many do not care what they will have to give up to get one. Whatever this desire for earthly salvation is, it is not new.

"In the ancient world," he observed, "individuals . . . sold themselves as slaves, in order to eat. So in society. Here is a witch-doctor who can save us from the sorcerers, a warlord who can save us from the barbarians, a Church that can save us from Hell. Give them what they ask, give ourselves to them bound and blindfold, if only they will! Perhaps the terrible bargain will be made again. We cannot blame men for making it. We can hardly wish them not to. Yet we can hardly bear that they should."

As Americans again hear the siren song of a federal government that offers to fulfill all their hopes and solve all their problems, these words are worth pondering. So are Lewis's many other writings on public life.

C. S. Lewis has much to offer the thoughtful citizen seeking to understand the nature of politics. He convincingly explains how people of faith can become involved in politics without sacrificing either their faith or their reason. He powerfully critiques political idealism that is untempered by prudent realism. And he reinforces with bedrock the moral underpinnings of limited government.

For an academic who once described himself as a cultural "dinosaur," C. S. Lewis's political voice still resonates strongly with relevance and prophetic power for our own day.

Michael Nelson (essay date Autumn 1996)

SOURCE: "'One Mythology Among Many': The Spiritual Odyssey of C. S. Lewis," in *Virginia Quarterly Review,* Vol. 72, No. 4, Autumn, 1996, pp. 619-33.

[*In the following essay, Nelson provides an overview of Lewis's literary career and intellectual development.*]

The student's name was Ben. He was a first-year student in his first week of college, and as I ate my lunch in the refectory I could see that he was waiting for me to finish so that he could approach my table. "I hear that you are a Christian," he said when, my tray pushed aside, he at last came up. I nodded. "Well," he said, in a rush, "I'm a Christian, too, and last night I got into a long discussion in the dorm with some other students and they were saying things that I didn't know how to answer and I was wondering if you could help." Instantly the scene of the night before unfolded in my mind. Ben, it was obvious, had gotten into his first college bull session and, as often is the case, the subject had been religion, science, evolution, and all the apparent conflicts and contradictions among them. He was a small town Alabamian from a small Baptist church and had found what the other students were saying very disturbing.

Ben and I agreed to meet and, when we did, there was no small talk. His first and only question was, "Do you think Genesis is true or is it just a myth?"

I smiled—having been down this road before, I knew exactly what to say. "Ben," I said, "I think Genesis is true *and* it's a myth. Myths aren't lies, even though the word is sometimes misused that way. Myths are stories that are told and retold because people find them helpful in making sense of the world and their place in it. I happen to think Genesis is a story that God gave us and that the truths in it are capital-T truths, not mere facts.

"Think what we learn from Genesis," I continued, warming up to my own eloquence. "We learn that God created everything and that it's good. We learn that God created us in his own image. We learn that God cares about how we behave and that there is a price to pay when we disobey. But we also learn that even then, even as he is banishing us from the garden, he's still with us to give us clothing and a pat on the back. Those are *truths,* Ben. How long it took to create things and whether or not there was really a garden of Eden—those are just details."

I sat back, pleased with myself, and waited. After a couple minutes, Ben looked up from his thoughts. "So what do you think?" he said, "Is Genesis true or is it just a myth?"

II

If I had been smart, I would have spared Ben my myth-is-truth rap and told him about C. S. Lewis.

Not everything about Lewis, of course—there is simply too much to tell. Does any other writer turn up on so many shelves of a good bookstore or library? In the literary criticism section one is likely to find, at a minimum, ***The Allegory of Love*** and ***English Literature in the Sixteenth Century,*** two books that, according to Norman Cantor's *Inventing the Middle Ages* (1993), were "bold, original, seminal works that rocked the transatlantic world of medieval studies" and had an "incalculable effect" on modern understandings of the Middle Ages. In literature we find ***Till We Have Faces,*** a retelling of the Cupid and Psyche myth that is arguably one of the finest English language novels of the 20th century. The religion shelves will be chock full, of course—books like ***Mere Christianity, The Screwtape Letters, The Problem of Pain,*** and ***Miracles*** continue to sell millions of copies each year. But then so will the science fiction shelves with Lewis's trilogy (***Out of the Silent Planet, Perelandra,*** and ***That Hideous Strength***), and the children's section, with his seven-volume ***Chronicles of Narnia,*** the most famous of which is ***The Lion, the Witch and the Wardrobe.*** And don't stop there—look in poetry for one of several collections of his verse, in biography for his spiritual autobiography ***Surprised by Joy,*** and in the section on death and dying for ***A Grief Observed,*** the nakedly powerful memoir of Lewis's tormented reaction to the death of his wife that provided the basis for the movie and play *Shadowlands.* If there is a book about great teachers to be found, it probably will contain a chapter on Lewis, a famously successful lecturer and tutor at Oxford and Cambridge Universities from the 1920's to the 1950's.

The Lewis I wish I had told Ben about, though, is one whose story has often been recorded but never fully understood. It is Lewis the spiritual pilgrim, the lifelong seeker of truth who rejected Christianity as a youth because it seemed "one mythology among many," embraced Christianity as a young man in part because it was mythic, then proclaimed Christianity to others for the rest of his life, most effectively through writings that are laden with mythology.

III

The young C. S. Lewis, born in Belfast, Northern Ireland, in 1898 to a middle-class family and schooled in England from his tenth birthday on, scorned Christianity because it seemed unreasonable. In ***Surprised by Joy*** Lewis records that although he had been raised (at least nominally) as a Christian, at the age of 13 he noticed that when his class studied, say, the *Aeneid,* the teachers' "accepted position seemed to be that religions were normally a mere farrago of nonsense, though our own, by a fortunate exception, was exactly true." This, on the face of it, struck him as absurd. His atheism gained intellectual grounding when, at age 16, he came under the influence of a private tutor, W. T. Kirkpatrick, who was much enamored of a new work by Sir James Frazer called *The Golden Bough.*

The Golden Bough was the product of Frazer's monumental survey of all the world religions and mythologies he could lay his hands on. In general, Frazer regarded religion as a human effort to make sense of the frightening and incomprehensible: thunder, pestilence, famine, death, and so on. In particular, Frazer found in human cultures a recurring story of a dying and resurrected god. This god usually was associated with agriculture and fertility—just as in the cycle of nature the plant is broken, the seed enters the ground, and life springs up, so is the god broken, buried, and restored. The Greek myth of Adonis is one such story. Adonis is a mortal beloved of both Aphrodite, the goddess of love, and Persephone, the goddess of the underworld, and each wants to possess him when he dies. Zeus arbitrates. For half the year, Adonis will inhabit the underworld with Persephone—on Earth, these will be the cold and barren months. Come

Spring, Adonis will return aboveground to be with Aphrodite, and warm weather and fertile fields will ensue. The comparable story from Egyptian mythology is of Osiris, who was slain and cut into fourteen pieces by his evil, desert-dwelling brother Set, then reassembled and brought back to life by Isis, his sister and wife. To the Egyptians, this story of death and resurrection was tied closely to the annual cycle of flood and fertility in the Nile delta.

Although Kirkpatrick was an atheist, he so instilled in Lewis the habit of taking nothing for granted that Lewis later credited him with making his eventual conversion to Christianity possible. Had he not been trained to keep his mind open to new ideas and evidence, Lewis wrote, he never would have considered Christianity seriously. But in the short term, Kirkpatrick's admiration of Frazer simply confirmed Lewis in the conviction that Christianity was as ridiculous as any other religion. In a letter to a Christian friend, written at age 18, Lewis disposed of Christianity as follows: "after the death of a Hebrew philosopher Yeshua (whose name we have corrupted into Jesus) he became regarded as a god, a cult sprang up, which was afterwards connected with the ancient Hebrew Jahweh-worship, and so Christianity came into being—one mythology among many, but the one that we happened to have been brought up in."

Lewis's boyhood experiences of church did little to soften this assessment. To be sure, he was taken to the local Anglican church by his parents, but worship there was as much a political act as a religious one—by attending the Church of England, Protestants in Northern Ireland let it be known that they were loyal subjects of the crown, not Roman papists. (Consider the criticism leveled by Lewis's brother Warner when Lewis later published some atheistic poetry: "it is obvious that a profession of a Christian belief is as necessary a part of a man's mental make up as a belief in the King, the Regular Army, and the Public Schools.") What Lewis found in church was arid, sterile, cold—"the dry husks of Christianity."

Reason uncontested by experience, then, led the young Lewis to reject Christianity. But other things were going on during Lewis's youth that, although devoid of explicit religious content, eventually would turn out to be of greater spiritual importance. These all may be grouped under the heading of the life of the imagination.

For one thing, Lewis loved stories. He was especially captivated by mythology. Even as an adult Christian, he said that in comparison to the stories of the Bible, "I like Greek mythology much better: Irish better still: Norse best of all."

In keeping with this love, Lewis wrote stories, many of them between the ages of six and eight. He and Warner, who was three years older, were kept inside most of the time to prevent their getting sick in the wet Irish climate. Warner recalled that their days were spent in the nursery where, from the window, they could see on the far horizon "the dim high line of the Castlereagh Hills—our world's limit, a distant land, strange and unattainable." Their imaginations fired by this landscape, the boys created an imaginary country called Boxen. The stories that Jack (for so, inexplicably, he insisted on being called) wrote "were an attempt to combine my two chief literary pleasures—'dressed animals' and 'knights in armour.' As a result, I wrote about chivalrous mice and rabbits who rode out in complete mail to kill not giants but cats."

An equally important part of Lewis's imaginative life as a child was the occasional experience of what he called "joy." Unpredictably, and for only moments at a time, Lewis would be overcome by an intense and exquisite yearning—"an unsatisfied desire which is itself more desirable than any other satisfaction." Joy might wash over him, as it once did, while he was reading a story like *Squirrel Nutkin,* or it might come with the memory of a toy garden fashioned of twigs and moss that his brother had made for him in the lid of a biscuit tin.

Lewis's most memorable experience of joy came while reading "Tegner's Drapa," a poem by Longfellow about the Norse god Balder. The story of Balder, a beloved figure among the Norse gods, was part of the death-and-resurrection genre that Frazer had found so pervasive in human cultures. In it Balder has dreams of death. When he shares those dreams with his fellow gods, they express their concern by swearing every being and object not to harm him. But Loki, a mischievous god who dislikes Balder, finds a mistletoe bush that the gods have overlooked and fashions one of its branches into a spear. Then, when the gods are enjoying the sport of throwing things at Balder and seeing them bounce off harmlessly, Loki arranges for Balder's brother to throw the mistletoe spear. It pierces Balder and kills him. Balder's death, the myth continues, triggers Ragnorak, the climactic twilight of the gods in which Balder returns to life to preside over a new world inaugurated by the first man and woman.

In reading Longfellow's poem, Lewis came upon these lines:

> I heard a voice, that cried,
> "Balder the beautiful
> Is dead, is dead!"
> And through the misty air
> Passed like the mournful cry
> Of sunward sailing cranes.

At that moment, Lewis records, "instantly I was uplifted into huge regions of northern sky, I desired with almost sickening intensity something never to be described . . . and then, as in other examples [of joy], found myself at the very same moment already falling out of that desire and wishing I were back in it."

IV

Lewis's passage to adulthood was more intellectual than imaginative. A precocious and successful student, he won a scholarship to University College, Oxford, earned first class degrees in Honour Mods (Greek and Latin texts), Greats (classical philosophy), and English language and literature. At age 27, after serving in the army during World War I, he was elected a fellow in English at Oxford's Magdalen College.

Through these years of academic progress, Lewis remained steadfast, even aggressive in his atheism. In 1917 he published a book of atheistic poems (the ones his brother objected to) called ***Spirits in Bondage.*** The title, which is drawn from *I Peter,* was meant to suggest the theme—namely, that religion keeps people in a state of spiritual enslavement. Lewis wrote that the book is "mainly strung around the idea . . . that nature is wholly diabolical and malevolent and that God, if he exists, is outside of and in opposition to the cosmic arrangements."

But even as a man, Lewis had occasional experiences of joy. At age 24, the old feeling of exquisite yearning was sparked during a visit home by a walk in the Castlereagh Hills, the very hills that had so enflamed his imagination as a boy. Four years later, just turning the pages of a dictionary of Norse mythology and seeing the old names was enough. Indeed, Lewis later wrote of this period in his life, "The two hemispheres of my mind were in the sharpest contrast. On the one side a many-islanded sea of poetry and myth; on the other a glib and shallow 'rationalism.' Nearly all that I loved I believed to be imaginary; nearly all that I believed to be real I thought grim and meaningless."

Not long afterward, while still a fellow at Magdalen, Lewis changed his mind about two things. First, he reluctantly concluded that there is a god. Emotions must have an object, he decided after reading Samuel Alexander's *Space, Time and Deity* (1920) and reflecting on his earlier study of Plato. The yearning that animates joy must be for a real thing. Letting go grudgingly of his atheism, Lewis tried out for a time the concept of the "Absolute Mind," which then was popular among the English Hegelians and which was quite different, he insisted, from "the God of popular religion." But he found in trying to teach the concept to students that the distinction between God and the Absolute Mind was so vague as to be meaningless. If there is a "superhuman mind," it must be a "Person." And what were his own efforts to understand the eternal truths of the Absolute Mind and bring his life into accord with them if not "what ordinary people call 'prayer to God'?"

Eventually, with all the enthusiasm of the mouse seeking the cat, Lewis gave way to theism. "You must picture me alone in that room in Magdalen," he later recalled, "night after night, feeling, whenever my mind lifted even for a second from my work, the steady, unrelenting approach of Him whom I so earnestly desired not to meet. That which I greatly feared had at last come upon me. In the Trinity Term of 1929 I gave in, and admitted that God was God, and knelt and prayed: perhaps, that night, the most dejected and reluctant convert in all England." To Lewis, belief in God was the only intellectually honest position he could take: "I am an empirical Theist. I have arrived at God by induction."

The second matter about which Lewis changed his mind was the resurrection of Jesus. He actually had begun entertaining the idea that the resurrection was a historical event before his conversion to theism. The catalyst was an offhand remark by T. D. Weldon, a fellow Oxford don and, like Lewis, an avowed atheist. "Rum thing, that stuff of Frazer's about the Dying God," Weldon said in casual conversation. "It almost looks as if it really happened once." Jarred by the remark and even more by its source, Lewis read the gospels closely and found them, "in their artless, historical, fashion," to be persuasive on the evidence. The gospels' avowedly historical character was telling, he concluded: unlike the other dying god stories, this one was painstakingly set in a particular time and place. Even more convincing to Lewis was what he did *not* find in the gospel accounts—namely, anything at all having to do with agriculture of fertility. What could it mean—a "corn god" story without the promise of corn?

Strange as it may seem, Lewis's newfound belief in God and the resurrection did not convert him to Christianity; indeed, he briefly flirted with Hinduism. Lewis did not like all the Christian talk about "'propitiation'—'sacrifice'—'the blood of the Lamb'—expressions which I could only interpret in senses that seemed to me either silly or shocking." Nor did he care much for Jesus. "Everyone told me that [in the gospels] I should find a figure I couldn't help loving," Lewis wrote in a letter. "Well, I could. . . . Indeed, some of His behaviour seemed to me open to criticism, e.g., accepting an invitation to dine with a Pharisee and then loading him with torrents of abuse." Above all, "What I couldn't see was how the life and death of Someone Else (whoever he was) two thousand years ago could help us here and now—except insofar as his *example* helped us."

On Sept. 19, 1931, Lewis vented his frustration to J.R.R. Tolkien and Hugo Dyson, two Christians and fellow scholars whom he was entertaining in his rooms at Magdalen. Whenever I encounter a dying god story in mythology, Lewis told them, I am "mysteriously moved, even though no one knows where he is supposed to have lived and died; he's not historical." The thrill was akin to that of watching "a diver, stripping off garment after garment, making himself naked, then flashing for a moment in the air, and then down through the green, and warm, and sunlit water into the pitch black, cold, freezing water, down into the mud and slime, then up again, his lungs almost bursting, back again to the green and warm and sunlit water, and then at last out into the sunshine, holding in his hand the dripping thing he went down to get." Why, Lewis wondered, am I not similarly moved by the gospels' historical accounts of Jesus's death and resurrection?

The answer, Lewis's colleagues told him, was to recognize that the gospel story was mythic and should be appreciated as such, "but with this tremendous difference that *it really happened*. . . . The dying god really appears—as a historical person, living in a definite time and place." As Lewis later wrote, "By becoming fact [the dying god story] does not cease to be myth: that is the miracle." But "it is God's myth where the others are men's myths: i.e. the Pagan stories are God expressing Himself through the minds of poets, using such images as He found there, while Christianity is God expressing Himself through what we call 'real things.'" The Christian story of the dying god, in other words, lay at the exact intersection of myth and history.

Lewis was persuaded by his friends' view, in part because it helped to resolve three other matters previously disturbing to him. One was the mundane literary style of the gospels, which he, like Saint Augustine, had previously found distasteful. Now Lewis realized that "if ever a myth had become fact, had been incarnated, it would be just like this," combining "the matter of the great myths" with an "artless, historical style."

Another was the seemingly inconsistent portrayal of Jesus in the gospels—"as real, as recognizable, through all that depth of time, as Plato's Socrates or Boswell's Johnson, . . . yet also numinous, lit by a light from beyond the world, a god." It now made sense to Lewis that Jesus was fully human—reflecting on Jesus's crucifixion eve despair and doubt in the garden of Gethsemane, he wrote, "How thankful I am that when God became man he did not choose to become a man of iron nerves: that would not have helped weaklings like and me nearly so much." (Lewis's letters show that he leaned heavily on the Jesus of Gethsemante when, years later, his wife was dying.) But he was equally appreciative of Jesus's divinity. To a correspondent who complained that divinity gave Jesus an unfair advantage, Lewis replied that, by that standard, "a man shd refuse a rope thrown to him by another who had one foot on the bank, saying 'Oh but you have an unfair advantage.' It is because of that advantage that He can help."

Lewis was perhaps most grateful for a third insight that accompanied his conversion, namely, that Christians should hold other mythologies and religions in high regard. (This was, of course, the opposite of his early teachers' views, which had turned him away from Christianity as a boy.) "Myth," Lewis wrote, "is the isthmus which connects the peninsular world of thought with the vast continent we really belong to"—indeed, "it was through *almost* believing in the gods that I came to believe in God." As for other religions, on the great issue of whether deity was real or not, "the whole mass of those who had worshipped—all who had danced and sung and sacrificed and trembled and adored—were clearly right." To declare Christianity true was not to declare all other religions false. Rather, Christianity was true because it was the answer to two vital questions: "Where has religion reached its true maturity? Where, if anywhere, have the hints of all Paganism been fulfilled?"

V

Lewis was, by temperament and (thanks to his tutor Kirkpatrick) by training the sort of person who, when he became convinced of something, could not resist sharing it with others. His vocational life at Oxford was the life of the mind, and most of the writing he had done since boyhood was of a scholarly kind. Not surprisingly, then, when Lewis turned his talents to spreading the gospel, he wrote numerous books and essays grounded in reason. "I am not asking anyone to accept Christianity if his best reasoning tells him that the weight of the evidence is against it," he wrote in ***Mere Christianity.***

Many people have found Lewis's apologetic works to be of great value. Most of them, I suspect, are people like me—people who were raised in the church, went off to college, then faced the challenge of reconciling faith with science and reason. To read a book by Lewis, whose intelligence sparkles on nearly every page of nearly everything he wrote, was enormously helpful in that effort. As Donald Williams once observed in *Christianity Today,* "the experience of discovering Lewis has formed an almost archetypal pattern in the lives of countless evangelical students. . . . First in this traditional pattern . . . came a period of gnawing doubt about the whole Christian faith. . . . Into this dark night of the soul swept whatever happened to be the student's first Lewis book. . . . And what he or she found there was not so much answers, though they were wonderful beyond all hope—but more, an irrefutable demonstration that at least one Christian *mind* actually existed."

Lewis's greatest gifts as a literary evangelist, however, are on display in his works of the imagination. Story and myth, after all, had marked his own journey of faith, especially his realization that myths not only could convey truth, but be truth. Lewis also realized that although a reasoned argument for Christianity might hold people's attention for as long as they were reading or hearing it, "the moment they have gone away from the lecture hall or laid down our article, they are plunged back into a world where the opposite position is taken for granted. Every newspaper, film, novel and textbook undermines our work. . . . [Thus w]hat we want is not more little books about Christianity, but more little books by Christians on other subjects—with their Christianity *latent.*" Practicing what he preached led Lewis to write his science fiction novels—***Perelandra,*** for example, in which the story of Eve's temptation is reenacted on a different planet, with a different Eve, and with a different result—as well as fantasies like ***The Great Divorce,*** an imaginative portrayal of the afterlife.

Lewis's crowning achievement was the ***Chronicles of Narnia,*** seven children's novels that, like *The Wind in the Willows* and *Charlotte's Web,* provide as much pleasure and satisfaction for the adults who read them aloud as for the children to whom they are read. Although Lewis was himself childless and had little experience of children, the enormous pleasure that successive generations of children have taken in the ***Chronicles*** is perhaps not altogether surprising. Given, as Lewis once wrote, that "the imaginative man in me is older, more continuously operative, and in that sense more basic than either the religious writer or the critic, . . . the fairy-tale was the *genre* best fitted for what I wanted to say." (Boxen revisited.) The circumstances of the five-year burst from 1948 to 1953 when he wrote all seven of the ***Chronicles*** also were helpful, albeit perversely. Having overworked himself into the hospital and, when his doctor prescribed a long rest, been forced instead to double up at home because his brother succumbed to alcoholism, Lewis seems desperately to have needed an escape into fantasy.

The ***Chronicles,*** taken as a whole, are an imaginative retelling of the entire Christian story. In them, Lewis wrote, "I say, "Supposing there was a world like Narnia, and supposing, like ours, it needed redemption, let us imagine what sort of Incarnation and Passion and Resurrection Christ would have there." He frankly hoped that children would not notice the books' Christianity, for fear for turning them off. (This is good for you, dear.) His own childhood experience of religion, after all, had been so shadowed by a lifeless, stained glass version of the faith that he had not been able to feel anything of the love for Jesus that he was repeatedly told he ought to fell. In the ***Chronicles,*** Lewis wrote, "I am aiming at a sort of pre-baptism of the child's imagination," so that when the child encountered the Christian story later, it would be more engaging.

Aslan, a lion, is the Christ of Narnia, and he is Lewis's greatest' literary creation. As Bede Griffiths has written, Aslan has all of the "hidden power and majesty and awesomeness which Lewis associated' with God, but also all his glory and the tenderness and even the humor which he believed belonged to him, so that children could run up to him and throw their arms around him and kiss him." In ***The Lion, the Witch, and the Wardrobe,*** the first of the ***Chronicles,*** four English schoolchildren enter a world of talking animals and mythological logical creatures ranging from fauns to Father Christmas. Tolkien hated the pastiche of fantastic characters but, according to the Lewis biographer George Sayer, Narnia was not unlike Lewis's view of heaven, "where all sorts of people could come together to celebrate, dance, and sing with fauns, giants, centaurs, dwarfs, and innumerable and very different animals." In Narnia, Aslan dies in order to spare one of the children from the full consequences of his sin, but is raised from death to triumph over the diabolical White Witch.

The six succeeding volumes of the ***Chronicles*** evoke other elements of the Christian story. "In ***Prince Caspian,***" Lewis wrote, "the old stories about [Aslan] are starting to be disbelieved. At the end of the [***Voyage of the***] ***Dawn Treader*** He appears as the Lamb. His three replies to Shasta [in ***The Horse and His Boy***] suggest the Trinity. In ***The Silver Chair*** the old king is raised from the dead by a drop of Aslan's blood. Finally in the ***Last Battle*** we have the reign of anti-Christ (the ape), the end of the world, and the Last Judgement." That quick summary makes the ***Chronicles*** sound far more formulaic than they are. Indeed, the chief pleasure of reading them lies not in the Christian elements themselves but rather in the stories and characters that make these elements seem—in the course of things, and without bold allegorical labels attached—appealing and exciting.

Near the end of ***The Magician's Nephew,*** for example, Aslan sings Narnia into creation. (The books are not chronological.) A voice—Aslan's voice—is heard, soon joined by a host of "cold, tingling, silvery voices" and a sky filled with stars. "If you had seen and heard it, you would have felt quite certain that it was the stars themselves who were singing, and that it was the First Voice, the deep one, which had made them appear and made them sing." Then a sun appears ("younger than ours—you could imagine that it laughed for joy as it came up"), revealing a landscape "of many colours: they were fresh, hot and vivid." Grass soon "spread out from the Lion like a pool. It ran up the sides of the little hills like a wave." Soon the land is "bubbling like water in a pot, . . . swelling into humps. They were of very different sizes, some no bigger than mole-hills, some as big as wheel-barrows, two the size of cottages. And the humps moved and swelled till they burst, and the crumbled earth poured out of them, and from each hump there came out an animal."

In ***The Silver Chair,*** the Queen of the Underworld traps and nearly convinces Puddleglum (a "marshwiggle") and some children, all of whom she has entranced with an incense-laden fire, that there is no Narnia, no sky, no Lion. To read this account is to experience what W. Fred Graham has called the "deadly asphyxiating stuffiness of life without the transcendent"; one cannot help but cheer when, in a final act of will, Puddleglum breaks the enchantment by bravely stamping out the fire with his bare feet. "The children's story pricks our imagination; it works," Graham observes, in a way that some of Lewis's more didactic writings—say, the proof he offers for God's existence in ***Mere Christianity***—do not.

One last example from the ***Chronicles:*** judgment day in Narnia, which is depicted in ***The Last Battle*** as a version of the parable of the sheep and the goats in Matthew 25. Emeth, a devout follower of the false god Tash who has never known Aslan, encounters him:

> [T]here came to meet me a great Lion. The speed of him was like the ostrich, and his size was an elephant's; his hair was like pure gold and the brightness of his eyes, like gold that is liquid in the furnace. . . . Then I fell at his feet and thought, Surely this is the hour of death, for the Lion (who is worthy of all honour) will know that I have served Tash all my days and not him. Nevertheless, it is better to see the Lion and die than to be Tisroc of the world and live and not to have seen him. But the Glorious One bent down his golden head and touched my forehead with his tongue and said, Son, thou art welcome. I said, Alas, Lord, I am no son of Thine but the servant of Tash. He answered, Child, all the service thou hast done to Tash, I account as service done to me. . . . [I]f any man swear by Tash and keep his oath for the oath's sake, it is by me that he has truly sworn, though he knows it not, and it is I who reward him. And if any man do a cruelty in my name, then though he says the name Aslan, it is Tash whom he serves and by Tash his deed is accepted.

VI

Inevitably, perhaps, Lewis has become something of a mythic figure himself. Lewis died, at age 65, on Nov. 22, 1963—a date that some now mark more for his passing than for that of President John F. Kennedy (or, for that matter, of Aldous Huxley). The mythmaking began almost immediately. In a 1967 book called *The Ring of Truth,* the distinguished New Testament translator J. B. Phillips blandly reported that a "rosily radiant" Lewis had visited him twice in his home shortly after he died and "spoke a few words which were particularly relevant to the difficult circumstances through which I was passing." Christian bookstores soon were filled with Lewis iconography, from the usual assortment of coffee mugs, T-shirts, and calendars to daily devotional books that consist entirely of excerpts from Lewis's writings and a coffee-table volume, titled *C. S. Lewis: Images of His* [sic!] *World,* that takes the reader on a photographic tour of the English byways that Lewis trod. The London and Broadway play *Shadowlands* and, especially, the popular 1993 movie (now on home video) have spread numinous images of Lewis to still wider audiences. Meanwhile, according to A. N. Wilson, rival Lewis cults have sprung up: at Wheaton College, the Marion E. Wade Center which "keeps alive the image of an evangelical Lewis . . . non-smoking and teetotaler" (in truth, Lewis smoked and drank to excess), while at the Anglo-verging-on-Roman Catholic C. S. Lewis Society in Oxford, "a High Church, celibate C. S. Lewis is reverenced," his inconvenient marriage notwithstanding.

Lewis, it is safe to say, would have been appalled by all of this. "Ever since I became a Christian," he wrote, "I have thought that the best, perhaps the only, service I could do for my unbelieving neighbours was to explain and defend the belief that has been common to nearly all Christians at all times." Having been led to Christianity along an avenue of myth and story, Lewis's sole purpose was to use his considerable gifts, notably of myth creation and story telling, to guide his readers in the same way. With a success matched or exceeded by few others—only Paul, Augustine, and Pascal come instantly to mind—he accomplished this purpose admirably.

Gilbert Meilaender (essay date August-September 1998)

SOURCE: "The Everyday C. S. Lewis," in *First Things,* No. 85, August-September, 1998, pp. 27-33.

[In the following essay, Meilaender examines Lewis's ability to illustrate the spiritual significance of commonplace experience. For Lewis, Meilaender notes, "the whole of life . . . every ordinary and everyday moment of it, every choice that we make, is charged with the significance of an eternal either/or."]

"One is sometimes (not often) glad not to be a great theologian. One might so easily confuse it with being a good Christian." Thus C. S. Lewis wrote in ***Reflections on the Psalms.*** Similarly, Lewis' religious writings are full of asides to the effect that he is not a theologian and that what he says is subject to correction by real theologians. In part, of course, let us recognize this for what it is: a smart rhetorical strategy that gets the reader on his side over against the presumably elitist theologians. But there is a worrisome sense in which Lewis' readers might be all too ready to hear such a message, all too ready to suppose that the faith is simple and clear, that theologians are largely in the business of making complicated what ought not be.

That is a temptation whose seductions we should resist. And indeed, in writing of "the everyday C. S. Lewis," I am not suggesting that Lewis' reflection is done at an everyday or unsophisticated level, but, rather, that he reflects religiously upon what is ordinary and everyday. Indeed, to the degree that Lewis is often characterized as a "popular" religious thinker, I am inclined to think the characterization misleading, and in part, I fear, a result of a peculiar academic prejudice against anyone who writes clearly and is widely read. Lewis' readers actually get a rather heavy dose of serious religious reflection, though generally in quite alluring literary style.

Nevertheless, theology is and must remain an elite activity. It is not, in fact, aimed at the masses. And there is a sense in which we might better say that Lewis' writing is "religious" rather than "theological." This sense is one that he would himself, I believe, affirm. He makes such a distinction, for example, in the incomplete, posthumously published essay **"The Language of Religion."** There he develops a distinction between ordinary language ("It was very cold") and two other kinds of language, each of which transforms ordinary language in the interest of certain purposes. Scientific language ("The temperature was -5 degrees Fahrenheit") seeks language that has a certain kind of precision lacking in our ordinary speech—a precision that we can quantify and test, that can be used to settle disputes about how cold it actually is. But this scientific language does not itself give us any sense of how a very cold day "feels," a sense of its "quality." If I have spent my entire life in a tropical climate, and you tell me that it is -5 degrees Fahrenheit where you live, such language will not help me feel what it's like to be there.

Ordinary language might do a little better in communicating this "feel." "Your ears will tingle." "It will hurt just to breathe." But poetic language exists in large part to try to improve ordinary language on just this point: to convey the quality, the feel, of experience. Lewis uses Keats' poem as illustration: "Ah, bitter chill it was! The owl, for all his feathers, was a-cold; The hare limped trembling through the frozen grass, And silent was the flock in wooly fold: Numb'd were the Beadsman's fingers." This language cannot be quantified or tested; but it may, Lewis suggests, convey information that can be given in no other way. Perhaps it may even convey the quality of experiences we ourselves have never had.

Religious talk, like all talk, begins with ordinary language, but, depending on our purposes, it may quickly turn in directions more like the scientific or the poetic. Theological language, as Lewis describes it, is, strictly speaking, an alteration rather like the scientific It seeks a precision that is needed and useful for clarifying uncertain or disputed points and for settling disagreements. As such, it is absolutely necessary. Elitist in a certain sense, it is, nonetheless, not to be belittled. Indeed, its precision can be a thing of beauty. But one thing it cannot do: it cannot by itself convey understanding of what in its very nature transcends our ordinary experience. For that we need language that is religious but not, in this sense, theological—language more like the poetic. To say "God is the Father of lights" is such language—religious, though not exactly theological.

A good bit of Lewis' success can, I think, be attributed to the fact that he actually writes relatively little "theology" in this technical sense. Clearly, he's read a good bit of it and been instructed by it—he does not in any sense belittle it—but he tends to seek language that captures and communicates the quality, the feel, of living and thinking as a Christian. As Austin Farrer put it: "[Lewis'] real power was not proof; it was depiction. There lived in his writings a Christian universe that could be both thought and felt, in which he was at home and in which he made his reader feel at home." That is the universe I want to explore. It illumines the everyday, so that we may find in it shafts of the divine glory that point to God, so that we may sense the eternal significance of ordinary life.

I

In his famous and powerful work *Fear and Trembling,* Søren Kierkegaard describes the "knight of faith" who has made the double movement of infinite resignation and of faith. Having given up the sense that anything is his possession to claim, having surrendered all for the sake of an immediate relation to God, the knight of faith nevertheless trusts that God will give it back—not in some future life, but in the here and now, in the finite realm. And, as a result, although he has made the first movement of infinite resignation, he is also able to savor the everyday. Kierkegaard describes him this way:

> Here he is. The acquaintance is struck, I am introduced. The moment I first set eyes on him I thrust him away, jump back, clasp my hands together and say half aloud: "Good God! Is this the person, is it really him? He looks just like a tax-gatherer." . . . I examine him from top to toe, in case there should be some crack through which the infinite peeped out. No! He is solid through and through. . . . One detects nothing of the strangeness and superiority that mark the knight of the infinite. This man takes pleasure, takes part, in everything, and whenever one catches him occupied with something his engagement has the persistence of the worldly person whose soul is wrapped up in such things. . . . He delights in everything he sees. . . .

The knight of faith is therefore, as Kierkegaard puts it, able "to express the sublime in the pedestrian absolutely."

That characterization—to express the sublime in the pedestrian—is an apt description of something that makes Lewis' religious writing so effective. "[O]nly supernaturalists really see Nature," Lewis says.

> You must go a little away from her, and then turn round, and look back. Then at last the true landscape will become visible. . . . Come out, look back, and then you will see . . . this astonishing cataract of bears, babies, and bananas: this immoderate deluge of atoms, orchids, oranges, cancers, canaries, fleas, gases, tornadoes, and toads. How could you have ever thought this was the ultimate reality?. . . She is herself. Offer her neither worship nor contempt.

The ordinary pleasures of life—both those simply given to us in nature and those derived from culture—play a large role in Lewis' thinking and account for much of the power of his writing.

He can make domesticity seem enticing—as when Peter, Susan, and Lucy share a meal with the Beavers. And, indeed, the best times in Narnia are not the times we read of in the stories, the times when momentous events are occurring. The good times are those when nothing "important" happens, when life goes on in its ordinary, everyday way. Similarly, Lewis finds—surely not by accident—that "cheerful moderation" is an important characteristic in the novels of Jane Austen. "She has, or at least all her favorite characters have, a hearty relish for what would now be regarded as very modest pleasures. A ball, a dinner party, books, conversation, a drive to see a great house ten miles away. . . ." He celebrates the appreciation of "middle things" that he finds in the writings of Joseph Addison. Granting that Addison does not stir one's soul as some writers do, Lewis nonetheless finds a kind of strength and goodness in Addison's affirmation of "the common ground of daily life." "If I were to live in a man's house for a whole twelve-month, I think I should be more curious about the quality of his small beer than about that of his wine; more curious about his bread and butter and beef than about either."

And few readers of ***Surprised by Joy*** are likely to forget Lewis' description of what was for him a "normal day" during the time he was living with and being tutored by Kirkpatrick.

> [I]f I could please myself I would always live as I lived there. I would choose always to breakfast at exactly eight and to be at my desk by nine, there to read or write till one. If a good cup of tea or coffee could be brought me about eleven, so much the better. A step or so out of doors for a pint of beer would not do quite so well; for a man does not want to drink alone and if you meet a friend in the taproom the break is likely to be extended beyond its ten minutes. At one precisely lunch should be on the table; and by two at the latest I would be on the road. Not, except at rare intervals, with a friend. Walking and talking are two very great pleasures, but it is a mistake to combine them. Our own noise blots out the sounds and silences of the outdoor world; and talking leads almost inevitably to smoking, and then farewell to nature as far as one of our senses is concerned. . . . The return from the walk, and the arrival of tea, should be exactly coincident, and not later than a quarter past four. Tea should be taken in solitude, . . . [f]or eating and reading are two pleasures that combine admirably. Of course not all books are suitable for mealtime reading. It would be a kind of blasphemy to read poetry at table. What one wants is a gossipy, formless book which can be opened anywhere. . . . At five a man should be at work again, and at it till seven. Then, at the evening meal and after, comes the time for talk, or, failing that, for lighter reading; and unless you are making a night of it with your cronies . . . there is no reason why you should ever be in bed later than eleven.

Such a life Lewis himself describes as "almost entirely selfish" but certainly not "self-centered." "[F]or in such a life my mind would be directed toward a thousand things, not one of which is myself." Lewis, of course, understands that an "almost entirely selfish" approach to life cannot really be recommended. He simply understands its attraction, and he sees that it may, in fact, be better in some respects than a life which seems less selfish.

> One of the happiest men and most pleasing companions I have ever known was intensely selfish. On the other hand I have known people capable of real sacrifice whose lives were nevertheless a misery to themselves and to others, because self-concern and self-pity filled all their thoughts. Either condition will destroy the soul in the end. But till the end give me the man who takes the best of everything (even at my expense) and then talks of other things, rather than the man who serves me and talks of himself, and whose very kindnesses are a continual reproach, a continual demand for pity, gratitude, and admiration.

In an epitaph he once composed, Lewis made the same point a little more playfully:

> Erected by her sorrowing brothers

In memory of Martha Clay.
Here lies one who lived for others;
Now she has peace. And so have they.

Thus, Lewis has a keen delight in the ordinary and the everyday. But I think this appreciation for the everyday goes yet a little further than simple delight—which, taken by itself after all, might be chiefly a matter of temperament. The deeper point is that the ordinary is the stuff of most of our lives most of the time. It is, therefore, where we most often find our callings, our opportunities for faithfulness, and our temptations.

Something like that is the point of Lewis' sermon **"Learning in War-Time,"** a sermon preached in the Church of St. Mary the Virgin on the evening of Sunday, October 22, 1939—when people in England had a genuine crisis, very much out of the ordinary, on their hands. Even such a moment of crisis does not, Lewis suggests, alter the fundamental situation in which we always find ourselves. For every moment of life is lived in the presence of the Eternal, in every moment of life we are "advancing either to Heaven or to Hell," and those high stakes are played out in the most mundane of decisions.

Lewis' ability to see that, and help us to see it, is part of the enduring power of ***The Screwtape Letters.*** Screwtape knows how much the ordinary and the everyday count for in our spiritual life. He knows, for example, of a human being who was once "defended from strong temptations to social ambition by a still stronger taste for tripe and onions." He knows that Wormwood has blundered badly when he permits his "patient" to read a book simply because he enjoys it, or to take a walk through country he enjoys. He knows that, when it comes to separating a human being from God, the ordinary can also be Wormwood's greatest ally. The important choices in life seldom present themselves in extraordinary appearance. "It does not matter how small the sins are, provided that their cumulative effect is to edge the man away from the Light and out into the Nothing. Murder is no better than cards if cards can do the trick. Indeed, the safest road to Hell is the gradual one—the gentle slope, soft underfoot, without sudden turnings, without milestones, without signposts."

This sense that eternal issues are at stake in the mundane choices of our everyday life helps, I think, to account for the fact that, in this country, Lewis has been so popular among evangelical Protestants. An analysis of the theological structure of his religious writings would, I am convinced, show clearly that this structure is more adequately described (to paint in broad strokes) as "Catholic" than as "Protestant." Faith as trust does not play a large role in his depiction of the Christian life. That life is not conceived primarily as a turn from consciousness of sin to the proclamation of grace. Instead, it is conceived as a journey, a process of perfection, and Jesus is the way toward that goal. From start to finish this journey is, to be sure, the work of grace, but that grace is primarily the power to finish the journey, not simply a pardoning word of forgiveness. The end of this journey is the beatific vision—to see God and to rest in God—and that vision is granted only to those who are perfected, to the pure in heart.

In good Aristotelian fashion, therefore, Lewis thinks of all the ordinary decisions of life as forming our character, as turning us into people who either do or do not wish to gaze forever upon the face of God. When "night falls on Narnia" and we get the great scene of final judgment, all the inhabitants of that world have no choice about one thing. All must march past Aslan and look upon him. Some see there the face they have always longed to see, which they have learned to love, and they enter Aslan's world. Others see there a face they can only hate, for that is the sort of person they have become. They go off into nothingness. Every choice counts. Every choice contributes to determining what we ultimately love.

Protestant readers may, I believe, be especially drawn to this picture because, though they might not articulate the matter this way, it supplies something that is often missing from standard Protestant talk of forgiveness and faith, pardon and trust. Lewis' picture suggests that our actions are important not only because they hurt or harm the neighbor, but also because—under grace—they form and shape the persons we are. There are, to be sure, some theological dangers embedded in such a vision of the Christian life, but in Lewis' hands we can also see its power and its allure.

If we ask ourselves, therefore, what accounts for the success Lewis' writings have clearly had in reaching a wide range of readers and in shaping a religiously informed vision of life, his appreciation of the everyday cannot be overlooked. His notion of the everyday comes, of course, with a distinctively British flavor, but that does not seem to have created insurmountable obstacles for his readers. It is not just that he appreciates the everyday, however; it is also that he understands and evokes its significance for our moral and spiritual life. In ordinary pleasures, shafts of the divine glory, God touches our lives to draw us to himself. In ***Surprised by Joy*** Lewis tells his own life story as one whose underlying theme is *Sehnsucht*—the longing for joy. As Augustine said that our restless hearts could find the rest they desire only in God, so Lewis suggests that the ordinary goods and pleasures of life draw us beyond themselves and beyond ourselves to the only One who is Goodness itself.

But, as Augustine also said in a passage that Lewis places as an epigraph at the start of the last chapter of ***Surprised***

by Joy, "It is one thing to see the land of peace from a wooded ridge . . . and another to tread the road that leads to it. "The ordinary and the everyday count immensely in our moral and spiritual life. In them God touches us to call us to himself. That means also, however, that the stakes there are very high, that seemingly minor decisions may help to shape a person who one day will say—with a tone of utter finality—either "*my* will be done," or "*thy* will be done." God calls to us in the pleasures of everyday life, but we can miss the message. We can refuse to let ourselves be called out beyond the ordinary, we can try to hang on to the everyday—ignoring what is terrible and mysterious about it. Then the manna that we have tried to save rots, the pleasures fade, and we are left with something less than the everyday: with only ourselves. Something like that, surely, is the picture Lewis paints in ***The Great Divorce.*** The choice is, finally and simply, between heaven and hell. But the choice is made, and eternal issues determined, in our everyday decisions and actions. Every moment of life is momentous—touched by and equidistant from the Eternal.

II

This is, I have suggested, part of the religious power of Lewis' vision of human life. But there is still more. If we take it only this far, in fact, we probably miss the most penetrating and compelling aspects of his thought. For the God who meets us in the ordinary and the everyday in order to call us to himself is not simply a God who makes us happy. To be sure, he will do that—will make us happier than we can even imagine. But Lewis offers no "feel good" religion, no books about how to live the abundant life. If there is a biblical theme that pervades all his writing it surely is: only the one who loses his life for Jesus' sake will find it. The ordinary pleasures of life give us just an inkling of what true pleasure must be, and Lewis is a master at using them to depict the happiness God will one day bestow on those who love him. But "it is one thing to see the land of peace from a wooded ridge . . . and another to tread the road that leads to it." And the road that leads to it may be painful indeed.

The Christian life hurts. God hurts. That's what Lewis really has to say, and it is, I think, the deepest reason for the power of his writing. "[T]he Divine Nature wounds and perhaps destroys us merely by being what it is," Orual reflects in ***Till We Have Faces.*** This theme—that God hurts—is perhaps most pronounced in some of Lewis' last works—especially in ***Till We Have Faces, A Grief Observed,*** and ***The Four Loves.*** And it is perhaps not insignificant that each of these three works, in different ways, was influenced by Lewis' acquaintance with and, finally, marriage to Joy Davidman Gresham. But, in fact, this theme was present in Lewis' writing almost from the very beginning. Near the end of ***The Pilgrim's Regress,*** John, the pilgrim who has finally made his way back to Mother Church, sings a song about "the tether and pang of the particular." It may not be great poetry. Despite Lewis' aspirations to be known as an epic poet, it turned out that his talent was for prose. Nevertheless, this very early poem makes clear how the turn (or return) to God wounds our nature.

> Passing today by a cottage, I shed tears
> When I remembered how once I had dwelled
> there
> With my mortal friends who are dead. Years
> Little had healed the wound that was laid bare.
>
> Out, little spear that stabs, I, fool, believed
> I had outgrown the local, unique sting,
> I had transmuted away (I was deceived)
> Into love universal the lov'd thing.
>
> But Thou, Lord, surely knewest Thine own plan
> When the angelic indifferences with no bar
> Universally loved but Thou gav'st man
> The tether and pang of the particular.
>
> Which, like a chemic drop, infinitesimal,
> Plashed into pure water, changing the whole,
> Embodies and embitters and turns all
> Spirit's sweet water to astringent soul.
>
> That we, though small, may quiver with fire's
> same
> Substantial form as Thou—not reflect merely,
> As lunar angel, back to thee, cold flame.
> Gods we are, Thou hast said: and we pay dearly.

Rather abstractly put, perhaps, but to the point. Lewis put flesh and bones on this abstraction in ***The Magician's Nephew,*** where Digory is forced to choose between obedience to Aslan's command and an action that may save the life of his dying mother. And, although the poem from ***Pilgrim's Regress*** surely betrays the influence of philosophical idealism on Lewis' thought, it also shows certain Christian assumptions about what it means to be human. We are created as both finite and free—made from the dust of the ground, tied to particular times and places, but also made for something more, a something more that is finally God.

Thus, the poem recognizes our finitude: We are not angels who love only universally, simply reflecting back the divine love. We also love particularly, with the tether and pang of the particular. We never outgrow "the local, unique sting," nor transmute it into universal love alone. Yet, we are also free, made for God. We must therefore learn how to love more universally—and, ultimately, how to love God, who is by no means ours alone. We live with this duality of our being, with our hearts both tied to what is local and unique and drawn toward the universal. Living within that tension, as the poem puts it, "we pay dearly."

The movie *Shadowlands* got it right, therefore, in a conversation it imagines between Lewis and Joy. During the period when her illness is in remission, Joy and Jack are on a trip and, taking shelter from the rain, suddenly find themselves talking about what lies ahead. Jack expresses his fear, fear of the pain he will feel when he loses her. To which Joy responds: "The pain then is a part of the pleasure now. That's the deal." The pleasure now is grounded in a particular commitment of the heart, and such a commitment makes us vulnerable. It sets us up to be hurt. But we can avoid that pain only by refusing right now to give our heart to anyone whom we might one day lose. We can, that is, avoid future pain only by retreating entirely into the self, by caring about nothing outside the self. But that, of course, would be hell—a retreat into the "ruthless, sleepless, unsmiling concentration upon self" that Lewis calls "the mark of Hell."

Even in his stories for children, Lewis does not hesitate to emphasize the appropriateness and necessity of suffering. When, in ***The Last Battle,*** "night falls on Narnia" and Aslan pulls down the curtain on Narnian history, the children who are friends of Narnia find themselves in Aslan's world—an even more wonderful place to be. But Lucy begins to cry at the thought of what they have left behind. "What Lucy!" Peter says. "You're not *crying?* With Aslan ahead, and all of us here?" To which Tirian, last of the kings of Narnia, who has come into Aslan's world with the children, replies. "Sirs, the ladies do well to weep. See I do so myself. I have seen my mother's death. What world but Narnia have I ever known? It were no virtue, but great discourtesy, if we did not mourn." Likewise, expressing and reflecting upon his own very deep personal anguish in ***A Grief Observed,*** Lewis writes that what he wants in his bereavement is to continue to live his marriage "well and faithfully" in and through his loss. "We were one flesh. Now that it has been cut in two, we don't want to pretend that it is whole and complete."

We could try to avoid this pain by holding on to the beloved—if only in memory—as if she were ours, our possession. That would, of course, be futile, but, still more important, it would be to miss the call of God that comes to us in and through the loved one. It would be to mistake the gift for the Giver. Or we could try to avoid this pain by telling ourselves that there has been no real loss. God's will has been done, and the loved one is now better off. But true though this is from one angle, it does less than justice to that "local, unique sting" that should and does characterize our loves. Lewis puts the point very directly and insightfully, again in ***A Grief Observed:***

> If a mother is mourning not for what she has lost but for what her dead child has lost, it is a comfort to believe that the child has not lost the end for which it was created. . . . A comfort to the God-aimed, eternal spirit within her. But not to her motherhood. The specifically maternal happiness must be written off. Never, in any place or time, will she have her son on her knees, or bathe him, or tell him a story, or plan for his future, or see her grandchild.

This theme—of the tension or rivalry between our natural loves and love for God—is given its most systematic treatment by Lewis in ***The Four Loves,*** a book that deserves, I believe, to be considered a minor classic in Christian ethics. The book is powerful because Lewis does not content "himself only with noting the possible rivalry between particular loves and love for God. With each of the loves that he takes up—affection, friendship, and erotic love—he begins where I began above: by depicting for us the sublime within the everyday.

Thus, he finds in each of the natural loves an image of what divine love itself is in part. We see one facet of God's love, for example, in the undiscriminating character of affection. Given familiarity over time, almost anyone can become an object of affection. Hence, this love manifests an implicit openness to the worth of every human being. Friendship, by contrast, is clearly a discriminating love, for we are friends only with certain people whom we have chosen for particular reasons. But, at the same time, friendship is, unlike affection, the least jealous of loves. Our circle of friends will be open to anyone who shares the interest that binds us together, and in that sense friendship is implicitly universal. If affection is jealous but undiscriminating, and friendship is discriminating but not jealous, eros is both discriminating and jealous. How, then, might it image for us divine love? In selfless devotion eros plants "the interests of another in the center of our being. Spontaneously and without effort we have fulfilled the law (towards one person) by loving our neighbor as ourselves. It is an image, a foretaste, of what we must become to all if Love Himself rules in us without a rival."

Lewis' first move is to evoke the beauty and the splendor of the natural loves, the way in which they give pleasure. And surely, part of the hold of this book upon several generations of readers has been its ability to evoke delight—to help us appreciate the beauty of the natural loves and find in them shafts of the divine glory. But Lewis' discussion never stops there. He never forgets that "the Divine Nature wounds and perhaps destroys us merely by being what it is. "And so, with each of the loves he notes also its insufficiency—the way in which, even and especially at its very best, it may go wrong. Affection is prone to jealousy and wants to possess the loved one. Still more, it needs to be needed. In affection we desire only the good *we* can give, which is not always the good the loved one needs. The love of friendship is always tempted to exclusivity. Rightly excluding those who do not share our special interests, we may easily take pride in our circle of friends and come to value exclusivity for its own sake. And so powerful, almost godlike, is the claim of eros upon us, that we may do great injustice in its name. Left to itself eros is likely to be fickle and unfaithful, to work harm and havoc in human life.

Therefore, each of the natural loves, beautiful and splendid as they are in themselves, must be transformed by charity, by love of God. They must be taken up into a life directed toward God and be reborn—transformed and perfected as "modes of charity." Lewis' concluding chapter on charity in ***The Four Loves,*** among the most powerful pieces of his generally powerful prose, is a haunting depiction of the way in which this needed transformation is likely to be painful. We say that the natural loves are transformed and perfected, but that language does not quite capture the truth of our experience. It may sometimes feel more like death—that the natural loves must be put to death so that a new life marked by charity can arise. With just such an idea in mind—namely, that the needed transformation of our natural loves may seem akin to dying—Josef Pieper once recalled that charity has been pictured by Christians as a consuming fire, and that it is therefore "much more than an innocuous piety when Christendom prays, 'Kindle in us the fire of Thy love.'"

At their very best, therefore, the natural loves fall short. In themselves they are good, but they were never meant to be simply "in themselves"—to be isolated from the God-relation, to be anything other than modes of charity. But in our sin we do isolate and idolize them, refusing to recognize that they are and must remain *creaturely* loves. Because we do so, we can only experience the transformation of our loves as painful. When God redirects them to himself, it hurts. We can, of course, say, with perfect justification, that this redirection is a restoration of them to what they are meant to be. It is a liberation of their true beauty and is in the service of their genuine flourishing. In the Augustinian language that underlies Lewis' treatment in ***The Four Loves,*** it is the restoring of inordinate love to right order. It is the restoration of harmony between nature and grace.

All true—and truly said. But we cannot always—perhaps not even often—experience this restoration as liberation and fulfillment. For all that is "far away in 'the land of the Trinity,'" and we remain pilgrims on the way. Along the way, nature may often seem wounded by grace. When, in the theological struggles to which the Reformation gave rise, Protestants depicted a nature so thoroughly corrupted by sin that death and rebirth were necessary, Catholics sometimes thought that this demonstrated an insufficient appreciation of the continuing goodness of creation, of its ability to point us to God. And so, Catholics responded by saying that "grace does not destroy nature, but perfects it." That is, over against an image of death and resurrection they set an incarnational image—not a destruction of the natural life and a new birth, but the natural life taken up into and perfected within a graced life.

Lewis, mere Christian that he seeks to be, sees the worth of both pictures of the Christian life—and sees it quite profoundly. As always in his view, the real truth of things is captured in the Catholic formulation: The natural life is God's good gift; he will not destroy but perfect it. The natural loves are transformed when they become incarnate as modes of charity. But the Protestant formulation captures something very important about the truth of our experience, about what this transformation may feel like. It hurts.

Lewis' most haunting depiction of nature wounded by grace must certainly be one of his least read books, ***Till We Have Faces.*** Before the story is over, Orual comes to see the harsh truth about her love for Psyche and others. It had been a "gnawing greed." She comes to see that the kingdom of Glome "was a web—I the swollen spider, squat at its center, gorged with men's stolen lives." Yet, her natural loves of affection, friendship, and eros were not mere selfishness. They were, in some ways, the natural loves at their best. As Lewis once put it in a letter to Clyde Kilby, Orual is an example of "human affection in its natural condition, true, tender, suffering, but in the long run tyrannically possessive and ready to turn to hatred when the beloved ceases to be its possession."

Sin builds its throne at the heart of what is best in our nature, and, then, when God draws us toward himself, it may feel the way it felt to Orual when the Divine surgeons went to work on her. What she experienced was loss and suffering—so great, indeed, that she finally cries out: "That there should be gods at all, there's our misery and bitter wrong. There's no room for you and us in the same world." Striving for independence, striving to isolate her natural loves from the only context in which they could ultimately flourish, Orual had been making war on the reality principle of the universe. How can the gods meet us face to face, she finally asks, till we have faces? She had to be broken to be transformed.

I do not believe there is any theme more central to Lewis' vision of human life in relation to God, and I think there are very few indeed who have managed as well as he to invoke simultaneously in readers both an appreciation for and delight in our created life, and a sense of the pain and anguish that come when that life is fully redirected to the One from whom it comes. "To love at all," Lewis wrote in ***The Four Loves,*** "is to be vulnerable. . . . The alternative to tragedy, or at least to the risk of tragedy, is damnation. The only place outside Heaven where you can be perfectly safe from all the dangers and perturbations of love is Hell." The whole of life, therefore, every ordinary and everyday moment of it, every choice that we make, is charged with the significance of an eternal either/or. Which means, I guess, that no moment is simply ordinary.

Here, I think, we find the truth behind the remarkable staying power of Lewis' writings. He is not really returning theology to the masses. In fact, in the strict sense, he can hardly be said to be writing theology. He gives us something better—the feel, the quality, of a life truly lived before God. He gives us the everyday—in all its splendor, terror, pain, and possibility. And through what is ordinary and everyday he invites us to enter into that "mystical death which is the secret of life."

J. I. Packer (essay date 7 September 1998)

SOURCE: "Still Surprised by Lewis," in *Christianity Today,* September 7, 1998, pp. 54, 56-60.

[*In the following essay, Packer discusses Lewis's literary career, religious beliefs, and popularity among Christians.*]

Yes, I was at Oxford in Lewis's day (I went up in 1944); but *no* I never met him. He was regularly on show as the anchorman of the Socratic Club, which met weekly to discuss how science, philosophy, and current culture related to Christianity; but as a young believer, I was sure I needed Bible teaching rather than apologetics, so I passed the Socratic by. The nearest I ever got to Lewis was hearing him address the Oxford theologians society on Richard Hooker about whom he was writing at that time for his assigned volume of the Oxford History of English Literature, the "Oh-Hell" as for obvious reasons he liked to call it. He spoke with a resonant Anglicized accent (you would never have guessed he was Irish), and when he said something funny, which he did quite often, he paused like a stage comedian for the laugh. They said he was the best lecturer in Oxford, and I daresay they were right. But he was not really part of my world.

Yet I owe him much, and I gratefully acknowledge my debt.

First of all, in 1942-43, when I thought I was a Christian but did not yet know what a Christian was—and had spent a year verifying the old adage that if you open your mind wide enough much rubbish will be tipped into it—***The Screwtape Letters*** and the three small books that became ***Mere Christianity*** brought me, not indeed to faith in the full sense, but to mainstream Christian beliefs about God, man, and Jesus Christ, so that now I was halfway there.

Second, in 1945, when I was newly converted, the student who was discipling me lent me ***The Pilgrim's Regress.*** This gave me both a full-color map of the Western intellectual world as it had been in 1932 and still pretty much was 13 years later, and also a very deep delight in knowing that I knew God, beyond anything I had felt before. The vivid glow of Lewis's scenic and dramatic imagination, as deployed in the story, had started to grab me. ***Regress,*** Lewis's first literary effort as a Christian, is still for me the freshest and liveliest of all his books, and I reread it more often than any of the others.

Third, Lewis sang the praises of an author named Charles Williams, of whom I had not heard, and in consequence I picked up *Many Dimensions* in paperback in 1953 and had one of the most overwhelming reading experiences of my life—though that is another story.

Fourth, there are stellar passages in Lewis that for me, at least, bring the reality of heaven very close. Few Christian writers today try to write about heaven, and the theme defeats almost all who take it up. But as one who learned long ago from Richard Baxter's *Saints' Everlasting* Rest and Bunyan's *Pilgrim's Progress* the need for clearly focused thought about heaven, I am grateful for the way Lewis helps me along here.

The number of Christians whom Lewis's writings have helped, one way and another, is enormous. Since his death in 1963, sales of his books have risen to 2 million a year, and a recently polled cross section of *CT* readers rated him the most influential writer in their lives—which is odd, for they and I identify ourselves as evangelicals, and Lewis did no such thing. He did not attend an evangelical place of worship nor fraternize with evangelical organizations. "I am a very ordinary layman of the Church of England," he wrote; "not especially 'high,' nor especially 'low,' nor especially anything else." By ordinary evangelical standards, his idea about the Atonement (archetypal penitence, rather than penal substitution), and his failure ever to mention justification by faith when speaking of the forgiveness of sins, and his apparent hospitality to baptismal regeneration, and his noninerrantist view of biblical inspiration, plus his quiet affirmation of purgatory and of the possible final salvation of some who have left this world as nonbelievers, were weaknesses; they led the late, great Martyn Lloyd-Jones, for whom evangelical orthodoxy was mandatory, to doubt whether Lewis was a Christian at all. His closest friends were Anglo-Catholics or Roman Catholics; his parish church, where he worshiped regularly, was "high"; he went to confession; he was, in fact, anchored in the (small-c) "catholic" stream of Anglican thought, which some (not all) regard as central. Yet evangelicals love his books and profit from them hugely. Why?

As one involved in this situation, I offer the following answer.

In the first place, Lewis was a *lay evangelist,* conservative in his beliefs and powerful in his defense of the old paths. "Ever since I became a Christian," he wrote in 1952, "I have thought that the best, perhaps the only service I could do for my unbelieving neighbors was to explain and defend the belief that has been common to nearly all Christians at all times." To make ordinary people think about historic Christianity, and to see and feel the strength and attraction of the case for it, was Lewis's goal throughout. All through his writings runs the sense that moderns have ceased to think about life and reality in a serious way and have settled instead for mindless drift with the crowd, or blind trust in technology, or the Athenian frivolity of always chasing new ideas, or the nihilism of knee-jerk negativism toward everything in the past. The Christian spokesman's first task, as Lewis saw it, is to put all this into reverse and get folk thinking again.

So his immediate goal in a sustained flow of didactic books, opinion pieces, children's stories, adult fiction and fantasy, autobiography, and poems, along with works of literary history and criticism, spread out over more than 30 years, was to stir up serious thought. About what? About the Christian values and perspectives that the people he once labeled the Clevers had left behind, and about the morasses one gets bogged down in once the Christian heritage is abandoned; and on from there. He would have agreed with the often-stated dictum of fellow evangelist Martyn Lloyd-Jones that the Christian is and must be the greatest thinker in the universe, and that God's first step in adult conversion is to make the person think.

Lewis was clear that, as he has Screwtape tell us in many different ways, thoughtlessness ruins souls; so he labored mightily by all kinds of stimulating persuasives—witty, argumentative, pictorial, fanciful, logical, prophetic, and dramatic by turns—to ensure, so far as he could, that death-dealing thoughtlessness would not flourish while he was around. His constant pummelling of his reader's mind was neither Ulster temperament nor Oxford didacticism, but the urgent compassionate expression of one who knew that the only alternative to grasping God's truth and seeing everything by its light is idiocy in one form or another.

And he believed, surely with reason, that his credibility as a Christian spokesman in an anticlerical age was enhanced by the fact that he had no professional religious identity but was just an Anglican layman earning his salt by teaching English at Oxford. As G. K. Chesterton was to himself simply a journalist with a significant Christian outlook, so Lewis was to himself simply an academic with a significant spare-time vocation of Christian utterance. Evangelicals appreciate lay evangelists of Lewis's kind.

Second, Lewis was a *brilliant teacher.* His strength lay not in the forming of new ideas but in the arresting simplicity, both logical and imaginative, with which he projected old ones. Not wasting words, he plunged straight into things and boiled matters down to essentials, positioning himself as a common-sense, down-to-earth, no-nonsense observer, analyst, and conversation partner. On paper he had a flair, comparable to that of the great evangelists in the pulpit (Whitefield, Spurgeon, Graham, for example), for making you feel he is in personal conversation with you, searching your heart and requiring of you total honesty in response. Never pontifical, never browbeating, and never wrapping things up, Lewis achieved an intimacy of instruction that is very unusual. Those who read today what he wrote half a century ago find him engaging and holding their attention, and when the reading is over, haunting them, in the sense that they do not forget what he said. At his best, Lewis is a teacher of great piercing power. What is his secret?

The secret lies in the blend of logic and imagination in Lewis's make-up, each power as strong as the other, and each enormously strong in its own right. In one sense, imagination took the lead. As Lewis wrote in 1954:

> The imaginative man in me is older, more continuously operative, and in that sense more basic than either the religious writer or the critic. It was he who made me first attempt (with little success) to be a poet. . . . It was he who after my conversion led me to embody my religious belief in symbolic or mythopoeic forms, ranging from Screwtape to a kind of theologized science-fiction. And it was of course he who has brought me, in the last few years, to write the series of Narnia stories for children . . . because the fairy tale was the genre best fitted for what I wanted to say.

The best teachers are always those in whom imagination and logical control combine, so that you receive wisdom from their flights of fancy as well as a human heartbeat from their logical analyses and arguments. This in fact is human communication at its profoundest, for in the sending-receiving process of both lobes of the brain (left for logic, right for imagination) are fully involved, and that gives great depth and strength to what is heard. The teaching of Jesus presents itself as the supreme example here. Because Lewis's mind was so highly developed in both directions, it can truly be said of him that all of his arguments (including his literary criticism) are illustrations, in the sense that they throw light directly on realities of life and action, while all his illustrations (including the fiction and fantasies) are arguments, in the sense that they throw light directly on realities of truth and fact.

G. K. Chesterton, Charles Williams, and to some extent Dorothy L. Sayers exhibit the same sort of bipolar mental development, and what I have said of Lewis's writings can be said of theirs, too. Such minds will always command attention, and when possessed, as the minds of these four were possessed, by the values and visions of Christian faith and Christian humanism, they will always make an appeal that is hard to resist; and that appeal will not diminish as the culture changes. Visionary didacticism, as in Plato, Jesus, and Paul (to look no further) is transcultural, and unfading in its power. Bible-loving evangelicals, who build their whole faith on the logical-visionary teaching of God himself via his servants from Genesis to Revelation, naturally seek and appreciate this mode of communication in their latter-day instructors, and the consensus among them is that no twentieth-century writer has managed it so brilliantly as did C. S. Lewis.

Third, Lewis projects a *vision of wholeness*—sanity, maturity, present peace and joy, and finally fulfillment in heaven—that cannot but attract, willy-nilly, the adult children of our confused, disillusioned, alienated, and embittered culture: the now established culture of the West, which we shall certainly take with us (or maybe, I should say, which will certainly take us with it) into the new millennium. Both Lewis's didactic expositions (think of ***The Problem of Pain, The Screwtape Letters, Mere Christianity, Miracles, The Four Loves, Letters to Malcolm: Chiefly on Prayer,*** and ***Reflections on the Psalms***) and his fiction (think of the three Ransom stories, the seven Narnia tales, ***The Great Divorce,*** and ***Till We Have Faces***) yield a vision of human life under God (or Maleldil, or Aslan, or the unnamed divinity who confronts Orual) that is redemptive, transformational, virtue-valuing, and shot through with hints and flashes of breathtaking glory and eternal delight in a world to come. To be sure, the vision is humbling, for the shattering of all egoistic pride, all Promethean heroics, and all the possessive perversions of love is part of it. In the text of all his Christian writings, and in the subtext, at least, of all his wider literary work, Lewis rings endless changes on the same story: a story of moral and intellectual corruption, embryonic or developed, being overcome in some way, whereby more or less disordered human beings, victims of bad thinking and bad influences from outside, find peace, poise, discernment, realism, fulfillment, and a meaningful future. Evangelicals love such writing: who can wonder at that?

Here we are at the deepest level of Lewis's creative identity. At bottom he was a mythmaker. As Austin Farrer, Lewis's closest clerical friend and Oxford's most brilliant theologian at that time, observed, in Lewis's apologetics "we think we are listening to an argument; in fact, we are presented with a vision; and it is the vision that carries conviction." Myth is perhaps best defined as a story that projects a vision of life of actual or potential communal significance by reason of the identity and attitudes that it invites us to adopt. Lewis had loved the pre-Christian god-stories of Norse and Greek mythology, and the thought that did most to shape his return to Christianity and his literary output thereafter was this: In the Incarnation, a myth that recurs worldwide, the myth of a dying and rising deity through whose ordeal salvation comes to others, has become a space-time fact. Both before Christ, in pagan mythology, and since Christ, in imaginative fiction from Christian and para-Christian Westerners, versions of this story in various aspects have functioned as "good dreams," preparing minds and hearts for the reality of Christ according to the gospel. With increasing clarity, Lewis saw his own fiction as adding to this stock of material.

Lewis knew that by becoming fact in Christ, the worldwide myth had not ceased to be a story that, by its appeal to our imagination, can give us "a taste for the other"—a sense of reality, that is, which takes us beyond left-brain conceptual knowledge. He found that what he now knew as the fact of Christ was generating and fertilizing within him stories of the same shape—stories, that is, that picture redemptive action in worlds other than ours, whether in the past, present, or future. In the fantasy novels (***Out of the Silent Planet, Perelandra, That Hideous Strength, Till We Have Faces,*** and the seven Narnias) he became what Tolkien called a "sub-creator," producing good dreams of his own that, by reflecting Christian fact in a fantasy world, might prepare hearts to embrace the truth of Christ. The vision of wholeness that these myths project, and of the God-figures through whom that wholeness comes (think here particularly of Aslan, the Christly lion), can stir in honest hearts the wish that something of this sort might be true, and so beget, under God, readiness to accept the revelation that something of this sort is true, as a matter of fact.

Lewis once described ***The Lion, the Witch and the Wardrobe*** as giving an answer to the question, "What might Christ be like if there really were a world like Narnia and he chose to be incarnate and die and rise again in that world as he actually has done in ours?" All the Narnia books elaborate that answer: Aslan's doings are a reimagining in another world of what Jesus Christ did, does, and will do in this one. George Sayer, Lewis's finest biographer, ends his chapter on Narnia by telling how "my little stepdaughter, after she had read all the Narnia stories, cried bitterly, saying, 'I don't want to go on living in this world. I want to live in Narnia with Aslan'"—and then adding the five-word paragraph: "Darling, one day you will." The power of Lewisian myth as Christian communication could not be better shown, and countless believers who have nourished their children on Narnia will resonate with Sayer here.

Nor is that all. Over and above its evangelistic, or pre-evangelistic, role, Lewisian myth has an educating and maturing purpose. Lewis's 1943 Durham University lectures, published as ***The Abolition of Man*** (whew!) with the cooler academic subtitle, "Reflections on education with special reference to the teaching of English in the upper forms of schools," is a prophetic depth charge (it has been called a harangue) embodying his acute concern about our educational and cultural future. Lewis's educational philosophy called for imaginative identification on the part of young people, with paths of truth and value foreshadowed in the Platonic tradition, focused in the biblical revelation, and modeled in such writings as Spenser's *Faerie Queene* and his own stories; and ***The Abolition of Man*** was the waving of a red flag at an oncoming juggernaut that would reduce education to the learning of techniques and so dehumanize and destroy it, tearing out of it that which is its true heart. (Could he inspect public education today, a half-century later, he would tell us that what he feared has happened.) His fiction, however, was meant to help in real education, moral aesthetic and spiritual—value-laden education, in other words—and it is from that standpoint that we look at it now.

A close-up on Lewis's philosophy of education is needed here. Its negative side is hostility to any reductionist subjectivizing of values, as if the words that express them signify not realities to discern and goals to pursue, but just feelings of like and dislike that come and go. As a long-term Platonist and now a Christian into the bargain, Lewis had for some time been troubled by the lurching of twentieth-century philosophy into this subjectivism, and ***The Abolition of Man*** begins as his assault on a school textbook that assumed it. Such subjectivizing, he says, produces "men without chests"; that is, adults who lack what he calls "emotions organized by trained habit into stable sentiments"—what we would call moral formation and moral character.

Positively, Lewis calls for adherence to the Tao (his term: *Tao* means *way*). The Tao is the basic moral code (beneficence, obligations and respect within the family, justice, truthfulness, mercy, magnanimity) that all significant religions and all stable cultures maintain, and that Christians recognize from the first two chapters of Romans as matters of God's general revelation to our race. Lewis sees this code as a unity, and as time-honored and experientially verified wisdom, and as the only safeguard of society in this or any age, so it is no wonder that he states its claim emphatically. Commenting on the fact that would-be leaders of thought dismiss some or all of the Tao in order to construct alternative moralities (think of Nietzsche, for instance), he declares:

> This thing which I have called for convenience the Tao, and which others may call Natural Law or Traditional Morality or the First Principles of Practical Reason or the First Platitudes is not one among a series of possible systems of value. It is the sole source of all value judgments. . . . The effort to refute it and raise a new system of value in its place is self-contradictory. . . . What purport to be new systems or (as they now call them) 'ideologies', all consist of fragments from the Tao itself, arbitrarily wrenched from their context in the whole and then swollen to madness in their isolation, yet still owing to the Tao and to it alone such validity as they possess. If my duty to my parents is a superstition, then so is my duty to posterity. . . . If the pursuit of scientific knowledge is a real value, then so is conjugal fidelity. The rebellion of new ideologies against the Tao is a rebellion of the branches against the tree: if the rebels could succeed they would find that they had destroyed themselves.

Lewis's novel ***That Hideous Strength,*** which tells of a devilish research organization called the N.I.C.E. taking over a British university in order to take over Britain in the name of science, seems to me as to others an artistic failure, but it is a striking success in the way that it pictures this process of moral rebellion and the self-destruction to which it leads—and that, I suspect, was the only success that Lewis cared about when he wrote it.

Now, Tao-orientation is an internalized mindset that has to be learned. Lewis invokes Plato on this: "The little human animal will not at first have the right responses. It must be trained to feel pleasure, liking, disgust and hatred at those things which really are pleasant, likable, disgusting, and hateful." Yes, but how? Partly, at least, through stories that model the right responses: poems like Spenser's *Faerie Queene,* one of Lewis's lifelong favorites (best read, he once affirmed, between the ages of 12 and 16), novels like those of George MacDonald, and myths like the ***Chronicles of Narnia.*** Doris Myers urges that the chronicles are a more or less conscious counterpart to the *Faerie Queene,* modeling particular forms of virtue in a Tao frame with Christian overtones across the spectrum of a human life. Affirming that "the didacticism of the ***Chronicles*** consists in the education of moral and aesthetic feelings . . . to prevent children growing up without Chests," Myers reviews them to show how in each one "a particular virtue or configuration of virtues is presented, and the reader is brought to love it through participating in the artistry of the tale." The child will thus absorb the Tao by osmosis through enjoying the story.

Specifically: in the first chronicle, ***The Lion, the Witch and the Wardrobe,*** Lewis works to "strengthen the Chest" by inducing an emotional affirmation of courage, honor, and limitless kindness, with an emotional rejection of cowardice and treachery. In ***Prince Caspian,*** the second, he highlights joy within responsible self-control, in courtesy, justice, appropriate obedience, and the quest for order. In the third, ***The Voyage of the Dawn Treader,*** the endragoning and dedragoning of Eustace, "the Boy without a Chest," is flanked by vivid images of personal nobility (Reepicheep the Mouse) and public responsibility (Caspian the captain), while a tailpiece tells us how Eustace after his dedragoning was seen to be improved—"you'd never know him for the same boy." (The image, of course, is of Christian conversion.) Numbers four and five (***The Silver Chair*** and ***The Horse and His Boy***) teach lessons on managing one's thoughts and feelings as one nears adulthood; number six (***The Magician's Nephew***) invites hatred for the life- defying development of knowledge and use of power apart from the Tao; and number seven (***The Last Battle***) inculcates bravery in face of loss and death.

Thus Lewis's Narnia links up with his attempt, in ***The Abolition of Man,*** to recall education to its Tao-grounded roots. The attempt was ignored, and today we reap the bitter fruits of that fact. The inner desolation and desperation that young people experience as subjectivist relativism and nihilism are wished upon them in schools and universities is a tragedy. (If you do not know what I am referring to, listen to the pop singers; they will tell you.) Yet Lewis's imaginative presentation in his tales of a life of wholeness, maturity, sanity, honesty, humility, and humaneness, fictionally envisaged in order that it might be factually realized, still has great potency for both conversion and character building, as Narnia lovers most of all will testify. And evangelical believers greatly appreciate potency of this kind.

This brings us to the fourth factor in evangelical enthusiasm for C. S. Lewis: namely, the power with which he communicates not only the goodness of godliness, but also the *reality of God,* and with that the reality of the heaven that exists in the fullness of God's gracious presence.

Lewis's power here stemmed from his own vivid *experience.* From childhood he knew stabbing moments of what he called *joy,* that is, intense delightful longing, Sweet Desire (his phrase), that nothing in this world satisfies, and that is in fact a God-sent summons to seek the enjoyment of God and heaven. The way he describes it is calculated (Lewis, like other writers, could calculate his effects) to focus in our minds an awareness that this experience is ours too, so that Augustine was right to say that God made us for himself and our hearts lack contentment till they find it in him, in foretaste here and in fullness hereafter. Having found Sweet Desire to be an Ariadne's thread leading him finally to Christ (the autobiographical ***Surprised by Joy*** tells us how), Lewis holds our feet to the fire to ensure, if he can, that the same will happen to us. "If we consider the unblushing promises of reward and the staggering nature of the rewards promised in the Gospels, it would seem that Our Lord finds our desires, not too strong, but too weak. We are half-hearted creatures, fooling about with drink and sex and ambition when infinite joy is offered us . . . We are far too easily pleased." Nothing must be allowed to distract us from staying the course with Sweet Desire.

Lewis's power to communicate God and heaven's reality was exerted through his marvelously vivid *rhetoric.* Rhetoric—that is, the art of using words persuasively—ran in the Lewis family, and C. S. Lewis himself was a prose poet whose skill with simple words, like Bunyan's, enabled him to suggest ineffable things to our imaginations with overwhelming poignancy.

Thus, in ***The Voyage of the Dawn Treader,*** a momentary breeze brought the three children "a smell and a sound, a musical sound. Edmund and Eustace would never talk about it afterwards. Lucy could only say, 'It would break your heart.' 'Why,' said I, 'was it so sad?' 'Sad!! No,' said Lucy.

"No one in that boat doubted that they were seeing beyond the End of the World into Aslan's country."

And this is how ***The Last Battle*** ends:

> "There *was* a real railway accident," said Aslan softly. "Your father and mother and all of you are—as you used to call it in the Shadowlands—dead. The term is over: the holidays have begun. The dream is ended: this is the morning."
>
> And as He spoke He no longer looked to them like a lion; but the things that began to happen to them after that were so great and beautiful that I cannot write them . . . we can most truly say that they all lived happily ever after. . . . All their life in this world and all their adventures in Narnia had only been the cover and the title page: now at last they were beginning Chapter One of the Great Story which no one on earth has read: which goes on forever: in which every chapter is better than the one before.

The knockout quality of such writing is more than words can express.

The combination within him of insight with vitality, wisdom with wit, and imaginative power with analytical precision made Lewis a sparkling communicator of the everlasting gospel. Matching Aslan in the Narnia stories with (of course!) the living Christ of the Bible and of Lewis's instructional books, and his presentation of Christ could hardly be more forthright. "We are told that Christ was killed for us, that His death has washed out our sins, and that by dying he disabled death itself. That is the formula. That is Christianity. That is what has to be believed." Then, on the basis of this belief and the future belief that he is risen and alive and so is personally *there* (that is, everywhere, which means *here*), we must "put on," or as Lewis strikingly renders it, "dress up as" Christ—that is, give ourselves totally to Christ, so that he may be "formed in us," and we may henceforth enjoy in him the status and character of adopted children in God's family, or as again Lewis strikingly puts it, "little Christs." "God looks at you as if you were a little Christ: Christ stands beside you to turn you into one." Precisely.

Not just evangelicals, but all Christians, should celebrate Lewis, "the brilliant, quietly saintly, slightly rumpled Oxford don" as James Patrick describes him. He was a Christ-centered, great-tradition mainstream Christian whose stature a generation after his death seems greater than anyone ever thought while he was alive, and whose Christian writings are now seen as having classic status.

Long may we learn from the contents of his marvelous, indeed magical, mind! I doubt whether the full measure of him has been taken by anyone as yet.

FURTHER READING

Criticism

Campbell, David C., and Dale E. Hess. "Olympian Detachment: A Critical Look at the World of C. S. Lewis's Characters." *Studies in the Literary Imagination* XXII, No. 2 (Fall 1989): 199-215.

Employs "attribution journal" methodology to the study of characters from *The Hideous Strength, Till We Have Faces,* and *Perelandra.*

Carnell, Corbin Scott. "Ransom in C. S. Lewis' *Perelandra* as Hero in Transformation: Notes Toward a Jungian Reading of the Novel." *Studies in the Literary Imagination* XIV, No. 2 (Fall 1981): 67-71.

Provides Jungian analysis of the Elwin Ransom character in *Perelandra.*

Christopher, Joe R. "C. S. Lewis, Love Poet." *Studies in the Literary Imagination* XXII, No. 2 (Fall 1989): 161-73.

Offers analysis of the structure, linguistic patterns, and romantic themes of Lewis's poetry.

Glover, Donald E. "The Magician's Book: That's Not Your Story." *Studies in the Literary Imagination* XXII, No. 2 (Fall 1989): 217-25.

Examines elements of plot, theme, and narrative presentation in "The Chronicles of Narnia" and *Till We Have Faces.*

Haigh, John D. "C. S. Lewis and the Tradition of Visionary Romance." In *Word and Story in C. S. Lewis,* edited by Peter J. Schakel and Charles A. Huttar, pp. 182-98. Columbia: University of Missouri Press, 1991.

Discusses Lewis's conception of the romance, as opposed to the novel, and its central themes and characteristics as delineated by critics and exhibited in Lewis's work.

Holbrook, David. *The Skeleton in the Wardrobe: C. S. Lewis's Fantasies: A Phenomenological Study.* Lewistown: Bucknell University Press, 1991, 298 p.

Explores Lewis's didacticism, Christian proselytizing, and menacing fantasies in "The Chronicles of Narnia."

King, Don W. "The Distant Voice in C. S. Lewis's *Poems.*" *Studies in the Literary Imagination* XXII, No. 2 (Fall 1989): 175-84.

Examines aspects of ambivalence and hesitancy in Lewis's poetic persona in *Poems.*

Petrik, James M. "In Defense of C. S. Lewis's Analysis of God's Goodness." *International Journal for Philosophy of Religion* 36, No. 1 (August 1994): 45-56.

Examines Lewis's conception of God's benevolence and the role of human suffering as outlined in *The Problem of Pain.*

Pittenger, Norman. "C. S. Lewis: Combative in Defense." *Studies in the Literary Imagination* XIV, No. 2 (Fall 1981): 13-20.

Offers a negative critique of Lewis's Christian perspective, dogmatism, and apologetic writings.

Robson, W. W. "C. S. Lewis." *The Cambridge Quarterly* 1, No. 3 (Summer 1966): 252-72.

Provides an overview of Lewis's religious and moral themes and critical discussion surrounding his work and literary reputation.

Schakel, Peter J. "Personal Writer of the Sixties: Reason and Imagination United." In *Reason and Imagination in C. S. Lewis: A Study of Till We Have Faces,* pp. 163-82. Grand Rapids, MI: William B. Eerdmans, 1984.

Discusses the reconciliation of intellectual detachment and creative imagination in Lewis's later writing.

Watson, Thomas Ramey. "Enlarging Augustinian Systems: C. S. Lewis' *The Great Divorce* and *Till We Have Faces.*" *Renascence: Essays on Values in Literature* XLVI, No. 3 (Spring 1994):163-74.

Examines the influence of Saint Augustine's theology and Christian typology in Lewis's fiction.

Additional coverage of Lewis's life and career is contained in the following sources published by Gale: *Authors and Artists for Young Adults,* Vol. 3; *Children's Literature Review,* Vols. 3, 27; *Concise Dictionary of British Literary Biography,* 1945-1960; *Contemporary Authors,* Vols. 81-84; *Contemporary Authors New Revision Series,* Vols. 33, 71; *Dictionary of Literary Biography,* Vols. 15, 100, 160; *DISCovering Authors; DISCovering Authors: British; DISCovering Authors: Canadian; DISCovering Authors Modules: Most-Studied, Novelists, and Popular Fiction and Genre Authors; Junior DISCovering Authors; Major Authors and Illustrators for Children and Young Adults; Major Twentieth Century Writers,* Vol. 1; *Something About the Author,* Vols. 13, 100; and *World Literature Criticism.*

Robert Lowell

1917-1977

American poet, dramatist, critic, and translator.

The following entry presents an overview of Lowell's career through 1997. For further information on his life and works, see *CLC,* Volumes 1, 2, 3, 4, 5, 8, 9, 11, 15, and 37.

INTRODUCTION

A foremost contributor to the development of "confessional" poetry, Robert Lowell is widely regarded as one of the most gifted and influential American poets of the postwar period. While his early verse in the Pulitzer Prize-winning volume *Lord Weary's Castle* (1946) is distinguished for its complex formalism and technical virtuosity, during the 1960s Lowell emerged as a leading innovator of the confessional mode. This highly charged, self-revelatory style of writing, heralded by his important collection *Life Studies* (1959), featured a new emphasis on intense, uninhibited discussion of personal, family, and psychological struggles. Though much of Lowell's poetry centers upon the autobiographic details of his New England upbringing, mental illness, and personal relationships, his erudition, mastery of conventional forms, and synthesis of private and public concerns separates him from other poets working in the confessional vein. Lowell's assiduous effort to discover new poetic forms through assimilation of traditional and modernist techniques is reflected in the impressive range and diversity of his work.

Biographical Information

Born Robert Traill Spence Lowell, Jr., to parents of prominent Boston families, Lowell descended from a long line of distinguished New Englanders, including literary relatives James Russell Lowell and Amy Lowell. Lowell's turbulent childhood, dominated by incessant tensions between his father, a naval officer, and mother, left deep and lasting emotional scars. He attended preparatory school at St. Mark's School in Southborough, Massachusetts, where he was a student of poet Richard Eberhart, Lowell's first literary mentor. At St. Mark's, Lowell also earned the nickname "Cal," a dual reference to Shakespeare's Caliban and the infamous Roman emperor Caligula. Lowell began studies at Harvard University in 1935, though left abruptly in 1937 to travel with English novelist Ford Madox Ford to the Tennessee home of poet Allen Tate and his wife, novelist Caroline Gordon. After spending a summer with the Tate's, Lowell followed Tate to Kenyon College in Ohio, where he enrolled and studied under John Crowe Ransom. While at Kenyon, Lowell met lifelong friends poet Randall Jarrell and short story writer Peter Taylor. Lowell graduated *summa cum laude* with a degree in classics in 1940 and, during the same year, converted to Roman Catholicism and married novelist Jean Stafford. The next year, Lowell attended graduate courses at Louisiana State University, where he studied under Robert Penn Warren and Cleanth Brooks. After brief employment with the Catholic publishing house Sheed and Ward in New York, Lowell took up residence with the Tate's in the Tennessee mountains, where he continued to write. A conscientious objector to military service during the Second World War, Lowell was imprisoned for six months during 1943 and 1944. He then published his first collection of poetry, *The Land of Unlikeness* (1944), followed two years later by *Lord Weary's Castle,* for which he was awarded a Pulitzer Prize. He also received a National Institute of Arts and Letters Award and a Guggenheim fellowship in 1947. In the period before the publication of his next volume, *The Mills of the Kavanaughs* (1951), Lowell divorced Stafford, abandoned the Catholic Church, and suffered a severe bout of manic depression, a psychological disorder that afflicted him for the rest of his life. Lowell married writer Elizabeth Hardwick in 1949. During the 1950s, he taught at several universities, maintained a friendship with William Carlos Williams, and traveled to California, where he encountered Allen Ginsberg and other Beat generation writers. Lowell settled in New York in 1960 and, from 1963 to 1970, commuted to Boston to teach at Harvard. He won a National Book Award in 1960 for *Life Studies* and a Bollingen Prize for *Imitations* (1961), a collection of verse translations, in 1962. Lowell also published *Phaedra,* a verse translation of Jean Baptiste Racine's tragedy, in *Phaedra and Figaro* (1961). During the mid-1960s, Lowell produced *For the Union Dead* (1964) and *The Old Glory* (1965), a trilogy of plays including *Endecott and the Red Cross* and *My Kinsman, Major Molineux,* both adapted from short stories by Nathaniel Hawthorne, and *Benito Cereno,* adapted from a novella by Herman Melville. Lowell also emerged as an outspoken critic of U.S. military involvement in Vietnam; he publicly declined an invitation by President Lyndon Johnson to attend the White House Festival of the Arts in 1965 and participated in the historic Pentagon march in 1967. His reaction to social and political upheaval during this time is the subject of *Near the Ocean* (1967) and *Notebook, 1967-68* (1969). Lowell moved to England in 1970 and taught at the University of Essex and Kent University. After divorcing Hardwick and marrying his third wife, British author Caroline Blackwood, in 1972, Lowell produced three additional volumes of poetry in 1973—*For Lizzie and Harriet, History,* and *The Dolphin,* for which Lowell received a second Pulitzer Prize in 1974. His final collection, *Day by Day* (1977), winner of the National Book Critics Award in 1978, was published days before Lowell suffered a fatal heart attack in a New York taxi.

Major Works

Lowell's early poetry is characterized by its Christian motifs and symbolism, historical reference, and intricate formalism, a trait cultivated by Lowell's early masters, the Southern New Critics Tate and Ransom. In *Land of Unlikeness,* introduced by Tate, Lowell responds to the chaos and brutality of the Second World War, his Catholic conversion, and renunciation of his Puritan heritage, often juxtaposing religious beatitude with the turmoil and vapidity of the modern secular world. The title of the collection, suggestive of Lowell's disillusionment, refers to Saint Bernard's idea that the human soul is unlike God and unknown to itself. Lowell incorporated many of these poems in his next volume, *Lord Weary's Castle.* Continuing the theme of rebellion, Lowell expresses his conflicted aversion to war, American imperialism, capitalism, and the legacy of New England Protestantism. In "The Quaker Graveyard in Nantucket," the most famous poem from this volume, Lowell rails against the corruption and lost innocence of America in an elegy for his cousin, Warren Winslow, who drowned while serving in the Navy during the Second World War. His next collection, *The Mills of the Kavanaughs,* marked a spiritual and stylistic crisis for Lowell. Under the influence of Robert Frost and Robert Browning, this volume contains several dramatic monologues and verse translations that, while indicative of Lowell's search for new poetic forms, are weighted with obscure symbolism and affected rhetoric. Lowell's major artist breakthrough came with *Life Studies,* in which he abandoned the rigid formalism of his previous poetry and shifted his focus to personal aspects of his life and family history. The malleable free verse and colloquial tone of this volume reveals the influence of William Carlos Williams. In "Skunk Hour," one of the best known poems from this volume, Lowell discloses his inner turmoil along with descriptions of a coastal Maine town and foraging skunks. The prose memoir "91 Revere Street," which represents the core of *Life Studies,* recounts Lowell's troubled childhood, including unflattering portraits of his parents and home life. The new openness of Lowell's poetry is also reflected in *Imitations,* a collection of loosely translated works by Homer, Sappho, Rainer Maria Rilke, Francois Villon, and Charles-Pierre Baudelaire, among others. Lowell continued in the confessional mode in *For the Union Dead,* whose title poem, originally delivered at the Boston Arts Festival in 1960, is regarded as one of his best. Beginning as a private meditation on his childhood memory of the Boston Aquarium, "For the Union Dead" commemorates the sacrifice of Colonel Robert Shaw, a Union officer killed while leading a regiment of black troops during the Civil War. Shifting between the historic past and present, Lowell laments the erosion of heroic idealism in contemporary America and technological encroachment. In *Near the Ocean,* written at the height of antiwar protest, Lowell returned to the formal metrical patterns of his earlier work. The polemical poetry of this volume, including verse translations of works by Horace, Juvenal, and Dante, derides American militarism and political leadership, as in the popular poem "Waking Early Sunday Morning." *Notebook 1967-68,* which began as diary, is an epic cycle of unrhymed sonnets loosely structured around the four seasons of the year. An amalgam of journal entries, historical observations, correspondence, and private meditations, these poems reflect Lowell's effort to harmonize his personal and public concerns; Lowell significantly revised and rearranged many of these poems in *Notebook* (1970). Lowell continued to work with unrhymed sonnets in his next three volumes—*For Lizzie and Harriet, History,* and *The Dolphin. For Lizzie and Harriet,* which consists of revised poems from *Notebook,* deals with Lowell's relationship with Elizabeth Hardwick and their daughter. *History,* also containing reworked poems from *Notebook* as well as many new compositions, evokes the broad sweep of Western civilization in fragmentary episodes and verse portraits of diverse historical and literary figures such as Juvenal, Maximilien-François Robespierre, Martin Luther King, Jr., and John Berryman. The new poems of *The Dolphin* center upon Lowell's relocation to England, his marriage to Lady Caroline Blackwood, and the birth of their son. In his final volume, *Day by Day,* Lowell abandoned the sonnet form for free verse and returned to the scrupulous honesty and autobiographic subjects reminiscent of *Life Studies.* The posthumously published *Collected Prose* contains Lowell's essays on various major poets and literary works, unfinished autobiographic sketches, and several interviews.

Critical Reception

Lowell is widely regarded as one of the most important American poets of the postwar era. Though famous for his role in the development of confessional poetry, his early verse in *Lord Weary's Castle* is highly regarded for its command of traditional forms and cerebral aesthetics. Lowell's preoccupation with religious themes in this volume and *Land of Unlikeness* also prompted some reviewers to classify him as a "Catholic poet." His transitional collection, *The Mills of the Kavanaughs,* is generally considered among his weakest, leading some reviewers to question the limitations of the New Criticism principles which Lowell inherited from his early teachers Tate, Ransom, Cleanth Brooks, and Robert Penn Warren. *Life Studies,* hailed as a major turning point in Lowell's career, is also considered a seminal work of contemporary American poetry. Through his example in this work, Lowell initiated the confessional genre and exerted a profound influence on subsequent American poets, including other first generation confessionalists such as Sylvia Plath and Anne Sexton. Lowell is also praised for his effective blend of autobiography and public history in the acclaimed poems "The Quaker Graveyard in Nantucket" and "For the Union Dead." During the late 1960s, Lowell received negative criticism for *Near the Ocean,* dismissed by many reviewers for its overt political rhetoric and what some perceived to be calculated accessibility. His artistic integrity was also called into question with the publication of *The Dolphin,* in which he incorporated verbatim transcripts of private correspondence with Elizabeth Hardwick and others, considered an egregious violation of personal trust by many of Lowell's critics and friends. Despite the wide influence of his poetry, Lowell's inseparable connection to the rise of confessional poetry has also elicited disapproval among critics who dismiss such writing as narrowly self-absorbed. Though critical interest in Lowell's work has diminished somewhat over recent decades, he is still highly regarded as one of the most brilliant and diversely talented American poets of the twentieth century.

PRINCIPAL WORKS

Land of Unlikeness (poetry) 1944
Lord Weary's Castle (poetry) 1946
Poems, 1938-1949 (poetry) 1950
The Mills of the Kavanaughs (poetry) 1951
Life Studies (poetry) 1959
Imitations [editor and translator] (poetry) 1961
Phaedra and Figaro [translator; with Jacques Barzun] (drama) 1961
For the Union Dead (poetry) 1964
The Old Glory (drama) 1965
Near the Ocean (poetry) 1967
Prometheus Bound [adaptor] (drama) 1967
The Voyage and Other Versions of Poems by Baudelaire [translator] (poetry) 1968
Notebook 1967-1968 [revised and republished as *Notebook,* 1970] (poetry) 1969
History (poetry) 1973
For Lizzie and Harriet (poetry) 1973
The Dolphin (poetry) 1973
Selected Poems (poetry) 1976
Day by Day (poetry) 1977
Collected Prose (prose) 1987
Collected Poems (poetry) 1997

CRITICISM

John Druska (essay date 9 December 1977)

SOURCE: "Aspects of Robert Lowell," in *Commonweal,* December 9, 1977, pp. 783-8.

[In the following essay, Druska provides an overview of Lowell's literary career, artistic development, and major themes in his poetry.]

I. His Career

The speaker of Robert Lowell's **"In the American Grain"** (***History***) announces at the close of the poem

> (') I am not William Carlos Williams. He
> knew the germ on every flower, and saw
> the snake is a petty, rather pathetic creature.'

Whether or not the speaker is Lowell—the poem is a direct quote, perhaps a letter to him—the sentiment is rarely his. Snakes, dragons, other biblical and/or allusive figures haunt Lowell's pages. In the early poems of ***Land of Unlikeness*** and ***Lord Weary's Castle*** he writes this most emblematic. "No ideas but in things," Williams proclaimed. Lowell's first works, for which he has lionized by much of the critical establishment, might well be saying, "Nothing but within my ideas of things":

> . . . I fear
> That only Armageddon will suffice
> To turn the hero skating on thin ice

When Whore and Beast and Dragon rise for air
From allegoric waters.

(**"To Peter Taylor on the Feast of the Epiphany,"** ***Lord Weary***)

The self-assurance of Lowell's poems in ***Lord Weary*** impressed. The difficulties they posed to be puzzled through impressed. Only a few objections have been recorded. Hayden Carruth dismissed the motifs in ***Lord Weary*** as lifeless tokens and many of the poems as "set pieces in a high style," a young poet's homage to his older masters; though among the purely "sententious" specimens Carruth discovered poems that include, under their "high gloss of artifice," urgent and moving autobiographical elements ("A Meaning of Robert Lowell," *Robert Lowell: A Portrait of the Artist in His Time,* 1970). And the artifice of Lowell's third volume, ***The Mills of the Kavanaughs,*** caused Williams to temper a favorable review:

> In his new book Robert Lowell gives us six first-rate poems of which we may well be proud. As usual he has taken the rhyme-track for his effects. We shall now have rhyme again for a while, rhymes completely missing the incentive. The rhymes are necessary to Mr. Lowell. He must, to his mind, appear to surmount them. ("In a Mood of tragedy . . . .": ibid.)

Did Williams's objection to rhyme echo a bit his lament that T. S. Eliot had set back irreparably the course of poetry in an American idiom?

Just as critics have stressed Eliot's religion, which never was more than a convenience to his poetry, many have made much of Lowell's temporarily-adopted (and adapted?) Catholicism and its influence on his early poetry. In retrospect, though, Lowell's true faith appears to have been in the Western tradition, T. S. Eliot pastor, rather than in the Catholic Church, which became, for a time, the exoskeleton of his emotions, ideas and images. And the farther we follow Lowell through his career the more we see his own mind, insofar as it assimilates the history and cultures of Western civilization as well as the data of his own experience, becoming his real church. Under its vault he worships not only the occasional order its rituals conjure, but the cracks in its walls, the dissolution implicit in accepting one's self in the world as the manifest sign of poetry. Thus his titles evolve from the symbolic prominence of ***Land of Unlikeness*** and ***Lord Weary's Castle*** to the pop-tune lyric, ***Day by Day.***

Wondering over the course of his poetry, Lowell says in one of his last poems (**"Unwanted,"** ***Day by Day***)

I was surer, wasn't I, once . . .
and had flashes when I first found
a humor for myself in images,
farfetched misalliance
that made evasions a revelation?

If those first poems were evasive, they were evading an audience already tantalized. If Lowell's marriage to his emblems was far-fetched, not many seemed to have noticed. Or his revelation sufficed.

But Lowell himself, long before his nostalgia in ***Day by Day,*** had reacted against the lineal descendants of his highly-praised ***Lord Weary*** works, in commenting upon poems he had been writing in the 1950's: "Their style seemed distant, symbol-ridden and willfully difficult . . . my own poems seemed like prehistoric monsters dragged down into the bog and death by their ponderous armor." (**"On Skunk Hour,"** *The Contemporary Poet as Artist and Critic,* 1964.) Later, after Lowell closed out the 50's with ***Life Studies,*** which made him as popular as any legitimate poet is likely to become today, and especially after his poems of the 1960's had accumulated in ***Notebook 1967-68,*** some critics saw a devolution in his poetry and enshrined ***Lord Weary*** as Lowell's masterwork. Others (including those for whom he became a confessional darling), and Lowell apparently came to regard ***Lord Weary's*** mode as some archaic-baroque shell of the poet's past.

Between the publications of ***Life Studies*** and ***Notebook 1967-68,*** Donald Hall, writing the introduction to the Penguin *Contemporary American Poetry* (1962), concluded: "When he wrote ***Life Studies,*** Robert Lowell sent his muse to the *atelier* of William Carlos Williams (from that of Allen Tate)." To Williams's *atelier,* though, just for diction lessons. Even after the shift from "rhetorical stanzas" to "common speech" (as Hall puts it), Lowell keeps us in a world skewed by his mind's impositions, an introverted mythos, rather than in the sort of garden of realized common-place that Williams gives us. As after his exit from Catholicism, figures of that faith (or the faith of his puritanical forebears) keep slithering through his lines, pets of the tradition he extends).

Following Lowell's break from rhetorical stanzas, his movement into freer verse forms, and his settling for a long while on blank verse sonnet-sections, he suffered less drastically from distaste for his own work. Change became a matter of shuffling lines, replacing words: rewriting became a prime writing method. Through the 60's, into the 1970's, Lowell rewrote incessantly, his poetry suggests, and the nature of this revision implies some amount of disintegration, off-centeredness in his evocations of the past, present and himself in relationship to himself—a difficulty in getting the equations right, a lack of perception. Yet it implies too Lowell's immense care for getting the poem right, his attention to focusing better, pulling his work, and so perhaps himself, together. Sometimes the changes perplex. Lines and sets of lines move from one poem to another in consecutive volumes; changing contexts as well, from historical to private or vice-versa. Lowell insists on our staying in his flux while he manipulates for us the data of history and memory in order to fix (but just momentarily?) his vision of his (our?) world. This is not Williams's *Paterson* regenerating itself beyond its designed end, but Lowell's notebook- history-life—Lowell's life become poem life, as Stephen Yenser claims—rehearsing as if unready to be apprised of its end.

In **"Randall Jarrell"** (***History***) Lowell has his fellow poet tell him, "You didn't write, you *re*wrote'." Lowell himself admitted to spending hours, days, choosing the proper word for a line. Farther and farther away from the devotional structures of his early poetry could Lowell hope to invest his work with any of the certainty whose lack his later poetry, as we've seen, seems on occasion to lament, in spite of his dismissing the "prehistoric monsters"?

> Those blessed structures, plot and rhyme—
> why are they no help to me now
> I want to make
> something imagined, not recalled?
> . . .
> We are poor passing facts,
> warned by that to give
> each figure in the photograph
> his living name.

From effects of stained glass to the snapshots with which Lowell ends **"Epilogue,"** last poem of ***Day by Day,*** his last book.

II. His Life, His Death: His Poetry

As much as history, legend and myth overshadow Lowell's work, he remains at the center of his poems, in the context of his life, from childhood to death and caught inextricably between.

Lowell's "childhood, closer to me than what I love" (**"Returning,"** ***History***) draws him, throughout his poetry, in its direction, at times back to encounters with his parents, at other times toward a life-force in his work, as well as in others': "the supreme artist, Flaubert, was a boy before the mania for phrases dried his heart" (**"Les Mots,"** ***Notebook***).

His fascination for childhood in places recalls Jarrell's. Even some of the same yearning for a child-like love occurs, as in Jarrell's brother-sister poems, or the folk tales he used to render:

> Here nature seldom feels the hand of man,
> our alders skirmish. I flame for the one friend—
> is it always the same child or animal
> impregnable in shell or coat of thorns
>
> (**"Long Summer,"** ***Notebook***)

And all Lowell's visions of childhood root in his own memories of Boston during the 1920's. In **"91 Revere Street,"** a rare piece of Lowell prose which serves as Part Two of ***Life Studies*** in the American edition, Lowell precisely details his family life as a child. The sketch ends with a joke, as obliquely as it began, neatly sliced. A joke, however, that aptly completes the poet's portrayal of himself. Lowell's father, in the piece, has been forced by his superior to spend nights away from home at the naval compound, and he is ribbed about this by an old Navy buddy: "I know why Young Bob is an only child."

But drawn in one direction by his childhood, Lowell is drawn even within the memories of his childhood in the other direction by death. "(A)lways inside me is the child who died," he says in **"Night Sweat"** (***For the Union Dead***), "always inside me is his will to die—" And, Lowell avers in **"Death and the Maiden"** ("Circles, 19," ***Notebook***), "A good ear hears its own death talking."

Death is the simple fact ("You were alive. You are dead.": **"Alfred Corning Clark,"** ***For the Union Dead***) that opens to the common mystery, the ultimate poet's question: "'But tell me, / Cal, why did we live? Why do we die?'" (**"Randall Jarrell,"** ***History***). It becomes in fact part of Lowell's grim bond with his fellow poets and the source of a wry recapitulation of his career:

> Ah the swift vanishing of my older
> generation—the deaths, suicide, madness
> of Roethke, Berryman, Jarrell and Lowell,
> 'the last the most discouraging of all
> surviving to dissipate ***Lord Weary's Castle***
> and nine subsequent useful poems
> in the seedy grandiloquence of ***Notebook.***'
>
> (**"Last Night,"** ***History***)

Consistently through Lowell's *corpus* death supplies a haunting keynote:

> Fifty-one years, how many millions gone—
>
> . . . hear it, hear the clopping
> of the hundreds of horses unstopping . . . each
> hauls a coffin.
>
> (**"Half a Century Gone, 5,"** ***Notebook***)

And at an extreme death grows to an embodiment of the

poet's work. In **"Reading Myself"** (***Notebook 1967-68***) Lowell shifts the metaphor of his work as honey-comb—"circle to circle, cell to cell, / the wax and honey of a mausoleum"—through that last image to the analogy, "this open book . . . my open coffin."

Even though his poetry virtually embalms him before our eyes, Lowell is not averse to gallows humor. Or is this the undertone of an unearthly wish?

sleep is lovely, death is better still,
not to have been born is of course the miracle.

(**"Heine Dying in Paris, I: Death and Morphine,"** ***Imitations***)

Impossible miracle for the child already born into life's continuum, prey to its inevitable changes: "They say fear of death is a child's remembrance / of the first desertion." (**"During a Transatlantic Call,"** ***The Dolphin***).

Yet even while chronicling his own aging in his poems, (while indulging in the delight and detritus of his marriages), Lowell retains an adolescent élan, at least wistfulness:

. . . it's the same for me
at fifty as at thirteen, my childish thirst
for the grown-ups in their open cars and girls. . . .

(**"Through the Night, 1,"** ***Notebook 1967-68***)

Growing old he does not, perhaps, grow adult. Writing for his adolescent daughter, Lowell sees her growing "too fast apace, / too fast adult; no, not adult, mature." (**"Growth,"** ***Notebook 1967-68***) He too, perhaps, matures without calcifying.

Born and bred of good Boston stock, Lowell set out, like Yeats, to do just one thing, to write poetry well, according to Hugh B. Staples, the first critic to deal with Lowell's poetry at book-length. Equipped with the wherewithal to live, and so the leisure to write, appropriately bull-headed (skeptical indeed of Yeats's achievement; what did Yeats really accomplish, he once told Staples, aside from leaving us "about four-hundred lyrics"), Lowell became a poet, discovering in the process that "Poets die adolescents" (**"Fishnet,"** ***The Dolphin***).

Are we, in fact, to regard him as a chronic adolescent? His precocious success with ***Lord Weary,*** his circling through his works the last decade, writing and rewriting, self-absorbed (insecure?), so seriously cocooning himself in the orbit of his psychic concerns—America's grand adolescent laureate?

III. His Reputation

Robert Lowell's persistent rewriting might have made us wonder at one time whether he would ever surpass the "four-hundred lyrics" he credited to Yeats. Yet today the critical writing on Lowell's position in American letters grows redundant. He has become for some a kind of American Yeats, not only bridging poetic tradition and the ragbone present, but turning out as well dramas that recast for us Classical and American myths, plays like those of the ***Old Glory*** trilogy that test our ancestral beliefs against our ancestors' and our own actions. In our present mood of eulogy, as in the wake of his lionization three decades ago, to evaluate Robert Lowell's work in a mode other than speculative is to attempt the common and the impossible.

What will come of the intellectual tradition that many have taken Lowell to represent? What of Robert Bly, called by some Lowell's most intransigent critic? Are his attacks on the *Kenyon Review* clique, Lowell included, and the anti-surrealist academics, along with his advocacy of "leaping poetry" (see *Leaping Poetry,* 1975), part of communist plot, or has Bly revealed the arc that will carry American poetry into its future? What of some voices who have been plainly showing us truths all along: Denise Levertov, David Ignatow, William Stafford, all poets in our world? And what do the Irish think of Yeats today anyway?

In its obituary of Robert Lowell last September 14, the Bangor (Me.) *Daily News* remarked, "James Russell Lowell, foremost American man of letters in his times, was Robert Lowell's great-grandfather. . . ." Born in 1819, James Russell Lowell died in 1891. In our time we remember too that Walt Whitman lived from 1819 to 1892.

So we might do well, at least for now, to think of Robert Lowell as a person and a poet in his own age, instead of as an idol for the ages.

While he attended Kenyon College in Gambier, Ohio, after a requisite year at Harvard, Robert Lowell roomed with Peter Taylor, today one of our finest storytellers. During their time under the tutelage of John Crowe Ransom (Jarrell appearing as Instructor for a year as well), Taylor, Lowell and a handful of hardy fellow-artists also survived the rigors of watching the frat-jock parades down Kenyon's famed Middle Path, where every Tuesday night's songfest included a lyrical toast to "The first of Kenyon's goodly race / . . . that great man Philander Chase." A friend who has just graduated from Kenyon assures me that not only was Philander Chase a real personage, but the parading and singing still go on along the Middle Path. As in Taylor's story of double romantic disillusionment, "1939," Lowell and his friends, reprobates all, continue to haunt Kenyon.

Lowell has written: "In truth I seem to have felt mostly the joys of living; in remembering, in recording, thanks to the gift of the Muse, it is the pain." (**"Afterthought,"** ***Notebook***)

Thanks to "1939" we see Lowell, even before he knows the harsh reality of love lost in Manhattan, in the self-consumed, self-consuming, sober attitude of the artist as youth that pervades his work, that causes us perhaps to call him a latter-day and peculiar Romantic, in this case the adolescent the father of the man:

> *We walked the country road for miles in every direction, talking every step of the way about ourselves or about our writing, or if we exhausted those two dearer subjects, we talked about whatever we were reading at the time. We read W. H. Auden and Yvor Winters and Wyndham Lewis and Joyce and Christopher Dawson. We read* The Wings of the Dove *(aloud!) and* The Cosmological Eye *and* The Last Puritan *and* In Dreams Begin Responsibilities. *(Of course, I am speaking only of books that didn't come within the range of the formal courses we were taking in the college.) On our walks through the country—never more than two or three of us together—we talked and talked, but I think none of us ever listened to anyone's talk but his own. Our talk seemed always to come to nothing. But our walking took us past the sheep farms and orchards and past some of the stone farmhouses that are scattered throughout that township. It brought us to the old quarry from which most of the stone for the college buildings and for the farmhouses had been taken, and brought us to Quarry Chapel, a long since deserted and 'deconsecrated' chapel, standing on a hill two miles from the college and symbolizing there the failure of Episcopalianism to take root among the Ohio country people. Sometimes we walked along the railroad track through the valley at the foot of the college hill, and I remember more than once coming upon two or three tramps warming themselves by a little fire they had built or even cooking a meal over it. We would see them may be a hundred yards ahead, and we would get close enough to hear them laughing and talking together. But as soon as they noticed us we would turn back and walk in the other direction, for we pitied them and felt that our presence was an intrusion. And yet, looking back on it, I remember how happy those tramps always seemed. And how sad and serious we were.*

Lauriat Lane, Jr. (essay date Winter 1980-81)

SOURCE: "Robert Lowell: The Problems and Power of Allusion," in *Dalhousie Review,* Vol. 60, No. 4, Winter, 1980-81, pp. 697-702.

[In the following essay, Lane discusses Lowell's use of allusion and metaphorical reference in "Man and Wife," "Sailing Home from Rapollo," and "For the Union Dead."]

Allusions, like symbols, can be divided broadly into explicit and implicit: separated, as Harry Levin says, by an equatorial line past which we can sail on problematically into the conjectural and, finally, the inadmissible. At the same time allusion to some entity otherwise wholly outside the text must be distinguished from reference to a similar entity which is actually presumed present within the world of the text. King Ahab is not present in *Moby Dick*; Captain Ahab is. Neither is present in Robert Lowell's **"The Quaker Graveyard at Nantucket,"** but both are alluded to: one explicitly, one implicitly. The allusions in Lowell's earlier, highly allusive poems such as **"The Quaker Graveyard"** have been glossed to the point where the reader's problem is not to reap but to winnow.

However, the referential content in Lowell's book, ***Life Studies,*** and in many subsequent poems, is so circumstantial and the style so direct that possible allusions are more likely to require discovery, juridical as well as analytic—witness Wilbur's, Nims's, and Berryman's well-known critiques of **"Skunk Hour"** and Lowell's response to their "discoveries." The very presence of such allusions may often be problematic. The following three examples serve to illustrate both the problem of distinguishing between references and allusion in poems by Lowell and the further problem of crossing from the explicit to the implicit and on to the conjectural and the inadmissible. They may also show the poetic power gained by affirming and explicating these problematic allusions.

I. Rahvs and Redskins

No one has ever doubted that in line 17 of **"Man and Wife"** Lowell alludes explicitly and semi-referentially to Philip Rahv and his wife who, if they do not literally inhabit the present world of the poem, inhabit the literal past of that present. For many critics, such as Marjorie Perloff, this allusion/reference contributes metonymically, as do many others in the poem, to establishing "the nature of the poem's milieu": "The 'rising sun' of line 2 becomes, in the diseased imagination of the poet who fears passion and vitality, an Indian savage in 'war paint' who 'dyes us red,' the pun on 'dyes' intensifying the death-in-life existence of the couple." At least one critic of Lowell, Steven Axelrod—and no doubt many others—has observed the general appropriateness to Lowell's personal and literary situation of Rahv's well-known categories of paleface and redskin. But has it been noted that in **"Man and Wife"** the combination of line 17, "outdrank the Rahvs in the heat," with line 2, "the rising sun in war paint dyes us red," constitutes a witty specific allusion to Rahv's essay, an essay which Rahv had gathered into *Image and Idea* at about the time of the scene being recalled by the monologist of the poem? Such an allusion would make Rahv's distinction not just generally pertinent to Lowell, as Axelrod has shown, but specially pertinent to this poem's issues. Man and wife, paleface and redskin—we may even wish to consider the thematic or biographical parallel of the poem's title and subject with Rahv's pair of categories, thus adding one more dimension to those that Perloff has explicated so thoroughly. This possible parallel may be further supported by Elizabeth Hardwick's recent "novel," *Sleepless Nights,* and even by the authorial stance of her *A View of My Own,* dedicated, incidentally, to Philip Rahv.

II. Frost at Midwinter

In the second half of **"Sailing Home from Rapallo,"** Lowell contrasts in his mind the actual Italian scene with a mental scene of his family cemetery in Dunbarton, H.H., where Lowell is now buried, in midwinter:

> where the burning cold illuminated
> the hewn inscriptions of Mother's relatives:
> twenty or thirty Winslows and Starks.
> Frost had given their names a diamond edge . . .

For Perloff these lines illustrate one significant strand of Lowell's "nexus of images": "Not only do winter and summer images regularly alternate in Lowell's poetry, but when the poet wishes to emphasize the isolation and death of the self, he merges the two clusters." Alan Williamson conjectures an implicit allusion: "It is Dante's Hell of ice, reserved for betrayal in intimate relationships; and the implicitly violent imagery of the passage suggests that Lowell holds his mother's Winslow coldness psychologically responsible for hastening his father's death." The conjectured allusion is certainly helpful, possible, and appropriate to all we know of Lowell's well-stocked poetic imagination. And Jerome Mazzaro has shown the importance of Dante to Lowell's earlier poetry.

But there is another allusion, another literary patron saint, much closer to home; an allusion that works more by metonymy than analogy or allegory. The capitalized frost of "Frost had given their names a diamond edge" directs us explicitly, if conjecturally, to another Frost of New Hampshire, "New Hampshire," and *New Hampshire,* that other Robert who inscribed himself Lowell's "friend in the art." That also "fatherless" Robert had written of New Hampshire, of the "burning cold" of fire and ice, and in **"The Generations of Men"** of two young "Starks" whose midsummer future Frost offered to us in terms ironically antithetical to those in which Lowell presents "Mother's relatives." Yet even Frost's young, hopeful couple can ask, "What will we come to / With all this pride of ancestry, we Yankees?", reply only partly facetiously, "I think we're all mad," but finally affirm, "What counts is the ideals, / And those will bear some keeping still about." This witty allusion, much like "Frost is in the stubble" in Wallace Stevens' "The Dwarf," clearly adds a significant allusive dimension to the metonymic and allegorical ones provided by previous commentators.

III. The Colonel's Bubble

Thus, allusions and references can be metaphorical or not; the same detail can be both a reference and an allusion, and it can be both literal and metaphorical. In lines 61-64 of **"For the Union Dead,"** the bubble on which Colonel Robert Gould Shaw, or his spirit, rides as "he waits / for the blessed break" has all these sometimes confusing dimensions, and more. With this poem and its commentators we are driven back to the world of Lowell's earlier poetry, where our problem is not to establish allusion but somehow to sort out, if we can, differing interpretations of reference and allusion, of metonymy and metaphor.

To judge from the commentators, our first problem is whether Lowell wishes us to "think"—for to "see" too vividly would, I feel, be aesthetically disastrous—Shaw as outside or inside "his bubble." Certain critics have glossed the bubble either as a "political bubble which drifts from the mouth of Leviathan," by the bursting of which Shaw, and Lowell, are to be freed from the state, or as one the breaking of which "might unveil truth" or bring about "an annihilation of the veil of Maya" and "a bursting of the amnion." However, we had better, to avoid compounding confusion, take the preposition "on" straightforwardly if still somewhat grotesquely, and leave the Colonel upon his enigmatic, polysemous bubble. For to have him both inside *and* outside the bubble would surely smash Empsonian ambiguity to chaotic rubble.

The bubble has its literal, contextual origin, of course, in the referential "bubbles / drifting from the noses of the cowed, complaint fish" of the South Boston Aquarium of Lowell's youth, which "my hand tingled / to burst." Remaining critical opinion has construed the bubble on which the Colonel rides variously as the world, hope, "the absolute zero of outer space," fame, illusion, idealism, the "boiling bubbles" of Hiroshima, and "the precarious ascendancy of a complacent civilization." Some of these are obviously explicit or implicit visual analogies to the bubble's roundness; others are conventional conceptual equivalents for its metaphorical fragility. Although these glosses may not be actually contradictory, some of us find their multiplicity formally and thematically distracting. Others may delight in their potentially deconstructive profusion.

Three possible separate but simultaneous allusions, however, do provide the esemplastic power to fuse these disparate significances into a single, complex, powerful poetic image, whose components need neither distract nor deconstruct. The first allusion, so obvious as to be almost explicit, puts Colonel Shaw in Shakespeare's fourth age of man, "Seeking the bubble reputation / Even in the cannon's mouth" (*As You Like It,* II. vii. 152-153). The second allusion, to Schopenhauer's *The World as Will and Representation,* may be implicit, even conjectural here, but was explicit in the epigraph of **"'To Speak of Woe That Is In Marriage,'"** in ***Life Studies.*** Both allusions to Schopenhauer, interestingly, combine an obvious literary source with a less obvious philosophical one. The passage from Schopenhauer most apposite to Colonel Shaw's bubble and to the Colonel's entire presence in the poem is as follows:

> Ultimately death must triumph, for by birth it has already become our lot; and it plays with its prey only for a while before swallowing it up. However, we continue our life with great interest and much solicitude as long as possible, just as we blow out a soap-bubble as long and as large as possible, although with the perfect certainty that it will burst.

The third and most conjectural allusion is to "Sintram in Fouqué's tale" and, to the best of my knowledge, was first implied by Steven Axelrod. It is a visual as well as literary allusion and translates the metaphorical bubble back to the iconographically stylized steed on which Shaw literally, in one sense, rides. For Saint-Gaudens' sculptor's vision of Colonel Shaw, which in turn inspired Lowell's poem, resembles the main figure of Albrecht Dürer's engraving, "The Knight, Death, and Satan." This engraving, in its turn, had inspired Baron Frederic de la Motte Fouqué's *Sintram and His Companions,* especially its final confrontation between the hero and these two other powers, from which the hero emerges chastened but whole. In some 19th-century translations of Fouqué. Dürer's engraving was modified to illustrate Sintram's final encounter with Death and with the Devil.

The simultaneity and fusion of these three allusions help us to cope with the image's troubling multiplicity of metaphorical reference and its possible grotesqueness. The conjectural allusion to Fouqué and, by extension, Dürer gives the awkward visual image of the bubble narrative, if fantastic, embodiment and heightens Shaw's existentially authentic fate by its ironic contrast with Sintram's German-Romantic love-honour turmoil. The almost explicit allusion to Jaques' speech fits Colonel Shaw's literal military heroism into the ethical pattern of Shakespeare's more traditional poetic images. It also links Shaw's heroism more unambiguously to Lowell's startlingly metaphorical bubble and ironically parallels Shaw's bubble with the cannon ball's real solidity. The allusion to Schopenhauer combines the differing thematic readings of the bubble's impermanence within a coherent philosophical framework significant in many ways to Lowell's poem and Shaw's fate. The result of this alliance of metaphor and allusion is, as I have already said, a single, complex, powerful poetic image.

Katharine Wallingford (essay date Fall 1986)

SOURCE: "Robert Lowell and Free Association," in *Mosaic,* Vol. XIX, No. 4, Fall, 1986, pp. 121-32.

[In the following essay, Wallingford examines free associational thinking as an important element of Lowell's creative process. Wallingford notes that free association, a technique derived from psychoanalysis, permits Lowell to both engage and reflect upon his own unconscious thoughts.]

In a letter he wrote in 1949 to George Santayana in Rome, Robert Lowell describes a process of thought which sounds remarkably like the psychoanalytic technique of free association:

> Dear Mr. Santayana:
>
> I was just nodding and I saw an image of a fat, yellowish dog receding down the center of a country road—the center was grass and the ruts clam-shells; so much for flux.
>
> I had hoped to send you a book of my poems as a sort of Christmas present; but no. One thing written brings up another—somewhat as the dog-image. Should one shut these things out? It seems safer to let them come, take one's time, to be helpless. . . .
>
> Vocation is love, I think: for beauty, or the Muse, or what you wish. . . . Now at 31 it's just there—I can't send it away for long or find alternatives. There's the power side, the making side, the craft one learns. But now I am struck by the other, the *powerless*—powerless, when it does not come;

> most of all powerless, when it does, like the dog taking you God knows where!

When Lowell pays attention to images which pop into his mind unbidden like the yellow dog, when he determines not to "shut these things out" but to "let them come," when he asserts his willingness to follow along as the dog takes him "God knows where," he might well be describing what Jacques Lacan has called "the forced labour of this discourse without escape, on which the psychologist (not without humor) and the therapist (not without cunning) have bestowed the name of 'free association'." Free association is a "forced labour" indeed, because in order to sneak through the bars of repression and gain access to the unconscious, a subject must be willing, in Freud's words, "entirely [to] renounce any critical selection . . . and say whatever comes into his head," to follow his associations wherever they lead, no matter how unpleasant such a process may be.

Lowell seems always to have been willing to submit himself to the uncontrolled flow of associational thinking. In his biography of the poet, Ian Hamilton quotes a prose piece which Lowell wrote while a student at Harvard:

> Sometimes, when we are in disorder, every pinprick and scraping blade of grass magnifies. A pebble rolls into the Rock of Gibraltar. I got a sunstroke regarding the gardener mow the lawn. He dumped matted green grass into a canvas bag and emptied the bag into a rut pond behind a clump of shrubbery. . . . I watched him dump grass on the surface where there ought to have been frogs. I smelled the odor of dried verdure in my sleep; tons of it, wet and lifeless, floating and stifling. At morning the grass tide rose up gruesome.
>
> The sea lay grass green and ever so serene. Sharks' fins ripped the ripe slick. The fish rhythmically approximated each others' courses and crossed at intervals. The water was toothed with their tusks. Oil dripped from the tusks. Short cropped grass drooped over their round eyes.

The prose piece continues for several paragraphs, its power issuing "from feverishly intent scrutiny," as Hamilton puts it, and from Lowell's apparent submission to the associational flow.

From time to time throughout his career Lowell would make poetry out of this free associational process, not necessarily with any conscious therapeutic intention, but rather because, as the prose piece and the letter to Santayana demonstrate, it was natural for him to think in this way. Of course the poet's use of associational material may differ from that of the psychoanalytic patient, who uses free association, in Stanley Leavy's words, to "disclose unconscious mental content, which has the power so long as it remains undisclosed of binding the patient-to-be in constraints." Robert Waelder explains that the "analysand is urged to abandon the ordinary habit of goal-directed thought, and instead to permit everything freely to enter his mind and to verbalize it as soon as it appears"; as a result of this process, "the unconscious begins to express itself." And although such raw data from the unconscious rarely qualified as poetry (although André Breton and the surrealists, as well as the Beat poets of the United States, made careers out of asserting just such an equation), Frederick Crews points out how closely the process approximates that of the artist, who "provisionally relaxes the censorship regnant in waking life, forgoes some of his society's characteristic defenses, and allows the repressed a measure of representation, though . . . only in disguised and compromised form."

Lowell himself described some of his poetry as surrealistic in the **"Afterthought"** to ***Notebook 1967-68:*** "I lean heavily to the rational, but am devoted to surrealism. A surrealist might not say, 'The man entered a house', but 'The man entered a police-whistle', or . . . make some bent generalization: 'Weak wills command the gods'. Or more subtly, words that seem right, though loosely in touch with reason: 'Saved by my anger from cruelty'. Surrealism can degenerate into meaningless clinical hallucination, or worse into rhetorical machinery, yet it is a natural way to write our fictions." The reader of ***Notebook,*** particularly one who tries to read the volume as a whole rather than to browse haphazardly among the individual sonnets, may well become impatient; some of the less successful poems indeed seem to "degenerate into meaningless clinical hallucinations, or worse into rhetorical machinery." For the most part, however, Lowell was able to transmute the associational material into successful poetry without losing the quality of spontaneity. In the **"Afterthought"** to the revised ***Notebook,*** he changed the word "surrealism" to "unrealism" and counterbalanced his warning about its dangers with the affirmation that "the true unreal is about something, and eats from the abundance of reality." Alan Williamson describes how the successful surrealistic poems work in ***Notebook:*** "Lowell's surrealistic poems turn . . . to the unruliness of the moment, showing us how many separate strands of sensation it contains, how weirdly the mind shuttles between them and its own equally abrupt and mysterious patterns of fantasy-thought. Lowell struggles . . . to deliver the feeling, if not the literal contents, of a basic mind-flux." The poems show us, in other words, how free association feels.

Consider **"Long Summer 3,"** the third in a sequence of fifteen sonnets in ***Notebook.*** Lowell begins by evoking in the reader the feeling of the state he describes:

Months of it, and the inarticulate mist so thick
we turned invisible to one another
across the room. . . .

Months of what? The preceding poem, ending with the image of a discarded boiled lobster and its "two burnt-out, pinhead, black and popping eyes," gives us no help. We are bewildered, in a fog, anxious. We are cut off from the poet, "invisible to one another / across the room" of the poem. And we are inarticulate: the words "inarticulate mist so thick" are hard to say because we falter and trip over the "s" and "t" sounds which are jammed together.

. . . the floor, aslant, shot hulling
through thunderheads, gun-cotton dipped in
pitch

And what now? The syntax has dissolved and the enjambment hurls us forward, but where are we?

Salmon-glow. . . .

Explosions from guns? Hell?

Salmon-glow as the early lighted moon

Not hell, but instead a respite from anxiety: a calm, lovely moment. But it cannot last.

Salmon-glow as the early lighted moon,
snuffed by the malodorous and frosted murk—
not now! . . .

Please not now. Not a return of the anxiety, the uncertainty, the fear.

. . . Earth's solid and the sky is light,
yet even on the steadiest day, dead noon,
the sun stockstill like Joshua's in midfield,
I have to brace my hand against a wall
to keep myself from swaying—

A moment of reflection, as the subject steps back from the pure flow of association, and rationally and coolly assesses his situation. The conclusion is not encouraging: although the physical world is stable and filled with light, the interior world threatens, and the subject totters. He is afraid. But free association is a "forced labour," and writer and reader have determined to submit themselves to it, to follow wherever the images lead.

. . . swaying wall,
straitjacket, hypodermic, helmeted
doctors, one crowd, white-smocked, in panic, hit
stop, bury the runner on the cleated field.

Panic indeed, as the images come so fast they blur into one another, threatening, pressing in, faster and faster, hospital, helmets, a wall of white, the quarterback about to be overwhelmed, the patient about to be subdued by force, terror, "in panic, hit, / stop." The moment and the momentum stop, the patient is knocked out, the runner is buried forever on the cleated field.

A poem like **"Long Summer 3"** works because Lowell is able, in Williamson's words, "to deliver the feeling, if not the literal contents, of a basic mind-flux." And poems like **"Long Summer 3"** abound not only in ***Notebook*** but throughout the body of his poetry. Williamson points out that "[i]n terms of the surrealists' ideal of a direct rendition of the flow of thought, conscious and unconscious, ***Lord Weary's Castle*** often succeeds brilliantly, where the later, 'confessional' writing often chooses to view psychological processes more remotely, in rational afterthought." Robert Hass, writing about **"The Quaker Graveyard in Nantucket,"** elaborates on this paradox:

> I still find myself blinking incredulously when I read . . . that those early poems "clearly reflect the dictates of the new criticism," while the later ones are "less consciously wrought and extremely intimate." This is the view in which it is "more intimate" and "less conscious" to say "my mind's not right" than to image the moment when
>
> The death-lance churns into the sanctuary, tears
> The gun-blue swingle, heaving like a flail,
> And hacks the coiling life out . . .
>
> which is to get things appallingly wrong.

A poem like **"The Quaker Graveyard"** is more "intimate" than many of the ***Life Studies*** poems in part because the speaker seems to have immersed himself in a flow of association rather than to have arranged images according to an esthetic or rational order—and this despite the fact that the early poems are more formal, bound by traditional meter and rhyme.

Williamson argues that "[i]ambic meters and rhyme, in Lowell, tend to produce, not neat rational statements, but a kind of trance," and he mentions the "intensity" with which symbols "arrive" in such poetry. The images in the early poems are charged with an energy that is often lacking in the poems of ***Life Studies.*** Compare, for example, images from **"Mother and Son,"** in ***Lord Weary's Castle,*** with images from **"My Last Afternoon with Uncle Devereux Winslow." "Mother and Son"** begins with a matter-of-fact statement describing the plight of an adult male still in thrall to his in thrall to his mother: "Meeting his mother makes him lose ten years, / Or is it twenty?" He is a boy again.

> . . . It is honest to hold fast
> Merely to what one sees with one's own eyes
> When the red velvet curves and haunches rise
> To blot him from the pretty driftwood fire's
> Facade of welcome. . . .

The red velvet curves and haunches are simultaneously seductive and repellent, and the image intervenes between the boy and the fire which promises but cannot deliver light and warmth. "Nothing shames / Him more than this uncoiling, counterfeit / Body presented as an idol"—and then, another terrible image:

> . . . It
> Is something in a circus, big as life,
> The painted dragon, a mother and a wife
> With flat glass eyes pushed at him on a stick;
> The human mover crawls to make them click.

A familiar child's push-toy appears to him as something gigantic and grotesque, and the implacable stresses in the penultimate line reinforce the threatening effect of the "flat glass eyes," pushing toward him.

With these images, effective and frightening, compare two from **"My Last Afternoon,"** in which the poet recalls impressions of himself as a small boy, "five and a half," spending an afternoon at the family farm with his uncle, who "was dying of the incurable Hodgkin's disease."

> No one had died there in my lifetime . . .
> Only Cinder, our Scottie puppy
> paralysed from gobbling toads.
> I sat mixing black earth and lime. (Lowell's
> ellipsis)

Here the adult speaker is not involved, not, to borrow Hass's phrase, "in the picture"; the paralyzed dog seems almost comic, evoking no emotion either in the reader or in the small boy who sits mixing earth and lime. At the very end of the poem, Lowell returns to the image of the boy:

> My hands were warm, then cool, on the piles
> of earth and lime,
> a black pile and a white pile. . . .
> Come winter,
> Uncle Devereux would blend to the one color.
> (Lowell's ellipsis)

We apprehend no intensity here, no element of submission to the flux of free association.

Yet the detached quality with which the adult speaker in **"My Last Afternoon"** looks back on his younger self is not sustained throughout the poem, much less throughout the volume ***Life Studies;*** indeed, throughout his career Lowell alternates, often within the course of a single poem, between a detached tone and the more intense, involved tone that seems to derive from a process like that of free association. And although we must be careful not to equate Lowell's use of free association with that of a patient in analysis, nevertheless we can borrow from psychoanalysis a concept which may help us to understand in Lowell's poetry the alternation in tone between detachment and involvement.

Psychoanalysis, or self-examination of any sort, implies a splitting of the "self" into that part which is to do the examining, and that part which is to be examined; in Otto Fenichel's words, the ego is split into "an observing and an experiencing part so that the former can judge the irrational character of the latter." Fenichel's "experiencing part," in an analysis, is "irrational" because it has been set free from the control of the rational, and allowed—indeed, encouraged—to roam freely. In *The Literary Use of the Psychoanalytic Process,* Meredith Skura describes the process of psychoanalysis as one in which "one part of the mind is freely associating" while the other part, the "observer," often "draws on the resources of logic and secondary process thinking discarded by free association, but its role is not to provide authoritative interpretations. . . . Instead it provides new perspectives, finds new relationships, reorganizes figure and ground, and changes emphasis." She associates this characteristic of the psychoanalytic process with literature: the "resemblance between psychoanalysis and literature lies in their dynamic interaction: the interaction between the free-ranging play of mind and the organizing response to it, and the continuing play which they contradict or confirm." Skura is primarily concerned with critical activity, the reading of literature, but we may extend her remarks to writing as well. May Sarton says that "a writer not only feels but watches himself feeling," and Ernst Kris applies this same concept to artists: "The process [of artistic creation] involves a continued interplay between creation and criticism, manifested in the painter's alternation of working on the canvas and stepping back to observe the effect. We may speak here of a *shift in psychic level,* consisting in the fluctuation of functional regression and control."

Although Kris is speaking of artistic creation in a spatial medium—painting—many critics have found in Lowell's poetry signs of a similar duality, which Jay Martin describes as "the analytic faculty of the poet's imagination overhearing the secrets of his personality." Steven Gould Axelrod, describing "Lowell's inner-outer view of his past self" in ***Life Studies,*** refers to "his use of a narratorial double-consciousness; the authorial awareness includes both the consciousness of the remembered child and that of the remembering adult poet." And Ian Hamilton records a similar view of the prose reminiscences upon which **"91 Revere Street"** and some of the poems in ***Life Studies*** are based: "Throughout there is a kind of double vision: the child's eye view judged and interpreted by the ironical narrator, with a good deal of adult invention around the edges."

This split in the ego of the poet, then, as we encounter it in Lowell's poetry, has itself a dual function: it permits the rational "observing ego" to observe the experiencing self, and to shape the materials of the experience into art. Each function enters into and affects the other. Skura has described how the observing ego "provides new perspectives, finds new relationships, reorganizes figure and ground, and changes emphasis"; in Lowell's poem **"Beyond the Alps,"** we can ourselves observe the observing ego as it performs these tasks.

"Beyond the Alps" begins ***Life Studies,*** and the name of the volume is instructive. The study of a life is a process; as the poem makes clear, it is the life of Robert Lowell—the experiencing self—that is being studied, and the observer self of Robert Lowell does the studying. The poem begins, as Irwin Ehrenpreis tells us, "with what look like random associations suggesting the real flow of a unique consciousness." The poet is both on a train, reading a newspaper while making a journey, and outside the train, watching:

> Reading how even the Swiss had thrown the
> sponge
> in once again and Everest was still unscaled,
> I watched our Paris pullman lunge mooning
> across the fallow Alpine snow.

Wyatt Prunty tells us that the train's "motion is analogous to Lowell's consciousness making constant revisions between a known past and an expected and unfolding future." The poet is making a journey through time and space from the Rome of his early Roman Catholicism to Paris, "our black classic," where he will have need of the new perspectives and new relationships which the observing ego can discern. "Life changed to landscape," he tells us. "Much against my will / I left the City of God where it belongs." Behind him he has left, among other things, the Pope, who has just "defined the dogma of Mary's bodily assumption" into heaven. The "old," believing Lowell might have accepted this dogma, but the "new," ironic Lowell has a different perspective:

> The lights of science couldn't hold a candle
> to Mary risen—at one miraculous stroke,
> angel-wing'd, gorgeous as a jungle bird!
> But who believed this? Who could understand?

Reorganizing figure and ground in a literal way, the observing Lowell tells us that "our mountain-climbing train had come to earth"; changing emphasis, no longer aspiring to unreachable heights, he says in a wry voice: "There were no tickets to that altitude / once held by Hellas." The poet who, in the early lines of the poem, had watched the train lunge forward, now turns around and watches, from a different perspective, "each backward, wasted Alp." And meanwhile, what of the experiencing self? "Tired of the querulous hush-hush of the wheels, / the blear-eyed ego kicking in my berth / lay still." A psychoanalyst might protest here that Lowell misuses the term "ego," but readers of the poem can recognize what is happening: the detached, rational part of the self is observing the experiencing self, and out of this process poetry is being written.

Lowell made poetry out of the process of free association throughout his career—from the tortured images of ***Land of Unlikeness*** and ***Lord Weary's Castle*** to the more serene poems of ***Day by Day,*** poems which, according to Axelrod, develop "through a process close to free association, [and] bring content from his unconscious into the light of consciousness." And from time to time Lowell wrote rather explicitly about the process itself. He begins **"Myopia: A Night"** (***For the Union Dead***) in a state of consciousness that is particularly conducive to free association, the state just before falling asleep.

> Bed, glasses off, and all's
> ramshackle, streaky, weird
> for the near-sighted, just
> a foot away.
>
> The light's
> still on an instant. Here
> are the blurred titles, here
> the books are blue hills, browns,
> greens, fields, or color.
>
> This
> is the departure strip,
> the dream-road. Whoever built it
> left numbers, words and arrows.
> He had to leave in a hurry.

For this myopic poet, the blur of books dissolves into a country scene of hills and fields, "the departure strip, / the dream-road" which he must travel, complete with "numbers, words and arrows" to point the way. Where does the road lead? As Stephen Yenser suggests, it leads directly to the study in which Lowell wrote his poems as a young man.

> I see
> a dull and alien room,
> my cell of learning,
> white, brightened by white pipes,
> ramrods of steam . . . (Lowell's ellipsis)

He sees the room clearly: the pipes, the steam; and the sight evokes the memory of a sound:

I hear
the lonely metal breathe
and gurgle like the sick.

This sound is unpleasant; this memory is going to be too painful, and for once Lowell turns back and refuses to follow the path of associations.

And yet my eyes avoid
that room. No need to see.
No need to know I hoped
its blank, foregoing whiteness
would burn away the blur,
as my five senses clenched
their teeth, thought stitched to thought,
as through a needle's eye . . . (Lowell's ellipsis)

Here past and present merge as the poet tries to shut out the memory of that "blank, foregoing whiteness" which he hoped might "burn away the blur" of approaching mania, that terrible condition in which the mind is bombarded by more sensation than it can accommodate, when associations succeed one another so quickly and so intensely that the mind feels stretched to the breaking point, painfully elongated.

I see the morning star.

Here, in a bedroom, looking through a window, he sees a star, the morning star: Lucifer, before the Fall.

Think of him in the Garden,
that seed of wisdom, Eve's
seducer, stuffed with man's
corruption, stuffed with triumph:
Satan triumphant in
the Garden! In a moment,
all that blinding brightness
changed into a serpent,
lay grovelling on its gut.

Satan is larger than life, like a young poet whose works have been roundly applauded, or like a manic patient proud of his sexual prowess, "stuffed" with man's corruption and with triumph, imbued with "blinding brightness" which never lasts, which always turns, "in a moment," into dust. And here? Now?

What has disturbed this household?
Only a foot away,
the familiar faces blur.
At fifty we're so fragile,
a feather . . . (Lowell's ellipsis)

Past and present, people and things, sickness and health, life and death, all combine and co-exist. As Lowell's many ellipses demonstrate, thoughts fade in and out, come and go. "We're so fragile." But, at least for now, we survive:

The things of the eye are done.
On the illuminated black dial,
green ciphers of a new moon—
one, two, three, four, five, six!
I breathe and cannot sleep.
Then morning comes,
saying, "This was a night."

In **"Myopia: A Night,"** Lowell's journey into the unconscious begins with the blurred sight of books, blue hills and browns, "the departure strip, / the dream road." The poem, like **"Eye and Tooth"** (***For the Union Dead***), is based on an extended pun on "I" and "eye," and Lowell makes clear the fact that what the eye sees may well lead one to investigate what the I feels. Something of the same relation obtains in psychoanalysis, as Theodor Reik tells us after relating an instance of his own free association: "These are my thoughts as I should tell them to a person in the room to whom I have to report them the moment they occur. It is clear that most of them are determined by the objects I see; the connections between them seem to be made only by the sight of the objects and by thoughts of the persons they remind me of."

Whether set into motion by the sight of an actual tangible object or by an image like that of the yellow dog that Lowell describes in his letter to Santayana, the associational process was crucial to Lowell in the writing of his poetry. "An image of a white house with a blotch on it—this is perhaps the start of a Williams poem," he says in an essay on William Carlos Williams—and might have said about his own poem **"Eye and Tooth."** Writing about his composition of **"Skunk Hour,"** he said that he "was haunted by the image of a blue china doorknob. I never used the doorknob or knew what it meant, yet somehow it started the current of images in my opening stanzas." According to Louis Simpson this passage describes "a process of evoking the unconscious"; the blue china doorknob "is like the image a therapist chooses from his patient's speech as he associates freely, in order to pursue it and see where it leads. It is a thread into the unconscious; tugged at, it brings other images in its train."

Although Lowell's interest in the associational process may well have derived in part from his experiences with psychotherapy and his general knowledge of psychoanalysis, his public remarks on the process invariably dealt not with psychoanalysis but with poetry:

> Almost the whole problem of writing poetry is to bring it back to what you really feel, and that takes an awful lot of maneuvering. You may feel the doorknob more strongly than some big personal event, and the doorknob will open into something that you can use as your own. . . . Some little image, some detail you've noticed—you're writing about a little country shop, just describing it, and your poem ends up with an existentialist account of your experience. But it's the shop that started it off. You didn't know why it meant a lot to you. Often images and often the sense of the beginning and end of a poem are all you have—some journey to be gone through between those things: you know that, but you don't know the details.

In a poem which he wrote for Elizabeth Bishop, Lowell created an image to stand for the poet on his journey through the poem:

> Have you seen an inchworm crawl on a leaf,
> cling to the very end, revolve in air,
> feeling for something to reach to something? Do
> you still hang your words in air, ten years
> unfinished, glued to your notice board, with
> gaps
> or empties for the unimaginable phrase—[?] ***(History)***

Even though he may have to grope his way along the path of associations, the poet nevertheless has faith that the blue doorknob will "open into something" that he can use. He has only to follow:

> Aroused, then sleeping, caught adrift . . . the
> voice
> singing to me in French, "*O mon avril.*"
> Those nasals . . . they woo us. Spring. Not
> theirs. Not mine.
> A large pileated bird flies up,
> dropping excretions like a frightened snake,
> its Easter feathers; its earwax-yellow spoonbill
> angrily hitting from side to side to blaze
> a broad passage through the Great Northern
> Jungle—
> the lizard tyrants were killed to a man by this bird,
> man's forerunner

The large pileated bird which flies up out of the poet's unconscious blazes "a broad passage" through which he can follow:

> I pick up stones, and hope
> to snatch its crest, its crown, at last, and cross
> the perilous passage, sound in mind and body . . .

Only by following the bird, with its earwax-yellow spoonbill-like the "fat, yellowish dog receding down the center of a country road"—can he cross "the perilous passage" and emerge, "sound in mind and body," able to write a passage of his own about the journey to be gone through between the beginning and the end of the poem and the life.

> often reaching the passage, seeing my thoughts
> stream on the water, as if I were cleaning fish.
> (**"Bird,"** ***Notebook***)

Don Bogen (review date 11 April 1987)

SOURCE: "Perfection of the Work," in *The Nation,* April 11, 1987, pp. 475-6, 478.

[*In the following review, Bogen offers positive evaluation of Lowell's* Collected Prose.]

Robert Lowell was probably the last American poet who might be described as formidable. His stylistic transformations—from dense formal elegies to free verse confessions, blank sonnets and diary-like musings—were *news* in a way that no poet's are today. Immersed in aesthetic debates and the controversies of public life, he held a commanding place in American culture even after his move to Britain in the late 1960s. That prominence has declined in the decade since his death. Lowell's choice of subject may be partly to blame here. A poet who writes a lot about his life is at the mercy of his biographer after his death, and Lowell was not served well by his. Ian Hamilton's *Robert Lowell: A Biography* is an exhausting compendium of letters, anecdotes and narration which presents, finally, a stock image of the poet as inspired madman: frenzied, often cruel, living life at superhuman intensity and, in the current version of the myth, a victim of his own aberrant brain chemistry. Lowell's ***Collected Prose*** should help correct that image. It reminds us that what matters is not how often the poet was in mental hospitals or how many affairs he had but what he wrote and thought.

Lowell seems to have struggled with his writing more than most, revising, as he put it, "endlessly." In his elegy for Lowell, the Irish poet Seamus Heaney compared him to a retiarius, the gladiator who fought with a net. Knotting, weaving, casting and recasting his mesh of words, Lowell produced a body of poetry that makes most poets' careers look facile and self-imitative. Though he wrote relatively little prose, the range of Lowell's net in this mode was wide. His ***Collected Prose*** contains autobiographical studies; essays on American, European and classical literature; reviews of contemporary poets and critics from I. A. Richards to Sylvia

Plath; and two interviews. Not all the material is equally well crafted or illuminating—sometimes the net has big holes in it. But what Lowell manages to capture in these pieces is well worth the occasional passage through empty air.

Lowell's prose was edited by his friend and publisher Robert Giroux, who provides a good introduction and careful, unobtrusive notes. A bit more than a quarter of the book consists of previously unpublished material, most of which is unfinished and still rough. The ideas are often fascinating here, especially Lowell's scattered comments on American writers in **"New England and Further,"** but we can see why the poet didn't find this work ready for print. A few of the unpublished pieces should probably not have been printed at all. The inclusion of Lowell's prep-school essay on the *Iliad,* for example, serves no purpose. Lowell was no Rimbaud; his term-paper, style sounds as windy and adolescent as any school boy's. Publishing the letter of protest Lowell wrote to President Roosevelt when he refused induction during World War II is perhaps more understandable, as there may be some biographical interest in seeing the actual "manic statement" mentioned in Lowell's ***Life Studies.*** But though his poems brilliantly capture the public climates of our time—particularly the cold war and Vietnam eras—this letter shows a muddled anticommunism that does him little credit. Like Yeats, Lowell used the ambiguities and tensions of verse to thread through the labyrinth of political life. Without them, he seems as lost as any of us.

But Lowell is not lost in the critical essays and reviews he wrote for publication. The ***Collected Prose*** brings those together well, juxtaposing his early and later pieces on central modernist figures such as T. S. Eliot and William Carlos Williams and poet-critics such as Randall Jarrell and John Crowe Ransom. In most of these pairings the first piece is an analytical review from the late 1940s, the second an overview and elegy some twenty years later. What's perhaps most striking in Lowell's criticism is his generosity of spirit. In dealing with poets' lives he has kind things to say about everyone. Even Robert Frost, a man possessing what Lowell termed "a heart of stonemason darkness," is treated with sympathetic understanding. Likewise his judgments of writers' work are appealingly eclectic, reminding us that the kinds of oppositions that shape a literary history—Williams versus Eliot, Stevens versus Frost—should not keep us from enjoying different kinds of poetry. Although he considered his essays "much sloppier and more intuitive" than standard criticism, Lowell rarely indulges in the bland poets' shoptalk that crops up all too frequently in literary magazines today. Rather he combines scholarly breadth and rigor with an insider's attention to the significant aspects of poetic practice. In his essay on Williams, for example, Lowell pinpoints the essence of the poet's free verse technique—"quick changes of tone, atmosphere, and speed"—which has escaped William's ubiquitous imitators. And his review of Elizabeth Bishop's first book, *North & South,* in 1947 defines the precise values that remained central throughout her career: variety and the ability to let description and reflection feed each other, to build poems that simultaneously show and think.

If Lowell as critic is perceptive in his praise, he is equally insightful in his put-downs. Here he is on a new translation of Ovid in 1955:

> A. E. Watts's translation of the *Metamorphoses* into five-foot couplets is admirable, steady, civilized—and impossible. Watts, you have to conclude, has chosen the wrong poem in the *Metamorphoses* because this work, as he says in his preface, is "the most complete exploration in verse of the resources of rhetoric." Unfortunately, the resources of rhetoric cannot be explored by academic piety and a photostat exhibition of devices and tropes. Once started on the job, however, Watts chose the wrong meter. No English poet has ever translated hexameters into adequate pentameter couplets. No poet since Chaucer has done a translation even of couplets into couplets that has turned out to be comparable to the original. No one *not* a poet has ever written readable couplets. No one in our century has written an interesting long poem in couplets. To make sure of mortally crippling himself, Watts has chosen to mix a gushing run-on line with the divided, antithetical, and end-stopped line of Pope and Dryden. The Watts couplet is freakishly stiff and floppy, a Minotaur, uneasy in both its natures; it brays without emphasis.

You can tell Lowell is having a good time here: a breezy wit animates the piece from the opening reversal through all those *no*'s below. But this is no cheap shot. Turning from what he calls "Watts-baiting" a paragraph later, Lowell spends the bulk of his review defining what makes Ovid so elusive in English. His discussion of what's wrong in just the first lines of English versions by Watts, Dryden and the Elizabethan translator Arthur Golding is an engaging tour de force, and his sense of Ovid's subtleties illuminates the entire essay. It's common enough to see a work of verse as untranslatable, but Lowell's review is finally encouraging to those who would attempt an English Ovid. By describing the original in all its protean energy, its shifts, as he puts it, "from Vergilian wonder to the flippant, forceful, jabbing worldliness of a letter writer," Lowell whets our appetite for a good translation. His concern with the intricacies of Ovid and Vergil is not merely antiquarian. For Lowell, modern America was a version of Augustan Rome: a republic gone to seed, peevish, imperialist, in constant search of reminders of its own greatness. In this regard the classics are as fresh as ever.

If the net of Lowell's verse caught much of our imperial petulance, it also dragged in great swaths of his own troubled life. It is interesting to see him examining parts of that life in two previously unpublished autobiographical essays from the late 1950s, **"Antebellum Boston"** and **"Near the Unbalanced Aquarium."** Though they complement the brilliant prose piece **"91 Revere Street,"** which Lowell included in ***Life Studies,*** they are not as well written. Their structures seem a little clunky, their ironies not as sharp as they could be. Instead of revising them extensively for publication, Lowell appears to have mined these essays for poems. In one section of **"Near the Unbalanced Aquarium,"** for instance, all the details of what will later become the poem **"Father's Bedroom"** arise in one dense paragraph. To read this is to appreciate Lowell's sheer craft in converting a mass of description and speculation into an incisive and purposeful work of verse. Elsewhere in these essays are some vivid depictions of illness: a childhood bout with croup, pervaded by the smell of benzoin and the hallucinations of three days without sleep; and Lowell's stay at the Payne-Whitney Clinic in 1954, which alternates between manic pranks and the medicated lethargy of "a diver in the full billowings of his equipment on the bottom of the sea."

But the best autobiographical piece in the ***Collected Prose***—and one of the finest essays of its sort in the last forty years—is **"91 Revere Street."** Weaving memories of boyhood incidents with family history and sketches of his parents and their friends, Lowell captures not just one life but a whole context of experience. The central event is Lowell's father's decision in 1927 to acquiesce to his wife's demands and resign his commission in the Navy. In tracing the man's pathetic attempts at explaining his action to his Navy buddies, Lowell builds a devastating vision of balding "boys" still checking out one another's "*figger* and waterline," frozen in adolescence by nostalgia and the petty rules and rewards of service life. Though the boy Lowell's sympathies are clearly with his mother (there is no shortage of Oedipal overtones here), the essay exposes her much-valued Old Boston taste as "middle-of-the-road," her social pretensions as laughable and her marital tactics as unscrupulous. Any pity we might feel for the only child of this union between New England snobbery and Annapolis juvenility is held in check by Lowell's depiction of himself as alternately aggressive and thick-skulled, enjoying his mother's attention and his role as a pawn in his parents' fights. As a study of the intricacies of domestic discord, **"91 Revere Street"** is cold, accurate and ferocious.

Lowell was a great poet of description, and one thing that makes the tensions so vivid in **"91 Revere Street"** is his startling treatment of inanimate objects, especially clothes and furniture. His picture of the Victorian furnishings the Lowells inherited from relatives is typical:

> Here, table, highboy, chairs, and screen—mahogany, cherry, teak—looked nervous and disproportioned. They seemed to wince, touch elbows, shift from foot to foot. High above the highboy, our gold National Eagle stooped forward, plastery and doddering. The Sheffield silver-plate urns, more precious than solid sterling, peeled; the bodies of the heraldic mermaids on the Mason-Myers crest blushed a metallic copper tan. In the harsh New England light, the bronze sphinxes supporting our sideboard looked as though manufactured in Grand Rapids.

Precise, evocative and ironic, Lowell gets *things* to say more about family life than most writers do with whole pages of dialogue. But domestic *angst* is, of course, not the only subject here. **"91 Revere Street"** is a study in mismatches: between furniture and its setting, between taste and wealth, between a husband and wife, and between the past and the present. The story of a naval engineer who decides to work for Lever Brothers has its interest, but the fact that the man's surname is Lowell gives his decline obvious ramifications. In taking apart his family history, exposing the shoddiness and awkward displacement behind the lofty facade, Lowell dissects the complex tissue of our New England "aristocracies." Puritan moral rectitude and family-tree exclusiveness go out the window. In a perfect touch near the end of the essay, Lowell imagines his great-great-grandfather Major Mordecai Myers (who, we are told, "had never frowned down in judgment on a Salem witch") announcing to his descendants, "My children, my blood, accept graciously the loot of your inheritance. We are all dealers in used furniture."

Latter-day Romans, inheritors of claptrap and loot—Robert Lowell was able to define better than most writers what we as Americans are. His reviews and essays have an almost old-fashioned element of intellectual responsibility to them. They reflect a time when critics actively interpreted poems and poets actually read what critics wrote. Lowell's attention to tradition, social issues and the subtleties of craft gives his ***Collected Prose*** energy and lasting value.

Donald Davie (review date 12 July 1987)

SOURCE: "Art, Evil, and the Poet," in *New York Times Book Review,* July 12, 1987, pp. 22-3.

[*In the following review, Davie offers favorable assessment of Lowell's* Collected Prose.]

This may be Robert Lowell's most winning book. But ***Collected Prose*** should not be read straight through, nor taken in big gulps. Robert Giroux, faced with more than 40 pieces, nearly all short and scrappy, some incomplete, has sorted them by subject matter into three sections and an appendix. On balance this arrangement is probably the best possible. But it has disadvantages. If we want to know what Lowell thought of William Carlos Williams, we find him taking three bites at the cherry—in 1947, 1948, 1962; and whereas we are enlightened about how he changed his mind (the two bites at John Berryman, eight years apart, are very illuminating in this way), we are confused about how far his second thoughts canceled out his first. At any rate, it's only by sorting out the chronology that we can construct a narrative of Lowell's life in and out of, but mostly in, literature.

We can read several plots in a narrative thus reconstructed. One might be called the defection from the South. The outline is well known: here it's documented in the famous **"Visiting the Tates,"** in a tribute in two parts to John Crowe Ransom (written 26 years apart) and in a piece on Ford Madox Ford, whose connections with the Old Confederacy drew the young Lowell southward in the first place. Without in the least minimizing the solidity of his educational grounding in New England (we have here an amazingly precocious essay on the "Iliad" by the 18-year-old Lowell at St. Mark's School). Lowell himself insisted that it was from Southerners, from Allen Tate and Ransom, that he imbibed the notion of the poetic calling as a strenuous and above all erudite discipline. Here the plot turns painful; for Tate, who never lost touch with his protégé and seems never to have complained of being betrayed, might well have done so. The drastic turnaround in taste that Lowell and Randall Jarrell (the latter himself a Southerner) effected in the 1950's left Tate for his last 25 years a poet bombinating into a void.

Did Lowell feel guilt at this defection? Between the lines there is some evidence he did. But he didn't dwell on it. Jarrell and he were right: however rigorously correct in the abstract Tate's and Ransom's poetics may have been, neither of them fathered a single poet writing to any purpose in their chosen and mastered styles. The revealing document is Lowell's 1953 essay on Robert Penn Warren's "Brother to Dragons," in which the author of ***The Mills of the Kavanaughs,*** an adept of New England gingerbread Gothic, sees through Warren's Southern Gothic—under a suave surface of respect and admiration. It is not just that Lowell and Jarrell read the signs of the times; they detected an obfuscating dishonesty in what was accepted as the appropriate rhetoric for poetry, particularly in the South. The Fugitives and the New Critics (often the same persons) had buttressed and vindicated that rhetoric by a poetic theory so sophisticated that Lowell and Jarrell, once indoctrinated in it, could never disprove it or disown it. But they themselves went by rule of thumb, by practice, and ignored or flouted the principles they could not deny.

Probably the strangest piece here is **"Art and Evil."** It was put together from a manuscript supplied by Elizabeth Hardwick, Lowell's second wife, with a continuation that turned up at Harvard. It is unfinished, but, since the last paragraph begins, "Finally," Mr. Giroux suggests only a couple of concluding sentences are missing. However, he must have felt, when he noted. "The manuscript breaks off at this point," that it could hardly have done anything else. For the discourse had become so wayward and rambling that any sort of drawing together was impossible. Some of it seems to date from the 50's, other parts from as much as 20 years later, but much of it surely was composed during the onset of one of Lowell's manic phases. And yet it has more than clinical interest. For the relation between Lowell's art and his apprehension of evil is for us the most vexing question about him (he shows himself aware of this). And that may have been his most strenuous attempt to explain himself to himself on this matter.

He begins with a brilliant and rapid survey of how the writers of his generation changed in their apprehension of evil from where they had started. They began with the posturing diabolism of the French and English 1890's, and of Jacobean playwrights seen through 90's spectacles, and only later perceived the black and sinister undersides of supposedly robust and wholesome writers like Shakespeare, Tennyson and Dickens. Then he turns to T. S. Eliot's 1933 essay "After Strange Gods," with its contempt—the easy and eager contempt of the lately converted—for all those to whom "the doctrine of Original Sin is not a very real and tremendous thing." Lowell thinks Eliot's "tremendous" gives the Devil too much dignity, or at least that it registers in the Devil's presence a *frisson* such as by the 50's no one could feel any longer; after Buchenwald and Hiroshima, Lowell suggests, we know the Devil as an old acquaintance in whose company we are more at home than with his heavenly Antagonist. There is some rewriting of history here; for in poems of strained religiosity like **"Colloquy in Black Rock,"** Lowell himself had made much play with "tremendousness."

After an airy excursus into theology and Christian apologetics, which assures us that Cain and Lucifer and Christ are alternative names for a figure called "the criminal," Lowell announces that the rest of his paper will be concerned with eight figures, catalogued two by two: Rimbaud and Milton's Satan; George Eliot's Grandcourt from "Daniel Deronda" and Virgil's Aeneas; Dickens's Sarah Gamp and Faulkner's Popeye; Goethe's Mephistopheles and Shakespeare's Iago. He considers on a par the historical person Arthur Rimbaud and the Satan of "Paradise Lost"; and Aeneas and Dido in the fourth book of the "Aeneid" are discussed quite as if we had access to them otherwise than through the sensibility of Virgil. Lowell blithely or flippantly reinstates one of the worst habits of the belletristic criticism from which L. C. Knights and Ransom, Cleanth Brooks and Warren and others, had for a time weaned him. Did he know what he was doing? I judge that he did, and didn't care. Give him credit, he never published this piece. But he was familiar with evil, no doubt of it.

Of course the old belle-lettrists, practicing their impressionist criticism, had their own ways of succeeding and delighting. And when Lowell wrote criticism, he did it as belles-lettres. There is a sparkling performance on Ovid's "Metamorphoses," where Lowell surpasses Jarrell at his best: an astonishing nine pages of lightly carried learning. Lowell professed not to take himself seriously as a critic; but here he must be taken very seriously indeed.

There is no poet now writing in English so well educated; this makes Lowell seem a figure from a lost age, the last of his kind. Often he refers to other writers to say obliquely something about himself and his work. A striking instance is an encomium of some late poems by Heine, interjected suddenly and fiercely into a conversation with Ian Hamilton in 1971; this throws a clear and self-justifying beam of light on Lowell's last four collections. Hamilton conscientiously needled Lowell about newly fashionable manifestations he was thought to have sponsored: confessional poetry, extremism, political mass violence, a welcome to popular song and verse. Lowell responded civilly and sourly; his fame, which he knows about, is for him a burden. We believe him, and think it does him credit.

And yet there were lacunae in Lowell's knowledge. Challenged as to living British poets, he remembers neither Basil Bunting nor Thom Gunn; among Americans, he has nothing to say of Charles Reznikoff or Carl Rakosi, George Oppen or Louis Zukofsky. The plot line called "defection from the South" twists in upon itself; the deafness of the New Critics to poets like these is one plank in the Southern rhetoricians' platform Lowell unfortunately did not reject.

He names me in talking to Hamilton, remarking on my escape to America almost simultaneous with his to England. "Davie and I," he says, "are taking vacations from our Furies." I have always felt honored that he thought me, at least in some respect, his peer.

Langdon Hammer (essay date Winter 1990)

SOURCE: "Robert Lowell's Breakdown," in *Yale Review,* Vol. 79, No. 2, Winter, 1990, pp. 172-87.

[*In the following essay, Hammer examines Lowell's artistic break from the influence of Allen Tate and the significance of Lowell's nervous breakdown as a metaphor for this schism as evident in* Life Studies. *"Lowell's 'breakdown' is itself a literary construction," according to Hammer.*]

In 1959, the year in which he published ***Life Studies,*** Robert Lowell remembered his first, unannounced arrival at the home of Allen Tate and Caroline Gordon as the beginning of his career: "My head was full of Miltonic, vaguely piratical ambitions. My only anchor was a suitcase, heavy with bad poetry. I was brought to earth by my bumper mashing the Tates' frail agrarian mailbox post. Getting out to disguise the damage, I turned my back on their peeling, pillared house. I had crashed the civilization of the South." And when we add that, before advancing any further on the Tates, Lowell stopped to mark the territory with a piss, we have recovered a ludicrous but instructive episode in the transmission of literary modernism. The young man carried with him "piratical ambitions," his juvenilia, and a car (no doubt manufactured in the North) that "mashes" the mailbox post of this Southern Agrarian household. Lowell's feeling, in retrospect, is of having conquered effortlessly and by accident. And yet the Southerners could plausibly construe this "strangest visitation" as a victory of their own. "Imagine," Gordon urged a friend, "a Lowell (yes, the poor boy's mother is a Cabot)—imagine one coming all the way from Boston to sit at Southern feet."

This was April 1937. The twenty-year-old poet had left behind him Harvard and the Cabots and the Lowells to pursue his study of literature under Tate and John Crowe Ransom. He was following the advice of Ford Madox Ford who, without informing his hosts there, had invited Lowell to visit him in Tennessee. It is very possible that Ford did not expect Lowell to take the invitation literally. Certainly Gordon and Tate did not expect him to when they told Lowell that if he wanted to stay, he would have to pitch a tent on the lawn—which, being both obedient and contrary, Lowell proceeded to do. The simple literal-mindedness of these gestures is telling, I believe, since the same kind of literalism would make Lowell both an obedient and a contrary student of Tate. For Lowell began his career by systematically appropriating the rigorous verse forms and cultural pessimism in Tate's work, writing poems that satisfied his mentor's demand for symbolic art that could stand apart from and above personal experience. But Lowell later rejected Tate's teaching by turning to events in his own life, and above all to the ordeal of his mental breakdown, in order to create a new kind of poetry, this one charged with the authority of fact. Lowell had destroyed Tate's symbols and discovered his own experience.

Or so Lowell came to understand his own career, and to narrate its progress. As I will suggest, the story that Lowell told—of generational struggle and succession, of obstruction, breakdown, and breakthrough—provided him and his readers with a way of organizing and interpreting the complex relations between modernist and postwar American poetry. According to this story, the initial, experimental authenticity of modernism had by the middle of the century been supplanted by a narrowly technical practice, sapping poetry of its creative vigor and oppositional force; and it remained for a new generation of poets to undo the restrictions on them by putting the violence of their lives into their work. This is an effective story, and it has been widely applied to poets as different from each other and from Lowell as Sylvia Plath and Allen Ginsberg. I want to challenge the historical accuracy of this account by calling attention to the ways in which it naturalizes—or reproduces as fact—the poetic fictions it is intended to explain. In particular, with Lowell's example before us, I want to question two closely related notions: that ***Life Studies*** enacts a definitive rupture with Tate, and that this breakthrough was a consequence of Lowell's nervous breakdown. My aim is to demonstrate the extent to which Lowell's "breakdown" is itself a literary construction—a fiction that misleadingly reduces the history of postwar American poetry to a particular moment of transformation in the same way that it reduces the history of Lowell's mental illness to a single moment of collapse.

Lowell's achievement, as Lowell himself saw in ***History,*** is radically uneven. But Lowell retains the status of a central or "representative" poet if only because he set out to become such a figure, and because he did so by allowing others to make him into the poet *they* wished him to be. Everyone knows that Lowell had a great influence on many poets; it is less often observed how many poets had a great influence on Lowell. Indeed, Lowell's writing is derivative in this incontestable and overwhelming sense: it continually uses other writers' words. Lowell formalized this principle of composition in ***Imitations,*** and then carried it to a new limit in verse transcriptions of the letters of his friends and—notoriously—the wife whom he had abandoned. It is possible to see Lowell's disregard for the conventional boundaries between one's own language and someone else's as a form of the psychosis that forced him to speak and act as if he really *were* someone else. But I would prefer to interpret Lowell's verbatim transcriptions as the expression of the "piratical ambitions" that led him to camp out on the Tates' lawn in 1937. Let me return to that episode now in order to describe the education Lowell got from Tate.

In **"Visiting the Tates,"** the memoir I have been citing, Lowell recalls that Tate immediately impressed upon his student the absolute importance of technical competence in traditional versification. A good poem, Lowell learned, "had nothing to do with exalted feelings or being moved by the spirit. It was simply a piece of craftsmanship, an intelligible or *cognitive* object." Therefore Lowell "turned out grimly unromantic poems—organized, hard, and classical as a cabinet." These exercises were meant to imitate and confirm Tate's own rejection of the romantic tradition in modern American poetry, including the examples of Hart Crane and William Carlos Williams, whose "exalted feelings" Tate saw as a neglect of craft, linking them in his mind with the amateurism and popular success of "slipshod Untermeyer anthology experimentalists." By requiring technical rigor and denigrating "experiment," Tate was seeking a successor who would, in effect, declare him the winner of this debate within modernism. This is the circular logic by which Tate prepared Lowell to be recognized as the rightful inheritor of T. S. Eliot, W. B. Yeats, and Ezra Pound—the modern poets whom Tate had held up to him for models. In the preface to Lowell's first volume, ***Land of Unlikeness,*** Tate could point as if with surprise to an event so far removed from the merely coincidental that Tate had himself supervised it: "T. S. Eliot's recent prediction that we should see a return to formal and even intricate metres and stanzas was coming true, before he made it, in the verse of Robert Lowell."

From our present distance, it is easy to see that the poems Tate taught Lowell to write share in the formalist poetics that came to prominence in the decade after the war—even if Lowell's versification was as "warped, fissured, strained, and terrific" as the handcrafted black cabinet that Tate exhibited to Lowell that first afternoon. More than a technical model, however, Tate transmitted to Lowell the reactionary anticapitalism behind his formal practice. In Tate's view, the received forms of literary tradition provided access to the so-called traditional cultures of prerevolutionary Europe and the antebellum South, and thus became a point of reference (and a source of authority) for his opposition to both bourgeois and communist states. Eliot, Yeats, and Pound—Tate understood these authors as representatives of an elite, antivernacular imagination, a timeless community he termed "the Republic of Letters" and Eliot simply called "tradition." Their membership in this "Republic" meant exile from the modern world in which these poets actually lived. And yet it also gave them autonomy, Tate argued, since it maintained the independence of aesthetic value from both popular taste and political interests, commerce and "causes."

In ***Land of Unlikeness*** and ***Lord Weary's Castle,*** Lowell took up Tate's ideas in an attack on something as generalized as the state of civilization itself. In fact, once again literal-minded and fierce, Lowell pushed Tate's dedication to formal disciplines further than Tate was at this point willing to commit himself: he converted to Catholicism. With this decision, which validated the prophetic vision of the first two books and gave them a vocabulary of apocalyptic symbols, Lowell acted on behalf of and in place of his teacher (who had debated this step from early in his career, and would not take it until 1950); it is as if Eliot had *also* predicted that we should see a return to formal and even intricate rituals and beliefs. On the one hand, Lowell's conversion completed the rejection of his Episcopalian upbringing in Boston—a remaking of himself that Lowell had initiated when he fought with his father, left Harvard, and drove south. On the other hand, Tate's political mythology invested Lowell's home with new meanings, marking Massachusetts as the site of a lost tradition, and giving Lowell the confidence that his name alone meant he was "part of a legend." As Gordon's preoccupation with the "poor boy's" genealogy confirms, "the old deadweight of J. R. Lowell was now an asset. Here, like the battered Confederacy, he still lived and was history."

It is hard to exaggerate the extent of Tate's influence. Indeed, as David Bromwich has remarked, "Tate may almost be said to have created Lowell. He gave him not only advice, friendship, and an idea of modernity, but a complete set of mannerisms to study, down to the very inflections of the Agrarian-Eliotic accent which Lowell picked up early and never wore out." And in turn Lowell gave Tate a son and heir—a poet who was capable of reproducing the sound of his own voice. But as Tate should have expected from a foster child who had knocked his real father down and then put himself up for adoption, Tate would become the object of Lowell's rebellion as well. In the course of that reversal, Lowell thrust upon Tate demonic versions of himself, turning on his teacher with a maniacal performance of the role that Tate had created for him.

The convulsive events of Lowell's first breakdown dramatize the process I have in mind. In 1949, Lowell summoned Tate, by telegram, to join him in New York "to fight evil." When Tate refused, Lowell took a train to see him and Gordon in Chicago. Tate described Lowell's state of mind in this way: "Cal is here, and in 24 hours has flattened us out. I do not know what we can do. . . . He constantly embraces us, and asks us to stand by him, since he is weak." Accounts differ about what happened next. According to the most spectacular (and least reliable), Lowell decided that Tate should repent of his sins and reported Tate's infidelities to Gordon. Then, to complete Tate's punishment, Lowell suspended his diminutive mentor from a second-floor window—while reciting Tate's most famous poem, "Ode to the Confederate Dead." Whether or not this last scene took place, we know that the police came and handcuffed Lowell as he shouted obscenities from the windows of Tate's home. Afterward, Tate could authoritatively reflect: "[Lowell] has a purification mania, which frequently takes homicidal form."

But Lowell's literary enactment of this attack on Tate is more famous, and famous precisely for effecting a "purification" of Lowell's style. There is a long-standing consensus among critics of the period that Lowell achieved "his own voice" in the middle of his career specifically by abandoning the traditional verse forms, religious symbols, and heroic rhetoric that Tate had taught him how to wield. It holds that Lowell made a significant break with his teacher; that in the autobiographical project of ***Life Studies,*** particularly, Lowell discovered a vital alternative to the formalism of the New Critics that was rapidly becoming institutionalized; and that Lowell thus established a definitively postmodern, or at least a postmodernist, practice in American poetry.

The consensus I am describing draws on the psychoanalytic thematics of a book like ***Life Studies*** itself in order to narrate the poet's passage beyond modernism as a story of oedipal violence in which new energies were released from confinement in old forms. This understanding of Lowell and his period not only revives the rhetoric of liberation once used to promote modernist poetry, it does so deliberately, with the suggestion that postwar American poetry restores the modernity of modernism. James E. B. Breslin, in a study called *From Modern to Contemporary* (1983), provides an especially clear example of this point of view: "At this moment of crisis, poetry once again became disruptive—critical of its culture, of its immediate past, of itself; by way of repudiating orthodox modernism, American poetry once again became modern, 'of the present.'" This passage is a generalization about American poetry in the late 1950s, but it specifically draws upon Lowell's view of the period. To be precise, Breslin is responding to an interview in which Lowell complained about the technical competence of the poets of "my generation." Their work, Lowell charged, had "become a craft, purely a craft, and there must be some breakthrough back into life." Here, of course, the meaning of "craft" is pejorative; it is an obstacle that must be broken down, or a wall that must be broken through, in order to recover the poet's unmediated contact with "life." But by 1961, when he formulated the problem in this way, Lowell had already made the kind of "breakthrough" that he claimed his "generation" of poets needed to make. The effect of Lowell's analysis is therefore to make his own career—or rather, Lowell's own *account* of his career—representative. And using this account, Breslin interprets ***Life Studies*** as a paradigm for an entire generation's rediscovery of literature's origin in life.

"I thought civilization was going to break down," Lowell later remembered, "and instead I did." This marvelously concise remark not only suggests that Lowell had to "break down" before he could see his own life as a subject capable of replacing the apocalyptic subject Tate had assigned him ("I thought civilization was going to break down"); it suggests that the "breakthrough" Lowell made at this pivotal moment—what he discovered for poetry—*was exactly his breakdown itself.* The analogy linking psychological and literary history here, which allows us to understand Lowell's "breakthrough" as a function of his breakdown, is essential to the story ***Life Studies*** tells, and essential to the story that critics tell about "confessional poetry" generally. Experience authenticates poetry in this analogy, and suffering authenticates experience. Although the life Lowell recovered in ***Life Studies*** remained something to be studied, not simply lived, it was his own, and it presented itself to his readers as fact. As we will see, though, the fact of Lowell's breakdown was never accessible outside of the poetic fictions Lowell created. And in this sense the phrase "Robert Lowell's breakdown" can only refer to an event in literary history, not in Lowell's life.

Let me develop this point by looking at Breslin's discussion in more detail, since it is typical of the critical consensus I mentioned earlier, especially in its view of the structure of ***Life Studies*** as a whole. For example, this is Breslin's account of the movement between parts 1 and 2 of the book: "The four poems of Part I describe cultural and historical disintegration in predetermined forms and all of these poems were written *before* Lowell's breakdown; in Part II Lowell begins again with the anecdotal prose of **'91 Revere Street'** dramatically breaking down the established boundaries of the literary—by moving toward the literal and contingent, the *data* of his own life." On one level, Breslin points to a thematic movement from cultural to personal "disintegration"; on another level, to a technical movement from "predetermined forms" to "anecdotal prose." By implication, at least, Breslin sees these events as analogous both to each other and to the breakdown Lowell suffered between the composition of the texts arranged in these two sections of ***Life Studies.*** The suggestion is that Lowell's breakdown allowed him to break down "the established boundaries of the literary."

Curiously, this line of argument represents the progress from one part of ***Life Studies*** to another as a record of events going on in Lowell's life. And the book's progress from verse to prose, which implicitly anticipates the direction of American poetry from the 1950s to the 1960s, is seen as the consequence of a particular psychological collapse. This is a misleading idea, if not simply an error, because it suggests that the cycles of mania and depression Lowell experienced before the one Breslin mentions never happened. As a result, Breslin's reading converts a series of chaotic episodes into a single, narratively accessible event. Behind this appeal to a conclusive moment of psychological change is the pressure of a particular interpretive framework. For it shows Breslin's desire to see ***Life Studies*** as a conclusive break with Lowell's prior ways of writing, and to imagine this break in terms of "the *data*" of Lowell's life—facts that Breslin then imagines according to the "data" ***Life Studies*** itself provides.

I dwell on Breslin's discussion because its deceptive use of Lowell's biography indicates one way in which ***Life Studies*** allows one to interpret the relation between Lowell's work and mania. But this is not the only way. It is true, for example, that a large portion of ***Life Studies*** was written after Lowell was hospitalized at the Payne Whitney Clinic in 1954, and that such famous poems as **"My Last Afternoon with Uncle Devereux Winslow"** were initially begun as part of the prose memoirs from which **"91 Revere Street"** derives. But it is also true that Lowell was hospitalized before he finished his previous book, ***The Mills of the Kavanaughs,*** and that Lowell was again hospitalized after he had written the poems about his family in ***Life Studies.*** Breslin interprets the family poems as signs that Lowell had survived a breakdown; Tate, as we will see, saw the same set of poems as the sign of an *approaching* breakdown. In a sense, Lowell's mania justified both of these claims. But my point is that ***Life Studies*** defines the meaning of Lowell's mental illness for his readers, and not the other way around.

To this extent, the changing ways in which Lowell and his family and friends interpreted his manic-depressive cycles are intimately tied to Lowell's changing definition of himself as a poet. In another autobiographical fragment, Lowell called the cause of his hospitalization in 1954 "an attack of pathological enthusiasm." This category is potentially broad and suggestive enough to describe not only the delusions and violence that led to Lowell's confinement and alienated Tate, but also Lowell's conversion and his refusal to serve during World War II—actions that were clearly connected to the Catholicism and pacifism of ***Lord Weary's Castle.*** Of course, I am not saying that Lowell was always—or merely—sick, but that the religious, political, and literary passions of Lowell's world entered his "enthusiasm" and gave it shape, making his madness a nightmarish recapitulation and distortion of the roles in which he ordinarily lived his life and wrote poetry. For this reason, Lowell's "enthusiasm" forced those who saw themselves as his literary allies, teachers, or peers to confront the features of the poet whom they knew and admired in the most fragmentary and caricatured of forms. At stake was the authority with which they had invested him, and the implications of Lowell's poetic claims to represent them and *their* experience.

Consider the episode that culminated shortly after he left Gordon and Tate in Chicago. It began during the winter of 1949 at Yaddo, the artists' colony, where Lowell had come to work on the manuscript that became ***The Mills of the Kavanaughs.*** The *New York Times* in February printed a report that a longtime guest of Yaddo, Agnes Smedley, was under official suspicion as having been part of "a Soviet spy ring in the Far East." A week later, the Army issued a retraction. At about the same time, however, FBI agents visited Yaddo and questioned the director, Elizabeth Ames, and two guests, Elizabeth Hardwick and Edward Maisel. The FBI's questions had concerned the politics of Smedley and other former Yaddo residents. Hardwick and Maisel discussed the interviews with Flannery O'Connor and Lowell, the only other guests at that time, and the group together resolved that "Mrs. Ames is somehow deeply and mysteriously involved in Mrs. Smedley's political activities." This sentence is Lowell's, and it comes from the massive transcript of the courtroom proceedings that he and the others caused the Yaddo Corporation to hold. Lowell stipulated and directed the form of these bizarre proceedings, during which he presented charges on behalf of the other guests, and then interviewed them himself. "I think two days will be necessary for a full hearing of this," Lowell said at the start, "and perhaps a meeting again in New York, on a Saturday or Sunday." And yet Lowell could produce little more "evidence" of Ames's political betrayal of Yaddo's artistic ideals than Hardwick's intuition—"that at times there is a discrepancy between Mrs. Ames' surface behavior and her true feelings"—and Ames's own unmysterious admission: "I sometimes do not dare to say what I think."

A much fuller report of these events is available in Ian Hamilton's biography of Lowell. Reading it, one is aware that the political hysteria Lowell participated in at Yaddo was sanctioned by the United States government and the national press. But it remains striking that the extraordinary zeal with which Lowell took on the role of anticommunist crusader would only later be recognized as pathological behavior. Instead, in his effort to protect Yaddo's artistic ideals from political interest, Lowell's "enthusiasm" seemed consistent with the righteous indignation of ***Lord Weary's Castle.*** As Robert Fitzgerald explained, the case against Ames was "vaporous," but Lowell and the other guests had determined "to strike hard, and there came into play an essential quality of his nature: the aggressive power that to the gentle must seem harsh and has indeed found, in his poems, violent images of strife: the harpoon that rips the sperm-whale's midriff into rags, the flintrock broken upon the father's skull." That is, Fitzgerald explained his friend's actions using images Lowell himself used in **"The Quaker Graveyard in Nantucket"** and **"Rebellion."** Fitzgerald needed the poet of ***Lord Weary's Castle*** to make sense of Lowell's mania.

Or it might be more accurate to say that Fitzgerald needed to defend the poet who wrote ***Lord Weary's Castle*** in the face of Lowell's subsequent, potentially discrediting actions. With this aim in mind, Fitzgerald argued that Lowell had simply acted out a struggle in the poems themselves "between the pure, living and creative spirit and an encrusted Mammon, the dry rot, *malitia,* and mammoth stupor of things." Fitzgerald recognized that the "evidences of Communist activity at Yaddo" were insubstantial, and he had no interest in pursuing them. What Fitzgerald wished to defend, rather, was Lowell's prophetic vision of "the great evil of the world": Lowell's anticommunism could in this case be seen as a misguided expression of Lowell's Christianity.

For Fitzgerald was above all concerned to defend Lowell's definition of himself as a Roman Catholic poet. Lowell had visited Fitzgerald after departing from Yaddo and announced his return to the church; by the end of the same week, Lowell had gone on a retreat with Trappist monks. Fitzgerald knew that Lowell was psychologically disturbed, but he wished to honor Lowell's claims "that God spoke through him and that his impulses were inspired." Lowell's prosecution of Ames was unsound, but it was motivated by the same impulses that inspired the poems. In fact, the incident had led Lowell to recover his Catholicism, and with it the visionary authority of ***Lord Weary's Castle.*** This authority, moreover, was sufficiently important to Fitzgerald to lead him to write to George Santayana explaining Lowell's already notorious behavior. Copies of this letter (from which I have been quoting) were then sent to Eliot, Tate, Ransom, and twelve other poets, fiction writers, and critics. Although not all of its recipients were sympathetic to Lowell, or even to each other, the letter put Lowell's crisis at the center of a distinguished community of authors. Its at least tacit assumption was that Lowell's reputation mattered to their own.

After treatment, Lowell wrote to Fitzgerald acknowledging his efforts, but Lowell's reconversion had passed with his mania, and the Catholic poet whom Fitzgerald wished to defend had all but ceased to exist. The poet Lowell would become was not fully evident until ***Life Studies*** was published in 1959. By that time Lowell had replaced his Catholicism with existentialism, as his commentary on the spiritual drama of **"Skunk Hour"** makes explicit: "This is the dark night. I hoped my readers would remember John of the Cross's poem. My night is not gracious, but secular, puritan, and agnostic. An existentialist night. Somewhere in my mind was a passage from Sartre or Camus about reaching some point of final darkness where the one free act is suicide." The point to be emphasized in these well-known remarks is this: that the extremity of Lowell's position, the "final darkness" he attains in **"Skunk Hour,"** is arrived at precisely by replacing St. John of the Cross with Sartre, and "The Dark Night of the Soul" with a dark night in Maine. It is not, in other words, that Catholicism stopped being important to Lowell's poetry, but that the poet of ***Life Studies*** generated new authority by abandoning it. In ***Lord Weary's Castle,*** Catholicism validates Lowell's formal discipline; in **"Beyond the Alps,"** the first poem in ***Life Studies,*** the church itself represents the "mammoth stupor of things." And to throw off its doctrines meant pushing one's self to the point "where the one free act is suicide"—to the point of demystification that **"Skunk Hour"** defines as breakdown.

"I thought civilization was going to break down, and instead I did." It is possible to see this turn of events as a rejection of the poetic identity Tate gave to Lowell, a role in which the poet enters into public discourse as the angry representative of a defeated and discredited tradition, speaking for an order of value and a way of life all but unrecognized by the modern world. In Tate, as in the modern poets with whom he aligned himself, modernity meant a crisis of culture; and Tate defined "the right kind of modernism" as that poetry which resisted the decay of aristocratic social orders by submitting the individual talent to the timeless and impersonal disciplines of a neoclassical literary tradition. In Lowell, by contrast, the reader is confronted less with a crisis of culture—social and political in nature—than with a crisis of mind, which is acted out in the private sphere of the family, and which is correctly observed through the lens of Freudian psychoanalysis. If ***Lord Weary's Castle*** marks a kind of limit to the apocalyptic rhetoric of "the right kind of modernism," ***Life Studies*** finds a way to go on by narrating the collapse not of tradition but of the individual talent.

Not surprisingly, Tate refused to sanction this development. And the ensuing conflict between Lowell and Tate not only looked like a family quarrel; it specifically concerned the family poems in ***Life Studies.*** As Tate told Lowell, "*All* the poems about your family . . . are definitely *bad,*" and these new poems were "bad" precisely because they lacked that "formal ordering of highly intractable materials" which marked Lowell's "fine poems in the past." Tate's advice was severe and direct:

> I do not think you should publish them. You didn't ask me whether you think they ought to be published, but I put the matter from this point of view to underline my anxiety about them. . . . The poems are composed of unassimilated details, terribly intimate, and coldly noted, which might well have been transferred from the notes from your autobiography without change.
>
> . . . Quite bluntly, these details, presented in *causerie* and at random, are of interest only to you. They are, of course, of great interest to me because I am one of your oldest friends. But they have no public or literary interest.

To others, Tate predicted that the loosening of Lowell's poetic structures and his immersion in family history demonstrated the mounting excitement and loss of control typical of Lowell's psychotic behavior. Tate's alarm, though, was not confined to the free-verse poems about Lowell's family. On his own copy of **"A Mad Negro Soldier Confined at Munich,"** a dramatic monologue in rhymed quatrains in which Lowell's GI exclaims, "'Oh mama, mama, like a trolley pole / sparking at contact, her electric shock—the powerhouse!'" Tate wrote in bewilderment or disgust, "author unknown."

By thus disowning Lowell, Tate refused to acknowledge the type of author who was created through Lowell's identification with figures like **"A Mad Negro Soldier,"** the "thoroughbred mental cases" in McLean Hospital, or "*Murder Incorporated's* Czar Lepke" in the West Street jail. What Tate did not foresee was that Lowell's new definition of himself as an author whose suffering had bound him to these social outcasts would be of *considerable* "public or literary interest." In fact, as the extraordinary reception of ***Life Studies*** and then ***For the Union Dead*** indicates, Lowell had created a hero who would be celebrated by his society precisely for his suffering. This is the scapegoat figure Ian Hamilton memorializes by quoting William Empson's commentary on *King Lear* at the end of his biography of Lowell: "The scapegoat who has collected all this wisdom for us is viewed at the end with a sort of hushed envy, not I think really because he has become wise but because the general human desire for experience has been so glutted in him; he has been through everything." It was this poet who had "been through everything" who emerged from ***Life Studies.*** He stood for no particular system of belief—he was not, in that sense, "wise"; rather, he had "collected" in his own life "the general human desire for experience." And the psychological violence through which Lowell acquired this kind of wisdom could therefore be seen as the result and proof of the disintegration of "the right kind of modernism"—it was the breakdown that had occurred while one was waiting for civilization to break down instead. By facing "final darkness" without the consolations of Roman Catholicism, aesthetic impersonality, or traditional verse forms, Lowell had abandoned the ideas his teachers had given him, and gained direct access to his experience, however bitter it might have been.

But it is also because he values "experience" in this way that Lowell finally redefines, rather than rejects, the poetic identity that Tate gave him. Lowell helps us to see why this is the case in the transcript of a talk that he gave not long after the publication of ***Life Studies.*** Lowell is speaking of the ideas he derived from his teachers in the late 1930s:

> We believed in form, . . . and for some reason we were very much against the Romantics. We would say that the ideal poet is Shakespeare, who is not a poet of ideology but a poet of experience, and tragedy, and the sort of villains to us were people like Shelley—that he used much too much ideology—and Whitman, the prophet, who was formless. And one felt that what poetry could do was have nothing to do with causes . . . ; and something like Aristotle's purging by pity and terror, that of going through a catharsis, that that is what was suitable, rather than to persuade people to do anything better or to make the world better.

In its efforts to inspire "pity and terror," rather than to urge others "to make the world better," ***Life Studies*** keeps faith with Tate's dedication to "experience" and his distrust of "ideology." Indeed, when he arrives at that point "where the one free act is suicide," Lowell may be felt to have realized—albeit ironically—the autonomy Tate demanded for art. And—again ironically—Lowell's validation of "experience" defends art against radical politics more successfully than the manic anticommunism of the Yaddo fiasco. What is changed here, of course, is that Tate's ideas themselves have taken the place of "ideology" in Lowell's thinking, and the kinds of poet whom Tate saw as "villains" now represent "experience." And for these reasons, I would argue, ***Life Studies*** is not a break with modernism but rather Lowell's self-conscious attempt to appropriate for his own uses the "exalted feelings" that he found in a poet like Crane, and that Tate had labeled the *wrong* kind of modernism.

"Words for Hart Crane" is an important poem in the volume, in this respect, because it makes explicit Lowell's intention to get outside the modernism of his teachers by identifying himself with a poet whom they themselves had cast out. Lowell would have known that Crane lived with Tate and Gordon as their guest about a decade before Lowell himself did, and that they had found Crane exhausting and intrusive, and had demanded that he leave. Lowell plays upon this story here specifically by imagining Crane as a sexual predator, as a man who has been victimized because of his homosexuality, and who therefore takes victims of his own. At the same time, Lowell specifically associates Crane's profession of excessive and prohibited desire with the "villains" in Tate's critical essays on Crane, Shelley, and Whitman.

> "When the Pulitzers showered on some dope
> or screw who flushed our dry mouths out with
> soap,
> few people would consider why I took
> to stalking sailors, and scattered Uncle Sam's
> phony gold-plated laurels to the birds.
> Because I knew my Whitman like a book,
> stranger in America, tell my country: I,
> *Catullus redivivus,* once the rage
> of the Village and Paris, used to play my role
> of homosexual, wolfing the stray lambs
> who hungered by the Place de la Concorde.
> My profit was a pocket with a hole.
> Who asks for me, the Shelley of my age,
> must lay his heart out for my bed and board."

The profligate's waste of talent is mythologized here as the cost of experience, and repressed powers, as in **"A Mad Negro Soldier Confined at Munich,"** return with the frank intensity of a starved appetite. This Crane, who was capable, Lowell felt, of including "the chaos of his life" in his poems, comes to the author of ***Life Studies*** as the demonic double of his own mentor, enabling Lowell to establish a point of view from which the chaos of his own life can be made into poems—with the effect of mocking the Pulitzer Prize-winning poet of ***Lord Weary's Castle.*** Thus the voice of a poet who is beyond or outside the boundaries of the New Critical discourse of the 1950s does indeed speak in ***Life Studies;*** and yet that poet, like Lowell's version of Crane, derived from Tate, can only speak within quotation marks. Tate believed that the author of ***Life Studies*** was unknown to him, but I have been suggesting that he helped to write that book himself.

Terri Witek (essay date December 1991)

SOURCE: "Robert Lowell's Tokens of the Self," in *American Literature,* Vol. 63, No. 4, December, 1991, pp. 712-26.

[*In the following essay, Witek examines Lowell's search for personal identity and Freudian themes relating to his parents in the poetry of* Life Studies *and his autobiographical prose writings.*]

Robert Lowell sold a large collection of manuscript materials to the Houghton Library in 1973, work which is just beginning to be made public, notably in Ian Hamilton's biography and in the 1987 volume of ***Collected Prose.*** Among the most interesting of these papers are over two hundred pages of autobiographical prose, many of which are still unpublished. This material, begun while Lowell was recovering from a mental breakdown following the death of his mother in 1954, offers dramatic evidence of his tendency to psychologize both his life and his method, and to conflate the two chronically and emblematically.

Lowell tells many bleakly humorous stories about dealing with the Payne Whitney Clinic's occupational therapy requirement while he was recuperating from the latest of what were beginning to be recognized as recurrent bouts of acute mania. Set to various artistic tasks, he found himself unable to translate thought into concrete form, a failure highly symbolic to someone whose life work is translating experience into language. In one account, the embarrassment of not being able "to think with my hands" inspires Lowell to lie that he has the doctors' permission to read *Kim* instead. More often he describes hopelessly botched products:

> Here for weeks I saw my abandoned pine-cone basket lying on the pile for waste materials. And as it sank under sawdust and shavings, it seemed to protest the pains Mr. Kemper, our instructor, had once taken to warp, to soak, to re-weave, to rescue it. And here in an old cigar box I saw my materially expensive, massively hideous silver ring, which Mr. Kemper had

> mostly forged and then capped off with an intaglio of
> an Iroquois corn shock ripening under the arrowy rays
> of a crescent moon.

Such adventures in translating thought into form are paradigms for Lowell's attempts to express the self in a world without the powerful figures of his parents, a quest which informs his work in the 1950s and finds its culmination in ***Life Studies.*** His chosen occupational therapy was finally not rings or baskets or even poetry but autobiographical prose, some of which has been collected by his longtime editor, Robert Giroux. The prose offers valuable evidence of his poetic process in ***Life Studies:*** some of that volume's most famous poems are revisions of the prose sources. But his autobiographical prose also contains a series of potent morality tales about the nature of the self. These stories expose his powerful ambivalence about the sources of his own identity and about the nature of that identity as it is expressed in language.

Lowell's anxiety about his position in a world without his earliest mentors is fueled by his conviction that the self is deeply, irreparably divided. This division ensures that he is perennially pulled in at least two directions: he is attracted both by the idea that the self should be a possession firmly within one's grasp and the idea that the self is an object which should be elusive, beyond the control of its possessor. In the autobiographical prose, Lowell often images these two possibilities as the figures of his own complex and embattled parents, each of whom offers a problematic alternative role model. His depiction of these two conflicting forces, each with its claim on him, is as painful as it is informative; his choices show the powerful dilemma into which the poet is thrust each time he tries to choose between alternative images of his own identity.

The allure of an identity which acquires its power through sheer pervasive immobility is represented in the autobiographical prose by Mother. Secure in the Boston of Lowell's youth, fixed forever by being dead, Charlotte Lowell is the unchanging star around whom the male Lowells group, set into motion by her changeless vigor. The prose which became **"91 Revere Street"** in the finished ***Life Studies*** volume includes an account of the Lowells' attempt to find a school for the problematic Bobby which is typical of the family dynamic: "I was promised an improved future and taken on Sunday afternoon drives through the suburbs to inspect boys' schools: Rivers, Dexter, Country Day. These expeditions were stratagems designed to give me a chance to know my father; Mother noisily stayed behind and amazed me by pretending that I had forbidden her to embark on 'men's work.'" Bob Lowell, Senior, does all the driving, but it is clear that from her Boston stronghold Charlotte is the family mover and shaker. She criticizes the results of these enforced male outings and goes back to interview the headmasters herself: "she expressed astonishment that a wishy-washy desire to be everything to everybody had robbed a naval man of any reliable concern for his son's welfare."

Lowell's many descriptions of Mother invoke her stability as the family's reigning presence; this one is a fragment from the "Miscellaneous worksheets":

> I might have been fifteen or I might have been thirty-five, my father might have been alive or he might have been dead, the location might have been our good (not grand) half a life-time's house in the Back Bay, or Mother's adequate Boston apartment, or Mother and Father's sprawly, slightly citified, unbalanced, battle-ship gray commuters' house in Beverly Farms, where they had migrated towards the end for a change, and of course changed as little as possible. Thus, one didn't start with a place or even a room that could be labelled such and such and no other. You had to begin with Mother's furniture, and *that* didn't change at all . . . if it did, the new or different pieces always managed to retell the same story.

The effect of this presence on the child and then man who is her son is nearly overwhelming: over and over again in the autobiographical prose, Mother's "furniture," symbols of her central presence, must be reckoned with. During Lowell's stay at Payne Whitney following his Mother's death, the poet seems to think of himself literally as an object confined within a more powerful structure. When he writes about Payne Whitney, the hospital architecture itself is perversely threatening. Looking out his window at the other buildings of the complex, he describes them as mysteriously female: "First I saw the hospital's architecture as a wedding-cake; no, not a wedding cake but the tall bride standing with her sacrificial silver knife beside the wedding cake; no, not the bride of flesh and blood, but a narrow, late Gothic bride, all arches, groins and stone lace-work; no bride, but a building. . . ."

Lowell writes himself away from dangerous associations by an effort of will in this passage, but it is well worth identifying the bride who seems to engulf him on all sides. In another version of this episode, the bridal building is linked to the bridal photograph Bob Lowell keeps on his dresser, and in the drafts of **"Sailing Home from Rapallo"** the dead Mother is also a bride. The powerful Mother thus seems to hold her son at the center of her being, but for him the position is fraught with peril: he is trapped almost as if he had been ingested by the bridal buildings of the New York Hospital which remind him of the all-powerful center of his own family.

It would appear that for Lowell an idea of the self as firmly positioned and rooted at the center of experience—the position of most power as it is described in terms of the family dynamic—is psychologically untenable because it would force a fatal identification with Mother. One possible coping mechanism might be an appropriation of her strategies, a tactic that Lowell enacts symbolically in those stories reported by Ian Hamilton in which young Bobby Lowell swallows a jewelry elephant (putting the coveted object in his own midmost regions) or drops a lost crucifix into the furnace, the center of his parents' house. While these defiances make the young Bobby feel powerful at the time, the results are rather ignominious, especially in the case of the elephant, which reappears after a few days in the obvious manner. Such defiances are the stratagems of a child, and the man who reports them seems to laugh at their naivete, or, rather, he reports that Charlotte Lowell certainly did: "I have no idea how Mother managed to mention the chamberpot, my movement, and the marvelous elephant all in one pure, smirking breath." No matter how bold or how devious the young boy's maneuvering, the only person who can control the center is Mother, a moral which is acted out by an incident Hamilton omits:

> This is my first remembered meeting with my grandfather, and I know that it was my birthday because I see him standing beside a present from my father, a flotilla of little camouflaged wooden warships that had been laid out along the mantelpiece. They had been purchased in the name of, and as a tribute to, my father who was off on sea-duty. Like later presents from my father, these toys had been bought with considerable pains and were a remarkable bargain, and very unfeminine. Made in Japan the boats were outrageously anti-German: the best boat was an American hostal ship magnificently marked with warning red crosses. By pressing a button on a cord, a concealed spring mouse-trapped shut and the cabins and turrets of the hospital ship collapsed on the floor—it had been hit by submarine's torpedo. [. . .] However, the toy was meant for adults and my mother soon robbed it of all allure. She snatched it from my hands, disembowelled it of its dangerous spring, and then gave its back, weightless and harmless, an insipid husk of its former warlike outrages.

Mother's action is clearly castrating, and the Father who is "off on sea duty" is so far away from the powerful center that he is unable to prevent the disemboweling (literally "taking away the guts," a pun which would not be lost on Lowell) of his "unfeminine" present. In this version of the story, the Father's ownership of the ships in the first place is obliquely called into question. "They were purchased in the name of, and as a tribute to, my father" implies that either the Mother bought them herself in the Father's name and then sabotaged them before her son's eyes or that the masculine present had something to do with the Grandfather's arrival. The latter reading suggests other versions of the incident, in which the maternal grandfather is upheld as the representative of Bobby's, and hence of masculine, interest: ". . . I still enjoy in recollection the feeling of relief I experienced when he scolded and teased Mother for ruining a flotilla of toy warships. . . ." In some versions the set is not only a bargain but "imperceptibly damaged," already flawed before Mother "ruins" it. And the flagship is described more clearly as a "hospital ship." When the spring works, "the hospital ship with all its gear, cabins, cots, stretchers and even red-cross nurses collapsed on the carpet." Mother thwarts this gory function when she gouges out the spring, taking away the ship's center—which may be a "mousetrap" but is also a weird escape mechanism for the inhabitants of the floating hospital. Her action suggests not only that Mother controls the center of power, but that she administers all escape routes as well. Of course the reference to "hospital" (in still other manuscripts the boat is a German U-boat) suggests Lowell's own various incarcerations. By removing the boat's spring for her own purposes Mother has absconded with both the powerful center and the only possibility for release from it. That the ship is a "hospital" suggests that what is at stake may be mental health. The woman who wields such authority must be actively resisted. Her presence is suggestively pervasive; in an unpublished fragment filed under the heading "Rock," she appears in the sitting room in pink nightclothes, and the son feels her inappropriate sexual pull: "Pink was to be held in Mother's bedroom. But here she was spilling out like a jack-in-the-box with too powerful a spring." Here the motif has been reworked to show that the Mother who possesses such a powerful "spring" is more dangerous than any toy: "I felt meshed and menaced."

Mother's control over Lowell's identity both as child and as adult seems complete in the powerfully symbolic stories of the ruined gift from the Father. But in the Christmas stories, the opposing presence of the Grandfather demonstrates not only Lowell's obvious admiration and affection for the family's most powerful male, but also what a firmly fixed masculine identity would look like. Arthur Winslow fearlessly chides the Mother on the child's behalf; even more important, he carries a potent talisman of the type young Bobby continually covets but only temporarily possesses:

> Arthur Winslow, my mother's father, paid us a surprise visit in 1919 a day or so before Christmas. I was almost three years old and I remember him distinctly. He was certainly wearing a white starched colar and a gray white tie-pin. Not only that, but he had a mysterious gold match-box dangling like the grapes of Tantalus from his gold

> watch chain. And I know that I wanted to own that match-box, and wasn't to be distracted by my legitimate Christmas present, a little flotilla a camouflaged wooden warships.

While Bobby Lowell is barred from the possession of this "mysterious" masculine talisman, he both yearns for it and feels responsible for it, as in this passage in which Lowell identifies the matchbox with that other dangerous object of central power from the Christmas when his father was "off on sea duty":

> Meanwhile my grandfather walked up and down in front of the fireplace and snapped his gold match-box open and shut. Somehow I imagined that the U-boat's spring was now inside the match-box, which had the added glories of being true gold, able to burst into flame, and none of the pettiness and unreality of objects solely designed as toys for children. I have a nightmare memory of the match-box disappearing. All morning I seem to have folding and unfolding a heavy sheet of brown wrapping paper. I kept holding the paper up to the fireplace and hoping to see the matchbox outlined against its brown translucentcy. I had a panicky feeling that my attitude and method of searching was wrong, that the match-box lay hidden somewhere in the paper, and that only my headlong, cllous temper prevented it from being promptly revealed. The matchbox never reappeared, and soon even its mechanics later seemed fabulous, improbable and impossible—a matchbox of gold that flew open by pressing a button and which lit like a cigarette-lighter. How often I used for the next six or seven years to introduce it unbelievable into questions addressed to my grandfather, whenever he was in a gay mood, nor would I ever be appeased by being alowed to handle his watch chain with a snake head hook, or even his watch itself.

In these incidents both Mother and her Father have acquired symbols of their power, whether by natural right of possession or, in the case of Mother, by a co-opting act. Lowell feels the lack of these objects acutely, and the suspicion is that the loss of them is somehow his fault. Whatever power they represent (and their similarity to the powerful objects which appear in order to rescue the heroes of fairy tales is no accident) the boy who must resort to devious questioning or downright stealth to obtain them does not feel he has the right to their potent magic. But in his grandfather he can see their power at work, even though he knows himself to be shut out from such power forever. Consequently, he yearns toward and longs to identify with his maternal grandfather as he must not identify with his Mother: "Grandpa! Have me, hold me, cherish me!" he cries in **"Grandparents,"** a poem from the completed ***Life Studies*** volume. But the grandfather is already implicated with the Mother (he is her "Freudian papa," Lowell claims in **"During Fever"**) and, like the Mother, he is far beyond the child's powers of imitation: Bobby is reduced to a version of femaleness rather than lifted to masculinity by this role model. In **"Dunbarton,"** the child persona "cuddled like a paramour" in his grandfather's bed, more like an illegal lover than the legitimate progeny of the powerful grandfather, whose fire-building skills in **"Dunbarton"** remind us of the manuscripts' hidden "matchbox."

Lowell also takes his search for elusive tokens of power beyond the family circle. In **"My Crime Wave"** he tells of various childhood "thefts": of stealing marbles, of tricking an acquaintance into trading valuable toy soldiers for worthless papier-mâché ones, of shoplifting a toy microscope. In each case the theft goes somehow awry, as if the child subconsciously knows such objects are not to be his: he is found out, or, in the case of the toy microscope, the elaborately acquired object doesn't work (this last contingency embroils him in a complicated plot to return the flawed microscope to the store for a refund). The fun Lowell pokes at his child persona is rather merciless in these manuscripts, as merciless as Mother's mention of young Bobby's treasure-filled bowel movement. The self-mocking tone leads to some painful effects, none more so than when Lowell claims that the thefts were less for the sake of the objects than to achieve solidarity with a confederate: "'Every day, in every way, I am becoming a better and better friend to Werner Ash,' this is how I ended my prayers each night." Here it seems as if the companion himself is the desired object, but the friendships gained by such "furtive, spectacular safe, risks" are as fleeting as the thrill of acquiring the objects themselves. The unsatisfactory thefts and friendships of **"My Crime Wave,"** like the hidden matchbox and the disgorged spring of the family stories, suggest again that while Lowell anxiously covets the talismans he associates with power, he knows they are not for him. Recovered by rightful owners or rendered inoperable in Lowell's possession, such objects, the suggestion is, must be kept from him: the center of power they represent must be hidden safely elsewhere to prevent co-option by the flawed but endlessly desiring self.

The many talismans of Lowell's autobiographical prose suggest a potent moral about the nature of authority. The powerful center he must not possess is imaged in Freudian terms as Mother, and to be free of her is to experience the partial loss of his own identity. To develop an identity which could stand on equal terms with Mother and yet remain wholly other is to be powerfully masculine: to be, in short, a Father. Lowell's maternal grandfather is the poet's candidate for the role; it is he who defends the absent father's Christmas present and is hung about with aggressively masculine symbols: tie-pin, matchbox, and, in other manuscripts, a phallic walking stick which the young Lowell "borrows." But this identification involves psychological risk for the boy who huddles, at the end of **"Dunbarton,"** in the bed of his Mother's "Freudian papa" as if he were not the grandfather's son but the Mother herself. To withstand the fatal temptation to identify with Mother, Lowell needs a Father who is not also Mother's Father, and to this end he tries on, in ***Life Studies,*** the often unprepossessing figure of Bob Lowell as the source of his identity.

Lowell said, much later, that the ***Life Studies*** poems were grouped around his Father, an assessment which seems skewed when the book is considered as a whole. It seems even more so in a consideration of the manuscripts, in which Mother's character is so pervasive: "Unanswerable Motherhood!" Lowell exclaims at one point, as if throwing up his hands at her character's perfect power. But while ***Life Studies*** often seems to orbit around the fixed center represented by Mother, the figure of Father acts as a counterstrategy for identification of the self. Lowell tries more than once to make Father the central object of the autobiographical prose. These efforts demonstrate the psychologically different problem incurred by putting his male parent at the center of power.

In one such story, Lowell describes himself writing a poem during his stay at the Payne Whitney Clinic, a process which is interrupted by "Prince Scharnhorst," a hospital inmate. The poet hides a piece of paper on which he'd written "the first and last lines of a sonnet entitled"

> TO MY FATHER
>
> You sailed to China, Father, and knew your math
> . . .
>
> Friendly to all, and loving none, perhaps.

The prose then switches into a detailed description of the Prince, and Father disappears from the text except for the presence in his stead of a toy boat, which the Prince offers to lend him because Lowell's father, "a naval man, had admired Count von Luckner, the Sea Devil." This miniature is another token provided in place of the absent Father, who is now dead in the present tense of the story itself. Like the other tokens, this one cannot be Lowell's own: it is to borrow, not to keep. Father himself has disappeared; the Prince takes over the text as the controlling presence of the story, and one which defies reason: "He flamed in my doorway, a sunbeam—a man so various in his moonshines and virtuosity that I half-imagined he was an apparition, an actor."

In this version of the prose which offers an embedded poem, Father has been superseded by the colorful Prince Scharnhorst, who now seems to control both the story and the talisman that recalls Father. If this appropriation acts as a sudden end to Father's power in the story, it is one prefigured by the poetry insert, itself a clandestine object. This "hidden" manuscript acts as its own cogent dismissal: the sonnet form has been reduced to a summary couplet, the first descriptive line of which is itself overpowered by the dismissive bite of the conclusion.

The unexpected force of this dismissal depends on the central paradox of Father's character. Unlike Mother, whose "furniture" never changes, the figure of Father—"Friendly to all, and loving none, perhaps"—is essentially mysterious. Appearances aren't useful, in his case, as keys to the inner man: the smile Lowell describes elsewhere as "anxious" and "repetitive" does not necessarily indicate love. If Father loves "none," then he is without tie to them; he is free from their power. But it is a terrible thing for a child, even a grown-up one, to acknowledge that his parent might not love him, and the man who writes the bitterly concise couplet provides only the most minimal of escape routes from the awful possibility in the last "perhaps." Robert Lowell, Senior, despite his seeming powerlessness in those sections of the autobiographical prose in which his ineffectiveness is contrasted with the power of Mother, emerges in this couplet as a figure who wields a mysterious authority of his own. While Mother is consuming and all identification with her is psychologically dangerous, Father is no help either against Mother or as an authoritative role model because he is an enigma, as inaccessible to his son as those mysterious talismans of his youth. At the period of Lowell's life in which he writes of his parents they are already dead, but as he structures the story of his life he situates his persona at every stage as a psychological orphan, one whose identity must be sequestered from Mother's at the same time that his rightful role model has effectually removed himself from the scene.

Lowell's efforts to put Father at the heart of ***Life Studies*** are showcased in **"91 Revere Street,"** the prose centerpiece of the finished ***Life Studies*** volume. Earlier manuscripts help get to the source of his ambivalence about his subject: **"91 Revere Street"** is a compilation of several manuscript sources, and Lowell combines and shapes them so they are loosely structured around the figure of Robert Lowell, Senior. Ruling all as an opening trope of the opening passages is a piece of Father's own "furniture": the ancestral portrait of a dashing progenitor, identified variously in the manuscripts but called Major Mordecai Myers in the published work. Thus **"91 Revere Street"** begins surprisingly auspiciously for Father, but the crucial ambivalence Lowell associates with this figure undermines the project from the start. The ambivalence surfaces in the text itself. The admired ancestor is somehow "double-faced"; while he looks quite dashing, Myers' "exotic" eye seems to have "shunned the outrageous." In one version of the story, Father tells young Bobby that Myers was actually a civilian, and the boy abandons the ancestor as a role model, much as Lowell seems to have abandoned his own father as a role model when that parent left the Navy at his wife's insistence. In the ***Life Studies*** version of **"91 Revere Street"** this effect has been softened considerably, and Lowell conveys pity with his dismissal of his father's ancestor: "Poor sheepdog in wolf's clothing!" But when he talks of Father's disappointing reality in contrast to pictures of the man in naval uniform, and then brings in Mother "to insist to all new visitors" that Bobby's "real LOVE" is his *toy* soldiers, the child's willed distancing of the "double-faced" Father is complete. Any hope that Bobby Lowell will be able to take Father as a powerful role model has thus been stifled within the opening movements of **"91 Revere Street,"** and the symbolic replacement of Father by a cartoonish "real" sailor at the end, much like his replacement by Prince Scharnhorst in the Payne Whitney story, is hardly surprising.

The elusiveness of the Father, frustrating as it is to the beleaguered son who describes him in the autobiographical prose, ultimately suggests that Lowell *does* identify with his father, albeit unwillingly, and that this identification is the source of his ambiguous descriptions and his damning dismissals. The figure of the Mother with whom he must be careful not to identify is both whole and forceful: she makes Bobby feel impotent, and in this Bobby is surely the son of the man Lowell identifies as Bob in the manuscripts. The source of identity needs to be unambivalently masculine for the boy to stay psychologically secure, and in this way the identification with his elusive Father is both problematic and absolutely necessary. Lowell makes the connection between Father and male sexuality the thinly veiled subject of the following passage from the "Rock" manuscripts. For the required masculine identification with Father to succeed, the compelling Mother must be forcibly displaced: "If I looked straight ahead into Mother and saw nothing, I found I could imagine Father with a swan's feather cockade in his hat and leaning on his sheathed sword, more rash than wise among the Templars."

The sword and cockade which adorn the father are unmistakably phallic, and the description of masculinity as soldiery is by this time a recurring motif in the autobiographical prose. The connection between successful sexual identification and Father is made again, and even more overtly, in the autobiographical prose which describes Mother as having "too powerful a spring." Once again, Lowell offers a type of willed replacement of the threatening object by a series of safer alternatives: "One way to get around Mother was to think of the man's colors, blue and tan. Father's chair was leather and oak. The water in his two photographs of the Battleships New York and the Pennsy, was a gray that stood for blue. I was a tower of muscle rushing into air and water. Then I did my best to look straight ahead and into Mother without seeing her."

Whatever the son does to displace Mother is a blow in favor of his own masculinity, and therefore in favor of his own identity. Bob stands in for Bobby in this regard, and if Father is portrayed as indecisive and fundamentally enigmatic, then the son who is even less of a real soldier shares in the fundamental ambivalence of the male Lowell line. Consequently, the problems of the Father are the problems of the son, an identification made again thematically in ***Life Studies*** when the persona himself becomes, at book's end, a problematic spouse and a "dim-bulb father." For the poet who tries to create an object that will adequately represent the self in his autobiographical prose, the dilemma remains wearyingly familiar, another version of the question of where to locate the source of one's identity and how to inhabit safely the center of one's work. In the Freudian scenario posed in the autobiographical prose, the unalloyed central power of Mother is both forbidden and dangerous to the identity; but the power of the Father is enigmatic and so highly ambiguous that it is impotent. Siding necessarily with Father despite his own sympathies, Lowell presents himself as caught between nearly impossible alternatives, owner of the chronically dispossessed identity which will become the identifying voice of ***Life Studies.***

Despite the pull toward a fixed identity Lowell describes as Mother, the poet who finds his way back into psychological and occupational health by his efforts in autobiographical prose must always identify with the less certain and infinitely more mysterious power of the Father. He can never, therefore, really possess the objects he seems to desire so intensely in the autobiographical prose. They represent the essential mystery of his own identity, a mystery he must safeguard in order not to be entrapped by an idea of the self as a permanent and changeless entity, fixed in its power and therefore dead at its very heart. As a writer performing occupational therapy, he must choose that idea of the self which corresponds to the fluidity and ambiguity of language as it represents an equally mysterious world. Despite his frustration and his chronic sense of loss, the position is not without unexpected compensations. As an adult, the poet who tells his story in the autobiographical prose does obtain a talisman reminiscent of his childhood yearning: "For the first time in the two months since my acceptance by the Clinic, I enjoyed 'sharps-priviledges.'" The nail clippers he recovers in the hospital are hardly the exotic tokens of childhood, the magical matchbox, or the toy boat with its dangerous spring. They are a homely reward for returning health: a weapon, the prohibition against them suggests, no longer in danger of being used against the self. But Lowell seems to have learned a lesson about the power such objects represent. As a child he was nearly sick with desire to own what he could not keep. As an adult writing his way into a new style of being, he knows the advantages of freeing things of the constrictions imposed by his identity: "I pulled the dingy, disfiguring adhesive tape marked 'Lowell' from my nail clipper, and saw the whole morning flash blindingly from the chromium surface." Here to strip his identity from the tokens of power is to be gifted with an almost Emersonian vision of the blinding wholeness of something outside the self, a vision which momentarily compensates for all loss.

William Doreski (essay date Winter 1994)

SOURCE: "War and Redemption in *Land of Unlikeness,*" in *Southern Humanities Review,* Vol. XXVIII, No. 1, Winter, 1994, pp. 1-14.

[*In the following essay, Doreski explores Lowell's effort to reconcile his aesthetic attraction to warfare and moral objection to the Second World War in the poetry of* Land of Unlikeness.]

In 1943, Robert Lowell, disturbed by the Allied bombing of German cities and facing induction, sent a "declaration of conscience" to President Roosevelt and the local draft board. Lowell declared himself unalterably opposed not to war itself but to the conduct of this war, particularly to the bombing of civilian populations and to the intransigence of the Allied requirement of unconditional surrender, which he felt would lead (as Versailles had) to an untenable post-war situation:

> The war has entered on an unforeseen phase: one that can by no possible extension of the meaning of the words be called defensive. By demanding unconditional surrender we reveal our complete confidence in the outcome, and declare that we are prepared to wage a war without quarter or principles, to the permanent destruction of Germany and Japan. (***Collected Prose***)

Although a conscientious objector in a limited sense, Lowell was not a pacifist since he indicated his willingness to fight in a purely defensive situation. Moreover, the poems he wrote in the early years of the war demonstrate that he was not only fascinated by modern warfare but determined to use it aesthetically. The poems of ***Land of Unlikeness*** (1944), his first book, show him struggling with two opposing desires: one, to embrace the coldly objective but enthralling beauty of modern warfare; the other, to subsume the imagery of war in tropes of penance and redemption.

Lowell faced two other difficulties in this early work. One was psychological—he was not a pacifist, was intrigued by war and drawn to it, so his impulse toward penance and redemption, insofar as they require the rejection of violence, was not wholehearted. The other problem was his failure to find an adequate trope or body of figuration (in Eliot's term, an objective correlative) for his desire for personal and national penance. His solution was to wrestle conventional Catholic iconography into contorted juxtaposition with the imagery of war, but the resulting grotesquerie supports rather than opposes the strong sense of cultural disintegration the poems convey. The central strategy of T. S. Eliot's version of modernism—the refusal of unmediated tradition and simultaneous embrace of the preconditions and privileges of tradition—shapes the poems, despite the poet's attempt to embrace a more Thomistic and hierarchical Catholic iconography. Thus in a "land of unlikeness" the more powerful but less holy aesthetic of Protestant resistance reshapes sacred imagery to its needs, and the poems achieve a partial and unwitting synthesis.

This essay will consider **"On the Eve of the Feast of the Immaculate Conception: 1942," "The Bomber," "Christmas Eve in the Time of War,"** and **"Cistercians in Germany"** to illustrate the tension between the poet's competing desires to acknowledge his fascination with war and to censure both war and his own unruly will. Lowell wanted to normalize modern warfare by imposing the language of classical and Napoleonic wars; his objections to the bombing of cities derive not only from conventional moral outrage but from his sense that the aesthetic continuity of war—which is an ethical as well as artistic construct—has been violated. Underlying this paradoxical dilemma is Lowell's recognition that war, like poetry, is a form of discourse, one that in this instance has been usurped by the ultra-rationality of post-Enlightenment thought, to which he instinctively opposes an almost medieval sense of the mystical power of religious discourse. Long before Michel Foucault would systematically delineate the failure of rational humanism (in studies such as *Madness and Civilization* and *The Order of Things*), Lowell's early poetry embodies a Nietzschean sense of the insidiously anti-human quality of the Enlightenment faith in reason.

In **"On the Eve of the Feast of the Immaculate Conception: 1942"** the primary figure of penance and redemption is the Virgin Mary, the "Mother of God, whose burly love / Turns swords to plowshares," while Eisenhower represents a Caesar-like secular heroism that has "won / Significant laurels." As with many of Lowell's early and later poems, the modifiers betray the tension between conflicting desires. That Mary's love should be "burly" indicates its worldly dimension, its bulk and brawn and utility; while Eisenhower's "significant laurels" link the present to the glorious history of warfare. Further, the wish to "make this holiday with Mars / Your feast Day" would bring Christian and pagan, military and religious worlds together in a suitably ecumenical manner. But the speaker must resist the kind of idealism that finds religious fervor and militaristic ambition compatible, acknowledge his ancestry in violence, and empathize with the victims of the war:

Bring me tonight no axe to grind
On wheels of the Utopian mind:
Six thousand years
Cain's blood has drummed into my ears,
Shall I wring plums from Plato's bush
When Burma's and Bizerte's dead
Must puff and push
Blood into bread?

Grinding an axe on wheels of the Utopian mind is undesirable not only because it would blunt both the speaker's distaste for and admiration of war, but because it would distance him from the blood and bread of war, the texture of suffering. As a poet he would find this loss of empathy intolerable; but any attempt to reconcile his conflicting desires might generate exactly the Utopian state of mind that would ease the rough and tumble of his imagery. Because the language is so jagged and aggressive (calling Mary a "nimrod," for example), the last two stanzas uncomfortably mingle holy communion, war, and cannibalism, which is certainly not Lowell's intention but rather a product of his fevered embrace of tactile and sanguinary images:

Oh, if soldiers mind you well
They shall find you are their belle
And belly too;
Christ's bread and beauty came by you,
Celestial Hoyden, when our Lord
Gave up the weary Ghost and died,
You shook a sword
From his torn side.
Over the seas and far away
They feast the fair and bloody day
When mankind's Mother,
Jesus' Mother, like another
Nimrod danced on Satan's head.
The old Snake lopes to his shelled hole;
Man eats the Dead
From pole to pole.

The poem seems at first to abandon its militaristic leanings and embrace a sentimental reconciliation in which Mary would simply comfort soldiers, heal them, and banish "The old Snake" to a "shelled hole," replaying the familiar old drama. The last two lines, however, shock the poem back into satire: "Man eats the Dead / From pole to pole," the speaker concludes—an image which Jerome Mazzaro sees as one of hope, but which might also be seen as an ironic suggestion that even with Satan banished, humankind continues to devour itself. This difficult juxtaposition of religious and geographical metaphors indicates the poem's failure to sustain the tension between religious fervor and war fever. Lowell's attempt to reconcile the two by making Mary the "belle / And belly too" of the soldiers produces a grotesque conflation of tactile and spiritual metaphors that reveals more fascination with the physical immediacy of war than with the spiritual glory of the Mother of Christ.

"The Bomber" seems a more straightforward attempt to satirize war and violence, ridiculing the bomber for assuming the role of God the avenger. Without the complementary role of redeemer, the bomber, despite its destructive force, merely plays at its role:

The Master has had enough
Of your trial flights and your cops
And robbers and blindman's bluff,
And Heaven's purring stops
When Christ gives up the ghost.

The bomber fails to understand that with godlike powers go the responsibilities of a god. To pretend to power one does not possess is childish, tolerable only until the Master tires of such antics. But the satire turns uneasy when the poem notes how cruelly effective this child's play is:

You nosed about the clouds
And warred on the wormy sod;
And your thunderbolts fast as light
Blitzed a wake of shrouds.
O godly Bomber, and most
A god when cascading tons
Baptized the infidel Huns
For the Holy Ghost . . .

Though intended to satirize with the language missionaries have used for centuries to rationalize the destruction of native peoples in the name of God, this passage also betrays Lowell's fascination with the destructive power of the bombings, and it is in part his own fascination that causes his revulsion. The language—"Blitzed a wake of shrouds"—describes a cartoon-like killing, too unreal to convince the reader that people are actually dying here. Lowell's hard Anglo-Saxon consonants may be intended to approximate the harsh mechanical grind of modern warfare, but the language is so removed from gruesome actuality that it privileges the bomber, however unwillingly, as having the only real function. One need only compare this to Randall Jarrell's "Eighth Air Force" poems (though they too have been criticized for their dreamlike distance from their subjects) to see how detached from reality this poem is, how comic-book-like, and how ambivalent.

The Yeatsian italicized refrain "*And* [or *When*] *Christ gave up the ghost*" adds a note of seriousness that the rest of the poem doesn't quite attain, partly because the poet, despite his rage at the way the "Freedoms" have chosen to "police the world," finds the bomber with its "goggled pilots" a figure of fascination as well as of irresponsible destruction. The "unlikeness" in this poem lies not only in the way in which the bomber is unlike the god its role suggests but in the ways the speaker is both repelled by and drawn to the figure of destruction. Again, modifiers reveal Lowell's ambivalence: "Daredevil" sky, "wormy" sod (privileging the sky-god bomber over the lowly earthlings), "thunderbolts fast as light." Caught up in admiration of the bomber's power, the speaker only half-recovers his censorious stance in the second and third stanzas, and as a result the pious refrain seems mawkish and insincere.

The central motif in **"Christmas Eve in the Time of War"** is the further torture of Christ by capitalist greed and the threat that war will inflict even worse agonies ("Tomorrow Mars will break his bones"). By juxtaposing Christian and classical figures the poem attempts to suggest that the war represents a conflict between opposing visions or versions of the world, a conflict that finds a psychological parallel in the speaker of the poem. According to the subtitle, this speaker is "A Capitalist" who "Meditates by a Civil War Monument." This capitalist longs for his materialist heroes (Santa Claus and Hamilton) to "break the price-controller's stranglehold" and by freeing capital to restore the pre-apocalyptic world of his childhood. Somewhat paradoxically, he also longs to "spare the Child a crust of mould" but cannot, because his world, even in his childhood, has been one in which money is an ethic that for him replaced religious consolation:

Twenty years ago
I strung my stocking on the tree—if Hell's
Inactive sting stuck in the stocking's toe,
Money would draw it out.

The argument in this poem is between the trope of suffering, which belongs to Christ but which the capitalist wants to claim for himself, and the trope of war-as-power, of Mars, which represents an ironic apocalypse (ironic because the trope also embodies the Christ of apocalypse with his drawn sword) that reflects the world's refusal of the consolations of the Redeemer:

Brazenly gracious, Mars is open arms,
The sabers of his statues slash the moon;
Their pageantary understanding forms
Anonymous machinery from raw men,
It rides the whirlwind it directs the drums.

Hardly any wonder that faced with this whirlwind the capitalist bawls "for Santa Claus and Hamilton," but he cannot conceal his awe, if not admiration, for the power of Mars. The capitalist himself, presumably on a smaller scale, has wielded such power by using his money to manufacture a different kind of "Anonymous machinery from raw men." **"Christmas Eve in the Time of War"** speaks in the voice of a persona; in its revised version, in ***Lord Weary's Castle,*** as **"Christmas Eve Under Hooker's Statue,"** the poem speaks in the voice of a poet musing to himself, a voice that however inwardly directed seems even more fiercely intent on confronting war with the fruitless history of war. The speakers of both versions, however, remain enthralled by the dumb power of war, the "blundering butcher."

The "unlikeness" at the heart of **"Christmas Eve in the Time of War"** is internalized in the figure of Christ, who though in danger of having his bones broken by Mars has "come with water and with fire" to assert his apocalyptic role. The child-Christ, like the child-capitalist, is subsumed in the absent figure of the capitalist's child . . . dead upon the field of honor," so the poem rightly concludes "woe unto the rich that are with child" because gold cannot compensate for the loss of a child, or even for the loss of childhood. In fact, venality is to blame for this state of loss, both the literal loss of the dead child and the lost childhood, corrupted early by the love of money and the belief that it constituted a bulwark against sin.

The trope of war-as-power dominates the poem by excluding the trope of redemption and absorbing the trope of suffering. The despairing note of the closure, though properly Old Testament-prophetic, suggests how much more appealing are the images of punishment than those of forgiveness and redemption. The theological paradox lies in the invocation of the Christ-child rather than God the Father, necessitating an uncomfortable conflation of the gentle child Jesus with the stern warrior-Christ of the Second Coming. But this conflation is precisely the point of the poem, which centers on the capitalist's loss of his childhood to money-love and his perception of the war as retribution (a just retribution?) for what this sacrifice of childhood implies about his religious stance. Since rejection of one's own childhood implies rejection of the childhood of Jesus, and with it the refusal of Christ's role of savior, the capitalist has left himself only the dour figure of apocalypse. The later version of the poem drops this melodrama and becomes a simpler and more focused meditation on the statue of Hooker (a Civil War hero) as an aesthetic embodiment of war and its consequences. The earlier version, however, better portrays Lowell's sense of cultural disintegration, and with dramatic effectiveness portrays the complex relationship between the social corruption that begins in childhood and its consequences for the adult.

In **"Cistercians in Germany"** the monks of the title are figures of penance and renunciation, for the sake of which "corpse and soul" *should* "go bare," but who have been functionally displaced by Hitler and his supporters. The opposing and central trope of the poem is embodied in the Nazi party's vulgar ideal of social order:

Here corpse and soul go bare. The Leader's
headpiece
Capers to his imagination's tumblings;
The Party barks at its unsteady fledglings
To goose-step in red-tape, and microphones
Sow the four winds with babble. Here the
Dragon's
Sucklings tumble on steel-scales and puff
Billows of cannon-fodder from the beaks
Of bee-hive camps, munition-pools and
scrap-heaps,
And here the serpent licks up Jesus' blood,
Valhalla vapors from the punctured tank.
Rank upon rank the cast-out Christians file
Unter den Linden to the Wilhelmsplatz,
Where Caesar paws the gladiator's breast;
His martial bumblings and hypnotic yawp
Drum out the pastors of these aimless pastures;
And what a muster of scarred hirelings and
scared sheep
To cheapen and popularize the price of blood!

Because renunciation is not the opposite but the complement to order, the poem presents, surely inadvertently, the possibility that the Nazi party, not the Cistercians, represents the only redemption available. The "cast-out Christians" seem both disenfranchised and deflated. The poem describes as "sheep" both the followers of Hitler—witless pawns—and the followers of Christ who deny the ego to save their souls. The speaker of the poem, we learn at the close, is one of the monks who "lift bloody hands to wizened Bernard, / To Bernard gathering his canticle of flowers," and assert the survival of the Christian ideal. But this vision of actual redemption arrives too late to save the poem from becoming a rather morbid dwelling upon the vicissitudes of totalitarian order, which seems to imply that for the common lot of humanity this secular cruelty is the only appropriate form of salvation:

Here
Puppets have heard the civil words of Darwin
Clang Clang, while the divines of screen and air
Twitter like Virgil's harpies eating plates,
And lions scamper up the rumps of sheep.
The Shepherd knows his sheep have gone to
market;
Sheep need no pastoral piping for the kill,
Only cold mutton and a fleecing.

Lowell's infatuation with puns not only generates the "fleecing" at the end of this passage but tempts him into confounding and then fusing disparate meanings of "sheep" and so deconstructing the religious center of the poem, the implied orthodox argument that submission leads to salvation. Fascinated against his will by the harsh images of order generated by his poem, Lowell admits that Christian passivity and meekness might submit too readily to Fascism. It is possible to claim that this poem demonstrates how complementary Christianity and Fascism are, though this observation violates the conscious ethical stance of the author. The ambiguity of his language, however, suggests how attractive Lowell found tropes of social and military power, how tenuous was his faith (his aesthetic faith, at any rate) in the figure of Christ the redeemer, how fragile that faith seemed when under the pressures of war.

The effect of this poem, then, is to appropriate sacred imagery—the image of Christ the Shepherd leading his flock to God—for the poet's need to somehow synthesize tropes of power and order and tropes of redemption into an aesthetic whole. The unsatisfactory nature of the result is clear in the way Lowell rewrote the conclusion of **"Cistercians in Germany"** to suit the new poem **"At the Indian Killer's Grave"** in ***Lord Weary's Castle.*** **"Cistercians"** concludes by invoking the figure of Bernard "gathering his canticle of flowers" and transforming his soul into "a bridal chamber fresh with flowers, / And all his body one extatic womb. . . ." This transcendental experience, though, awkwardly mixes sexual overtones by confusing genders, abstracting the metaphor too far from concrete actuality. It confounds a quasi-sexual moment of religious ecstasy with one of unwitting transvestism, as if the masculine world of war, power, and imposed order had crushed the last vestiges of manliness from the saint and driven him to the embrace of his anima. Though this reading may seem forced, the poem invokes it by inadequately dramatizing the transition from scabrous social vision to transcendent metaphor. Because the earlier imagery has been so dramatic, one might expect comparable dramatization of the ecstasy of Bernard as he escapes, through the gathering of flowers (itself a sexual dramatization), the violent quotidian world. Unfortunately, such dramatization requires visualization, and this sort of religious imagery is intended to touch the spirit rather than the senses. That is, one should experience it with the meditative faculty rather than the perceptual one. But Lowell has already committed his poem to the imagery and language of dramatic excess. He somewhat mitigates this excess by the capitalization of Shepherd, which warns us that we are moving toward the world of religious allegory. But the conclusion occurs too abruptly, and attempts to depart too radically from the tone and movement of the bulk of the poem. Lowell's purpose is to draw a violent contrast between the frenzied order of Nazi Germany and the somewhat abstract world of contemplation occupied by the monks; however, the imagery of the early part of the poem is so strong and engaging that the effect is to make Bernard's meditative ascension seem faintly ridiculous. Lowell has not yet learned how decisively the tone of a short poem, once firmly established, shapes the reading of the whole.

Only a year or so later, when he revised the closure of **"Cistercians"** for **"At the Indian Killer's Grave,"** a much stronger poem, Lowell would demonstrate how apt was John Crowe Ransom's comment in 1945: "I don't know who has grown up in verse more than you, these last few years" (Lowell papers). **"At the Indian Killer's Grave"** shows how early Lowell began to move toward a more personal poetics of testimony. Here the voice of the poem seems coincident with the voice of the poet, so the reader may understand the concluding moment of religious vision as an expression of a psychologically verifiable presence rather than as an inchoate attempt to portray a saint's peculiar experience:

I ponder on the railing at this park:
Who was the man who sowed the dragon's
teeth,
That fabulous or fancied patriarch
Who sowed so ill for his descent, beneath
King's Chapel in this underworld and dark?
John, Matthew, Luke and Mark,
Gospel me to the Garden, let me come
Where Mary twists the warlock with her
flowers—
Her soul a bridal chamber fresh with flowers
And her whole body an ecstatic womb,
As through the trellis peers the sudden
Bridegroom.

Because the soul and womb are now Mary's, rather than the visionary's the sexual content no longer requires our special indulgence. It remains somewhat awkward (especially in the phrase "Gospel me to the Garden"), but placed in a less insistently violent and dramatic yet more historically situated meditation it seems a fit conclusion to a poem concerned with the religious and social hypocrisy of early New England. The Catholic vision of Mary, however fraught, in this instance, with overstated sexuality, is an appropriate rebuke to the Protestantism that motivated the excesses of cruelty and the self-deluded rationalizations of the Puritans.

However, when Lowell revised his poems for ***Lord Weary's Castle*** most of the overt references to the war disappeared, along with poems like **"The Bomber,"** not because they suddenly seemed dated but because, possibly, Lowell realized how difficult it was for him to control a seductive and compelling language of violence and power. Allen Tate in his introduction to ***Land of Unlikeness*** correctly observes that Lowell is "consciously a Catholic poet"; but unconsciously Lowell demonstrates a fascination with violence, imposed order, and unchecked power. The real source of unlikeness is not the land but the mind of the poet, and Lowell would eventually recognize that for himself and turn to the writing of more frankly autobiographical, self-exploratory poems. Once the poet began, like Wordsworth, to contemplate his own development, he had no difficulty portraying his early and ongoing fascination with war and his propensity for violence:

There was rebellion, father, when the mock
French windows slammed and you hove
backward, rammed
Into your heirlooms, screens, a glass-cased clock,
The highboy quaking to its toes. You damned
My arm that cast your house upon your head
And broke the chimney flintlock on your skull.

(**"Rebellion,"** ***Lord Weary's Castle***)

And I, bristling and manic,
skulked in the attic,
and got two hundred French generals by name,
from A to V—from Augereau to Vandamme.
I used to dope myself asleep
naming those unpronounceables like sheep.

(**"Commander Lowell,"** ***Life Studies***)

In much of the early work, Lowell writes in an impersonal voice and finds himself wrestling with unlikenesses that impose conflicting languages of varying but unequal strength, and very often poems of religious intention veer perilously close to becoming paeans to arbitrary power. But with the fashioning of ***Lord Weary's Castle***—building on strong first-person poems from ***Land of Unlikeness*** such as **"In Memory of Arthur Winslow"**—it seems clear that Lowell's proper voice—his surest and most controlled—was not that of a dramatic figure or persona but what Eliot calls "the voice of the poet" either talking to himself or "addressing an audience."

This is not simply a matter of Lowell's suddenly discovering himself, either as person or poet, since he would continue to evolve in sometimes radical ways as both poet and citizen for the rest of his career. Rather it is a matter of rhetoric. Lowell's poems needed to learn to persuade themselves before they might persuade an audience, and to do this they needed the fiction of a central speaking consciousness, not the picture of a division between consciousness and unconsciousness. In time-honored lyric tradition, Lowell found that fiction most readily embodied in the first person speaker, especially when that speaker could be firmly placed in a landscape. If Lowell at the time of ***Land of Unlikeness*** was writing work that, as Stephen Yenser argues, "assumes a disjunction of the verbal symbol and the actual world" and "ignores the incorrigible referential function of words," he found this excursion into "pure poetry" unsatisfactory, and gradually moved toward a poetics more firmly rooted in experience.

Consider the difference between the openings of **"Cistercians in Germany"** (quoted above), with its generalized if vivid social description, and the opening of the "Five Years Later" section of **"In Memory of Arthur Winslow,"** which establishes the speaker's consciousness at the center of the poem:

This Easter, Arthur Winslow, five years gone,
I come to bury you and not to praise
The craft that netted a million dollars, late
Mining in California's golden bays
Then lost it all in Boston real estate;
Then from the train, at dawn,
Leaving Columbus in Ohio, shell
On shell of our stark culture struck the sun
To fill my head with all our father won
When Cotton Mather wrestled with the fiends
from Hell.

Lowell still entwines considerable social commentary into the latter passage, but he also establishes a particularized consciousness to testify to the psychological authenticity of these perceptions. Perhaps more than many other poets, Lowell would require this centering to control the tendency of his rhetoric to assume a life of its own and expose fascinations too politically or socially unkempt, and perhaps too inauthentic. The war poems of ***Land of Unlikeness*** reveal much more about the modern fascination with violence, power, and imposed order than Lowell probably intended, and reveal as well how thin a veneer was his Catholicism, which he gave up only a few years later. They also reveal his first tentative movement toward the conflation of self and history, a decisive rejection of the Enlightenment belief in objectivity and the conventional limitations of genre.

Most interestingly, perhaps, these early poems reveal how powerfully the rhetoric of war grips the modern (and postmodern) mind, how firmly entrenched are the tropes of violence, how readily they overwhelm tropes of religious consciousness and vision. Language, not reason, shapes the controlling ethos of poems like **"The Bomber."** To overcome the tendency of language to plummet to the very bottom of the unconscious, Lowell would have to face it "without face" in the naked first person, the exposed romantic ego of ***Life Studies*** and ***The Dolphin,*** who would eventually admit in **"Facing Oneself"** how constructed that ego is, how necessarily unrepentant and honest, and even how unreligious:

After a day indoors I sometimes see
my face in the shaving mirror looks as old,
frail and distinguished as my photographs—
as established. But it doesn't make one feel
the temptation to try to be a Christian.

(***The Dolphin***)

Lowell's struggle to face himself, which required a temporary surrender of epic and satiric ambitions in favor of lyric or meditative intimacy, was as hard-fought as any of the other struggles of modern literature. In writing ***Land of Unlikeness*** he hadn't yet learned that this struggle, not the attempt to satirize America and the world back to sanity, would consume most of his career; but already by 1944 his language was pushing him inward, toward the only source of fragile stability he would ever find.

Richard Tillinghast (essay date Winter 1994)

SOURCE: "Damaged Grandeur: The Life of Robert Lowell," in *Sewanee Review,* Vol. CII, No. 1, Winter, 1994, pp. 121-31.

[*In the following essay, Tillinghast provides an overview of Lowell's literary career, artistic development, and critical reception.*]

A meteorologist of late twentieth-century American poetry, noting changes in the literary climate, tuning his awareness to the shifting winds of reputation and ideology, will be aware of at least one major cooling trend. I am speaking of the decline in estimation of Robert Lowell's poetry. He is still taught, his importance is acknowledged, but I wonder how many younger poets actually read him anymore? During his lifetime it was quite another story. Early in Lowell's career Peter Viereck had judged him "best qualified to restore to our literature its sense of the tragic and the lofty." When ***Life Studies*** appeared in 1959, John Thompson wrote in the *Kenyon Review* that "the great past, Revolutionary America, the Renaissance, Rome, is all contemporary to him. He moves among its great figures at ease with his peers. . . . This is why, perhaps alone of living poets, he can bear for us the role of the great poet, the man who on a very large scale sees more, feels more, and speaks more bravely about it than we ourselves can do."

Largeness of scale was part of Lowell's makeup. He came into the world with a sense of grandeur: "Like Henry Adams, I was born under the shadow of the Dome of the Boston State House and under Pisces, the Fish, on the first of March 1917. America was entering the First World War and was about to play her part in the downfall of five empires." Thus begins Robert Lowell's unfinished autobiographical piece, unpublished during his lifetime but appearing in a slightly different form in his posthumously published ***Collected Prose*** under the title **"Antebellum Boston."** The two sentences I have quoted wonderfully capture Lowell's essence. If the dramatic self-proclamation seems presumptuous—well, the phenomenon of Robert Lowell was awe-inspiring. The juxtaposition of the personal with a crucial historical moment became a trademark of his poetry—"These are the tranquillized *Fifties* / and I am forty"—a delusion of grandeur that was perhaps not a delusion at all.

Robert Lowell has, as a historical poet, few rivals among modern writers. History! Few poets have the erudition (not to speak of the brazenness) to link their births with a world war and the decline of the British, German, Hapsburg, Czarist Russian, and Ottoman empires. But Lowell's preoccupation with historical turning points was an expression of his psychological makeup. Lowell suffered from manic-depressive mental illness (bipolar disorder), in which the manic flights took the form of highly excited identifications with powerful figures from history, such as Napoleon, Alexander the Great, Churchill, Stalin, Hitler. This tendency began in childhood:

> And I, bristling and manic,
> skulked in the attic,
> and got two hundred French generals by name,
> From *A* to *V*—from Augereau to Vandamme.
> I used to dope myself asleep,
> naming those unpronounceables like sheep.

An obsession with Napoleon runs through Lowell's madness, an enthusiasm he shared, or so he claims in **"Antebellum Boston,"** with his mother when she was a girl: "She began to bolt her food, and for a time slept on an Army cot and took cold dips in the morning. In all this she could be Napoleon made over in my grandfather's Prussian image. It was always my grandfather she admired, even if she called him Napoleon." Napoleon is a pint-sized image of domination. "Mother, her strong chin unprotected and chilled in the helpless autumn, seemed to me the young Alexander, all gleam and panache. . . . Mother, also, was a sort of commander in chief of her virgin battlefield." Alexander was another of Lowell's favorite tyrants: Robert Silvers recalls that "at Mt. Sinai [hospital] he talked in a wandering way about Alexander the Great—how Philip of Macedon had been a canny politician but Alexander had been able to cut through Asia." His manic attacks were sometimes heralded by his wearing a medallion of Alexander the Great around his neck, or reading *Mein Kampf* (Jonathan Miller writes that Lowell kept a copy of it inside the dustjacket of Baudelaire's *Les Fleurs du Mal*), or buying a bust of Napoleon and displaying it on his dining room table in his apartment on West 67th Street in New York.

If we will better understand Robert Lowell's life and art, we need first of all to examine at least briefly some of the preconceptions engendered by what has so far been the only biography of him available, Ian Hamilton's large, handsomely turned-out, but often misleading, work. As with Lawrance Thompson's biography of Robert Frost, many readers—even if they have not read the book—have a sense of the poet which they assume to be accurate. The Hamilton biography makes it too easy to come to conclusions about Lowell's megalomania. Even when the book was being written, I had my doubts about it. Ian Hamilton phoned me in 1980 or 81 to make an appointment for an interview, which he later broke. That made me wonder whether his research might not be hasty and hit-or-miss.

Certainly he reports on the more sensational aspects of Lowell's public life, rather than on the extraordinary life of the mind that gave Lowell's poetry its depth. In addition he thanks Jason Epstein of Random House "for commissioning the book," suggesting that he was hired to undertake the project rather than initiating it on his own. This makes one question his personal stake in the project. Despite adopting a consistently snide and carping tone throughout the book, Hamilton by the end becomes overwhelmed by the air of damaged grandeur associated with Lowell's life. The book ends with a quotation from *King Lear:* "We that are young / Shall never see so much, nor live so long."

Hamilton is a professional biographer who has gone on to write a book about J. D. Salinger and another called *Writers in Hollywood*—and to edit *The Faber Book of Soccer.* It's unfortunate that the "definitive" biographer of Robert Lowell, the subtleties of whose poems are extremely hard to grasp outside the American context, should not be an American. As an Englishman, Hamilton simply lacks the ear to interpret, or misses the tone of, much of the material he is confronted with. He presents Lowell's grandfather Arthur Winslow as "a Boston boy who had made his middle-sized pile as a mining engineer in Colorado . . . almost ridiculously proud of his descent from the New England Winslows who had supported George III," as though Winslow were some sort of jumped-up, socially insecure nouveau riche, not a typical Bostonian of good family. I've never heard the expression a *Boston boy* in my life. And the suggestion that Arthur Winslow had anything to worry about socially is ridiculous.

If Sylvia Plath's *Ariel* is as Lowell says in introducing that book, "the autobiography of a fever," Hamilton's biography of Lowell is the biography of a psychosis. But Lowell was, like Hamlet, "but mad north-north-west"; when the wind was southerly he too knew "a hawk from a handsaw." His attacks, and the subsequent recovery periods, typically lasted one to two months. Hamilton devotes roughly one-fourth of his account of Lowell's adult life to the poet's madness, thereby giving readers of the biography the impression that

Lowell was off his rocker about twice as much of the time as he actually was. What astounded Lowell's friends was how quickly and substantially he was able to recover from his manic episodes: "In between, as you know," Blair Clark wrote, "Cal [Lowell's nickname from prep school on, inspired by his resemblance both to Shakespeare's Caliban and to the mad Roman emperor Caligula] functions brilliantly, and I mean this to apply not only to his writing but to his personal and family life." Writing for *Robert Lowell: Essays on the Poetry* (1986), which he also edited, Steven Gould Axelrod endeavors to explain why Hamilton's book has left readers with the sense that having read it, they know what there is to know about Robert Lowell: "First, of course, Hamilton's ability to persuade Lowell's intimates and executors to help him has seemed to give his book an official imprimatur. Second, Hamilton does indeed reveal more information about Lowell's private life, especially its scandalous side. . . . But I believe another factor has played a crucial role in the book's success. Hamilton's genius is in relating the most sordid personal details in a tone of effortless, agreeable superiority. Reading *Robert Lowell: A Biography* is like reading the *National Enquirer* firm in the conviction that one is actually perusing the *Times Literary Supplement.*"

Lowell's second wife, Elizabeth Hardwick, who was in the best, or worst, position to speak of his attacks and recoveries, has written that:

> . . . it seemed so miraculous that the old gifts of person and art were still there, as if they had been stored in some serene, safe box somewhere. Then it did not seem possible that the dread assault could return to hammer him into bits once more.
>
> He "came to" sad, worried, always ashamed and fearful; and yet there he was, this unique soul for whom one felt great pity. . . . Out of the hospital, he returned to his days, which were regular, getting up early in the morning, going to his room or separate place for work. All day long he lay on the bed, propped up on an elbow. And this was his life, reading, studying and writing. The papers piled up on the floor, the books on the bed, the bottles of milk on the window sill, and the ashtray filled. . . . The discipline, the dedication, the endless adding to his *store,* by reading and studying—all this had, in my view, much that was heroic about it.

To reverse the terms of the old Aristotelian chestnut, Lowell had the qualities of his defects. He had not only that sense of self-confidence without which it's hard to see how anyone writes poetry at all, but also the luck to have been born with a name and family tradition that lent authority to his utterances. Elizabeth Bishop put it this way: "I am green with envy of your kind of assurance. I feel I could write in as much detail about my uncle Artie, say—but what would be the significance? Nothing at all. . . . Whereas all you have to do is put down the names! And the fact that it seems significant, illustrative, American etc. gives you, I think, the confidence you display about tackling any idea or theme, *seriously,* in both writing and conversation. In some ways you are the luckiest poet I know!" And the unluckiest. Both as poet and man, Lowell presents an awesome spectacle of great gifts, great luck, and great misfortune.

The young Lowell was notorious for his singlemindedness, ambition, lack of humor, and belief in aristocratic ideals. "I am not flattered by the remark that you do not know where I am leading or that my ways are not your ways," he wrote at age twenty-three to his tyrannical mother: "I am heading exactly where I have been heading for six years. One can hardly be ostracized for taking the intellect and aristocracy and family tradition seriously." As a teenager he had prescribed for his friends not only a reading and self-improvement program, but even, during a summer on Nantucket with two schoolmates, the daily menu: "We had dreadful health food all the time. The diet was eels—cooked by me, badly—and a dreadful cereal with raw honey. All decided by Cal."

Lord Weary's Castle, Lowell's first major collection, can be seen as a proud, forbidding citadel that the poet erected around himself. The title was already a good indication that here was a poet who would concern himself with the exercise of power, both on the personal and political levels. Robert Hass, in the essay "Lowell's Graveyard" from *Twentieth Century Pleasures,* writes: "**'The Quaker Graveyard'** is not a political poem. I had assumed that it was, that its rage against the war and Puritan will and the Quakers of Nantucket who financed the butchery of whales was an attack on American capitalism. But a political criticism of any social order implies both that a saner one can be imagined and the hope or conviction that it can be achieved. . . . I went back to the poem looking for the vision of an alternative world. There is none." If optimism about alternative political solutions is the sine qua non of political poetry, then we conclude that Lowell was never a political poet at all. But I would have to disagree with Hass's strictures on political poetry. While remaining pessimistic about change, Lowell constantly engaged himself with the world of politics and power. His view of the radical alternatives to capitalism was just as dark as his critique of capitalism.

Received opinion has it Lowell started writing "personal" poetry only with ***Life Studies***—a view that Robert Hass counters brilliantly in his essay:

> I still find myself blinking incredulously when I read—in almost anything written about the poetry—

that those early poems "clearly reflect the dictates of the new criticism," while the later ones are "less consciously wrought and extremely intimate." This is the view in which it is "more intimate" and "less conscious" to say "my mind's not right" than to imagine the moment when

> The death-lance churns into the sanctuary, tears
> The gun-blue swingle, heaving like a flail,
> And hacks the coiling life out . . .

which is to get things appallingly wrong.

Lowell's manner in **"The Quaker Graveyard at Nantucket"** is to manhandle the iambic pentameter with strong spondees and enjambments learned from Milton, and to express an extreme mental derangement through violent imagery and logical absurdities. Speaking of the lines "Where the heelheaded dogfish barks its nose / On Ahab's void and forehead," Hass comments: "The lines depend on our willingness to let barking dogs marry scavenging sharks in the deep places where men void and are voided. To complain about this is not to launch an attack on 'consciously wrought' but the reverse." So much for the fiction that in ***Life Studies*** Lowell conformed to a culture-wide shift from the cooked to the raw, from paleface to redskin—though he himself publicly made the case for such a view. For poets like Galway Kinnell, Robert Bly, and Adrienne Rich, free verse really does mean what the name implies. For Lowell what are erroneously called fixed forms meant freedom and madness, while free verse meant prose, sanity, and control.

In the deepest part of his psyche, Lowell was, I suspect, that tyrant, that pure id that always longed to "break loose," to dominate, to be the entire world. Writing "imitations" of poets from Homer to Pasternak, for example, he "Lowellized" (Hamilton's term) his originals, making their poems sound like his own. There was not a drop of Wordsworthian "wise passivity" in his veins. In a poem written later in life, he addressed a bit of light but telling raillery to his wife and daughter: "I hope, of course, you both will outlive me, / but you and Harriet are perhaps like countries / not yet ripe for self-determination."

His personality was far from monolithic. In person he could shamelessly bully the weak and even the strong, often charmingly. But the tyrant shared a bed with the rebel, as Lowell himself understood. His sense of humor—and Hamilton gives us little sense of it—was mischievously subversive. In **"Grandparents,"** written when he inherited his grandfather's summer place, he grieves for his grandfather, who is "Never again to walk there, chalk our cues, / insist on shooting for us both," but he concludes "I hold an *Illustrated London News*—; / disloyal still, / I doodle handlebar / mustaches on the last Russian Czar." Being both dictator and revolutionary allowed him a unique view of politics. Given the contradictions inherent in this position, he naturally was a pessimist. His lines on Stalin could have referred to himself: "What raised him / was an unusual lust to break the icon, / joke cruelly, seriously, and be himself." Prometheus, in Lowell's ***Prometheus Bound,*** sums up the position: "It is impossible to think too much about power."

Lowell as a political poet remains, for all his brilliance and insight, something of a creature of the 1960s, together with the Kennedys, Eugene McCarthy, Che Guevara, and Lyndon Johnson, all of whom appear in his poems. Pronouncements on America from those years have a way of sounding, in retrospect, excitedly and unjustifiably apocalyptic. Hamilton's evaluation is sound: "His difficulty was that his image of America was not too sharply different from his image of himself." On the other hand it was Lowell's own violent nature, perhaps, that made him healthily skeptical of the glibness with which many of us promoted a potentially violent revolution during that giddy decade. If James Atlas's "Robert Lowell in Cambridge: Lord Weary" is accurate, Lowell's comments on former students who like me—fictionalized as Leonard Wiggins—had been swept up in left wing politics, were rather caustic but not unfair:

> "What about Leonard Wiggins?" I said. He had gone out to California for the semester and "been through a lot of heavy changes," he reported in a letter I now quoted to Lowell.
>
> "Yes, I gather he's brimming with revolutionary zeal," Lowell said, leaning forward to concentrate on my words. (What a keen pleasure that was!) He loved news of anyone he knew. "I like his early poems, but I can't follow what he's writing now. You wonder if there isn't too much California in it." (He always switched from "I" to "you," as if attributing his opinions to someone else.)

The side of Lowell's personality that needed to dominate was balanced by a side that liked to be led. Writing about his acrimonious home life with his parents, John Crowe Ransom (quoted in Steven Gould Axelrod's *Robert Lowell: Life and Art,* which contains some documentation Hamilton seems not to have seen) calls it "a bad hurt for a boy who would have revered all his elders if they were not unworthy." In the forties both Ransom and Allen Tate were to some degree surrogate fathers to Lowell, though Tate was extremely uncomfortable being called Father Tate.

Randall Jarrell, Lowell's elder by only three years (Lowell's pet name for him was the Old Man) always, though a lifelong close friend, remained a distant and austere critic of Lowell's poetry: "I have never known anyone who so connected what his friends wrote with their lives, or their lives with what they wrote. This could be trying; whenever we turned out something Randall felt was unworthy or a falling off, there was a coolness in all one's relations with him. You felt that even your choice in neckties wounded him." His relationship with Jarrell, who had the surest taste in poetry of anyone in his generation, is another example of Lowell's wonderful luck.

An even more important bit of luck was his marriage to Elizabeth Hardwick. Hardwick's acerbic wit, in conversation and in print, is famous if not notorious, and she is not, thank God, the saint that some readers of this biography might imagine. But she married, took care of, and tolerated all manner of outrageous behavior from a man who could be insufferable. (Though this is the image of him that predominates in Hamilton's book, most of the time Lowell was a fascinating conversationalist, very funny, affectionate and touchingly loyal to his friends.) Part of what made Hardwick stick with him was love; part must have been a dedication to literature. Jarrell expressed what many people thought: "You feel before reading any new poem of his the uneasy expectation of perhaps encountering a masterpiece." It's clear that Lowell needed something like Hardwick's astringency to keep his native wildness under control: "your old-fashioned tirade— / loving, rapid, merciless— / breaks like the Atlantic Ocean on my head." He had also loved the gift his first wife, Jean Stafford, had for malicious gossip and slander. "Calumny!", he would shout delightedly. "Here comes the black tongue!" Readers with a Freudian inclination will not be surprised to learn that Lowell's mother also had a wickedly sharp tongue.

It was inevitable, though, that Lowell would bite the hand that fed him. "O to break loose!", the opening of **"Waking Early Sunday Morning,"** could have been his motto. After he left Hardwick, he wrote her: "What shall I say? That I miss your old guiding and even chiding hand. Not having you is like learning to walk. I suppose though one thing worse than stumbling and vacillating, is to depend on someone who does these things." Yet the sense of breaking loose that accompanied Lowell's estrangement from Elizabeth Hardwick and his move to England eventually brought personal unhappiness and confusion rather than clarity. His third marriage, to Caroline Blackwood, turned into a disaster. On the fourteen-line poems (it is not accurate to refer to them as sonnets) that he began writing in 1967 for ***Notebook,*** and continuing through 1973, that constitute ***History, For Lizzie and Harriet,*** and ***The Dolphin,*** I am inclined to agree with Ian Hamilton: "The death of Randall Jarrell had removed the one critical voice that Lowell was in fear of—What will Randall think of *this*? had always been one of his first worries. It is possible that Jarrell might have found most of these new fourteen-liners slack, near-journalistic, or too much like casual diary jottings; they might have seemed to him too mumblingly unrhetorical, too self-indulgent. This is guessing; but there *is* a sense in which Lowell's new surge of eloquence is also a surge of truancy from the idea of some absolute critical authority, a 'breaking loose' from the requirement *never* to write badly."

Part of what is wrong with the fourteen-liners is a formal problem. Lowell's willfulness led him to think that if he could convince himself of the truth of something, then that was all that needed to be done. The fourteen-liners were little molds into which he could pour whatever. The mere fact that they *resembled* sonnets was enough to make them do what sonnets have traditionally done in English poetry. In an afterthought to ***Notebook 1967-68*** he avers: "My meter, fourteen line unrhymed blank verse sections, is fairly strict at first and elsewhere, but often corrupts in single lines to the freedom of prose. Even with this license, I fear I have failed to avoid the themes and gigantism of the sonnet." He was guarding the wrong flank: the poems need more, not less, of the traditional virtues (which he derides as "gigantism") of the sonnet sequence. The gigantism came not from his approximation of the sonnet form, but from his own megalomania.

"Those blessed structures, plot and rhyme— / why are they no help to me now / I want to make / something imagined, not recalled?" Lowell asks in his last book, ***Day by Day.*** Perhaps they *would* have been a help to him, if he had the discipline and deliberation to return to them. Hamilton identifies another problem of the "sonnets" as one of tone: "There is something glazed and foreign in their manner of address, as if they sense an audience too far-off, too blurred to be worth striving for." Lowell at his best is a very grounded, personal writer, and his prefatory remark to ***Notebook 1967-68,*** "Accident threw up subjects, and the plot swallowed them—famished for human chances," suggests an impersonality far from his genius. ***Notebook*** and its later incarnations have been seen by some critics as attempts to rival John Berryman's *Dream Songs.* If this was the case, Lowell might have done well to emulate the *Dream Songs*' formal division into stanzas. Furious debate surrounded the ethics of Lowell's having included the letters, telephone conversations, etc., of Elizabeth Hardwick in his late books, ***The Dolphin*** and ***For Lizzie and Harriet.*** His friend William Alfred was strongly against it. W. H. Auden said he would never speak to Lowell again if he published the Hardwick material. Elizabeth Bishop wrote him an impassioned letter trying to dissuade him: "That is 'infinite mischief,' I think. The first one, page 10, is so shocking—well, I don't know what to say. . . . One can use one's life as material—one does, anyway—but these letters—aren't you violating a trust? IF you were given permission—IF you hadn't changed them . . . etc. *But art just isn't worth that much. . . .* It is not being "gentle" to use personal, tragic, anguished letters that way—it's cruel." To Lowell, though, life and art were one. His loyalties were, finally, to his work, to the idea that, as Frank Bidart has written, "the only thing posterity will not forgive you for is a bad book."

But in his last book, ***Day by Day,*** Lowell seems to say that he has botched not only his life but his poetry as well. Perhaps he was writing his own epitaph when he addressed these words to his namesake: "yours the lawlessness / of something simple that has lost its law, / my namesake, not the last Caligula." He could perhaps have endured the pain of inflicting pain on his family. In fact in the last poem of ***The Dolphin*** he shoulders that responsibility:

> I have sat and listened to too many
> words of the collaborating muse,
> and plotted perhaps too freely with my life,
> not avoiding injury to others,
> not avoiding injury to myself—
> to ask compassion . . . this book, half fiction,
> an eelnet made by man for the eel fighting—
> my eyes have seen what my hand did.

Writing in the *American Poetry Review* in 1973, Adrienne Rich delivered the harshest condemnation of the three books of "sonnets." Harsh as these words are, it is hard to disagree with Rich's assessment of the lines I have just quoted, except that what she sees as vindictiveness is more truly a colossal thoughtlessness: "I have to say that I think this is bullshit eloquence, a poor excuse for a cruel and shallow book, that it is presumptuous to balance injury done to others with injury done to myself—and that the question remains, after all—to what purpose? The inclusion of the letter poems stands as one of the most vindictive and mean-spirited acts in the history of poetry, one for which I can think of no precedent: and the same unproportioned ego that was capable of this act is damagingly at work in all three of Lowell's books."

Lowell was not completely written out when he died at sixty. The poems in ***Day by Day*** demonstrate that he had abandoned the crutch the fourteen-line form had become for him during the period of ***History;*** the anguished candor of the new poems suggests that, had he lived, he might have achieved another poetic breakthrough as important as the one he brought off in ***Life Studies.*** Sixty might, in some people, seem a ripe enough age to die. Not for Lowell, of whom one can say that he "should have died hereafter." In the meantime one looks forward to a better biography of Robert Lowell, one that will give readers a more rounded picture of the Cal his friends put up with, laughed about, became exasperated with, but always admired and deeply loved. To say that his friends laughed about him may sound cruel; but, sad as his life in some ways was, why not grant the man the credit of being one in a long line of aristocratic Boston eccentrics? Keith Botsford, who accompanied Lowell on a Congress for Cultural Freedom junket to South America, would visit Lowell in the hospital in Buenos Aires during one of his attacks: "I was brought up as a composer, and all he wanted me to do was whistle. Sometimes it was "Yankee Doodle Dandy" or "The Battle Hymn of the Republic." Or it was Brandenberg concertos, Mozart piano concertos, anything. It was the one thing he craved, the one thing that would calm him. I'd be there two or three hours, just whistling until I was dry in the mouth. I'd whistle all the parts in the Ninth Symphony, or whatever, and he'd say, 'Yeah, but do the tympani bit.'"

I leave the last word to Peter Taylor, one of Lowell's oldest friends:

> As poet, as man, he approaches the great mystery playfully and seriously at the same time. From the very beginning or from the time when I first knew him in his later teens, he seemed determined that there should be no split in his approach to understanding profound matters. He was searching for a oneness in himself and a oneness in the world. He would not allow that any single kind of experience denied him the right and access to some opposite kind. . . . He would boast at times that he had never lost a friend. He never even wanted to give up a marriage entirely. He wanted his wife and children around him in an old fashioned household, and yet he wanted to be free and on the town. Who *doesn't* wish for all that, of course? But he *would* have both. He wanted it all so intensely that he became very sick at times. . . . When one heard that he was dead and how he died in the back seat of a New York taxi cab, one could not help feeling that he had everything, even the kind of death he had always said he wanted.

William Doreski (essay date March 1994)

SOURCE: "'One Gallant Rush': The Writing of Robert Lowell's 'For the Union Dead,'" in *New England Quarterly,* Vol. LXVII, No. 1, March, 1994, pp. 30-45.

[*In the following essay, Doreski traces the creative evolution of "For the Union Dead" and offers alternative interpretations. According to Doreski, the poem "centers not in its public language of history and heroism, as some critics would have it, but in its tropes of memory and psychological alienation."*]

In 1969 Robert Lowell drafted a statement on his poem **"For the Union Dead"** to be included in an anthology edited by Whit Burnett and entitled *This is My Best.* Each poet was to select the most outstanding poem from his or her own work and then explain that choice. Though Lowell hedged on declaring **"For the Union Dead"** his best poem, in choosing it for the collection he confirmed what many of his readers had felt, that if not his "best," this was certainly one of his most attractive, compelling, and characteristic poems.

Lowell's statement touches on the composition and the thematic center of the poem. Those who have not read his account of its origins may find his assessment surprising. As originally drafted, Lowell's remarks read as follows:

> If I knew my best poem, I think I would be too elated to reveal the secret; like some powerful chemical formula, this knowledge should be guarded and sipped by stealth. Anyway, I have no idea. Each poem was meant to be alive and new, and many were once ambitious. I chose **"For the Union Dead"** partly because of its length, neither overmodest nor hoggishly long for this collection. All one winter, I cut, added and tinkered. Some of my better lines came to me a few days before I read the poem at the Boston Public Garden Festival
>
> He rejoices in man's lovely,
> peculiar power to choose life and die.
>
> I have written nothing else for an occasion, and feel no desire to try again. The demands helped and even encouraged me to try to pull three incoherent sketches together. One was about an aquarium, one about a parking lot, one about a Boston club. I do not regard ambitious interpretations of his own poems as one of the poet's most useful chores. I wished to give my own structure to the free verse I had learned from my friend, William Carlos Williams. My poem may be about a child maturing into courage and terror. My lines are on the dry and angry side, but the fish and steam-shovels are Tahitian. In 1959 I had a message. Since then the blacks have perhaps found their "break," but the landscape remains.

Within this statement, I have suspected, lie subtle directions for those seeking to interpret **"For the Union Dead."** It is my intent, then, briefly to trace the process by which Lowell pulled his "incoherent sketches together" and combined them with the Ur-poem called "One Gallant Rush" to create "Colonel Shaw and the Massachusetts 54th," now entitled **"For the Union Dead."** I will also consider the implications of Lowell's ingenuous suggestion that his poem "may be about a child maturing into courage and terror," which implies that the finished poem **"For the Union Dead"** centers not in its public language of history and heroism, as most critics would have it, but in its tropes of memory and psychological alienation. Lowell wrote (or, perhaps more accurately, completed) his poetic performance to be delivered at the Boston Arts Festival of 1960. This annual event, for many years held every June in the Public Garden, featured paintings and sculpture displayed among the plantings and a reading by a prominent poet. The year that Lowell read his poem, Boston Common, directly across Charles Street, had been partially dug up for construction of a massive underground parking garage. Because of the scale of the excavations, the State House and the Shaw Memorial, two hundred yards up the slope of Beacon Hill, required substantial bracing to stabilize them against vibrations, as Lowell notes in his completed poem. Yellow power shovels and other heavy equipment, idled for the evening, stood in full view of the reading site.

Lowell recognized the dangers of writing occasional poetry, and, consciously resisting conventional pitfalls, he cast his autobiographical-psychological study of historical self-presence (that is, a poem that places the self at the center of history) within the framework of a Horatian ode. He thereby makes room for his own revisionary approach to modernism, which abandons Eliot's doctrine of impersonality and restores a Wordsworthian faith in the signature of individual experience.

"The Old Aquarium"

Lowell's "incoherent sketches" are drafts of two separate poems, one about the old South Boston Aquarium and the other about Colonel Shaw. The parking lot sketch and the Boston club sketch in surviving drafts have already been incorporated into "The Old Aquarium," the five draft pages of which illustrate Lowell's attempt to combine the strongest elements of one half-finished sketch with the other. "The Old Aquarium" opens, "Remember how your nose crawled like a snail on the glass, / your hand, a child's, tingled / with careless confidence." A penciled "my" over the first "your" indicates that even at this early stage Lowell was making the decision to filter experience through a first-person speaker.

The fourth stanza of the draft contains the remainder of the otherwise lost sketch about the Boston club:

> The curator, once the city's foremost citizen,
> the pillar and sustainer of its symphony,
> stands, a judge and beggar, in the doorway. His
> white scar,
> a trophy of the Civil War, is like a jawbone.

The subject of the portrait is Henry Lee Higginson, Civil War veteran and founder of the Boston Symphony Orchestra, who had died when Lowell was two years old. Perhaps in the original Boston club sketch Higginson had been portrayed with more historic verisimilitude, but identifying him as the "curator" of the aquarium is, of course, an act of fancy, irony, and satire. While in this draft-poem Lowell's purpose in conflating the imaginary and the real is unclear, Higginson's historical presence will serve to facilitate Lowell's imaginative leap when, some drafts hence, he brings together the aquarium and the Shaw Memorial as civic monuments of dissimilar public status but comparable personal significance.

Certainly Higginson was the archetypal old Boston club member, a partner in Lee, Higginson, and Co., investment bankers, and a wealthy benefactor of schools and cultural institutions. The "club" to which Higginson belonged is no particular institution but rather that class of powerful and well-educated men who once ran the city of Boston but who, by the time he died, were losing control to Irish and Italian politicians. Lowell seems to imagine Higginson in reduced circumstances, as "curator" of a broken-down, snow-shrouded aquarium, ironic emblem of cultural and educational institutions now bereft of their purpose and dignity. But Higginson retains his sense of self:

> Blunt humor and blunt severity
> alternately puff from his chewed cigar;
>   /bitten
> his exquisite, taut face,
> a grayhound's, trembles with robustness.

In spite of his longing for the antebellum world, he seems to understand that its utopian qualities have flourished only in his own mind:

> "No one I've ever met," he sighs,
> even remembers the code duello,
> man's peculiar and lovely power
> to deny what is and die."

Here Higginson, the Civil War survivor, offers a romantic view of combat that Lowell would later apply to Colonel Shaw. Higginson, a friend of Shaw's, was a member of the Massachusetts Second Regiment, Shaw's second military unit and the first in which he served as an officer. Although Lowell proceeded no further with "The Old Aquarium" (subsequent drafts comprise his efforts to merge it with "One Gallant Rush"), he already had hit upon one of the essential strategies of his finished poem: to bridge the gap between the historically distant, heroic self-sacrifice of Colonel Shaw and the human degradation of an unheroic present through the medium of individual perception and memory. Higginson, who survived into the new century, embodies the Civil War experience and draws it closer to our own time. As such, he serves as a transition between the long-lost personal experience of Shaw and that of the contemporary, first-person speaker, who views Shaw only as a historical figure.

"*One Gallant Rush*"

In rhetorical terms, Lowell, in "One Gallant Rush," overlays a meditative lyric on the structure of a historical narrative. The earliest draft so called derives several of its phrases and scenes from Luis F. Emilio's *A Brave Black Regiment: History of the Fifty-Fourth Regiment of Massachusetts Volunteer Infantry* (1891), and the title is almost certainly drawn from Frederick Douglass's famous words, "The iron gate of our prison stands half open, one gallant rush . . . will fling it wide."

The draft begins as a critique of modern war: "Fort Wagner uselessly cannonaded all day / like the French English and German trenches." As in *Henry V*, the pageantry of the battlefield almost conceals the futility of armed conflict:

> and you on the far right of your negros,
> sword out, now ankle deep, now knee deep,
> as the waves slapped the sand,
> the white flag of Massachusetts in front,
> the national flag to the rear.

But pageantry isn't combat, and once the gunfire breaks out, Shaw's sense of predestination, as Lowell imagines it, prepares him for his fate, perhaps even causes it. The syntax propelling the Colonel to his death relies on infinitives, which suggest a continuing expectancy. The event itself concludes so abruptly that the poem, failing to catch the moment, simply notes that it is "all over."

> The . . . cannon and muskets,
> your men holding their fire,
> everywhere dropping,
> then the moment it was all about,
> the moment you'd been expecting,
> three days, perhaps all winter since
> you took the command,
> at last the instant, powder-lit,
> sword in hand, crouched like a cat—
> all over.

The poem's argument, insofar as it makes one, is, of course, the rather well-worn observation that war is hell, modern war somewhat more hellish than those of earlier days. The black soldiers who stormed Fort Wagner have no role in this pageant-poem other than to hold their fire and die. On a separate page, however, probably written as an afterthought to the first draft, Lowell begins to complicate his poem. He had adhered too closely to his single source. He needed to multiply the dimensions of his poem so that it would spring to life. He would do so by extending his concerns into his own century.

The first lines of the fragment undercut the futility the first draft projects by presenting Shaw's death as a moment that somehow transcends momentariness:

> Because that fine moment ended abruptly,
> it never ended.
> It shines on distinct like a target.
> Or is it a loaded and leveled gun?

The question links the historical figure with contemporary black civil rights leaders; nonetheless, Lowell argues, Shaw is "to[o] perfect for the moment" to be of use in the present struggle, for his willingness to sacrifice, his embrace of the heroic imperative, involved not only himself but the black soldiers he led. Shaw is thus a pivotal figure, his military-heroic values rooted in the past, his democratic sympathies, though grounded in the New England aristocrat's natural sense of leadership, expanding to encompass a grander ideal of human equality.

Finding the proper symbolic framework to embody the complexities of Shaw's relationship with the contemporary world would eventually require Lowell to privilege the meditative, first-person speaker and to wind the plot of the poem through the speaker's associations. It is central to Lowell's aesthetic that the most profound links with history are revealed by means of an associative process so personal that it can only be justified by acknowledging the peculiarities of individual perception.

But before making that important leap in the composition process, Lowell again reworked his straightforward historical sketch in yet another draft of "One Gallant Rush." Focusing on Shaw's experience, it suggests that blacks and whites have been so divided since the Civil War that Shaw's personal qualities are irrelevant to the contemporary civil rights movement. Too much a product of the war and of heroic idealism, Shaw exists, in a sense, only because he chose not to. If he had lived, he would have gone "on like a Strulbug," in a state of death-in-life.

Finding a bronze immortality ill suited to his purposes, Lowell marshalls some historic anecdotes to soften the effect. The martyr is addressed: "you shaved your beard / and mustache and passed for a girl at the ball" (the incident is apparently true), and "at your mother's nagging you packed / the colonels uniform you wouldn't wear at your wedding." Drawing upon such domestic details helps humanize Shaw, and it permits Lowell to begin imagining a larger but more personal context in which the figure of Shaw is subsumed, but not lost, in a more contemporary meditation.

The rest of this draft concentrates on the heroic act itself. Calling the Civil War "the first modern war" (a historical truism, although some historians give the Crimean War precedence), Lowell resorts to desultory melodramatics of a sort he would never have allowed himself to publish:

> your general, soon mortally wounded,
> on his great bay charger, saying:
> "I am a Massachusetts man myself,"
> then turning and asking,
> "if the flag-bearer fall,
> who will carry the fla[g]?"
> And you tense and watchful,
> affable, easy in your movements,
> parsimonious in speech, saying:
> "I will."

Clearly this melodramatic language (taken word for word from Emilio's book) wouldn't do. Lowell realized he had to find a way to link the past to the present, to follow the line of development suggested in his opening stanza. He would look no further than his last work to find his strategy.

In ***Life Studies,*** published shortly before he began working on "One Gallant Rush," Lowell had committed himself to a personal, autobiographical aesthetic. While such an aesthetic functions naturally in poems about one's family life and childhood—and even about one's stay in a mental hospital—**"For the Union Dead"** would significantly extend the range of the approach beyond the personal, even beyond perceivable space and time, into shared history.

In the next, fragmentary draft of "One Gallant Rush," Lowell introduced some poignant domestic lines about his daughter's guinea pigs. Although incorporated in a full-length draft of **"For the Union Dead,"** the passage was eventually dropped, only to find its way into **"Fourth of July in Maine"** three or four years later. The lines were probably intended to provide a meditative setting and therefore fulfill the same function as the childhood and present-tense landscapes of aquarium and Boston Common in the finished poem:

> Always this itch for the far away,
> the excessive, the decadent!
> Even on this dead June afternoon,
> when the air has stopped still,
> and my daughter has just brought home
> a baby guinea pig and its mother from school
> to board with us till fall,
> I dream of some flash of powder or whiff of
> grapeshot
> to destroy the chaff of day.

Lowell would have quickly seen the awkwardness of allowing two guinea pigs to trigger a meditation on war, but the draft justifies the connection by means of an analogy between Shaw's childhood and Lowell's, Harriet being the intermediary. As a boy Shaw had altogether too much in common with the inhabitants of the twentieth century to excite our envy or admiration, Lowell argues, so we can be "grateful" that in his subsequent martyrdom he "managed to supersede / those fond, early out of key anecdotes."

The anecdote, cited by Lowell and recounted in detail by Peter Burchard, refers to Shaw's ballroom cross-dressing. Though probably a typical jest of the period, it is hardly the sort of story we expect to hear about a Civil War hero, since it calls into question the rigidly conventional, nineteenth-century ideal of manhood. In war, whatever its social or political justifications, men distinguish themselves by demonstrating courage and military prowess. How could a boy amused by an activity that implicitly rejects the phallic power and privilege of manhood have become, only six or seven years later, a martyr to the cause of abolition and the republic? And Shaw was, it seems, still young enough to be "nagged" by his "abolitionist mother / into packing the colonel's uniform [he] wouldn't wear to [his] wedding."

The problem with "One Gallant Rush" was that it failed, despite Lowell's tinkering, to bridge the historical gap between the narrator and his subject. For Lowell, naked historicism was unacceptable; only through its personal dimensions could the intellectual experience of history be authenticated and only through the language of the senses could it be adequately conveyed. The attempt autobiographically to place "One Gallant Rush" on a "dead June afternoon" didn't work. But combining it with the aquarium sketch would locate it within a landscape of loss and destruction, one more richly endowed with personal memory-images and public sociopolitical dimensions.

From "The Old Aquarium" to "Colonel Shaw and his Men"

Reworking passages from the aquarium sketch and combining them with passages from "One Gallant Rush," Lowell began to fashion his poem into the four-line free verse stanzas of the finished version. Almost immediately, the opening lines take shape:

> The old South Boston aquarium stands
> in a sahara of snow now. The broken windows
>   are boarded,
> the bronze weathervane carp has lost half its scales,
> the seedy tanks are dry.
>
> Once my nose crawled like a snail on the glass,
> my hand, a child's, tingled
> with careless confidence to burst
> the bubbles drifting from the noses of the cowed,
> compliant fish.

Establishing the essential rhythm in these two stanzas was Lowell's most important single step toward completing the poem. "One Gallant Rush" was dogged and flat-footed in its cadence; the new stanzas provided a far more effective rhythmic template which subsequent stanzas could follow or play upon.

Another central concern was to position the speaker in relation to his material, and here Lowell still has some problems. The two subsequent stanzas, which deal with Shaw (and mention for the first time the "bell-cheeked negro infantry"), both begin with "Later," as Lowell hesitates to bring his childhood self and his contemporary persona into conjunction. "Once" places the child comfortably in the past, but only in the next draft would Lowell devise the stanza that relinquishes his childhood and valorizes the role of the Shaw Memorial in linking historical past, memory, and the present:

> The Aquarium is gone. Here in the heart of
> Boston
> the Shaw Civil War Memorial
> still immortalizes the immortal moment,
> and stick[s] like a fishbone in the City's throat.

Extending this draft generated new problems but also fresh images that would survive in the finished poem, images like the "bell-cheeked negro infantry" and the memorial as a hook, later a fishhook, finally a fishbone in the throat of the city. A version of lines that would eventually conclude the poem—

> giant finned cars nose on like fish,
> a savage servility slides by on grease

—appears at this stage, but in subsequent drafts Lowell would bury them in the middle of the poem.

Lowell now embarks on five successive complete drafts, the first two entitled "Robert Shaw and his Men" and "Colonel Shaw and his Negro Regiment," the rest **"Colonel Shaw and the 54th,"** the title under which the poem would appear in the first paperback edition of ***Life Studies.*** These drafts all contain the essential tensions of the finished poem, the historical conversation between past and present, the violence of modern life and the dignity of Shaw's enterprise, the ironic awareness that Shaw's battle remains unconcluded. Not until the fifth complete draft, however, would Lowell finally end his poem.

Driving the giant finned cars to the rear of the poem, Lowell refuses any hint of resolution and leaves the reader with an image of sharks schooling, as if they had grown from the modest little fish the child once observed in the South Boston Aquarium. It is because of this ending that

Lowell could argue successfully that his poem is about that child's maturation; the poem is about the maturation of a point of view, a widening of observation from a child's wonderment at the contained natural world to a critically informed understanding of the relationship between history and the present. Moving to giant finned cars from cowed, compliant fish completes the trope of observation and maturation that opens the poem.

Before he settled on an adequate conclusion to what had become a slightly unwieldy poem, Lowell made several attempts to close with his historical material rather than with the present:

> Unable to bend his back, he leads
> his men to death, and seems to wince
> at pleasure, suffocate to be alone.
> They all died for the Republic.
> [Complete draft #1]
>
> . . . .
>
> A gay, droll gentleman—he) had no leisure (to distrust
> (nature at ease,) the resolute disorder
> of his bronze, bell-cheeked negro infantry,
> their eternal lubberly slogging past the Statehouse steps.
> [Complete draft #3]

Besides generating (or rediscovering) the eventual ending, Lowell's five drafts produce another essential image—that of the Mosler safe and the atomic explosion at Hiroshima. This key image of modern warfare provides the historical balance against which to weigh the individual heroism of Shaw and his troops and with which to return to the present. With the other key image, also found in these drafts, of the speaker's hand drawing back not from cowed fish but from "negro school children" seen on television (who, too, are cowed like the fish), the poem is largely complete, though many penciled notations on the final draft indicate further polishing. This last of the Houghton drafts still differs enough from the published version of the poem to warrant reproduction here, with the kind permission of the Lowell Estate and of Houghton Library. I make no attempt to correct the spelling nor to take into account the marginal notations, some of which will be incorporated into the finished poem:

> COLONEL SHAW AND THE MASSACHUSETTS' 54TH
>
> Relinquunt omnia servare rem publicam
>
> The old South Boston Aquarium stands
> in a Sahara of snow now. Its broken windows are boarded.
> The black weathervane cod has lost half its scales.
> The airy tanks are dry.
>
> Once my nose crawled like a snail on the glass;
> my hand tingled
> to burst the bubbles
> drifting from the noses of the cowed, compliant fish.
>
> My hand draws back now. I often sigh
> for the dark, downward and vegetative kingdom
> of the fish and reptile. One morning last March,
> I pressed against the new, barbed and galvanized
>
> fence on the Boston Common. Behind their cage,
> yellow dyosaur steamshovels were grunting
> as they cropped up tons of mush and grass
> to build the mammoth parking lot.
>
> Everywhere, the purr of commercial optimism
> rises to the clang of desecration. Orange,
> Thanksgiving-colored pumpkin-colored girders
> brace the tingling Statehouse.
>
> A steel frame reinforced
> Colonel Shaw
> and his bell-cheeked negro infantry
> on St. Gaudens' Civil War relief . . .
>
> The monument sticks like a fishbone
> in the City's throat;
> its Colonel is as lean
> as a compass-needle.
>
> He has an angry wrenlike vigilence,
> a greyhound's gentle tautness;
> he seems to wince at pleasure,
> and suffocate for privacy.
>
> When he leads his negro volunteers to death,
> he cannot bend his back—
> he is rejoicing in man's lovely,
> peculiar power to deny what is and die.
>
> Outside Boston,
> the old white churches hold their air
> of sparse, sincere rebellion; transparant flags quilt
> the graveyards of the Grand Army of the Republic;
>
> it[s] ramrod-witted stone Union Soldiers
> grow slimmer and younger each year—
> wasp-waisted, they doze over muskets,

and muse through their sideburns.

Here in this city, a girdle of girder;
the terminus of turnpikes,
there are no bronze monuments for the last war.
A felt, authentic commercial photograph

of Hiroshima rising like a cloud
above an American safe that survived the blast
says no thief
will break into our treasure.

The aquarium is gone. My hand draws back.
When I crouch to my television set,
the terrorized faces of negro schoolchildren
flash like bubbles on the screen.

Colonel Shaw is riding on his bubble,
he waits for the blessed break.

Everywhere,
giant finned cars nose forward like fish;
a savage servility
slides by on grease.

Before publishing the poem Lowell added two lines to the penultimate stanza, revised the stanza about the stone Union soldiers to give them a little more dignity, eliminated "terminus of turnpikes," changed the "mammoth parking lot" to an "underworld garage," replaced "commercial optimism" with "parking spaces" that "luxuriate like civic / sand piles," eliminated the awkward lines "says no thief / will break into our treasure," and generally rendered the poem more euphonious and rhythmically satisfying.

At the Boston Arts Festival Lowell would say (reading a prepared statement), "My poem, **'The Union Dead,'** is about childhood memories, the evisceration of our modern cities, civil rights, nuclear warfare and more particularly Colonel Robert Shaw and his negro regiment, the Massachusetts 54th. I brought in early personal memories because I wanted to avoid the fixed, brazen tone of the set-piece and official ode." Later, in drafting his statement for the Burnett anthology, Lowell would recognize how deeply personal he had made his poem, how far from the "official ode" it is. In examining these drafts we can see how consistently the poem moves from wooden impersonality toward a more vivid, more openly autobiographical moment, a progress consistent with Lowell's strengths as a lyric and meditative poet. History and autobiography mingle deeply and subtly in Lowell's creative process, and perhaps we can now more fully understand that when later he wrote, "the age burns in me," he spoke not as a megalomaniac but as an artist whose very personality plumbed the vagaries of history and the contemporary American social scene.

Richard Tillinghast (essay date Summer 1994)

SOURCE: "Robert Lowell's *Day by Day:* 'Until the Wristwatch is Taken From the Wrist,'" in *New England Review,* Vol. 16, No. 3, Summer, 1994, pp. 54-63.

[*In the following essay, Tillinghast discusses Lowell's death and offers critical evaluation of* Day by Day.]

To read Robert Lowell's last book, ***Day by Day,*** published shortly before his death in 1977, is to accompany the poet on a valedictory retrospective of his life and work. This is the most elegiac book of one of our great elegists. In poem after poem he says goodbye not only to old friends but to old ideas—the ruling ideas of the time in which he lived. He continues to feel ambivalent about the third of his troublesome marriages, wondering whether he had made a mistake in leaving his second wife Elizabeth Hardwick, to marry the Anglo-Irish novelist Lady Caroline Blackwood. Ambivalence was Lowell's characteristic stance—a stance that positioned him ideally to exemplify many of the conflicts of his period. When he died in a taxicab on the way to Hardwick's apartment in Manhattan after a flight from London, he was carrying, wrapped in brown paper, the famous portrait of Caroline Blackwood, *Girl in Bed,* which had been painted by her first husband, Lucian Freud. In an interview in the September, 1993, issue of *Town and Country,* Blackwood reveals that attendants at the hospital had to break Lowell's arms to remove the picture from his grasp.

Day by Day has the overall effect of an almost posthumous work: On the last page of Ian Hamilton's biography of Lowell, William Empson's words on *King Lear* are invoked:

> The scapegoat who has collected all this wisdom for us is viewed at the end with a sort of hushed envy, not I think really because he has become wise but because the general human desire for experience has been so glutted in him; he has been through everything.
>
> We that are young
> Shall never see so much, nor live so long.

The use of the verb "see" in the quotation from *King Lear* turns out, as I shall make clear, to be quite relevant to this unusually visual poet's experience. In the last section of the book he attempts to enunciate a visually based aesthetic, which is only partially substantiated in his practice. As to the length of his life: In terms of an ordinary human lifetime, Lowell was not really so old—he died at sixty. But he filled his consignment of years with more involvement, personal and public, than most people manage to do. Elizabeth Bishop chided Lowell for what she saw as a premature embrace of old age: "Please, *please* don't talk about old age so much, my dear old friend! . . . I wish Auden hadn't gone on about it so his last years, and I hope you won't." From the vantage-point of his relatively early death her remarks seem unprescient. Both friends had much less time than Bishop, the older of the two, could guess. She herself would die in 1979. Lowell's premonition that his own life span would be cut off early, as his parents' had been, turns out to have been uncannily accurate.

Far from the unseemly denial of ageing and death that many engage in, Lowell was almost in a hurry to get old and even to die. In ***For the Union Dead,*** written before he had reached fifty, he was ready in **"The Flaw"** to elegize Elizabeth Hardwick and himself:

> Old wives and husbands! Look, their gravestones
> wait
> in couples with the names and half the date—
> one future and one freedom. In a flash,
> I see us whiten into skeletons,
> our eager, sharpened cries, a pair of stones,
> cutting like shark-fins through the boundless
> wash.

Perhaps, to an extent, Lowell even romanticizes their deaths. Ten years later, on the contrary, the grim details of a hard-to-diagnose illness, rather than an appealing and idealized notion of death, recommend themselves to the poet's attention in the poem **"Day by Day."** A preternatural "seriousness," a brutal realism, have consistently been part of this poet's arsenal, so his accuracy in rendering the symptoms of what look like foreshadowings of his fatal heart disease should not come as a surprise. In **"Our Afterlife II,"** addressed to his old friend Peter Taylor, he chills us with his clarity:

> My thinking is talking to you—
> last night I fainted at dinner
> and came nearer to your sickness,
> nearer to the angels in nausea.
> The room turned upside-down,
> I was my interrupted sentence,
> a misdirection tumbled back alive
> on a low, cooling table.

Faced with the direst of eventualities, his directness, the accuracy of his words, are at the ready. The writer's image of himself as an interrupted sentence is a humorous and lovely figure. One might well imagine how his cousin Harriet Winslow, paralyzed, an invalid for years, must have appreciated **"Soft Wood,"** his ***For the Union Dead*** poem to her, not only for its affectionate tone but for its unsentimentalized acknowledgment of her illness:

> I think of you far off in Washington,
> breathing in the heat wave
> and air-conditioning, knowing
> each drug that numbs alerts another nerve to
> pain.

In **"Endings"**—one of the many poetic farewells to family members and friends which give ***Day by Day*** its deep elegiac tone—Lowell, older now, relates his own symptoms to hers:

> You joked of your blackouts,
> your abstractions,
> comic and monumental
> even for Washington.
> You woke wondering why
> you woke in another room,
> you woke close to drowning.
> Effects are without cause;
> your doctors found nothing.
> A month later you were paralyzed
> and never unknotted . . .

Because, as the last poem in the book puts it, "We are poor passing facts," we are "warned by that to give / each figure in the photograph / his living name." The accuracy of observation, the determination to do justice to fact—though it is highly questionable how faithful Lowell was to fact even when he thought he was—can in places give the realism of these poems a certain heroic air:

> A small spark tears at my head,
> a flirting of light brown specks in the sky,
> explosive pinpricks,
> an unaccountable lapse of time.

One's final response to ***Day by Day*** is likely to be complicated and therefore hard to describe. A certain awe when faced with the last work of a great artist is part of the complication. That this is the last work Lowell left, that there will never be a new Lowell poem to read, informs part of our response, prompting us to look back over the entire *oeuvre.*

These feelings of retrospective awe are complicated by a sense that many of the poems are off-puttingly oblique. Some of them read more like notes for poems than inspired utterances. The opening of **"Phillips House Revisited,"** which finds Lowell hospitalized for a heart condition in the same place his grandfather died, sounds undeveloped, jotted down in haste: "Something sinister and comforting / in this return after forty years' arrears / to death and Phillips House . . ." Many of these writings are willful. In some of them the logic is opaque. And then there is the suspicion that often, no sequential logic is intended. I am not speaking of the "difficulty" that good poems often achieve. Perhaps the most intriguing aspect of the book is that the poems' obliquity, their lack of interest in "making sense" is guided, at least ostensibly, by a consistent aesthetic. Interestingly, this aesthetic is announced only in the last few poems in the book. **"Shifting Colors"** ends with these lines:

I am too weak to strain to remember, or give
recollection the eye of a microscope. I see
horse and meadow, duck and pond,
universal consolatory
description without significance,
transcribed verbatim by my eye.

This is not the directness that catches
everything on the run and then expires—
I would write only in response to the gods,
like Mallarmé who had the good fortune
to find a style that made writing impossible.

Renunciation of memory, "description without significance," then, consoles. The next stanza offers a ready example of the obliquity I mentioned above. How does this brand of description differ from "the direction that catches / everything on the run and then expires"? The next line seems to say that Lowell would always rather write only under the urging of inspiration.

Too many of the poems in this book read as if they were written just for the sake of writing. This circumstances does not, one must quickly add, exclude brilliant images, observations and lines. If the last two lines are not simply a joke not meant to be looked at too closely, do they mean that Lowell thinks he would be happier giving up poetry altogether? That strains credibility: this is a man whose existence without his writing would be impossible to imagine.

Another poem, **"Grass Fires,"** asserts baldly:

In the realistic memory
the memorable must be forgone;
it never matters,
except in front of the eyes.

If Lowell really believes that memorable events "must be forgone," he would have to throw out most of what he had written. On the other hand, a poet so wholeheartedly dedicated to the new would relish the task. Still, put briefly, Lowell's various statements on observation, memory, and the imagination are just too contradictory to form a consistent position. Is a poet required to take a consistent position? No. But this is Lowell's most discursive book; it markedly takes positions on poetics and thus asks to be responded to intellectually.

Earlier Lowell had been bothered that students of his poems found it too easy to find "keys" to the work. He expressed reservations about Freudian readings of his work. "Maybe I throw in too much Freud," he wrote in a letter in 1969. "I try to use him two thirds (?) skeptically and playfully. Even then [while writing ***Life Studies***] I found his Faith harder to take straight than the Pope's." Yet Lowell was in therapy with a Freudian analyst for several years preceding ***Life Studies,*** and had, it seems to me, absorbed more of Freud's point of view than he knew.

As early as 1965, in the original version of **"Waking Early Sunday Morning,"** which appeared in *The New York Review of Books,* Lowell was questioning the very notion of significance, of "great subjects," of meaningful symbols, in his poetry:

I lie here on my bed apart,
and when I look into my heart,
I discover none of the great
subjects: death, friendship, love and hate—
only old china doorknobs, sad,
slight, useless things to calm the mad.

The china doorknob held his attention in an almost obsessive way. Almost as soon as he had put the Freudianism of ***Life Studies*** behind him, he began trying to come to terms with the notion that whatever attracted his eye would become the true subject of his poetry. The eye becomes the arbiter of what he will write about, the eye tyrannizes him in a way, as is clear from the ***For the Union Dead*** poem **"Eye and Tooth":** "No oil / for the eye, nothing to pour / on these waters or flames." Significantly, these lines are followed directly by his famous statement, "I am tired. Everyone's tired of my turmoil."

Again, in **"Dolphin,"** the final poem in the book of the same name, Lowell evokes sight as a way of acknowledging action: "my eyes have seen what my hand did." The verb tenses, interestingly, have their own story to tell. Sight, for which the present perfect tense is employed, continues from the past into the present; action occurs in the past definite, and is final. Since Lowell's **"Epilogue"** to the book is brief, and since it sums up his aesthetic of writing at the end of his life, I will quote it whole:

"Epilogue"

Those blessed structures, plot and rhyme—
why are they no help to me now
I want to make
something imagined, not recalled?
I hear the noise of my own voice:
The painter's vision is not a lens,
it trembles to caress the light.
But sometimes everything I write

with the threadbare art of my eye
seems a snapshot,
lurid, rapid, garish, grouped,
heightened from life,
yet paralyzed by fact.
All's misalliance.
Yet why not say what happened?
Pray for the grace of accuracy
Vermeer gave to the sun's illumination
stealing like the tide across a map
to his girl solid with yearning.
We are poor passing facts,
warned by that to give
each figure in the photograph
his living name.

This announced eschewal of plot and rhyme represents a renunciation of artificiality both in concept and style. Lowell wrote often of plot in ***The Dolphin,*** most notoriously in the line, "one man, two women, the common novel plot . . . ." The same poem ends with words apparently quoted out of a letter from Elizabeth Hardwick: "*Don't you dare mail us the love your life denies; I do you really know what you have done?*" A good question; there is something heartless and dangerous about speaking of one's own life as though it were a novel.

The sense of the poem becomes problematic almost immediately when the author announces his allegiance not to memory but to the imagination. By arguing that the painter's vision "trembles to caress the light," Lowell gives realism an emotional coloration. Then he goes on to lament that his own realism too much resembles photography and not painting—"paralyzed by fact." It's hard to say exactly what he means by "All's misalliance." I think he means, consciously or not, that he can't make his ideas fit his practice. If, to paraphrase Yeats, we make rhetoric out of our quarrels with others, and poetry out of our quarrels with ourselves, certainly this poem arises from a quarrel with the self. "Yet why not say what happened?" he asks with a sort of exasperated shrug. It is meant, one would think, to be a rhetorical question.

But one is provoked to speak up and answer: If you just say what happened, then you lose the interest of readers who don't find your own life as urgently fascinating as you do. Lowell's reply in the last eight lines of the poem is that an inspired "accuracy" amounts to "grace." Because our mortality and the brevity of our lives is in itself so poignant, then memorialization—which takes up much of this book, as well as much of Lowell's whole *oeuvre*—is inherently valuable. This despite his having earlier declared in **"Grass Fires"** that "In the realistic memory / the memorable must be forgone." An extreme example of poetry as just jotting down whatever comes to mind is **"Wellesley Free."** The poem wanders aimlessly from the leaf-blower operating outside, to a fleeting memory of the poet's school days, to a description of the room where he is sleeping. Then he tells us "I cannot read," and later that "I cannot sleep solo, / I loathe age with terror" and finally trails off: "70 outside, / and almost December." This is a poem that should have been edited out of the collection.

The uncritical embrace of writing as process, which made the unrhymed "sonnets" lose focus and almost turn their backs to their readers, became a serious problem for the poet from ***Notebook*** on. Daniel Hoffman, as friendly a reader as one can imagine, characterizes the ***Notebook*** period in these terms: "The yawning monster wouldn't stop—he soon revised and enlarged the book, republishing the new version as ***Notebook,*** and that also to be revised, enlarged, in an endless flood of unrhymed sonnets. By 1973 the machine had disgorged several hundred poems . . ." One would hardly want to tar Robert Lowell with the brush of "poetry as therapy," but, oddly, he was not untouched by this confusion that has put serious art and basket weaving in the same category. He had even benefitted from it: he had started writing **"91 Revere Street"** as a prose memoir suggested by his psychiatrist, and ***Life Studies*** poems like **"My Last Afternoon with Uncle Devereux Winslow"** had begun as prose. At the end of "Unwanted," a critique of his tendency to see poetry as therapy, which I will look at in more detail later, Lowell asks an unanswerable and desperate question: "Is getting well ever an art, / or art a way to get well?"

The fusion of life and art that had been Lowell's genius from ***Life Studies*** on apparently blinded him to something essential that goes into a poem. Good poems have enough magnetism as objects or events to engage the reader. They stand on their own without reference to the author's biography. Lowell more and more presumed his readers' knowledge of his life. He seems to have subsumed the act of writing so thoroughly into the personal realm that he lost the artist's edge. An indication that writing had become simply an activity rather than a means to the end of making poems with a life of their own, is suggested by Lowell's question to a doctor at the asylum where he was hospitalized in England:

"These days of only poems and depression—
what can I do with them?
Will they help me to notice
what I cannot bear to look at?"

If his poems are "only poems," if they are only meant to help their author, one can hardly wonder why they might lose their attraction for the reader. And then if the poet posits the supremacy of pure observation, one is much closer to understanding what is missing in Lowell's late poetry.

There are plenty of times when his confidence in his newly formulated philosophy of writing wavers. **"Unwanted"** is the poem that most closely resembles the ***Life Studies*** belief in psychological causality:

I read an article on a friend,
as if recognizing my obituary:
"Though his mother loved her son consumingly,
she lacked a really affectionate nature;
so he always loved what he missed."
This was John Berryman's mother, not mine.

The way Lowell follows up on this psychological clue is reminiscent of the insistent self-analysis of his most Freudian period: "Often with unadulterated joy, / Mother, we bent by the fire / rehashing Father's character." Here it is Lowell's own character getting rehashed. The difference now, though, is that Lowell analyzes his habit of self-absorbed analysis: "Alas, I can only tell my own story— / talking to myself, or reading, or writing, / or fearlessly holding back nothing from a friend."

What one can't help noticing, though, is how much of what Lowell was able to bring to ***Life Studies*** is missing even in the poems in this book that resemble the earlier book. The detailed panorama of social life, for instance—as though Lowell were an anthropologist of his own culture, noticing everything and rendering the feel of it with percepts and images, gossipy anecdotes, cameo appearances, and pitch-perfect quotations from his characters. The question is not: "Yet why not say what happened?" The question is how finely, in what detail, with what humor, with how well-rendered "surround" one says what happened.

Yet this is a meaty book, informed by an acute historical sense, full of moving retrospectives, the reflections on ageing which I have already discussed, poems to old friends. Lowell's world-weary tone is earned, as suggested by the allusion to *King Lear* I quoted at the beginning of this essay. No one is in a better position that Robert Lowell, after a lifetime's involvement with psychiatry, to chronicle the decline in the influence of Freud's ideas: "Dreams," he comments, "they've had their vogue, / so alike in their modernist invention." In **"Since 1939"** Lowell even anticipates the end of Communism. The *frisson* of W. H. Auden's early poems forms a backdrop for the poem's insights into a curious phenomenon of our times: the obsolescence of a political doctrine that promised the end of history, seen through the eyes of the generation who came of age in the immediate postwar period:

We missed the declaration of war,
we were on our honeymoon train west;
we leafed through the revolutionary thirties'
Poems of Auden, till our heads fell down
swaying with the comfortable
ungainly gait of obsolescence . . .

Having elsewhere defined history as that which we cannot see, Lowell labors to make visible the transition of ideas from revolutionary to outmoded: "I see another girl reading Auden's last book. / She must be very modern, / she dissects him in the past tense." His ironic use of the word "modern" here reinforces how difficult it is for our century, whose chief cultural movements all defined themselves under the banner of Modernism, to see itself as re-entering that elusive continuum called history. Auden "is historical now as Munich, / and grew perhaps / to love the rot of capitalism." The poem brilliantly captures the confused sense of suspension experienced by those who have experienced and assented to the doctrines of Communism and Modernism: "In our unfinished revolutionary now, / everything seems to end and nothing to begin."

Though capable of the insight and economy of that formulation, this poet, who has applied himself to the task of understanding history more assiduously than anyone since Pound, is clearly at a loss where to go next. So he ruminates aimlessly:

England like America has lasted
long enough to fear its past,
the habits squashed like wax,
the gay, the prosperous,
their acid of outrage.

His style fails him here. If one is going to generalize and make pronouncements, as the Augustan poets did, rhyme and meter can at least lend shapeliness and sonority to the enterprise. Lowell accomplished this in the rhyming stanza he used in ***Near the Ocean:***

No weekends for the gods now. Wars
flicker, earth licks its open sores,
fresh breakage, fresh promotions, chance
assassinations, no advance.
Only man thinning out his kind
sounds through the Sabbath noon, the blind
swipe of the pruner and his knife
busy about the tree of life . . .

Perhaps I have been too vigorous in pointing out the book's flaws, though. ***Day by Day*** contains great elegiac moments, and these are its lasting achievement. **"Our Afterlife I,"** the first of the two poems addressed to Peter Taylor, begins with an image of two Tennessee cardinals in migration—Taylor is a native Tennessean, and some of Lowell's apprentice days as a poet were spent in that Southern state.

Following through on the image of the birds, the poem ends with a moment of pure elegiac transcendence:

We are things thrown in the air
alive in flight . . .
our rust the color of the chameleon.

He notes the "rust" of age and other natural processes, like the rain's "simmer of rot and renewal" and the "triangular blotch / of rot on the red roof" in a earlier poem, **"Eye and Tooth,"** in a poem about Milgate, Caroline Blackwood's ancestral manor house. Lowell characteristically celebrates decay and decline as few other poets do: "It is a natural life. Nettles / subdue the fugitive violet's bed, / a border of thistles hedges the drive." He is also capable of startlingly original images, such as New York as a cigarette lighter:

Now the lifefluid goes
from the throwaway lighter,
its crimson, cylindrical, translucent
glow grows pale—

From a Brazilian *ex voto* sent to him by Elizabeth Bishop, a primitive head meant to be offered in church as a thanks-offering, Lowell spins a touching little poem which expresses his relief at being himself again after one of his manic attacks: "Something has been taken off, / a wooden winter shadow— / goodbye nothing. I give thanks . . ." Described, it comes alive:

its shallow, chiseled ears,
crudely healed scars lumped out
to listen to itself, perhaps, not knowing
it was made to be given up.

With the wooden head as an emblem, Lowell deftly turns the object around to himself: "This winter, I thought / I was created to be given away."

That kind of directness and clarity were too often lacking in the three books that preceded ***Day by Day.*** Of the poet's last book, a sympathetic reader would like to agree with Louis Simpson that "In his new book ***Day by Day*** . . . we are back with the fascinating, superbly gifted poet of ***Life Studies*** and ***For the Union Dead.***" Simpson's statement perhaps embodied a wish more than a certainty. Certainly Lowell had turned a corner and at the moment of death, when "the wristwatch is taken from the wrist," was on the way back to finding himself as a poet. Had he lived, it is impossible to predict what poetic self he would have found. The features of this new self would surely have taken his readers by surprise, because self-transformation was Lowell's *forte.* As Elizabeth Bishop wrote in her elegy on him,

You left North Haven, anchored in its rock,
afloat in mystic blue . . . And now—you've left
for good. You can't derange, or re-arrange,
your poems again. (But the Sparrows can their song.)
The words won't change again. Sad friend, you
cannot change.

At the same time he was on the way back to his second wife, who had stood by him through it all, when he was struck down by a heart attack in the taxi from the airport in New York. As Peter Taylor has written, he got the kind of death he always said he wanted: "a natural death, no teeth on the ground, no blood about the place." But, tragically, he died before he had the chance to pull off another of those startling poetic metamorphoses that made him the most innovative poet of the age.

Hilene Flanzbaum (essay date March 1995)

SOURCE: "Surviving the Marketplace: Robert Lowell and the Sixties," in *New England Review,* Vol. LXVIII, No. 1, March, 1995, pp. 44-57.

[*In the following essay, Flanzbaum discusses Lowell's literary fame, political protest, and critical reception during the 1960s. Flanzbaum contends that Lowell's public ambition "should not be understood as a venal thirst for fame but rather as a result of his yearning to find common ground with the large American audience."*]

In the 1960s, Robert Lowell took his career in an unexpected direction. Having won the Pulitzer Prize and inspired the devotion of literary critics and fellow practitioners in the previous two decades, he had established himself as the leading poet of his generation. But in the sixties, more than being warmly appreciated by a small elite audience, Lowell became a sensation: an American celebrity and a figure of political influence. In a few short years, he joined a select group of American poets who had bridged the great divide between academic and popular culture. This extraordinary stage in Lowell's career deserves wider critical attention than it has yet received, for it sheds significant light not only on his personal poetics but on the workings of America's literary and cultural history.

Scion of a dynastic American family, Lowell had always garnered more public attention than other modern poets, who, as we know, spent much of their time composing essays about the disappearance of their audiences. While the publication of ***Life Studies*** in 1959 guaranteed Lowell's critical reputation and reaffirmed his position as the preeminent poet of his generation, it also foreshadowed his dramatic rise to national prominence a mere five years later.

The story of Lowell's ascent begins in 1964, when President Lyndon Baines Johnson asked him to read at the White House Arts Festival. Citing his objections to LBJ's policies on Vietnam, Lowell declined. He also sent a copy of his letter of refusal to the *New York Times,* whose editors, knowing that a Lowell could always make news, decided to print it on the front page. Furious, Johnson responded, accusing Lowell of publicity seeking and grandstanding. When many of the nation's most important writers and artists lined up behind Lowell, the stage was set for a media battle between literati and the executive branch that took almost three months to play out and whose echoes could be heard now and again in the ideological war that raged for the better part of a decade.

Lowell's opposition to the Vietnam War constituted the first and perhaps most essential ingredient in the hash of political and social changes in which he served himself up to the public sphere. Politically he had always been a renegade—a conscientious objector to World War II and a persistent and harsh critic of American capitalism—yet the growing unpopularity of the Vietnam War, and the cultural revolution spawned in the wake of protests against it, found Lowell closer to mainstream American ideology and appetites than he would ever have thought possible. Abruptly, Lowell's iconoclasm was chic.

In 1965, Lowell wrote and directed ***The Old Glory,*** an off-Broadway production that targeted the hypocrisy of American government and institutions; it ran for three years and won an Obie award for best play. In the years between 1964 and 1967, four of Lowell's dramas were staged and two books of his poetry published. His 1964 volume ***For the Union Dead,*** issued just months before the LBJ letter, had been applauded by the critics. By 1967, he drew thousands of anti-war protestors to the steps of the Pentagon and narrowly avoided being arrested with Norman Mailer. In 1968, Lowell frequently dined with Jacqueline Kennedy, and he joined presidential candidate Eugene McCarthy on the campaign trail.

Lowell found that when he walked his dog on the streets of Manhattan, paparazzi trailed him. While it has been argued that he abjured this particular aspect of celebrity, he had to be pleased, nonetheless, to see the entire texts of **"The Quaker Graveyard in Nantucket"** and **"Memories of West Street and Lepke"** reprinted in *Life* magazine, his portrait featured on the covers of *Time* and *Newsweek,* and articles touting his political views spreading to all corners of the world.

Despite Lowell's undeniable fame, curiously enough his career has never been appreciated, nor has his poetry been read, as a product of his lifelong ambition for popular, as well as critical, approbation. For it was not solely Lowell's political actions that brought him celebrity and influence; not every war resister, not even those who were poets, became stars. While certain external circumstances made Lowell popular—the turbulent political times, his maverick stance juxtaposed against his Brahmin background—Lowell's celebrity does not proceed simply from a serendipitous combination of biology and global events. Rather, Lowell is exceptional because he had skillfully mastered the formula for media attention.

A close friend of Lowell's, Blair Clark, explained the tremendous impact of the White House letter this way:

> Lowell had a shrewdness in handling his public persona, and the "LBJ letter" was an example of his brilliant timing. . . . Cal, the public figure. He knew what he was doing. I'm sure there were people who were terribly envious of his ability to manipulate himself as a public figure. He did it without any pomposity—but he definitely believed he was a public figure.

Yet Lowell's prodigious talent for finding the spotlight should not be understood as a venal thirst for fame but rather as a result of his yearning to find common ground with the large American audience. Critics have mistakenly seen Lowell's gesturing to a popular audience as evidence of his poetic misprision instead of as a premeditated maneuver to widen his literary domain and to make contact with an audience that had become deeply alienated from most modern poetry. Lowell did manage his career shrewdly, but mere celebrity was not his aim: he wanted to be more than the poet literary critics acclaimed; he *also* wanted to be the poet the American people looked to for wisdom. While this conclusion has been occasionally and hurriedly noted in biographies of the poet, I believe that understanding Lowell means appreciating precisely how his conflicting ambitions directed his career decisions and affected the poetry he wrote.

For instance, many critics note that Lowell's career was a string of continual rebirths. A phoenix from the ashes, again and again Lowell reinvented his poetic persona with seeming ease: the student of obscure and inaccessible New Critical methods in ***Lord Weary's Castle*** transformed himself into the accessible, confessional poet of ***Life Studies,*** then turned himself into the political and public poet of ***History,*** then reinvented himself once more as the morose and withdrawn journalist of ***Day by Day.*** Critics have located the germs of these poetic evolutions in Lowell's tumultuous psychological profile, but they have failed to measure how his aspiration simultaneously to engage both an academic and a popular audience took its toll on him. Because the mass market and canonical poetry, especially in the post-Eliotic haze of high modernism, have always appeared implausible conspirators, literary scholars have been slow to recognize the degree to which marketplace pressures have driven American poetry. In Lowell's case, when the marketplace and the academy briefly reconciled, that oversight has resulted in a missed opportunity to examine the inner workings of literary history as well as precluded a thorough understanding of many of Lowell's greatest poems.

"For the Union Dead," published in 1964 in a volume of the same name and considered one of Lowell's most important poems, has attracted substantial critical attention. Commentators have fully explicated Lowell's resemblance to the iron-clad hero of the poem, Robert Gould Shaw, who led the first black battalion of the Civil War into a conflict that sent more than half his fighting men to their deaths and ended in defeat. The romantic hero who accepts the challenge of political responsibility in a doomed cause is a recurring paradigm in Lowell's work. Throughout his career, Lowell was intrigued by individualists and idealists, even those on apparently misconceived missions. Thus, critics have long debated how **"For the Union Dead"** treats Shaw's particular task. Is Lowell celebrating Shaw's bravery? or is he criticizing his foolhardiness?

Stalled in progress, this debate has prevented literary criticism from opening other avenues of inquiry. I argue that **"For the Union Dead,"** written just as Lowell is about to take centerstage in American culture, anticipates and showcases his conscious decision to abandon the neglected poet's pulpit and engage fully in American public, political, and economic life. Alan Williamson has noted that Shaw "represents a compromised, but still living, still responsible connection between ideology, or image and realities." While Williamson's articulation of Lowell's "compromise" is apt, by noticing neither that the "hero" of the poem is the statue and not the man nor that the statue is placed in a specific physical context, Williamson and other critics have failed to recognize a crucial facet of the poem: **"For the Union Dead"** presents more than a political crisis; it embodies an artistic one as well. And the compromise to which Williamson refers extends beyond the presentation of Shaw to encompass how Lowell will manage his own career.

In **"For the Union Dead,"** technology and commercial opportunism threaten the artifact, "St. Gauden's shaky Civil War relief," which depicts Shaw on horseback among his black foot soldiers. Sited on the Boston Common, "the heart of Boston," and facing the "tingling State House," directly across Beacon Street, the nineteenth-century masterpiece has been rocked by excavations for a new parking garage. Thus, the poem treats the fate of the art work, left either to stand or perish when brought to the center of civic action. Shaw's metallic glance not only reflects his problematic idealism but it peers directly into all that is most hostile to American art.

"For the Union Dead" does not open with the image of Shaw, however. Neither the statue nor Shaw himself appears until stanza six. Lowell carefully sets the scene with the destruction of another romantic icon, the Boston Aquarium. More resigned to his fate than the speaker in "The Waste Land," who still prays for rain, the speaker in **"For the Union Dead"** expects no relief: He writes, "The Old South Boston Aquarium is waterless; the bronze weather vane has lost half its scales." The poet longs for "the dark downward vegetating kingdom of the fish and reptile," an image of artistic fertility; he instead finds a "new(ly) barbed and galvanized world" where "yellow dinosaur steamshovels . . . crop up tons of mush and grass / to gouge their underworld garage."

These opening images suggest a vision of hell, inhabited by the unearthly monsters of technological advance. But Lowell warns that the statue faces more than one local excavation; it gazes out upon the larger contemporary horizon—the barbed wire fence and dinosaur steam shovels and the commercial photographs of television and advertising. The juxtaposition of the statue with commercial art suggests a previously unrecognized theme in the poem. The art that seems more expressive of and appropriate to sixties culture is "a commercial photograph / (that) shows Hiroshima boiling / over a Mosler safe." As Lowell presents it, the statue appears out of its element, for it shows signs of physical as well as thematic antiquity. Indeed, that it is "shaky" and needs "prop(ping) by a plank split against the garage" symbolizes the poet's uncertainty about its ability to survive amidst the increasingly threatening aspects of commercial culture.

After evoking an artistic field from which the subject has disappeared and only the artifact remains in its compromised form, the poet announces Shaw's death, stating peculiarly that "he is out of bounds now." At Shaw's death, his "father wanted no monument / except the ditch / where his son's body was thrown." In these lines, Lowell both repudiates the power of art adequately to measure contemporary reality and sounds the note of alarm for which his poem is destined. If the ditch is the fitting grave for Shaw, it is because it symbolizes the necessary and paradoxical nobility of abasing oneself in order to lead the nation. Just as Shaw's burial in a ditch serves a more important function than a ceremonious entombment might have, Lowell believes that his own descent into the pit of American commercialism has now become the most important contribution he can offer to the people, for only then can he lead them out of their morass. Lowell's insistence that "The ditch is nearer" ominously precedes his account of the barbarity of modern civilization. Critics have from the start acknowledged that "the ditch" is, in the words of one, a "many-layered symbol, that brings together nuclear annihilation, the absolute zero of outer space, the blank terror in the faces of the Negro schoolchildren, and the hollowness of ideals out of touch with real circumstances." They have not noted, however, that Lowell's identification with his character, Shaw, extends to his venturing into that ditch.

Just as he has described the position of Shaw's statue, so Lowell now places himself eye to eye with the political realities of his time, indicating his readiness to participate in the world of commercial transaction. Even while identifying with Shaw's compromised idealism and the statue's compromised ability to speak to a new age, Lowell nonetheless prepares to carry himself and his artistic creations into the center of civic action. In fact, in **"For the Union Dead"** Lowell is proclaiming that only a compromised artistic vision *can* endure among the brutally realistic symbols of a highly technological and commercialized culture. Taking his lesson from the compromised statue of Shaw, which still maintains its tenacious hold on Boston Common, Lowell decides to do what he must to turn his art public.

Lowell's interaction with the marketplace of the sixties culminated with the publication of ***Near the Ocean.*** The volume, hurried to the stores by both a determined Lowell and an opportunistic publisher eager to cash in on the heyday of the poet's prestige, stands as a telling marker of Lowell's aspirations. Of the many clues in his career that he sought to influence the larger culture and earn the plaudits of a wide audience, none is more revealing than the collection of poems that appeared in January 1967. Strongly critical of American ideology and policy, the poems in ***Near the Ocean*** expose the corruption of America's leaders and preach an end to imperialist violence.

The message cannot be missed: the poems do not hide their meanings in dense metaphors or obscure references; they mask neither their political nor their commercial intentions. A conventionally popular form, rhyming couplets maximize the oral potential of the poems and thus their public quality; we can be read before crowds, they announce, or chanted and remembered. In **"The Fourth of July,"** Lowell writes "dinner waits / in the cold oven, icy plates— / repeating and repeating, one / Joan Baez on the gramophone." The reference to Joan Baez reveals the immediacy of Lowell's intentions and also identifies the poet with youth culture, a youth culture that might adapt his verse to song.

"Waking Early Sunday Morning," the first poem in the volume, became "*the* political poem of the sixties," according to critic Richard Howard. When read aloud, it included a stanza that regularly received howls of delight from Lowell's audiences and represented one of his most Ginsberg-like moments:

> O to break loose. All life's grandeur
> is something with a girl in summer . . .
> elated as the President
> girdled by his establishment
> this Sunday morning, free to chaff
> his own thoughts with his bear-cuffed staff,
> swimming nude, unbuttoned, sick
> of his ghost-written rhetoric!

The poem ends with a generalized plea against all war, but listeners could not help but hear the relevance to their own decade's aggression and imperialism:

> Pity the planet, all joy gone
> from this sweet volcanic cone;
> peace to our children when they fall
> in small war on the heels of small
> war—until the end of time
> to police the earth, a ghost
> orbiting forever lost
> in our monotonous sublime.

Other poems in the volume also take swipes at the American military. In Lowell's imitation of Juvenal's **"The Vanity of Human Wishes,"** the poet rewrites the classic to make it more topical and pertinent to his own decade:

> barbarian commanders march; for these they
> pledge their lives
> and freedom—such their thirst for fame, and such
> their scorn of virtue.
> For who wants a life
> a virtue without praise? Whole nations die
> to serve the glory of a few; all lust for honors . . .

Even more remarkable than the overt politics of the poems it contained was the physical appearance of the volume itself. ***Near the Ocean*** looked like, as a handful of reviewers dared mention, "a coffee table book." At 10 inches by 8 inches, it was larger than a standard-sized collection of poetry; Sidney Nolan had illustrated the poems with impressionistic pen-and-ink drawings; the lines were double spaced and the pages held at most sixteen lines—a markedly unserious and unliterary format. While the poems of ***Near the Ocean*** may or may not stand with his best work, in the context of Lowell's career, the appearance of a coffee table book is a significant piece of literary history. This volume evidences just how much Lowell labored to influence the wider culture; and more important, perhaps, the critical reception of the volume reveals the fate of the literary artist who struggles to satisfy a commercial market. Lowell's biographer cautiously suggests that Lowell may have decided to issue a new collection of poetry at this stage of his career because "he felt himself to be at something of a dead end, or that the public or occasional aspects of poems like **'Waking Early Sunday Morning'** made him see the book as his timely contribution to the intensifying antiwar campaign." But in making his case so tentatively, Hamilton, like many Lowell scholars, underemphasizes the poet's commercial aspirations. Indeed, most critics have failed to recognize that ***Near the Ocean*** was Lowell's deliberate and premeditated attempt to ensconce his literary productions among the paraphernalia of the American household and to inscribe his message into American hearts and minds. Instead, the book has been viewed as an anomaly, virtually wished out of existence by supportive critics. To others, it has simply confirmed that Lowell's career was finished.

With the exception of Richard Howard, who, writing in *Poetry,* called the book "devastating" and **"Waking Early Sunday Morning"** a masterpiece, reviewers for high culture publications panned ***Near the Ocean.*** Helen Vendler, writing in the *Massachusetts Review,* called it sensationalistic, shrill, and full of doggerel. Charles Philbrick, in the *Saturday Review,* dubbed it "the disappointment of the season." David Kalstone generously noted in the *Partisan Review* that "the slick coffee-table design of the volume entirely misrepresents the poems, which, at their best, challenge things that are shiny and bright."

The reviewer for the *New Yorker,* Louise Bogan, condemned ***Near the Ocean*** for its "coldness and theatricality, its will towards pure shock and its horrifying illustrations that disqualify it as a coffee table object," although ultimately Bogan admits the book "is in that class." Explaining that a reviewer had "good reason to be annoyed with Robert Lowell's new book," Hayden Carruth, commenting in the *Hudson Review,* elaborated on its many commercial aspects:

> It is a pretentious volume; printed on expensive paper, bound in heavy cloth and stamped in three colors, decorated with twenty-one drawings, designed lavishly and wastefully in out-size format, jacketed in varnished sixty-pound stock—in short, a very self-conscious-looking collector's item. . . . The price has been announced progressively at $4.95, $5.50 and $6.00.

Despite the American literary establishment's dismay, ***Near the Ocean*** was widely and enthusiastically reviewed in both the British and American mass media. The *London Times* complained that "niggling critics were treating the book too harshly and that it was an important complement to [Lowell's] work"; Donald Davie, in the *Manchester Guardian Weekly,* said several poems were "elating and invigorating." In the American media, the book accumulated more plaudits: *Life* titled its review "The Poet as Folk Hero"; the *New York Times* and the *New York Herald Tribune Book Week* responded positively; and in the *Chicago Tribune of Books,* William Stafford claimed, that Lowell's new book had immediate relevance to the national mood.

Only *Life* magazine grasped the obvious: in ***Near the Ocean,*** Lowell's project had changed—he wanted to be a folk hero. No longer seeking to please the academician exclusively, Lowell tried his hand at poetry that advanced a political cause. Yet the critical reception of ***Near the Ocean*** proved that the large majority of reviewers for high culture publications could not tolerate Lowell's shift in intentions. Theatricality, doggerel; pretentious, sensationalistic: detractors used such descriptions to suggest that Lowell was no longer writing poetry worthy of serious attention. American critics, who had no criteria for the evaluation of, and no interest in, popular poetry, could only condemn a collection so blatantly commercial and aggressively political.

While the cultural revolution of the sixties opened a space for the critical recognition of certain popular art forms, it was not of the sort to accommodate ***Near the Ocean.*** Poetry designed exclusively for success in the political and commercial market not only suffered the slings and arrows of elite culture; it could not survive in a de-politicized mass culture. A modest fad in the sixties, Lowell's poetry soon succumbed to the fate of most timely products. By 1970, the anti-war movement had lost its steam with the election of Richard Nixon and the slow withdrawal of American troops. Lowell's politics and his poetry had outlived their usefulness. ***Near the Ocean*** was out of print by the early seventies, and in the 1990s critics dismiss the collection as containing his least important poetry.

Yet the volume is central to an understanding both of Lowell's ambitions and conflicts and of the relationship between poetry and American culture. ***Near the Ocean*** marks the apex of a personal career perched on the brink of marketplace success, and, however fleetingly, it also represents a rare phenomenon in recent literary history: an academically credentialed, canonical poet exerting wide cultural influence and political leadership. On its own terms, ***Near the Ocean*** succeeded. It demonstrated that poetry could be relevant; it brought Lowell and his politics before the public; and it provided, with **"Waking Early Sunday Morning,"** a poetic cry to ignite and rally war resisters.

Despite these notable accomplishments, Lowell would never think of himself as a success. He had gained cultural prominence and political stature, but he had sacrificed too much. In a sonnet for Robert F. Kennedy, composed in 1968, Lowell had written, "For them like a prince, you daily left your tower / to walk through dirt in your best clothes. Untouched." In 1964, Lowell had considered himself to be like Shaw, an aristocrat bending down to carry the people towards glory. But by 1968, Lowell's clothes, supposedly unlike those of Shaw and the equally heroic aristocrat RFK, *were* dirty; Lowell had tumbled farther into the ditch than he had believed possible. Literary critics had turned their backs on him; RFK had been assassinated; the anti-war movement had spawned its own regrettable violence; and he had been dragged into one distasteful partisan controversy after the next in which his motives and his methods were impugned. Indeed, "his commitment to see the whole thing through" waned as the anti-war movement wound down and as he became a target for "New Left" bashers. Diana Trilling and Lowell had argued in the politically conservative pages of *Commentary.* Their acrimonious volley extended for several months and encompassed more than just their disagreement about the United States' involvement in the Vietnam War. Trilling had attacked Lowell for his "grandstanding" and "opportunism" during the student strikes at Columbia, and Lowell was deeply troubled by her reproach, the violence that erupted at Columbia during the demonstrations, and the critical indifference to his work.

But just as the critics forsook Lowell after ***Near the Ocean,*** he forsook them, and the general reading audience as well. A poet who until this point catered to critical trends and anticipated, public appetites, Lowell used his last three volumes to chasten himself for fashioning his career to win public approval. Thus, after accomplishing what he always thought he wanted—securing a podium to preach his convictions and a popular audience to appreciate his poetry—Lowell retreated to a manor house in England. Like a wounded warrior at the end of a ravaging and futile battle, he repudiated the national crusade. And his bitterness towards the critics he believed had misunderstood him and the American public he thought had abandoned him haunt the final poems of his career.

FURTHER READING

Criticism

Axelrod, Steven G. "Robert Lowell and the New York Intellectuals." *English Language Notes* XI, No. 3 (March 1974): 206-9.

Discusses Lowell's response to critical attacks in his poem "The New York Intellectuals."

Bromwich, David. "Reading Robert Lowell." *Commentary* 52, No. 2 (August 1971): 78-83.

Provides an overview of Lowell's literary career, major works, and critical reception.

Brumleve, Eric Marie. "Permanence and Change in the Poetry of Robert Lowell." *Texas Studies in Literature and Language* X, No. 1 (Spring 1968); 143-53.

Examines Lowell's preoccupation with the "flux of experience" in his poetry, especially aspects of unity and multiplicity surrounding his presentation of time, death, and history.

Doherty, Paul C. "The Poet As Historian: 'For the Union Dead' by Robert Lowell." *Concerning Poetry* 1, No. 2 (Fall 1968): 37-41.

Examines Lowell's subjective response to the historical past in "For the Union Dead."

Eddins, Dwight. "Poet and State in the Verse of Robert Lowell." *Texas Studies in Literature and Language* XV, No. 2 (Summer 1973): 371-86.

Explores Lowell's political perspective and reaction to governmental power and contemporary historical events.

Hart, Henry. "Robert Lowell and the New Critical Sublime." *Southern Review* 28, No. 2 (April 1992): 353-70.

Examines Lowell's expression of the sublime in paradoxical aspects of power, evil, and war, especially as influenced by the literary theories of New Criticism.

———. "Robert Lowell and the Psychopathology of the Sublime." *Contemporary Literature* XXXII, No. 4 (Winter 1991): 496-519.

Explores Lowell's conception of the sublime and the personal and cultural significance of Oedipal conflicts in his poetry.

Hoffman, Michael. "The Accents of Adequate Praise." *Times Literary Supplement* (10 July 1987): 746-7.

A positive review of Lowell's *Collected Prose.*

Holloway, John. "Robert Lowell and the Public Dimension." *Encounter* XXX (April 1968): 73-9.

Offers positive assessment of *Near the Ocean,* drawing attention to Lowell's historical perspective and public concerns.

Lindsay, Geoffrey. "Robert Lowell's 'Common Novel Plot': Names, Naming, and Polyphony in *The Dolphin.*" *Dalhousie Review* 75, No. 3 (Winter 1996): 351-68.

Examines Lowell's undisguised incorporation of real people and their private communications in *The Dolphin.*

Logan, William. "Lowell in the Shadows." *New Criterion* 13, No. 4 (December 1994): 61-7.

Provides an overview of Lowell's life and literary career through review of Paul Mariani's biography *Lost Puritan: A Life of Robert Lowell* (1994).

Petersen, Donald. "The Legacy of Robert Lowell." *New Criterion* 1, No. 5 (January 1983): 9-29.

Provides an overview of Lowell's life and literary career through review of Ian Hamilton's *Robert Lowell: A Biography* (1982).

Tillinghast, Richard. "Robert Lowell on Native Ground." *Virginia Quarterly Review* 71, No. 1 (Winter 1995): 86-100.

Discusses Lowell's artistic preoccupations and offers personal recollection of Lowell as a poet and teacher at Harvard.

Veitch, Jonathan. "'Moondust in the Prowling Eye': The *History* Poems of Robert Lowell." *Contemporary Literature* XXXIII, No. 3 (Fall 1992): 458-79.

Examines Lowell's historical imagination and psychological themes in *History.*

Vendler, Helen. "The Poet and the City: Robert Lowell." In *Literature and the Urban Experience: Essays on the City and Literature,* edited by Michael C. Jaye and Ann Chalmers Watts, pp. 51-62. New Brunswick: Rutgers University Press, 1981.

Discusses the personal, historical, and aesthetic significance of urban settings and landscapes in Lowell's poetry.

Williamson, Alan. "Looking Back at Robert Lowell." *American Poetry Review* 24, No. 3 (May-June 1995): 35-8.

Provides an overview of Lowell's life and literary career through review of Paul Mariani's *Lost Puritan: A Life of Robert Lowell* and Richard Tillinghast's *Robert Lowell's Life and Work: Damaged Grandeur* (1995).

Additional coverage of Lowell's life and career is contained in the following sources published by Gale: *Contemporary Authors,* Vols. 9-12R, 73-76; *Contemporary Authors Bibliographical Series,* Vol. 2; *Contemporary Authors New Revision Series,* Vols. 26, 60; *Dictionary of Literary Biography,* Vols. 5, 169; *DISCovering Authors; DISCovering Authors: British; DISCovering Authors: Canadian; DISCovering Authors Modules: Most-Studied and Novelists; Major Twentieth Century Writers,* Vol. 1; *Poetry Criticism,* Vol. 3; *World Literature Criticism.*

Jean Rhys
1890-1979

West Indian-born English novelist, short story writer, and autobiographer.

The following entry presents an overview of Rhys's career through 1990. For further information on Rhys's life and works, see *CLC,* Volumes 2, 4, 6, 14, 19, and 51.

INTRODUCTION

With the publication of *Wide Sargasso Sea* (1966), a critically acclaimed reinterpretation of Charlotte Brontë's *Jane Eyre,* Jean Rhys suddenly emerged from more than two decades of obscurity. A noted Left Bank literary figure and author of four novels during the 1920s and 1930s, Rhys ceased to publish and disappeared from the public eye until her work was rediscovered in the late 1950s. Her highly regarded novels and short stories are distinguished for their spare, understated prose and complex psychological portraits of dispossessed though determined women who struggle unsuccessfully against poverty, loneliness, and humiliating dependencies on loveless men. Praised as a master stylist, Rhys is also identified as a powerful commentator on the exploitative social structures and sexual power dynamics that reduce women to despondency and self-abasement.

Biographical Information

Born Ella Gwendolen Rhys Williams in Dominica, a British-held island in the West Indies, Rhys was the fourth of five children of Rhys Williams, a Welsh physician, and Minna Lockhart, a Dominican Creole who descended from a long line of slaveholding planters. The island's lush tropical environment, native culture, and racist colonial legacy, particularly that of her maternal ancestors, was deeply imprinted in Rhys's psyche during her formative years. A lonely and introspective child, she received her early education at a Catholic convent school, where she began to write poetry and, for a time, wished to become a nun. At age sixteen Rhys left Dominica for England to live with her aunt in Cambridge and studied at the Academy of Dramatic Art beginning in 1908. When her father's death in 1910 deprived her of financial means, she refused to return to Dominica, opting instead to support herself as a chorus line girl and demimondaine. During the same year, she began an affair with Lancelot Smith, a well-stationed, middle-aged Englishman whose rejection in 1912, the first of several significant romantic betrayals in her life, caused Rhys to plunge into suicidal despair and a series of self-destructive liaisons. In 1919 Rhys married her first husband, John Lenglet, a Dutch writer, singer, and artist who, unknown to Rhys, doubled as a French intelligence agent and black market financier. The couple moved from Holland to Vienna, Paris, and Budapest during the early 1920s and had two children; only the second, daughter Maryvonne, survived infancy. Returning to Paris in 1924, Rhys was introduced to Ford Madox Ford, who adopted her as his protégé and exposed her to the expatriate literary circles of Gertrude Stein and Ernest Hemingway. Her first published work, an excerpt from the story "Suzy Tells" (renamed "Triple Sec"), appeared in the December 1924 issue of Ford's journal *Transatlantic Review.* When Lenglet was arrested and imprisoned for fraud, Rhys moved in with Ford and his girlfriend Stella Bowen, with whom she became enmeshed in an exploitative menage a trois. Rhys's sketches from the 1920s were collected and published as *Left Bank and Other Stories* (1927) with an enthusiastic introduction by Ford. Rhys then moved to Amsterdam with her newly released husband, though they separated before the publication of her first novel, *Postures* (1928), republished as *Quartet* the next year. Rhys left for London and moved in with literary agent Leslie Tilden Smith, whom she married in 1934. Though producing three additional novels during the 1930s, her most productive years, Rhys suffered increasingly from severe depression and alcoholism, causing her to cease writing after the publication of *Good Morning, Midnight* (1939). Following Smith's death in 1945, Rhys remarried his cousin, Max Hamer, and steadily declined in obscurity. She was briefly imprisoned in 1949 for attacking a neighbor in a drunken rage, and the next year Hamer was incarcerated for illegal financial dealings. However, interest in Rhys's writing was suddenly revived after actress Selma Vaz Dias contacted her to arrange an BBC radio adaptation of *Good Morning, Midnight,* which aired in 1957. With a new contract from Deutsch editor Francis Wyndham, Rhys returned to an early draft for the novel *Wide Sargasso Sea,* which she took six years to complete. Her efforts were rewarded with a W. H. Smith Award, Heinemann Award, and Arts Council of Great Britain Award for Writers in 1967. Rhys continued to write and publish new works until her death in 1979 at age eighty-four, including short stories in *Tigers are Better-Looking* (1968) and *Sleep It Off, Lady* (1976), and the three autobiographic sketches of *My Day* (1975). Her unfinished autobiography was posthumously published as *Smile Please* (1979).

Major Works

Rhys's trademark fiction is noted for its controlled detachment, shifting perspective, surreal episodes, laconic tone, and vivid psychological profiles of outcasted women. A typical Rhys heroine is a passive, emotionally fragile woman on the verge of homelessness and destitution who clings desperately to a façade of respectability and her ever failing feminine charms. Though not strictly autobiographic, much of Rhys's fiction draws directly from events and circumstances in her own life—particularly her Caribbean upbringing, her precarious existence on the fringes of London and Parisian society, and unhappy relationships with various men. *The Left Bank and Other Stories* consists of impressionistic fragments and vignettes that describe bohemian life in Paris during the 1920s, introducing the distinct style, themes, and victimized female prototypes of her subsequent fiction. The story "La Grosse Fifi," for example, relates the demise of an aging, self-conscious woman who is murdered by the young gigolo she selflessly supports. *Quartet* is a fictionalized version of Rhys's relationship with Ford during the mid-1920s; the original title, *Postures,* was used at the publisher's insistence to prevent against a libel suit. Set in Paris, the novel revolves around protagonist Marya Zelli, a former chorus girl who is helpless and alone after her reckless husband, Stephen, is jailed. Befriended by H. J. and Lois Heidler, a middle-aged couple who offer comfort and security, Marya soon becomes entangled in a manipulative love triangle that reveals the predatory nature of her male host and the self-serving passivity of his wife. Through recurring metaphors and dreamlike imagery that contrast with the narrative's realism, Rhys evokes an atmosphere of entrapment and disorientation that corresponds to Marya's psychic decline and attendant issues of moral ambiguity. Even more pessimistic than *Quartet, After Leaving Mr. Mackenzie* chronicles the dissolution of Julia Martin, an abandoned, profligate woman whose daily survival depends upon the reluctant generosity of friends and former lovers. Rejected by the title character, Julia leaves Paris for London, where she visits her sister Norah and enters into a failed relationship with Mr. Horsfield. Norah's role as the dutiful caretaker for their dying mother is contrasted with Julia's reckless drinking and promiscuity. Returning to Paris, Julia finally confronts Mr. Mackenzie, whose condescension and cruelty toward her reflects the contemptible status of women in patriarchal society. Through distancing techniques and shifting narratorial perspectives, Rhys examines the imposture and self-deception that dominate relations between the sexes. *Voyage in the Dark,* derived from Rhys's early notebooks, traces the emotional deterioration of protagonist Anna Morgan, a naïve, Dominican chorus girl who finds temporary security in an affair with an older Englishman named Walter. When Anna is cast off by Walter, she descends into a vagabond existence and prostitution, resulting in a life-threatening abortion. The first person narrative relates Anna's cycle of despair and delirium though memory sequences and imagery that juxtapose the vibrant environment of her tropical childhood with the cold desolation of England. *Good Morning, Midnight* features Sasha Jansen, a composite of Rhys's previous protagonists, though older and further bereft. Set in Paris on the eve the Second World War, the novel follows Sasha's efforts to recuperate from the death of her infant child and a failed marriage. She is pursued by a charming gigolo, René, whom she spurns, and finally succumbs to an ambiguous sexual encounter with her neighbor. As in earlier novels, Rhys blurs the division between hallucination and reality, past and present, through the interplay of memory, self-conscious meditation, and imagistic description of the external world. Unlike the contemporary European settings of her previous novels, *Wide Sargasso Sea,* an interpretative prequel to Brontë's *Jane Eyre,* is set almost entirely in the West Indies during the mid-nineteenth-century. Through alternating first person perspectives, the complex narrative recounts the traumatic Caribbean childhood of Antoinette Mason and her marriage to an unnamed Englishman whose repressive temperament further weakens her fragile mental state. Their strained relationship is reflected in the foreboding tropical atmosphere, voodoo curses, and the pervasive threat of violent reprisal by the island's newly emancipated slaves. In the last section of the novel, Antoinette accompanies her husband to England, where it is revealed that he is Edward Rochester, Jane Eyre's beloved, and that Antoinette represents Bertha, Rochester's mad first wife who is secretly locked in the attic.

Critical Reception

Since the resurrection of Rhys's literary career in the late

1960s, critical reevaluation of her fiction has focused primarily on *Wide Sargasso Sea.* Generally regarded as her most significant work, *Wide Sargasso Sea* is praised for its haunting tropical setting, facile appropriation of Brontë's plot and characters, insightful critique of Western imperialism, and stark evocation of psychological isolation. The novel has also received comparison to the work of Ann Radcliffe, Edgar Allen Poe, and William Faulkner for its gothic tone. Rhys's four prewar novels, though well received upon their original publication, have only recently begun to attract serious critical scrutiny. As with *Wide Sargasso Sea,* they are praised for their penetrating studies of female alienation, technical virtuosity, bitter irony, and multilevel themes surrounding male-female relationships and the construction of female self-identity. Though often overlooked as an innovative modernist writer, many critics note similarities between Rhys's terse, direct style and that of Hemingway. Commentators frequently draw attention to Rhys's disturbing treatment of victimized women and the social significance of their suffering and acquiescence. While some critics dismiss her heroines as self-pitying and sentimental, most appreciate their depth and emotional complexity. Feminist scholars in particular find in Rhys's fiction a prescient elucidation of female persecution and anxiety in a male-dominated society. As Rosalind Miles notes, "Through the power of her analysis, Jean Rhys was one of the few women writers able to make explicit the link between the sex war and the class struggle." Despite the highly personal nature of her fiction, *Smile Please,* Rhys's unfinished autobiography, received unfavorable reviews for failing to provide greater insight into the author's life.

PRINCIPAL WORKS

The Left Bank and Other Stories (short stories) 1927
Postures [republished as *Quartet,* 1929] (novel) 1928
After Leaving Mr. Mackenzie (novel) 1931
Voyage in the Dark (novel) 1934
Good Morning, Midnight (novel) 1939
Wide Sargasso Sea (novel) 1966
Tigers Are Better-Looking (short stories) 1968
My Day: Three Pieces (prose) 1975
Sleep it Off, Lady (short stories) 1976
Smile Please: An Unfinished Autobiography (autobiography) 1979
The Collected Short Stories (short stories) 1987

CRITICISM

Anthony E. Luengo (essay date April 1976)

SOURCE: "*Wide Sargasso Sea* and the Gothic Mode," in *World Literature Written in English,* Vol. 15, No. 1, April, 1976, pp. 229-45.

[*In the following essay, Luengo discusses gothic themes and motifs in* Wide Sargasso Sea, *especially the significance of landscape, the occult, and the characterization of victim and villain. "In the final analysis," writes Luengo,* "Wide Sargasso Sea *must be read as a novel about anxiety.*"]

Critics have so far failed to place ***Wide Sargasso Sea*** within its proper literary context, the Gothic mode of fiction. This is not to say that it should be considered a Gothic novel in the traditional and strictest sense of the term. More than time separates its author from the late eighteenth century world of such quintessentially Gothic novelists as Ann Radcliffe and "Monk" Lewis. Nowhere as sentimental as Radcliffe, much less sensationalistic than Lewis, Rhys moves much deeper than either into the unstable mental world of her characters, much as Charlotte and Emily Brontë were to do when they helped to transform the tired clichés and conventions of the Gothic into powerful tools for exploring the turbid depths of the human spirit.

One might perhaps hazard the term "neo-Gothic" to describe novels such as *Jane Eyre, Wuthering Heights,* ***Wide Sargasso Sea*** and the numerous American writers of fiction from Charles Brockden Brown through Hawthorne, Poe and Melville to Faulkner, Capote and McCullers who, as one important commentator on the "American Gothic" sub-species puts it, deal:

> . . . with the exaggerated and the grotesque, not as they are verifiable in any external landscape or sociological observation of manners and men, but as they correspond in quality to our deepest fears and guilts as projected in our dreams or lived through in "extreme situations."

It is tempting, of course, to use the term "Caribbean Gothic" with reference to ***Wide Sargasso Sea*** but in the absence of a body of West Indian writing in a similar vein, the term remains largely meaningless. The novel must therefore be discussed within the wider context of the Gothic tradition. While no definite sources can be accurately pinned down, one finds in Rhys much that is reminiscent of writers as widely separated in time and place as Emily Brontë and William Faulkner. In recognizing such similarities, one is simply recognizing the literary richness of the novel.

Like all novels in the Gothic and neo-Gothic mode, ***Wide Sargasso Sea*** is remarkable in its evocation of landscape. Both narrators of the novel evince, to slightly paraphrase Ramchand, a "sensuous feel" for a land that is at once overpoweringly beautiful and mysteriously menacing. At the most superficial level this makes the work intoxicatingly "atmospheric." Colours and smells predominate as indeed they do in the many scenes of pastoral charm strewn throughout Radcliffe's writings. Compare, for example, Rochester's account of his sensations as he stands on the veranda of the honeymoon retreat at Granbois for the first time with one of Radcliffe's typical descriptions of the Mediterranean lowlands at the foot of the Alps. Here is Rochester:

> Standing on the veranda I breathed the sweetness of the air. Cloves I could smell and cinnamon, roses and orange blossom. And an intoxicating freshness as if all this had never been breathed before.

Here is Radcliffe's more mannered prose:

> The gay tints of cultivation once more beautified the landscape; for the lowlands were coloured with the richest hues, which a luxuriant climate, and an industrious people can awaken into life. Groves of orange and lemon perfumed the air, their ripe fruit glowing among the foliage; while, sloping to the plains, extensive vineyards spread their treasures.

But even as unprofound a writer as Radcliffe attempts to make her carefully wrought landscape pictures perform more than merely a decorative function. In short, her landscapes are made to convey, in however uncomplex a way, the subjective states of her characters, especially those of her overly sensitive young heroines such as Emily (*The Mysteries of Udolpho*): gloomy, precipitous heights reflect her terror, sunlit, gentle valley slopes and pasturelands her peace of soul. This "projective method" of landscape description, as we have already noted above, becomes a valuable tool in the hands of neo-Gothic writers in England and America, and Rhys, working in the same tradition, uses it to great effect. As Rochester ascends towards Granbois (shades of Emily ascending to the gloomy pile of Montoni's castle!), the sense of impending danger is conveyed thus:

> The road climbed upward. On one side the wall of green, on the other a steep drop to the ravine below. We pulled up and looked at the hills, the mountains and the blue-green sea. There was a soft warm wind blowing but I understood why the porter had called it a wild place. Not only wild but menacing. These hills would close in on you.

The subjective nature of landscape description in the novel has been recognized by Ramchand though, ever preoccupied with psycho-historical factors, he fails to acknowledge Rhys's indebtedness to Gothic and neo-Gothic fiction for the method. Thus the dense tropical forest which symbolises the increasing gloom and confusion of Rochester's mind should be seen as a latter-day descendent of the many dark woods that appear in the novel's late eighteenth and early nineteenth-century literary ancestors. In desperate search of the truth, Rochester moves through the forest:

> I had reached the forest and you cannot mistake a forest. It is hostile. The path was overgrown but it was possible to follow it. I went on without looking at the tall trees on either side. . . . How can one discover truth I thought and that thought led me nowhere. . . . I found that the undergrowth and creepers caught at my legs and the trees closed over my head. . . .

The sense of menace is here more pronounced that it is in similar scenes in Radcliffe owing, I feel, to the greater importance given the function of the forest in neo-Gothic fiction, especially as it developed in America. Fiedler makes the point that the haunted forest provided a handy solution to a basic problem that faced the Gothic in the New World: what to substitute for the centuries-old castle of the European Gothic writers? Hawthorne, perhaps the most quintessential of American Gothic writers, exploits to the full the symbolic implications of the dark forest in such superb allegories on the nature of good and evil as *The Scarlet Letter* and "Young Goodman Brown." Rhys's technique is much the same: her Caribbean jungles at once provide a strikingly visual and textured terror and a convenient mirror in which to reflect the inner turmoil of her two main characters. Thus we can trace Rochester's changing moods by his "changing attitudes to a seemingly changing land." Antoinette, in contrast, is unnervingly consistent in her view of the forest: it is an absolutely diabolical force that presses close on the walls of her Edenic garden (her recurring erotic dream at the convent), and which, in fact, is seen at one point early in the narrative to actually overwhelm the garden at her beloved Coulibri:

> Our garden was large and beautiful as that garden in the Bible—the tree of life grew there. But it had gone wild. . . . Underneath the tree ferns, tall as forest tree ferns, the light was green. Orchids flourished out of reach or for some reason not to be touched. One was snaky looking. . . .

As in American Gothic then, nature, especially in its wilder aspects, takes on in ***Wide Sargasso Sea*** the importance that had in original Gothic fiction been given to architecture. In his vastly informative if not very profound history of the Gothic novel, Montague Summers rightly stresses the central role played by the many castles, manors, convents and abbeys in the novels of Walpole, Radcliffe, Lewis and the many less adept practitioners of Gothic fictional art. By the time of the Brontës, architecture (Wuthering Heights, Thornfield Hall) takes second place to the portrayal of character, especially as reflected in the natural landscape. In

America, Poe liberated neo-Gothic fiction even further from the confines of the original "haunted castle." Not surprisingly, ***Wide Sargasso Sea*** provides little in the way of haunted interiors. Coulibri is, if anything, a place of refuge for Antoinette from the outside darkness, as indeed is the convent in its own morbid way, ". . . my refuge, a place of sunshine and of death." The shabby cottage at Granbois is more pathetic than frightening, ". . . more awkward than ugly, a little sad as if it knew it couldn't last," though at times one can feel Rhys pushing description in the direction of the traditional Gothic:

> But the feeling of security had left me. I looked round suspiciously. The door into her room could be bolted, a stout wooden bar pushed across the other. This was the last room in the house. . . . I went back into the dressing-room and looked out of the window. I saw a clay road. . . . Beyond the road various half-hidden outbuildings.

One quality that Coulibri and Granbois very definitely share is their extraordinary remoteness, a geographical isolation which, of course, symbolises the spiritual separation of the protagonists from the mainstays of normality. Antoinette's mother suffers because of the isolation of Coulibri (her favourite word is "marooned"), and this eventually turns her mad. Granbois is even more remote, high in the hills, shut in by the forest, on an island inhabited, according to Antoinette, by four "hermits."

The presence of ruins in ***Wide Sargasso Sea*** should also be seen in terms of the book's literary ancestry. As in the European Gothic novel, they are expressive not so much of the end of a feudal order (in the West Indian context, the plantation system) as they are of a romantic statement of deeper, more universal significance of the kind made by Radcliffe in the following passage:

> The view of the ruins was very striking; the three chief masses, great and solemn, without being beautiful. They spoke at once to the imagination, with the force and simplicity of truth, the nothingness and brevity of this life—"generations have beheld us and passed away, as you now behold us and shall pass away: they thought of the generations before them as you now think of them, and as future ages shall think of you. We have witnessed this, yet we remain; the voices that revelled beneath us are heard no more, yet the winds of Heaven still sound in our ivy."

Much the same kind of romantic, contemplative mood (though much more is left implied than actually stated) descends on Rochester in the midst of his desperate trek through the forest referred to above:

> Here were the ruins of a stone house and round the ruins rose trees that had grown to an incredible height. At the back of the ruins a wild orange tree covered with fruit, the leaves a dark green. A beautiful place. And calm—so calm that it seemed foolish to think or plan.

The ruins, to be sure, fulfill a definite purpose in the narrative: they embody the increasingly terrifying enigma of Antoinette, her ancestry and her island which Rochester is finding he cannot solve. At the same time, the almost mind-annihilating calm which they momentarily induce in him broaden the meaning of the scene: what is suggested, I believe, is a Radcliffean or romantic apprehension of mutability.

Brief yet striking, the "ruins scene" in ***Wide Sargasso Sea*** is typical of the economic and effective use that Rhys makes of the conventional machinery of the Gothic. Her narrative remains uncluttered with the prodigious use of much of the traditional claptrap. Fearsome approaching footsteps; shadowy figures and flickering lights in the dark; strange voices and music form out of nowhere; mysterious portraits; doors suddenly slamming or grating bloodcurdlingly on their rusty hinges: all that is left out. Tempestuous atmospheric conditions in which, as one historian of the Gothic has correctly noted, the Gothic spirit delighted, makes an appearance only once (and this in the hurricane zone!).

One must not forget either the moon which inevitably provided the dim illumination for the Gothic night as, for example, in the following passage from Lewis's *The Monk,* a description rich with the stock ingredients of the traditional Gothic:

> The castle, which stood full in my sight, formed an object equally awful and picturesque. Its ponderous walls, tinged by the moon with solemn brightness; its old and partly ruined towers, lifting themselves into the clouds. . . .

Rhys does not indulge in such stagey effects, but rather connects the moon with terrifying intimacy to the subjective states of her two main characters. Thus Antoinette relates to Rochester the incident in which she sleeps in a hammock on the veranda under the full moon. She concludes the account with the question:

> "Do you think that too," she said, "that I have slept too long in the moonlight?"

The question is indirect but its meaning is nonetheless clear. Rhys is consistent in her application of the moon image to Antoinette, the climactic and most horrifying flicker (superbly pinpointing her deteriorated mental state) coming when Rochester refers in the final section of his narration to her "blank hating moonstruck face." The same consistency of application holds with regard to Rochester, though the moon takes on a different resonance in his case. It is made to express his sense of desperate alienation, "Not night or darkness as I knew it but night with blazing stars, an alien moon. . . ." He also associates it with the heavily scented river flowers which hold promise of an intense, almost self-annihilating dark sexuality:

> I was longing for night and darkness and the time when the moonflowers open.
>
> Blot out the moon,
> Pull down the stars.
> Love in the dark, for we're for the dark
> So soon, so soon.

Rhys has here moved way beyond the calculated theatricality of the traditional Gothic. To her credit, she comes close in spirit at this point to that outstanding achievement of nineteenth century neo-Gothic, Emily Brontë's *Wuthering Heights.*

Rhys's use and control of the machinery of, what Summers has called, the "terror-Gothic" is even more remarkable in the area of magic and superstition. Here she makes more lavish use of the materials available to her but they are at no time allowed to get out of hand. She completely avoids both the lurid diablerie of Lewis's *The Monk* and the reneging "explained supernatural" of Radcliffe. In ***Wide Sargasso Sea*** discussion of obeah revolves around the figure of Christophine. As a child, Antoinette hears the talk of the other servants concerning Christophine's supposed necromantic activities and, not surprisingly, her already fevered imagination conjures up terrors whenever she enters the servant's room:

> I was certain that hidden in the room (behind the old black press?) there was a dead man's dried hand, white chicken feathers, a cock with its throat cut, dying slowly, slowly. Drop by drop the blood was falling into a red basin and I imagined I could hear it.

This is as sensational as Rhys ever becomes in her treatment of obeah (and this is purely *imagined*). Antoinette sees "the girls from the bay-side" bringing suspicious offerings of fruit and vegetables to Christophine, and seemingly more reliable proof of evil doings comes to Rochester in the warning of Daniel and the letter from Fraser. But Daniel's vindictiveness and Fraser's vague reference to Christophine's "nonsense" make their testimony not very trustworthy. Even when Antoinette turns in desperation to Christophine for some kind of magical cure to the unbearable tensions between Rochester and herself, the reader is not made privy to the consultation; the sly words of Christophine are calculatedly chosen to create a sense of ambiguity:

> "So already you frightened eh?" And when I saw her expression I took my purse from my pocket and threw it on the bed.
>
> "You don't have to give me money. I do this foolishness because you beg me—not for money."
>
> "Is it foolishness?" I said, whispering and she laughed again, but softly.
>
> "If *béké* say it foolishness, then it foolishness. *Béké* clever like the devil. More clever than God. Ain't so? Now listen and I will tell you what to do."

We never in fact hear what Antoinette is told. We only know that she departs with something wrapped in a leaf "cold and smooth" against her skin, some kind of natural drug as it turns out which she gives to Rochester in a glass of wine. But this is hardly black magic. Far from being a wicked devil-woman in the mould of Lewis's Matilda (*The Monk*) Christophine comes across as the most sane, perceptive and dignified character in the novel. If she does dabble in obeah, we can surmise that it is mainly for practical purposes, her forte a kind of natural bush medicine for which the authorities (quite irrationally) have little sympathy.

Obeah is also used in the novel to heighten the enigma of Antoinette and her island which, as pointed out above, disorients Rochester. Thus when he comes upon the ruins of the stone house in the forest, he finds propitiatory bunches of flowers strewn on the ground; questioning the unsmiling Baptiste soon after he receives only brief, elusive answers. In this way then Rhys, as with the figure of Christophine, makes her materials narratively purposeful and essential to the thematic import of her fiction.

Still drawing upon elements from the realm of magic and superstition, Rhys puts to good service that eerie visitant to the nighttime world of the Gothic and neo-Gothic—the ghost. To be sure, she does not, as Lewis does, present us with actual ghosts. Neither does she follow the practice of Gothic writers like Walpole and Radcliffe who, as Railo has correctly noted, talk a lot about ghosts (especially hinting at their imminent appearance), but never actually introduce them. Radcliffe's ghosts, like so much else that is apparently supernatural in her work, are either explained away or discussed in the spirit of eighteenth century rationalism as, for example, in the discussion between the Baron de Saint Foix and Count De Villefort in the last volume of *The Mysteries of Udolpho.*

For Rhys a ghost is a mental phenomenon, the product, like Macbeth's dagger, of the "heat-oppressed brain." It thus becomes, like the landscape, an expression of the anguish of her main characters. In the midst of her recurring dream of conflagration at Thornfield Hall, Antoinette sees the ghost of a "woman with streaming hair . . . surrounded by a gilt frame but I knew her [her mother]." Antoinette herself becomes a ghost in the eyes of Rochester a death-in-life figure as she sinks deeper and deeper into madness:

> She was only a ghost. A ghost in the gray daylight. Nothing left but hopelessness. *Say die and I will die. Say die and watch me die.*

In becoming a ghost, she is becoming for Rochester one with her ancestors, themselves ghosts with their "White faces, dazed eyes, aimless gestures, high-pitched laughter." It is appropriate that Rochester should end his section of the narrative with such spectral images as he faces head-on the full horror of his situation.

In transforming the conventional machinery of the "terror-Gothic" Rhys gives new life as well to the conventions of characterization (in other words, to the stereotypes) of the Gothic and neo-Gothic that have come down to her. In her portrayal of Rochester and Antoinette she works with four important character types: the Gothic villain, the young hero, the "persecuted woman" or "maiden in flight," and the *femme fatale.* We must now discuss her use of these types before we can reach a conclusion concerning what the novel is ultimately all about.

The Gothic Villain, as many literary historians and critics have indicated, is the closest literary ancestor of the type that was to become known in the Romantic period as the "Byronic Hero." Rochester, as he is portrayed in *Jane Eyre,* comes definitely out of this mould: he has been a guilt-haunted wanderer, "harsh . . . grim . . . almost histrionically cynical," his face marked with the standard features of his type (prominent forehead, full, black, well-defined eyebrows and piercing dark eyes, grim mouth and chin, black whiskers). ***In Wide Sargasso Sea***, Rhys gives us a more youthful Rochester, an initially self-deluding, fortune-hunting Englishman who comes to a gradual and deeply unsettling realisation of his Creole wife's mental instability. As he first presents himself to us, he is a romantic suitor, ". . . I bowed, smiled, kissed her hand, danced with her," to outward appearances like many another colourless and virtuous young hero (more calculating than most, perhaps) from the world of Gothic and neo-Gothic fiction: Theodore and Edmund in *The Castle of Otranto,* Valancourt in *The Mysteries of Udolpho,* Edgar Linton in *Wuthering Heights* but to name a few. They serve in their respective novels as foils to the darker (and more memorable) personalities of Manfred, Montoni, Heathcliff and the many other Gothic villains and near villains who achieve a kind of apotheosis in Byron's work. In ***Wide Sargasso Sea,*** however, Rochester does not remain the young hero for long, as he pointedly states: "A short youth mine was." Subjected to shock after shock, he goes through a metamorphosis, not only psychologically in the direction of neurosis, but, from a purely literary standpoint, in the direction of the Gothic/Byronic villain/hero type.

A foreshadowing of the transformation that is to take place comes early in Rochester's narration when he sees himself as a Faustian figure:

> I have sold my soul or you [his father] have sold it, and after all is it such a bad bargain?

The reference is fleeting but no doubt calculated, introducing as it does the "diabolic bargain" (the willing choice of damnation) which, as Fiedler has perceptively pointed out, is at the center of the Gothic novel and its descendents. Later in the narrative, Christophine, in anger, accuses Rochester of being "wicked like Satan self," an accusation hardly justified in terms of the action itself, but which in the light of the literary tradition in which the author is working is highly connotative. Finally, there is Grace Poole's account of her reaction to Rochester's offer of extra remuneration for keeping the mad Antoinette: "I don't serve the devil for no money." Rochester has by this time become the Byronic figure, "misery in his eyes," who is much more fully developed in *Jane Eyre.* Rhys, it can be seen, had Brontë's Rochester very much in mind as she created her own version of the character. She is careful to have her Rochester anticipate what he is to become in later life and in another fiction. From the viewpoint of characterization then, Rhys's Rochester needs the complement of Charlotte Brontë's if he is to be fully understood.

Rhys's Antoinette, in contrast, has only the most tenuous relationship with the grotesquely insane "Bertha" of Brontë's novel. As depicted in ***Wide Sargasso Sea,*** she is not the type of raging mad woman, but rather a complex amalgam of two stock figures of Gothic and neo-Gothic fiction: the "persecuted woman" and the *femme fatale.*

The most immediate literary ancestor of the "persecuted woman" of Gothic fiction, as Praz has pointed out, was Richardson's Clarissa Harlowe, the gentle, virtuous, melancholic maiden, pursued, persecuted and seduced by the lecherous Lovelace. Walpole and Lewis retained the frankly sexual nature of the pursuit, though Radcliffe, not surprisingly, considerably toned down the erotic element. Typical of her general method, Rhys internalises the image of flight in order to make it speak of the terrible anguish of her heroine. She begins with the external, objective depiction of persecution and flight, the recurring scenes early in the book in which the hapless Antoinette is harassed by the recently freed blacks:

> I never looked at any strange negro. They hated us. They called us white cockroaches. Let sleeping dogs lie. One day a little girl followed me singing, "Go away white cockroach, go away, go away." I walked fast but she walked faster. "White cockroach, go away, go away. Nobody want you. Go away."

As the external menace gives way to a steadily deepening anxiety, the images become charged with eroticism, welling up in Antoinette's recurring nightmare in which she is followed into the forest near Coulibri by one man, "his face black with hatred." Antoinette exists, in effect, in a state of continuous flight, from the blacks, from Rochester himself (her initial resistance to marriage and, later on, her flight to Christophine), from the terrors of her own soul.

To be sure, Antoinette is more than merely a Radcliffean innocent in danger. The complexity of her characterization comes in Rhys showing her to be at once victim and *femme fatale.* In Rochester's eyes she becomes understandably very much the latter, a dangerous woman, like her ancestors before her, who must be watched:

> The way they walk and talk and scream or try to kill (themselves or you) if you laugh back at them. Yes, they've got to be watched. For the time comes when they try to kill. . . . She's one of them. . . .

As it is, she robs him of his youth and peace of soul (forgetting for the moment the happiness which he does eventually find in *Jane Eyre*). At one point in the narrative she even mocks his God:

> "You are always calling on God," she said. "Do you believe in God?"
>
> "Of course, of course I believe in the power and wisdom of my creator."
>
> She raised her eyebrows and the corners of her mouth turned down in a questioning mocking way.

This is not to call Antoinette Satanic after the fashion of, say, Lewis' Matilda: that would be to exaggerate, Matilda is presented as a witch, a woman actively in the service of the Devil. Rhys, as we have noted already, avoids Lewis' excesses. Her method is much more subtle. She creates around Antoinette, as she does around Rochester, a sense of damnation that grows naturally out of the narrative action. Again, a process of internalisation takes place: Antoinette is first told by the servants (early in the book, first by Godfrey, then by Myra) that she and her kind are destined to hell. In time, she herself comes to believe this, dreaming of damnation at the convent and even embracing it in fits of ecstatic self-condemnation:

> All the same, I did not pray so often after that and soon, hardly at all. I felt bolder, happier, more free. But not so safe.

But such moments of desperate, heaven-defying happiness predictably give way to a state of unrelieved inner torment from which her only release can be death:

> "Say die and I will die. You don't believe me? Then try, try, say die and watch me die."

In the final analysis, ***Wide Sargasso Sea*** must be read as a novel about anxiety. This is to be expected. As Praz has commented:

> . . . an anxiety with no possibility of escape is the main theme of the Gothic tales. . . .

But the anxiety conveyed in Rhys's novel goes much deeper than the shallow fears and terrors felt by the one-dimensional characters in the novels of Walpole, Radcliffe and Lewis. The anxiety that haunts Rochester and, especially, Antoinette is caused by the disintegration of the self. In Rochester's case an initial self-deluding confidence is rapidly undermined and he feels, for the first time in his life, a dreadful sense of alienation. In Antoinette's case the dilemma is stated specifically in terms of a crisis of identity:

> "It was a song about a white cockroach. That's me. That's what they call all of us who were here before their own people sold them to the slave traders. And I've heard English women call us white niggers. So between you I often wonder who I am and where is my country and where do I belong and why I was ever born at all."

One is reminded here of the character of Joe Christmas in Faulkner's *Light in August* who, like Antoinette, lives in a nightmare world because he does not know who he is or where he belongs. To create this nightmare of identity adrift, both Faulkner and Rhys make imaginatively powerful and deeply meaningful use of the conventions of the Gothic mode. Thus, like all good writers, they at once relate to literary tradition and make a statement that is relevant to their own time.

Dennis Porter (essay date Autumn 1976)

SOURCE: "Of Heroines and Victims: Jean Rhys and *Jane*

Eyre," in *Massachusetts Review,* Vol. XVII, No. 3, Autumn, 1976, pp. 540-52.

[*In the following essay, Porter examines Rhys's portrayal of alienated and dispossessed female protagonists and the interrelationship of* Wide Sargasso Sea *and* Jane Eyre.]

Between 1927 and 1939 Jean Rhys published four novels and a collection of short stories. The novels all have in common a central figure who is an alienated woman and a modern setting, chiefly the years between the two world wars in Paris and London. Whether or not they are actually written in the first person, they adopt the point of view of their solitary heroines, of women who are more or less attractive and more or less mature, but who remain enigmatic and remote. Dependent on but invariably abandoned by men, they seem obscurely destined to drift from man to man and from one dingy hotel room to another. Although they come close to breakdown—this is most apparent in the fortyish Sasha Jansen of ***Good Morning, Midnight***—the novels end characteristically with an abrupt gesture that stops the action short before breakdown can occur. Such, however, is not the case with Jean Rhys's latest heroine, the first wife of Charlotte Bronte's Rochester. In the remarkably new departure in her art that is ***Wide Sargasso Sea,*** which was first published in England in 1966, Jean Rhys follows her central character beyond the self-imposed limits of her earlier fiction and, as a result, gives fresh significance to her whole *oeuvre.* At the same time she subjects *Jane Eyre* itself to a provocatively new critical reading.

As Ford Madox Ford observed on the occasion of the publication of her earliest volume of short stories in 1927, Jean Rhys naturally assumes the point of view of the underdog. In her latest novel it is point of view she consciously carries to an extreme. If all her heroines are in one way or other victims of men, the mad captive of Thornfield Hall is interpreted as the most hideous example of the power exercise by men over women. Jean Rhys's implied point of departure for ***Wide Sargasso Sea*** is Charlotte Bronte's description of Bertha Rochester as seen properly for the first time by Jane Eyre:

> In the deep shade, at the farther end of the room, a figure ran backward and forwards. What it was, whether beast or human being, one could not at first sight tells it grovelled, seemingly, on all fours; it snatched and growled like some strange wild animal: but it was covered with clothing, and a quantity of dark, grizzled hair, wild as a mane, hid its face.

Such "madness" is accepted by Jane Eyre, though not altogether by her author, as a given. The subhuman creature is explained in terms of a degenerate heredity; she is the mad daughter of a mad mother. But Jean Rhys takes us back to the beginnings of the journey that led from birth in Jamaica to the attic cell at Thornfield. The thematic continuity with Jean Rhys's preceding novels resides in the fact that she affirms in ***Wide Sargasso Sea*** that Bertha Rochester was not born mad but made so, and made so, both singly and collectively, by men.

Unlike her other novels with a contemporary setting, ***Wide Sargasso Sea*** derives its leading characters and their situation from another work of art. *Jane Eyre* provides the impulse for an imaginative *tour de force* and at the same time dictates a mode and a style that are new in Jean Rhys's fiction. This time she has written an historical novel with an exotic setting; in the words of a blurb on the paperback edition, it is "a novel of unforgettable romance and terror. A 'triumph' of Caribbean Gothic!" And the reasons for such a setting and such a mood are clear. In order to comment effectively on *Jane Eyre* and extend its meaning in previously unperceived ways, Jean Rhys had to create a novel that would be largely continuous with Charlotte Bronte's work in terms of style and period and would stand comparison with the original. Thus although ***Wide Sargasso Sea*** is not a fully autonomous novel because an understanding of its meaning depends on our knowledge of *Jane Eyre,* it achieves its purpose because it is a remarkable work of art in its own right.

To begin with, since in Jean Rhys's striking interpretation the anguish which only ends with the burning of Thornfield has its origins in the realities of colonial society, she had to find a way of suggesting the deep differences and the hidden connections between nineteenth-century England and the Antilles. The Gothic of moor and manor in *Jane Eyre* had to be set off against the lush and stranger horror of the Caribbean islands during the heyday of colonialism. And just as Charlotte Bronte found it appropriate to use the first person in order to heighten the suggestiveness of her work, so Jean Rhys recreates the islands in the consciousness of her two narrators. She invents a prose not for Jane Eyre but for the first Mrs. Rochester and Rochester himself, one that would differentiate their voices from each other and from that of Charlotte Bronte's heroine. The nature of the Creole girl and of the husband she will share with the English governess are to be revealed as significantly different from the way they seem in the original work.

As a result, there emerges a subtle analysis of the relations between the sexes in the age of colonialism, of the multiple hidden connections among class, race, and sex. That Jane Rhys succeeds so well is due in the first place to a use of the language that is new for her. Thus, on the one hand, ***Wide Sargasso Sea*** often employs a lyricism that is resolutely avoided in the novels set between the wars, but it is a functional lyricism that incorporates both beauty and terror and simultaneously defines the limited consciousness of the two narrators. The speech of the girl who will become the first Mrs. Rochester is generally swift and elliptical. It is in no way that of a madwoman, but is shaped by the author to suggest the naivete and the hope, the terrors and the longings that haunt her.

On the other hand, at the same time that Jean Rhys invents a language that expresses the form and content of the consciousness of her two leading characters, she also uses extensively the Creole speech of the black population. Whether or not it is historically accurate insofar as it is a precise transcription of the spoken language of black Jamaicans and others in the nineteenth century, Jean Rhys's Creole convinces of its authenticity both because it possesses the characteristic of all pidgin and Creole language to simplify and eliminate redundancies in the standard language, and because it has the energy and precision of a vehicle that satisfies all the communication needs of its speakers. As used particularly by the black servant, Christophine, and by Antoinette Cosway's self-proclaimed half-brother, Daniel Mason, it establishes itself as an alien and powerful medium when set against the relatively pedestrian standard English of Rochester.

Central to Jean Rhys's vision of the nineteenth-century Antilles is her sense of the ubiquity of suspicion, fear, and hate. A colonial society that had institutionalized slavery means a society deeply divided according to a complicated caste system founded on gradations of skin color and place of birth. Colonialism fosters the myth of irreconcilable differences between groups, objectified, for the writer, in the very speech which is the medium of her art. Jean Rhys gives a specific concrete form to the knowledge that the history of colonialism is written into the varieties and levels of human speech. In the words of a contemporary linguist, the very existence of pidgins and Creoles is "largely due to the process—discovery, exploration, trade, conquest, slavery, migration, colonialism, nationalism—that have brought the peoples of Europe and the peoples of the rest of the world to share a common destiny."

That experience which is mirrored in language of races thrust together but culturally and socially separate within the same limited living space is also present in the earliest perceptions of the little girl whose life will end in Thornfield Hall in faraway England. Her earliest consciousness is of differentness and isolation. As a Creole girl whose mother is from another island, she is despised not only by blacks and the native-born English but also by the Creole ladies of Jamaica. She is a "white cockroach" to the former and a "white nigger" to the latter. For Antoinette Cosway, in the beginning is a sense of loss and degradation: though white, she is less than "English"; as the daughter of a former slave-owning planter, she is mocked by the ex-slaves as a poor white; finally, her mother rejects her female offspring in favor of the half-wit brother.

When Rochester comes into her life, she is an odd blend of knowledge and innocence, having perceived far more than she can fully apprehend. And Rochester's failure to care enough for the feelings and the fate of his vulnerable child-bride is represented by Jean Rhys as a paradigm of male cruelty towards women. For in her version, it is not Rochester who is the innocent party; it is not he who is deceived and trapped into an alliance with a mad heiress, but she who is sought out by a fortune hunter and his family, sexually exploited for a time, and when once she has grown dependent on his love and his lovemaking, rejected: ". . . you make love to her till she drunk with it, no rum could make her drunk like that, till she can't do without it. It's *she* can't see the sun anymore. Only you she see. But all you want is to break her up."

In ***Wide Sargasso Sea,*** therefore—and here the facts are taken straight from *Jane Eyre*—Rochester provides an example of how the colonial system operated for the benefit of England's established families. As the younger son of a father determined to preserve the integrity of his wealth and property by bequeathing it all to his first male child, Rochester is required to seek his own fortune by marrying the daughter of a wealthy plantation-owner from the West Indies. Marriage to Antoinette Cosway is looked upon as a business arrangement by means of which caste and class are traded off against a substantial sum of cash. The fortune of the plantation-owner's daughter is exported to the homeland after having first been "washed" through marriage into an appropriate family. Rochester's affluence will in part be founded on slavery.

If the fate of the first Mrs. Rochester is bound up with her colonial origins, as is barely hinted in *Jane Eyre,* it is also determined by the character of male sexuality and the cultural modes through which such sexuality finds expression. Rochester, of course, has been taken to be the most conventional figure in Charlotte Bronte's novel, an embodiment of the darkly brooding Byronic hero stricken with romantic melancholy, on the one hand, and as a wish-fulfillment figure, a dominant highly sexualized male, on the other. By the very fact that she adopts his point of view, Jean Rhys to some extent demythifies the figure; to see the West Indies through his eyes is to see what a relatively conventional and class-conscious nineteenth-century English gentleman might well have perceived. But Jean Rhys is not simply reductive. The journey to the Antilles to procure a rich wife is also in her handling a journey to Rochester's own heart of darkness—a journey for which even in *Jane Eyre* he will eventually be called to account.

The two themes of colonialism and male sexuality come together most strikingly during the meeting between Rochester and the demonic Daniel Mason. The latter's letter is by itself a brilliant piece of writing that suggests the profound deviousness and complex self-hate of the social outcast which turns him into an informer and a destroyer of other people's happiness. It is, in any case, Daniel Mason's function to play Iago to Rochester's swaggering Othello, only on this occasion, in terms of color, the roles are reversed. It is Daniel Mason who confirms the white male's buried fears in relation to his colonial bride. Thus, the concluding remarks of Rochester's embittered interlocutor reverberate in a mind that is suspicious both of his wife's blood and of her physical attractiveness: "'Give my love to your wife—my sister,' he called after me venomously. 'You are not the first to kiss her pretty face. Pretty face, soft skin, pretty colour—not yellow like me. But my sister just the same. . . .'"

Daniel Mason's claims mean that for Rochester his wife is double contaminated. In the first place, she is henceforth associated with the yellow-skinned Daniel; she is derived at the very least from a perverted source, from a lecherous, alcoholic father who had sexual relations with black women. In the second place, he is haunted with the idea that she was not pure but sexually experienced before he married her. The play on the word "pretty" suggests the psychic mechanism through which he will now reject her. Hers is a prettiness made squalid by his own obsessions, that face which had made her attractive to him is now her ugliest feature; since it arouses desire, it becomes the face of desire. To look at her is to be reminded of her double impurity. Therefore, since he cannot be rid of her, she will be shunned, broken and finally shut away.

Although the relationship of ***Wide Sargasso Sea*** to *Jane Eyre* is not entirely reciprocal—the one is fully autonomous, the other it not—there is reciprocity to the degree that Jean Rhys's novel constitutes a formidable critical essay on the nineteenth-century work. The modern author alerts us to latent meanings in the original that remind us of its singular power. ***Wide Sargasso Sea*** may develop hints from her own work in ways that would have surprised Charlotte Bronte, but it is the genius of the nineteenth-century novelist to have created a symbolic structure that accommodates itself easily to the insights of the twentieth-century writer. Now that the shibboleths of nineteenth-century realism have been discarded and the rather narrow modernist view of "the art of the novel" significantly modified, it is impossible to dismiss *Jane Eyre* patronizingly as a form of Gothic sport or as the wish fulfillment of frustrated sexuality. ***Wide Sargasso Sea*** pays homage to what modern French critics refer to as "the plurality" of substantial literary texts by bringing to consciousness some of the hidden implications of *Jane Eyre,* which it both develops and challenges.

To begin with, the secret that is for so long hidden away at Thornfield is finally revealed to Jane, but its meaning is not interpreted. From Jean Rhys's point of view, Jane Eyre's own question concerning the mystery receives no satisfactory answer in Charlotte Bronte's novel: "What crime was this, that lived incarnate in this sequestered mansion, and could neither be expelled nor subdued by the owner?—what mystery, that broke out, now in fire and now in blood, at the deadest hours of night? What creature was it, that, masked in an ordinary woman's face and shape, uttered the voice, now of a mocking demon, and anon of a carrion-seeking bird of prey?" Jean Rhys's answer, as has already been noted, is that the "creature" was once an ordinary woman, who had the misfortune to be raised in Jamaica in the 1830's and 1840's, a white planter's white daughter, who discovered she did not belong where she was born and had no place else to go, a woman put up for sale by one man and purchased for his own purposes by another.

In the light of ***Wide Sargasso Sea,*** the mad Bertha Rochester of *Jane Eyre* can be seen as a living image of Rochester's shame and guilt that he can neither destroy nor forget, though he has the power to lock it away out of sight of the world. As a member of the colonial *nouveaux riches,* she is felt to be inferior to England's fine old families; as a daughter of a former slave-owning plantation-owner, she is a living reminder of the sordid origins of his affluence; as an exotic and beautiful woman raised on a tropical island, she is associated with a sensuality that both tempts and torments Rochester; as a Creole, the racial purity of her blood will always remain suspect in Rochester's eyes. No wonder Thornfield (Thorn-field, Thorn-filled) appears so malevolent; its grandeur disguises greed and concupiscence and pride. The purifying fire that destroys it and the incarnation of Rochester's guilt is in *Jane Eyre* a necessary prelude to the harmonious relationship achieved at the end. Rochester has to be punished and Jane herself put to a further test before their successful union is possible. It is a remarkable tribute to the force of Charlotte Bronte's insights that in spite of her professed Toryism she intimates how the manor house is a monument raised on the foundation of human exploitation. For the sake of his soul Rochester has to give up his baronial dwelling, the symbol of a power rooted in sex and class arrogance.

The difference between Charlotte Bronte and Jean Rhys as far as Rochester is concerned is, first, that the latter explicitly adds race, where the former perceives sex and class, and second, that the modern author sees him as unredeemable, whereas her nineteenth-century predecessor demonstrates how he might be reformed. The harsh pessimism of Jean Rhys concerning relations between the sexes confronts a relative optimism in the Victorian author that is founded on faith in moral energy and the regenerative power of human feelings. Charlotte Bronte's mythic tale embodies the tragedy of an overreacher, a Byronic rebel, who like Faust himself is saved through the power of a woman's love. The robust originality of the English novelist's work, however, resides in the fact that her heroine is far more complex than Goethe's loving and passively suffering Gretchen, and if she avoids the fate of Jean Rhys's women, it is because in her own patiently determined was she learns how to resist and survive. It is paradoxically the Victoria author who furnishes the model of a woman who triumphs in a male dominated society, triumphs, moreover, in ways that are not attributable to authorial wish-fulfillment, but to a series of concrete choices that the heroine makes on the basis of her sense of what is right for herself.

Above all, the secret of Jane Eyre's triumph resides in her instinctive understanding of the fact that, especially when coupled with a sense of class superiority, male sexuality is a potentially destructive force. She is both drawn to and frightened by the energy of the wild rider who falls from his horse in an opening encounter that prefigures the end. But until what is merely a temporary physical disability in the beginning becomes a permanent condition of the whole man at the denouement, she never fully gives herself to Rochester. For a long time her apparent submissiveness as social inferior and as a woman disguises a determination not to submit to his will to possess and dominate. The sexual teasing to which she subjects him during the period of their first engagement is not simply a matter of Victorian hypocrisy. She does not shelter behind the exigencies of nineteenth-century morality merely to excite the more. The game she plays is vital, since it enables her to retain control over a potentially dangerous situation; it is dictated by an instinct for self-preservation. And the same thing is true of her decision not to become Rochester's mistress. To have yielded to him in that way would have been to give herself completely into his power. As the fate of Jean Rhys's Antoinette Cosway suggests, under such circumstances Rochester could not be trusted not to break what he so completely possessed.

It is not finally until Thornfield has been destroyed and Rochester has been obliged to put away the aggressive accoutrements of his sex and class—the horse and those weapons, spurs, boots and crop, by means of which one mounts and dominates it—that Jane Eyre finally consents to be his bride. Consequently, the blindness and maiming that Rochester experiences as a consequence of the burning of Thornfield are not simply a matter of his punishment for past sins—whether those committed in connection with Bertha, as Jean Rhys would have it, or, in the more conventional view, because of his decision to commit bigamy. Rochester has to be spiritually humbled and physically impaired before marriage between him and Jane Eyre on the basis of equality is possible.

The form the punishment takes is itself significant because it suggests that in Charlotte Bronte's work, too, the cause of the suffering in the past and its avoidance in the future are related to the character of Rochester's sexuality. The fire in the blood which drew him to his Creole wife and later to his foreign mistresses—to Parisian and Viennese women in the two contemporary European capitals of sexual pleasure—has to be controlled without being extinguished. Yet the idea of an asexual, passionless marriage that St. John Rivers proposes is felt by Jane Eyre to be as sad as the merely sexual unions that characterize Rochester's past. The implication is that love without sexual consummation is as destructive of human happiness as the sexual drive that seeks to dominate and humiliate and finds its ultimate expression in a rape. Sex, as both Charlotte Bronte and Jean Rhys remind us, *can be* dehumanizing and demonic. Consequently, Rochester loses the sight of those eyes which saw and in seeing, desired, and of one of the two hands that caressed and overpowered. From henceforth the only beauty he will experience is that which can be felt and heard; he will know only the warmth of a physical presence and the sweetness of a disembodied voice. Rochester's is such an extreme case that it requires the radical surgery of blindness before he can see fully through Jane's outward plainness in order to appreciate an inner beauty that is nevertheless of the body.

Whether or not we approve of all the implications of Rochester's impaired potency, Jane Eyre is no simple "castrating female." She is prepared to have Rochester only on terms of equality. Only a marriage founded on mutual respect and mutual need could hope to prove happy and durable. Before he could become a husband and a father—see in this respect his previous treatment of Adele—Rochester had first to suffer and to be taught how to love. In her novel of the orphan/governess turned wife, therefore, Charlotte Bronte creates one of the great portraits of women in literature, next to whom Jean Rhys's characters appear as almost willing victims. In Jane Eyre's extraordinary instinct for survival and self-affirmation, a balance is struck between spirited independence and loving solicitude, tough-mindedness and generosity. She has the strength of character to resist the power of men in a society dominated by men and to choose the right man a the right time on terms that fulfill her own deepest needs.

It may be, as ***Wide Sargasso Sea*** provocatively implies, that Jane Eyre's ultimate happiness is founded on the suffering of another woman that Bertha Rochester's madness and horrible death were necessary in order to chasten Rochester's male arrogance. There is certainly something uncharacteristic about the way in which Jane Eyre leaves he husband's version of his first wife's past unexamined. It may even be that she herself unconsciously harbors a combination of nineteenth-century parochialism and racism that made it normal for her to associate colonial living with the idea of degeneracy and madness. Nevertheless, the man she marries is profoundly different from the one whom Jean Rhys regards as the tormentor of Bertha.

Whether Jean Rhys fully intended it or not, the contrast between the two women characters is, in any case, highly instructive. Although Jane Eyre begins as apparently the most disadvantaged, she has a resourcefulness and a positive sense of self that are altogether lacking in Antoinette Cosway. It is perhaps providential that she is without face or fortune and, as a consequence, is the object of neither male cupidity nor, for a long time, of desire. But there is far more than providence involved. From the memorable opening chapter of Charlotte Bronte's novel, Jane Eyre is revealed as someone who knows she must fight back to survive. At the same time, although the English girl may be an unloved orphan, she has the rich cultural resources of the Victorian middle-class available to her—in that same opening chapter, in resisting her tyrannical boy cousin she can call upon Goldsmith's *History of Rome* for support. The Creole girl, on the other hand, grows up in a milieu without books and finds support in a traditional value system only briefly during the years of her convent education. Elsewhere she encounters the bitter cultural conflicts and moral ambiguities of colonial life.

There is thus a singular appropriateness in Jane Eyre's situation as *govern-ess,* since the very word implies the way in which she finally forces respect for her situation and her sex. The enlightened self-discipline of her conduct invests the word's root with an unexpected significance, and the suffix itself is suggestive of a proud acceptance of her womanhood. Unlike the heiress, whose status derives from another and is therefore alienable, the penniless orphan is self-possessed as well as self-made; since she owes nothing to anyone, she is owned by no one. Her triumph is perhaps all the more remarkable, but it is grounded in Charlotte Bronte's firm sense of the complex interrelatedness of socioeconomic and psychic realities. Jane Eyre is not, as has sometimes been suggested, the heroine of a fairy tale. Hers may be the triumph of a plain, middle-class woman over the obstacles of wealth and class and beauty, as well as over the antithetical demons of aggressive male sexuality (Rochester) and inhuman religious fervor (St. John Rivers), but it is a triumph that is fully motivated in psychological and socioeconomic terms. If Jane Eyre negotiates a course that leads to self-fulfillment in the face of great odds, it is because she is first made independent by circumstances—a poor orphan is socially and economically as well as psychologically a completely autonomous individual—and earns the difficult art of maintaining will, intelligence, and feelings in delicate equilibrium. Unlike Antoinette Cosway, Jane Eyre knows how to govern as well as to give and which, under changing circumstances, is the humanly appropriate choice.

The difference between the two characters is perhaps revealed most strikingly in the use made by both authors of names. It is characteristic of Jean Rhys's compressed insights that she should invent a new name for Charlotte Bronte's Bertha Rochester. In that way, not only is her Antoinette Cosway, like all women, seen to give up her father's name for her husband's—thus implicitly acknowledging how, legally and psychologically, her identity derives from a man—Rochester also requires her to change her own first name. By substituting the dullness of Bertha for the French-flavored prettiness of Antoinette, he is, in Jean Rhys's version, insisting that his wife is his creature who must conform her conduct to the name he bestows on her. To name, as we know, is magically to possess.

Jane Eyre, on the other hand, never gives up her name. In the combination it suggests of plainness in the outward form ("plain Jane") and spirited inwardness (air, eyrie), it continues to define her even after her marriage. Therefore, although as we learn in the concluding chapter, her autobiography was written after ten years of happy marriage to Rochester, the title of her story is not that *Mrs. Rochester* one might have expected but *Jane Eyre.* To the end, her independent but loving female identity remains unsubdued by the Roman severity of her husband's name (Roche = rock, chester < castrum). It is, in fact, he who as husband gives up his peremptory surname—so suggestive of male forthrightness and self-sufficiency and with echoes of the rhyming word "Master"—for the gentler Christian name, Edward.

Wide Sargasso Sea illuminates and is illuminated by *Jane Eyre* Perhaps the most fascinating aspect of this relationship is the way in which Charlotte Bronte's novel plays a generative role in the creation of a work that had previously eluded Jean Rhys. It is apparently through the mediation of *Jane Eyre* that the contemporary novelist found a satisfactory way to distance and objectify early experiences that had only surfaced briefly and intermittently in her previous fiction What, given its origin in literature, looks like the least personal of Jean Rhys's novels is, in fact, a deeply mediated work that has an intensely personal character. That this is the case is confirmed by the light ***Wide Sargasso Sea*** sheds on all Jean Rhys's earlier works. The turbulent tale of the nineteenth-century Creole girl is crucial to an understanding of the author's frequently enigmatic modern heroines.

To read the first four novels is to be aware that the stories they tell concern a fundamentally similar woman at different stages on the journey from early womanhood into middle age. But beyond that, one comes to perceive the existence of an itinerary which, since she returns to it with an obsessive insistence, seems to be deeply rooted in Jean Rhys's own experience. Yet, through the objectifying power of her art, it achieves an almost mythic generality. Nowhere completely written-up in a single novel, the itinerary exists as a kind of structural model that can be abstracted from the novels taken together and that reflects back revealingly on any given novel. Although the typical Jean Rhys work may be said to start at a point beyond hope—it concentrates on the problems of minimal living without expectation and recounts a few final desperate gestures that serve only to confirm despair—a whole past is suggested either through swift and elliptical flashbacks or through brief meetings with those whom the heroine once knew intimately. Often as a consequence only of hints and suggestions, there emerges a well-defined portrait of a woman's life in time. It is an itinerary from which, until ***Wide Sargasso Sea,*** the earliest and the final movements are largely missing.

In the beginning is the memory of a birth on a sun-drenched but haunted island. There follows the uprooting and removal to England, the usually unacknowledged absence of a father, the experience of rejection by a distracted mother who confers her remaining love on a younger sibling, youth in England in a vaguely respectable but relatively poor middle-class family, the departure from home and the restless wanderings in search of happiness in an inhospitable island, the early love affairs and disappointments, the attachment to a foreigner who takes the woman into exile to the continent, the unhappy experience of exile and the failure of the marriage and, finally, total alienation and self-destructive despair. Beyond that lies madness.

The significance of ***Wide Sargasso Sea*** is that it shows so clearly for the first time the sources of the life experience that ends with alienation in Paris. In all of Jean Rhys's novels with a modern setting, the heroines are shown during the final stages of their journey. They are by then largely passive women who permit themselves to be manipulated and exploited by men. Their only revenge is irony and their only resistance an occasional gesture of violence that is directed at themselves often as at others. Deep within they seem to harbor a gloomy form self-hate that draws them to men who are not good for them, like the Heidler and the Stephan Zelli of ***Quartet***—to successful, well-connected men who briefly enjoy their bodies or to marginal social types like themselves who share their own rootlessness and vulnerability. Yet it is only finally through the intense scrutiny to which she subjects Charlotte Bronte's profoundly Victorian novel in her own that Jean Rhys reveals so sharply the roots of the behavior she evokes in her pre-World War II fiction.

What in the novels from ***Quartet*** through ***Good Morning, Midnight*** is presented as predicament without cause, almost as a woman's destiny within a world made immutably by men, is shown to have its origins in a life begun in colonial society. Those women who wander the streets of a Paris that is so unlike Hemingway's "moveable feast" carry within them a sense of homelessness and of worthlessness that is socioeconomic, racial and even political before it is existential. Their mature experience of sexism reinforces an early but undeclared familiarity with colonialism. As well as daughters of absent fathers and unloving mothers, Jean Rhys's women are also "white niggers" without a homeland. They have learned to believe they deserve little and they get no more than they believe they deserve.

That is why their situation is expressed most poignantly in a lament by the character whose even greater misfortune was to have been born a Creole girl in nineteenth-century Jamaica: "So between you both I often wonder who I am and where is my country and where do I belong and why was I ever born at all." All Jean Rhys's modern women are victims, sisters of that Antoinette Cosway who in a transaction between men is taken into exile and transformed into Bertha Rochester. The heroic alternative model suggested by Charlotte Bronte's Jane Eyre is not entertained in Jean Rhys's fiction because the heroism that against all odds fashions its own fate is founded on self-esteem. The contrasting experiences of the two Mrs. Rochesters suggest the mechanisms according to which a plain and abused English orphan might regard herself more highly than a beautiful colonial heiress.

Clara Thomas (essay date April 1978)

SOURCE: "Mr. Rochester's First Marriage: *Wide Sargasso Sea* by Jean Rhys," in *World Literature Written in English,* Vol. 17, No. 1, April, 1978, pp. 342-57.

[*In the following essay, Thomas examines the narrative structure and psychological dynamics of the relationship between Rochester and Antoinette in* Wide Sargasso Sea.]

Antoinette Bertha Cosway Mason is the mad wife of Mr. Rochester, imprisoned in the attics of Thornfield Hall, cared for and guarded by Grace Poole. In ***Wide Sargasso Sea*** Jean Rhys tells her story, from her earliest memories of fear and loss as the Creole daughter of a former slave owner in Jamaica, to her final dream, after uncounted days and years in Thornfield Hall:

> Now at last I know why I was brought here and what I have to do. There must have been a draught for the flame flickered and I thought it was out. But I shielded it with my hand and it burned up again to light me along the dark passage.

The book does not require a knowledge of *Jane Eyre*—a reader who had never heard of Charlotte Brontë or her work could find it a self-contained, haunting, tragic story. But it is nonetheless cross-referenced to *Jane Eyre* at many points, climaxing with the final lines which precede the catastrophe of fire at Thornfield Hall, the death of Bertha Mason and the blinding of Rochester. At the same time the character of Rochester as Charlotte Brontë drew it is immensely extended by Rhys's study of Rochester in ***Wide Sargasso Sea.*** Here we see the reasons for his black bitterness. Here is charted the growth of suspicion and distrust into a tangle of love and hate towards his Creole wife and, finally, into a wild bitterness of damaged pride and vindictiveness that is at least as mad as Bertha Mason's lost desperation. Rochester is a victim of his own Englishness—of the pressure on a younger son to marry well and so to a mass his fortune; of his inexperience and built-in conditioning to despise and distrust blacks and abhor the thought of English blood "tainted" by black; of the attitudes of his time towards purity in women, so confused by the realities of sexuality in both men and women. Most of all he is victimized by his own pride; like Browning's Duke, he "does not choose to stoop," and he becomes both monstrous in vindictiveness and increasingly vulnerable to the torments of jealousy. Finally he is separated from human contact with everyone—and this is the Rochester we first met in *Jane Eyre.* In *Jane Eyre,* Rochester appears to the reader as a victim of his wife's tragic madness; in ***Wide Sargasso Sea*** there is, finally, no clear decision possible between his madness and hers, though clearly, at the end he is his own victim, motivated by pride and hate, and she is irreparably victimized by him.

Antoinette Cosway, the daughter of a Jamaican slave owner, a Creole—a white-skinned West Indian—has never known anything but fear, loss, and, in even her happiest moments, a pitiful pretense of security. She can't believe in the safety of love, because she has always known betrayal and always expects it—and in this she is proved right over and over again. Yet she knows that a safe love could save her. In the first days of her honeymoon she has it very briefly and she blossoms briefly into a happy woman, but her blood, her birth, and her background all make her a pre-fated victim. When the catastrophe's betrayal comes, from within her marriage and from the outside as well, Antoinette loses all hope of safety forever and, in the friendless hell of her confinement at Thornfield Hall, she does become irrevocably mad. She is finally like a zombi, the West Indian spectre that Rochester, in spite of himself, superstitiously fears: "A zombi is a dead person who seems to be alive or a living person who is dead. . . . They cry out in the wind that is their voice, they rage in the sea that is their anger."

Few novels that I have read answer Henry James's form and content, needle and thread metaphor as perfectly as does ***Wide Sargasso Sea.*** The story and the structure become one and inseparable, an interweaving of causality in the story with reinforcing narrative techniques that enhance the story's credibility and make its outcome a tragic inevitability. As the composition of certain paintings can be seen to rest on a solid geometric substructure, so this novel is built on a dramatic substructure that forms Part II of the book, a tragedy in seven scenes, marked off one from the other by asterisks in the text. The structure of this tragic action is perfectly symmetrical: three scenes rise to a betrayal scene and three scenes follow it; scene six is the longest in the book, the climax and catastrophe that, for both Antoinette and Rochester, bring them to their moments of unbearable truth; scene seven is a falling away into despair. The closest dramatic correlative to Part II is *Othello.* With a reversal in races, Rochester and Antoinette are ruined by a combination of irreconcilable cultural differences, personal insecurities, and the pride, jealousy, and betrayal that destroy Othello and Desdemona. Daniel Cosway is the outside agent of their tragedy, motivated, like Iago, by a malign destructiveness that is complicated, in Cosway's case, by greed. In this central tragic drama of Part II, there are only three major actors, Rochesters, Antoinette, and Christophine, her nurse, though there are many minor parts. Christophine is rock-solid, while the other two sway and break with their passion. In scene six, the catastrophe, it is finally Christophine's voice that dominates, speaking truth, with love for Antoinette and with contempt and accusation for Rochester. The centrality of the tragic hero is removed, however, from ***Wide Sargasso Sea,*** since the drama of Part II is enclosed by Antoinette's story in Parts I and III. Part I, Antoinette's childhood, is the prologue to this action; Part III, at Thornfield Hall, is its epilogue.

Built on this powerful dramatic substructure, the success of Jean Rhys's novelistic superstructure lies in her use of narrative voice and point of view. Part I is in the voice of Antoinette; six of the seven scenes of Part II are narrated by Rochester, the seventh by Antoinette; Part III is introduced by Grace Poole, then Antoinette's voice takes over and ends the novel. Rhys has thus set up an alternating current between the voices and points of view of Rochester and Antoinette, holding the reader in sympathy with each one of them and, simultaneously, in tension between them. Grace Poole's voice brings us back to Thornfield Hall and the world of *Jane Eyre,* to finally enclose the tragedy of Antoinette and Rochester undiminished. For now the reader has experienced their tragedy in their own words and in its own setting. The end of ***Wide Sargasso Sea,*** moments before the fire in *Thornfield Hall,* is finally their release from the circumstantial bond in which, long after the catastrophe of their marriage, they have remained imprisoned.

In Part I Antoinette tells the story of her life and her losses to a time just before she meets Rochester. That time is exactly indicated; it is 1839; Antoinette is recalling her past as she lies safely in bed in the convent after a dream of following a menacing stranger through a forest. This is the second time she has dreamed this dream, a nightmare of fear to her. Sister Maria Augustine has comforted her and put her back to bed: "Think of calm, peaceful things and try to sleep.

Soon I will give the signal. Soon it will be tomorrow morning." Her memories begin with her mother, a Martinique girl, second wife to Mr. Cosway, a plantation owner, who like many others has been impoverished by the emancipation of the slaves. Memory begins after Cosway's death, on the run-down Coulibri estate near Spanish Town where she and her mother and her crippled younger brother live, still waited on by three servants who have not deserted them. The destitution encroaching on the lives of these people is not described, but evoked in a series of brief, dramatic memories. Her mother and their neighbour, Mr. Luttrell, were still waiting for the compensation promised by the English when the Emancipation Act was passed. "How could she know that Mr. Luttrell would be the first who grew tired of waiting? One calm evening he shot his dog, swam out to sea and was gone for always." Her mother still planned, hoped, and kept up appearances, riding every morning, ". . . not caring that the black people stood about in groups to jeer at her, especially after her riding clothes grew shabby (they notice clothes, they know about money)." Then one morning Antoinette found her mother's horse, poisoned. "'Now we are marooned,' my mother said, 'now what will become of us?'"

To Antoinette the Coulibri estate was beautiful even though it had gone wild, the green light underneath the tree ferns, the smell of dead flowers mixed with a fresh living smell, the purple octopus orchid, beautiful but fearsome. "No more slavery—why should *anybody* work? This never saddened me. I did not remember the place when it was prosperous." But everything else around her was a frightening mystery. Her mother grew thin and remote after the Spanish Town doctor came to see her brother: ". . . She pushed me away, not roughly, but calmly, coldly, without a word, as if she had decided once and for all that I was useless to her." Antoinette wanted to love and trust Christophine, her black nurse from Martinique, and yet her mother did not trust Christophine. "Christophine stayed with me because she wanted to stay. She had her own very good reasons you may be sure. I dare say we would have died if she'd turned against us and that would have been a better fate." Everyday she played with Tia, the daughter of Christophine's friend. In Antoinette's memories Tia is her "friend," but when they play, Tia tricks her and when they argue, she calls Antoinette "white nigger" and takes her dress: "Old time white people nothing but white nigger now, and black nigger better than white nigger." Surrounded by fear and often afraid herself, when she was still a child at Coulibri Antoinette dreamed her first dream of being lost and menaced in a dark forest.

Antoinette's mother seems to be saved when she marries Mr. Mason, a rich Englishman, but in fact this marriage precipitates her tragedy. Antoinette hates the people who come to see them, laughing and gossiping behind her mother's back and calling Christophine an Obeah woman, a witch. She rejects her stepfather, although he is kind to her. But the worst is that he does not understand the menace around Coulibri and he doesn't move them away in time, in spite of the angry insistence of Antoinette's mother, supported by her sister, Aunt Cora.

> "You have lived alone far too long, Annette. You imagine enmity which doesn't exist. Always one extreme or the other. Didn't you fly at me like a little wild cat when I said nigger. Not nigger, nor even negro. Black people I must say."
>
> "You don't like, or even recognize, the good in them," she said, "and you won't believe in the other side."
>
> "They're too damn lazy to be dangerous," said Mr Mason.
>
> "They are more alive than you are, lazy or not, and they can be dangerous and cruel for reasons you wouldn't understand."

Antoinette's mother is right. The blacks burn Coulibri, Pierre dies of the effects of the fire, and Antoinette is ill for weeks after having been hit on the forehead by a jagged stone thrown by Tia, her "friend." When she is well she finds that her mother is mad and violent, detained in a house with a black man and woman as her keepers.

The convent where Antoinette is sent to school is her refuge after the breakup of her home and family life. Even the streets are filled with menace for her, with children chasing her, calling her crazy girl and taunting her about her mother. When she is seventeen Mr. Mason comes to tell her that she is to live with him and that he has asked some English friends to visit next winter. On the evening of his visit she has her second nightmare. This time the unknown menace has become a man who is leading her in the forest: "I follow him, sick with fear but I make no effort to save myself; if anyone were to try to save me, I would refuse. This must happen." Part I ends with safety in bed and comfort from the nuns—the dream has unlocked the memories that make up the narrative of Part I.

All the elements of Antoinette's tragedy are established here—loss, fear, rejection, betrayal, withdrawal from people, distrust even of Christophine, her nurse, who sometimes is tainted in her mind with the mysterious menace of Obeah. Reconstructed by her memory, the events of her childhood memories move from stagnation to catastrophe because of the arrival of Mr. Mason. He is a controlling and eventually hated figure in her mother's life and, as a rich stepfather, he becomes a controlling figure to Antoinette. She cannot forget the causes of her mother's ruin and degradation though she does not completely understand them. She dreads the same fate for herself but at the same time, in a doomed way, she expects it.

> Then, not so far off, I saw Tia and her mother and I ran to her, for she was all that was left of my life as it had been. . . . When I was close I saw the jagged stone in her hand but I did not see her throw it. I did not feel it either, only something wet, running down my face. I looked at her and I saw her face crumple up as she began to cry. We stared at each other, blood on my face, tears on hers. *It was as if I saw myself. Like in a looking-glass.* (emphasis mine)

Events prove her right. What happened to the mother in Part I will happen to the daughter in Part II, with Rochester the activating agent of her tragedy and with the agony of hindsight on her mother's life added to her sense of helplessness.

Antoinette's memories and her two dreams both introduce and foreshadow the drama of Part II, the story of her uneasily happy honeymoon with Rochester and its catastrophic ending. This section is 110 pages long as against Part I's 60 pages and Part III's 12 pages. In all of its seven scenes the narrators are looking back and remembering from the last despairing moments of Part II when everything is lost. Antoinette is beaten and hopeless, "I know nothing about you, and I cannot speak for you . . . ," and Rochester is cold in his hate of Antoinette and of the land: "I hated its indifference and the cruelty which was part of its loveliness. Above all I hated her. For she belonged to the magic and the loveliness. She had left me thirsty and all my life would be thirst and longing for what I had lost before I found it."

In scene one, Rochester remembers the beginning of their honeymoon near a village called Massacre in one of the Windward Islands. The house, Granbois, is high up in the hills. It is run-down and lonely, but it had belonged to Antoinette's mother and she loves it as a place of safety and remembered childhood happiness. This scene establishes Rochester's strangeness to everything and everyone around him, and indicates his barely dormant suspicion that he has been duped by Mr. Mason, married to a girl who perhaps has a taint of colour and perhaps madness in her blood. He also has to deal with his own self-contempt, the recognition, that following his father's instructions, he married for money—he was bought.

> Creole of pure English descent she may be, but they are not English or European either. And when did I begin to notice all this about my wife Antoinette? . . . Not that I had much time to notice anything. I was married a month after I arrived in Jamaica and for nearly three weeks of that time I was in bed with fever.

Rochester is weary with travel, half-sick with bitterness towards his father and brother and disgust with himself.

> Everything is too much, I felt as I rode wearily after her. Too much blue, too much purple, too much green [these are the colours Antoinette loves and always chose to paint with in the convent]. . . . Dear Father. The thirty thousand pounds have been paid to me without question or condition. . . . I have a modest competence now. I will never be a disgrace to you or to my dear brother, the son you love. . . . I have sold my soul or you have sold it, and after all is it such a bad bargain? The girl is thought to be beautiful, she is beautiful. And yet . . .

Rochester is as damaged by his father's failure to love him as Antoinette is by her mother's, but neither one of them is in the least able to comprehend that about the other.

In scene two, Rochester remembers his brief courtship of Antoinette and their marriage: "I played the part I was expected to play. . . . Every movement I made was an effort of will and sometimes I wondered that no one noticed this. . . . I remember little of the actual ceremony." What he does remember vividly is her last minute "I'll trust you if you'll trust me. Is that a bargain?" The word trust is bitterly ironic—neither one of them has any basis of personal security or understanding of the other on which to build trust.

In scene three he recalls, with both longing and bitterness, their brief honeymoon happiness: "It was very late when I poured out two glasses and told her to drink to our happiness, to our love and the day without end which would be tomorrow. I was young then. A short youth mine was." Even on their first morning Christophine's entrance with their coffee, Antoinette's familiar treatment of her, and Antoinette's whims, which to Rochester are so exotic and therefore troubling, bring distrust and suspicion into their idyll.

On its one side, theirs becomes an idyllic honeymoon in an Edenic setting with Antoinette losing her fears by day and confiding them to Rochester by night. On its other side, however, is the constant menace of the strange exotic land, the people he distrusts and something secret that he cannot fathom in Antoinette. Here in his recollections we begin to get signals suggesting a real disturbance in Rochester's mind. What secret is he talking about? How disturbed *is* he as he remembers their lovemaking?

> Die then, Sleep. It is all that I can give you. . . . I wonder if she ever guessed how near she came to dying. In her way, not in mine. It was not a safe

> game to play—in that place. Desire, Hatred, Life, Death came very close in the darkness. Better not know how close.

Earlier Rochester has mentioned his "confused impressions"; "There are blanks in my mind that cannot be filled up." Subsequently, Jean Rhys indicates certain blanks in his recollections by four dots, and others by the omission of key words in a sentence. She does not do this often, but sparingly, and because of that the reader is all the more aware of ellipses in Rochester's memories—or in his admission of his memories.

The catastrophe, always immanent, is set in motion in scene four. Its agent is a long letter from Daniel Cosway who claims to be Antoinette's brother, the illegitimate son of her father and a Negress. Antoinette, he says, has "bad blood on both sides." Her father died from drink, "raving and cursing," and her mother is shut away for trying to kill Mason—"madness not being all either." Rochester has been the victim of a plot to marry him to a girl who will certainly go mad as her mother did before her: *"Money is good but no money can pay for a crazy wife in your bed."* This is the betrayal from outside of two people who are so vulnerable within themselves that they have no hope of withstanding it. Daniel Cosway writes that it is his "Christian duty" to write his accusations to Rochester. Henceforth the image of the cock crowing is used repeatedly in Part II, as Cosway's malicious betrayal of Antoinette is reinforced by Rochester's own accumulating betrayals.

For Antoinette, her mother's pattern of ruin is beginning to repeat itself. As Coulibri was burned by the blacks who laughed at them poor and hated them rich, so Cosway is burning with envy and eager to destroy the fragile structure of her happiness. ". . . [T]hey are white, I am coloured," he writes. "They are rich, I am poor . . . ." Her father and mine was a shameless man and of all his illegitimates I am the most unfortunate and poverty-stricken." As for Rochester, it was as if he had been expecting the letter. "I felt no surprise." It was brought to him by Amélie, the coloured maid who had attracted him from the start—"a lovely little creature, but shy, spiteful, malignant perhaps, like much else in this place." Henceforth Amélie is open in her betrayal of Antoinette, and can only be intimidated by Christophine. In the culmination of the ensuing see-saw between Rochester's rage and Antoinette's desperation, he takes Amélie to bed in the room adjacent to his wife's, where she cannot fail to hear them.

What we have been reading in ***Wide Sargasso Sea*** is, in contemporary terms, psycho-biography, presented as a reconstruction of the past by the two main characters. There is no authorial voice intervening between their voices and our understanding and, therefore, we increasingly accept their voices as immediate and contemporary to our own. Rhys's swing-back to the classic use of a letter to initiate the catastrophe is a startling and, in context, a brilliant device, pushing us back into the nineteenth century and the world of *Jane Eyre* where such a letter, at least in literary convention, could indeed wreak such havoc. Furthermore, we have been prepared for the letter convention by the various snatches of letters that Rochester has drafted to his father.

Everything now moves swiftly and inexorably towards the final catastrophe. Having betrayed, Amélie now defies Antoinette and calls her "white cockroach," singing the song that was used to taunt the Cosways on the Coulibri estate. Antoinette, enraged, first attacks Amélie and then repeats a part of the pattern of breakup she saw as a child. As her Aunt Cora had torn her petticoat in strips to bind up the burns Pierre suffered in the fire, so she tears a sheet into strips in an outburst of rage that is also a symbolic preparation for the binding of her wounds. Then she retreats into another pattern of her childhood, shutting herself away in silence. Rochester drinks rum punch and then wanders in the forest. This is the point at which their mutual ruin becomes inevitable—at this crucial point each one of them is impelled to take a further and further diverging path until there is no hope of trustful communication between them. Everything that Antoinette does from now on looks to Rochester like the confirmation of Cosway's accusation: to the reader everything she does is also explained by the knowledge given us of her memories in Part I. The patterns were shown to us then from a time when she was safe and at peace, in no sense mad, though totally vulnerable to her future. From here on, it is only Christophine who is a rock of strength and sanity. Though also, because she cannot be other than herself, a product of her place, her race and her background, she is also unwittingly an activator of further disaster. She leaves Antoinette and goes up to her house in the hills.

Scene five is narrated by Antoinette, desolate and desperate, but not beaten yet. She goes to Christophine for advice and from her she gets the advice she won't take: "You ask me a hard thing, I tell you a hard thing, pack up and go." Antoinette's pride may well be as strong as Rochester's; it may even be stronger than her need for love! "No, I will not, then everyone, not only the servants, will laugh at me." What she also gets, because Christophine loves her and cannot refuse her desperation, is a love potion, a mixture of the Obeah medicine that had always frightened and also fascinated Antoinette. Antoinette still has the will to fight for her marriage, but the means she uses, coming out of the only culture she knows, are doomed to be disastrous.

The 40-page scene six, narrated by Rochester, is the drama's painful climax. Throughout, he swings wildly between love and its gentle impulses and hate and its vindictive ones. Amélie plants more suspicion in his mind about Antoinette's behaviour with her cousin, Sandi Cosway. He goes to see Daniel Cosway who is after money to keep silent and he leaves in rage and disgust. He listens to Antoinette who talks to him as she had promised Christophine, telling him something of her mother's ruin and its causes. But essentially his mind is made up to her madness and his tone is one of cold reason, though he cannot listen without suffering and regret: "I began to wonder how much of all this was true, how much imagined, distorted. . . . But my heart was heavy as lead." The reader knows that what she tells him is completely true to her memories, but since Rochester has not that corroboration we can also understand his confusion and doubt. He never loses our sympathy to become, simply, a heartless monster. But instead we are given a terrifying record of a man progressively losing his hold on sanity and any capacity for the trust that might have saved them both. After he has listened to Antoinette's story of her mother's ruin he first begins to call her Bertha—for him, Antoinette no longer exists. For her it is troubling and finally terrifying to be called by another name: "Will you come in and say goodnight to me?' 'Certainly I will, my dear Bertha.' 'Not Bertha tonight,' she said. 'Of course, on this of all nights you must be Bertha." From here on the agonizing split in Rochester's mind is made more and more evident. On the one hand is love, pain, and remorse:

> She poured wine into two glasses and handed me one but I swear it was before I drank that I longed to bury my face in her hair as I used to do. . . . She need not have done what she did to me, I will always swear that, she need not have done it.

On the other hand there is his pride that makes him hard, the self-contempt that makes him harder still and his suspicions, by now extending to everyone around him. He makes love to Antoinette one last time but wakes up sick, full of self-disgust and sure that he has been poisoned. He takes Amélie to bed but wakens the next morning ". . . satisfied and peaceful, but not gay . . . no, by God, not gay." "And her skin was darker, her lips thicker than I had thought."

From this time onward Rochester is outwardly invulnerable, but inwardly well along in the process of disintegration. Amélie he pays off—her betrayal has worked for her as she hoped and she now has the money to go to Rio. She also has pity for both her victims: "As she was going I could not resist saying, half longing, half triumphant, 'Well Amélie, are you still sorry for me?' 'Yes,' she said, 'I am sorry for you. But I find it in my heart to be sorry for her too.'" Rochester, however, is beyond compassion for Antoinette, Christophine, or most important, for the blundering humanity in himself. He arms himself with power over Christophine by soliciting and receiving a letter from Mr. Fraser, an English magistrate: "[I] consider her a most dangerous person. . . . I have written very discretely to Hill, the white inspector of police in your town. If she lives near you and gets up to any of her nonsense let him know at once." When Antoinette returns, distraught and drunk on the rum that Christophine has given her to deaden her despair, Rochester is drinking rum too. But he chooses to see and judge his wife only by the fact of her drunkenness, not its causes. When she accuses him, in taking Amélie, of being as bad as the old slave owners he pretended to despise, he slips away into cold abstraction. "'Slavery was not a matter of liking or disliking, 'I said, trying to speak calmly. 'It was a question of justice.'" When Antionette says of Amélie, "Is she so much prettier than I am? Don't you love me at all?" he says, "'No, I do not.'" Always, now, he calls her Bertha, or "my wife," and he remembers, when Christophine accuses him, that in the cold passion of his last lovemaking he called her "Marionette." "'That word mean doll, eh? Because she don't speak, You want to force her to cry and to speak.'"

The climax of scene six is Christophine's confrontation with Rochester, when she accuses him and pleads for Antoinette. Here we see the strength of Christophine. Though Antoinette's love for her has always been mixed with a superstitious fear, Christophine's love for Antoinette is strong and without a trace of self-interest or betrayal. This is a powerful and a disturbing scene, as evocative of pity and terror as Lear on the heath or Othello in his torment of jealousy. Outwardly Rochester maintains a calm and supercilious superiority as she accuses him and pleads for Antoinette.

> ". . . Nobody is to have any pride but you. She have more pride than you and she say nothing.
>
> . . . Everybody know that you marry her for her money and you take it all. And then you want to break her up, because you jealous of her. She is more better than you, she have better blood in her and she don't care for money—it's nothing for her. Oh I see that first time I look at you. You young but already you hard. You fool the girl. You make her think you can't see the sun for looking at her."

To himself, Rochester admits that it was like that. He listens to "her judge's voice" telling him what he has done and what he should do now to win her back, but inside he is convinced it is all hopeless: "I should stop this useless conversation, I thought, but could only listen, hypnotized, to her dark voice coming from the darkness."

Finally, however, Rochester is enraged by Christophine's suggestion that Antoinette might, if free, marry again. He is also alerted and hardened to his course by her talk of money. Christophine talked to Antoinette about money, too, and by now we, the readers, know that she is innocent of self-interest—but all Rochester's resentment of Cosway's attempt at blackmail springs alive, as well as all of the self-interest which made him marry for a fortune, which he admits but despises. About money, Rochester is always defensive. Therefore he becomes "alert and wary, ready to defend myself," dismisses Christophine with contempt, "you ridiculous old woman," and threatens her with the police unless she leaves.

This scene of confrontation is so dramatically powerful that one hears and sees it all as one reads, the black woman, the white Englishman, the chasm between them in cultural identity marked by accent and attitude, Rochester outwardly strong but inwardly disintegrating and Christophine—"her eyes were undaunted." It ends with Christophine's summary accusation—he wants her money but not Antoinette, he will say she is mad, her brother, Richard Mason, will corroborate him, and she will indeed become like her mother.

> . . . "You do that for money? But you wicked like Satan self!"
>
> I said loudly and wildly, "And do you think that I wanted all this? I would give my life to undo it. I would give my eyes never to have seen this abominable place!"
>
> She laughed, "And that's the first damn word of truth you speak. You choose what you give, eh? Then you choose. You meddle in something and perhaps you don't know what it is." She began to mutter to herself. Not in patois. I knew the sound of patois now.

This final chilling foreshadowing of the future blinding of Rochester is spoken by Christophine when, transformed by rage and pain for Antoinette, she has taken upon herself the mysterious and prophetic Obeah woman role.

After she leaves Rochester turns to rum for solace and he rages in torment between vindictive jealousy and agonized loss:

> She'll not laugh in the sun again. She'd not dress up and smile at herself in that damnable looking-glass. . . .
>
> . . . Made for loving? Yes, but she'll have no lover, for I don't want her and she'll see no other.

At the very base of this passion there is his torment that he never knew Antoinette, was always separate from her: "I could not touch her. Excepting as the hurricane will touch that tree—and break it." Even now if she would capitulate to his drive for power and mastery over her by so much as one tear, he would relent, he swears: "She's mad, but *mine, mine*. . . . Antoinette—I can be gentle too. Hide your face. Hide yourself but in my arms. You'll soon see how gentle. My lunatic. My mad girl." The terrible recognition that builds in the reader through Part II and is finally confirmed in this climax is that of all the chasms between them, the differences in culture are deep, but sexuality is deeper still. Rochester cannot cope with either Antoinette's sexuality or his own. He can only tolerate a relationship in which he is the master. A mutual delight in free sexuality is beyond him. Since he has not been able to dominate Antoinette's own sexuality, he will either condescend to keep and enjoy her as his mad girl, or he will shut her away from all loving and possibilities of loving.

In scene seven, as he recalls their final departure from Granbois, there is no trace of such a sign of submission from Antoinette. Her whole life's experience has been a preconditioning to this ruin, and furthermore, as Christophine has warned him, she in her way is at least as proud as he in his. As for Rochester, he swings wildly in his mind from love and regret to hate and revenge, "Again the giddy change, the remembering, the sickening swing back to hate," until finally the hate irrevocably takes over:

> . . . My hate is colder, stronger, and you'll have no hate to warm yourself. You will have nothing.
>
> I did it too. I saw the hate go out of her eyes.
>
> I forced it out. And with the hate her beauty. She was only a ghost.

But with that last exercise of his will in hate, Rochester has also forced everything out of himself. His mastery is empty, because he, too, has become like a zombi, one of the living dead. When the young boy cries at being left behind, Rochester speaks one last line out of his own emptiness: "Who would have thought that any boy would cry like that. For nothing. Nothing."

After the power and the passion of Part II, Part III locks ***Wide Sargasso Sea*** into the final action of *Jane Eyre*. The pathos of the lost girl in the attic is acknowledged by Grace Poole, who pities her and who is the first speaker in Part III, gossiping to Leah, the maid. But Grace Poole needs the double salary she is paid for being wardress and besides, to Mrs. Fairfax who hired her, Rochester is the one who has been wronged: "Don't ask me to pity anyone who had a hand in that." As for Antoinette, she is Bertha to the few who know of her existence. The madness that she feared, that Rochester thought he saw in her, has now been forced upon her by her confinement. Her only tangible link with Antoinette and the islands is her red dress: "The scent that came from the dress was very faint at first, then it grew stronger. The smell of vetivert and frangipanni, of cinnamon and dust and lime trees when they are flowering. The smell of the sun and the smell of the rain." The thoughts and memories of Antoinette as she gives them in Part III are not lucid and consecutively ordered as they were in Part I. They are snatches and fragments and when she has been violent, as when Richard Mason comes to see her, she does not remember. Constantly she is troubled by one question, "Why have I been brought here?" and "What must I do?" Her third dream gives her the answer, the ending to the two dreams she remembered in Part I. The flight of steps and the terrifying stranger lead to this room with a lighted candle and her keeper asleep beside the gin bottle. Antoinette takes the candle and goes out into the hall: "I shielded it with my hand and it burned up again to light me along the dark passage." Just as Coulibri, her home, was destroyed by fire long ago, so must she now burn Thornfield Hall, her alien prison.

Sociologically, ***Wide Sargasso Sea*** is a novel about the tragic effects on individuals of mass cultural conditioning among peoples and between sexes. It can be read as a parable about the terrible damage that an imperial power, by asserting its drives and values as unalterable law, does to its own and its colonized people. It is a novel of cultural determinism—both Antoinette and Rochester are caught in a limbo between two cultures, helpless to move, change, or understand each other. Only Christophine knows exactly who and where she is. She warns Antoinette, who has always had a fantasy dream of England, even a foreshadowing of her final loneliness there. England is alien, it is a "cold thief" place, and Christophine doubts its existence: "If there is this place at all, I never see it, that is one thing sure." Behind the culturally-trapped individuals, money is the activating evil in the novel. Rochester does marry for money, Antoinette is, effectively, sold for money, Daniel Cosway betrays for money as does Amélie, Grace Poole is enticed to Thornfield Hall for money, Antoinette's ruin is complete because, once married, her fortune is Rochester's. And when Rochester thinks wrongly that Christophine is after money, he becomes adamant, to "defend himself," as he says. He seals Antoinette's ruin and his own.

The novel is also a study in environmental and climatic determinism. Jean Rhys's sense of place is very strong and she evokes the sights, sounds, and scents of the islands with haunting power. Antoinette's love of the islands must also be the author's remembered love, but Rhys also understands and communicates Rochester's uncase in a landscape which, because it is strange to him, he takes to be hostile. Antoinette loves the blues, greens, and purples that are the colours of the Jamaican hills, and the brilliance of the flamboyant tree: "If you are buried under a flamboyant tree, your soul is lifted up when it flowers, Everyone wants that." She cannot imagine snow, except as torn pieces of white paper or floating white feathers. To Rochester, on the other hand, the islands are all too much: the hills are menacing and an "extreme green"—"that green menace. I had felt it ever since I saw this place." He soon tires of the sunsets and waits for night, but the night is still foreign, with "strange noises" and "an alien moon." Where Antoinette sees a familiar village, he sees desolation, "the sad leaning coconut palms, the fishing boats drawn upon the shingly beach, the uneven row of whitewashed huts." Many, many such examples of contrasting reaction to environment occur throughout the text.

The name, ***Wide Sargasso Sea,*** takes its reference from the terrible, overpowering conditions of culturally-imposed separation that effectively paralyze the wills of individuals trapped within them. It is a haunting title, with strong echoes of Arnold's "salt, estranging sea" of course, but beyond that it signifies the vast, dead centre to which Rochester and Antoinette drift and from which they have not the power to escape. One of the O.E.D.'s citations for Sargasso is this definition, from Maury's Physical Geography of 1855: "There is in each ocean a Sargasso into which all drift matter finds its way." The line could well serve as an epigraph for Jean Rhys's novel.

Technically, Jean Rhys set herself an enormous challenge in writing this novel. To build a contemporary work into another, classic novel of the nineteenth century is to invite a hypercritical approach from readers and critics who are consciously or unconsciously defensive about a trespass into familiar and protected territory. She succeeded because her depth of concern for, and understanding of, her characters was complemented by a stunning achievement in narrative technique—and also (constantly at work within her narrative), because of the dazzling success of her ambivalent evocation of place.

Helen Tiffin (essay date April 1978)

SOURCE: "Mirror and Mask: Colonial Motifs in the Novels of Jean Rhys," in *World Literature Written in English*, Vol. 17, No. 1, April, 1978, pp. 328-41.

[*In the following essay, Tiffin discusses the portrayal of exploitative male-female relationships, distorted female self-identity, and imperialism in Rhys's fiction.*]

Since Wally Look Lai's illuminating study of ***Wide Sargasso Sea,*** the importance of West Indian history and character in Jean Rhys's writing has been generally recognized, though both he and later critics such as Dennis Porter tend to regard ***Wide Sargasso Sea*** as a "new departure" rather than a culmination of moods and motifs. Rhys's fiction in its entirety, however, presents a complex picture of the mind of a people uniquely isolated by the vagaries of history and winning a grip on their "postage stamp of native soil" not, like Faulkner's Southerners, by revolutionary war but from the

Sargasso Sea of an ambiguously divisive yet shackling colonial history.

All of Rhys's heroines, whether ostensibly English or actually Creole, share a recognizably colonial sensibility, and since this sensibility is the product of a relationship between at least two peoples and two places, it is generally expressed and explored in liaisons between individuals whose world views differ and who are bound in a destructive relationship involving dominance and dependence. In *Palace of the Peacock* Wilson Harris traces a process of psychic decolonization whereby "the oldest uncertainty and desire in the world, the desire to govern or be governed, rule or be ruled forever" is abrogated in favour of a union between all sexes and all races through the agency of the spirit of place. In her novels Jean Rhys works towards a comparable solution to this colonial dilemma; and if ultimately she lacks Harris' confidence, it is because the white West Indian has the double problem of rejecting former affiliations and power structures and of being accepted into a community from which she seems irretrievably excluded by the hostilities of a history which is, and yet is not, her own.

The white Creole is, as a double outsider, condemned to self-consciousness, homelessness, a sense of inescapable difference and even deformity in the two societies by whose judgements she always condemns herself. "White nigger" to the Europeans and "white cockroach" to the Blacks, she sees herself as a gauche, immature distortion of the Europeans on the one hand, and a pale and terrified "deformed" reflection of her Black compatriots on the other. As the distorted reflection of two images, neither of which is really her but which beckon and taunt her with their normality, the Rhys heroine relies on mirrors and mirror images, and they are central to Rhys's depiction of her dilemma.

Enable to judge their own worth, Rhys's heroines are obsessed with mirrors and the need for outside opinion. All are inevitably outsiders in the European worlds through which they drift, and all rely for financial survival and physic support on Englishmen who are usually much older than themselves. Indeed their whole sense of identity or conviction of self-worth is entirely dependent, as is their fate, on these men and on external accoutrements. Though the Rhys heroine usually has sufficient sensitivity to despise the arrogant complacency of her English lover, she remains shackled to his every whim. In fact it seems that it is dependence itself to which the women are addicted. When the men tire of the liaison, it is abruptly terminated, and independence is foisted on the reluctant mistress whose unhealthy, child-like need for support has only been exacerbated by the association.

The men of Jean Rhys's novels also share certain characteristics: as Englishmen these lovers are almost by definition cold, cautious, hypocritical, and joyless. They are self-absorbed and self-assured, firmly rooted in a world which mirrors their every characteristic—an urban world of perpetually dark streets, actively hostile look-alike houses, and grim cheerless interiors where reluctantly kindled fires shed no warmth. These men patronize their mistresses, encourage their child-like dependence, but readily abdicate ultimate responsibility for their fate. By contrast to the women they exploit, they have little interest in the impression they make on outsiders, although they are devoted nevertheless to keeping up appearances and to "playing the game." But this insistence is intimately connected with the survival of the values of a closely-knit group rather than with personal survival or identity. These men share a total tack of interest in anything that is not English and not, therefore, immediately comprehensible to them. Their reserved, aloof outlook contrasts with the women's open acknowledgement of emotion, which the men consequently find "fantastic" and "hysterical," and condemn as evidence of lack of maturity and self-control.

The liaison is of secondary or even tertiary importance in the life of the man, while it forms the very texture of the woman's existence. The women rarely influence the men; indeed their daily thoughts and actions are a complex and painful mixture of their own undervalued resources and the usually low (and undiscriminating) opinions held of these resources by the men. The parallel between destructive male/female relationships and between imperial nation and colonial underdog is obvious.

In ***Quartet*** and ***After Leaving Mr. Mackenzie*** the nature of the colonial dilemma is established in the portrayal of the aimless, drifting, dependent lives of Marya and Julia. In ***Voyage in the Dark*** the historical basis of the personality and way of life of the earlier heroines is made explicit, and the first step towards an exit from this impasse is posited, ***Good Morning, Midnight*** reappraises and reestablishes the original situation of the eternal exile and continues the exploration of the relationship between outcasts rather than between the outcast and "organized society" that was explored in the first two novels. ***Wide Sargasso Sea*** at last offers the revolutionary alternative to the aimless, sargasso drift of the heroines of the earlier works.

In ***Quartet*** Marya, almost inexplicably an outsider, is forced after her husband's imprisonment into living with the Heidlers, an English couple, and with Lois' apparent connivance, into becoming Heidler's mistress. Marya's three most frequent "postures" provide the reader with illuminating images of her relation to the Heidlers.

It is only after her husband Stephan goes to prison that Marya falls prey to this couple, and the joy Stephan had introduced into her sombre world is extinguished. She is frequently shown visiting him in prison, and as they sit facing each other with bars between them, the couple are now mirror images of each other, for just as the *Santé* has extinguished Stephan's joy, so Marya's "imprisonment" by the Heidlers crushes her spirit. Like Stephan, Marya is now a "caged animal" and the cool, cautious, joyless Heidler replaces the mercurial Stephan, Confined by Heidler's hypocritical decorum, her longing for joy is

> like some splendid caged animal roused and fighting to get out. It was an unborn child jumping, leaping, kicking at her side.

Since Lois Heidlers regards Marya as "some strange animal that might be dangerous" the conclusion that joy itself is terrifying to the English and so must be confined, is inescapable. A "captive attached to somebody's chariot wheels," Marya feels "the fright of a child shut up in a dark room. Fright of an animal caught in a trap." This wild animal-child fears that enslavement to Heidler's world will result in her domestication, and the extinction of even the faint inner spark of rebellion she retains. Both "prisons" are now "familiar," and the mirror image of Stephan's cowered spirit haunts her.

Not just Stephan but Lois provides a mirror image for Marya's condition. In their common subjugation to Heidler, Marya sees a reflection of her own trapped condition in Lois who has the eyes of a "well trained domestic animal." The second memorable image of Marya in the novel is of her sitting side by side with Lois, crying, although this rare communion of victims is only a temporary aberration. Both Lois and Marya know that they are Heidlers victims, yet they make the common tragic mistake of underdogs—tearing each other to pieces instead of attacking the source of their domestication and imprisonment in the greed and self-absorption of the dominant male.

Looking into Heidler's hypnotic blue eyes is Marya's third and most frequent posture in ***Quartet.*** It is here that her "desire to be governed . . . to be ruled," and Heidler's complementary one to "rule" and "govern" meet to express the subtleties of the ties that bind colonizer and colonized. "The way men look with their hard greedy eyes. . . . When he touched her she felt warm and secure, then weak and so desolate that tears came into her eyes." Even though Marya knows he almost despises women and love, she still cannot resist the desire to depend, and to please, to "live up to his idea of her" as his "petite femme." She feels she is a "marionette," all strings pulled by Heidlers who, significantly, "looks exactly like a picture of Queen Victoria." "Convincing, impressive, and full of authority." H. J. clearly believes that "victims are necessary so the strong may exercise their will and become more strong."

In ***Quartet,*** then, though Marya ostensibly is English, the relationship between Heidler and Marya deliberately duplicates that between imperial power and colonized people, and while Marya shares her slave status with Lois, their common plight cannot unite them. The Heidlers live on the Avenue de l'Observatoire, and against Heidlers, invulnerable observer and judge, Marya has almost "no chance."

In ***After Leaving Mr. Mackenzie*** the central character, Julia Martin, is again English, and is the "black sheep" of a poverty-stricken middle-class family dominated by the Heidler-like figure of Uncle Griffiths who once "had represented to the family the large and powerful male." Even now when he has aged into a self-centred distance, "he appeared solid and powerful, and she felt a great desire to please him, to make him look kindly at her." Neither her uncle nor her sister Norah is pleased to see her, and during her stay in England she remains "outside the sacred circle of warmth." Norah, from whom she had hoped for a little affection, regards her, as the Heidlers did Marya, as "something out of the zoo," and again an ostensibly English character remains almost puzzlingly alien, her unconventional looks and wanderings the apparent source of her ostracism.

Julia's mother however was not English; she had been "transplanted" from Brazil. The very-English Norah obviously associates the mother's origins with what she regards as the family malaise, pointing out "That there's something wrong with our family. We're soft, or lazy, or something." In the central episode of the novel, Julia's mother, already paralysed, dies.

Earlier in the novel Julia had been deeply affected by the Modigliani painting of

> a woman lying on a couch, a woman with a lovely, lovely body. Oh, utterly lovely. . . . A sort of proud body, like an utterly lovely proud animal, And a face like a mask, a long, dark face, and very big eyes. The eyes were blank, like a mask, but when you had looked at it a bit it was as if you were looking at a real woman, a live woman.

The painting seems to be telling Julia, "I am more real than you. But at the same time I *am* you. I'm all that matters of you." The dark, proud animal of the portrait is the felt reflection of Julia's own inner self, and the first indication that a Rhys heroine might escape her paralysing devotion to an outside reflection and judgement and thus eventually eschew the dependence that is symptomatic of her "colonial" condition. Further associating Julia with the Modigliani print and with the perpetual search of the Rhys heroine for a darker skin are Julia's "blackened eyelids" which particularly incense Norah.

But the Modigliani print has more immediate significance

in its application to Julia's mother herself. In the cold, grey, English environment to which she has been transplanted, Julia's mother frequently appears to be "sickening for the sun. Julia remembered her saying: "'This is a cold, grey country. This isn't a country to be really happy in.'" The mother, like the Modigliani woman with whom Julia had already identified herself, is "dark skinned" and "beautiful, as and animal would be in old age." It becomes obvious that Julia, like her mother, in spirit if not in fact, is the dark, wild, transplanted foreigner and that this is what marks her off from her erstwhile English "relatives."

In her relationships with the shadowy Mr. Mackenzie, whose brief cafe appearances open and close the novel, and with the even more unpleasantly self-absorbed Mr. Horsfield, Julia is again the subservient child that Marya of ***Quartet*** was, and Mackenzie and his lawyer in their invulnerable insensitivity are seen by Julia to represent "organized society." She is again the outside, the wild animal caged, and when she sees this reflection of herself in *their* solidly respectable eyes, she loses her confidence in the implicit approval the portrait woman seems to give to her own character. The problem for Julia is still, whose mirror?

Norah is the domesticated slave-sister reflection of the "wild" heroine. Julia's presence in Norah's domestic establishment triggers a momentary spark of rebellion in her and inspires her with the desire to hurt Julia's whose "caged" fires remind her only too well of the potential within her which is now largely extinguished. "Everytime she looked at Julia she felt a fierce desire to hurt her or to see her hurt and humiliated. . . . It was as if meeting Julia had aroused some spirit of rebellion to tear her to bits." This instinct arises in Norah as she is (coincidentally) reading *Almayer's Folly:*

> The slave had no hope, and knew of no change. She knew of no other sky, no other water, no other forest, no other world, no other life. She had no wish, no hope, no love. . . .

Again domestic and tamed wild animals sit side by side and attack each other, instead of directing their attention to their shared fate, or to the root cause of their enslavement, which in this case is less directly a single, representative individual than the grey life of English caution to which the mother had been transplanted and which imposes its cold male judgements on women and colonies alike.

In ***Voyage in the Dark*** the Creole colonial background of the heroine, implicit in the earlier novels, is made explicit, and the contrasting viewpoint against which Marya and Julia were judging Europe and finding it wanting is given specific form in Anna Morgan's West Indian world. While this is the land and the climate Anna loves, and the society to which she would dearly like to belong, her childhood is by no means a total contrast with her adult European experiences, as both involve rejection by a majority community which finds her unacceptable.

Anna's abortive attempt in childhood to identify with the black Creole community by burning her white skin black in the Caribbean sun (an attempt which ironically results in a fever) is paralleled by her similarly abortive attempt later to "fit in" with the English, though she would vastly prefer acceptance by the former community. But her experiences with Walter Jeffries and with a series of itinerant lovers leave her again friendless, nomadic, and dependent, a prey to European and American whims. The pattern of her life mirrors her own Caribbean history of European conquest, flirtation, and desertion, and the resultant dependence of the colonial on the colonizer.

The imprisonment of the alien colonial in the ideals of the almighty "Motherland," and yet the unreality of that land, is expressed in Anna's dream of the ship which sails in a doll's sea, "transparent as glass."

> Somebody said in my ear, "That's your island that you talk such a lot about." And the ship was sailing very close to an island, which was home except that the trees were all wrong. These were English trees, their leaves trailing in the water. I tried to catch hold of a branch and step ashore, but the deck of the ship expanded. Somebody had fallen overboard.

With the characteristic irrationality of dreams, a doll-like boy-bishop who has cruel associations for the dreamer emerges from a coffin to render the dreamer powerless, and thoroughly fatigued, she is left attempting to negotiate a deck that is slippery and lacks any solidity. As a pawn in a power game so remote as to be meaningless, West Indian Anna has been checkmated by King's bishop and is left to wallow in a volitionless Sargasso Sea.

If the thraldom that this dream expresses is ever to be broken, Anna's only chance seems to be to identify with the members of the black Creole community. She feels she shares their fate even if they (like Lois or Marya or Norah) are reluctant to acknowledge the relation, seeing Anna, instead, as part of the white European establishment, to which, it is made painfully clear in another context, she most definitely does not belong. History is responsible for her plight and for that of her ex-slave compatriots.

Forced to act as puppet reflections of their owners, black slaves masked their hatred of their white masters with diurnal submission and nocturnal satire, which, in post-emancipation days, emerged as the Masquerade which Rhys depicts in ***Voyage in the Dark.*** The mask in which the blacks dance is a satirical mirror in which the white Creoles, had they sufficient sensitivity, would see themselves in shocking caricature. Instead, they reject the "wild" behaviour of the blacks as typically animalistic and thus avoid confronting the message of the mask.

The mask had been for the child Anna a terrifying reminder of the chasm which yawned between black and white West Indians, when Anna's nurse Meta terrified her charge by poking her tongue at her from behind the mask. Later in the Masquerade, the masks the blacks wear to satirize the whites are understood by Anna to express the deeply felt hatred of one section of the community for the other. It is only after an experience or reenactment of slave history that she is able at the end of ***Voyage in the Dark*** to arrive at an unself-conscious emotional identity with the Black masqueraders and overcome in the final scenes the typical violence between exiles and underdogs. It is interesting to note how the mask gradually replaces dependence on the mirror for the Rhys heroine in later novels as both the path to association with other victims and as a way to unapologetic self-assertion and even criticism of the colonizer.

Anna's English "master," Walter Jeffries, is first associated with slave owning when he admires Anna's teeth and then leaves her money. Later, when Anna is humiliated by Walter and his brother Vincent, she retaliates with what is almost a parody of the typical slave act of burning the great house. She burns Walter's hand with her cigarette. Comic in its comparative inefficacy, it nevertheless stresses the pathos of her powerlessness, and the depth of her hurt. Petty and almost parodic as these hints of slave experience are, they do provide a demonstrable link between white and black Creole.

Finally, identifying with the black West Indians involves Anna's change of stance from the "I" of white observer to the "we" of black participator.

> *I was watching them from between the slats of the jalousies dancing along dressed in red and blue and yellow the women with their dark necks and arms covered with white power—dancing along to concertina-music dressed in all the colours of the rainbow and the sky so blue. . . . I'm awfully giddy—but we went on dancing forwards and backwards backwards and forwards whirling round and round.*

The black community does not in actual fact accept her, but she overcomes her fear of their hatred, and unself-consciously identifies with them as fellows in oppression, dancing with them their joy and their satire. Significantly this dream communality occurs as the adult Anna is having the abortion which is the inevitable result of her failure to effect a mature and satisfying relationship with a hostile Europe.

The white heroine, through her immersion in the black world, however, may gradually overcome her initial passivity and arrive at the twin possibilities which the masks express: retaliation against former masters and true communality with colonial compatriots. But this thoroughly hopeful prognostic has been qualified by the earlier mention of the fate of the Caribs, who chose extermination over the alternative of domestication by the British, and the Caribs as much as the Blacks are colonial sisters of the white West Indian.

In ***Good Morning, Midnight,*** the heroine is again ostensibly English, and irretrievably the insecure and exploited outsider. This novel again records the state of colonial "impasse" where, in the dream Sasha has at the beginning there seems no "exit," and all corridors lead only to the "Exhibition," the familiar double exposure of the heroine to critical observation. Another caged and exhibited animal, the ageing Sasha, formerly a resident on the Continent, has returned to Europe, and painfully retraces many of her earlier steps. She remembers her dismissal by an English employer, Mr. Blank, who shares the recognizably characterless but domineering qualities of Heidler, Uncle Griffiths, and Mr. Mackenzie. Yet Mr. Blank's relation to his employee is less important than Sasha's liaison with the gigolo and with the strange man in her adjacent hotel room, both of whom she meets on this return visit. Here then Rhys turns her attention to recording the nature of hostilities between underdogs and suggests a tentative exit from this particular branch of the colonial impasse. No movement forward in possible with the "Mr. Blanks," but as in ***Voyage in the Dark,*** progress is made towards a colonial brother/sisterhood in suffering.

The gigolo whom Sasha encounters is, like herself, one of *La Legion Étrangère,* and like Sasha, is selling his affections. Of obscure origin and no fixed abode he is obviously a reflection of herself, but Sasha sees in this soul brother not the potential for rebellion against the organized society which has brought them to this "impasse," only an opportunity for retaliation.

> I had meant to get this man to talk to me and tell me all about it, and then be so devastatingly English that perhaps I should manage to hurt him a little in return for all the many times I've been hurt.

To achieve this, she casts herself in the familiar role of ruler and slave-owner, and admires his teeth. "'Very nice, very nice indeed. Beautiful teeth,' I say in an insolent voice." In her exquisitely subtle exploration of the moves and counter moves of these wary underdogs, Rhys traces the slow growth of Sasha's respect for her mirror image. The culmination of this mood is her acceptance of the man in the white dressing gown as her lover, without despising as she had previously done, all underdogs, including herself.

Colonial implications are evident not only in Sasha's imaginary conversation with Mr. Blank about his exploitation of her labour, but also in the difficulties of deciding what colour to dye her hair:

> Shall I have it black? Now black—that would be startling. Shall I have it blond cendré? But blond cendré, madame, is the most difficult of colours. It is very, very rarely, madame, that hair can be successfully dyed blond cendré. . . . First it must be bleached, that is to say, its own colour must be taken out of it—and then it must be dyed, that is to say, another colour must be imposed on it. (Educated hair. . . . And then, what?)

It is obvious that this technique of hair re-education, is, like many seemingly incidental images and motifs in Rhys's earlier works, an appropriate metaphor for the processes of colonization. But here it expresses not only the general colonial dilemma but the specifically white West Indian one: communal identification with people of a different colour who may refuse to accept her "colour change" even after the difficult denaturing and reconstructing process.

Just as the situation of Sasha seems a general summation of the condition of Marya, Julia, and Anna, so the image of the colonial state more vividly realized in Anna Morgan's dream of the islands and the boy-bishop emerges here as once again the colonial is "plunged in a dream, when all the faces are masks and only the trees are alive and you can almost see the strings that are pulling the puppets."

Wide Sargasso Sea provides the summation and climax of Rhys's explorations. In the marriage between Antoinette Cosway and Edward Rochester, the imperial/colonial relation is clear. What were purely metaphoric expressions for psychic states in the earlier novels are actual in ***Wide Sargasso Sea.*** Antoinette is literally Rochester's prisoner in England. She is friendless, has lost her own name, and is regarded as a wild animal who must be restrained by her captors. Earlier heroines felt they were being exposed in a zoo, but Antoinette actually has a keeper in the formidable Grace Poole, a confessed "underdog" herself. This attitude toward Antoinette, like those of the Englishmen in the earlier novels, is directly ascribable to fear of, and inability to tolerate what cannot be comprehended.

While the ultimate implications of that always-destructive colonial/imperial relation are now laid bare, so too are the very real similarities between Antoinette's fate and that of black slaves in European hands. Antoinette is bought for profit, and is regarded as exotic, hysterical, and incomprehensible by her buyer. He changes her name to a more comfortably English one, and she is dependent on him for her very existence. When she seems to show signs of rebellion she is cruelly punished, though the evidence against her is at best circumstantial. Finally she is reviled as a wild animal and confined in a cruelly uncongenial prison. Antoinette Cosway is thus shown to share the history which apparently divided her from the Blacks.

As a child, Antoinette was pulled between the prejudices of the white and black communities, as Anna Morgan was, and though she subconsciously realizes her affinity with Blacks as victims of history, the divisive stereotypes created by that history continued to thwart her attempts at identification with them. Her embryonic friendship with Tia is shattered when, feeling cheated by Tia, she reacts with automatic white prejudice and dubs Tia "cheating nigger." Yet her conviction that Tia is her soul-mate persists, though Tia forcibly rejects her former playmate when Antoinette's family home is fired by the Blacks. Though Tia utterly rejects Antoinette here, it is noteworthy that in Antoinette's memory of the incident all violence is repressed, and what is shared is emphasized. Antoinette, like Sasha in the end, can reach beyond the immediate violence of the relation between "underdogs" to perceive their common condition. Victims of history, one is the true sacrificial mirror image of the other.

> As I ran, I thought, I will live with Tia and I will be like her. . . . When I was close I saw the jagged stone in her hand but I did not see her throw it. I did not feel it either, only something wet, running down my face. I looked at her and I saw her face crumple up as she began to cry. We stared at each other, blood on my face, tears on hers. It was as if I saw myself. Like in a looking-glass.

Here at last is a mirror in which Antoinette can perceive herself, not the English distortion of self.

After her confinement in Thornfield Hall, Antoinette has suffered in fact a fate comparable with the black Creole one, and her reaction to her confinement is not the "sweet peace of giving in" of Marya of ***Quartet,*** but the typical slave retaliation in the firing of the great house. In this final, controversial section of the novel, Antoinette's red dress provides a striking and supremely important contrast to the black dress of the earlier Rhys heroines. Black there represented the ideal of male European taste: "'She wore black. Men delighted in that sable colour, or lack of colour.'" The women believed that the black dress provided camouflage, protecting them from the critical observation of others, and it was also frequently seen as a potential talisman which might ward off evil. But the black dress ultimately provides no armour against judging European eyes: It never provides the woman with the darker identity she seeks either. Her skin remains insistently pale, and the black dress only mirrors the cold, sad, northern world; it cannot invoke the warm gaiety of a tropical one.

The red dress is different. Beautiful, and strangely alive, it is both an effective mask and an integrated reflection of Antoinette's personality. Like the masks of Masqueraders, it is a satirical comment on an English character which fears and so represses any outbreak of spontaneous warmth, joy, or colour, and which tries, like Grace Poole, to force others into its "grey wrapper." The dress has its own obeah to ward off those who are now by *its* definition outsiders. Its charm works effectively against the English spell of darkness cast over former Rhys heroines, and which they were generally powerless to resist. For Marya, Julia, Anna, and Sasha only "the darkness of the streets had meaning." Antoinette's red dress is the antidote. "Something you can touch and hold like my red dress, that has a meaning." This meaning is the unashamed expression of a tropical riot of felt experience, the sights, sounds, and scents of the West Indian environment which had made the aggressively English Hester of ***Voyage in the Dark*** "faint" and which so appalled Edward Rochester. This red dress which has been locked away by her English captors is the true and undistorted image of Antoinette's personality.

> As soon as I turned the key I saw it hanging, the colour of fire and sunset. The colour of flamboyant flowers. "If you are buried under a flamboyant tree," I said, "your soul is lifted up when it flowers. Everyone wants that." She [Grace Poole] shook her head but she did not move or touch me.
>
> The scent that came from the dress was very faint at first, then it grew stronger. The smell of vetivert and frangipanni, of cinnamon and dust and lime trees when they are flowering. The smell of the sun and the smell of the rain.

Significantly Grace Poole cannot "touch her" while she communes with the dress which casts its charmed circle round her.

Though Antoinette's identification with Tia, and thus her genuine absorption by the black Creole community remains ambiguous to the end, the red flowers of fire and beauty which have blossomed out of Antoinette's actual experience of slave suffering promise that her choice of Tia's invitation to jump, rather than live as Rochester's captive, is the correct one. Though initially "faint" the "scent" of the red dress has been strengthened by this suffering, and in death she will at last be accepted and lifted up by her childhood environment through the myth of rebirth that "Everyone" shares. The fire which consumes Thornfield Hall that Antoinette sees in her dream is both the promise of a flamboyant rebirth and the culmination of her shared slave experience with the Blacks. Jumping to the still slightly taunting Tia, she rejects Rochester and the old imperial associations, choosing instead the fate of her Carib "ancestors." Along the dark passage that has been the experience of England for the Rhys heroine, Antoinette has at last found, in the mask of the red dress, the talisman that lights her way.

In the final scenes then, it is important that the altar of gold (empire profit, the boy-bishop, the Mr. Blanks) be destroyed by the combined powers of Christophine and the red dress (that unite to protect Antoinette as well) for this is a ceremonial, a religious reconciliation of a woman and her land. As in *Palace of the Peacock,* this ultimate union of the forces of a divisive historical destiny is achieved through the "magic" of the spirit of place, and its promise is an integrated, upright personality to annihilate at last the stunted reflection of a beguiling dream.

Frank Baldanza (essay date Fall 1978)

SOURCE: "Jean Rhys on Insult and Injury," in *Studies in the Literary Imagination,* Vol. XI, No. 2, Fall, 1978, pp. 55-65.

[In the following essay, Baldanza provides analysis of the recurring themes, narrative strategies, and female protagonists in Rhys's fiction.]

In discussing the seeming monotony of tone in the work of many distinguished literary figures, Alberto Moravia remarked that most major writers have only one string to their lute, so that the fundamental question ought not to be one of the variety of their effects, but of the complexity and intensity with which they do what they do well. Although few readers outside coteries would call Jean Rhys a major writer, Moravia's remark is nevertheless quite apposite to her fiction. Miss Rhys works, in terms of both theme and technique, in a severely limited range—but, since another essay in this collection discusses her Impressionist methods, I shall concentrate on her thematic complexity and intensity and shall try to avoid, insofar as possible, analysis of technique.

The "archetypal" career of the Rhys protagonist—which can be pieced together from glimpses of variously named characters at various phases of similar lives in her five novels and three collections of short stories—closely resembles the few scraps of biographical information now available about the author, though we have no warrant for a reverse extrapolation from fiction to life. It is in the context of this career that we find her most deeply-felt values and most typical thematic concerns.

We first encounter a sensitive, anti-social, reclusive—nearly misanthropic—West Indian girl whose severe alienation seems self-contained and *sui generis,* though many exterior factors reinforce her withdrawal. In the social sphere, she belongs neither to the stuffily rigid colonial society of her English father nor to the economically precarious but proudly exclusive circles of her Creole mother, a woman of marginal nervous stability. Her only instinctive alliance, and one her mother disapproves of, is with a black servant girl, an omen of her later adult alignment with "the insulted and injured" out cast in Europe. But even here, the general hostility of the subservient natives as a class is a constant source of tension for a girl uncertain of her social identity. In terms of pubescent sexual experience, the girl's passive acceptance of an elderly eccentric's salacious talk and furtive pawing convinces her that she is naturally bad and therefore outside the whole structure of conventional convent-taught morality. (In the deeply felt **"Goodbye Marcus, Goodbye Rose,"** a recently published sketch, the girl bids farewell to her own two pretend-children, about whom she and her classmates had heretofore fantasized.)

The apparent ease and simplicity of this self-judgment, along with her unreflecting passivity, remain highly typical traits throughout her career—the epistemological sanction for most judgments of self and others is simply emotive, never discursively rational, sometimes barely conscious. This passive-emotive decision-making reaches a frozen impasse when one protagonist decides on whether or not to go from France to England to visit an ailing mother by the chance of a taxi horn's blowing before she counts to three. And the most frequent charge against persons she dislikes is their incapacity to feel, their refusal, in effect, to experience emotion. Many characteristics of the protagonists' epistemology bear a remarkable resemblance to those illustrated in the second half of Dostoevsky's "Notes from Underground," in itself a *locus classicus* for tense moods of reclusive alienation. One of the Rhys protagonists, in fact, disagrees with her uncle in his facile dismissal of Dostoevsky's world view, in a scene that constitutes one of the author's most acute confrontations between the alienated and the solidly bourgeois.

After a convent education in the West Indies and a brief period at an English girls' school just before World War I, the girl decides on a stage career on the basis of several scraps of praise for her portrayal of Autolycus in a school production of *A Winter's Tale.* Typically, the girl includes in her performance words and phrases which some of the teachers wanted to censor. Already we sense the Rhys protagonist's virulent hostility to the ranks of the respectable.

The girl launches herself on an independent course, after a short period at the Royal Academy of Dramatic Art, with the partly grudging, partly relieved permission of distant relatives, by joining the chorus for the provincial tour of an English musical comedy. From this point on, the Rhys protagonist's career is fairly stable in its typicality and predictability, if rather unstable in terms of economic and emotional security. "Reckless, lazy, a vagabond by nature" (***Quartet***), the girl seems to accept with a quiet passivity, after a brief initial revulsion, the attentions of well-off young bachelors; partly schooled by more experienced fellow-chorines, partly induced by an insatiable delight in luxurious clothing and a need to feel protected, she goes from one fairly deep emotional involvement through a series of liaisons to a madcap marriage with a dashing, free-wheeling, pettily criminal young man whose appeal is his capacity to live entirely in the present moment. At this point, the early 1920's, she discovers in the Left Bank a more congenial *ambiance* than the gray streets of London.

She may briefly attempt to work as a manicurist, an artist's model, a teacher of English, or a mannequin, but never for more than a few days at a time, since the slightest contact with middle-class regularity shatters her nerves. Essentially, her life, following the death of a baby and the departure of her husband after he has served a jail sentence, is that of a drifting mistress, sometimes kept for a period of time, sometimes dependent on casual street encounters. When she receives a windfall payment from a present or former lover, new clothes are the first concern; but she has also learned to live with hunger. This lust for new clothes is largely a matter of keeping up street appearances before the implacable phalanxes of the respectable; it recalls the machinations of Dostoevsky's underground man to obtain a new beaver collar for his coat when he plans to go out and jostle the elegant strollers on the Nevsky Prospect.

The tone of her experience becomes the sour, rebellious despair of an aging outcast in Europe, given to the false consolations of alcohol and veronal, occasionally begging from former lovers or disapproving relatives, but still retaining token independence and defiance, as her beauty wanes. The Rhys protagonist is giving a local habitation to the same concerns as Dostoevsky's underground man, who asks within his own context of experience whether a man who takes a perverse pleasure in his own humiliation can possibly retain any degree of self-respect. Much of the direct aim of Miss Rhys's writing, especially at this state of the protagonist's career, is to communicate the emotional states of a rudderless beggar-drifter in Paris—the depressing wallpaper of cheap hotels, the care to avoid *cafes* where one has wept openly or made a scene, the spiritless encounters with casual men in which the woman depends on a gradually diminishing charm in order not to reveal too soon in the evening her desperately passive dependence on the man's gratuity—either to him or to herself.

The author herself aims cleanly and taciturnly at communication of emotion, though various readers will respond to the presentation of these emotional states in ways suggested by their own experience, education, and values: Marxist, feminist, formalist, or clinically-psychological readers will place differing emphases; at least one of the feminist reviewers already on record uses the dilemma of the protagonist to illustrate assumptions about society that in themselves have no source whatsoever in the Rhys text. However, if there is a thematic core to the whole varied body of work, it is the evocation of the radical loneliness and despair of a woman who has always been outside the pale of ordinary respectability, tinged with a defiant determination not to let defenses down, not to give an inch of advantage to the enemy in spite of poverty and hopelessness.

From a sociological viewpoint, Miss Rhys gives voice to a class and type of person rarely heard in English writing since the eighteenth century, but her works do not supply enough exterior detail to be hailed as documentary in any sense. The closest analogue I can find for the peculiarly desperate, passive, haunting, hopelessly melancholy loneliness of these pages is in the lady diarists of Heian Japan—Lady Murasaki's *Tale of Genji* and Sei Shonagon's *Pillow Book,* but most particularly The Mother of Michitsuna's *The Gossamer Years* (*Kagero Nikki*). Both the Heian diarists and Miss Rhys present the impasse of a helpless woman entirely dependent on the casual whims of male attention, who must maintain a mask of elegant indifference and unruffled economic security as she desperately watches both her material means and her personal beauty decline.

In this world, there are certain constants. Paris grants anonymity and even the possibility of positive pleasure in youth, whereas England's cold climate and darkly oppressive streets constitute an inferno for the Rhys woman. One must have money to buttress respectability, which she early discovers to be the single, massive anathematic force in her experience. Meanly spying landladies and policemen are the immediate agents of the hypocritically punctilious, emotionlessly calculating, penny-pinching majority, who can kill with a glance. The only escape from this dour army are the well-off bachelors who are willing to support a mistress in lodgings and supply pretty clothes, good times, and an occasional weekend in the country as long as their initial passion lasts.

Miss Rhys's first publication, ***The Left-Bank, Sketches and Studies of Present-Day Bohemian Paris,*** includes a few West Indian vignettes along with Paris material, some of which show up in fuller form in later fiction—for example, the sketch **"From a French Prison"** parallels certain chapters of her first novel, ***Quartet.*** The most impressive piece is **"La Grosse Fifi,"** detailing narrator Roseau's observations of fat, vulgar Fifi's stormy amours with a young gigolo, who later murders her when she objects to his proposed marriage to a young girl. The refraction of Fifi's life through the mind of Roseau guarantees instant and implicit sympathy, since Roseau, despite her morose manner, is herself a similar (if quieter) outcast from respectability whom Fifi tries to resuscitate. In Roseau's allying with Fifi rather than with her snobbishly disapproving friends the upright Olsens, Miss Rhys initiates a strategy that becomes familiar in later works—if the focus is not on the experience of the protagonist/narrator herself, it is frequently transferred to another derelict. In one of Miss Rhys's most recent sketches, **"Night Out, 1925,"** Suzy overpays a pair of whores from the wallet of her stingy escort to compensate them for failing to interest the couple. When Suzy's escort abandons her, she drapes a medallion given her by one of the whores over a discarded red hat in a gutter. This image, by no means as sentimental as it may sound in summary, combines her sympathy for the unlucky whores with an extension to whoever lost the red hat in whatever sad circumstances.

Though slightly marred by explicit "description" of characters here and there, Miss Rhys's first long work, ***Quartet,*** presents the absolute confrontation between the outcast and the respectable in a taut domestic situation. Marya Zelli, without resources during the imprisonment of her husband for fraud in the sale of art works, is taken in by Hugh and Lois Heidler, rich dilettantes of the Left Bank who repeatedly "adopt" vagabonds and repeatedly quarrel with them. Although at first the offer is simply one of succor, it soon becomes evident that Hugh is overmastered by a passion for Marya, in which his wife, Lois, is prepared to acquiesce for his sake, though she extracts her price in insisting Marya show up at social functions to quell gossip about the affair; she habitually practices mean little cruelties that would reduce Marya to the status of a family rag doll.

After a nasty domestic squabble, Hugh removes Marya to a cheap hotel as an occasional mistress. The Heidlers' attempt almost literally to enslave Marya is balked when she leaps from a taxi, after her husband's release from prison, in her determination to be with him despite the Heidlers' disapproval.

The epigraph to this work, a verse by R. C. Dunning, warns against having any doings with Good Samaritans, and despite Miss Rhys's taciturn cleanliness of narration, the deck is stacked fairly heavily against the Heidlers—Hugh wants passion, but not at the cost of breaking with Lois, the perfect snobbish party hostess; Lois thinks she wants Hugh to have his fling, but she erupts in crying spells and endless petty cruelties to Marya. The Heidlers want to dabble in Bohemia without renouncing one bit of respectability.

From all the evidence given in the text, Marya is a helpless victim: at each important early juncture in the relationship, she would prefer not to take up with Hugh and Lois, but their indomitable bossing, coupled with her imprisoned husband's advice to take advantage of their largesse, pushes her into the menage. Once committed, she develops a hopeless love for Hugh, though apparently despising his character throughout. Frequently, the Rhys woman's position as a guest at a bourgeois household or celebration (a weekend in the country with the Heidlers) is generally similar to that of Dostoevsky's underground man at the farewell dinner for Zverkov, the sulking, resentful, brooding intruder whose enraged eruptions and denunciations are simply dismissed by the irritated host. To be sure, Miss Rhys presents such situations with certain differences due to a feminine protagonist and a set of manners removed from nineteenth-century St. Petersburg. And Marya is also much more passively helpless than the underground man, to a degree that taxes my own sympathies: if one frequently behaves like a rag doll, one's right to complain about rag-doll treatment is therefore qualified.

In the two years that intervened before her next novel, Miss Rhys's art matured remarkably; ***After Leaving Mr. Mackenzie*** is a poignant, masterful evocation of her peculiar blend of desperation, loneliness, and defiance. There is even less emphasis on narrative trajectory than in the slight "story" of the first novel, and a consequent emphasis on mood-moments and individual confrontations. Julia Martin, having broken with rich Mr. Mackenzie in Paris, is cut off from her monthly stipend by a lump payment, which she angrily tears up; then, she taps his cheek with her gloves in a restaurant. The bulk of the rest of the novel concerns her return to London to visit her dying mother while maintaining an acquaintance with Mr. Horsfield, a tepid interim lover. Always just a pound or two away from total poverty, abandoned, rejected, and despised, Julia nevertheless maintains an admirably integral grittiness, as assertion of her own autonomy in the face of impossibly bleak prospects and outright hatred by smugly respectable relatives. Her virtues are, without much exaggeration, those that sustain people who keep dignity in the face of incurable illnesses or prison death sentences.

The presentation is one of subtle nuance, in which juxtaposition of extremely short scenes often serves an expressive function. For example, we know that before the opening of the novel, Julia made a loudly hysterical scene at the Restaurant Albert; we then observe her second encounter with Mr. Mackenzie, when she follows him to the same restaurant, he fearing a recurrence of the same ugliness, but getting off more easily with a soft slap. At the conclusion of the novel, perhaps in unconscious gratitude for her restraint at the restaurant, he actually goes over to Julia in the street, after her return from London, congratulating himself on his liberality in even acknowledging her existence, and when she asks him for a small sum, he cavalierly hands her most of the change from his pocket. The complexity of situational irony at this juncture is overwhelming, because in the meantime Julia has in part sustained herself on handouts from Mr. Horsfield, the only man in the Restaurant Albert who observed the slap and who followed her that evening out of interest at her pluck. There is an interesting implicit contrast between Mackenzie and Horsfield in themselves: the former is a very upright, respectable businessman whose general probity carries him through in bourgeois circles, despite the minor weaknesses of having written a few poems and having indulged in the secret liaison with Julia; Horsfield, by contrast, had earlier felt the same kind of smug superiority, the same self-satisfaction in using and discarding unfortunate victims, until wartime experience obliterated his sense of the categorical difference between exploiter and victim. At an important juncture in their London meetings, Julia remarks that seeming benefactors often extract one's life story in lurid detail, and then take subtle pleasure in refusing to give one a penny. Horsfield responds that the pleasure is not subtle, it is direct and brutal, but that he has learned it is also mistaken and cruel. Julia mentioned this kind of situation because she had just asked money of her uncle, who is even more summarily cruel than Mr. Mackenzie; after pumping her for details of her failed marriage, he refuses her absolutely, only relenting to the extent of one pound to pay her fare back to France. Perhaps the most trenchant focus for the oppositeness of Julia and her uncle is in his puzzled opacity in the face of her assertion that Dostoevsky saw man's condition clearly.

The Marya of ***Quartet*** was at a somewhat younger phase, when her physical appeal still gave her a minimal confidence; whereas Julia has begun to sense the onset of middle age—indeed, one aggressive young Parisian pursues her vigorously until he catches a close look at her face in a good light and then departs muttering, "*Oh, la, la . . . Ah, non, alors.*" As she walks through the tawdry Halles quarter, she no longer feels a quick sympathy for tired horses or doorway drunks: Julia realizes that through an accumulation of troubles, she has ended up where most hard-hearted, respectable people begin, with an impassive coldness toward the suffering of others. This sense of both physical and spiritual aging gives peculiarly painful poignancy to the closing lines, "The street was cool and full of grey shadows. Lights were beginning to come out in the cafés. It was the hour between dog and wolf, as they say."

In her fourth work, ***Voyage in the Dark,*** Miss Rhys gives us her typical protagonist, now named Anna Morgan, at a much earlier stage in her career, two years after her arrival in England from the West Indies. The work teems with minor characters, complexity of perceived detail, and an increased emphasis on story line—altogether thicker in texture than any of the preceding novels. In addition, the psychological complexity of Anna's presentation is augmented by sudden recalls of fairly lurid, frightening details from her

Caribbean childhood. The substance of the narration concerns Anna's loss of virginity during her chorus-girl phase, and the subsequent breakup of this first love attachment, followed by a brief period as manicurist to a masseuse and a series of brief liaisons and one-night encounters.

The previous novel treated in an elegiac tone the onset of middle age for a vagabond woman; now the author is looking back to a protagonist who recalls her first menstruation, undergoes sexual initiation and later disillusionment, culminating in a lonely, nightmarish, fear-ridden abortion. From the outset, Anna always instinctively turns toward others outside received society rather than to their respectable persecutors: as a child, she is obsessed by the very name of a slave in family estate records; she is only happy with the black cook Francine, and fervently wishes *she* could be black; perplexed by her first menstruation, she goes immediately to Francine, who reassures her gently, but her fears are revived in a subsequent talk with her mother. Even as an adult, when the forty-year-old masseuse takes her to a cinema in Camden Town, Anna sympathizes totally with Three-Fingered Kate, the burglaress, and feels the audience always applauds in the wrong places, as when the police arrive to arrest Kate.

As she makes her first encounter with the edges of English society, she shows little of the *savoir-faire* of her more seasoned comrades and their playboy admirers, and despite their best efforts to initiate her, she persists in her own peculiar non-conformity. She frequently looks sad, withdrawn, and contemplative in situations where a chorine is uniformly expected to be chipper and sparkling, again like the underground man at Zverkov's banquet. She repulses the attentions of men who do not stimulate her romantically, but when she does find the right man, Walter Jeffries, she relates herself to him in terms of a loving equal, despite what all the pulp fiction, fellow *artistes,* and even the playboys themselves tell her about the evanescence of the man's interest. Indeed, one of Walter's reasons for tiring of her is that Anna burdens him like a heavy stone, rather than taking vigorous advantage of his offer of singing lessons and professional contacts. Unlike her more astute friends, she never saves a penny, and when Walter breaks with her, Anna impulsively refuses help (just as Julia tore up Mr. Mackenzie's parting check). This passive failure of the instinct of self-advancement again demonstrates that the Rhys protagonist hasn't a bourgeois bone in her body.

In Part Two, when Anna has come on desperate times, she is appropriated by the masseuse Ethel Matthews, who takes her up on the impressive strength of her owning a fur coat. But after an occasional success with men like a rich visiting American businessman, Anna's seeming lumpish passivity culminates in a pregnancy that is three months advanced before she seeks help. Ethel abandons her in anger and exasperation.

In contrast to the narration itself, my summary runs the danger of moralizing, to the degree that it incorporates as explicit statement certain value-conclusions which are presented in the text as extremely subtle implicit meanings. Miss Rhys's own emphasis is on the reader's participatory sharing in Anna's sensibility, without generalization. The most masterful effects are in the juxtaposition of present emotional states and recalled childhood traumas, with the hallucinatory abortion at the end as a general recall of previous imagistic *leit-motivs.* In the flow of Anna's contemporary experience, the implicit meanings are carried by scraps of songs or conventional pictures on the walls and especially by images of walls and streets associated with the stern, repressive grayness of English morality. The Caribbean memories, like that of the face of a noseless victim of yaws, tend toward drama and horror.

A morose verse of Emily Dickinson provides the title of Miss Rhys's fourth novel, ***Good Morning, Midnight,*** which takes us forward in the protagonist's career to 1937. This work moves along on a rich flow of perceived detail, even fuller than in the preceding novel, though the narrative progress is considerably less evident; indeed, this seems by far the most episodic of all her novels. In other works, there is a surface commitment to the detached moment, but one senses the steady flow of the story underneath—in ***Voyage in the Dark,*** for example, the stages in the initiation of a young girl. In this novel, seemingly random street encounters and lengthy reminiscences take up the first three parts. Sasha Jansen, the protagonist, is in Paris for a brief rest, financed by a London friend who wishes to rescue her from her immersion in alcohol. The novel ends, in Part Four, on Sasha's tense, dramatic, shattering confrontation with the gigolo René—a devastating impasse which, even if it does seem to stem from the cliché comic encounter of a gigolo and a street walker, is handled with masterful power and gripping emotion that give it profound human significance.

On reaching this final scene, the reader senses a structural ambiguity in the work that may be either a weakness or a strength, perhaps depending on the depth of his sympathy for Sasha's whole world-view. One feels the final scene concentrates the essence of Sasha's whole experience, and yet the drifting, episodic character of much of the previous material does not encourage one to expect a definitive conclusion. In short, the loose structure may be an organic expression of living from moment to moment.

Part One sketches out situation and mood, along with preliminary recall of earlier passages in Sasha's life; Part Two is entirely taken up by an encounter with a subduedly disillusioned Russian who introduces her to an eccentric Dutch painter. Part Three consists of Sasha's memories of her earlier vagabond marriage to the ebullient Enno, and her loss of a baby. To be sure, Sasha first meets René at the end of

Part One, but the reader barely distinguishes him from the texture of other random encounters.

What *may* serve to hold together the exceedingly disparate materials of the first three parts—and may even weld them to the climactic fourth part—is the common theme of down-and-outers, of people at the end of the tether, derelicts at the edge of desperation, like the tramp in a Halles-quarter *café* who tried to eat his glass to earn a drink. The material makes one think of the James Purdy of "63: Dream Palace" or *Eustace Chisholm and the Works.*

Sasha herself, in recalling her humiliating days as a receptionist at a *haute couture* establishment, dwells on her English employer's spite (the animus against the English is strong in all these novels): perhaps his type has the power to cut off one's legs at one blow, but should he then have the right to ridicule the cripple? She later recalls a grim period when she was living at a cheap hotel. On leaving a *cafe* with a casual escort, Sasha staggered from drunkenness, saying she'd not eaten in three weeks; as a result, the man slammed the taxi door in her face and raced off. A train of such incidents illustrates the hideous irony that the more desperate one is, the more cruelly people treat one; the more one needs help, the less one gets. As a capstone to this kind of reminiscence, the Dutch painter recalls finding a sobbing, drunken mulatto woman in his hallway during a London sojourn in Notting Hill Gate. She had lived for two years with a man she didn't love, who only tolerated her for her cooking. She almost never went outdoors because one time when she entered the street at twilight, a child shouted, "I hate you and I wish you were dead."

This emphasis on the lacerating pain of such humiliations raises a central issue of interpretation and of value in Rhys. The financially, socially, and mentally secure middle-class reader may have difficulty understanding the point of such anecdotes. If one steps out of a suburban home and the child next door shouts such a remark, one either laughs it off or gives the parents the name of a good psychiatrist. It becomes obvious that the reference to Dostoevsky in ***After Leaving Mr. Mackenzie*** is not just window dressing: the narrator of "Notes from Underground" has the same open-wound sensitivity to slights like being jostled on the street. It would be too facile to dismiss both Dostoevsky and Rhys as chroniclers of a certain cast of neurotic sensibility (though the observation is true); the value of their art lies in its achievements in inducing readers to extend imaginative sympathy toward "the insulted and injured."

But if we recall how Dostoevsky's protagonist got revenge for his many humiliations—by seeming to redeem a prostitute by genuine love, and then cruelly debasing her—the final section of this novel becomes clearer. Sasha indeed tells herself when she first meets René that his tales of service in the Foreign Legion are lies, but she will lead him on with the lure of her fur coat (the same bait that drew the masseuse in the preceding novel) into thinking her a lonely rich woman and will then slap him down to get revenge for her own humiliations.

In Part Four, in the final confrontation in her room, Dostoevskian ironies proliferate. Sasha refuses René's overtures (though she has been ambivalent about his sexual appeal), and he threatens violence because, though an obvious gigolo, his male pride is piqued. Sasha offers him money from her purse if he will only leave, and when he discovers that this *is* all the money she has, he departs. There is a very subtle suggestion that each of the down-and-outers comes to see the other's wretchedness, though the multiple ambiguities leaves open many paths of interpretation.

But the *tone* of the ending is certainly not one of tender sympathy triumphant. In another Dostoevskian reversal, Sasha lies naked on her bed with the door open hoping against hope that René will return and take her passionately. Instead, the repellent traveling salesman from the next room, a man who has despised and vilified her, enters and takes her as she moans Molly-Bloom yeses.

Miss Rhys's latest novel, ***Wide Sargasso Sea,*** receives full treatment in Todd Bender's essay in this issue, so I shall simply remark that this attempt to right Charlotte Brontë's apparent prejudice against the West Indies in *Jane Eyre* carries forward typical thematic interests. For one thing, the experience of the protagonist fits interestingly into the standard Rhys pattern of what Ford Madox Ford called her "underdog" sympathies. The vindication of Rochester's mad wife, a bit like Anna Morgan's cheering on Three-Fingered Kate at the movies, does not express itself as partisan pleading or tourist brochure blurbs; by simply inducing the reader to share the experience of an outcast, Miss Rhys puts her faith, as she does in all her works, in the proverb *Tout comprendre, c'est tout pardonner.*

Gail Pool (review date Spring 1981)

SOURCE: "Jean Rhys: Life's Unfinished Form," in *Chicago Review,* Vol. 32, No. 4, Spring, 1981, pp. 68-74.

[*In the following review, Pool offers negative analysis of* Smile Please, *citing flaws in the book's lack of structure and Rhys's unreflective content.*]

> "Smile please," the man said. "Not quite so serious."

He'd dodged out from behind the dark cloth. He had a yellow black face and pimples on his chin.

I looked down at my white dress, the one I had got for my birthday, and my legs and the white socks coming half way up my legs, and the black shiny shoes with the strap over the instep.

"Now," the man said.

I tried but my arm shot up of its own accord.

"Oh what a pity, she moved."

"You must keep still," my mother said, frowning.

Smile Please

Those who are familiar with the work of Jean Rhys will recognize in this opening passage of her autobiography the defining characteristics and world view of the central character of her fiction. Repeatedly, Rhys's heroine—a vulnerable, intelligent, perceptive, helpless woman—is told what to do, tries to do it, fails, and is looked upon with a combination of pity and disapproval. It is certainly not inconsequential that what the child in this episode fails to do is to smile; one of Rhys's themes is that one ought to try to "make the best of things," and that she never really manages to do so. The impotence, the self-doubt, the self-consciousness, the failure, the disapproval, the pity, the acute and intelligent awareness of the entire scene, which takes place moreover in the realm of appearances—all describe what we find over and over again in the novels.

The opening passage is one of the best in ***Smile Please: An Unfinished Autobiography,*** published in 1979, after Rhys's death, a book that only intermittently gathers energy and never manages to sustain it. That the book is not in itself successful is. I think, evident, and the reasons for its lack of success relate interestingly to the way that Rhys's fiction works. In part, the relationship contrasts the form of fiction with the formlessness of life, an issue which frustrated Rhys. In part, the problem hinges on Rhys's approach both to fiction and to life. That she was neither reflective nor analytical limits the statements she can make about her life. Interestingly, too, what we discover moving back from the autobiography to the fiction, which uses much of the same material, is how little we know about Jean Rhys personally.

It is well known that Rhys's fiction was largely autobiographical. As Diana Athill, Rhys's editor who wrote the foreword to her autobiography, remarks, the process of fictionalizing "never took her a great distance from the experience." However, Rhys did fictionalize, and the process was to create form: she changed episodes from their reality to meet the aesthetic requirements of the work at hand.

"I like shape very much," said Rhys. "A novel has to have a shape and life doesn't have any." Indeed, form is the quality that characterizes almost all of Rhys's fiction from the earliest, written in the 1920s, to the latest. It may be that ***Quartet,*** her first novel, is not strong, but its weakness is certainly not a lack of form. In ***Quartet*** and the three fine novels which follow it, ***Voyage in the Dark, After Leaving Mr. Mackenzie,*** and ***Good Morning, Midnight,*** the overall structure of the fiction is tight as a fist—and that tightness is its strength and its power. It is almost as if Rhys saw and felt her work in shapes, and what she created and offered us was precisely those shapes; thus, her form was not merely integral to the work, but to some degree was the work itself.

But if the essence of fiction, to Rhys, was form, did autobiography have to be formless? ***Smile Please*** is a series of vignettes and sketches that serve to create impressions. What form the work has is its time frame, since it presents the chronological sequence of her life, and it is an artificial, imposed form—one that might have worked, but didn't, because it was not really consistent with the way Rhys viewed her life. What might have saved the structure was some sense of linkage or causality. But we do not have the sense that Rhys's early years were crucial, causally, to the later years, or even related to them. None of the sections are critically linked.

It is true that the autobiography was not finished when Rhys died, and it is difficult to evaluate critically an unfinished work, especially if the writer is a craftsman, in which case unfinished is as good as not done at all. The work was moving away from the vague sketches toward a narrative form, which might have proved more effective. But revision alone might not have solved the problems of the work. The autobiography is divided into two parts. "Smile Please," and "It Began to Grow Cold"; and it is the latter of the two that Athill identifies as truly unfinished. Yet it comes more fully to life than the former. It may be that "finishing" this particular work would not have improved it, that further refinement would have further deadened it.

Why the lifelessness? This is not a quality one finds in Rhys's fiction. Athill suggests that the autobiography was weak because the material had already been used up in the novels, written out, and had grown too stale to bear repetition. Yet I wonder if this is the case. If we turn from the autobiography to the fiction, we find that of the novels that take place in London and Paris, each, read singly, is a stunning rendition of a story that Rhys never seemed to tire of telling. The story in each of these novels is essentially the same, but each time it strikes with fresh and painful force. It does not seem likely that she would either write this material out or use it up.

The major part of ***Smile Please*** takes place in Dominica, where Rhys was born and where she remained until the age of sixteen, when she was sent to school in London. The West Indian material had always been to some degree intractable, and not because it had been "written out." ***Sleep It Off, Lady,*** a work which in a number of ways strongly resembles ***Smile Please,*** is a collection of stories which was published in 1976; drawn from Rhys's life and arranged in chronological order, the stories offer an overview of the life (though explicitly not an autobiography), beginning with stories set in the West Indies and concluding beyond death with the heroine's appearance as a ghost. The collection is of uneven quality, but the weakest of the stories are those which take place in the West Indies; they are diffuse, tedious, and disoriented.

One has the sense that Rhys did not have anything pressing she wanted to say about her West Indian childhood. Because the setting was dramatic, it must have appealed to her to try to work with it, but unlike Lowry's Mexico, which was not only the background of an obsession but a part of it. Rhys's Dominica in her stories and in her autobiography is simply there, a picturesque backdrop rather than a living part of the play.

Rhys used the tropical setting effectively in ***The Wide Sargasso Sea,*** the least autobiographical of her writings, which suggests that Rhys's problem was not the setting itself, but that she had no precise ideas about or attitudes toward its significance in her own life. In the novel, a brilliant interpretation of the life of Mrs. Rochester, the wife of the hero of *Jane Eyre,* the West Indies serves to create the character. But in ***Smile Please,*** we hear that Rhys feared insects, went to numerous carnivals and religious processions, that she was in a convent, that her nurse practiced witchcraft—details that do not possess intrinsic interest. That the events occur in an exotic setting does not suffice to make them exotic. We need a perspective that would make the details significant.

The listless quality of the West Indian material points us toward the kind of writing Rhys did not do, the ways in which she did not think, which are useful for defining who she was. For what there was to write about in Dominica, it seems, was the political and social, uneasiness, the relations between colonials and blacks, the position of Rhys's own parents on the island, the interplay between the religious elements (Catholic and pagan)—all of which appear but are not explored in depth in either Rhys's fiction or her autobiography. That they hover in the background, potential sources of a power never achieved, makes clear that Rhys was neither a political nor, directly, a social writer. She was aware of these forces, but they were not what mattered in her life, they were not what determined her life.

It is unfortunate that Rhys held such a strictly chronological concept of autobiography that compelled her, both in ***Sleep It Off, Lady*** and in ***Smile Please,*** to start at the beginning in Dominica and proceed through to the end, for her energy is diffused in the tropics long before she reaches the chapters of her life which seem to have interested her more. Only in London and Paris did Rhys find a subject that did not dry out and that engaged her interest, a subject which that world symbolized and provided material for: life on the edge.

Life on the edge, struggle, compromise, defeat—these are what Rhys depicts best in her fiction and what must have related most powerfully to her own life. Not in the West Indies but in this world of cheap hotels, pick-ups, and kept women Rhys found the arena in which she would play out her life struggles. It is easy to see Rhys as the heroine of her novels. What is unusual about the character who inhabits this world is her intelligence, her perception, her ability to size up her situation—clearly Rhys's own talents and skills. But if it is easy to attribute the character's intelligence to Rhys, one must be wary of ascribing attributes at random. There is always the form: Rhys changed what needed to be changed, and one does not really know how far to read.

One is dealing in part with events and in part with experience. Rhys was concerned in her autobiography to set straight the events of her life, but perhaps the experience was the more confusing element. Most perplexing, perhaps, is Rhys's attitude toward women and the position of women. Her central characters reveal an odd combination of intelligence and foolishness. For all their intelligence, their solutions to the problems in which they find themselves are inane. They seem truly to believe that if one only had a new coat, one would surely get a good job. A new hat, a new dress, a new pair of shoes are seen as bridges to a new life.

It is fair to say that intelligence will not in itself ward off disintegration: one may perceive acutely why one is falling apart and be unable to prevent it. In addition, Rhys understands the fear her heroines endure; for the most part, they are too frightened to make the moves they must make to get themselves out of the holes they are in. But it is clear that the intelligence of Rhys's heroines is neither reflective nor analytical. They analyze perceptions, not ideas; they move in an area of sensibility.

The emphasis on the world of superficial appearances throughout the fiction is striking. That the heroine has no decent hat, that she has put on weight, that her hair at any particular moment might be out of place are factors that take on disproportionate significance. One becomes aware that the heroine's world does not extend far beyond her own body, that to some degree it is circumscribed by her physicality. One could not imagine a male weighing his situation in such terms; this is a part of the female situation which Rhys depicts so terrifyingly.

But what about Rhys herself? Could she have saved her heroines? Could she have provided them with the solutions they could not find? Did she merely depict what was real, the reality of women's lives?

Rhys did not see fiction's role as offering judgments; they would have diminished the power of her work by delineating heroes and villains in a simplistic fashion. Thus, the refusal to judge was a part not only of her style but of the meaning of her work. But I had always believed that Rhys presented so clearly and painfully the rut into which her heroine's solutions led because she meant for us to conclude that the solutions were inane, that the position of women in the world was inane.

Smile Please offers a different view of Rhys. For here, in the realm of non-fiction, what Rhys relates about lives and her own experience is precisely that world of appearances: what one looked like, what one wanted to look like, what the effects of looking like that were, what the effects of looking like what one wanted to look like would have been. And suddenly, looking at the pictures of Rhys, a beautiful woman with enormous eyes, one realizes that she must have cared terribly about appearance, that she did feel it was of crucial significance, and that possibly she did not view her heroines' solutions as inane; that perhaps there was no judgment in the fiction because—there was no judgment.

That Rhys herself was caught in the situation she so accurately describes in no way diminishes the power of her description. However, her refusal to analyze does restrict her access to her life. Without analysis, she can only offer details; without reflection, she cannot shape the details for us. The techniques which are so effective in the fiction simply do not work in the autobiography. The vignettes, the snippets, the flip and witty asides seem to hide more than they reveal. While this is intriguing in fiction, it is irritating in autobiography. I do not read fiction to find out about a life; I do read autobiography because I want to know about a particular life, and I am resentful if I am not given entry, having paid the price of a ticket.

What drew Rhys to the project of writing an autobiography? She was 86 when she began to work on the book; she had a heart condition, her hands were too severely crippled to write, and she had a drinking problem. In a reminiscence published in *Paris Review* (number 76, 1979) that is excessive, tasteless, and finally pointless, David Plante (who worked with Rhys on this autobiography) reveals but this one useful fact: that Rhys was in no shape to write anything, let alone give form to the material that had been her life.

According to Athill, the idea of writing an autobiography did not really "attract" Rhys; it was not "the kind of writing that came to her naturally." This is most probably true. Autobiography requires reflection, the formulation of an overview Rhys was either unwilling or unable to make. She did not work this way in her fiction, and it seems to have been a mode of thinking she found alien.

If the idea of writing an autobiography did not attract Rhys, if the type of writing was not what she enjoyed, if her health was poor, and if she had already in ***Sleep It Off, Lady*** presented a good deal of the material, what on earth drew Rhys on to undertake this work? "Because she was sometimes angered and hurt by what other people wrote about her, she wanted to get the facts down," Athill says. If this was her main motivation, it is unfortunate; for although there are numerous facts in the work (including those she wanted to get down to set the record straight), they are for the most part lost for lack of a perspective that might have given them coherence. The events are clarified only to fall into oblivion.

Interestingly, as a result of reading ***Smile Please,*** I began to question the autobiographical aspects of her work. Much of the autobiography appears to be the writing out of a persona: it is not material that is untrue, but it represents a set of characteristics Jean Rhys had decided were Jean Rhys. Since much of this material appears in the fiction as well, I began to wonder where one might find reality. To be tough, as Rhys is about the London-Paris years, or to be nostalgic, as she is about her early years, is not necessarily to be open about the experience. Perhaps Rhys imposed more form than she was aware of upon life itself and gave it a shape after all.

There are things one might have wanted to know about Jean Rhys's life, about her attitudes toward women or toward writing, that probably never could have been known—because she herself didn't know them. The Rhys we see in ***Smile Please*** did not ask herself questions about her attitudes and philosophy; there seem to have been modes of analysis she had no patience for. She did not want to reflect in certain ways about her life—or if she did, she fully intended to keep those reflections to herself. Indeed, reading her autobiography one comes to the conclusion that for an author who wrote almost exclusively about herself, Jean Rhys revealed remarkably little about Jean Rhys.

Linda Bamber (essay date 1982)

SOURCE: "Jean Rhys," in *Partisan Review,* Vol. XLIX, No. 1, 1982, pp. 92-100.

[*In the following essay, Bamber provides an overview of Rhys's fiction, literary career, and critical reception.*]

Jean Rhys, who died in 1978 at age eighty-four, lived long enough to ride the wheel of literary fashion full circle. Taken up by Ford Madox Ford in the twenties, she was completely forgotten two decades later. In 1958 a British radio producer advertised for news of her whereabouts; Rhys herself answered the ad from Devon and subsequently resumed her literary career. Since the publication of ***Wide Sargasso Sea*** in 1966, there has been a steady growth of interest in her stories and novels. One by one all her books of the twenties and thirties have been reissued and enthusiastically reviewed; the final accolade came several years ago when A. Alvarez, writing in the *New York Times,* called her "the best living English novelist." Recently, articles of literary criticism have begun to appear on Rhys. Her readers seem confident that the job of evaluation is over and that her books may be treated as classics.

It would be interesting to know Rhys's own attitude towards her second wave of literary success. It was clearly gratifying to her at some level; under its influence she wrote the later stories published in the *New Yorker* and collected in ***Sleep It Off, Lady*** (1976). But Rhys was a woman more comfortable with failure than with success, and she apparently met her admirers with suspicion and some bitterness. She saw herself as an outsider, someone beyond the pale of respectable society; it is not surprising that she picked up on the unpleasant, rather than the pleasant, parts of her growing fame. Miriam Levine, the poet, interviewed Rhys in 1977 and reports that her conversation was, at least initially, prickly and self-protective. Rhys is quoted as follows:

> I did a satiric piece on interviews called **"Building Bricks Without Straws."** They did a terrible piece about me in *Women's Wear Daily.* Mizener lied about me in his book on Ford. Some critic sent me this long article comparing me to Ann Radcliffe. You're not going to call me a Gothic novelist, are you?

Rhys is here playing the role she is most familiar with: Establishment Victim, in this case the victim of the literary establishment. Yet the literary establishment these days is unanimous in its enthusiasm for her work.

Rhys's sense of being an outsider must certainly have its roots in her personal history. Born in Dominica of a Welsh father and a Creole mother, she ran away to England at sixteen, married a French-Dutch poet and moved to France. In England she studied briefly at the Royal Academy of Dramatic Arts; then she went on the road as a chorus girl. With Jean Lenglet, the first of her three husbands, she led an irregular life, borrowing money and sleeping on other people's couches, often in some sort of trouble with the authorities. A contemporary describes the world Lenglet shared with Rhys as "an underworld of darkness and disorder, where officialdom, the bourgeoisie and the police were the . . . enemies and the fugitive the . . . hero." In one of her fitful efforts to make some money Rhys at one point translated a few of Lenglet's feature articles into English and peddled them to Paris-based representatives of British newspapers. It was while she was acting as Lenglet's agent that she was herself "discovered" as a writer. The sympathetic wife of a *London Times* correspondent read Rhys's journals, typed them up for her, and sent them on to Ford Madox Ford, at that time the editor of the *Transatlantic Review.* Ford became Rhys's literary mentor, her lover, and the subject of her future work. ***The Left Bank*** (1927) is a collection of stories that Ford helped into print; ***Quartet*** (1928) is a about the period of time during which Rhys lived in a *ménage à trois* with Ford and his wife, Stella Bowen; and ***After Leaving Mr. Mackenzie*** (1930) looks back on the affair after its unpleasant ending. Her last prewar novel, ***Good Morning Midnight*** (1939), was written more than a decade after her relations with both Ford and Lenglet were over. At this point, Rhys was remarried to Leslie Tilden Smith, reader for a British publishing company. Yet in the novel Rhys returns to the events of her early married life, replaying them in the memory of her aging heroine.

Rhys's novels, all of them autobiographical, have one subject: the victimization and self-victimization of a woman drifting along the edges of artsy-bourgeois society. The Rhys heroine has no money, no family to speak of, no particular talents. Out of sexual desperation (for she is always spurned by the man she loves) she picks up men who turn out to be cads or gigolos. These encounters usually take place in Bloomsbury or the Left Bank; the atmosphere is of a café life, of cosmopolitan sterility. The heroine lives entirely in the present, and her ambition for the future is to get through the afternoon without crying. When she fails she says to herself, "Now, I'm a gone coon. I've begun crying and I'll never stop." The world shrinks to the size of the heroine's rented room—from which she makes pathetic forays for a brandy and to which she returns, as like as not, to be bullied for her failures by the landlady.

Notably absent from Rhys's account of her heroine is any analysis of her plight in political terms. The Rhys heroine is a natural victim, not a victim of sexual politics or class oppression. As an exile of obscure origins she is more or less classless; and although she certainly feels brutalized by men, she insists that "I'm even more afraid of women." The problem is extremely general: "People are such beasts, such mean beasts," says the heroine of ***After Leav-***

ing Mr. Mackenzie. Elsewhere the formula is simply "life is cruel and horrible to unprotected people." The social analysis of Rhys's work stops with the assertion that there are outsiders and insiders, and that the one is entitled to resent the other. But even the resentment is fitful and limp. The Rhys heroine knows that she is largely responsible for her own unhappiness. Whenever something good comes her way—money, a man, the possibility of a good time—she instantly loses it through laziness, obsessiveness, or a kind of petty anger arising from her sense that it isn't enough.

Another notable absence in Rhys's work is the sense of place. We are told that we are in Paris rather than London, or vice versa, but it seems to make little difference. The outside world has withdrawn from the Rhys heroine. As long as there is a room, a street, or a restaurant for her to occupy, she doesn't bother much about the details. That is, of course, Rhys herself, in sympathy with her heroine's depression, makes no effort to find correspondences between the inner and the outer life. Her heroines experience the thinness of life and Rhys means for her readers to do likewise. Ford Madox Ford tells in the preface to ***The Left Bank*** how he tried to get Rhys to "introduce some sort of topography. . . into her sketches. . . ." He goes on to say:

> But would she do it? No! With cold deliberation, once her attention was called to the matter, she eliminated even such two or three words of descriptive matter as had crept into her work. Her business was with passion, hardship, emotions.

Rhys does sometimes include material that is interesting for its own sake: there are descriptions of the life of a Paris manikin, of a Bloomsbury group's horrible country vacation, of Left Bank parties. And in the first section of ***Wide Sargasso Sea*** she quite brilliantly works up the landscape of Dominica, where all relationships are as decadent as the lush, rotting vegetation. But the monotony of the heroine's feelings is more likely than not to fill the whole frame, foreground and background.

Ford's description of Rhys's "business" is worth pausing over. According to Ford, and to many of Rhys's contemporary readers, the point of Rhys's work is the intensity of the heroine's inner life. From time to time Rhys will indeed claim a kind of energy for her heroine; in ***Quartet,*** for example, the "longing for joy" is said to be a "mad thing in her heart . . . like some splendid caged animal roused and fighting to get out." But the characteristic gesture in Rhys's novels is actually the *withdrawal* of emotional presence in times of crisis, not the enactment of fierce emotional needs. The following exchange between heroine and her lover is typical:

> "I want to help you; I want you to get on. You want to get on, don't you?"
>
> "I don't know," I said.
> "But my dear, how do you mean you don't know? . . . What would you really like to do?"
>
> I said, "I want to be with you. That's all I want."
>
> "Oh, you'll soon get sick of me." He smiled, a bit as if he were sneering at me.
>
> I didn't answer.
>
> "Don't be like that," he said. "Don't be like a stone that I try to roll uphill and that always rolls down again."
>
> "Like a stone," he said. It's funny how you think, "It won't hurt until I move." So you sit perfectly still. Even your face goes stiff.

The withdrawal here is twofold. The heroine, Anna, withdraws from the lover, her face stiff with pain; and Rhys withdraws from the reader into ellipsis and Hemingway-style understatement. Neither gesture seems compatible with mad, splendid longings for joy. Both the author and the heroine characteristically avert their eyes from precisely the "passion, hardship [and] emotion" that Ford thought central to Rhys's project.

A more recent admirer of Jean Rhys, A. Alvarez, explains the novelist's technique as follows:

> She is . . . far too pure an artist to allow herself the luxury of self-pity . . . The moments of drama and confrontation—when the subterranean terror and despair seem about to burst through-remain strictly moments, done briefly, without comment or fuss from the outside. Her mind flicks away from them, quick as a fly, and settles on some small detail off to one side: her makeup is wrong, the light falls oddly, a bell rings, a car hoots. . . . And this . . . is far more unnerving than any full-throated howl of anguish can ever be.

To Alvarez, the withdrawals of consciousness are precisely the point. According to Alvarez, it is just when the author abandons the effort to render the heroine's feelings that they become most vivid to us, just when the heroine abandons her claims on life that we become aware of the depth of her needs. And yet as we can see from the dialogue leading up to Anna's withdrawal, the disappearances of the heroine and her author do not come at "moments of drama and confrontation—when the subterranean terror and despair seem about to burst through." They come at moments when the linguistic and emotional energy is already low. Anna can't get a job, can't want a job, can only throw herself on the mercy of her helpful/superior lover: "I want to be with you. That's all I want." When Anna averts her eyes from the inevitable response to her meagerness, her withdrawal is not a sudden and striking gesture of giving up. It is another step in the continuous retreat that is the form and content of Rhys's work.

Anna is the heroine of ***Voyage in the Dark,*** Rhys's first novel. This book describes Rhys's first love affair and was initially written in journal form. In ***Smile Please*** (1978), Rhys's posthumously published autobiography, she comments on that affair as follows:

> When my first love affair came to an end I wrote this poem:
>
> I didn't know.
> I didn't know.
> I didn't know.
>
> Then I settled down to be miserable.
>
> But it still annoys me when my first object of worship is supposed to be a villain. . . .
>
> On the contrary, I realise now what a very kind man he must have been. I was an ignorant girl, a shy girl. And . . . I realise I was also a passive, dull girl. Though I couldn't control my hammering heart when he touched me, I was too shy to say "I love you." It would be too much, too important I couldn't claim so much.

Rhys here describes both her biographical self and the heroine of her autobiographical novels. Like her heroines, Rhys couldn't claim much. That is, she could not make her claims directly; she based them on her weaknesses and failures rather than on her strengths. Stella Bowen, Ford's wife at the time of his liaison with Jean Rhys, tells us that, in life as in her fiction, Rhys self-consciously played the role of the loser:

> Ford's girl was by no means without generous instincts and her world had its own standards of chic. . . . Yet here I was cast for the role of the fortunate wife who held all the cards, and the girl for that of the poor, brave, and desperate beggar who was doomed to be let down by the bourgeoisie. I learned what a powerful weapon lies in weakness and pathos and how strong is the position of the person who has nothings to lose, and I simply hated my role! I played it, however, until the girl was restored to health and a job materialized, since we appeared to represent her last chance of survival.

Bowen's analysis rings true, right down to the constant sense of "last chance" that Rhys creates in her novels. The final disaster, desertion or death, is always just around the corner. In ***Quartet*** Rhys explicitly claims pathos as her defining mode, commenting on the Ford and Bowen figures as follows:

> Of course, there they were: inscrutable people, invulnerable people, and she simply hadn't a chance against them, naive sinner that she was.

The outside world is knowing and invulnerable, the Rhys heroine is "naive," innocent in spite of her sins, pure because helpless.

Rhys's helplessness is often a kind of "weapon" in her fiction just as it was in her life. Her silences are not, unfortunately, the true absences that Alvarez takes them for but a form of pressure for the reader's sympathy. Rhys's retreats have a double message. We cannot be such beasts, she seems to say, as to refuse our sympathy to someone with such poverty of artistic means, someone so helpless to make her own case. There is a kind of emotional blackmail to Rhys's technique: she is like a woman who leaves the room in silent agony, indicating in every line of her body an absolute demand to be followed.

What is particularly disturbing is that Rhys seems to equate her femininity with her pathos, the one reinforcing the other. In ***Good Morning, Midnight,*** for instance, we hear of a "thin, scraggy and hunted" kitten: "Well, all the male cats in the neighborhood were on to her like one o'clock. She got a sore on her neck and the sore got worse. . . . In the glass just now my eyes were like that kitten's eyes." The heroine is called romantic names like Antoinette, Petronella, Julia, Sasha, Roseau. She is as vulnerable as the kittens, sad children, and gentle prostitutes who so often cross her path; there is no question but that the feminine should be protected. The men who don't pay up, the lovers who fail to provide a haven for the heroine, practically perceive *themselves* as cads and slink ignominiously from the novels. The one time a Rhys heroine is satisfied with the behavior of "people" in general is when they do homage to her femininity during a pregnancy:

> My face is pretty, my stomach is huge. . . . People are very kind to me. They get up and give me their seats in buses. *Passe, femme sacrée.*

"*Passe, femme sacrée,*" of course, is offered ironically; and yet to Rhys it is a kind of tragedy when, as so often, the feminine is *not* held sacred.

Rhys's last book, ***Smile Please,*** is a curious phenomenon. It was apparently undertaken to correct false impressions about the author's life. There were rumors that one of her two children was Ford's; not so, Rhys wanted us to know, both were Lenglet's. Her first lover was, as we have seen, a kind man, not a villain; Lenglet was arrested for currency violations, not robbery. But what developed from this impulse to set the record straight is a collection of fragments which are pointless, at best, and at their worst, quite ugly. Rhys finished only the first half of the book, the part on her childhood in Dominica; but even if we confine ourselves to that we must be surprised at what we are offered. Our attention is claimed for what cannot possibly interest us. We learn that Rhys had *petits pains* for breakfast while she was in convent school, not *croissants;* that she cannot remember how her father defined Nirvana; that when she first got a clothing allowance she bought herself a red tam-o'-shanter; that she loved the word "wisteria" and hated the word "cold." It is when she comes to the matter of race relations in Dominica that her book seems worse that shapeless. Rhys records her discovery that she was disliked by a black fellow student in tones of undisguised self-pity; and she includes this lethargically mean-spirited comment on the contemporary Caribbean situation:

> When years later I paid a short visit to Dominica I went to the library of course. Instead of being empty it was crowded, a long queue before the librarian's desk. At first I thought it was a very touching sight, all the black hands, eagerly stretched out, holding books. Then I noticed how all the librarian, whom of course I knew, looked. As people filed past her she'd take the book, stamp it and give it back. No one looked at her and no one thanked her. They seemed to think that she was a machine and indeed there was something robotlike about the way she was working. Book after book and with each one she seemed to get more tired, look more ill. I wasn't at all surprised when I heard a few days later that she was dead.
>
> I seem to be brought up willy-nilly against the two sides of the question. Sometimes I ask myself if I am the only one who is; for after all, who knows or cares if there are two sides.

Ludicrously, Rhys seems to imply that the spread of culture to the third world will result in the death of the Culture-keepers, overworked librarians. She doesn't mean it, of course; but what does she mean?

Smile Please includes an admiring foreword by Rhys's editor at Harper and Row, Diana Athill, and is followed by a chronology of Rhys's life and a bibliography of her books. In the middle are pictures of Rhys's grandfather's church in Wales, Rhys's first and second husbands, and Rhys's return to Dominica in the thirties. In other words, the book treats Rhys as a classic author. There is something incongruous in the contrast between the featherweight text and the solemn superstructure that surrounds it. As Phyllis Rose points out in the *Yale Review,* "her autobiography will win her no new readers." And yet it has been, for the most part, reviewed as respectfully as it has been packaged. Rose is one of the few reviewers as to admit that this book "demonstrates how *not* to write an autobiography" and that Rhys's talents as a writer have clearly been undermined by the fact that she was "frequently soused" while writing the book. Rhys, who was awarded the CBE (Commander of the Order of the British Empire) in 1978, is an institution. We have apparently learned from her the trick of silent withdrawal from her failures.

Jean Rhys had a hard life. She grew up imagining that life was elsewhere—in England; when she got to England it was dingy, cold, and hostile to her ambition to become an actress. The most appealing picture of Rhys in ***Smile Please*** shows her posed in a tableau vivant with other young and pretty members of her troupe. But the energy and good humor of this moment faded during a grueling and humiliating tour of the north of England, and Rhys came to think of herself mostly in terms of her unsatisfactory relationships with men. Her first marriage ended in divorce; her second husband died seven years after her marriage to him. She lost a child, she herself was in poor health for the last fifteen years of her life. For the biographical woman who suffered all this we can have only sympathy. We are indeed "mean beasts" if we refuse to recognize in her an example of common human misfortune. But towards the heroine of her novels, towards the woman as she imagines herself, we may surely be permitted to feel some irritation and disapproval. Her unhappiness does not seem awful and inevitable, as Rhys's own unhappiness was. It is worn as a badge of honor, claimed as a position of power. The Rhys heroine considers her unhappiness a brilliant distinction. Sasha, the heroine of ***Good Morning, Midnight,*** tells us:

> I'm not talking about the struggle when you are strong and a good swimmer and there are willing and eager friends on the bank waiting to pull you out at the first sign of distress. I mean *the real thing.* You jump in with no willing and eager friends and when you sink you sink to the accompaniment of loud laughter. [my italics]

To sink is more interesting than to swim, to be friendless is to experience *the real thing.* If only Sasha would value her pathos a little less than she does, perhaps she would become less pathetic. The great modern poets of our futility and choicelessness persuade us, against our wills, that there is no alternative to our difficulties. The Rhys heroine, however, proudly *refuses* alternatives. Her situation, therefore, is not necessarily ours. Within the shelter in *Endgame* is the whole of the modern world; we cannot escape it. But we need only visit the rented rooms of Rhys's novels when we are feeling low or broke or pissy. Who would do time there if she could help it? Not Rhys, certainly, who remarked in an interview:

> When I was excited about life, I didn't want to write at all. . . . You see, there is very little invention in my books. What came first with most of them was the wish to get rid of this awful sadness that weighed me down.

The desolation in Rhys's work, then, is not to be mistaken for the whole story. It is only how things look when we feel bad. The novels powerfully evoke a mood, but it is a mood we would ordinarily do much to avoid: depression. There is very little here to distance us from the bad mood of her work. This is the thing itself, much as we might hear it from a friend in trouble or, if we were in the business, from the couch.

Arnold E. Davidson (essay date Summer 1984)

SOURCE: "The Art and Economics of Destitution in Jean Rhys's *After Leaving Mr. Mackenzie,*" in *Studies in the Novel,* Vol. XVI, No. 2, Summer, 1984, pp. 215-27.

[*In the following essay, Davidson offers analysis of the characters, narrative structure, and thematic concerns of* After Leaving Mr. Mackenzie.]

Jean Rhys published her first four novels to little notice in the 1920s and 1930s and then passed into a long oblivion but one that she survived to see herself proclaimed in 1974 as "quite simply, the best living English novelist." However, as Elizabeth Abel subsequently observed, a belated recognition of Rhys's genius as a writer does not itself do full justice to that genius, and, "despite her exceptional technical skill and the relevance of her subject matter to the women's movement," her fiction "has [still] received little critical attention." Moreover, Rhys is commonly viewed, in Todd Bender's wording, as "the author of one masterpiece [and] four less interesting novels." ***Wide Sargasso Sea,*** the acknowledged masterpiece and Rhys's fifth and final novel, has, of course, received the preponderance of critical attention. Bender observes, too, that a general critical concern with Rhys's "topicality . . . carries its own dangers," one of which is a tendency to overlook how "seriously [she was] engaged in the modernist movement in literature."

The present essay is intended to address some of the imbalances suggested in the previous paragraph. Rhys's fiction does merit continued critical attention, and it particularly merits such attention because, as Bender implies, the artistic principles and procedures of this author have not yet been adequately assessed. Abel, in fact, practices an odd version of the critical neglect she early deplores. She first maintains that "although Rhys describes her heroines' progressive degeneration, often in excruciating detail, she fails to provide an adequate explanation for this process," and then argues that "a closer look at Rhys's recurrent heroine" gives us an explanation in the form of the protagonist's "schizophrenia." But Abel's delineation of the incipient madness in the characters misses the covert method in the plots—a method that also "rationalizes" most of the evidence of irrationality upon which Abel's argument rests. In short, the "closer look" must be at the individual novels themselves and more specifically at just how carefully Rhys depicts in her "sparse and repetitive narratives" (Abel's phrase) a particular protagonist's declining fortunes and to what ends. I therefore propose to examine one test case, and for my present purposes I pick not the first novel, ***Quartet,*** which does admittedly evince a number of the flaws that first novels are commonly heir to, but the second, ***After Leaving Mr. Mackenzie.*** In this work we can see how quickly Rhys achieved a characteristic artistic control of her essential subject matter. We can also see how capably she exercised that control and how much her second novel is not at all what a recent critic has called it, a "book [which] does not give its heroine's desolation the quality of art."

Like Rhys's other longer fictions, ***After Leaving Mr. Mackenzie*** is the story of a woman more left than leaving. The novel begins, it will be remembered, in Paris in the springtime. But in that hallowed romantic setting, the protagonist, Julia Martin, a "*jeune dame*" of thirty-six, enjoys no April rejuvenation. Julia's fall, Rhys demonstrates through an unobtrusive chronology carefully worked into the novel, continues into spring and beyond. Left early in October by Mr. Mackenzie, her latest lover, Julia has lived for six months on the weekly allowance that he has continued to provide. Her first crisis is a substantially larger check (fifteen hundred francs instead of the usual three hundred) and the promise that there will be no more. Julia seeks out Mackenzie in his favorite restaurant, slaps him, and flings back at him his money. While doing so, she is observed by Mr. Horsfield, an Englishman vacationing in Paris, who soon becomes Mackenzie's successor and who almost immediately provides Julia with the same sum that she has just thrown away. That money returned enables her to journey to London to see her family (a dying mother, a jealous sister, a selfish uncle), to seek financial help from the wealthy older man who was her first lover (he had promised that they would always be friends), and to continue her affair with Mr. Horsfield. All three objectives come to nothing. Ten days after her voyage to England Julia returns to Paris; ten days after her return to Paris she once more encounters Mr. Mackenzie, who buys her a drink, sadly observes how "suddenly" she has gone "phut," and obliges her when she requests a "loan" of one hundred francs. On that declining note the novel ends.

The argument of the plot thus summarized is not promising, and yet Rhys everywhere gives her story unexpected depth and complexity. We might note, for example, how ***After Leaving Mr. Mackenzie*** opens with a half-reversal of the usual fate of the usual demimondaine protagonist. Instead of ending with this foreordained victim seduced and abandoned, we commence that way. Or more accurately, we half commence that way. Julia Martin was not exactly seduced in that she readily acceded to Mackenzie's original advances. She is not exactly abandoned in that, six months after he decided to take himself out of her life, he is still paying her three hundred francs a week, which is enough for her to go on living modestly in Paris. But not exactly living either. For the six months following Mackenzie's departure, Julia has immured herself in a room in a cheap hotel seeking mostly "a good sort of place to hide in . . . until the sore and cringing feeling, which was the legacy of Mr. Mackenzie, had departed." Her refuge is also the setting for a sustained but hopeless rage. Often she would "walk up and down the room consumed with hatred of the world and everybody in it. . . . Often she would talk to herself as she walked." As Thomas Staley has observed, references to ghosts run throughout the novel. The first ghost is Julia herself haunting her quarters and her own empty existence.

There is a definite point to the protraction of that haunting, which is to say that Rhys has her reasons for beginning the book with the aftermath of a crucial parting and not with the preliminary relationship or even the parting itself. In the first place, the separation is standard, predictable, part of the normal course of affairs. Why note what has often happened before? What has not happened before is Julia's sense of being "done for" after being put down yet another time. The reader might therefore wonder at first what was so special about Mr. Mackenzie (we never learn his first name) that his loss mattered so much. The answer, the novel soon shows, is nothing; Mackenzie is no different from his numerous predecessors; he treats Julia no differently than they all have done. But that "no difference" finally makes a difference, and Julia breaks after being dropped once more in just the same fashion as she has been dropped numerous times before. The retreat from life, the emotional debilitation, the futile rage that Julia sees as "the legacy of Mr. Mackenzie" is also the legacy of all who have preceded him. One unlikely reaction sums up the previous course of a too common life.

Rhys also uses her protagonist's initial contradictory reaction—such a minor cause, such a major effect—to suggest something of the contradictions inherent in that protagonist's previous life. Julia, we are one time told, had gone from "artist's model" to "mannequin" to "principally living on the money given to her by various men." That third mode of supporting herself on the basis of her good looks occasions a delicate question as to this character's actual profession just before the beginning of the novel. Is she a woman selling herself to a limited clientele and for no set price, or is she a woman too ready to fall in love with some man from whom she can then accept assistance because financial gifts are tokens of his love for her? Is she essentially a mercenary or essentially a romantic? The answer, of course, is that she must be both and neither. Physical survival demands the former and precludes the latter. Psychic survival demands the latter and precludes the former. Furthermore, these fine considerations would not apply if the woman were simply a prostitute. Cash received for no services rendered would then pose no problem. But Julia's problem, at the beginning of the novel, is that she must insist that her dealings with Mackenzie were not primarily commercial despite the fact that she is still being paid. Such sustained pretense, incidentally, is also required for the greater satisfaction of her customers. The men in Julia's life are as determined as she to define their dealings with her as affairs of the heart, not affairs of the pocketbook.

We might also note that Julia originally thought that "a week or perhaps a fortnight" would suffice as a post-letdown recovery period. Six months later she is no nearer a cure. That contradictory conjunction of an optimistic prognosis and a prolonged devastation reflects Julia's basic strategy of surviving crises through the odd ploy of both denying and indulging them. Indeed, Rhys suggests her protagonist's capabilities as a victim-endurer even with the first sentences in the novel: "After she had parted from Mr. Mackenzie, Julia Martin went to live in a cheap hotel on the Quai des Grands Augustins. It looked a lowdown sort of place and the staircase smelt of the landlady's cats, but the rooms were cleaner than you would have expected." The cheapness of the hotel is countered by the grand address; the rooms, cleaner than you would have expected, are not necessarily as clean as you might have wished, and the stairway smells of cat. So is the hotel acceptable, bearable, or not? The question is hard to answer, and that surely is the point. What I am arguing is that Rhys, in portraying her protagonist and her protagonist's situation, strikes from the very start a strained balance correlative to the way Julia balances herself on the edge of her profession. We have the facts of Julia's physical and psychological destitution and countering those facts we have the ploys whereby Julia attempts to retain some semblance of self-respect. Note, in this context, the very first words of the novel and how the deliberately indefinite formulation, "After she had parted from . . ." serves to suggest, as does the title itself, that Julia has left Mr. Mackenzie without exactly denying that he has thrown her out.

Julia's careful balancing allows her to live on the limited resources available to her. Yet that same balancing, we soon see, sometimes costs more than this character can afford. There is, therefore, a double irony to the author's double entry bookkeeping of her character's psychological and social losses and gains. Even the first entries, the claims Julia makes for herself—the hotel is not so bad, she has not yet become the "hideous" old woman upstairs—attest by their very paltriness to her desperate plight. But that plight becomes even more desperate when yet another transaction must be doubly entered. Julia receives Mackenzie's unexpectedly large last check. That same night she seeks him out and makes a scene. She does not need his money, she must insist, precisely because it is all she will receive and she needs it more than ever.

There are still other contradictions in this charged encounter. The scene with Mackenzie will punish him for abandoning her, first as his lover and then as his officially abandoned lover. But punishing him, she also, with clear Freudian implications, punishes herself, first for allowing herself to be bought when she entered into the relationship and second for allowing herself to be paid off when he exited from it. With such gestures as returning Mackenzie's money or returning herself to London and to the family and former lover who all want her elsewhere, Julia enforces a subconscious sentence against herself. In short, Rhys shows that even as her protagonist acts to deny a crisis ("I am an honorable woman and I won't take your [Mackenzie's] money"), she also acts to make it worse ("I am a destitute woman and must accept whatever money you [Horsfield] will give me and on whatever terms you give it"). In the duplicity of that double action Julia both penalizes herself for how low she has fallen and demonstrates the justice of her punishment.

Consciously, of course, Julia would vociferously deny the verdict that she, in effect, passes. She is, she would have it, mostly the victim of circumstances, circumstances being mostly a shortage of cash. "You see," she had one time argued with Mackenzie, "a time comes in your life when, if you have any money, you can go one way. But if you have nothing at all—absolutely nothing at all—and nowhere to get anything, then you go another." She thereby asserts that she is not responsible for the expedients she has been forced to embrace. Yet that rationalization, Rhys shows, takes Julia farther down the road she would have supposedly preferred not to take and serves substantially to make her into the woman whom she claims only circumstances forced her to become.

Rhys early incorporates into the novel a calculated reference to a still larger dichotomy implicit in her protagonist's story. When Julia encounters Mackenzie at the restaurant she gives vent to her hitherto repressed anger: "It was like a flood which has been long dammed up suddenly pouring forth." Yet he is not at all moved by the torrent of her grief and rage: "He listened, half-smiling. Surely even she must see that she was trying to make a tragedy out of a situation that was fundamentally comical. The discarded mistress. . . . A situation consecrated as comical by ten thousand farces and a thousand comedies." He would make a farce of her tragedy, and furthermore the whole weight of cultural tradition supports him, not her. After all, how can all those farces and comedies be wrong? Rhys's task, of course, is to show that they are wrong, that we have all been conditioned to evaluate romances gone astray in ways favorable to the men thereby discomforted. This author would have us read Julia's story to correct the conventional misreading of that story. The protagonist's suffering demands attention, not the "Mackenzieish" dismissal of "well, what did she expect if she chose to live that way?"

Rhys gives substance to a story of suffering by giving it form. What might otherwise be merely the ongoing saga of Julia's setbacks—a kind of soggy revelling in protracted sorrows—is subtly cast into a three-part tale that circles back, appropriately, to its own approximate origins. That three-part progression is, it should also be noted, underlined by the geographic progress of the plot. The first four chapters constitute Part One and, beginning with Julia abandoned in Paris by Mr. Mackenzie, tell of her crucial encounter with him, her subsequent meeting with Mr. Horsfield who gives her the same amount of money that she insisted on returning to Mackenzie, and of her decision (made possible by the recouping of that loss) to return to London. Part Two, the bulk of the novel, chronicles in fourteen chapters her misadventures in London. We see her disappointed by her family, by her elderly first lover (she has believed his long ago parting admonition that if she should ever need . . .), and finally by Horsfield himself. In Part Three, only three chapters long and hence the briefest section of the book, she is back in Paris again and in retreat in another cheap hotel very much like the one in which she was originally in hiding.

Yet the concluding three chapters do not quite balance the opening four. Julia's world, small as it was, has contracted still more, and her options are even more limited than they originally were. To return again to London, for example, is, at the end, quite out of her reach. The form traced out during the course of the novel is not, then, a circle—a line of narrative bent round to return to its own origin as does, say, James Joyce's *Finnegans Wake*. Instead, Rhys's narration bends back to its beginning but falls short of it, which gives us, to translate the novel into spatial terms, a geometric figure that corresponds to one full turn of a spiral. The ending of the circled novel is totally open; the action portrayed in the plot can be imaginatively extended in endless repetition. The spiralled novel is both open and closed. The plot imaginatively extended can be represented as a single line of action often repeated but still circling toward its own vanishing point. The resultant figure of a vortex descending to nothingness is also clearly suggested in the novel itself. At one point Julia stands looking long "at a picture representing a male figure encircled by what appeared to be a huge mauve corkscrew. At the end of the picture was written, '*La vie est un spiral, flottant dans l'espace, que les hommes grimpent et redescendent très, très, très serieusement.*'"

Form substantiates the story, and details substantiate the form. For example, Rhys provides a number of seemingly minor facts to conjoin the first part with the third one while also differentiating them one from the other. Thus the gift of fifteen hundred francs that brought Mr. Horsfield into Julia's life is not exactly matched by the later gift of ten pounds that apparently takes him out of her life. Or Mr. Mackenzie's final large sum which she returns to him in the first section is partly returned to her as his small "loan" of one hundred francs in the third section. And to consider all of her men and their money, we can note that Julia boasts to Mr. Horsfield, in Part One, about her London friend, "a very rich man," and how readily "he'd help me." The friend is Mr. James; the help is all of twenty pounds, which serves only to take Julia back to Paris and Part Three.

Two noteworthy chapters, "The First Unknown" in Part One and "The Second Unknown" in Part Three, provide another example of Rhys's unequal balancing to achieve connective contrasts between the novel's beginning and its end. In each case Julia is approached by a man who intends a pick-up in the streets. She denounces the first stranger for his presumptuous insult of, in effect, labelling her a prostitute. He denies the charge: "Not at all. . . . I have some money and I am willing to give it to you. Why do you say that I am *ignoble.*" For him, obviously, ignobility and insult lie in proposing to enjoy the favors of an unknown lady without at least offering to pay. Yet Julia is still buoyed up by this encounter, and back in her room "her forebodings about the future were changed into a feeling of exultation." She can think, as "she looked at herself in the glass . . . 'After all, I'm not finished. It's all nonsense that I am. I'm not finished at all.'" It is the second stranger who finishes her when he sees her more clearly during the course of the second pass: "'*Oh, la la.*' he said. '*Ah, non, alors,*' [and] he turned about and walked away." His look of "deadly and impartial criticism" strikes her like "a blow over the heart." The blow is her recognition of her value in his eyes, even though she had no intention of bargaining with this prospective buyer either. Nevertheless, a non-transaction still leaves her both sold out and worthless at the end of the novel. The further irony is that it is unknown men, not the known men in her life, who most determine what her value must be.

As earlier noted, Rhys does not validate what would be the conventional reading of her protagonist's story. But neither does she validate her protagonist's own reading of her own story. Just as the unequal balance between the first part and the third gives us the form of the novel, the two chapters, "The First Unknown" and "The Second Unknown," are the fulcrum upon which that balance turns. It is through these two unknowns that we best know Julia, for it is her failures to read these readings (and the men who provide them—as unknown to her as she is to them) that show her reading of herself. Essentially, she is, throughout most of the novel, a blank page upon which others can inscribe whatever value they wish and that then is her value. So the two episodes in which Julia is differently priced by two nameless men appropriately frame most of the action in the novel even as they also emphasize what we might term the protagonist's "commodityness" and provide a paradigm for her dealings with all other characters. Rhys's point is clear. Having no money of her own, Julia is worth just what some man (even a total stranger) will pay to have or not to have—it does not matter which—her company. Valuing herself in this fashion, as she does until the very end of the novel, Julia seems no more disposed to take control of her own life or even to determine the direction of her fall than is a leaf in the wind.

Yet Rhys also shows that the obvious fecklessness of Julia's life is not the whole story, and that this character's resolute refusal to admit to motives does not prove that she hasn't any. "I don't know why I came. A sort of impulse, I suppose," is how Julia at one point "explains" her return to London. Admittedly, her decision to make the journey was consciously made on less than rational grounds:

> She thought: 'If a taxi hoots before I count three, I'll go to London. If not, I won't.'
>
> She counted, 'One . . . Two . . .' slowly. A car shrieked a loud blast. (ellipsis in the original)

Yet we still note the fudging here—the slow count, the fact that a "car" is not necessarily a "taxi"—and note also how fortuitously chance pushes Julia in the direction she will not admit she wishes to travel. She had already decided that she "must go away," that some escape from the mess she has made of things in Paris was "the only thing to be done." The money recently acquired from Horsfield makes that escape possible. Even better, it means that she can go home in some semblance of style, not as an obviously abject and defeated woman. Still more important, Julia wants to meet again with both her mother and her first lover as a kind of symbolic coming to terms with her own beginnings as both a woman and a certain kind of woman. And that large purpose serves a still larger one. A disastrous present prompts a return to the past which might provide the basis for a different future. In short, Julia is making a desperate attempt at some kind of rebirth.

It does not work; the journey to London comes to nothing;

the return to Paris marks the three-part structure of the book and establishes the pattern of Julia's life. Implicit in that pattern is one of Rhys's subtlest ironies, for it is the protagonist's covert effort to alter the course of her existence that most attests to the downward spiral characteristic of her previous life. That life had been, of course, a round of men. Each man had represented a possible new beginning, a chance that this time it might be different, although it never was. In short, things after leaving Mr. Mackenzie continue to be much as they were before meeting him, and the specific setbacks Julia suffers in her attempt to escape, even briefly and geographically, the failure she has made of her life are themselves, as a brief analysis can show, versions of that failure.

To consider her first London failure, from the very beginning Julia's efforts to reestablish a relationship with her family are muddled. In need of validation, she also needs the badges of an assumed success. And again Rhys shows how her protagonist's desperate remedies only compound the problems they were intended to cover over. Because the older sister has spent most of her money on clothes, she must plead poverty to Norah when they first meet in the cheap, dingy hotel room that Julia can barely afford. Resentful of the sister who has not sacrificed herself for their dying mother ("And who's better dressed—you or I?"), Norah refuses Julia's implicit and explicit requests. She will not lend her any money; she will not even allow her sister to stay a few days in the family flat. Norah already has "a friend . . . a trained nurse" living with her to help with the mother, "and there's not a scrap more room in the place." Julia thus becomes an occasional bystander to her mother's dying; her limited role is directed not just by Norah but also by Norah's mannish friend, Miss Wyatt; the end result is a bitter quarrel with Norah immediately after the mother's death. That quarrel ends with one of the protagonist's saddest setbacks, Julia "being put out of her mother's house by a stranger." Which gives us one of Rhys's grimmer "home truths": Home, when you have to go there, is not always the place where they have to take you in.

Julia is dispossessed even during those times she can spend with her dying mother. The daughter never consciously acknowledges to herself what she wants (a ploy that obviously serves to blunt her disappointment when, as she suspects will be the case, her want is thwarted), but it is clear that she hopes for some sign of concern, acceptance, love. When the unconscious mother is beyond making such a sign, the most the daughter can do is to recollect a past that does not provide a base for some brave new beginning in her unhappy present. Julia's earliest memories of how as "a very young child she had loved her mother" who had then been "the warm center of the world" are inextricably mixed with memories of how she had been pushed at age six from the center of this world by the birth of her baby sister. Another female took her place in a crucial pairing (the story of Julia's life); that first pairing inverted still persists, with Norah now babying their dying mother in a manner that leaves no place for Julia. Witness, for example, the end of the first meeting with the mother: "Sometimes anybody strange seems to upset her. Go on; you'd better go," Norah orders, and "Julia went out of the room listening to Norah's crooning and authoritative voice. 'Don't cry, my darling. Don't cry, my sweet. Now, what is it? What is it you want?'"

Paralleling Julia's return to her young childhood past is her return to her young womanhood past, which is also an attempt to come to terms with another crucial abandonment. After the long afternoon spent with her unconscious mother, Julia pays an evening call on W. Neil James, the man with whom she had, at age nineteen, her first affair. Here too, Rhys hints, her protagonist has certain covert expectations. Again, Julia wants a sign. And this time she receives it, but the sign received is not exactly the sign she wanted. Indeed, the scene between these two former loves covertly at cross-purposes shows us Rhys at her tragicomic best. Mr. James treats Julia as an old friend even though he is thinking how "tactless" are such "resurrections of the past." She is uncomfortable in his presence, as if he were an "important person" to whom she was appealing and not an old friend. His polite request as to how she is doing elicits the honest answer that such a question is not intended to provoke. She would briefly describe the downward tenor of her life after she and he parted, in the hope that such a confession might be a possible preliminary to some from of absolution. He does not want to hear, for the saga of her setbacks can hardly gratify his vanity, considering his role in the tale. She wishes for some evidence of real concern but, with her characteristic inability to articulate to others or herself just what she wants, can only hint of money. Or perhaps the confusion lies elsewhere. After all, money is, in Julia's world, the best proof of concern. In any event, he is angered by her not so covert plea but also relieved. The promise of money can shut her up, and he promises. So she does receive a sign that he cares and what he mostly cares for, in the present as in the past, is to preserve his own equanimity. The sense of self-complacency that his twenty pounds purchases is cheap at the price. That twenty pounds defines her too—in the present as in the past. The gift received is, as were, undoubtedly, "gifts" before it, a payment for services rendered—not for sex this time but for a kind of masturbatory stroking of his ego. Just as it was with the mother, so is it with the lover. Julia's attempt to find in a problematic past a retreat from an impossible present gives her a parodic version of both her present and her past that is more demeaning than either was in its original form.

A spiral, however, spins both ways, and if the picture of the corkscrewed man sets forth a transsexualized synecdoche of the novel, it should also be remembered that the sentence appended to that painting observed that men clamber up as well as slide down life as a spiral. In different terms and in keeping with the double entry "bookkeeping" whereby Julia conducts her life and Rhys portrays it, we can observe that just as Julia's small triumphs often come at large cost, so too can her major setbacks bring her unexpected dividends. In this context, let us look again at Julia's London failures, starting with her inability to establish any connection with her family and with the breach between the two sisters.

When the two women first meet after a ten year separation, each reads in the other the other's story of the intervening years. Norah notes that Julia "doesn't even look like a lady now." But Norah too "was labelled for all to see." "Trained to certain opinions which forbid her even the relief of rebellion against her lot," Norah is exactly what Julia is not, the quintessential "good girl" who will act just as she is supposed to act. The novel dramatizes the differences between the two women, and it also dramatizes how little difference that difference makes. If Norah, then, represents, for Julia, the accepted and expected road, the road Julia has not taken, what Julia and the reader both see during the course of the older sister's attempt to ground herself again in her family and her past is Julia's justification for having struck out on her own. Admittedly, she ended up lost, but, as she later also admits, she at least "had a shot at the life I wanted." Norah has had the invalid mother for six years and a life she sums up as "like death . . . like being buried alive."

The contretemps with Norah serves to dispel any possible sad regrets regarding a misspent life by forcing Julia to contemplate in Norah the proper woman whom Julia herself might have been. The reencounter with Neil James provides another corrective disillusionment. As we have seen, Julia had considerably romanticized her first affair. But Rhys also shows how Julia is brought to revise her earlier self-gratifying revision of what were the facts of the case. Shortly after the final meeting with Mr. James, Julia observes to Mr. Horsfield that she really knows little about the other man—then or now. "You see, he never used to talk to me much. I was for sleeping with—not for talking to." It is not a flattering assessment, but she does at last know where she stands, and where she stood.

It is this knowledge that partly redeems the conclusion of ***After Leaving Mr. Mackenzie.*** When Julia, back in Paris, asks Mackenzie for a "loan," there is a continuing element of self-deception in the terminology that she employs. Nevertheless, she then knows what she is after. She wants the money as money, not as a sign of something else (his continuing concern, say). Although Julia is finally reduced to obvious mendicancy, asking solely for the cash, she is also more successful than when she earlier asked for something more. Presumably she will continue with that greater success in a game more demeaning (she is now a beggar) and less (she is no longer, in effect, hypocritically prostituting herself), which is another reason why the ending of the novel is not irredeemably bleak. Julia sits alone with the second drink Mr. Mackenzie bought her: "The street was cool and full of grey shadows. Lights were beginning to come out in the cafés. It was the hour between the dog and wolf, as they say." This poetically suggestive final sentence moves, as does the symbolic spiral, in two directions. Darkness is descending, but Julia, with a drink and some cash, is partly provided for, and there are some lights to counter the coming night. The hour of the wolf has not yet arrived (the reference here is not to men as sexual "wolves"—that time has come and gone—but perhaps to the finally untamable aspects of life, to the mother howling and dying as an animal); meanwhile Julia is somewhat more adept at managing the dogs in her life.

There is one final turn to the ending that Rhys appropriately appends to this subtly plotted work. The symbolic spiral in the painting was "*flottant dans l'espace.*" It was supported by nothing, rested on nothing. And as Helen Nebeker especially observes, nothing is, indeed, a key issue in the novel. Julia's earliest memories are of being happy because of nothing and then of being frightened by nothing. At one point in Part One she describes one of her failures to give an account of herself: "And I felt as if all my life and all myself were floating away from me like smoke and there was nothing to lay hold of—nothing." By the end of the novel, she better knows the nothing that pervades her life. More specifically, she knows that her role in her family is nothing; that her dreams of her first love were nothing; that her hopes for her next affair have already come to nothing. But if Julia does not quite become, with that awareness, a forerunner of Camus' Sisyphus who can happily roll the rock of her own nothingness up the mountain of the nothingness of existence, neither is she crushed between the weight of those two voids. In that strained survival we see again how completely Rhys envisions the bleak life of her protagonist right down to the small sustaining victory achieved through the way in which Julia finally confronts the unredeemed darkness of her fate, and we also see how carefully the author structures the novel to sum up the emptiness of both the defeats and the victory.

Rosalind Miles (essay date 1987)

SOURCE: "Man the Enemy," in *The Female Form: Women Writers and the Conquest of the Novel,* Routledge and Kegan Paul, 1987, pp. 132-47.

[In the following excerpt, Miles discusses the depiction of female alienation and social subjugation in Rhys's fiction. "In the work of Jean Rhys," writes Miles, "female self-distrust and despair finds its extremest voice."]

> 'Men—they're so funny—they simply must have you,' said Estelle. 'It's all they want—you. It's imperative they make love to you there and then or, well, they'll die. And then whoops, it's all over and they're not even sure why you're there, in the bed beside them, taking up so much room. It's not that they lied to you in the first place. It's just that they're different. We don't want the sex all *that* much—although it's perfectly nice—we want the love afterwards. We make love to win love, and they to lose it'.
>
> Sally Emerson, *Listeners* (1983)
>
> A curse from the depths of womanhood,
> Is very salt, and bitter, and good.
>
> Elizabeth Barrett Browning, 'A Curse for a Nation'

'The man, the male, the important person, the only person who matters.' This phrase, from 1928, might have been taken straight from the pages of any of the feminist publications of the 1960s and 1970s. Those who complained of the 'stridency' of that wave of feminist protest might have reflected upon the length of time during which women had been stating their case to an overwhelming silence from a deaf world. In all her work Jean Rhys was to be found making weary but still spirited gestures in the direction of the opposite sex. But with a subtler and tenderer gift than Ivy Compton-Burnett's, she constantly directs our attention towards the casualties in the sex war rather than the mechanisms by which it has operated. All her work is illuminated by what Ford Madox Ford, in his preface to her first volume of short stories, ***Left Bank*** (1927), called her 'terrific . . . almost lurid!—passion for stating the case of the underdog'. Ford saw this as part of Jean Rhys's sympathy with the 'left bank' of life itself, the sinister, the frightening, the out of order. Most of Jean Rhys's characters live among 'the fools and the defeated', on that shabby fringe of society where the need for money, for release, for some assertion of the self as a necessity to survival, leads to financial and social offences and hence into conflict with the organised sections of the community. These offences are not presented as morally culpable; the money difficulties in **'Vienne',** the drunk and disorderly out bursts of the young West Indian girl in **'Let Them Call It Jazz',** two key stories in ***Left Bank,*** are set down without comment as symptoms of moral, social, and personal debility, a cry for help rather than an onslaught on the fabric of society.

But it is not always necessary to outrage the bourgeoisie to find yourself in trouble, as Jean Rhys sees it. Hers is a world where it is an offence to be old, ugly, or stupid, so harsh are the operations of the established and administrative classes. **'From a French Prison',** in ***Left Bank,*** gives us an old man and a boy waiting in a queue of visitors. The prison itself, with its bored, preoccupied guards, serves as a microcosm of a society which is both indifferent and incomprehensible to its members. The old man is confused and apprehensive; he doesn't speak the language (always a significant metaphor for this writer, whose work concentrates on the dispossessed inhabitants of several major European cities, notably Paris and London). He fails to hand in his permit, and is deprived of it in tears and fear, unable to grasp what is happening. Even in this early study of impotence, later to prove a major concern in Jean Rhys's work, the rich use of metaphor and symbol, and the evocative choice of location, are remarkable and distinctive features.

In the main, though, it is women who suffer, Jean Rhys does not indict the social system in vague or general terms. She always highlights its malfunction through some specific insult to one person in particular, almost invariably a female. Typically Jean Rhys sees woman as a creature both frail and robust. She is handicapped in the daily battle by the inferiority of her weapons and by her crippling inner sensitivity. Yet at the same time she is fortified by a determination to survive, and by a compulsion to show no outward sign of 'softness', for she believes that to show softness automatically provokes hardness in others. ***Postures*** (1928), republished in 1969 as ***Quartet*** with a regrettable loss of the social and sexual innuendo in the original title, offers the prototype Rhys anti-heroine. Marya Zelli is a bewildered expatriate whose marriage to a foreigner has robbed her of her own sense of nationality without providing a new one. Her reluctant association, through his shady and unsuccessful dealings, with the world of petty crime, precipitates her initiation into the dreary round of money shortage, letters home, appeals to men, subsistence on coffee and croissants. The dingy hotel room and the insolence of the waiters are a continuous bitter mockery of better times.

Below the surface realism of the detail, the vein of expressionism in Jean Rhys's work accounts for much of the reverberation of her writing. The linking of Marya's life with crime is a grim symbol of her 'offence' against society, her inability to fit in with the conventional, the acceptable and safe. The 'punishment', deprivation of cash, food, and a place to live is, with nightmarish circularity, a further continuation of the 'crime'. In the course of things the experience of rejection becomes internalised; in the work of Jean Rhys female self-distrust and despair finds its extremest voice. All her heroines are run down by the lives they lead to the point of serious debility, almost illness. They can only endure each day by nursing themselves through it, like invalids. Here is Sasha, in ***Good Morning, Midnight*** (1939), returning to Paris:

> I have been here five days. I have decided on a place

to eat in at midday, a place to eat in at night, a place to have my drink in after dinner. I have arranged my little life.

The stress on the 'realities' of life serves to highlight the narrator's acquaintance with the terrible underworld, the sub-culture inhabited by those without income, security, function. There is a dreamlike quality to the prose here, with a consistent use of dislocation techniques; the heroine looks into a mirror and sees through it the movement of her past, as in the moment of drowning. In this treatment of the sensations of the excluded, the progress through perplexity to panic, the exhausting emotional oscillation between the frenetic and the torpid, Jean Rhys is often reminiscent of Kafka. Like Kafka's K, the Rhys heroine is broken on the wheel of repeated hopeless attempts to placate the implacable, the impenetrable and inexorable machine of authority. There is, too something Kafkaesque about Jean Rhys's irony, her feeling that the whole of life is just one long unspeakable practical joke. A characteristic moment occurs when one of Marya's complacent acquaintances advises her that she should try to 'retrieve' her damaged fortunes by becoming a '*femme nue*' in a nightclub.

As this 'joke' suggests, the work of Jean Rhys has certain affinities with that of Camus. But for her the Outsider is always female. It is her recurrent, almost obsessive theme, that women are permanent and perpetual victims of masculine society. Not only will they be oppressed by individual male bullies; they are everywhere confronted by institutionalised masculine hostility in the shape of the law, the professions, the police and the bureaucrats of every country. Through the power of her analysis Jean Rhys was one of the few women writers able to make explicit the link between the sex war and the class struggle. To be female is to inhabit, without hope of escape, the lowest class of all in a sexist structure. Men may work, singly or in groups, to improve their own position on the social scale, or to revolutionise the situation which forces them to deal in these terms. Women, denied any such recourse, flit about on the edges of the 'real' world, dependent on men for maintaining even the most unsatisfactory existence within it.

One of her most deeply-felt attacks on the system is couched in the form of a mental monologue by Sasha, who has just been humiliated and dismissed by her employer. Note how the economic factor in female dependence is brought out, as well as the enfeeblement of the victim of such treatment:

> Well, let's argue this out, Mr Blank. You, who represent Society, have the right to pay me four hundred francs a month. That's my market value, for I am an inefficient member of Society, slow on the uptake, uncertain, slightly damaged in the fray, there's no denying it. So you have the right to pay me four hundred francs a month, to lodge me in a small, dark room, to clothe me shabbily, to harass me with worry and monotony and unsatisfied longings till you get me to the point when I blush at a look, cry at a word. We can't all be happy, we can't all be rich, we can't all be lucky—and it would all be so much less fun if we were. Isn't that so, Mr Blank? There must be the dark background to show up the bright colours. Some must cry so that others may be able to laugh the more heartily. Sacrifices are necessary. . . . Let's say you have this mystical right to cut my legs off. But the right to ridicule me afterwards because I am a cripple—no, that I think you haven't got. And that's the right you hold most dearly, isn't it? You must be able to despise the people you exploit. But I wish you a lot of trouble, Mr Blank, and just to start off with, your damned shop's going bust. Alleluia! Did I say all this? Of course I didn't. I didn't even think it.

Sasha speaks here for all the exploited, all the underpaid and helpless. But it is Jean Rhys's talent to be able to change the focus from the general to the particular at will. Her portrayal of Sasha also offers some painful images of specifically female despair, like crying in the *lavabo* under the gaze of the attendant, or feeling at best 'saved, rescued, fished-up, half-drowned, out of the deep, dark river, dry clothes, hair shampooed and set'. And few women writers have so skilfully summed up the accelerating needs and anxieties of the ageing woman:

> Now, money, for the night is coming. Money for my hair, money for my teeth, money for shoes that won't deform my feet (It's not easy now to walk around in cheap shoes with very high heels), money for good clothes, money, money. The night is coming.

In Sasha's consciousness, her 'film-mind' as she calls it, males play varying but always hurtful parts. At one stage she is tormented by a whore's dream of an *apache:*

> I am in a little whitewashed room. The sun is hot outside. A man is standing with his back to me . . . I am wearing a black dress, very short, and heelless slippers. My legs are bare. I am watching for the expression on the man's face when he turns round. Now he ill-treats me, now he betrays me. He often brings home other women and I have to wait on them, and I don't like that. But as long as he is alive and near me I am not unhappy. If he were to die I should kill myself.

Later she is shaken by a harsh blast of self-disgust and caricatures herself viciously as aged and sexually pretentious:

'What an amusing ten days! Positively packed with thrills. The last performance of What's-her-name And Her Boys or It Was All Due To An Old Fur Coat. Positively the last performance. . . .' The irony in the last phrase is made clear in the novel's stunning climax in which the man who offers sex offers also death and in full awareness Sasha embraces the two experiences, which have for her always been one.

After the appearance of ***Good Morning, Midnight*** in 1939, Jean Rhys ceased publishing for many years. Her subsequent reemergence with the stunning ***Wide Sargasso Sea*** (1966) from this self-imposed silence, outlined in Carole Angier's sensitive biographical portrait, *Jean Rhys* (1985), showed that her major preoccupations had developed, but not changed. Womanhood remained, to her, a nightmare dystopia, since a deep fear and hatred motivate the behaviour of men towards women. Male seeks female as his natural adversary; sex *is* war. In the context of this theme, the wartime setting provides more than a historical backdrop to **'I Spy a Stranger'**; it acts as a continuing image of the relations between the sexes, where polarisation determines opposing roles and makes impossible any sort of civilised or humane living. Male aggression reduces the female by stages to foreigner, enemy, refugee; she may resist, but she cannot win.

The victim in this case is Laura, who because of the fighting in Europe has been forced to give up her life there and return to England to lodge with a married cousin for the duration. Here she arouses the hostility of the cousin's husband, who persecutes her and finally drives her into a geriatric asylum. Laura is thus the victim of male belligerence twice over; she loses home, friends, lover, through the external conflict, and refuge, sanity, freedom through her defeat on the domestic front; and Jean Rhys makes it plain which of the two she considers to be the real war. Such is the nature of this war, Jean Rhys implies, that certain women need do nothing in order to draw male fire. They provoke simply by what they are, Laura never offers any insult to the husband. But she challenges him indirectly by displaying many characteristics which are traditionally if unconsciously felt as offences in a female; she is single, she is 'brainy', and she is old. Because she has lived abroad she is regarded as suspiciously un-English—these two features are united in the abusive village nickname for her, 'the witch of Prague'. Further, she is by temperament reclusive and literary, and her actions and preferences in this respect are subtly used to increase her isolation and to stress its pathos. We see her writing endless letters, keeping a diary, cutting out newspaper reports and sticking them into a scrapbook. As in Doris Lessing's *The Golden Notebook,* where the heroine does the same thing as her breakdown gathers momentum, this activity is seen as an apt evocation of the fragmentation of her life, its final resolution into the sensational and ephemeral.

All this is the work of men, the enemy. At times we seem to be in an inverse Strindbergian landscape, and Jean Rhys insists on her interpretation with a rather rigid contrivance by which none of the male characters is permitted any warmth, gentleness, or even common human decency (this recalls Strindberg's treatment of the female characters in *The Father, The Dance of Death,* and *The Stronger*). The husband, Ricky, as his name suggests, is conceived in the diminutive, the perennial schoolboy, emotionally retarded at the stage of truculence towards and inability to cope with the female sex.

Male humour is the first weapon with which Ricky seeks to prove and to place Laura. Jean Rhys's bitter assessment of the reality of intersex warfare emerges nowhere so clearly as in this sequence, where Ricky is vulgarly cruel under the mask of geniality and goodwill. Annoyed by Laura's attempts to obtain news of her friends in occupied Europe, Ricky decides to 'laugh her out of it'. He offers as a joke the idea of 'the Gestapo getting her sweetheart'. Her reaction to this confirms him in his view that 'the old girl's got no sense of humour at all'. Part of the joke for Ricky lies in the thought of an 'old girl' having a 'sweetheart', though we are told that Laura has; this is an important theme in Jean Rhys, the continuance of love among those whom orthodox society feels are, or rightly should be, beyond it.

At last verbal persecution gives way to the physical violence which it has for some time been hiding. Becoming increasingly paranoid about Laura, Ricky details his wife to tell her that she must go, simultaneously exposing both his cowardice and his immaturity in the retreat behind the female. As she is leaving, Ricky decides to speed the parting guest. Approaching her with one of his crass jokes—'It's moving day'—he takes her arm to hurry her downstairs. At his touch she breaks down, screaming and swearing. She clings to the bannisters and Ricky attacks her, hitting and kicking, and drags her downstairs. Beaten, dazed, and more than half mad, she is whirled away in a taxi. But even in the grim asylum of his choice Laura is not safe from Ricky's malice—he announces that she can only stay there as long as her own money lasts—and the reader is left to speculate upon a future which Jean Rhys has managed so that it presents not a spark of hope.

All of the other men in the story are introduced to reinforce the effect of male brutality. A friend of Ricky's Fluting (the name indicates the author's derisive view of his capacities), is used to illustrate Jean Rhys's concept of that area of the masculine mentality in which sexual and military matters unite with a peculiarly indecent flourish. This is principally brought out through the symbolism of weapons—obscene letters threaten 'A Gun for the Old Girls', and the old cliché is given a new significance in the remark of his wife that Ricky has 'got his knife into Laura'. Fluting is an underwear man. He tells Laura that 'the Waafs up at the station smelt', and waxes 'sarcastic about their laundry allowance'. In the general context of this piece, Laura's vigorous counter-attack—'Sir, they smell; you stink'—seems not a victory but a defeat, a descent to Fluting's level. Further, the direct echo of one of Dr Johnson's most famous remarks highlights Laura's pathos and frailty by the evocation of the vigorous and articulate Great Cham of English Literature.

And males band together, Jean Rhys warns. The crisis for Laura comes symbolically at the height of the worst air-raid of the war, when her neglect of her blackout curtain unites against her the forces of law and order in the attentions of the air-raid warden and the police. The police are doubly enemies, of sex and class, as males and as custodians of the male social order. They have 'a good laugh' (male humour again) over Laura's diary-scrapbook, and Ricky gives orders that it must be destroyed. Even the doctor, who might be thought impartial, comes to Laura not in his office of healer but because Ricky sends for him in order to get Laura certified. The doctor refuses this, but out of professional cussedness, not true sympathy. The level of his concern for his patient is shown in the following exchange:

> Pratt asked her if she was willing to go to a sanatorium for a rest and she said 'Why not?' Ricky shouted at her 'You get off to your sanatorium pronto. You ought to have been there long ago.' 'You're being inhuman,' Pratt said. Ricky said, 'Well, will the bloody old fool keep quiet?' Pratt told him he'd guarantee that.

Set against this efficient male bonding, even between men who are antipathetic to each other, like Ricky and Pratt, is the inability of women to offer even the most elementary support for one another. Laura's cousin, Mrs Hudson, cannot help her, though aware of her sufferings. This woman is implicated in Laura's story not only through the narrative connection, but structurally, by Jean Rhys's use of a framing device by which Mrs Hudson relates the events to her sister, Mrs Trant.

A key passage makes clear the interaction of all the women's lives. The diary writing, the only part of Laura that we encounter directly, is used to convey her sense of the reduction of life and the erosion of her personality. She feels 'like a cog in a machine'; she sees herself as 'shamming dead'. But above all she is alienated and finally destroyed by the English man's attitude to women. This piece involves the sisters in Laura's plight, drawing added importance from the fact that Laura's voice is reaching us from the grave of the asylum, and through the mist of the incomprehension of the two women who are reading it together:

> There is something strange about the attitude to women as women. Not the dislike (or fear). That isn't strange of course. But it's all so completely taken for granted, and surely that is strange. It has settled down and become an atmosphere, or, if you like, a climate, and no one questions it, least of all the women themselves. There is *no* opposition. The effects are criticized, for some of the effects are hardly advertisements for the system, the cause is seldom mentioned, and then very gingerly. The few mild ambiguous protests usually come from men. Most of the women seem to be carefully trained to revenge any unhappiness that they feel on each other, or on children—or on any individual man who happens to be at a disadvantage. In dealing with men as a whole, a streak of subservience, of servility, usually appears, something cold, calculating, lacking in imagination.
>
> But no one can go against the spirit of a country with impunity and propaganda from the cradle to the grave can do a lot.

This powerful statement stands at the centre of the story. It has been prepared for by the account of Laura as outsider and victim, and partly serves to describe her own condition. But it moves on to become a savage indictment of the situation of all women, including the two sisters. They too have regarded Laura as an enemy because of her refusal to accept the inevitability of male domination as they do. But they have enough of her in them, in every sense, to feel her misery. Their failure to help her is seen as a failure of sex loyalty as well as of kinship, since both turn against her mainly under pressure from their husbands. So Laura's thoughts are deeply relevant to them, and they are glimmeringly alive to this. Mrs Hudson has 'moments' when she agrees with Laura. Mrs Trant finds it 'nonsense', but her thoughts turn anxiously to her favourite daughter, who not only liked Laura, but opposed her father in standing up for her. Mrs Trant had taken the slave's covert delight in any defiance of the master, but now feels that it was bad: 'A girl ought to play safe, ought to go with the tide, it was a bad sign when a girl liked unpopular people. The duty of young females to make themselves acceptable overcomes her. She fearfully imagines Judy growing up to be unhappy (another Laura, perhaps) and considers her sister a 'sterile old fool' for offering the view that Judy is 'tough'. This further extension of the web of hostility between women is not only Jean Rhys's way of supporting and developing Laura's pronouncement. It also explains why they cannot unite against the enemy in mutual help.

A final touch neatly catches up this aspect of the theme. The 'home', says Mrs Hudson, where Laura has gone, has a golf links for the patients. '"But does she play golf?" said Mrs Trant. "Let's hope," said Mrs Hudson, "let's hope"...' The sentimentalist may find in that a comforting reassurance of the unfailing warm concern of the gentler sex for one another. It seems more likely, however, that it is intended to emphasise not only the hopelessness of Laura's fate, but also the dismal prospect for the women who 'survive'. Hope is all they have. It is standard currency among the hopeless. Jean Rhys invites us all to appreciate the joke.

In this suggestion that there is no real possibility of individual freedom for women, since they are moulded from their earliest years into conventionally acceptable forms, Jean Rhys touches a central nerve of much of women's writing in the twentieth century. . . .

Kathy Mezei (essay date Summer 1987)

SOURCE: "'And it Kept its Secret': Narration, Memory, and Madness in Jean Rhys' *Wide Sargasso Sea,*" in *Critique: Studies in Modern Fiction,* Vol. XXVIII, No. 4, Summer, 1987, pp. 195-209.

[*In the following essay, Mezei examines the narrative structure and presentation of Antoinette's madness in* Wide Sargasso Sea. *According to Mezei, Antoinette's deteriorating mental state is linked to her inability to remember and recount her story.*]

> Very soon she'll join all the others who know the secret and will not tell it. Or cannot. Or try and fail because they do not know enough. . . . She's one of them. I too can wait—for the day when she is only a memory to be avoided, looked away, and like all memories a legend. Or a lie. . . . (***Wide Sargasso Sea***)

With these vengeful words, Rochester closes his narration, the disturbing story of his marriage in Jamaica to Antoinette Cosway (Mason), the first Mrs. Rochester. Soon enough Rochester has transformed Antoinette from a speaking subject into an object, an other, a locked-away madwoman—a lie. As a character and a narrator, Rochester has committed one kind of narratorial lie, but, according to Jean Rhys, the author of *Jane Eyre,* Charlotte Brontë, had engendered another, equally serious lie:

> The Creole in Charlotte Brontë's novel is a lay figure—repulsive which does not matter, and not once alive which does. She's necessary to the plot, but always she shrieks, howls, laughs horribly, attacks all and sundry—*off stage.* For me (and for you I hope) she must be right *on stage.* She must be at least plausible with a past, the *reason* why Mr. Rochester treats her so abominably and feels justified, the *reason* why he thinks she is mad and why of course she goes mad, even the *reason* why she tries to set everything on fire, and eventually succeeds. (Personally, I think *that* one is simple. She is cold—and fire is the only warmth she knows in England). (***Letters, 1931-1966***)

Rochester's sin was to impose his point of view on both the narrative and Antoinette: Charlotte Brontë's was a narratorial omission: in *Jane Eyre,* Antoinette (Bertha) is not permitted to speak. Instead, it is Jane who speaks for her when she admonishes Rochester, "you are inexorable for that unfortunate lady . . . she cannot help being mad." To rectify the situation, Jean Rhys in her novel, ***Wide Sargasso Sea,*** allows Antoinette to narrate her own story. Thus, despite Rochester's malediction, Antoinette does "tell it," and the telling of her secret, her memories, and her story mirrors her desperate effort to save herself from a lie.

How, as subject, does Antoinette tell her story? And does her narration hold a clue to her madness? In fact, Jean Rhys was uncertain how best to present Antoinette's point of view:

> It can be done three ways. (1) Straight, Childhood, Marriage, Finale told in first person. Or it can be done (2) Man's point of view; (3) Woman's ditto both first person. Or it can be told in the third person with the writer as the Almighty. Well that is hard for me. I prefer direct thoughts and actions.
>
> I am doing (2). (***Letters***)

As the novel reveals, Rhys decided to begin with Antoinette's narration, then to shift to Rochester's, and finally to close with Antoinette's disintegrating narration, introduced and contextualized by the disembodied voice of Grace Poole.

But, as Rochester feared, there are secrets shadowing Antoinette and her narration. Since the suspense in this essay lies in what I will say about the secrets, not in what they are, let me immediately alleviate the reader's suspense. First, hidden within the narrative is the textual secret representing the hidden or deferred meaning, which is the nature of Antoinette's ultimate "marooning," a secrecy as deep and seductive as the pools she swims in, but as dangerous as the madness in which she finally drowns. This "marooning" is gradually disclosed by the deliberate sequence of her opening narrative. The structural secret, which is the secret the reader must discover as he or she travels through the text, consists of Antoinette's desire (and need) for sequence. Her very sanity is tied to her ability to narrate, and here being "marooned" has consequences for both her narrative and her state of mind.

There is also, finally, the secret shaping the entire narrative—the secret of the narrative. In describing the tales of Henry James, Tzvetan Todorov observed:

> we now know that Henry James' secret . . . resides precisely in the existence of a secret, of an absent and absolute cause, as well as in the effort to plumb this secret, to render the absent present. ("The Secret of Narrative")

Inevitably, the hunt for such a secret initiates, propels, and in effect creates the narrative. Quite simply the secret of ***Wide Sargasso Sea*** is Antoinette's valiant, heroic attempt to tell her story. The secret of the narrative is not her descent into madness in the figure of the madwoman locked in the attic, or her lack of madness and conventional society's excess of it, but her *reason* for engaging in the act of narration. Antoinette and the others "keep" their secret from Rochester (and perhaps the reader), because Rochester does not pause to unravel the story Antoinette is telling: he resists the structures and the function of her narrative, as well as its *histoire;* he is neither an ideal listener nor an ideal reader.

To prevent a false telling of her story by others—the lie—Antoinette must tell herself in the first person following the conventions of narrative order. When the narrative disintegrates, as it does in Part Three, so does Antoinette. When the narrative stops, Antoinette dies. By her act of narration, she retains her tenuous fragile hold on sanity, on life itself, since to narrate is to live, to order a life, to "make sense" out of it. If "narrative is a strategy for survival" (Daphne Marlatt, *How Hug a Stone*), Antoinette survives only as long as she creates narratives.

Although, according to Kenneth Burke, the construction of symbolic actions such as the telling of stories is the "defining feature of human beings," (*Language as Symbolic Action*) for women narrators, this symbolic action may be a necessary strategy for survival. Antoinette joins Penelope, Scheherazade, the wicked stepmother in *Snow White,* and countless female narrators whose only form of control is through the weaving of words, the plotting of stories, the constructing of plots, and the telling of their own story in their voice as narrating subject, not narrated object. What is interesting about Antoinette's narration is how desperately and ingeniously she uses narrative techniques such as the "illusion of sequence" (W. J. T. Mitchell, Foreword, *On Narrative*) and linear chronology to delay the final secret, climax, closure of her story—her descent into madness and death.

As long as Antoinette can remember and order the events of her memories into a temporal or causal sequence, create even an illusion of sequence and maintain a measured sense of space and time, then she can hold her life and self together. Her act of narration becomes an act of affirmation and cohesion, a nod to the world and its conventions, an attempt to prevent herself from dissolving. When, in Part Three, Antoinette lies encaged in Thornfield Hall's dark, cold attic, the threads that hold her to the reality that the world perceives as sanity finally break. These threads are the elements of conventional narrative: linear chronology, sequence, narratorial lucidity, distance. She herself admits at this point that "time has no meaning"; sequence disintegrates into a confusion of present and past and ultimately into a dream which narrates her future. The relation between text-time (*récit*) and story-time (*histoire*) blurs, creating anachrony (Gérard Genette, *Narrative Discourse*). She can neither "remember" what has happened in the past, nor what it is she must do in the future. Like her sense of time, her sense of space becomes distorted; "that afternoon we went to England" she says, describing a brief foray from her attic. Her attic is not England, a place, but a configuration of her mind, an enclosure. Finally, no longer in control of her narration, she must end it.

Rhys is a deliberately elusive writer, whose elusiveness differs from the lucid strategies of Joyce or Nabokov. She is also a modernist writer who polishes and hones her texts with a perfectionist's obsessions, and whose modernism is reflected in her method of paring away at authorial presence so that her characters may speak and act without intrusive authorial judgments and commentary. Unlike some of her contemporaries in the 1960s, she is not experimenting with the concept of narrative or narrator; her struggle with point of view and focalization concerns her desire to present a consciousness sincerely rather than to question the structures of presenting consciousness. We need, therefore, to dip and borrow and construct our own approach to her narrative, beckoned as it were by the text itself. With this in mind, we can now turn to narration in ***Wide Sargasso Sea*** and its relation to memory and madness.

An earlier version of Part One of ***Wide Sargasso Sea*** was published in *Art and Literature,* March 1964, and this and the endless agonizing revisions of this manuscript that took over ten years to complete, are witness to her search for perfection and purity of presentation. The changes to the earlier manuscript show her building a stronger case to justify Antoinette's state of mind and subsequent actions. Rhys removes verbs like "seem" or "thought" to allow Antoinette to speak directly, and omits "and," "but," and "then" in order to make Antoinette's discourse more disjointed and associative, to undermine the illusion of sequence. Certain deletions are indicative of her intention to allow Antionette to proffer her experiences with a greater immediacy through less commentary, therefore creating the sense of a highly impressionistic, troubled mind. For example, the earlier version had Antoinette commenting on her childhood. "I got used to a solitary life and began to distrust strangers . . . ," which is unnecessary commentary whose signification is more effectively revealed by Antoinette's reactions to ensuing events. Similarly, the final version cuts "but it was understood that she would not approve of Tia," leaving "My mother never asked me where I had been or what I had done" to stand as an even more poignant indictment of her mother's neglect.

Rhys also adds several scenes in her final version—the poisoned horse, the first "forest" dream, a visit to her imprisoned mother, all of which strengthen the case of a troubled past for Antoinette. Despite Rhys' authorial elusiveness, by looking closely at the structures of these narrative acts, we can see how narrative becomes, for Antoinette, a strategy of survival, an attempt to maintain her hold on reality, to constrain dissolution into madness and how, finally, the act of retention helps her to remember what act (other than narration) she must commit in the future.

Part One is Antoinette's narration and the narrating (present) self seems to be speaking from the perspective (place and time) with which her narration closes—the convent, in the early hours of the morning as she falls asleep again. In this case, the narrating and experiencing self merge in the present time with which Part One closes. This first narration covers the period from Antoinette's childhood at Coulibri to age seventeen at the convent just prior to her marriage to Rochester. The narrating self is engaged in an act of memory, creating a pattern like Aunt Cora's colorful patchwork counterpane out of significant moments of her childhood. Although there is little dissonance between the two selves, for the narrating self rarely judges or comments on her younger self, there are several significant occasions in which the narrating self explicitly draws attention to her present state. At these moments, we are made aware of Antoinette's urgency, her hysteria, her desperation as if her world were closing in.

Since Antoinette is a child of silence, to whom communication, words, speech bring only unhappiness and rejection (her mother continually orders the child to leave her alone), it is a heroic effort for her to speak, even to herself. On two occasions—the poisoning of her mother's horse, and Mr. Mason's intimation of the prospect of her marriage—she shows her suspicion of words: "for I thought if I told no one it might not be true." To speak something raises it to the level of concrete reality. On the other hand, it is not her *passive* silence that causes her the greatest perturbation and the eventual division into two disassociated selves, but the act of being silenced. She is silenced first by her mother, who denies her existence, and then again by Rochester who refuses to be the reader of her story. He "reads" Daniel Cosway's letter-version, but is reluctant to listen to Antoinette's version. As the couple departs from Granbois, he refuses the healing act of communication: "No, I would say—I know what I would say 'I have made a terrible mistake. Forgive me.'" But he never says it, never releases her from her imprisoning silence.

Although Part One is narrated retrospectively in the past tense, it is in the moments when Antoinette slips into the present that we catch a glimpse of the older, narrating Antoinette and the secret of her narrative. The novel opens with the ominous "They say when trouble comes close ranks, and so the white people did." Although "say" is in the gnomic present, and functions as a reminder of the outside, anonymous world of clichés, it also serves to remind us that there is a present voice, a narrator who sometimes lapses into the present. Already the troubled presence of the present is felt.

At the beginning of her story, Antoinette describes her mother:

> Once I made excuses to be near her, when she brushed her hair, a soft black cloak to cover me, hide me, keep me safe.
>
> But not any longer. Not any more.

The repetition of "not any" and the slight change from "longer" to "more" implies that the second phrase is spoken by the present narrating self brooding on her loss-of her mother, of feeling "safe" and that, in the narrator's mind, past and present blur, a blurring which occurs repeatedly in Part Three and suggests a disassociated mind. Like conventional narrative, sanity apparently requires clarity of sequence and distinction.

Further along in her narrative, just before the burning of Coulibri, Antoinette slips again into a gnomic present:

> There are more ways than one of being happy, better perhaps to be peaceful and contented and protected, as I feel now, peaceful for years and long years.

"As I feel now" probably refers to her sense of the convent as a refuge (or possibly to the attic, where locked in the refuge of her mind, she feels safe). She digresses from retrospection again in that same section when she remarks in the only noticeable judgment of her younger experiencing self "All this was long ago, when I was still babyish and sure that everything was alive."

The most striking emergence into the present occurs as

Antoinette describes her sojourn' in the convent, after Coulibri was burned and her mother locked away: "Quickly while I can, I must remember the hot classroom." Why the sense of urgency? Why must she remember? The phrase "must remember" recurs in Part Three and is in fact the secret or hidden figure of her last narrative, her link to sanity, and the motivation of her entire narrative. Must it be told quickly because soon her narrative will be taken over by another narrator and/or because she is in danger of forgetting (losing) her mind?

After Mr. Mason hints that he has a suitor for her, Antoinette enters, for the second time, a recurring nightmare where she wanders in a menacing forest, pursued by someone characterized by the fact that he hates her. This dream is narrated in the present tense. It is then an *aide mémoire,* spoken by Antoinette in the attic, to help her to remember what it is she must do at Thornfield, since the dream clearly shifts from Jamaica to England: "We are no longer in the forest but in an enclosed garden surrounded by a stone wall and the trees are different trees." Or is the narrator, speaking from the convent, shifting from a past dream to a premonition of her future English nightmare? Then she wakes and continues in the present tense to describe Sister Marie Augustine giving her chocolate and their ensuing enigmatic discussion. Her recollection of chocolate causes a digression into the past to her mother's funeral, chocolate being the trigger of this memory. "Now the thought of her is mixed up with my dream." Antoinette's narration concludes as she goes back to bed to sleep, to dream; the last words she hears are the Sister's which lead into the future and into Rochester's narration: "Soon I will give the signal. Soon it will be tomorrow morning." This anticipation of the future is paralleled by the ending of Part Three which propels the reader into true closure only in *Jane Eyre.* The entire narrative ends with the future which remains, of course, to be narrated. The intertextuality of sequence between Brontë's and Rhys' novels is as significant as the intertextuality of the *histoire.*

Before we can leave Antoinette's narrative, there remain further secrets hidden in her story and in her telling that call for disclosure. First, her narrative appears to have certain characteristics of a monologue, of what Dorrit Cohn calls the "autobiographical monologue" in which "a lone speaker recalls his own past and tells it to himself—in chronological order" (*Transparent Minds*), or even of a "memory monologue." In order to describe the memory monologue Cohn quotes Claude Simon's remarks on his novel *La Route des Flandres:*

> this author undertakes less. . .to tell a story than to describe the imprint left by it on a memory and a sensibility. (*Transparent Minds*)

Cohn then suggests that the model is not autobiographical communication (telling one's story) but the self-involvement of memory and that this imitation of a solipsistic process imposes not only a fractured chronology but also a fragmentary coverage. Cohn again quotes Simon: "I do not fill in the blanks. They remain, like so many fragments." The movement of the narration is determined not by chronology but by associative memory.

Is then Antoinette's narration not a narrative but a monologue, an autobiographical or memory monologue? I think not. Antoinette has structured her narrative deliberately and, although as we shall see, the sequence of events are connected by associative memory rather than by temporality or causality, Antoinette's narrative is forcibly contained by a motif that determines her memories and her retelling of them. Conversely as stated earlier, she herself is held together by the act of narrating. Therefore, there is a deliberate narrative presentation and strategy. Moreover, as a narrator, she is always seeking to restrain her story within the boundaries of conventional narrative temporality such as sequence, linear chronology, plausible duration. This is why she so carefully sprinkles dates and sets out duration of time throughout her telling: a date of 1839 when she enters the convent, a reference to "the first day I had to go to the convent," and explanation that "During this time, nearly eighteen months my stepfather often came to see me." These are signposts of sanity. To measure time is a measure of how closely one is in touch with reality. Accordingly, Antoinette makes an effort to measure time and to progress from childhood, to school, to marriage. Rochester called her "a lunatic who always knows the time. But never does." Pulling against chronology is her mind's tendency to work by association, to digress to the present, to compress time. After describing how she "knew the time of day when though it is hot and blue and there are no clouds, the sky can have a very black look," she pauses and begins a new section, a new time: "I was a bridesmaid when my mother married Mr. Mason." Surely this is the memory association of a bride who has learned to equate marriage with tragedy and blackness. The narrating self has invaded the experiencing self and imposed her perceptions upon the younger mind. While Antoinette's strategy as narrator is to compose a conventional narrative, the boundaries of the narrative are continually under threat of disintegrating—as is Antoinette herself. For Rhys and her narrator, freedom, iconoclasm, innovation imply danger, isolation, alienation: the tenets of modernism do not hold out liberation for a bound mind, they only release that mind into a further and more horrible entrapment, particularly if that mind is female, and by definition, not free.

A monologue, whether autobiography or memory, is suitable for a mad, rambling, or childish mind that free-associates and thus reveals itself (as Benjy does in *Sound and Fury,* or Vardaman in *As I Lay Dying*), but when a narrator like Antoinette makes such a formidable effort to structure a narrative and abide by the rhetorical principles of narrative, the difference between monologue and narrative becomes the difference between madness and sanity.

Rhys, in fact, originally intended to present Antoinette in monologue, but then changed her mind, her story, and as a consequence offered the reader a more complex fiction, a fiction with a secret to be discovered:

> The book began with a dream and ended with a dream (though I didn't get the last dream right for a long time). All the rest was to be a long monologue. Antoinette in her prison room remembers, loves, hates, raves, talks to imaginary people, hears imaginary voices answering and overhears meaningless conversations outside. The story, if any, to be implied, never told straight. . . . I remembered the last part of ***Voyage in the Dark*** written like that—time and place abolished, past and present the same—and I had been almost satisfied. Then everybody said it was "confused and confusing—impossible to understand, etc." and I had to cut and rewrite it (I still think I was right and they were wrong, tho' it was long ago). Still I thought "if they fussed over one part of a book, nobody will get the hang of a whole book written that way at all" or "A mad girl speaking all the time is too much!" And anyway there was a lot left to be done and could I do it? I think I was tired. Anyway after a week or two I decided to write it again as a story, a romance, but keeping the dream feeling and working up to the madness (I hoped). (***Letters***)

Because there is a psychological motivation for narrative, Antoinette's discourse, even if spoken, even if directed to herself (and really to whom else does she ever speak?) must be received as narrative.

Although her narrative unfolds primarily in the past, and although there is the appearance of consonance between the narrating and the experiencing selves, between the young woman of the present and the lonely child of the past, the heavy hand of present consciousness is felt throughout. But this is where Rhys is so elusive. Although in retrospective narratives, the relationship between narrating and experiencing selves varies from primary focalization on the experiencing self (and childhood) as in *Great Expectations,* to focalization on the present consciousness as it engages in the act of interpreting its past, and analyzing the present in the context of this past (Proust's *A la recherche du temps perdu*), Rhys' deliberate blurring of the two selves through allowing the present (and disturbed) consciousness of Antoinette to overtly and covertly intrude upon the narration, sows seeds of warning about the precarious state of the narrating consciousness. While Part One is evidently narrated in the past, we in fact learn as much about the present state of her mind. Antoinette's inability at times, particularly in Part Three, to distinguish between her past and present self is simultaneously a sign of her increased disturbance and of the breakdown of narrative presentation.

In Part One, Antoinette succumbs to certain narrative habits that are revelatory of her present disturbed mind. She repeats the adverbs "always" and "never." Within the opening pages, Mr. Luttrell "was gone for always"; Pierre's doctor "never came again"; Antoinette "never went near" the orchid in the wild garden at Coulibri; "The Wilderness of Coulibri never saddened me"; Christophine "never paid them"; "I never looked at any strange negro"; "My mother never asked me where I had been or what I had done." In one sense the use of "always," along with the repetition of "still," ("she still rode about every morning") and "sometimes" ("sometimes we left the bathing pool at midday, sometimes we stayed till late afternoon") is iterative and durative, implying continuity over a certain duration of time in the past. However, the plaintive echo of "still," "sometimes," "usually," "always," and "never" intimates a presentness in that adverbs like "still" reach *into* the present, and that "always," and more strongly "never" affect the present narrating Antoinette who has suffered the consequences of the string of "always" and "never" in her childhood, and now exists in a state of neverness—always. Moreover the finality and negativity of "never" (and, in the context of her discourse, of "always") imply a continual, progressing closure as her world narrows, closes in on her, and freedom, safety, and happiness are progressively cut off from her.

In other words, the repetition of adverbs (whose very repetition would connote iterativity) in fact implies the opposite—closure, a finality. The frequency and persistence of repetition evokes this sense of finality and desperate sadness.

With similar effect, Rhys often resorts to the verbal auxiliary "would." In reporting angry conversations between her mother and Mr. Mason, Antoinette describes their dialogue by reporting "he would say," "she'd speak,"; "would" is here used in the habitual mode. The impression the reader receives is again iterative—this argument occurred over and over again. Antoinette also creates this effect by remembering that "Mr. Mason *always* said." This use of the iterative has a psychological effect upon the reader, in that Antoinette's narration takes on a timeless urgency as if it were a universal or apocalyptic tale whose signification extends beyond the narrator and her experience, or to put it another way, the narrator's life and experience are not merely personal but also symbolic.

As Antoinette draws her narrative to its first conclusion, as she falls into her first sleep, and she seems to narrate from a region in which she is either just entering sleep or waking, a pre- or subconscious state where "only the magic and the dream are true," she sounds her most foreboding note. She has just woken from her nightmare, and asks the Sister who tends to her "such terrible things happen I said, 'why? why'?" If the reader reflects back on Part One, Antoinette's narrative has consisted entirely of the telling of "terrible things" one after the other; her narrative is obsessed with safety, her understandable desire to find refuge, the progressive diminishment of any feeling of safety, and conversely her increasing sense of isolation or, to use Antoinette's more poetic phrase, being "marooned." Rejected (and betrayed) by her mother, by Tia, the local blacks, and eventually by Mr. Mason, as first he abandons her to Rochester, and secondly, dies making her abandonment complete, Antoinette becomes increasingly marooned.

While Antoinette's narrative appears to follow a linear sequence, its deep structure is not linear but associative. Conscious of the need to present her story convincingly (even to herself), she appears to maintain a chronology, the illusion of sequence. Yet, if we look carefully at the sequence of events, we see their connexity is associative rather than temporal or causal, and that the associations are based on Antoinette's obsessions—her fear of the loss of safety, her sense of desertion and isolation—so that each episode she narrates becomes an amplification of these obsessions. She begins her story with an oblique reference to the Emancipation Act, "when trouble comes close ranks," continues with the anecdote of Mr. Luttrell's suicide, then recounts the poisoned horse incident (each episode "marooning" them further), and moves on to Pierre's feebleness, and a description to the wild garden. Eden destroyed. Safety for Antoinette implies evasion, burial, escape, enclosing oneself away from the world by assigning signs of safety to parentheses "(My father, visitors, horses, feeling safe in bed—all belonged to the past)." For a time, she feels safe in her bed, Coulibri, the convent, and Granbois. Gradually, however, each refuge is progressively destroyed: the safety of her bed and Coulibri ruined by fire and by her mother's marriage to Mr. Mason and the invasion of the blacks, the sanctuary of the convent by the imminent arrival of a suitor and another invasive marriage which, like her mother's, culminates in fire and madness. Her final evasion is within her own mind, disassociated from time, from people, even from her own self of which the attic, dark, cold and lightless, is a perfect sign.

Antoinette's narrative in Part One ends as she falls into sleep, and another narrator, Edward Rochester, who remains unnamed although his personal signature is strongly stamped on his discourse. Rhys wanted a "cold factual" narrator to contrast with Antoinette's "emotional" account (***Letters***); she also felt sympathy for Rochester's plight and gave him a chance to justify himself. His narration then, unlike Antoinette's is not a confession or a matter of survival, but a self-justification, an attempt at a rational, analytic explanation of the breakdown of his marriage and of his wife. It is appropriate that the narrative now falls into his hands since, at the point when Antoinette closes her narrative, she is experiencing greater and greater distress and disassociation. Like her mother, she is suffering a division of the self where she undergoes what she calls the real death, the death of the mind, and becomes blank, doll-like, inhuman, in waiting for the second death, the death of the body. Since she is now outside herself, her story, appropriately, is told from the outside by an outsider. Rochester has married her, taken possession of her, and made her *his* wife, and so he now tells *her* story and the story of their marriage which has become *his* story and no longer hers. Instead of narrating her own story, Antoinette becomes a character in his narration. She does, however, resist complete marital and narratorial possession by Rochester for on two occasions she breaks into Rochester's narrative to present her point of view.

In contrast to Antoinette's narrative, Rochester's narrating self (and his narration takes the shape of a letter to his father that he will never send) is close in time to his experiencing self, and the immediacy of his language reflects the shocks suffered by his experiencing self. He speaks of "this morning" as he begins, slipping into the present because there is so little temporal distance between his two selves: "So this is Massacre," "Everything is too much." Despite Rochester's intention of presenting a reasoned explanation of the events, he is overwhelmed by the magic and sensuality of Granbois and his wife and crushed by his sense of betrayal by his own family and Antoinette's in saddling him with a mad wife. As a consequence, his mind loses its apparent clarity. His discourse, which in the beginning, although reflecting his unease, was at least ordered, becomes by the end of his narrative disjointed, wild, fragmented, impressionistic. "The tree shivers. Shivers and gathers all its strength. And waits." Unlike the Antoinette of Part One, he loses control of his narration and the structure of his narrative presentation disintegrates. This loss of control is manifested through Antoinette's invasion of his narration, first in what Rhys calls the interlude, but more pointedly, into his thoughts, her invasion is delivered in italics, between parentheses."

> *(I lay awake all night long after they were asleep, and as soon as it was light I got up and dressed and saddled Preston. And I came to you. Oh Christophine. On Pheena, Pheena, help me).*

If to narrate is a sign of lucidity, who then has lost his mind?

It is in Rochester's narration that the author's presence as manipulator and organizer is most strongly felt since Rhys permits Antoinette to interrupt Rochester's narrative and tell her story. After Rochester receives Daniel Cosway's incriminating letter condemning Antoinette and her mother to madness, Rochester turns against his wife. At that point, Antoinette wakes from one of her sleeps and temporarily takes on the telling of her own story. Here there is dissonance between the narrating and experiencing self; this narrating Antoinette is speaking from her English attic since, in a digression, she refers to England, focalizing on her experiencing self: "I will be a different person when I live in England," but then quickly reveals her knowledge of England, a knowledge that can only come from living there and thus from the narrating self: "Summer. There are fields of corn like sugar-cane fields, but good colour and not so tall. After summer the trees are bare, then winter and snow." Thus, the narrating self asserts its disturbing and disturbed presence. As she closes her interlude, it is the narrating Antoinette speaking in the present from her attic room, with its one window high up, who observes:

> but now I see everything still, fixed for ever like the colours in a stained-glass window. Only the clouds move.

Rhys also ensures that Antoinette's point of view and voice are heard even in the midst of Rochester's narrative, through extended passages of dialogue between the two that allow Antoinette to explain her past and clarify the sequence of events of her own life. Rochester reports one of their dialogues ("'Now come for a walk,' she said, 'and I will tell you a story'" in which Antoinette describes her dream of the watching rats and her moonlight sleep to explain her present state of mind.

Rochester's narration of their dialogues also becomes a mode for her clarification of sequence:

> ". . . Is your mother alive?"
>
> "No, she is dead, she died."
>
> "When?"
>
> "Not long ago."
>
> "Then why did you tell me she died when you were a child?"
>
> "Because they told me to say so and because it is true. She did die when I was a child. There are always two deaths, the real one, and the one people know about."

In a disturbed, fragmented state of mind, Rochester simultaneously concludes his own narrative (and Antoinette remains forever silenced and absent) and leaves that place with "its beauty and magic and the secret I would never know" (172). Antoinette's mind is broken (to use Christophine's phrase) and Rochester vows:

> I too can wait—for the day when she is only a memory to be avoided, locked away, and like all memories a legend. Or a lie. . . .

His vow is prophetic, for in the end all Antoinette has is her memory which becomes her life line, her death, and almost the death of Rochester. Antoinette as a remembering consciousness absorbed not in retrospection, but in the *act* of recollection, acts out of that memory to burn Thornfield to the ground, and to die she has become another of the heroines killed into art, noted by Gilbert and Gubar in *The Madwoman in the Attic.* Once she has recollected the past (those moments that she wants and needs to recollect)—retention, and recollected the future (that which she must do next)—protention, Antoinette transforms memory from a passive to an active mode.

In Part Three, after a brief narrative by Grace Poole, which brings the reader to England and into the darkness, prison, or shelter where Antoinette dwells, Antoinette once again takes up her own story. In contrast to her earlier narration, she now speaks in the present, digresses into the past (analepsis), and into the future through a dream (prolepsis) that foretells the events that follow after the narrative concludes, for a narrator presumably cannot describe her own death.

As she begins this her final narrative, she says: "In this room, I wake early and lie shivering for it is very cold." The present tense indicates that the judicious distance of her first narrative is obliterated. She has lost all sense of measured time and place for she refuses to believe "this is England," and of self for she does not recognize the woman with streaming hair, surrounded by a gilt frame as herself. The structures of narrative have broken down and she is faltering, shivering, an absence. Her memory which gave her a tenuous connection to reality and her narrative its surface structure, also eludes her. An Antoinette who can no longer remember is no longer Antoinette; she has lost her true self, her centre no longer holds. The narrating self has dissolved into a completely experiencing self. She had told Rochester "I am not a forgetting person." But here, in the attic, she has forgotten.

Her last narrative act is the story of her struggle to remember, and the phrases "to remember" and "must remember" recur continually. At first she remarks: "and to wonder why I have been brought here. For what reason? There must be a reason. What is it that I must do?" Then, "when I got back into bed, I could remember more and think again." Slowly, in a disjointed manner, she makes a tremendous effort to remember, to disclose the secret locked in her past, and to complete her story; her mind works again by feverish association—"Looking at the tapestry one day I recognized my mother. . ."; "I remember watching myself"; "We lost our way to England. When? Where? I don't remember, but we lost it." Since her state of wakedness only seems to confuse her, she sinks into dream and when she wakes from it, she finally remembers: "Now at last I know why I was brought here and what I have to do." Through dreaming and submission to her subconscious, her memory has been restored. Now, by jumping to her death, she commits one of her few acts, other than narration, and closes her life and her story.

Deprived of light and warmth and love, she has made the supreme effort of will in sleeping, in dreaming, and in waking to narrate her own story, and to bring it to conclusion herself. The secret is thus told and the telling is the secret.

Helen E. Nebeker (essay date 1990)

SOURCE: "The Artist Emerging," in *Critical Perspectives on Jean Rhys,* edited by Pierrette M. Frickey, Three Continents Press, 1990, pp. 148-57.

[*In the following essay, Nebeker discusses the presentation of female archetypes, mythic patterns, and shifting perspective in* After Leaving Mr. Mackenzie.]

In her second novel, ***After Leaving Mr. Mackenzie,*** Jean Rhys presents a work so complex that it defies discussion. This complexity has led critics to a consistent oversimplification and misconstruing of the novel's impact. The plot is at once deceivingly simple in thrust and complicated in detail. The setting is April in Paris, the heroine Julia Martin, the time some ten years after World War I. As the story opens, Julia is living in a cheap room, recovering from psychic wounds incurred six months earlier, when Mr. Mackenzie had ended their love affair. A "decent Englishman," Mackenzie has been sending Julia a weekly allowance of three hundred francs, but now, in April, having sent her a severance check of fifteen hundred francs, he abjures further responsibility. Julia, in a rage, seeks him out in a nearby restaurant and, in an embarrassing public scene, melodramatically returns his check. Later the same evening, she meets George Horsfield, a young Englishman, and accepts from him, during the course of a platonic evening, fifteen hundred francs. George sympathetically encourages Julia to return to London, where she hopes to gain financial aid from her first lover, W. Neil James. The rest of the plot concerns Julia's ten-day sojourn in London, where she visits James and her family—a sister, a paternal uncle, and an invalid mother who dies during the visit. On the night of the funeral, after having buried her mother and quarreled with her sister and uncle, Julia sleeps with George for the first and last time, Then, having received twenty pounds as a brush-off from the ex-lover, James, Julia returns to Paris. Ten days later, roused from a lethargy of despair by George's gift of ten pounds, ecstatically planning the new wardrobe she will buy with it, Julia goes out into the evening, encounters Mackenzie, and on the spur of the moment borrows from him one hundred francs.

This meager plot belies the novel's aesthetic complexity. The major difficulty—and perhaps defect—lies in Rhys's seemingly diffuse thematic purpose, a confusion which reflects her struggle to construct a viable, personal philosophy within the changing social framework of her time. Actually, once sorted out, one sees that Rhys has managed to evoke in the complexities a panoramic view of changing twentieth-century philosophy. This changing philosophy, almost imperceptible in Rhys's own life, was rising phoenix-like from the ashes of a dying, patriarchal social structure. In this Victorian milieu, man's superior role was clearly defined. Woman, man's adjunct, was at once his creation, his wife, his servant or his mistress. Man's role was certain, secure; woman's was predictable, but tenuous and stifling.

Rhys's main problem in this, her second novel, was to find the means of communicating both the reality she saw and her feelings about that reality, without risking contemptuous denial. She had attempted this difficult communication in her first novel, ***Quartet.*** Marya, her protagonist, facing the problem of revealing the starkness of woman's life—a revelation for which she anticipated either vehement repudiation or vilification—repeatedly questioned: "How can you understand? What can you know?" But, in ***After Leaving Mr. Mackenzie,*** Rhys, the emerging artist, chances upon the archetypal metaphor. Through that metaphor, she can express what was formerly inexpressible. Combining a basic mythic pattern with a shifting narrative focus—a focus criticized by many as a disturbing defect, because they do not understand its purpose—Rhys reveals the truth as she sees it, even as she honestly acknowledges that "truth" must always be suspect, multifaceted as it is.

2

Rhys's archetypes are immediately obvious in the details of Julia's hotel room in Paris. The room is "sombre," with a "one-eyed aspect," because the solitary window "was very much to one side." The wallpaper depicts a large, open-beaked bird on the branch of a tree, faced by a "strange, wingless creature, half-bird, half-lizard," also open-beaked and belligerent. The branch on which they perch sprouts "fungus and queerly shaped leaves and fruit." Alerted to the purpose of the story by these images, we know that from the "room" of her private thoughts, Rhys is going to communicate through her "window"—off-sided though it may be—her vision of woman, the strange wingless creature undergoing metamorphosis, threatened by man, the large bird (a symbol of transcendence) with open beak. Perched together on the phallic branch of the tree (a tree is an archetype for life) which sprouts only fungus and *distorted* fruits and leaves (all sexual symbols), the wingless creature, driven by its instinct for survival, faces the larger menace belligerently.

Further archetypes emerge in the red plush sofa, the spotted gilt-framed mirror, which reflects the bed and an "unframed oil-painting of a half-empty bottle of red wine, a knife, and a piece of Gruyere cheese." The reflection is "slightly distorted and full of obscure meaning. The picture and the sofa were linked in her mind . . . The picture stood for the idea, the spirit, and the sofa stood for the act." The reader now sees, far more clearly than can Julia, the essence of reality of her life. Julia links the economics of life (food, drink, the phallic blade) with the "spirit" or essence and knows they are achieved by the act (everything associated with the red-plush sofa). Thus Julia, prostituting herself for the necessities of life, sees the distortion of her life and hates it, but, in the end, she will be unable to reject it.

Archetypes continue to unfold in details of Julia's life. Financially secure, physically unexploited during the six months of Mackenzie's support, Julia is "not altogether unhappy." "Locked in her room," she feels safe. But sometimes she is confused and frightened by her thoughts. Lying in bed, she hates the world and everybody in it. She feels "horribly fatigued." The "rumble of life [is] like the sound of the sea . . . rising gradually around her." Her memory is filled with images of trees, dark shadows, dark, purple seas. Critics have seen in these details only Julia's submersion in her sexual urges. But Rhys's muted strokes deny such simplification, evoking awareness of deeper significance. These are Jungian images of the primal consciousness, the collective-unconscious archetypes of sea and shadow and tree and sunshine. The conflict within Julia is her "unconscious" urging her toward psychic illumination, toward the process of "individuation" in which the conscious comes to terms with the inner center or SELF. This unconscious yearning of Julia for psychic wholeness pains the reader. He senses the implicit irony and pathos as Julia, unconsciously yearning for identity, constantly powders her face, grieves over her fatness and her old coat, plans a new wardrobe. Woman's only sense of worth, implies Rhys, is in terms of physical attractiveness and sexual desirability. But, as Julia sits in a cafe drinking Pernod, planning her "new clothes with passion and voluptuousness," her vision of Mackenzie's "cool and derisory smile" fills her with "dreary and abject humiliation," and we know that Julia, too, is aware of the degradation she suffers.

3

Having examined, if only superficially, Rhys's emerging mythic patterns, we can turn our attention to her use of a multiple narrative focus, through which she develops levels of characterization and, by extension and implication, levels of truth. Furthermore, through this focus, all characters emerge as archetypes, reinforcing her mythic framework. Thus, in the character of Mackenzie, Rhys delineates the prototype of the economically secure, upper-middle-class, late-Victorian male. His mind is "tight and tidy . . . adapted to the social system." He lives by a "certain code of morals and manners from which he seldom departs." Nevertheless, he, too, is undergoing metamorphosis; he has published in his youth a book of poems; he is drawn to "strangeness and recklessness;" he feels haunted by "ungenerous action;" and he pities Julia, even though he rejects her irresponsibility and her lack of self-control. If one remembers Heidler in Rhys's first novel, ***Quartet,*** Rhys's artistic growth is obvious. For in permitting Mackenzie these contradictory qualities—a consideration Rhys was unable to extend to her earlier arch-villain—Rhys suggests that man, like woman, is vulnerable and a product of his social system, though he struggles against it.

Parenthetically, it is through Mackenzie that Rhys will develop a major theme which she has been intellectually formulating since her first novel. That is, the seeds of man's essential hatred and fear of woman lie in the financial and emotional demands which she makes upon him. The burden of these demands is powerfully demonstrated in a scene where Julia is berating Mackenzie over the unfairness of woman's life. Helplessly he mentally expostulates: "'No, of course life isn't fair. It's damned unfair, really . . . but what does she expect me to do about. I'm not God Almighty.'" And, in the end, abjuring responsibility for her situation and rejecting her emotional and financial pleadings, Mackenzie has "no pity for her; she [is] a dangerous person." Only after she leaves and he has eaten hot food and drunk good wine, secure in his unthreatened world, is he again able to pity her. "'Poor devil,' he thought. 'She's got damn all.'"

Because we are permitted to view Julia and her existence from a shifting vantage point, Rhys convinces us that communication is a many-leveled process and that the "truth" of any communication must be highly suspect. Although Julia reveals to Mackenzie the tawdry facts of her life—marriage, the child that dies, divorce (though perhaps she had never been married at all, as Mackenzie thinks to himself)—one questions the truth. We are aware that Julia recites the script she thinks Mackenzie expects from her "sort of woman" who, he knows, "would be certain to tell you lies anyhow." Typically, Julia mistakes her script for tragedy, but Mackenzie sees only comedy. Rhys's multiple narrative voice operates further to show that men, as well as women, play predetermined roles, which in turn condition their response to others.

Having introduced Julia and Mackenzie, Rhys continues both character development and mythic reference, as she contrasts Mackenzie with young George Horsfield. Both are English, but Mackenzie is of medium height and coloring, whereas George is "the dark young man." While Mackenzie is the stock "capitalist," wealthy and retired at the age of forty-eight, George seems to have inherited only a temporary financial windfall which has permitted him to spend six months kicking up his heels. Unlike cynical Mackenzie, George is romantically sensitive, pitying Julia. George senses that much of life is fantastic, dreamlike, distorted, as in a poor looking-glass, like Julia's vision in the opening scene of the novel. He is tolerant, not a "cold hypocrite" like Mackenzie. He is cautious, ponderous, childish, but, at root, genuine. Having known disillusionment and poverty, George can sympathize with Julia as Mackenzie cannot. Thus his vision of life permits Julia to confide details of her life—real or imagined—which she could not voice to Mackenzie. She can play to the hilt, with George, her role of impotent, suffering womanhood. To him she reveals her wanderings with men, her experience with an older woman, her youthful desire for adventure—and in her adventure, "men were mixed up, because they had to be." And hearing all these details of her life, George oozes warm humanity, thinking, "'Hang it all, one can't leave this unfortunate creature alone to go and drink herself dotty." But even as he listens to Julia's rambling, sentimental story, he is irritated by her vagueness concerning her role: ". . . She spoke as if she were trying to recall a book she had read or a story she had heard and Mr. Horsfield felt irritated by her vagueness, 'because,' he thought, 'your life is your life, and you must be pretty definite about it. Or if it's a story you are making up, you ought at least to have it pat.'" Ironically, at the end of their evening together, George's last thoughts of Julia are in terms of a bawdy song: "Roll me over on my right side, "Roll me over slow; Roll me over on my right side, cause my left side hurts me so." Thus, through Horsfield, Rhys reveals a sympathetic but sharp perception of Julia: she gets kicked around like a dog, but she keeps asking for it!

Unfortunately, George cannot fully transcend the hold of the past, so even as Julia unfolds the supposed reality of her life, we are left unsure of its veracity. Because everything revealed by Julia is filtered through the mirror of George's comprehension, flawed as it is by the myths which work upon him as a male, all that he understands must be questioned. To emphasize the specious nature of George's perception, Rhys introduces the sculptress, Ruth, Julia's older female friend. Through Ruth, Rhys suggests that the "female perception" can be understood only by another sensitive, artistic female. In Julia's seeking communion with another woman—an archetype for the unconscious—we are returned to Rhys's theme of the symbolic search for the SELF. But in Julia's account of her attempt to tell Ruth the truth about herself, that it had been as if she were standing before a judge who didn't believe a word she had said, Rhys suggests two more diffuse but basic themes: (1) that women cannot really hope for rapport with other women, antagonists that they are; (2) at a deeper level, that one cannot fool the unconscious with conscious rationalization. In Rhys's extended imagery, "real" or archetypal woman lies couched, "like an utterly lovely proud animal," behind a mask-like, long, dark face with blank eyes. And in this introduction of the mask image, to be explored at both the literal and the mythic level, Rhys's emerging aesthetic and technical power cannot be challenged.

4

Before Julia can address the mystery of woman's mask, she must make the archetypal "journey of discovery" from Paris to London. Rhys prepares us, as she has done before, for the ultimate results of that experience. Archetypally, the usual "journey into awareness" is a night sea journey from west to east (a symbolic journey from death to life). But Julia's journey is from east to west and Rhys emphasizes the train journey, avoiding completely the sea crossing. In this way, she foreshadows Julia's inability to effect change in her life.

Julia's return to her old haunts in London discloses details of her former life as well as her meetings with five significant people who fall into recognizable patterns. The former lover, W. Neal James is typical Victorian-male stereotype. Preparing for their meeting, Julia remembers that when he had ended their affair, James had been "eternally grateful" for her "sweetness and generosity" and had subsequently "lent" her a "good deal of money." He is, she thinks, "so kind, so cautious, so perfectly certain that all is for the best." But meeting him seventeen years later, Julia realizes the truth. "Because he has money, he's a kind of God. Because I have none I'm a kind of worm." For Julia, James now represents the system which corrupts and the sex which exploits, the male "capitalist" who has created her reality, who controls her vision of herself. With him there can be no communication, no playing the role of impotent, suffering womanhood, no sentimentalizing of her dead little son—real or imagined. His only response would be—and as Rhys structures it, this may well be Julia's dialogue with herself—"Look here, I don't believe that; you're making it up." As Julia admits to Horsfield later, "'I was for sleeping with—not talking to. And quite right, too, I suppose.'" So in the face of her knowledge, Julia plays yet another role, the role in which she believes James has cast her. Good sport, corruptible woman. Then she lapses into her role of helpless, fatalistic woman: "She said: 'Anyhow, I don't know how I could have done differently . . . Do you think I could have done differently?'"

Surprisingly, James, by implication a believer in the Victorian view that working women are naturally corruptible, that they inevitably seek out their own fate as surely as good women control their destiny, replies: "'Don't ask me. I'm not the person to ask that sort of thing, am I? I don't know. Probably you couldn't." Then we find that the war has changed James, given him the perspective to understand that some "really decent guys" don't "get on," simply because of "bad luck": "'. . . some women too. Though mind you, women are a different thing altogether. Because it's all nonsense; *the life of a man and the life of a woman can't be compared.* They're up against entirely different things the whole time. What's she use of talking nonsense about it?'" (Emphasis added.) Which shows that James understands everything and understands nothing!

That James is a predecessor of Mackenzie is obvious in his age, his attitudes, his affluence which is seemingly not rooted in the competitive capitalistic system. In the same way, Uncle Griffiths, older than James—sixty-five, though he looks much younger—represents an older, patriarchal order from which James, Mackenzie, and George derive. Almost Norse in description, broad, short, unwrinkled, red complexioned, "solid and powerful," Uncle Griffiths represents to Julia and her family "the large and powerful male," Because he is practical, self-concerned, Julia feels contempt for him, perhaps unjustly. For Julia has violated the order in which he is rooted—the patriarch family. In his rational view, Julia has made her bed and must now lie in it. Rhys does not condemn Uncle Griffiths, as does Julia, for being unfeeling, hard. She permits him a sense of humor, love for his wife, whom he had married, impulsively, without subsequent regret. She emphasizes that he provides for himself and his wife, a burden upon no one, and would help Norah, Julia's sister, if he could. Furthermore, he knows a truth of life: "'Of course, everybody has to sit on their own bottoms. I've found that out all my life. You mustn't grumble if you find it out too.'"

But wise though he appears, Uncle Griffiths is at best a benevolent despot. After the funeral of Julia's mother, comfortable, well-fed, surrounded by his "audience of females": ". . . He talked and talked. He talked about life, about literature, about Dostoevsky. He said: 'Why see the world through the eyes of an epileptic?'" or of a "woman" he might just as easily have substituted. And when Julia mechanically says, "'But he might see things very clearly, mightn't he? At moments.'" Griffiths can only reply: "Clearly? Why clearly? How do you mean clearly?" To which, of course, there is no answer.

Patriarchal Uncle Griffiths can, however, understand and approve of Julia's younger sister, Norah, who has chosen to stay within the family framework, to measure up to the responsibility of caring for her invalid mother, "making do" as best she can, expecting no better life. Cliché though her type might be, Norah emerges in the capable hands of Rhys as a sympathetic character for whom we have compassion and even hope. Since Norah represents that which Rhys rejected in her own life, one must admire both her artistic control and her intellectual maturity in developing the character.

Norah, dark like Julia, is tall, strongly built, straight-backed. Her face wears an expression of endurance and her voice is sweet "with a warm and tender quality," although Julia sees her face "cold as though warmth and tenderness were dead in her." She is, in Julia's eyes, plainly labelled "middle class, no money . . . all the daintiness and prettiness perforce cut out . . . brought up to certain tastes, then left without the money to gratify them . . . [forbidden] even the relief of rebellion against her lot. . . ." Norah is similarly shocked by Julia. She thinks, "'She doesn't even look like a lady now.'"

At the meeting of the sisters in the home of the dying mother, the pull between compassion and hatred is masterful. Julia's visible emotion for her sister touches us. Her gentleness with Norah—now on the defensive about the sordidness of her own life—is in sharp contrast with Norah's desire to see Julia hurt and humiliated. But the reader understands Norah's need to strike out when the starkness of her life unfolds. She reads from a book: "The slave had no hope, and knew of no change . . . no other world, no other life. She had no wish, no hope, no love . . . The absence of pain and hunger was her happiness, and when she felt unhappy she was tired, more than usual after the day's labour . . ."; we realize that this is the truth of Norah's existence. But when Rhys forces upon us, through narrative manipulation, the knowledge that this is also the reality of Julia who has sought to escape the fate of her sister, we feel a stab of pain for woman's lot. This is narrative focus employed at its best.

Norah, however, has no room for compassion. She only knows that she is "tall and straight and slim and young—well, fairly young," and that her life is "like being buried alive." "It isn't fair, it isn't fair," she sobs. Julia's return home has forced Norah to realize that in the nine years of caring for her mother, her youth has vanished, her soft heart grown hard and bitter and that the only voices of approval are those of "beasts and devils," the same "beasts and devils" that torture Julia in her vastly different life.

But at least, for Norah, there will be recompense for her years of duty; the will her mother has made will make her financially secure—the *sine qua non* of both men and women in Rhys's view—and at the death of her mother, Norah will begin her own quest for fulfillment. But before this, she and Julia have a fight in which all the animosities of their lives are unleashed in verbal violence. In that scene, which follows the funeral, Rhys reveals, as she has done before, the irony of women able to see each other only in those stereotypes *created by men.* Hence, women cannot reach out in sisterhood, understanding the pain and frustration they all endure as women. Rather, they must seize arms, do battle against each other, engaged as they are in the fight for economic survival. "Good" Norah, once without financial hope for herself, must triumph over penniless Julia, provoking her to anger and incoherence, even though inwardly both sisters desire communication. "Bad" Julia must hate and rage against her sister, who symbolizes the "mean beasts," the good, respectable people" whom she at once envies and hates.

5

It is in the relatively minor character of Julia's mother that Rhys completes her theme of woman's search for SELF or archetypal woman—the creature behind the mask. Brazilian born, "transplanted" from a warm world of "orange trees" to the "cold, grey country" of England, the dark-skinned, high-cheek-boned, dying mother seems to Julia "still beautiful as an animal would be in old age." In sorrow and confusion, she remembers when her mother had been "the warm centre of the world," only to change and become "a dark, austere, rather plump woman . . . worried," unreasonable, whom Julia had grown to fear, dislike, ignore, tolerate, and finally, to sentimentalize as her mother. In the final look at her now dead mother, who had struggled and fought for every tortured breath, Julia senses that "something in the poise of her body and in her serene face was old, old, old . . . [The] sunken face, bound with white linen, looked frightening—horribly frightening, like a mask. Always masks had frightened her."

With the reference to "masks," all Rhys's overtones coalesce. This "beautiful" woman—"more beautiful than either of us," as Julia has said to Norah—emerges as a mother archetype, Earth-Mother, bearer of life and source of love, the female principle personified. But though she was "old, old, old" (timeless, that is) and had fought long after her body was paralyzed and useless, she is now dead. And her only offspring are Norah—symbol of a kind of light or virtue—who had done the best for her mother that she could; and Julia, at whom the dying woman had looked with "recognition and surprise and anger." These two "realities"—the one rooted in a kind of depressing "duty" and deprivation (the results of the pressures of the superego or the Zeitgeist), the other in egocentrism and an aline, distorted vision (the manifestation of the ego)—will never measure up to the progenitor, the great archetypal woman. As Norah has said: "We're soft, or lazy, or something." But Rhys knows the problem is deeper than that. Ancient, archetypal woman, long since an anachronism (just as is patriarchal Uncle Griffiths), is dead. There is no return to the security of that "sweet, warm centre." If there is to be any hope for woman at all, says Rhys, she must throw off her paralysis and face life without dependency, void though it may seem.

But Julia, on the verge of recognizing the truths synthesized in the person of her mother, is ultimately frightened by the "mask" and all that it entails. Her final gesture of unconscious understanding is the bouquet of roses she buys for her mother's funeral with her last ten shillings;, a token of love for that which was beautiful but, like the roses, fragile and transitory. From this point on, Julia can only grapple with the idea of "nothingness," that is for her the truth of existence.

Although the theme of nothingness is central to understanding the intellectual complexity of this novel, unfortunately, limitations of space prevent discussion here. Suffice it to say that Rhys wrestles masterfully with existentialism, that canker in the soul of twentieth century man: the realization that "*nothing* matters" because "nothing *matters.*" This agonizing awareness dominates Julia's final evening with Horsfield, finally overwhelming her so that she sends him away. But as Julia lies on her bed, cold and hostile, hating him, Rhys lets us know that George Horsfield is not the enemy. An enlightened male, he understands Julia's misery and he hates the people and the system which control both their lives. Returning to his "pleasant, peaceful, spacious" book-lined room after leaving Julia at the hotel, he sees with startling clarity what the reader must also see if he is to avoid a grievous over-simplification of Rhys's art: ". . . 'I don't see how I can bring her here exactly . . . I can't bring her here.' Suddenly he saw Julia not as a representative of the insulted and injured, but as a solid human being . . . She must have a bed to sleep in, food, clothes, companionship—or she would be lonely; understanding of her own peculiar point of view—or she would be aggrieved."

Horsfield knows, as does Rhys, at least unconsciously, that woman cannot be transported into a world of peace and order simply because one pities her, as we have seen George pity his cat. She is not a pathetic abstraction; she is an individual, a human being who wants the same things George wants: economic security, friendship (not sexual exploitation). Above all, an understanding of her "reality" as valid.

But just as Rhys will not make George the villain, neither will she give him the role of Saviour. Though he symbolizes enlightened, evolving man, and though he sympathizes with Julia's plight, it is "in a cold and theoretical way." Seeing all that he has with "great clarity," he is nevertheless "appalled" and ultimately will not "be rushed into anything." Rhys seems to tell us that man's own need for survival precludes involvement beyond a sentimental pity and a gratuitous handout. From this point, Rhys never again in her novels takes up the idea of man's evolution.

The final section of ***After Leaving Mr. Mackenzie*** is anticlimactic. Julia returns from her journey, having changed not at all. She still sees woman as prisoner, confined to her bedroom. Contemplating employment for which she has no references and is in no way prepared, she receives a letter from George containing ten pounds and another brush-off. She leaves her confining room to walk the streets thinking of new clothes, of "love," denying "age." Later she sees a "slim woman with full soft breasts" to whom she longs to talk—again the symbolic urge to communicate with the unconscious. Later still, she thinks, "After all, what have I done? I haven't done anything," which is, for the true existentialist, the only sin. All of this we have heard before.

Then Rhys makes a final mythic statement, in a tense scene between Julia and a young man who stalks her on the street. Wanting to tell the "boy" to leave, she cannot and they "walk on side by side—tense like two animals." In the light she sees that he is a . . . boy—wearing a cap, very pale and with very small, dark eyes set deeply in his head. He gave her a rapid glance, "'*Oh, la la,*' he said. '*Ah, non alors.*' He turned about and walked away. 'Well,' said Julia aloud, 'that's funny. The joke's on me this time.'" She walks on seeing nothing but the "young man's little eyes, which had looked at her with such deadly and impartial criticism. She thought again: 'The joke was on me that time.'"

Patently this scene has more significance than just a rejection by a "boy" walking the streets looking for a pick-up (particularly in view of the brief scene which follows where Julia gazes "indifferent and cold, like a stone," on a poor, drooping skeleton of a man). This 'boy" is both Julia's "animus" (that masculine half of the soul image) and, more importantly, the archetypal "trickster," who though dominated by physical appetite, often evolves to become a guide, an initiator into the unconscious. Julia, however, is not yet ready for initiation into even limited truth and the "boy" must reject her, his eyes "deadly and impartial" in their perception. As Rhys has foreshadowed in her first pages, Julia must continue to believe that woman is victimized by man's sexual demands. She will be unable to admit that it is woman who seeks sexual attention; that it is woman who demands both sexual abasement and economic support, protesting all the time, "'That is not what I meant at all, that is not it at all.' YOU BEASTS!"

Rhys concludes this statement in Julia's' final scene with Mackenzie, where she takes him for another hundred francs and goes out into the streets at "the hour between god and wolf, as they say."

To summarize further the ideas suggested in ***After Leaving Mr. Mackenzie*** is impossible; the complexity of Rhys's vision is yet to fully emerge, both intellectually and technically. But the power is there; each detail in this novel works to purpose; her myth is assuming outline. The later novels will refine and process the wheat from the chaff. This process is discussed in totality in my book: *Jean Rhys: Woman in Passage,* Montreal, Canada: Eden Press, 1981.

Jan Curtis (essay date Spring 1990)

SOURCE: "The Secret of *Wide Sargasso Sea,*" in *Critique: Studies in Contemporary Fiction,* Vol. XXXI, No. 3, Spring, 1990, pp. 185-97.

[*In the following essay, Curtis examines the use of paradoxical imagery and metaphor to portray Antoinette's death and transformation in* Wide Sargasso Sea.]

In **"Making Bricks Without Straw,"** Jean Rhys remembers a typical question-and-answer game she played with many journalists who interviewed her. Before long, the game gently pushed her into her "predestined role, the role of victim." This means, says Rhys, that "I have never had any good times, never laughed, never got my own back, never dared, never worn pretty clothes, never been happy, never known wild hopes or wilder despairs. . . . Wailing, I have gone from tyrant to tyrant; each letdown worse than the last. All this, of course, leads straight to Women's Lib." As the game went on, Rhys shocked the interviewer when she said that she "didn't like the suffragettes much" and told how one threw herself in front of a horse. Rhys could only feel sorry for the horse. No doubt the woman was wonderful—she wanted to be a martyr, but the horse did not: "He had to be shot." Inevitably, some will interpret Rhys's sympathy for the horse in terms of the now-worn-out statement that Rhys sympathized with the underdog because she herself was a victim.

Critics persist in not so gently pushing Rhys and her heroines into the predestined role of victim. In 1983, Selma James argued from a feminist perspective that Rhys's novels are "about how women are aliens; how we don't stand a chance because the cards are stacked against us." The heroines have in common "hopelessness," "defeat," and "isolation"; each of the heroines is a personification of the "female condition," that is, alas, "the perfect victim, unable or unwilling to defend herself." In an excellent 1982 study of Rhys's work, Jane Aschom made a similar statement: "Rhys's novels describe a female consciousness passive and impotent in a world where men have all the power." In the same year, Linda Bamber included Rhys with her fictional heroines when she described Rhys as a "woman more comfortable with failure than with success" and the novels as autobiographical, having one subject: "the victimization and self-victimization of a woman drifting along the edges of artsy-bourgeois society." But she is a certain kind of victim; she is a "natural victim, not a victim of sexual politics or class oppression." Bamber, like Angela Williams, makes little distinction between the author and her fictional heroines when she claims that "Rhys's helplessness is often a kind of 'weapon' in her fiction just as it was in her life." Where does this helplessness originate? Williams provides an answer: "perhaps the Jean Rhys heroine, the perennial victim, originates from Jean Rhys's own childhood background." In 1979, Elizabeth Abel adopted a "psychological framework," derived from R. D. Laing's approach to schizophrenia, "to explain the perversely self-destructive reactions of Rhys's heroines." The diagnosis is that Rhys's heroines are not really in-sane but fit into the "category sometimes referred to as ambulatory schizophrenia and sometimes as the schizoid (as opposed to the schizophrenic) state." The picture we now have of Rhys and her heroines is that of a passive, impotent, self-victimized schizoid who, comfortable with failure, wields her helplessness like a weapon—all as natural as being female.

The tendency to see Jean Rhys and her heroines as natural perennial victims is found in many of the critical essays on ***Wide Sargasso Sea,*** particularly in the interpretations of Antoinette's dream of her own death. Anthony Luengo, in his study of the similarities between ***Wide Sargasso Sea*** and the Gothic mode of fiction, describes Antoinette as at "once victim and *femme fatale*" and argues that Rhys "creates around Antoinette, as she does around Rochester, a sense of damnation that grows naturally out of the narrative action." Luengo supports this argument by recalling how the servants (Godfrey and Myra) told Antoinette "that she and her kind are destined to hell." Gradually, Antoinette believes this, "dreaming of damnation at the convent and even embracing it in fits of ecstatic self-condemnation." Luengo uses the following quotation from ***Wide Sargasso Sea*** to illustrate his argument: "All the same, I did not pray so often after that and soon, hardly at all. I felt bolder, happier, more free. But not so safe." At no time at the convent does Antoinette dream of or ecstatically embrace damnation. She does, however, pray for death so that she may attain the blessed attributes or transcendent beauty, but she is told that it is a sin—the sin of despair—to pray for death. In time, she learns to "gabble without thinking as the others did," but as any sensitive woman would be dissatisfied with gabbling, she stops praying such gabble. While she is "bolder, happier, more free," she never stops longing for the blessed attributes. Surely this is not evidence that Antoinette dreams of damnation and even embraces it in "fits of ecstatic self-condemnation."

While biographical, psychiatric, and feminist approaches are valuable and enlightening, none of these approaches totally reveals the secret of ***Wide Sargasso Sea,*** which depends upon the language of poetry and paradox. What is the secret of ***Wide Sargasso Sea,*** of Antoinette's dream of her own death, and of too, too beautiful Granbois? What is it about Antoinette that disturbs Rochester, and why, as Rochester asks, is there always this talk about death? What is the secret, and how does Rhys reveal it?

"Only the magic and the dream are true—all the rest's a lie. Let it go. Here is the secret. Here." The secret of ***Wide Sargasso Sea*** lies in the paradox that "Desire, Hatred, Life, Death came very close in the darkness. . . . Not close. The same." Mad moonstruck Antoinette, the "orchid" heroine of Rhys's novel, discovers, like the narrator of Wilson Harris's *Palace of the Peacock,* that "every boundary line is a myth" and that she cannot escape the "ancestral and twin fantasy of death-in-life and life-in-death." In ***Smile Please,*** Rhys makes a similar discovery, and she is accused of madness. But if she has everything within her—life and death, good and evil—then so must strength be within her if only she knew how to get to it. Perhaps every Rhys heroine lives on the edge of the "abyss of sincerity," trying to get to this strength, this secret that life and death come so close in the darkness—"Not close. The same."

Each Rhys heroine struggles to heave herself out of the wide Sargasso sea found in every Rhys novel. Clara Thomas cites the *OED* when she points out that "there is in each ocean a Sargasso into which all drift matter finds its way." Sasha Jansen describes a similar dead center, one of hate and indifference—the wide Sargasso of ***Good Morning, Midnight:*** "Too sad, too sad. . . . It doesn't matter, there I am, like one of those straws which floats round the edge of a whirlpool and is gradually sucked into the centre, the dead centre, where everything is stagnant, everything is calm." It is not until ***Wide Sargasso Sea*** that the Rhys heroine overcomes the Sargasso and discovers her strength in a fallen world of fractured consciousness and failed relationships by overcoming what Harris's narrator describes as the "need in the world to provide a material nexus to bind the spirit of the universe" (*Palace*). ***Wide Sargasso Sea*** is the tale of intuitive Antoinette, the lunatic who always knows, yet never knows, the time, the lunatic who envisions a metaphysical wedding of magic and reality, of time and eternity.

In the beginning, there is a garden as "large and beautiful as that garden in the Bible," a sacred space where Antoinette hugs to herself the secret hidden in Coulibri. "There is the tree of life in the garden and the wall green with moss. The barrier of the cliffs and the high mountains. And the barrier of the sea. I am safe. I am safe from strangers." Coulibri itself is a "sacred place. It was sacred to the sun." The obvious allusions to the garden of Genesis are associated with the equally obvious fall when the garden has gone wild, gone to "bush" and the "smell of dead flowers mixed with the fresh living smell." For a time, Rhys lingers in a lost world of wholeness and holiness, but the focus of ***Wide Sargasso Sea*** is on the tragic loss of a place sacred to the sun and the need to "re-enter 'lost' origins, 'lost' heavens, 'lost' divinity." Rhys, like Harris, hungers for "renewed visions of creation" in which the boundary line between life and death—the "smell of dead flowers" and the "fresh living smell"—is no more. In *Palace of the Peacock,* such a vision is "radical and disruptive of all material conviction." No gulf exists between consciousness and the world, materiality and divinity. They are the same.

This radical disruptive vision is symbolized by the conflagration in the final dream of ***Wide Sargasso Sea*** when Antoinette sees the sky and the tree of life in flames. "It was red and all my life was in it." Lunatic Antoinette in phoenix flame symbolizes a rediscovery of "lost origins." The rediscovery happens only after Antoinette remembers what it is she must do; it is an act of remembering, a bringing to mind once again that which is lost. At the end of the novel, in the image of Antoinette standing at the edge of the battlements that Tia calls "you afraid?" Rhys describes a moment similar to that which Auden describes in *The Sea and the Mirror:*

> Yet, at this very moment when we do at last see ourselves as we are, neither cosy nor playful, but swaying out on the ultimate wind-whipped cornice that overhangs the unabiding void—we have never stood anywhere else—when our reasons are silenced by the heavy huge derision—there is nothing to say. There never has been.

Although Auden is writing from a Christian perspective, this moment has a secular parallel in ***Wide Sargasso Sea.*** Antoinette sways out on the "ultimate wind-whipped" battlements of the "unabiding void" that disrupts the material conviction of Thornfield Hall. At this moment, overhanging the "abyss of sincerity," she reaches the strength that is born of the secret that death and life are the same. To reach this strength is perhaps to experience "the inseparable moment within ourselves of all fulfillment and understanding" (*Palace*).

Rhys prefigures this moment when Coco the parrot falls from the glacis railing, all on fire. It is bad luck to watch a parrot die, perhaps because in West Indian folklore, the parrot is a symbol of the soul. Fire destroys Coco in the burning of Coulibri and also destroys, but re-creates, the soul as Antoinette discovers what it is she must do. She has broken away from the imitation of life in Thornfield Hall and has chosen to shield the flame, the strength, that transforms her soul in phoenix flame. In all Rhys's novels, fire is an image of beauty and strength. The light from the sun is gold in the Dominica of ***Voyage In The Dark,*** and "when you shut your eyes you see fire color." Marya, in ***Quartet,*** envisions dreams that are "many-colored and dark shot with flame"; the flame in Marya kicks like an "unborn child." In ***Good Morning, Midnight,*** Sasha wants more of the miracle of "fire and wings." Julia Griffiths in ***After Leaving Mr. Mackenzie,*** like Rhys in ***Smile Please,*** thinks "if I could get to the end of what I was feeling it would be the truth about myself and about the world and about everything that one puzzles and pains about all the time." Strength must be in her if only she can get to it. For a moment, she does: ". . . in a miraculous manner, some essence of her was shooting upwards like a flame. She was great." She is not only *like* a flame; she *is* a flame, defiantly "shooting upwards not to plead but to threaten." But the moment vanishes: the "flame sank down again, useless, having reached nothing." It is moonstruck Antoinette who finally experiences the miracle of "fire and wings." Some essence of her miraculously shoots upward. For a moment, the candle flickers, but Antoinette shields the flame with her hand, and it burns brightly to light her along the dark passage. Antoinette, like Robin in that old song Rochester thought he had forgotten, paradoxically shines bright in death: "Hail to the queen of the silent night, / Shine bright, shine bright Robin as you die."

Antoinette's dream of her own death has been variously interpreted as a triumph, a nihilistic embrace of nothingness, or an agnostic cry for redemption. To interpret Antoinette's death negatively, however, is to ignore the fact that ***Wide Sargasso Sea*** depends upon paradox. For example, Aschom argues that because Antoinette dies in the conflagration, she necessarily wants "not merely retaliation but personal annihilation. So much of herself has she lost already that to lose all is best." This interpretation is justified only if we accept a literal reading of the novel, but death and life come so close in ***Wide Sargasso Sea*** that every boundary line is a myth. Rochester knows that Antoinette has the secret hidden in wild, untouched Granbois: Granbois, where "everything is too much. . . . The flowers too red, the mountains too high, the hills too near." It has a "disturbing, secret loveliness. And it kept its secret." But Antoinette knows: "Always this talk of death. (Is she trying to tell me that is the secret of this place? That there is no other way. She knows. She knows)." Later, Rochester realizes that everything he has "imagined to be true was false. False." Is this the secret? "Always this talk of death." Always the coexistence of death and life, shadow and light, death and beatitude. When Antoinette was a child, Christophine sang to her "about the cedar tree flowers which only last for a day," but, at the same time, Antoinette was "sure everything was alive, not only the river or the rain, but chairs, looking-glasses, cups, saucers, everything." ***Wide Sargasso Sea*** so depends upon the co-inherence of life and death and the crossing of familiar barriers between dream and reality that Antoinette's death can be understood in terms of the web of paradox in the novel.

Antoinette comes to her own understanding of the paradox inherent in Christianity during her stay at the convent, a "place of sunshine and death" where "everything was brightness, or dark." The co-inherence of opposites suggests the paradox that Rhys explores: "That was how it was, light and dark, sun and shadow, Heaven and Hell, for one of the nuns knew all about Hell and who does not? But another one knew about Heaven and the attributes of the blessed, of which the least is transcendent beauty." For a long time, Antoinette prays to die so that she can experience the ecstasy of the blessed. Underlying her prayer is the belief that death is necessary for rebirth. But she is told that it is another sin—"presumption or despair"—to pray for death and transcendent beauty. Sin or not, she prays for the blessed attributes to transform the motif of death that permeates convent life: after the meal, there is always the prayer "now and at the hour of our death, and at midday and at six in the evening, now and at the hour of our death. Let perpetual light shine on them." Her mother "hated a strong light and loved the cool and the shade"; thus, Antoinette refuses to say "Let perpetual light shine on them." Outside, the "shifting shadows [are] more beautiful than any perpetual light could be." The co-inherence of death and beatitude, of "great splashes of sunlight" and the "shadows of trees" fires Antoinette's soul. The blessed attributes cannot be symbolized by perpetual light or disembodied essence but by "something tangible," like the brilliant silk roses Antoinette colors green, blue, and purple or the fire-red dress with which she later identifies. Antoinette discovers happiness in "the blazing colours of flowers" in a "place of sunshine and death" and finds her identity in "the colour of fire and sunset. The colour of flamboyant flowers." She wonders and soon forgets about happiness but thinks "about changing now and the hour of our death for it is all we have."

To change now and the hour of our death is to discover the blessed attributes, not in the glaring perpetual light of the absolute but in "something you can touch and hold." Antoinette longs to discover in earthly existence, "In all poor foolish things that live a day, / Eternal beauty wandering on her way." Where among the pale flowers too fragile to resist the wind is the rose that has never faded? At the convent, Mother St. Justin tells the story of a saint who brings a rose to her earthly lover from the Garden of the Eternal Spouse: "'Here Theophilus is a rose from the garden of my Spouse, in whom you did not believe.' The rose he found by his side when he awoke has never faded. It still exists. (Oh, but where, where?)." While the flowers fade and fall in a day, Antoinette looks for the never-fading rose from the sensuous sacred garden of spousal love. Mother St. Justin's story combines immortality and earthly existence in the symbol of the rose that never fades. It *exists*. It combines "immateriality and mysterious substantiality" (*Palace*). Perhaps like Antoinette, who knows yet never knows the time, the rose also knows but never knows time. No dichotomy exists between immortality and mortality, magic and reality, sunlight and shadow. To find the rose from the Garden of the Eternal Spouse is, paradoxically, to know eternity in time and to transform now and the hour of our death.

Antoinette longs for the metaphysical wedding of opposites, but in her marriage to Rochester she does not find the eternal rose from the sacred garden. But there are roses. At the honeymoon house when Hilda brings coffee, there are "always two roses on the tray." One day, when Rochester touches the full-blown pink rose and its petals drop at his touch, he wonders, "Is that poem true? Have all beautiful things sad destinies?" It can be almost any poem, perhaps one such as this:

> But pleasures are like poppies spread,
> You seize the flower, its bloom is shed;
> Or like the snow falls in the river,
> A moment white—then melts for ever.

For Rochester, the sentiment of that poem is true. He finds the secret hidden in Granbois and is determined to keep it, to hold it fast, as he would hold Antoinette. But as he seizes the secret of the rose, "its bloom is shed." And always, Antoinette is the solitary queen of the silent night whose "long, sad, dark, alien eyes" never reveal their secret. She is like the solitary mountain bird: "Oh, a heartstopper is the solitaire's one note—high, sweet, lonely, magic." "She was silence itself," as silent as this "beautiful place—wild, untouched, above all untouched, with an alien, disturbing, secret loveliness. And it kept its secret."

Derek Walcott aptly describes that wild silence in his poem "Jean Rhys":

> In that fierce hush
> between Dominican mountains
> the child expects a sound
> from a butterfly clipping itself to a bush
> like a gold earring to a black maid's ear.

The "fierce hush" disturbs Rochester. Neither the landscape nor Antoinette can (or will) break the silence; "No one would tell [him] the truth." Rochester's image of Antoinette—the orchid—symbolizes the paradox that life and death not only come close in the darkness but are the same. Paradoxically, the orchid, one of the most beautiful flowers, lives from dead and decaying matter. As Rochester "passed an orchid with long sprays of golden-brown flowers," he remembers telling Antoinette that the orchids are like her. Because no one will tell him the secret the orchid symbolizes, however, he breaks one of the long sprays and tramples it in the mud: "Its bloom is shed." Always there is talk of death; always there is the orchid's silence, as hushed as the child's sigh in Walcott's "Jean Rhys":

> And the sigh of that child
> is white as an orchid
> on a crusted log
> in the bush of Dominica.

Rochester comes to hate beautiful Granbois, its magic and indifference, and the secret he will never know. Above all, he hates Antoinette because "she belonged to the magic and the loveliness." She is intuitive, even prophetic, but certainly not matter-of-fact; she is undecided and uncertain about facts. Moonstruck Antoinette overcomes the usual limitations of space and time and, in the final conflagration, destroys the "cardboard" security of Thornfield Hall. Like Julia Griffiths, she strains to "see what is behind the cardboard." During her mother's funeral, Julia thinks that "she was so close to seeing the thing that was behind all this talking and posturing, and that the talking and the posturing were there to prevent her from seeing it." The false security of Thornfield Hall, like the posturing of ritual, hides the darkness and death within. It is women such as Grace Poole, Mrs. Eff, and Leah who refuse to confront their own darkness, who cling to a "shelter from the world outside which, say what you like, can be a black and cruel world to a woman." For some of Rhys's characters, "the secret of life was never to go too far or too deep," and for others, the "shadow can be more important than the substance." In ***Quartet,*** the Heidlers believe that life should have a "surface of grace, lightness, and gaiety"; but Antoinette knows that we are "neither cosy nor playful" but swaying out on the "cornice that overhangs the unabiding void." In confronting that void, that death, she learns what it is she must do: the secret is all about changing now and the hour of our death, for that is all we have.

Antoinette is like the swimmer in Margaret Avison's "The Swimmer's Moment," who recognizes the whirlpool and "dare[s] the knowledge." "For everyone / The swimmer's moment at the whirlpool comes," but many, like Grace Poole, refuse to contest the "deadly rapids" and choose, rather, to remain on the "rim of suction." Those "bland-blank faces," which refuse to go beyond all the talking and posturing, also shrink from the struggle for what Harris calls "that harmonious rounded miracle of spirit which the world of appearances has never truly known" (*Palace*). Avison writes about a similar experience, using different images. Those who refuse the whirlpool are not only saved from contesting the rapids but never emerge in "the mysterious, and more ample, further waters." The swimmer who descends into the "black pit" may be one of the few who experiences the rounded miracle of spirit—those who come to "the silver reaches of the estuary." Rhys and Avison use the familiar paradox of life in death so that the images in ***Wide Sargasso Sea*** and "The Swimmer's Moment" suggest resurrection and triumph in death rather than a nihilistic embrace of nothingness. But if only a few come to the "silver reaches of the estuary," what happens to those who dare the knowledge, yet do not emerge in the mysterious further waters? They are the ones who are "whirled into the ominous centre which seals up / For them an eternal boon of privacy": they are sealed in their own silence, not able to speak their knowledge. We turn away from them "with a despair, not from their deaths, but for / Ourselves, who cannot penetrate their secret." Rochester turns away from Antoinette, and very soon, he says, she will join all those who dare the knowledge, "who know the secret and will not tell it. Or cannot. Or try and fail because they do not know enough."

Antoinette's secret is as sealed as the pirates' knowledge of treasure; those who find the jewels never tell "because you see they'd only get one-third then: that's the law of treasure." The pirates want it all, so it is better not to tell, not to speak of the treasure. For a moment, before they leave England, Rochester wistfully imagines that they can be like the swaggering pirates who make the most and worst of what they have, that perhaps one day they will watch the sunset and see the "Emerald drop" of the sky, but Antoinette is as silent as "an orchid / on a crusted log."

Antoinette's knowledge is born of dream and madness. The line Rochester draws, Antoinette crosses out; the barriers he builds, she destroys. Her secret and her madness frustrate Rochester's sane need to provide a material nexus to bind her spirit, a need that is illustrated by his childish scribble of a woman standing in a third-floor room of a large house. Presumably this is Antoinette imprisoned in Thornfield Hall. But the lines of such a house cannot contain the secret and the dream. Rhys uses a sequence of dreams not only to foretell and to parallel Antoinette's experience but to reveal how Antoinette's knowledge transcends ordinary perception.

In the first fragment of her dream, Antoinette is walking in a forest where someone who hates her follows out of sight. In the second fragment, it is Antoinette who follows the man, whose face is "black with hatred." She is sick with fear, but "if anyone were to try and save [her, she] would refuse. This must happen." Soon Antoinette and the man are no longer in the forest "but in an enclosed garden surrounded by a stone wall and the trees are different trees." She touches a tree and tries to hold on, but it sways as though it were trying to cast her off. These images recall Anna Morgan's dream in ***Voyage In The Dark,*** in which Anna is on a ship "sailing very close to an island, which was home except that the trees were all wrong. These were English trees." Antoinette's dream foretells her voyage to England. The voyage into darkness is inevitable; it must happen so that finally Antoinette is the only one, among Grace Poole and the others, who does not accept the thick walls of Thornfield Hall. She "lives in her own darkness," but "I'll say one thing for her, she hasn't lost her spirit. She's still fierce."

But Antoinette's prophetic knowledge is not only articulated in dreams. In Part Two, she consciously foretells the future in an intuitive remembrance: "For I know that house where I will be cold and not belonging, the bed I shall lie in has red curtains and I have slept there many times before, long ago. How long ago? In that bed I will dream the end of my dream." For Antoinette, time is not linear, but fluid. Like the narrator of *Palace of the Peacock,* we may ask

> Was it possible that one's memory and apprehension of a tragic event would strike one's spirit before the actual happening had been digested? Could a memory spring from nowhere into one's belly and experience? I knew that if I was dreaming I could pinch myself and wake. But an undigested morsel of recollection erased all present waking sensation and evoked a future time, petrifying and painful, confused and unjust.

Antoinette's "undigested morsel of recollection" evokes the future when she will dream the end of her dream and finally answer, "What is it that [she] must do?"

In Part Three, the red dress, "the colour of fire and sunset," suggests "the colour of flamboyant flowers. 'If you are buried under a flamboyant tree,' I said, 'your soul is lifted up when it flowers. Everyone wants that.'" The paradox of the buried, then flowering soul has all the conventional connotations of phoenix, rebirth, and resurrection, but it also recalls the importance Rochester assigns the tree image. The hurricane months are not far off when he imagines the trees striking their "roots deeper, making ready to fight the wind." Some, like the royal palms, take the hard way; they defy the wind, but the bamboos bend to the earth and cry for mercy: "the contemptuous wind passes, not caring for these abject things." Rochester himself will not touch Antoinette, "excepting as the hurricane will touch that tree—and break it." Rhys carries the tree image into Antoinette's final dream, where the tree of life is in flames: this is Antoinette, a defiant flame shooting upward, not an abject creature crying mercy against a contemptuous wind. It is an image that combines the resurrection theme associated with the flamboyant tree, the paradox inherent in the symbol of fire, and Antoinette's earlier prayer for death and the blessed attributes.

Antoinette's longing for the lifting up of the soul is analogous to that "immortal passion" in Yeats's "The Travail of Passion":

> When the flaming lute-thronged angelic door is
> wide;
> When an immortal passion breathes in mortal clay;
> Our hearts endure the scourge, the plaited thorns,
> the way.

The theme of immortal passion is a perennial one, one to which Leonardo da Vinci alluded when he compared man with moths flying into the candle flame; for man's longing to return to his origins contains the seeds of his destruction, and yet it is the essence of life. Rhys symbolizes this paradox in the "procession of moths and beetles fly[ing] into the candle flame": they are attracted to the light but to their deaths as well. Rochester is drawn to the flame, longing for the secret, but he is rather like the bird-like moth that "blundered into one of the candles, put it out and fell to the floor," whereas Antoinette, at the end of the novel, shields the flame, and it burns brightly.

William MacNamara tells a story that provides an interesting parallel to Rhys's story of Antoinette:

> I think of the young novice in the desert who went to the elder, the holy man of God, and said: "father, according as I am able, I keep my little Rule, and my little fast, my prayer, meditation, and contemplative silence; and according as I am able, I strive to cleanse my heart of thoughts. Now, what more should I do?" The elder rose up in reply and stretched out his hands to heaven, and his fingers became like ten lamps of fire. He said: "Why not be totally changed into fire?"

Antoinette ventures a jail break, a transformation at the hour of her death when she refuses to live as Rochester's marionette: "Marionette, Antoinette, Marionetta, Antoinetta." This is a redeeming change from the Marya of ***Quartet,*** who to the very end "felt like a marionette, as though something outside her were jerking strings." Marya cannot get to her strength, but Antoinette reaches the flame and is totally changed into fire. Perhaps Antoinette would say, like Margaret Avison, "nobody stuffs the world in at your eyes. / The optic heart must venture: a jail-break / And recreation."

The pattern of images in ***Wide Sargasso Sea*** suggests that Antoinette's death is a re-creation. Obviously and literally, death is death, and there is the end; but, because Rhys focuses upon the paradox of transforming the hour of death, Antoinette's death should probably be read in terms of transformation and paradox. If everything is within her all along, Antoinette perhaps discovers, like the characters in *Palace of the Peacock,* that "each of us now held at last in his arms what he had been forever seeking and what he had eternally possessed." But Antoinette's death is neither absolute triumph nor absolute failure. Rather, the image of death in her final dream mixes the "twin fantasy of death-in-life and life-in-death," the smell of dead flowers and the fresh living smell, the buried but flowering soul, the prayer for death and the blessed attributes, and the immortal passion that draws the moth to the candle flame. Here is the secret. When Antoinette awakens from her dream, her strength guides her along the dark passageway, and she knows in the moment of epiphany that no one on "earth can truly understand the fortune of love and the art of victory over death without mixing blind joy and sadness and the sense of being lost with the nearness of being found" (*Palace*).

FURTHER READING

Criticism

Berry, Betsy. "'Between Dog and Wolf': Jean Rhys's Version of Naturalism in *After Leaving Mr. Mackenzie.*" *Studies in the Novel* 27, No. 4 (Winter 1995): 544-62.

Offers critical analysis of *After Leaving Mr. Mackenzie,* drawing attention to Rhys's stylistic connection to French naturalism.

Borinsky, Alicia. "Jean Rhys: Poses of a Woman as Guest." *Poetics Today* 6, Nos. 1-2 (1985): 229-43.

Examines the characterization of female protagonists in Rhys's fiction.

Erwin, Lee. "'Like in a Looking-Glass': History and Narrative in *Wide Sargasso Sea.*" *Novel: A Forum on Fiction* 22, No. 2 (Winter 1989): 143-58.

Discusses the historical underpinnings of *Wide Sargasso Sea,* particularly Rhys's portrayal of racism, nationalism, and divided self-identity in the West Indies after the Emancipation Act of 1833.

Howells, Coral Ann. *Jean Rhys.* New York: St. Martin's Press, 1991.

Book-length critical study of Rhys's novels and short stories, including discussion of her placement as a feminist, colonial, and modernist author.

Kendrick, Robert. "Edward Rochester and the Margins of Masculinity in *Jane Eyre* and *Wide Sargasso Sea.*" *Papers on Language and Literature* 30, No. 3 (Summer 1994): 235-56.

Considers Edward Rochester's inadequacies and redefinition of patriarchal male identity through his interactions with Jane Eyre and Antoinette Cosway in the complimentary texts of Brontë and Rhys.

Kloepfer, Deborah Kelly. "*Voyage in the Dark:* Jean Rhys's Masquerade for the Mother." *Contemporary Literature* 26, No. 4 (Winter 1985): 443-59.

Examines the significance of the mother-child relationship, the absence of mothers in Rhys's fiction, linguistic alienation among women in *Voyage in the Dark,* and the novel's revision.

Neck-Yoder, Hilda van. "Colonial Desires, Silence, and Metonymy: 'All Things Considered' in *Wide Sargasso Sea.*" *Texas Studies in Literature and Language* 40, No. 2 (Summer 1998): 184-208.

Discusses aspects of narrative authority and the repression of colonial impulses in *Wide Sargasso Sea.*

Nixon, Nicola. "*Wide Sargasso Sea* and Jean Rhys's Interrogation of the 'nature wholly alien' in *Jane Eyre.*" *Essays in Literature* XXI, No. 2 (Fall 1994): 267-84.

Provides analysis of Bertha's madness in *Jane Eyre* and Rhys's corresponding portrayal of female alienation and patriarchal imperialism in *Wide Sargasso Sea.*

Roe, Sue. "'The Shadow of Light': The Symbolic Underworld of Jean Rhys." In *Women Reading Women's Writing,* edited by Sue Roe, pp. 229-62. New York: St. Martin's Press, 1987.

Examines Rhys's narrative style, characterization of victimized women, paradoxical themes of suffering and resignation, and the significance of imagery in her fiction.

Streip, Katharine. "'Just a Cérébrale': Jean Rhys, Women's Humor, and Ressentiment." *Representations,* 45 (Winter 1994): 117-44.

Refutes the perception of women as "humorless" through analysis of Rhys's ironic wit and double-edged comedy in *Good Morning, Midnight.*

Wilson, Lucy. "'Women Must Have Spunks': Jean Rhys's West Indian Outcasts." *Modern Fiction Studies* 32, No. 3 (Autumn 1986): 439-48.

Examines Rhys's social critique of racism and domination through analysis of black West Indian characters in her fiction, including Christophine Dubois in *Wide Sargasso Sea* and Selina Davis in "Let Them Call It Jazz."

Additional coverage of Rhys's life and career is contained in the following sources published by Gale: *Concise Dictionary of British Literary Biography,* 1945-1960; *Contemporary Authors,* Vols. 25-28R, 85-88; *Contemporary Authors New Revision Series,* Vols. 35, 62; *Dictionary of Literary Biography,* Vols. 36, 117, 162; *DISCovering Authors Module: Novelists; Major Twentieth-Century Writers,* Vol. 1; and *Short Story Criticism,* Vol. 21.

John Steinbeck
1902-1968

American novelist, short story writer, playwright, non-fiction writer, journalist, and screenplay writer.

The following entry presents an overview of Steinbeck's career. For further information about his life and works, see *CLC,* Volumes 1, 5, 9, 13, 21, 34, 45, and 75.

INTRODUCTION

A Nobel Prize laureate and widely popular novelist, John Steinbeck is among the most enduring American authors of the twentieth century. Best known for *Of Men and Mice* (1937), *East of Eden* (1952), and his Pulitzer prize-winning masterpiece *The Grapes of Wrath* (1939), Steinbeck is distinguished for his lucid prose, engaging naturalistic descriptions, forceful symbolism, and examination of the myth of America as Edenic paradise. Sympathetic to the plight of the impoverished and downtrodden, his Depression-era fiction offers poignant depiction of socioeconomic conditions and human realities in the American West during the 1930s. Though controversial for the overt socialist views evinced in much of his work, he continues to receive critical acclaim for his best-selling novels, several of which were adapted into successful motion pictures and plays. The distinctly American perspective and journalistic realism of Steinbeck's social protest novels struck an emotional chord with the reading public and exerted an important influence on contemporary literature.

Biographical Information

Born in California's Salinas Valley, which serves as the backdrop for much of his work, Steinbeck was one of four children of Olive Hamilton Steinbeck, a teacher, and John Ernst Steinbeck II, the treasurer of Monterey County. Steinbeck intermittently attended Stanford University for five years but never received a degree. During and after college he worked variously as a reporter, bricklayer, surveyor, store clerk, ranch hand, and laborer. These jobs, particularly the time spent working for the Spreckels Sugar Company during a period of worker unrest, served as the crucible in which Steinbeck formed his pro-labor views. In 1930 Steinbeck met Edward F. Ricketts, a marine biologist whose theories influenced Steinbeck's developing "biological" world view of mankind. After seven rejections, Steinbeck published his first book, *Cup of Gold* (1929), a historical novel based on the life of Henry Morgan, a seventeenth-century buccaneer. He followed with *The Pastures of Heaven* (1932) and *To a God Unknown* (1933). From 1933 to 1936, Steinbeck and his first wife, Carol Henning, lived in Pacific Grove, California. During this time, Steinbeck often visited Ricketts at his laboratory on Cannery Row in Monterey and later fictionalized the experience in *Cannery Row* (1945). Steinbeck became known to the American public in 1935 with the publication of *Tortilla Flat* (1935), which was a best-seller. His meeting with two union organizers in 1934 led to *In Dubious Battle* (1936), a novel about labor unrest in a California orchard. Soon afterward Steinbeck wrote a series of articles for the *San Francisco News* about the mass exodus of thousands of migrants from the Dust Bowl to California. This experience led to *The Grapes of Wrath*, for which he was awarded the Pulitzer Prize the next year. In 1943, he married his second wife, Gwyndolyn Conger, with whom he had two children. During the Second World War, Steinbeck went overseas as a war correspondent for the *New York Herald-Tribune* and wrote propaganda pieces for the United States government, including the novel *The Moon is Down* (1942), which he adapted as a play, and *Bombs Away* (1942), a non-fiction work about the U.S. Air Force. In 1948 Steinbeck suffered a double loss—his friend

Ricketts was killed and his second wife left him. The emotional strain affected his work and he published nothing until two years later, when he married Elaine Scott and produced *Burning Bright* (1950), a study of a troubled marriage, followed by *East of Eden*. Steinbeck received the Nobel Prize for Literature in 1962. He died of a heart attack in New York City in 1968.

Major Works

Noted for his descriptions of the search for the American dream and sympathy for the plight of the working class, Steinbeck's works typically describe ordinary men and women who come close to achieving greatness only when faced with a trial that requires them to join with others for the greater good. Steinbeck's brand of literature, mixed with social commentary, was influenced by his teleological view of people as parts of a larger whole who must work in concert to improve the lot of humanity. In *Tortilla Flat,* the first of many novels set in the Salinas Valley, a group of paisanos form an Arthurian round table and experience several seriocomic adventures. They attempt to escape a materialistic society but in the end their pursuits are not enough to hold the brotherhood together and it dissolves. *"The Red Pony,"* (1937) a group of four stories in the short-story collection *The Long Valley* (1938), is a coming-of-age story about Jody, a boy who learns about birth, life, and death through his experiences with a colt given to him by his father which sickens and dies; his contact with an old man who lives on his father's ranch and leaves in order to die in the mountains; the death of a mare who dies while giving birth to a colt; and his interaction with his aging grandfather. Another initiation story, "Flight," involves a boy who commits murder in a fit of rage and achieves manhood in an aborted attempt to escape the law in the mountains. *Of Mice and Men,* which Steinbeck later made into a highly successful play, involves George and Lennie, two ranch hands who hope to escape the ranch for a place of their own where they can live an idyllic existence. George watches out for the simple-minded Lennie, a grown-up child who doesn't understand his own strength and cuddles mice and puppies to death. Their dreams of escape are destroyed when Lennie accidentally kills the ranch owner's wife and George must shoot him to prevent an angry mob from brutally murdering him. *The Grapes of Wrath,* Steinbeck's most famous work, chronicles the exodus of the Joad family, led by the matriarch Ma Joad, from the Dust Bowl to the supposed Eden of California. They are joined by Jim Casy, a Christ archetype who sparks their evolution from a self-contained, self-involved family unit to a part of the migrant community which must work together for the greater good. Steinbeck alternates the Joads's story with intercalary chapters illustrating the conditions faced by the migrant group during their forced flight. During the course of their travels, the family's grandmother and grandfather die and Rose of Sharon, the Joads's married and pregnant daughter, is deserted by her husband. The Joads make their way to California only to become exploited workers in a migrant camp. Casy tries to organize the workers and is murdered by thugs who work for the farm owners. Finally, the migrants face a disastrous flood, during which Rose of Sharon's baby is stillborn. In the ultimate affirmation of the Joads's recognition of their membership in the human family, Rose of Sharon gives her breast milk to a starving migrant man in order to save his life. Steinbeck intended *East of Eden,* an epic retelling of the Cain and Abel story, to be his masterpiece. It chronicles the stories of the Trask family and his real-life mother's family, the Hamiltons. Adam Trask marries Cathy Ames, a cold, malevolent woman who deserts Adam and her twin sons, Cal and Aron, who grapple for their father's favor and attention. When Aron, the innocent son, discovers his mother's true nature it destroys him, while Cal realizes he is free to choose between good and evil. Steinbeck's last novel, *The Winter of Our Discontent* (1961), indicts American society for its focus on materialism and individual's disregard for the family of man. Shortly afterwards he published *Travels With Charley* (1962), an account of his cross-country peregrinations with his poodle, Charley.

Critical Reception

Critical assessment of Steinbeck's work varied widely throughout his career and was often influenced by its political content. Some critics expressed surprise when the Nobel Prize Committee honored Steinbeck in 1962, many years after his literary star had fallen. While many reviewers praised Steinbeck's optimistic view of humanity and its quest for improvement and redemption, others claimed that his characters, especially women, were largely one-dimensional and symbolic. Steinbeck is renowned for the clarity of his natural descriptions, especially those of his native California, which pervade his most effective work. Much critical attention is directed at the prominent sociological concerns, allegorical motifs, themes of initiation, and Christian archetypes in his novels. His most successful fiction, particularly *Of Mice and Men* and *The Grapes of Wrath,* is praised by most for its universality, though faulted by others for excessive sentimentalism and melodrama. Reception of *The Grapes of Wrath* was distorted because the book caused a maelstrom of political controversy due to its castigation of agribusiness and the governmental system that contributed to the Dust Bowl predicament. The press and politicians attempted to discredit Steinbeck's book, accusing him of socialist sympathies. As a result *The Grapes of Wrath* became one of the most commonly banned books in America. Critics were disappointed with his post-*Grapes of Wrath* work, particularly after the publication of *East of Eden.* Most considered Steinbeck's attempts to experiment with the literary form in *East of Eden* to be a failure. They denounced the uneven structure, obvious symbolism, and flat characterization. Though Steinbeck's reputation was in decline when he died, he remains one of the most widely read and anthologized American writers of the twentieth century.

PRINCIPAL WORKS

Cup of Gold: A Life of Henry Morgan, Buccaneer, with Occasional References to History (novel) 1929
The Pastures of Heaven (novel) 1932
To a God Unknown (novel) 1933
Tortilla Flat (novel) 1935
In Dubious Battle (novel) 1936
Nothing So Monstrous (short stories) 1936
Saint Kay the Virgin (short stories) 1936
Of Mice and Men (novel) 1937
Of Mice and Men: A Play in Three Acts [with George S. Kaufman] (drama) 1937
The Red Pony (novella) 1937
The Long Valley (short stories) 1938
The Grapes of Wrath (novel) 1939
The Forgotten Village (novel) 1941
Sea of Cortez: A Leisurely Journal of Travel and Research (travel book) 1941
The Moon is Down (novel) 1942
The Moon is Down: Play in Two Parts (drama) 1942
How Edith McGillicuddy Met R.L.S. (short stories) 1943
Cannery Row (novel) 1945
The Pearl (novella) 1947
The Wayward Bus (novel) 1947
Burning Bright: A Play in Story Form (novel) 1950
East of Eden (novel) 1952
Viva Zapata! (screenplay) 1952
Sweet Thursday (novel) 1954
The Crapshooter (short stories) 1957
The Short Reign of Pippin IV: A Fabrication (novel) 1957
The Winter of Our Discontent (novel) 1961
Travels with Charley: In Search of America (nonfiction) 1962

CRITICISM

Carroll Britch and Cliff Lewis (essay date 1989)

SOURCE: "Growth of the Family in *The Grapes of Wrath*," in *Critical Essays on Steinbeck's The Grapes of Wrath*, edited by John Ditsky, G. K. Hall, 1989, pp. 97-108.

[*In the following essay, Britch and Lewis examine the solidarity and self-preservation of the Joad family in* The Grapes of Wrath. *According to Britch and Lewis, "if ever the mettle of the American spirit has been tested and found strong, it has been so with the Joads."*]

> Resistance to innovation indicates, in the eye of nature, senility and senility is doomed to be discarded. . . . That nation thrives best which is most flexible, and which has fewer prejudices to hamper adaption.
>
> —Brooks Adams

Although it addresses issues of great sociological change, ***The Grapes of Wrath*** is at its core about the family and the struggle of its members to assert their separate identities without breaking up as a family. In his treatment of the Joads, Steinbeck manages to delineate "kid-wild" Winfield through "growed-up" Tom to "lecherous" Grampa in ways that gain each an individualized life beyond their inherited roles in the family hierarchy as well as beyond the symbolic roles they serve as an "over-essence of people" to amplify the argument of the plot. The argument, as Steinbeck writes in his "Journal," is that the Joads and those like them must abandon their felt notions of individualism and move toward an "I to We" relationship with the other migrants if they are to survive the economic and spiritual challenge of their displacement. Hence, the central question of the narrative is whether or not the Joads can act on Casy's principle "to love all people" and still remain as Ma would have it "one thing . . . the fambly . . . whole and clear."

Contrary to some prevailing views, it is our contention that 1) the Joad family does not break up so much as grow up; 2) that its members are less altruistic than self-protective; and 3) that they articulate the argument of the plot precisely because they achieve in the novelistic sense a convincing human reality. In order for the central question to sustain its tension throughout the four odd months of the Joads' wanderings, it is crucial that they as individuals and as a family unit confront the challenge of the transformation from "I to We" in terms of the emotional logic and ethic that characterized their everyday life in Oklahoma. For if the Joads were to embrace Casy's principle just because it seems a nice idea, their being and his idea would pale for lack of credibility.

As Brooks Adams implies in his thoughts about "resistance to innovation," people are slow to change—if at all. And were it not for the intolerable conditions that the Joads encounter on the road, they as a group would likely fall prey to the "senility" that dooms Muley Graves, not to mention Grampa. In a letter to the literary critic Joseph Henry Jackson, Steinbeck argues the motive that leads those like the Joads to growth and change: "The human like any other life form will tolerate an unhealthy condition for some time, and then will either die or will overcome the condition either by mutation or by destroying the unhealthful condition.

Since there seems little tendency for the human race to become extinct, and since one cannot through biological mutation overcome the necessity for eating, I judge that the final method will be the one chosen." Most of the Joads survive because they do like to eat, but work to keep on eating because they have a dream. Like the turtle and the seeds it carries on its journey, the Joads take the souls of themselves with them west. Their will to move may have been born of necessity, but their movement is sustained by the down-to-earth hopes of better days that have often seen Americans through to prosperity. For Uncle John especially, the initial "unhealthful condition" is the self-pity that issues from a distorted sense of sin concerning his part in a calamitous childbirth. At times Rosasharn and Pa suffer in just about the same way for similar reasons. Nevertheless, the external unhealthiness of flood, famine, and economic injustice spurs them on to do eventually what, as Ma says of Tom, is "more'n" themselves.

Uprooted, the fundamental dream they share is that of stability and self-respect. On the farm the family enjoyed both. They slide from being land owners to being renters. True. But that slide still afforded them the dignity to serve as hosts. And on the road Ma intends that they do not backslide into the wretchedness that has destroyed the humanity of many in Hooverville. In show of her fundamental spirit she accepts Casy into the family because the Joads just do not refuse "food an' shelter or a lift on the road to anybody that ask[s]." Her dream of "a little white house" and Rosasharn's dream to "live in a town" to make it "nice for the baby" bespeak their ethic to re-establish a home, out from the protection of which they can in the pride of true deed care for themselves as well as for others in need.

All of the blood-Joads, excepting Noah, display a healthy sense of themselves. If Steinbeck had not created them so, they could hardly be used to work out the "I to We" theme either within the family or within the large social unit that the family comes to represent. As proud as it is of its pioneering background, the family is not *a* Joad but a unit—a *we*—made up of several singular "I's" who answer to the name if Joad. At Uncle John's the staging area and jump-off point of the journey, each family member in his or her own way answers also to the call of pulling together to make the trip happen. Apart from moments of negative self-involvement (which is only human), when it comes to serving the family unit each Joad, with the exception noted, displays a "we" attitude throughout. Even Ruthie and Winfield, who are just too young to consider much other than their own ego-demands, help to pick peaches and do domestic chores. Ma's sense of *we-ness* seems always to have extended beyond the immediate family. And, as evidenced by the famous milk-sharing scene of the final chapter, it is boundless. She exists as the essence of Casy's principle, and is "so great with love," hence fearlessness, that she makes even him feel "afraid an' mean." Her capacity to care marks the measure of her self-respect. As the action progresses, her caring does not change in kind but rather grows in breadth and intensity. But even at that, her family comes first. Steinbeck reveals it as a training ground for an expanded social consciousness. However, with Ma at the head the family harbors no armchair philosophers or bleeding-hearts.

"Citadel" of the family, Ma defines its membership in terms of those who can defend it against disorganization, dishonor, sickness, broken-down transportation, meanness, lack of food, and want of shelter. Well before Tom arrives at Uncle John's to announce his parole and surprise homecoming, the able members of the family have joined in work to prepare for life on the road. Al, the young "tom-catter," has made a good buy on a Hudson that Pa Joad is finishing converting to a truck when Tom does arrive. Uncle John is in town selling off odds and ends to help finance the trip. On the eve of the journey Noah, the first-born, and Tom, the second-born, slaughter the pigs to eat on the way. Casy helps Ma to salt them. His doing "woman's work" foreshadows the reversal of roles the general uprooting engenders, illustrates his personal need to repay his hosts, and demonstrates through actual deed his preachings about love and service to people in need. Rosasharn packs the family clothes and stacks for loading many of the larger household goods. Granma and Grampa and the kids do little but eat and sleep. The narrator does not mention Connie by name as doing anything other than squatting in place with the other men during the family conference, and before that he was off "nestin" with Rosasharn at his folks' place. However, for the Joads work is pride. Al's work with the Hudson earns him not only his "first participation in the conference" but also the compliment from Grampa and big brother Tom that he has "done good." At sixteen, Al may "think of nothin' but girls and engines"; nevertheless, it is that very thinking that helps to get his folks to California, gets him a wife, and will likely make his dream of getting a job in a garage a reality. In essence, Al is a family man. That he leaves his Ma and Pa to make a life of his own with Wainwright is, even in hard times, a good and healthy thing to do—and it in no way hurts his blood-kin or spoils his relationship with them. In reference to the marriage, Ma says "we're glad. We're awful glad."

Given the plain fact that old folks normally fight to stay put and that children struggle to cut the cord to make a life of their own, the Joads as families go are no more split up at the start than at the finish of the novel. Speeding up the normal process is the fact that the highway becomes "their home and movement their medium of expression." Granma and Grampa die en route as casualties of old age, displacement, and exhaustion. Once in the ground they are hardly mentioned by anyone again. Faced with the immediate needs of the living, especially with feeding Ruthie and Winfield and with soothing Rosasharn after Connie leaves, Ma realizes that she must "forget" the dead. The ones who depart of their own accord, including Al, do so because they cannot sustain their sense of selfhood if they stay.

Tom's motives for leaving are exceptional. And they are mixed. Wanted for murder and in hiding, he can be of no practical use to the family if he stays. A man of action, Tom exhibits few self-doubts. Near the end of the novel he decides that "long as [he's] a outlaw anyways," he might just as well carry on Casy's work in organizing the strikers, and in that way help the plight of his family from afar. Anyway, as things happen, Ruthie gets into a kid-fight over Cracker Jacks, and to save face she blabs about Tom's having "kil't two fellas," and in light of this brag Tom is forced to leave to save his skin. Unlike Noah and Connie, Tom goes with Ma's blessing and her gift of seven dollars to help him on his way.

By choice Noah is the first to go. He worked all his life on the family farm and helped to ready things for the journey. But as "a stranger to all the world" he has never really dwelt within the bosom of the family. With the words "Listen, you goddamn fool—" Tom is the only one to see Noah off down the Colorado River, and when he is barely out of eyesight Tom lies down to sleep. Ma worries a bit about how Noah will eat, but at Weedpatch she dismisses him from her mind, saying, "Maybe he'll have a nice time by the river. Maybe it's better so." Incapable of wrath and amazed by its appearance in others, Noah is Steinbeck's boldest example of the self-involved and self-contained "I." He is the total opposite of his brother Tom, Ma's favorite. He could never find comfort dwelling in Tom's shadow or in the "embarrassed eyes" of his Pa. And he would most certainly shy away from the common cause that Ma supports and that Tom comes to embrace. Marked by a "twisted" birth, and with "no sexual urges," making it on his own is about the most grown-up thing Noah could try.

Connie Rivers is the next to go. He sneaks off without so much as a "so long" to anyone. In chapter 10 the narrator states that he is "a good hard worker and would make a good husband," but that he is "frightened and bewildered" by Rosasharn's pregnancy. Well, the reader never sees him work. But the reader does see him frightened. The fact of Hooverville is just too much for him. Of a "Texan strain" and not a Joad, Connie brags too much, specifically about how he is going to study radio by mail and get Rosasharn a house and car. Whether he leaves to study up on radios or tractors is anyone's guess. But that he leaves his wife halfway through her pregnancy for the truly illusory dream of making a success of himself through "home study" marks him a failure as a man and husband. He has witnessed Pa Joad lose his place as head of the family because of poverty and Ma's demands, and he no doubt knows that he can in no way live up to Rosasharn's dream of motherhood. He leaves to save face. Aside from Rosasharn, the greater family does not miss him. Pa Joad concludes that "Connie wasn' no good. I seen that a long time. Didn' have no guts, jus' too big for his overalls." Ma agrees, and tells Pa to act as if Connie were "dead."

Now, although Connie and Noah have vanished like deserters from the heat of battle, the essential family structure is still intact, and stronger without them. They were on the fringe at best. And better men have replaced them. Foreshadowing the good luck it has in securing room at Weedpatch and work on the road, the family is strengthened by the chance meeting of Tom and Casy. It will be remembered that, back in Oklahoma, Casy teamed up with Tom on Tom's way "home," and that both arrived at Uncle John's out of the blue and just in time to join the family for the trip West. On behalf of the younger members of her family, Ma would have gone without Tom. Even before the family "shove[d]" off their homestead and their house was "all pushed out a shape," Tom was all but dead to them. During his four years of imprisonment, he received one Christmas card from Ma and one from Granma, and that is all. Released, Tom brings new life into the family, and in a very material way prefigures the virtual death of his brother Noah, whose knowledge of the outside world and modern machinery is zero. And his gift of Casy to the family, who is an outsider but brother to all, prefigures the demise of Connie, whose behavior as a brother-in-law leaves much to be desired. It may be a bad pun but it is no accident that Steinbeck has Connie *Rivers* and Noah (whose name is associated with the destruction of the world by flood) disappear within a few days of one another along a river and well before the hardship of the flood the family undergoes at the end of the narrative. In short, without Noah and Connie, as without Granma and Grampa, the family as Ma defines it is better equipped to survive the agony ahead, of which Hooverville in all its meanness of spirit is but an initiation.

As a reflection of the sorry spectacle, it is at Hooverville that Uncle John comes face to face with his own lack of self-honor and life-purpose. Having witnessed Casy just go right up to be arrested by a deputy by saying straight out that he clobbered one of them makes Uncle John "feel awful." He knows that he could have stepped in and helped Tom and Floyd, and taken the blame on himself. But he "slipped up," and so goes off by himself to get drunk. Not until the flood and the miscarriage of Rosasharn's baby does Uncle John find himself. He sets the apple box that serves as the baby's coffin afloat in the flood waters and says, "Go down an' tell em. Go down in the street an' rot an' tell 'em that way." Given his shy nature, it is fitting that he attacks the system that helped to kill the baby alone and without the need of congratulation from anyone. He does "more'n" himself. Although the gesture may go unheeded, he consciously aligns himself with the struggle of the "We." And he does so in a manner no less creative than, and every bit as shocking as, Rosasharn's baring her breast to nurse a starving man.

If the dead baby were not blood kin, and the stab of injustice personal, he may never have been moved to express his wrath against the general condition. Like John, Pa Joad is moved to action for personal reasons. He wants his family to stay dry. But he needs help. He cannot build a dike alone. Wainwright, Al's future father-in-law, thinks in a waste. But Pa persuades him and others by saying, "Well, we ain't doin' nothin'. . . . We can do her if ever'body helps." The day before the flood Pa feels that his life is "over an' done." Building the dike renews his spirit, and teaches him that there is much to be gained through the "We" attitude. The dike does break, but it holds just long enough for Rosasharn to deliver, and for that Pa is moved to laugh "in triumph."

It will be recalled that when Casy went off to jail at Hooverville he did so with a "smile" and "a curious look of conquest" on his face. Shortly before his arrest he had confessed to Tom that he wanted to "go off alone" because he was "a-eatin" the family food and "doin' nobody no good" in return. Hence, like Pa and John, who knowingly or not follow his example, Casy triumphs over his doubts of self-worth by acting in behalf of others in need. For most of the Joads, his spirit does indeed take hold. It shows up in the "smile" of Ma when she gives her blessing to Al to "stay" in the boxcar with Aggie while she leads the rest of the family to higher ground. En route, the spirit even takes hold of Ruthie, who finally realizes that there is little fun in playing alone, and so shares the petals of a wild geranium with her brother Winfield. And it positively radiates from the face of Rosasharn as the "mysterious smile" that concludes the narrative. Finding self-worth through sharing and cooperating with kin and outsiders is what keeps the Joads, with the exceptions noted, from falling apart as a family and failing as migrants.

What probably causes some readers to conclude that the Joads break up is Tom's mission, Al's engagement, and Ma's complaint at the Hooper ranch that "There ain't no fambly now." Yet her family is in fact with her, and those who are able are doing their share of work in the orchard. Her complaint focuses on the "wildness" of the kids to Pa's "lost place" as head of the family. However, it is calculated to persuade Tom to "stay an' help." Tom stays, but he is in no condition to do anything but rest and hide from the vigilantes. In short, Ma at this point is just plain depressed, and so uses every trick of motherhood she knows to delay the inevitable departure of her favorite son, whose spirit she trusts, and whom she has come to lean on as the male leader of the family. Earlier, she told Tom straight out how she felt about him as opposed to the rest of the family; "Them others—they're kinda strangers, all but you. . . . Ever'thing you do is more'n you." And now, at Hooper's, she wants his moral support. They are soul mates. From the strength of that bond she can when the time comes see him off, and say to Pa "I—sent 'im away." During the flood, as mentioned above, she does the same for Al—that is, without emotional blackmail, she releases Al to grow on his own with a new family. And although the narrative is open-ended, Al will likely stay around the boxcar for a few weeks to start the Hudson, for none of the vehicles will dry out until then. Yet, beyond the practical help the Joads lend one another, the basic thing that makes them a family is what George explains to Lennie in chapter 1 in ***Of Mice and Men:*** "We got somebody to talk to that gives a damn about us."

The Joad who talks the most, and whose thoughts are directed toward putting into action the "I to We" principle, is Tom. He is the one Joad capable of the violence needed to combat the "unhealthful condition" that violates the dignity and very survival of the migrants. The motive source of his tendency to violence is personal. Like Muley Graves, who is ready to kill any of "them sons-a-bitches" that threaten to push him around, Tom is quick to protect his pride and person. He admits that prison did not reform him, saying, "if I seen Herb Turnbull comin' for me with a knife right now, I'd squash him down with a shovel again. . . . Do her before I could figure her out. . . . That sort of senselessness kind a worries a man." Yet prison taught him how to survive in any environment. He receives an early release for good behavior because he learned how to handle the inmates and the officials without having to use violence to protect his dignity. It is turtlelike willpower and determination to survive that brings Tom back to the family, but it is his ability to change and adapt to a reality even tougher than prison that enables him to view the means by which the Okies will survive. He is capable of picking up on Black Hat's thoughts about the five thousand Akron strikers who "jes' marched through town with their rifles. An' they had their turkey shoot . . . ain't been no trouble sence then."

On the road Tom evolves from just a guy who wanted to enjoy his whiskey, smokes, whores, and home-cooked meals to a figure expansive enough to represent the essence of the American spirit, what Steinbeck later described as the "national character." "I thought," he wrote, "that if we had a national character and national genius, these people, who were beginning to be called Okies, were it. With all the odds against them, their goodness and strength survived." If Tom and his kin had not run out of cash, he would likely not have become Steinbeck's realistic version of the questing knight in search of the lost grail:

the American Dream of justice, democracy, and the opportunity to live in dignity.

As illustrated by his angry gesture of crushing the "hard skull-like head" of a grasshopper in response to the nosey truckdriver who pushes him to admit that he is an ex-convict, Tom is dangerous to anyone who would tarnish his sense of self-dignity. His greatest enemies, of course, are those wanting cheap labor. But with economic individualism doomed, Tom and his like no longer have a power base from which to defend their rights. Hence, to maintain at least the sense of personal power and self-worth, Tom and the others take strength from their subconscious memories or dreams. Steinbeck writes in an editorial chapter that they "seemed to be part of an organization of the unconscious. They obeyed impulses . . . ."

However, some of Tom's more violent impulses have to be restrained. His re-education begins with Muley Graves, a former neighbor, and at the very place of his birth where, on a smaller scale, Tom gets a glimpse of the more powerful militant forces that he will face in California. He learns from Muley of Willy Feely, a former cotton farmer, who drives a "cat" for the powerful forces who now own the land. Why hold this demeaning job? Willy remarks: "I got two little kids. . . . What happens to other folks is their look-out." Like his kind in California Willy has become a deputy sheriff, and Tom learns that he can no longer approach the Willys of the land as an equal. Rather than get "pushed around," Tom would "lots rather take a sock at Willy." After Muley explains that Willy may use his gun, Tom realizes his present plight. By challenging Willy and his power structure, "I ain't got a thing in the worl' to win, no matter how it comes out." Later, at the "half a buck" campgrounds in New Mexico, when the proprietor calls Tom a bum, he shows that he has not forgotten Muley's lesson, saying, "It's a hard thing to be named a bum. I ain't afraid . . . I'll go for you an' your deputy with my mitts—here now, or jump Jesus. But there ain't no good in it." However, in California, when stopped on route to Weedpatch, he would have clobbered a whiskey-smelling Legionnaire with a jack handle if Ma had not restrained him. The Legionnaire calls him a "goddamn Okie" but Tom backs down from a fight by assuming a "servile whine" in asking directions to Tulare. Good thing. The Legionnaires are "armed with pick handles and shotguns."

At Weedpatch Tom joins a committee to prevent hooligans from the Cattle and Growers Associations from starting a riot at the Saturday night dance. With but the show of force the committee escorts the troublemakers out of camp without hurting them. Beyond the obvious lesson that there is strength in a will united, Tom gains also from the experience the good sense that, even outside of prison, there can be dignity in a nonviolent approach to people who would put him down. Happily, he carries that attitude to Hooper Ranch—a false Eden—which the Joads enter for work picking peaches, ignorant that they are strike breakers. The orchard is a virtual prison. Tom wants to get outside to discover what is going on. Neither Pa nor Al will go with him, so he tries alone. An armed guard challenges him. Tom backs away. But he does not whine. In reflection of the Weedpatch strategy, he remains cool, declaring, "If it's gonna cause a mess, I don't give a darn. Sure, I'll go back." He escapes. Unfortunately, he then walks into a real "mess." And, for the second time in his life, he kills a man.

Prone to violence though he is, it is important to see Tom's gentler side. For example, the turtle that some motorists try to hit, Tom treats as a pet and as a worthy gift for Ruthie and Winfield. On his way to Uncle John's, a gopher snake crosses his path. Tom says, "Let him go." Tom is neither instinctively cruel nor destructive. When he drives the Hudson he feels no remorse in running over the dangerous rattlesnake, but his reaction to hitting the frightened jackrabbit is telling: "Gives me a little shakes ever' time." And he confesses to Al that he is sorry he killed young Turnbull "'cause he was dead." Al, obviously proud of his brother Tom, sums him up at Hooverville in the declaration that he is just "as nice as pie till he's roused, an' then—look out." Tom will not be reduced to the level of a turtle.

Beyond direct threat to his person, what rouses Tom the most is the fact that law has become a tool of the fascistic Association of Farmers. He assures Ma more than once that he is not a "Floyd" who attacks society out or personal bitterness. He explains: "if it was the law they [land owners] was workin' with, why, we could take it. But it *ain't* the law. They're a workin' away at our spirits . . . . tryin' to break us." The few moments that Tom spends with Casy in the ravine of his bloody murder gives Tom a glimpse of the possibility of organizing the Okies to challenge the power structure. Hence, when the agents of that structure beat Casy down, they in effect attack the new hope in Tom that friend Casy inspired. There is an ugly irony in the fact that the very tool of the laborer, a new pick handle, is used against Casy. Tom is enraged. A man like his brother Noah or brother-in-law Connie would have fled. But Tom wrests the pick handle away from the murderer, and then strikes him not once but five times. The brutality in this overkill demystifies Tom: he is cruel beyond what is necessary to save himself. And now to survive he must run.

With his face looking like the raw meat of a prizefighter's, the last we see of Tom is in chapter 28, what we call the "harvest" chapter. Like Rose of Sharon, he takes counsel with himself in a "cave of vines." There he explains to Ma his new resolve, the harvest of his hard knocks: since he's an "outlaw anyways" he will be present, if not in fact then in spirit, to lead the "fight so hungry people can eat"—this because the struggle for mere self-survival is not enough, for a "fella ain't no good alone." He has grown to realize that the rewards of life must be harvested in the here and now, and that hope in the religious hereafter will not cure the present misery. He and the others of his lot must work together to drive back the oppressors who would break their spirit. Tom is not alone in holding this vision. Floyd Knowles at Hooverville and Black Hat at Weedpatch express the same ideas. But Tom's temperament, passion, and particular circumstance make it probable that he will become in word and deed a strike organizer. On the run he has little to lose and much to gain from working underground. Being joined to the just cause of his people will make him a good outlaw.

Al assumes Tom's role as male leader of the family. From the youth who was chastised by Pa for having been away two weeks when preparations for the trip were under way, Al at journey's and is hardly recognizable. He proves Tom's faith in the resurgence of the Okie spirit. He has heeded the big brother who said, "Al, don' keep ya guard up when nobody ain't sparrin' with ya." Hence, when he announces his decision to marry Aggie, his defiant speech is directed not so much against the two families as it is against the outside economic forces that lurk to ambush his dream of a job, a marriage, and a house: "they ain't nobody can stop us." And when a stranger threatens Pa somehow to even the score for having been talked into working on the flood wall that broke, Al's defense of his father is as vigorous as Tom's might have been: "You're gonna fight your way in." Pa restrains Al as Ma restrained Tom and deals in a peaceful manner with the intruder.

After the rains stop it is Al who makes the plans on how to protect both families from the rising flood. Casy or Tom could be speaking: "I been a-thinkin.'" While Al and Ma plan on building a platform to shield the families from the water, Ma's eyes open from her sleep and "She crie[s] sharply in warning, 'Tom! Oh, Tom! Tom!'" Then she lapses back into her dream. It is dawn. Whether or not her warning saves her favorite in his travail, it seems to summon Al to take Tom's place of leadership—for upon the instant he sets to work to keep the family high and dry. Finishing the job, Al makes a conscious stand as leader by requesting of Pa that he go buy food for breakfast: "I need some meat."

The Joads and the Wainwrights have a new warrior. As such, Al accepts the responsibility of guarding his family's possessions as well as his wife-to-be. His harvest does not include the larger questions of social justice that feed Tom. For it will be remembered that at the peach orchard "Al looked away." But his passion for an honest piece of the American pie is undeniable, and, in terms of the family ethic, praiseworthy. As Ma says, "I couldn't want for a better boy." And she sallies forth to nurture Winfield and Ruthie, who, as the seedlings of the family, have a way to go in weathering the hazards of Self and the outside world before reaching the height of Al, Tom, and Rosasharn. That Ma ushers them into "the tool shed" at the close of the narrative is telling. For such is the emblem of the migrant family, and the hope of their lot.

Although the narrative is open-ended, the Joads on the whole have demonstrated that their "fears" of the general "unhealthy condition" have in effect evaporated in their dreams of better days, acts of sharing, and gestures of "wrath." Noah, Connie, and the grandparents never grow beyond their old ways of thinking. But the rest have shown themselves as bright innovators and forward thinkers. Dashed hopes and sudden changes have not broken their spirit. A happy and normal change is that Al has become the star figure of two families. A change of mixed feeling is that the older men have come to accept themselves as well as their deflated status in the family hierarchy. Uncle John has ceased complaining about his old "sins" and Pa does the shopping, even if what he buys displeases Ma. Despite the changes, the family has not, as the critics cited in note 4 insist, broken up. Rather, it has restructured itself to meet the challenge of new life in changing times. Ma gives orders to keep "the family unbroke" because the family is her pride and best means of security. And, in another reversal of family habit, she and Rosasharn earn that security by working in the fields and orchards right alongside of the men. Uncle John and Pa take the orders because they no longer have the particular distinction of being the only family members to bring home the bacon. They stay because the family is their friend, and the best they have.

Each, the kids included, has experienced the intentional meanness of landlords, the indiscriminate fury of the flood, the anger of strangers, and the self-doubts of their own worth. But, excepting Ruthie, they have also reached out in kindness to strangers, and as strangers have accepted kindness. Through it all they have come to know or to sense that their plight is not unique, and that some others are far worse off than themselves. That Pa and Uncle John gaze "helplessly" at the sick man Rose of Sharon feeds bespeaks not only their feeling of vulnerability but also their impulse to help. With the only means they have at hand they do help: Pa, especially, puts aside his authority as the male elder and forgoes any word of sarcasm or defeatism; in silence both men acquiesce to the extraordinary thing Ma urges the daughter to do. They, like Ma and Rosasharn, indeed do "more'n" themselves, and in ways that declare their individuality and their role as "essence people," both. Finally, if every the mettle of the American spirit and family has been tested and found strong, it has been so with the Joads.

Louis Owens (essay date 1989)

SOURCE: "The Culpable Joads: Desentimentalizing *The Grapes of Wrath,*" in *Critical Essays on Steinbeck's The Grapes of Wrath,* edited by John Ditsky, G. K. Hall, 1989, pp. 108-16.

[In the following essay, Owens draws attention to Steinbeck's effort to evoke sympathy for the Joad family without sentimentalizing their plight. According to Owens, Steinbeck incorporates panoramic interchapters to offset over-identification with the Joad family.]

The Grapes of Wrath is one of John Steinbeck's great experiments, perhaps his greatest, a novel that exploded upon the American conscience in 1939, bringing home to American readers both the intimate reality of the Joads' suffering and the immense panorama of a people's—the Dust Bowl migrants'—suffering. In spite of howls of outrage from opposite ends of the novel's journey—both Oklahoma and California—America took the Joads to heart, forming out of ***The Grapes of Wrath*** a new American archetype of oppression and endurance, survival if not salvation. So warmly did readers embrace the Dust Bowl Okies, in fact, that critics began almost immediately to accuse Steinbeck again of sentimentality in his portrayal of the downtrodden proletariat. Edmund Wilson was one of the first serious critics to take such a position, declaring that in this novel Steinbeck learned much from films, "and not only from the documentary pictures of Pare Lorentz, but from the sentimental symbolism of Hollywood." Bernard De Voto had anticipated Wilson when he complained that the novel's ending was "symbolism gone sentimental." Still a third major American critic, R. W. B. Lewis, found Steinbeck's fiction "mawkish" and "constitutionally unequipped to deal with the more sombre reality a man must come up against. . . ."

As Steinbeck's most imposing and both popularly and critically successful work, ***The Grapes of Wrath*** has been studied from a multitude of angles, with critics focusing on its historical, political, philosophical, religious, symbolic, structural, and stylistic aspects. Steinbeck's great formal experiment in this novel—the interchapters—has been often studied and commented upon. What has been little noted in this novel, however, is the care Steinbeck takes to counterbalance the narrative's seemingly inevitable drift in the direction of sentimentalism as the story of the Joads and of the migrants as a whole unfolds in all its pathos. While Steinbeck is undeniably intensely sympathetic in this novel to the suffering of the croppers and to the plight of the seemingly powerless "little people" caught up in the destructive path of corporate America, he is at the same time painstakingly careful *not* to sentimentalize these figures, a fact of utmost importance to a critical understanding of ***The Grapes of Wrath.***

A primary means by which Steinbeck attempts to unsentimentalize this story of displacement and suffering is through his use of interchapters. As has been often noted, the most obvious value of the intercalary chapters is to provide the big picture, to ensure the reader's awareness of the panoramic dimensions of this socioeconomic tragedy. At the same time, the narrative chapters focusing on the Joad family stem from Steinbeck's self-professed awareness that "It means very little to know that a million Chinese are starving unless you know one Chinese who is starving." Through the interchapters we feel the scope and dimension of the Dust Bowl drama; through the narrative chapters we experience the tragedy of one family on a personal, intimate level. A second very important function of the interchapters, however, one that has gone largely unnoticed, is that of offsetting the intimacy of the narrative chapters, of creating necessary distance between the reader and Steinbeck's representative family, the Joads. Steinbeck uses the interchapters skillfully as a means of preventing the reader from identifying too closely with the Joads. Again and again, just as we begin to be drawn fully into the pain of the Joads' experience, Steinbeck pulls us away from the intimate picture into the broad scope of one of the interchapters, reminding us that these are merely representative people, that the scale of suffering is so great as to dwarf the anguish of one small group such as Ma Joad's family. Chapter 18 ends, for example, with the Joads about to descend into the promised land of California's Central Valley, weighted with the emotionally charged burden of the dead Granma. The heartbreaking courage of Ma, who has lain beside Granma all night to ensure that the family gets "across," is deeply moving, and as the Joads drive down into the highly stylized Eden of the valley the reader must respond emotionally to the courage and suffering of the family. Immediately, however, with the opening lines of chapter 19, Steinbeck shifts the reader's focused away from the Joads onto a broad, impersonal sweep of California's agricultural history culminating in a view of the Hoovervilles and a generic portrait of the migrants. The Joads' suffering is put into perspective as we realize once again that this family's tragedy is every migrant's, that there must be a thousand Granmas and as many Ma Joads, and that the family is about to descend into a sea of families in precisely the same circumstances and facing their predicament with roughly the same proportion of courage and cowardice. In place of the familiar voices of Tom and Ma Joad and reader now hears the voice of history, and the perspective is readjusted once again. It is more difficult to become sentimental about the fate of the individual when one is simultaneously aware of the fate of the species.

In addition to the depersonalizing distance achieved through the movement from narrative chapter to interchapter, Steinbeck also takes advantage of a more familiar device to desentimentalize his treatment of the downtrodden sharecropper in this novel: the objective authorial stance that he exploited so successfully in the earlier study of oppressed workers, ***In Dubious Battle.*** In that novel, published just three years before, Steinbeck was careful to underscore the failings of the migrant workers as well as those of the oppressors—both sides are greedy, selfish, lazy, bloodthirsty, and ignorant. These are simply aspects of the human character, says Steinbeck in that strike novel, simply the way it is, nonteleologically. In ***The Grapes of Wrath,*** Steinbeck does not assume the purely objective stance of the narrative voice of ***In Dubious Battle,*** choosing not to become "merely a recording consciousness, judging nothing" as he claimed to be in the earlier strike novel. In ***The Grapes of Wrath,*** Steinbeck allows his authorial voice the freedom to intrude in the guise of a modern Jeremiah, judging, condemning. However, once again in spite of his sympathies with the displaced Okies, as he did in ***In Dubious Battle*** in ***Grapes*** Steinbeck takes care to similarly undercut the nobility and "goodness" of the migrants.

Tom, for example, is a loner who begins the novel looking out only for number one, as his solitary initial appearance and his aggressive manipulation of the witless truck driver indicate. Only gradually, through the tutoring of Casy, does the unsympathetic Tom grow into his role of proletarian savior. Throughout the novel, Pa Joad is self-centered and weakwilled, too ineffectual to assume the role of leadership demanded of him, a character thoroughly incapable of igniting the reader's sympathy, as Tom makes clear when he tells Casy late in the novel "Think Pa's gonna give up his meat on account a other fellas?" Tom's brother Al is concerned chiefly with his own concupiscence, eager even near the end of the novel to abandon his family and strike out on his own with his wife-to-be, Rose of Sharon's husband, Connie, proves himself to be a selfish and soft-minded believer in the American Dream advertised in comic books and a deserter of his pregnant wife. Rose of Sharon, in turn, forces the reader to suffer through hundreds of pages of whining self-pity before her miraculous conversion near the novel's end. Even Ma, larger-than-life Earth Mother and obvious heroine of this novel, demonstrates her limitations as she rambles on pointlessly about "Purty Boy Floyd," repeating herself tediously the way real people really do as she intones one of the folkmyths of Oklahoma and the Dust Bowl region.

While the trials of the Joads engage us, even excite our admiration and pity, Steinbeck takes pains to deny is the luxury of sentimental attachment. The Joads, including even the ultimately heroic and Christ-like Casy, are no better, no greater, no less human than they should be. Nor are any of the other migrants in the novel.

More important than either Steinbeck's illumination of the human failings of his characters on such limited levels or his use of the interchapters as distancing devices is his care to emphasize the migrants' culpability, their portion of responsibility for what has happened to the land and to themselves. Certainly Steinbeck makes it clear that the sharecroppers are victimized by an inhuman economic monster that tears at the roots of Jeffersonian agrarianism. However, when Steinbeck causes his representative migrant voice to plead with the owners for a chance to remain on the land, he qualifies the celebrated Jeffersonian agrarianism and love-for-the land by tainting the croppers' wish: "Get enough wars and cotton'll hit the ceiling," the cropper argues. A willingness to accept war and death as the price for further cottoning out of the land is difficult to admire on any level. And Steinbeck goes a step further, to make it clear that the migrants are firmly fixed in a larger, even more damning American pattern. Though the tenants have tried to persuade the owners to let them hang, one hoping for a war to drive up cotton prices, the tenant-voice also warns the owners: "But you'll kill the land with cotton." And the owners reply: "We know. We've got to take cotton quick before the land dies. Then we'll sell the land. Lots of families in the East would like to own a piece of land." With their words the westering pattern of American history is laid bare: we arrive on the Atlantic seaboard seeking Eden only to discover a rocky and dangerous paradise with natives who aggressively resent the "discovery" of their land; the true Eden must therefore lie ever to the west, over the next hill, across the next plain, until finally we reach the Pacific Ocean and, along with Jody's grandfather in ***The Red Pony,*** we end up shaking our fists at the Pacific because it stopped us, breaking the pattern of displacement, a pattern put into focus in Walt Whitman's poignant query in "Facing West from California's Shores": "But where is what I started for so long ago? / And why is it yet unfound?"

That the croppers are part of this pattern becomes even more evident when the representative tenant voice informs us that their fathers had to "kill the Indians and drive them away." And when the tenants add, "Grampa killed Indians, Pa killed snakes for the land," we should hear a powerful echo of the Puritan forebears who wrested the wilderness from the Satanic serpent and his Indian servants, killing and displacing the original inhabitants of the new Canaan.

It is difficult to feel excessive sorrow for these ignorant men who are quite willing to barter death to maintain their place in the destructive pattern of American expansion, a pattern that has ravaged a continent. That Steinbeck thought long about the American phenomenon of destroying the Garden just discovered in the search for an even better Garden is suggested in his declaration more than a decade later that in ***East of Eden,*** his great investigation of the myth of American, "people dominate the land, gradually. They stripe it and rob it. Then they are forced to try to replace what they have taken out."

The tenant and owner voices are wrong, of course: you cannot "kill the land." The land can be altered, made inhospitable for the sons of Cain who inhabit it, but it will survive. The epic perspective with which the novel begins suggests the enduring nature of this earth, the land which "abideth forever."

The first paragraph of ***The Grapes of Wrath*** opens with an impressionistic swath of color reminiscent of Stephen Crane as Steinbeck intones, "To the red country and part of the gray country of Oklahoma, the last rains came gently, and they did not cut the scarred earth." He continues:

> The plows crossed and recrossed the rivulet marks. The last rains lifted the corn quickly and scattered weed colonies and grass along the sides of the roads so that the gray country and the dark red country began to disappear under a green cover. In the last part of May the sky grew pale and the clouds that had hung in high puffs for so long in the spring were dissipated. The sun flared down on the growing corn day after day until a line of brown spread along the edge of each green bayonet. The clouds appeared, and went away, and in a while they did not try any more. The weeds grew darker green to protect themselves, and they did not spread any more. The surface of the earth crusted, a thin hard crust, and as the sky became pale, so the earth became pale, pink in the red country and white in the gray country.

A close look at this paragraph shows that following the panoramic, generalized opening, the paragraph begins to focus, to zoom in: "The plows crossed and recrossed the rivulet marks." And finally, from the impressionistic opening image our vision has closed the distance to focus very closely upon not just "the growing corn" but the "line of brown" that spreads "along the edge of each green bayonet." At once the narrative eye begins to pan back to register broader details of clouds and generalized "weeds" until the paragraph ends where it began, with a panoramic image of the earth, which "became pale, pink in the red country and white in the gray country." "In the second paragraph, the camera's eye again zooms in for a close-up: "In the water-cut gullies the earth dusted down in dry little streams." And again this paragraph expands to end with a panorama: "The air was thin and the sky more pale, and every day the earth paled."

In these first paragraphs, Steinbeck is introducing the pattern upon which ***The Grapes of Wrath*** will be structured; a pattern of expansion and contraction, of a generalized panoramic view of the plight of the migrants in the interchapters followed in the narrative chapters by a closeup of the plight of the representative individuals, the Joads. As early as the novel's opening paragraph, the reader is being subliminally programmed for this movement in the novel, and he is being introduced to the idea that beyond the Joads is the pattern made up of the migrants and the Dust Bowl phenomenon as a whole; beyond the seeming tragedy of the drought and the cropped-out land is the pattern made up of the panoramic earth itself. The shifting focus is designed to remind us that the individual tragedies are played out against a backdrop of enduring life. In teleological terms, as defined by Steinbeck and Ed Ricketts in ***The Log from the Sea of Cortez,*** the drought, the Dust Bowl, and the tragedy of the migrants seem immeasurable disasters for which blame must be assigned; in nonteleologically terms, however, we are reminded by the panoramic sweep of the author's brush that we are seeing only part of the picture, partial indices of what the ***Log*** defined as "all reality, known and unknowable."

Paradoxically, such a nonteleological perspective serve to make the Dust Bowl a tragedy only insofar as it is judged according to transient, human values. From a distance, the drought-wasted land is lovely, a sweeping panorama of pastels; up close, the picture becomes one of horror, but only in human terms. For the sharecroppers this is a tragedy; the larger picture suggests that the tragedy is limited, transient, that the earth abides beyond man's errors and shortsightedness. To believe, as the croppers and landowners in this novel do, that one can "kill the land" is to see only part of the picture, to commit the error Joseph Wayne commits in Steinbeck's early novel ***To a God Unknown*** of believing that the land can die. The biblical prose style of these opening paragraphs, recalling the incantatory force of Genesis, also underscores the power of primal creation that precedes man and exists beyond man's ability to effect or effect. Like the people who, drawing their strength from the earth, "go on," the earth cannot be destroyed, and Steinbeck's style and tone in these first paragraphs is designed to reinforce that message.

If Steinbeck's message in the opening paragraphs is that the land cannot die, he nonetheless begins as early as the second sentence of the novel to subtly imply human responsibility for the disruption of the drought. In the second sentence, he tells us that "The plows crossed and recrossed the rivulet marks," superimposing an ultimately self-destructive human patter—the erosion-inducing plow lines—upon the natural watershed pattern. The rivulet marks are a sign of the earth's flow, cycle, continuum; their crossing and erasure is a sign of a failure of human understanding. The wheels that "milled the ground," and the hooves that "beat the ground" until "the dirt crust broke and the dust formed" further underscores man's responsibility for the human tragedy depicted in the first paragraphs and developed throughout the novel. By the novel's end, the rain will come again in a great, destructive, cleansing flood, erasing in its turn the pattern of human failure set upon the edenic valleys of California.

Steinbeck also foreshadows in these opening paragraphs the fate of the migrants. The "weed colonies" that are "scattered . . . along the sides of the roads" suggest the colonies of migrants that will soon be scattered the length of Route 66; and the minuscule ant lion trap, a funnel of finely blown sand from which the ant simply cannot escape, serves as a naturalistic image to define the situation of the sharecroppers. They have no further in the cropped-out region of blowing dust and sand; they have sealed their fates should they stubbornly struggle to remain. Muley Graves, whose name hints strongly at his character and fate, chooses to remain in the trap, a "graveyard ghos'" without a future.

Through this burnt country cut the tracks of walking men and machines, raising dust clouds as signs of their passage. When Tom Joad appears, he will be the representative walking man, the individual who must accept responsibility for what man has done to himself and to the earth. Along with Tom, the Joads and all of the migrants will be sent on the road on a quest to rethink their relationship with humanity as well as with the land itself. What Warren French has aptly termed the "education of the heart" is a journey toward a new national consciousness, one that may, Steinbeck seems to imply, finally break the grip of the westering pattern in this country, causing Americans to free themselves from the delusive quest for a New Eden and this from the destructive process of exploitation and removal entailed in such a pattern.

Once the Joads and their fellow migrants have reached California, they can go no farther. The Joads are the representative migrants, and the migrants are the representative Americans. The migrants' westward journey is America's, a movement that encapsulated the directionality of the American experience. The horrors of the California Eden confronting the migrants have been brought on by all of us, Steinbeck implies; no one is innocent. When Uncle John releases Rose of Sharon's stillborn baby upon the flood waters with the words, "Go down an' tell'em," Steinbeck is underscoring the new consciousness. This Moses is stillborn because the people have no further need for a *Moses.* The Promised Land has long ago been reached, and there is nowhere else to go, no place for a Moses to lead his chosen people. The American myth of the Eden ever to the west is shattered, the dangers of the myth exposed. The new leader will be an everyman, Tom Joad, who crawls into a cave of vines—the womb of the earth—to experience his rebirth and who emerges committed not to leading the people somewhere else but to making this place, this America, the garden it might be. The cleansing, destructive flood that prepares for the novel's concluding tableau rises not merely around the threatened migrants but over the entire land.

The Grapes of Wrath is Steinbeck's jeremiad, his attempt to expose not only the actual, historical suffering of a particular segment of our society, but also the pattern of through, the mindset, that has led to this one isolated tragedy. In this novel, Steinbeck set out to expose the fatal dangers of the American myth of a new Eden, new Canaan, new Jerusalem, and to illuminate a path toward a new consciousness of commitment in place of removal, engagement instead of displacement. And in making his argument, Steinbeck was careful not to sentimentalize his fictional creations, careful to emphasize the shared guilt and responsibility—there are no innocents; a new sensibility, not sentimentality, is Steinbeck's answer.

Louis Owens (essay date 1989)

SOURCE: "The Story of a Writing: Narrative Structure in *East of Eden,*" in *Rediscovering Steinbeck: Revisionist Views of His Art, Politics, and Intellect,* edited by Cliff Lewis and Carroll Britch, Edwin Mellen Press, 1989, pp. 60-76.

[In the following essay, Owens examines the plot, central themes, and characters of East of Eden. *Tempering his earlier unfavorable criticism of the novel, Owens writes, "*East of Eden *is, I believe, Steinbeck's greatest experiment, and one that succeeds more than some of us have thus far suspected."]*

When I said, in my recent study of Steinbeck's fiction, that ***East of Eden*** fails "unmistakably," it seemed to me that it was so. Now I have bent close with a glass over the fine print of the novel and reread the footnotes, and I wonder if it is true.

Most readers of ***East of Eden*** will recognize in the above statement a rather unsubtle paraphrase of Steinbeck's own comments within the novel concerning the nature of his creation called Cathy Ames Trask. It is a paraphrase designed to call to mind the manner in which Steinbeck enters into this novel, becoming not merely the omnipresent "I" who remembers the Salinas Valley and its inhabitants, but the laconic narrator who feels free to step back and comment upon and modify his fictional construct when the desire or whim seems to strike him. And with its emphasis upon the text itself, this paraphrase should also call to mind the acutely self-conscious nature of ***East of Eden.***

In 1927, E.M. Forster, in his *Aspects of the Novel,* passed judgment upon this idiosyncrasy on the part of the novelist, asking,

> . . . may the writer take the reader into his confidence about his characters? . . . better not. It is dangerous, it generally leads to a drop in the temperature, to intellectual and emotional laxity. . . . It is like standing a man to a drink so that he may not criticize your opinions. . . . To take your reader into your confidence about the universe is a different thing. It is not dangerous for a novelist to draw back from his characters, as Hardy and Conrad do, and to generalize about the conditions under which he thinks life is carried on. It is confidences about the individual people that do harm, and *beckon the reader away from the people to an examination of the novelist's mind.* [My italics.]

The slow, sprawling, omnivorous quality of ***East of Eden*** has long disturbed some readers, as have the obvious drops in temperature, the intellectual and emotional laxity, and the novel's tendency to split into dual narratives that don't seem to come together for every critic in a convincing manner. A question arising from the narrative difficulties posed by this novel, especially in light of Steinbeck's obvious awareness of what he was doing, as is demonstrated in ***Journal of a Novel,*** is, why? What is Steinbeck up to in this large novel that would move him to do what Forster and so many readers have found to be so dangerous?

As John Ditsky pointed out in 1977, in his monograph entitled *Essays on East of Eden,* Steinbeck "knew what he was doing." And Ditsky provides another valuable hint in how to read the novel when he says, in this monograph, "It takes no stretching of the point to conclude that, for Steinbeck, this most planned of his novels is most genuinely his portrait of the artist as a mature man." While Ditsky focuses primarily upon Steinbeck's relationships with his home territory—the Salinas Valley—and sees a kind of cathartic force operating in the novel, it may be that the portrait of the artist in this novel functions on a different, aesthetic level as well. It may well be, in fact, that in ***East of Eden*** Steinbeck is quite consciously and intentionally, in Forster's words, beckoning "the reader away from the people [and thus the mimetic convention of the novel] to an examination of the novelist's mind." In fact, what Steinbeck may be beckoning us to in this great, rather unwieldy novel is the study of the creative process itself, with the focus being the mind of John Steinbeck.

It is possible and profitable, I think, to read ***East of Eden*** as another of the large number of novels that are, to a significant extent, concerned with their own creation; to read it to a certain degree, that is, as a self-conscious novel. That John Steinbeck would arrive at such a work in the early 1950's should not be surprising, given the eagerness to experiment with form evident throughout his career and his self-expressed doubts concerning the limitations of both the conventional novel and realism itself. It should be remembered that, as early as 1933, Steinbeck was confessing, "I never had much ability for nor faith nor belief in realism." ***East of Eden*** is, I believe, Steinbeck's greatest experiment, and one that succeeds more than some of us have thus far suspected. A key to this reading of ***East of Eden*** can be found in the opening paragraphs of the novel, in which Steinbeck begins with his usual method of carefully establishing his setting before introducing his characters, but in which he quickly and deftly goes beyond such a mechanical formula to move from geography to symbol:

> I remember that the Gabilan Mountains to the east of the valley were light gay mountains full of sun and loveliness and a kind of invitation, so that you wanted to climb into their warm foothills almost as you want to climb into the lap of a beloved mother. They were beckoning mountains with a brown grass love. The Santa Lucias stood up against the sky to the west and kept the valley from the open sea, and they were dark and brooding—unfriendly and dangerous. I always found in myself a dread of west and love of east. Where I ever got such an idea I cannot say, unless it could be that the morning came over the peaks of the Gabilans and the night drifted back from the ridges of the Santa Lucias. It may be that the birth and death of the day had some part in my feeling about the two ranges of mountains.

In this paragraph, Steinbeck illustrates the way in which a kind of psychic topography grows out of an untutored, intuitive response to natural symbols: the setting and rising sun. We find here a delineation of the symbolic landscape that dominates Steinbeck's writing, from early to late, and we find a hint of what Clifford Lewis has termed the split in the American consciousness—the almost Manichaean sense of opposed absolutes: good and evil, life and death. Here, the dualism is introduced which will quickly become the structural center of the novel, and the focus is not merely upon the landscape but upon the consciousness responding to that landscape: the developing consciousness of the artist.

As perhaps every reader has discovered, ***East of Eden*** is about man's struggle for full knowledge, for the freedom of will implied in Steinbeck's interpretation of *timshel:* "thou mayest." He who accepts his fallen state—the Ishmael who embraces full knowledge—has the potential to survive in this world and, perhaps, to grow to greatness. Samuel Hamilton is such a man, and Cal Trask is becoming one—the everyman, Steinbeck's "sorry" man. He (or she) who does not attain this fullness of vision will perish, literally and/or spiritually. Adam, Aaron, Charles, and Cathy represent two sides of the American consciousness at war, and in these doomed characters the twain never meet.

What Steinbeck is suggesting in the opening paragraphs is the way in which this sense of opposed absolutes rises from deep within man, represents something profound and inevitable in human consciousness. The central theme of ***East of Eden*** appears to grow naturally and quickly out of a child's—little Johnny Steinbeck's—response to his environment, and out of the effect of that remembered response upon the mind of the mature, creative artist. Steinbeck is demonstrating the way fiction itself is created, how it rises out of the deepest feelings for place, and how what the artist knows—place, family—can become transformed into a fictional structure. In the opening chapter of ***East of Eden,*** the so-called American Myth, so powerfully embedded in the American psyche, the myth of the new garden in which the American Adam squares off against evil, seems to emerge out of a convergence of feelings for place, and out of this intuition comes a structure.

From place, the microcosmic Salinas Valley, Steinbeck moves rapidly in the opening pages of the novel to introduce his family, the Hamiltons out of whom the creative source of the novel—John Steinbeck—springs. Steinbeck tells us that "Once, fifty miles down the valley, my father bored a well" and he recounts his wonder at what was found beneath the fertile valley, adding, "And it seemed to me sometimes at night that I could feel both the sea and the redwood forest in it [the valley]." In these lines, Steinbeck lays bare the creative process again, for out of this "real" memory will come Samuel Hamilton's fictional discovery of the fallen star that precedes the Trask twins' birth and symbolizes the merger of "dark violence" and great beauty deep in the valley. Since the long-vanished sea beneath the valley floor, with its rich, dark strata must, like all Steinbeckian seas, bring to mind the unconscious, the fallen star may also suggest a plunge into the unconscious. Whereas the conventional novelistic method is to allow imaginative sources to disappear behind the text, Steinbeck brings his sources into full light in these opening pages, allowing the reader a rare glimpse of the raw materials of fiction.

A few paragraphs after we have been told of his father's well and his own dark thoughts concerning the valley, Steinbeck introduces his grandfather, Samuel Hamilton, followed by the introduction of another *fact* about the valley: the cycles of flood and drought, the latter of which "put a terror on the valley" reminiscent of the violence Samuel intuits when he looks down on the edenic bottom land. Steinbeck declares that "it never failed that during the dry years the people forgot about the rich years, and during the wet years they lost all memory of the dry years." In this passage, Steinbeck is simply remembering the way it was, and *is,* in the valley, and he is simultaneously underscoring the dangerous inability of the valley's inhabitants to hold in mind seemingly contradictory realities. The man who can accept the reality of both the rich years and the terror of the drought will be the "balanced man" of Melville's *Moby Dick,* the man with a Catskill eagle in his soul. Steinbeck continues in this first chapter to remember in a casual, lyrical tone what the valley was like, offering a list of place names with easy-paced commentary in keeping with the tone and style of this introductory chapter. The list of place names ends casually with "Corral de Tierra for a fence of earth; Paraiso because it was like Heaven." Those who have read ***The Pastures of Heaven*** may recall that Pastures of Heaven is Steinbeck's ironic name in that novel for the actual valley called Corral de Tierra, and that the inhabitants of this paradisiacal valley suffer from dangerous delusions. These casually juxtaposed place names underscore in ***East of Eden*** the duality of vision already introduced: the same plot of earth may fence in earthly imperfections or may, through another peephole, seem paradise.

Once the dualism at the heart of this novel has been deftly introduced in this opening, reminiscent chapter, Steinbeck brings in the whole Hamilton clan in Chapter Two, beginning with the autobiographical statement: "I must depend upon hearsay, old photographs. . . ." Conveniently, the Hamilton ranch nestles in the Gabilan Mountains to the east of the valley, the mountains of life described in the opening paragraphs, and, also conveniently, "From their barren hills the Hamiltons could look down to the west and see the richness of the bottom land and the greenness around the Salinas River. . . ." Obviously, Steinbeck is again simply telling us what is—the Hamilton Ranch, now known by another name, really is there in the Gabilan Mountains, a bone-dry ranch of hard-scrabble rounded hills, and from these hills one *can* look down on the richness of the river valley and across the valley to the dark wall of the Santa Lucias where the sun descends into blackness. Because of their location, however, the Hamiltons become strongly identified with the life force in this novel, the life force associated with the eastern mountains in the opening paragraphs of the book. Samuel Hamilton becomes a force for good, a kind of savior, water-witch, grail knight, and non-teleological visionary all rolled into one, and when he bends to grasp a handful of the dry, seemingly barren earth, Samuel is demonstrating his bond with these hills.

With the introduction of the Hamiltons—that aspect of Steinbeck's autobiography which he, like Ben Franklin, the author of another book about America, would purportedly record for his sons—Steinbeck has introduced the soil from which the artistic consciousness of the novel will grow. What remains is for Steinbeck to create the fictional structure necessary to make this the story of America, and out of this need grows the Trask narrative. And as if the beginnings of the Hamilton narrative have indeed prepared the way for the allegorical Trasks, Chapter Two, the first Hamilton chapter, ends with the introduction of Adam Trask in a single line: "Such a man was Adam Trask."

In conjoining the Trask and Hamilton narratives, Steinbeck was fully aware of the risks he was taking. Critics would complain he predicted, putting the words in the mouth of a hypothetical editor: "The book is out of balance. The reader expects one thing and you give him something else. You have written two books and stuck them together." Steinbeck's well-known answer is, "No, sir. It goes together. I have written about one family and used stories about another family as well as counterpoint, as rest, as contrast in pace and color." The same editor complains: "Right in the middle you throw in a story about your mother and an airplane ride. The reader wants to know where it ties in and, by God, it doesn't tie in at all. That disappoints a reader." Finally, Steinbeck responds coyly to his invented editor, saying, "Yes, sir. I guess you're right. Shall I cut out the story of my mother and the airplane?"

Steinbeck foresaw correctly. Again and again, critics have lamented the structural outrage of this novel, focusing particularly upon the lamentable episode of Olive Hamilton's airplane ride. Typical is my own reaction: "Completely out of place in whatever thematic unity the novel possesses, this episode is reminiscent of the most damaging of Steinbeck's sentimental writing in the war dispatches later published as ***Once There Was A War.***"

If Steinbeck knew with such certainty that this would be labeled a structural flaw, why did he do it? And why, since chapters focusing exclusively upon the Hamiltons constitute less than ten percent of the entire novel, did he insist upon including the Hamiltons? The contrast in pace and color offered by the Hamilton narrative is minimal and disappears entirely in the fourth book of the novel. Whatever contrast in pace and color exists in the final book comes only through Steinbeck's authorial intrusion to tell us what he believes, what the collective "we" felt about the war, and how "we" responded to it along with the Trasks. That such a small portion of the novel as the Hamilton narrative could appear to have such an impact is remarkable, and is to be explained largely by the fact that the Hamiltons are the novel's round, human characters, those characters which transcend the role of "symbol people" Steinbeck assigned to the Trasks. Thus the story of Tom and Dessie, a poignant tale of two cases of arrested emotional development coming together in their loneliness, over-balances the Trask drama, steals its thunder.

It may also be that Steinbeck took the risk he did with the Hamiltons out of a desire, in this novel, to keep the reader fully aware of the so-called "real" world out of which fiction grows. "In fact," Steinbeck told Pat Covici in the ***East of Eden*** letters, "all of the Hamilton stories are true." The one Hamilton who slips away from the "real," however, is Samuel. In Samuel, the Hamiltons produce their one figure of suspect reality, a larger-than-life patriarch with shining aura, a freer-of-waters and restorer of wasted lands, a flawed man so good that he tips the scale.

The reason for Samuel's growth toward Trask-like symbolhood is precisely Samuel's growing involvement in the Trask narrative in which Steinbeck is operating in the realm of idea, of allegory, with little concern for making his symbol-people believable. What, in an earlier reference to ***The Red Pony,*** Steinbeck called the "stream underneath," is all that counts and with the Trasks—the story of the prelapsarian Adam and very fallen Eve—the stream flows rapidly above the surface of the story itself. When Samuel becomes involved with Adam Trask, Samuel immediately begins to grow beyond the dimensions of Steinbeck's remembered grandfather to fill a vacuum in the larger story—he grows into the heroic dimensions required to fill the need for a non-teleological visionary, a balanced man. One could say that Samuel is stolen from the Hamilton narrative and transfers his allegiance as a fictional construct to the allegorical realm of Trask. And it seems very likely that Steinbeck wants us to be aware of this theft.

Samuel's transformation from remembered grandfather to fictional creation is highlighted for the reader in Steinbeck's treatment of Samuel's supposed long-lost love back in Ireland. In the beginning pages of the novel, Steinbeck tells us of Samuel's past, saying, "There was a whisper—not even a rumor but rather an unsaid feeling—in my family that it was love drove him out [of Ireland], and not love of the wife he married. But whether it was too successful love or whether he left in pique at unsuccessful love, *I do not know*" [my italics]. Steinbeck follows this a page later with the declaration, "I think there must have been some other girl printed somewhere in his heart, for he was a man of love and his wife was not a woman to show her feelings." By Chapter Twenty-four, more than three hundred pages later, Steinbeck has allowed that early conjecture and the character called Samuel to grow to the point that Samuel is able to tell Adam of the vision of love that has come to him "night after month after year, right to the very now," adding, "And I think I should have double-bolted my mind and sealed off my heart against her, but I did not. All of these years I've cheated Liza . . . ."

Samuel is the point of contact between "real" and fictional worlds in the novel, the bridge. How much of Samuel is created and how much remembered? Just past midpoint in the novel, Steinbeck breaks in to state, "And Samuel was wise, but I think he knew only one side of Tom." Given his obvious freedom to invent Samuel, why doesn't Steinbeck know everything Samuel knows? Of Uncle Tom, Steinbeck intones, "What I set down about him will be the result of memory plus what I know to be true plus conjecture built on the combination. Who knows whether it will be correct?" And to impress upon us this limited, autobiographical approach to Tom Hamilton, Steinbeck uses the expression, "I remember" or a slight variation of that expression, eleven times in three brief paragraphs as he begins to tell us about Tom. Similarly, of Dessie's tragedy, Steinbeck writes, "I do not know any details of her love affair. . . . All I know is. . . ."

Steinbeck is obviously deciding when and where to disguise his fiction-making within the hidey-hole of autobiography, a great freedom which his presence in the novel, and the presence of the Hamilton narrative, allows him. However, in the character of Samuel, Steinbeck is, more importantly, demonstrating the way in which fiction grows out of the real. What happens to Samuel is that he is contaminated by the fictional Trask narrative and its demands in a way the other Hamiltons are not. And Steinbeck, by repeatedly entering the novel to remind us of the creative process, attempts to ensure that we see this process taking place. We are allowed behind the curtain of the author's workshop to watch Samuel's transformation.

Just before he introduces Samuel to Adam Trask, Steinbeck begins his chapter with a sermon on the freedom essential to the creative mind: "And this I believe: that the free, exploring mind of the individual human is the most valuable thing in the world. And this I would fight for: the freedom of the mind to take any direction it wishes, undirected." Here, Steinbeck may be anticipating the new direction the character of Samuel will take as the author's "free, exploring mind" explores the conflict between good and evil, between self-imposed blindness and the human need to attain full knowledge. Very quickly, Samuel will spin out of his Hamilton orbit and into that of the Trasks and, with this declaration, Steinbeck may well be preparing the reader for this new creative freedom.

Throughout the novel, Steinbeck breaks into his narrative to remind us of his authorial presence, addressing his reader directly, as when he writes, "You can see how this book has reached a great boundary that was called 1900"; or ruminating upon those beliefs he holds most dear; or mimicking the collective voice of the nation; or even analyzing his characters and then coming back to qualify and contradict himself. To introduce Horace Quinn's role in the Trask narrative, for example, Steinbeck enters the story, saying, "We could not imagine anyone else being sheriff," and later, as Cal prepares to take Abra on their important picnic, Steinbeck adds, "We knew—or at least we were confident—that on May Day, when all the Sunday School picnics took place in Alisal, the wild azaleas that grew in the skirts of the streams would be in bloom." By this point, near the end of the novel, autobiography and fictional narrative have merged completely, with the authorial voice joining the authorial constructs as a participant—a character—within the fiction.

A consideration of ***East of Eden*** as a self-conscious fiction may also allow us to come to terms with one of the major problems often cited by critics: Cathy Ames Trask. Is Cathy the C.A.T. a genetically misshapen monster who simply is predetermined to be evil because of something she lacks? Or is she more psychologically complex than this as her early and late obsessions with the Wonderland Alice seem to suggest? Why, if *timshel* must apply to all of us, does it seem not to apply to Cathy or Adam, or even Charles, who is incapable of feeling sorry? If this novel is designed to mark the end of an era—naturalism with its emphasis upon pessimistic determinism—as John Ditsky has persuasively suggested, why does Steinbeck create absolutists such as Adam and Cathy who seem, for most of the novel, incapable of free will?

An answer may be that in the course of this long novel the implied author—the voice creating the characters and plot—changes, grows, and learns, as Steinbeck suggests in the opening line in ***The Log from the Sea of Cortez*** when he declares that "The design of a book is the pattern of a reality controlled and shaped by the mind of the writer." At first Steinbeck states that Cathy is a monster, declaring simply, "I believe there are monsters born in the world. . . . Later, he qualifies: "It doesn't matter that Cathy was what I have called a monster. . . ." And finally, he writes: "When I said Cathy was a monster it seemed to me that it was so. Now I have bent close with a glass over the small print of her and reread the footnotes, and I wonder if it was true." Steinbeck is reminding us that to create is to learn and, furthermore, with his allusion to the "small print" of his character, reminding us that as readers we, too, are involved in the process of fiction-making, that Cathy has existence only on the page.

Very subtly, in his introduction of Cathy, Steinbeck also illustrates for us the way in which a fictional creation takes form. At the beginning of Chapter Eight, the authorial voice declares its belief that not only are "monsters born in the world" but that "Cathy Ames was born with the tendencies or lack of them, which drove her all her life. . . . She was not like other people." Following the clear statement of the author's conception of his character, we are given a description of that character: "Her nose was delicate and thin, and her cheekbones high and wide, sweeping down to a small chin so that her face was heart-shaped. Her mouth was well shaped and well lipped but abnormally small. . . . Her ears were very little, without lobes, and they pressed so close to her head that even with her hair combed up they made no silhouette. They were thin flaps sealed against her head." Cathy's resemblance to a serpent must be obvious to anyone reading such a description, and to ensure that we don't miss the Satanic suggestion, Steinbeck adds: "Her feet were small and round and stubby, with fat insteps almost like little hoofs." If we pay close attention to the process taking place here, we should become aware that we are being allowed to watch as the character's form rises quite clearly out of the artist's conception of that character. The Cathy we begin to see conforms to the author's idea of Cathy defined for us a few lines earlier. Because at this point in the novel the implied author conceives of Cathy as predetermined to evil, inherently depraved, she takes a snake-like form. Later, Cathy's form will change as the author's conception of her changes.

In ***East of Eden,*** Steinbeck first illustrates the way the sense of opposed absolutes at the heart of the American myth grows out of an intuitive response to environment. Then, he demonstrates the way in which this dualism is manifested in everyday life—the flood-drought cycle, the Fence of Earth-Paradise juxtaposition. Next, he introduces the Hamiltons and bares the autobiographical sources of his fiction: his father's well-drilling, for example. At this point, he brings in the Trask narrative, overlaying the autobiographical narrative with the allegorical fiction. He gradually allows Samuel to be drawn into the fiction, leaving the remaining Hamiltons firmly fixed in the realm of autobiography. Samuel becomes, thus, the highly charged point of contact between autobiography and fiction, a role most appropriate to the eloquent artificer and teller of tales at his forge. In this role, Samuel becomes a proto-Daedalus, from whom John Steinbeck, the artificer of this amazing novel, will descend.

And finally Steinbeck, or the implied author called John Steinbeck, enters the novel as not simply the "recording consciousness" of such an earlier work as ***In Dubious Battle,*** but as interpreter and creator, one who creates the "reality" of the novel as he records it, learning as he records and changing as he learns. As he comes to know more about the idea called Cathy/Kate, his feelings change. He qualifies and contradicts his earlier self. The disclosure process of conventional novels is altered so that the novel discloses itself to the author as well as reader in the process of its creation. What the reader, what America itself, must learn in the course of this novel is what the author learns: a belief in absolutes, an Ahabian monomania, is dangerously delusive; the pursuit of Eden leads to the destruction of whatever earthly paradise may be possible. The author, too, must learn the necessity for balance, the danger of staring too long into the fire. Steinbeck's method resembles that described by Austin Wright as the creation of a "narrator-controlled world," one in which "the autonomy of the fictional world breaks down the inventive/narrative distinction: in effect, the inventor's manipulations have become the teller's, implicitly seeming to reflect the latter's creative, expressive, or rhetorical needs."

Of this novel, written at the height of his career, Steinbeck declared, "This is my most complicated and at the same time, my most simple sounding book." And he added, "Jesus am I going to catch critical hell for it. My carefully worked out method will be jumped on by the not too careful critic as slipshod. For it is not an easy form to come on quickly nor to understand immediately." Finally, Steinbeck lamented in frustration, "I don't know why writers are never given credit for knowing their craft." Given the general failure of early reviewers to comprehend the carefully worked out methods of such simple-seeming works as ***The Pastures of Heaven, To a God Unknown, Tortilla Flat,*** and ***Cannery Row,*** Steinbeck's frustration is more than understandable.

In 1979, in his book *Fabulation and Metafiction,* Robert Scholes made this surprising observation concerning John Steinbeck: "For the last decade of his life, one of America's finest writers in the realistic/naturalistic tradition was engaged in a serious artistic struggle through which he sought to come to terms with fabulation." Scholes is speaking here specifically of ***The Acts of King Arthur and His Noble Knights,*** but Scholes goes on to ponder, "What moved Steinbeck toward fabulation? What but the same impulse that was moving younger writers in the same direction—the sense that the positivistic basis for traditional realism had been eroded, and that reality, if it could be caught at all, would require a whole new set of fictional skills."

East of Eden, long viewed as problematic, may well stand as sharp evidence of both Steinbeck's dissatisfaction with the tradition Scholes names and Steinbeck's desire to experiment and, in so doing, expose a kind of metaphysics of fiction-making. Like many of Steinbeck's works, ***East of Eden*** may be a much more subtle and complex construction than we are at first prepared to believe, one deserving of more careful scrutiny than we have yet brought to bear.

M. R. Satyanarayana (essay date 1989)

SOURCE: "'And Then the Child Becomes a Man': Three Initiation Stories of John Steinbeck," in *John Steinbeck: A Study of the Short Fiction,* edited by R. S. Hughes, Twayne, 1989, pp. 181-8.

[In the following essay, Satyanarayana examines the theme of initiation in "The Raid," The Red Pony, *and "Flight."]*

In his introduction to *John Steinbeck* (1965) Joseph Fontenrose observes: "Myth has been a more consistent factor, profoundly affecting the form and content of all his (Steinbeck's) novels since 1929. In most of them we see a palimpsest upon which Steinbeck has inscribed a realistic tale of contemporary men." Yet, in his actual interpretation of the works, Fontenrose makes no reference to the use of myth in three stories from ***The Long Valley:* "The Raid,"** ***The Red Pony*** cycle and **"Flight."** He considers only ***The Red Pony*** as a story of initiation in which the hero passes from "naive childhood to the threshold of adulthood through knowledge of birth, old age, and death, gained through experience with horses." As a matter of fact all the three works are about the growth of boys into men, each different from the others, in its use of myth. **"The Raid"** is an excellent example of a sociological initiation, in which the boy hero is initiated to an altogether new social order. In ***The Red Pony*** the hero's initiation is brought about within the same social order into which he is born, with a view to preserving the traditions cherished by that order. Further, the hero is also introduced to the existential aspects of pain, age, and death. **"Flight"** is somewhat complex as an initiation story. It deals with the improper initiation of the hero leading to tragedy as in the myth of Phaëton; and at the same time it is a story of the hero's magic flight and the mystic return to the origin.

I

The structure of **"The Raid"** falls neatly into four parts: (1) the hero's severance from the mother, (2) the revelation of the mystery of adult experience, (3) the ordeal, and (4) the symbolic death and rebirth. Root, the hero goes through all the well-known rites of passage except the change of name.

The story begins with Dick, the initiator, and Root, the novice, walking away from the well-lit streets to a dark and lonely place where they expect to hold a radical meeting. Severance from the mother has already taken place for the boy, he having been thrown out by the father for his radical views. The boy looks back in regret at his childhood innocence, and is at the same time anxious to experience a new life. This state of confusion, typical of all the novices, is symbolically expressed by an old tune, "Come to me my melancholy baby," which haunts the boy, and try as he might, he is unable to get it out of his head. Passing through the dark streets he observes that "it's a good night to get away if anything happens." The dark night is the mother whose protection the boy seeks. The novice is quickly pulled back to the road by Dick (father-surrogate) who holds out the threat of a denial of the much desired new experience. He warns Root that his party would have nothing to do with cowards.

In the second part we find Dick and Root in a lonely store lit by a small kerosene lamp. They put up the picture of their leader on the wall, along with a certain red symbol on a white background. As they wait for their audience Root becomes more and more nervous. He asks for the time of the night thrice in three quarters of an hour. He keeps on pestering the senior man as to how it would be to face a group of vigilantes. He is scared of them and the cops, having heard of their brutality. Although annoyed and irritated by the boy's questions Dick allays his fears by kind words. With the picture of the leader presiding over the ceremony, the initiator passes on the magic formula (the *mantra*) to the novice, a formula he himself had been taught in similar circumstances: "The men of little spirit must have an example of stead—stead-fastness. The people at large must have an example of injustice." And therefore no sacrifice is too much and the initiate must remember that "If some one busts you, it isn't him that's doing it, it's the System. And it isn't you he's busting. He's taking a crack at the Principle." This initiatory ceremony is observed on the lines followed by secret societies like the Free Masons.

The tension caused by anxiety and suspense is itself an ordeal. But the real test for the initiate is physical torture which includes bleeding also. Just as the male adults of the Australian tribes surround the initiate and beat him up, Root is buffeted by the vigilantes when they raid the place. As he begins the prepared text of his speech he is knocked down by a blow on the side of the head. When he struggles to his feet, "his split ear spill[ing] a red stream down his neck," he is no longer a boy. "His breath burst passionately. His hands were steady now, his voice sure and strong. His eyes were hot with an ecstasy." As he goes down again under a wave of violence he cries, "You don't know what you're doing."

When Root falls unconscious he goes through the last phase of the initiatory rites, symbolic death, from which he emerges a new being. The last words of the boy before he falls down unconscious, add a new dimension to the story. His death and rebirth become a re-enactment of Christ's death and resurrection. Later, in the hospital, Root recalls how he felt like saying those words of Christ to his killers. Written in 1934, **"The Raid"** reveals Steinbeck's interest in some of the most devoted radicals he knew. Root is also a symbol of all the good Christians, who in the 1930's looked toward Russia for an answer to the economic questions which the democratic Europe had failed to solve. This same Root, who appears as Jim in ***In Dubious Battle,*** "grows" to become the radical Christ, Jim Casy in ***The Grapes of Wrath.***

II

In ***The Red Pony*** the boy Jody Tiflin is initiated to the chores of an agrarian life on his father's ranch. Here there is no sudden severance from the childhood links for the boy. It is a slow transition from childhood innocence to experience, and the transition takes place without a change of scene. His initiators are his parents and Billy Buck, the ranch hand. And because it is a transitional type of initiation the ordeal is spread over a considerable length of time. Jody's loss of innocence occurs when the shock of realization of death comes upon him. "Perhaps this is the first adulthood of any man or woman," as Steinbeck puts it. "The first tortured question 'why?' and then acceptance, and then the child becomes a man."

In "The Gift," Jody's initiation begins with the gift of a pony by his father. The boy's curiosity is excited. But severe restrictions are laid down to thwart his enthusiasm to ride the pony. He must scrub the pony, polish the saddle, and feed the animal, but he should not ride him yet. In the course of his training under Billy Buck the boy experiences pain and horror, which invariably accompany the rites of passage. When the pony catches a severe cold an operation becomes necessary. To help the animal breathe a hole is drilled in his throat. Jody is made to watch and help in the operation. He keeps a close watch over the ailing pony and witnesses his futile struggle against death. With the death of the pony, Jody is entrusted with greater responsibility. In "The Promise," he is placed in charge of the mare Nellie. He is asked to get her bred, and to take good care of the mare during the gestation period, if the newborn colt is to be his. Once again an operation becomes necessary. To save the colt the mare has to be killed. The boy is made to watch Billy Buck take a hammer and knock down the animal, saw through her belly, and bring out a dripping bundle of a colt. With this ritualistic killing of the mare the novice realises that birth and death are only phases in a continuous process of life.

The horse is the central symbol in ***The Red Pony,*** as in D. H. Lawrence's "St. Mawr." All knowledge of pain, suffering, old age, death, and even the knowledge of sex comes to Jody through the three horses in the story. The proud red pony gives him the first glimpse of death, which is repeated in the death of the mare Nellie. The mating of the mare and the stallion provides a vicarious lesson in sex for the boy. In "The Great Mountains," there is the horse Easter, which had served the master faithfully for years, but is now disliked by the master Tiflin for being old and useless. Tiflin equates the old horse with Gitano, an old paisano, who seeks shelter on the ranch. Tiflin is not impressed by the fact that the paisano was born on the ranch long before he bought it and now wishes to die on the place. He has no feeling for either the old horse or the old man. Luckily for Jody he has, as models, the defence of the old horse by Billy Buck and his mother's sympathy for the paisano. It is through Billy Buck and his mother that Jody gets a proper initiation to the right understanding of other's sorrows. For there is a repetition of the father's rudeness and the compassionate response of Jody's mother and Billy Buck in the fourth section of the story cycle. It is here, in "The Leader of the People," that Jody shows signs of growth. In the teeth of his father's opposition he asks his grandfather to tell stories about "Injuns" (Indians), which he had told a number of times. Tiflin considers his father-in-law a bore. The story ends with the efforts of the boy in consoling the grandfather who has been insulted by his father. It is as though Jody were the grown-up man, and the grandfather a child. (He offers to get a lemonade for the old man). The growth of Jody to adult experience is suggested by a humorous change of his name into Mr. Big Britches.

III

Unlike the initiation of Root and Jody the initiation of Pepé takes place overnight. It is actually a case of improper initiation, and reflects "the pathos of inverted emphasis" in the United States where, as Joseph Campbell observes, "The goal is not to grow old, but to remain young; not to mature away from Mother, but to cleave to her." Although nineteen years old and the father dead, Pepé is not called upon to shoulder the responsibility of the adult male. An early initiation would have been the most natural thing in his case. Instead we find Mama Torres dismissing her son's claim to manhood as that of a "foolish chicken." Yet, it is not as though she is unaware of the need for boys to grow up in time. For she tells her second son (after Pepé rides away for the first time by himself) that "A boy gets to be a man when a man is needed. Remember this thing. I have known boys forty years old." But, in spite of this wisdom she goes on waiting for a need to arise. Initiation rites are meant to prevent precisely this sort of danger, men of forty remaining boys, by preparing the boys to be ready for adult life well in advance. What actually happens is that Pepé finds himself unprepared when the need at last arises.

Pepé rides to town. He has been allowed to use his father's saddle. He carries with him his father's knife, which has always been with him. In Monterey he drinks wine with some people. Some one calls him names and makes a gesture of attack. And Pepé throws the knife at him as unerringly and as thoughtlessly as he had been throwing at a redwood post in a playful manner. The knife "went almost by itself. It flew, it darted before Pepé knew it." Like Phaëthon he is ignorant of the proper use of the weapon (the bridle of Phoebus), and he has to pay for it with his life. Taken by surprise at his own action Pepé rushes back to the protective mother. Mama Torres ruefully realises that the son has attained manhood. She prepares him for his flight into the mountains. With the severance of her son from her imminent, she takes on the role of an initiator for a brief time. She gives Pepé her husband's black coat, and rifle. She gives him food and water. And she gives good advice concerning the dangers on the way and how to surmount them. When at last he rides away she raises a formal death wail: "Our beautiful—our brave, he is gone." With this Pepé completes the rite of severance from the mother, and a symbolic death, and enters upon the next stage of the great ordeal.

So far it has been a story of maturation. With the commencement of the hero's ordeal the story gathers a new dimension. Pepé's ordeal is his flight; and the flight becomes the magic flight of the mythical hero. In his flight (ordeal) Pepé does not encounter the elders of the tribe or a father-surrogate in person. The hurdles he crosses and the physical torture he undergoes are not due to any human agency. (The flight itself is caused by human pursuers, who are not on the scene of action). For three days and nights he flees, gradually losing his hat, horse, the coat, and the rifle. He is incapacitated by hunger, thirst, and a poisonous wound. Finally, he gives up the struggle and stands up to welcome death. In all his ordeals Pepé is alone, without a sympathetic initiator. The initiator, if there is one, is his dead father, represented by his black coat, the hat, the rifle, and the saddle. When all these articles are lost the hero is ready to die. The unseen but ever-present father, then, puts his son to a severe ordeal after the severance from the mother. At the end of the ordeal the son becomes himself the father. There is no return to the normal world for him who achieves an atonement with the father. Having shed all "infantile illusions of 'good' and 'evil'" the hero is purged of hope and fear, and at peace in the understanding of the revelation of being."

Pepé's flight is an inversion of the mythical hero's magic flight. In the latter's flight the hero discards objects which grow in size and delay the pursuers. For instance, a discarded hairbrush grows to be a huge wooded mountain. But here Pepé leaves behind him, quite unintentionally, articles which are of great use. The coat or the hat or the rifle, instead of delaying his pursuers, serve only as clues in the chase. This is so because the hero is not fleeing *from* anything. He is only making "a return to the origin."

Steinbeck's use of the symbolic *regressus ad uterum* lends a third dimension to the story **"Flight."** According to Mercea Elaide the mythical hero is swallowed by a sea monster and re-emerges breaking through the monster's belly; or the hero goes through an "initiatory passage through a *vagina dentata,* or the dangerous descent into a cave or a crevice assimilated to the mouth or the uterus of Mother Earth." Pepé's passage belongs to the latter type. But unlike the adventures of the mythical hero, which are accomplished physically, Pepé adventures are symbolic in the oriental tradition. Pepé descends into narrow dark valleys three times, and when he meets his death, he rolls down the mountain and is covered over by an avalanche of rocks, thus entering the womb of the Mother Earth. Further these initiatory adventures of the spiritual type do not end in the hero becoming, even spiritually, a new being; they end in the searcher becoming one with "the Primordial Great-One," as visualized by the oriental mystics for whom "the goal ceased to be beginning a new life again here below, on earth, and became 'going back' and reconstituting the Primordial Great-One."

I believe there are many ways of looking at this most interesting story. It is possible to see in it the murderer, pursued by his sense of guilt and failing to shake it off, finally welcome death as proper wages for his sin. It is also possible to see in it "the emergence of Man from the primeval darkness."

John H. Timmerman (essay date Autumn 1989)

SOURCE: "The Squatter's Circle in *The Grapes of Wrath,*" in *Studies in American Fiction,* Vol. 17, No. 2, Autumn, 1989, pp. 203-11.

[*In the following essay, Timmerman discusses the function and significance of the squatter's circle as a symbol of patriarchal authority and unity.*]

In John Steinbeck's ***The Grapes of Wrath,*** the indomitable Ma Joad emerges as a hero and the leader of, in her words, "the fambly of man." In so doing, however, she also displaces Pa Joad from his traditional position of authority in the family. While several critical studies have examined those qualities of Ma Joad that direct her leadership—qualities of humor, a steadfast vision, and a resilient ability to bend and adapt to new situations without breaking—Pa Joad has disappeared from critical scrutiny as if of no account. In fact, Steinbeck very carefully directs the reversal of leadership roles through the use of the "squatter's circle" motif.

That the migrant family of the 1930s was strongly patriarchal has been demonstrated by Tom Collins' detailed reports on California migrant camps during the late 1930s. Collins was the manager of the Kern County Migrant Camp and was also Steinbeck's most profitable source of information about migrant traditions. He personally escorted Steinbeck through both the established government camps and the squatters' camps. More importantly, Steinbeck took back with him to Los Gatos hundreds of pages of Collins' reports and assessments of migrant families. These reports figured directly into Steinbeck's composition of his novel.

Collins' weekly reports from Kern County's Arvin Camp, prototype for the Weedpatch Camp in ***The Grapes of Wrath,*** testify that these migrant families, while traditionally patriarchal, were experiencing a revolution of matriarchal uprising. As the men foundered in the bewildering tides of joblessness, indirection, and poverty, the women assumed dominant authority in the family.

One of the most revealing parts of Collins' reports in this matter of family authority appears in his weekly entry entitled "Bits of Migrant Wisdom." Here Collins diverges from his statistical information, his detailed accounts of camp activities, and his necessarily objective analysis to satisfy the governmental bureaucracy, to probe intimately the nature of migrant lives. Frequently such musings and probings focus upon marital relationships. After recounting at some length in his report for June 6, 1936, one protracted and often violent lover's quarrel, Collins observes: "We just let her cry. In fact we encouraged her to cry and bawl to her hearts [sic] content. That's what she wanted to do. Migrant women are that way." But he does not leave the portrait with this traditional depiction of the weakly crying woman. There is tougher stuff in the camp women, and one has an idea that Collins appreciates the woman he quotes two paragraphs further in the story: "A woman neighbor summed the incident thusly; 'She aint ole nuf ter u'stand men folks. She'll larn sum day. What she shuld adun was ter kick him plenty in the fanny, only she wont.'" Collins observes, "we believe she will do that soon." While he portrays the migrant women in their customary matriarchal roles of canning, housekeeping, and sewing, he also senses a tide of revolution sweeping through them.

A second observation of Collins, appearing in his report for June 13, 1936, recounts a specific example of a woman revolting against the patriarchal system:

> Reversing the usual migrant system whereby the man is the master of the house, the bride in this instance rules the roost. She can be heard every evening after the boy's return from work, laying down the law. On one occasion we saw her sitting down giving him orders on proper dish washing and later, instructions regarding sweeping out the tent and doing the family wash. He grunted a lot but went about the task as "ordered."

Collins closes with a terse reflection: "Maybe a new day has dawned for the migrant woman, eh?" If it had, nowhere would it be more evident than in Ma Joad's reversal of the patriarchal role in the family.

In ***The Grapes of Wrath,*** Ma Joad rises as the force that unifies and directs the disintegrating family. In order to do so, however, on several occasions she stands up to and eventually displaces Pa from his family role. The first such incident occurs on the road to California, when Ma brandishes a jack handle and orders Pa to keep the family together. Tom Joad has offered to lay over with Al to repair the blown connecting rod on the Wilson car, while the others travel ahead. Ma's rebellion is forthright and undeniable:

> And now Ma's mouth set hard. She said softly, "On'y way you gonna get me to go is whup me." She moved the jack handle gently again. "An' I'll shame you, Pa. I won't take no whuppin', cryin' an' a-beggin'. I'll light into you. An' you ain't so sure you can whup me anyways."

Repeatedly, she defies and threatens Pa, and he finds himself bewildered in the face of her assertion of authority. Tom Joad wonders, "Ma, what's eatin' on you? What ya wanna do this-a-way for? What's the matter'th you anyways? You gone johnrabbit on us?" To which Ma replies with the first annunciation of her vision of the primacy of the family: "Ma's face softened, but her eyes were still fierce. 'You done this 'thout thinkin' much,' Ma said. 'What we got lef' in the worl'? Nothin' but us. Nothin' but the folks.'" The effect is undeniable: "The eyes of the whole family shifted back to Ma. She was the power. She had taken control."

Certainly there is steely resolve in this woman's spine. When the family camps along the Colorado River, and Granma lies hallucinating in the unbearable heat of the tent, Ma has her care of Granma interrupted by a pompous law officer who tries to threaten her. Ma stands up to him, brandishing her skillet like a war club. When Ma recounts the scene to Tom, he responds, "'Fust you stan' us off with a jack handle, and now you try to hit a cop.' He laughed softly, and he reached out and patted her bare foot tenderly. 'A ol' hell-cat,' he said." Truly Ma can be "a ol' hell-cat." Once before she lit into a tin peddler with a live chicken, beating the peddler until "they wasn't nothing but a pair a legs in her han." Ma's standing up to Pa Joad, however, is not a fit of pique, nor a momentary explosion of temper; rather, it is a standing up for a vision and a dream of her family.

This struggle for the family becomes clear in the second major episode of Ma's assertion of authority. Having enjoyed the comforts of the Weedpatch Camp for some time, having been solaced in the compassion of its members so that, in Ma's words, "I feel like people again." Ma nonetheless insists that the family move on. The family is disintegrating through lack of challenge and work; its dependency, in her view, breeds a slovenliness of spirit. Ma's order is terse and to the point: "We'll go in the mornin'." Pa remonstrates: "'Seems like times is changed,' he said sarcastically. 'Time was when a man said what we'd do. Seems like women is tellin' now. Seems like it's purty near time to get out a stick.'" But his comments are no more effective against Ma's steely will than they were earlier. When Pa and Uncle John wander off, Tom remains to question Ma: "You jus' a-treadin' him on?" Work, Ma believes, absolves worry. Pa has had too much time to ponder; insufficient opportunity to provide: "Take a man, he can get worried an' worried, an' it eats out his liver, an' purty soon he'll jus' lay down and die with his heart et out. But if you can take an' make 'im mad, why, he'll be awright."

A third time Ma Joad asserts her dominance over the family. After Tom strikes one of the landowners' goons and has to go into hiding, Ma again makes the decision to go. This time Pa readily accedes: "Come on now. Le's get out to her. Kids, you come he'p. Ma's right. We got to go outa here." He capitulates to her authority, but not until his own authority has been hopelessly battered. In fact, the Joad family has no reasonable place to go; all order seems destroyed.

Huddled in a boxcar, afflicted by the deluge of winter rains, Pa reflects: "Funny! Woman takin' over the fambly. Woman sayin' we'll do this here, an' we'll go there. An' I don' even care." Pa himself recognizes the transference of authority, and in response to this recognition Ma delivers her eloquent and compassionate eulogy to the power of the woman: "'Woman can change better'n a man,' Ma said soothingly. 'Woman got all her life in her arms. Man got it all in his head. Don' you mind. Maybe—well, maybe nex' year we can get a place.'" She adds, "man, he lives in jerks—baby born an' a man dies, an' that's a jerk—gets a farm an' loses his farm, an' that's a jerk. Woman, it's all one flow, like a stream, little eddies, little waterfalls, but the river, it goes right on. Woman looks at it like that." At this final, bleak scene, a thoroughly defeated Pa, like a bewildered child, seeks the restorative comfort of Ma Joad, whose spirit flows like the river.

That moving description of man and woman by Ma Joad, however, also underlies the displacement of authority in the novel from thinking man to spiritual woman, from a rational life jerked apart to a life led by the heart that bends and flows like the river. To demonstrate this, Steinbeck parallels Ma's rise to authority with Pa's displacement from, and the destruction of, the squatter's circle. In the novel Steinbeck depicts the traditional physical posture for decision-making among the male leaders of the family as squatting on the haunches in a circle. It represents a high formality among the migrant men and functions in the novel as a testament to rational order and male authority.

In his typical pattern of introducing an event or condition in its broadest scope in the intercalary chapters and then focusing upon the microcosmic unit of the Joad family in the narrative chapters, so too Steinbeck introduces the traditional posture of the squatter's circle in Chapter 5, an overview of the dispossession of the migrant families. As the landowner's spokesmen come to evict the tenant farmers, "the tenant men stood beside the cars for a while, and then squatted on their hams and found sticks with which to mark the dust." The farmers band together in the face of adversity, drawing upon each other's strength to plot a course of action. When the owners drive away, the men are left to consider matters on their own. Steinbeck provides the first carefully ordered description of the squatter's circle according to the male hierarchy in the tenant family:

> The tenant men squatted down on their hams again to mark the dust with a stick, to figure, to wonder. Their sun-burned faces were dark, and their sun-whipped eyes were light. The women moved cautiously out of the doorways toward their men, and the children crept behind the women, cautiously, ready to run. The bigger boys squatted beside their fathers, because that made them men. After a time the women asked, What did he want?

In this instance, all their pondering and figuring prove ineffective, as the monstrous roar of Joe Davis' son's tractor drones over the land, destroying the homes, despoiling the family's hope. From the start of the novel, the male authority structure is threatened.

While the intercalary chapters introduce the large, universal, macrocosmic scenes, the narrative chapters place the particular instance of the Joads within that pattern. A more detailed rendition of the squatter's circle is delivered in Chapter 10 as the Joad family prepares to leave Oklahoma. Here each male member assumes his hierarchical position in the squatter's circle, the women and children rimmed around its edges:

> Pa walked around the truck, looking at it, and then he squatted down in the dust and found a stick to draw with. One foot was flat to the ground, the other rested on the ball and slightly back, so that one knee was higher than the other. Left forearm rested on the lower, left, knee; the right elbow on the right knee, and the right fist cupped for the chin. Pa squatted there, looking at the truck, his chin in his cupped fist. And Uncle John moved towards him and squatted down beside him.

Grampa Joad comes out of the house and, too old to bend physically to the squatter's circle, takes his seat of preeminent authority on the running board of the old truck. That, Steinbeck writes, "was the nucleus," the three male heads of the family. But Tom and Connie and Noah "strolled in and squatted, and the line was a half-circle with Grampa in the opening." After them, Ma, Granma, and the children come: "They took their places behind the squatting men;

they stood up and put their hands on their hips." It is a careful order in a careful ritual, this pattern of the dominance of male authority. As the only non-family member, Jim Casy has the good sense to stay off to the side; only after the decision is made to include him on the journey may he come over and squat on the sidelines, a member of the male ruling hierarchy but still an outsider.

The squatter's circle represents several things in ***The Grapes of Wrath.*** First, the circle represents the hierarchy of male authority in the family. The men are ranged from the ruling eldest to the youngest or newest members; women and children are excluded from it as bystanders who only await the decisions. Second, it represents order, both a physical order in which the combined strength of the males unifies against the world, and a rational order in which decisions affecting the family may be discussed and decided. Third, it represents a chain of human unity; the members, within the hierarchy of authority, are one body. Within the circle there may be discussion and dissension, but when a decision is made the body is of one mind.

The squatter's circle is an emblem of unity, a physical testament to the preservation of old ways and the freedom to make choices. In his journalistic reports on the migrants, written for the *San Francisco News,* Steinbeck assessed this unique spirit of the migrants: "They are men who have worked hard on their own farms and have felt the pride of possessing and living in close touch with the land. They are resourceful and intelligent Americans who have gone through the hell of the drought, have seen their lands wither and die and the top soil blow away; and this, to a man who has owned his land, is a curious and terrible pain." Despite their travail and oppression, Steinbeck asserts that "they have weathered the thing, and they can weather much more for their blood is strong." Elsewhere in his journalistic entries, Steinbeck discourses on the most devastating blow to the migrants: the loss of dignity. The disruption of the squatter's circle in ***The Grapes of Wrath*** is also a dissolving of the fragile fabric of human dignity; as the circle breaks down, so too do the independence, freedom, and dignity of the migrants.

All levels of significance for the squatter's circle are severely tested in the drama of the story. The dissolution of the Joad family's squatter's circle lies in direct correlation to Ma Joad's assumption of authority. When the Wilson car breaks down and Tom proposes his idea of laying over to repair it while the others go ahead, Pa and Uncle John automatically drop to their hams in a makeshift squatter's circle to discuss it. This time, however, Ma Joad makes her defiant gesture of threatening Pa with the jack handle, thereby disrupting the circle.

The raw conditions of the long journey and the rough introduction to California also serve to break up the circle. At the first California camp, Tom and Al help Floyd repair his car. About them men are squatting in small circles, driven to the solace of the unit as they try to figure out the woeful working conditions. When a man drives up to contract workers, all the squatting groups move up and gather around him. The squatter's circles disrupt under the authority of the landowner, but the men also coalesce as a larger unit than that of the family. Floyd tries to galvanize the separate units of men into one unit, encouraging them to stand with one circle against the contractor.

In the larger artistic pattern of the novel, Steinbeck has anticipated this scene in intercalary Chapter 14, Here, too, men squat around, lamenting their common loss, trying to determine what action to take. The scene parallels the action of the California camp:

> And in the night one family camps in a ditch and another family pulls in and the tents come out. The two men squat on their hams and the women and children listen. Here is the node, you who hate change and fear revolution. Keep these two squatting men apart; make them hate, fear, suspect each other. Here is the anlage of the thing you fear. This is the zygote. For here "I lost my land" is changed; a cell is split and from its splitting brews the thing you hate—"We lost *our* land." The danger is here, for two men are not as lonely and perplexed as one.

In the California camp, Floyd's voice is the echo of this. And indeed this is the thing the landowners hate. They fight back with the indictment "he's talkin' red, agitating trouble." Under this banner they are free to disperse any group of men, disrupt any unit, abort any zygote. In the California camp, the collection of men remains simply that: a collection. No cohesive unity cements their spirits together. The disruption in the Joad family is poignantly encapsulated in one sharp portrait where Ma fries potatoes over a hissing fire and "Pa sat nearby hugging his knees," almost as if Pa, in a degraded stance of the squatter's posture, clings futilely to a position now much diminished.

Just as the later stay at the Weedpatch Camp is restorative to the Joad family spirit, so too it restores the dignity of the menfolk, particularly when they do unify here against the threat of outside aggression. Not surprisingly, the squatter's circles appear frequently in the narration as old routines are restored for a time. Yet, none of the men can escape the reality of joblessness. As if to turn their shoulders in protection against the fear, the men huddle frequently in the squatter's circle. At one point, the men squat by the porch of the manager's office. Pa opens the speculation on work, and the frightening reality of no work to be had. The mood of the circle changes; these men are res-tive, nervous. The strength of the circle has dissipated. Steinbeck repeats a grim refrain: "The squatting men moved nervously"; "The circle of men shifted their feet nervously." The squatter's circle is no longer a hierarchical arrangement of authority, vision, and, unity; it is a nervous assembly of men huddling in fear.

On the evening of the Joads' departure, the men fall back into the routine of the circle: "The evening dark came down and Pa and Uncle John squatted with the heads of families out by the office. They studied the night and the future." The future they see is grim indeed: the squatter's circle is a communion in despair. Only Ma's steely will drives them on. She makes the decisions. She instills order. She possesses the hope for the future. The family moves once again.

As the cold rains inundate the California valley, Pa and a body of men, unnamed and disorganized now that the family order has been ruptured, band together in a battle against the floods. The people's spiritual enervation and the depletion of male authority have already been established in intercalary Chapter 29. There Steinbeck establishes an overview of the dismal rains scouring California's valleys and depicts the men, weak and dejected, before the onslaught: "On the fields the water stood, reflecting the gray sky, and the land whispered with moving water. And the men came out of the barns, out of the sheds. They squatted on their hams and looked out over the flooded land. And they were silent. And sometimes they talked very quietly." The silence of the men is profound; here there is no purpose, no decision to be made, no work to go to. Only the vast desolation of the rain speaks.

This overview focuses in Chapter 30 upon Pa and a ragged band of migrants in their individual battle against the flood. That final warfare of male strength is paralleled neatly by the turbulent events of Rose of Sharon's birth and ultimately paves the way for her ascendancy to a position of authority as she changes from a naive, egocentric young girl to one who mysteriously rises to share Ma Joad's vision of the family of man. That ascendancy happens only with the thorough dissolution of Pa's preeminence in the squatter's circle.

After slogging in the mud all night, bending his physical strength with a rag-tag band of warriors against the onslaught of the flood, Pa staggers into the boxcar where Rose of Sharon has just given birth. In one explosive passage, Steinbeck clenches the transference of authority: "Pa walked slowly to Rose of Sharon's matters. He tried to squat down, but his legs were too tired. He knelt instead." Pa tries, terribly hard, to adopt the squatter's pose, his old position of authority and order, before Ma and Rose of Sharon, but he cannot. Weariness staggers him and he falls to his knees *before* them. From a position of authority he falls to a position of abnegation and supplication. He bends now before the authority of Ma. And Ma offers him the solace of her compassion: "Ma looked at him strangely. Her white lips smiled in a dreaming compassion. 'Don't take no blame. Hush! It'll be awright. They's changes—all over.'"

That transference also signals the victorious thematic closure to the novel, for Ma once more goads the family to action. She directs, gives orders. When the battered family enters the barn, Ma commands the men to get out. But there is no commanding of Rose of Sharon; there is only the mystical passing of authority based upon human giving, the needy giving all they have to the needy. Ma and Rose of Sharon look deeply into each other, and Rose of Sharon murmurs, "Yes." It is more than assent to Ma's will and authority. She ascends to this new order, not of protecting the one family, as in the male-ordered squatter's circle, but of giving to others in the "fambly of man."

Rose of Sharon does not squat. Hers is not the posture of authority and order as in the squatter's circle. Bearing one of the names of Jesus from the Canticles (2:1), she enacts the Christ-like posture of laying down her life for another. The Rose of Sharon of the Canticles is described as having "breasts . . . like clusters of the vine," and here she gives the new wine, not the grapes of wrath, but the wine of human compassion and nurture to the starved father next to her. Once, perhaps, he too held his place of authority in the squatter's circle. And just as Pa Joad kneels before Ma's benediction of compassion, this man too is nurtured by the one who bends down beside him.

The pattern of displacement in ***The Grapes of Wrath*** is from the male-dominated squatter's circle of hierarchical authority to Ma Joad's vision of caring for the "fambly of man" and Rose of Sharon's physical enactment of it. That pattern also undergirds the thematic heart of the novel. In his reports for the *San Francisco News,* Steinbeck observed that "a man herded about, surrounded by armed guards, starved and forced to live in filth loses his dignity; that is, he loses his valid position in regard to society, and consequently his whole ethics toward society." In ***The Grapes of Wrath,*** the migrant male does indeed lose his position, but not his ethics, for those ethics are nurtured by the ascension to authority of Ma Joad and her ethical vision of the family of man.

David Cassuto (essay date Winter 1993)

SOURCE: "Turning Wine into Water: Water as Privileged Signifier in *The Grapes of Wrath,*" in *Papers on Language and Literature,* Vol. 29, No. 1, Winter, 1993, pp. 67-95.

[In the following essay, Cassuto examines the symbolic and socioeconomic significance of water as a scarce resource and commodity in The Grapes of Wrath, *particularly in relation to the history of agriculture in the American West.]*

> Eastward I go only by force; but westward I go free.
>
> —Henry David Thoreau

The Old Testament describes wilderness as "a thirsty ground where there was no water." When the Lord wished to punish, He threatened to "turn the rivers into islands and dry up the pools and . . . command the clouds that they rain no rain upon it." When granting redemption in Isaiah, God promises instead that "waters shall break forth in the wilderness and streams in the desert" and that "the desert and dry land shall be glad" (Deut 8:7, 15; Isaiah 5:6, 35:1, 6, 43:20). The Garden of Eden provided the antithesis of desert wilderness, a place where water flowed freely and bounty of all sorts lay ready to spring out of the ground. This is the legacy which spawned what Henry Nash Smith termed the "myth of the garden" in the American West. At the dawn of the common era, John offered Jesus his baptism in the River Jordan. Two millennia later, Casy baptized Tom Joad in an irrigation ditch.

I will argue that ***The Grapes of Wrath*** represents an indictment of the American myth of the garden and its accompanying myth of the frontier. The lever with which Steinbeck pries apart and ultimately dismantles these fictions is a critique of the agricultural practices that created the Dust Bowl and then metamorphosed into a new set of norms which continued to victimize both the land and its inhabitants. Both nineteenth-century homesteading (based on the Homestead Act of 1862) and agribusiness, its twentieth century descendant (born from the failure of the Homestead Act), relied on the (mis)use of water to accomplish their respective goals. And both policies resulted in ecological disaster.

The Plains were called upon to supply grain for the international war effort in 1914 and to feed a hungry nation whose population continued to multiply exponentially. Throughout the nation, industrialization held sway as the isolationism of the nineteenth century gave way to the globalism of the twentieth. These transitions required great expenditures of resources and, in the grain belt, the resource most in demand was water. As farmers poured their short-term profits back into land and seed, their fates became ever more dependent on the availability of water. When the climatic pendulum swung back toward aridity, Plains farmers had to declare hydrological bankruptcy, though neither they nor the federal government would abandon the myth of the garden. As the government scrambled to dam rivers and force water into the desert, farmers clung fast to their vision of uncountable abundance amidst a green world.

Water was a commodity, symbol of wealth and expanding capabilities. Admitting its unattainability involved acknowledging the limited productive capabilities of the land. Such an admission also meant conceding the limitations of the nation and its people, a prospect that remained anathema to a culture steeped in the dominant myths. Myra Jehlen notes that "the conviction that farming brought reason and nature together (since man and nature had the same reasons) inspired cultivation . . . but made it particularly difficult, in fact, contradictory to contemplate basic changes in agrarian policy." Instead of abandoning the American Dream, the dream itself underwent an ideological shift. The myth of the garden remained intact but its form evolved from an Edenic Xanadu to a neo-Baconian Atlantis which no longer awaited manna from heaven but wrested it instead from the grips of Nature.

Water's primacy as both commodity and signifier in the Southwest arose through a combination of its scarcity and utility. Its privileged place in the biotic schema predates its commodification by the state and corporate apparatus, but the two forces are by now inseparable in the history and mythology of the American West. The social and environmental conditions in the Southwest made water an ideal unit of exchange and this led to its concurrent fetishization. As Gregory Jay characterizes commodity fetishism, "Capitalism structures symbolic exchange so as to elicit desire, manipulate its character, and teach it to find sublimity in prescribed objects." Since water is necessary to a number of human biological functions, in an arid region a dominant state apparatus would need to expend relatively little effort to transform water into a commodity whose scarcity would privilege it as well as its controllers. Once established as a commodity, any item of exchange value acquires symbolic value, connoting power and wealth and thereby enhancing the prestige of its possessor. In this sense, water becomes not just a measure of economic value, but a culturally powerful symbol as well.

The class stratification depicted in ***The Grapes of Wrath*** arose from corporate control over the region's most precious resource. However, the region's aridity made water an *absent* signifier. Both in the novel and in the desert itself, water's conspicuous absence is what makes it so powerful. The flooding that climaxes the novel is thematically situated to provide maximum counterpoint to the drought which originally forced the Joads to migrate west. Disenfranchised and dehumanized, the Joads can only curse the rising floodwaters even as they once prayed for a deluge to feed their parched crops. The cycle of alienation appears complete; people whose humanity was once integrally tied to the land and the weather now care nothing for the growing season or the health of the earth. Their survival has come to depend on shelter from the elements rather than the elements themselves. They have become components of the factory-farming process, economically distant from their bourgeois oppressors but closely tied to the industrial ethos which rewards the subjugation of nature. The primary difference between the growers and the migrants now lies in their respective relationships with the privileged signifier. The growers—owners of the irrigation channels, centrifugal pumps, and watertight mansions, control it—while the Okies, starving and drenched, are at its mercy.

In ***The Grapes of Wrath,*** Steinbeck presents an archetypal Plains family caught in the modernization of the American dream. Forced to adapt to the realities of a closed frontier and a desert in the country's midsection, Americans retrofit their dominant myths to encompass corporate capitalism and, in so doing, accepted water's scarcity and preeminence as commodity in the western region. This shift in ideology completed the antiquation of the Joads' way of life. Ecological realities had long ago proven their lifestyle quixotic, but it took the formidable alliance of the Dust Bowl and corporate agribusiness to dislodge the Okies from their land and homes. Later in his life, Steinbeck returned to criticize the America-as-Eden myth by writing ***East of Eden,*** a novel whose very title suggests alienation from paradise. It is in ***The Grapes of Wrath,*** however, that he is most concerned with the hydrological causes for that estrangement.

Steinbeck acknowledges water's primacy in the West by documenting the social ramifications of the ideology which permits its monopolization and waste. At the same time, his abiding affection for the yeoman agricultural ideal forms a strong undercurrent throughout the novel. Donald Worster feels that this nostalgia comes at the expense of a coherent critique of the water-based oligarchy primarily responsible for the ecological demise of the Southwest and its accompanying human suffering. While Worster's criticism has substantial merit, it fails to address the symbolic power attached to water that pervades the novel. From the drought in Oklahoma to Noah's refusal to leave the river in Arizona to the raging floodwaters that climax the text, Steinbeck weaves water into the novel's structure as well as virtually every thematically significant event.

This tendency to privilege water, either by absence or surfeit, appears frequently in the Steinbeck canon. For example, ***Of Mice and Men*** opens and closes on the banks of a river; ***The Log From the Sea of Cortez,*** with its fascination with tide pools, offers the clearest presentation of Steinbeck's eco-philosophy; and ***The Wayward Bus,*** like ***The Grapes of Wrath,*** utilizes floodwaters in the desert to spur its characters to action and the acquisition of wisdom. That in ***The Grapes of Wrath*** Steinbeck chose to stress his affection for the yeoman tradition rather than explicitly condemn modern hydraulic society does not detract from the book's acknowledged success in subverting that same hydraulic apparatus. The reactions of the state and federal governments to the book's publication as well as that of the oligarchy-controlled media clearly demonstrate the novel's effectiveness. Vehement condemnations of the book and its author followed shortly after its publication in 1939 and continued for years afterward. That the most vociferous denunciations came from the water-barons and their political allies demonstrates that, contrary to Worster's contention, Steinbeck did indeed understand the politics of water-use and that his novel attacked it successfully.

I

Water's dominance in the cultural and agricultural hierarchy of the arid region is neither new nor surprising. Not just in the Hebrew Bible but throughout history, the habitability of any region has traditionally been determined by the availability and accessibility of its water. The Spanish explorers who first traversed the Southwest deemed it an inhospitable wasteland, unfit for human settlement except by those savages already content to scrape an existence from the unforgiving rock. American trailblazers including Lewis and Clark and Zebulon Pike held little hope that the arid region could sustain American settlements. Such criticism, however, quickly disappeared in the storm of patriotism that surged through the new United States. Parallel visions of world dominance and transcendental bonding with nature created a unique blend of ideologies which sought to simultaneously sustain an extractive economy and an unspoiled, untrammeled frontier. Not till near the turn of the twentieth century did the inexorable collision of these visions loom close enough to draw the notice of the nation's policymakers. The resulting tension between ecosystemic requirements and the modes of production caused a "transformation in consciousness and legitimating worldviews," a phenomenon Carolyn Merchant has termed an "ecological revolution."

Settling a "virgin land" offered Americans the chance to reincarnate themselves in a world whose history had no relevance to their inherited Eurocentric worldviews. This rugged new continent, rather than representing a continuation of European cultural hegemony, offered a singular destiny for those brave enough to seize it. Without an acknowledged history, America offered a new beginning wherein land and settler could merge into a single corporate entity and recover, through diligence, husbandry, and mettle, the lost paradise of Eden. Myra Jehlen argues that this vision reified the American tendency to merge selfhood into a collective national ideal while preserving a uniqueness defined by one's own relationship to the land:

> The American incarnation fused continent and civilization, nation and citizen, man and nature to constitute a universe where oppositions amounted to different versions each of which was the other's cathartic, so that their difference was itself transmuted into "necessary" means to the emergence of the single and unchanging truth.

For nineteenth-century settlers in the Southwest, that truth lay in the juxtaposition of aridity with the Jeffersonian yeoman ideal. The synthesis of these two poles created the "truth" of the yeoman Plains farmer.

American history shows that people traditionally migrated to the Plains during periods of high rainfall. When the rains subsided to typical levels, people retreated or pressed on. But by the 1920s, the frontier was closed and Americans had bought solidly into the notion that technology and God would see to it that the Great Plains became the agricultural capital of the world. Unable to accept that meeting the grain demands of a global market economy in a region where annual rainfall fluctuated between seven and twenty inches made little ecological sense, Dust Bowl residents lashed out at the weather, believing it caused their woes. There was not enough water, they complained; the weather had failed them. Such an argument is analogous to blaming the mint for not making people enough money. I do not mean to belittle the very real human tragedy of the Dust Bowl nor to deny the nobility of many of those who suffered through it. Nevertheless, the Dust Bowl's ecosystemic catastrophe was both avoidable and remediable except that neither option was palatable to the region's residents. Worster describes the typical Plains farmer's position as follows:

> . . . [F]ail to anticipate drought, underestimate its duration when it comes, expect rain momentarily, deny that they are as hard hit as outsiders believe . . . admit that some help would be useful, demand that the government act and act quickly . . . without strings . . . pooh-pooh the need for major reform . . . eagerly await the return of "normalcy" . . . But whenever the New Deal tried to become new and innovative, plainsmen turned hostile. The fate of the plains lay in the hands of Providence, and Providence, not Washington, would see them come out all right.

It is precisely this sort of stubborn adherence to traditional values while implementing ecologically pernicious agricultural methods which brought on the "dirty thirties."

The Joads' saga offers a fictional version of the consequences of this myth of the garden and the accompanying myth of the American Frontier. Both were driven by a perceived superabundance of resources, a national fantasy that prodded the Joads towards Oklahoma and then later to California. Belief in an infinite national trust fueled the American dream of individual wealth and world dominance amidst a rugged land which would never cease testing all those attempting to wrest an existence from it. West of the 99th meridian, water's scarcity threatened to undermine this popular vision of America as a limitless Edenic paradise. Rather than permit a subversion of the prevailing value system, Americans bought heavily into a myth of hydro-abundance promulgated by Western ideologues such as William Gilpin. Gilpin and his followers' insistence that "rain follows the plow" and boasts that the West contained infinite supplies of minerals and timber convinced people like Grampa and Gramma Joad to move west, settle in the arid region, and take up the yeoman agricultural ideal first written into American mythology by Thomas Jefferson.

Jefferson, however, lived in Virginia. His philosophy stemmed from his unquestioned intimacy with farming practices in the humid region, yet he was profoundly ignorant of agricultural techniques west of the Mississippi. A century later, John Wesley Powell labored for close to thirty years to bring American western land use policies closer to terrestrial and hydrological realities. Only after Powell's death in 1902 did the regional and federal governments begin acknowledging that agricultural practices in the arid lands required severe retooling. By then, however, powerful corporate interests already dominated the region's economy. The conflict between misguided government policies, yeoman land-use ideals, and geographical realities had expanded to include the profit-centered machinations of agribusiness concerns.

Early in the novel, Steinbeck establishes the fundamental conflict between the yeoman farmer and the land and then diagrams the imperialist maneuverings of corporate agribusiness:

> Grampa took up the land, and he had to kill the Indians and drive them away. And Pa was born here, and he killed weeds and snakes. Then a bad year came and he had to borrow a little money. An' we was born here
>
> . . . our children born here. And Pa had to borrow money. The bank owned the land then. . . . Sure cried the tenant men, but it's our land. We measured it and broke it up. We were even born on it, and we got killed on it, died on it. Even if it's no good, it's still ours. . . . That makes ownership, not a paper with numbers on it.

The above passage reveals several of the guiding principles governing life in the Plains. First, the term "bad year" refers to inadequate rainfall and an accompanying water shortage, a cyclical reality of Plains life that formed one of the bases for the collapse of the yeoman lifestyle. Second, right of ownership was established through displacing the native peoples. That act in and of itself constituted (in the farmer's eyes) a right of title. Last, birthing and dying on the land created a blood-right of succession that no financial transaction could negate. And most importantly, working the land formed the litmus test of possession. The quotation reveals the teller's sadness that the laws of the country conflict with the laws of the land. The agrarian ideology held that only those who work and love the land can truly own it:

> If a man owns a little property, that property is him, it's part of him and it's like him. If he owns property only so he can walk on it and handle it and be sad when it isn't doing well, and feel fine when the rain falls on it, that property is him. . . . Even if he isn't successful he's big with his property.

Such feelings descend directly from the dual myths of the frontier and the garden. The frontier myth posited that land in the West was uninhabited by anybody with legal rights and that the strength of the nation lay in its boundless and unsettled western frontier. The myth of the garden held that the land would yield bountiful harvests to any American willing to work it. Rain would fall in direct proportion to the farmer's needs. Any failure in these natural laws was necessarily transitory and had no lasting relevance. This supposed law of nature was disproven by the Okies' experiences in both Oklahoma and California. After a prolonged drought revealed the unsustainability of their farming methods and drove them from their homes, the wet/dry cycle in California nearly caused their demise.

Not only did meteorological laws conflict with the yeoman belief system, the Okies also found their way of life colliding with the policies of a nation committed to corporate capitalism. Empiricism and a bottom line mentality created rigid parameters for the decision-making process. While for agrarians land constituted a part of themselves and their culture—something for which the term "market value" lacked a referent—banks and corporations translated it into assets on a balance sheet. Where the Joads spoke of "bad years," account managers acknowledged the reality of sparse rainfall and a semi-arid climate. Historical climatic patterns decreed that "bad years" for rainfall were the norm for the Plains, a fact which made tenant farmers a poor investment. For banks, it became a matter of short-term profit at any cost. Years of drought and over-reliance on nutrient-draining cash crops had left the land ecologically devastated. Those keeping accounts looked to squeeze out every vestige of production before abandoning it for more lucrative investments:

> But you'll kill the land with cotton.
>
> We know. We've got to take cotton quick before the land dies. Then we'll sell the land. Lots of families in the East would like to own a piece of land.

The sight of faceless corporate "monsters" intentionally destroying the land's fertility moved the tenants to violence. Yet the Joads and their neighbors had often planted cotton and were at present sharecropping frenziedly in order to build up a stake to take west: "The whole bunch of us chopped cotton, even Grampa." The differences between the Okies and the banks lay more in scale and philosophy than methodology and eventual result. Both sides participated in the capitalist mechanism, but the banks had better adapted to thrive within it.

Mining the land of nutrients and leaving it for dead demonstrates a new, production-oriented allegiance to the frontier myth. Treating the nation's breadbasket as an expendable resource necessarily assumes an infinite resource reservoir from which to replace it. Short-term profiteering, by its very nature, posits that the future will take care of itself. Such a position depends on a telos of inexhaustible plenty, a concept central to the frontier and garden myths. This pattern of behavior again shows that the onset of the Industrial Age and accompanying supremacy of corporate capitalism did not eradicate the dominant myths, but simply adapted them to twentieth century exigencies. Richard Slotkin offers an intriguing explanation for this transition. He argues that the systems of myth and ideology that developed in this country depended on a positive association with physical migration which revolved around two geographical poles: the "Metropolis" and the "Frontier." The Metropolis must have a negative association or no one would want to leave, while the Frontier need offer riches enough to satisfy all of our dreams. Emigrants suffer in the wilderness while temporarily regressing to a more primitive state. The results, though, more than compensate for the ephemeral loss of civilization's comforts:

> The completed American was therefore one who remade his fortune and his character by an emigration, a setting forth for newer and richer lands; by isolation and regression to a more primitive manner of life; and by establishing his political position.

This discussion offers striking parallels to the Joads' saga. Slotkin's analysis takes the city or the "Metropolis" as the emigrant's point of departure, but we can substitute the Dust Bowl region without interfering with the argument. Since the trappings of the Industrial revolution came late to the Plains, the region lacked the large, mechanized urban areas that pose such an effective antipode to the wilderness frontier. Instead, mechanization and factory farming—both consequences of industrialization—provided the major impetus that drove families like the Joads from their homes. In the Dust Bowl, wage-slavery and the specter of starvation resulting from technological and economic displacement offered the negative contrast to the frontier. Not present was the traditional coupling of those factors with the dense population centers that characterized urban industry. The Okies' choices, in Steinbeck's view, were either to drive a tractor through their neighbors' homes while raping the land with machinery and cash crops, or to leave.

When the Joads first emigrated to the Sallisaw, they endured isolation and primitive conditions while homesteading their land and seeking to fulfill their yeoman ideals. Aridity and untenable agricultural practices caused the dream's collapse, forcing thousands of people like Steinbeck's Joads to again move west. This time they settled in California, the geographical border of the once limitless frontier, now a privatized corporate fiefdom. Once more the Okies suffered primitive, dehumanizing conditions while attempting to exercise their supposedly inalienable human rights. The growers' cartel, however, had disenfranchised them even before they arrived, forcing them into a nomadic existence designed to destroy the homesteading instinct so central to the Frontier Myth.

Despite uncountable acres lying fallow, no land was available for the Okies, a reality Steinbeck often demonstrates. Their dreams of subsistence farming were fundamentally incompatible with the market economy that allowed a select few to grow vastly wealthy on the toil of disenfranchised adherents to the old American Dream. What ultimately kills Casy and exiles Tom is—just as in Slotkin's paradigm—an urgent desire to participate in the political process. They do not succeed, for the moment, because the growers' control over water rights allows them complete dominion over the local government and media. I will discuss this phenomenon at greater length later in the essay. Its relevance here stems from water's role in the third major cause for the Okies' westward migration: inadequate irrigation and a perceived drought.

II

Steinbeck's humanistic bent impelled him to focus on the human side of the agricultural morass that drove the Okies west. However, the underlying motivation for both the Okies' behavior and that of the agribusiness concerns can ultimately be analyzed in hydrological terms. Rainfall in the Southwest in the 1930s fell well within historical norms; cycles of drought are more common than periods of heavy rain. Drought did not cause the Dust Bowl; a more accurate description of the region's troubles should instead focus on the Depression and local agricultural mismanagement. The Depression, though, did not seriously affect the Great Plains until the onset of the Dust Bowl. If local farmers had been able to continue planting and harvesting cash crops at the rate they had in the 1920s, the plains might have escaped the worst of the Depression. Unfortunately, by the end of the decade, they had borrowed heavily and expanded their acreage to maximize annual yields. When the crops failed and the "black blizzards" came, the national plague of poverty and joblessness infected the Plains states as well.

By the 1930s, Plains farmers had plowed under virtually all the region's grasslands. Without sod and other vegetation to hold the topsoil in place, the land became extremely vulnerable to ecological disturbance. When the drought hit, the land had no natural defenses with which to keep its topsoil intact. The resulting dust storms stripped the land bare. Yet, if the region had retained its indigenous vegetation, the drought would have had little long-term effect on the land. Profit-oriented agriculture and ecological ignorance turned a cyclical shortfall of water into a disaster.

High-yield monoculture is a dubious ecological proposition even in humid regions, but in the Southwest such methods become disastrous. When Grampa Joad cleared the land and put it to plow, he hoped to fulfill the traditional yeoman ideal. Barring precipitation shortfalls, the average homestead proved more than adequate for subsistence farming. The region could not, however, sustain the rigors of a capitalist-based agriculture, a task which the metamorphosis of the American Dream soon demanded. Steinbeck condemns what he sees as a dissolution of the values so cherished by the people who settled the region: connectedness to the land coupled with love and gratitude for its sustaining them. Such reverence became obsolete with the ascension of factory farming.

> The driver sat in his iron seat and he was proud of the straight lines he did not will, proud of the tractor he did not own or love, proud of the power he could not control. And when that crop grew, and was harvested, no man had crumbled a hot clod in his fingers and let the earth sift past his fingertips. No man had touched the seed, or lusted for the growth. Men ate what they had not raised, had no connection with the bread. The land bore under iron, and under iron gradually died. . . .

Steinbeck mourned this change in values but could offer no viable solutions. Even as they cursed the technology that drove them west, the Okies traveled in cars bought through the trade of their mules and watched with sadness as tractors did their work in a fraction of the time. The yeoman farmer was an anachronism; the American ideal had to be modified to meet the evolving needs of society.

The Okies formed the pivot point for the western land's transition from earth mother to degraded resource. As the yeoman ideal gave way to the wages of capitalism, the Okies adapted their methods to meet the parameters of a market-based economy. Even as they clung tenaciously to their pre-industrial, terrestrial reverence, they grudgingly accepted the new dominance of the capitalist shift. Muley Graves, unable to relinquish his ties to the land, cannot go with his family when they move west. Rooted to the place where he was born, Muley rages against the dual inequity of bad land and evil bankers:

> 'Cause what'd they take when they tractored the folks off the lan'? What'd they get so their margin a profit was safe? . . . God knows the lan' ain't no good. Nobody been able to make a crop for years. But them sons-a-bitches at their desks, they just chopped folks in two. . . . Place where folks live is them folks. They ain't whole, out lonely on the road in a piled-up car. Them sons-a-bitches killed them.

For Muley, the link with the land still stained with his father's blood is stronger than his ties to wife and family. He cannot leave even as he acknowledges that he is a living anachronism ("You fellas think I'm touched?"). Sadly, Muley's protestations held little weight with a population caught up in the quasi-divine status allowed them by technological advance. It did not matter if the land was poor because human ingenuity could and would transform it. No longer need the land yield forth its bounty, it will instead be mined and harvested. Modern agriculture provided the means to merge Henry Adams' classic juxtaposition of the dynamo and the virgin. Through this synthesis, the earth ceased to be a virgin and became a wife. Similar phenomena occur often both in the American landscape and literary corpus. The masculine, aggressive machine assaults and reshapes the idyllic, feminine landscape.

As farmers were forced more and more to mistreat their holdings, they degraded it further to sexual plaything and chattel. This ideological evolution progressed naturally from the dominant myths. As industrialism began to dominate the West, the accompanying mindset fit a unique niche in the American dream of rugged individualism and merit-based achievement.

Bacon, anticipating the Industrial Revolution, advocated reclaiming Eden through industry and science; a century later, Americans embraced the challenge as their destiny. Westerners could reclaim the garden but it involved literally "reclaiming" their place in paradise through diligence and industry. Men would finish what Nature had begun. Eden, ideologues hastened to point out, was after all an irrigated garden. Adam fell; Americans will stand tall. The Reclamation Act of 1902 established the Bureau of Reclamation, intending to fulfill Powell's credo of "rescuing" and "redeeming" the land from its arid state. The true meaning of the word "reclamation" lost all significance in the technological assault on the region's hydrology. The verb "to reclaim" infers prior ownership; the people seeking to irrigate the desert could make no such claim. Nevertheless, whatever needed to be done would be done to get water to the land and restore it to its imagined, bountiful state. Any water that ran into the sea without serving some agricultural purpose was "wasted," a Providential oversight correctable through human diligence.

Denying the hydrological realities of the Southwest while modernizing the dominant mythology permitted Westerners to reject the implication that all is not within the grasp of any perspicacious American. Henry Luce's *Time* magazine trumpeted the rediscovered limitlessness that irrigation technology brought to the frontier: "Irrigation experts are now convinced that the rapidly growing U.S. can expand indefinitely within its present boundaries." This quotation is pregnant with the contradictions inherent to the American and specifically western dream of infinite abundance. The notion of indefinite expansion within acknowledged boundaries is fundamentally self-contradictory. Attributing this ability to accomplish the impossible to the calculations of irrigation experts beautifully underscores the incongruities within western water policy. Western land barons relied on irrigation to accomplish the impossible and ignored or destroyed anyone or anything that interfered with their pursuit of that grail. The Joads and their contemporaries were ill-equipped for the ramifications of the growers' zeal. They clung fast to traditional yeoman values even while participating in the market economy. Caught between two worlds, they could not linger in Oklahoma and set out instead for the land where corporate growers had remanufactured the traditional Myth of the Garden to entice exodusters westward.

As they traversed the migrant highway, the Joads met many who, like themselves, had readily believed the leaflets spread by agents of the California growers.

> "Why, I seen han'bills how they need folks to pick fruit, an' good wages, Why, jus' think how it's gonna be, under them shady trees a-pickin' fruit an' takin' a bite ever' once in a while. . . . An' with them good wages, maybe a fella can get hisself a piece a land an' work out for extra cash. Why, hell, in a couple a years I bet a fella could have a place of his own."

That the Great Plains could no longer sustain the yeoman

ideal did not necessarily spell the death of the American dream for a dispossessed people, barely literate and ready to jump at any hope of salvation. The California growers cartel, already enmeshed in a cycle of wage-slavery, remained convinced that additional workers could only lengthen their profit margins. They recruited Dust Bowl refugees with promises of a vast, temperate paradise wherein they might recreate the homesteads they had been forced to leave. This new myth of the garden presented an even more seductive exterior than the Plains by adapting the Jeffersonian ideal to a region where husbandry was allegedly secondary to the munificence of Nature. Grampa, before becoming overwhelmed by his attachment to the land he cleared and raised his family on, fantasized about bathing in a washtub full of grapes where he would "scrooge aroun' an' let the juice run down my pants." But this vision of unchecked abundance was less a cultural phenomenon than a calculated product of the growers' propaganda mills. The agribusiness consortia dangled visions of their own wealth and massive land-holdings before the Okies in order to fuel their (the cartel's) hegemony. And the irony of that vision, as Steinbeck depicts it, is that the growers were as alienated from their land-wealth as they forced the Okies to be:

> And it came about that the owners no longer worked their farms . . . they forgot the land, the smell and the feel of it, and remembered only that they owned it. . . . And the owners not only did not work the farms any more, many of them had never seen the farms they owned.

The California growers had become immensely wealthy and powerful as the result of an uneasy but mutually profitable alliance with the Bureau of Reclamation. Having already incarnated themselves in the image of the new garden which depended heavily on the tools of the technocracy to subdue the land, they looked to consolidate their holdings by enacting the Social Darwinism which fueled their telos of industry. They had managed to consolidate the dual definitions of "garden" into one highly profitable vision of production and wealth. No longer could "garden" signify either a region of natural, providential splendor or an area of human-created agrarian abundance; the Edenic garden propounded by Gilpin and his nineteenth-century allies was completely replaced by its opposing Baconian definition of a human-engineered paradise achieved through work and intellect. Humans—specifically men—had invented the tools necessary to subjugate nature. Those tools had brought water to the desert via centrifugal pumping and, more importantly, through the diversion of rivers.

By shaping the perceived objectivity of science to fit the needs of western agriculture, an elite group's control over the dissemination of knowledge led to dominion over the region's geography. Literally overnight, worthless land became incredibly valuable through shady, often illicit dealings that brought subsidized water to the region. The men whose schemes created this technological garden stood to profit most from its enactment and it was they who formed the powerful growers' cartel that enslaved the migrants. Those who controlled the water controlled the entire regional economy, and that domination bled into every other facet of life.

Californian agribusiness's command over nature required large temporary workforces while the capitalist regime necessitated that this transient labor force be paid very little. The growers had traditionally indentured immigrants and other disenfranchised groups since little public outcry arose from their mistreatment. However, the arrival of the Okies, a large, skilled, English-speaking labor force whose migrant status left them bereft of any governmental protection, appeared to be a tremendous windfall to the growers cartel. In the novel, however, the latent power of the oppressed becomes the looming threat to the water-based oligarchy. The Okies come to embody Marx's concept of alienated labor. Their corporate oppressors force them to work ever harder and faster in order to eke out a subsistence, yet each hour worked and each piece of fruit harvested bring them that much closer to unemployment and starvation. They must further compete against each other by underbidding fellow workers in a futile attempt to participate in an exclusionary economic system. Conversely, growers must dehumanize the workers, degrading them as they do the land so that their acts of subjugation can be perpetrated on objects beneath contempt. In ***In Dubious Battle,*** Steinbeck treats the worker/grower relationship as a matter strictly related to class struggle. In ***The Grapes of Wrath,*** he elevates it to the realm of epistemology, viewing the schism between workers and land barons as symptomatic of the larger issue of human alienation from the earth and as a catalyst for the synthesis of humans and their surroundings into the all-encompassing organismic one.

> Three hundred thousand, hungry and miserable; if ever they know themselves, the land will be theirs. . . . And the great owners, who had become through their holdings both more and less than men, ran to their destruction, and used every means that in the long run would destroy them.

The cycle of poverty imposed on the Okies contained a seasonal period of starvation during the rainy season. Water again, this time through super-abundance, became the immediate threat to the Okies' survival. When Rosasharn goes into labor, the men outside labor frantically to erect a dam to keep the boxcar shelters dry. Water, priceless commodity and building block of life, endangers the birthing process and threatens to starve an entire class of people. Both attempts—the birth and the dam—are unsuccessful. As the floodwaters force the Joads to flee, Uncle John is assigned the task of burying the stillborn child. Rather than do so, he coopts the water, using it and the dead child to spread his message of despair and defiance:

> Go down an' tell 'em. Go down in the street an' rot an' tell em that way, That's the way you can talk. . . . Go on down now an' lay in the street. Maybe they'll know then.

Driven from Oklahoma where widespread refusal to acknowledge water's scarcity resulted in an unsustainable way of life, the Okies found themselves in a new region with an already intact and sophisticated capitalist infrastructure with water at its plinth. As a disenfranchised and powerless class, the migrants had no opportunity to gain control over water rights and consequently could not participate in the dominant discourse. John's act represented an ephemeral yet powerful appropriation of the preeminent unit of capital. Using water to convey a message of worker defiance strikes at the heart of the power structure: if the Okies were to gain actual control over the region's water, the growers' cartel would collapse and the legions of migrants could seize power and redistribute the land according to need and fairness.

The dual hopes for the migrants, according to Steinbeck, are class alliance and worker control over the tools of domination. When Tom takes over the task of organizing the Okies from the martyred Casy, the class struggle takes a symbolic step forward. When Uncle John seizes control over the water that enslaves his people and threatened their lives, he takes another major step towards toppling the ruling class. Shortly after Uncle John's act of defiance, Rosasharn's gift of her maternal milk to another starving Okie demonstrates that both Tom's and John's acts will eventually bear fruit. Sheltered from the water by a barn, itself a potent symbol of the yeoman agricultural ideal, Rosasharn's offering her breast to a fellow migrant demonstrates the class cohesion that will ultimately topple the ruling class. While her stillborn infant rots in the town below, Rosasharn breast-feeds an old man whose advanced state of starvation has caused him to regress to a pre-lingual state. Her act and the old man's condition represent the succoring of the infant movement toward social change. Each act, while primarily symbolic, is also genuinely subversive. In these small acts of defiance and hope, suggests Steinbeck, lie the restoration of traditional ties between people and between people and the land. So, despite their socialization into a culture in which water is both hoarded and feared, the Okies have not completely acquiesced to their role in the factory-farm mechanism. They retain their dreams of an idyllic land where the family farm reigns supreme and water and land are distributed according to need and connectedness to the land rather than amassed corporate capital and political dominance.

In the final analysis, however, the migrant dream of resurgent family farms reclaiming their place as the preeminent agricultural ideal cannot work in the arid lands. Water reclamation projects, because of their expense and complexity, require the participation of an elite, educated class. The projects therefore become political pawns. The family farmer, allied with a subsistence ideology and unwilling to exploit the land past its carrying capacity, cannot compete with wealthy, powerful, corporate interests. For this reason, the novel, though hopeful, does not offer any quantifiable hope. Worster feels this lack of an attainable goal to be the novel's major failing. Decrying the system of land distribution without explicitly condemning the accompanying hydrological autocracy leads to the specious conclusion that simply putting the land in the hands of the migrants will solve the region's agrarian morass. In a section of *Rivers of Empire* entitled "The Grapes of Wealth," Worster argues:

> Nowhere in ***The Grapes of Wrath*** does Steinbeck draw attention to the elaborate hydraulic apparatus that has been required to create the California garden. . . . Grapes, carrots, cotton and the like are the products, it would seem, of spontaneous nature, not the contrivances of advanced water engineering and the social organization it has required.

Since Steinbeck failed to acknowledge the inherent oligarchic nature of irrigation-based societies, he creates the false impression that equitable land distribution and a classless society will return the region to ecological stability. Historically, there are no precedents for this vision being realizable. In fact, returning the family farm to the arid region without altering the national capitalist infrastructure will, given the Plains example, cause devastating ecological harm.

Worster's critique does raise the problematic issue of Steinbeck's unrepentant affection for the family farm but does not, as I mentioned earlier, address the powerful critique of hydraulic society implicit in the novel's structure. That he used water throughout the novel as an absent signifier suggests that Steinbeck was well aware of its power and complicity in the region's power hierarchy. When, at novel's end, Steinbeck suddenly introduces water as a tangible presence and powerful symbolic force, it empowers the migrants by demonstrating their class cohesion and latent strength. Structuring the novel in this manner permitted Steinbeck to criticize the extant hydraulic society more effectively than he could through overt polemics. Indeed, the novel's reception, both locally and nationally, bears witness to its powerful subversive nature, a fact which underscores the most crucial flaw in Worster's argument. If the novel caused both the government and the nation-at-large to reevaluate federal irrigation subsidies for corporate growers, clearly it must have effectively criticized the inequity and corruption infusing California's water-appropriation schema.

The migrants' struggle became a national *cause celebre* and the novel's verisimilitude was debated at the highest levels of government. The Hearst-Chandler-Copley yellow press pilloried the novel and its author throughout California. Only after a *Life* magazine expose and Eleanor Roosevelt's endorsement of the book's veracity did the tide of public opinion begin to turn in Steinbeck's favor. The rage and furor from agribusiness conglomerates and their allies arose because ***The Grapes of Wrath*** shook the very foundations of the water-based oligarchy. Worster himself acknowledges this:

> Up to the very end of the decade, both the Bureau [of Reclamation] and the Department of the Interior were placidly moving forward . . . avoiding any cause for alarm on the part of the growers in California . . . What changed all of that undoubtedly was . . . the publication in 1939 of ***The Grapes of Wrath*** . . . Suddenly, it became rather difficult for a liberal government in Washington to give subsidized, unrestricted water to groups like the reactionary Associated Farmers, to underwrite their labor policies and their concentration of wealth.

Nevertheless, despite a temporary surge in popular and governmental concern, neither the novel nor the reform movement it generated achieved any lasting change in western water policy. Porkbarrel appropriations bills continued to subsidize corporate growers who continued to couch their greed within the rubric of a technologically controlled Eden which they believed would and should form the destiny of the West. The migrants' struggle faded into the background with the outbreak of World War II. U.S. entry into the conflict stoked the fires of nationalism and the nation turned to the West once again to fuel the American war machine. The Okies benefited from the wartime surge in production, finding work in munitions factories and other war-related industries. Relieved, the growers turned once again to immigrant labor, a class of people they could be relatively certain of keeping disenfranchised and powerless. So, the cycle of exploitation resumed after only a brief hiatus. Public interest in the issue peaked again two decades later when Cesar Chavez briefly managed to organize the Migrant Farm Workers Union into an effective national lobby.

Only in the 1990s, after a prolonged drought and numerous aborted attempts at reform, has the Californian agricultural machine seemingly run dry. Faced with a severe, unremitting drought and a recession-locked nation unwilling to finance any more quixotic reclamation projects, the Californian growers now face a complete embargo on federally supplied water. Years of drought and insupportable agriculture in an arid land are seemingly on the verge of accomplishing what neither Powell nor Steinbeck nor any individual person could accomplish on his own: decanonization of the myth of the garden and its accompanying myth of the frontier. These two myths, dominant since the birth of the nation, eventually ran headlong into the realities of a closed frontier and a finite hydrology. Steven Goldstein, spokesman for Interior Secretary Manuel Lujan, aptly summed up the situation when announcing the curtailment of further water-subsidy, saying: "We recognize . . . what a hardship this will be. But we cannot make it rain."

Nicholas Visser (essay date Spring 1994)

SOURCE: "Audience and Closure in *The Grapes of Wrath*," in *Studies in American Fiction,* Vol. 22, No. 1, Spring, 1994, pp. 19-36.

[*In the following essay, Visser discusses the historical context of* The Grapes of Wrath, *Steinbeck's persuasive depiction of social injustice, and narrative strategies employed to present a politically radical message to a large public audience.*]

Although ***The Grapes of Wrath*** continues to be regarded as Steinbeck's major achievement, changing critical fashions have ensured that the novel's status remains uncertain. The novel's standing came under pressure as early as the decades immediately following its publication, as literary studies with the onset of the Cold War intensified a longstanding tendency in modern poetics to strip literary texts of social and political implications. It was not difficult to decontextualize most of the literature of earlier times, but because the thirties were part of living memory, and because so much of the decade's literature was politically leftwing, the need to depoliticize it was particularly urgent. Where critics could not manage that task, if only because social content was too firmly in the foreground to be obscured, they simply declared such literary works unworthy of serious attention. So strong were these pressures that one of the first critics to write a full-length study of Steinbeck, Harry T. Moore, later wrote an epilogue to the second edition of his book recanting his earlier approval. Why he would have bothered to publish a second edition is unclear.

Recent criticism has done little to reverse the situation. Poststructuralist critics generally ignore, when they do not derogate, writers who presume to represent actual material conditions and social processes; accordingly a writer like Steinbeck, particularly the Steinbeck of ***In Dubious Battle*** or ***The Grapes of Wrath,*** has little to offer them. Even recent Marxist criticism has largely ignored Steinbeck. Eager to demonstrate its intellectual respectability, which apparently requires that in order to distance itself sufficiently from the Stalinist penchant for socialist realism it repudiate representation altogether, recent Marxist criticism, particularly that current which has responded to the powerful gravitational tug of poststructuralist theory, has generally shunned politically explicit literature. What all this has meant is that ***The Grapes of Wrath*** has been either ignored or disparaged.

Since what follows seeks to examine the interplay of politics and form in the novel and as a consequence of that endeavor points to certain unresolved or incompletely resolved formal problems raised by ***The Grapes of Wrath,*** I am concerned that my comments will seem to grant attention to the novel at the cost of issuing in yet another negative assessment. There are problems in ***The Grapes of Wrath,*** even large problems, but no more so than in any number of more politically conservative novels of the same period that have enjoyed critical esteem. Furthermore, David Craig and Michael Egan are surely correct in their view that Steinbeck is "incomparable at presenting [working people's] way of life, with an attention to people's manual skills and their self expression which is signally missing from nearly all literature to date," and that the "bulk of [***The Grapes of Wrath***] is unrivaled in Western literature for describing, dramatizing, and *explaining* a large socio-historical process." These are hardly insignificant achievements.

A substantial part of the novel's achievement lies in the way Steinbeck both renders such processes and simultaneously shields the novel from the abstraction and generalization such a description would seem to entail. Even in the interchapters, much of the purpose of which is to generalize the particular experiences of the Joads, the emphasis is on rendering process rather than abstractly describing it. And for the Joad family, socio-historical process is not something consciously perceived as trends and circumstances prevailing in the society in which they live—the Depression, the dustbowl in the southwest of the United States and the mass migration to California, the increasingly rapid transformation of American farming into the highly mechanized, capital-intensive agribusiness of today, and the like. Rather, such broader processes are experienced as daily pressures in their lives. The farm which they once owned but on which they have been reduced to labor tenancy is lost through events and means that remain largely mysterious to them. They undertake their exodus to the false promised land of California through decisions both deliberately (and therefore apparently freely) taken by the family and utterly constrained by their material and social conditions. And when they arrive in California, the extreme exploitation to which they are subjected baffles them and destroys them as a family. Indeed, lacking analytical categories like "socio-historical process," the Joads and others in their situation feel an urgent need for some way of making these pressures more immediately present, more concrete and personal, so that they can attempt to gain some sort of purchase on them.

For all that it passionately castigates the social and political conditions under which the Joads live, there may be reasons for questioning just how politically radical ***The Grapes of Wrath*** ultimately is. At the same time, however, the generative context for the novel is the international left-wing political culture of the 1930s, and Steinbeck's novel takes its place among the radical novels produced by that culture. In rendering the efforts of the Joads to cope with the collapse of their world, ***The Grapes of Wrath*** brings to the surface two problems that arise repeatedly in politically radical novels. First is the obvious, but usually overlooked, question of how radical novels manage to gain access to an audience. What formal or discursive strategies do they adopt to that end? Second is the question of how radical novels conclude, especially when, as in ***The Grapes of Wrath,*** the "large socio-historical process" of which Craig and Egan speak had not ended when the novel was published.

The problem of audience for politically radical fiction was succinctly identified by Engels in his famous letter to Minna Kautsky written in November 1885. After indicating that he is "not at all an opponent of tendentious writing as such," Engels nevertheless urges Kautsky to avoid revealing an overtly political stance in her novels on the entirely practical grounds that "the novel primarily finds readers in bourgeois circles, circles not directly related to our own." Accordingly, Engels suggests something quite different from the notion that radical literature should be directly insurrectionary. We may infer from what Engels says that in his view it is not properly the function of the "socialist tendentious novel" to mobilize the oppressed, since for practical reasons such as the lack of disposable leisure time, of the privacy and quiet needed to spend long periods reading, and in some cases even of the requisite levels of literacy, the oppressed are not realistically available as an audience. Instead, the project of the radical writer should be to act on the audience that is available for novels; more specifically, Engels writes, to shatter "the optimism of the bourgeois world," thereby "causing doubt about the eternal validity of the existing order." The argument is persuasive, but there is one important consideration it does not address. Why, especially given the glut of novels which endorse bourgeois optimism, would bourgeois readers bother to read radical novels? How, then—to put the problem another way—does the radical novelist gain access to that actually available audience?

A good part of the answer to these questions lies in the contexts of a work's production and initial reception. In times of social and political crisis, for instance, the readership for politicized literature typically expands, if only for the duration of the crisis. At the same time, the awareness that authors gain of prevailing material and social forces and constraints can prompt them to develop formal strategies designed to win over readers, or at least to allay their suspicion and resistance. The strategies of ***The Grapes of Wrath*** derive from Steinbeck's understanding of what audience he was addressing and in what relation to it he wished to stand.

Much of the early debate over the novel hinged on the question of address, the opposing positions revealing how intimately address is understood to be bound up with the political position the novel stakes out. Peter Lisca examines expressions of the two standard views, one from an early attack entitled *The Truth about John Steinbeck and the Migrants* and one from an established critic, Stanley Edgar Hyman. The author of the first says that he "can think of no other novel which advances the idea of class war and promotes hatred of class against class . . . more than does ***The Grapes of Wrath.***" Hyman disagrees: "Actually . . . the central message of ***The Grapes of Wrath*** is an appeal to the owning class to behave, to become enlightened, rather than to the working class to change its own conditions." Warren French sides with Hyman, arguing that Steinbeck does not advocate revolution; rather "he speaks as an observer, warning what *may* happen—what it *regrettably* appears *will* happen." He goes on to suggest that any apparently revolutionary passages in the novel

> are not rabble-rousing speeches inciting an outraged proletariat to rise against its oppressors; rather they are warnings to a comfortable and negligent propertied class to awaken it to what is happening around it. ***The Grapes of Wrath*** in its treatment of contemporary events is a cautionary tale.

Both views misconstrue Steinbeck's handling of address in the novel. That the oppressed themselves are not the object of address—even accepting that Steinbeck could have made the mistake of assuming it was possible to address that audience directly—can be inferred from, among other things, the strongly "anthropological" mode of the novel, much of which is devoted to (re)presenting one social group to another. Hence the use of dialect and the explanations offered for details of daily life. Much of the novel's effect derives from giving the impression that it is engaged in revealing the hitherto unknown to an audience socially and culturally distant from the novel's characters.

The assertion that the "owning" or "propertied" class is the audience directly addressed is superficially more plausible but ultimately fails to account for much that goes on in the novel, especially the sustained and impassioned attack on "big business." Calling ***The Grapes of Wrath*** a "cautionary tale," as French does, links it with the long tradition of English-language reformist fiction in the manner of Dickens and Gaskell. Steinbeck shares much with the conventions of reformist or ameliorative fiction, but he differs sharply in one significant respect. Reformist fiction not only addresses the dominant class, it also depicts the dominated classes from a vantage point outside and above their own experience. That perspective is largely absent from ***The Grapes of Wrath.*** Instead, even though the anthropological mode of the narrative at times entails an exterior view, just as the occasional lapses into sentimentalism similarly establish a narrating position above the represented people, that discursive situation is never permitted to persist for long or to stray far from the textures of daily experience. For most of its course the novel, as Craig and Egan indicate, penetrates fully into the way of life, the everyday habits and skills and even the self-expression of the characters portrayed.

If oppressed social groups are not the prospective audience for the novel, they may nevertheless assert their presence not as a directly addressed group but as what Sartre called a virtual public, made up of dominated groups who lack access to "high" or official culture. Since awareness of this virtual public typically exerts a certain pressure on progressive writers, Sartre's notion can tell us something about an author's alignment if not something directly about the actual or intended audience. They are the group an author would wish to address if that were practicable, or on whose behalf an author writes. Responding to a virtual public would have been consonant with Steinbeck's developing feelings about the people he was depicting in his novel. His first effort to write ***The Grapes of Wrath*** resulted in a satire which he felt obliged to withdraw even though his publishers had already announced its impending release. He wrote to his publishers:

> I know that a great many people would think they liked this book. I, myself, have built up a hole-proof argument on how and why I liked it. I can't beat the argument, but I don't like the book . . . My whole work drive has been aimed at making people understand each other and then I deliberately write this book, the aim of which is to cause hatred through partial understanding.

Useful though the concept of virtual public is in grasping the puzzling modes of address in radical fiction, it is necessarily silent about the social bloc whose attention and interest Steinbeck did wish to engage. His conception of his audience stemmed from his awareness that in a time of acute social and economic crisis, the bourgeois audience of which Engels writes is unusually fractured, so that a much larger than usual segment of it is, temporarily at least, susceptible to the appeal of politically progressive ideas. As Sartre puts it: "If the real public is broken up into hostile factions, everything changes." Steinbeck frames his novel neither, strictly speaking, for the oppressed groups, necessarily present only as a virtual public, nor for the owners. Instead he writes with a peculiarly modern notion of audience that comes into existence with the modern nation state and the forms of communication and cultural practice (including, centrally, the novel) that construct and sustain notions of national identity. He writes, in short, in the effort to influence "public opinion." The discursive situation Steinbeck imagines is not a bilateral relation between author and a readership but a triadic relation of author, audience, and owners. He seeks to influence public opinion to put pressure on a putatively beneficent national government to ameliorate the impossible conditions which big business and greedy landowners have imposed on the landless migrants in California. He is not, in other words, supposing that he is directly addressing the owners in the cautionary mode suggested by French, nor is he addressing the migrants: he may write *for* them as virtual public, but he does not, if only because he cannot, write to them.

The wish to influence public opinion makes it all the more urgent for Steinbeck to ensure that his project does not fail to reach its audience. Public opinion, after all, can equally be influenced to ignore or reject his message. One of the devices he employs to overcome the expected difficulties is attempting to gain control over the operative definitions of the words "Okies" and "reds." To reach his audience, Steinbeck had to find some way of bridging the social and cultural distance between them and his characters. An anthropological mode of discourse can create and even sustain interest in unknown social groups, but Steinbeck required more than interest. For his project to succeed he needed active sympathy: he needed his readers to wish so wholeheartedly for the amelioration of the conditions suffered by the migrants that public opinion would be swayed in their favor. One way of accomplishing that end was to neutralize the terms of contempt with which dominant groups label those they dominate.

The migrants are in one respect unusual as objects of prejudice: they lack a history of victimization. Because prejudice is not something they have grown up with, they actually have to be taught the meaning of the term used to vilify them.

> "You gonna see in people's face how they hate you. What the hell! You never been called 'Okie' yet."
>
> Tom said: "Okie? What's that?"
>
> "Well, Okie use' ta mean you was from Oklahoma. Now it means you're a dirty son-of-a-bitch. Okie means you're scum. Don't mean nothing itself, it's the way they say it."

For those who use the word, "Okies" functions to establish the greatest possible distance between themselves and those to whom it is applied, to constitute the latter as utterly different, absolutely other. Our privileged position as readers enables us to see the inadequacy of such labels and the descriptions which accompany them, to see how self-serving they are, how they end up blaming the victims for their oppression, how they seek to dehumanize the migrants and wind up instead desensitizing and dehumanizing those who use them. By situating us within the ambit of the migrants' experience, the novel decisively separates us from those who would use such words, from the landowners and their retainers.

If constituting readers as people who would not use a word like "Okie" shows canny insight into ways of managing social prejudice, Steinbeck, with equal canniness, recognizes that access to an audience as abstract, impermanent, and vacillating as "public opinion" requires anticipating and neutralizing anything likely to prompt rejection of his project. All it would take would be for one of the customary charges of the period—"radical" or "communist sympathizer," in short, "red"—to be convincingly leveled, and even the more open-minded members of his audience would shun the novel. The Joads begin to hear about troublemakers and agitators and reds even before they arrive in California. A campsite owner who regularly swindles the migrants retaliates when Tom Joad jokes bitterly about the owner's money-grubbing:

> The chair-legs hit the floor. "Don't you go a-sassin' me. I 'member you. You're one of these here trouble makers."
>
> "Damn right," said Tom. "I'm bolshevisky."
>
> "They's too damn many of you kinda guys aroun'." Tom laughed as they went out the gate.

Laughter on the reader's part is exactly the desired effect. It comes partly from Tom's mangling of the word Bolshevik or Bolsheviksi: his ignorance is transparently his innocence. More important, the reader already knows Tom, and of course also knows the owner. The perspective of the narration ensures that accusations are subsumed under the valuings that have already been established for characters.

The same management of perspective shapes the reader's

response to a later incident. The Joads leave a migrants' camp shortly before local vigilantes and hired goons violently destroy it. The newspaper story reporting the event reads:

> Citizens, angered at red agitators, burn squatters' camp. Last night a band of citizens, infuriated at the agitation going on in a local squatters' camp, burned the tents to the ground and warned agitators to get out of the county.

Because we have vicariously experienced the camp in the company of the Joads, we reject the report as an outrageous distortion. We might be inclined to assume from such passages that Steinbeck's point is that the Joads are not reds. But more is at issue. The crucial insight is provided by Tom immediately after he reads the newspaper account: "I watched it a long time. There's always red agitators just before a pay cut. Always." The accusation is a deliberate effort to discredit the migrants through a word so powerfully charged that once deployed it can usually be counted on to issue in stock responses. Such attempts to discredit the characters are equivalent to and anticipations of attempts to discredit the novel through using the same epithets. In devising strategies to deflect the one, Steinbeck seeks to deflect the other.

The discussion of the newspaper story continues until finally the migrants themselves are able to grasp what is going on in the accusation. When Tom asks, "What the hell is these reds anyway?" he is told a story about another man who had asked his boss the same question. The boss replied:

> "A red is any son-of-a-bitch that wants thirty cents an hour when we're payin' twenty-five!" Well, this young fella he thinks about her, an' he scratches his head, an' he says: "Well, Jesus, Mr. Hines. I ain't a son-of-a bitch, but if that's what a red is—why, I want thirty cents an hour. Ever' body does. Hell, Mr. Hines, we're all reds."

After hearing this, "Tom laughed. 'Me too, I guess.'" Once again, then, laughter, our own as well as Tom's, is the response, but behind Tom's laughter and that of the other migrants is a growing political consciousness, an increasingly developed realization of how the owners and their hirelings deploy all the resources at their disposal, including discursive resources, to entrench and expand their domination of the migrants.

The interrogation of the word "reds" leads finally to a roundabout but unmistakable association of the word with Christ. As Tom tells Ma of Casy's murder, he relates Casy's last words, which, in keeping with the Biblical parallels established in the novel, closely echo Christ's last words on the cross:

> "Casy said: 'You got no right to starve people.' An' then this heavy fella called him a red son-of-a-bitch. An' Casy says: 'You don' know what you're a-doin'.' An' then this guy smashed 'im."
>
> Ma looked down. She twisted her hands together.
>
> "Tha's what he said—'You don't know what you're doin'?'"

In probing and contesting the meanings attached to "Okies" and "reds" Steinbeck seeks to disarm the discursive authority of the holders of social power, whose control over meanings is a powerful tool in maintaining social hegemony. To undermine the discursive practices of the dominant group is to steal their ideological magic, as it were. By prizing words out of their customary associations and valuings and laying bare the interests served by certain usages, thereby hampering efforts by the powerful to maintain control over meanings, Steinbeck makes it more difficult for public opinion to be turned against his project. It will not be enough to count on the social distance between audience and represented, nor will it be enough to dismiss the book as "red." Without those two weapons, the owners and those who labor for them in the management of public opinion are reduced to having to claim not that "Okies" are unworthy of sympathy—a tactic as likely to backfire as to succeed—or that Steinbeck is a "red," but that he gets his facts wrong, that he misrepresents the experience of the migrants in California. They are forced, in other words, to shift the terrain of dispute from a straightforward ideological plane to an empirical plane. And in the event empirical claims were easily dismissed.

Efforts to resolve disputes over a novel by attempting to verify or falsify what it depicts may seem odd—even, in light of the way notions of reference are called into question by current literary theory, frivolous. Yet such efforts not only makes sense in relation to ***The Grapes of Wrath,*** they disclose a significant dimension of the novel's relation to its audience. Central to the reading experience of ***The Grapes of Wrath*** is the acceptance that what the narrative relates actually occurs in the life-world. In the absence of a tacit but absolutely binding contract between author and reader that the reader can rely on the novel's general veracity, the novel would be almost entirely lacking in meaning. Moreover, if it could be established that Steinbeck *had* distorted the truth, the novel would be felt to lose a substantial component of its value, and not just its value as social documentation (a function I would not wish to disparage) but its value as a novel, for who would read it today, when its documentary value alone could not count for much, if it had been successfully exposed as a fraud? At stake here, then, is not a question of the putative lifelikeness or verisimilitude of the realistic novel. We may not ordinarily feel compelled to ask of novelists if the events they depict can be matched to events of the real world; in the case of ***The Grapes of Wrath,*** however, the relationship between reader and text depends on the reader's conviction that people in the dustbowl actually lost their land when banks foreclosed on their loans, migrant camps really were raided and burned out, goons and vigilantes really were used to harass migrants and stymie efforts to organize labor unions, owners and their organizations genuinely colluded to drive down wages, and so on. Steinbeck revealed his sensitivity to the demands of the tacit contract with his readers in a letter: "There's one other difficulty too. I'm trying to write history while it is happening and I don't want to be wrong." Being discovered to be wrong, especially deliberately wrong, would have proved fatal to the success of the book.

Even leaving aside whether it is theoretically possible for a novel (or any other discursive form) to give the reader access to the real, it is at least a challenge to the adequacy of such theorizing about reference to note that certain literary works, for all their fictiveness, depend for their import as well as their impact on successfully securing the reader's acceptance that reference is being actively accomplished. There should not be anything particularly surprising about such a conclusion. To cite just one example, Solzhenitsyn's *One Day in the Life of Ivan Denisovich* absolutely requires that its readers grant a referential axis of meaning, for in the absence of certain beliefs about Stalinist labor camps, not to mention the belief that the author experienced those camps at first hand, the novel could have no meaning. Similarly, the relationship which ***The Grapes of Wrath*** continues to establish with its audience, even long after the circumstances it depicts have been transformed, depends on readers accepting that those circumstances once actually existed.

Steinbeck's handling of his relation with his audience is one of the most interesting and successful features of ***The Grapes of Wrath.*** Somewhat less successfully handled is the other major formal challenge of the novel: how to end the narrative. Radical novels regularly encounter difficulties with closure. Although it is obviously not part of the project of radical novels to promote defeatism, they nevertheless repeatedly end either inconclusively or in failure. To cite just a few representative cases from among the many radical novels written in the same period as ***The Grapes of Wrath,*** Richard Wright's *Native Son* ends with the death of Bigger Thomas, while the insurrectionary movements of Andre Malraux's *Man's Fate* and Ignazio Silone's *Fontamara* end in crushing defeat. The list could be expanded to cover practically the entirety of radical fiction. Part of the problem stems from the customary attachment of radical fiction to the external world, to history. Since in most cases the material conditions and social iniquities portrayed in radical novels have not been resolved in the external world, or where they have been resolved they have issued in the defeat of progressive forces rather than in their victory, and since the success of the political project undertaken in a political novel hinges on persuading the reader that these conditions and iniquities actually exist or have existed, closure becomes a significant problem at a juncture where the formal properties of the novel and the political project undertaken in radical fiction converge.

Many things could be said about Steinbeck's ending, and it has probably as many defenders as detractors. But whether we find the moment when Rose of Sharon offers her breast to the starving stranger genuinely moving in the way it enacts the compassion the novel has promoted throughout, or painfully mawkish in the way it entraps the reader in a position tantamount to voyeurism, it remains the case that closure is operating on an entirely personal level. The intensely intimate moment is obviously not generalizable in any literal sense, and even if it is given a more abstract form, the form, say, of "Do unto others," it shifts the arena of values from the social and economic and political to the personal and private and ethical, and does so without indicating how the one may be actively linked to the other. In short, the final moments end up telling the oppressed and exploited the old story: social justice can emerge only when there is a universal change of heart, only when people decide to be kinder to each other—a message which has always consoled those who gain advantage from the *status quo* more than it has those who bear the costs of social inequity.

Why does a novel which has required the destruction of the bonds of family and neighborliness so that a broader collectivity can take their place suddenly, at the very last moment, provide resolution only at the most intimate, most personal level? Even Ma, the normative center of familial values in the novel, comes finally to comprehend that the family must give way to broader affiliations if the conditions confronted by the migrants are ever to be overcome: "Use' ta be the fambly was fust. It ain't so now. It's anybody. Worse off we get, the more we got to do." Rose of Sharon's moment of exemplary humanity in feeding the stranger, especially since it is the first generous action of a hitherto utterly self-absorbed person, may at first appear to enact that "more"; however, up to this point the novel has intimated that the social lesson being proffered is not the parable of the good Samaritan but the Aesopean fable of the bundle of sticks or the three-fold cord of Ecclesiastes, exempla rarely invoked by those in positions of religious or secular authority as models for social conduct precisely because, unlike the more frequently cited "golden rule," they disclose the potential strength of the group acting in concert and on its own behalf.

The move towards collective political action promises, ultimately falsely, to be the central trajectory of the novel's meanings. The destruction of the family, the developing political consciousness, the beginnings of an organized labor movement, the instilling of cooperative values in the Joad children during their stay at the government camp—all these and more in the novel ascribe preeminent value to collective social action. Such action would seem the logical culmination of the prophetic threats and warnings strewn throughout the novel. Whether they are "rabble-rousing speeches inciting an outraged proletariat to rise against its oppressors," the prophetic passages are explicit, pointed, and sustained. Not just obscurely phrased dire warnings to the powerful that if they do not act promptly to regain legitimacy something terrible may happen (terrible in the narrator's view as well in the view of the owners), the passages declare apocalyptically that, unless there is rapid, radical social change, this is what is coming. That at least seems to be the force of passages like the following:

> Here is the node, you who hate change and fear revolution. Keep these two squatting men apart; make them hate, fear, suspect each other. Here is the anlage of the thing you fear. This is the zygote. For here "I lost my land" is changed; a cell is split and from the splitting grows the thing you hate—"we lost *our* land." The danger is here, for two men are not as lonely and perplexed as one. And from this first "we" there grows a still more dangerous thing: "I have a little food" plus "I have none." If from this problem the sum is "We have a little food," the thing is on its way, the movement has direction. Only a little multiplication now, and this land, this tractor are ours. . . . This is the thing to bomb. This is the beginning—from "I" to "we."

A later passage in a similar vein adds, "if they ever know themselves, the land will be theirs."

Eventually the warnings of what will eventuate when isolated individuals and families join together in mass political action connect with the novel's title, a device which endows them with immense centrality, particularly since the title derives from a patriotic song ("Battle Hymn of the Republic") which in turn draws on the Bible. As the migrants approach the limit of what can be humanly endured, we read: "In the souls of the people the grapes of wrath are filling and growing heavy, growing heavy for the vintage."

These rumblings of ancestral voices prophesy revolution repeatedly in the novel (though much more in the interchapters than in the main narrative), but pointed and sustained as they are, they do not converge in or project any particular insurrectionary endeavor. They are prophecies without outcomes (even outcomes projected into the future)—portentous, apocalyptic, stirring, but finally never more than rhetorical. The gap they leave between prophecy and praxis is particularly clear in one feature of the narrative language of the passages: throughout, the reference is to what "they" will do; the threatened course of action is never unambiguously endorsed, never transformed into a "we" that includes the narrating voice. Of course, the anthropological mode of the novel presumes that Steinbeck's social locus is closer to his audience than to the social group he depicts. Nevertheless, not even optatively does the novel ever fully identify itself with any revolutionary action that might be undertaken by the oppressed; there is always a sense of holding back at the last moment, of taking fright at the very possibilities for widespread uprising which the novel discloses. What is promised in the interchapters is withdrawn in the main narrative, and particularly at its conclusion. What prevents Steinbeck from carrying prophecy through to action is not only that "history"—the material and social circumstances both within which and about which he writes—had not yet provided a solution to the problems he investigates. He is incapable of *imagining* a resolution. He is confident enough at a purely oratorical level, but the level of actual social initiative is another matter. The source of his difficulty in the analysis he provides of existing American society and the vision he projects of an alternative to it.

From both the novel itself and statements he made at the time concerning his growing compassion for the migrants in California, we might reasonably infer that Steinbeck saw his role in writing ***The Grapes of Wrath*** as contributing to an effort to change their immediate conditions rather than providing in addition a critique of the social and economic structures and relations that create and maintain such conditions. At the same time, the novel has to account for the situation in which the migrants find themselves. The prolonged drought in the southwest accounts in part for why the migrants undertake their exodus, but it cannot on its own explain how they lose their land or make sense of what they experience once they arrive in California. For their suffering to be more than adventitious, the narrative has to provide some sort of explanation. The furthest Steinbeck is able to go to satisfy this narrative demand is to place blame on impersonal business and financial institutions and greedy landowners.

What he is unable to account for is how such institutions and individuals are able not only to act the way they do, but to persist in their actions. Where are the laws that could constrain them? How are they able to use the police to assist their efforts? Why is there no speedy *political* resolution to the growing conflict? Steinbeck makes it all but impossible to confront such issues once he carefully dissociates the state from the injustices he depicts. Throughout the novel, the state is assumed to be outside and above the causes of the migrants' suffering. Responsibility for all injustices falls to business corporations and avaricious individuals. The state is not only deemed separate from capitalism, the defining and enabling context of these institutions and individuals; it is seen (in a distinctively American strain of political populism) as positively antithetical to capitalism and the social relations it produces. Nowhere is this made clearer than in the government camp in which the Joads find temporary refuge. Discussing the actions of the owners and the police, one inhabitant of the camp says: "An' that's why they hate this here camp. No cops can get in. This here's United States, not California."

This view of the state is entirely consistent with, and might even be entailed in, the way Steinbeck defined his project. Only a neutral state, available for the role of impartial social arbiter, or a benevolent state, eager to remedy social ills once they are identified (Steinbeck hovers between the two views), can be envisaged as open to the influence of an awakened public opinion. Conceiving the state in these terms, however, thoroughly mystifies the deeply complicit relation between the state and capital, which in turn means that the narrative can provide no coherent account for the oppression and exploitation depicted. At no point does Steinbeck raise the obvious question: if the federal government is as well disposed towards the migrants as the government camps would suggest, why has it not already intervened to end oppression and relieve the migrants of their suffering? Such a government would not require a novel designed to outrage public opinion to be written before it responded. Paradoxically, then, the very act of writing ***The Grapes of Wrath*** refutes the analysis of American society on which the novel is based.

From the opening moments of the novel, when the issue of how Tom could have been so unjustly imprisoned is almost but never quite made explicit, to the conclusion, when the inaction of the state permits the wholesale destruction of migrant families, questions like these continually threaten to rise to the surface of the narrative, only to be pushed back out of sight. So consistently does Steinbeck decline to engage with the questions his narrative provokes that the question of bad faith eventually arises, for it is difficult to imagine any other way of accounting for how the novel ultimately issues in the familiar message: "The fundamental institutions of society are not bad, just certain individuals and isolated practices. Once these are corrected, things will be just fine." A novelist who gives every appearance of writing from a social and political perspective somewhere on an axis of left-liberal to radical socialist nevertheless produces a narrative which ultimately endorses the existing scheme of things (barring a few unfortunate anomalies) and declines to contemplate the possibility that the scheme itself needs overthrowing. Instead of seeing the novel as an expression of bad faith, however, we might more fruitfully think of it, with its radical impulses and less than radical projections, as a "fellow-traveling" novel, bearing in mind Trotsky's important insight:

> As regards a "fellow-traveler," the question always comes up—how far will he go? This question cannot be answered in advance, not even approximately. The solution of it depends not so much on the personal qualities of this or that "fellow-traveler," but mainly on the objective trends of things.

Steinbeck's inability to confront the most profound implications of his own narrative leaves him no way to end the novel, since the social horrors he has been depicting with such compassion require at the very least giving serious thought to a form of redress he is incapable of imagining except, as in the prophetic passages, in the most abstract and oratorical way. Unable to resolve the novel at the level of the social, economic, and political iniquities he renders in such compelling detail, he withdraws at the conclusion of the narrative to the merely interpersonal.

So reluctant is Steinbeck to confront the depredations of capitalism analytically rather than emotionally that he undermines still another dimension of his project. Implicitly or explicitly, the kind of novel Steinbeck has written, for which Craig and Egan have proposed the suggestive term "social tragedy," projects an alternative to the depicted social order, a social and political "possible other case." That projection is a vital part of the utopian impulse of social tragedy as it gestures towards a realm beyond necessity. Deducing Steinbeck's projected alternative, at least in its broad features, seems at first glance a simple task. Most of the novel would seem to imply that a new social order would have to be built on collective principles and would have to exclude economic practices which depend on exploitation. Property would no longer be presumed as an absolute right, since accumulation would have to be regulated to ensure that land did not again fall into the hands of a few. Profit would have to give way to or at least be modified by notions of social benefit, so that people would no longer have their homes confiscated. No one would be permitted to have wealth beyond a certain level, and the gap between the richest and poorest in society would be kept fairly narrow. The rights of workers to a living wage, to organize in labor unions, and to strike would be placed above the claims of owners. Or so the novel implies.

Yet surprisingly, whatever the society ultimately prefigured in the novel, it is certainly not any form of socialist or even social-welfare society. Tom's farewell to his mother—one of the few times the portentous tone of the prophetic passages, for the most part restricted to the interchapters, enters the main narrative—reveals in its closing sentence the boundaries of Steinbeck's vision of an alternative America: "An' when our folks eat the stuff they raise an' live in the houses they build—why, I'll be there." This is Steinbeck's alternative social order, a reiteration of Jefferson's vision of a society made up of independent small farmers eating the food they grow and living in the houses they build. Where in this is collective social life? How, if it was necessary for the family to be destroyed in order for people to discover their collective destiny, do the nuclear families return who will presumably inhabit these houses and grow the food? Where in the reconstituted household economy of small farms will be the space for what is ostensibly projected as a new status for women, achieved at such cost? All such considerations are overwhelmed by the "ache of ownership" which, far from rejecting in favor of collective ownership, Steinbeck gladly ratifies.

A second strand to Steinbeck's vision of an alternative order emerges earlier in the same conversation, at the point where Tom remembers something Casy had once related to him: "Says one time he went out in the wilderness to find his own soul, an' he foun' he didn't have no soul that was his'n. Says he foun' he jus' got a little piece of a great big soul." Here, as collectivity gets absorbed into the ideas of yet another seminal American thinker with the barely veiled reference to Emerson's conception of the oversoul, Tom's memory takes on a regressive quality, for at this point the novel doubles back on its own development in character and action. Tom recalls not Casy the labor organizer, who late in the novel, just before he becomes the victim of violent reaction, speaks eloquently and lucidly of revolution and counter-revolution, but the Casy of their first encounter, who at the outset of the action was the prophet of the oversoul.

Tom's final conversation with Ma reveals the strains and confusions of the proffered resolutions of the novel's conflicts as the concluding chapters work to contain and defuse the revolutionary implications of the depiction of mounting class conflict. For all that Steinbeck may be linking his narrative to notions deeply embedded in American hegemonic cultural traditions, Jeffersonian and Emersonian ideas are inadequate to the weight placed upon them. The oversoul suggests something entirely different from revolutionary action; indeed it suggests no action at all, only some state of being exempt from the immediacies of the social and historical. Similarly, collective life is negated by the Jeffersonian ideal, a negation which can be felt in the contradictory quality of statements like "All work together for our own thing—all farm our own lan'." To further complicate matters, by the time of the conversation between Tom and Ma near the end of the novel, the appeal of the Jeffersonian ideal has long since been diminished by repeated suggestions of the guilty secret behind the land the farmers till—the violent dispossession of the Indians whose land it once was.

The difficulties Steinbeck had with closure in ***The Grapes of Wrath*** may stem in part from the very success he had in gaining access to his audience. Appealing to public opinion entails granting a measure of legitimacy to the social order the presumptive audience inhabits. Appealing to specifically *American* cultural tradition further confirms legitimacy. Once legitimacy is granted, any revolutionary implications arising from the narrative must be curtailed, even if that means skirting some of the narrative's most profound insights into how the social order is actually constructed and in whose benefit it operates. What is involved here is not a question merely of an author's intention, even broadening that notion to include how authors of radical novels define for themselves the political projects in which they are engaged. At issue here is the very possibility of writing a novel that both reaches a wide audience and remains politically radical. Victor Serge's *Birth of Our Power,* a major radical novel of the 1930s, is remarkable among other things for the way it succeeded in keeping its leftist politics intact, but it did so perhaps at the cost of remaining all but unknown for many years. From its original publication to today it has probably not sold as many copies as ***The Grapes of Wrath*** sells in an average year. One conclusion we can draw from Steinbeck's example is that the advice Engels gave Minna Kautsky about eschewing overtly "tendentious writing" in order to reach the "bourgeois circles" who are the only available audience may understate the consequences of the techniques novelists may have to use to accomplish that task. Reaching that audience might entail the simultaneous (and intimately related) dilution of the novel's politics and distortion of its form.

Lorelei Cederstrom (essay date 1997)

SOURCE: "The 'Great Mother' in *The Grapes of Wrath,*" in *Steinbeck and the Environment: Interdisciplinary Approaches,* edited by Susan F. Beegel, Susan Shillinglaw, and Wesley N. Tiffney, Jr., University of Alabama Press, 1997, pp. 76-91.

[*In the following essay, Cederstrom examines the significance of archetypal maternal figures and feminine values in* The Grapes of Wrath. *According to Cederstrom, "An archetypal analysis of Steinbeck's novel reveals that in assessing the economic problems of the 1930s he had, perhaps unconsciously, arrived at an alternative to the dominant structures of Western civilization."*]

Pagan cultures identify the earth, with its seasonal cycles of birth, growth, death, and renewal, with a feminine principle. Such cultures worship an earth goddess, on whose fecundity and compassion men depend, and depict her as a maternal figure, a "Great Mother." In The Grapes of Wrath, *the Joad family, with Ma Joad as matriarch, adopt the Great Mother's ethos and iconography. On the road to California, they become a matriarchy valuing family and nurture, a social system with roots deep in a primitive time when men lived in harmony with the land and in direct opposition to the patriarchal forces driving the Dust Bowl disaster. The novel's famous final image, in which Rose of Sharon gives her breast to a starving man, is not Christian iconography but the culmination of the pagan, earth-directed values of the Great Mother.*

In his depiction of the destruction of the fertile earth and the lives of those who have depended upon her abundance, John Steinbeck in ***The Grapes of Wrath*** presents a visionary foreshadowing of the universal ecological disaster that looms so prominently on the horizon today. Equally visionary is his evocation of the primordial alternative to the patriarchal structures and attitudes that are destroying the earth. Throughout the novel, he describes the reemergence of the archetypal feminine and asserts the importance of matriarchal cultures that understand the relationship between the cycles of their lives and the natural world. An archetypal analysis of Steinbeck's novel reveals that in assessing the economic problems of the 1930s he had, perhaps unconsciously, arrived at an alternative to the dominant structures of Western civilization.

This alternative surfaces among the people who are the first victims of the decline of the old order, the migrant families. The failure of Western civilization to provide the necessities for these disinherited wanderers leads them to establish a more primitive social order based upon feminine values and matriarchal structures. Concurrent with the development of the matriarchy is the irruption of images, patterns, and attitudes associated with the primitive and transformative forms of the matriarchal deities. Throughout the novel, patriarchal culture and its attitudes give way to manifestations of the presence of the archetypal "Great Mother."

The powerful closing scene of the novel in which Rose of Sharon suckles a starving man at her breast provides an iconographic image of the Great Mother: "Rose of Sharon loosened one side of the blanket and bared her breast. 'You got to,' she said. She squirmed closer and pulled his head close. 'There!' she said. 'There!' Her hand moved gently in his hair. She looked up and across the barn, and her lips came together and smiled mysteriously." The haunting power of this image indicates the presence of a powerful archetype. Sensing an archetypal pattern, critics have related Rose of Sharon to the Madonna, and her nurturing gesture has been seen as a manifestation of Christian love. One must keep in mind, however, that Rose of Sharon is not a mother suckling her child; her baby was born dead, "a blue shriveled little mummy." At her breast is a starving stranger, a fellow refugee from a rising flood that has already destroyed many homes and families. This archetypal gesture and mysterious smile are, nonetheless, the fitting conclusion to the novel, for it is in this affirmation of the power to give life and to take it, to nourish even while surrounded by the death and destruction she has wrought, that the full power of the Great Mother is evident. A detailed analysis of the archetypal Great Mother as she appears throughout the novel reveals more clearly the iconographic significance of this scene.

It is necessary to define the limits of this archetype as Steinbeck has used it, for in her many facets, the Great Mother encompasses virtually everything. "Woman=body=vessel=world," is the formula Erich Neumann uses to define the all-inclusive quality of the archetypal feminine. In ***The Grapes of Wrath,*** the Great Mother appears in both her elementary and transformative characters. In the former, she can be seen as a primordial spirit behind both the positive and negative forces of nature, manifesting herself in soft sunlight and scourging drought, in gentle rain and destroying flood, in food and shelter as well as famine and deprivation. In her elementary character she is also present in the home and in the cultural activities that grow out of the establishment of facilities for sleep, food preparation, and so on. In her transformative character, the Great Mother is a force for change in the individual and society; this change may involve growth or destruction, rebirth or death, for both are within her domain.

This last point must be emphasized, for destruction is as much a part of the Great Mother as is creation; she who gives life can also bring death to the natural world or the individual. A well-known icon of the Great Mother, the nineteenth-century Indian statue of Kali dancing on Shiva, indicates both aspects of her character; Kali holds a sword of destruction in her upraised hand and holds out a bowl of nourishment in the other. Similarly, among the dual mother goddesses of Central America we find the Mayan earth goddess who "gives all life, all food—and then cries in the night for human blood, her food." Even the more familiar Near Eastern goddesses like Isis, Astarte, Ishtar, Artemis, and Diana have a dark face in which they represent the "womb-tomb, abysmally prolific with children and with death." This same ambivalence is present throughout Steinbeck's novel and is profoundly expressed in the paradoxical situation of the final scene, when the man near death by starvation and flood, two disasters particularly associated with primitive earth goddesses like the Great Mother, is given the nourishing breast, the most elementary symbol of her life-giving quality.

On the most basic level, the Great Mother as the giver of life or death appears as a personification of the Earth itself. In Steinbeck's earlier novel, ***To a God Unknown*** (1933), the earth is constantly imaged as a female presence, a presence that like "an ancient religion" might "possess" those who come to know her. The Indian, Juanito, shares with homesteader Joseph Wayne his understanding of this ancient power: "My mother said how the earth is our mother and how everything that lives has life from the mother and goes back into the mother." Joseph spends his entire life trying to understand the Great Mother as she is manifest in the earth he tends. Indeed, he can be seen as a priest assisting in her mysteries, as he works to ensure the fertility of the earth. He views these priestly duties as "the heritage of a race which for a million years had sucked at the breasts of the soil and co-habited with the earth."

It is apparent from the beginning of ***The Grapes of Wrath*** that man has lost awareness that the earth is both sacred and living. Mother Earth is still fertile, but the crops are covered with dust. The land has been raped, and growing the same crop year after year under these conditions has destroyed the ability of the earth to nurture those who treat her this way. The Joad family suffers because they too have been guilty of this kind of neglect: "'Ever' year,' said Joad, 'Every year I can remember, we had a good crop comin' an' it never came. Grampa says she was good the first five plowin's, while the wild grass was still in her.'" The novel opens many years after the last of the wild grass; the land is not even owned by people any more but by banks or corporations.

The matriarchal consciousness has also been lost, for as Neumann notes, it is dependent upon man's "participation mystique with his environment." The participation mystique has been replaced by an attitude of unemotional domination: "No man touched the seed, or lusted for the growth. Men ate what they had not raised, had no connection with the bread. The land bore under iron, and under iron gradually died; for it was not loved or hated, it had no prayers or curses." The land is worked by a "machine man" who sits on an iron seat on an iron horse. Steinbeck has embodied the lack of connection to the land in a number of small details as well. Tom Joad, returning to his home, discovers that all the artifacts that symbolize a life close to the earth are askew. The well is dry; there are no weeds under its trough. The house is aslant, all of the windows are broken, and there is a hole where there once was a stovepipe. The machine man's lunch is another detail of this kind. It is wrapped in waxed paper, and all his food is processed: Spam, white bread, "a piece of pie branded like an engine part." The result of this process of alienation from the earth, the Great Mother, is separation and exile. The machine man "goes home, and his home is not the land"; the Joads have lost both home and land.

Both the male and female characters in the novel are depicted in terms of their relationship to the Great Mother. The women are divided between those who have no relationship to the earth, land, or a natural life and those whose lives demonstrate the many faces of the archetypal feminine. The female counterparts of the machine men are defined by the objects with which they surround themselves: big cars, cosmetics, clothing and potbellied husbands. Their feminine attributes are disguised: breasts are confined, "stomachs and thighs straining against cases of rubber."

These women are also distinguished in terms of their relationship to time. The matriarchal consciousness is at work when a woman lives in tune with the cycles of nature. Mircea Eliade in *Cosmos and History* notes that primitive peoples experience the sacredness of life by living in tune with seasonal cycles and the recurrence of crops. In opposition, our contemporary world measures life linearly, as history, a progress from one point to another, stamping masculine measurements upon feminine cyclicality. Women, even in an industrial society, experience themselves at least in terms of biological cycles. Steinbeck's nameless women on the road, however, have accepted linear time and have lost the regenerative capacity that comes from recognizing oneself as part of an eternally recurring pattern. Steinbeck is explicit about this: the eyes of these women are "sullen, disliking sun and wind and earth, resenting food and weariness, hating time that rarely makes them beautiful and always makes them old."

In contrast, the Joad women are linked to the cyclicality of the archetypal feminine. Granma, Ma, and Rose of Sharon manifest the three ages of the Great Mother: hag, mother, and nubile daughter. The youngest girl, Ruthie, remains outside; she has not yet achieved her initiation into womanhood, so she merely watches and learns. Granma is shrill, ferocious, and assertive, true to her mythical forebears, Hecate, or Athene as Crone. She once shot off one of Grampa's buttocks, an act that indicates her tendency toward matriarchal dominance. Her power is apparent; she outlasts her mate, without succumbing to grief. Her acceptance of death as a part of a pattern of renewal is indicated by Ma's assertion that Granma "always et a good meal at a funeral." As her own death approaches, Granma becomes "like a little baby." A sense of her involvement in the recurrent cycles of life is suggested by the mysterious whisperings between dying Granma and pregnant Rose of Sharon.

Tom describes Ma as the "citadel of the family, the strong

place that could not be taken." Neumann describes numerous instances in which the primordial Great Mother is similarly depicted as an encompassing shelter. Ma is the center and source of the family and its emotions; Tom sees her position as "great and humble." Her beauty arises out of her services within the family: "From her position as healer, her hands had grown sure and cool and quiet; from her position as arbiter she had become as remote and faultless in judgment as a goddess." At the center of the humble recurring cycles of family life, Ma continually reflects the many aspects of the nurturing force of the Great Mother.

The first time we see Ma she is cooking pork, food from an animal that is associated with her throughout the novel. Neumann notes that "the pig is a symbol of the archetypal feminine and occurs everywhere as the sacrificial beast of the Earth Goddess." It is the pork that Ma has salted and prepared that keeps the family alive on the road. Like Granma, Ma lives in tune with recurrent cycles and is contrasted with the male characters. On the road, the men are concerned with maps, miles, and time: "From Sallisaw to Gore is twenty-one miles and the Hudson was doing thirty-five miles an hour. From Gore to Warner thirteen miles; Warner to Checotah fourteen miles; Checotah a long jump to Henrietta—thirty-four miles, but a real town at the end of it." Ma sees the journey differently: "it's jus' the road goin' by for me. An' it's jus' how soon they gonna wanta eat some more pork bones."

Before the journey, Ma was just one voice among many in making group decisions. As the novel progresses, Ma becomes more dominant. She forces the men to accede to the human needs of the family and decides when they will stop and go on. Pa threatens to reestablish patriarchal dominance with a shovel to the side of her head but acquiesces to her rule every time. Off the land, yet unable to relate to industrial society, the lives of the Joads are organized around primitive, matriarchal cultural activities. Preparing food and making shelter are their most immediate concerns, and Ma is the prime mover in creating the rituals of this primitive civilization. Ma also instructs Pa and the others about the importance of the family over property and the superiority of cyclic time over linear. A conversation between Pa and Ma establishes their separate priorities:

> *"Funny! Woman takin' over the fambly. Woman sayin' we'll do this here, an' we'll go there. An' I don' even care."*
>
> *"Woman can change better'n a man," Ma said soothingly. "Woman got all her life in her arms. Man got it all in his head. Don' you mind. Maybe—well, maybe nex' year we can get a place."*
>
> *"We got nothin', now," Pa said. . . . "Seems our life is over and done!"*
>
> *"No it ain't," Ma smiled. "It ain't, Pa. An that's one more thing a woman knows. I noticed that. Man, he lives in jerks—baby born, an' a man dies, an' that's a jerk. Woman, it's all one flow, like a stream, little eddies, little waterfalls, but the river, it goes right on. Woman looks at it like that. We ain't gonna die out. People is goin' on—changin' a little, maybe, but goin' right on!"*

Ma is also a purveyor of matriarchal folk wisdom. She knows about burial rites, for example; Grampa is sewed neatly into his shroud, coins traditionally placed on his eyes. Ma also presides at births, acting as midwife, and she initiates Rose of Sharon into womanhood by piercing her ears: "Does it mean sompin?" Rose of Sharon asked. "Why course it does, . . . course it does," Ma replied. Everything Ma does is in accord with her function as an archetypal mother. She experiences herself as a provider of nourishment; others experience her as a source of strength. Her character has a positive effect on those around her for it is firmly rooted in the generating spirit of the Great Mother.

Rose of Sharon in her preoccupation with her pregnancy represents the transformative and life-giving power of the Great Mother. From the beginning of the novel, Steinbeck links Rose of Sharon to fertility: "The world was pregnant to her; she thought only in terms of reproduction and motherhood." This pregnancy transforms her husband, Connie, as well. Steinbeck describes both Rose of Sharon and Connie as drawn together in contemplation of this central female mystery: "The world had drawn close around them and they were in the center of it, or rather Rose of Sharon was in the center of it with Connie making a small orbit about her. Everything they said was a kind of secret." "Fecundation," Neumann notes, "makes the woman into a numinous being for herself and for the male."

Removal from their home and land disrupts their relationship and focus on the child to be. Uprooted, Connie and Rose of Sharon both attempt to adjust to the patriarchal structures of the larger world. Connie begins to dream of a new life in the machine age, hoping to work in a store or a factory or to learn a technical trade, and eventually, he deserts the family in pursuit of these fantasies of power in the world of men's work. Rose of Sharon hopes to have her baby in a hospital, attended by doctors, rejecting traditional female wisdom by her willingness to accept male authority over female functions. Rose of Sharon's defection is strongly punished, however, for Connie abandons her, and her child is stillborn. Her recovery is directed by her mother as she reinitiates Rose of Sharon into the female mysteries of life and death: "Ma lay close to Rose of Sharon. Sometimes Ma whispered to her and sometimes she sat up quietly, her face brooding."

It is at Ma's direction that Rose of Sharon transcends her individual suffering by giving her breast to the starving man. Neumann notes that the production of milk is an archetypal transformation mystery, involving a woman's transition from nubility to motherhood and focusing a woman's awareness of herself as a nurturing force. As she holds the starving man in her arms, Rose of Sharon develops into full womanhood. She moves from the inturned self-obsession of her adolescent passion for Connie to an understanding of selfless maternal love. Her smile reflects her recognition of the Great Mother within.

The male characters in the novel also experience the transforming power of the Great Mother. Speaking of the power of the feminine to act as a catalyst in men's lives, Neumann notes that "the male experiences . . . the feminine directly and indirectly as provocative, as a force that sets him in motion and impels him toward change." The details that surround the various transformative experiences in the novel indicate clearly that the change is brought about as characters realign their former patriarchal attitudes in accordance with matriarchal values, rather than as the result of Christian conversion or the development of social consciousness. Steinbeck has created strong patriarchs in his other novels, but one looks in vain for sustained masculine attributes in either Pa or Grampa. Grampa, for example, was a force to be reckoned with until he left the land; it took only a few days of separation from his vital relationship to the earth for him to die. Pa, too, as we have noted, off the land becomes more and more an auxiliary of Ma, indicating a consistent dependence on the feminine whether manifested in land or woman.

Pa's attitude toward the archetypal feminine remains a troubled one, characterized by fear and misunderstanding, a fault for which he pays. Although Mother Earth fed him, he did not know how to ensure the fertility of his land; the constant raising of the same crop contributed to the failure of his farm and the removal of his family from their roots. In the scene that describes the birth of his first son, Noah, Pa is depicted as someone who fails to understand the fundamental transformation mystery of birth. Noah is sacrificed to his father's impatience and fear of the natural functions of the feminine:

> *For on the night when Noah was born, Pa, frightened at the spreading thighs, alone in the house, and horrified at the screaming wretch his wife had become, went mad with apprehension. Using his hands, his strong fingers for forceps, he had pulled and twisted the baby. The midwife, arriving late, had found the baby's head pulled out of shape, its neck stretched, its body warped; and she had pushed the head back and molded the body with her hands. But Pa always remembered and was ashamed.*

As a result, Noah is strange, aloof and alienated from the rest of the family. Halfway to California, however, Noah undergoes a symbolic rebirth, a baptism that brings him back into connection with the Great Mother. The rite of passage takes place in one of the domains associated with the feminine, a river where the men have come to wash and cool themselves. The river is too shallow to allow them to submerge their heads, signifying that their masculine consciousness will impede them from receiving the full benefit of their experiences in the female element and must be left behind. Noah's limited intelligence is a benefit in this case, and he is the first to respond to the call of the instinctual life promised by the Great Mother in the river. He tells the others: "I was in that there water. An' I ain't a-gonna leave her. I'm a-gonna go now, . . . down the river. I'll catch fish an' stuff, but I can't leave her. I can't." Noah's use of the feminine pronoun is significant here. When told that Noah is gone, Pa does not understand, and his failure places him in the position of a child in the family, subservient to Ma, who seems to understand everything.

The case for the centrality of the Great Mother in the novel is challenged by the frequent and obvious association of Jim Casy with Christ. It is obvious that Casy not only shares Christ's initials but also delivers the Christian message of love and professes a willingness to sacrifice himself for his fellow man. His relationships with women, however, reveal him as a truer disciple of the Great Mother than follower of Christian dogma. Casy tells Tom that he is no longer a preacher because love of God and religious ecstasy led him to express that love physically. "Tell you what," he said, "I used ta get the people jumpin' and talkin' in tongues, an' glory-shoutin' till they just fell down and passed out. . . . An' then—you know what I'd do? I'd take one of them girls out in the grass, an' I'd lay with her. Done it ever' time." This combination of religious ecstasy and sexuality causes Casy to question how the so-called working of the devil could be present when a woman felt full of the divine spirit and leads to his abandonment of his ministry. Sexuality is, of course, perfectly compatible with the worship of the Great Goddess and has always played a part in her rituals.

Casy's concept of spirituality also departs from the narrow Christian view and emphasizes a unity between body and soul, in which sex and food reflect spiritual mysteries. His attempt to define a divine principle that includes both body and spirit leads to something akin to the oversoul of cosmic consciousness: "Maybe it's all men an' all women that we love; maybe tha's the Holy Sperit—the human sperit—the whole shebang. Maybe all men got one big soul ever'body's a part of." He explicitly separates his spiritual ideas from Christianity, asking, "Why do we got to hang it all on God or Jesus?"

Casy's views seem very similar to those that Steinbeck himself expressed. Robert Bennett, in *The Wrath of John Steinbeck; or, St. John Goes to Church,* reports that when Steinbeck was in college, he could not refrain, upon visiting a church, from responding to the minister's comments on the necessity of nourishing the soul: "A lot of crap," he remarked rather loudly. "If the soul is immortal, why worry about it—it's the body that—" Casy, too, respects the body; although he expresses guilt at betraying his Christian principles through his sexuality, his experience of woman as a "holy vessel" leads him to take her to the grass time and again. Casy also feels alienated by the sexual prudery of Christianity and enjoys laughing at the old joke about the bull and the heifer.

Unlike the Father whom Jesus worshiped, Casy's god is a god unknown. Moreover, it is a divine principle that expresses itself through a feeling of unity with the natural world and an unqualified maternal love. Casy's rejection of formal religion is apparent in the scene when Granma asks him to bless their food. Here he explains his reluctance to participate in rituals of Christian tradition but agrees to present a more general blessing based upon a redefinition of holiness in terms of the central functions of the Great Mother, food, and love:

> *Sometimes I'd pray like I always done. On'y I coudn' figure what I was prayin' to or for. There was the hills, an' there was me, an' we wasn't separate no more. We was one thing. An' that one thing was holy. . . . An' then I got thinkin' I don't even know what I mean by holy. . . . I can't say no grace like I use' ta say. I'm glad of the holiness of breakfast. I'm glad there's love here. That's all.*

As Casy travels with the Joad family he becomes more and more closely attached to Ma and is initiated by her into some of the mysteries of the Great Mother. His first communal gesture is to help slaughter a pig, which is, as mentioned earlier, one of the Great Mother's sacrificial beasts. For the other men, this slaughter is simply part of their ordinary work, but Casy involves himself in the women's task of salting down the meat, thereby becoming an initiate in one of the fundamental mysteries of the Great Mother, that of food transformation. Ma is dubious about his participation at first: "It's women's work," she protests. "It's all work," the preacher replies. "They's too much of it to split it up to men's and women's work."

In the final analysis, interpreting Casy as a Christ figure leaves out too much of his fundamental earthiness. If he is seen as the unconscious prophet of a primitive earth goddess, both his sexuality and his feeling that "all that lives is holy" and "what people does is right" can be taken into account. Nor do Casy's sacrifices of himself take him beyond the realm of the Great Mother, for she has always demanded sacrifices in her honor; pain and deprivation are associated with her most primitive rituals. Casy's first sacrifice was for the Joad family, the second for the family of man. Casy's last words are reminiscent of Christ's as he tells the men who are attacking him: "You don't know what you're a doin." But his rationale for this remark is not that they do not know they are killing a son of god but that they do not know that they are "starvin' kids," a basic concern of the matriarchs and the Great Mother.

Tom Joad is more nearly a Christ figure than Casy, but he is even more profoundly the son of his mother. He is badly abused by the patriarchy both before the novel opens and later in the work camps and rejects the hierarchies of patriarchal society as well as the violence toward the weak that sustains those structures. After each confrontation with men and authority, he returns to his mother for support and spiritual nourishment. Before he leaves the family, he undergoes an initiation into the mysteries of the Great Mother. The initiation begins with a symbolic reentry into the womb, as he hides in the maternal, cavelike darkness of a culvert. His mother brings nourishment to him, and he discusses with her his plans to aid the other migrants by organizing them. He envisions an apotheosis for himself, one in which he is absorbed into a maternal darkness, maintaining a transcendent presence at food rituals: "I'll be all aroun' in the dark. I'll be ever' where—wherever you look. Whenever they's a fight so hungry people can eat, I'll be there." His transformation from bitter ex-con to fighter for humanity is the result of his developing matriarchal consciousness in which the needs of the family, the earth, and those who live close to it are primary.

Unlike Tom, Casy, and Noah, Uncle John has been transformed before the novel opens. He has been punishing himself with drink and celibacy for contributing to the death of his wife, suffering in atonement for his sins against the Great Mother. He remains in the background for the most part, a living reminder of the failure of patriarchal rule and values. Ma gives him a bit of appropriate and useful advice when she warns him not to burden others with his crimes against life: "Don't tell'em," she warns. "Go down the river an' stick your head under an' whisper'em in the stream." John does not take her advice at this point, but at the end of the novel, he performs a ritualistic sacrifice in the river that can be seen as an act of reparation to the Great Mother for all of their sins. He takes Rose of Sharon's dead baby and casts it on the stream as a warning to others that they are betraying life: "Go down an' tell 'em. Go down in the street an' rot an' tell 'em that way. That's the way you can talk. . . . Maybe they'll know then."

Beyond the manifestations of the transformative power of the Great Mother in the central characters, Steinbeck's descriptions of the migrant camps also indicate a strong matriarchal principle at work: "In the evening, a strange thing happened: the twenty families became one family, the children were the children of all." The highlights of life in these camps, culminating in the Weedpatch camp, are the rituals that develop around the basic functional spheres of the feminine. Birth and death incite community celebrations: "And it might be that a sick child threw despair into the hearts of twenty families, of a hundred people; that a birth there in a tent kept a hundred people quiet and awe-struck through the night and filled a hundred people with the birth-joy in the morning."

Food preparation and laundry are social events on a smaller scale. Ma, for example, finds herself feeding twenty or more waifs in one campground. She is also told about the laundry rituals: "You wait till the women get to washing . . . . know what they did yesterday, Mrs. Joad? They had a chorus. Singing a hymn tune and rubbing the clothes all in time. That was something to hear, I tell you." The principles on which families are established in the camps are based on the needs of women and children. The legal aspects of marriage, invented so that men can pass on their names and property, are no longer useful. The rules are simple: "a man might have a willing girl if he stayed with her, if he fathered her children and protected them. But a man might not have one girl one night and another the next, for this would endanger the worlds."

This last custom, the development of a matrilinear principle, is responsible for Al leaving the Joads. Like Connie, Al had previously been a man of the new age. With his mechanical abilities he performed several small miracles in keeping the car on the road between Oklahoma and California. By the last scene of the novel, however, he has been absorbed by matriarchal principles and matrilinear necessities. His mechanical abilities fail at last, and he leaves his own family for the family of his wife, a custom demanded by the matriarchal world of migrant living. This is not regarded as a desertion of the family but a reestablishment of the basic principles on which the family can continue.

Steinbeck makes it clear that life in the migrant camps does not represent an emergent Christian communism. Rose of Sharon is frightened by a dour Christian woman who warns her against the sinful dances and wicked plays that are held in the camp, insisting that "they ain't but a few deep down Jesus-lovers left." During the dancing, the "Jesus-lovers" remain aloof and keep their children under close scrutiny, safely protected from these pagan celebrations. Ma, however, urges husbandless Rose of Sharon to attend the festivities, telling her that she will be especially welcome because "it makes folks happy to see a girl in a fambly way."

Thus, although the concluding scene has generated much debate, Rose of Sharon's nurturing of the starving man is the appropriate culmination of the many manifestations of the Great Mother throughout the novel. Critics who fail to see the importance of the developing matriarchal consciousness and to recognize the transformative power of the feminine interpret Steinbeck's final image in naturalistic terms, seeing the helpless humans at the mercy of the elements when the diminished family—Ma, Pa, Rose of Sharon, Ruthie, and Winfield—are driven from their boxcar home by the rising river. Other critics, unwilling to accept the implications of the ending for their theories about the Christian or communistic patterns, have tended to concur instead that "the ending is intentionally inconclusive," albeit generally supportive of an optimism about the survival of the family of man. In its poetic and paradoxical completeness, however, the image of Rose of Sharon nursing the stranger while the flood moves to engulf the family unites both the naturalistic and optimistic views.

Failure to recognize the culmination of the archetypal pattern in this has led to such realignments of the final message as John Ford's replacement, in the film version of ***The Grapes of Wrath,*** of the powerful iconographic image of Rose of Sharon with Tom's farewell speech to his mother. Although the film's final scene, perhaps at Steinbeck's insistence, focuses on Ma Joad, the young Tom Joad, portrayed by rising star Henry Fonda, is the hero. Concluding the film with Tom's assertion of his ubiquitous, God-like presence "all around in the dark . . . ever' where—wherever you look," with its echoes of Christ's "insomuch as you do it to the least of them you do it unto me" restores an emphasis to patriarchal values and Christian masculinist perceptions of spiritual power that the novel undercuts.

Steinbeck, however, had no ambivalence about the conclusion of the novel, feeling its correctness, although he did not fully express the reasons for his decision. He certainly intended to take the predominant social attitudes to task, and whether he articulated it intellectually or not, the archetypal alternative to Western patriarchal values comes to the surface in the novel. Each of the characters is forced to choose between patriarchal and matriarchal attitudes toward the natural world and each other. Muley Graves provides an example at the beginning of the novel when he refuses to be driven from the garden by the appearance of the man on the machine. He will not leave the land that has been soaked by the blood of his father or the grass on which he first "laid with a girl." So he remains, living in caves and eating wild rabbits, thereby aligning himself with the vestiges of the Great Mother in nature, as he haunts the machine men who ride unfeelingly over the living earth.

The Joads confront the Great Mother within: the women learn to understand themselves as a part of the natural cycles of life and death; the men are forced to atone for their sins against life and are either transformed or die in the process. In each case, the Great Mother is experienced as a dual power, a womb/tomb that can nurture or destroy. In a brief scene toward the end of the book, Steinbeck reinforces this message, as Ruthie teaches Winfield a stern lesson about the gifts of the Great Mother. When Winfield attempts to grab a flower from Ruthie, she bangs "him in the face with her open hand." Winfield is learning early that the gifts of the Great Mother cannot be taken by force but must be earned by virtue of a reverent attitude toward nature and the feminine. He is also learning that she can withhold or bestow her gifts at will. The image of Rose of Sharon with the starving man at her breast expresses the paradoxical power of the Great Mother completely. Sword in one hand, bowl in the other, Kali, like Rose of Sharon, wears a smile.

Marilyn Chandler McEntyre (essay date 1997)

SOURCE: "Natural Wisdom: Steinbeck's Men of Nature as Prophets and Peacemakers," in *Steinbeck and the Environment: Interdisciplinary Approaches,* edited by Susan F. Beegel, Susan Shillinglaw, and Wesley N. Tiffney, Jr., University of Alabama Press, 1997, pp. 113-24.

[*In the following essay, McEntyre discusses the self-knowledge and compassion acquired by Jim Casy in* The Grapes of Wrath *and Doc in* Cannery Row *through solitary communion with nature. According to McEntyre, "In these two figures, Casy and Doc, Steinbeck incorporates a complex vision of wisdom derived from attentiveness to the natural world."*]

Steinbeck's prophets, men of broad understanding and acceptance, draw their vision from the natural world. Jim Casy, a lapsed preacher and wise counselor to the Joad family, finds new faith in love of nature and renewed purpose through his involvement with the people of the earth. At the center of Cannery Row, *is Doc, marine biologist, whose holistic vision and compassionate attention to human needs are similarly drawn from close observation of his environment and nature. Through a nonteleological acceptance of what is, both the rigorous scientist and the intuitive preacher recognize the interconnectedness of creation.*

Steinbeck's indebtedness to the American transcendentalists, particularly Emerson and Whitman, has been noted frequently. That relationship lies partly in his way of looking upon the natural world as a source of knowledge, a text to replace or expand upon Scripture, which teaches those who have eyes to see and ears to hear. For Steinbeck, as for his predecessors, the wise man was above all else defined by his discerning relationship to the natural world, allowing it to inform his understanding of human relations and enterprises.

In several of Steinbeck's novels we encounter variations on the type of the wise man—a character whose self-knowledge, compassion for human frailty, and sharp intuitions come from close association with the natural world. Two of the most notable of these are Casy, the preacher in ***The Grapes of Wrath,*** and Doc in ***Cannery Row.*** Both are solitaries who take frequent "flights into the wilderness" but who live among people who rely upon them for guidance. Both understand themselves and others with an insight that at times seems prophetic, and indeed in the motley circles they frequent they are accorded special status as counselors and wise men. Both are more educated than those around them, but each in his way has rejected the institutional forms and frameworks that endowed him with professional credentials and lives as a maverick of sorts, moving easily among circles of people to none of which he belongs. Both are explicitly linked with images of Jesus, though neither is conventionally religious. Both are "nonteleological thinkers" in the sense in which Steinbeck claimed that he himself viewed the world: not in terms of defined purposes, but with what he called "is thinking"—acceptance without second-guessing of the divine plan.

For each, the source of wisdom and virtue appears to lie in communion with nature. And each, communing with nature, assumes the status and role of prophet in his community. Indeed it might be said that in these characters Steinbeck is working out a definition of prophecy and the importance of the prophet in modern life, not as one who calls for specific acts of repentance and return to a convenantal tradition, but as one who sees into the heart of nature and speaks forth what lesson it teaches. In doing so he, in effect, issues a warning call to turn away from those forms of civilized life that remove us from what Robinson Jeffers, Steinbeck's contemporary and fellow Californian, called "the great humaneness at the heart of things." And like Jeffers, he writes as one who is himself a visionary trying to find a language for the ultimate interconnectedness of all creation as a means for understanding what as humans we must do.

Steinbeck's most explicit articulation of this vision is given in ***Sea of Cortez,*** where he describes "nonteleological thinking" as a way of understanding the natural and thence the social world independent of the causal relations and presumed purposes we so readily posit to satisfy our need for comprehensible meaning. Freeman Champney sums up nonteleological thinking as "a mixture of philosophical relativism, the rigorous refusal of the scientist to be dogmatic about hypotheses, and a sort of moral fatalism." Steinbeck himself explains, "Nonteleological thinking concerns itself primarily not with what should be, or could be, or might be, but rather with what actually 'is'—attempting at most to answer the already sufficiently difficult questions *what* or *how*, instead of *why*."

To think in such a way entails a kind of humility related to Jeffers's idea of "unhumanism"—a rejection of the myopic anthropocentrism that distorts our understanding of the functioning of whole systems, the large patterns of evolution, the nature of natural and human communities as organic wholes that transcend the life and purposes of any individual within them. This capacity for "whole sight," as well as what Champney sees as relativism, antidogmatism, and ultimate acceptance of what is, defines the prophet in Steinbeck's world. In ***The Grapes of Wrath*** it is Casy, the unpretentious fellow traveler in the Joads' pilgrim band and maverick Christian in self-imposed exile from institutional religion, who embodies the nonteleological or "is" thinker capable of prophesying and ultimately enacting a larger truth than those around him are able to grasp.

Casy, who was once a preacher, now makes it a point of honor to reject his status and its privileges, assuring the Joads, who receive him as a kind of family chaplain, that he doesn't pray any more. But the habit of prayer is as ingrained in him as the way of life he leaves behind on the road to California: "'Fella gets use' to a place, it's hard to go,' said Casy. 'Fella gets use' to a way a thinkin', it's hard to leave. I ain't a preacher no more, but all the time I find I'm prayin', not even thinkin' what I'm doin.'" His prayer is no longer a petition to an omnipotent God but a way of being and a largeness of awareness that comes to him in moments of solitude in the wilderness. He recognizes in himself a natural kinship with the Jesus who fled the crowds and went up into the high desert to pray:

> *I been in the hills thinking, almost you might say like Jesus went into the wilderness to think his way out of a mess of troubles. I ain't sayin' I'm like Jesus, . . . But I got tired like Him, an' I got mixed up like Him, an' I went into the wilderness like Him, without no campin' stuff. Nighttime I'd lay on may back and look up at the stars; morning I'd set and watch the sun come up; midday I'd look out from a hill at the rollin' dry country; evenin' I'd foller the sun down. Sometimes I'd pray like I always done. On'y I couldn't figure what I was prayin' to or for. There was the hills, an' there was me, an' we wasn't separate no more. We was one thing. An' that one thing was holy.*

The idea of the holy has expanded for Casy since his rejection of the church. It springs from an awareness of nature honed and trained by his frequent retreats, his attitude of receptivity, and a habit of mind that links what he knows of the unconscious natural world to a deepening intuition about the ways of human nature. To be in the wilderness "without no campin' stuff" is to be in more direct sensual contact with the earth than those for whom the multilayered insulations of clothing and shelter dull the raw sensate experience of nature. Casy's reflection here also traces a line of thinking that begins in Christian typology and ends in a rejection of that tradition in favor of a universalistic mysticism removed from the claims of any institution. Like Emerson, the transcendentalist who left his pulpit and went out among the people, and like Thoreau, who turned eccentricity to high purposes, Casy opens his heart to a wider calling than the pulpit afforded—to return to the earth and live close to it and the people who till the soil and to learn from them:

> *I ain't gonna baptize. I'm gonna work in the fiel's, in the green fiel's, an' I'm gonna be near to folks. I ain't gonna try to teach 'em nothin'. I'm gonna try to learn. Gonna learn why the folks walks in the grass, gonna hear 'em talk, gonna hear 'em sing. . . . Gonna lay in the grass, open and honest with anybody that'll have me. Gonna cuss an' swear an' hear the poetry of folks talkin'. All that's holy, all that's what I didn' understand'. All them things is the good things.*

In both these speeches there are echoes of transcendentalism, Protestant theology, and Whitmanian democracy. Frederick Carpenter points out the rich soil and deep roots that underlie Casy's philosophical statements as he "translates American philosophy into words of one syllable." And Peter Lisca comments that in these same articulations, Casy moves "from Bible-belt evangelism to social prophesy." As a social prophet, however, his task is to prophesy to a particular and peculiar people. It is in his shared life with the Joad family that he works out his destiny and mission, often in terms reduced to their own simpler way of understanding what he is about.

Despite Casy's protestations, the Joads and others continue to take him for a preacher. The title sticks, and in that assigned role Casy assumes a place in but not of the Joad family, increasingly committed to a vision of things and a version of action that might be described as natural Christianity. His models for prayer and action come from Jesus, but his epistemology emerges not from any organized doctrine but from observation of, trust in, and love for the natural world and the people who live close to the earth.

"I can see it like a prophecy," Casy says, prognosticating about the fate of the people when tractors have made work "so easy that the wonder goes out of work, so efficient that the wonder goes out of the land and the working of it, and with the wonder the deep understanding and the relation." Like his Old and New Testament prototypes he sees the broad connections among things, understands the ominous signs of destruction of the natural order, and longs to save "the people" from the legal and economic machinery that is devouring their lives and driving them off their land. "If ya listen," he says, "you'll hear a movin' an' a sneakin', an' a rustlin', an'—an' a restlessness. They's stuff goin' on that the folks doin' it don't know nothin' about—yet. They's gonna come somepin onto all these folks goin' wes'—outa all their farms lef' lonely. They's gonna come a thing that's gonna change the whole country."

Casy knows these things because he watches and listens and understands signs and portents. He stays awake nights, watching the stars and listening to the sounds of animals in their burrows. He frequently speaks what he knows in parables drawn from nature:

> *But they's somepin worse'n the devil got hold a the country, an' it ain't gonna let go till it's chopped loose. Ever see one a them Gila monsters take hold . . . ? Grabs hold, an' you chop him in two an' his head hangs on. Chop him at the neck and his head hangs on. Got to take a screwdriver an' pry his head apart to get him loose. An' while he's layin' there poison is drippin' an' drippin' into the hole he's made with his teeth.*

Casy's sense of the enormity of the evil coming upon the people is commensurate with his great reverence for creation. At Grampa Joad's funeral he quotes, "All that lives is holy." He has little respect for the laws of man, returning repeatedly to simple expressions of natural law as the only reliable guide for human action: "Law changes," he says, "but' got to's' go on. You got the right to do what you got to do."

His understanding of human nature as well as his rudimentary awareness of the profound involvement of human emotions and desires and needs in the life of the physical body as well as the body politic make him a healer. When Grampa falls sick, Ma finds Casy and asks him simply, "You been aroun' sick people. . . . Grampa's sick. Won't you go take a look at him?" Significantly enough, he can't fix a car, though he can administer comfort, healing, and leadership. All he can do when the car breaks down is shine the light for Tom and Al to see by. His work is with matters of "the sperit."

As the awareness of evil grows on Casy, so does his sense of mission. "I hear the way folks are feelin'," he says. "Goin' on all the time. I hear 'em an' feel 'em; an' they're beating their wings like a bird in an attic. Gonna bust their wings on a dusty winda tryin' ta get out." Casy eventually dies by the principle of natural law, leading a strike, telling his attackers, "You got no right to starve people," and then, "You don' know what you're a-doin'"—final words that powerfully recall Jesus' words, "Father, forgive them, for they know not what they do."

Casy's homegrown natural theology has been the subject of much critical comment, especially the Emersonian echoes in his much- cited insight that "maybe all men got one big soul ever'body's a part of." It is from this essentially pantheistic vision that his politics derive. Ownership makes little sense to him beyond the natural claim to what one needs. The arbitrariness of man-made boundaries seems not simply to ignore but to violate natural laws of distribution and interdependence. Frederick Carpenter in his essay "The Philosophical Joads" sums up Casy's story in this way: "Unorthodox Jim Casy went into the Oklahoma wilderness to save his soul. And in the wilderness he experienced the religious feeling of identity with nature which has always been the heart of transcendental mysticism. . . . the corollary of this mystical philosophy is that man's self-seeking destroys the unity or `holiness' of nature."

Casy's cosmic perspective on human affairs, his involvement in the immediacies of human needs, and his deep attention to the natural world as a source of wisdom are all reiterated in a new key in the character of Doc, the wise man of ***Cannery Row.*** Robert Benton has pointed out that the "ecological" cast of Steinbeck's thinking is reflected in his characterization of Doc—a way of thinking that "causes him to see man as an organism related to a vast and complex ecosystem." In chapter 2 of that book, the narrator pauses characteristically to take a step back from the canvas on which he is painting the colorful local scene and take a cosmic perspective. He sees Lee Chong the grocer and Mack and the boys "spinning in their orbits." The short chapter ends with a prayer: "Our Father who art in nature, who has given the gift of survival to the coyote, the common brown rat, the English sparrow, the house fly and the moth, must have a great and overwhelming love for no-goods and blots-on-the-town and bums, and Mack and the boys. Virtues and graces and laziness and zest. Our Father who art in nature."

In light of this presentation of natural religion as the ideological backdrop to the narrative, Doc's close and attentive knowledge of nature endows him with not only professional but also prophetic credibility. In subsequent chapters the virtues of a good naturalist, as attributes of Doc's character, are manifestations of virtue in a much larger sense; Doc's patience in observing and collecting specimens for study, his steady commitment to objectivity, and his curiosity itself are seen as forms of compassion. He answers Hazel's desultory questions with more seriousness than they deserve because "Doc had one mental habit he could not get over. When anyone asked a question, Doc thought he wanted to know the answer. That was the way with Doc. He never asked unless he wanted to know and he could not conceive of the brain that would ask without wanting to know." The simplicity and straightforwardness of his scientific habit of mind appear as an almost child-like innocence, a quality of guilelessness that wins him universal trust among the ragged crowd who surround him.

At times Doc's steadiness of focus is broken by a kind of whimsy, itself related to wider spiritual vision. When Hazel, observing a crowd of stinkbugs on the ice plant, asks "What they got their asses up in the air for?" Doc's first answer is, "I looked them up recently—they're very common animals and one of the commonest things they do is put their tails up in the air. And in all the books there isn't one mention of the fact that they put their tails up in the air or why." Pressed further with "Well, why do *you* think they do it?" Doc answers, "I think they're praying," and to Hazel's shocked response adds, "The remarkable thing . . . isn't that they put their tails up in the air—the really incredible thing is that we find it remarkable. We can only use ourselves as yardsticks. If we did something as inexplicable and strange we'd probably be praying—so maybe they're praying." The exchange speaks volumes about the way Doc brings together observation, research, deductive and inductive reasoning, contemplation, and a gentle humor that seems to proceed out of a detachment from the entangled human perspective that few men achieve.

Steinbeck's narrators take whole chapters to give voice and color to the natural environments the characters inhabit, embedding in those descriptions much philosophy about the right relation between earth and its creatures. But it is in these small exchanges that draw attention to the minute designs of the natural world that the novels reveal how nature shapes vision and character, how a place known intimately—a farm, a field, a tidepool—can become, as Casy puts it, "a way of thinkin'."

Doc's general wisdom, like Casy's spills over the boundaries of professional definition. At various times he has to remind petitioners that he is neither a medical doctor nor a veterinarian nor a psychiatrist. Like the Joads with their proprietary expectations of Casy as personal chaplain, Doc's cohorts expect him to be all of these things as well as spiritual counselor, confessor, and source of ready money:

> *Now Doc of the Western Biological Laboratory had no right to practice medicine. It was not his fault that everyone in the Row came to him for medical advice. Before he knew it he found himself running from shanty to shanty taking temperatures, giving physics, borrowing and delivering blankets and even taking food from house to house where mothers looked at him with inflamed eyes from their beds, and thanked him and put the full responsibility for their children's recovery on him. When a case got really out of hand he phoned a local doctor and sometimes one came if it seemed to be an emergency. But to the families it was all emergency. Doc didn't get much sleep. He lived on beer and canned sardines.*

Doc maintains his own spiritual and mental health by means of frequent retreats into music, poetry, and nature. His scrupulously scientific habit of mind is a counterpart to Casy's broadly intuitive epistemology but expresses the same deep reverence for what can be learned from the natural world.

> *Doc had to keep up his collecting. He tried to get to the good tides along the coast. The sea rocks and the beaches were his stock pile. He knew where every thing was when he wanted it. All the articles of his trade were filed away on the coast, sea cradles here, octopi here, tube worms in another place, sea pansies in another. He knew where to get them but he could not go for them exactly when he wanted. For Nature locked up the items and only released them occasionally. Doc had to know not only the tides but when a particular low tide was good in a particular place. When such a low tide occurred, he packed his collecting tools in his car, he packed his jars, his bottles, his plates and preservatives and he went to the beach or reef or rock ledge where the animals he needed were stored.*

Doc doesn't even need a clock but lives by a tidal pattern: "He could feel a tide change in his sleep." His knowledge has penetrated to his very body and bones. This kind of knowledge depends on humility, attentiveness, and long fidelity to the habit of patient contemplation—qualities that are also the basis of Doc's legendary compassion. But committed as he is to scientific accuracy and truth-telling, he has also had to learn that "people didn't like you for telling the truth." Once, he recalls, on a walking trip through the South, he repeatedly encountered people who asked him why he was walking through the country but were disturbed by his honest answer:

Because he loved true things he tried to explain. He said he was nervous and besides he wanted to see the country, smell the ground and look at grass and birds and trees, to savor the country, and there was no other way to do it save on foot. And people didn't like him for telling the truth. They scowled, or shook and tapped their heads, they laughed as though they knew it was a lie and they appreciated a liar. And some, afraid for their daughters or their pigs, told him to move on, to get going, just not to stop near their place if he knew what was good for him.

And so he stopped trying to tell the truth. He said he was doing it on a bet—that he stood to win a hundred dollars. Everyone liked him then and believed him. They asked him in to dinner and gave him a bed and they put lunches up for him and wished him good luck and thought he was a hell of a fine fellow. Doc still loved true things but he knew it was not a general love and it could be a very dangerous mistress.

The recognition in this passage that the solitary poses a subtle but vividly felt threat to the community recalls some of well-known stories about the suspicions Thoreau encountered among his fellows in Concord or, more dramatically, the association of intimacy with nature with witchcraft and occultism. Hawthorne's Roger Chillingworth in *The Scarlet Letter* illustrates this latter point; an herbalist whose compendious knowledge of the healing powers of herbs derives from long association with Indians and a solitary life dedicated to this study appears as a practitioner of "dark arts." More benevolent images like that of "Johnny Appleseed" still mark as an eccentric the individual who forsakes community life and communes with nature.

Doc understands this common suspicion, and with a diplomacy that is the measure of his great charity he takes care to foster his own needs in a way that does not threaten or alienate him from the community that depends on him. His understanding of the natural order, like Casy's, informs his social behavior. Much of Doc's activity among his cohorts on Cannery Row is a kind of pastoral subterfuge. Like Casy he is a shrewd assessor of human nature and calculates his demands and concessions accordingly. He also serves as a hub that draws people together in a way that makes community possible. He understands, like Casy, the wide web of interdependency that binds the things of this world and makes a mockery of short-sighted ideas of ownership. His generosity has a character of matter-of-fact common sense to it; it is simply the way of nature.

We do get an occasional ironic comment on the effects of such natural sanctity on the more commercially minded: "Lee was indebted to Doc—deeply indebted. What Lee was having trouble comprehending was how his indebtedness to Doc made it necessary to give credit to Mack." But Doc knows that somehow things even out, like water seeking its own level. He trusts some principle of natural distribution as a basis for all moral action: people do what they can do, they act on what they can understand, and as long as they act in harmony with their nature things even out and we learn from one another. Thus his admiration for Mack and the boys escapes condescension because he understands the necessity of their presence in a world that needs just such a corrective. "Look at them," he says:

They are your true philosophers. I think . . . that Mack and the boys know everything that has ever happened in the world and possibly everything that will happen. I think they survive in this particular world better than other people. In a time when people tear themselves to pieces with ambition and nervousness and covetousness, they are relaxed. All of our so-called successful men are sick men, with bad stomachs and bad souls, but Mack and the boys are healthy and curiously clean. They can do what they want. They can satisfy their appetites without calling them something else.

Chapter 31 of ***Cannery Row,*** which details the life and frustrated enterprises of a gopher, serves as a parable to describe Doc's solitary, industrious life in the face of the social changes and chances that defeat his human ambitions. The gopher, like him, is busy, solitary, in the prime of life. He burrows into rich soil "on a little eminence" where he could watch Mack and the boys. He prepares an elaborate place for a female to join him and raise a family, but no female appears. He goes out to court one but comes back bitten. Finally, "he had to move two blocks up the hill to the dahlia garden where they put out traps every night." Doc is, finally, the gopher in the dahlia garden. He adapts to an environment diminished in natural richness, unsympathetic to his higher ends but livable. He is a prophet unhonored by a mechanized, commercialized, secular culture, quietly, stubbornly cherishing ideals that culture has begun to threaten.

In these two figures, Casy and Doc, Steinbeck incorporates a complex vision of wisdom derived from attentiveness to the natural world. The best of what we call human virtue—compassion, forgiveness, clarity, flexibility—comes from the habit of attention. And in characters like these he would seem to be suggesting that nature teaches us what we need to know—and that our best teachers are those who have learned her lessons.

FURTHER READING

Criticism

Davis, Robert Murray. "The World of John Steinbeck's Joads." *World Literature Today* 64, No. 3 (Summer 1990): 401-4.

Examines the Joad family's migratory route and provides an overview of the central social themes in *The Grapes of Wrath.*

McKay, Nellie Y. "'Happy[?]-Wife-and-Motherdom': The Portrayal of Ma Joad in John Steinbeck's *The Grapes of Wrath.*" In *New Essays on The Grapes of Wrath,* edited by David Wyatt, pp. 47-69. Cambridge: Cambridge University Press, 1990.

Provides analysis of sex roles and gender stereotypes in *The Grapes of Wrath,* particularly in Steinbeck's presentation of Ma Joad as an archetypal Earth Mother figure.

Mitchell, Marilyn H. "Steinbeck's Strong Women: Feminine Identity in the Short Stories." In *John Steinbeck: A Study of the Short Fiction,* edited by R. S. Hughes, pp. 154-66. Boston: Twayne, 1989.

Examines the sexual psychology and gender roles of female characters in two stories from *The Long Valley*—"The Chrysanthemums" and "The White Quail."

Railton, Stephen. "Pilgrim's Politics: Steinbeck's Art of Conversion." In *New Essays on The Grapes of Wrath,* edited by David Wyatt, pp. 27-46. Cambridge: Cambridge University Press, 1990.

Examines Steinbeck's effort to effect social awareness and revolutionary change through presentation of socioeconomic degradation in *The Grapes of Wrath.*

Salter, Christopher L. "John Steinbeck's *The Grapes of Wrath* as a Primer for Cultural Geography." In *Critical Essays on Steinbeck's The Grapes of Wrath,* edited by John Ditsky, pp. 138-52. Boston: G. K. Hall, 1989.

Examines the significance of social, economic, and demographic information in *The Grapes of Wrath* for sociocultural analysis of the Dust Bowl migrations.

Simpson, Hassell A. "Steinbeck's Anglo-Saxon 'Wonder-Words' and the American Paradox." *American Literature* 62, No. 2 (June 1990): 310-7.

Examines Steinbeck's paradoxical vision of America in *The Winter of Our Discontent,* alluded to in an Anglo-Saxon passage from the Bible contained in the novel.

Timmerman, John. "Steinbeck's Environmental Ethic: Humanity and Harmony with the Land." In *Steinbeck and the Environment: Interdisciplinary Approaches,* edited by Susan F. Beegel, Susan Shillinglaw, and Wesley N. Tiffney, Jr., pp. 310-22. Tuscaloosa: University of Alabama Press, 1997.

Discusses Steinbeck's ethical perspective concerning human use and preservation of the environment, particularly as revealed in *America and Americans, Travels with Charley,* and *Sweet Thursday.*

Tuttleton, James W. "Steinbeck Remembered." *The New Criterion* 13, No. 7 (March 1995): 22-8.

Offers an overview of Steinbeck's critical reputation, literary career, and recent writings on his life and work.

Yarmus, Marcia. "The Picaresque Novel and John Steinbeck." In *Rediscovering Steinbeck: Revisionist Views of His Art, Politics, and Intellect,* edited by Cliff Lewis and Carroll Britch, pp. 79-103. Lewiston: Edwin Mellen Press, 1989.

Examines the literary influence of Cervantes's *Don Quixote* and the conventions of Spanish picaresque novels on Steinbeck's fiction.

Additional coverage of Steinbeck's life and career is contained in the following sources published by Gale: *Authors and Artists for Young Adults,* Vol. 12; *Concise Dictionary of American Literary Biography,* 1929-1941; *Contemporary Authors,* Vols. 1-4R, 25-28R; *Contemporary Authors New Revision Series,* Vols. 1, 35; *Dictionary of Literary Biography,* Vols. 7, 9; *Dictionary of Literary Biography Documentary Series,* Vol. 2; *DISCovering Authors; DISCovering Authors: British; DISCovering Authors: Canadian; DISCovering Authors Modules: Dramatists, Most-Studied, and Novelists; Major Twentieth Century Writers,* Vol. 1; *Short Story Criticism,* Vol. 11; *Something about the Author,* Vol. 9; and *World Literature Criticism.*

□ Contemporary Literary Criticism

Indexes

Literary Criticism Series
Cumulative Author Index
Cumulative Topic Index
Cumulative Nationality Index
Title Index, Volume 124

How to Use This Index

The main references

Camus, Albert
1913-1960 . . . .**CLC 1, 2, 4, 9, 11, 14, 32, 69; DA; DAB; DAC; DAM DRAM, MST, NOV; DC2; SSC 9; WLC**

list all author entries in the following Gale Literary Criticism series:

BLC = *Black Literature Criticism*
BLCS = *Black Literature Criticism Supplement*
CLC = *Contemporary Literary Criticism*
CLR = *Children's Literature Review*
CMLC = *Classical and Medieval Literature Criticism*
DA = *DISCovering Authors*
DAB = *DISCovering Authors: British*
DAC = *DISCovering Authors: Canadian*
DAM = *DISCovering Authors Modules*
DRAM = *dramatists;* ***MST*** = *most-studied authors;* ***MULT*** = *multicultural authors;* ***NOV*** = *novelists;* ***POET*** = *poets;* ***POP*** = *popular/genre writers;* ***DC*** = *Drama Criticism*
HLC = *Hispanic Literature Criticism*
LC = *Literature Criticism from 1400 to 1800*
NCLC = *Nineteenth-Century Literature Criticism*
PC = *Poetry Criticism*
SSC = *Short Story Criticism*
TCLC = *Twentieth-Century Literary Criticism*
WLC = *World Literature Criticism, 1500 to the Present*
WLCS = *World Literature Criticism Supplement*

The cross-references

See also CA 89-92; DLB 72; MTCW

list all author entries in the following Gale biographical and literary sources:

AAYA = *Authors & Artists for Young Adults*
AITN = *Authors in the News*
BEST = *Bestsellers*
BW = *Black Writers*
CA = *Contemporary Authors*
CAAS = *Contemporary Authors Autobiography Series*
CABS = *Contemporary Authors Bibliographical Series*
CANR = *Contemporary Authors New Revision Series*
CAP = *Contemporary Authors Permanent Series*
CDALB = *Concise Dictionary of American Literary Biography*
CDBLB = *Concise Dictionary of British Literary Biography*
DLB = *Dictionary of Literary Biography*
DLBD = *Dictionary of Literary Biography Documentary Series*
DLBY = *Dictionary of Literary Biography Yearbook*
HW = *Hispanic Writers*
JRDA = *Junior DISCovering Authors*
MAICYA = *Major Authors and Illustrators for Children and Young Adults*
MTCW = *Major 20th-Century Writers*
NNAL = *Native North American Literature*
SAAS = *Something about the Author Autobiography Series*
SATA = *Something about the Author*
YABC = *Yesterday's Authors of Books for Children*

Literary Criticism Series Cumulative Author Index

Author Index

Literary Criticism Series Cumulative Topic Index

This index lists all topic entries in Gale's *Classical and Medieval Literature Criticism, Contemporary Literary Criticism, Literature Criticism from 1400 to 1800, Nineteenth-Century Literature Criticism,* and *Twentieth-Century Literary Criticism.*

Contemporary Literary Criticism
Cumulative Nationality Index

Nationality Index

CLC-124 Title Index

Title Index

ISBN 0-7876-3199-X

90000

9 780787 631994